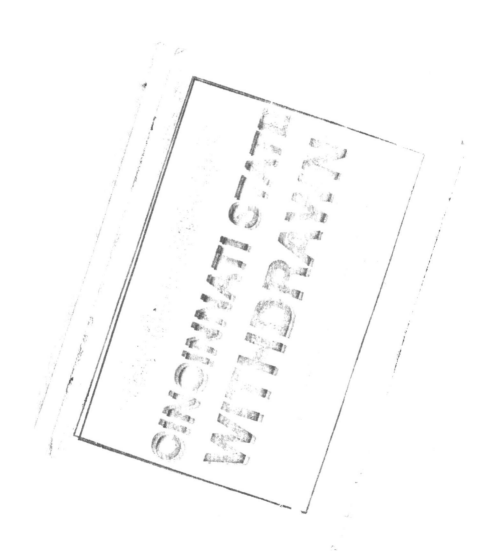

The Handbook of Hearing and the Effects of Noise

ERRATA

1. The phrase identifying ownership of copyright should be omitted from the following figure legends: Figures 2.4, 2.8–2.17, 2.19, 2.20, 3.6, 3.7, 3.11, 3.12, 4.12, 5.2, 5.3B, 5.7, 5.10, 5.13, 5.18–5.21, 5.23–5.25, 5.27, 5.33, 5.35, 6.1, 6.11, 6.13, 6.14, 6.16–6.21, 6.23, 6.26, 6.29, 6.30, 9.8, 9.20, 10.1, and 10.5.

2. On page 188, Equation (5.2) should read

$$L_{\mathrm{Aeq8h},\, n_1} = L_{An_1} - 10 \log (28{,}800/t), \mathrm{dB}.$$

3. On page 188, Equation (5.5) should read

$$L_{\mathrm{Aeq8h,osha},\, n_1 \cdots n_x} = 10 \log 10^{(L_{\mathrm{Aeq8h,osha},\, n_1} + \cdots + n_x/10)}.$$

4. On page 257, the legend to Figure 5.28 should read as follows: (A) Normal stereocilia extending from hair cells (from Angelborg and Engstrom, 1973); (B) noise damaged stereocilia (from Nilsson *et al.*, 1982); (C) organ of corti torn (curled up) from basilar membrane, following exposure to intense impulses (from Hamernik *et al.*, 1985).

The Handbook of Hearing and the Effects of Noise: Physiology, Psychology, and Public Health

Karl D. Kryter

ISBN: 0-12-427455-2

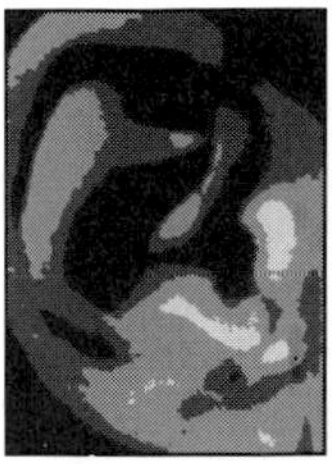

The Handbook of Hearing and the Effects of Noise

Physiology, Psychology, and Public Health

Karl D. Kryter
San Diego State University
San Diego, California

Academic Press
San Diego New York Boston
London Sydney Tokyo Toronto

This book is printed on acid-free paper. ♾

Academic Press, Inc.
A Division of Harcourt Brace & Company
525 B Street, Suite 1900, San Diego, California 92101-4495

United Kingdom Edition published by
Academic Press Limited
24-28 Oval Road, London NW1 7DX

Library of Congress Cataloging-in-Publication Data

Kryter, Karl D.
The handbook of hearing and the effects of noise / by Karl D. Kryter.
p. cm.
Includes bibliographical references and index.
ISBN 0-12-427455-2
1. Noise--Physiological effect. 2. Hearing. 3. Deafness, Noise induced. 4. Noise pollution. I. Title.
QP82.2.N6K798 1994
612.8'5--dc20 94-10454
CIP

PRINTED IN THE UNITED STATES OF AMERICA
94 95 96 97 98 99 EB 9 8 7 6 5 4 3 2 1

For my wife, Grace Irene,
and our family:
Dianne, Victoria, Kathryn,
Myron, Richard, Zachary,
Samuel, Abraham, Jessica,
and Richard II

Contents

Preface

The Handbook of Hearing and the Effects of Noise presents the methods and the results of research for quantitatively describing the major attributes of hearing and the effects of sound and noise on people. This book is intended for students, researchers, and professionals in the fields of experimental psychology, physiology, audiology, otolaryngology, and public health. It contains information of interest to government decision makers, architects, and engineers concerned with criteria, guidelines, and standards for acceptable and safe levels of sound and noise.

Chapters 1–3 cover the basic nature and measurement of sound, the structure and functioning of the ear, and auditory sensations and perceptions. Chapters 4–7 are devoted to research methods and findings pertaining to noise-induced hearing loss, speech communications in noise, assessments of hearing handicaps, compensation for hearing loss, and the conservation of hearing. Chapters 8–10 review and evaluate research findings and theoretical concepts related to: (1) mental and psychomotor work performance in noise, (2) nonauditory system physiological reactions, and sensations in nonauditory sense modalities, from exposure to sound and noise, and (3) psychological reactions and stress-related health disorders in noisy work and residential areas.

This book is dedicated to J. C. R. Licklider, S. S. Stevens, L. L. Beranek, and Halloway Davis, men who are responsible for much of the science of psychological and physiological acoustics, and, as colleagues, greatly influenced my own research interests and career. Since 1939, the author has been engaged in research and teaching related to the neurology of hearing, and psychological and physiological acoustics at: the University of Rochester; Harvard University; Washington University; Bolt, Beranek, and Newman, Inc.; Stanford Research Institute; and during the preparation of this book, as an adjunct professor and lecturer at San Diego State University.

I wish to thank the many authors and publishers who have given me permission to use figures from their publications, and to James R. Young for his counsel on several mathematical expressions presented in the book.

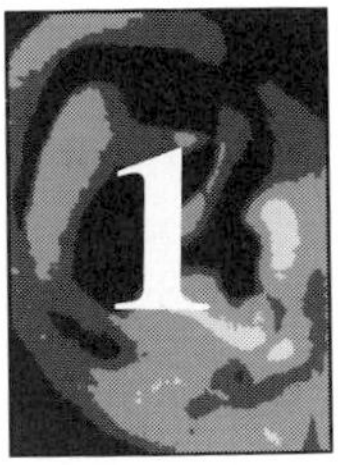

Definitions and Measurement of Noise and Sound

NOISE

In the fields of physics, electronics, neurophysiology, and communication theory, *noise* means signals that bear no information and whose intensities usually vary randomly in time. The word *noise* is used in that sense in physical acoustics. But for our purposes, noise will be defined as audible acoustic energy (or sound) that is unwanted because it has adverse auditory and nonauditory physiological or psychological effects on people.

A large share of the research conducted on the effects of sound as noise is concerned with adverse physiological effects on the ear and hearing that accrue in individuals from exposure to intense sound. In the present book, the adverse psychological effects of sound as noise are the annoyances due to (1) inherently unpleasant sensations of loudness, pitch, duration, and impulsiveness; and (2) interferences with auditory communications, sleep, work performance, and general behavior.

Sounds may be wanted by some people, or in some contexts, when they contain learned information that is of either aesthetic or practical interest (e.g., music, speech); while for other people, or in other contexts, the same sounds may be considered as noise because they interfere with sleep or the hearing of other sounds. In either case, some such sounds may also be capable of causing loss in hearing sensitivity. Such losses are to be evaluated in this book.

Although much of the scientific research on noise has been on fundamental physiological, perceptual, and behavior-interference aspects, there are suspected sequela on mental and general health. Research, to be discussed in the later chapters of the book, has been conducted to explore whether annoyances and stress from the behavior-interference effects, and related social interactions are correlated with physiological stresses that are a putative cause of some mental and bodily health disorders.

SOUND

Frequency

Before it is anything else, noise is sound—a succession in time of varying-intensity waves of pressure. The diaphragm of a loudspeaker creates sound when, in moving outward, it pushes air particles at that place in space closer together, and when, in moving backward, it leaves a partial vacuum and rarefaction of air particles at that place (see Fig. 1.1). This positive air pressure, compared with normal, followed by a reduced air pressure, compared with normal, travels through the air like a wave that may push back and forth an eardrum on which it falls. Acoustical pressure waves can be transmitted by particles in air, solids, or liquids.

Sound can be generated by any vibrating physical object, such as a violin string, parts of a truck, the column of air puffing from the exhaust of a jet engine, the muzzle of a gun, or the mouth of a person talking. The number of times per second the air pressure increases above, then decreases below, and then returns to normal pressure is defined as the frequency in hertz (Hz) [also referred to as *cycles per second* (cps)]. For the human listener, *sound*

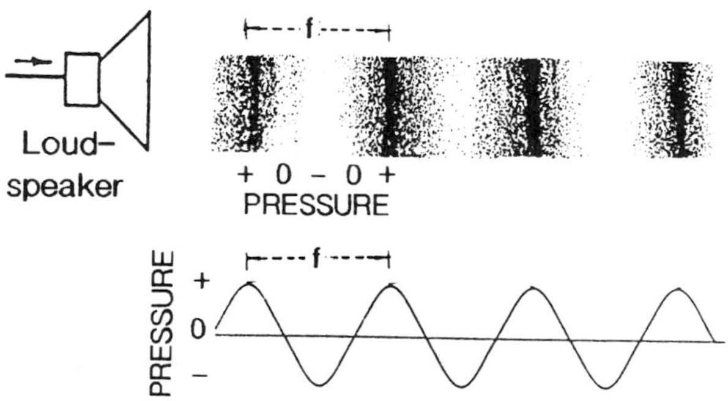

FIGURE 1.1 Upper segment: Illustration of condensation and rarefaction of air particles in time from movement of loudspeaker diaphragm. Number of cycles per second pattern repeats and is called frequency, *f*, expressed in hertz (Hz). Lower segment shows pressure, relative to ambient-air pressure, exerted by air particles on microphone of a SLM during condensation–rarefaction phases.

is defined as acoustic energy between 2 and 20,000 Hz, the typical frequency limits of the ear. The lowest frequency of sound that has a pitch-like quality is ~20 Hz.

Strictly speaking, sound can be said to exist only when the acoustical waves have stimulated and been perceived, or responded to, by an organism. The word *sound* is commonly applied to both the psychological perceptions of hearing (e.g., the sound of a whistle, the sound of music), and the physical, acoustical disturbance (sound wave of pressure). As indicated above, in the context of this book, the word *noise* will refer to unwanted sound.

Sound Pressure

The degree to which the particles of air at a point in space (e.g., at the eardrum of a person) are compressed and rarefied from their normal ambient state is called the pressure p of sound at an instant i in time pi [see Fig. 1.2 and Eq. (1.1)]. According to standards (ANSI, 1983; IEC, 1965, 1973), pressure is measured in newtons per square meter, or pascals (Pa). The reference pressure used with standardized sound-level meters (SLMs) is 20 μPa. Physical and other subjective quantities or attributes of sound are generally measured relative to (abbreviated as "re" throughout) a reference amount of that quantity or attribute, as shown for pressure by the vertical ordinate of Fig. 1.2.

$$P_t^2 = 1/x(pi_1^2 \cdots + pi_x^2), \tag{1.1}$$

where t is a specified period of time and x is the number, 1 through x, of instants (i s) of pressures p samples of pressures taken over the specified period of time. This is the average of the instantaneous pressures squared for the specified period of time. (Definitions of *instantaneous* are generally related to a system of measurement. An electron beam on an oscilloscope

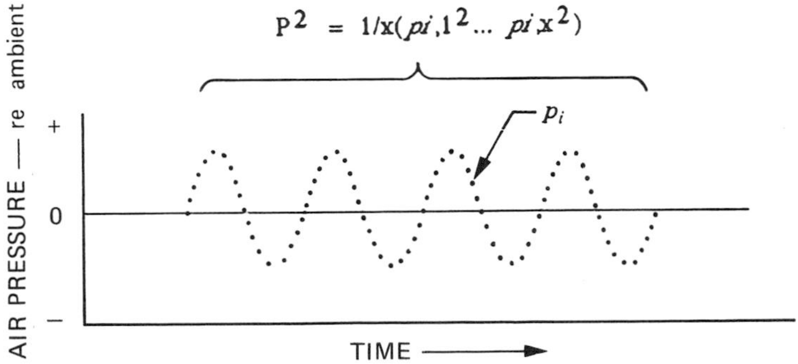

FIGURE 1.2 Representation of samples 1 through x of instantaneous sound pressures pi. Summing and averaging the instantaneous sound pressures squared over a specified period of time gives the root-mean-square (rms) pressure P in that period of time.

is a means of measuring nearly instantaneous sound pressures. However, as will be discussed in later chapters, the frequency bandwidth of sound over which the ear is responsive and the response characteristics of the sensory–neural elements therein are such that sound pressure need be measured, for even extreme conditions, by a sample taken over no less than about a 0.00002-s interval of time. In the formulas and discussions to follow, *i* is used generically as a symbol for a time interval used for sampling sound pressures. Throughout the text, except as otherwise noted, s, second; min, minute; and h, hour.

Sound Energy

Sound energy is used here in the general sense of the ability to force, over time, particles of air in a unit of space a specified distance and with a specified velocity. The pressure and frequency components as measured generally adequately express, for the sense of hearing, all but the temporal variable in sound energy. The integral of $pi^2\, dt$ is proportional to physical sound energy, and is labeled *p,* and capital *P* (or *sp* and *SP*) with lowercase, italicized *p* and *pi* reserved for an instantaneous pressure. The act of squaring *pi* reflects the fact that the work required to rarefy the air (the negative pressure) is the same as that to compress (the positive pressure) the air by a like amount. As far as the sense of hearing is concerned, it is the energy from the pressure exerted over the approximate square centimeter of the eardrum that is effective.

The mean, or average [root mean square (rms)] of the squared pressures, pi^2 at a number of instants in a longer period of time, labeled *P,* or *SP,* is proportional to the sound energy in the given period of time. Even an "instantaneous" sound pressure requires some finite period of time and contains energy.

According to Fourier's mathematical theorem of spectrum analysis, the sampling rate *n* or instants in time *pi* is measured must be at least 2 times the highest frequency in the sound signal in order to have the measurement properly reflect the energy in all frequencies present in the signal. This summing and averaging process is accomplished, with varying degrees of accuracy, by means of standard sound level meters.

For our purposes, the air—over practical ranges of temperature and humidity conditions—is presumed to act as a pure resistance to sound waves of different audible frequencies. The basic period of time traditionally used for most measurements of sounds and noise in terms of how they affect people is 1 s. However, as will be discussed later, 0.5 s is a more appropriate, general, interval because of certain response characteristics of the ear to sound.

It is common practice to express sound pressure level (SPL, or simply *L*) in a unit called the *decibel* (dB). In acoustics the decibel is 10 times the logarithm, base 10, of the ratio of two entities, such as pressure, that are related to sound energy and sound power. For sound pressure, these entities are the measured pressure, P_{meas}, and the reference pressure, 20 μPa. Throughout this book, unless otherwise specified, logarithms are to the base 10.

$$\text{SPL, dB} = 10 \log_{10} (P^2_{meas}/20\ \mu\text{Pa}^2), \tag{1.2}$$

where P is the rms over a specified period, e.g., 1 s, 0.5 s, or the actual duration, if shorter, of instantaneous pressures, *pi*.

The relations between SPL in decibels and various units in which pressure P can be expressed are shown in Fig. 1.3. It is often the maximum 1-s level that occurs during a relatively long-duration noise event that is of interest. This is designated as SPL_{max} (or L_{max}) in decibels. For sake of brevity in mathematical formulas, L will generally be used, when appropriate, to express level; but in the text, depending on context, the term *sound-pressure level* (or SPL) will be used unless accompanied by a numerical value, e.g., L 70 dB, L 70, or simply 70 dB.

For some purposes, as will be done later, it is common practice to also calculate decibels for other quantities related to the energy in an exposure to a sound event. For example, the number of seconds of duration of exposure to a given intensity relative to a specified reference duration, and/or the number of exposures to noises of the same intensity and duration.

Effective Sound Energy

The concept of effective sound energy, as distinct from physical sound energy, is an important key to the understanding of the hearing process and the effects of noise on hearing. Adjustments to these physical sound measurements necessary to properly express their effective energy with respect to hearing are developed in later chapters.

MEASURES OF SOUND EVENTS

The following measures of sound have been developed for the general purposes of relating, with respect to its effects on people, the amount of sound energy of (1) a single sound event or (2) a number of events over time, such as a day, or even years.

1. *Event exposure level L_{ex} in decibels.* Most sounds or noises are of duration longer than 1 s (i.e., >1-s duration), and their effects on people are related to not only their highest level of intensity in 1 s or less (≤1 s) but also to some degree of summation of the energy over time, e.g., the sound of an airplane flying overhead, or of an automobile passing by. The term L_{ex} is generally used to indicate the overall energy of such noise events. *Sound*

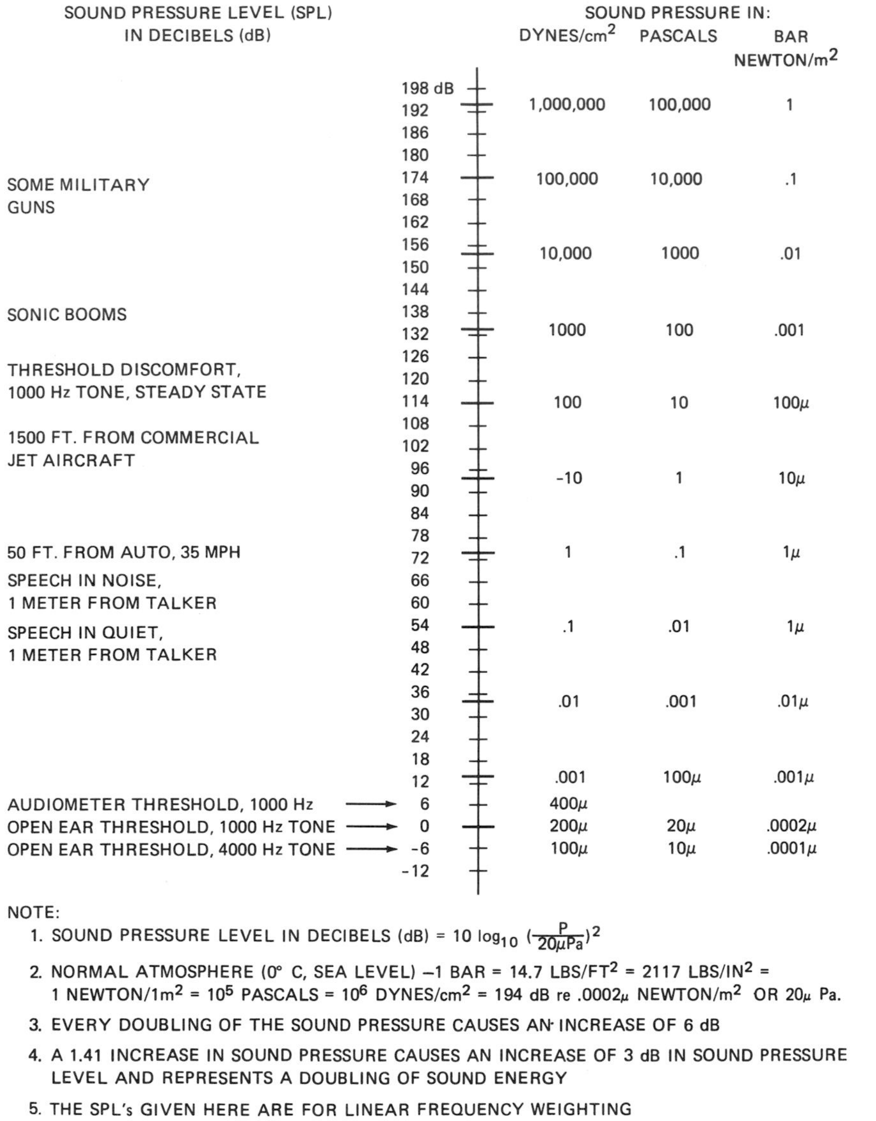

FIGURE 1.3 Sound-pressure level in decibels as a function of various units of sound pressure. Approximate SPLs for certain sounds and noises are indicated.

exposure level (SEL) and *single-event-noise exposure level* (SENEL) are other names for L_{ex} to be found in the literature.

$$L_{ex,N} = 10 \log(10^{(L_{N_1} + \cdots + L_{N_x}/10)}), \quad \text{dB} \tag{1.3}$$

where N_1 is the SPL in the first second and N_x is the SPL in the last second, of the sound event. For practical reasons related to the logarithmic character of decibels, as well as other reasons to be discussed later, it is sometimes sufficient and appropriate to sum only SPLs between the times the sound is within 10 dB of the maximum, or peak, SPL reached by the sound.

2. *Multiple-event sound equivalent level, in decibels*. The cumulative effects of the energy in repetitions of the same or different sounds within a day, or even over days and years of exposure, are often of primary concern in the assessment of real-life noise environments. For these purposes, a quantity labeled L_{eq} has been developed.

This measure of exposure is proportional to the sum of the sound energy in 1 s, or 0.5 s, if so indicated, SPLs summed over a fixed, specified longer period of time (e.g., 1 h, 8 h, 1 day, 1 year) and then averaged by the total duration, in seconds, or, half-seconds, of the specified period of time. Again, it is understood that the SPLs in this process represent average (rms) of samples of the instantaneous pressures in the short-term intervals, 1 s, 0.5 s, or other, as specified. (The specification of the short-term intervals becomes especially important, as will be discussed later, in the evaluation of methods of assessing the effects of so-called impulse noise on hearing loss.)

Accordingly, $L_{eq,T}$ is the level that would have had to be present during the specified long period of time T at a continuous, steady intensity in order to add up to, or be equivalent to, the total amount of sound energy actually present during that entire period, of noise(s) that were of either a steady or irregular level of intensity. In decibels, L_{eq} can be expressed in ways such as the following:

$$L_{eq,T} = 10 \log(1/x\ 10^{(L_{1\,s} + \cdots + L_{xs})/10)}, \text{ dB}, \tag{1.4}$$

where $L_{1\,s}$ is the SPL in the first second, and $L_{x\,s}$ is the SPL in the last second during a specified period of time in seconds (synonymous with $L_{ex,N}$ for continuous noise).

$$L_{eq,T,N1} = L_{ex,N1} + 10 \log x + 10 \log (1/T), \tag{1.5}$$

where $L_{ex,N1}$ is the level of similar noise events occurring during the specified period of time T in seconds, and x is the number of such occurrences. Table 1.1 can be used to find the number of decibels (10 log x) corresponding to a given number of similar events.

$$L_{eq,T,N_1} - N_x = 10 \log(1/T^{(10(L_{ex,N1} + \cdots + L_{ex,N_x})/10)}, \text{ dB}, \tag{1.6}$$

where $L_{ex,N1}$ is the first L_{ex} value and L_{ex,N_x} is the last L_{ex,N_x} value for each $L_{ex,N}$ present during the specified period of time T in seconds.

The reason for using the decibel is that the very large ranges of sound pressures (from less than 20 millionths' of a Pascal to over a hundred thousand Pascals, see Fig. 1.3), and times (fractions of a second to years of exposure) are compressed into a smaller scale of numbers. Numerically equally-sized steps in the compressed decibel scale reflect exponentially-increasing sized steps in the units of the quantity, pressure or time, being measured.

TABLE 1.1 For Adding Decibel Levels of Sounds with Random Phase Relations

Difference between L_1–L_2	Add, to higher level	Difference between L_1–L_2	Add, to higher level	Difference between L_1–L_2	Add, to higher level	Difference between L_1–L_2	Add, to higher level
0.0–0.1	3.0	1.7–1.9	2.2	4.1–4.3	1.4	8.0–8.6	0.6
0.2–0.3	2.9	2.0–2.1	2.1	4.4–4.7	1.3	8.7–9.6	0.5
0.4–0.5	2.8	2.2–2.4	2.0	4.8–5.1	1.2	9.7–10.7	0.4
0.6–0.7	2.7	2.5–2.7	1.9	5.2–5.6	1.1	10.8–12.2	0.3
0.8–0.9	2.6	2.8–3.0	1.8	5.7–6.1	1.0	12.3–14.5	0.2
1.0–1.2	2.5	3.1–3.3	1.7	6.2–6.6	0.9	14.6–19.3	0.1
1.3–1.4	2.4	3.4–3.6	1.6	6.7–7.2	0.8	19.4->	0.0
1.5–1.6	2.3	3.7–4.0	1.5	7.3–7.9	0.7		

Step 1: Find the difference between the number of decibels to be added together.
Step 2: Find the amount in above table corresponding to this difference.
Step 3: Add this amount to the highest of the two levels to find the decibel sum.

To add a third decibel level, find the difference between the sum, as found, between the first two levels and the third level and find the amount in above table corresponding to this difference. Add this amount to the sum of the first two levels. Proceed with additional levels as needed.

In the text to follow, the units for L(SPL), $L_{ex,N}$, and $L_{eq,T}$ will always be in decibels (dB). For this reason, the dB label following the number of decibels of L, $L_{ex,N}$, or $L_{eq,T}$ will be understood and generally not given, i.e., L 70 dB, $L_{ex,N}$ 70 dB, and $L_{eq,T}$ 70 dB will usually be expressed as L 70, $L_{ex,N}$ 70, and $L_{eq,T\,70}$. *Note:* L_{eq} is sometimes written without the T component indicated when discussing sound events of similar, understood durations, or the levels summed over similar, understood overall durations.

FREQUENCY-BAND MEASURES OF SOUND ENERGY

Pure Tones and Complex, Broadband Sounds

When the sound pressure varies in a very regular way at the same unvarying frequency, a pure tone is said to be present. When more than one tone, or frequency, is present, the sound has a complex waveform (see Fig. 1.4). Most everyday sounds and noises, such as speech, music, from the operation of machinery, the firing of guns, etc. have broadband spectra. By this is meant that the sound contains low-, middle-, and high-frequency components. If the components are sufficiently separated, a number of tonal pitches can be heard; if one of these components is more intense than the others, a somewhat predominating tonal character to the overall sound is generally perceived.

One way of illustrating this frequency band spectrum of a sound, or noise, is to consider the kind of sound that comes from a piano when a large number of the keys are simultaneously struck, each key causing a different tonal frequency to be emitted. The noise of an airplane engine, caused by many different vibrating parts and air exhausts, will usually have different and

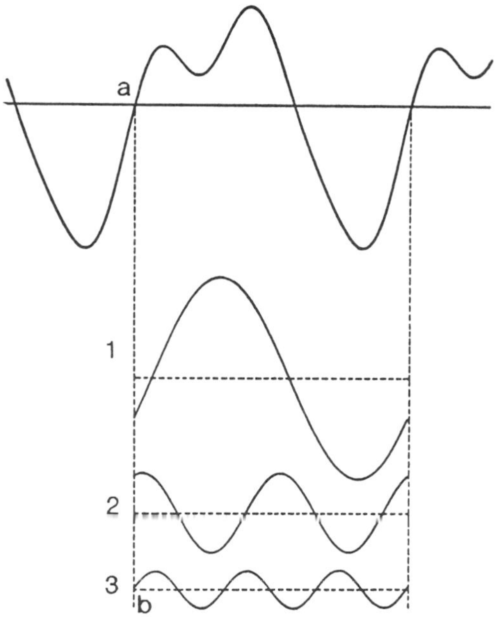

FIGURE 1.4 Waveforms of pure tones singly and in combinations to form a complex sound or noise. By shifting the phase relations (the time of start of positive movement from ambient pressure) of any of the pure-tone components (1, 2, or 3) with respect to each other, the envelope of the complex waveform (top, a) would change, but its frequency content would not. (From Miller, 1926.)

time-varying amounts of energy at more frequencies in its spectrum than the sound of the piano, even with all strings struck simultaneously. However, both of these sources emit a broadband spectrum sound. This is not to say that a single frequency or tone is not, at times, considered as a noise, even a very objectionable one, but that, by and large, most sounds and noises are broadband in nature.

OVERALL FREQUENCIES WEIGHTING METHOD

The ear has the ability to hear individual parts of broadband sounds and also to respond to the sound over all frequencies. However, the ear is more responsive to some frequencies in the sound spectrum than to other frequencies. Figure 1.5 shows the results of experiments in which subjects were presented with, one at a time, individual $^1/_3$-octave bands of sound frequencies (shown by the small horizontal bars) and asked to adjust its intensity level until it sounded as noisy (solid curve) or as loud (dashed curve) as the $^1/_3$-octave band centered at 1000 Hz. The higher-frequency bands (1000 Hz) had to be made physically less intense (lower SPL in decibels) than the

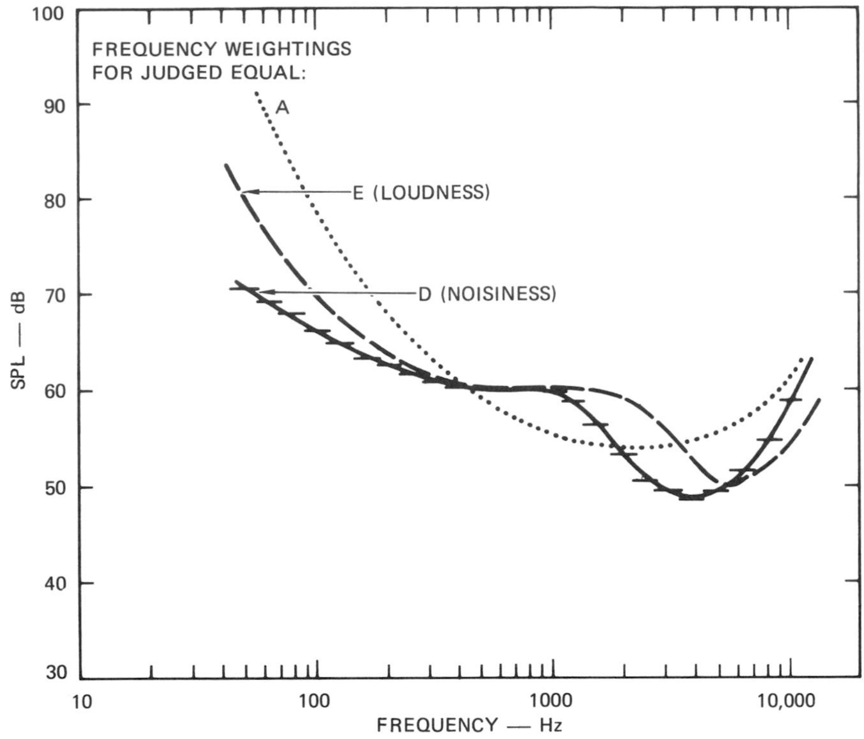

FIGURE 1.5 Relative frequency weightings for loudness, perceived noisiness, and *A*-weighting of SLM. The short horizontal bars on the noisiness contour represent narrow-frequency band judged for loudness and noisiness. The D_2 weighting differs from D_1 in that it is modified at frequencies below 355 Hz to better agree with judgments based on critical bandwidths than 1/3-octave bands.

lower-frequency bands in order to sound equal in noisiness and loudness to the band centered at 1000 Hz. The frequencies included in each 1/3-octave band are given in the left-hand column of Table 1.2.

Sound-level meters (SLMs) are built to integrate, over brief moving windows of time, the energy in all the frequencies in the sound. This "window" is usually $\leq$1 s long, depending on the meter setting (the "slow" setting supposedly is for about 1 s). SLMs are also built with filter networks that allow different weightings to be given to the intensity found in different parts of the frequency spectrum of a sound. The relative values of a standardized frequency weightings are given in Table 1.2. Although incorporated in standard SLMs, the *B*-weighting is not used for most noise-assessment purposes.

As shown in Fig. 1.5, the *A*-weighting follows somewhat the relative shape of the equal-loudness and equal-noisiness contours and has become the most widely used method of measuring broadband sounds to predict how loud they will sound. Accordingly, two noises that have the same *A*-weighted

TABLE 1.2 Cutoff Frequencies and Center Frequencies of Preferred 1/3-Octave-Band Filters and Frequency Weightings for Sound-Level Meters

Cutoff frequencies, Hz	Center frequencies, Hz	*A*-Weighting, dB	*B*-Weighting, dB	*C*-Weighting, dB	D_1-Weighting, dB	D_2-Weighting, dB
45–56	50	−30.2	−11.7	−1.3	−12	−19
56–71	63	−26.1	−9.4	−0.8	−11	−17
71–90	80	−22.3	−7.4	−0.5	−9	−14
90–112	100	−19.1	−5.7	−0.3	−7	−11
112–140	125	−16.2	−4.3	−0.2	−6	−9
140–180	160	−13.2	−3.0	−0.1	−5	−7
180–224	200	−10.8	−2.1	0	−3	−5
224–280	250	−8.0	−1.4	0	−2	−3
280–355	315	−6.5	−0.9	0	−1	−2
355–450	400	−4.8	−0.6	0	0	0
450–560	500	−3.3	−0.3	0	0	0
560–710	630	−1.9	−0.2	0	0	0
710–900	800	−0.8	−0.1	0	0	0
900–1,120	1,000	0	0	0	0	0
1,120–1,400	1,250	0.5	−0.1	−0.1	2	2
1,400–1,800	1,600	1.0	−0.1	−0.1	6	6
1,800–2,240	2,000	1.2	−0.2	−0.2	8	8
2,240–2,800	2,500	1.2	−0.3	−0.3	10	10
2,800–3,550	3,150	1.2	−0.5	−0.5	11	11
3,550–4,500	4,000	1.0	−0.8	−0.8	11	11
4,500–5,600	5,000	0.5	−1.3	−1.3	10	10
5,600–7,100	6,300	−0.2	−2.0	−2.0	9	9
7,100–9,000	8,000	−1.1	−3.0	−3.0	6	6
9,000–11,020	10,000	−2.5	−4.3	−4.3	3	3

A

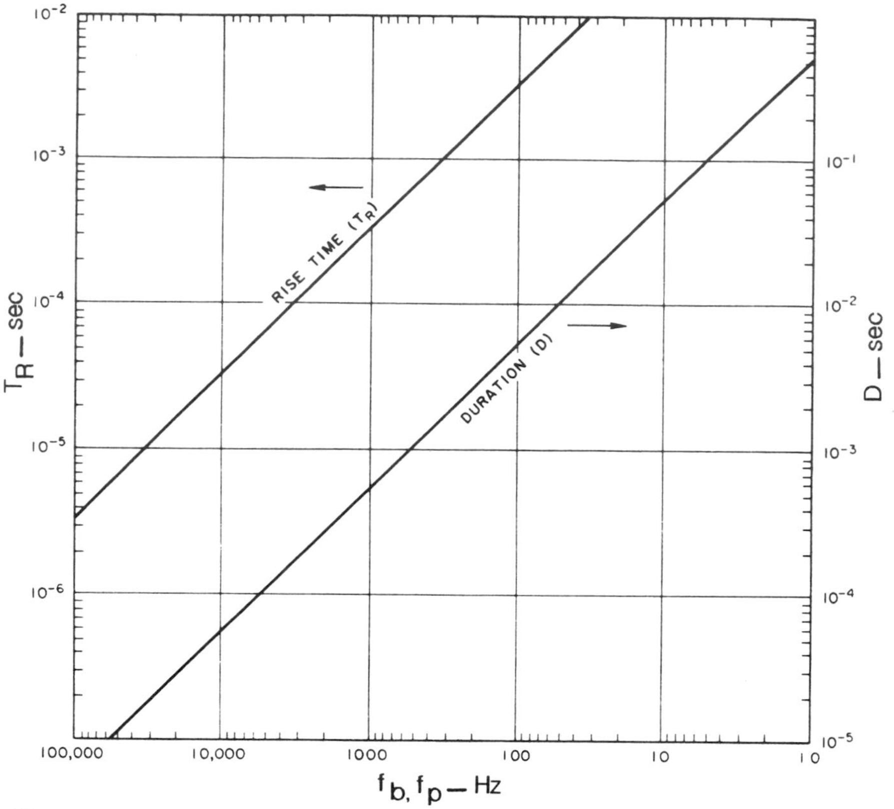

10^{-2}
10^{-3}
10^{-4}
10^{-5}
10^{-6}
T_R — sec
10^{-1}
10^{-2}
10^{-3}
10^{-4}
10^{-5}
D — sec
RISE TIME (T_R)
DURATION (D)
100,000
10,000
1000
100
10
1.0
f_b, f_p — Hz

B

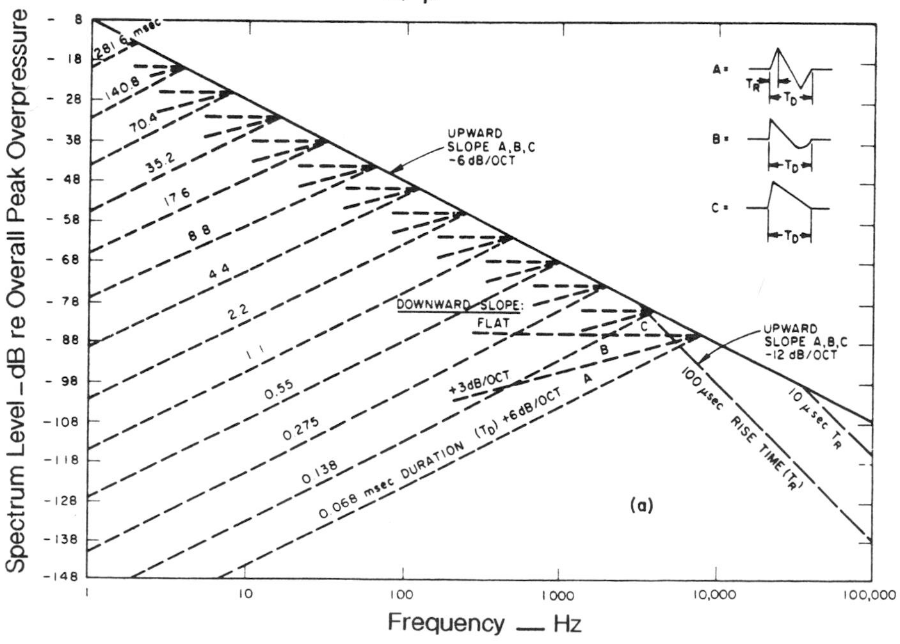

Spectrum Level – dB re Overall Peak Overpressure
- 8
- 18
- 28
- 38
- 48
- 58
- 68
- 78
- 88
- 98
- 108
- 118
- 128
- 138
- 148
281.6 msec
140.8
70.4
35.2
17.6
8.8
4.4
2.2
1.1
0.55
0.275
0.138
0.068 msec DURATION (T_D) +6 dB/OCT
UPWARD SLOPE A, B, C -6 dB/OCT
DOWNWARD SLOPE: FLAT
+3 dB/OCT
A
B
C
UPWARD SLOPE A, B, C -12 dB/OCT
100 μsec RISE TIME (T_R)
10 μsec T_R
A =
T_R
T_D
B =
T_D
C =
T_D
(a)
1
10
100
1000
10,000
100,000
Frequency — Hz

level will presumably sound equally loud to the average listener. Some of the limitations to this generalization are discussed in Chapter 3. For a number of strictly acoustical purposes, it is often more appropriate to use the more linear, "flat," or *C*-weighting networks.

In order to avoid ambiguity when decibel values are cited, frequency-weighting letter designation should be given: SPL_A, L_A, dB_A; SPL_C, L_C, dB_C *C*-weighting represents, for the measurement of sound with respect to its effect on typical hearing range (50–10,000 Hz), essentially linear, or uniform, weighting over that effective spectrum. As such, it is common practice, in that context, to refer to the level as dB, rather than dB_C.

A further shorthand designation is to attach, when appropriate, the subscript "max" or "pk" to the unit (e.g., $L_{A\,max}$, max dB_A or $dB_{A\,max}$, $dB_{A\,pk}$) when referring to the maximum or peak 1-s SPL that occurs during a noise event. Without a letter identification, *L* indicates linear, or equal-for all-frequencies weighting, or as noted, because of the limited-frequency bandwidth of the ear, *C*-weighting. The reader will often find in the literature the quantities L_A; L_{ex}; L_{eq}; dB_A written plainly without italics or subscripting, i.e., LA; Lex; Leq; dBA and dB(A).

In the text to follow, the frequency weighting used in the measurement of *L* of the quantities L_{ex} and L_{eq} is indicated by adding the letter designation, if any, after *L*, such as L_{Acx}, L_{Dcx}, L_{cx}, and L_{ex}. Again, because the units will always be decibels, the dB label following the number of decibels of L_{ex}, L_{Aex}, L_{Aeq}, etc. need not be given; thus L_{Cex} 70 dB, L_{Aeq} 70 dB, etc. may be expressed as L_{Cex} 70, L_{Aeq} 70, and so on.

The frequency range covered by most SLMs is from about 15 to 11,020 Hz (1/3-octave band center frequencies of 20–10,000 Hz). L_C is sometimes referred to as *overall (frequencies) sound-pressure level* (OASPL) and *L*, linear, because over that range the different frequencies are equally weighted; however, a linear setting on a meter usually covers a wider range of unweighted frequencies. [The use of the designation "OASPL" without a letter designation is, however, deprecated.)

ONE-THIRD-OCTAVE-BAND METHOD

A common procedure for measuring broadband noises, besides that of overall frequencies with a standard SLM, is the following: (1) transduce, by a microphone, a broadband sound into an electrical signal that can be filtered by electronic means into, and measured as the SPL, in decibels, in 1/3-octave bands; (2) adjust the SPL for each band in accordance with the *A*-, or *C*- (if desired) weighting pertaining to each frequency band (Table 1.2); and (3) sum, on an energy basis, these 1/3-octave-band SPLs.

FIGURE 1.6 (A) Frequencies as function of duration *D* and rise time T_R. (B) General spectrum envelope of various waveforms (inserts *a*, *b*, and *c*); see text. (From Kryter, 1985.)

To add these decibel values on an energy basis, the sum of their antilogs must first be found, and then converted back to a decibel level. However, this process can be avoided through the use of Table 1.1. The result is the weighted SPL in decibels over all frequencies, as would also be measured on an SLM with *A*- or *C*-weighting. The individual band values give the noise control engineer or equipment designer more insight than overall SLM readings into what design changes might be made in order to effect a noise spectrum that is less loud or noisy. The band spectra have, as we shall see, some other advantages and disadvantages.

IMPULSES

A sound is often called "impulsive" when its intensity increases at a very rapid rate and is of brief duration. As will be noted latter, in terms of subjective loudness, perceived noisiness, or loss of hearing, an impulse is defined as a segment of sound of <0.5 s duration that exceeds the preceding, or succeeding (or both) 0.5-s segment(s) by ≥ 5 dB; all other sounds are considered as nonimpulsive.

Impulsiveness is determined largely by the phase relations among the waves of its frequency components. By phase relations is meant the relative position to a point in time of the zero-pressure points of the different frequency components in a complex sound (see Fig. 1.4). When there are a large number of components they coalesce, or may be forced to coalesce, to give waveforms such as seen in the insert in Fig. 1.6B. Gunfire, sonic booms, sharp blows on metal, etc. are examples of sounds with special phase relations among its frequency components.

The spectral content, an important determinant of the loudness and damage effect of an impulse, can be approximated from the graphs given in Fig. 1.6. This is done by entering the top graph of Fig. 1.6 with the rise time T_R and duration D to find, from T_R, the frequency f_b of the point at which the upward slope of the spectrum level (the intensity in hertz) "breaks" from -6 to -12 dB per octave, and, from D, the frequency f_p at which the spectrum reaches its peak intensity (see Fig. 1.6B.) The nature of the negative part, if any, of the illustrated impulses *A, B,* and *C* in Figure 1.6B, influences the rate at which the spectrum level decreases below the frequency of peak intensity. The spectrum levels of the frequencies encompassed under a set of thus determined points and slopes is approximately that of the impulse.

For detailed discussion of physical acoustical theory and measurements the reader is referred to texts and handbooks of Beranek (1949, 1954) and Harris (1957, 1979, 1991), and, for impulsive sounds, Hamernik and Hsueh (1991).

References

ANSI (1983). S1.4-1971. "American National Standard Specification for Sound Level Meters." Am. Natl. Stand. Inst., New York.

Beranek, L. L. (1949). "Acoustic Measurements." Wiley, New York.

Beranek, L. L. (1954). "Acoustics." McGraw-Hill, New York.

Hamernik, R. P., and Hsueh, K. D. (1991). Impulse noise: Some definitions, physical acoustics and other considerations. *J. Acoust. Soc. Am.* **90,** 189–196.

Harris, C. M., ed. (1957, 1979, 1991). "Handbook of Noise Control." McGraw-Hill, New York.

IEC (1965, 1973). "Recommendations for Precision Sound Level Meters," Publ. No. 179. Int. Electrotech. Comm., Geneva.

Kryter, K. D. (1985). "The Effects of Noise on Man," 2nd Ed. Academic Press, Orlando, Florida. (Orig. publ., 1970.)

Miller, D. C. (1926). "The Science of Musical Sounds." Macmillan, New York.

2 Structures and Functions of the Ear

OUTER, MIDDLE, AND INNER EAR

Figure 2.1A is a sketch of the main parts of the human ear. Sound waves, normally reaching the eardrum through the external ear canal, cause the small bony ossicles in the middle ear to vibrate and set into motion the fluid (perilymph) in the cochlea. It is also possible to transmit sound energy to the inner ear via the bone in which the cochlea is imbedded, and thereby set the perilymph fluid into motion. This fluid action causes nerve fibers on the basilar membrane to send neural impulses to higher nerve centers where they are perceived, or "heard," as sound. Figure 2.1B is a more detailed schematic of the coupling of the eardrum of the outer ear to the cochlea of the inner ear by means of the ossicles of the middle ear.

In classical auditory theory, the principal analysis of sound with respect to the physical dimensions of frequency, intensity, and phase takes place in the inner ear, or cochlea. The sound frequencies, and their relative intensities, that reach the cochlea are limited largely by the outer and middle ear. This is shown in Fig. 2.2A for the outer ear and in Fig. 2.2B for the middle ear. As seen in Fig. 2.2A, the outer ear amplifies frequencies above ~1500 Hz, relative to lower frequencies; and the middle ear somewhat flattens the frequency response for frequencies above ~500 Hz. Thus, it appears that

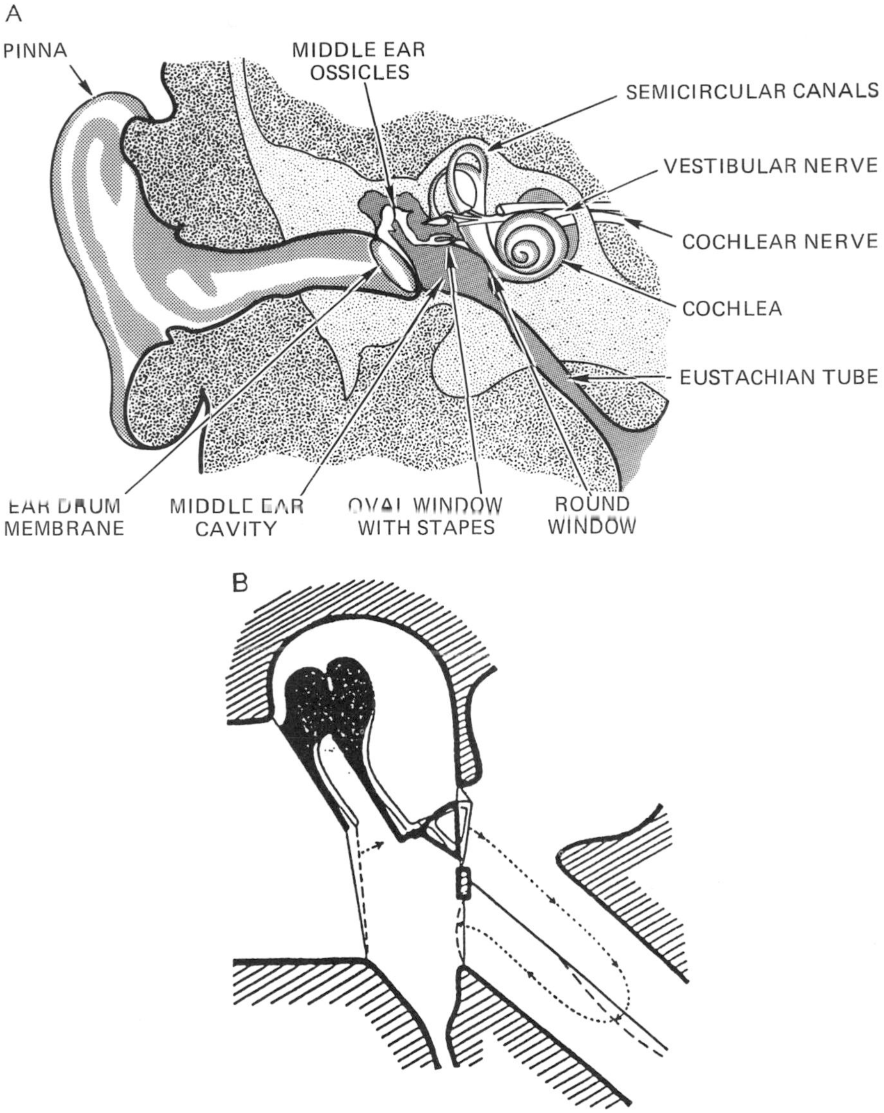

FIGURE 2.1 (A) Parts of the external, middle, and inner ear. (After Zemlin, 1968). (B) Schematic diagram of tympanic, drum, membrane, ossicles, and basilar membrane in cochlea. Solid lines show positions of those structures at rest, dash lines show their position following inward displace of drum by a sound wave. (From Stevens and Davis, 1938).

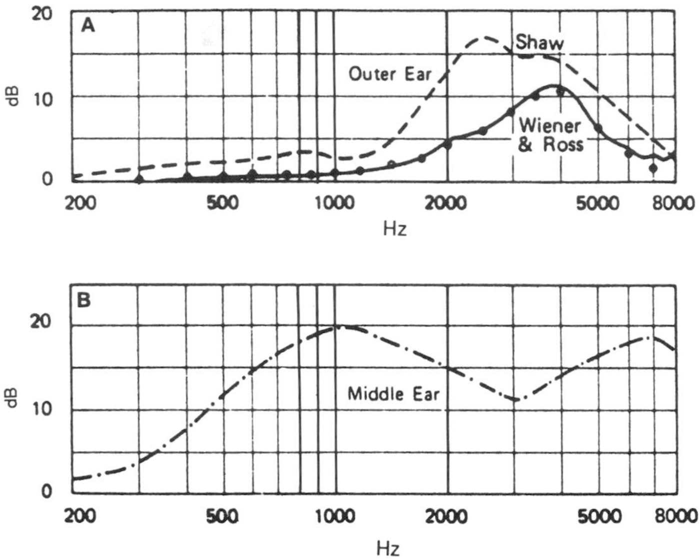

FIGURE 2.2 Frequency transmission characteristic of the (A) outer ear, upper graph; (B) middle ear, lower graph (after Møller, 1965; from Bruel, 1977).

the differential sensitivity of the ear found for different sound frequencies is determined primarily by acoustical resonance and diffraction of sound around the head and in the outer ear, and by the sound transmission characteristics of structures of the middle ear.

The outer and middle ear not only transmit the pressure waveform of the sound to the inner ear, but in so doing also protect the inner ear from very intense sounds. In that regard, the middle ear (1) prevents the transmission to the inner ear of slow, low-frequency, pressure waves because the slowly developing wave reaches the middle-ear cavity and inner surface of the eardrum via the mouth and eustachian tube approximately in phase with the pressure wave at the outer surface of the drum via the ear canal, although somewhat attenuated in level; this tends to prevent a normal inward movement of the drum from the pressure in the ear canal; (2) by rupturing of the eardrum so that, usually until it heals, it does not transmit sound as efficiently; and (3) when presented with fairly high-intensity pressure waves, small muscles in the middle ear can contract and stiffen the ossicular chain and attenuate the transmission of some frequencies of sound. This action, called the *aural reflex,* will be discussed later.

Also, with very intense sound, the ossicular chain appears to rotate from its normal axis in a way that limits, or even reduces, the pressure level reaching the inner ear. The mass and stiffness of the ossicular chain prevent transmission of a pressure wave with a rise time of $<50\ \mu s$. The time durations, from 200 ms to $50\ \mu s$, correspond to the period of the frequencies of 5–20,000 Hz.

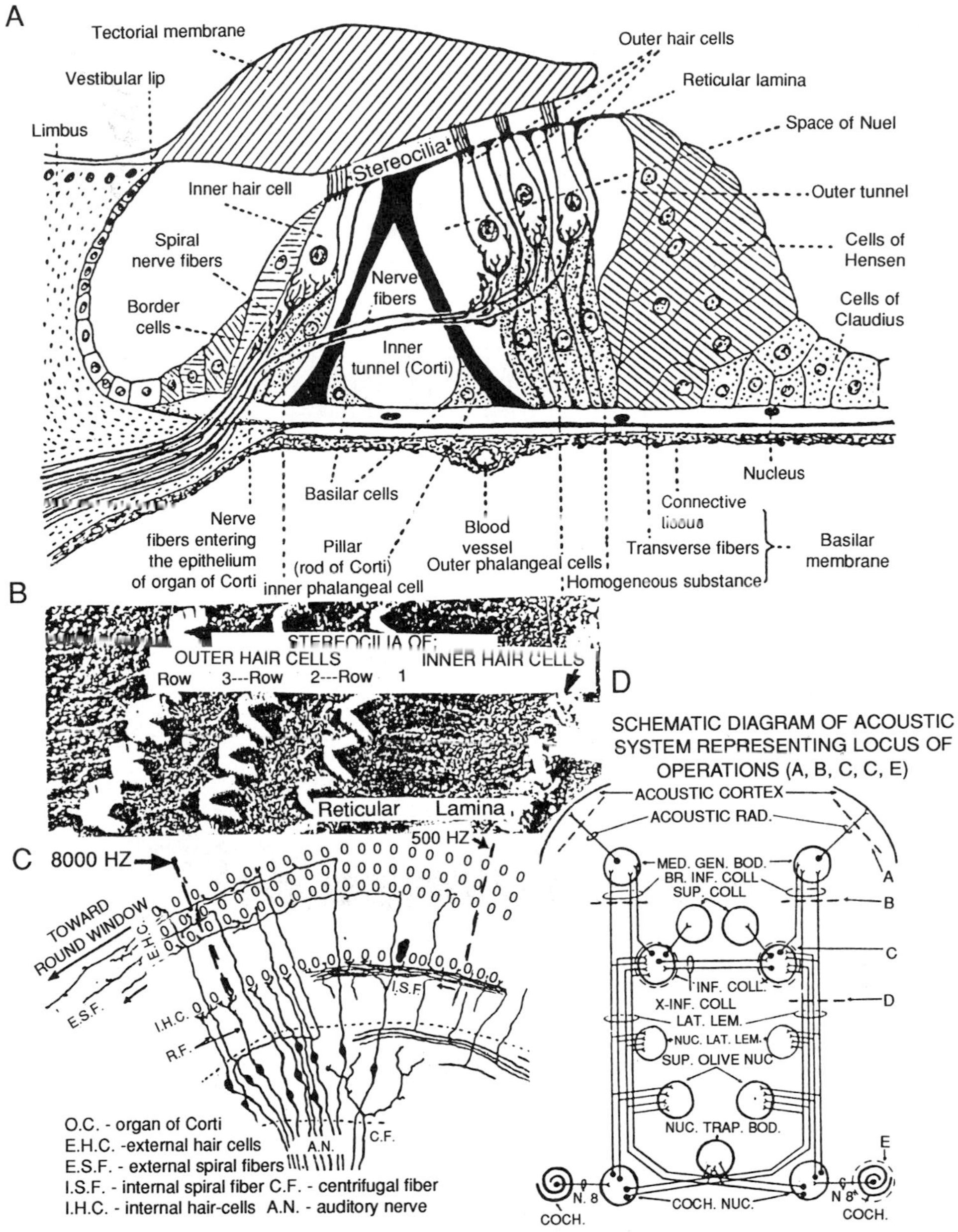

FIGURE 2.3 (A) Drawing of enlarged cross section of the cochlea. (From Rasmussen, 1947). (B) Downward view, by electron microscopy, of reticular lamina of basilar membrane with stereocilia, white structures, of hair cells emerging upwards. Tectorial membrane has been removed. (After Kessel and Kardon, 1979). (C) Diagram of the innervation of hair cells on organ of corti. (From Lorento de No, 1933.) (D) Schematic of auditory system nerve centers. (From Kryter and Ades, 1943).

Inner Ear

A schematic drawing of a side view of a transverse slice of the basilar membrane of the cochlea is shown of Fig. 2.3A. Figure 2.3B is an electron-micrographic view of the top of the cilia protruding from inner and outer hair cells in the basilar membrane, and Fig. 2.3C is a diagram of the innervation of the hair cells. It is believed that the cilia on these hair cells are bent or moved by turbulences created in the cochlear fluid from traveling waves caused by pumping action on that fluid by the ossicles in response to sound waves moving the eardrum back and forth.

As a result, nerve fibers attached to the hair cells somehow cause, or allow to be generated, neural–electric impulses that are transmitted to the auditory centers of the brain stem and brain. There are approximately 30,000 hair cells spread out from the base to apex (*helicotrema*) of the basilar membrane. These hair cells are arranged in three outer, or external, rows and one inner row as shown in Fig. 2.3B. (Some of the neurophysiology and theory of this process will be discussed further in Chapter 5).

CODING OF INFORMATION BY THE EAR

Except for certain startle reflexes, the pitches, loudness, or other sensations of sounds as they occur in time depend on stimulations of neural centers in the brain. The role of the ear is, of course, to deliver to the brain, and to a limited extent some other systems of the body, information of the changing frequency–intensity content of sound as needed to generate auditory sensations. However, a neural impulse is an all-or-nothing event with, for similar-sized nerve fibers, undistinguishing features that would allow for identification by higher neural centers, of the sensory receptor initiating the impulse—whether in the ear, eye, skin, or muscle. Energy specific to the neural system, and not to the sound or other stimulating agent, is all that is available to the brain.

Accordingly, various explanations of how the brain "hears" different pitches and loudnesses when the ear is stimulated have been offered over the years (see Stevens and Davis, 1938; Wever, 1949; Zwislocki, 1981; see also compilations of theoretical reviews in Tobias, 1970; Tobias and Schubert, 1981; Møller, 1973). In the simplest concepts, the attribute of loudness is ascribed to the number and/or rate at which neural impulses are generated at specific places on the basilar membrane; that of pitch to stimulation of specific points or areas in the higher auditory nerve centers that are coupled to specific regions on the basilar membrane of the cochlea, plus action of efferent connections among hair cells and auditory neural centers.

Von Békésy (1943) demonstrated that when different frequencies are introduced into the cochlea, resonant-type turbulences are created at different locations along the basilar membrane, with higher frequencies causing turbulences that stimulate the sensorineural hair cells located near the base of the cochlea, with the lower frequencies causing fluid disturbances at progressively greater distances from the base, towards the apex. Figures 2.4A and 2.4B illustrate these findings and the location of general frequency regions along the basilar membrane.

The auditory system is capable, however, of perceiving pitch changes, trills, beats, etc., from frequency changes in an acoustic stimulus that are much narrower than the gross hydromechanical patterns observed by von Bekesy. This ability can be explained by theories that neural networks in the cochlea, brain stem, and brain allows for audible discriminations among

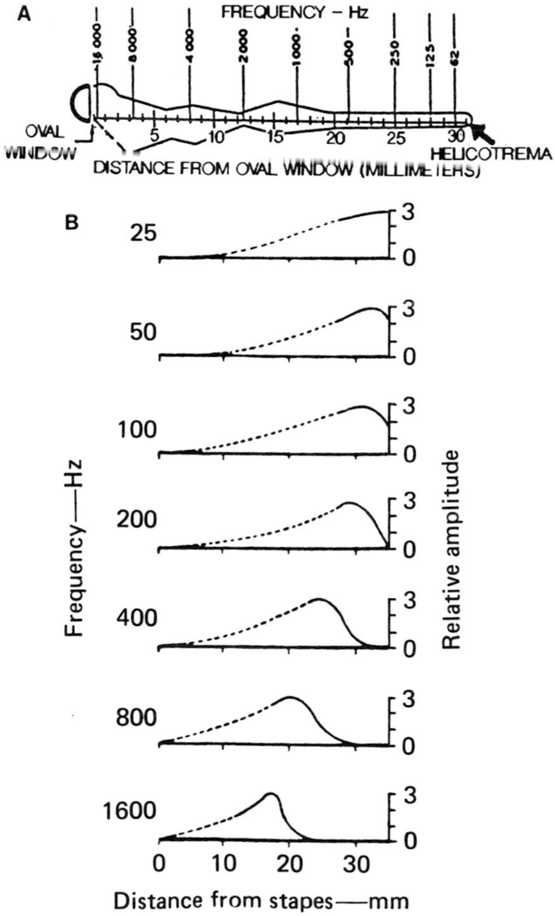

FIGURE 2.4 (A) Approximate distance from oval window of place on basilar membrane of maximum turbulence from different frequencies. (B) The stapes were driven at a constant amplitude at different frequencies. The maximum displacement amplitude moves toward the apex, heliocotrema, as the frequency is decreased. (From von Békésy, 1943. Copyright 1943 by the American Psychological Association. Adapted by permission of the author.)

the components of complex sounds through autocorrelation functions that are based on temporal cues and periodicities within complex acoustical signals (Licklider, 1959; Zwislocki, 1986; Duifuis *et al.*, 1988; Plomp, 1988; Zwicker, 1988.)

These theories would seem to describe satisfactory mechanisms for mediating pitch perception and discrimination and leave the number of impulses generated at a particular spot or region as the neural code for intensity or loudness. By itself, however, this concept seems inadequate to explain some

TABLE 2.1 Hypothetical System for Pitch and Loudness Perception. Code for Loudness Based on Combination of: (1) Place of Stimulation (Row), and (2) Number (Rate) of Neural Impulses Elicited from a Given Row.

Hair cell	SPL tone (dB)	Number of impulses in hair cell-nerve complex	Perceived loudness (sones)
Outer hair cell			
Row 1	−10	25	0.125
(most easily stimulated,	20	50	0.25
fatigued, or damaged)	30	100	0.5
	40	200	1
Outer hair cell			
Row 2	50	25	2
(2nd most easily	60	50	4
stimulated, fatigued, or	60	100	8
damaged)	80	200	16
Outer hair cell			
Row 3	90	25	32
(3rd most easily stimulated,	100	50	64
fatigued, or damaged)	110	100	128
	120	200	256
Inner hair cell			
Row 4	130	25	512
(least easily stimulated,	140	50	1024
fatigued or damaged)	150	100	2048
	160	200	4096

Notes: 1. A given sound frequency stimulates neural impulses from a locus, or "stripe," of four hair cells, across the basilar membrane (stripes for a 500 Hz tone and an 8000 Hz tone illustrated on Figure 2.3C). The frequency(s) of the sound determines which stripe(s) are most stimulated, and the intensity determines: (1) which row within a stripe is most stimulated, and (2) the number, within limits, of neural impulses per second that are emitted.

2. It is presumed that the higher brain centers perceive the loudness of a sound from the number of impulses per unit of time, as well as from their row(s) of origin, and the pitch from the locus stripe(s) of origin of the impulses on the basilar membrane and locus of termination in the brain. The number of neural impulses from a single cell can increase up to a rate of, say, about 200 per s, as the intensity of a stimulus is increased.

3. Destruction, or reduced functioning, of the weaker hair cells would not reduce the number of impulses from the respective stronger, intact hair cell-nerve units. That is, recruitment—the loss of loudness of weak intensity sounds with normal, or near normal, loudness of higher intensity sounds is maintained.

of the phenomena of masking in normal ears, and the hearing in ears that have lost sensitivity because of exposure to intense noise. This latter behavior refers to the fact that while persons with partially noise-damaged cochlea lose some ability to hear weak-intensity sounds, sounds above their elevated thresholds appear to them to normally loud. This hearing response, called *recruitment,* will be discussed again later.

Recruitment indicates that it must be not only the number of impulses being generated in the cochlea that determine the loudness of a sound, but also the particular hair-cell unit that is responding. After all, if the ear has reduced sensitivity due to damaged sensorineural cells, the number of impulses being transmitted to the brain, and resulting loudness, must also be reduced. As indicated, this does not happen when recruitment is operative. The hypothesized place plus the "number of impulses for loudness" concept, as perhaps needed to explain recruitment, is demonstrated in Table 2.1.

There are electroneurologic data in cats, dogs, and monkeys indicating that the mechanism outlined in Table 2.1 is projected, as would be needed for it to work, to specific "pitch" (Licklider, 1941, Licklider and Kryter, 1942) and "loudness" (Tunturi, 1952) points in the auditory brain center. Figure 2.5 shows that, similar to the cochlea, there are (1) "stripes" of brain cells connected to stripes of hair cells located in regions along the basilar membrane that are stimulated by different sound frequencies and (2) stripes of brain cells on the basilar membrane are segmented into different "rows" that respond to different intensities that are connected to rows of cells within the frequency stripes of cells in the cortex of the brain.

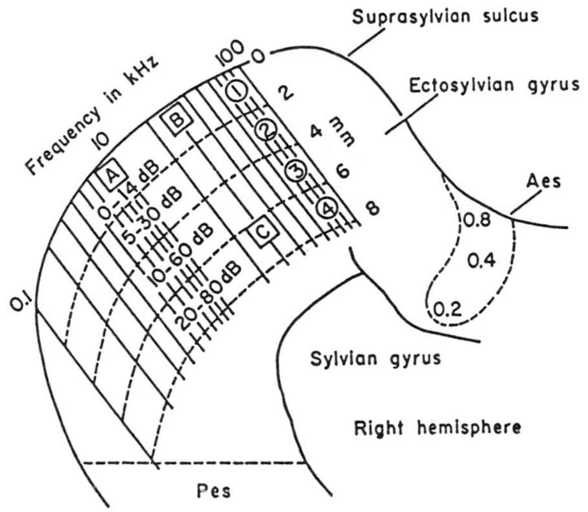

FIGURE 2.5 Arrangement of efferent connections to ectosylvian area of right hemisphere of brain of dog and relation of intensity of stimulation along isofrequency contours. (After Tunturi, 1952.)

This hypothetical model is schematically illustrated in Fig. 2.6. It is emphasized that this "model" is an oversimplification of what is now known about the neurology of the cochlea. For example, the inner and outer hair cells have somewhat different efferent nerve connections, which suggest a somewhat different, or at least expanded role for the inner (compared to the outer) hair cells in the hearing process.

It is to be noted that although the integration of hearing with cognition and the other sensory systems of the body depends on the upper brain, the auditory system has neural processing centers in the mid-brain and brain stem, as shown in Fig. 2.3D. These centers not only permit the organism to respond to sound at a more primitive level, they undoubtedly also contribute to the analysis of the complex acoustical signals received in the cochlea. Cats with their auditory neural system intact at the inferior colliculus (Inf. Coll.) level, but not below, will give near normal thresholds of hearing. (Kryter and Ades, 1943), and superthreshold intensity discriminations (Raab and Ades, 1946).

CRITICAL BANDWIDTH OF THE EAR

As conceived by H. Fletcher (1940) the concept of filtering actions within the ear having what are called *critical bandwidths* has proved to be significant. This concept has furnished a basis for explaining some auditory behavior with respect to speech perception, noise-induced hearing-loss loudness, pitch

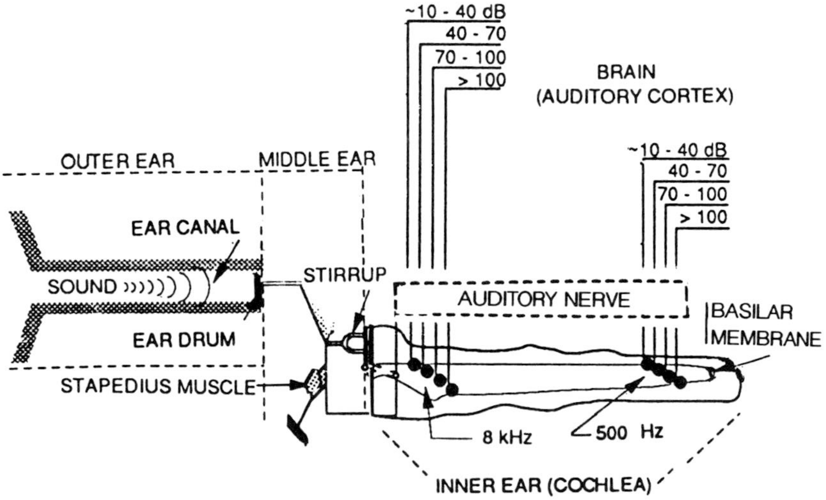

FIGURE 2.6 Schematic drawing of ear, place on basilar membrane for frequency locus, and hair-cell row for intensity place, stimulation, and projection to places in higher brain centers. Based on hypothesis of place and neural nets for frequency, pitch discrimination, and place plus number of impulses for intensity loudness, discriminations.

perception, and masking. Basically, the cochlea and its associated nerve nets often seem to behave as a very large set of overlapping bandpass filters connected in parallel. The concept is compatible with the resonance curves observed by von Békésy (1943) (see Fig. 2.3B).

These filters have skirts above and below the primary passband of frequencies that are not sharp (Schafer *et al.,* 1950). Their bandwidths change as a function of frequency, and they become broader when the signal intensity is increased. In particular, it seems that at high intensity levels the upper skirt of the filter becomes much less steep than the lower skirt. The critical-band concept indicates that increasing the bandwidth of a masking noise beyond a certain width does not increase the degree to which a pure tone located at the center of the band is masked. Only the energy at frequencies nearer the center frequency contribute to the analysis and masking of the tone at the center.

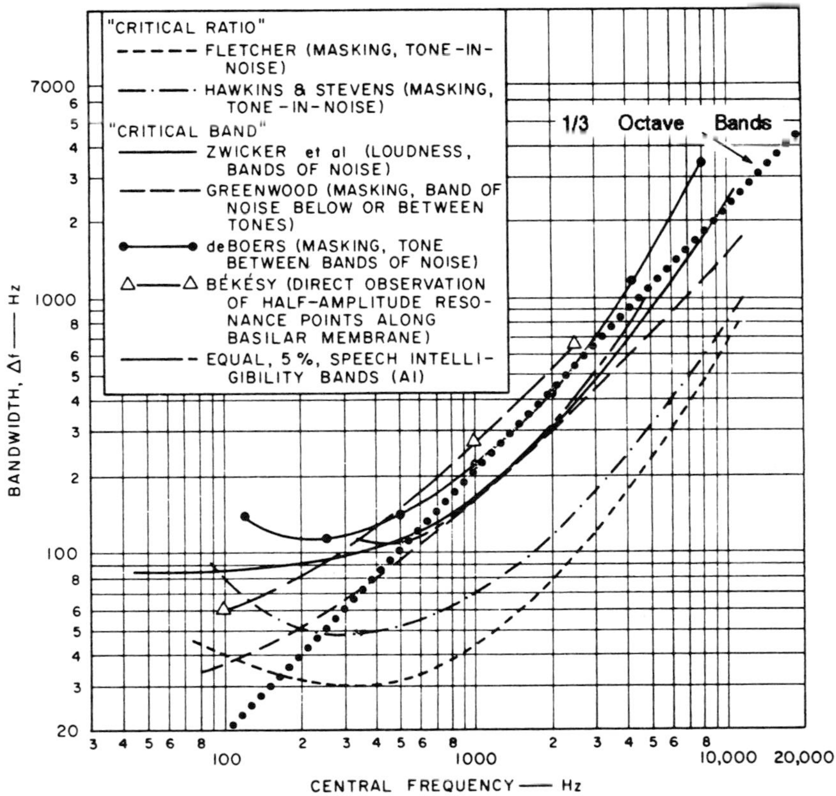

FIGURE 2.7 Bandwidth and position on basilar membrane of sounds as function of band center frequency for various parameters. "Equal, 5% Speech Intelligibility" curve from Freuch and Steinberg, 1947. (From Kryter, 1985.)

Studies by Fletcher (1940), Hawkins and Stevens (1950), and Bilger and Hirsh (1956) are experiments in which the intensity level of a pure tone, presented with a broadband random noise, was adjusted until the tone was just audible. This process was repeated with pure tones of different frequencies. Swets *et al.* (1962) conducted a similar experiment in which a narrow band of noise was masked with a wider band. Masking is said to occur when a tone or other signal is rendered inaudible to a listener because of the presence of another sound or noise. The results in Fig. 2.7 show that the width of the critical band and critical ratio vary as a function of frequency.

For the two bottom curves in Fig. 2.7, *critical band* is defined as the ratio (called the *critical ratio*) between the spectrum level (level per hertz) of white noise and the pure tone at a masked threshold. That is, the critical band was defined as the band of noise around a pure tone, at center frequency, whose acoustic power equaled that of the pure tone when at masked threshold. It has been found that when the critical band was measured directly in a variety of perceptual judgment tests (von Gassler, 1954; Zwicker, 1958; Zwicker *et al.*, 1957; Hamilton, 1957; Greenwood, 1961a,b; Scharf, 1961; de Boer, 1962; Plomp and Levelt 1965), its bandwidth varied more or less as a function of frequency, as did the critical band when measured indirectly by the masking of a pure tone by a white noise. However, the width was about 2.5 times greater when measured directly (see Fig. 2.7).

TIME CONSTANT OF THE EAR

Just as in the frequency domain where there is a critical bandwidth over which the ear processes sound energy to achieve an audible loudness, there is a critical time period over which the ear processes sound energy to achieve an audible loudness. This time period, called the *time constant* of the ear, is ~0.2–0.5 s for detection of the thresholds in quiet, changes in loudness, or noisiness in the presence of a masking noise. The time constant for the detection of a change in the loudness of a complex sound when it is at suprathreshold levels and with masking noise present is taken to be ~0.5 s.

The critical summation time is also shown by the fact that sound energy occurring outside a time frame of ~0.5 s does not contribute to the loudness of a sound perceived for that period of time. This is, of course, analogous to the critical frequency bandwidth of the ear where sound energy present outside the critical bandwidth does not contribute to the loudness of the sound perceived in the critical band. Data relevant to the time constant of the ear as found by masking and loudness judgments, are shown in Fig. 2.8.

A general theory (Zwislocki, 1960) of the physiological basis of the time constant is that (1) sensorineural excitation of a receptor unit from a sound stimulus perseverates for some brief period and aids in, or is added, by continuing sound stimulation; (2) excitation that occurs in a sensorineural

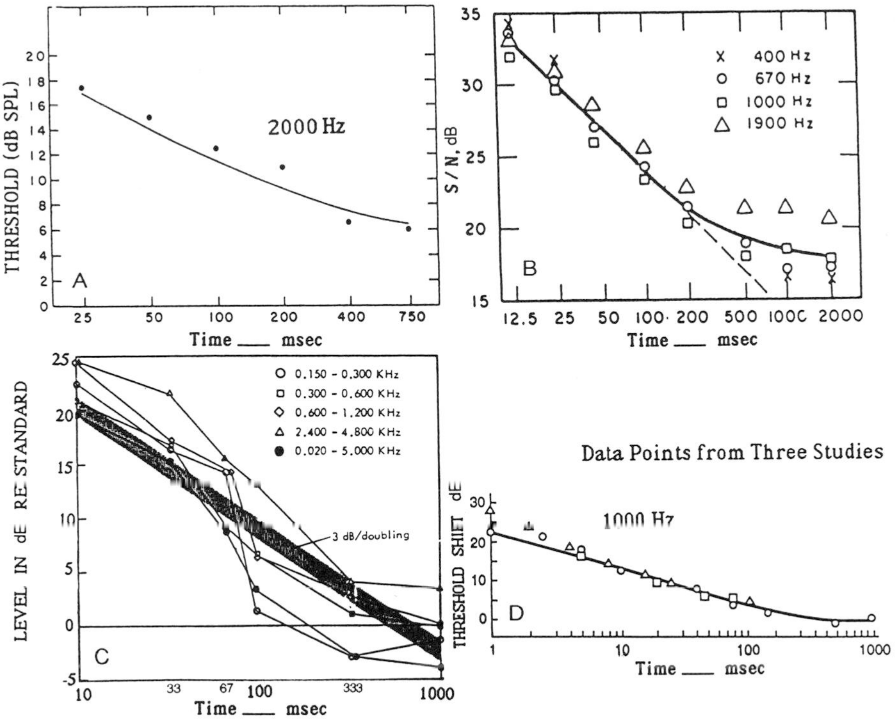

FIGURE 2.8 (A) Threshold as function of duration of a 2000-Hz signal with a 5-ms rise–fall time. Solid curve based on formula with a time constant of 0.346 s. (From Henderson, 1969.) (B) Relation between masked threshold of a pure tone in a broadband noise and duration of the tone. The dashed line represents linear integration. (From Garner and Miller, 1947.) (C) SPL of band of noise when equal in perceived noisiness as a reference standard band from 0.6 to 1.2 kHz and duration of 1000 ms. (From Fidell *et al.*, 1970. Copyright 1970 by the American Psychological Association. Adapted by permission of the author.) (D) Threshold of audibility of a 1000-Hz tone in the quiet as a function of its duration. (After Zwislocki, 1960. Copyright 1960 by the American Psychological Association. Adapted by permission of the author.)

receptor unit from a sound stimulus starts to decay after a period of 0.2–0.5 s; and (3) accordingly, a stable amount of neural excitation is reached in about 0.5 s from a continuing sound presented at a constant, stimulating level of intensity. Because of the adding- and decaying-excitation processes simulataneously occurring, the amount of sensorineural activity elicited by sound is proportional to the average of the squared instantaneous sound pressures occurring over the 0.5 s period.

The implications of the time constant and a minimum duration required for the measurement of sound in order to estimate its effects on loudness and hearing loss will be discussed in Chapters 3 and 5.

MASKING

The nature of the hearing process is similar, if not the same, under the condition of so-called auditory masking and that of sensorineural loss in hearing sensitivity. With masking, the presence of sound energy from one source is made inaudible by the presence of sound energy from another source; that is the sensorineural cell(s) normally responsive to one source do not respond because they are occupied with responding to the sound from the other source. In sensorineural hearing loss, the sensorineural cell(s) normally responsive to a particular intensity sound do not respond because they are incapable as a result of damage or fatigue.

In a sense, noise is always present during the hearing process—it is the internal, physiological noise floor of the auditory system, whether it is that of (1) a normal ear, or an abnormal ear with a temporary or permanent thresholds shift; or (2) an ear with thresholds elevated because of external noise. The effects of noise on speech communication because of direct masking by noise, and indirectly because of noise-induced hearing loss, are also of particular importance to behavior in everyday life. Various aspects of their effects on speech understanding, and its consequences, will be discussed in some detail in Chapters 6, 7, and 8.

Direct and Frequency-Spread Masking

The general method used for measuring masking of tones or bands of noise is as follows. The threshold of audibility is determined at a number of pure tones or narrow bands of frequencies for the listener in the quiet. Then, while a masking tone or a band of noise is presented, the listener redetermines his or her threshold of audibility for the tones or narrow bands of noise. The increase in level required for the tones or narrow bands of noise to be audible represents the amount of masking caused by the masking tone or band of noise.

Wegel and Lane (1924), Egan and Hake (1950), Ehmer, 1959a,b; Zwicker *et al.*, (1957), Saito and Watanabe (1961), and Carter and Kryter (1962) measured the masking pattern of pure tones or narrow bands of noise. Typical examples of the results obtained are shown in Fig. 2.9, which shows that the masking pattern from narrow bands of noise is smoother at the vicinity of the center frequency of the masker than those found with pure tones; the latter masking functions are disturbed by audible beats that occur between the probe tone and the masking tone and its harmonics. These harmonics are introduced by nonlinear distortion in the transmission of sound in the ear.

The curves in Fig. 2.9 reveal the following characteristics of direct masking:

(1) The band of noise causes more masking around its center frequency than does the pure tone. Increased masking near the center frequency of the masker band of noise would, of course, be expected from the integrative

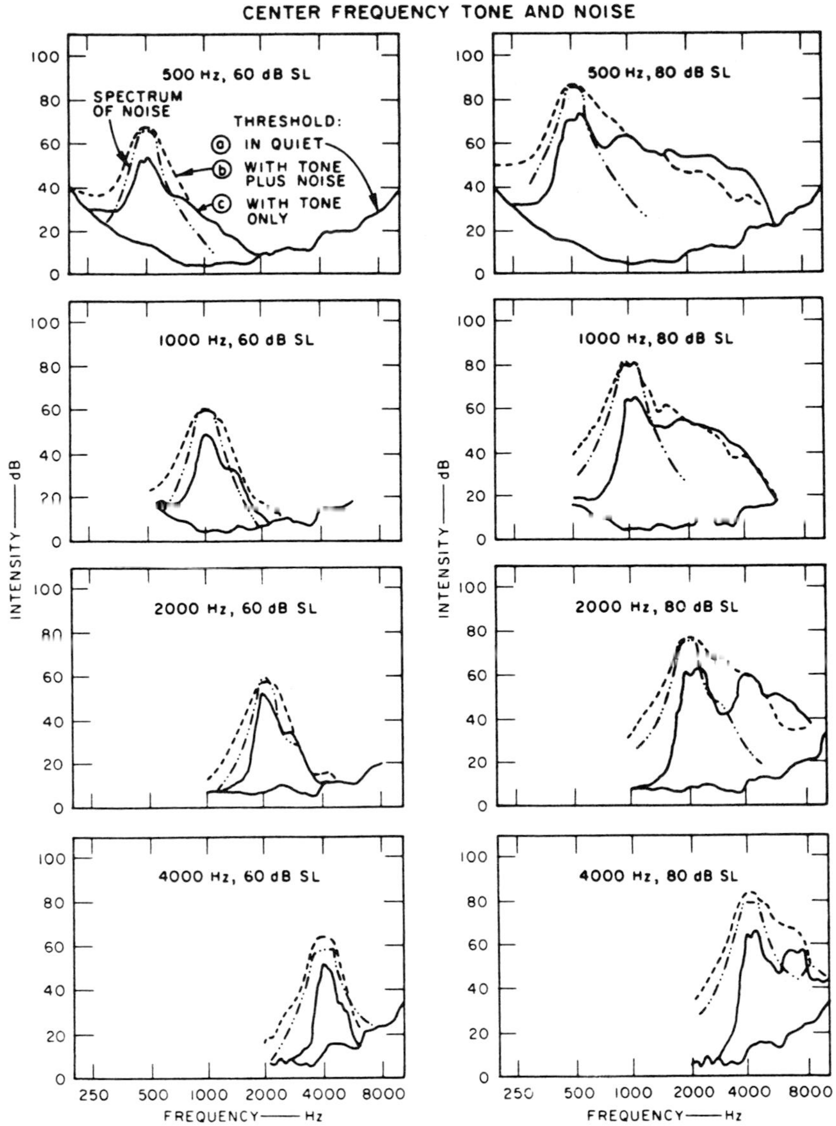

FIGURE 2.9 Masked thresholds for pure tones and narrow bands of noise. The center frequency and sensation level (SL) of the tone and noise are parameters. (From Ehmer, 1959b. Copyright 1959 by the American Psychological Association. Adapted by permission of the author.)

action of the critical bandwidth of cochlear functioning. Also, as Egan and Hake (1950) and Ehmer (1959a,b) suggest, the pure-tone masking may be only apparently lessened at the locus of the masking tone, because beats between the probe and masking tone cause a false measurement of the threshold of the tone.

(2) There is an asymmetrical upward spread of masking that becomes more severe at higher intensity levels. von Békésy's (1943) observations of asymmetrical resonance patterns along the basilar membrane offer an apparent mechanism to explain the asymmetrical upward spread of masking.

Of particular interest are the masking patterns obtained with intense low-frequency tones ranging from 10 to 50 Hz (see Fig. 2.10). The masking pattern for a tone as low as 25 Hz and an intensity level of 130 dB appears to extend

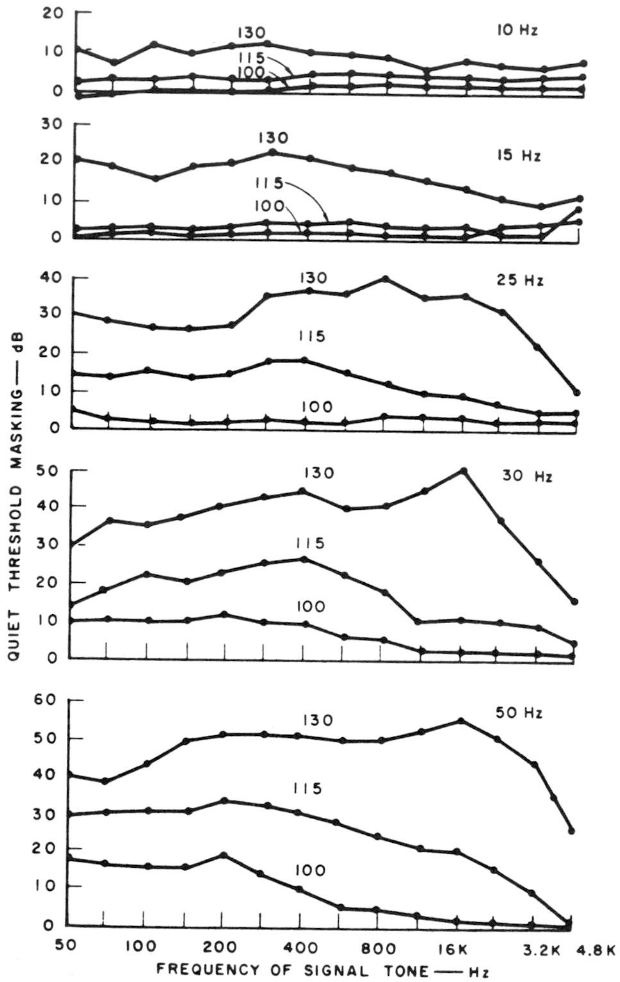

FIGURE 2.10 Masking with low-frequency pure tones (10, 15, 25, 30, and 50 Hz) and three intensity levels (100, 115, and 130 dB). The ordinate shows masking in decibels relative to the quiet threshold. The abscissa shows the frequency of the signal tone in hertz. The parameter is the SPL of the masking tone in decibels. Each point is the average masking for five listeners. (From Finck, 1961. Copyright 1961 by the American Psychological Association. Adapted by permission of the author.)

from almost flat to as high as 4000 Hz. The masking effects of tones as low as 50 Hz on speech will be discussed subsequently.

It is of some interest to consider what, if any, effect masking noise has on loudness and on the ability of the ear to discriminate, or detect, changes in signal level. This detection of change is called the *difference limen for intensity*. It is a generality, as is also shown in experiments on the intelligibility of speech in noise, that the signal-to-noise ratio (S/N), not the absolute level of the masking noise (up to ~110 dB), determines the detectability of changes in signal intensity. Figure 2.11 shows that the difference limen for intensity ΔI for an octave band of noise is essentially constant for sensation levels above 20 dB.

Figures 2.12 and 2.13 demonstrate that the loudness of a sound grows, recruits, much more rapidly above its threshold in noise than in quiet. Loudness grows, or recruits, for intense signals in the normal ear when in the presence of a noise, as it does in the abnormal ear with a sensorineural loss

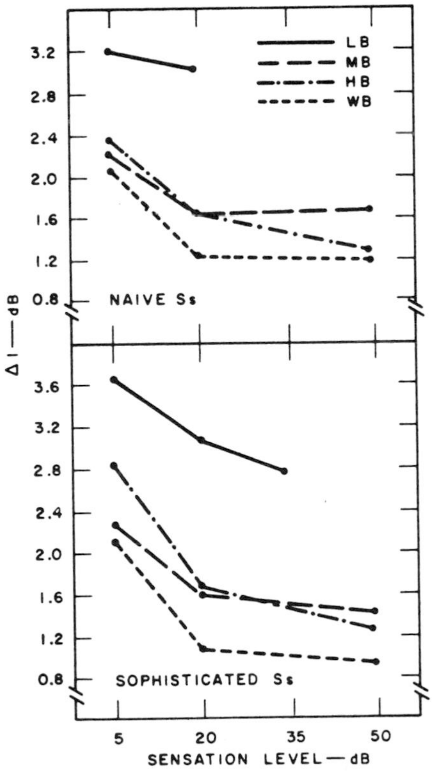

FIGURE 2.11 Mean decibel increase in frequency for naive and sophisticated subjects to detect a change in intensity of octave bands of noise. Each point represents 44 threshold determinations in the upper panel and 24 in the lower panel. (From Small *et al.*, 1959. Copyright 1959 by the American Psychological Association. Adapted by permission of the author.)

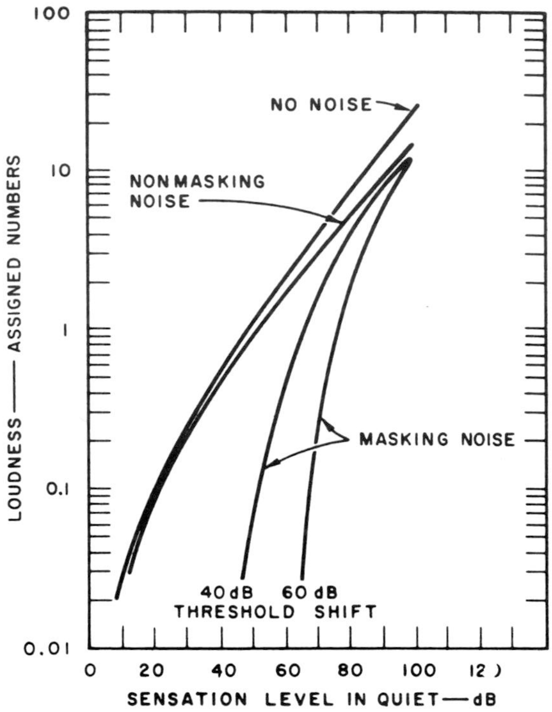

FIGURE 2.12 Monaural–loudness curves without masking and in the presence of a nonmasking noise. (From Hellman and Zwislocki, 1964. Copyright 1964 by the American Psychological Association. Adapted by permission of the author.)

(see circles, ○, in Fig. 2.13). That is, recruitment occurs in both cases, further illustrating the similarity of behavior of the ear with sensorineural loss and the normal ear with noise masking.

Pitch Changes with Direct Masking

A number of investigations (Corso, 1954; Egan and Meyer, 1950; Webster *et al.*, 1952) have reported that the pitch of a tone may change when heard in the presence of a band of noise. If the band of noise is of a higher frequency than the tone, the pitch decreases slightly; if the noise is of a lower frequency than the tone, the pitch increases. Both of these effects occur only when the loudness of the tone and the noise are about the same.

Egan and Meyer (1950) offer a convincing explanation of why these pitch changes may occur. The argument, put forth also by de Boer (1962), is that the locus or central tendency of the area on the basilar membrane that has the highest S/N determines what pitch is perceived. This concept, which is a general model for direct masking in the cochlea, is illustrated in Fig. 2.14, which shows that the point on the frequency scale enjoying the maximum

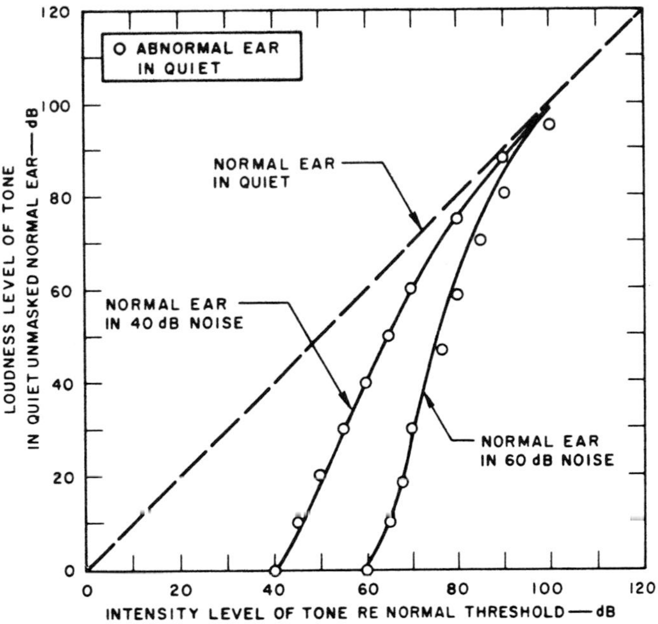

FIGURE 2.13 Loudness-level curves of a partially masked tone in normal ears compared to those for abnormal (sensorineural) ears exhibiting recruitment. (After Hellman and Zwislocki, 1964. Copyright 1964 by the American Psychological Association. Adapted by permission of the author.)

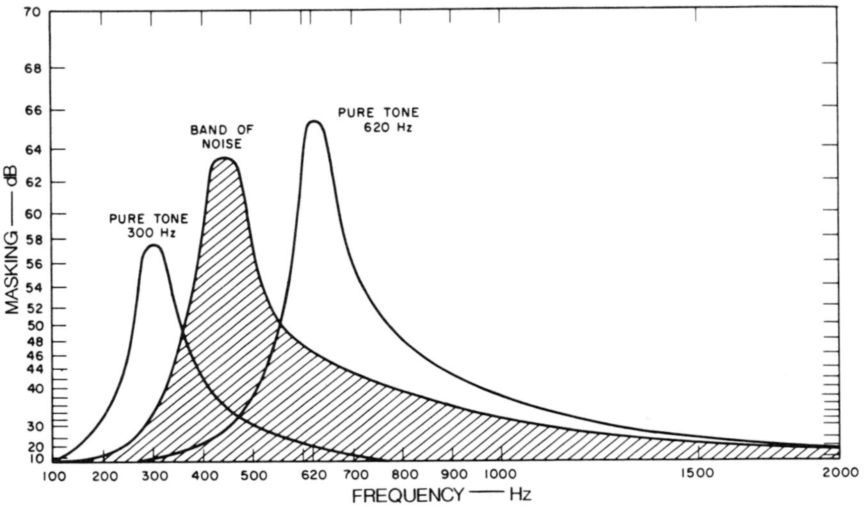

FIGURE 2.14 Loudness pattern curves. The coordinates are such that when the amount of masking produced by a stimulus is plotted as a function of frequency, the area under the resulting curve is proportional to the loudness of that masking stimulus. (From Egan and Meyer, 1950. Copyright 1950 by the American Psychological Association. Adapted by permission of the author.)

S/N is not the center frequency of the pure tone, but is lower in frequency for the tone below the band of noise and higher for the tone above the band of noise.

Remote Masking

Remote masking refers to the fact that a high-frequency band of noise, provided it is sufficiently intense, will elevate the audibility threshold for pure tones of low frequency (Bilger and Hirsh, 1956). This is shown in Fig. 2.15. It is usually presumed that this masking is direct masking caused by the presence of low-frequency-distortion products resulting from the amplitude distortion that occurs when the signal strength is sufficiently intense to overload the ear. Bilger (1966) demonstrated remote masking with subjects whose intraaural muscles had been cut. This result seems to rule out masking as the result of attenuation of low-frequency sounds due to the reaction of the aural muscles to intense sound.

Temporal Masking

Since the pioneer work of Samojlova (1959), Pickett (1959), and Chistovich and Ivanova (1959), considerable attention has been given to the temporal

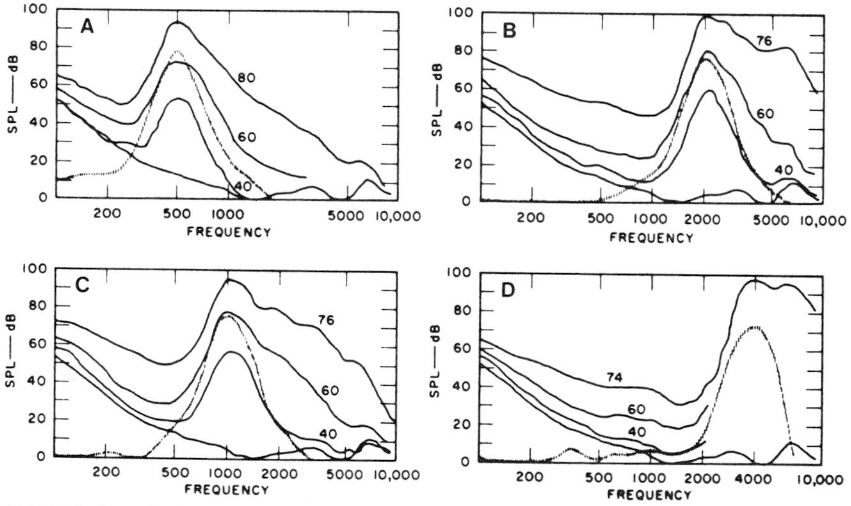

FIGURE 2.15 Solid curves represent the average binaural pulsed pure-tone thresholds in quiet (bottom curves) and in the presence of several levels of noise centered at (A) 500, (B) 1000, (C) 2000, and (D) 4000 Hz. The spectrum level (level per hertz) of the noise producing each threshold curve is shown as the parameter in each figure. The hatched curve in each figure shows the spectrum of the noise at the maximum level used. All data obtained with the same five subjects. (From Spieth, 1957. Copyright 1957 by the American Psychological Association. Adapted by permission of the author.)

pattern of masking. In these investigations, a probe tone of very brief duration is presented both before and after a masking tone or noise. Figure 2.16 shows typical results; the small amount of masking for dichotic listening (probe tone in one ear, masking tone in opposite ear) indicates that temporal masking is primarily of a direct, or at least ipsilateral (occurring on same side), sort. Forward masking in time is not surprising—it could be a manifestation of temporary auditory fatigue or some sort of refractory period due to the previous stimulation. But how can a masker elevate the threshold of a sound preceding it in time? Zwislocki (1960) and Wright (1964) suggest that the effect is due to a restriction in the time available for the auditory system to summate the energy and loudness of the tone or a click preceding the masking noise.

Apparently, according to this theory, a given length of time is required because of a stimulus–intensity–neural-response time factor wherein, it is hypothesized, the neural impulses from the much more intense masking noise reach the brain sooner than the impulses resulting from the test tone or click at threshold. Presumably, the growth of the perception of a signal is the integral of the distribution of impulses in the various neural pathways from the cochlea to the higher centers. Since the weaker, preceding sound activates the slower pathways, its growth of loudness occurs at a slower rate than that of the later, more intense masking sound.

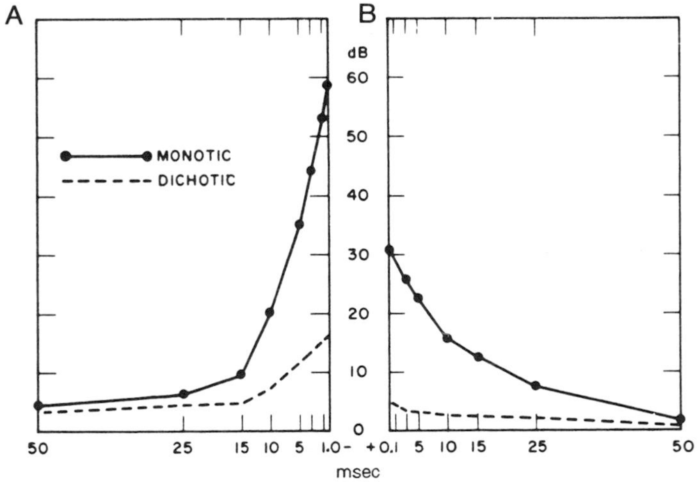

FIGURE 2.16 Backward and forward masking under conditions of 90-dB masking and 5-ms probe tone duration. The abscissa represents the masking interval (maskers not present) with the positive values of forward masking (A) and the negative time values of backward masking (B). The vertical ordinate represents the amount of masking in decibels, i.e., the difference between masked threshold and unmasked threshold of the probe. Data on the monotic listening condition are shown by the solid line, and the dotted line represents dichotic listening. (From Elliott, 1962. Copyright 1962 by the American Psychological Association. Adapted by permission of the author.)

Temporal masking is obviously a factor in the detection of temporal order of two stimuli. Hirsh (1959) found that a 10–20-ms separation is required between two sounds for the human observer to correctly detect which of the two sounds came first. With only a 2–3-ms delay, a separation between two sounds was heard, but the order in which the two sounds came could not be identified.

BINAURAL EFFECTS

The basis for the detection of minimal differences among auditory signals are generally ascribed to variations in phase relations of the frequencies in a sound, or sounds, at both ears. Following the work of Licklider (1948), Hirsh (1948), Pollack (1948), Jeffress *et al.* (1952), Jeffress (1965), others have extended the knowledge of how both ears work together in terms of signal detection in noise. Recent research and theories have also revealed somewhat similar signal detection phenomena with monaural listening (Green, 1988).

For some unknown reason, if two signals are presented simultaneously to both ears, they mask each other by the minimal amount if one signal is in phase with respect to itself at the two ears and the other is out of phase with respect to itself at the two ears. However, if the phases are the same at the two ears for both signals (i.e., both in or both out of phase), mutual masking is increased from 0 to 16 dB, depending on the frequency spectra involved. Intermediate degrees of phase correlations cause intermediate effects (Jeffress *et al.,* 1952). Thus, certain obvious advantages may be gained in communication systems, as is discussed in Chapter 6, when control of the signal- and-noise- phase relations at the two ears is possible.

The conclusions described above are for the binaural presentation of the signal and the noise. Also of interest are the conditions under which the noise is presented to one ear or to both ears. In both of these cases, the signal is presented only to one ear. A somewhat startling finding, as shown in Fig. 2.17, is that adding noise to the ear opposite the ear receiving both the tone signal and the noise reduces the masking of the tone when the tone is at a sensation level of more than ~10 dB above its threshold in the quiet. That is, the addition of noise at the opposite ear improves the detection of the signal. This phenomenon has been labeled *masking-level difference* (MLD)—the difference in the level of the tone at the detection threshold when being masked by noise in the same ear and when masked by noise in both ears.

These binaural phase effects are clearly caused by an analysis process going on in the central nervous system—a process that is also consciously recognized as a locus of the signal and the noise in so-called phenomenal space. Phenomenal space is the locus, on introspection, of the source of a sound. For example, when a recording of a musical instrument is played via

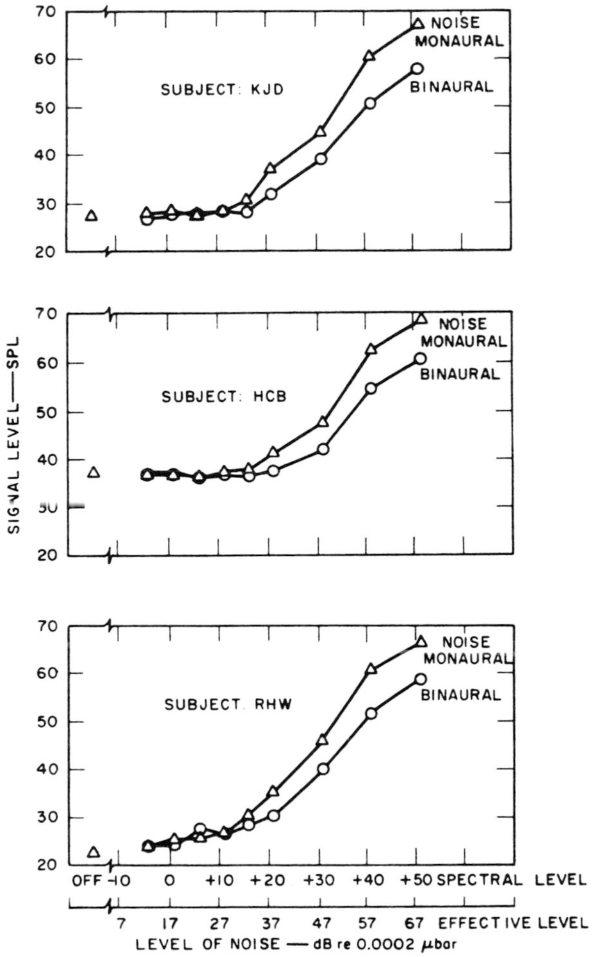

FIGURE 2.17 Masked thresholds (required level of signal to be audible in presence of noise) for one ear vs. noise level in that ear, or noise in both ears. (From Blodgett *et al.*, 1962. Copyright 1962 by the American Psychological Association. Adapted by permission of the author.)

earphones with the signal in phase at both ears, the impression is that the sound is centered in the middle of the head. Changing the phase relations between the two ears tends to externalize the source and place it to the side of the head where the lower-frequency components in the signal lead in phase.

Finally, under binaural listening, it should be mentioned that in addition to phase differences for a signal or signals at both ears, intensity differences also make important contributions to the detection and localization of sound in space. Phase differences between tonal signals in the presence of noise improve detection for frequencies only below 2000 Hz, and pressure-level differences between the two ears increase detection for all frequencies above ~500 Hz (Gardner, 1962).

Localization (perhaps a better term is *lateralization*) of the source of impulsive sound with respect to the listener is, apparently, based on at least two cues. The first of these is the well-known precedence effect [first investigated by Wallach *et al.* (1949), but known as the "Hass effect" in architectural acoustics (Gardner, 1968)], where the position of the source of sound is ascribed to the side of the person, or ear, first receiving the sound. The second cue consists of phase and intensity differences between the sound at both ears. The precedence and intensity cues were investigated by Freedman and Pfaff (1962). They found that a 25–45-ms (depending on the experimental method used) temporal difference for a click at both ears was equivalent to about a 1-dB difference in dichotic intensity with respect to lateralization of the source of the clicks.

A practical interest in these binaural effects lies in the fact that noise-induced hearing loss, as will be discussed, may be severe for one ear but not the other ear of a person. For that condition, the person's ability to hear and understand speech in real-life noise could be considerably degraded relative to that of a person with two normal ears, even though both persons could hear speech coming from a frontal source equally well when listening in the quiet.

AURAL REFLEX

The tympanic and stapedius muscles in the middle ear mediate the so-called aural reflex and thereby play a role in audition when intense sound is present. The aural reflex can influence the effects of noise with regard to masking, loudness, and auditory fatigue. The tympanic and stapedial muscles contract when one or both ears is exposed to a sound that is about 80 dB above threshold level, although the contraction in the sound-stimulated ear is somewhat stronger than that in the nonexposed ear.

Some people are able to voluntarily activate their aural reflex (see Fig. 2.18). These people are apparently not aware of a reduction in the loudness level of some sounds, but they may hear the sound made by the contraction and relaxation of the intraaural muscles. It is estimated that 1–2% of people have this ability, and that others can be trained (Reger *et al.,* 1963). In humans, the reflex action is inferred from

1. An increase in the threshold of hearing at different frequencies due to an activating stimulus in the contralateral ear
2. Physical measurements of changes in the volume of the external ear canal
3. Changes in the acoustic impedance of the eardrum

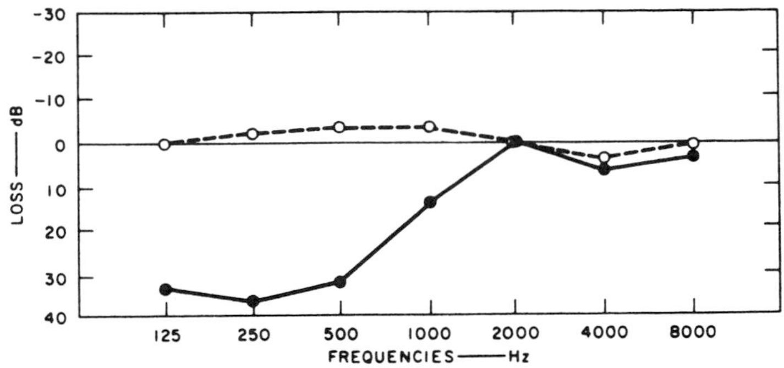

FIGURE 2.18 The dotted line shows the average hearing level of eight selected ears. The solid line shows the average hearing level of the same ears during maximum contraction of the middle-ear muscles. (From Reger *et al.*, 1963.)

The contralateral threshold shift method is accomplished as follows. Sound at an intensity sufficient to elicit the aural reflex is presented to one ear and, at the same time, the listener is tracking his or her threshold for pure tones in the opposite ear (Ward, 1961). When activated, the reflex, being bilateral, will cause a rise in the threshold at some frequencies in the "quiet" ear. It is, of course, necessary that the frequency content of the sound used to elicit the reflex be sufficiently different in frequency from the tones being tracked, so as not to mask, via bone conduction, the threshold of the probe tone.

Up to a point, as the intensity of the sound increases, the degree of contraction increases (Richards and Goodman). It appears that the reflex is more responsive to broadband sounds than to pure tones, and is more responsive to lower frequencies than to higher frequencies. The reflex returns to a normal, quiescent state within a second or so after an effective stimulus is terminated (see Fig. 2.19A). It appears to adapt or relax in the presence of continued stimulation after about 15 min of exposure to an intense steady-state noise (see Fig. 2.19B.)

That this adaptation is not due to fatigue of the aural muscles is shown by the fact that the reflex can be reactivated by changing the acoustic stimulus (Wersall, 1958). The aural reflex seems to be most readily activated and maintained by intermittent, intense impulses of noise. Latency of the reflex is ~35–150 ms, depending on the intensity of the stimulus, and relaxation time following an impulse of noise is reported to be as long as 2–3 s for complete relaxation, with most of the recovery probably occurring within about 0.5 s. The reflex is involuntary, and, except to the specially trained subject, its occurrence is not subjectively detected by the listener. It can apparently be conditioned to light and other stimuli (Loeb and Riopelle, 1960).

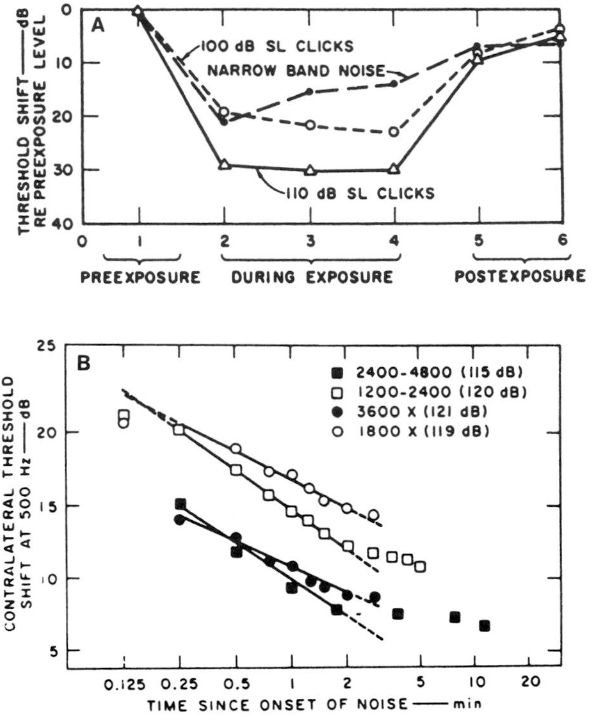

FIGURE 2.19 (A) Contralateral threshold shift at 500 Hz produced by aural reflex from exposure to several acoustical stimuli. Time in minutes. (From Fletcher and Loeb, 1962.) (B) Adaptation of contralateral threshold shift due to aural reflex. (From Ward, 1961. Copyright 1961 by the American Psychological Association. Adapted by permission of the author.)

It is reasonable to think that the aural reflex serves to stiffen the movement of the bones of the middle ear so that they do not transmit very intense sound as effectively as sounds of lower intensity. Something like this must occur, but it affects the transmission of sounds mostly below ~2000 Hz (see Fig. 2.18)—frequencies, as will be shown, that are the most resistant anyway to loss from exposure to intense sounds (Ward, 1962a,b).

Fletcher and Riopelle (1960) elicited the reflex with a click and a band of noise, presented 200 ms before exposing the ear to the impulse from the firing of a gun. They measured the threshold shifts, which were temporary, after 200 rounds of firing. A second experimental condition was the same as that just described except the click or band of noise was withheld prior to each round of firing. Presumably, the aural reflex was not active in the latter case when the gun noise reached the ear. Figure 2.20 shows that the aural reflex afforded as much as 15 dB of protection from temporary threshold shift (TTS). Somewhat similar amounts of protection from TTS by the aural reflex were obtained by Fletcher (1961) and Fleer (1963).

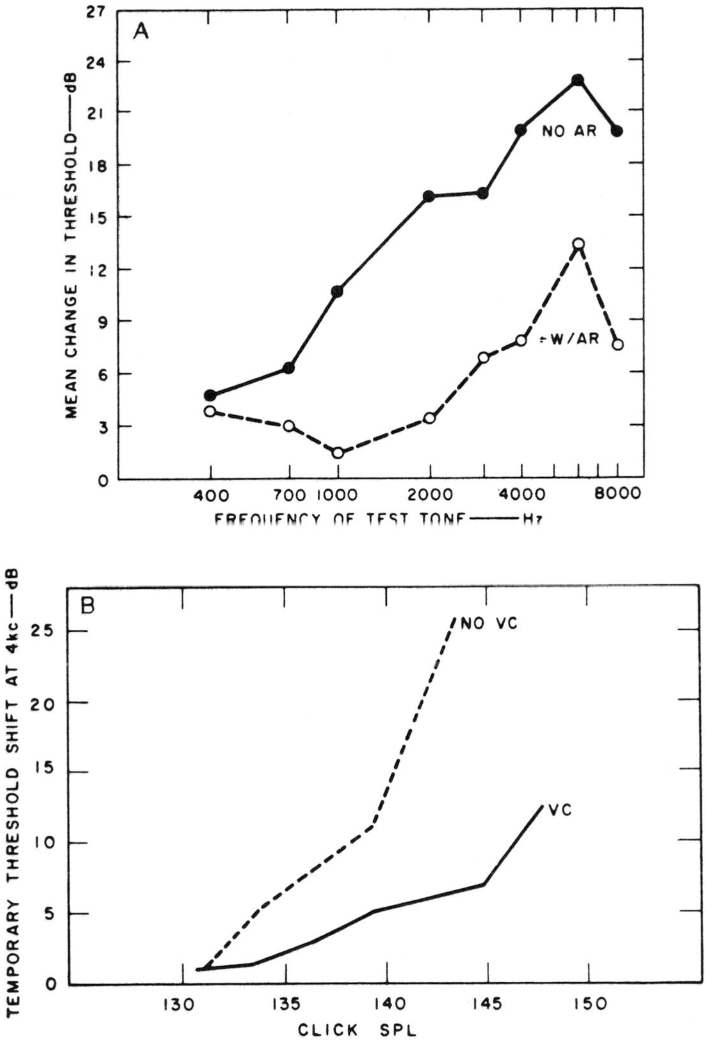

FIGURE 2.20 (A) Mean temporary threshold shifts (TTS), in decibels, at various frequencies for two experimental conditions: W/AR—with aural reflex; No AR—no aural reflex. (From Fletcher and Riopelle, 1960. Copyright 1960 by the American Psychological Association. Adapted by permission of the author.) (B) Average growth of TTS with successive exposures to increasing pulse levels with and without voluntary contraction (VC) of middle-ear muscles. The attenuation produced by VC is represented by the amount by which the function generated with VC is shifted to the right of that with "No VC." (From Fleer, 1963.)

Aural Reflex in Persons with Hearing Loss

The aural reflex is used as a means of diagnosing certain types of hearing disorders (Jepsen, 1963). In particular, its absence indicates conductive difficulties in the middle ear. Terkildsen (1960) found that persons in industry with significant hearing losses as a result of exposure to traumatic noise had somewhat weaker aural reflexes than in persons with normal hearing.

On the other hand, Hecker and Kryter (1964) found that soldiers with large permanent hearing losses, presumably due to exposure to gunfire, showed greater aural reflexes than soldiers with normal hearing. These investigators also found that the men with greater reflex activity showed less TTS on exposure to gunfire than was exhibited by men with lesser aural reflexes; however, this difference may have been because of the decreased sensitivity (larger permanent hearing losses) of the former group relative to the latter, and not because of some increased protection afforded by the aural reflex, although this latter is a possibility.

The aural reflex is of primary interest as a potential factor in the possible retardation of noise induced hearing loss, and will be discussed further in that context in Chapter 5. Detailed reviews of research on the aural reflex are to be found in Møller (1974), Borg and Odman (1979), Zakrisson (1979), Brask (1979), and Silman (1984).

Differential Thresholds for Frequency and Intensity

The ability of the auditory system to respond to changes in the frequency (corollary of pitch) or in the intensity (corollary of loudness) of a sound depends somewhat on the rate at which the changes take place, as well as the degree of the change. Studies have shown that the optimum rate for the auditory detection of a shift in frequency is approximately 2–3 per second (Shower and Biddulph, 1931). It is to be noted that this means a duration of ~0.33–0.5 s at each of the unshifted and shifted-to frequencies. As might be expected, this result is consistent with the time constant of the ear for intensity or loudness, as discussed earlier.

Figure 2.21A shows the differential threshold, or limen, (ratio of the amount of shift to initial frequency) required for a change to be detected in the frequency of a tone when heard at different sensation levels. (Sensation level is defined as the number of decibels a sound is above its intensity at threshold.) It is seen, for example, that a change in frequency and pitch has taken place when the frequency of a 1000 Hz tone at a sensation level of 5 dB is shifted about 10 Hz, and with a shift of no more than ~2–3 Hz, at sensation levels above ~40 dB.

Figure 2.21B shows the minimum changes in the intensity of different pure tones (in dB) that are required for the intensity and loudness to change when the tones are heard at different average sensation levels. At sensation

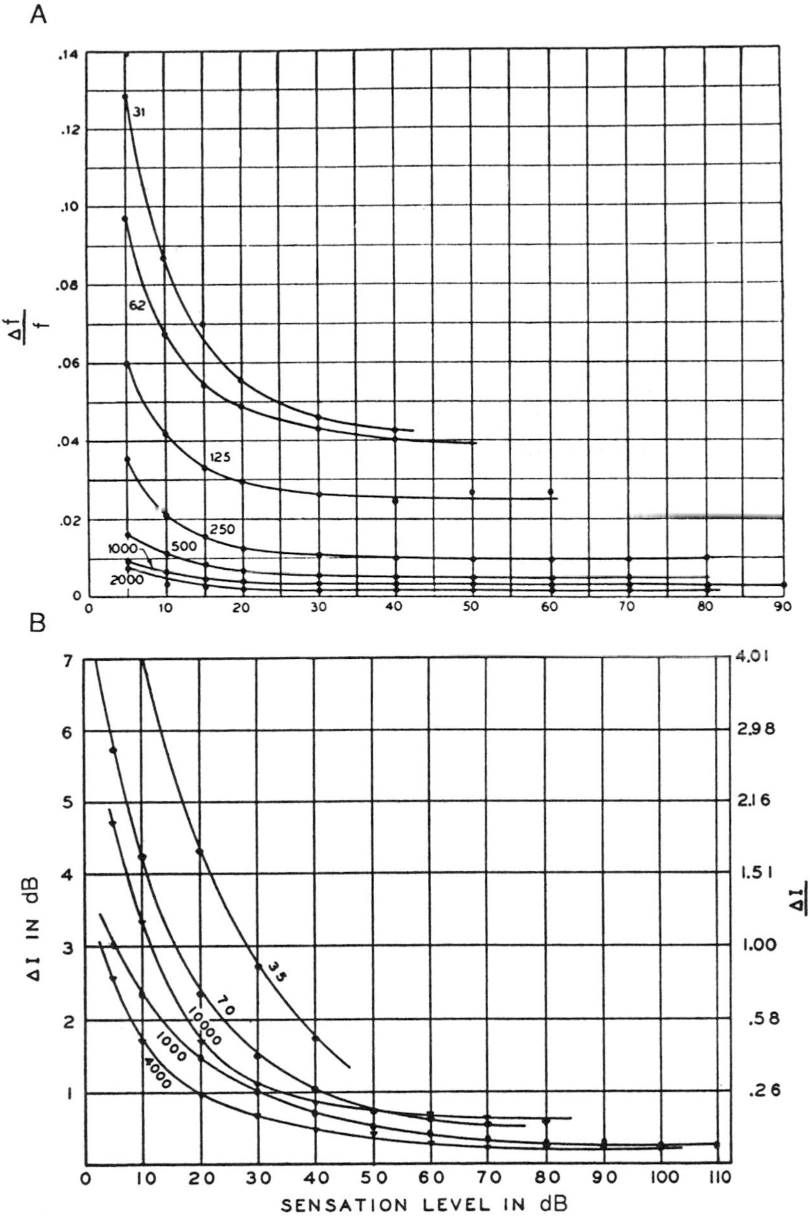

FIGURE 2.21 (A) Difference limens for a change in frequency and (B) for a change in intensity of pure-tones as a function of their sensation level. Frequencies in Hz shown by numbers attached to curves. [From Stevens and Davis (1938); after Shower and Biddulph data (1931, (A), and Riesz data (1928), (B).]

TABLE 2.2 Difference-Limen for Intensity, 1000 Hz Tone, 40 dB Sensation Level. Method: Tone Switched from First to Second Intensity.

Condition	Decibels	$\Delta I/I$
1. Switch not controlled by subject, one comparison, half-second interval between tones	0.8	0.200
2. Same, except no interval between tones	0.6	0.150
3. Repeated comparison, no interval between tones	0.4	0.096
4. Switch controlled by subject, repeated comparisons, no interval between tones	0.2	0.047
5. Sinusoidal variation (continuous presentation) (cf. Riesz).	0.5	0.120

From Stevens and Davis, 1938.

levels above ~40 dB, the typical difference limen is ~0.5 dB. The data in this graph were obtained by a method in which intensity change was identified by a "beat", a sensation heard when the intensity of two identical frequency tones is slightly different. These findings are similar to those found when the difference limen is measured by methods in which the subjects judge

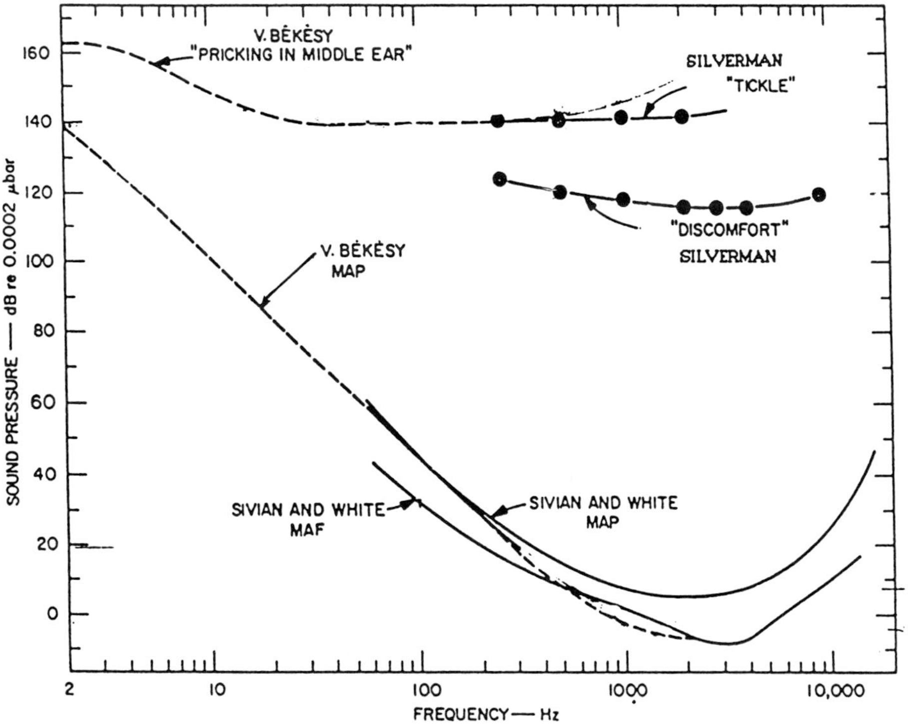

FIGURE 2.22 Thresholds of audibility and feeling from sound. MAP, minimum audible pressure in ear canal; MAF, minimum audible pressure in a free sound field, measured at the place where the listener's head had been. Upper curves show the approximate upper boundary of the auditory realm, beyond which sound gives rise to nonauditory sensations of tickle and discomfort and pain in the ear.

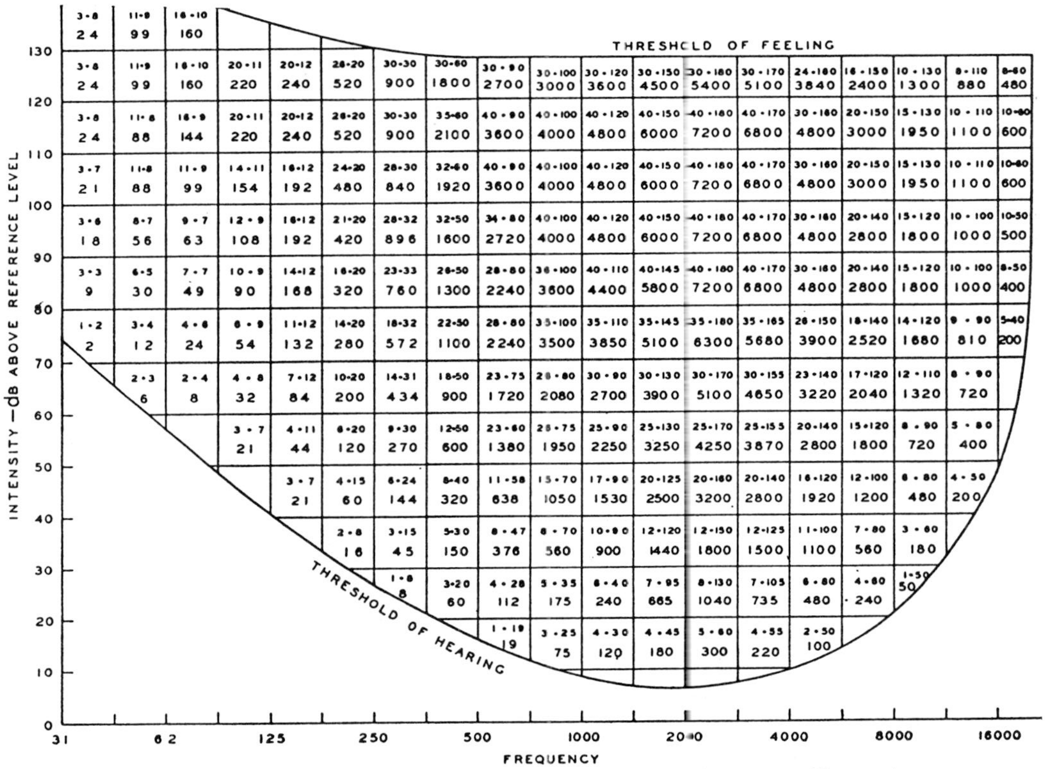

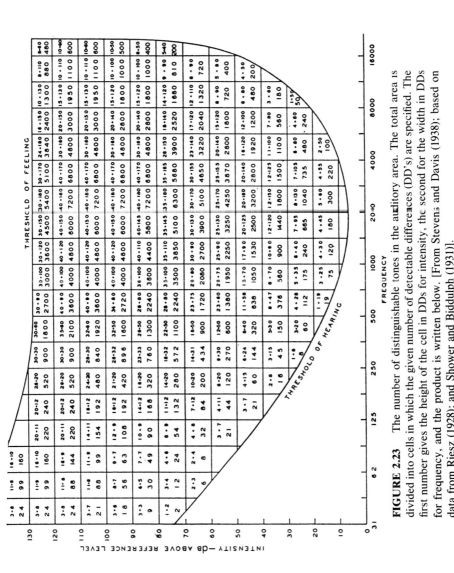

FIGURE 2.23 The number of distinguishable tones in the auditory area. The total area is divided into cells in which the given number of detectable differences (DD's) are specified. The first number gives the height of the cell in DDs for intensity, the second for the width in DDs for frequency, and the product is written below. [From Stevens and Davis (1938); based on data from Riesz (1928); and Shower and Biddulph (1931)].

any changes in the loudness as brief as 1 s and segments of the same sound are presented sequentially in time but at slightly different levels of intensity, as shown in Table 2.2.

Area of Auditory Sensitivity

The range of audible, pure-tone frequencies and intensities of the normal, young adult ear are shown in Fig. 2.22. The minimum audible pressure (MAP) in ear canal intensity curve refers to the pressure measured in the ear canal for threshold of detection or threshold of sensitivity of the ear at a given frequency. The minimum audible pressure in a free sound field (MAF) curve is for the same subjective threshold with the sound pressure being measured in the field position of the ear but without the ear present. Less threshold pressure is required with open-field measurements because of differences in acoustic resonances in the ear canal and difraction around the head of different sound frequencies. The subjective sensations of "pricking," "tickle," and "discomfort" reported at very high intensities of sound are not considered auditory, but they are believed to be due to receptors in the eardrum.

The magnitude of a shift in the frequency of a tone to be detected, or the change in its intensity necessary for detection, varies over different regions of the audible frequency scale and range of effective intensities. It has been found that when intensity is held at a medium level, the normal ear can distinguish approximately 1500 noticeable steps in frequency and pitch, and when frequency is held to a medium range, approximately 325 steps in intensity and loudness are detectable (Stevens and Davis, 1938). Figure 2.23 illustrates that approximately 340,000 just noticeable differences (JNDs) in frequency and intensity can be detected by the normal ear.

References

von Békésy, G.; Rosenblith, W. A. (1960). The mechanical properties of the ear. *In* "Handbook of Experimental Psychology" (S. S. Stevens, ed.), pp. 1075–1115. Wiley, New York.

von Békésy, G. (1935). Uber akustische Reizung des Vestibularapparates. *Pfluegers Arch. Gesamte Physiol.* **236,** 59–76.

von Békésy, G. (1936a). Uber die Herstellunh und Messunh langsamer sinusformiger Luftdruckschwankungen. *Ann. Physik.* **25,** 413–432.

von Békésy, G. (1936b). Uber die Horschwelle und Fuhlgrenze langsamer sinusformiger Luftruchschwankungen. *Ann. Physik.* **26,** 5554–566.

von Békésy, G. (1943, 1949). Uber die Resonanzkurve und die Abklingzeit der verschiedenen Stellen der Sehneekentrennwand (on the resonance curve and the delay period at various points on the cochlear partition). *Acustica* **8,** 66–76. (Available in English translation, *J. Acoust. Soc. Am.* **21,** 245–254.)

Bilger, R. C. (1966). Remote masking in the absence of intra-aural muscles. *J. Acoust. Soc. Am.* **39,** 103–108.

Bilger, R. C., Hirsh, L. J. (1956). Masking of tones by bands of noise. *J. Acoust. Soc. Am.* **28,** 623–630.

Blodgett, H. C., Jeffress, L. A., and Whitworth, R. H. (1962). Effect of noise at one ear on the masked threshold for tone at the other. *J. Acoust. Soc. Am.* **34,** 979–981.

Borg, E., Odman, B. (1979). Decay and recovery of the acoustic Stapedius reflex in humans. *Acta Oto-Laryngol.* **87,** 421–428.

Brask, T. (1979). The noise protection effect of the Stapedius reflex. *Acta Oto-Laryngol. Suppl.* No. 360, 116–117.

Bruel, P. V. (1977). Do we measure damaging noise correctly? *Noise Control Eng.* **8**(2), 52–60.

Carter, N. L., and Kryter, K. D. (1962). Masking of pure tones in speech. *J. Aud. Res.* **2,** 68–98.

Chistovich, L. A., and Ivanova, V. A. (1959). Backward masking by short sound pulses. *Biofizika* **4,** 170–180.

Corso, J. F. (1954). Historical note on the thermal masking noise and pure tone pitch changes. *J. Acoust. Soc. Am.* **26,** 1078.

de Boer, E. (1962). Note on the critical bandwidth. *J. Acoust. Soc. Am.* **34,** 985–986.

Duifhuis, H., Horst, J. W., and Wit, H. P., eds. (1988). "Basic Issues in Hearing." Academic Press, San Diego.

Egan, J. P., and Hake, H. W. (1950). On the masking pattern of a simple auditory stimulus. *J. Acoust. Soc. Am.* **22,** 622–630.

Egan, J. P., and Meyer, D. R. (1950). Changes in pitch of tones of low frequency as a function of the pattern of excitation produced by a band of noise. *J. Acoust. Soc. Am.* **22,** 827–833.

Ehmer, R. H. (1959a). Masking patterns of tones. *J. Acoust. Soc. Am.* **31,** 1115–1120.

Ehmer, R. H. (1959b). Masking by tones vs. noise bands. *J. Acoust. Soc. Am.* **31,** 1253–1256.

Elliott, L. L. (1962). Backward masking: Monotic and dichotic conditions. *J. Acoust. Soc. Am.* **34,** 1108–1115.

Fidell, S., Pearsons, K. S., Grignetti, M., and Green, D. M. (1970). The noisiness of impulsive sounds. *J. Acoust. Soc. Am.* **48,** 1304–1310.

Finck, A. (1961). Low-frequency pure tone masking. *J. Acoust. Soc. Am.* **33,** 1140–1141.

Fleer, R. (1963). Protection afforded against impulsive noise by voluntary contraction of the middle ear muscles. *Semin. Middle Ear Funct.* (J. L. Fletcher, ed.), Rep. No. 576. U.S. Army Med. Res. Lab., Fort Knox, Kentucky.

Fletcher, H. (1940). Auditory patterns. *Rev. Mod. Phys.* **12,** 47–65.

Fletcher, J. L. (1961). TTS following prolonged exposure to acoustic reflex eliciting stimuli. *J. Aud. Res.* **1,** 242–246.

Fletcher, J. L., and Loeb, M. (1962). The influence of different acoustical stimuli on the tympanic reflex. *Acta Oto-Laryngol.* **54,** 33–47.

Fletcher, J. L., and Riopelle, A. J. (1960). Protective effect of the acoustic reflex for impulsive noises. *J. Acoust. Soc. Am.* **32,** 401–404.

Freedman, S. J., and Pfaff, D. W. (1962). Trading relations between dichotic time and intensity differences in auditory localization. *J. Aud. Res.* **2,** 311–317.

French, N. R., and Steinberg, J. C. (1947). Factors governing the intelligibility of speech sounds. *J. Acoust. Soc. Am.* **19,** 90–119.

Gardner, M. B. (1962). Binaural detection of single-frequency signals in the presence of noise. *J. Acoust. Soc. Am.* **34,** 1824–1830.

Gardner, M. B. (1968). Historical background of the Haas and/or precedence effect. *J. Acoust. Soc. Am.* **43,** 1243–1248.

Garner, W. R., and Miller, G. A. (1947). The masked threshold of pure tones as a function of duration. *J. Exp. Psychol.* **37,** 293–303.

Green, D. M. (1988). "Profile Analysis." Oxford Sci. Publ., New York.

Greenwood, D. D. (1961a). Critical bandwidth and the frequency coordinates of the basilar membrane. *J. Acoust. Soc. Am.* **33,** 1344–1356.

Greenwood, D. D. (1961b). Auditory masking and the critical band. *J. Acoust. Soc. Am.* **33,** 484–502.

Hamilton, P. M. (1957). Noise masked thresholds as a function of tonal duration and masking noise band width. *J. Acoust. Soc. Am.* **29,** 506–511.
Hawkins, J. E., Jr., and Stevens, S. S. (1950). The masking of pure tones and speech by white noise. *J. Acoust. Soc. Am.* **22,** 6–13.
Hecker, M. H. L., and Kryter, K. D. (1964). "A Study of Auditory Fatigue Caused by High-Intensity Acoustic Transients" Rep. No. 1158. Bolt, Beranek, & Newman (Avail. from DTIC as AD 450 707.)
Hellman, R. P., and Zwislocki, J. (1964). Loudness function of a 1000-cps tone in the presence of a masking noise. *J. Acoust. Soc. Am.* **36,** 1618–1627.
Henderson, D. (1969). Temporal summation of acoustic signals by the chinchilla. *J. Acoust. Soc. Am.* **46,** 474–475.
Hirsh, I. J. (1948). The influence of interaural phase on interaural summation and inhibition. *J. Acoust. Soc. Am.* **20,** 536–544.
Hirsh, I. J. (1959). Auditory perception of temporal order. *J. Acoust. Soc. Am.* **31,** 759–767.
Jepsen, O. (1963). Middle Ear Muscle Reflexes in Man. *In* "Modern Developments in Audiology" (J. Jerger, ed.), pp. 194–237. Academic Press, New York.
Jeffress, L. A. (1965). "Masking and Binaural Phenomena." DRL-A-245. Def. Res. Lab., Univ. of Texas. (Avail. as NASA CR-64362.)
Jeffress, L. A., Blodgett, H. C., and Deatherage, B. H. (1952). The masking of tones by white noise as a function of the interaural phases of both components. 1. 500 Cycles. *J. Acoust. Soc. Am.* **24,** 523–527.
Kessel, R. G., and Kardon, R. H. (1979). "Tissues and Organs: A Text-Atlas of Scanning Electron Microscopy." Freeman, San Francisco.
Kryter, K. D. (1985). "The Effects of Noise on Man," 2nd Ed. Academic Press, Orlando, Florida. (Orig. publ., 1970).
Kryter, K. D., and Ades, H. (1943). Function of acoustic nervous centers in the cat. *Am. J. Psychol.* **56,** 501–536.
Licklider, J. C. R. (1941). An electrical study of frequency localization in the auditory cortex of the cat. *Psychol. Bull.* **38,** 727.
Licklider, J. C. R. (1948). The influence of interaural phase relations upon the masking of speech by white noise. *J. Acoust. Soc. Am.* **20,** 150–159.
Licklider, J. C. R. (1959). Three auditory theories. *In* "Psychology: A Study of a Science" (S. Koch, ed.), pp. 41–144. McGraw-Hill, New York.
Licklider, J. C. R., and Kryter, K. D. (1942). Frequency-localization in the auditory cortex of the monkey. *Fed. Proc. Fed. Am. Soc. Exp. Biol.* **1,** 51.
Loeb, M., and Riopelle, A. J. (1960). Influence of loud contralateral stimulation in the threshold and perceived loudness of low-frequency tones. *J. Acoust. Soc. Am.* **32,** 602–610.
Lorento de No, R. (1933). Anatomy of the eighth nerve. *Laryngoscope* **43,** 327–350.
Møller, A. R. (1965). An experimental study of the acoustic impedance of the middle ear and its transmission properties. *Acta Oto-Laryngol* **60,** 129–138.
Møller, A. R., ed. (1973). "Basic Mechanisms in Hearing." Academic Press, New York.
Møller, A. R. (1974). Function of the middle ear. *In* "Handbook of Sensory Physiology" (W. D. Keidel and W. D. Neff, eds.) Springer-Verlag, Berlin.
Pickett, J. M. (1959). Backward masking. *J. Acoust. Soc. Am.* **31,** 1613–1615.
Plomp, R. (1988). A personal view on tone perception research. *In* "Basic Issues in Hearing." (H. Dufius, J. W. Horst, and H. P. Wit, eds.), pp. 12–13. Academic Press, San Diego.
Plomp, R., and Levelt, W. J. M. (1965). Tonal consonance with critical bandwidth. *J. Acoust. Soc. Am.* **38,** 548–560.
Pollack, I. (1948). Monaural and binaural threshold sensitivity for tones and for white noise. *J. Acoust. Soc. Am.* **20,** 52–57.

Raab, D. H., and Ades, H. W. (1946). Cortical and midbrain meditation of a conditioned discrimination of acoustic intensities. *Am. J. Psychol.* **59,** 59–83.

Rasmussen, A. T. (1947). "Outlines of Neuroanatomy." W. C. Brown, Dubuque, Iowa.

Reger, S. N., Menzel, O., Ickes, W. K., and Steiner, S. J. (1963). Changes in air conduction and bone conduction sensitivity associated with voluntary contraction of middle ear musculature. *Semin. Middle Ear Funct.* (J. L. Fletcher, ed.), Rep. No. 576. U.S. Army Med. Res. Lab., Fort Knox, Kentucky.

Richards, A. M., and Goodman, A. C. (1977). Threshold of the human acoustic Stapedius reflex for short-duration burst of noise. *J. Aud. Res.* **13,** 183–189.

Riesz, R. R. (1928). Differential intensity sensitivity of the ear for pure tones. *Phys. Rev.* **31,** 867–875.

Saito, S., and Watanabe, S. (1961). Normalized representation of noise band masking and its application to the prediction of speech intelligibility. *J. Acoust. Soc. Am.* **33,** 1013–1021.

Samojlova, I. K. (1959). The masking effect of short signals as a function of the time between the masked and masking sound. *Biofizika* **4,** 550–558.

Schafer, T. H., Gales, R. S., Shewmaker, C. A., and Thompson, P. O. (1950). Frequency selectivity of the ear as determined by masking experiments. *J. Acoust. Soc. Am.* **22,** 490–496.

Scharf, B. (1961). Complex sounds and critical bands. *Psychol. Bull.* **1,** 705–717.

Shaw, E. A. G. (1966). Ear canal pressure generated by a free sound field. *J. Acoust. Soc. Am.* **39,** 465–470.

Shower, E. G., and Biddulph, R. (1931). Differential pitch sensitivity of the ear. *J. Acoust. Soc. Am.* **3,** Suppl. I, Part 2, 275–287.

Silman, S., ed. (1984). "The Acoustic Reflex." Academic Press, Orlando, Florida.

Silverman, S. R. (1947). Tolerance for pure tones and speech in normal and defective hearing. *Ann. Otol. Rhinol. Laryngol.* **56,** 658–677.

Sivian, L. J., and White, S. D. (1933). On minimum audible sound fields. *J. Acoust. Soc. Am.* **4,** 288–321.

Small, A. M., Jr., Bacon, W. E., and Fozard, J. L. (1959). Intensive differential thresholds for octave-band noise. *J. Acoust. Soc. Am.* **31,** 508–510.

Spieth, W. (1957). Downward spread of masking. *J. Acoust. Soc. Am.* **29,** 502–505.

Stevens, S. S., and Davis, H. (1938). "Hearing—Its Psychology and Physiology." Wiley, New York.

Swets, J. A., Green, D. M., and Tanner, W. P., Jr. (1962). On the width of critical bands. *J. Acoust. Soc. Am.* **34,** 108–113.

Terkildsen, K. (1960). The intra-aural muscle reflexes in normal persons and in workers exposed to intense industrial noise. *Acta Oto-Laryngol.* **52,** 384–396.

Tobias, J. V., ed. (1970). "Modern Foundations of Auditory Theory," Vol. 1. Academic Press, New York.

Tobias, J. V., and Schubert, E. D., eds. (1981). "Hearing Research and Theory," Vol. 1. Academic Press, New York.

Tunturi, A. R. (1952). A difference in the representation of auditory signals for the left and right ears in the iso-frequency contours of the right middle ectosylvian auditory cortex of the dog. *Am. J. Physiol.* **168,** 712–727.

von Békésy, G. (1943). Über die Resonanzkurve und die Abklingzeit der ver sehiedenen Stellen der Sehneekentrennwand. (On the resonance curve and the delay period at various points on the cochlear partition.) *Acustica* **8,** 66–76; Engl. transl. *J. Acoust. Soc. Am.* **21,** 245–254 (1949).

von Békésy, G., and Rosenblith, W. A. (1960). The mechanical properties of the ear. *In* "Handbook of Experimental Psychology" (S. S. Stevens, ed.), pp. 1075–1115. Wiley, New York.

von Gassler, G. (1954). Über die Horschwelle fur Schallereignisse mit Verschiec Breitem

Frequenzspektrum. (On the threshold of hearing for sound with different spectrum width.) *Acustica* **4**, 456–462.
Wallach, H., Newman, E. B., and Rosenzweig, M. R. (1949). The precedence effect in sound localization. *Am. J. Psychol.* **62,** 315–335.
Ward, W. D. (1961). Studies of the aural reflex. I. Contralateral remote masking as an indicator of reflex activity. *J. Acoust. Soc. Am.* **33,** 1034–1045.
Ward, W. D. (1962a). Studies on the aural reflex. II. Reduction of temporary threshold shift from intermittent noise by reflex activity: Implications for damage-risk criteria. *J. Acoust. Soc. Am.* **34,** 234–241.
Ward, W. D. (1962b). Effect of temporal spacing on temporary threshold shift from impulses. *J. Acoust. Soc. Am.* **34,** 1230–1232.
Webster, J. C., Miller, P. H., Thompson, P. O., and Davenport, E. W. (1952). The masking and pitch shifts of pure tones near abrupt changes in a thermal noise spectrum. *J. Acoust. Soc. Am.* **24,** 147–152.
Wegel, R. L., and Lane, C. E. (1924). The auditory masking of one pure tone by another and its probable relation to the dynamics of the inner ear. *Phys. Rev.* **23,** 266–285.
Wersall, R. (1958). The tympanic muscles and their reflexes. *Acta Oto-Laryngol, Suppl.* No. 139.
Wever, E. G. (1949). "Theory of Hearing." New York.
Wiener, F. M. (1947). On the diffraction of a progressive sound wave by the human head. *J. Acoust. Soc. Am.* **19,** 143–146.
Wiener, F. M., and Ross, D. (1946). The distribution in the auditory canal in a progressive sound field. *J. Acoust. Soc. Am.* **18,** 401–408.
Wright, H. N. (1964). Temporal summation and backward masking. *J. Acoust. Soc. Am.* **36,** 927–932.
Zakrisson, J. E. (1979). The effect of the Stapedius reflex on attenuation and post-stimulatory auditory fatigue at different frequencies. *Acta Oto-Laryngol. Suppl.* No. 360, 118–121.
Zemlin, W. R. (1968). "The Ear, Speech and Hearing Science: Anatomy and Physiology." Prentice-Hall, Englewood Cliffs, New Jersey.
Zwicker, E. (1958). Über psychologische und methodische Grundlagen der Lautheit. *Acustica,* **3,** 237–258.
Zwicker, E. (1988). Psychophysics and physiology of peripheral processing in hearing. *In* "Basic Issues in Hearing." (H. Dufuis, J. W. Horst, and H. P. Wit, eds.), pp. 24–25. Academic Press, San Diego.
Zwicker, E., Flottorp, G., and Stevens, S. S. (1957). Critical band width in loudness summation. *J. Acoust. Soc. Am.* **29,** 548–557.
Zwislocki, J. J. (1960). Theory of temporal auditory summation. *J. Acoust. Soc. Am.* **32,** 1046–1060.
Zwislocki, J. J. (1981). Sound analysis in the ear: A history of discoveries. *Am. Sci.* **60,** 184–192.
Zwislocki, J. J. (1986). Analysis of cochlear mechanics. *Hear. Res.* **22,** 155–169.

Auditory Sensations and Perceptions

INTRODUCTION

A *sensation* is defined as a mental event that innately, and normally, occurs as the result of a physical or chemical energy stimulating a sensory system of the body. A *perception* is defined as the act of recognizing a sensation, or a complex of sensations, caused by such energies. For a comprehensive review of the different philosophies involved in the development of scientific concepts of measuring sensations and perceptions see Boring (1942).

The major problem that has faced sensory psychology has been that of establishing a so-called psychophysical law that shows an invariant, quantitative relation between a stimulating physical agent and some subjective sensation and perception. The psychophysical law now most widely accepted is, in its simplest terms, that "equal ratios of stimulus energy produce equal ratios of subjective magnitude" of a sensation (Stevens, 1957a, 1959a).

Auditory Sensations

To qualify, each auditory sensation—or attribute, as they are sometimes called—must have a characteristic quality and a measurable magnitude that is associated with a quantifiable physical variable. The most fundamental auditory sensations and their magnitudes are those of (1) *loudness*—weak to strong; (2) *pitch*—low to high; and (3) *duration*—brief to long.

As noted earlier, the attribute of loudness is primarily a corollary of the averaged intensity of variations in sound pressure, quantified in decibels; that of pitch, with the frequency of the variations, quantified in hertz; and duration of a sequence of pressure variations, usually measured in seconds or part of a second. Those three physical dimensions are involved to some extent in any and all stimulations of hearing, regardless of the sensation perceived.

As will be outlined below, it has been proposed that an inherent sensation of ''unwantedness'' is elicited by sounds having certain physical characteristics. Whether the human brain perceives sensations other than loudness and pitch, such as unwantedness, that can be quantitatively related to the intensity, frequency, and duration of a sound is a matter of some controversy in the field of psychoacoustics.

Perceived Noisiness

The subjective unwantedness felt from a sound, independently of any meanings or effects it may have, is defined as perceived noisiness, or, more simply, noisiness. It is scaled in degrees from minimal to extreme.

The term *loudness* has often been used as a synonym of *perceived noisiness*. However, loudness does not always sufficiently characterize the inherent unwantedness of some kinds of sounds. Perceived noisiness may at times be based on one, or a combination, of the sensations of (1) loudness; (2) tonality; (3) duration; and, as separate aspects of duration, (4) impulsiveness and (5) variability. Further, the term *loudness,* strictly speaking, has no necessary pejorative connotation as, appropriately, does *noisiness*—a low level of loudness can be judged as desirable, wanted, or pleasant, whereas, by definition, a low level of unwantedness is still unwanted sound, or noise.

Feelings of annoyance felt because of meanings associated with given sounds could, of course, bias judgments made of any inherent unwantedness a sound may have because of particular physical characteristics. This fact requires that measurements of perceived noisiness, as a separate sensation of sound, be based on experiments in which the effects of such biases are minimized or are, at least, about the same for nearly all people.

Laboratory research on perceived noisiness has often used the word *annoyance* when asking listener-subjects to judge possible noisiness or unwantedness of meaningless tones and narrowband, and broadband sounds. The phrase ''perceived noisiness'' was chosen in an attempt to avoid some of the ambiguity possible with the word *annoyance*. When the word annoyance is used in laboratory tests of perceived noisiness it is generally defined as referring to the "unwantedness, objectionableness, bothersomeness, etc." of a sound, independently of any meaning the sound may convey.

Also, noises in real life may involve annoyances due to the way they interfere with speech, sleep, and other behaviors. These annoyances are to be evaluated separately, or as constants, in the assessment of a general sensation of perceived noisiness. All types of annoyances from sound—learned biases, behavior interferences, and perceived noisiness—are, of course, factors to be considered in the overall evaluation of noise environments. These factors will be considered in Chapters 9 and 10.

Defining perceived noisiness as a sensation inherently related to certain physical characteristics of sound appears to be inconsistent with two commonly held physiological and psychological tenets of hearing. The first is that all peripheral neural information is presumed to be coded for loudness and pitch discrimination; as a result, there is no neural information available from the cochlea on which to base a sensation such as noisiness. Second, and accordingly, a feeling of noisiness from a stimulation must mean that a cognitive, learned, association is involved, so that the "feeling" is not a sensation as such; it is conventionally presumed that a learned relationship is not involved in the sensations of loudness and pitch.

Answers, if available, to such questions are to be found in empirical data. If some seemingly invariant relations between the physical aspects of sound and a human perception of noisiness or unwantedness can be reliably demonstrated, those relations may have practical usefulness, independently of whether an explanation of "why" can be offered. One perhaps plausible explanation is, nevertheless, suggested.

It is conjectured that perhaps the organism somehow senses when it is being stimulated by a sound such that the sensorineural receptors in the cochlea are being, or will be, unduly fatigued and that loss in hearing sensitivity may ensue. It is perhaps this sensing that gives rise to the unlearned sensation of unwantedness, noisiness, or annoyance, independent of and in addition to, any negative, or positive, learned meanings that the sound in question may convey to the listener. The aspects of sound cited above that appear to be correlated with the perceived noisiness—loudness (intensity), tonality, duration, and impulsiveness—are to varying degrees also correlated to temporary and permanent hearing loss. Research data related to this possibility will be presented later.

Other Sensations Related to Hearing and the Ear

Musicality in sound is often thought of as an inherent auditory sensation, one, however, that may also be involved with learning and training. Discussion of musicality is, however, beyond the scope of the present book.

Feelings of "discomfort" are observed when sound intensity reaches about L_C 120, "pain" when the level reaches about L_C 140, with feelings of "touch," "tickle," and "pricking" at intermediate levels (Silverman, 1947) (Fig. 2.21). However, these are considered to be nonauditory sensations due to stretching of receptors in the skin and other tissues in the outer and middle ear.

LOUDNESS

Loudness is defined as the subjective intensity of a sound. The loudness level of a complex sound is normally correlated with the intensity, averaged over 0.5 s-segments of time, tones, or critical bands of frequencies are above threshold level. That time segment is appropriate for most narrow- and broadband sounds, but can be as short as ~0.2 s for a pure tone (see Fig. 2.1).

Equal Loudness Frequency Contours

Fletcher and Steinberg (1924) and Fletcher and Munson (1933) appear to have made the first major attempts to measure the intensity levels required for equal loudness of different sound frequencies. Fletcher and Munson (1933) specified a 1000-Hz tone as the standard sound against which other tones would be judged for loudness.

Since those of Fletcher and Munson's, a number of studies have been conducted in which the intensities have been found for equal loudness of pure tones and narrow frequency bands of noise relative to a tone or brand of noise centered at 1000 Hz. For all intents and purposes, the *A*-, *D*-, and *E*-weighting contours shown in Fig. 1.5, and the perceived noisiness level (PNL) and loudness level contours shown in Fig. 3.1, fairly represent the findings. Figure 3.1 compares the shapes of various equal loudness and equal noisiness contours.

Growth of Loudness as a Function of Intensity

Stevens (1955) suggested that the unit of loudness be called the *sone* and that 1 sone be ascribed to a 1000-Hz tone set at a sound-pressure level (SPL) of 40 dB. On the sone scale, a sound twice as loud as a sound of 1 sone is given a value of 2 sones; four times as loud, 4 sones; etc.

Scaling the growth of loudness of a sound of a given duration and frequency as a function of changes in its intensity into steps that are subjectively equal in size has been a somewhat controversial problem. Reviews of the work in this area have been made by Stevens (1959b; Gzhesik *et al.*, 1961; Kryter, 1966, Scharf *et al.*, 1977). Three general methods have been used for scaling the growth of loudness of a sound, usually a 1000-Hz tone, as a function of changes in sound pressure level: (1) monaural vs. binaural loudness, (2) magnitude and ratio estimation, and (3) equal section or equal interval.

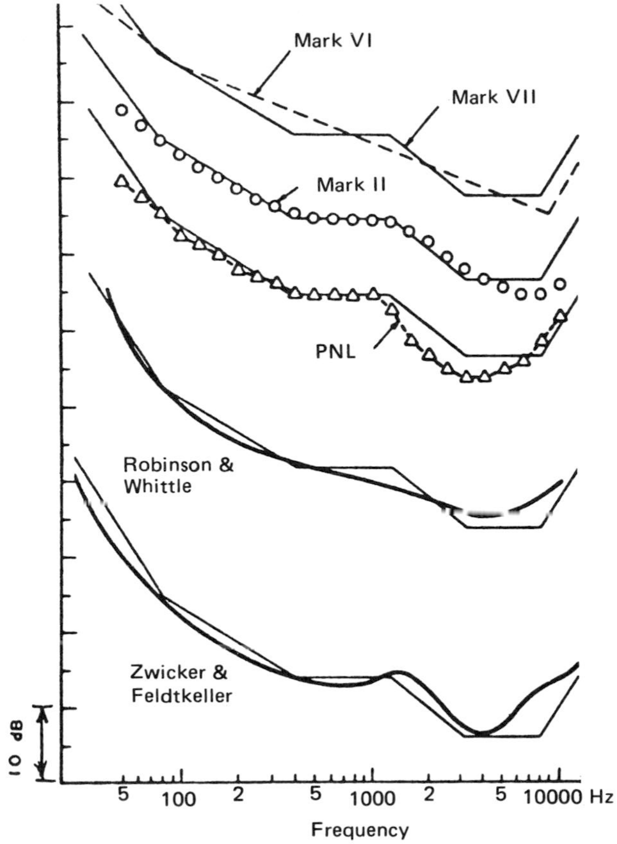

FIGURE 3.1 Comparison of equal-loudness contours (in phons), and equal-noisiness contours (PNL in PN_{dB}) (Robinson and Whittle, 1964; Zwicker and Feldtkeller, 1967; Kryter and Pearsons, 1965). Mark II, VI, and VII, proposed by Stevens (1961, 1972). Level of 1000-Hz reference band was 40dB for all contours, separated here to improve legibility (From Stevens, 1972.)

Monaural versus Binaural Loudness

The monaural–binaural loudness argument used by Fletcher and Munson (1933) was that a given sound when presented to two ears should appear to be twice as loud as when presented only to one ear (this argument followed from their assumption that loudness was proportional to the number of auditory nerve impulses reaching the brain per second). Fletcher and Munson (1933) found that the level of the monaurally presented tone had to be set about 10 dB higher in level than the level of an equally loud binaurally presented tone. Thus, they concluded that over at least the middle range of loudness levels, loudness (and the number of neural impulses generated in the auditory system) about doubles for each 10-dB increase in the sound pressure level of a sound.

Reynolds and Stevens (1960) found that the loudness scale for monaural listening was somewhat different from the loudness scale for binaural listening. However, Hellman and Zwislocki (1963) later found nearly perfect, within experimental error, interaural summation of loudness, as shown in Fig. 3.2.

Magnitude and Ratio Estimation

The monaural–binaural equal-loudness scale is very similar to the average of those developed on the basis of magnitude estimations of the loudness of

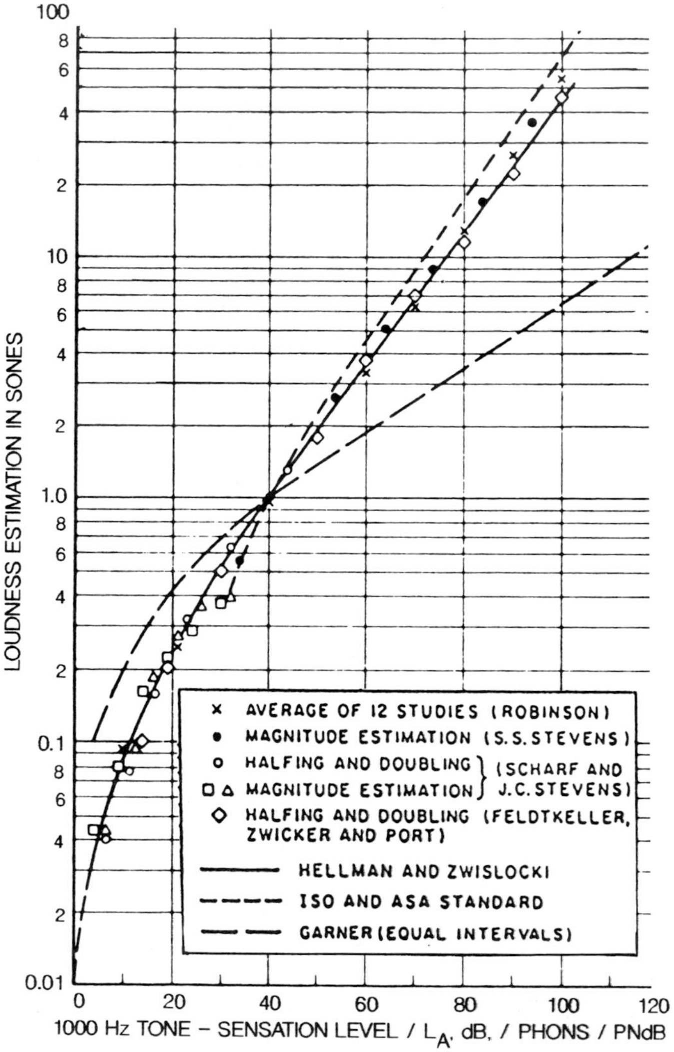

FIGURE 3.2 Comparison of binaural loudness growth functions. Results of several investigators. (From Kryter, 1966).

sound presented only monaurally or only binaurally. In this method, the subjects assign a number—say, 100—to a tone at a particular SPL—say, 100 dB; they are then asked to assign the number 50 to the tone when it sounds half as loud as it did at 100 dB. Another method is to estimate loudness ratios or fractions; here the subjects may adjust the level of a tone until it is one-half, one-tenth, etc. as loud as a standard or reference level.

Results of studies by various investigators using the magnitude estimation and ratio judgment methods differ rather widely. Garner (1959) suggested that differences among these results are due in part to context effects. That is, subjects' judgments about what appears half as loud are different when they know the total range of levels available to them for judgment and when they do not.

In reviewing loudness scaling procedures, Stevens (1959b) suggests that the best method is "magnitude production" in which each subject is allowed to choose a number scheme and then results are averaged across subjects, after normalizing the results for individual differences in the choice of numbers used. Others have since employed this, or related, methods in a number of studies of the growth of loudness as a function of intensity (see, e.g., Hellman, 1981, 1988).

Equisection Loudness Scale (Equal Intervals)

In addition to the monaural versus binaural, and the methods of magnitude and ratio estimation, the method of equal intervals, or equisections, has been suggested as a suitable method for deriving a scale of loudness. In this method, the subjects hear a tone presented at, in the simplest case, two different levels of intensity. The subjects are then told to adjust the third level of the same tone so that the difference in loudness between the second and third levels is equal to that between the first and second levels. Using this method, Wolsk (1964), Kwiek (1953), and Garner (1954), measured equal intervals over various ranges of intensity of a 1000-Hz tone.

Unlike the magnitude and ratio estimation methods, the results obtained by various investigators using the method of equal intervals agree closely with each other. However, no real knowledge is obtained from the equal interval method as to what changes in level are required in order for the listener to report a subjective sensation of, for example, the doubling or halving of the loudness of a sound. Because the loudness scale derived by the equal-interval method is so different from the scales derived by other methods (see Fig. 3.2), we must choose one or the other for a practical use.

It would seem reasonable to choose the form of loudness function on the basis of how the loudness scale is to be used. If, for example, we intend to say that sound A is twice (or some portion) as loud as sound B, then we are obliged to use a loudness scale based on ratio or magnitude judgments. On the other hand, if we want to decide whether the difference in loudness between sounds A and B is equal to the difference in loudness between B and C, then the Garner (1954, 1958)–Kwiek (1953) equal-interval loudness scale would be more meaningful. The general interest in loudness judgments in real-life situations is probably more in terms of apparent magnitude or relative loudness than in terms of equal intervals, and thus the loudness scale based on magnitude estimation seems the more appropriate for general use.

Standard Scale of Loudness as Function of Intensity Level

The scaling of subjective loudness of a sound in sones as a function of its intensity in phons, or decibels of sound pressure level of an equal loud reference sound has been standardized on a national and international basis (ANSI, 1986; ISO, 1975). These are in approximate agreement with the results of magnitude and halving–doubling methods of estimation (see short dashed curve in Fig. 3.2). It is seen that in terms of sound pressure level, in decibels, a doubling, or 100% increase, of loudness occurs with an increase of about 10 dB (actually closer to 9 dB), or phons, in sound pressure level. As a rule of thumb, each 1-dB increase in SPL of a noise causes a 10% increase in its loudness.

Because sound energy, in decibels, is a logarithmic function, to the base 10, of sound pressure squared, an increase of sound pressure by a factor of 1.41 ($\sqrt{2}$) causes an increase of 3 dB in sound pressure level. However, a 3-dB increase in SPL results in an increase of only about 30% in loudness, or sones. An increase of 1.41 in sound pressure, or 3 dB in SPL, occurs when the power output of a single source is doubled, or when two of those sources are "turned on." Turning on 10 such sources would cause an increase in SPL of 10 dB at the position of the listener and about a doubling, or slightly more than a 100% increase, in loudness. In brief, while a ratio-change in the intensity of a sound will be perceived as about a same-sized change in loudness, physical intensity is measured in units that are scaled differently than are the units of subjective loudness.

Standard Scale of Perceived Noisiness as Function of Intensity Level

As will be discussed below, the same scale for growth of loudness has been found in early laboratory tests to be appropriate for perceived noisiness. However, the maximum level of intensity employed in those test, and in the development of the loudness scale were somewhat limited. Note, for example, that in Fig. 3.2 the highest intensity apparently judged for the loudness scale was $L_A \sim 100$ dB for a 1000-Hz tone, the standard reference frequency employed.

As seen in Fig. 3.3A, up to peak phons or perceived noisiness in decibels (PN_{dB}) the rate, or slope, of the scaled growth of judged noisiness of the aircraft noises increased as a function of intensity level up to L_{Aex} levels of $\sim \leq 100$ dB, in fairly close accordance with the standard rate that has been established for loudness and perceived noisiness. However, as seen in Fig.

3.3B, above about that level perceived noisiness grew at a somewhat greater rate. Although loudness judgments, as such, were not obtained it is hypothesized that they would have shown the same growth functions displayed in Figs. 3.3A and 3.3B for perceived noisiness.

The width and shape of the spectra of the aircraft noises cause their L_A levels to be numerically lower than their phon or PN_{dB} values, which, as seen in Fig. 3.2, are the same in the case of a tone, or narrowband noise, centered at 1000 Hz. As will be discussed later, a procedure for adjusting the levels of ultra high-intensity noises to take into account this accelerated growth of noisiness (and presumed loudness) at those intensities is proposed.

Effect of Bandwidth on Loudness

The scaling of growth of loudness of a given spectra sound as a function of its intensity has been a relatively straightforward matter. Scaling the loudnesses of sounds whose frequency bandwidths differ is more complicated.

Fletcher and Munson (1933) proposed a procedure for calculating from physical measurements the loudness of a complex sound consisting of a number of tones that was not used because of its complexity. Churcher and King (1937), and later Beranek *et al.* (1951) proposed that a simple summation in sones of the loudness of octave bands of sound would give a reasonable approximation to the perceived loudness of a complex sound consisting of one or more octave bands of random noise. For these purposes, an octave band of random noise having the same overall SPL as a pure tone of the same center frequency was assumed to be equally loud.

Since those earlier proposed methods, two major approaches were developed. One, that of Stevens (1955; 1957a, 1957b) is based on empirical judgment-scaling data of sensory magnitudes. The second, that of Zwicker (1958, 1960) involves, in addition to some such scaling, the use of functions derived from experiments on masking. The results of numerous experimental studies, to be presented later, indicates that sound measurements based on these two procedures predict with about equal accuracy, on the average, the judged loudness and perceived noisiness of noises under laboratory and real-life listening conditions.

Stevens' Methods

Stevens (1956, 1957b, 1961, 1972) published procedures for evaluating the total loudness of sounds with broad, continuous spectra. Stevens' procedures were ostensibly more accurate in predicting the judged loudness of complex sounds consisting of bands of random noise than the method of simply adding together the sone values of individual octave bands.

Stevens' general formula, the terms of which were derived from curve-fitting analyses, is to add to the sone value of the loudest band a fractional

A

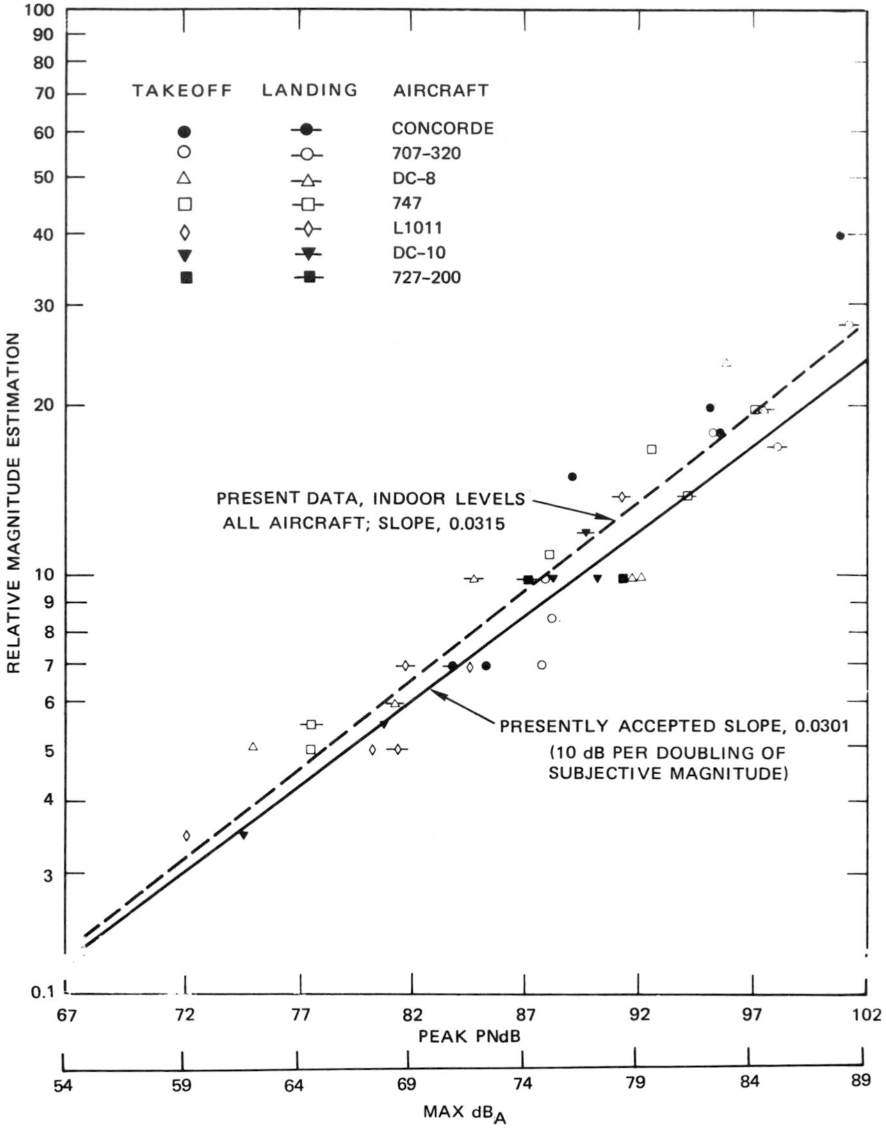

FIGURE 3.3 Magnitude estimations of aircraft noises judged relative to reference aircraft flyover noise at (A) level of L_{Aex} 80, and assigned magnitude of 10; and (B) L_{Aex} of 97, and magnitude of 10. Noises presented via high-fidelity loudspeakers to 15 adult subjects in test chamber from recording of actual aircraft flyovers. (From Kryter and Poza, 1977.)

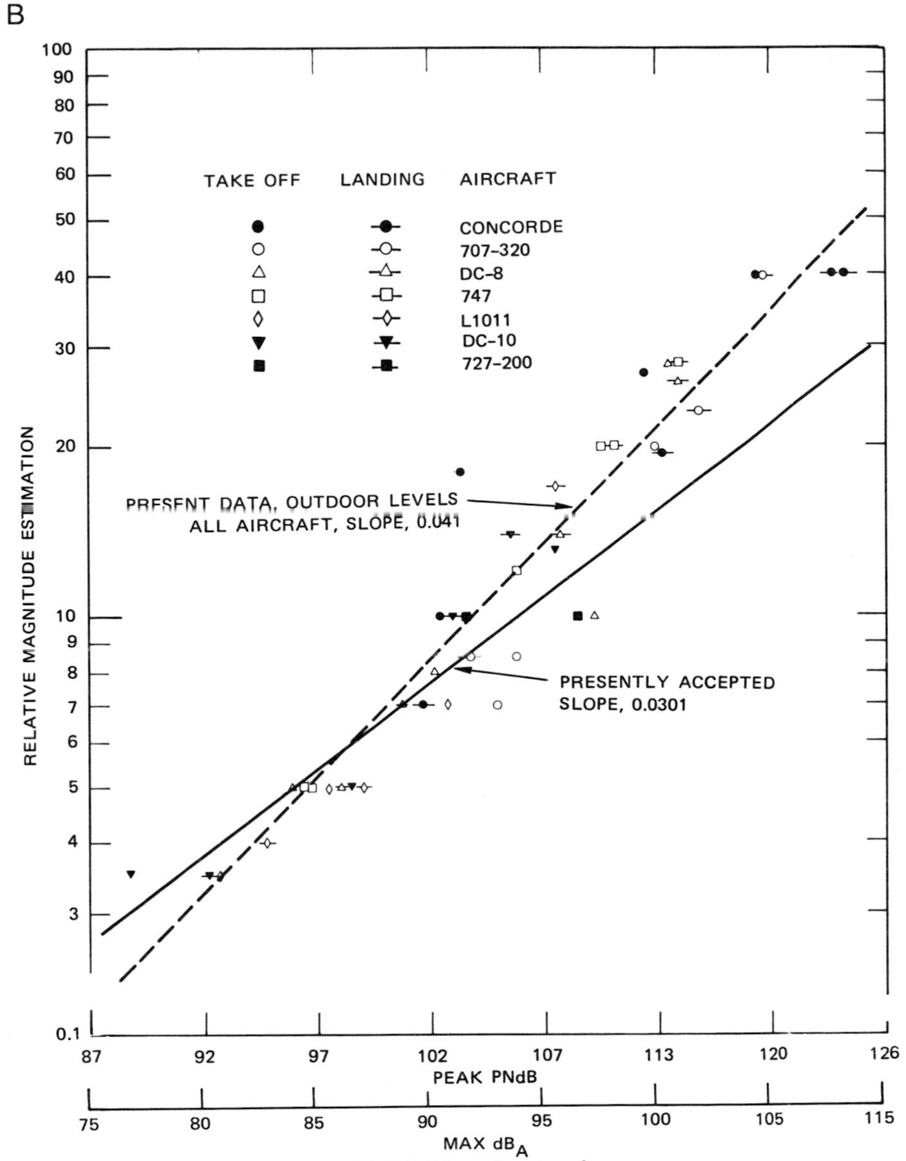

FIGURE 3.3 *Continued.*

portion of the sum of the sone values of the remainder of the bands: loudness = $S_{max} + f\,(S_{all} - S_{max})$, where S is sones, and f is a fraction dependent on bandwidth. Stevens derived the fraction to be applied when the spectrum of the sound was measured in either full-octave (f = 0.3), ½-octave (f = 0.2), or ⅓-octave (f = 0.15) bands.

However, instead of expressing loudness in terms of sones, it is general practice to express the loudness of a given sound in terms of a SPL, in decibels. For this purpose, Stevens used a reference sound, usually a tone or narrowband centered at 1000 Hz, when it is as loud as the given sound. The result is called *loudness level in phons,* or, in German, *bark.* The unit phon can be calculated from psychological units, sones, but not directly from physical measurements of sound pressure because the relation between SPL and loudness varies with frequency differently at different levels of intensity.

Stevens (1961) slightly modified his earlier method of calculating loudness (Stevens, 1957b) and named this new method "Mark V1." Mark V1 has been adopted by the American National Standards Institute (ANSI, 1986) as the procedure to be used for the calculation of loudness of noise measured in either octave, 1/2-octave, or 1/3-octave bands. The International Standardization Organization (ISO, 1975) has recommended Mark V1 as the method to be used for calculating the loudness of sounds measured with octave band filters, and Zwicker's (1958; 1960) method, described below, when the sounds are measured with 1/3-octave band filters.

Zwicker's Method

As previously mentioned, Fletcher and Munson (1933) suggested that loudness is proportional to the number of neural impulses per second reaching the brain from the auditory nerve fibers. Further, they noted that two tones competing for the attention of a single nerve fiber could mutually contribute to its stimulation and, therefore, components within a certain frequency band should be grouped together and treated as a single stimulating component.

The width of these frequency bands was estimated by Fletcher and Munson (1933) to be 100 Hz wide for frequencies below 2000 Hz, 200 Hz wide for frequencies between 2000 and 4000 Hz, and 400 Hz wide for frequencies between 4000 and 8000 Hz. From subjective tests of loudness and masking, Zwicker *et al.* (1957) also determined frequency groupings, "frequenzgruppen," that take place in the cochlea of the ear (see Fig. 2.6). Frequenzgruppen are similar to critical bands as conceived by Fletcher and Munson (1933).

Zwicker (1958) determined the spread of masking for narrow bands of noise, the threshold of audibility of pure tones, and the change in level of a 1000-Hz tone to obtain a doubling (or halving) of loudness. His results for equal loudness contours as a function of frequency are much like those found by Stevens (1957b) and Robinson and Whittle (1964) (see Fig. 3.1). His published results for spread of masking for narrow bands of noise are similar to the spread of masking data obtained by Egan and Meyer (1950), Ehmer (1959), and Carter and Kryter (1962). Zwicker's assumption that there is a functional correspondence between masking and loudness is well substantiated by data on the critical bandwidth of the ear.

On the basis of these concepts, Zwicker (1960) developed a graphic method for depicting and calculating the loudness of a complex sound. For calculation purposes, he prepared 10 graphs (covering both diffuse and free-field conditions; see Fig. 3.4 for an example) in which the horizontal ordinates are marked off in equal frequenzgruppen (approximated for practical purposes by 1/3-octave steps above 280 Hz), with the vertical divisions for each frequenzgruppen, in phons, being proportional to sones.

The short-dash curves show the area covered by the upward spread of masking. Plotting a sound spectrum on Zwicker's graph and drawing in the lines for spread of masking are supposed to show what proportion of available "nerve impulse units" are made operative as the result of exposure of the ear to a given sound. Accordingly, this area on the graph should be proportional to total loudness.

PERCEIVED NOISINESS

Equal Noisiness Frequency Contours

In 1956 or thereabouts, the question arose as to why the flyover sound of a jet aircraft with a peak sound pressure level of around LC 100 sounded so much louder and obnoxious than that from propeller-driven aircraft with the same C-weighted sound pressure level. At that time, C-weighting, essentially linear as far as the auditory system is concerned, was the standard method used for the assessment of the loudness of such broad band noise. This was done in accordance with some then existing equal loudness contours for pure tones when presented at moderate to high levels of intensity.

Some early research on the judged annoyance of tones (Laird and Coye, 1929), and narrow bands of white noise (Reese *et al.*, 1944; Kryter, 1948) indicated that noise with larger amounts of pure tone energy in the higher than lower frequencies, as was the case with jet aircraft, would be heard, as being inherently more "annoying" than a noise with predominately low frequencies, such as from propeller-driven aircraft. On the basis of those early data, plus the results of a newly conducted laboratory study, it was suggested that the phrase "perceived noisiness" should be used to identify the immediate sensation of annoyance or unwantedness elicited by broadband sounds with different shaped spectra at the higher frequencies.

It is interesting to note that Rich (1916) observed that tones can be perceived as having an apparent "size" or "extensiveness"—low tones of an pipe organ sound "bigger in space" (voluminous) than high tones, and Stevens (1934a,b) measured as a function of frequency: (1) equal "volume" (size) contours and (2) conversely, "density." High-frequency tones are sometimes said to be more "piercing" than low-frequency tones. "Roughness" (Zwicker, 1989), "shrillness" (Weber, 1990), and "sharpness" (von Bismark, 1974; Aures, 1985b, in narrow bands or tones have been

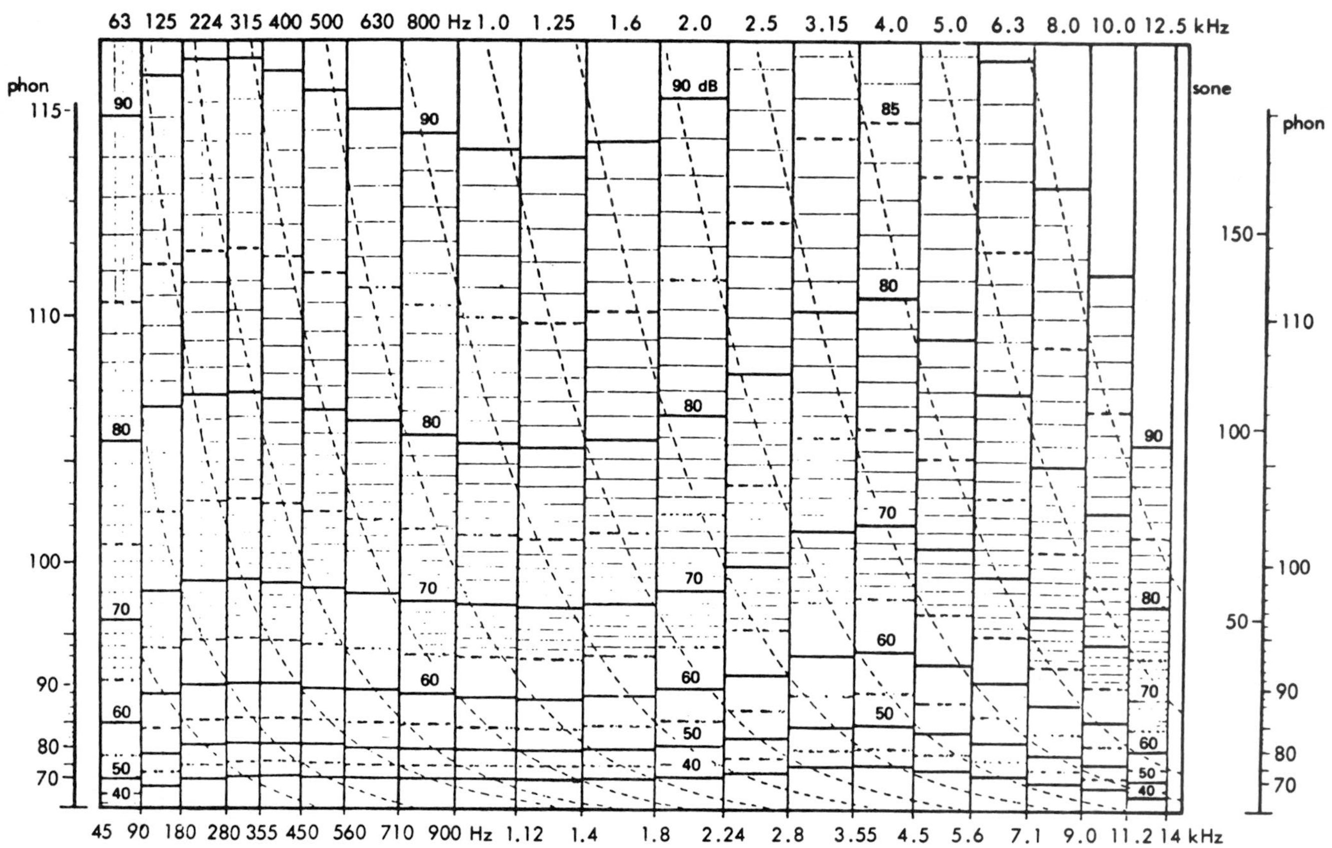

FIGURE 3.4 Example of loudness computation graph, range 70–115 (in phons). (After Zwicker, 1960.)

proposed as contributing to unbiased annoyance sensation from sounds. (If one felt oblidged to believe that these judgments refer to inherent, unlearned sensations, on a par with loudness, pitch etc., it would be appropriate to attempt to rationalize the existence of the involvement of some neural information unique to the sensations. It is perhaps not unreasonable to suggest that possibly, among other things, the extents of the basilar membrane, cochlea, and brain involved during sound stimulations are somehow comparatively sensed by the auditory system.)

Contours for Pure Tones and Narrow Bands

The early studies of judged annoyance that showed a difference between equal loudness and equal annoyance frequency-contours were conducted with pure tones and narrow bands of filtered white noise (Reese et al. 1944; Kryter 1948). Subsequent studies with 1/3-and full-octave bands of noise showed that the difference between the annoyance and loudness contours of sound, as a function of frequency, was not as large as found with narrow bands or pure tones (Kryter and Pearsons, 1963, 1964).

Wells (1967) obtained a set of equal-noisiness contours with 1/3-octave and full-octave bands of noise. Stevens (1972) compiled composite equal-loudness and equal-noisiness contours from various published loudness and noisiness contours, and labeled the contours perceived level, Mark V11. These contours and the contours of Wells (1967) and Ollerhead (1969) are similar in general shape to those obtained later by Kryter and Pearsons (1965) as shown in Fig. 3.1.

It must be concluded, the author believes, that the pitch of 1/3-octave, or wider, bands of sound does not cause there to be any significant difference between equal-noisiness and equal-loudness contours as a function of frequency. However, such a difference does appear to exist when narrowband or predominately tonal spectra are involved.

Perceived Noisiness, in PN_{dB} and L_D

It was suggested that a unit called PN_{dB}, calculated from 1/3-octave band levels, and a *N*- (later labeled *D*-) weighting for use in a sound-level meter be used to estimate the perceived noise level of a sound (Kryter, 1959). These calculations utilized Stevens' (1972) concepts and general band integration procedures, but equal noisiness, in lieu of his equal loudness, contours.

It was proposed that the subjective unit of noisiness be called the *noy*, parallel to the sone for loudness. A sound of 2 noys was said to be subjectively twice as noisy as a sound of 1 noy; 4 noys, to be four times as noisy as a sound of I noy; etc.. PN_{dB} (perceived noisiness in decibels) was coined to be analogous to the phon for loudness. The same scale as that for the growth of loudness as a function of SPL was adopted—an increase of the slightly less than 10 PN_{dB} was equivalent to about a doubling of the noy value, or perceived noisiness of a sound.

However, as discussed above, data obtained with aircraft noise indicate that the standard growth scale for loudness is appropriate for intensity levels less than a peak level of L_{Aex} ~85 (L_{PNdBex}, $L_{phon,ex}$ ~97; see Fig. 3.3), indicating that perceived noisiness grows at a somewhat greater rate at higher levels of intensity. Table 3.1 has not been modified to reflect this change.

PN_{dB} is calculated as

$$PN_{dB} = 40 + 33.3 \log N, \text{ where } N = \text{noy}_{\text{max band}} + 0.15[\Sigma_{\text{noy}_{1/3\text{-octave bands}} - \text{noy}_{\text{max band}}}].$$

Table 3.1 give noy values, as further developed by Kryter and Pearsons (1964), as a function of SPL, for the 24 1/3-octave bands, center frequencies from 50 to 10,000 Hz.

It was proposed as a modification for the calculation of PN_{dB}, that 1/3-octave bands below 400 Hz be combined to make the measured low-frequency energy more consistent with the critical bandwidths of the ear at those frequencies. That is, the sound energy in 1/3 bands of center frequencies 25, 32, 50, 63, 80, and 100 Hz are combined, and the resulting SPL assigned to a band frequency of 63 Hz; 1/3-octave bands of 125, 160, and 200 Hz are combined, and assigned to a band frequency of 160 Hz; and 1/3-octave bands of 250 and 315 Hz, are combined, and assigned to band frequency of 315 Hz (Kryter, 1970b). A D_2-weighting reflecting those modifications was also tentatively proposed and used to some extent.

PN_{dB} and L_D are only two units of physical sound measurement that can be related to subjective noisiness—L_A, phons, or other units can be used to predict perceived noisiness of many sounds and noises, just as PN_{dB} and L_D in their basic form can be used to predict the aspect of perceived noisiness called loudness. Stevens (1972) proposed that the average of a number of equal-loudness and equal-noisiness contours be standardized and used for the calculation, from 1/3 octave bands, of the 'perceived level' in PL_{dB}, and an E-weighting, L_E, be used in a sound-level meter for approximating P_{ldB} (see Fig. 1.4.)

COMPLEX SPECTRAL AND TEMPORAL FACTORS

The relation between some frequency-weighted SPLs of broadband sound and judged loudness and noisiness are, for practical purposes, about the same when other acoustical factors are kept constant. However, variations in several other physical features of sound appear to differently affect their perceived noisiness and loudness, for example: (1) spectral complexity, or concentration of energy in pure tones or narrow frequency bands within a broadband spectrum; (2) duration of the sound; (3) duration of the increase in level prior to the maximum level of nonimpulsive sounds; and (4) impulsiveness of a sound of <0.5-s duration.

Some physical aspects that might seem important appear to have very secondary effects on people compared with the four noted above. Examples of such unimportant factors are Doppler shift (the change in the frequency and sometimes noted pitch of a sound as the sound source moves toward, and away from, the listener (Rosinger *et al,* 1970; Ollerhead, 1968), and modulation of pure tones [Pearsons (1966); data to be presented below], "sharpness," and "roughness" [Angerer *et al.* (1991); data to be presented below].

'Roughness' of sounds due to modulation of their intensity or frequency, regular or random, is sometimes thought to contribute to the perceived noisiness of sounds and has led to the development of binaural measurement-analysis instruments and techniques for its quantification. Such irregularities can, of course, be suggestive of a lack of 'quality' in the source of the sound (Genuit, 1991). In that context, it is suggested, that a "meaning" of some inappropriate or incorrectly operating parts of an engine or machine is involved rather than an inherent sensation of auditory unwantedness.

Before discussing the results of experiments on these various spectral–temporal features, a few issues pertaining to research methods involved should be mentioned. In particular, the instructions to the subjects are a matter of importance.

Instructions to Subjects

Pearsons and Horonjeff (1967) investigated the influence different words had on subjective ratings of motor vehicle and aircraft noises. Their findings are shown in Fig. 3.5. It is academic to try to explain the rather small range of differences shown in Fig. 3.5, and whether these words used really meant different things to different people in the context of the experiments. In any event, there is no apparent reason why listeners should not be asked to rate sounds in terms of their unwantedness, unacceptability, annoyance, or noisiness, especially if all, or several of such words, are used as synonyms.

The virtue of the use of a group of synonyms is that this, hopefully, tends to make clear that the sound of the sound, rather than a learned meaning the sound may have to the individual listener, is the judgment desired. Although the term *loudness* may be included in the instructions, with experiments requiring repeated judgments among many different sounds, subjects may tend to make their task easier, and more reliable, by rating only the most obvious sensation from a sound, which is usually its loudness, rather than an overall perception of its unwantedness. An example of an apparent result of this kind is given later for experiments of the loudness and noisiness of impulsive sounds.

Berglund *et al.* (1975) have also conducted studies on the effect of different

TABLE 3.1 Noy as a Function of Sound-Pressure Level in 1/3-Octave Bands (Band Center Frequency in Kilohertz)

	Frequency, kHz																							
SPL, dB	0.05	0.06	0.08	0.10	0.13	0.16	0.20	0.25	0.32	0.40	0.50	0.63	0.80	1.0	1.2	1.6	2.0	2.5	3.1	4.0	5.0	6.3	8.0	10.0
29																			1.0	1.0				
30																		1.0	1.1	1.1				
31																		1.1	1.1	1.1	1.0			
32																	1.0	1.1	1.2	1.2	1.1			
33																	1.1	1.2	1.3	1.3	1.2	1.0		
34																1.0	1.2	1.3	1.4	1.4	1.3	1.1		
35																1.1	1.3	1.4	1.5	1.5	1.4	1.2		
36																1.2	1.3	1.5	1.6	1.6	1.5	1.4		
37																1.3	1.4	1.6	1.8	1.8	1.6	1.5	1.0	
38															1.0	1.3	1.5	1.8	1.9	1.9	1.7	1.6	1.1	
39															1.1	1.4	1.6	1.9	2.0	2.0	1.9	1.8	1.2	
40										1.0	1.0	1.0	1.0	1.0	1.2	1.5	1.7	2.0	2.2	2.2	2.0	1.9	1.4	
41										1.1	1.1	1.1	1.1	1.1	1.3	1.6	1.8	2.2	2.4	2.4	2.2	2.0	1.5	1.0
42									1.0	1.1	1.1	1.1	1.1	1.1	1.3	1.7	2.0	2.4	2.6	2.6	2.4	2.2	1.7	1.1
43									1.1	1.2	1.2	1.2	1.2	1.2	1.4	1.8	2.2	2.6	2.8	2.8	2.6	2.4	1.8	1.2
44								1.0	1.1	1.3	1.3	1.3	1.3	1.3	1.5	2.0	2.4	2.8	3.0	3.0	2.8	2.6	2.0	1.4
45								1.1	1.2	1.4	1.4	1.4	1.4	1.4	1.6	2.1	2.6	3.0	3.2	3.2	3.0	2.8	2.2	1.5
46							1.0	1.2	1.3	1.5	1.5	1.5	1.5	1.5	1.7	2.3	2.8	3.2	3.4	3.4	3.2	3.0	2.4	1.7
47							1.1	1.3	1.4	1.6	1.6	1.6	1.6	1.6	1.8	2.4	3.0	3.4	3.6	3.6	3.4	3.2	2.6	1.8
48						1.0	1.2	1.4	1.5	1.7	1.7	1.7	1.7	1.7	2.0	2.6	3.2	3.6	3.9	3.9	3.6	3.4	2.8	2.0
49						1.1	1.3	1.5	1.6	1.9	1.9	1.9	1.9	1.9	2.1	2.8	3.4	3.9	4.1	4.1	3.9	3.6	3.0	2.2
50						1.2	1.4	1.6	1.7	2.0	2.0	2.0	2.0	2.0	2.3	3.0	3.6	4.1	4.4	4.4	4.1	3.9	3.2	2.4
51					1.0	1.3	1.5	1.7	1.9	2.1	2.1	2.1	2.1	2.1	2.4	3.2	3.9	4.4	4.7	4.7	4.4	4.1	3.4	2.6
52					1.1	1.4	1.6	1.9	2.0	2.3	2.3	2.3	2.3	2.3	2.6	3.5	4.1	4.7	5.0	5.0	4.7	4.4	3.6	2.8
53				1.0	1.2	1.5	1.7	2.0	2.1	2.5	2.5	2.5	2.5	2.5	2.8	3.7	4.4	5.0	5.3	5.3	5.0	4.7	3.9	3.0
54				1.1	1.3	1.6	1.9	2.1	2.3	2.6	2.6	2.6	2.6	2.6	3.0	4.0	4.7	5.3	5.7	5.7	5.3	5.0	4.1	3.2

55				1.2	1.4	1.7	2.0	2.3	2.4	2.8	2.8	2.8	2.8	2.8	3.2	4.3	5.0	5.7	6.1	6.1	5.7	5.3	4.4	3.5
56			1.0	1.3	1.5	1.9	2.2	2.4	2.6	3.0	3.0	3.0	3.0	3.0	3.5	4.6	5.3	6.1	6.5	6.5	6.1	5.7	4.7	3.7
57			1.1	1.4	1.7	2.0	2.4	2.6	2.8	3.2	3.2	3.2	3.2	3.2	3.7	5.0	5.7	6.5	7.0	7.0	6.5	6.1	5.0	4.0
58			1.2	1.5	1.8	2.2	2.6	2.8	3.0	3.5	3.5	3.5	3.5	3.5	4.0	5.3	6.1	7.0	7.5	7.5	7.0	6.5	5.3	4.3
59			1.3	1.7	2.0	2.4	2.8	3.0	3.2	3.7	3.7	3.7	3.7	3.7	4.3	5.7	6.5	7.5	8.0	8.0	7.5	7.0	5.7	4.6
60		1.0	1.4	1.8	2.2	2.6	3.0	3.2	3.5	4.0	4.0	4.0	4.0	4.0	4.6	6.1	6.0	8.0	8.7	8.7	8.0	7.5	6.1	5.0
61		1.1	1.5	2.0	2.4	2.8	3.2	3.5	3.7	4.3	4.3	4.3	4.3	4.3	5.0	6.5	7.5	8.7	9.3	9.3	8.7	8.0	6.5	5.3
62		1.2	1.7	2.2	2.6	3.0	3.5	3.7	4.0	4.6	4.6	4.6	4.6	4.6	5.3	7.0	8.0	9.3	10.0	10.0	9.3	8.7	7.0	5.7
63		1.3	1.8	2.4	2.8	3.2	3.7	4.0	4.3	4.9	4.9	4.9	4.9	4.9	5.7	7.5	8.7	10.0	11.0	11.0	10.0	9.3	7.5	6.1
64	1.0	1.5	2.0	2.6	3.0	3.5	4.0	4.3	4.6	5.3	5.3	5.3	5.3	5.3	6.1	8.0	9.3	11.0	11.0	11.0	11.0	10.0	8.0	6.5
65	1.1	1.6	2.2	2.8	3.2	3.7	4.3	4.6	5.0	5.7	5.7	5.7	5.7	5.7	6.5	8.7	10.0	11.0	12.0	12.0	11.0	11.0	8.7	7.0
66	1.2	1.8	2.4	3.0	3.5	4.0	4.6	5.0	5.4	6.1	6.1	6.1	6.1	6.1	7.0	9.3	11.0	12.0	13.0	13.0	12.0	11.0	9.3	7.5
67	1.4	2.0	2.6	3.3	3.7	4.3	5.0	5.4	5.9	6.5	6.5	6.5	6.5	6.5	7.5	10.0	11.0	13.0	14.0	14.0	13.0	12.0	10.0	8.0
68	1.6	2.2	2.8	3.6	4.0	4.6	5.4	5.9	6.4	7.0	7.0	7.0	7.0	7.0	8.0	11.0	12.0	14.0	15.0	15.0	14.0	13.0	11.0	8.7
69	1.8	2.3	3.0	3.9	4.3	5.0	5.9	6.4	6.9	7.5	7.5	7.5	7.5	7.5	8.7	11.0	13.0	15.0	16.0	16.0	15.0	14.0	11.0	9.3
70	2.0	2.5	3.3	4.2	4.6	5.4	6.4	6.9	7.5	8.0	8.0	8.0	8.0	8.0	9.3	12.0	14.0	16.0	17.0	17.0	16.0	15.0	12.0	10.0
71	2.2	2.8	3.6	4.6	5.0	5.9	6.9	7.5	8.0	8.6	8.6	8.6	8.6	8.6	10.0	13.0	15.0	17.0	19.0	19.0	17.0	16.0	13.0	11.0
72	2.3	3.0	3.9	5.0	5.4	6.4	7.5	8.0	8.7	9.2	9.2	9.2	9.2	9.2	11.0	14.0	16.0	19.0	20.0	20.0	19.0	17.0	14.0	11.0
73	2.5	3.3	4.2	5.4	5.9	6.9	8.0	8.7	9.3	9.8	9.8	9.8	9.8	9.8	11.0	15.0	17.0	20.0	21.0	21.0	20.0	19.0	15.0	12.0
74	2.8	3.7	4.6	5.9	6.4	7.5	8.7	9.3	10.0	10.6	10.6	10.6	10.6	10.6	12.0	16.0	19.0	21.0	23.0	23.0	21.0	20.0	16.0	13.0
75	3.0	4.1	5.0	6.4	6.9	8.0	9.3	10.0	11.0	11.3	11.3	11.3	11.3	11.3	13.0	17.0	20.0	23.0	24.0	24.0	23.0	21.0	17.0	14.0
76	3.3	4.5	5.4	6.9	7.5	8.7	10.0	11.0	11.0	12.0	12.0	12.0	12.0	12.0	14.0	19.0	21.0	24.0	26.0	26.0	24.0	23.0	19.0	15.0
77	3.7	5.0	5.9	7.5	8.3	9.3	11.0	11.0	12.0	13.0	13.0	13.0	13.0	13.0	15.0	20.0	23.0	26.0	28.0	28.0	26.0	24.0	20.0	16.0
78	4.1	5.4	6.4	8.3	9.1	10.0	11.0	12.0	13.0	14.0	14.0	14.0	14.0	14.0	16.0	21.0	24.0	28.0	30.0	30.0	28.0	26.0	21.0	17.0
79	4.5	5.9	6.9	9.1	10.0	11.0	12.0	13.0	14.0	15.0	15.0	15.0	15.0	15.0	17.0	23.0	26.0	30.0	32.0	32.0	30.0	28.0	23.0	19.0
80	5.0	6.4	7.5	10.0	11.0	11.0	13.0	14.0	15.0	16.0	16.0	16.0	16.0	16.0	19.0	24.0	28.0	32.0	35.0	35.0	32.0	30.0	24.0	20.0
81	5.5	6.9	8.3	11.0	11.0	12.0	14.0	15.0	16.0	18.0	18.0	18.0	18.0	18.0	20.0	26.0	30.0	35.0	37.0	37.0	35.0	32.0	26.0	21.0
82	6.1	7.5	9.1	11.0	12.0	13.0	15.0	16.0	17.0	19.0	19.0	19.0	19.0	19.0	21.0	28.0	32.0	37.0	40.0	40.0	37.0	35.0	28.0	23.0
83	6.8	8.3	10.0	12.0	13.0	14.0	16.0	17.0	19.0	20.0	20.0	20.0	20.0	20.0	23.0	30.0	35.0	40.0	42.0	42.0	40.0	37.0	30.0	24.0
84	7.5	9.1	12.0	13.0	14.0	15.0	17.0	19.0	20.0	21.0	21.0	21.0	21.0	21.0	24.0	32.0	37.0	42.0	45.0	45.0	42.0	40.0	32.0	26.0
85	8.3	10.0	13.0	14.0	15.0	16.0	19.0	20.0	21.0	23.0	23.0	23.0	23.0	23.0	26.0	35.0	40.0	45.0	47.0	47.0	45.0	42.0	35.0	28.0
86	9.1	12.0	13.0	15.0	16.0	17.0	20.0	21.0	23.0	24.0	24.0	24.0	24.0	24.0	28.0	37.0	42.0	47.0	50.0	50.0	47.0	45.0	37.0	30.0
87	10.0	13.0	14.0	16.0	17.0	19.0	21.0	23.0	24.0	26.0	26.0	26.0	26.0	26.0	30.0	40.0	45.0	50.0	55.0	55.0	50.0	47.0	40.0	32.0

(*continues*)

TABLE 3.1 *(Continued)*

SPL, dB	Frequency, kHz 0.05	0.06	0.08	0.10	0.13	0.16	0.20	0.25	0.32	0.40	0.50	0.63	0.80	1.0	1.2	1.6	2.0	2.5	3.1	4.0	5.0	6.3	8.0	10.0
88	11.0	13.0	15.0	17.0	19.0	20.0	23.0	24.0	26.0	28.0	28.0	28.0	28.0	28.0	32.0	42.0	47.0	55.0	60.0	60.0	55.0	50.0	42.0	35.0
89	12	14	16	19	20	21	24	26	28	30	30	30	30	30	35	45	50	60	63	63	60	55	45	37
90	14	15	17	20	21	23	26	28	30	32	32	32	32	32	37	47	55	63	67	67	63	60	47	40
91	15	16	19	21	23	24	28	30	32	34	34	34	34	34	40	50	60	67	71	71	67	63	50	42
92	16	17	20	23	24	24	30	32	35	37	37	37	37	37	42	55	63	71	75	75	71	67	55	45
93	17	19	21	24	26	28	32	35	37	39	39	39	39	39	45	60	67	75	80	80	75	71	60	47
94	19	20	23	26	28	30	35	37	40	42	42	42	42	42	47	63	71	80	86	86	80	75	63	50
95	20	21	24	28	30	32	37	40	42	45	45	45	45	45	50	67	75	86	93	93	86	80	67	55
96	21	23	26	30	32	35	40	42	45	49	49	49	49	49	55	71	80	93	100	100	93	86	71	60
97	23	24	28	32	35	37	42	45	47	52	52	52	52	52	60	75	86	100	108	108	100	93	75	63
98	24	26	30	35	37	40	45	47	50	56	56	56	56	56	64	80	93	108	116	116	108	100	80	67
99	26	28	32	37	40	42	47	50	55	60	60	60	60	60	69	86	100	116	125	125	116	108	86	71
100	28	30	35	40	42	45	50	55	60	64	64	64	64	64	74	93	108	125	133	133	125	116	93	75
101	30	32	37	42	45	47	55	60	64	69	69	69	69	69	79	100	116	133	142	142	133	125	100	80
102	32	35	40	45	47	50	60	64	69	74	74	74	74	74	84	108	125	142	150	150	142	133	108	86
103	35	37	42	47	50	55	64	69	74	79	79	79	79	79	91	116	133	150	162	162	150	142	116	93
104	37	40	45	50	55	60	69	74	79	84	84	84	84	84	97	125	142	162	173	173	162	150	125	100
105	40	42	47	55	60	64	74	79	84	91	91	91	91	91	104	133	150	173	108	108	173	162	133	108
106	42	45	50	60	64	69	79	84	91	97	97	97	97	97	111	142	162	186	200	200	186	173	142	116
107	45	47	55	64	69	74	84	91	97	104	104	104	104	104	119	150	173	200	215	215	200	186	150	125
108	47	50	60	69	74	79	91	97	104	111	111	111	111	111	128	162	186	215	232	232	215	200	162	133
109	50	55	64	74	79	84	97	104	111	119	119	119	119	119	137	173	200	237	250	250	232	215	173	142
110	55	60	69	79	84	91	104	111	119	128	128	128	128	128	147	186	215	250	266	266	250	232	186	150
111	60	64	74	84	91	97	111	119	128	137	137	137	137	137	158	200	232	266	284	284	266	250	200	162
112	64	69	79	91	97	104	119	128	137	147	147	147	147	147	169	215	250	284	300	300	284	266	215	173
113	69	74	84	97	104	111	128	137	147	158	158	158	158	158	181	232	266	300	324	324	300	284	232	186
114	74	79	91	104	111	119	137	147	158	169	169	169	169	169	194	250	284	324	346	346	324	300	250	200
115	79	84	97	111	119	128	147	158	169	181	181	181	181	181	208	266	300	346	372	372	346	324	266	215
116	84	91	104	119	128	137	158	169	181	194	194	194	194	194	223	284	324	372	400	400	372	346	284	232
117	91	97	111	128	137	147	169	181	194	208	208	208	208	208	239	300	346	400	430	430	400	372	300	250
118	97	104	119	137	147	158	181	194	208	223	223	223	223	223	256	324	372	430	464	464	430	400	324	266

119	104	111	128	147	158	169	194	208	233	239	239	239	239	239	274	346	400	464	500	500	464	430	346	284
120	111	119	137	158	169	181	208	223	239	256	256	256	256	256	294	372	430	500	532	532	500	464	372	300
121	119	128	147	169	181	194	223	239	256	274	274	274	274	274	315	400	464	532	568	568	532	500	400	324
122	128	137	158	181	194	208	239	256	274	294	294	294	294	294	338	430	500	568	600	600	568	532	430	346
123	137	147	169	194	208	223	256	274	294	315	315	315	315	315	362	464	532	600	648	648	600	568	464	372
124	147	158	181	208	223	239	274	294	315	338	338	338	338	338	388	500	568	648	692	692	648	600	500	400
125	158	169	194	223	239	256	294	315	338	362	362	362	362	362	416	532	600	692	744	744	692	648	532	430
126	169	181	208	239	256	274	315	338	362	388	388	388	388	388	446	568	648	744	800	800	744	692	560	464
127	181	194	223	256	274	294	338	362	388	416	416	416	416	416	478	600	692	800	860	860	800	744	600	500
128	194	208	239	274	294	315	362	388	416	446	446	446	446	446	512	648	744	860	928	928	860	800	648	532
129	208	223	256	294	315	338	388	416	446	478	478	478	478	478	549	692	800	928	1000	1000	928	860	692	560
130	223	239	274	315	338	362	416	446	478	512	512	512	512	512	588	744	860	1000	1064	1064	1000	928	744	600
131	239	256	294	338	362	388	446	478	512	549	549	549	549	549	630	800	928	1064	1136	1136	1064	1000	800	648
132	256	274	315	362	388	416	478	512	549	588	588	588	588	588	676	860	1000	1136	1200	1200	1136	1064	860	692
133	274	294	338	388	416	446	512	549	588	630	630	630	630	630	724	928	1064	1200	1296	1296	1200	1136	929	744
134	294	315	362	416	446	478	549	586	630	676	676	676	676	676	776	1000	1136	1296	1384	1384	1296	1200	1000	800
135	315	338	388	446	478	512	588	630	676	724	724	724	724	724	832	1064	1200	1384	1488	1488	1384	1296	1064	860
136	338	362	416	478	512	549	630	676	724	776	776	776	776	776	891	1136	1296	1488	1600	1600	1488	1384	1136	928
137	362	388	446	512	549	588	676	724	776	832	832	832	832	832	955	1200	1384	1600	1720	1720	1600	1488	1200	1000
138	388	416	478	549	588	630	724	776	832	891	891	891	891	891	1024	1296	1488	1720	1856	1856	1720	1600	1296	1064
139	416	446	512	588	630	676	776	832	891	955	955	955	955	955	1098	1384	1600	1856	2000	2000	1856	1720	1384	1136
140	446	478	549	630	676	724	832	891	955	1024	1024	1024	1024	1024	1176	1486	1720	2000			2000	1856	1488	1200
141	478	512	588	676	724	776	891	955	1024	1098	1098	1098	1098	1098	1261	1600	1856					2000	1600	1296
142	512	549	630	724	776	832	955	1024	1098	1176	1176	1176	1176	1176	1351	1720	2000						1720	1384
143	549	588	678	776	832	891	1024	1098	1176	1261	1261	1261	1261	1261	1488	1856							1856	1488
144	588	630	724	832	891	955	1098	1176	1261	1351	1351	1351	1351	1351	1552	2000							2000	1600
145	630	676	776	891	955	1024	1176	1261	1351	1448	1448	1448	1448	1448	1663									1720
146	676	724	832	955	1024	1098	1261	1351	1448	1552	1552	1552	1552	1552	1783									1856
147	724	776	891	1024	1098	1176	1351	1448	1552	1663	1663	1663	1663	1663	191[illegible]									2000
148	776	832	955	1098	1176	1261	1448	1552	1663	1783	1783	1783	1783	1783	204[illegible]									

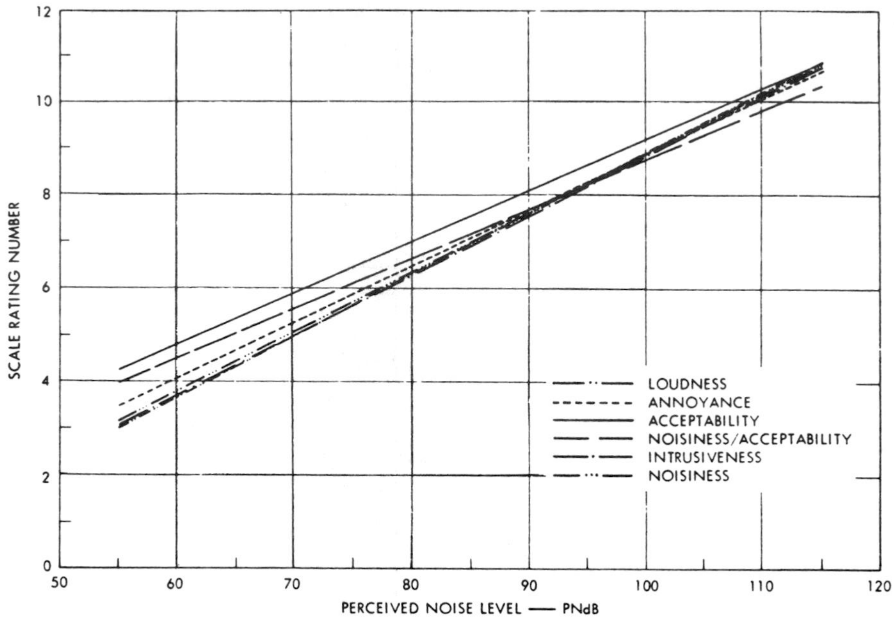

FIGURE 3.5 Mean response ratings of noise stimuli in laboratory for different instruction-words to define perception of relative acceptability. (From Pearsons and Horonjeff, 1967.)

instructions (loudness, noisiness, and annoyance) on the judgments of aircraft noise relative to a broadband random (white) noise of 10-s duration. The aircraft noise durations varied from about 4 to 34 s between the points in time the noises were 10 dB below their maximum level.

Their results indicated that aircraft noise at a maximum level L_A 70 is judged equal in loudness to a 10-s sample of white noise at L_A 70, but that the aircraft noise at L_A 20 would be judged as annoying as the white noise at L_A 70 (see Fig. 3.6). At L_A 20, the aircraft noise would be barely audible in the absolute quiet. These investigators also found that the duration of the sounds had no apparent affect on how they were judged. Such differences between this and other studies on this subject ostensibly arise from differences in the instructions given to the subjects. Bergland *et al.* (1975) defined: (1) loudness as "the perceptual aspect that is changed by turning the volume on a radio set"; (2) noisiness as "the quality of the noise. A jackhammer . . . or motorbike. Music may be loud but not noisy"; and (3) "Annoyance as the nuisance aspect of a noise. Imagine you hear the noise after a hard day's work . . . intending to read your newspaper."

It is possible that some of the independent effects of intensity, frequency, tonality, and/or duration on judgments of perceived noisiness are not properly determined because of inadequate instructions or motivation of the subjects. Consider, for example, tests where several hundred comparative

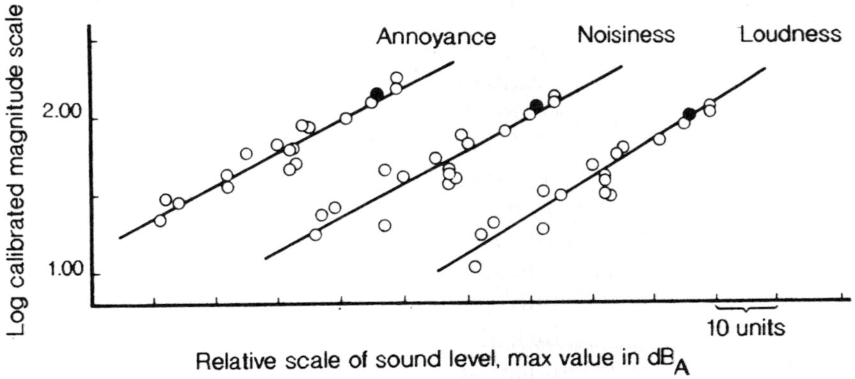

FIGURE 3.6 Psychophysical relations for the three attribute scales. Filled symbols refer to the standard white noise. The regression lines are fitted by the method of least squares. (From Berglund *et al.*, 1975. Copyright 1975 by the American Psychological Association. Adapted by permission of the author.)

judgments, or magnitude estimates, of a number of different sounds are requested in order to evaluate the effects of physical variations in their structure.

While the subjects may initially respond to how each of the total events is perceived (taking duration, tonal components, as well as peak loudness into account), research experience indicates that, after making a number of subjective judgments, many subjects will focus their attention on the most predominate characteristics that the various sounds have in common. This will usually be that of the noise when at its peak level. This response tendency is presumably based on the subject's desire to make the task easier and the responses consistent.

It can, of course, be maintained that if the effect of some physical aspect does not emerge from the data, the results are, practically speaking, valid. However, under real-life, or less arduous, listening conditions, the judgments of relative acceptability to a person of a broadband noise with a high-frequency tonal component versus about the same bandwidth noise without the tonal component, or of a noise of 10 s versus the same noise of, say, 5 s in duration, can be expected to reveal preferences even when the noises reach equal peak levels.

TONAL ASPECTS

Noisiness is often judged to be greater for broadband sounds that contain relatively high concentrations of energy in narrowbands (≤1/3-octave wide) than for broadband sounds with energy distributed rather evenly over frequency. The judged perceived noisiness of the sounds that have energy concentrated in tones or in narrow bands that exceed adjacent band levels can be estimated approximately, through corrections applied to the measured SPLs normally used in calculating perceived noisiness (Kryter and Pearsons, 1963, 1965; Kryter *et al.*, 1965; Pearsons *et al.*, 1965; Pearsons, 1968; Parnell *et al.*, 1967). Parenthetically, a greater saliency, or effectiveness, of pure tones in comparison to broadband sounds, is also found with respect to the relative intensity levels required of those sounds to cause hearing loss and arousal from sleep. Data on these phenomenon are presented in Chapters 6 and 9.

Tonal "Correction" Procedures

A procedure for correcting the SPL of frequency bands containing strong tonal components to their effective, according to judged perceived noisiness, level is given in Fig. 3.7. Little (1961) suggested another method for correcting calculated PNL of sounds that contain pure tones. Unlike the procedure outlined in Fig. 3.7, only one correction is added to a sound even though more than one pure-tone component is present, and the magnitude of the correction is independent of the absolute intensity of the bands of noise. Sperry (1968) quantified the Little method for use by the Federal Aviation Administration (FAA).

Wells and Blazier (1962) also proposed a method to account for the effect of pure-tone components on judged noisiness. In the Wells and Blazier (1962) approach, the value of one of a family of frequency-weighted contours (given in published graphs) that is tangentially closest to a given sound spectrum

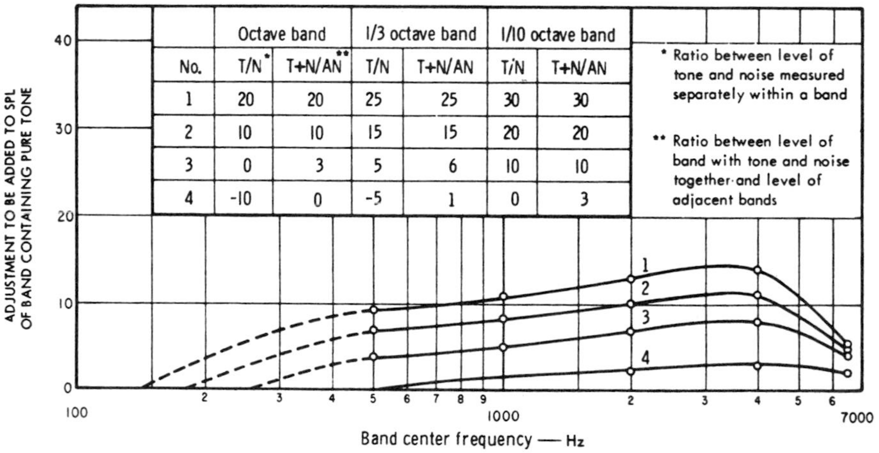

No.	Octave band T/N*	Octave band T+N/AN**	1/3 octave band T/N	1/3 octave band T+N/AN	1/10 octave band T/N	1/10 octave band T+N/AN
1	20	20	25	25	30	30
2	10	10	15	15	20	20
3	0	3	5	6	10	10
4	-10	0	-5	1	0	3

FIGURE 3.7 Correction, in decibels, to be applied to the SPL of a broadband sound containing a pure tone or very narrow band of energy. (From Kryter and Pearsons, 1965. Copyright 1965 by the American Psychological Association. Adapted by permission of the author.)

is assigned to the actual spectrum of the sound in question. The value is, however, corrected according to the number of 1/3-octave bands within 5 dB of the highest contour tangent to the sound spectrum.

Test of Tone Corrections

Tests were conducted of the perceived noisiness of sounds containing single and multiple steady-state and modulated tones relative to a standard, or reference, sound. Figure 3.8 illustrates the general spectra of the different sounds. The findings, shown in Fig. 3.9, indicate that perceived noise levels (PNL), in PN_{dB}, calculated with tone corrections based on the procedures in Fig. 3.7 resulted in PN_{dB}s for the comparison noises that were comparable to that of the standard sound judged to be equally noisy. Without tone corrections the PN_{dB} values differed considerably.

However, for the results of some tests of pure tones and aircraft flyover sounds that contained some pure-tone components, tone corrections were not always necessary for obtaining the best estimates of judged perceived noisiness (Kryter *et al.*, 1965; Kryter, 1970a). Part of the difficulty appeared to be related to the unreliability that is introduced in the detailed band-level measurements required for making the tone corrections. From their assembly

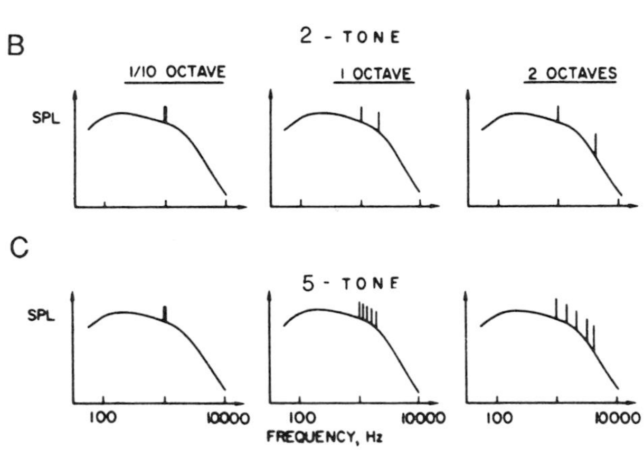

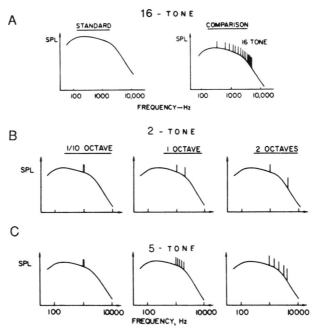

FIGURE 3.8 Spectrum of standard and 16-tone comparison stimuli (upper graphs) and samples of spectra of 2- and 5-tone comparison stimuli (lower graph). (From Pearsons, 1968.)

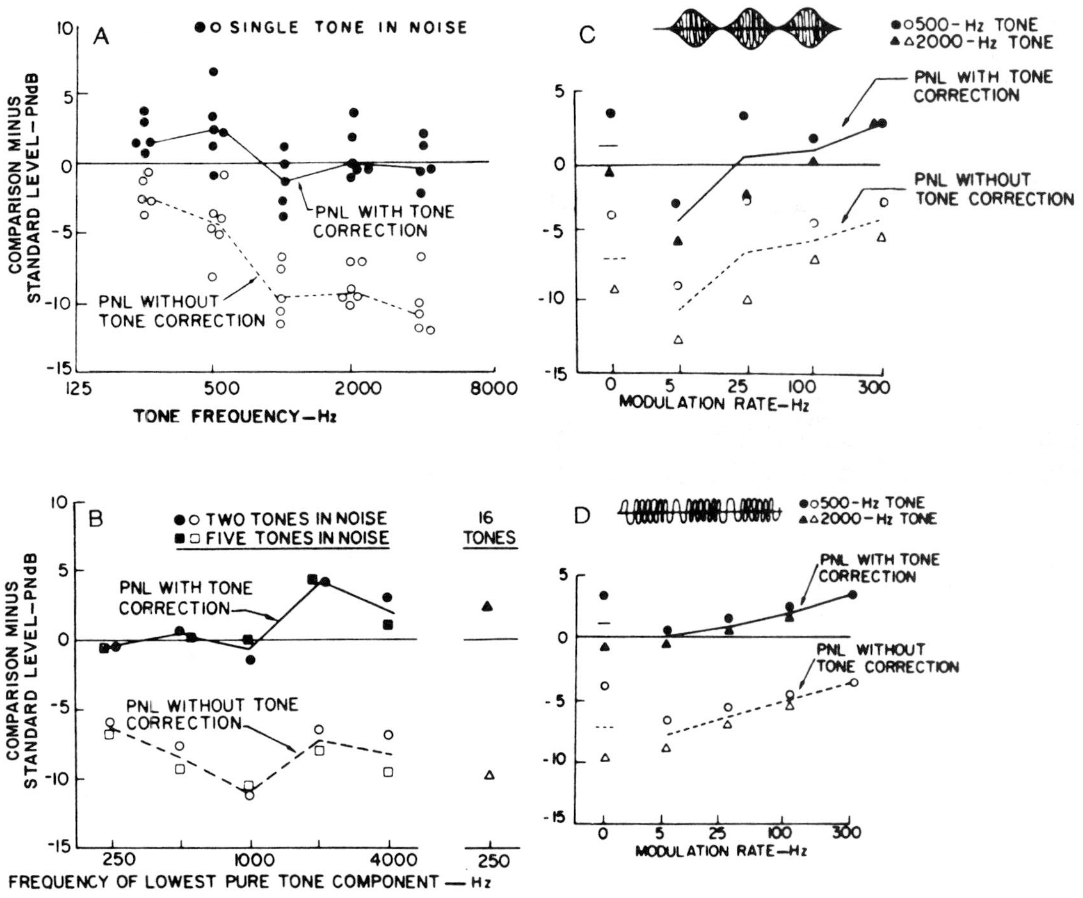
A
●○ SINGLE TONE IN NOISE
COMPARISON MINUS STANDARD LEVEL–PNdB
PNL WITH TONE CORRECTION
PNL WITHOUT TONE CORRECTION
TONE FREQUENCY—Hz
C
●○500-Hz TONE
▲△2000-Hz TONE
PNL WITH TONE CORRECTION
PNL WITHOUT TONE CORRECTION
MODULATION RATE–Hz
B
●○ TWO TONES IN NOISE
■□ FIVE TONES IN NOISE
16 TONES
COMPARISON MINUS STANDARD LEVEL–PNdB
PNL WITH TONE CORRECTION
PNL WITHOUT TONE CORRECTION
FREQUENCY OF LOWEST PURE TONE COMPONENT — Hz
D
●○500-Hz TONE
▲△2000-Hz TONE
PNL WITH TONE CORRECTION
PNL WITHOUT TONE CORRECTION
MODULATION RATE–Hz

of data from studies of broadband noises, a few of which contained some tonal components, Scharf *et al.* (1977; Scharf and Hellman, 1979) also calculated that various tone-correction procedures did not significantly improve predictions of the judgments. Some more recent data on this matter are given below.

Recent Studies of Tone Corrections of Aircraft Noise

McCurdy (1988, 1989, 1990, 1991, 1992) conducted a series of laboratory tests of judged perceived annoyance, defined as unwanted, objectionable, etc., of recorded aircraft flyover noise. The variability, as well as consistencies, among the findings are evidenced by the following excerpts from some of the conclusions reached in the different studies. It is to be noted that different types of aircraft engines (pure-jet, turboprops, etc.), and their mode of operation were involved in the different studies, so that a broad variety of noises were tested:

- Duration corrections improved annoyance prediction . . . Limiting tone corrections to tones at or above 500 Hz improved annoyance prediction (McCurdy, 1988).
- The annoyance prediction ability of the noise metric was improved by . . . a duration (and tone) correction (McCurdy, 1989).
- L_A with duration and tone corrections provided the most accurate annoyance prediction (McCurdy, 1990).
- L_A with duration and tone corrections provided the most accurate annoyance prediction (McCurdy, 1991).
- Of the noise metrics considered (PNL, phons Stevens and Zwicker, L_A L_D) PNL with no tone . . . correction (was best). The optimum duration-correction magnitude is approximately 1 dB per doubling of effective duration instead of 3 dB . . . for takeoff and landing noise (McCurdy, 1992).

Angerer *et al.* (1991) obtained, under laboratory conditions, magnitude estimates of the annoyance, defined as "How unpleasant, objectionable, disturbing, or unwanted" were the sounds of recordings of the interior noise of (1) present-day turbofan aircraft, and (2) of advanced propeller-driven aircraft of the future. Each of some 240 noises were presented steady state for 15 s with on-set and offset times of 2 s.

FIGURE 3.9 Difference in perceived noise level (PNL, in PN_{dB} when comparison and standard sounds are judged to be equally noisy. (A, B) Standard noise without tones, comparison with single and multiple tones. (C) Frequency modulated tones. (D) Amplitude modulated tones. Tone corrections made according to method shown in Fig. 3.7. (From Pearsons, 1968.)

The experimenters compared the regression functions between the $\log_{10}$ of magnitude estimates and (1) L_C labeled as OASPL; (2) L_A; (3) $\log_{10}$ Zwicker sones, labeled as "loudness"; (4) $\log_{10}$ Zwicker sones modified for "tonality"); (5) "sharpness" as calculated for a spectrum by methods of von Bismark (1974) and Aures (1985c); (5) "tonality"; as calculated for a spectrum by a method proposed by Aures (1985c); and (6) "roughness", calculated for a spectrum by a method proposed by Aures (1985c). Loudness was calculated by means of a computer program (von Paulus and Zwicker, 1972), based on Zwicker's method as given in ISO (1966).

Tonality, sharpness, and roughness are sensations of a 'sensory euphony model' propounded by Aures (1985b). Sharpness was defined as an indication of a sound's timbre, and roughness as an unpleasant auditory sensation elicited when sounds contain relatively rapid amplitude fluctuations. The procedures involved in casting physical measures of sound into units that will supposedly predict those sensations are not given by Angerer *et al.* (1991), except by reference to publications by Aures (1985) and von Bismark (1974).

Figure 3.10 clearly shows that as far as common units of sound measurement are concerned, the unit most highly correlated with judged annoyance was L_A, followed by loudness (Zwicker), with the usual poor showing of OASPL (frequency unweighted sound-pressure level, L_C). The units calculated for sharpness and roughness are very poorly related to judged annoyance. The loudness–tonality model (lower left graph in Fig. 3.10) appears to be correlated with judged annoyance as well as, perhaps slightly better, than L_A. This would seem to indicate that tonality, from relatively intense pure tone components, contributed to annoyance beyond that due to the loudness of the aircraft noise. Unfortunately, how this unit was calculated is not discussed by the authors.

DURATIONAL ASPECTS

Duration: Effective Energy for Perceived Noisiness

When a sound is near its masked threshold, the ear best perceives loudness, or a change in loudness, after it averages, effectively, sound intensity over a period of ~0.5 s. Judged loudness, or delectability of the sound, does not increase for durations longer than ~ 0.5s (see Fig. 2.7). (A fuller discussion of the acceptance and integration of sound energy by the ear is given in Chapter 6 in relation to auditory fatigue from sound stimulation.)

Indeed, if one ear is exposed continuously for a time to a sound, and the other not exposed, when both ears are subsequently exposed to the same sound, its loudness is greater in the previously unexposed ear (Egan, 1955). It is not clear whether the effect is due to receptor equilibration, fatigue, or a purely perceptual loudness adaptation in the previously exposed ear, or some combination of all three.

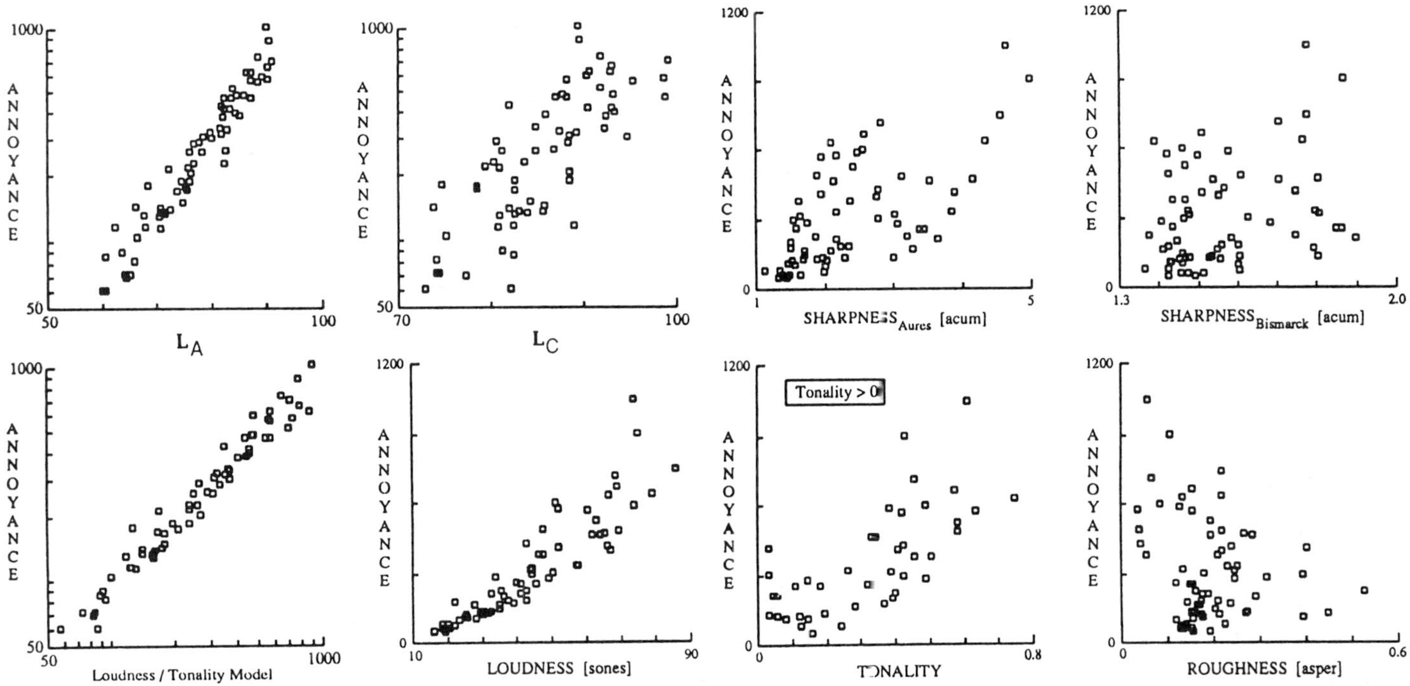

FIGURE 3.10 Geometric means of annoyance judgments plotted on log–log coordinates against L_A, L_C, sones, and various tonality-sharpness-roughness models. (From Angerer *et al.*, 1991.)

On the other hand, judgment tests show that perceived noisiness continues to increase as duration is increased at least up to ~100 s (see Fig. 3.11). That is, equal energy gives approximately equal judged noisiness. Note that some of the apparent bend in best-fit-to-data-point curves in Fig. 2.7C and Fig. 3.11 may be related to judgments being influenced to some extent by durations of the reference signals, 1 and 12s, respectively.

Subjective judgment data also show that energy in a sound event that is 10 to 15 dB lower than the maximum level in the event does not appear to contribute significantly to the perceived noisiness of the event (Kryter and Pearsons, 1963; McCurdy, 1992). (Incidentally, for everyday noises of practical interest, little, or no, difference is found in the L_{Aex} values of a noise event from measurement of (1) the integrated energy level above a threshold of noisiness, or (2) the maximum level plus a duration correction calculated by the "10 dB-downpoint rule," where L_{Amax} + 10 log (0.5 × duration in 0.5 s). This applies to noises where the intensity increases to a maximum and then decreases at about the same rate (e.g., the noise from aircraft flyovers or ground-based vehicle passbys).

Fuller and Robinson (1975) asked subjects to judge the annoyance, unpleasantness, loudness, distractiveness, etc., of recorded traffic noise at essentially a constant level of L_A 85 for durations varying from 5 to 60 min. The overall results were consistent with an increase in the subjective unwantedness equivalent to 2 dB for a doubling of duration. This finding, something less than the 3-dB energy rule, is rather like the shape of the data-fit function from about 20 to 60 sec shown in Fig. 3.11. The findings of McCurdy (1992) from tests of aircraft noise, see above quotations, varied in this regard from about 1 to 3 dB.

Hiramatsu *et al.* studied the effect on judged annoyance of the duration (30 ms to 90 s) of white noise at four levels of intensity. Kuwano *et al.* (1980) investigated the judged noisiness of 16 kinds of intermittent and 22 kinds of steady-state noises. The results of the Hiramatsu *et al.* (1978) indicated that there was some interaction between the effects of level and duration, but that, taken overall, the slope of the duration effect was 3.4 dB per doubling of duration. Kuwano *et al.* (1980) report that energy (3 dB per doubling of duration) was appropriate for expressing the duration effect on the noisiness of steady-state noise, but not entirely so for intermittent noise. For the latter noise its mean energy level plus 10 times the common logarithm of the number of pulses was cited as being more appropriate.

Multiple Events

Equal energy, frequency weighted for loudness, seems to be a valid indicator of the relative perceived noisiness due to noises of different durations. This question will be addressed, for the most part, in Chapter 10. As will be seen in Chapter 10 from attitude survey data in real life, this equal-energy concept

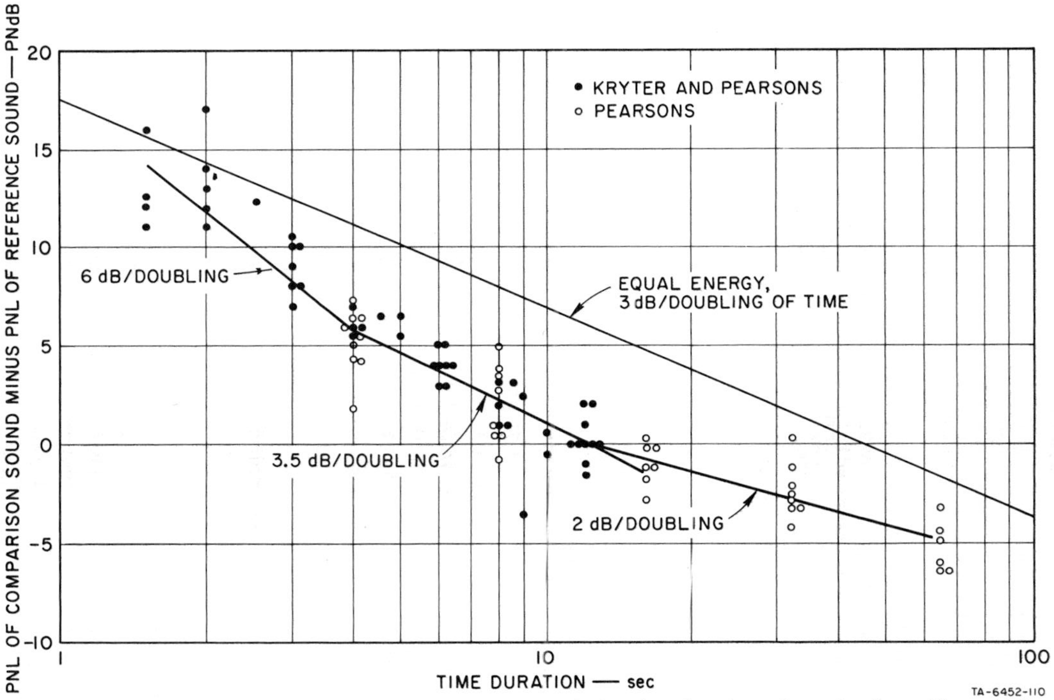

FIGURE 3.11 Relative effect on perceived noise level of changing duration of a noise from 12 sc. (After Kryter and Pearsons, 1965; Copyright 1965 by the American Psychological Association. Adapted by permission of the author; Pearsons, 1966.)

can, within limits, be extended to the summation of annoyance from multiple events.

Duration of Onset of Nonimpulsive Sound

Rosinger *et al.* (1970) reported that a sound that increases slowly to a given peak level and then decreases rapidly is much more objectionable than one of the same total duration and maximum intensity that increases rapidly and then decreases slowly in intensity (see Fig. 3.12). Comparison of the results for the first pair in Fig. 3.12 (an intensity but no frequency shift (versus those for the second pair (intensity as well as frequency shift) reveals that a shift in frequency, such as would be present with an actual moving sound source (the Doppler shift), does not appear, as mentioned above, to have a significant effect on the results.

Rosinger *et al.* (1970) reported that to be judged equally acceptable, the level of signal *A* of Fig. 3.12 had to be about 7 dB less than signal *B*. These investigators suggest that as long as a sound is increasing in intensity, listeners presume that the source of the sound is approaching and may come dangerously close. Therefore, the onset portion of the sound is judged noisier than the portion that is decreasing in level, even when these two portions are of equal duration and equal energy.

The trend in the judgments of these noises is also consistent with the "time error" of subjective judgments. That term is used to describe the phenomenon that the more recent of two physically equal stimuli is subjectively judged to be the more intense. Accordingly, the sound whose peak level occurred closest (at the end of a sound) might be judged the more intense by an amount equivalent to 1–2 dB, other things being equal. However, fear of an oncoming source and, particularly, the longer uncertainty felt by the

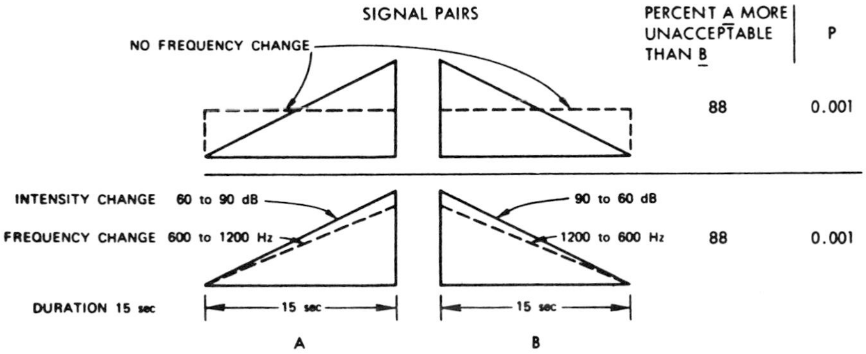

FIGURE 3.12 Temporal intensity and frequency patterns of pure tone signals used in judgment tests and test stimuli. (From Rosinger *et al.*, 1970. Copyright 1970 by the American Psychological Association. Adapted by permission of the author.)

listener concerning how intense an increasing noise may seem more reasonable explanations for the phenomenon found by Rosinger *et al.* (1970). In addition, the effect is generally greater than could usually be explained by the subjective time error.

Because of the meager amount of data available regarding this phenomenon, the development of a correction to integrated noisiness does not seem justifiable at this time. Also, insofar as these judgments of noisiness are at least partially based on fear of an increasing closeness to a dangerous source, they are clearly not based on as inherent a sensation of perceived noisiness as the other aspects discussed above.

BACKGROUND NOISE FOR JUDGMENT TESTS

However, if the onset duration is a factor to be considered in judged perceived noisiness, then the degree to which the standard reference at its maximum level exceeds its initial level will influence its onset duration and noisiness. Obviously, the higher the background noise level, the shorter the onset of an intruding noise, regardless of its final absolute level, and therefore, the lesser the annoyance to be expected from the intruding noise.

For that reason, it is recommended that in laboratory testing with a standard reference sound, a background noise be continuously present during the judgment tests of the standard reference sound and any comparison sounds. The level of the background noise should be at least 15 dB below the maximum level at all frequencies of the standard reference and comparison sounds, or at least at a threshold level for noisiness.

Combined Noises and Long-Duration Test Periods

When aircraft noise is heard in the presence of background or competing noises of sufficient intensity, the background noise can be expected to mask to some extent the aircraft noise. Related to this question are some experiments conducted by Namba and Kuwano (1979) in which they independently varied the level of background and intrusive aircraft noise. Subjects were asked to rate on a 7-point scale (from "not noisy at all" to "intolerably noisy") the noises from moment to moment and also after a 10-min session of listening.

Figure 3.13A shows that the judged noisiness increased with L_{Aeq} but that in some conditions, the judged noisiness was somewhat less than that expressed from the same L_{Aeq} of background noise alone. This would seem to suggest that not only did one noise somewhat mask the other but also the overall noisiness was decreased somewhat. This finding seems contrary to the steady growth of noisiness as a function of L_{Aeq} of either noise alone.

From a practical point of view, it is to be noted that the aircraft noises were varied over rather low levels of intensity (peak levels ranging from 55 to 75 dB_A) and that at the higher L_{Aeq} this possible phenomenon seems to

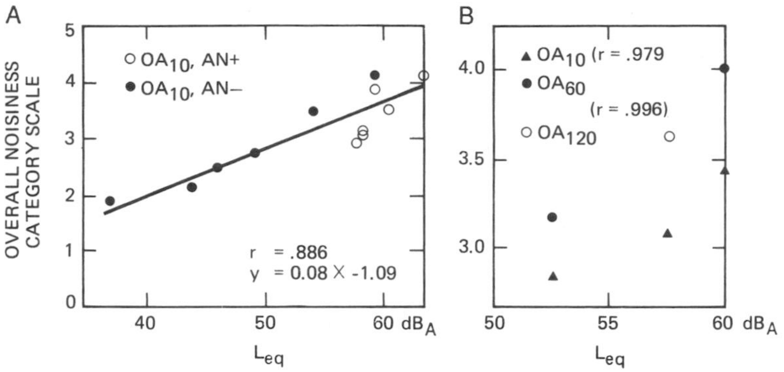

FIGURE 3.13 Judgments of overall noisiness. (A) After 10-min exposures to background noise alone (AN −) and background noise plus aircraft flyover noises (AN +). (B) After 10-, 60-, and 120-min exposure to background noise with and without aircraft flyover noise. (From Namba and Kuwano, 1979.)

disappear. That is, for the three values of L_{Aeq} above ~58 dB, the combined noise environment is judged to be about equal to, or worse than, the background noise alone of equal L_{Aeq}.

Namba and Kuwano (1979) also conducted experimental sessions of 10-, 60-, and 120-min duration, some of which contained only steady-state background noise, and some contained background plus an aircraft noise every 2 min. After each session the subjects rated, among other things, the noisiness overall for each session. Figure 3.13B shows that the overall ratings for sessions of a given duration follow the L_{Aeq} hypothesis (that the total energy, regardless of source, controls the judged noisiness) within a session, but that the 60- and 120-min sessions were judged overall to be somewhat noisier than the 10-min session. It is noteworthy that the judgments of noisiness were quite reliable; correlations between ratings made one month apart of $r = .89–.99$ for the different combinations of test conditions.

PERCEIVED NOISINESS OF IMPULSES

Impulsiveness

As defined in Chapter 1, impulses are measured as the rms intensity, above some specified absolute level, of 0.5-s segments of sound that differ by 10 dB, or more, from preceding, succeeding, or both, 0.5-s segments of time. Typically impulses are sounds of <0.5-s duration, but, by this definition, they may be the first and/or last, 0.5-s segment of a nonimpulsive sound. The choice of 0.5 s is predicated on the time constant of the ear. The 10-dB change in level within 0.5 s and the absolute-level qualifications are based on empirical observations and evidence to be discussed in this chapter, and data in Chapter 6 concern hearing loss from impulses.

An object traveling through the air at speeds faster than that for sound, about 700 miles per hour (mph) under typical atmospheric conditions, creates an impulse of sound from the leading and trailing edge of the object. This impulsive pressure wave shows a very rapid increase above ambient air pressure, followed by a slower decline in level to a negative pressure level, followed by a second rapid increase from the negative "bottom" to ambient pressure. So-called sonic booms from aircraft traveling at supersonic speeds and gunfire are examples of such impulses. Impact impulses may occur when an object with various structural resonance stresses (such as in a sheet of metal) is struck by another object. All impulses have complex spectra, even a pure tone gated, within 0.5 s, on, or off, from reasonably high levels, will have a relatively broadband spectrum.

Whatever their cause, impulse sounds can be decomposed into a number of different frequency components having certain phase and intensity relations with each other. By means of nomographs given in Chapter 1 (Figs. 1.3A and 1.3B) the relative intensities of the frequency components are approximately specifyable from the rise time and duration of the pressure intensity envelope.

As discussed in Chapter 2, the ear also performs a frequency–intensity analysis of sounds, be they impulsive or nonimpulsive, as herein defined. For this reason, it should perhaps be expected that the intensity of an impulsive sound summed over 0.5 s should be predictive of its perceived noisiness when frequency-weighted according to the equal noisiness, or loudness, contour functions found with nonimpulsive sounds.

However, common experience indicates that impulsive sounds of high intensity seem inordinately loud and annoying. Much of the latter is often due to startle reactions that involve nonauditory neural and muscular systems of the body. As will be discussed in Chapter 8, the major amount of nonauditory startle reaction is attributable to psychological unexpectedness and presumed danger from the source of the sound. With continued exposure to such noises, the unexpectedness, and nonauditory startle reactions also diminish, or adapt-out.

The rate at which the intensity envelope increases to peak level within the 0.5-s segment appears to enhance the perceived noisiness of impulses. Harris (1990) concluded that with changes of level of very low-flying aircraft noise somewhere between 2.2 and 11 dB/s impulsiveness was noticed, and at a rate of 15 dB/s, a "correction penalty" was appropriate. Brambilla and Carretti (1990) identify the presence of an impulse when the difference between the L_{Aex} levels measured with a "fast" and "slow" time weighting is greater than 4 dB. An impulse "increment descriptor" is specified as the positive-going difference between successive short-term L_{Aex} (10-ms) levels.

Brambilla and Carretti (1990) found, using recordings of impulsive and nonimpulsive real-life noises, that when the increment descriptor value exceed 10 dB, a 12-dB penalty to equate annoyance value of the noise relative to nonimpulsive road noise at L_A 35, but the penalty required fell to near 1 dB when the impulsive and nonimpulsive noises were presented at L_A 70. However, such effects of rise-time and amount of increment-above-ambient of impulses may be due to spectral changes ensuing from the shortened rise times, rather than rate or amount of rise time, per se.

Perceived Noisiness as Function of Level of Intensity of Sonic-Boom Impulse

With the possibility of significant numbers of commercial aircraft operating at supersonic speeds over populated areas in the late 1960s and early 1970s, a number of research studies were undertaken to assess the adverse impact, if any, the sonic booms created might have on people and animals. The principal findings, in those regards, of a number of these studies in the United States and other countries are summarized by Kryter (1969).

An extensive field study was undertaken at a major U.S. Air Force and National Aeronautics and Space Administration research facility in southern California (Edwards Air Force Base). One primary goal of the research study was to determine the intensity levels of the flyover noise from jet aircraft, when operating at typical subsonic speeds and altitudes, that were judged equal in relative acceptability, or conversely unwantedness, to sonic booms of known intensity.

The rationale for the studies was that with such an equation established one could reasonably well predict the attitudes and ratings of annoyance that would be experienced in communities exposed to specified numbers of sonic booms per day at specified levels of intensity. This would be made feasible by availability of well-documented judgment tests, community attitude surveys, and complaint behaviors in communities now exposed to known numbers of commercial jet aircraft flyover noises of specified levels of intensity. Figure 3.14 shows photographs of the site for the judgment tests, some subjects at an indoor location, and a schematic of overall operations.

The subjects, some located indoors and some outdoors, were exposed to the flyover noise and sonic booms in pairs, with approximately 1–2 min between the members of each pair, and 4–5 min between pairs. The houses were new structures and fully furnished. Each experimental condition was repeated 4 times, twice with sound *A* of the pair given first in the sequence, and twice with sound *B* of the pair given first. Excerpts from the printed instructions for that were given, and also read to, the subject's instruction are:

> The primary purpose of the tests being conducted is to determine, if possible, how people feel about the *relative* acceptability of one type of aircraft noise when compared with a second type or level of aircraft noise. . . . You will hear a series of sounds from aircraft. Some of the sounds will be sonic booms and some will be the sound made by a subsonic jet aircraft. The sounds will

FIGURE 3.14 (A) Photograph of Edwards Air Force Base Test Site. (B) Photograph of some indoor subjects at Edwards Tests. (C) Schematic diagram of test site and aircraft flight path. (From National Sonic Boom Evaluation Office, 1967.)

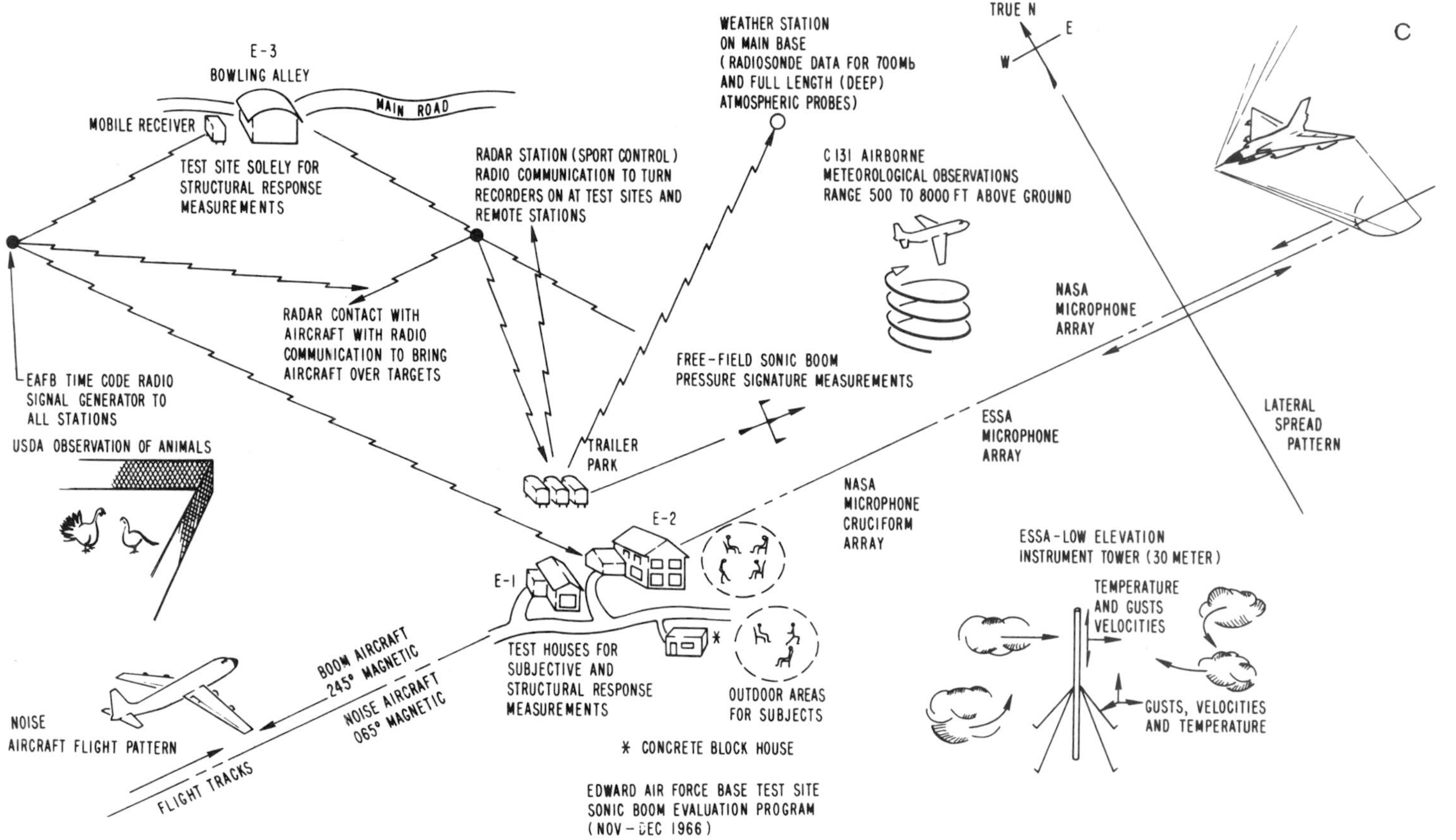

C
TRUE N
E
W
E-3
BOWLING ALLEY
MAIN ROAD
MOBILE RECEIVER
TEST SITE SOLELY FOR STRUCTURAL RESPONSE MEASUREMENTS
RADAR STATION (SPORT CONTROL) RADIO COMMUNICATION TO TURN RECORDERS ON AT TEST SITES AND REMOTE STATIONS
WEATHER STATION ON MAIN BASE (RADIOSONDE DATA FOR 700Mb AND FULL LENGTH (DEEP) ATMOSPHERIC PROBES)
C 131 AIRBORNE METEOROLOGICAL OBSERVATIONS RANGE 500 TO 8000 FT ABOVE GROUND
RADAR CONTACT WITH AIRCRAFT WITH RADIO COMMUNICATION TO BRING AIRCRAFT OVER TARGETS
NASA MICROPHONE ARRAY
FREE-FIELD SONIC BOOM PRESSURE SIGNATURE MEASUREMENTS
EAFB TIME CODE RADIO SIGNAL GENERATOR TO ALL STATIONS
USDA OBSERVATION OF ANIMALS
TRAILER PARK
ESSA MICROPHONE ARRAY
LATERAL SPREAD PATTERN
NASA MICROPHONE CRUCIFORM ARRAY
E-2
E-1
ESSA-LOW ELEVATION INSTRUMENT TOWER (30 METER)
TEMPERATURE AND GUSTS VELOCITIES
BOOM AIRCRAFT 245° MAGNETIC
NOISE AIRCRAFT 065° MAGNETIC
TEST HOUSES FOR SUBJECTIVE AND STRUCTURAL RESPONSE MEASUREMENTS
OUTDOOR AREAS FOR SUBJECTS
GUSTS, VELOCITIES AND TEMPERATURE
NOISE AIRCRAFT FLIGHT PATTERN
* CONCRETE BLOCK HOUSE
FLIGHT TRACKS
EDWARD AIR FORCE BASE TEST SITE SONIC BOOM EVALUATION PROGRAM (NOV-DEC 1966)

FIGURE 3.14 *Continued.*

occur in 'pairs' and your tasks is to judge which sound in each pair if heard in or near your home during the day and/or evening when you are engage in typical, awake activities.

After you hear each pair of sounds please quickly decide which of the two you feel would be more acceptable to you . . . if the second circle *B* on the answer sheet for that pair, and . . . *A* if you think the first is more acceptable than the second. . . . There are no "right" or "wrong" answers . . . nor do we expect people to agree with each other.

An announcement will be made before each pair is to occur. The sounds may be separated in time by several minutes, but usually by less than one minute. During the test period be attentive and quiet. Give us your best judgment and imagine that you are listening to these sounds in or near your own home.

In keeping with the definition that judgments of perceived noisiness should be as free as possible from unexpectedness and fear from any unfamiliarity or the like, a number (142) of the subjects were chosen because they were residents at Edwards AF Base. As such, they had been exposed to typical some subsonic aircraft takeoff and landing noise and over the previous four years an average of four to eight sonic booms per day. The biographical data for all the subjects are summarized in Table 3.2.

TABLE 3.2 Biographical Data for Three Groups: Edwards, Fontana, Redlands

	Edwards	Fontana	Redlands
Sex and marital status			
Single male	1%	4%	12%
Married male	12%	21%	28%
Total male	13%	25%	40%
Single female	3%	4%	7%
Married female	84%	71%	53%
Total female	87%	75%	60%
Male occupations			
Air Force	79%	4%	0%
Retired	16%	25%	46%
Other	5%	71%	54%
Female occupations			
Housewife	94%	92%	75%
Retired	1%	0%	11%
Other	5%	8%	14%
Average age (years)			
Male	36.9	44.0	50.8
Female	33.7	38.7	49.2
Total	34.2	40.0	49.8
Education (average years completed)			
Male	12.3	13.1	13.2
Female	11.8	11.9	13.1
Total	11.8	12.2	13.1
Total biography cards	142	98	153

The data points, and lower curve drawn thereto, of Fig. 3.15 show the intensity level of the sonic booms judged by Edwards' subjects to be as acceptable as the subsonic aircraft noise if heard in or near their homes. (The relation between levels of typical jet aircraft noise in residential areas near airports and their ratings of annoyance and unwantedness will be presented in Chapter 10.)

As shown by the upper curves in Fig. 3.15, subjects unfamiliar with sonic booms found them to be the equivalent of about 10 dB in level less acceptable than the noise of subsonic aircraft than did the subjects who were familiar with sonic booms as part of their living environment. These subjects were

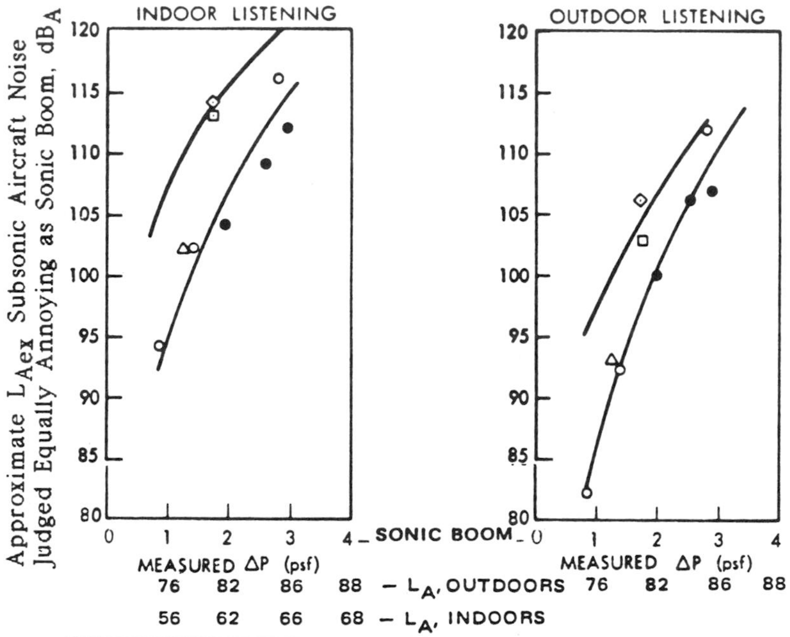

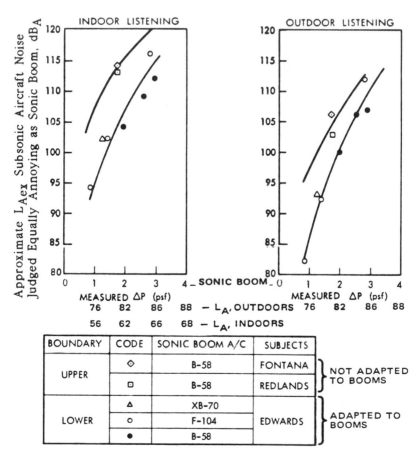

BOUNDARY	CODE	SONIC BOOM A/C	SUBJECTS	
UPPER	◇	B-58	FONTANA	NOT ADAPTED TO BOOMS
	□	B-58	REDLANDS	
LOWER	△	XB-70	EDWARDS	ADAPTED TO BOOMS
	○	F-104		
	●	B-58		

FIGURE 3.15 Level of subsonic aircraft noise when judged to be equal in acceptability to sonic booms when heard by subjects indoors and subjects outdoors. Edwards' subjects were adapted to booms from average of year's exposure to average of 6 booms per day. The abscissa is the level of sonic boom in pounds per square foot (lb/ft^2) and L_{Aex} ($L_{A0.5s}$). All levels given are as measured outdoors. (After Kryter *et al.*, 1967.)

251 adults bused in from communities that had not been exposed to sonic booms.

Perceived Noisiness as Function of Intensity Level of Artillery Fire, Glass Breaking, and Air-Horn Impulse

Young (1976) conducted a study to measure the perceived noisiness of the following sounds presented at different levels of intensity: (1) simulated artillery fire; (2) breaking glass; (3) air horn; and (4) jet aircraft noise following takeoff, and during approach to landing. The first two sounds were less than 0.4 s in duration and impulsive, the air horns were somewhat longer, 0.4 and 0.8 s, and the aircraft noise was definitely nonimpulsive, 8–16 s in duration. The artillery fire was simulated by mechanically driving (with a cam-operated plunger) one wall of the test room. The other sounds were from recordings played over a high-fidelity loudspeaker in the test room, or, for the air horn, placed outside the room.

In this study, the judgments were magnitude estimations made by 30 subjects (tested a few at a time) following the presentation of each sound. The number 10 was assigned as the relative acceptability of the noise of a 747 aircraft following takeoff, having an L_{Aex} of 78. This noise, called the *reference standard,* was periodically repeated for judgments throughout a series of judgments of the other noises. The instruction to the subjects were, in summary, as follows:

> The purpose of the test is to determine the relative acceptability or tolerability of various noises heard by people in or near their homes.
>
> We want you to judge the noises you will hear as though you were listening to them in your home when engaged in typical, everyday, activities, such as reading, conversing with friends, etc. It is important that you judge each noise in its entirety, from beginning to end as an overall noise occurrence.
>
> You may like or dislike any of the noise you hear. . . . Several times during each test session you will be presented with a flyover noise from an aircraft to which you will listen and assign the number *10*. Please score all other noises relative to the reference noise. If, for example, a noise sounds to you twice as bothersome, noisy, unwanted or disturbing as the reference noise, score the noise as having a value of *20;* since the reference noise had a score of *10.* However, if the noise appears one-half or, one-quarter as noisy or unwanted as the reference noise mark your answer sheet accordingly: if *one-half;* its score is *5;* if *one-quarter,* its score is *2.5*.
>
> There are no right or wrong answers and we do not expect people to agree with each other.

The L_{Cex} and L_{Aex} levels, and magnitude estimates of the noises are given in Table 3.3. (For an impulsive sound, L_{eq}, L_{ex} and $L_{0.5\ s}$ values are, of course, the same). The means of the magnitude estimates are shown in Fig. 3.16, plotted on a log scale, as a function of the L_{Aex} of the various noises.

TABLE 3.3 Magnitude Estimations of Judged Noisiness (Annoyance) of Various Impulsive and Nonimpulsive Sounds

Noises	L_{Cex}*	L_{Aex}*	$L_{Cex} - L_{Aex}$ Difference	Magnitude Noise/Annoyance
Simulated artillery 1	78.0	57.3	20.8	2.4
Simulated artillery 2	81.5	62.3	19.3	3.6
Simulated artillery 3	93.8	74.8	19.0	22.8
Simulated artillery 4	93.5	74.8	18.8	26.7
Simulated artillery 5	90.8	73.5	17.3	20.0
Simulated artillery 6	96.8	77.8	19.0	34.4
Simulated artillery 7	99.8	81.8	18.0	41.9
Simulated artillery 8	104.8	86.5	18.3	62.6
	Average difference = 18.8			
Glass 1	80.8	78.3	2.5	10.7
Glass 2	87.3	85.3	2.0	13.1
Glass 3	85.3	80.0	5.3	17.5
Glass 4	90.3	87.3	3.0	16.0
	Average difference = 3.2			
Air horn 2	91.8	92.0	−0.3	83.4
Air horn 1	93.3	93.5	−0.3	62.9
	Average difference = −0.3			
747 (TO) 1	64.8	58.3	6.5	3.4
747 (TO) 2	74.8	68.3	6.5	6.2
747 (TO) 3	84.8	78.3	6.5	10†
747 (TO) 4	94.8	88.3	6.5	26.2
747 (TO) 5	104.8	90.3	14.5	49.1
	Average difference = 8.1			
DC-8 (L) 1	64.3	57.3	7.0	2.9
DC-8 (L) 2	74.3	67.3	7.0	5.9
DC-8 (L) 3	84.3	77.3	7.0	11.0
DC-8 (L) 4	94.3	87.2	7.0	29.9
DC-8 (L) 5	104.3	97.3	7.0	55.4
	Average difference = 7.0			

Note: TO = takeoff; L = landing. * L_{Cex} and L_{Aex} values of noise events inside test room. † Numbers assigned to other sounds relative to 10, assigned as reference, to magnitude of perceived noisiness or annoyance of this sound. After Young (1976).

Also shown on Fig. 3.16 are magnitude estimates of the sonic boom at levels of 3.2, and 1 psf (pounds per square foot) or $L_{A0.5\ s}$ of 86, 82, and 76 dB respectively, and curves of visual best fit to (1) nonimpulsive sounds, solid and dashed; and (2) impulsive sound, the dot–dash segment. Oscillographic tracings of these various impulsive sounds and spectrum levels of sonic booms are shown in Fig. 3.17.

The magnitude estimates for the sonic-boom data were derived in accordance with the assumption that the noise from the subsonic aircraft, against which the booms were judged in the Edwards study, would also deserve a 10 when their L_{Aex} was 78 dB and other levels would have been subjectively

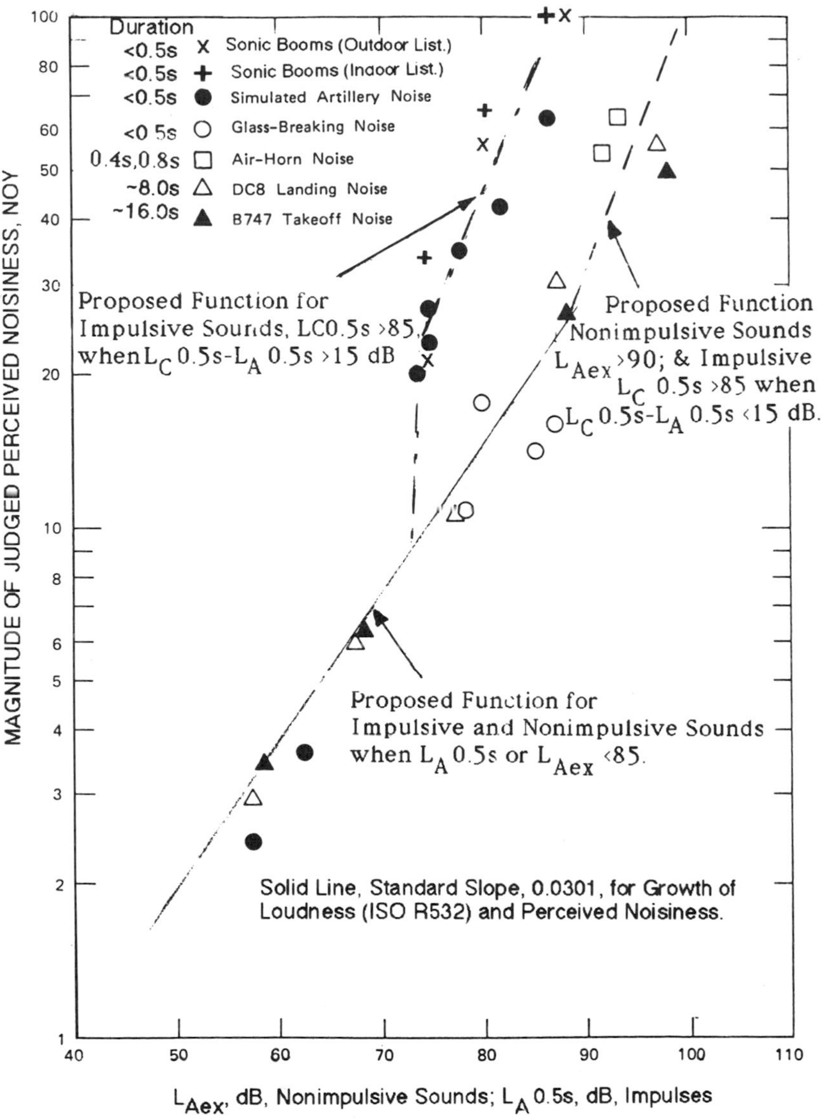

FIGURE 3.16 Magnitude of judged perceived noisiness (relative acceptability), on log scale, as function of L_{Aex} of nonimpulsive and impulsive noises as found by Young (1976), and for sonic boom by Kryter *et al.*, 1967.)

scaled accordingly. This follows the fact that the L_{Aex} 78 of the reference noise in the Young (1976) experiment was scaled as having a magnitude of relative acceptability of 10, with less acceptable noises being given a higher number. The steps in this derivation, and some various measures of the aircraft noise and sonic boom are given in Table 3.4.

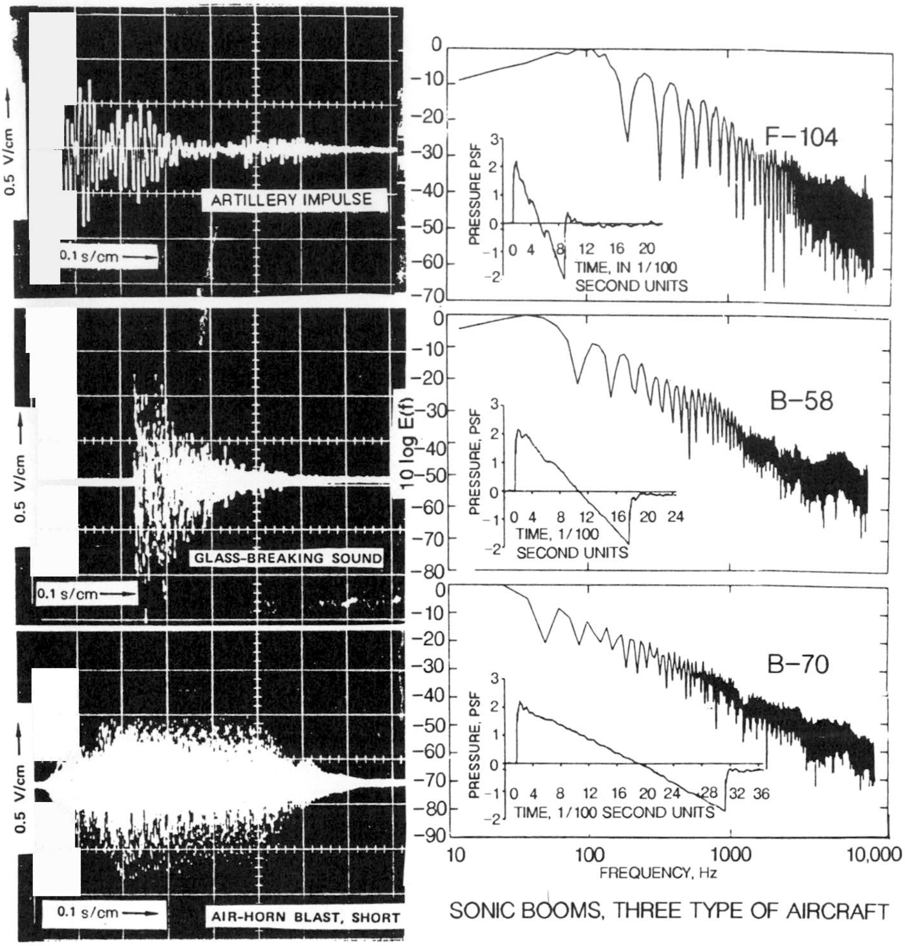

FIGURE 3.17 Oscillographic tracings of time histories of pressure changes of brief-duration sounds studied by Young (1976) left graphs, and, inserts on right graphs, of sonic booms in study of Kryter *et al.* (1967). Also shown are spectrum levels of sonic booms.

Schomer, 1977, and the Committee on Hearing, Bioacoustics and Biomechanics (CHABA, 1977) proposed that, for the evaluation of environmental noises, $L_{C\text{ex}}$ be used to measure impulsive sounds when $L_C > 85$ dB, and $L_{A\text{ex}}$ to measure nonimpulsive sounds with $L_{A\text{ex}} > 85$. However, when the data for the impulses are looked at separated from the nonimpulsive noise data (see Fig. 3.18), it is seen that some impulses exceeding the magnitude of judged noisiness depends not only on the L_C 85 but also on the $L_C : L_A$ ratio.

These findings would seem to indicate that in addition to the L_C 85 level as a minimum for an impulse correction, imposing a ratio of 15 dB between

TABLE 3.4 Levels of Sonic Booms and Jet Aircraft Noise Judged to Be Equally Noisy, or Acceptable; Also, Derived Magnitude-Scaled Judgments of Noisiness for Sonic Booms Resulting From Aircraft Noise

Subsonic jet aircraft noise					Sonic Boom			
PN_{dBpk}	L_{Cpk}	L_{Cex}	L_{Aex}	Magnitude Perc. N.*	lb/ft²‡	$L_{C0.5\,s}$†	$L_{A0.5\,s}$†	Magnitude Perc. N.*
				Listeners outside houses				
113	105	99	103	100	3	107	86	100
105	94	91	95	55	2	101	82	55
90	80	76	83	20	1	95	76	20
	$L_{Cex} - L_{Aex} = 7$					$L_{C0.5\,s} - L_{A0.5\,s} = 21$		
				Listeners inside houses				
118	108	104	108	100	3	107	86	100
111	101	97	101	68	2	103	80	68
97	87	83	90	33	1	95	74	33

* Magnitude of perceived noisiness based on average judgment data for similar subsonic jet aircraft flyover noises as scaled by Young (see Table 3.3 and Fig. 3.16).
† Levels of sonic boom found to be equally acceptable as subsonic aircraft noise of specified subjective magnitude. (Kryter *et al.*, 1967; see also Fig. 3.16).
‡ Pounds per square foot, typical measure of sonic-boom intensity.

L_C and L_A or so as an additional requirement for the impulse adjustment is justified. Perhaps this is somewhat related to the greater activation of the reflex to the higher than lower frequencies, as is also reflected in the greater weight given the higher than lower frequencies by the *A*-weighting, e.g., ~15 dB for frequencies between 1000 and 4000 Hz, as compared to the frequencies from about 50 to 1000 Hz. Spectra with energy predominate in these lower frequencies are typical (see spectra of sonic booms in Fig. 3.17).

Proposed Adjustments to L_{Aex}, L_{Dex}, L_{Phonex}, or LPN_{dBex} for Very High Exposure Levels and Impulsiveness

Figure 3.19 shows functions for correcting, or adjusting the exposure level of a broadband noise event for the perceived noisiness that exceeds that attributable to the present loudness function, as reflected on L_{Aex}, L_{Dex}, L_{phonex}, LPN_{dBex}, or their counterpart units. It is deduced that these adjustment are needed because of (1) an accelerated growth in perceived noisiness, or unwantedness, of nonimpulsive sounds when their event exposure level exceeds that comparable to an L_{Aex} of ~85; and (2) a near, apparently, stepwise increase in perceived noisiness of impulsive sounds when their $L_{C0.5\,s}$ level exceeds 85 dB and their $L_{A0.5\,s}$ level by 15. These adjustments would be in addition to any adjustments that may have been made to these measurements for tonality. These functions are based largely on the data of Fig. 3.16.

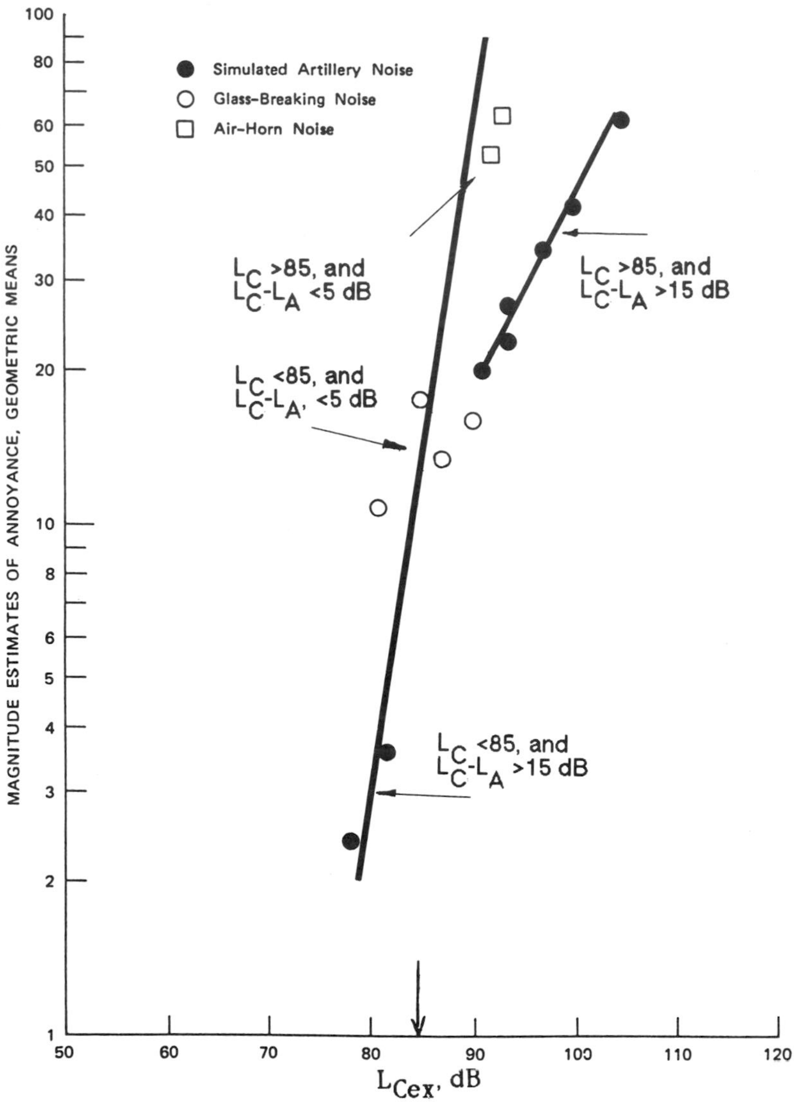

FIGURE 3.18 Dissimilarity of growth function of annoyance for impulses having $L_C >$ 85 dB and with $L_C : L_A$ ratios $>$ 15 dB, compared to that for (1) impulses with $L_C >$ 85 dB and $L_C : L_A$ ratios of either >15 or <15 dB; and (3) nonimpulsive sound at $L_{Aex} >$ 90 dB. (After Young, 1976; see also Fig. 3.16.)

Judgments of the relative loudness and annoyance of recordings of the noise from a passing car and impulses from weapons were obtained from 51 subjects, mean age of 40 years. The subjects were tested individually in a laboratory "living" room, with the various test noises played to the listeners at levels measured in the field. The listener adjusted the level of a 3-s duration

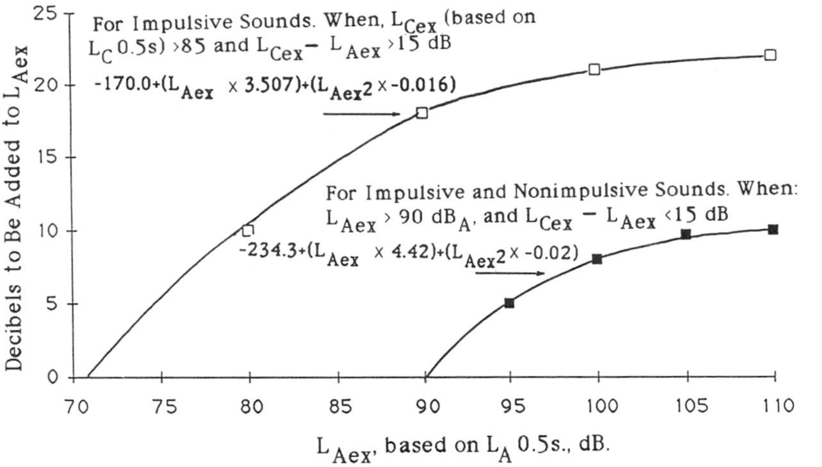

FIGURE 3.19 Proposed adjustments for accelerated, above present standard, growth of perceived noisiness for: *upper curve*, when impulsive sound > L_{Cex} 85 dB, and $L_{Cex} : L_{Aex}$ ratio > 15 dB; and *lower curve*,for impulsive or nonimpulsive sounds when L_{Aex} > 90 dB. Based on functions in Fig. 3.16.

pink noise, with a gradual on–off, temporal pattern, until it was equal in "disturbance" (from no disturbance = 0, to strong disturbance, = 10) to a test noise (Meloni and Krueger, 1993).

The results, shown in the upper graph Fig. 3.20, L_{Aex} (SEL_{dBA}) fairly well predicts the judged noisiness (or disturbance) for these nonimpulsive and impulsive noises. Comparison of the dB_A abscissa of Fig. 3.20A, with that of Fig. 3.20B dB_C, shows that latter levels were not >15 dB greater than the dB_A levels, nor, except for two small exceptions, were the dB_A levels in excess of 90, the requirements for application of any impulse correction according to Fig. 3.19. At the same time, dB_C leads to a much more inconsistent estimate of judged disturbance level than does L_{Aeq} (SEL_{dBA}).

Repeated Impulses

The findings of Izumi (see Fig. 3.21) show that for each doubling of a number of impulses of a constant duration required that the burst energy level be decreased by about 3 dB to maintain equal subjective loudness. This is in agreement with earlier data on loudness of 1-ms triangular transients of varying rise times and repetition rates (Carter, 1972). Izumi's data show a similar relation for judged perceived noisiness, but that the impulses were apparently judged to be 2–3 dB noisier than loud (Izumi, 1975, 1977a,b).

Impulsive sounds coming from helicopters (the "blade slap") has been studied in the context of practical procedures for assessing aircraft noise. It is somewhat difficult to generalize the results from the various studies. A detailed review of helicopter noise studies through about 1978 is given in

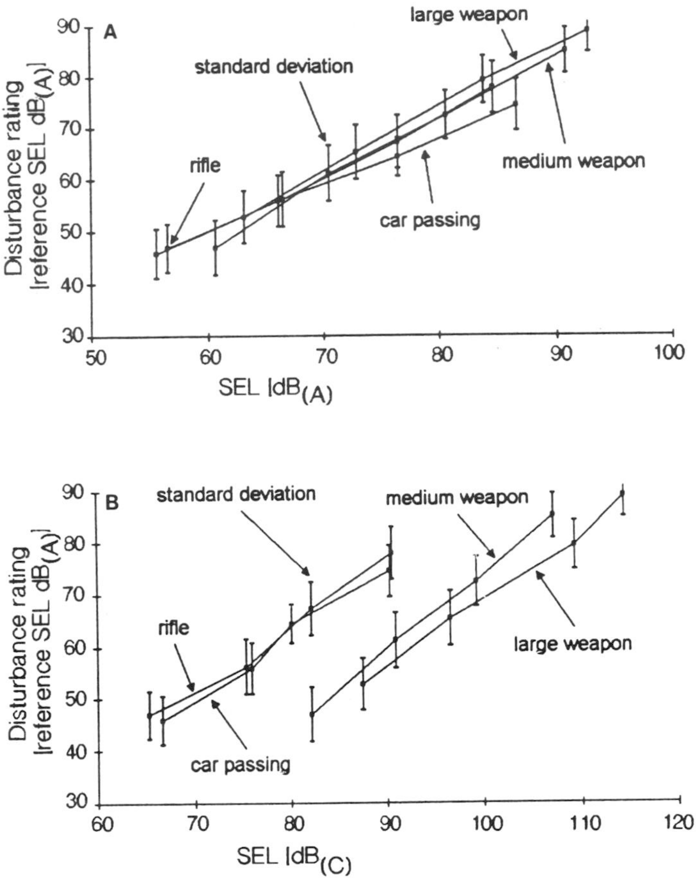

FIGURE 3.20 Relative disturbance ratings given a nonimpulsive and impulsive noises as a function of their level in (A) L_{Aex} (SEL_{dBA}) and (B) L_{Cex} (SEL_{dbC}). (From Meloni and Krueger, 1993.)

Sutherland and Burke (1979). It appears from the results of these studies that a correction to the L_{Aex} of helicopter noise with blade slap relative to helicopter noise without blade slap ranges from about −2 to 8 dB.

This underestimation by L_{Aex} of perceived noisiness with blade slap present is, perhaps, not necessarily because of impulsiveness per se, but because *A*-weighting underweights the relative contribution to loudness and noisiness of the low frequencies (see Fig. 1.4). Blade slap noise augments the level in frequencies as low as 10–30 Hz or so. In fact, when sound level is expressed as LPN_{dBex} or L_{Dex}, which more appropriately weights the ultra-low-frequency spectrum, the required correction becomes 2 to −4 dB rather than the above-noted average 2–8 dB_A (Powell, 1978; Galloway, 1978; Powell, 1981; Powell and McCurdy, 1982). Some further references to research on helicopter noise are presented in Chapter 10.

Rate and On–Off Times

Izumi (1975) conducted a study of the effects of the rate and duration of interruption on the relative perceived noisiness of a 20-s period of pink noise (onset and offset times of 30 and 200 ms, respectively, i.e., impulsive sounds). In these tests, 20-s periods of uninterrupted pink noises were judged against 20-s periods of the noise with all combinations of on times from 0.125 to 1 s and off times from 0.125 to 1 s. Peak levels of the uninterrupted reference noise were 60, 70, and 80 dB_A.

Izumi (1975) developed graphic and mathematical formulas to show the contribution to perceived noisiness of the parameters of burst time-fractions (BTFs), equal to on time divided by on time plus off time, and repetition rate (RR), as found in his studies. The following formula represents results he obtained in a later study (Izumi, 1977a) with interrupted vs. uninterrupted 10-s periods of pink noise: $L_{RB} = 6 \log_{10}\mathrm{BTFG}\ (10 \log_{10}\mathrm{RR}10)(1 - e^{-15T_{off}})$, where L_{RB} is relative A-weighted noise level of burst, dB; BTF is burst time fraction; RR is repetition rate, s^{-1}; T_{off} is off time, s.

Also, for multiple, brief (<1 s) impulses such as those studied by Izumi (1977b) the aural reflex could possibly affect judged loudness and noisiness in somewhat confusing ways. That is, the aural reflex, as discussed in Chapter 2, could be activated to different degrees for given BTFs depending on the actual durations of the off time between impulse bursts of differing durations.

ROUND-ROBIN STUDY OF LOUDNESS OF IMPULSES

A special study was conducted under the auspices of the International Standardization Organization (ISO) in which a variety of recorded impulsive sounds were administered to subjects in 21 laboratories in 11 different countries (Pedersen *et al.*, 1977). The subjects were asked (Pedersen *et al.*, 1977, p. A9) "to compare the loudness, but not the noisiness or any other factor" of the impulsive sounds with respect to that of a reference sound. By varying in successive presentations the intensity level of the either the comparison sound and keeping the level of other reference constant, or vice versa, the relative intensity levels of the two for equal loudness was established. The impulse sounds tested, and their durations, are shown in table on Fig. 3.22. Some of the impulses of 1.0-s duration (e.g., Nos. 7 and 8) were made that long by repeating shorter duration impulses within the 1.0 s as needed.

Level Comparisons with Reference Signals

The decibel attenuation required in the level of a comparison impulse so that a subject considered the comparison impulse equal in loudness to the reference signal was called the *equal-loudness attenuation* (ELA). The results for the ELAs averaged for the various panels of subjects are shown in Fig. 3.22. Except for the group iii impulses, the data show a large (15–

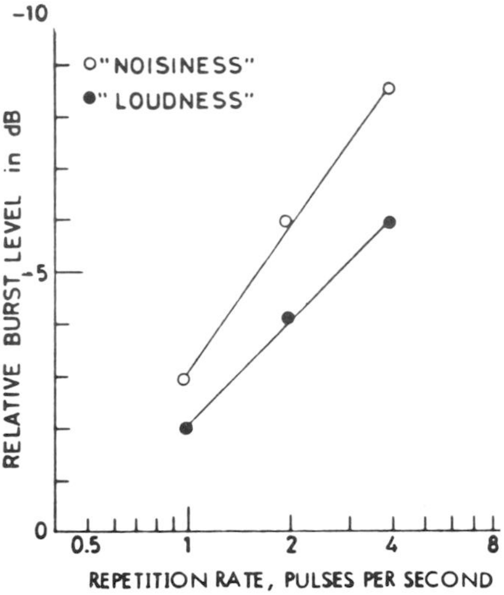

FIGURE 3.21 Comparison of loudness and noisiness versus repetition rate for a burst-time fraction (on-time divided by on-time plus off-time) of 0.063. (From Izumi, 1977b).

20-dB) range in ELA for a given impulse among the 21 different panels of subjects.

In Fig. 3.22, the group iii impulses and reference signal consisted of a burst of a 1-kHz tone, with the reference signal being twice the duration of the comparison. Whereas group i and ii noises, consisting of impulses of complex frequency spectra and repetitions, were judged against either a $^1/_3$-octave band of filtered random noise, or a 1 kilohertz tone of the same duration as the comparison noise. It is hypothesized that since the group i and ii impulses were more complex than those in group iii, their relative differences from the reference signals with respect to noisiness were more clearly perceived by some of the subjects.

It is suggested that the instructions to the subjects were unfortunate in the context of this study because the word *loudness,* and its counterparts in other languages, can be interpreted ambiguously. Some subjects may have taken the instruction to mean that they should judge the peak physical intensity in the noise in relation to the reference noise; others may have judged the summed or averaged subjective intensity of the comparison versus the reference noises; other subjects might well have interpreted that the intent of the study was to have them judge how unacceptable they felt the impulses

---

FIGURE 3.22 (A) List of noise and reference signals in round-robin study. (B) Mean values of equal loudness attenuations (ELA) from subjective measurements (level of L_A 75) as reported in round-robin study. The separate lines represent the findings of each of the 22 laboratories administering the same tests. (From Pedersen *et al.*, 1977.)

A

Group	Noise no.	Noise		Reference	
		Source	Duration, msec	Signal	Duration, msec
i	1	Puncher	1000	1/3 octave noise	1000
	2	Cement mill	↓	↓	↓
	3	Teletype			
	4	Pneumatic hammer (silenced)			
	5	Pneumatic drill			
	6	Outboard motor			
	7	Hammer and anvil			
	8	Ram			
	9	Puncher			
ii	10	Typewriter		1-kHz tone	80
	11	Hammer and anvil			320
	12	Ram			160
	13	Gun			10
	14	Sonic boom			320
iii	15	1-kHz tone	160	1-kHz tone	320
	16	↓	80	↓	160
	17		40		80
	18		20		40
	19		10		20
	20		5		10
	21	1-kHz tone	1000	1/3 octave noise	1000

B

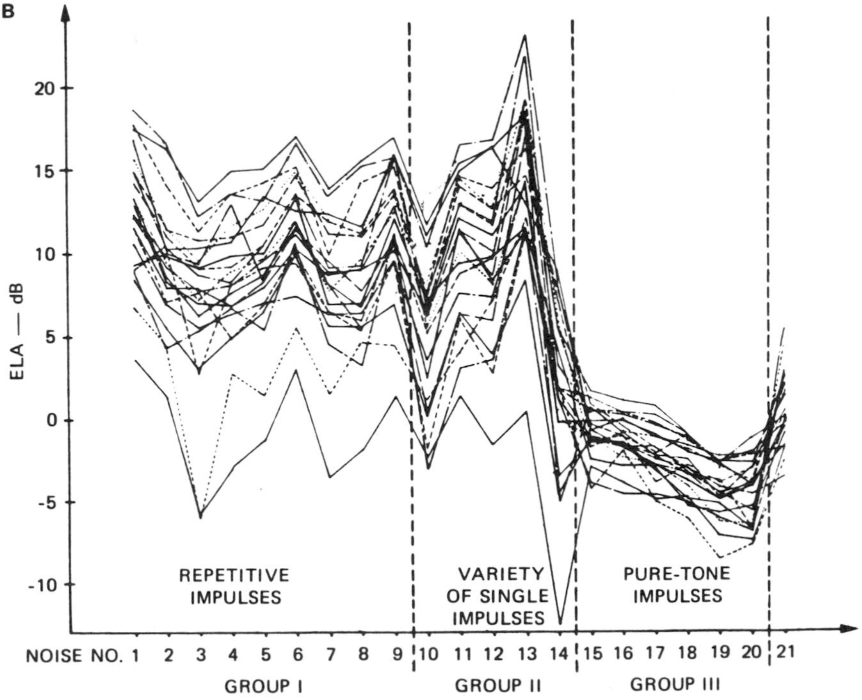

were relative to the reference stimulus. Note that Izumi found a consistent difference of several decibels between loudness and noisiness judgments of impulses, with the noisiness being greater than the loudness (see Fig. 3.21).

Relative Contributions of Spectra and Duration

Although in the round-robin experiments the subjective aspect of impulsiveness per se was possibly a floating variable among the different panels of subjects, the relative effects of spectra and duration on the judgments were fairly consistently revealed. That is, the relative differences (increases and decreases) in ELA between different impulses were somewhat similar for all the panels of subjects (see Fig. 3.22).

The investigators used different statistics for expressing the variability of the ELA data; one was called a variance *shape deviation criterion* (log S^2) and the other, a mean-square (log MS) deviation criterion. These results, shown in Fig. 3.23, demonstrate several things that in general agree with previous studies on these matters:

1. Overall, the meter response characteristics of "sort time" and "1-s integration" performed the best, with "slow," "impulse," and "peak" the worst.

2. Stevens and Zwicker phons are generally more accurate in predicting subjective judgments than are overall frequency weightings, such as linear, *A, B, C,* or *D,* apparently because the phon is calculated from band spectral measures and thereby reflects the contribution to the subjective judgments of relative differences in the bandwidths of the different noises.

3. The *D*-weighting is generally more accurate in predicting the loudness judgments according to the mean square deviation criterion than the *A*-weighting or any of the other overall frequency weightings for the quasistationary noises (Fig. 3.23(c) or for the single pulses (Fig. 3.23(d). However, with variability scores based on the variance shape criterion, the *A*-weighting predicts the judgments of quasi stationary noises with somewhat more accuracy than do the other frequency weightings, except when using impulse and peak meter functions. The superior performance of the *D*-weighting over the other weightings, when it occurs, is probably because the other weightings do not reflect, as does *D,* the approximate 10-dB "hump" found in equal loudness and noisiness contours for frequencies in the ~1500–4000-Hz region.

In spite of these results, in the report of the Round Robin study the *A*-weighting is recommended for the assessment of environmental noise in general for the following reasons: (1) a sound-level meter with an overall frequency weighting is much more practical for everyday use than the instrumentation required to obtain the spectral data needed to calculate phons;

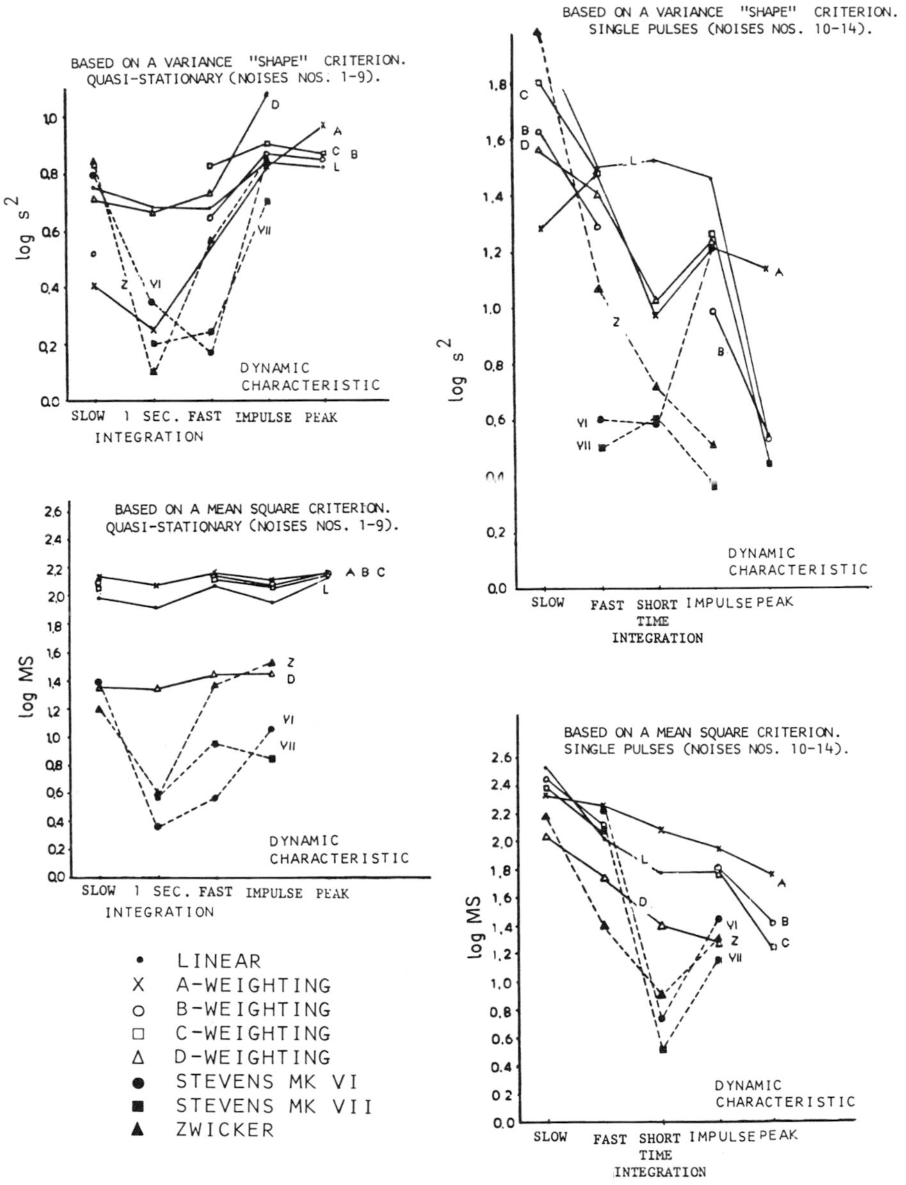

AGREEMENT BETWEEN OBJECTIVE AND SUBJECTIVE RESULTS

FIGURE 3.23 Relation between two error criteria and dynamic characteristics of sound-level measurements, including integrated energy. Parameter in frequency weighting procedure. (A) Quasistationary impulses, variance shape criterion; (B) single impulses, variance shape criterion; (C) quasistationary impulses, mean-square criterion; (D) single impulses, mean-square criterion.

and (2) the *A*-weighting is generally used as a standard method for the assessment of steady state noises. However, the *D*- and *E*-weightings, although not incorporated in most sound-level meters, assess the perceived loudness and noisiness of many steady-state broadband noises as well as, and narrowband steady-state noise better than, does the *A*-weighting, as discussed somewhat earlier and summarized below.

ACCURACY OF DIFFERENT PROCEDURES FOR ESTIMATING LOUDNESS AND NOISINESS

Scharf *et al.* (1977) reached the following conclusion with respect to overall frequency weightings, and calculation procedures:

> One important conclusion, based on a total of over 600 spectra, was that the band calculation procedures predicted subjective magnitude (of loudness and/or noisiness) with less variability and with greater validity than did the frequency weightings.
>
> Among the six frequency weightings studied, the *B*- and *C*-weightings were the poorest predictors of subjective magnitude while the D_1-, D_2-, and *E*-weightings were the best predictive weighting functions. It was also noted that the *A*-weighting was less than 0.5 dB more variable than the D_1-, D_2-, and *E*-weightings. Among the five calculation procedures studied, Steven's' Mark [VI] (1961), Mark [VII] All (1972), and Zwicker's (1958) loudness calculation procedures were the least variable but Perceived Noise Level (Kryter, 1959) was almost as reliable. Tone-corrected Perceived Noise Level (following the FAR 36 procedure, 1969) was a somewhat poorer predictor. Mark and Perceived Noise Level yielded the calculated values that were closest, on the average, to the observed or judged values, although all of the frequency weightings and computational procedures examined were about equally variable in this respect.

Table 3.4 shows that, consistent with Scharf's overall conclusions given above, the *A*-weighting to be the least accurate predictor of the loudnesses of a wide variety of narrow- and wideband noises by various simple overall frequency weighting and 1/3-octave-band calculation schemes. Quinlan (1990) has calculated the enormous (>40 dB) differences that are possible between dB_A levels of selected sounds of equal loudness, in phons, as calculated by the Zwicker (1958) method.

However, as discussed earlier, and also shown in Table 3.5, *D*-, *E*-, and particularly *A*-weighting, can predict the relative noisiness of aircraft noises, when judged against each other, better than the band methods used for phons and PN_{dB}. Such results are perhaps to be expected only when reasonably similar and complex noises are judged relative to each other. This is presumably possible when noises are broad in spectrum, with energy both above and below 1000 Hz. Under these circumstances, the underestimation, relative to 1000 Hz, by the *A*-weighting of the impact of sound energy above 1000 Hz is being compensated for by an overestimation, relative to 1000 Hz,

TABLE 3.5 Calculated Minus Observed Loudness or Perceived Noisiness*

	L_A	L_{D_1}	L_{D_2}	L_E	Stevens Phons, VI	Stevens Phons, VII	Zwicker Phons	PN_{dB}
All units calculated without duration or tone "corrections"								
				Variety of narrow and broadband noises				
Mean of differences, dB	−12.1	−5.3	−5.8	−6.8	−1.2	−8.6	3.1	−1.4
Standard deviation differences, dB	4.8	4.0	4.3	4.1	3.2	3.2	3.0	3.1
Range of differences	16.0	12.6	13.7	12.6	11.6	11.1	8.8	10.8
				Turboprop and turbofan jet aircraft noises				
Standard deviation differences, dB	2.7	3.4	3.1	3.4	3.8	3.5	3.4	3.3
Standard deviation differences, dB	2.2	2.9	2.6	2.8	3.2	3.1	2.9	2.9

* Upper table: based on published studies of 335 noises of wide variety of spectra, after Scharf *et al.* (1977). Lower table: judgments of noise from turboprop and turbofan jet aircraft; average of two experiments, Table VI, McCurdy (1990).

of the impact from the sound energy below 1000 Hz (see Fig. 1.5). The superiority of the band methods becomes apparent when comparisons are to be made among sound of with considerably different band widths and/or spectrum shapes.

SUMMARY

Spectral, intensity and temporal aspects of sounds are related to sensations of loudness, tonality, duration, impulsiveness, and to a perception of auditory unwantedness, defined as perceived noisiness. These sensations and perceptions were studied, as far as possible, independently of the effects of (1) any psychological, learned meanings (including unexpectedness) a sound may have and (2) any interference effects of the sound with other auditory behavior or nonauditory system arousals. The complex nature of the psychological and acoustical variables involved has made data and theory in this problem area somewhat controversial.

One theory offered for perceived noisiness is that the magnitudes of some physical dimensions of sound that emerged as indicative of thresholds of unwantedness are approximately the same magnitudes as when at the threshold of causing a temporary decrease in the sensitivity of hearing. A factor contributing to the perceived unwantedness of impulses could be described as physiological startle reactions to sounds that might typically be considered as "warning signals" of potential danger.

It is concluded that the perceived noisiness of broadband sounds, independently of their meanings is generally predictable, depending upon the variety in the sounds to be thus evaluated, from the following physical measures:

1. One-third or critical band adjusted, spectra, frequency, and bandwidth weighted for loudness according to Zwicker or Stevens phons, or PN_{dB}; or overall spectra *D*-, *E*-, or *A*-weighted.
2. Loudness-weighted spectra corrected for tonal unwantedness
3. Sound-event energy spectrum weighted for loudness and tonality, over duration of event measured in 0.5-s segments.
4. Sound-event frequency weighted and tonality energy corrected for accelerated growth of perceived noisiness (loudness) at ultrahigh levels of intensity.
5. Loudness weighted spectra of $\leq$0.5-s, duration impulses of sound corrected for the unwantedness of the sensation of impulsiveness.

References

Angerer, J. R., McCurdy, D. A., and Erickson, R. A. (1991). "Development of an Annoyance Model Based upon Elementary Auditory Sensations for Steady-State Aircraft Inter Noise Containing Tonal Components," NASA TM-104147. NASA Langley Res. Cent., Hampton, Virginia.

ANSI (1986). S3.4-1980. "American National Standard Procedure for the Computation of Loudness of Noise." Am. Natl. Stand. Inst., New York (Mar. 26, 1968).

Aures, W. (1985a). Ein Berechnungsverfahren der Rautigkeit. *Acustica* **58,** 268–281.

Aures, W. (1985b). Der Sensorische Wohlklang als Function psychoakusticscher Empfindungsgrössen. *Acustica* **58,** 282–290.

Aures, W. (1985c). Berechnungsverfahren für den sensorischen Wohlklang beliiebiger Schallsignale. *Acustica* **59,** 130–141.

Beranek, L. L., Marshall, J. L., Cudworth, A. L., and Peterson, A. P. G. (1951). Calculation and measurement of the loudness of sounds. *J. Acoust. Soc. Am.* **23,** 261–269.

Berglund, B, Berglund, U., and Lindvall, T. (1975). Scaling loudness, noisiness and annoyance of aircraft noise. *J. Acoust. Soc. Am.* **57,** 930–934.

Boring, E. G. (1942). "Sensation and Perception in the History of Experimental Psychology." Appleton, New York.

Brambilla, G., and Carretti, M. R. (1990). Evaluation of annoyance due to impulsive sound. *Proc. NOISE-CON 90* pp. 279–284.

Broadbent, D. E., and Robinson, D. W. (1964). Subjective measurements of the relative annoyance of simulated sonic bangs and aircraft noise. *J. Sound Vib.* **1,** 162–174.

Carter, N. L. (1972). Effect of rise time and repetition rate on the loudness of acoustic transients. *J. Sound Vib.* **21,** 227–239.

Carter, N. L., and Kryter, K. D. (1962). Masking of pure tones and speech. *J. Aud. Res.* **2,** 68–98.

CHABA (1977). "Guidelines for Preparing Environmental Impact Statements on Noise," Rep. WG 69. Comm. Hear., Bioacoust., Biomech., Natl. Res. Counc., Washington, D.C.

Churcher, B. G., and King, A. J. (1937). Performance of noise meters in terms of the primary standard. *J. Inst. Electr. Eng.* **81,** 59–90.

Egan, J. P. (1955). Perstimulatory fatigue as measured by heterphonic loudness balances. *J. Acoust. Soc. Am.* **27,** 111–120.

Egan, J. P., and Meyer, D. R. (1950). Changes in pitch of tones of low frequency as a function of the pattern of excitation produced by a band of noise. *J. Acoust. Soc. Am.* **22,** 827–833.

Ehmer, R. H. (1959). Masking by tones vs. noise bands. *J. Acoust. Soc. Am.* **31,** 1253–1256.

Fletcher, H., and Munson, W. A. (1933). Loudness, its definition, measurement and calculation. *J. Acoust. Soc. Am.* **5,** 82–108.

Fletcher, H., and Steinberg, J. C. (1924). The dependence of the loudness of a complex sound upon the energy in the various frequency regions of the sound. *Phys. Rev.* **24,** 306–317.

Fuller, H. C., and Robinson, D. W. (1975). "Tempora! Variables in the Assessment of an Experimental Noise Environment," NPL Acoust. Rep. Ac-72. Br. A.R.C., Teddington, England.

Galloway, W. J. (1978). "Subjective Evaluation of Helicopter Blade Slap Noise. Helicopter Acoustics," NASA CP-2052, Part 11, pp. 403–418. NASA Langley Res. Cent., Hampton, Virginia.

Garner, W. R. (1954). A technique and a scale for loudness measurement. *J. Acoust. Soc. Am.* **26,** 73–88.

Garner, W. R. (1958). Half-loudness judgments without prior stimulus context. *J. Exp. Psychol.* **55,** 482–485.

Garner, W. R. (1959). The development of context effects in half-loudness judgments. *J. Exp. Psychol.* **58,** 212–221.

Genuit, K. (1991). Binaural technique for the objective measurement of subjectively perceived sound quality. *NOISE-CON 91* pp. 451–458.

Gzhesik, Y., Lempkovski, A., Turchinski, B., Fazonovich, Y., and Shimchik, K. (1961). Comparison of methods for evaluating loudness from data published during the period 1930–1957. *Sov. Phys.—Acoust.* **6,** 421–441.

Harris, C. S. (1990). Effects of military training route noise on human annoyance. *Proc. NOISE-CON 90* pp. 297–302.

Hellman, R. P. (1981). Stability of individual loudness functions obtained by magnitude estimation and production. *Perception and Psychophysics.* **29,** 63–70.

Hellman, R. P. (1988). Loudness functions in noise-induced and noise-simulated hearing losses. *In* "Noise as a Public Health Problem., Proc. Int. Congr., 5th," (B. Bergland, U. Berglund, J. Karlsson, T. Lindvall, eds.). Vol. 2, pp. 1–5 and 110.

Hellman, R., and Zwislocki, J. (1963). Monaural loudness function at 1000 cps and interaural summation. *J. Acoust. Soc. Am.* **35,** 856–865.

Hiramatsu, K., Takagi, K., and Yamamoto, Y. (1978). The effect of sound duration on annoyance. *J. Sound Vib.* **59,** 511–520.

ISO (1975). R 532. "Methods for Calculating Loudness Level: Method A, Method B." Int. Organ. Standardization, Geneva.

Izumi, K. (1975). Two aspects of the perceived noisiness of intermittent sounds. *Inter-Noise 75 Proc.* (K. Kido, ed.), pp. 453–456. Tohoku Univ., Sendai, Jpn.

Izumi, K. (1977a). Two experiments on the perceived noisiness of periodically intermittent sounds. *Noise Control Eng.* **9**(1), 16–23.

Izumi, K. (1977b). The startle effect and the perceived noisiness of periodically intermittent sounds. *Inter-Noise 77—Noise Control: Eng. Responsibility* (E. J. Rathe, ed.), pp. B 363–B 368. Swiss Fed. Inst. Technol., Zurich.

Kryter, K. D. (1948). Loudness and annoyance-value of bands of noise. *Oralism Auralism: Trans. Annu. Meet. Natl. Forum Deafness Speech Pathol., 30th, St. Louis* pp. 26–28.

Kryter, K. D. (1959). Scaling human reactions to the sound from aircraft. *J. Acoust. Soc. Am.* **31,** 1415–1429.

Kryter, K. D., and Pearsons, K. S. (1963). Some effects of spectral content and duration on perceived noise level. *J. Acoust. Soc. Am.* **35,** 866–883.

Kryter, K. D., and Pearsons, K. S. (1964). Modification of noy tables. *J. Acoust. Soc. Am.* **36,** 394–397.

Kryter, K. D., and Pearsons, K. S. (1965). Judged noisiness of a band of random noise containing and audible pure tone. *J. Acoust. Soc. Am.* **38,** 106–112.

Kryter, K. D., Pearsons, K. S., and Woods, B. (1965). "Preliminary Study on the Effect of Multiple and Modulated Tones on Perceived Noise," NASA CR-69606. NASA Langley Res. Cent., Hampton, Virginia.

Kryter, K. D. (1966). "Review of Research and Methods for Measuring the Loudness and Noisiness of Complex Sounds," NASA CR-422. NASA Langley Res. Cent., Hampton, Virginia.

Kryter, K. D., Johnson, P. J., and Young, J. R. (1967). "Psychological Experiments on Sonic Booms. Annex B of Sonic Boom Experiments at Edwards Air Force Base," Stanford Res. Inst., NSBEO-1-67 (Contract AF 49(638)-1758), CFSTI, U.S. Dep. Commer. (July 28, 1967).

Kryter, K. D. (1969). Sonic booms from supersonic transport. *Science* **163,** 359–367.

Kryter, K. D. (1970a). "The Effects of Noise on Man." Academic Press, New York.

Kryter, K. D. (1970b). "Possible Modifications to the Calculation of Perceived Noisiness," NASA CR-1636. NASA Langley Res. Cent., Hampton, Virginia.

Kryter, K. D., and Poza, F. (1977). "Study of Relative Acceptability of Takeoff and Landing Noises of Concorde and Other Commercial Aircraft," Rep. to Port Authority of New York and New Jersey (Mar.). (Unpubl.)

Kuwano, S., Namba, S., and Nakajima, Y. (1980). On the noisiness of steady state and intermittent noises. *J. Sound Vib.* **72,** 87–96.

Kwiek, M. (1953). Investigation of the relation between the hearing sensitivity and intensity of sinusoidal tones by differential methods. *Friends Sci. Soc., Poznan, Ser. A* **6,** 329.

Laird, D. A. and Coye, K. (1929). Psychological Measurements of Annoyance as Related to Pitch and Loudness. *J. Acoust. Soc. Am.* **1,** 158–163.

Little, J. W. (1961). Human response to jet engine noises. *Noise Control Shock Vib.* **7**(3), 11–13.

McCurdy, D. A. (1988). "Advanced Turboprop Aircraft Flyover Noise: Annoyance to Counter-Rotating-Propeller Configurations with A Different Number of Blades on Each Roto—Preliminary Results," NASA TM-100636. NASA Langley Res. Cent., Hampton, Virginia.

McCurdy, D. A. (1989). "Advanced Turboprop Aircraft Flyover Noise: Annoyance: Comparison of Different Propeller Configurations" (AIAA Aeroacoust. Conf., 12th), AIAA 89–1128. San Antonio, Texas.

McCurdy, D. A. (1990). "Annoyance Caused by Advanced Turboprop Aircraft Flyover Noise," NASA TP3027. NASA Langley Res. Cent., Hampton, Virginia.

McCurdy, D. A. (1991). "Annoyance Caused by Advanced Turboprop Aircraft Flyover Noise—Comparison of Different Propeller Configurations," NASA TP-3104. NASA Langley Res. Cent., Hampton, Virginia.

McCurdy, D. A. (1992). "Annoyance Caused by Aircraft En Route Noise," NASA TP-3165. NASA Langley Res. Cent., Hampton, Virginia.

Meloni, T., and Krueger, H. (1993). Loudness perception and annoyance of impulsive noise measured in the laboratory. *Noise Public Health Probl. Proc. Int. Congr. 6th* (M. Vallet, ed.), Vol. 2, pp. 601–602. l'INRETS, 94114 Arcuil Cedex, France.

Namba, S., and Kuwano, S. (1979). An experimental study on the relation between long-term annoyance and instantaneous judgment of level-fluctuating sounds. *Proc. Inter-Noise 79* (S. Czarnecki, ed.), Vol. 11, pp. 837–842. Inst. Fundam. Technol. Res., Polish Acad. Sci., Warsaw.

National Sonic Boom Evaluation Office (1967). "Sonic Boom Experiments at Edwards Air Force Base, Interim Report." Prepared by Stanford Res. Inst., Contract AF 49(638)-1758. (Avail. from Clearing House for Fed. Sci. Tech. Inf., U.S. Dep. Commer., Springfield, Virginia.)

Ollerhead, J. B. (1968). "Subjective Evaluation of General Aviation Aircraft Noise," Tech. Rpt. No. 68-35. Federal Aviation Administration, Washington, D.C.

Ollerhead, J. B. (1969). "The Noisiness of Diffuse Sound Fields at High Intensities." FAA-No.-70-3. Federal Aviation Administration. Washington, D.C. (Avail. from DTIC as AD 708 816.)

Parnell, J. E., Nagel, D. C., and Parry, H. J. (1967). Growth of Noisiness for Tones and Bands of Noise at Different Frequencies," FAA-DS-67-21. Fed. Aviat. Adm., Washington, D.C.

Pearsons, K. S. (1966). "The Effects of Duration and Background Noise Level on Perceived Noisiness," ADS-78. Fed. Aviat. Adm., Washington, D.C. (Apr. 1966).

Pearsons, K. S. (1968). "Assessment of the Validity of Pure Tone Corrections to Perceived Noise Level. Progress on NASA Research Relating to Noise Alliviation of Large Subsonic Jet Aircraft," NASA SP-189. NASA Langley Res. Center, Hampton Virginia.

Pearsons, K. S., and Horonjeff, R. D. (1967). "Category Scaling Judgment Tests of Motor Vehicle and Aircraft Noise," FAA-DS-67-8. Federal Aviation Administration, Washington, D.C.

Pearsons, K. S., Woods, B., and Kryter, K. D. (1965). "Preliminary Study on the Effect of Multiple and Modulated Tones on Perceived Noisiness," Rpt. 1265, NASA CR-1117. NASA Langley Res. Center, Hampton, Virginia.

Pedersen, O. J. Lyregaard, P. E., and Poulsen, T. (1977). "The Round Robin Test on Evaluation of Loudness Level of Impulsive Noise," ISO/TC 43/SC 1/SG 'B' (Secretariat-15) 23. Acoustics Lab. Tech., Univ. of Denmark.

Powell, C. A. (1978). "A Subjective Field Study of Helicopter Blade-Slap Noise," NASA TM-78758. NASA Langley Res. Cent., Hampton, Virginia.

Powell, C. A. (1981). "Subjective Field Study of Response to Impulsive Helicopter Noise," NASA TP-1833. NASA Langley Res. Cent., Hampton, Virginia.

Powell, C. A., and McCurdy, D. A. (1982). "Effects of Repetition Rate and Impulsiveness of Simulated Helicopter Rotor Noise on Annoyance," NASA TP 1969. NASA Langley Res. Center, Hampton, Virginia.

Quinlan, D. (1990). Numerical analysis of Zwicker's loudness method. *Proc. NOISE-CON 90* pp. 285–290.

Reese, T. W., Kryter, K. D., and Stevens, S. S. (1944). "The Relative Annoyance Produced by Various Bands of Noise," I.C.-65. Psycho-Acoust. Lab., Harvard Univ., Cambridge, Massachusetts.

Reynolds, G. S., and Stevens, S. S. (1960). Binaural summation of loudness. *J. Acoust. Soc. Am.* **32,** 1337–1344.

Rich, G. J. (1916). A preliminary study of tonal volume. *J. Exper. Psychol.* **1,** 13–22.

Robinson, D. W., and Whittle, L. S. (1964). The loudness of octave-bands of noise. *Acustica* **14,** 24–35.

Rosinger, G., Nixon, C. W., and Von Gierke, H. E. (1970). Quantification of the noisiness of "approaching" and "receding" sounds. *J. Acoust. Soc. Am.* **48,** 843–853.

Scharf, B., and Hellman, R. (1979). "Comparison of Various Methods for Predicting the Loudness and Acceptability of Noise. Part 2: Effects of Spectral Pattern and Tonal Components," Rep. EPA-550/9-79-102. U.S. Environ. Prot. Agency, Washington, D.C. (Avail. from NTIS as PB 82-138 702.)

Scharf, B., Hellman, R., and Bauer, J. (1977). "Comparison of Various Methods for Predicting the Loudness and Acceptability of Noise," Rep. EPA-550/977-101. U.S. Environ. Prot. Agency, Washington, D.C.

Schomer, P. D. (1977). Evaluation of C-weighted L dn for assessment of impulse noise. *J. Acoust. Soc. Am.* **62,** 396–399.

Silverman, S. R. (1947). Tolerance for pure tones and speech in normal and defective hearing. *Ann. Otol. Rhinol. Laryngol.* **56,** 658–677.

Sperry, W. C. (1968). "Aircraft Noise Evaluation," Rep. FAA-NO-68-34. Fed. Aviat. Adm., Washington, D.C. (Avail. from DTIC as AD 676 230.)

Stevens, S. S. (1934a). The volume and intensity of tones. *Am. J. Psychol.* **46,** 397–408.

Stevens, S. S. (1934b). Tonal density. *J. Exp. Psychol.* **17,** 585–592.

Stevens, S. S. (1955). The measurement of loudness. *J. Acoust. Soc. Am.* **27,** 815–829.

Stevens, S. S. (1956). Calculation of the loudness of complex noise. *J. Acoust. Soc. Am.* **28,** 807–832.

Stevens, S. S. (1957a). On the psychophysical law. *Psychol. Rev.* **64,** 153–181.

Stevens, S. S. (1957b). Concerning the form of the loudness function. *J. Acoust. Soc. Am.* **29,** 603–606.

Stevens, S. S. (1959a). The quantification of sensation, Daedalus. *J. Am. Acad. Arts Sci.* **88,** 608–621.

Stevens, S. S. (1959b). On the validity of the loudness scale. *J. Acoust. Soc. Am.* **31,** 995–1003.

Stevens, S. S. (1961). Procedure for calculating loudness: Mark VI. *J. Acoust. Soc. Am.* **33,** 1577–1585.

Stevens, S. S. (1972). Perceived level of noise by Mark VII and decibels (E). *J. Acoust. Soc. Am.* **51,** 575–601.

Sutherland, L. C., and Burke, R. E. (1979). "Annoyance, Loudness, and Measurement of Repetitive Type Impulsive Noise Sources," Rept. EPA-550/9-79-103. U.S. Environ. Prot. Agency, Washington, D.C. (Avail. from NTIS as PB 82-138 785.)

von Bismark, G. (1974). Sharpness as an attribute of the timbre of steady sounds. *Acustica* **30,** 159–172.

von Paulus, E., and Zwicker, E. (1972). Programme zur automatischen Bestimmung der Lautheit aus Terzpegeln ode Frequenzgruppenpegeln. *Acustica* **27,** 253–266.

Weber, R. (1990). Acoustical parameters causing the annoyance of shrilling chalk noise. *Proc. NOISE-CON 90* pp. 275–278.

Wells, R. J. (1967). Recent research relative to perceived noise level. *J. Acoust. Soc. Am.* **42,** 1151.

Wells, R. J., and Blazier, W. E., Jr. (1962). "A Procedure for Computing the Subjective Reaction to Complex Noise," Congr. Rep. I: *Int. Congr. Acoust., 4th, Copenhagen* Organ. Comm., Pap. L24.

Wolsk, D. (1964). Discrimination limen for loudness under varying rates of intensity change. *J. Acoust. Soc. Am.* **36,** 1277–1282.

Young, J. R. (1976). "Measurement of the Psychological Annoyance of Simulated Explosion Sequences (Second Year)," Contract DACA 23-74-C-0008. Stanford Res. Inst., Menlo Park, California.

Zwicker, E. (1958). Uber Psychologische und Methodische Grundlagen der Lautheit. *Acustica* **8,** 237–258.

Zwicker, E. (1960). Ein Verfahren zur Berechnung der Lautstarke. *Acustica* **10,** 304–308.

Zwicker, E. (1989). On the dependence of unbiased annoyance on loudness. *Proc. 1989 Int. Conf. Noise Control Eng. Newport Beach, California.* pp. 809–814.

Zwicker, E., and Feldtkeller, R. (1967). "Das Ohr als Nachrichtenempfanger," Aufl. 2. Hirzel, Stuttgart.

Zwicker, E., Flottorp, G., and Stevens, S. S. (1957). Critical band width in loudness summation. *J. Acoust. Soc. Am.* **29,** 548–557.

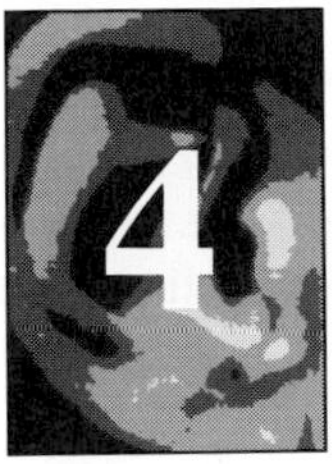

Normal Hearing, Sociocusis, Nosocusis, and Hearing Loss from Industrial Noise

INTRODUCTION

Loss in hearing sensitivity as the result of exposure to sound has been recognized for many years as a disease affecting persons in noisy occupations in industry and the military services. It is also realized that most members of the general population suffer varying degrees of sound-induced hearing loss, or *sociocusis*.

Most previous studies of noise-induced hearing loss involved perceptually unwanted sounds from industry and the firing of guns. However, as far as damage to the peripheral ear is concerned there is no physical basis for making a distinction between perceptually wanted and unwanted sounds. It is sound per se that causes the losses. In deference to custom, the term *noise-induced permanent threshold shift* (NIPTS) will be used in the discussions that follow to mean sound-induced permanent threshold shift.

Pure-tone audiometry is the most widely used medical procedure for the assessment of loss in hearing sensitivity. The minimum SPL of a pure tone at the threshold of audibility of the average young adult ear, free of ear disease and exposure to intense noise, has been labeled *audiometric zero* for that tone. The thresholds are typically determined by earphone presentation in otherwise quiet listening conditions. The threshold SPLs required for different pure-tone frequencies are labeled HL (hearing level) with reference to audiometric zero.

A problem for the assessment of loss in hearing sensitivity from an occupational noise, NIPTS, has been the identification of the separate effects on the threshold of hearing of (1) aging (*presbycusis*), (2) exposure to non occupational noise (sociocusis), and (3) certain ear diseases (*nosocusis*). In an attempt to circumvent this problem, a number of research studies have been conducted in which the hearing levels of a control group of supposedly non-noise-exposed office and factory workers are compared to the hearing levels of a comparable-age group of factory workers exposed to high levels of factory noise.

The tenets of this approach are (1) the effects of presbycusis, sociocusis, and nosocusis, whatever they might be, would be about the same for both the noise-exposed and control groups, and, accordingly, (2) any differences between the distributions of hearing levels for the two groups could be attributed to the industrial noise. However, as will be shown, this approach is not reliable. A more valid method is to determine NIPTS by comparisons made between the hearing levels of similar-age (presbycusis-controlled) groups of noise and non-noise-exposed workers who have been screened to be free from sociocusis and nosocusis. Under those conditions, any differences between the hearing levels of the two groups should be attributable to the effects of the noise at the workplace.

However, even when the latter method has been employed, the screening of the subjects for sociocusis and nosocusis in a number of studies conducted in industries has been less than adequate. Also, as we shall see, in an industrial study presently used internationally as a basis of standards for noise control, there appears to have been a significant bias in the data due to the method used to obtain subjects from higher, as compared to the lower, levels, of workplace noise.

Research Data to Be Examined

The specification of quantitative relations between exposures to workplace noise and hearing loss has been a difficult and controversial process over the past 45 or so years. The hearing-level data of published major studies of NIPTS from typical 8-h workday exposures to steady and impulse and/impact industrial noises are analyzed below. These analyses will serve, it is believed, to place into perspective the validity of past and present standard procedures for predicting hearing loss from industrial noise and also to provide a partial basis for the development of a new procedure for that purpose.

A major study is defined as one for which quantitative information regarding the intensities and durations of workplace noise exposures and the sex and ages of a large number of exposed workers are specified. In this process, some adjustment of some of the published data was required to allow for comparative interpretation of the findings. These adjustments, and the rationales for them, are given immediately below, followed by results and discussion of more direct interest.

METHODS OF MEASURING HEARING LEVEL

Audiometer Zero

Early surveys of hearing levels employed manual audiometers calibrated to the United States ASA (1951) standard. That standard differs from the more recent ISO 389, 1964-(1985), ANSI S3.6-(1969), and the roughly equivalent British (BSI, 2497 (1954) standards for audiometric zero. For all data used herein that were based on ASA (1951), the hearing levels were, or had been by others, converted to levels re ISO 389 (1985) by the addition of the following number of decibels to the reported level: 500 Hz, 14 dB; 1000 Hz, 10 dB; 2000 Hz, 8.5 dB; 3000 Hz, 8.5 dB; 4000 Hz, 6 dB, 6000 Hz, 9.5 dB. Threshold sound pressure levels specified in ISO 389 (1985), ASA (1951), and ANSI (1969), are given in Table 4.1A.

Why the ASA (1951) levels for audiometric zero are so different from the other standards is something of a mystery. Questions have been raised regarding possible bias due to the selection of limited samples from the total database and uncertainties about presbycusis effects, see discussion by Noble (1978).

Manual versus Self-Recording Audiometry

Besides the problem of recognizing and making adjustments for differences in audiometric zeros prescribed by different standards, systematic differences are found in the hearing levels measured by manual, as compared to self-recording, audiometers. This creates some difficulty in a comparative analysis of hearing levels in that most studies of presbycusis were obtained with so-called manual audiometers, whereas the hearing levels of noise exposed workers in a number of studies were measured with so-called self-recording audiometers.

With the manual instrument, the intensity at which the subject hears the presence of a pure tone no more than twice out of three, or three out of four presentations, is usually selected as the threshold level of hearing sensitivity, such as a 67–75%—say, 70%—correct criterion of threshold. With self-recording (also called *Bekesy-type*) audiometers, the threshold level is typically taken to be the level halfway between the extremes (audible–inaudible) of the recorded trace of the changes in the level of the tone. This could be called the 50% correct threshold, as distinct from the 70% correct threshold of manual audiometry.

Because the range in intensity from inaudible to audible levels, and reverse, on the self-recording audiometers is typically 10 dB (Rudmose, 1963),

TABLE 4.1A Recommended Audiometer-Zero Reference Sound-Pressure Levels, Measured with Specified Earphone–Coupler Combinations, by ISO 389 (1985), ASA, 24.5, (1951), and ANSI S3.6 (1969) and Differences between Levels Specified in the Two Latter Standards Manual Audiometry Presumed Method for Measuring Subjective Thresholds.

	Audiometric zero, 0 dB								
	ISO 389 (1985)					Reference equivalent threshold SPL, dB			
Frequency Hz	Reference equivalent threshold SPL, dB					Frequency Hz	ASA, 1951	ANSI, 1969	Difference
125	44.5	47.5	47.0	45.5	55.0	125	54.5	45.5	9.0
250	27.5	28.5	28.0	24.5	33.0	250	39.5	24.5	15.0
500	11.5	14.5	11.5	11.0	14.5	500	25.0	11.0	14.0
1000	5.5	8.0	5.5	6.5	8.5	1000	16.5	6.5	10.0
1500	4.5	7.5	6.5	6.5	8.5	1500	16.5*	6.5	10.0
2000	4.5	8.0	9.0	8.5	9.0	2000	17.0	8.5	8.5
3000	6.0	6.0	8.0	7.5	10.5	3000	16.0*	7.5	8.5
4000	8.0	5.5	9.5	9.0	11.5	4000	15.0	9.0	6.0
6000	17.0	8.0	8.0	8.0	18.5	6000	17.5*	8.0	9.5
8000	14.5	14.5	10.0	9.5	9.5	8000	21.5	9.5	11.5
Earphone:	Audio 15	Beyer DT 48	S.T.C. 4026-A	W.E. 705A	T.D.6	Earphone:	W.E. 705A	W.E. 705A	
Coupler:	C.N.E.T.	NBS 9-A +P.T.B.	B.S. 2042	N.B.S. 9-A	IU-3	Coupler:	N.B.S. 9-A	N.B.S. 9-A	
Country:	France	Germany	U.K.	U.S.A.	U.S.S.R.	Country:	U.S.A.	U.S.A.	

* Interpolation, not in 1951 standard.

the difference between the 50% point of the level trace and the 70% correct manual threshold would be of the order of 2.5 dB, with the manual threshold being the higher of the two. Whatever the reasons might be, a difference of that magnitude has been generally found in studies of thresholds obtained by these two methodologies, as shown in Table 4.1B.

To make comparisons among the databases as direct as possible, all reviewed hearing-level data that were obtained with self-recording audiometry (see, e.g., Lempert and Henderson, 1973; Taylor *et al.,* 1984) are increased by 3 dB, per Table 4.1B, to make them comparable to manual audiograms. An exception to this are the data of Burns and Robinson (1970). These investigators employed self-recording audiometers, but corrected their own

TABLE 4.1B Comparison of Mean Threshold Hearing Levels Taken with Self-Recording (Bekesy-Type) vs. Manual Audiometers

	Frequency, Hz					
Study	500	1000	2000	3000	4000	6000
1	−1.1	3.1	1.1	1.8	1.1	0.8
2	1.7	5.3	6.2	6.2	4.8	3.9
3	0.0	0.0	3.0	3.0	4.0	0.0
4	1.0	3.4	4.6	3.7	3.4	−1.6
5	2.2	3.5	4.0	3.6	3.8	2.4
6	2.9	3.2	0.8	−4.0	3.7	3.3
7	3.0	2.1	3.2	3.3	3.7	3.7
8	1.3	4.6	5.7	1.9	2.6	0.0
9	2.8	2.7	3.0	3.0	2.8	2.8
Mean	2	3	4	3	3	2
Prop. diff.	3	3	3	3	3	3
10	−3	−3	−3	−3	−3	−3

Note: A positive value indicates lower-value, more sensitive, hearing level, found with self-recording audiometers.

Studies:

1. Burns and Hinchcliff (1957): 20 subjects tested twice each method.
2. Rudmose (1963): data taken at Wisconsin State Fair.
3. Harris (1964): comparison of groups tested on different audiometers.
4. Rice and Coles (1966): 370 ears. Table IV, groups tested on different audiometers.
5. Knight (1966): manual HLs were reduced by 2.5 dB on the assumption of "a linear distribution of thresholds over the imposed 5 dB class interval." This procedure is seldom applied in manual audiometry and reduction restored here. Comparison based on Table II. 66 S's.
6. Jokinen (1969): Tables 1 and 2; groups 3 and 4 at 4 kHz, Table 1, excluded.
7. Stephens (1971): HLs at 3 and 6 kHz estimated here; 38 subjects, Fig. 50.
8. Burns and Robinson (1970): Table 16.1, differences between their control group, self-recording Audiometry, and Hinchcliff group, Manual audiometry.
9. Robinson and Whittle (1973): 128 subjects, Table 8.
10. Clark and Popelka (1989): 540 subjects tested on conventional manual and Micro Audiometrics Earscan II self-recording audiometer.

data for the apparent difference in threshold hearing levels due to audiometric techniques, see study 8, Table 4.1B.

Contrary to the findings discussed above, Clark and Popelka (1989) reported that the hearing levels of 540 railroad train workers were, on the average, 3 dB higher when measured by a self-recording audiometer, than by manual audiometry, see Table 4.1B. However, with the particular self-recording instrument used for their study, the threshold was automatically recorded, according to the manufacturer, as being the level where the listener indicated twice in succession that the tone was audible, i.e., equivalent to the highest point reached by the intensity trace on self-recording audiometers. This would correspond to a 100% correct threshold, instead of the 50% point of conventionally scored self-recording audiometers. Even so, the 3-dB correction found with this particular instrument seems somewhat larger than one would expect.

The direction and magnitude of the differences found among the manual and various self-recording thresholds appear to be due primarily to threshold scoring criteria, rather than differences in the methods of stimulus presentation, per se, by the different instruments.

Mean and Median (50th Percentile)

Because of upward skewing in distributions of the hearing levels of, particularly, older and noise-exposed groups of people, the mean of a given distribution is typically about 1–2 dB higher than its median. The medians, and other percentile points, of the distributions of the hearing levels for the various studies were used to cross-compare and combine the data of the various studies. For those instances where only mean levels were published, the central tendency of mean hearing levels were reduced by 2 dB, to their estimated median counterparts. In documents concerned with distributions of hearing levels, the median is commonly referred to as the *fiftieth percentile*. In the tables, figures, and remaining text of this chapter, "50%ile" will be generally used as a short label for the fiftieth percentile, or median, "25%ile," for the twenty-fifth percentile, etc.

ASSESSMENT OF PRESBYCUSIS, SOCIOCUSIS, AND NOSOCUSIS

Presbycusis

The increases in hearing levels of people in industrialized societies that are due to aging, presbycusis, are to be found in ISO Standard 7029 (1984). (The second column for females, and third for males, of the distributions of 50%ile hearing levels in Table 4.2, which gives the distributions for the 10%ile, 50%ile, and 90%ile of these populations). These data represent the average of a number of studies in which the subjects were, for the most part, thoroughly screened for nosocusis and exposure to industrial and gun noise

TABLE 4.2 50%ile HLs, ISO 389, for "Control" Groups for Studies of NIPTS in Industry and Presbycusis in Noise-Free Society ("Av.R,LE" = Average Hearing for Right and Left Ears)

	Screened for nosocusis and exposure to gun and excessive work noise								Unscreened nosocusis and (except R&S) noise				Oto-screened	
	General populations			Professional	Factory-worker populations				General populations				Noise-free society	
	Av.R.LE	Av.R,LE		Av.R,LE	Av.R,LE		Av.R,LE	Av.R,LE	Better Ear	Av.R,LE	Av.R,LE	Av.R,LE	Av.R,LE	
Age, years	Female, Hinch[a]	Female, 7029[b]	Male, 7029[b]	Male, G&N[c]	Female, Yerg[f]	Male, Yerg[f]	Male, L&H[d]	Male, R&S[e]	Male, G&R[g]	Female, G&R[h]	Male, G&R[h]	Male, S&G[i]	Female, Rosen[k]	Male, Rosen[k]
500 Hz														
25	1	0	0		4	6	8	14	6	9	9	6	−1	1
30	1	1	1	Data	5	5	9	13	7	10	10	7	1	0
35	2	1	1	not	5	5	10	13	8	10	11	8	1	0
40	2	2	2	available	6	6	11	14	8	10	12	8	3	2
45	3	3	3		7	6	12	14	9	12	12	10	5	3
50	4	4	4		8	7	13	14	10	14	13	11	4	4
55	6	5	5		10	8	14	na	11	16	13	12	4	5
60	7	6	6		na	na	na	na	12	18	16	13	5	6
1000 Hz														
25	1	0	0	10	2	5	9	10	0	4	3	3	0	0
30	1	1	1	10	4	3	9	9	0	3	4	4	0	0
35	2	1	1	10	5	3	10	10	2	4	5	5	0	0
40	2	2	2	10	5	4	11	10	3	4	6	5	0	1
45	4	3	3	11	5	5	12	10	4	5	7	7	1	2
50	5	4	4	11	7	7	13	11	5	6	9	9	2	2
55	6	5	6	11	8	9	14	na	6	8	9	10	4	2
60	6	6	7	12	na	na	na	na	6	10	10	11	5	3

(continues)

TABLE 4.2 *(Continued)*

	Screened for nosocusis and exposure to gun and excessive work noise							Unscreened nosocusis and (except R&S) noise					Oto-screened	
	General populations			Professional	Factory-worker populations				General populations				Noise-free society	
	Av.R.LE	Av.R,LE		Av.R,LE	Av.R,LE		Av.R,LE	Av.R,LE	Bter Ear	Av.R,LE	Av.R,LE	Av.R,LE	Av.R,LE	
Age, years	Female, Hinch[a]	Female, 7029[b]	Male, 7029[b]	Male, G&N[c]	Female, Yerg[f]	Male, Yerg[f]	Male, L&H[d]	Male, R&S[e]	Male, G&R[g]	Female, G&R[h]	Male, G&R[h]	Male, S&G[i]	Female, Rosen[k]	Male, Rosen[k]
2000 Hz														
25	0	0	0	6	1	3	7	9	1	3	4	2	0	0
30	0	1	1	7	5	5	8	8	2	4	5	3	2	0
35	1	2	2	7	6	7	9	8	3	5	6	5	3	0
40	3	3	3	8	6	9	9	10	4	7	8	6	2	1
45	4	4	5	9	6	9	10	14	6	8	10	9	5	1
50	6	6	7	10	8	13	11	16	8	10	12	11	5	3
55	7	8	10	11	11	17	13	na	9	12	15	14	5	5
60	9	11	12	14	na	na	na	na	10	14	18	16	6	6
3000 Hz														
25	1	0	1	7	2	7	8	18	7	6	10	6	2	0
30	2	1	2	9	5	10	9	16	9	8	12	7	3	2
35	4	2	3	10	9	14	12	22	11	9	15	10	5	4
40	6	4	6	13	9	15	13	25	13	10	18	13	7	5
45	8	6	8	15	9	17	17	28	16	11	21	19	10	5
50	10	8	12	16	12	22	20	28	19	13	25	24	8	7
55	12	10	16	17	16	28	24	na	25	17	32	29	7	9
60	15	13	20	23	na	na	na	na	30	21	40	34	8	10
4000 Hz														
25	1	0	1	7	1	11	10	23	8	15	11	6	3	−2
30	4	1	2	10	6	13	13	16	10	18	15	11	4	0
35	5	3	5	12	11	15	16	26	14	19	21	15	4	2
40	5	4	8	15	13	22	19	26	17	21	28	20	7	3
45	9	7	12	17	16	22	23	31	16	23	29	28	9	3
50	13	9	16	19	18	37	26	32	26	25	30	35	8	6
55	16	12	22	21	20	41	31	na	31	28	38	40	8	8
60	19	16	28	27	na	na	na	na	36	28	46	45	10	9

6000 Hz															
25	2	1	1	8	7	15	12	29	13	15	20	8	3	2
30	4	2	3	12	10	18	16	24	18	18	24	14	4	3
35	5	4	5	16	13	17	20	32	21	19	28	18	5	4
40	6	6	9	18	15	23	24	29	24	21	32	22	8	7
45	9	9	13	21	18	28	29	34	28	23	35	29	11	9
50	11	12	18	24	22	35	33	35	31	25	39	36	15	9
55	17	16	25	26	27	40	35	na	39	30	45	42	19	9
60	22	21	32	35	na	na	na	na	46	35	54	47	20	10
	Average age 25–60 years				Average age 25–55 years			25–50 years	Average ages 25–60 years					
0.5–2 kHz	3	4	4	10	6	7	11	12	6	8	9	8	3	2
3–6 kHz	8	7	11	16	12	21	21	27	21	19	28	22	10	5

[a] Hinchcliff (1959): rural population Scotland. Otologically screened for nosocusis. Manual audiometry, HL per BSI.

[b] ISO 7029, also Annex A, ISO 1999: ears screened for exposure to noise and, otologically, nosocusis. Based on analysis by Robinson and Sutton of data from 11 studies. Manual audiometry, N = ~2300.

[c] Glorig and Nixon (1962): professional research workers and otolaryngologists screened, by questionnaire, for nosocusis and exposure to noise. Manual audiometry, $N = 286$.

[d] Lempert and Henderson (1973): otologically screened for nosocusis and excessive noise (workers in <80-dBA noise, and some gun noise). HLs 500 Hz reduced 5 dB, for apparent calibration problem; 3 dB added all HLs for self-recording audiometry, $N = 380$.

[e] Rosenwinkel and Stewart (1957): male office workers with <2 years' exposure to factory noise. Not screened for nosocusis or use of guns; 50%ile = means (as published)—2 dB. Manual audiometry, $N = 2789$.

[f] Yerg *et al.* (1978): factory workers oto-screened for nosocusis. Screening for gun noise not specified. Controls in <75 dB_A factory noise. Manual audiometry, 50%ile = means (as published)—2 dB. Data interpolated ages 30, 40, and 50 years, $N = 96$.

[g] Annex B, ISO 1999 (1990): better (Bter)-ear HLs based on Glorig and Roberts (1965), USPHS survey. Random sample of U.S. males, unscreened for nosocusis or exposure to noise. Manual audiometry, N = approximately 3300.

[h] Glorig and Roberts (1965): USPHS survey. Average of right and left ears.

[i] Sutherland and Gasaway (1978): unscreened (?) civilian males working in "noisy" jobs Air Force bases. Manual audiometry, $N = 18{,}136$.

[j] Robinson (1988): derived from G&R and S&G data as typical for unscreened males, industrial society. Manual audiometry, average for right and left ears.

[k] Rosen *et al.* (1962): HLs in noise-free, non-industrial society (Mabaan) per HLs 15-year olds, Manual audiometry, N = 226 female, 748 male ears.

(Robinson and Sutton, 1978). However, in some of those studies some unspecified amount of exposure to workplace noise may be the cause, seen at the higher frequencies, of greater hearing loss in male, as compared to female subjects. For example, Kell *et al.* (1979) one of the studies included in Robinson and Sutton's screened groups, involved some men working in noise in bakeries (L_A 79), in a food-processing factory (L_A 81–92), and in fishing-boat cabins (L_A 99).

Table 4.2 also gives the 50%ile hearing levels that have been used, or proposed for use as comparison, control, group data for estimating NIPTS in industrial workers. Figure 4.1 for males, and Fig. 4.2 for females, graphically show, as a function of age, differences in hearing sensitivities at different frequencies for the screened populations of ISO 7029, and the screened and unscreened control groups selected from factory workers.

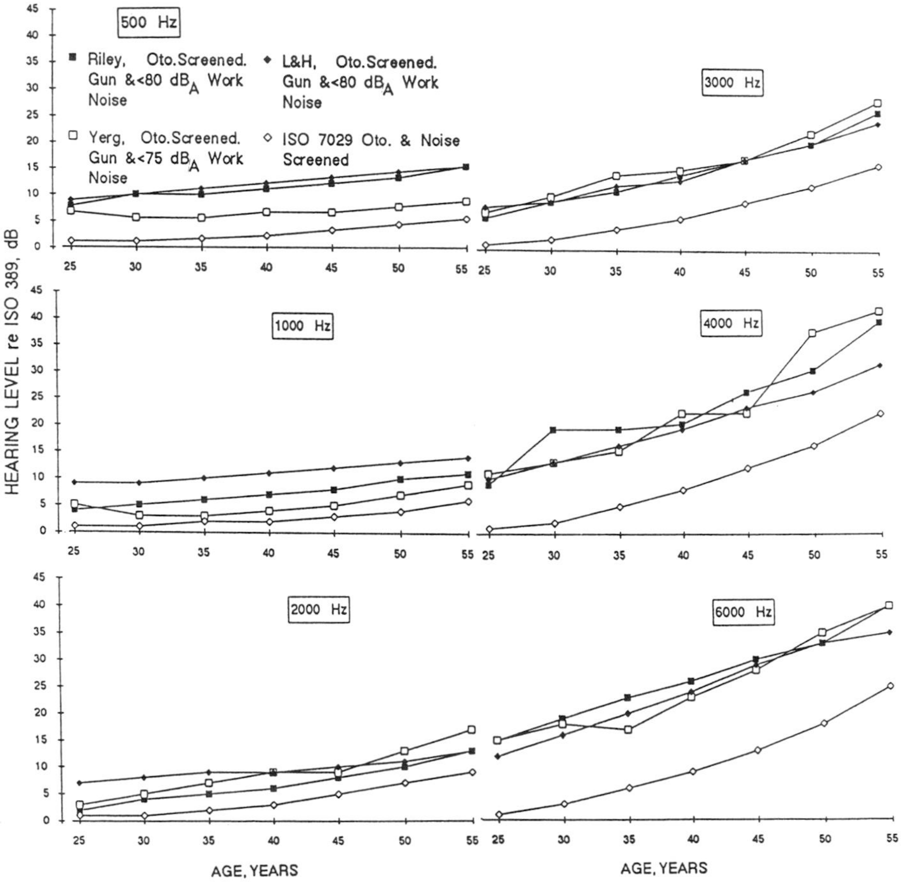

FIGURE 4.1 Comparison of 50%ile hearing levels of male workers who have been screened for nosocusis and exposure to intense workplace, but not gun noise, with 50%ile hearing levels of general-population males screened for nosocusis and exposure to noise ISO 7029 (1984).

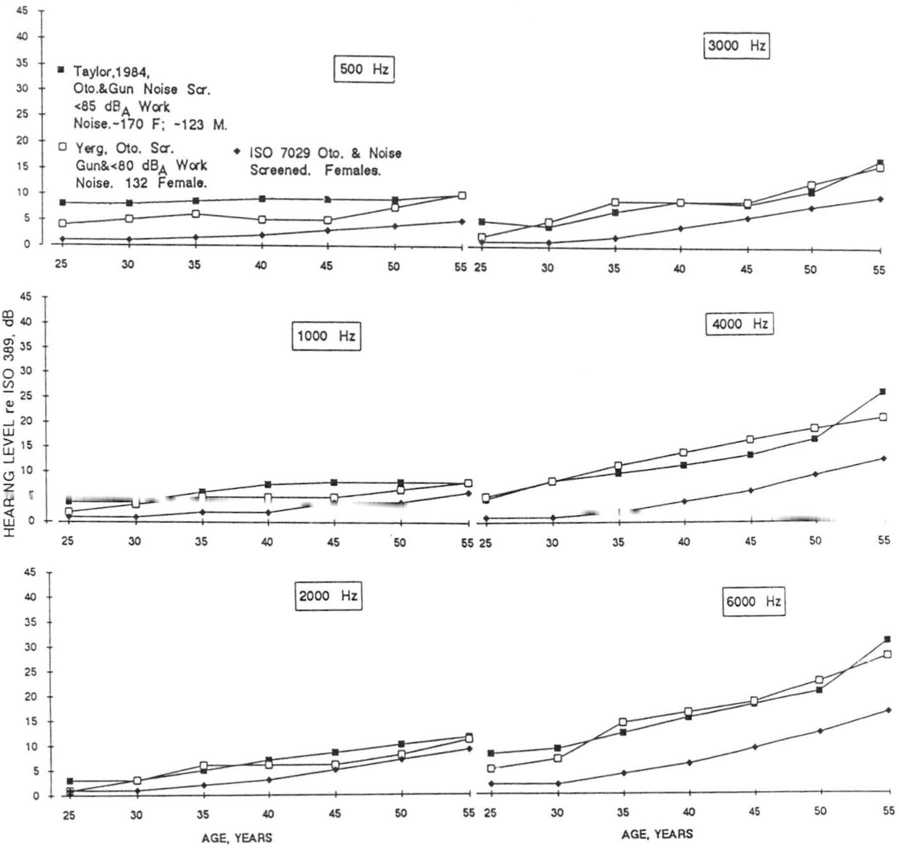

FIGURE 4.2 Comparison of 50%ile hearing levels of female workers who have been screened for nosocusis and exposure to intense workplace noise, with hearing levels of general-population females screened for nosocusis and exposure to noise (ISO, 7029 1984) .

"Pure" Presbycusis and Sociocusis

Everyday sounds and noise appear to be a source of some NIPTS, or sociocusis, in the population of industrial societies. Figure 4.3A shows the 50%ile hearing levels, at 4000 Hz, for different age–decades of factory noise and nosocusis-screened people in industrialized societies (ISO 7029), and nosocusis-screened people of a non-industrialized and noise-free society, the Mabaans of the Sudan (Rosen *et al.*, 1962).

It is seen that in industrialized societies, by the age of 60 years, hearing losses of about 28 dB, 50%ile at 4000, accrue in males, and about 16 dB in females. For the Mabaans, the loss by that age is about 9 dB for either males or females, and is presumably attributable solely to aging, or "pure" presbycusis. Inasmuch as both groups were screened for ear disease, the

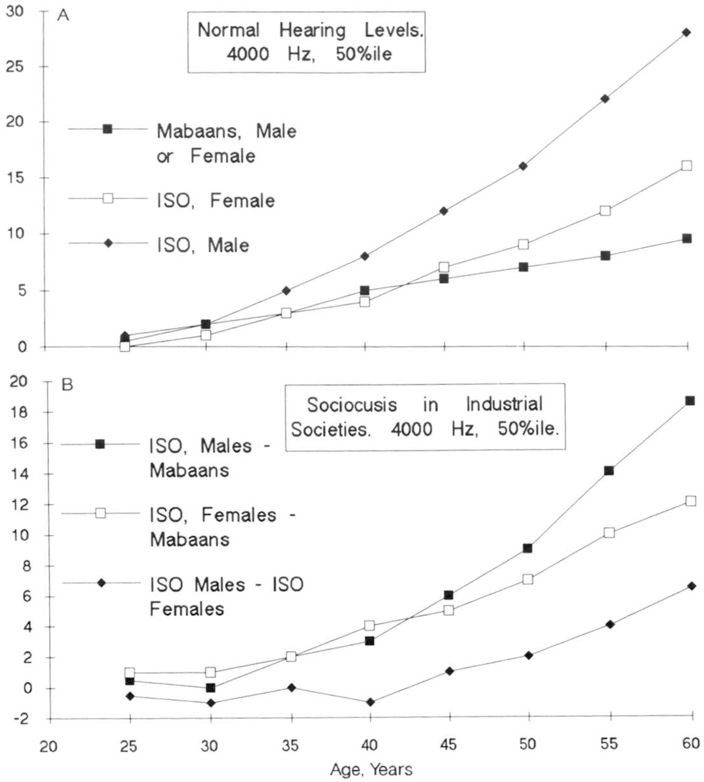

FIGURE 4.3 (A) Hearing levels of nosocusis- and noise-screened females and males in industrialized societies (ISO 7029 1984), and hearing levels of nosocusis-screened males and females from a noise-free primitive society, Mabaans (Rosen *et al.,* 1962). (B) Amount of sociocusis between Mabaans and females and males of industrialized societies, and between males and females of industrialized societies.

differences (see Fig. 4.3B) in the hearing levels for males and for females between the Mabaans and the industrialized society groups can presumably be attributed to sociocusis from the everyday sounds and noises in industrialized societies. Bergman (1966) notes that the growth of presbycusis in the 10% of the U.S. population with the best hearing is about the same as that for the Mabaans. This might indicate that those persons represent the part of the U.S. population exposed to the least amount of "everyday" noise. [Questions raised by Bergman about the hearing levels of young Mabaans are discussed by Kryter (1983).]

It is clear that in modern industrial societies, males experience more sociocusis than females. The 50%ile, 4000 Hz, data in Table 4.2 and Fig. 4.2 show that males have higher hearing levels than females—of about 1 dB at 25 years, and 12 dB at 60 years. Note in this regard that the hearing levels of boys and girls do not differ, at least up to the age of 11 or so years. Above the age of 11 years, both boys and girls are progressively exposed to greater amounts of noise, but more so for boys than girls (see Fig. 4.4B).

Screened Control Groups

Data from Glorig and Nixon (1962) (G&N) in Table 4.2 show that the 50%ile hearing levels, average over all ages, of a group of professional men questionnaire-screened for exposure to noise and nosocusis are some 5 dB higher, averaged over all test frequencies, than those of the screened populations represented in ISO 7029. A possible reason for this difference is that some members of the professional group, although screened by questionnaire, were perhaps actually not completely free of nosocusis nor exposure to noise.

Particular attention is invited to the some 10 dB differences between the hearing levels, average for 3000, 4000, and 6000 Hz, of males, over all ages, of ISO 7029 versus those reported for the Yerg *et al.* (1978), Lempert and Henderson (1973) (L&H), and the Riley *et al.* (1961) studies. These differences (see Table 4.2 and Fig. 4.1) are unexpected in that the subjects in all these distributions were otoscopically screened for nosocusis, and question-

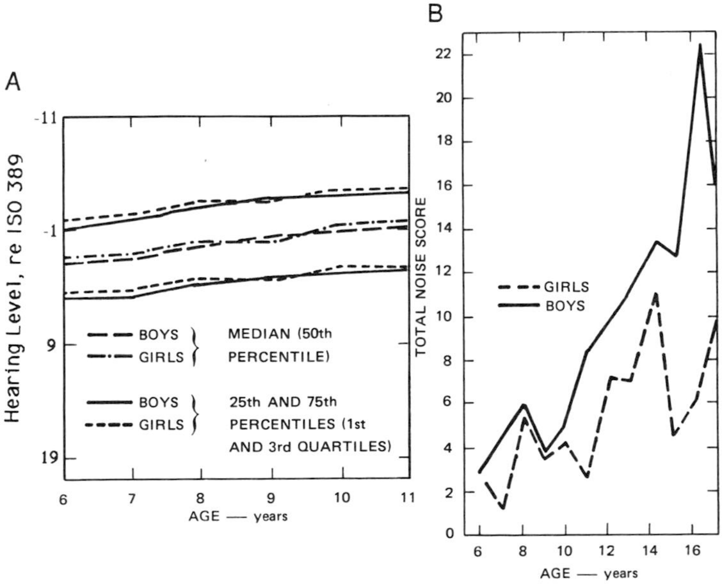

FIGURE 4.4 (A) Percentile hearing levels of children 6–11 years of age, average at 500, 1000, and 2000 Hz. (From Roberts and Huber, 1970.) (B) Median total noise score, 6-month intervals, obtained from questionnaires (higher scores indicate greater exposures to noise). (From Roche *et al.*, 1977.)

naire-screened for exposure to "excessive" noise. However, the screening of the control subjects in these studies allowed the inclusion of persons who had been exposed to gun noise and low levels of factory noise.

In the Lempert and Henderson (1973) investigation, the subjects were considered as non-noise-exposed if they worked in noise that did not exceed L_A 80, and had no more than 100 days' exposure to military guns, or up to 1000 rounds of sport gunfire for more than one year, or up to 500 rounds per year for no more than 4 years. In the Yerg *et al.* (1978) study, the control subjects were considered as non-noise-exposed if they worked in noise that did not exceed L_A 75, and no mention is made of screening for exposure to gun noise. In the Riley *et al.* (1961) study, no mention is made of screening for gun noise per se, and work noise levels of 80 dB were taken to be, for NIPTS, effectively quiet.

The hearing levels, at the higher frequencies, between oto-screened (otoscopically screened) females as given in ISO 7029 vs. those for oto-screened, control group females of the Yerg *et al.* (1978) study averaged 5 dB, and 8 dB vs. a mixture of oto-screened females and males in the control group of the Taylor *et al.* (1984), study. However, in the Yerg *et al.* study control subjects were taken, as previously noted, from noise work areas with noise up to L_A 75, in the Taylor *et al.* (1984) study from areas up to L_A 85, and there was no screening in either study for exposure to gun noise.

Unscreened Control Groups

Annex B of ISO 1999 is a tabulation of the better-ear hearing levels found in a survey by Glorig and Roberts (1965) of 6672 U.S. adults unscreened for nosocusis or exposure to noise (these data for males, and the average of the right and left ears of females from that survey, are shown in Table 4.2). Robinson (1988) proposed that the average of right and left-ear hearing levels found in the surveys of Glorig and Roberts and Sutherland and Gasaway (1978) would better represent those of unscreened populations of industrialized societies, than does ISO 1999 (1990), Annex B.

However, the Sutherland and Gasaway (1978) study was of 18,136 civilian employees of the U.S. Air Force, unscreened for nosocusis but screened to include only persons considered to be exposed to potentially hazardous noise at their work. Rather than representing the general population unscreened for exposure to noise, this sample of employees was screened to be those exposed to potential hazardous noise. Data from these surveys of unscreened populations are also given in Table 4.2. Lutman *et al.* 1993, proposed that the better ear hearing levels of a randomly selected, and questionnaire screened to be free of undue noise exposure and ear disease be considered as appropriate for control group purposes. Their data will be discussed at the end of the chapter.

Gun Noise Sociocusis

Significant amounts of NIPTS at frequencies above 1000 Hz are present in industrial workers due to gun noise from military service, hunting, and target shooting (Chung *et al.*, 1991; Prosser *et al.*, 1988; Kryter, 1991). This creates a significant problem for the identification of NIPTS from workplace noise. It appears that gun noise, from military service and hunting is equivalent to exposures to industrial noise of ~89 L_{Aeq8h} (Johnson and Riffle, 1982; Kryter, 1991) (L_{Aeq8h} is a commonly used unit for the measurement of sound, or noise):

$$L_{Aeq8h} = 10 \log ((1/28{,}800)10^{L_{A_1} \cdots L_{A_{28,000}}/10}), \quad (4.1)$$

Where L_A is a weighted sound, and 1 . . . 28,800 are seconds of time during the typical 8-h workday, that is, the total sound energy in the 8 h averaged over the seconds in the 8 h and converted to a decibel level.

It is found, see Table 4.3, that the overall amount of NIPTS from exposure to railroad noise and gunfire is about that which would arise from the sum of the sound energy in the two noises. If, as has been estimated to be the case, the railroad and gun noise each has about the same effective L_{Aeq8h} exposure level, the effective L_{Aeq8h} for the group of railroad workers who used guns could be expected to be about 3 dB higher than for the group who did not use guns. Further, if each of the noises by itself can cause an NIPTS of 12 dB, an NIPTS of about 16 dB is to be expected when exposures to

TABLE 4.3 HLs and NIPTSs, per ISO (1984) 7029, for Gun-Noise Exposed and Non-Gun-Noise-Exposed Railroad Workers

	HL, average, right and left ears, dB		NIPTS, dB (HL − HL, ISO 7029)		
Average ages >25–64 years	Prosser *et al.** Mean average 2, 3, 4 kHz	Kryter† 50%ile average 3, 4, 6 kHz	Prosser *et al.* Mean–50%ile average 0.2, 3, 4 kHz	Kryter 50%ile–50%ile average 3, 4, 6 kHz	Average
Used guns	23.0	18.9	16.7	15.6	16.1
Used no guns	17.8	15.5	11.4	12.2	11.8
Difference	5.2	3.4	5.2	3.4	4.3
Used guns	N = 133	N = 6734			
Used no guns	N = 82	N = 3044			
Percent used guns	62%	69%			

From Prosser *et al.* (1988) and Kryter (1991).

* All subjects otologically screened.

† Hearing levels adjusted for nosocusis.

both are involved (there being, in this range, about 1–2 dB of NIPTS per 1 dB of sound pressure level).

In brief, NIPTS is a function of the effective sound energies in all the noise exposures imposed on a person, and is not the sum of the decibels of NIPTS to be expected from each noise alone. This fact has adverse implications for the assumption implicit in some industrial studies of NIPTS—namely, that NIPTS from the industrial noise is represented by the difference between the hearing levels of a group of workers exposed to workplace plus, for some of the group, gun noise, versus the hearing levels of a control group exposed to no significant amount of workplace noise, but, for some of the control group, to gun noise. As will be further discussed later, the workplace noise can cause significantly more NIPTS than would be deduced from such differences.

The "equivalent" exposure level of gun noise is, of course, an estimated value representing the population of typical gun users, with wide variations among individuals with respect to number of gun shots experienced per year, years of exposure, types of guns used, etc. Prosser *et al.* (1988) found that there is an increase in the difference between left- and right-ear hearing levels (generally indicative of gun usage) as a function of number of shots per year and years of exposure (see Fig. 4.5), and Chung *et al.* (1991) found a similar increase between the ears of industrial workers as a function of years of shooting. The subjects in the Chung *et al.* and Prosser *et al.* studies did not, and, presumably for the most part, in the Johnson and Riffle (1982) and Kryter (1991) studies, wear ear protection when shooting.

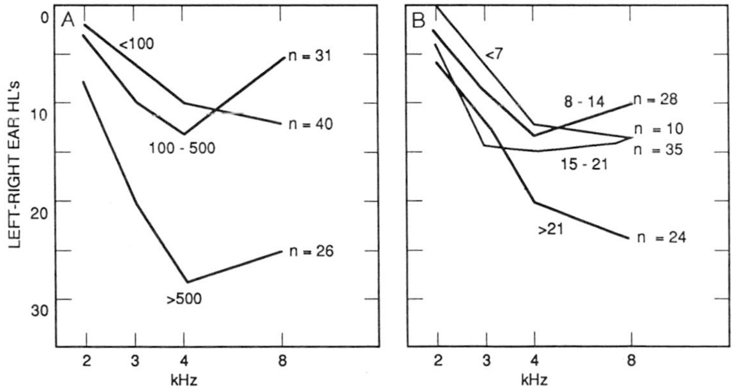

FIGURE 4.5 Interaural threshold differences (left–right) in hunters as function of test frequency. (A) Number of shots per year, and (B) years of exposure. (After Prosser *et al.*, 1988.)

L_{Aeq8h} Workplace Plus Equivalent L_{Aeq8h} Gun Noise

For some of the studies analyzed below, the workplace noise exposure levels are, when appropriate, adjusted upward, on an energy basis. The adjustment is calculated in accordance with an estimate that 50% of male workers are exposed to gun noise, and that the typical L_{Aeq8h} from shooting is equivalent to 89 L_{Aeq8h}. The result is labeled $L_{Aeq8h(wg)}$ (work and gun noise), the effective total noise energy received by the workers as a group.

The estimate that 50% of male industrial workers are significantly exposed to gun noise is based on the following data: about 12% of workers in various U.S. factories (Lempert and Henderson, 1973); 57% of workers in U.S. coal mines (NIOSH, 1976); 50% of workers in British Columbia noisy industries (Chung *et al.*, 1991), 69% of U.S. railroad train workers (Kryter, 1991). The criteria for the identification of "gun users" varied among these studies, from exposures to the rather large numbers of daily or annual rounds of gunfire in the Lempert and Henderson and NIOSH (1976) data, to, for the other cited studies, mere acknowledgment of hunting and target shooting, or having been in military service. For the present analyses, the phrase "uses" or "used guns" probably means more than about 250 rounds of gunfire a year for three or more years.

Adjustments for Nosocusis

The term *nosocusis,* or loss of hearing from diseases of the ear, properly includes sensorineural damage from exposure to noise, as reflected by shifts in hearing thresholds. However, the pervasiveness of NIPTS in modern society justifies its discussion as a separate disease entity, and that the term nosocusis can be used to cover the effects of ear diseases other than NIPTS.

With that definition in mind, it appears that, as far as the hearing levels for relatively large groups of people are concerned, nosocutic shifts in hearing thresholds are typically due to disorders that reduce the sound conductive ability of the eardrum and middle-ear structures. The prevalence and effects of other disorders of the auditory system, such as those caused by oto-toxic drugs, are assumed to be insufficient to have had any significant effect on the distributions of hearing levels found in the various studies of NIPTS.

Among the factors that could be considered in efforts to interpret the impacts of nosocusis on the results of studies of NIPTS are (1) the prevention of some NIPTS, because of sound attenuation due to eardrum and middle-ear disorders (assuming that the sound conductive loss preceded or was concomitant with damage from exposure to noise); (2) to the extent that both sensorineural and conductive loss have been incurred, the effects on hearing level, in decibels, should probably be additive, because different structural parts of the hearing mechanism are involved; and (3) anamnestic histories of ear disease and related medical matters (herein called *question-*

naire screening), do not adequately identify persons with ears that have or have not suffered, threshold shifts due to typical ear diseases.

It was found that the differences between the hearing levels of railroad workers with and without nosocusis, according to a questionnaire, differed by less than one-half the amount found between the hearing levels of steel workers with and without nosocusis according to otoscopic examination of the ear canal and ear drum (see Table 4.4). Clearly, it cannot be assumed that screening for nosocusis by questions pertaining to a history of ear disorders identifies all the people in a group who have suffered some amount of nosocusis; nor that all recalled "ear problems" represented a disorder that could affect hearing.

Table 4.4 indicates that the amount of conductive nosocusis, detected by otoscopic examination, increases from about 5 dB in young people to 9 dB by the age of 60–65 years. From these limited data, it was estimated that the percentage of persons with this form of nosocusis increased from ~20% in young people to ~40–50% in the 60–65-year age group (Kryter, 1991).

The factors cited in the preceding three paragraphs indicate there is no simple means of equating the hearing levels of groups of subjects differently screened for nosocusis. Nevertheless, some minor adjustments are made, in accordance with the lower section of Table 4.4, in the hearing levels found in two studies of Nixon and Glorig, and Gallo and Glorig, to be analyzed later, where the workers were screened for nosocusis only by questionnaire.

Effective Energy of Years of Exposures to Workplace Noise, EE_A

A wide variety of intensities and years of exposures are represented in different studies of NIPTS. For this reason, the valid expression, in a single unit, of the relative impact on hearing sensitivity of different combinations of daily L_{Aeq8h} levels and years of exposure are needed to allow for uniform integration and interpretation of the data from these different studies.

The relative contributions to NIPTS of noise energy due to L_{Aeq8h} level in decibels [(10 log sound pressure)^2] and to years of exposure in decibels (10 log years) were found by multiple regression and subjective graphic analysis techniques for those studies that provided data capable of such analysis. The results are shown in Table 4.5 and in Figs. 4.6A and 4.6B. Scheiblechner (1974), as shown in Table 4.5, found the years-of-exposure regression factor for NIPTS from factory noise, relative to that of L_{Aeq8h}, to range from 0.6 to 0.91, depending on audiometric test frequency. It is suggested that differences seen in Table 4.5 among the ratios for different test frequencies are due to experimental chance, and not to differences in responses of the ear to the daily noise energy variable for different sound spectra.

As shown in Table 4.5, relative to L_{Aeq8h}, the average scale factor for years of exposure is 0.80; or, 8 log years of exposure compared to 10 log *A*-weighted sound pressure. For present purposes, a measure of career noise

TABLE 4.4 Differences between HLs for Ears of Children and Steel Workers with, versus without, Nosocusis According to Clinical Exam, for Railroad Workers, According to Questionnaire [after Kryter (1991)] and Adjustments for Nosocusis in Present Analysis

Age, years: Frequency Hz	Oto-screened 10–12 Mean*	Railroad workers (questionnaire-screened)† 55–64				Steel workers‡ (Oto-screened) 60–65			
		10%ile	50%ile	90%ile	Mean	10%ile	50%ile	90%ile	Mean‡
500	5	1.3	2.7	6.1	2.5	1.2†	8.2†	20.4†	10.4
1000	5	1.3	2.9	9.6	4.1	1.2	8.2	20.4	11.0
2000	3	1.5	0.8	9.2	5.6	1.2	8.2	20.4	13.9
3000	5	7.1	9.8	12.8	7.8	7.5†	9.8†	15.2†	12.8
4000	5	2.2	4.5	6.2	6.7	7.5	9.8	15.2	12.0
6000	4	0.4	2.8	10.5	9.1	7.5	9.8	15.2	12.3
Av. all Freq.§	4.5	2.3	3.9	9.1	6.0	4.4	9.0	17.8	12.1

* Based on Figs. 6 and 7 in Roberts and Frederico (1972).

† From Table V, Kryter (1991).

‡ Data for average .5, 1 & 2 kHz and 3, 4 & 6 kHz are from Table 5, weighted for *N* values, Table 1. Means given for each frequency, in Table 2. Tables 1, 2, and 5 in Burns *et al.* (1977).

§ Averages for all frequencies.

Corrections to Hearing Levels, 500–6000 Hz, for Nosocusis

Age, years	Estimated % nosocusis	Corrections, dB* 10–25%ile		50–75%ile		90%ile	
		Qu. Scr	Unscr.	Qu. Scr	Unscr.	Qu. Scr	Unscr.
<45	25	1	1	1	2	2	4
>45–<60	35	1	2	2	3	3	6
>60	40	2	3	3	5	4	9

* Corrections to be subtracted from percentile hearing levels, at all frequencies, of subjects questionnaire-only screened (Qu. Scr.) and subjects totally unscreened (Unscr.), for nosocusis, on the assumption that the estimated percentages would be found by otoscopic examination to have nosocusis.

TABLE 4.5 NIPTS as Function 10 Log Years (Decibels) of Exposure with L_{Aeq8h} (dB) Constant and L_{Aeq8h} (dB) with Years of Exposure Constant [YE = Years of Exposure (to Noise); z = Standardized Scores]

Graphic: Ratio of linear trend lines of NIPTS vs. 10 log years' exposure and NIPTS vs. L_{Aeq8h} (see Fig. 3.5)

	N&G*	Baughn	N&G*	R*	L&H*	L&H*	L&H*	L&H*	L&H*	L&H*	Rop‡
Audiometer test frequency, kHz:	2	4	4	4	0.5	1	2	3	4	6	1 + 2 + 3
NIPTS per dB YE	0.64	1.20	1.60	0.80	0.54	0.54	1.10	2.04	1.52	1.80	0.115z
NIPTS per dB L_{Aeq8h}	1.00	1.70	2.40	0.96	0.82	0.44	1.40	2.20	1.71	2.00	0.135z
NIPTS per dB YE dB L_A	0.64	0.71	0.67	0.83	0.66	1.22	0.79	0.93	0.89	0.76	0.85

Multiple regression: ratio of ratios of $\beta^{\dagger}$ weights for NIPTS vs. 10 log YE and vs. L_{Aeq8h}

	Lempert & Henderson						N&G		Baughn	R
β_{NIPTS} vs. dB YE, kHz:	0.5	1	2	3	4	6	2	4	4	4
β_{NIPTS} vs. L_{Aeq8h}	[2.7]	[1.7]	[1.1]	1.04	0.76	0.82	0.72	0.38	0.57	0.83

	Scheiblechner¶							
β_{NIPTS} vs. dB YE, kHZ:	0.25	0.5	1	2	3	4	6	8
β_{NIPTS} vs. dB L_{Aeq8h}	0.86	0.56	0.59	0.92	0.85	0.60	0.91	0.77

Averages over all studies and both methods

NIPTS per dB YE, kHz:	0.25	0.5	1	2	3	4	6	8	Average
NIPTS per dB L_{Aeq8h}	0.86	0.61	0.88	0.82	0.92	0.67	0.88	0.77	0.80

* N&G, Nixon and Glorig (1961); L&H, Lempert and Henderson (1973); R, Robinson (1968); Fig. 10.7 in Burns and Robinson (1970).

† $\beta_{12.3} = r_{12} - r_{13}r_{12}/1 - (r_{23})^2$; $\beta_{13.2} = r_{13} - r_{12}r_{23}/1 - (r_{23})^2$.

‡ Data from Table II in Rop *et al*. (1979).

§ [ ] Apparent anamolous data points created very curvilinear regressions. Results not included in averages.

¶ Data from Table V in Scheiblechner (1974). Precise frequencies tested: 256, 1024, 2048, 2896, 5792, 8142.

exposure level is derived. It is called EE_A (effective energy, A-weighted), and its unit, edBy.

$$EE_A = L_{A\mathrm{eq8h(wg)}} + 8 \log_{\text{calendar year's exposure}}, \; e\mathrm{dB}y, \tag{4.2}$$

where $L_{A\mathrm{eq8h}}$ is a typical exposure-day level, and one calendar year = 250 workdays, or 250 days of exposure. (Two nonworkdays per week, and 15 or so vacation days, being about 250 days, of the 365-day year.)

The term $L_{A\mathrm{eq8h}}$, and the unit edBy, are for use with continuous 8-h exposures to steady-level workday noise. For that condition $L_{A\mathrm{eq8h}}$ is numerically the same as the unit $EL_{A\mathrm{eq8h}}$, to be defined in Chapter 5. The terms edBy and edBy, units also to be defined in Chapter 5, make explicit that the units, while involving a decibel sound pressure level, refer to effective, e, levels of a daily noise, n, and long-term exposures relative to a year, y.

As will be presented later, Robinson (1968, 1970) proposed, as is consistent with an equal-energy concept, that 10 log, rather than 8 log, years be calculated to equate years of exposure with average SPL. The explanation for the 8, rather than 10 scaling factor for years-of-exposure, probably rests on the fact that the estimated 250 workdays per year represent about 70% of the 365 day year.

ANALYSIS OF DATA FOR NOISE-EXPOSED AND CONTROL GROUPS

With discussion of those methodological and data treatment matters completed, the NIPTS data are considered next. A search of the literature revealed eleven major studies of NIPTS, the results of which leant themselves to rather uniform analysis. Four of these studies (see Table 4.6) involved subjects unscreened for nosocusis or exposure to adventitious noise, and seven studies involved subjects who had been screened, to varying degrees, for nosocusis and exposure to adventitious noise. Age of subjects, noise exposures, 50%ile hearing level, and NIPTS values derived herein for the subjects in these studies, are given in Tables 4.7 through 4.10.

Some of these hearing-level data, and others to be presented latter, are available only in the form of published graphs (ANSI, 1954; Rosenwinkel and Stewart, 1957; Lempert and Henderson, 1973; Gallo and Glorig, 1964; and, to some extent, Taylor *et al.*, 1984). The values of those data are estimates based on viewings of enlargements made by the writer of the published graphs.

Comparison of NIPTS for Screened and Unscreened Male Subjects

Figure 4.7 shows considerable variability in the amount of NIPTS, 50%ile, 4000 Hz, found, as a function of EE_A, among these nine studies of screened and unscreened male workers. It is clear in Fig. 4.7 that NIPTS is generally

A

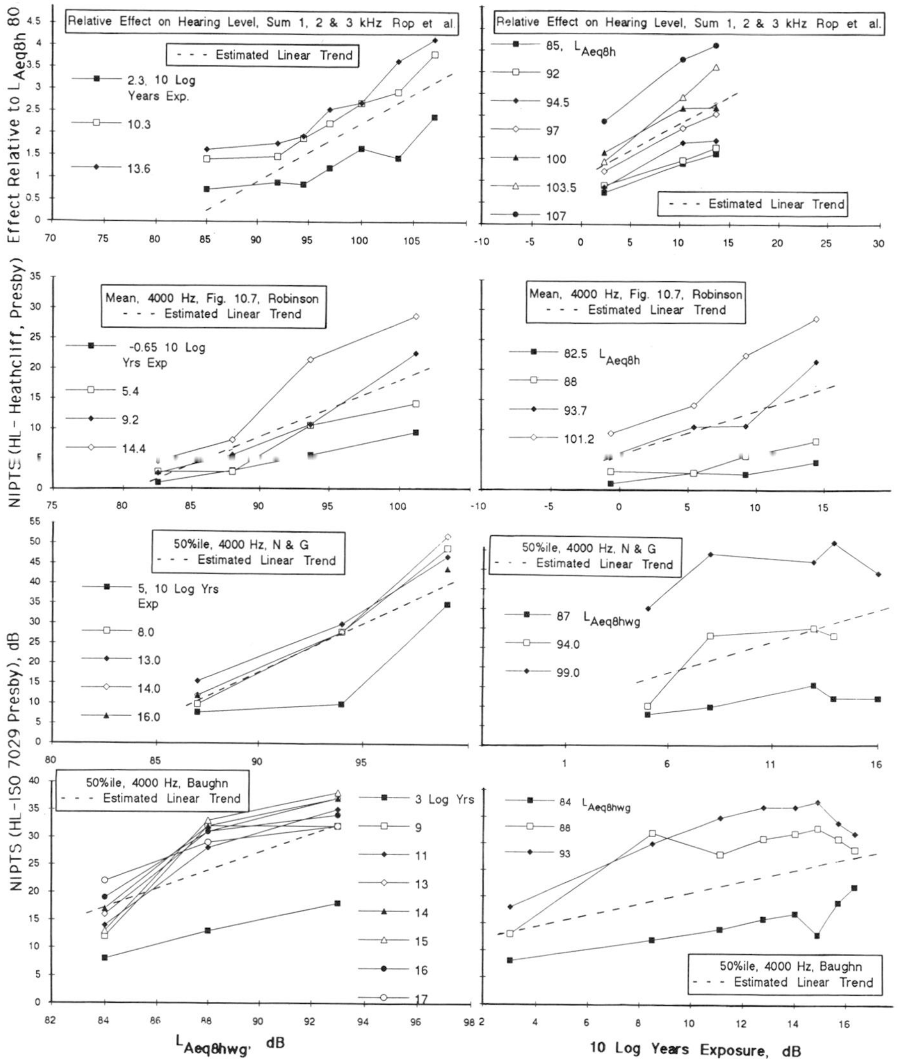

FIGURE 4.6 (A) NIPTS, as found by different investigators, for various frequencies, as functions of (1) $L_{Aeq8h(wg)}$, left-hand graph, and (2), 10 log years of exposure, right-hand graph. (B) NIPTS, as found by Lempert and Henderson, for different frequencies, as functions of (1) $L_{Aeq8h(wg)}$ and (2), 10 log years of exposure.

considerably larger at EE_A levels below, but not above, ~100 *e*dB*y* for unscreened, than for screened subjects. This is not, of course, a surprising finding because, as will be discussed more fully later, the effects of the

B

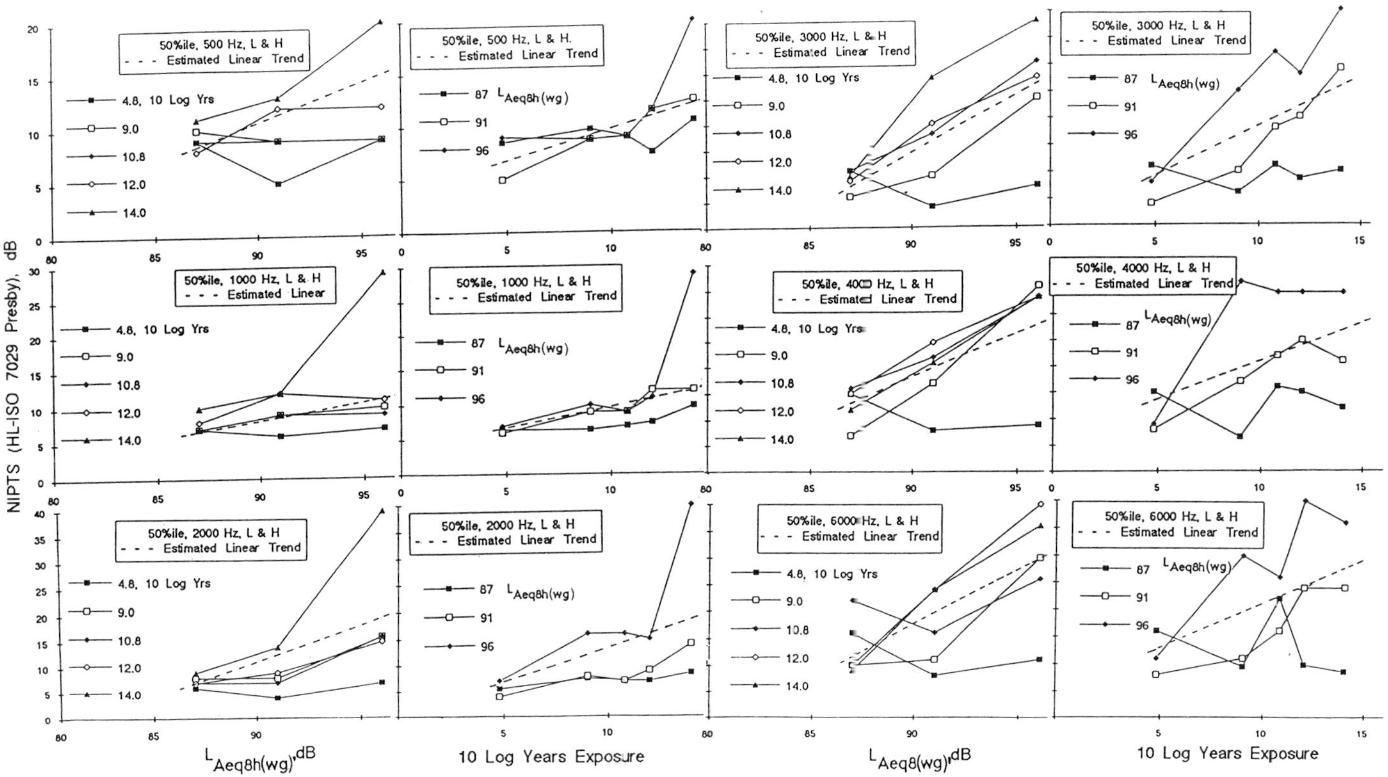

FIGURE 4.6 *Continued*

TABLE 4.6 Studies to Be Analyzed for Hearing Levels (HLs) and Noise-Induced Permanent Threshold Shift (NIPTS) in Industrial Workers

			Experimental subjects					Control subjects			
Study	YE	Range of levels dB_A	No., sex experimental Ss	Criteria for selection of experimental Ss	Time of HL testing	HL data from	Audiometer	No., sex control Ss	Criteria for selection of control Ss	Time of HL testing	Audiometer
Studies with Subjects Exposed to Steady Noise and Controls Unscreened for Nosocusis and Exposure to Adventitious Noise											
ANSI (1954)	2–44	78–100	200, M; ? F	No other intense noise exposure	Not given	Figs. 8–10	Manual ASA A24.5	N ?, M & F	General population hearing surveys	Not given	Manual ASA A24.5
Rosenwinkel and Stewart (1957)	3–34	84	270, M Av. L,RE	Worked only in specified noise	Start workday	Fig. 2	Manual ASA A24.5	290, M	Office workers, <2 YE some exposed to gun noise	Start workday	Manual ASA A24.5
Baughn (1973)	5–40	86–92	6783, presume M	No other intense noise exposure	During workday	Table 9	Manual ASA A24.5	852, M	Worked in 78 dB_A noise, some exposed to gun noise	During workday	Manual ASA A24.5
Kylin (1960)	10–15	81–100	72, M Av. L,RE	Worked only in specified noise	Start workday	Table 19	Manual BSI 2497	29, M 22, M	Worked in <75 dB_A noise, some exposed to gun noise	Start workday	Manual BSI 2497
Studies with Subjects, Exposed to Steady Noise and Controls Screened for Nosocusis and Varying Degrees of Exposure to Adventitious Noise											
Lempert and Henderson (1973)	3–30	85–95	792, M; Av. L,RE	Full oto-screen; < 100 days Mil. guns, <1000 rnds/yr hunt	Start workday	Fig. 9	Self-recording ISO 389	380, M	Full oto-screen; <80 dB_A work noise; <100 days Mil. guns; <1000 rnds/yr hunt	During workday	Self-recording ISO 389
Yerg *et al.* (1978)	3–30+	82–92	154, M; 192, F	Full oto-screen; no previous noise exposure >75 dB_A; gun noise not specified	Start workday	Table 8	Manual ISO 389	95, M; 132, F	Full oto-screen; <75 dB_A work noise; gun noise exposure not specified	During workday	Manual ISO 389

Nixon and Glorig (1961)	4–36.6	85–99	2559, M; Av L,RE	No history nosocusis or noise gun noise not specified	Not given	Table 1	Manual ASA A24.5	253, M	No history nosocusis, exposure to noise prof. men (Glorig and Nixon, 1960)	During day	Manual ASA A24.5
Gallo and Glorig (1964)	1–39	98	400, M; 90, F	No history nosocusis or noise; gun noise not specified	Start workday	Figs. 3–8	Manual ASA A24.5	253, M	No history nosocusis exp. noise prof. men (Glorig and Nixon, 1960)	Not given	Manual ASA A24.5
Taylor *et al.* (1965)	1–52	101	251, F	Full oto-screen; no exposure to other noises	Start of week	Table I	Manual BSI 2497	326, M; 319, F	Female rural population, oto-screened. (Hinchcliff, 1959)	Not given	Manual BSI 2497
Burns and Robinson (1970)	15–50	81–101	422, M; 337, F	Full oto-screen; no gun or other noise	Start workday	Table 5, R&S	Self-recording	326, M; 319, F	Female rural population, oto-screened. (Hinchcliff, 1959)	Not given	Manual BSI 2497
Study with Subjects Exposed to Impact-Impulsive Noise and Controls Screened for Nosocusis and Some Adventitious Noise											
Taylor *et al.* (1984)	1–37	99–108	716, M	Full oto-screen; no scr. gun n., ear protection worn ≤4 years	<2 h start of day	Tables XII, XV	Self-recording ISO 389	170, F; 123, M	Office and canteen workers exposed to <85-dB_A noise; full oto-screen; no scr. gun n.	During workday	Self-recording ISO 389

Abbreviations: Ss—subjects; YE—years of exposure (to noise); Av. L,RE—average for left and right ears; M—male, F—Female; Mil.—military; Full oto-screened—Fully otoscopically screened; no scr. gun n.—not screened for exposure to gun noise; rnds/yr hunt—(gun) rounds per year from hunting.

TABLE 4.7 HL and NIPTS for Males Unscreened for Nosocusis and Exposure to Adventitious Noise

NIPTS per ISP 7029 Males, Unscreened. No Adjustments for Nosocusis or Exposure to Gun Noise

Z24-X-2 — Test frequency 4000 Hz

Noise age/exp.	L_{Aeq8h} 93 EE_A	HL*	NIPTS	L_{Aeq8h} 100 EE_A§	HL*	NIPTS
30/10	101	24	26	108	32	34
40/20	103	42	34	110	42	34
50/30	105	52	36	112	62	46
55/35	106	59	38	113	68	46

* Mean HL, Fig. 10, Z24-X-2 (ANSI, 1954). Man. Audiometry per ISO 389 (ISO, 1985). HL presbycusis function, Fig. 2, Z24-X-2 (ANSI, 1954), corrected to ISO 7029 (ISO, 1984).

Baughn — Test Freq., 4000 Hz

Noise age/exp.	L_{Aeq8h} 78 EE_A§	HL*	NIPTS	L_{Aeq8h} 86 EE_A§	HL*	NIPTS	L_{Aeq8h} 92 EE_A§	HL*	NIPTS
21/2	80	10	9	88	15	13	94	20	19
27/7	85	15	13	93	35	33	99	33	31
33/13	87	20	15	95	34	29	101	41	36
39/19	88	26	18	96	41	33	102	47	39
45/25	89	32	20	97	47	35	103	52	40
51/31	90	39	23	98	52	36	104	57	41
57/37	91	46	24	99	58	31	105	61	39
62/43	91	55	27	99	62	34	105	65	37

* 50%ile HL, Table 9, Baughn (1973). Manual audiometry per ISO 389 (ISO, 1985). right ear.

NIPTS per Same Industry Controls and ISO 7029. 50%ILE Males Unscreened. Adjustment to L_{Aeq8h} for Gun Noise

Rosenwinkel and Stewart	Control groups*. N = 270 HL—frequency, Hz*						$L_{Aeq8h}/L_{Aeq8h(wg)}$† 85/88.5			Noise-exposed groups*. N = 290 HL/NIPTS per control group—frequency, Hz				
Age/years	500 HL	1000 HL	2000 HL	3000 HL	4000 HL	6000 HL	Age/years exp‡	EE_A§	500 HL/1/2¶	1000 HL/1/2	2000 HL/1/2	3000 HL/1/2	4000 HL/1/2	6000 HL/1/2
25	14	10	9	18	23	29	24/3	93	15/1/14	11/1/10	10/1/9	23/5/22	26/3/25	34/5/33
30	13	9	8	16	16	24	30/7	96	13/0/13	11/2/10	14/6/13	22/6/20	31/15/29	34/10/31

34	13	10	8	22	26	32	35/11	97	16/3/14	14/4/12	18/10/16	34/1/30	37/11/32	39/7/33
39	14	10	10	25	26	29	40/16	99	14/0/12	10/0/8	11/1/8	34/9/28	37/11/29	39/10/30
44	14	10	14	28	31	34	45/21	100	15/1/12	13/3/10	20/6/8	46/19/37	46/15/34	44/10/29
49	14	11	16	28	32	35	51/27	100	16/2/12	16/5/12	28/12/21	48/20/36	55/23/39	54/19/36

* Data 50%iles, based on Rosenwinkel and Stewart (1957), Fig., 2: 2 dB. Control group HLs for men in same industries with less than 2 years in "noisy jobs."

Kylin control groups*. $N = 51$ Approx. age 36 years					Noise-exposed groups*. $N = 89$ HL/NIPTS per control group—frequency, Hz					
Frequency, Hz	HL†	Age/years exp‡	L_{Aeq8h}†/$L_{Aeq8h(wg)}$	EE_A§	500 HL/1/2¶	1000 HL/1/2	2000 HL/1/2	3000 HL/1/2	4000 HL/1/2	6000 HL/1/2
500	4									
1000	4	36/12	79/83	92	5/1/3	3/−1/1	3/0/1	10/0/6	12/−3/7	20/−1/14
2000	3	36/12	84/89	98	4/0/2	5/1/[illegible]	5/2/3	20/11/16	34/19/29	38/17/32
3000	10	36/12	89/91	100	3/−1/1	4/0/[illegible]	7/4/5	24/14/20	37/22/32	41/20/34
4000	15	36/12	97/98	107	6/2/4	8/4/[illegible]	17/14/15	49/39/45	49/34/44	55/34/49
6000	21	36/12	102/102	111	5/1/3	11/7/9	16/13/14	40/30/26	56/41/51	54/33/48

* HL data from Kylin (1960), Table 18. Controls = average of "control group" and "H" group (<70 L_{Aeq8h} factory noise).

† The first L_{Aeq8h} value in each pair is for workplace noise, the second is for workplace noise plus estimated effective level, L_{Aeq8h} 89, for gun noise with estimated 50% of workers, in these studies, exposed to gun noise: $L_{Aeq8h(wg)} = 10 \log ((10^{L_{Aeq8h,\ work\ noise}/10}) + ((^1/_2\ 10^{L_{A8h,\ gun\ noise}/10})$.

‡ Approximate age, years / years of noise exposure.

§ $EE_A = L_{Aeq8h(wg)} + 8 \log$ years of exposure.

¶ $HL_{1/2}$: HL per ISO 389 (ISO, 1985); 1 = NIPTS per same industry controls; 2 = NIPTS per ISO 7029 (ISO, 1984).

TABLE 4.8 50%ile HL and NIPTS, ISO 7029; Males Nosocusis and Adventitious-Noise-Exposure Screened; also for L & H and YERG, NIPTS per Control (Ctrl) Groups, Table III, Same Industry

Lempert and Henderson		500 Hz NIPTS per:			1000 Hz NIPTS per:			2000 Hz NIPTS per:			3000 Hz NIPTS per:			4000 Hz NIPTS per:			6000 Hz NIPTS per:		
L_{Aeq8h} 85/88.5† Age/exp.‡	EE_A§	HL*	Ctrl	ISO	HL	Ctrl	ISO	HL	Ctrl	ISO	HL	Ctrl	ISO	HL	Ctrl	ISO	HL	Ctrl	ISO
25/3	93	12	4	12	10	1	10	9	2	9	15	7	14	19	9	18	20	8	19
32/8	96	14	5	13	11	2	11	12	4	11	12	2	10	13	0	10	17	0	14
39/12	96	14	4	13	12	1	11	13	4	10	20	7	15	27	8	20	34	10	26
47/16	99	14	1	11	14	2	11	16	5	10	22	4	12	32	7	18	29	−2	14
57/25	100	19	5	14	19	5	13	22	9	12	31	7	14	40	9	15	40	5	13
								L_{Aeq8h} 90/91											
24/3	95	8	0	8	9	0	9	7	0	7	8	0	8	12	2	11	12	0	11
32/7	98	13	4	12	13	4	12	12	4	11	16	6	14	23	10	20	18	1	15
39/14	100	14	4	13	14	3	12	13	4	10	27	14	22	33	14	26	28	4	20
47/20	101	18	5	15	18	6	15	18	7	12	33	15	23	42	17	29	43	12	28
57/23	102	21	7	16	21	7	15	27	14	16	50	26	33	49	18	25	55	20	28
								L_{Aeq8h} 95/96											
24/3	100	12	4	12	10	1	10	10	3	10	12	4	12	13	3	12	15	3	14
32/8	103	13	4	12	14	5	13	20	12	19	31	21	29	42	29	39	37	20	34
39/13	105	14	4	13	14	3	12	22	13	19	41	28	36	45	26	38	38	14	30
47/16	106	18	5	15	17	5	14	24	13	18	41	23	31	51	26	38	59	28	44
59/30	108	29	15	23	39	25	32	55	42	43	63	39	44	65	34	38	71	36	41

* Data 50%iles L & H, Lempert and Henderson (1973), Fig. 9. HLs reduced by 5 dB at 500 Hz due to apparent calibration problem. HLs, all frequencies, increased 3 dB for self-recording audiometry. Av. R,L male ears, $N = 792$.

Yerg *et al.* L_{Aeq8h} 87/90† Age/exp.‡	EE_A§	500 Hz NIPTS per: HL*	Ctrl	ISO	1000 Hz NIPTS per: HL	Ctrl	ISO	2000 Hz NIPTS per: HL	Ctrl	ISO	3000 Hz NIPTS per: HL	Ctrl	ISO	4000 Hz NIPTS per: HL	Ctrl	ISO	6000 Hz NIPTS per: HL	Ctrl	ISO
25/5	96	4	−2	3	3	−3	3	5	1	5	8	0	7	14	1	13	16	−3	15
35/15	99	6	1	5	5	2	4	5	−2	3	15	0	12	20	5	15	25	7	20
45/25	101	5	−2	2	7	2	5	11	−1	6	31	15	23	39	18	27	41	13	28
55/35	102	11	3	6	13	4	7	13	−3	3	37	1	21	49	13	27	50	9	25

* Data 50%iles. Means from Yerg *et al.*, Table 8 −2 dB. Manual audiometry Av. R,L male ears, N = 154.

Nixon and Glorig*	NIPTS per ISO 7029														
	L_{Aeq8h} 85/88.5†					93/94†					99/99†				
		2000 Hz		4000 Hz			2000 Hz		4000 Hz			2000 Hz		4000 Hz	
Age/exp.‡	EE_A§	HL¶	NIPTS	HL¶	NIPTS	EE_A§	HL¶	NIPTS	HL	NIPTS	EE_A§	HL¶	NIPTS	HL¶	NIPTS
28/3	93	9	9	11	9	98	13	13	13	11	103	14	13	38	36
33/7	96	10	9	16	12	101	13	12	34	30	106	15	13	55	51
44/18	99	11	6	30	19	104	19	14	44	33	109	38	33	61	50
49/28	100	16	9	33	18	105	23	16	45	29	110	45	38	69	54
57/36	101	20	9	35	10	106	na	na	na	na	111	52	42	68	44

* Data 50%iles from Nixon and Glorig (1961), Table 1. Manual audiometry. Av. R,L male ears, N = 2559.

(continues)

TABLE 4.8 *(Continued)*

Gallo and Glorig*		NIPTS per ISO 7029											
L_{Aeq8h} 98/98†		500 Hz		1000 Hz		2000 Hz		3000 Hz		4000 Hz		6000 Hz	
Age/exp.‡	EE_A§	HL¶	NIPTS	HL¶	NIPTS	HL¶	NIPTS	HL¶	NIPTS	HL¶	NIPTS	HL¶	NIPTS
20/2	100	11	11	6	6	8	8	16	16	14	14	9	9
30/10	106	14	14	11	10	12	11	34	32	39	37	29	26
40/20	108	16	14	16	14	22	19	45	39	53	45	45	36
50/30	110	16	12	18	14	29	22	48	36	55	39	49	31
60/40	111	19	13	22	15	34	22	48	28	56	28	50	18

* Data 50%iles Gallo and Glorig (1964), Figs. 3–8. Manual audiometry Av. R,L male ears, $N = 400$.

† The first L_{Aeq8h} value in each pair is for workplace noise, the second is for workplace noise plus estimated effective level, L_{Aeq8h} 89, for gun noise with estimated 50% of workers, in these studies, exposed to gun noise: $L_{Aeq8h(wg)} = 10 \log [(10^{L_{Aeq8h\ work\ noise}/10}) + (10^{L_{Aeq8h\ work\ noise}+L_{Aeq8h\ gun\ noise}/10)/2})]$.

‡ Approximate age, years/years of noise exposure.

§ $EE_A = L_{Aeq8h(wg)\ (work+gun\ noise,\ if\ any)} + 8 \log$ years exposure.

¶ HL = HL −1 dB, ages <45; −2 dB, ages >44 years; adjustment questionnaire nosocusis screening.

TABLE 4.9 50%ile Hearing Levels and NIPTS for Female Workers, and for Male Workers Exposed to Impact and Impulse Noise

Taylor *et al.* (1965)		Females exposed to steady, continuous factory (weaving shed) noise											
L_{Aeq8h} 101		500 Hz		1000 Hz		2000 Hz		3000 Hz		4000 Hz		6000 Hz	
Age/exp.[a]	EE_A[f]	HL[e]	NIPTS[e]	HL	NIPTS	HL	NIPTS	HL	NIPTS	HL	NIPTS	HL	NIPTS
25/4	106	2	2	2	2	4	4	9	9	21	20	14	13
30/7	108	6	5	3	3	8	8	20	19	34	32	22	20
40/17	111	11	9	10	8	19	16	45	41	50	46	35	30
50/27	112	10	12	21	17	29	23	5[illegible]	46	60	51	46	34
60/37	113	17	16	19	12	57	46	6[illegible]	53	70	54	63	42

[e] HL, ISO 7029 (1984), + NIPTS. NIPTS, Taylor *et al.* (1965), Table II, corrected for ISO 7029 (1984)—Hinchcliff (1959).

Yerg *et al.*		Females exposed to steady, continuous factory noise																					
		500 Hz				1000 Hz				2000 Hz				3000 Hz				4000 Hz				6000 Hz			
L_{Aeq8h} 87		Exp	Ctrl	NIPTS per:		Exp	Ctrl	NIPTS per:		Exp	Ctrl	NIPTS per:		Exp	Ctrl	NIPTS per:		Exp	Ctrl	NIPTS per:		Exp	Ctrl	NIPTS per:	
Age/exp.[a]	EE_A[f]	HL*	HL	Ctrl	ISO	HL	HL	Ctrl	ISO	HL	HL	Ctrl	ISO	HL	HL	Ctrl	ISO	HL	HL	Ctrl	ISO	HL	HL	Ctrl	ISO
25/5	96	6	4	−3	6	5	2	3	5	3	1	2	3	4		2	4	6	5	1	6	8	7	1	7
35/15	99	5	6	−1	4	3	5	−3	1	3	6	−3	1	6	[illegible]	−3	4	11	11	−1	8	13	14	−2	9
45/25	101	7	5	1	4	6	5	1	3	8	6	3	4	11	[illegible]	2	5	16	16	1	9	16	18	−2	7
55/35	102	10	10	0	5	10	8	2	5	13	11	2	5	19	[illegible]	3	9	26	20	6	14	30	27	4	14

* Data 50%iles. Means from Yerg *et al.* (1978), Table 8 −2 dB. Manual audiometry. Av. R,L female ears, $N = 192$.

† $EE_A = L_{Aeq8h} + 8 \log$ years of exposure. Little or no exposure to gun noise assumed for female subjects.

(*continues*)

TABLE 4.9 (*Continued*)

Taylor *et al.* (1984) — Males exposed to impact noise

Press-forge operators, L_{Aeq8h} = 99 (L_A 100.8), EL_{Aeq8h} (e_{dBn}) = 99.4[c]

N = 211		500 Hz				1000 Hz				2000 Hz				3000 Hz				4000 Hz				6000 Hz			
		Exp	Ctrl	NIPTS per:		Exp	Ctrl	NIPTS per:		Exp	Ctrl	NIPTS per:		Exp	Ctrl	NIPTS per:		Exp	Ctrl	NIPTS per:		Exp	Ctrl	NIPTS per:	
Age/exp.[a]	EE_A[d]	HL*	HL*	ISO	Ctrl	HL*	HL*	ISO	Ctrl	HL*	HL*	ISO	Ctrl	HL*	HL*	ISO	Ctrl	HL*	HL*	ISO	Ctrl	HL*	HL*	ISO	Ctrl
29/1.3	100.2	8	8	7	0	3	4	2	−1	6	3	5	3	12	4	10	8	14	8	12	6	20	9	17	11
28/2.7	102.7	10	8	9	2	8	4	7	4	6	3	5	3	14	4	12	10	21	8	19	13	23	9	20	14
30/5.3	105.0	11	8	10	3	8	4	7	4	12	3	11	9	22	4	20	18	30	8	29	22	28	9	25	19
37/10.6	107.4	11	9	9	2	8	8	6	0	16	7	14	9	40	9	35	31	45	11	39	34	45	15	35	30
47/19.7	109.6	9	9	6	0	10	8	7	2	22	10	16	12	50	11	40	39	58	16	44	42	61	20	55	41

Taylor *et al.* (1984) — Males exposed to impulse noise

Drop-hammer operators, L_{Aeq8h} = 108 (L_A 109.8), E_{LAeq8h}, (e_{dBn}) = 99.5[e]

N = 505		500 Hz				1000 Hz				2000 Hz				3000 Hz				4000 Hz				6000 Hz			
		Exp	Ctrl	NIPTS per:		Exp	Ctrl	NIPTS per:		Exp	Ctrl	NIPTS per:		Exp	Ctrl	NIPTS per:		Exp	Ctrl	NIPTS per:		Exp	Ctrl	NIPTS per:	
Age/exp.[a]	EE_A[f]	HL*	HL*	ISO	Ctrl	HL*	HL*	ISO	Ctrl	HL*	HL*	ISO	Ctrl	HL*	HL*	ISO	Ctrl	HL*	HL*	ISO	Ctrl	HL*	HL*	ISO	Ctrl
26/1.3	100.3	10	8	9	2	7	4	6	3	8	3	7	5	11	4	10	7	15	8	14	7	17	9	16	8
28/2.5	102.5	10	8	9	2	9	4	8	5	9	3	8	6	17	4	15	13	22	8	20	14	2	9	20	14
32/5.1	105.0	12	8	11	4	12	4	11	8	14	3	13	11	23	4	21	19	28	8	26	20	27	9	24	18
39/11.2	107.7	15	9	13	6	20	8	18	12	40	7	37	33	49	9	43	40	52	11	44	41	45	15	36	30
49/20.9	109.9	21	9	17	12	33	8	29	25	51	10	45	41	60	11	48	49	63	16	47	47	65	20	47	45
55/36.6	111.8	31	11	26	20	53	8	47	45	50	13	41	37	69	23	53	46	74	34	52	40	79	40	54	39

[a] Age/years of exposure.

[b] HLs increased 3 dB, all frequencies, for self-recording, midtrace-scored, audiometer. Data from Tables VIII, XII, XV of Taylor *et al.* (1984).

[c] Eight 20-min breaks and 0.5-h lunch = 5 h exposure to 0.5-s impact noise. L_{Aeq8h} changed to EL_{Aeq8h} (effective), edB*n*.

[d] Impacts: EE_A, edB*y* = edB*dn* + 8 log years of exposure = L_A − 20 log [57,600/38,400 (eight 40-min work periods) − (2.5 + 3.95 log 8 [*i*, > 15 s, at 20-min breaks]) + 20 log [(38,400 + 17,082)/38,400], where 38,400 is 0.5 s in eight 40-min exposure periods, and 17,082 = 2 × (8533 interruptions >0.5 s + 8 *i* >15 sec/*t*, 0.5). Interruptions from impulse/impact every 2.35 s during 5 h of exposure to noise. Factor 2 based on 1-s residual after-effect.

[e] Total 5 h daily exposure to ~0.065-s impulse noise. Measured L_{Aeq8h} changed to EL_{Aeq8h}, edB*n*.

[f] Impulses: EE_A, edB*y* = edB*dn* + 8 log years of exposure edB*dn* = L_A (0.5-s interval level) − 8.9 dB. 8.9 dB = 10 log 0.065/0.5, where ~0.065 is duration of impulse in 0.5 s. Adjustments for interruptions same as for impacts. The procedures for calculating EE_A for steady and nonsteady noises and exposures are to be presented later.

Hearing-level data from Yerg *et al.* (1965) and Taylor *et al.* (1984).

TABLE 4.10 Percentile Hearing Levels

Taylor *et al.* (1984): press operators, EL_{Aeq8h} 99.3; HL data from Fig. 8, +3 dB for self-recording audiometry

Age, Mid Decade	10%ile HL	25%ile	50%ile	75%ile	90%ile	10%ile	25%ile	50%ile	75%ile	90%ile	10%ile	25%ile	50%ile	75%ile	90%ile
			500 Hz					1000 Hz					2000 Hz		
25	3.5	5.5	8.0	12.0	14.0	−0.5	2.0	4.0	7.0	9.0	−0.5	2.0	6.0	9.0	11.5
35	4.0	7.0	10.5	14.0	20.0	0.0	4.0	8.0	11.0	20.0	2.0	5.0	11.0	19.0	31.0
45	1.0	5.5	10.5	18.0	23.0	1.0	3.5	10.5	16.0	22.0	3.5	6.5	17.0	33.0	42.0
55	5.5	7.0	11.0	16.0	20.0	5.5	9.0	12.0	18.0	26.0	7.0	10.0	23.0	41.0	55.0
			3000 Hz					4000 Hz					6000 Hz		
25	1.0	3.5	10.8	17.0	43.0	8.0	12.0	15.0	25.0	43.0	8.0	10.0	14.0	22.0	36.5
35	7.0	11.0	19.0	37.5	50.0	11.0	19.0	30.0	41.0	57.0	17.0	21.0	28.0	42.0	54.0
45	15.0	22.0	40.0	49.0	58.0	27.0	38.0	46.0	57.0	64.0	26.0	33.0	48.0	59.0	66.0
55	23.0	38.0	49.0	59.0	77.0	37.0	47.5	48.5	68.0	74.0	37.0	53.0	62.0	70.0	77.0

Taylor *et al.* (1984): hammer operators, EL_{Aeq8h} 99.4; HL data from Fig. 7, +3 dB for self-recording audiometry

Age, Mid Decade	10%ile HL	25%ile	50%ile	75%ile	90%ile	10%ile	25%ile	50%ile	75%ile	90%ile	10%ile	25%ile	50%ile	75%ile	90%ile
			500 Hz					1000 Hz					2000 Hz		
25	6.0	8.0	10.5	15.0	18.0	−0.5	4.0	8.0	11.0	13.5	−1.0	3.0	8.0	12.0	18.0
35	4.0	7.0	10.5	15.0	20.0	3.0	6.5	9.0	15.0	26.0	3.0	7.0	11.0	24.0	41.0
45	7.0	8.5	15.0	23.0	33.0	7.0	8.5	19.0	33.0	42.0	8.0	13.0	33.5	52.0	59.0
55	9.0	15.0	22.0	33.0	47.0	15.0	20.0	34.0	47.0	60.5	17.5	36.0	51.0	59.0	74.0
			3000 Hz					4000 Hz					6000 Hz		
25	2.0	4.5	10.0	17.0	29.0	3.0	9.0	15.0	24.0	39.0	7.0	11.0	20.0	28.0	47.0
35	7.0	12.0	20.5	36.0	53.0	10.0	18.0	28.0	44.0	57.5	17.0	21.0	24.0	27.0	53.0
45	16.0	25.0	47.0	59.0	71.0	19.5	35.0	49.5	62.0	73.0	20.0	28.0	41.0	66.0	75.0
55	28.0	47.5	55.0	68.5	78.0	51.0	54.5	64.0	74.0	81.0	33.0	48.0	63.0	72.0	84.0

Gallo and Glorig (1964), $L_{Aeq8h(wg)}$ 98, data from Figs. 3–8, approximate age decades

			500 Hz					1000 Hz					2000 Hz		
25	2.0	7.0	11.0	16.0	17.0	−1.0	2.0	6.0	12.0	15.0	−3.5	−2.0	7.5	12.5	19.0
35	4.0	9.0	14.0	18.0	21.0	0.0	3.0	11.0	18.0	25.0	−1.5	0.5	9.8	16.8	25.3
45	5.0	11.0	16.0	20.0	29.0	4.0	12.0	16.0	24.0	36.0	4.0	11.5	22.0	33.5	45.0
55*	6.5	12.0	17.5	24.0	30.0	7.0	13.0	20.0	29.0	42.5	9.0	18.0	31.5	46.0	50.5
			3000 Hz					4000 Hz					6000 Hz		
25	3.0	8.0	16.0	30.0	41.5	−4.0	5.5	14.0	29.0	37.0	−1.0	2.0	9.0	25.0	36.0
35	11.0	19.0	34.0	51.0	64.5	14.0	26.0	39.0	53.0	62.0	7.5	13.5	29.0	36.5	55.5
45	19.0	33.0	45.0	59.5	70.0	27.5	40.5	53.0	59.0	72.0	13.0	27.5	45.0	57.0	65.0
55*	23.0	36.5	48.0	59.5	69.0	30.0	43.0	55.5	62.5	70.0	25.0	36.0	49.5	61.5	67.0

* Average age groups 50 and 60 years.

Lempert and Henderson (1973), $L_{Aeq8h(wg)}$ 96; HL data from Fig. 9, +3 dB for self-recording audiometry; approximate age decades

			500 Hz					1000 Hz					2000 Hz		
25	3.0	8.0	12.0	16.5	18.0	7.0	8.0	10.0	15.0	18.0	5.0	6.0	10.0	13.0	19.0
35	4.0	9.0	13.0	26.0	45.0	8.0	10.0	14.0	19.0	48.0	7.0	8.0	20.0	33.0	54.0
45*	6.3	10.3	16.0	23.5	27.0	8.5	10.8	15.5	22.0	30.0	7.3	10.8	23.0	36.3	57.0
55	15.0	19.0	29.0	43.0	57.0	18.0	27.5	39.0	58.0	64.0	19.0	30.0	55.0	68.0	81.0
			3000 Hz					4000 Hz					6000 Hz		
25	4.0	7.5	12.0	23.0	38.0	5.0	8.0	13.0	24.5	48.0	5.0	9.5	15.0	32.0	58.0
35	5.0	17.0	31.0	48.0	67.0	8.0	23.0	42.0	55.0	64.0	8.0	15.0	37.0	55.0	69.0
45	13.5	26.8	41.0	55.5	63.0	17.0	28.8	48.0	56.8	69.0	16.5	27.5	48.0	59.0	73.5
55	36.0	57.0	63.0	78.0	88.0	47.0	57.0	65.0	79.0	88.0	42.0	64.0	71.0	85.0	89.0

* Average for ages 35–51 years.

From Taylor *et al.* (1984), Gallo and Glorig (1964), and Lempert and Henderson (1973).

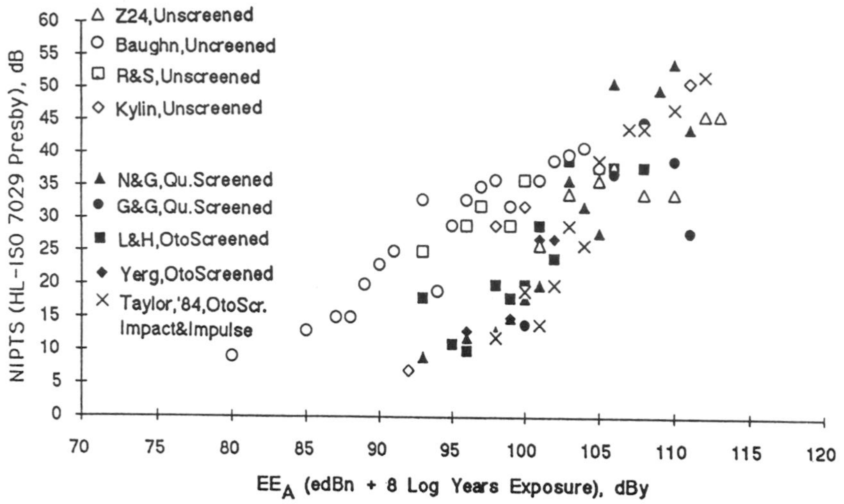

FIGURE 4.7 Fiftieth-percentile NIPTS, 4000 Hz, per ISO 7029, as function of EE_A. Hearing levels of male subjects, screened (closed symbols) and unscreened (open symbols) for nosocusis.

everyday noises in unscreened subjects causes measurable sociocusis NIPTS only when the workplace noise is at lower levels of intensity.

NIPTS Based on Comparisons Made with Same-Industry Controls

For five of the selected studies, NIPTS is derived from comparisons made of the hearing levels of noise exposed workers with the hearing levels of control groups selected from the same industries (Rosenwinkel and Stewart, 1957; Kylin, 1960; Lempert and Henderson, 1973; Yerg *et al.*, 1978; Taylor *et al.*, 1984). There was no screening for nosocusis or exposure to gun noise in either the control or work-noise-exposed groups in the Rosenwinkel and Stewart and Kylin studies. There was otoscopic screening for nosocusis of all subjects in the Lempert and Henderson, Yerg *et al.*, and Taylor *et al.* studies, but, as discussed earlier, screening for exposure to low-level factory noise and gun noise was lacking, or not very rigorous, in these studies.

It was assumed that 50% of the men in all five of these studies used guns, and that their L_{Aeq8h} levels of work noise were increased to $L_{Aeq8h(wg)}$ on that assumption. Because of the high intensity levels involved (L_{Aeq8h} 99 and 108, see Table 4.9), the assumed additional noise from guns contributes an insignificant amount to the total effective L_{Aeq8h} noise level in the Taylor *et al*, (1984) study.

Attention is invited to the fact that in the Taylor *et al.* (1984) study the noises were impact and impulsive in nature, and during every work hour there was a 20-min rest break in relative quiet. These conditions are considerably different than the nominal 8-h workday exposures to steady noise present in all the other studies of NIPTS examined in the present analysis. The $E'L_{Aeq8h}$ for the Taylor *et al.* (1984) study is calculated in accordance with procedures described in footnote on Table 4.9 and in Chapter 5. The NIPTSs deduced for male subjects in all these five studies are shown in Fig. 4.8 as a function of EE_A for test frequencies of 500–6000 Hz.

The NIPTS found from comparisons of noise-exposed workers with controls from the same industries are judged to be fairly consistent for all the studies, whether the subjects were, or were not, screened for nosocusis. This suggests that the effects of nosocusis, at least in these samples of subjects, are not differentially interactive with NIPTS from work-noise exposure levels. Visually drawn trend lines drawn on Fig. 4.8 intercept 0-dB NIPTS for 500 Hz at 100 *e*dB*y*: 1000 Hz, 97; 2000 Hz, 93; 3000, 91; 4000 Hz, 90; and 6000 Hz, 92.

As will be shown later, for nosocusis screened workers, with noise exposure levels adjusted for gun noise, the EE_A thresholds for NIPTS at the different test frequencies are about 4–10 dB lower, depending on test frequency, than those in Fig. 4.8, but reach about the same NIPTS values with the higher EE_A exposure levels. These findings can again be attributed to the fact that gun or other adventitious noise energy has a measurable influence on NIPTS only when workplace noise is of a relatively low exposure level.

Influence of Gun Noise on Amount of NIPTS Found for Factory Noise

As noted, the effects of gun noise on NIPTS in factory-noise-exposed workers will depend on the sum of the energies of the $L_{Aeq8h,w}$ (work noise) and estimated 89 $L_{Aeq8h,g}$ (gun noise) to which different subgroups of the workers are exposed. This makes somewhat problematical the interpretation of the contribution of specified levels of factory noise to hearing levels and NIPTS. This is revealed by the following examples. It is assumed, for these examples, that 12%, 25%, and 50% of the noise-exposed workers used guns, and that the equivalent L_{Aeq8h} level of the gun noise is 89.

It is seen from the following table that: (1) when the workplace noise is $L_{Aeq8h,w} \leq 280$, total effective exposure level of the group is essentially set by the exposures to the gun noise; (2) when the workplace noise is $L_{Ae98h,w} \geq 90$, the total exposure level of the group is essentially that of the workplace noise; and (3) the total exposure level of the group between the levels of $L_{Aeq8h,w+g} \sim 80\text{–}{\sim}90$ is a joint function of the workplace and gun noise exposures. These facts could perhaps explain the relatively small differences in hearing levels found by Yerg *et al.* (1978) between their "quiet" ("q") control groups (selected from factory areas with background noise levels up to $L_{Aeq8h\text{“}q\text{”}}$ 75), and their experimental groups exposed to workplace

Workplace noise exposure level of group $L_{Aeq8h,w}$	% of groups exposed to gun noise, $L_{Aeq8h,g}$			Total effective exposure level with different % of group also exposed to gun noise[b]		
	12%	25%	50%	12%	25%	50%
60[a]	80	83	86	80	83	86
70[a]	80	83	86	80	83	86
75[a]	80	83	86	81	83	86
80[a]	80	83	86	83	85	87
85	80	83	86	86	87	89
90	80	83	86	90	90	91
100	80	83	86	100	100	100

[a] Levels up-to L 75–80 considered as "Quiet" for control groups in some studies of NIPTS
[b] $L_{Aeq8h,w+g} = 10 \log[10^{L_{Aeq8h,w}/10} + ((n/N)10^{L_{Aeq8h,g}/10})]$ where N is the total number in group exposed workplace noise; and n is the number in group also exposed to gun noise.

noise of $L_{Aeq8h,w}$ 82 and 92, with no specified screening for exposure to gun noise. (Procedures for calculating an effective daily exposure level, EL_{Aeq8h}, for impulses, such as gunfire, will be developed in Chapter 5 to follow. Those procedures indicate that about 10 firings with peak $L \sim 140$ dB, per day, for 25 days per year, for 3 or more years, will have an EL_{Aeq8h} of about 89 dB. As mentioned, the NIPTS data are for open-ear listening, conditions presumed to be typical for the era in which the NIPTS involved was incurred.)

On the basis of such findings as those seen in Fig. 4.8, it has been suggested for many years (see e.g., Botsford, 1969; Yerg *et al.*, 1978) that the threshold exposure level for NIPTS is around 85–90 L_{Aeq8h}. Such a conclusion is unjustified, especially with respect to the assessment of work-noise-induced hearing loss possibly experienced by those workers who do not use guns. With work-noise exposures of $< L_{Aeq8h}$ 85–90, those workers could be experiencing significant amounts of NIPTS from the work noise, and those workers who used guns could be experiencing a few more decibels in loss of hearing sensitivity because of the gun noise (or conversely, because of the workplace noise), see Table 4.3.

SYNTHESIS FUNCTION FOR NIPTS

In view of the above findings, it was decided that for the development of a synthesis function for NIPTS, to use only data from the studies in which the noise-exposed subjects had been (1) screened for exposure to adventitious noise, and, if not screened specifically for gun noise, to estimate group total noise exposure levels from workplace plus estimated gun noise, and (2) otoscopically and/or questionnaire-screened for nosocusis. Seven such studies are listed in the lower sections of Table 4.6 (Lempert and Henderson,

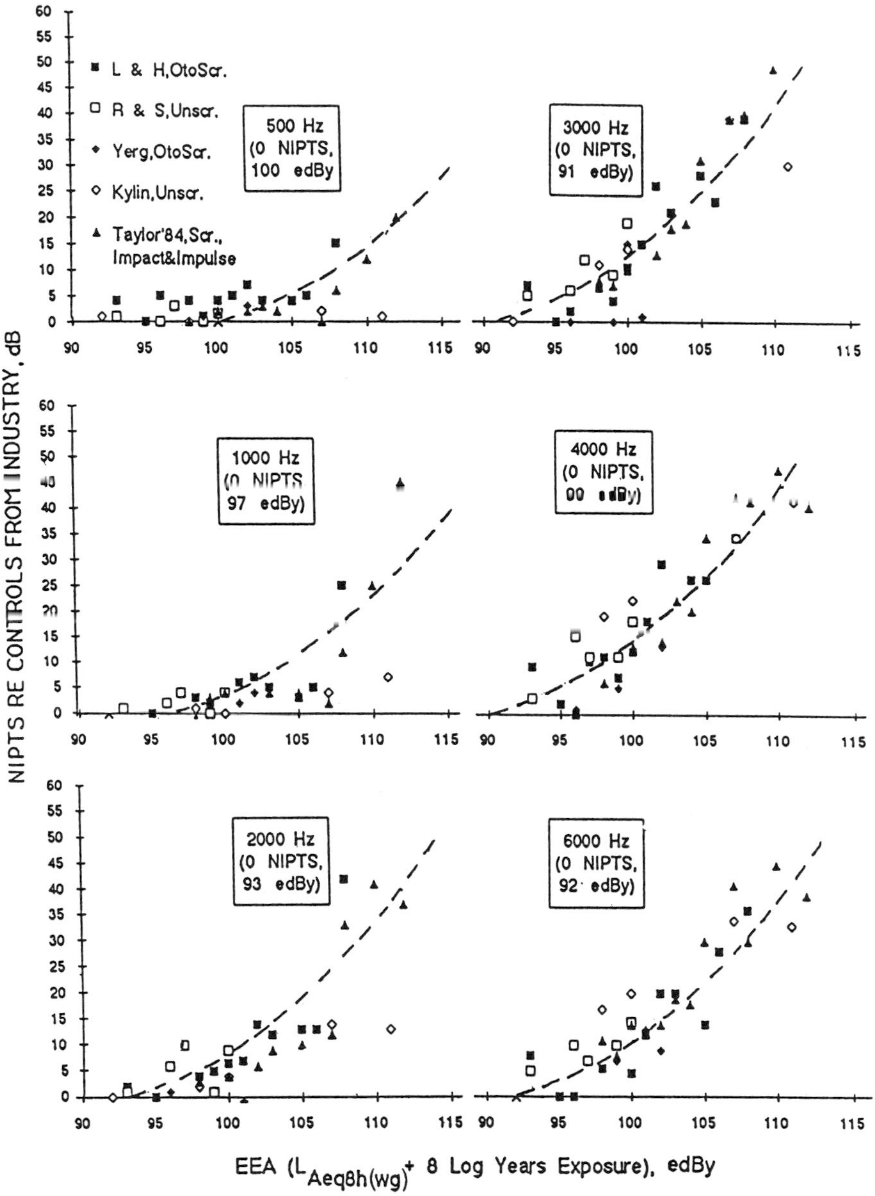

FIGURE 4.8 Fiftieth-percentile NIPTS, 500–6000 Hz, as function of EE_A. Hearing levels of screened (closed symbols) and unscreened (open symbols) noise-exposed male workers per control groups from same industry as noise-exposed subjects.

1973; Yerg *et al.,* 1978; Nixon and Glorig, 1961; Gallo and Glorig, 1964; Burns and Robinson, 1970; Taylor *et al.,* 1965, 1984). Yerg *et al.* and Burns and Robinson studied both males and females, and Taylor *et al.* (1965) only females. Only males were studied in the other investigations.

Six of these seven studies involved only more-or-less steady-state, continuous, 8-h workday noise-exposure conditions, whereas in the Taylor *et al.* (1984) study, as afore noted, the noises were impact and impulsive, and in every hour the workers received a 20-min break. The reductions in daily noise dosages due to typical workday lunch and restroom breaks are not, it is assumed, capable of measurably reducing NIPTS, and, in any event, represent a "constant" for all the studies.

Burns and Robinson Study and Robinson's E_A Formulation

The Burns and Robinson (1970) study deserves special attention because it represents an extensive study of NIPTS in industry, and because the findings differ, as will be shown, significantly from those found for the other selected industrial studies. In addition, the results of their study formed a partial basis for an internationally standardized procedure, ISO 1999 (1990), for the determination of the amount of NIPTS to be expected from exposure to industrial noises, to be discussed in the Appendix to this chapter.

In the Burns and Robinson study, the subjects were rigorously screened for nosocusis and, more so than in any of the other studies, exposure to gun, or other, adventitious noises. On the bases of the data collected, Robinson (1968, and 1970) formulated certain generalizations and mathematical equations for estimating NIPTS from exposure to steady-state noise.

The observed hearing levels for 427 male and 337 female noise exposed subjects of this study were (1) converted into NIPTS values by subtracting the 50%ile presbycusis levels for females, as found by Hinchcliffe, see Table 3.2; and (2) then corrected for the noted differences in audiometer-zero in the Hinchcliffe and the Burns and Robinson (1970) surveys. On the basis of trial and error fittings of plots of the thusly treated hearing level data of the noise exposed workers, Robinson (1968, 1970) came to the conclusions that: (1) the growth of NIPTS at 4000 Hz as a function of E_A can be described by a relatively simple mathematical function and (2) that function is the same for test frequencies from 500 to 6000 Hz, but with somewhat different points of origin on the E_A scale of exposure.

Robinsons's predictive mathematical formula is

$$\text{(Eq): NIPTS} = 27.5[1 + \tanh\{(E_A + \text{k} - \text{f} + \text{u})/15\}] + \text{u} \qquad (4.3)$$

where k is sex parameter (1.5 for males, and -1.5 for females); f is a value dependent on test frequency (see under "Shift," Fig. 3.8); u is a normally distributed percentile parameter around the median, 50%ile, with a standard deviation of 6 dB. The hyperbolic curve of the above-bracketed argument in Eq. (4.3), z, $= 1 + (e^{z} - e^{-z})/\Sigma(e^{z} + e^{-z})$, where e is natural logarithm. For the 50%ile, the resulting function has a symmetrical shape around HL 27 dB and becomes asymptotic at HL 0 dB, and at its upper end, HL 54 dB.

This NIPTS function is shown in Fig. 4.9A, drawn on the plot of points for normalized (frequency-shifted) data cells it is supposed to represent. Figure 4.9B shows individual data points for 581 subjects used in Robinson's (1968, 1970) analysis, along with the NIPTS function from Fig. 4.9A, based on a total of 759 subjects, and some 50 %ile points, marked as x's, determined by the writer for E_A cells, steps of 2.5 dB, in Fig. 4.9B.

Prediction of NIPTS by E_A, R_2

Before comparing NIPTS predicted by E_A with that found in the other studies, two factors involved in the development and application of the E_A method are considered. First is that of the use by Robinson (1968) of presbycusis corrections for females with the hearing levels of males. This procedure made the amount of NIPTS deduced for males somewhat larger, at some test frequencies and ages, than would have been found with presbycusis corrections based on male data. This is seen by comparison, in Table 4.2, of the Hinchcliffe (1959) hearing levels for females, with those given in ISO 7029 for males. Over all ages and frequencies, the average hearing level is 2 dB higher for the males than the females (1 dB, average for test frequencies 500–2000 Hz, and 3 dB, average for 3000–6000 Hz).

Robinson (1968) found that 1.5 dB had to be added to, and 1.5 dB subtracted from, E_A exposure levels in order to predict the NIPTS of, respectively, his male and female subjects when considered as separate groups [the sex factor k in the predictive formula, Eq. (4.3)]. That difference of 3 dB may, at least partially, be a reflection of an overestimation of NIPTS, in males, due to the use of the female presbycusis data for both female and male subjects in the initial data processing.

In order to compensate for this possible overestimation by the E_A method, E_A is used here without adding or subtracting the prescribed 1.5 dB. For middle levels of E_A, this omission reduces predicted NIPTS for males by about 2 dB, approximately compensating for the 2-dB increase believed to be present in the E_A formulation from the use of female presbycusis data when correcting the hearing-level data of male subjects for presbycusis. The modified procedure (omission of the k factor) is labeled R_2 in the discussion and figures to follow.

E'_A

As discussed, analyses of available data, including some from the Burns and Robinson (1970) study, indicate that 8 log years' exposure (EE_A) rather than

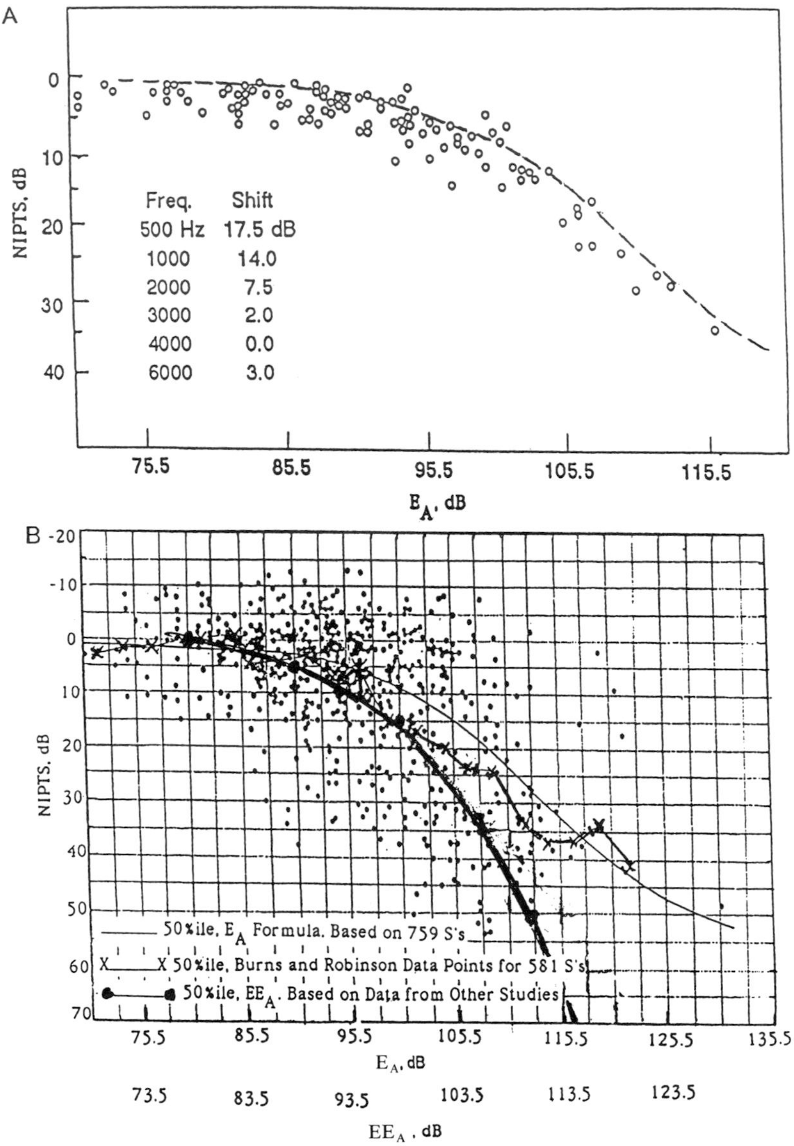

FIGURE 4.9 (A) Plot of 50%ile NIPTS values for 20 cells (Four levels, L_{Aeq8h}, ×5 durations, in years). Used for postulating a single function (the dashed curve) for relation between E_A and 50%ile NIPTS at different frequencies, when normalized by indicated E_A axis shifts. Hearing levels for 759 subjects. (After Fig. 10.13 in Burns and Robinson, 1970.) (B) (1) Thin solid curve function from part A (2) NIPTS data points at 4 kHz found for 581 individual subjects, from Fig. 11.3 in Burns and Robinson, (1970). The x's represent 50%ile points for cells of E_A 2.5 dB wide, calculated by writer from enlargement of Fig. 11.3 (3) Heavy solid line is EE_A-NIPTS function.

10 log calendar years' exposure (E_A) is proportional to the effectiveness of L_{Aeq8h} as a cause of NIPTS. To place the E_A-NIPTS function, and the EE_A-NIPTS data from the other selected studies, on a single set of coordinates, the E_A scale is shifted downward by 2 dB. The result is labeled E_A' (see Fig. 4.10). This does not, of course, change the shape of the E_A' vis à vis the E_A function, but accounts for the 20% difference between the 10- and 8-scale factors used with the logarithms of calendar years of exposure.

NIPTS, Male and Female Subjects

NIPTS is plotted on Fig. 4.10 as a function of career exposure level for noise exposed male and female workers who were otoscopically and/or

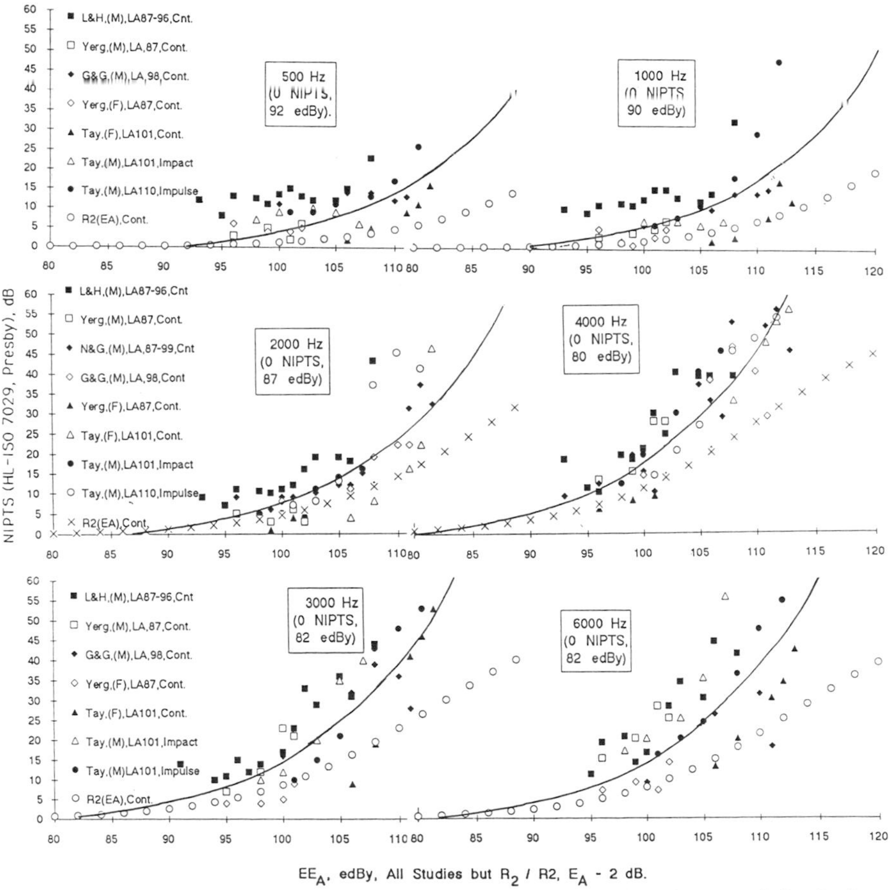

FIGURE 4.10 Fiftieth-percentile NIPTS, 500–6000 Hz, as function of EE_A, and, for R_2 data, E_A'. Hearing levels of nosocusis-screened, noise-exposed males per ISO 7029. Dashed curve, estimated trend of approximate average of the data points and R_2 curve at 4000 Hz, is laid on the graphs for the other test frequencies starting at the indicated EE_A levels for 0 dB NIPTS.

questionnaire-screened for nosocusis, and screened, to varying degrees, for exposure to adventitious noises. Where appropriate, studies of Nixon and Glorig (1961) and Gallo and Glorig (1964) hearing levels of the workers have been somewhat reduced (by 1 or 2 dB depending on age) for estimated (somewhat ineffective) questionnaire-only screening for nosocusis.

Some EE_A levels were increased because of estimated exposure to gun noise for some L_{Aeq8h} levels in five sets of the data for male workers. This adjustment presumably provided the $L_{Aeq8h(wg)}$ noise exposures actually experienced, rather than merely the level reported for the factory noise. This was done for all the selected studies except R_2, where the subjects were screened for gun noise and Taylor *et al.* (1984) where, as previously noted, the factory noise levels were so intense presumed gun noise would not have increased calculated L_{Aeq8h}. It was assumed that exposure to gun noise was not a significant condition for the female subjects in any of the studies.

Even with these adjustments, which lessened the NIPTS to be deduced for certain levels of factory noise, it is seen that as functions of EE_A and E'_A, the R_2 function predicts some 10–15 dB less NIPTS at the higher exposure levels than the great majority of the data points plotted on Fig. 4.10. Possible reasons for these differences will be discussed later.

NIPTS, Female Subjects

The 50%ile hearing level and NIPTS data for female workers are given in the top section of Table 4.9. Figure 4.11 shows NIPTS, measured per ISO (1984) 7029, for these female ears and that predicted by EE_A, based on data for screened male and female ears. The Taylor *et al.* (1984) data suggest that the female ear is somewhat more resistant than the male ear to NIPTS, at the lower frequencies and EE_A levels, than do the data of Yerg *et al.* (1978). At the higher noise exposure levels (with female data available only from the Taylor *et al.* study), NIPTS for females becomes about equal to or exceeds that predicted by EE_A.

Comparison of the hearing levels in the Yerg *et al.* (1978) study of the noise exposed females with those of controls selected from the same industries shows negligible amounts of NIPTS (see Table 4.9). One possible explanation is that some small percentage of the female control and noise-exposed workers in that study suffered some NIPTS from exposure to adventitious noises that prevented detection of any NIPTS from the rather low-intensity factory noise involved.

As seen in Fig. 4.2 and Table 4.9, female, as well as the male in Table 3.8, control subjects in the Yerg *et al.* (1978) study had significantly higher hearing levels, as a function of age, than is to be expected according to ISO 7029 (1984). This occurred even though all these subjects had been otoscopically screened for nosocusis. The most likely explanation, as dis-

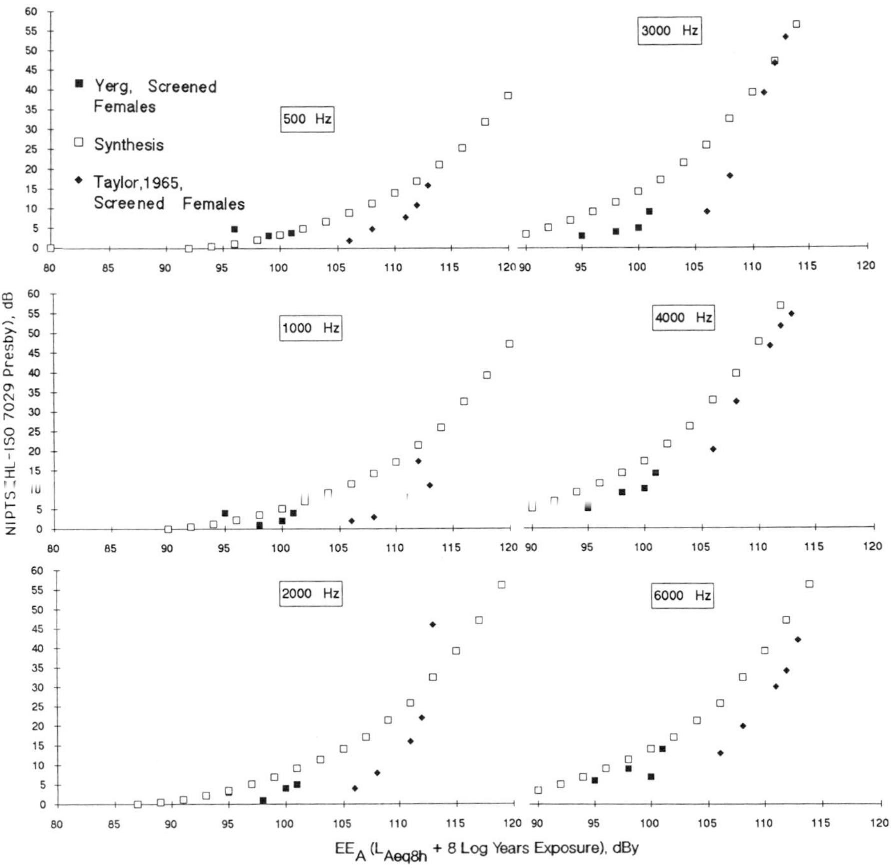

FIGURE 4.11 Fiftieth-percentile NIPTS, 500–6000 Hz, per ISO 7029, of synthesis curve and as found for female factory workers as function of EE_A. NIPTS for females based on hearing-level data from Yerg *et al.* (1978) and Taylor *et al.* (1965) for otoscopically screened, factory-noise-exposed females.

cussed previously, is that the presence of sociocusis in the control groups prevented the detection of NIPTS from the relatively low intensity levels of workplace noise.

It is concluded from these two studies that, for practical purposes, male and female ears probably do not differ significantly in regard to susceptibility to NIPTS. As mentioned, Robinson's (1968) analysis of the Burns and Robinson (1970) data indicated that they do, but this finding could have been, at least partially, due to the procedure used by Robinson to correct male hearing levels for presbycusis.

Synthesis Curve and EE_A

The synthesis curve for 4000 Hz (solid line in Fig. 4.10) is a visual estimate of the midtrend of the other-than-R_2 data points. Except for those from the Taylor *et al.* (1984) study, these points are from those studies in which the noise was more-or-less steady and continuous throughout 8 work-hours. The predictions of NIPTS by R_2 (E_A') are believed by the writer to be too much lower than warranted to be considered in the placement of the synthesis curve. The reasons for this decision will be given later. The synthesis curve is reasonably well fitted by the formulas.

$$80\text{–}100 e\text{dB}y = 206.927 + (-5.308(e\text{dB}y + 0.6)) + (0.034(e\text{dB}y + 0.6)^2)).$$
$$101\text{–}118\ e\text{dB}y = 1418.261 + (-29.186(e\text{dB}y)) + (0.152(e\text{dB}y)^2) \qquad (4.4)$$

Examined over all frequencies, the data plotted in Fig. 4.10 support Robinson's (1968) observation that the growth, whatever it may be, of NIPTS as a function of years of exposure is similar for all test frequencies, provided exposure level is a like amount above the NIPTS threshold level for a given frequency. As shown by the solid curves in Fig. 4.10, the synthesis curve drawn for 4000 Hz was placed on the graphs for the other frequencies, starting at the exposure level that appeared to be the threshold level for NIPTS at that frequency. The basic curve was drawn for the 4000-Hz results because the widest range of exposure-level NIPTS values is found at that frequency.

Attention is invited to the somewhat lesser variability of the data points around the trend lines for 500, 1000, 2000, and 6000 Hz than for 3000 and 4000 Hz. This is believed to be due to the grossness of an overall frequency level for measuring industrial noises. Such noises can differ considerably with respect to the intensity of their low-, and high-, frequency content, while the middle-frequency content remains rather the same for a given $A-$, or other, weighted overall level. As a result, the NIPTS at 3000 and 4000 Hz tend to be more alike than they are at lower and higher test frequencies with exposures to given overall levels of differing spectra noises.

The selected EE_A threshold levels, with one year of exposure, for the different test frequencies, and the differences in threshold levels from that for 4000 Hz, are 500 Hz, 92 *e*dB*y*, 12-dB difference; 1000 Hz, 90 *e*dB*y*, 10-dB difference; 2000 Hz, 87 *e*dB*y*, 7-dB difference; 3000 Hz, 82 *e*dB*y*, 2-dB difference; 4000 Hz, 80 *e*dB*y*, 0-dB difference; 6000 Hz, 82 *e*dB*y*, 2-dB difference. The threshold levels for each of these test frequencies are also indicated on Fig. 4.10. According to the EE_A formula, the level for threshold of NIPTS at 4000 Hz would be an L_{Aeq8h} of about 66 with 50 years of exposure. Inasmuch as typical daily exposure levels to everyday sound and noise is of the order of L_{Aeq24h} 73 (Kono *et al.*, 1982), a threshold level for long-term exposures to workplace noise of L_{Aeq8h} 66 seems unrealistically low. However, because of the intermittent and temporal nature of everyday sounds and noises, their effective level as a cause of NIPTS is estimated to be 10 dB or so less than is indicated by their L_{Aeq24h} levels.

Possible Reasons for Differences between E_A Predictions and NIPTS Data

There are several possible alternative explanations for the lesser amounts of NIPTS predicted by E_A than was generally found for the other selected studies.

1. The E_A-NIPTS function is driven by a perhaps somewhat unjustifiable hyperbolic tangent function.
2. The hearing level data collected in the Burns and Robinson (1970) survey are biased because workers with the higher amounts of NIPTS were inadvertently not tested.
3. The subjects in the Burns and Robinson survey were more resistant to NIPTS than those of the other studies, and/or the screenings of subjects for nosocusis and sociocusis in the other studies were grossly inadequate.

Fitting of Hyperbolic Tangent Curve to Data

First, with respect to the fitting of the hyperbolic tangent curve, as seen in Fig. 4.9, the curve representing NIPTS predicted by the E_A method appears to have been set somewhat higher than it might have been to better fit the midrange of the data for all 759 subjects (Fig. 4.9A) or the separate data points for 581 individuals of those subjects (Fig. 4.9B). Second, above an E_A of ~115, the data are, arguably, too sparse to justify the inflection of the curve toward an asymptote dictated by the hyperbolic tangent function. [As will be discussed in Chapter 6, this hyperbolic function is similar in general shape to a Gompertz function employed by Lutman and Robinson (1992) and Lutman *et al.* (1987) in other contexts.]

Selection of Subjects

The EE_A-NIPTS function approximates NIPTS as measured in studies other than that of Burns and Robinson (1970). In three of these studies, those of Gallo and Glorig (1964) Nixon and Glorig (1961) and Taylor *et al.* (1984), the hearing-level data were taken from routinely collected medical records for all workers, with the subjects selected by the investigators on the basis of noise exposure and other factors. In the Yerg *et al.* (1978) study, workers selected on the basis of their noise exposures and medical history, were asked to serve as subjects, with but a "few" refusing to do so. In the Lempert and Henderson (1973) study, attempts were made to test the entire workforce in plants with fewer than 500 employees, and in the larger plants subject selection was done on a random basis.

In the Burns and Robinson (1970) study, a printed handout was provided to factory management. This handout advised that the British government was undertaking a research program to "help the Minister of Pensions and National Insurance in considering whether . . . industrial deafness might attract benefit under the Industrial Injuries Act. . . . The Medical Research Council team will visit this factory soon and ask a few selected people to help them by answering a simple questionnaire and submitting to an ear examination." Workers were assured of no loss of pay, and confidentiality of the test results.

For actual testing, workers were selected by management from among those who had expressed a wish to participate. This selection was to eliminate those "whose present noise exposure was not amenable to quantitative description" or "whose past noise exposure was different from that of their present occupation."

These selection procedures are clearly well intended. However, they seem more likely, than the procedures used in the other studies, to provide a sample of subjects that is not representative of the population of workers exposed to a given level of workplace noise. It is hypothesized that these procedures may have served to eliminate workers who were suffering from the higher amounts of NIPTS.

A factor contributing to that end would be a reluctance to volunteer on the part of those workers, who knew, or suspected that they had a significant hearing handicap. This on the belief that the results might reduce peer esteem, or might prejudice their employment status. To illustrate: it was found in a study conducted in Canada that hearing-impaired workers were reluctant to acknowledge their hearing difficulties, and workers with hearing difficulties were stigmatized as being deaf, especially by coworkers (Hétu *et al.,* 1990). It is also possible that managers tended to exclude those volunteers with the more obvious hearing handicaps on unjustified beliefs that the handicaps were perhaps due to factors other than on-the-present-job noise environments.

The biasing influence of subject self-selection has been found, in the opposite direction, in the distributions of hearing levels obtained from self-selected subjects tested at large gatherings of people, such as at Fairs and shopping malls (Steinberg *et al.,* 1940; Glorig *et al.,* 1954; Webster, *et al.,* 1950; Royster and Thomas, 1979). Under these conditions there appears to be a tendency for those persons most concerned about their hearing abilities to participate in free testing being offered, without, of course, any attendent adverse consequences. Biasing in the distributions of data from volunteer, or volunteered, subjects is an ever-present threat to the validity of epidemiological studies.

In any event, it is clear that the subjects in the Burns and Robinson (1970) study were workers selected by work supervisors from those who came forward as willing to have their hearing tested, and were then screened for nosocusis and sociocusis and tested by research personnel. Whereas in all the other studies of NIPTS, the hearing-level data were (1) for all, or nearly all, the workers in each particular noise situation; or (2) for subjects selected and screened by research personnel on a random basis from the workers in each particular noise situation.

Alternative Hypotheses Concerning Burns and Robinson's Subjects

It is conceivable that the hearing-level data for the Burns and Robinson (1970) study came from a population of workers that had significantly greater resistance to NIPTS than did the workers in the other studies. Or, perhaps, that the screening for nosocusis and the adjustments for gun-noise exposure, which were exemplary in the Burns and Robinson study, were essentially inadequate in the other studies of screened workers. However, there is no basis at all for a "greater resistance" hypothesis.

The supposition of inadequate nosocusis screening and gun-noise adjustment in the other studies is a possible explanation for the difference of only a few decibels of NIPTS between NIPTS-E_A and the synthesis curve at the lower levels of noise exposure. However, it can hardly explain the differences of $\geq$10–15, dB of NIPTS seen in Fig. 4.10, at the higher noise-exposure levels, where the effects of the factory noise, and not nosocusis or sociocusis, could be expected to be the dominating factor controlling hearing levels.

The data for one of those other studies, Taylor *et al.* (1965) (females exposed to the noise in weaving sheds), required no adjustments and provide for a more direct test of the magnitude and reliability of the conjectured bias on the distribution of the hearing levels measured by Burns and Robinson (1970). As in the Burns and Robinson study, the subjects in the Taylor *et al.* study were screened for exposures to adventitious noise, and questionnaire- and medically screened for nosocusis. NIPTS was measured in both studies by comparison of the hearing levels of noise-exposed workers with those of females as found by Hinchcliffe (1959). In the Taylor *et al.* study, the hearing levels were measured by manual audiometry, so that no adjustments were required in the comparison made with the Hinchcliffe data.

A difference between the two studies, but one presumably immaterial to the prediction of NIPTS by E_A, is that in the Taylor *et al.* (1965) study, only one intensity level, L_{Aeq8h} 101, was involved, with years of exposure being varied, whereas Robinson (1968) developed the E_A formulation from exposures inseparably expressed as a joint function of intensity level and years of exposure. Fortunately, whether this difference could be a differentiating factor affecting the results can also be tested through an analysis of some of the data published by Burns and Robinson (1970) for a sample of 581 subjects. In particular, NIPTS was reported by Burns and Robinson for conditions comparable to those in the Taylor *et al.* study, i.e., different numbers of years of exposure to an L_{Aeq8h} also of 101. These data are shown in Fig. 4.12A.

Fig. 4.12B shows that the generalized E_A underpredicts by 5–20 dB measured NIPTS with ≥3 years of exposure to weaving noise of L_{Aeq8h} 101. As also seen in Fig. 4.12B, the Burns and Robinson (1970) NIPTS data for L_{Aeq8h} 101 (Fig. 4.12A) are consistent with the E_A formulation, and similarly show significantly less, up to ~20 dB, NIPTS than did the Taylor *et al.* (1965) subjects from exposure to L_{Aeq8h} 101. The one difference between these two

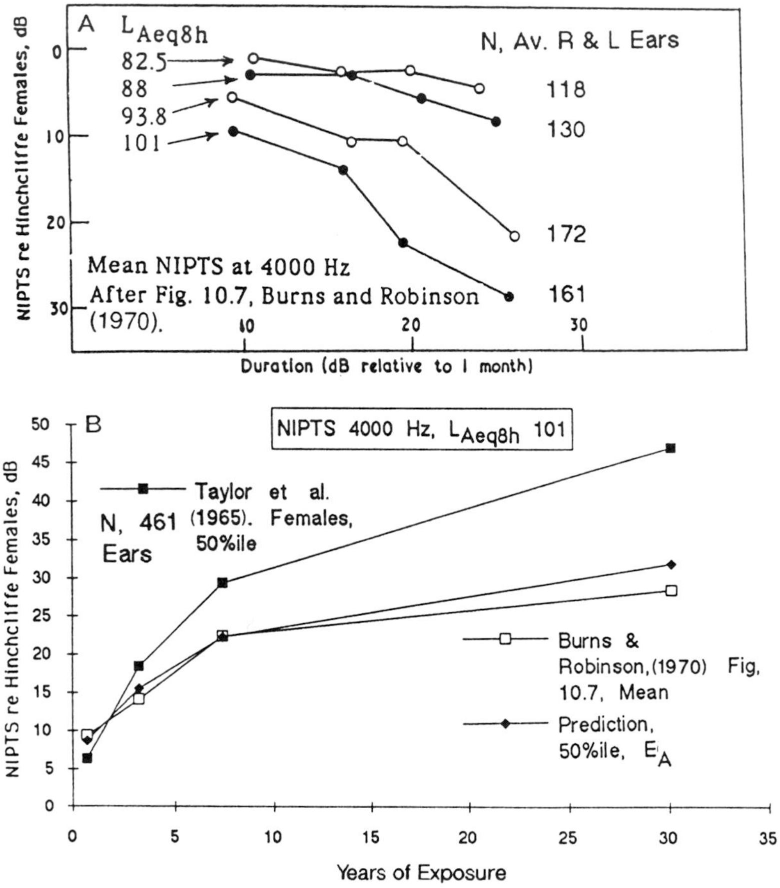

FIGURE 4.12 (A) E_A for females, and raw data from Burns and Robinson (1970), (B) (1) NIPTS found for females from noise exposure condition in study of Taylor *et al.* (1965). Copyright 1965 by the American Psychological Association. Adapted by permission of the author. (2) NIPTS as found for same exposure condition by Burns and Robinson (1970); and (3) NIPTS as predicted by E_A for same noise exposure condition.

studies that could ostensibly have produced the differential findings is that in the Taylor *et al.,* (1965) study, 100% of the workers in the noise area investigated, group III, were tested, whereas in Burns and Robinson, the hearing levels of only self- and management-selected subjects were tested.

Hyperbolic Function Atypical for Physiological Condition of Interest

Hearing threshold elevation resulting from excessive stimulation and aging typically proceed on a monotonic exponential course until the upper limit of normal operation is reached, rather than on the course of the hyperbolic tangent function with a point of negative inflection. The hyperbolic function, on the other hand, becomes asymptotic at a relatively low hearing level. For example, with exposure for 10 years to an 8-h workday noise of 120 L_A, E_A equals 130 (the allowable maximum), and predicts for 50%ile, age 30 years, 1000 Hz, an NIPTS of 40 dB, and HL 42 dB. Of course, HL 42 dB (the 50%ile maximum predicted by E_A) is far below the 102 dB, per ISO 389, upper threshold level of 50%ile, normal hearing (AAOO-AMA).

The deceleration in rate of growth of NIPTS beyond the 27-dB point prescribed by the E_A hyperbolic tangent function is believed to be inconsistent with general principles of growth, as a function of intensity of exposure, of sensory fatigue, or stimulation, for that matter, in a distribution of sensory receptors. One would expect the number of receptors capable of response to progressively decrease toward the extremes of a distribution of receptors, especially when the stimulus variable is expressed in terms of the logarithmetically compressed decibel scale. The same reasoning applies, of course, when dealing with the distribution of the hearing levels of an unbiased sample of persons who have been exposed to noise, and is seen to operate for all the NIPTS data except for that of Burns and Robinson (1970).

However, the E_A tangent would appear from group data if the workers with the greater losses in hearing sensitivity were, because of the suspected Burns and Robinson subject selection procedures, not tested. Because such subjects could be expected to be increasingly present in the workers exposed to the increasingly higher levels of noise, the lack of their hearing-level data would perforce show a progressive slowing in the rate of growth of NIPTS for the groups with the higher levels of noise exposure. The "x" curve added to Fig. 4.9 clearly shows this to be the case when the E_A level exceeds ~100.

DISTRIBUTIONS OF PERCENTILE PRESBYCUSIS AND NIPTS

Robinson and Sutton (1978) developed formulas for calculating the percentile hearing levels to be expected in the general male and female populations with normal ears as a function of age. Tables of 1%ile to 99%ile, in 1%ile steps, presbycusis-corrected hearing levels calculated by these formulas are to be found in Shipton (1979).

In documents published by Burns and Robinson (1970), Robinson (1968), Shipton (1979), and ISO 7029 (1984), lower percentile values are assigned to the higher-valued hearing levels and NIPTS's of such distributions, and higher valued percentiles are assigned to the lower-valued hearing levels and NIPTSs. For example, "99%ile" refers, in those documents, to the 1% of the persons with the lowest hearing levels, most sensitive ears. The reverse is believed to be a more common practice, at least in the United States, and is followed in this book. As appropriate, the percentiles for Robinson and ISO data to follow have been converted to conform with this latter procedure.

Lempert and Henderson (1973), Gallo and Glorig (1964), and Taylor *et al.* (1984) provided hearing levels for the 10%ile, 25%ile, 50%ile, 75%ile, and 90%ile of their distributions of hearing-level data at each of these percentiles (see Table 4.10). NIPTS values at these percentiles were calculated by the writer by subtracting the percentile hearing levels of same-aged males as given in ISO 7029 (1984). The hearing levels at these percentiles for normal ears as given in ISO 7029 (1984), and the NIPTS data averaged over the three industrial noise studies, are given in Table 4.11. Also shown in Table 4.11 are the ratios of NIPTS at 10%ile, 25%ile, 75%ile, and 90%ile to that at 50%ile for each test frequency and age group, and the average over age and test frequency.

Distribution of Normal HL and NIPTS per 50%ile Values

As seen in the bottom section of Table 4.11, the ratios, per 50%ile, for NIPTS averaged over the adult years and test frequencies, are, respectively, for 10%ile, 25%ile, 75%ile, and 90%ile: 0.3, 0.6, 1.5, and 2.0. Figure 4.13 shows these findings, and a formula that can be used to estimate the approximate amount of NIPTS to be expected, given a specified 50%ile NIPTS value, at any percentile, from 10%ile to 90%ile, of a population of similarly noise-exposed workers.

It is seen in Fig. 4.14A that susceptibility, average for the ages of 25–55 years, to presbycusis increases rather sharply for persons with the worse (90%ile) hearing, compared with that for persons with better (10%ile) hearing. The differences between the 10%ile and 90%ile hearing levels range from about 15 dB for 500 Hz to 30 dB for 6000 Hz. The amount of estimated typical sociocusis at a given percentile over this age range, average age 40 years, is estimated to be equal to the differences between hearing levels at 500 Hz and the higher frequencies, as indicated by the bracket in the panel. The supposition being that sociocusis is not found at 500 Hz and lower frequencies (Kryter, 1983).

Figure 4.14B shows an apparent lesser increase in susceptibility to NIPTS than presbycusis as a function of distribution percentile. The differences, averaged for subjects 25–55 years of age, between 10%ile and 90%ile range from about only 5 dB at 500 Hz to 20 dB at 6000 Hz. Figure 4.13 also illustrates the relatively small range in NIPTS, compared to that for prebyscusis, between the 10%ile and 90%ile points on the respective distributions. Figure 4.14C shows the actual hearing levels for the average of the three studies.

Distributions of NIPTS in Ears with High Hearing Levels

The top right-hand panel on Fig. 4.15 shows, with 4000 Hz as an example, that hearing levels rise from the joint effects of presbycusis (top left-hand panel) and the NIPTS for the three studies cited (bottom left-hand panel) to ~80 dB. However, when presbycusis and NIPTS together elevate hearing levels to more than ~65 dB, the resulting level is somewhat less than the sum of the elevations expected from each factor operating alone. This is expressed, in the lower panels of Fig. 4.15, as a decreasing reduction in NIPTS. It occurs, for the average intensity condition involved, L_{Aeq8h} 100, only at 3000, 4000, and 6000 Hz, in 90%ile, and to some extent 75%ile, ears in subjects aged ≥35 and years of exposure >15.

Beyond a hearing level of ~65 dB, these two causes of loss in hearing sensitivity appear to be competing for what hearing capacity remains in the ear. Some further hearing losses due to NIPTS can, of course, accrue. As noted earlier, in a young normal (50%ile) ear, an NIPTS of 102 dB, or total deafness, could occur.

Formula for Estimating Percentile HL of Populations with NIPTS

The following formula is proposed for use with EE_A for the estimation of HL (predicted hearing level) for percentiles of populations with predicted percentile NIPTS:

$$\text{HL}' = \text{HL(normal, ISO 7029)} + 65 + (\text{NIPTS} - 65) \qquad (4.5)$$

where HL and NIPTS are matched for population age and percentile.

ISO (1990) 1999 adopted, the following formula for that purpose (see also Robinson, 1991):

$$\text{HL}' = \text{HL (ISO 7029)} + \text{NIPTS} - (\text{HL} \times \text{NIPTS})/120). \qquad (4.6)$$

Using data in Table 4.11, HL′ was predicted by the ISO method and compared to HL as measured for 50%ile, 75%ile, and 90%ile, at 3000, 4000, and 6000 Hz, respectively. For these data, the ISO 1999 procedure underpredicted measured HL an average of 5.3 dB (see Table 4.12). Since NIPTS equaled measured HL minus normal HL, the EE_A procedure shows, by definition, no differences between predicted and measured HL.

TABLE 4.11 Percentile HL, ISO 7029, HL, and HL and NIPTS, per ISO 7029, for Average of Three Studies of Table 4.10; Ratios of 10%, 25, 75, and 90%ile / 50%ile Average over Age, Frequency, and Age and Frequency, for Average HL of Three Studies

ISO 7029 (ISO, 1984), presbycusis data from Shipton (1979), Table M

Age, Mid Decade	10%ile HL	25%ile	50%ile	75%ile	90%ile	10%ile	25%ile	50%ile	75%ile	90%ile	10%ile	25%ile	50%ile	75%ile	90%ile
			500 Hz					1000 Hz					2000 Hz		
25	−6.2	−3.2	0.2	4.3	8.1	−6.2	−3.2	0.2	4.4	8.1	−7.2	−3.6	0.3	5.3	9.8
35	−5.7	−2.5	1.0	5.4	9.4	−5.6	−2.4	1.2	5.6	9.7	−6.3	−2.4	2.0	7.5	12.4
45	−4.9	−1.4	2.6	7.4	11.8	−4.7	−1.1	2.9	7.9	12.4	−4.6	0.0	5.1	11.5	17.3
55	−3.7	0.3	4.8	10.4	15.4	−3.3	0.9	5.5	11.2	16.4	−2.2	3.4	9.6	17.3	24.3
Average	−5.1	−1.7	2.2	6.9	11.2	−5.0	−1.5	2.5	7.3	11.7	−5.1	−0.7	4.3	10.4	16.0
			3000 Hz					4000 Hz					6000 Hz		
25	−7.7	−3.8	0.6	6.0	10.9	−8.1	−3.9	0.8	6.6	11.9	−9.2	−4.4	0.9	7.5	13.5
35	−6.2	−1.7	3.3	9.6	15.2	−6.0	−1.0	4.6	11.6	17.9	−6.9	−1.1	5.2	13.1	20.3
45	−3.4	2.2	8.4	16.1	23.1	−2.2	4.4	11.7	20.8	29.0	−2.6	4.9	13.1	23.4	32.7
55	0.6	7.8	15.7	25.7	34.7	3.4	12.1	21.9	34.1	45.1	3.7	13.6	24.6	38.4	50.8
Average	−4.2	1.1	7.0	14.4	21.0	−3.2	2.9	9.8	18.3	26.0	−3.8	3.3	11.0	20.6	29.3

Average ratios HL over age and frequency: 10%ile/50%ile = −0.7; 25%ile/50%ile = 0.1; 75%ile/50%ile = 2.1; 90%ile/50%ile = 3.1.

Average HL, Taylor *et al.* (1967), Gallo and Glorig (1964), Lempert and Henderson (1973)

Age, Mid Decade	10%ile HL	25%ile	50%ile	75%ile	90%ile	10%ile	25%ile	50%ile	75%ile	90%ile	10%ile	25%ile	50%ile	75%ile	90%ile
			500 Hz					1000 Hz					2000 Hz		
25	3.6	7.1	10.4	14.9	16.8	1.3	4.0	7.0	11.3	13.9	0.0	2.3	7.9	11.6	16.9
35	4.0	8.0	12.0	18.3	26.5	2.8	5.9	10.5	15.8	29.8	2.6	5.1	13.0	23.2	37.8
45	4.8	8.8	14.4	21.1	28.0	5.1	8.7	15.3	23.8	32.5	5.7	10.4	23.9	38.7	50.8
55	9.0	13.3	19.9	29.0	38.5	11.4	17.4	26.3	38.0	48.3	13.1	23.5	40.1	53.5	65.1
Average	5.4	9.3	14.2	20.8	27.4	5.1	9.0	14.8	22.2	31.1	5.4	10.3	21.2	31.8	42.6
			3000 Hz					4000 Hz					6000 Hz		
25	2.5	5.9	12.2	21.8	37.9	3.0	8.6	14.3	25.6	41.8	4.8	8.1	14.5	26.8	44.4
35	7.5	14.8	26.1	43.1	58.6	10.8	21.5	34.8	48.3	60.1	12.4	17.6	29.5	40.1	57.9
45	15.9	26.7	43.3	55.8	65.5	22.8	35.6	49.1	58.7	69.5	18.9	29.0	45.5	60.3	69.9
55	27.5	44.8	53.8	66.3	78.0	41.3	50.5	58.3	70.9	78.3	34.3	50.3	61.4	72.1	79.3
Average	13.3	23.0	33.8	46.7	60.0	19.4	29.0	39.1	50.9	62.4	17.6	26.3	37.7	49.8	62.8

Average NIPTS, per ISO 7029 (ISO, 1984), Taylor *et al.* (1967), Gallo and Glorig (1964), Lempert and Henderson (1973)

			500 Hz					1000 Hz					2000 Hz		
25	9.8	10.3	10.2	10.6	8.7	7.5	7.2	6.8	6.9	5.8	7.2	5.9	7.6	6.3	7.1
35	9.7	10.5	11.0	12.9	17.1	8.4	8.3	9.3	10.2	20.1	8.9	7.5	11.0	15.7	25.4
45	9.7	10.2	11.8	13.7	16.2	9.8	9.8	12.4	15.9	20.1	10.3	10.4	18.8	27.2	33.5
55	12.7	13.0	15.1	18.6	23.1	14.7	16.5	20.8	26.8	31.9	15.3	20.1	30.5	36.2	40.8
Average*	10.5	11.0	12.0	13.9	16.3	10.1	10.4	12.3	14.9	19.4	10.4	11.0	17.0	21.4	26.7
			3000 Hz					4000 Hz					6000 Hz		
25	10.2	9.7	11.6	15.8	27.0	11.1	12.5	13.5	19.0	29.9	14.0	12.5	13.6	19.3	30.9
35	13.7	16.5	22.8	33.5	43.4	16.8	22.5	30.2	36.7	42.2	19.3	18.7	24.3	27.0	37.6
45	19.3	24.5	34.9	39.7	42.4	25.0	31.2	37.4	37.9	40.5	21.5	24.1	32.4	36.9	37.2
55	26.9	37.0	38.1	40.6	43.3	37.9	38.4	36.4	36.8	33.2	30.6	36.7	36.8	33.7	28.5
Average*	17.5	21.9	26.8	32.4	39.0	22.7	26.1	29.3	32.6	36.4	21.3	23.0	26.8	29.2	33.5

* Ratios for 500, 1000, and 2000 Hz, age 25 years, and 3000, 4000 and 6000 Hz, age 55 years not included in averages.

Ratios: 10%/50%; 25%/50%; 75%/50%; and 90%ile/50%ile HL. Aver. of Taylor *et al.* (1967), Gallo and Glorig (1964), Lempert and Henderson (1973)

HL, Hz	10/50	25/50	75/50	90/50		HL	10/50	25/50	75/50	90/50	
500	0.4	0.7	1.5	1.9	Average ratios, HL over age	25 Yrs	0.2	0.5	1.7	2.6	Average ratios, HL over frequency
1000	0.3	0.6	1.5	2.2	" " "	35 Yrs	0.3	0.6	1.5	2.2	"
2000	0.2	0.4	1.6	2.2	" " "	45 Yrs	0.4	0.6	1.3	1.7	"
3000	0.3	0.6	1.5	2.1	" " "	55 Yrs	0.5	0.8	1.3	1.5	"
4000	0.4	0.7	1.4	1.9	" " "	Average	0.4	0.6	1.5	2.0	Average ratios, HL, frequency and age
6000	0.4	0.7	1.4	2.0	" " "						
Average	0.3	0.6	1.5	2.0	Ratios, HL over age and frequency						

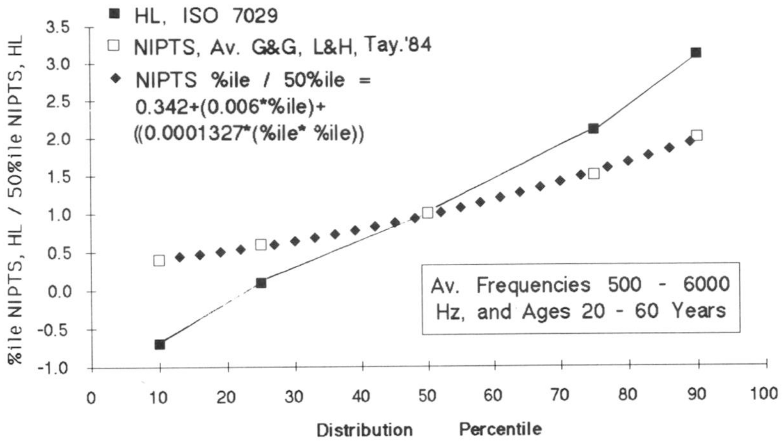

FIGURE 4.13 Ratios of NIPTS for 10%ile, 25%ile, 75%ile, and 90%ile to NIPTS for 50%ile of distribution of NIPTS averaged over studies of noise-exposed, nosocusis-screened subjects; and the same ratios for hearing levels (HLs) of nosocusis screened population (ISO, 1984 7029).

ISO 1999 (1990)

The ISO Standard 1999 (1990) for the estimation of noise-induced hearing loss from exposure to occupational noise is based in part on the E_A model and, in part, on an analysis by Passcheir-Vermeer (1977) of other data of NIPTS from exposure to industrial noise. A critique of ISO 1999 is given in the Appendix to this chapter. Additional discussion of applications of ISO 1999 for the prediction of NIPTS are provided in Chapters 5 and 7.

As discussed in detail in the Appendix, the analyses of NIPTS data by Passcheir-Vermeer (1977) significantly underestimate NIPTS to be expected from exposure to industrial noise. The primary reason for the underestimations is that the control, supposedly non-noise-exposed, groups against which the hearing levels of screened noise-exposed workers were compared represented unscreened hearing levels. ISO 1999 generally underestimates NIPTS according to the present analysis and the EE_A method.

ISSUES OF CONTROL GROUP AND OVERESTIMATIONS OF EXPOSURES

As discussed, the magnitude of deduced NIPTS depends on the use of control groups free of NIPTS from unknown noise exposures. At the same time, an issue sometimes raised is whether the screened subjects in the studies used

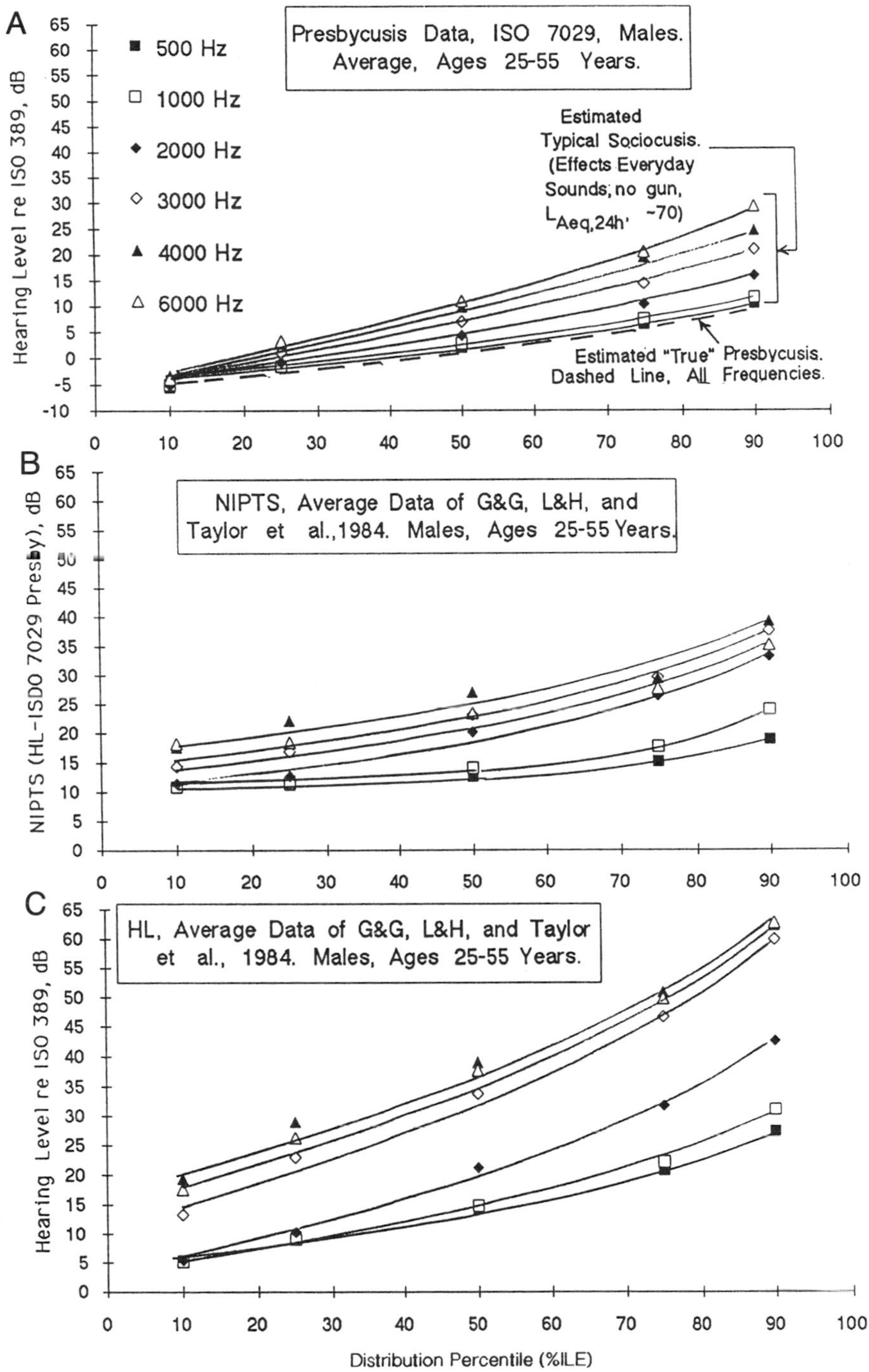

FIGURE 4.14 (A) 10–90%ile hearing levels, normal males (ISO, 1984 7029), average age 40 years; (B) 10–90%ile NIPTS for nosocusis-screened male workers, average age 40 years, average noise exposure 100 L_{Aeq8h}; (C) 10–90%ile hearing levels of the noise-exposed workers. Parameter is test frequency on all graphs.

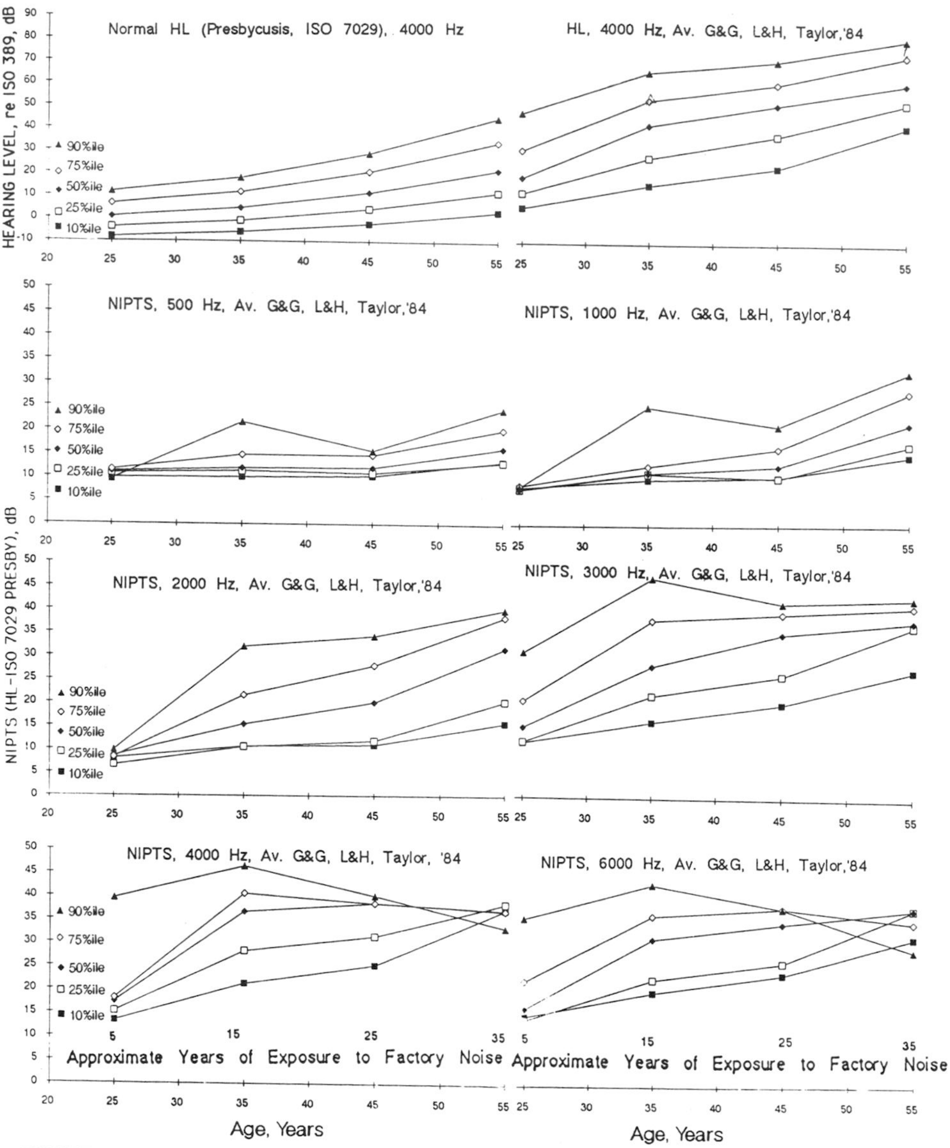

FIGURE 4.15 Hearing level, 4000 Hz, as function of age for male presbycusis (ISO, 7029 (1984)), and for nosocusis-screened males exposed to average of EL_{Aeq8h} 100 work noise (average for three studies). Also, NIPTS, 500–6000 Hz, same conditions and average same studies. Parameter is distribution percentile.

TABLE 4.12 Measured HL and Predicted HL′ (ISO Method) at 50, 75, and 90%ile for 3000, 4000, and 6000 Hz; HL_M and $NIPTS_M$ Are Measured Average of Three Studies, per Table 4.11

Age	HL_M	HL, normal	50%ile $NIPTS_M$	HL′	HL_M	HL, normal	75%ile $NIPTS_M$	HL′	HL_M	HL, normal	90%ile $NIPTS_M$	HL′
3000 Hz												
25	12.2	0.6	11.6	12.1	21.8	6.0	15.8	21.0	37.9	10.9	27.0	35.4
35	26.1	3.3	22.8	25.5	43.1	9.6	33.5	40.4	58.6	15.2	43.4	53.1
45	43.3	8.4	34.8	40.8	55.8	16.1	39.6	50.4	65.5	23.2	42.4	57.4
55	53.8	15.7	38.0	48.7	66.3	25.7	40.5	57.5	78.0	34.7	43.3	65.5
Average	33.9	7.0	26.8	31.8	46.8	14.4	32.4	42.3	60.0	21.0	39.0	52.9
HL_M − HL′*				2.1				4.4				7.1
4000 Hz												
25	14.3	0.8	13.4	14.1	25.6	6.6	13.7	19.5	41.8	12.0	29.8	38.8
35	34.8	4.6	30.1	33.5	48.3	11.6	36.6	44.7	60.1	17.9	42.2	53.8
45	49.1	11.7	37.4	45.5	58.7	20.8	37.9	52.1	69.5	29.0	40.5	59.7
55	58.3	21.9	36.3	51.6	70.9	34.1	36.8	60.4	78.3	45.1	33.1	65.8
Average	39.1	9.8	29.3	36.2	50.9	18.3	31.3	44.2	62.4	26.0	36.4	54.5
HL_M − HL′*				3.0				6.7				7.9
6000 Hz												
25	14.5	0.9	13.6	14.4	26.8	7.5	19.3	25.6	44.4	13.5	30.9	40.9
35	29.5	5.2	24.3	28.4	40.1	13.1	27.0	37.2	57.9	20.3	37.6	51.5
45	45.5	13.1	32.4	42.0	60.3	23.4	36.8	53.0	69.9	32.7	37.2	59.8
55	61.4	24.6	36.8	53.9	72.1	38.4	33.7	61.3	79.3	50.8	28.4	67.2
Average	37.7	11.0	26.8	34.7	49.8	20.6	29.2	44.3	62.9	29.3	33.5	54.9
HL_M − HL′*				3.1				5.6				8.0

HL_M − HL′ ISO-predicted, average of 3000, 4000, and 6000 Hz at 50, 75, and 90 %lile = 5.3 dB.

* HL′, ISO = HL, normal, ISO 7029 (ISO, 1984) + $NIPTS_M$ − (HL, ISO 7029 × $NIPTS_M$ / 120).

in the Robinson and Sutton (1978) presbycusis analysis (adopted for ISO 7029) represent the hearing of a truly random sample of noise-free members of the general population.

Lutman and Spencer (1991) and Lutman *et al.* (1993) reported the differences in the hearing levels of persons exposed to estimated levels of occupational and leisure noise, including gunfire. The 1968 subjects were randomly selected adults from Great Britain and matched in groups by age and gender. Estimates of cumulative noise exposure, noise emission level (NEL) or E_A, were made on the basis of responses obtained in interviews structured separately for occupational noise, leisure noise, and gunfire. The exposures were classified into four levels: NEL (E_A): <97; 97–107; 107–117; and >117. Hearing levels were obtained by manual audiometry. Subjects with air–bone gap >5 dB, average at 0.5, 1, and 2 kHz, and a history of use of oto-toxic drugs were excluded.

Lutman *et al.* (1993) found that the hearing levels for their estimated noise exposed subjects were similar to those predicted by E_A, but their younger, especially those under 45 years old, non-noise exposed subjects, had hearing that was several decibels worse than the non-noise subjects, ISO (1990) 7029, used for the E_A model. However, these data are not definitive as recognized by the investigators with respect to the effect of noise exposure on hearing loss.

In the first place, the E_A noise exposure levels for each person were estimates made by the experimenters after questioning the subjects about their occupations and experience with gunfire and exposure to recreational noise. As such, it is speculated that they may represent some considerable overestimations of total effective exposures in that: (1) Some exposure conditions assuming peak dB_A was accurately remembered may not have been continuous at that level for 8-h workdays. The L_{Aeq8h} exposures, especially the effective EL_{Aeq8h} exposures, were in reality possibly often less than one would estimate from peak levels because of interruptions and sound barriers present in many noise environments. (2) Months of exposure in different noise levels are perhaps more likely to be reported as longer, than actual or shorter durations. (3) Ear protection was perhaps worn by a number of the subjects at higher levels of noise. (4) Lutman *et al.* (1993) reported hearing levels only for the better ear of each subject.

The hearing levels of noise-free, control subjects with average ages of 25–65 years in the Lutman *et al.* (1993) study showed worse hearing than the ISO 7029 control subjects by ~2 dB (average hearing levels at 0.5, 1, and 2 kHz) and ~5 dB (average 3,4, and 6 kHz), see Fig. 4.16. Their control groups below the age of 45 years show about one-half the amount (average 0.5, 1, and 2 kHz) and one-quarter the amount (average 3, 4, and 6 kHz) of apparent "sociocusis" than the control groups of oto-screened groups se-

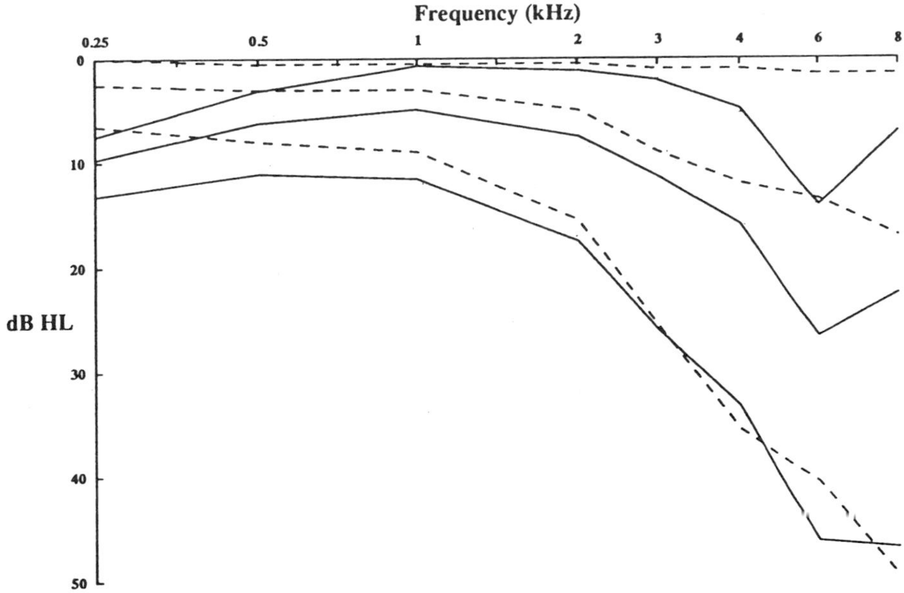

FIGURE 4.16 Hearing level (HL) estimated from the present study (solid curves) for noise-free males in non-manual occupations at ages (from top to bottom) of 25, 45, and 65 years. Equivalent data from ISO (1984) 7029 shown by dashed curves. (From Lutman *et al.* 1993.)

lected from factory "noise-free" groups. The data for the latter studies of NIPTS are given in Table 4.2.

It is probable that the noise-free control group of the Lutman *et al.* (1993) study reflects some effects of noise, sociocusis, and is not a totally proper baseline for determining the effects of noise exposure on loss in hearing sensitive subjects. However, this control group is more appropriate than control groups from industry as a baseline, and could have application in the process of adjudicating responsibility for industrial, noise-induced hearing losses. The greatest obstacle to valid and reliable estimates of hazard to hearing loss from exposure to noise is perhaps the overestimation of the *effective* exposure levels to which some workers are, or have been, exposed.

ADDITIONAL RESEARCH STUDIES

As indicated, only research data were analyzed that lent themselves to the depiction of generalized functions of NIPTS as related to noise exposure level. However, a number of other studies have been published in recent years that contain findings relevant to that matter, and to various other research issues related to sensorineural hearing loss. Immediately following the references for this chapter, selected bibliographies of that material are presented in the following areas: (1) additional studies of sociocusis and industrial NIPTS; (2) ultra- and infrafrequencies, blasts, and vibration; and (3) susceptibility to NIPTS.

APPENDIX

This appendix presents a critique of ISO Standard 1999 (1990) determination of occupational noise exposure, and estimation of occupational noise-induced hearing impairment.

Introduction

The International Organization for Standardization (ISO) is supported by government agencies and technical societies of the industrialized countries of the world. ISO Standard 1999, approved and published in its present form in 1990, specifies a method for calculating NIPTS to be expected in adult populations exposed to various levels and durations of noise.

ISO 1999 utilizes *A*-weighted, average energy per second, for the calculation of equivalent exposures to noise levels, $\pm$ 2.5 dB, of daily durations of $\leq$8 h. The resulting unit L_{Aex8h} is comparable to L_{Aeq8h}. Formulas are provided for calculating percentile NIPTS to be expected from a given number of years of exposure to L_{ex8h} or L_{Aeq8h}.

Shown in Fig. 4A.1 are the amounts of NIPTS predicted for 10, 20, 30, and 40 years of 8-h workday exposures to L_A 85, 90, 95, and 100 dB by (1) ISO 1999, and (2) by the *A*-weighted effective energy, (EE_A) prediction procedure derived in the main text of this chapter from some of the same database as that used with ISO 1999. It is seen that, at the higher levels of exposure, the ISO procedure systematically predicts less NIPTS than does EE_A. An examination of the material used in the preparation of ISO 1999 was undertaken to find possible reasons for the differences seen in Fig. 4A.1 between NIPTS predicted by ISO 1999 (1990) and EE_A.

Database of ISO 1999 (1990)

ISO 1999 cites two documents (Johnson, 1978; Passchier-Vermeer, 1977) as the sources of research findings underlying the procedures specified. These two documents are summaries and averagings of NIPTS predicted by the E_A (energy, *A*-weighted), and the Passchier-Vermeer (P-V) models. As discussed in the main text of this chapter, E_A is based on a study of NIPTS in British industry (Burns and Robinson, 1970). The P-V model was derived from an analysis of a number of studies of hearing in industrial workers.

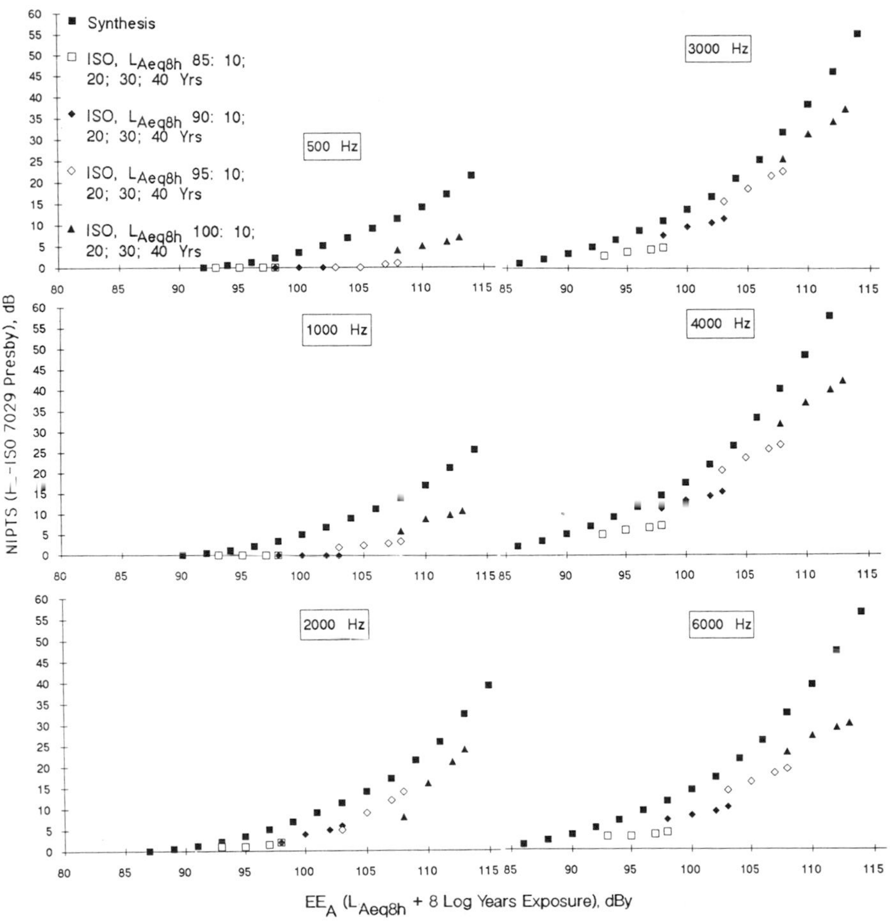

FIGURE 4A.1 Synthesis curve 50%ile NIPTS, 500–6000 Hz, from exposure to noise, 8 h per workday, as functions of EE_A, and as predicted by ISO 1999 (1990). The L_{Aeq8h} and years of exposure for which EE_A values were calculated are given in upper right part of the figure.

Johnson Summary Report

In presenting the E_A predictions of NIPTS, Johnson (1978) modified the EA procedures on the argument that the E_A prediction of some amount of NIPTS after years of exposure to steady noise $<L_A$ 75 is incorrect. However, in an attempt to avoid presumed overestimates of NIPTS by E_A values that involve intensity levels $<L_A$ 75, Johnson applied a "correction" procedure that reduced predicted NIPTS for all levels of intensity, not just for L_A 75.

What Johnson (1978) did was to subtract the NIPTS predicted by E_A for

L_{Aeq8h} 75 with a given number of years of exposure, from the amount of NIPTS predicted for any higher intensity noise, but with the same number of years of exposure. The following, using 40 years of exposure, 4000 Hz, 50%ile for an example, illustrates the steps involved in this process:

Step 1: An exposure for 40 years to a level of L_{Aeq8h} 75 gives an E_A of 91, and E_A 91 predicts, according to the Robinson and Shipton (1977) tables, 3 dB NIPTS.

Step 2: That prediction was reduced by 3 dB to 0 dB NIPTS (on Johnson's belief that a level of L_{Aeq8h} 75, no matter with how many years of exposure, will cause no NIPTS).

Step 3: An exposure for 40 years to noise at a level, for example, of L_{Aeq8h} 95 gives an E_A of 111, and E_A 111 predicts, according to the Robinson and Shipton tables, 24.8 dB NIPTS.

Step 4: On the basis of the finding in step 1 for L_{Aeq8h} 75, 40 years of exposure, the E_A 111 prediction for L_{Aeq8h} 95, 40 years of exposure, was also reduced by 3 dB, from 24.8 to 21.8 dB NIPTS.

Application of this procedure reduces E_A predicted NIPTS by 1.4 dB after 10, 2.0 dB after 20, 2.5 dB after 30, and 3.0 dB after 40 years of exposure for L_{Aeq8h} levels 75, 80, 85, 90, 95, and 100, not just 75; see Table 4A.1 for examples. Johnson cites no justifications for the reductions made when the L_{Aeq8h} levels are >75.

The final summary recommendations in the Johnson (1978) report to ISO 1999 working group (ISO, 1990) consisted of the average of his modified EA predictions of NIPTS with predictions of NIPTS made according to the model of Passchier-Vermeer (1977) for L_{Aeq8h} 85, 90, 95, and 100, with 10, 20, 30, and 40 years of exposure. It is also to be noted that, as discussed in the main text of this chapter, even without Johnson's modification, the E_A procedure appears to significantly underestimate NIPTS from the higher levels of noise exposure.

TABLE 4A.1 Examples of Differences in NIPTS, 50%ile, 4000 Hz, as Predicted by E_A in Robinson and Shipton (1977) (R&S), and by E_A as Modified by Johnson (1978) (J)

	10 YE* NIPTS, E_A		20 YE NIPTS, E_A		30 YE NIPTS, E_A		40 YE NIPTS, E_A		Average difference
L_{Aeq8h}	R&S	per J	R&S	per J	R&S	per J	R&S	per J	R&S − J
75	1.4	0.0	2.0	0.0	2.5	0.0	3.0	0.0	2.2
90	8.7	7.3	12.1	10.1	14.6	12.2	16.3	13.3	2.2
100	23.0	21.6	28.4	26.4	32.0	29.4	33.8	30.8	2.3

* Years of exposure (to noise).

Passchier-Vermeer Summary Report

A similar approach was taken by Passchier-Vermeer (1977) in her summary report to the ISO 1999 working group (ISO, 1990), except that the Passchier-Vermeer model predictions were averaged with unmodified EA predictions, as given in the Robinson and Shipton (1977) tables.

Passchier-Vermeer Model

Passchier-Vermeer (1977) tabulated NIPTS based on (1) graphs showing 50%ile NIPTS, frequencies 500–8000 Hz, as a function of L_{Aeq8h}, or the equivalent, after 10 and 40 years of exposure, and (2) graphs showing differences between 50%ile and higher and lower percentile NIPTS values. For distributions of hearing levels, showing normal presbycusis, Passchier-Vermeer used functions derived by Spoor (1969). These functions are, for practical purposes, the same as those later standardized in ISO 7029 (ISO, 1984). The graphs, derived by Passchier-Vermeer (1968) and, in part, by Passchier-Vermeer (1974), are based on data from the following studies: (1) Burns *et al.* (1977); (2) Gallo and Glorig (1964); (3) ASA Z24-X-2 (1954); and (4) Rosenwinkel and Stewart (1957); (5) Nixon and Glorig (1961); (6) Taylor *et al.* (1965); (7) Kylin (1960); (8) F. van Laar (unpublished).

Passchier-Vermeer (1974) specified that (1) those studies were selected on the basis that the workers were "without any ear damage or clinical ear abnormalities . . ."; [however, this was not the case for the, Z24-X-2 (ASA, 1954), the Rosenwinkel and Stewart (1957) and Kylin (1960) studies, where the workers were not screened for ear disease or abnormalities]; and (2) "All hearing levels have been converted to ISO Standard, if necessary (ISO 1985/R389)." However, this conversion was not done for the Gallo and Glorig (1964), Nixon and Glorig (1961), and Rosenwinkel and Stewart (1957) studies, all of which were done with audiometers calibrated to ASA (1951) standard.

Rather, NIPTSs for the Gallo and Glorig (1964) and Nixon and Glorig (1961) studies were taken as the difference between hearing levels of the medically ear-disease-screened noise-exposed workers and those of like-aged, non-noise-exposed ears as measured by Glorig and Nixon (1960), also with ASA (1951) audiometers. Accordingly, it was presumed by Passchier-Vermeer that conversion of none of these hearing-level data to ISO (1985) 389 was needed (personal correspondence, August 6, 1992, from Dr. Passchier-Vermeer to the writer). NIPTS for the Rosenwinkel and Stewart (1957) study appears to have been taken as the difference between their factory-worker control group and noise-exposed workers.

Unfortunately, the hearing levels of the Glorig and Nixon (1960) non-noise-exposed, control, subjects are considerably higher than Spoor (1969) or ISO 7029 (ISO, 1984) normal hearing levels. Comparison of the Rosenwinkel and Stewart (1957) control group hearing levels with ISO 7029 levels shows even larger differences. It follows, of course, that the NIPTS found

TABLE 4A.2 Underestimation of 50%ile NIPTS, per Spoor, as Interpreted by Passcheir-Vermeer for Data of Nixon and Glorig (1961), and Gallo and Glorig (1964) Compared to NIPTS Found When Data from Those Studies Converted to Be per ISO 389 (ISO, 1985)

	1000 Hz	6000 Hz	Database: Gallo and Glorig					Database: Gallo and Glorig				
Age, years	HL, males spoor*	HL, males spoor*	1000 Hz apprx. yrs. exp/age¶	G&G HL¶	NIPTS (HL data per spoor)	NIPTS (HL P-V per spoor)§	Difference data − P-V	6000 Hz apprx. yrs. exp/age§	G&G HL§	NIPTS (HL data per spoor)	NIPTS (HL P-V per spoor)§	Difference data − P-V
22	0	0	2/20	10	10	0	10	2/20	12	12	3	9
25	0	2	4/23	10	10	0	10	4/23	15	13	5	8
30	1	4	7/25	11	11	2	9	7/25	23	19	9	10
35	1	8	10/30	12	11	2	9	10/30	30	22	18	4
40	2	12	14/35	15	13	3	10	14/35	44	33	21	12
45	3	17	17/38	17	14	5	9	17/38	51	35	24	11
50	5	22	23/45	20	16	5	11	23/45	49	28	24	4
55	6	28	31/56	21	15	5	10	31/56	53	26	18	8
			Average NIPTS data per ISO − NIPTS P-V = 10					Average NIPTS data per ISO − NIPTS P-V = 8				
			ASA (1951) to ISO 389, 0, 1 kHz = 10 dB					ASA (1951) to ISO 389, 0, 6 kHz = 9.5 dB				

Age, years	2000 Hz HL, males spoor*	HL, males 7029[†]	Database: Nixon and Glorig 2000 Hz apprx. yrs. exp/age[‡]	N&G HL[‡]	NIPTS (HL data per spoor)	NIPTS (HL P-V per spoor)[§]	Difference data − P-V	Database: Gallo and Glorig 2000 Hz apprx. yrs. exp/age[¶]	G&G HL[¶]	NIPTS (HL data per spoor)	NIPTS (HL P-V per spoor)[§]	Difference data − P-V
22	0	0	2/28	10	10	0	10	2/20	5	5	−1	6
25	1	0	6/34	11	10	0	10	4/23	7	7	−1	8
30	1	1	10/40	12	9	1	9	7/25	9	8	2	6
35	2	2	15/40	13	10	0	10	10/30	14	12	3	9
40	3	3	19/45	12	6	0	6	14/35	15	12	4	8
45	6	5	23/49	13	5	0	5	17/38	27	21	11	10
50	9	7	28/50	18	9	4	5	23/45	28	20	12	8
55	11	10	37/57	22	11	5	6	31/56	24	13	17	−4
			Average NIPTS data per ISO − NIPTS P-V = 8					Average NIPTS data per ISO − NIPTS P-V = 6				
			ASA (1951) to ISO 389, 0, 2 kHz = 8.5 dB					ASA (1951) to ISO 389, 0, 2 kHz = 8.5 dB				

Age, years	500 Hz HL, males spoor*	3000 Hz HL, males spoor*	Database: Gallo and Glorig 500 Hz apprx. yrs. exp/age[¶]	G&G HL[¶]	NIPTS (HL data per spoor)	NIPTS (HL P-V per spoor)[§]	Difference data − P-V	Database: Gallo and Glorig 3000 Hz apprx. yrs. exp/age[¶]	G&G HL[¶]	NIPTS (HL data per spoor)	NIPTS (HL P-V per spoor)[§]	Difference data − P-V
22	0	0	2/20	14	14	0	14	2/20	18	18	11	7
25	0	1	4/23	15	15	2	13	4/23	24	23	14	8
30	1	2	7/25	17	17	2	15	7/25	33	31	24	8
35	1	4	10/30	18	17	3	14	10/30	35	31	23	8
40	2	7	14/35	18	17	1	16	14/35	43	36	26	10
45	3	10	17/38	18	16	3	13	17/38	45	35	35	0
50	5	13	23/45	19	16	1	15	23/45	49	36	31	5
55	7	18	31/56	20	13	1	12	31/56	48	30	28	2
			Average NIPTS data − NIPTS P-V = 14					Average NIPTS data − NIPTS P-V = 6				
			ASA (1951) to ISO 389, 0, 0.5 kHz = 14 dB					ASA (1951) to ISO 389, 0, 3 kHz = 8.5 dB				

(*continues*)

TABLE 4A.2 *(Continued)*

	4000 Hz		Database: Nixon and Glorig					Database: Gallo and Glorig				
Age, years	HL, males spoor*	HL, males 7029†	4000 Hz approx. yrs. exp/age‡	N&G HL‡	NIPTS (HL data per spoor)	NIPTS (HL P-V per spoor)§	Difference data − P-V	4000 Hz approx. yrs. exp/age¶	G&G HL¶	NIPTS (HL data per spoor)	NIPTS (HL P-V per spoor)§	Difference data − P-V
22	1	0	2/28	12	11	1	10	6/25	26	25	17	8
25	1	1	6/34	17	16	4	12	10/30	42	40	35	5
30	3	2	10/40	25	22	11	12	14/35	51	45	40	5
35	6	5	15/40	26	20	10	10	17/38	54	46	42	4
40	10	8	19/45	31	21	14	7	23/45	55	41	39	2
45	14	12	23/49	31	17	11	6	31/56	55	32	34	−2
50	18	16	28/50	35	17	16	1	38/63	55	25	19	6
55	23	22	37/57	37	14	11	3	Average NIPTS data − NIPTS P-V = 4				
			Average NIPTS data − NIPTS P-V = 8					ASA (1951) to ISO 389, 0, 4 kHz = 6 dB				
			ASA (1951) to ISO 389, 0, 4 kHz = 6 dB									

* Spoor presbycusis data, per ISO 389, after Passcheir-Vermeer (1977). Screened males.

† Presbycusis ISO 7029 (ISO, 1984), 50%ILE, per ISO 389, screened males. Shown, by examples 2 and 4 kHz, to be similar to Spoor (1969) functions.

‡ Nixon and Glorig (1961), Table 1, 85 dB_A noise HLs corrected (+8.5 dB, 2000 Hz, +6 dB, 4000 Hz) per ISO 389; 1948 males screened. Nixon and Glorig published data only for audiometric test frequencies 2000 and 4000 Hz.

§ Passcheir-Vermeer (1968; 1974), Figs. 2, 3; 1968, Pages R 35-3, -4, -5 (Study E1, Nixon and Glorig, 1961; Study B, Gallo and Glorig, 1964).

¶ Gallo and Glorig (1964), Fig. 1 and, for age vs. years' exposure, Fig. 2. HLs corrected (+8.5 dB, 2000, 3000 Hz, +6 dB, 4000 Hz) per ISO 389; 400 males screened.

by Passcheir-Vermeer (1974) was less than would have been found by comparison of the noise-exposed workers hearing levels, converted to ISO 389 audiometric zero, with the presbycusis hearing levels of Spoor or ISO 7029, also per ISO 389.

Table 4A.2 shows (1) NIPTS for the Gallo and Glorig (1964) and Nixon and Glorig (1961) studies per Passchier-Vermeer (1974), (2) NIPTS found from subtracting Spoor (1969) presbycusis data from the measured hearing levels for the Gallo–Glorig and Nixon–Glorig studies corrected to ISO 389 and (3) the differences between the Passchier-Vermeer predicted and the measured NIPTS values. It is seen that (1) the NIPTS's per Passchier-Vermeer are, averaged over all age groups, 6–14 dB, depending on test frequency, smaller than is found by comparison of the hearing levels for the noise exposed workers with the Spoor presbycusis hearing levels; and (2) the differences are generally similar in magnitude to the decibel corrections required to convert hearing levels per ASA (1951) to ISO 389 (1985) standards, which should have made them suitable for comparison, for purposes of determining NIPTS, with Spoor or ISO 7029 presbycusis hearing levels.

The latter corrections are, on the average, but 1 dB greater than the NIPTS per P-V and the NIPTS per converted hearing-level data minus Spoor (1969) presbycusis. This finding indicates that whatever Passchier-Vermeer (1974) did with the Gallo and Glorig (1964) and Nixon and Glorig (1961) data it was not the equivalent, as claimed, of conversion of their hearing level data to ISO (1985) 389 audiometric zero for comparison to Spoor or ISO 7029 presbycusis data to estimate NIPTS. As seen in Table 4A.2, significantly larger NIPTS values are found when the hearing levels for these two studies are converted to the ISO 389 audiometric standard, and then compared to ISO 7029, or Spoor for NIPTS, than were deduced by Passchier-Vermeer.

CONCLUSION

ISO 1999 (1990) formulas for predicting NIPTS from exposure to occupational noise are based on empirical research data, or analyses thereof, that appear to be flawed in certain respects. For these reasons, it appears that less than appropriate amounts of NIPTS from exposure to steady noise will be estimated by the procedures prescribed for that purpose in ISO 1999. Restrictions regarding the application of ISO 1999 for assessment of impact and impulse noise are discussed in Chapter 5.

References

ANSI S3.6 (1969). "American National Standard for Audiometers." Am. Natl. Stand. Inst., New York.

ASA Z24.5 (1951). "American Standard Specification for Audiometers for General Diagnostic Purposes." Am. Stand. Assoc., New York.

ASA Z24-X-2 (1954). "The Relations of Hearing Loss to Noise Exposure." Am. Natl. Stand. Inst., New York.

Baughn, W. L. (1973). "Relation Between Daily Noise Exposure and Hearing Loss Based on the Evaluation of 6,835 Industrial Noise Exposure Cases," AMRL-TR-74-53. Joint EPA/USAF Study. 6570th Aerosp. Med. Res. Lab., Wright-Patterson AFB, Ohio.

Bergman, M. (1966). Hearing in the Mabaans—A critical review of related literature. *Arch. Otolaryngol.* **84,** 441–445.

Botsford, J. H. (1969). Prevalence of impaired hearing and sound levels at work. *J. Acoust. Soc. Am.* **45**, 79–82.

BSI (1954) 2497. "The Normal Threshold of Hearing for Pure Tones by Earphone Listening." Br. Stand. Inst., London.

Burns, W., and Hinchcliff, R. (1957). Comparison of the auditory threshold as measured by individual pure tone and the Bekesy audiometer. *J. Acoust. Soc. Am.* **29,** 1274–1277.

Burns, W., and Robinson, D. W. (1970). "Hearing and Noise in Industry." HM Stationery Off., London.

Burns, W., Robinson, D. W., Shipton, M. S., and Sinclair, A. (1977). "Hearing Hazard from Occupational Noise," NPL Acoust. Rep. AC 80. Nat. Phys. Lab., Teddington, England.

Chung, D. Y., Gannon, R. P., Willson, G. N., and Mason, K. (1991). Shooting, sensorineural loss, and worker's compensation. *J. Occup. Med.* **23,** 481–484.

Clark, W. W., and Popelka, G. (1989). Hearing levels of railroad trainmen, *Laryngoscope* **99,** 1151–1157.

Gallo, R., and Glorig, A. (1964). Permanent threshold shift changes produced by noise exposure and aging. *Am. Ind. Hyg. Assoc. J.* **23,** 237–245.

Glorig, A., Wheeler, D., Quiggle, R., Grings, W., and Summerfield, A. (1957). "1954 Wisconsin State Fair Hearing Survey: Statistical Treatment of Clinical and Audiometric Data." Amer. Academy Ophthalmology and Otolaryngology and Research Center on Noise in Industry, Los Angeles.

Glorig, A., and Nixon, J. (1960). Distribution of hearing loss in various populations. *Ann. Otol. Rhinol. Laryngol.* **69,** 497–516.

Glorig A., and Nixon, J. (1962). Hearing loss as a function of age. *Laryngoscope* **72,** 1596–1610.

Glorig, A., and Roberts, J. (1965). "Hearing Levels of Adults by Age and Sex, United States, 1960–1962," Rep. PHS-PUB-1000-SER-11-11. U.S. Dep. Health, Educ. Welfare, Washington, D.C.

Harris, J. D. (1964). Bekesy audiometry at 20 frequencies from .2 to 6 kc/sec (L). *J. Acoust. Soc. Am.* **36,** 1954–1964.

Hétu, R, Riverin, L, Getty, L, Lalande, N. M. and St-Cyr, C. (1990). The reluctance to acknowledge hearing difficulties among hearing impaired workers. *Br. J. Audiol.* **24,** 265–276.

Hinchcliffe R. (1959). The threshold of hearing as a function of age. *Acustica* **9,** 303–308.

ISO 7029. (1984). "Acoustics—Threshold of Hearing by Air Conduction as a Function of Age, and Sex for Otologically Normal Persons," Int. Organ. Stand., Geneva.

ISO 389 (1985). Acoustics—Standard Reference Zero for the Calibration of Pure Tone Air Conduction Audiometers," Int. Organ. Stand., Geneva.

ISO 1999 (1990). "Acoustics—Determination of Occupational Noise Exposure and Estimation of Noise-Induced Hearing Impairment." Int. Organ. Stand., Geneva.

Johnson, D. L. (1978). "Derivation of Presbycusis and Noise Induced Permanent Threshold Shift (NIPTS) to be Used for the Basis of a Standard on the Effects of Noise on Hearing," AMRL-TR-78-128. Aerosp. Med. Res. Lab., Wright-Patterson AFB, Ohio.

Johnson, D. L., and Riffle, C. (1982). Effects of gunfire on hearing level for selected individuals of the Inter-Industry Noise Study. *J. Acoust. Soc. Am.* **72,** 1311–1314.

Jokinen, K. (1969). Presbycusis 1. Comparison of manual and automatic thresholds. Acta Otolaryngol. **68,** 327–335.

Kell, R. L., Pearson, J. C., and Taylor, W. (1979). Hearing thresholds of an island population in north Scotland. *Int. Audiol.* **18,** 334–348.

Knight, J. (1966). Normal hearing threshold determined by manual and self-recording techniques (L). *J. Acoust. Soc. Am.* **39,** 1184–1185.

Kono, S., Sone, T., and Nimura, T. (1982). Personal reaction to daily noise exposure. *Noise Control Eng.* **19,** 4–7.

Kryter, K. D. (1983). Presbycusis, sociocusis, and nosocusis. *J. Acoust. Soc. Am.* **73,** 1897-1919; addendum and erratum (L), *J. Acoust. Soc. Am.* **74,** 1907-1909 (1983).

Kryter, K. D. (1991). Hearing loss from gun and railroad noise—relations with ISO Standard 1999. *J. Acoust. Soc. Am.* **90,** 3180–3195.

Kylin, B. (1960). Temporary threshold shift and auditory trauma following exposure to steady-state noise. *Acta Otolaryngol., Suppl.* No. 152.

Lempert, B. L., and Henderson, T. L. (1973). "Occupational Noise and Hearing," NIOSH-TR-201-74. Natl. Inst. Occup. Saf. Health, DHEW, Washington, D.C.

Lutman, M. E.; Brown, E. J.; Coles, R. R. A. (1987). Self-reported disability and handicap in the population in relation to pure-tone threshold, age, sex and type of hearing loss. *British. J. Audiol.* **21,** 45–58.

Lutman, M. E., and Spencer, H. (1991). Occupational noise and demographic factors in hearing. *Acta Otolaryngol: Suppl.* 476, 74–84.

Lutman, M. E.; Robinson, D. W. (1992). Quantification of hearing disability for medicolegal purposes based on self-rating. *British J. Audiol.* **26,** 297–306.

Lutman, M. E., Davis, A. and Spencer, H. (1993). Interpreting NIHL by comparison of noise exposed subjects with appropriate controls. *In "Noise as a Public Health Problem., 6th Proc. Int. Congr."* (M. Vallet, ed.), Vol. 3, pp. 114–121. l'Interets, 94114, Aruil Cedex, France.

NIOSH (1976). "Survey of Hearing Loss in the Coal Mining Industry," PB-271-811. Natl. Inst. Occup. Saf. Health, Cincinnati.

Nixon, J. C. and Glorig, A. (1961). Noise induced permanent threshold shift at 2000 and 4000 cps. *J. Acoust. Soc. Am.* **17,** 904–908.

Noble, W. G. (1978). "Assessment of Impaired Hearing—A Critique and a New Method," Academic Press, New York.

Passchier-Vermeer, W. (1968). "Hearing Loss Due to Exposure to Steady-State Broad Band Noise," Rep. 35. Res. Inst. Public Health Eng. Delft, Netherlands.

Passchier-Vermeer, W. (1974). Hearing loss due to continuous exposure to steady-state broad-band noise. *J. Acoust. Soc. Am.* **56,** 1585–1593.

Passchier-Vermeer, W. (1977). "Hearing Levels of Non-Noise Exposed Subjects and of Subjects Exposed to Constant Noise During Working Hours," Rep. B367. Res. Inst. Environ. Hyg., Delft, Netherlands.

Prosser, S., Tartari, M. C., and Arslan, E. (1988). Hearing loss in sports hunters exposed to occupational noise. *Br. J. Audiol.* **22,** 85–91.

Rice, C., and Coles, R. (1966). Normal threshold of hearing for pure tones by earphone listening with a self-recording technique (L). *J. Acoust. Soc. Am.* **39,** 1185–1187.

Riley, E. C., Sterner, J. H., Fassett, D. W., and Sutton, W. L. (1961). Ten years' experience with industrial audiometry. *Am. Ind. Hyg. Assoc. J.* **22,** 151–159.

Roberts, J., and Frederico, J. V. (1972). "Hearing Sensitivity and Related Medical Findings Among Children," Ser. 11—No. 114, DHEW Publ. No. (HSM) 72-1046. Natl. Cent. Health Serv. Res. Dev., U.S. Dep. Health, Educ., Welfare, Washington, D.C.

Roberts, J., and Huber, P. (1970). "Hearing Levels of Children by Age and Sex," Ser. 11—No. 102, DHEW Publ. Natl. Cent. Health Serv. Res. Dev., U.S. Dep. Health, Educ., Welfare, Washington, D.C.

Robinson, D. W. (1968). "The Relationships Between Hearing Loss and Noise Exposure," NPL Aero Rep. Ac 32. Natl. Phys. Lab., Teddington, England.

Robinson, D. W. (1970). Relationships between hearing loss and noise exposure, appendix 10. *In* "Hearing and Noise in Industry" (W. Burns and D.W. Robinson, eds.), pp. 100–151. Her Majesty's Stantionery Office, London.

Robinson, D. W. (1988). Threshold of hearing as a function of age and sex for the typical unscreened population. *Br. J. Audiol.* **22,** 5–20.

Robinson, D. W., and Shipton, M. S. (1977). "Tables for the Estimation of Noise-Induced Hearing Loss," NPL Acoust. Rep. Ac 61, 2nd Ed. Natl. Phys. Lab., Teddington, England.

Robinson, D. W., and Sutton, G. J. (1978). "A Comparative Analysis of Data on the Relation of Pure-Tone Audiometric Thresholds to Age," NPL Acoust. Rep. Ac84, Natl. Phys. Lab., Teddington, England.

Robinson, D., and Whittle, S. (1973). A comparison of self-recording and manual audiometer. *J. Sound Vib.* **26,** 42–62.

Roche, A. F., Siervogel, R. M., Himes, J. H., and Johnson, D. (1977). "Longitudinal Study of Human Hearing," Rep. AMRL-TR-76-110. Wright-Patterson AFB, Ohio. (Avail. from DTIC as AD A040 168.)

Rop, I., Raber, A., and Fischer, G. H. (1979). Study of hearing losses of industrial workers with occupational noise exposure, using statistical methods for the analysis of qualitative data. *Audiology* **18,** 181–196.

Rosenwinkel, N. E., and Stewart, K. C. (1957). The relationship of hearing loss to steady state noise exposure. *Am. Ind. Hyg. O.* **18,** 227-230.

Rosen, S., Bergman, M., Plester, D., El-Mofty, A., and Satti, M. (1962). Presbycusis study of a relatively noise-free population in the Sudan. *Ann. Otol. Rhinol. and Laryngol.* **71,** 727–743.

Royster, L. H., and Thomas, W. G. (1979). Age effect hearing levels for a white nonindustrial noise exposed population (NINEP) and their use in evaluating industrial hearing conversation programs. *J. Am. Ind. Hyg. Assoc.* **40,** 504–511.

Rudmose, W. (1963). Automatic audiometry. *In* "Modern Developments in Audiology" (J. Jerger, ed.) Chap. 2. Academic Press, New York.

Scheiblechner, H. (1974). The validity of the 'energy principle' for noise-induced hearing loss. *Audiology* **13,** 93–111.

Shipton, M. S. (1979). "Tables Relating Pure-Tone Audiometric Threshold to Age," NPL Acoust. Rep. Ac94. Natl. Phys. Lab., Teddington, England.

Spoor, A. (1969). Presbyacousis values in relation to noise induced hearing loss. *Int. Audiol.* **6,** 48–57.

Steinberg, J. C., Montgomery, H. C., and Gardner, M. B. (1940). Results of world's fair hearing tests. *J. Acoust. Soc. Am.* **12,** 291–301.

Stephens, S. (1971). "Occupational Hearing Loss" (D. Robinson, ed.), Academic Press, New York.

Sutherland, H. C., and Gasaway, D. C. (1978). "Current Hearing Threshold Levels for Noise-Exposed U. S. Air Force Personnel: One Year's Reportings," SAM-TR-78-39. USAF Sch. Aerosp. Med., Brooks AFB, Texas.

Taylor, W., Pearson, J., Mair, A., and Burns, W. (1965). Study of noise and hearing in jute weavers. *J. Acoust. Soc. Am.* **38,** 113–120.

Taylor, W., Pearson, J., and Nair, A. (1967). Hearing thresholds of a non-noise exposed population in Dundee. *Br. J. Ind. Med.* **24,** 114–122.

Taylor, W., Lempert, B., Pelmear, P., Hemstock, I., and Kershaw, J. (1984). Noise levels and hearing thresholds in the drop forging industry. *J. Acoust. Soc. Am.* **76,** 807–819.

Webster, J. C., Hines, H. W., and Lichtenstein, M. (1950). San Diego County Fair hearing survey. *J. Acoust. Soc. Am.* **22,** 473–483.

Yerg. R., Sataloff, J., Glorig, A., and Menduke, H. (1978). Inter Industry Noise Study—The effects upon hearing of steady state noise between 82 and 92 dBA. *J. Occup. Med.* **20,** 361–358.

Selected Bibliographies

1. Additional studies of sociocusis and industrial NIPTS

Abel, S. M., and Haythornthwaite, C. A. (1984). The progression of noise-induced hearing loss. A survey of workers in selected industries in Canada. *J. Otolaryngol. Suppl.* No. 13, 2–36.

Bauer, P., Korpert, K., Neuberger, M., Raber, A., and Schwetz, F. (1991). Risk factors for hearing loss at different frequencies in a population of 47,388 noise-exposed workers. *J. Acoust. Soc. Am.* **90,** 3086–3098.

Bergstrom, B., and Nystrom, B. (1986). Development of hearing loss during longterm exposure to occupational noise. A 20-year follow-up study. *Scand. Audiol.* **15,** 227–234.

Catalano, P., and Lewin, S. M. (1985). Noise-induced hearing loss and portable radio with headphones. *Int. J. Pediatr. Otorhinolaryngol.* **9,** 59–67.

Chavalitsakulchai, P., Kawakami, T., Kongmuang, U., Vivatjestsadawut, P., and Leongsrisook, W. (1989). Noise exposure and permanent hearing loss of textile workers in Thailand. *Ind. Health* **27** (4), 165–173.

Chen, T. J., Chiang, H. C., and Chen, S. S. (1992). Effects of aircraft noise on hearing and auditory pathway function of airport employees. *J. Occup. Med.* **34,** 613–619.

Chung, D. Y., Mason, K., Willson, G. N., and Gannon, R. P. (1983). Asymmetrical noise exposure and hearing loss among shingle sawyers. *J. Occup. Med.* **25,** 541–543.

Counter, S. A., and Klareskov, B. (1990). Hypoacusis among the Polar Eskimos of northwest Greenland. *Scand. Audiol,* **19,** 149–160.

Dobie, R. A. (1992). The relative contributions of occupational noise and aging in individual cases of hearing loss. *Ear Hear.* **13,** 19–27.

Dufresne, R. M., Alleyne, B. C., and Reesal, M. R. (1988). Asymmetric hearing loss in truck drivers. *Ear Hear.* **9,** 41–42.

Erlandsson, B., Hakanson, H., Ivarsson, A., Nilsson, P., and Sheppard, H. (1983). Hearing deterioration in shipyard workers. Serial audiometry over a four-year period. *Scand Audiol.* **12,** 265–271.

Gerling, I. J., and Jerger, J. F. (1985). Cordless telephones and acoustic trauma: a case study. *Ear Hear.* 6, 203–205.

Guyot, J. P. (1988). Acoustic trauma caused by the telephone. Report of two cases. *ORL J. Otorhinolaryngol. Relat. Spec.* **50,** 313–318.

Hessel, P. A., and Sluis-Cremer, G. K. (1987). Hearing loss in white South African goldminers. *S. Afr. Med. J.* **71,** 364–367.

Karlovich, R. S., Wiley. T. L., Tweed, T., and Jensen, D. V. (1988). Hearing sensitivity in farmers. *Public Health Rep.* **103,** 61–71.

Kawada, T., Koyama, H., and Suzuki, S. (1990). Decrease of hearing aciuity from use of portable headphones. *Jpn. J. Public Health.* **37,** 39–43.

Kristensen, S., and Gimsing, S. (1988). Occupational hearing impairment in pig breeders. *Scand. Audiol.* **17,** 191–192.

Kunov, H., Dajani, H., and Seshagiri, B. (1993). Measurement of noise exposure from communication headsets. *Noise Public Health Probl., Proc. Int. Congr., 6th* (M. Vallet, ed.), Vol. 2, pp.165–168. l'INRETS, 94114 Arcuil Cedex, France.

Lee, P.C., Senders, C. W., Gantz, B. J., and Otto, S. R. (1985). Transient sensorineural hearing loss after overuse of portable cassette radios. *Otolaryngol.—Head Neck Surg.* **93,** 622–625.

Macrae, J. H. (1991). Permanent threshold shift associated with overamplification by hearing aids. *J. Speech Hear. Res.* **34,** 403–414.

Mori, T. (1985). Effects of record music on hearing loss among workers in a shipyard. *Int. Arch. Occup. Environ. Health* **56,** 91–97.

Neuberge, M., Korpert, K., Raber, A., Schwetz, F., and Bauer, P. (1992). Hearing loss from industrial noise, head injury and ear disease. A multivariate analysis on audiometric examinations of 110,647 workers. *Audiology* **31,** 45–57.

Oishi, I., Ino, T., Koga, K., and Hanamoto, M. (1986). TTS2 after exposure to music by open-type headphones. *Audiol. Jpn.* **29,** 164–170.

Orchik, D. J., Schmaier, D. R., Shea, J. J., Jr., Emmett, J. R., Moretz, W. H., Jr., and Shea, J. J., 3d (1987). Sensorineural hearing loss in cordless telephone injury. *Otolaryngol. Head Neck Surg.* **96,** 30–33.

Ostri, B., and Parving, A. (1991). A longitudinal study of hearing impairment in male subjects—an 8-year follow-up. *Br. J. Audiol.* **25,** 41–48.

Ostri, B., Eller, N., Dahlin, E., and Skylv, G. (1989). Hearing impairment in orchestral musicians. *Scand. Audiol.* **18,** 243–249.

Plakke, B. L., and Dare, E. (1992). Occupational hearing loss in farmers. *Public Health Rep.* **107,** 188–192.

Polpathapee, S., and Chiwapong, S. (1986). Sensorineural hearing loss in longtailed motor boat drivers. *J. Med. Assoc. Thai.* **69,** 672–678.

Rice, C. G., Breslin, M., and Roper, R. G. (1987). Sound levels from personal cassette players. *Br. J. Audiol.* **21,** 273–278.

Rosenhall, U., Pedersen, K., and Svanborg, A. (1990). Presbycusis and noise-induced hearing loss. *Ear Hear.* **11,** 257–263.

Royster, J. D., Royster, L. H., and Killion, M. C. (1991). Sound exposures and hearing thresholds of symphony orchestra musicians. *J. Acoust. Soc. Am.* **89,** 2793–2803.

Thiery, L., and Meyer-Bisch, C. (1988). Hearing loss due to partly impulsive industrial noise exposure at levels between 87 and 90 dB (A). *J. Acoust. Soc. Am.* **84,** 651–659.

2. Ultra- and infra-frequencies, blasts, and vibration

Acton, W. I. (1983). Exposure to industrial ultrasound: hazards, appraisal and control. *J. Soc. Occup. Med.* **33,** 107–113.

Casler, J. D., Chait, R. H., and Zajtchuk, J. T. (1989). Treatment of blast injury to the ear. *Ann. Otol. Rhinol. Laryngol., Suppl.* No. 140, 13–16.

Grzesik, J., and Pluta, E. (1986). High-frequency-noise-induced hearing loss: a field study on the role of intensity level and accumulated noise dose. *Int. Arch. Occup. Environ. Health* **57,** 127–136.

Grzesik, J., and Pluta, E. (1986). Dynamics of high-frequency hearing loss of operators of industrial ultrasonic devices. *Int. Arch. Occup. Environ. Health* **57,** 137–142.

Hamernik, R. P., Ahroon, W. A., Davis, R. I., and Axelsson, A. (1989). Noise and vibration interactions: effects on hearing. *J. Acoust. Soc. Am.* **86,** 2129–2137.

Iki, M., Kurumatani, N., Hirata, K., Moriyama, T., Satoh, M., and Arai, T. (1986). Association between vibration-induced white finger and hearing loss in forestry workers. *Scand. J. Work Environ. Health* **12**(4, Spec. No.), 365–370.

Juntunen, J., Matikainen, E., Ylikoski, J., Ylikoski, M., Ojala, M., and Vaheri, E. (1987). Postural body sway and exposure to high-energy impulse noise. *Lancet* No. 8553, 261–264.

Kile, J. E., and Wurzback, W. F. (1980). Temporary threshold shifts induced by vibratory stimulation. *Sound Vib.* **14,** 26–29.

Miyakita, T., Miura, H., and Futatsuka, M. (1987). Noise-induced hearing loss in relation to vibration-induced white finger in chain-saw workers. *Scand. J. Work Environ. Health* **13,** 32–36.

Pyykko, I., Pekkarinen, J., and Starck, J. (1987). Sensory-neural hearing loss during combined noise and vibation exposure. An analysis of risk factors. *Int. Arch. Occup. Environ. Health* **59,** 439–454.

Pyykko, I., Aalto, H., and Ylikoski, J. (1989). Does impulse noise induce vestibular disturbances? *Acta Otolaryngol., Suppl.* No. 468, 211–216.

Roberto, M., Hamernik, R. P., and Turrentine, G. A. (1989). Damage of the auditory system associated with acute blast trauma. *Ann. Otol. Rhinol. Laryngol., Suppl.* No. 140, 23–34.

Starck, J., Pekkarinen, J., and Pyykko, I. (1988). Impulse noise and hand–arm vibration in relation to sensory neural hearing loss. *Scand. J. Work Environ. Health* **14,** 265–271.

Ylikoski, J., Juntunen, J., Matikainen, E., Ylikoski, M., and Ojala, M. (1988). Subclinical vestibular pathology in patients with noise-induced hearing loss from intense impulse noise. *Acta Otolaryngol.* **105,** 558–563.

3. Susceptibility to NIPTS

Attias, J., and Pratt, H. (1984). Auditory evoked potentials and audiological follow-up of subjects. *Audiology* **23,** 498–508.

Attias, J., and Pratt, H. (1985). Auditory-evoked potential correlates of susceptibility to noise-induced hearing loss. *Audiology* **24,** 149–156.

Barrenas, M. L., and Lindgren, F. (1990). The influence of inner ear melanin on susceptibility to TTS in humans. *Scand. Audiol.* **19,** 97–102.

Barrenas, M. L., and Lindgren, F. (1991). The influence of eye colour on susceptibility to TTS in humans. *Br. J. Audiol.* **25,** 303–307.

Bergman, M., Najenson, T., Korn, C., Harel, N., Erenthal, P., and Sachartov, E. (1992). Frequency selectivity as a potential measure of noise damage susceptibility. *Br. J. Audiol.* **26,** 15–22.

Conlee, J. W., Abdul-Baqi, K. J., McCandless, G. A., and Creel, D. J. (1986). Differential susceptibility to noise-induced permanent threshold shift between albino and pigmented guinea pigs. *Hear. Res.* **23,** 81–91.

Conlee, J. W., Abdul-Baqi, K. J., McCandless, G. A., and Creel, D. J. (1988). Effects of aging on normal hearing loss and noise-induced threshold shift in albino and pigmented guinea pigs. *Acta Otolaryngol.* **106,** 64–70.

Kleinstein, R. N., Seitz, M. R., Barton, T. E., and Smith, C. R. (1984). Iris color and hearing loss. *Am. J. Optom. Physiol. Opt.* **61,** 145–149.

Pye, A. (1987). Comparison of various short noise exposures in albino and pigmented guinea pigs. *Arch. Otorhinolaryngol.* **243,** 411–416.

Sikora, M. A., Morizono, T., Ward, W. D., Paparella, M. M., and Leslie, K. (1986). Diet-induced hyperlipidemia and auditory dysfunction. *Acta Otolaryngol.* **102,** 372–381.

Yanz, J. L., Herr, L. R., Townsend, D. W., and Witkop, C. J., Jr. (1985). The questionable relation between cochlear pigmentation and noise-induced hearing loss. *Audiology* **24,** 260–268.

Derivation of a General Theory and Procedure for Predicting Hearing Loss from Exposure to Sound

INTRODUCTION

Chapter 4 describes the E_A and EE_A procedures for predicting hearing loss from exposure to industrial noises that are more-or-less continuous throughout the workday. More useful, of course, would be a method for predicting hearing loss from daily exposures to sounds in general—either continuous or interrupted, steady or impulsive in nature.

In this chapter, a modified EE_A model for this more general purpose is developed. This procedure is based on theory and data, from both humans and animals, about (1) transmission and transformation of spectral sound energy by the outer and middle ear; (2) excitation, in time, of sensorineural elements in the inner ear; and (3) recovery, in time, from auditory 'fatigue' (metabolic and/or structural) resulting from this excitation. The ability of this new EE_A, compared to the equal energy and the OSHA models, to predict temporary (TTS) and permanent (NIPTS) threshold shifts from exposure to continuous, and interrupted, steady and impulsive sound is demonstrated. Approximate "true" and "practical" thresholds of effective quiet—the maximum level of exposure that will not cause a threshold shift—are also derived.

First, however, the history and theory of the A-weighted equal-energy (E_A) and the initial effective-energy (EE_A) procedures are briefly reviewed.

EQUAL- AND EFFECTIVE-ENERGY MODELS FOR PREDICTING NIPTS

Equal-Energy Models

In 1956 the U.S. Air Force published a regulation, AFR 160-3, aimed at the protection of the hearing of civilian and military workers at Air Force bases (AFR, 1956). This regulation was based on the proposition that the potential adverse effect of noise on the threshold of hearing was a function of the amount of energy in daily exposures to noises above a certain total level (Eldred *et al.*, 1955). Accordingly, exposure time and sound intensity were taken to be equally proportionally hazardous to hearing sensitivity, i.e., a doubling of the intensity of a noise, and keeping its duration the same, would cause the same amount of NIPTS as would doubling its duration, and keeping its intensity the same. The equal-energy concept holds that the effects of an amount of sound energy are equivalent when they are from either (1) a continuous sound over a specified period of time or (2) the sum of segments of sound occurring during the specified period of time. The quantity proposed in the Air Force regulation was labeled *equivalent exposure time* (EET).

On the basis of a study conducted by the British government (Burns and Robinson, 1970), this equivalent-, or equal-, energy theory was enlarged to include energy from work-years of exposure as a predictor of threshold shifts from a career of working in noise. As was discussed in Chapter 4, using the data from that study, Robinson (1968, 1970) developed an A-weighted equal-energy quantity, called E_A, for predicting NIPTS. The rather widely used Passchier-Vermeer (1974, 1977) and ISO 1999 (1990) procedures for estimating NIPTS, discussed in Appendix A of Chapter 4, are also based on the equal-energy concept.

It is the custom, as shown in Chapter 1, to (1) integrate the squared instantaneous sound pressures, divided by a squared reference pressure, sampled over a specified period of time; (2) divide that sum by the number of seconds in the period of time; and (3) convert the results to decibels (the logarithm, base 10, of the result multipled by 10). Equivalent A-weighted level L_{Aeq}, is the amount of varying-intensity sound energy in a specifed period equivalent to that of a continuous sound of the same 1-s level for the entire specified period. That period of time is typically chosen to be 8 h, the duration of exposure in the usual workday. Mathematical expressions for exposure energy, according to the concept of equal energy in steady continuous sounds (or, equivalent-to-continuous energy, with interrupted or intensity-varying sounds) are

$$L_{Aeq,n_1,} = L_{An_1} - 10 \log (T/t), \text{ dB}. \qquad (5.1)$$

where L_{An_1} is a level ±2.5 dB, of 10 log (*A*-weighted $sp^2/20\ \mu Pa^2$), above a threshold level of L_A for NIPTS after a work career of exposure; *T* is the number of seconds in the specified period; and *t* is number of seconds L_A is present during the specified period. As given in Chapter 1, *P* refers to the integrated samples of squared instantaneous sound pressures, $pi,^2$ averaged over, usually, 1-s intervals, and SPL (*L*, L_A) refers to 10 times the logarithm of that average divided by 400, the square of the reference pressure, and instantaneous, *i*, is taken to be as 0.00002 s. The range of ±2.5 dB is a common allowance for inherent variability encountered in the measurement of sound by sound-level meters, and is so specified in ISO Standard 1999 (1990).

$$L_{Aeq8h,n_1} = 10 \log (28{,}800/t), \text{ dB}, \tag{5.2}$$

where 28,800 is the number of seconds in 8 h.

$$L_{Aeq8h,n_1 \cdots nx} = 10 \log 10^{(L_{Aeq8h,n_1} + \cdots nx)/10)}, \text{ dB} \tag{5.3}$$

where $n_1 \cdots n_x$ are levels of L_A, in 5-dB steps, above some specified long-term threshold for NIPTS.

AFR 160-3, and ISO Standard 1999, follow the equal-energy rule in the calculation of L_{Aeq8h} exposure levels for estimating the effects on NIPTS of interrupted and <8-h durations. Accordingly, the preceding equations are applicable to noise environments consisting of a single continuous, or of a number of individual nonimpulsive, broad-frequency spectrum "steady" noise events, during an 8-h workday. It is recognized that "L_{Aeq8h}" for industrial noise exposures actually cover about 9 clock hours, when lunch and other breaks are included. These interval are seldom included in industrial noise-exposure calculations for practical reasons.

OSHA "5-dB Rule," an Effective-Energy Method for Predicting NIPTS

The U.S. Occupational Safety and Health Administration (OSHA. 1969, 1981, 1983) adopted a noise quantity which, compared to the equal-energy, L_{Aeq8h}, quantity underrates the hazard to be expected from intermittent and < 8-h noise exposures. This metric, called *time-weighted average* (TWA), is proportional to, herein labeled, $L_{Aeq8h,osha}$:

$$L_{Aeq8h,osha,n} = L_{An} - 16.6 \log (28{,}800/t), \tag{5.4}$$

where *n* is an L_A level, ±2.5 dB, above 90 : 28,800 is the number of seconds in 8 h, and *t* is the number of seconds during the 8-h day that n is present.

$$L_{Aeq8h,osha,n_1 \cdots n_x} = 16.6 \log 10^{(L_{Aeq8h,osha,n_1} + \cdots n_x/10)}, \tag{5.5}$$

where $n_1 \cdots n_x$ are levels of L_A, in 5-dB steps, above 90.

It appears from a report of the National Institute of Occupational Safety and Health (NIOSH, 1972), that the OSHA "5-dB rule" is an estimate based on, primarily, qualitative results of some field studies of NIPTS, and laboratory studies of TTS, due to exposures to intermittent noise. The data from some of the laboratory studies will be shown later.

EE_A, an Effective Energy Method for Predicting NIPTS

The equal-energy concept holds that the time between interrupted noise events during a day does not reduce hazard to hearing sensitivity, provided the total amount of energy received during the day is kept constant. However, most TTS and PTS data for noncontinuous noise conditions are at odds with the equal-energy concept.

As an alternative to the equal-energy concept, an *effective-energy* concept, has been proposed (Kryter, 1970, 1973, 1985). In keeping with that general concept, it was concluded that the effective, for the generation of TTS and NIPTS, energy per workday from steady noise is proportional to the quantities, or their equivalents, $E''L_{Aeq8h,n}$ and $E''L_{Aeq8h,n_1} \cdots n_x$:

$$E''L_{Aeq8h,n_1} = L_{A,n_1} - 20 \log(28{,}800/t),\ e\mathrm{dB}''n_1 \qquad (5.6)$$

where n is an L_A, ±2.5 dB, above L_A 60; 28,800 is number of seconds in 8 h; and t is number of seconds L_{A,n_1} is present in the 8 h. In the calculation, or measurement, of an edB″n, the seconds of time the noise level n is present during the 8-h day are not necessarily consecutive. The bases for choosing L_A 60 as a suitable threshold level for n, threshold of effective noise for threshold shift, will be presented later in the Chapter. The -20 log (T/t) term, where T is usually 28,800 s, represents an effective energy principle. Research findings in support of that term will be presented later.

$$E''LAeq8h,n_1 \ldots n_x = 10 \log 10(e\mathrm{dB}''n_1 \ldots e\mathrm{dB}''n_x)/10,\ e\mathrm{dB}''n_1 \ldots e\mathrm{dB}''n_x. \qquad (5.7)$$

where $n_1 \cdots n_x$ are levels of L_A, in 5-dB steps, above L_A 60.

For equal hazard of NIPTS, L_{Aeq8h}, equal energy, allows a 3-dB reduction, $L_{Aeq8h,osha}$ allows a 5-dB reduction, and $E''L_{Aeq8h,\ \mathrm{effective\ energy}}$ allows a 6-dB reduction in sound-pressure level with each halving of on-time duration of a noise during an 8-h workday. The terms L_{Aeq8h}, $L_{A8h,osha}$, and $E''L_{Aeq8h}$ are all, of course, numerically equal when applied to an 8-h, or other fixed, period of continuous exposure to steady-state noise. Some further extensions to $E''L_{Aeq8h,n_1}$, [Eq (5.6)] and $E''L_{Aeq8h,n_1 \cdots n_x}$ [Eq (5.7)] are developed later in this chapter to allow for prediction of hearing loss from exposures to temporally complex noise environments.

RESPONSE CHARACTERISTICS OF THE EAR TO STIMULATION

The relative effects on TTS and PTS of variations in the spectral content of sound on sensorineural activity have been reasonably well researched and quantified. However, the effects on TTS and PTS of variations in the distribution of sound energy in the temporal domain are not as well understood (Ward, 1991). Nevertheless, information useful to the quantification of various temporal effects, and the development of a model for their prediction from physical measures of noise, are extracted below from data pertaining to some basic functional characteristics of the auditory system.

The 0.5-s Time Constant of the Ear and Sensorineural Activity

Figure 2.8 showed that increasing the duration of a sound beyond 0.5 s, keeping intensity constant, does not result in an apparent increase in subjective loudness, or in the ability to discriminate among loudnesses. This fact, presumably, indicates that with a constant input intensity of sound a stable rate of neural response activity is generated at, and beyond, that duration.

Figure 2.8 shows that the duration at which this temporal integration process becomes constant is somewhat different for different frequencies. However, in view of the relatively small differences involved, and for the purpose of simplifying sound measurements, this time constant is taken for present purposes to be 0.5 s for all frequencies and intensities.

As was also seen in Fig. 2.8, to maintain equal loudness detectability (and presumably equal sensorineural activity) the intensity of sounds of <0.5-s duration must be increased proportionately to the reduction in their duration times below 0.5 s. That is, with stimulation durations of less than ~0.5 s, it is not the sums of the squared instantaneous pressure intensities, but the averages of the sums of squared instantaneous pressure intensities [including zeros] sampled at a specified rate over an entire 0.5 s that must be equal for equal response.

It is estimated that the upper left-hand terminus of a curve on Fig. 2.8 for lowest audible frequencies would be reached with a minimum duration of ~0.012 s. The ultimate terminus of the upper left-hand point is presumed to be reached with a minimum duration commensurate with the highest audible frequency (around 20,000 Hz, or 0.00002 s). Note that a sound of <0.012-s duration will have a low-frequency roll off below ~20 Hz, the lower limit of audibility for pitch, and with a rise time of less than 0.00002, a high-frequency roll off above 20,000 Hz (see Fig. 1.6).

Empirical data will be presented later that demonstrate the efficacy of measuring the energy averaged over 0.5 s as the basic unit for estimating the effective, as a cause of threshold shift of frequency-weighted steady or impulsive sounds. As was shown in Chapter 3, the 0.5-s time constant is also an important aspect of the elicitation of the subjective sensations of loudness and perceived noisiness.

Definitions of Continuous and Interrupted Steady and Impulse Sounds

Although it is a somewhat arbitrary definition, an impulse of sound is said to occur when the *A*-weighted, rms level of a sample of pressures in near-instantaneous "slices" of time within a 0.5-s segment of time is ⩾10 dB higher than the rms level of an adjacent 0.5s segment of time. All other segments of sounds, whether of 0.5 s or longer in duration, are classified as steady. The response characteristics of the ear shown in Fig. 2.8 indicate that it would be appropriate to thusly define sounds for purposes of predicting amounts of sensorineural activation.

In accordance with the time constant of the ear, it is postulated that the effective energy for sensorineural auditory stimulation as related to loudness, perceived noisiness, auditory fatigue, and, possibly, other auditory phenomena, is the average, rms, of instantaneous samples of pressure taken over 0.5-s segments of time. For perceived noisiness, auditory fatigue, and certain other auditory phenomena (but not for loudness, which tends to remain at a steady level, see Chapter 3) of sounds that last for more than 0.5 s, the total effective energy is proportional to the sum of the effective energies in the 0.5-s segments.

Continuous steady or impulsive sound is defined as occurring over the period of time when the effective level in consecutive 0.5-s segments ($L_{A0.5\,s}$) does not vary more than ±2.5 dB. The effective energy of exposures of continuing steady or impulsive segments of sound longer than 0.5 s (L_{Aex}) depends on the particular attribute or effect studied (loudness, perceived noisiness, auditory fatigue).

For the period(s) of time, the effective sound level, 0.5-s segments, becomes 5 or more dB less than the immediately preceding 0.5-s effective level, the previous effective noise level is said to be interrupted. For interrupted exposures, the effective energy is taken to be, with some modifications to be described, as

Step 1: 10 log of the sum of the effective energies in the 0.5-s segments the sound is present in a period of time
Step 2: That sum minus 20 log of the number of 0.5-s intervals the sound is not present in that period of time [see Eq. (5.6)]

These relations are expressed in formulas (given below) that are applicable to the assessment of the effective energy level of either steady or impulsive sounds. Further, they are to be used with either continuous or, with limits to be specified later, interrupted nature. The quantities of sound energy are given in decibels. In measuring sound energy, pressure intensities should be sampled at about twice the rate per second of the highest significantly audible frequency components involved. For practical reasons, as has been discussed, A-weighting is cited in the following formulas. However, other frequency weightings may also be appropriately used.

Formulae for Modified E″LAeq8h

The units and terms of the E″LAeq8h formulas are modified as follows:

$$L_{A0.5s,n_1} = 10 \log ((^1/_x)10^{(L_{A,1_i} \,.\,.\, L_{A,x_i}/10)}), \text{ dB.} \qquad (5.8)$$

Where n is a specified LA level, ±2.5 dB; $LA,1_i$ is the first, in the 0.5 s interval (10 log of A-weighted instantaneous pressure-sample, 1 pi^2, divided by 20 μPa^2) and LA,x_i, is the last sample, xpi^2, in the 0.5 s interval. Note: 7500 samples of pi per 0.5 s is generally considered as an adequate, practical number to be measured, or estimated for A-, or similarly weighted, sounds inasmuch as such weightings are designed to progressively diminish energy in frequencies >~5000 Hz, and a sampling rate of 1.5 per 0.5 s of the highest frequency of interest is considered to be an adequate rate.

$$E''L_{Aeq,n_1} = L_{A0.5\ s,n_1} - 20\log(T/t) = edB''n_1 \tag{5.9}$$

where T is a specified period of time in seconds, and t is number of 0.5 s $L_{A0.5\ s,n_1}$ is present during the specified period of time [The empirical basis for the -20 log (T/t) term will be presented later.]

$$E''L_{Aeq8h,n_1} = L_{A0.5\ s,n_1} - 20\log(T/57{,}600) = edB''n_1, \tag{5.10}$$

where 57,600 is 0.5 s intervals in 8 h, and t is number of 0.5-s intervals that $edB''n_1$ is present during the 8 h.

$$E''L_{Aeq,8h,n_1-x} = 10\log 10^{(edB''n_1 + \ \cdots\ edB''n,x)/10} = edB''n_1 - n_x, \tag{5.11}$$

where $n_1 \cdots n_x$ represents levels of $edBn_1 \ldots n_x$ present during 8 h that differ from each other by ⩾5 dB.

In the text, tables and figures to follow, measured, calculated, and estimated sound levels will be based on the 0.5-s unit of time, unless otherwise specified. When only steady sounds longer than 1 s are to be evaluated, the more common 1-s rms levels and T = 28,800 s may, of course, be used with $edBn$ and $E''L_{Aeq8h,n}$.

Examples of the application of Eq. (5.8) for estimating the effective energy of different numbers of 0.012-s duration noise bursts in a 0.5-s segment of time are

Level L_A* in 0.012s Slice(s)	Number of slices with $L_{A0.012\ s}$ 100 and $L_{A\ 0.012\ s}$ 60 of other slices	Effective energy 0.5 s†
L_A 100, impulse	1, others <60 L_A	84, $edBn$,0.5s
L_A 100, impulse	10, others <60 L_A	90, $edBn$,0.5s
L_A 100, impulse	20, others <60 L_A	93, $edBn$,0.5s
L_A 100, impulse	41.7, All 100 L_A‡	100, $edBn$,0.5s

* $L_{A0.012\ s}$ = 10 log $(1/x(pi,1^2 \cdot\cdot pi,x^2/400))$, $edB_{0.0125\ s}$·; x = no of samples in 0.012 s.
‡41.7, 0.012-s intervals in 0.5 s. $edBn = 10\log((1/47.1)10^{(L_A0.0125 + \cdot\cdot\ L_A0.55)10)}$, edB_n.

RECOVERY CHARACTERISTICS OF THE EAR AND MODIFICATIONS OF MODEL

Recovery from Sensorineural Fatigue

Auditory fatigue is said to be present when sensorineural receptors have not returned to a normal state of responsiveness at some given time after they have been stimulated by sound. It is postulated that the amount of TTS found at a given moment in time after stimulation is an index to the relative amount of sensorineural activation, and generation of fatigue, that has taken place. It is presumed that recovery from such fatigue is achieved through the expenditure of metabolic energy at the sensorineural level. The losses in hearing sensitivity due to structural damage within the cochlea may also be involved, as will be discussed later.

It appears that there are three broad recovery processes that need to be considered with respect to the development of TTS and PTS: (1) that during exposure, (2) that between exposures during a day, and (3) that between days of exposure. The quantification of the third factor is believed to be approximately expressed by the term 8 log (12,500/days of exposure), as derived in Chapter 4. (12,500 days, 50 years, with an average of 250 days of exposure to a given noise environment per year).

Recovery during Exposure

In order for the ear to maintain a continuing level of sensorineural response activity during prolonged stimulation, some recovery from auditory fatigue must, ostensibly, occur during stimulation. If so, it would follow, that the longer the exposure time, the less would be the TTS measurable at termination of equal energy exposures. That is, because there would be more time for recovery during stimulation, there should be less fatigue at the end of a longer duration, lower intensity than a shorter duration, higher intensity, equal energy exposure. That proposition is supported, to some degree, by data from several experiments.

Figure 5.1 shows TTS in human subjects from uninterrupted exposures to octave band and pink noise (random noise having octave bands of equal sound pressure levels), and TTS in chinchillas exposed to an octave band of noise. For humans, the TTS grew, on the average, at a rate of about 1.2 dB of intensity, and about 1.6 dB per "decibels" of time (10 log seconds) from exposure to an octave band of noise, and respectively, 1.5 and 1.7 dB from exposure to pink noise. The human ear appears to not respond equally, but nearly so, to time and intensity as measured.

For the chinchilla, TTS grew at the rate of about 0.9 dB per decibel of intensity, and ~3.0 dB per decibel of time. The rate of growth of TTS in the chinchilla appeared to accelerate somewhat when the durations were longer than ~200 min. These data show a large difference between the human and

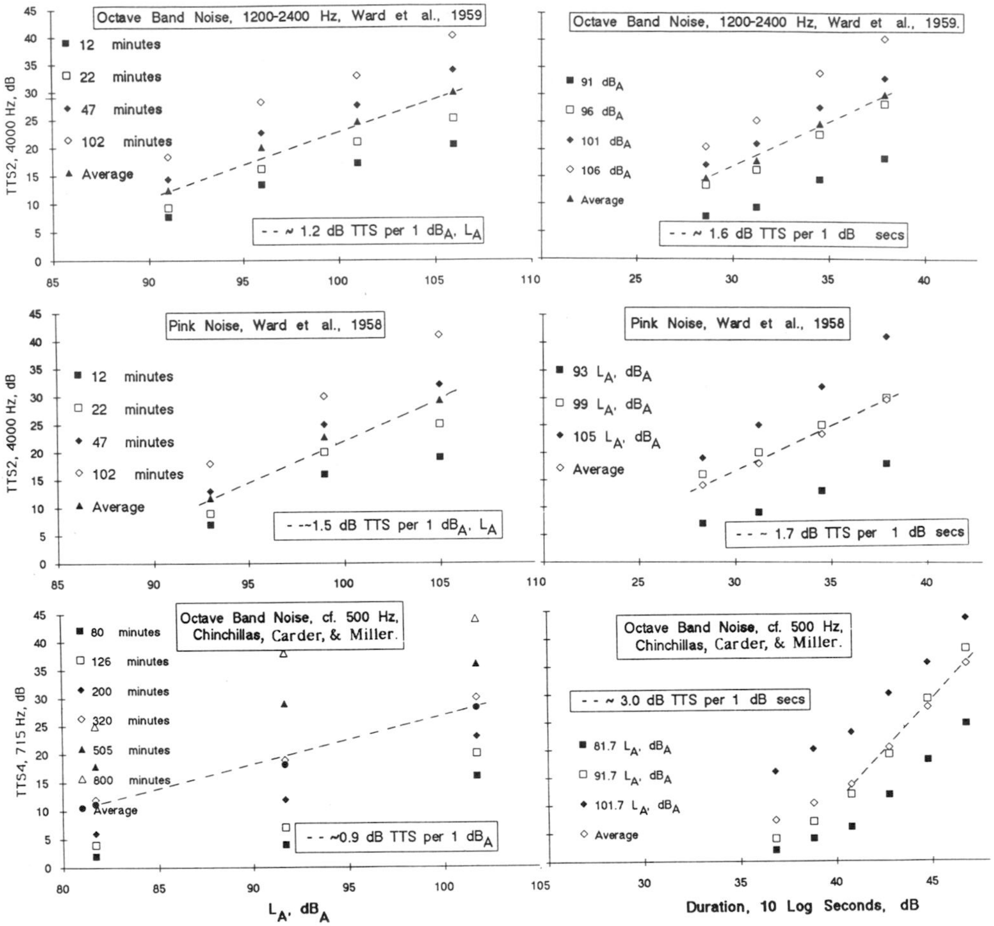

FIGURE 5.1 Growth of TTS from exposure to octave-band noise in humans and in chinchillas as functions of (left-hand graphs), intensity, with duration as parameter; and (right-hand graphs), exposure duration, with intensity as parameter.

chinchilla ear with respect to differential sensitivity to intensity energy versus duration energy of sound in causing TTS. This finding possibly illustrates the need for some caution in generalizing data among animal species.

Other studies with humans have shown that TTS's from exposures to intense tones and broadband sounds of relatively short duration are significantly greater than the TTSs from longer-duration, but equal-energy, exposures to the same sounds (Davis *et al.*, 1943; Spieth and Trittipoe, 1958). The data tabulated on the upper right corner of Fig. 5.2 show this result; For instance, sounds of 16 versus 32 min duration: the latter were 3 dB greater in duration energy but gave about the same TTS at a given post

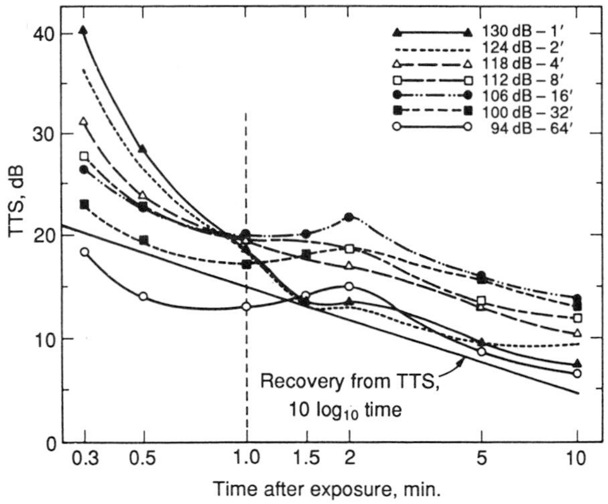

FIGURE 5.2 Threshold shifts at 4000 Hz following exposure to each of the conditions listed. (From Spieth and Trittipoe, 1958. Copyright 1958 by the American Psychological Association. Adapted by permission of the author.)

exposure time even though the intensity of the latter was 6 dB less, 106 versus 100 dB.

An implication of the data in Figs. 5.1 and 5.2 is that some recovery from auditory fatigue ensues during auditory stimulation. At the very least, these data indicate that the equal energy hypothesis, which predicts equal TTS from equal exposure level, is not compatible with the growth and recovery of TTS during noise stimulation. However, the equal-energy concept was based largely on PTS, not TTS data. Whether PTS and TTS are similarly related to exposure level is a question to be discussed later.

Recovery between Exposures during a Day (Off-Time Periods)

Consider packaging equal amounts of sound energy so that, in one case, one-fourth of the energy is due to pressure intensity spread over three-fourths of an 8-h day, and, in a second case, one-fourth of the energy is due to duration and three-fourths to pressure intensity. Obviously, there is less off-time in the first case than in the second for recovery from possible auditory fatigue (2 as compared to 6 h).

For these examples of equal-energy sounds, the 20 log off-time term [-20 log T/t of Eqs. (5.6) and (5.10)], reduces the magnitude of the effective exposure level, $E''L_{Aeq8h,n}$ of the second case relative to that of the first. This provides more allowance for recovery experienced during (1) off-time periods of a noise; and (2) prolonged-, relative to short-, duration exposures than that is given in the 10 log off-time term used in the calculation of equal energy exposure level, $L_{Aeq8h.}$

The -20 log term is predicated on the hypothesis that the amount of sensorineural activity, and generation of fatigue, is proportional to the amount of effective energy of the sound as a stimulus, and that recovery is proportional to the sum of recovery in on- and off-times. Support for the $E''L_{Aeq8h}$ formula with respect to TTS is shown in the graph in Fig. 5.3A. That graph illustrates the growth of TTS as a function of duration of exposures to noise for 4 h in the morning work-hours (8–12 AM), and afternoon (1–5 PM) at 92 and 98 L_A, and for 8 h (8–12 AM plus 1–5 PM) at levels, in 3-dB steps, from L_A 86 to 104. Also shown are typical rates of recovery from TTS following those exposures.

The straight-line growth of TTS functions on Fig. 5.3A are based on a formula fitted by Ward *et al.* (1959) to the data points shown in Fig. 5.3A. The formula is TTS $= 0.61(L - 70)(\log t + 0.33)$-9.5, where t is exposure time in minutes. The straight-line recovery functions in Fig. 5.3a are based on a formula fitted by Ward *et al.* (1959a) to the data shown in the left graph of Fig. 5.3B. The formula is $\text{TTS}_t = \text{TTS}_2(1 - {}^{(\log (t/2)/(1.5 + 0.045\ \text{TTS}_2))}$. The recovery functions in Fig. 5.3A, where TTS_2 exceeded 40 dB, are estimates based on recovery data such as shown in right graph of Fig. 5.3B, from Ward, 1970.

It is very unusual to find situations in industry, the military services, or elsewhere, where a single, typical day's exposure to noise will cause more than 40 dB TTS_2. Accordingly, it is realistic, it is believed, to consider the

A

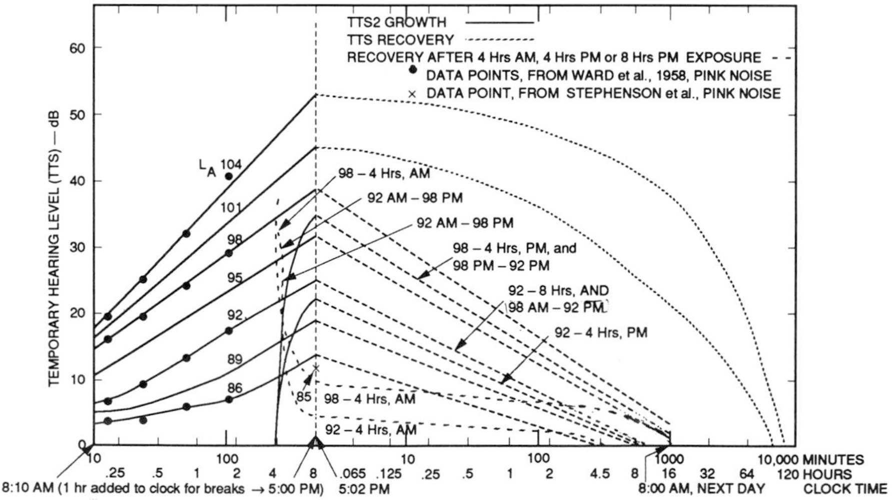

FIGURE 5.3A Idealized growth of, and recovery from, TTS at 4000 Hz, from uninterrupted exposures for 4 and 8 h to broadband noise.

B

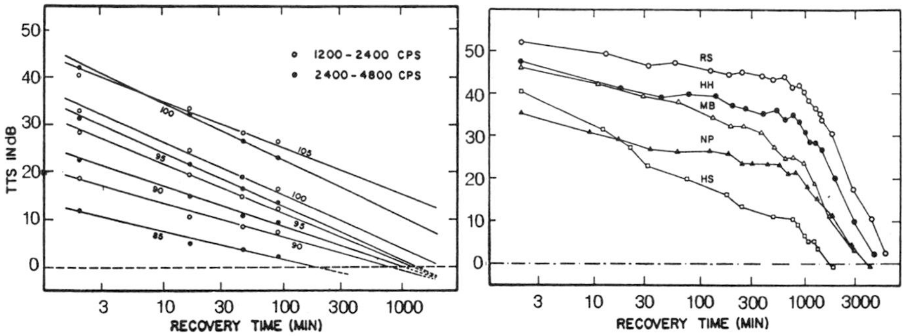

FIGURE 5.3B Left graph: course of recovery from TTS at 4000 Hz following exposure to various, indicated, levels of noise at 1200–2400 Hz (open circles), and 2400–4000 Hz (solid circles). (From Ward *et al.*, 1959. Copyright 1959 by the American Psychological Association. Adapted by permission of the author.) Right graph: the average course of recovery from TTS at 3000 and 4000 Hz, right and left ears combined, for 5 subjects, following exposure to 105-dB SPL at 1200–2400 Hz band of noise whose duration was sufficient to produce 30-dB TTS_2 at either 3000 or 4000 Hz in one of the two ears of a given subject. (From Ward, 1961. Copyright 1961 by the American Psychological Association. Adapted by permission of the author.)

TTS growth and recovery functions for maximum TTS_2 of less than ~40 dB to be suitable for comparisons to be made later with NIPTS data.

Note in Fig. 5.3A that before any recovery, the amount of TTS2 after 4 h PM exposure at L_A 98 is greater than after 8 h to noise at a level of 3 dB less, L_A 95. According to the equal energy concept the TTS_2 for these exposure should be equal. This again demonstrates the afore discussed recovery-during-exposure phenomenon that longer duration exposures cause less auditory fatigue than do shorter, but equal-energy, exposures. For the exposures causing TTS_2 of less than ~40 dB, the growth and recovery curves shown in Fig. 5.3A are nearly symmetrical.

It is not, of course, only TTS_2 that is of potential value for estimating eventual NIPTS. The assessment of the amount of residual auditory fatigue that will be present the next day, at the start of a repeated noise-exposure cycle, may be crucial to the accumulation of a NIPTS. It could be argued that if there were no measurable TTS present when subsequent noise exposures were imposed on the ear, no NIPTS could be expected. This position may be unwarranted, however, in that audiometric thresholds do not necessarily reveal incipient permanent effects of auditory fatigue.

As seen in Fig. 5.3A, immediate auditory fatigue, TTS_2, increased by ~4 dB (from ~35–39) when intensity was 3 dB greater, but duration of 3 dB less (e.g., L_A 95 with 8 h of exposure, versus L_A 98 with 4 h of exposure). In addition, residual TTS was somewhat greater for the shorter-duration, higher-intensity combination by the end of the day and by the start of the next day.

Short-time (<2-s and >15-s) Postexposure Recovery Factors

It seems clear that TTS, and presumably PTS, are significantly influenced by recovery from stimulation both during and after stimulation. Auditory fatigue, at least TTS, from intermittent noise is also influenced by (1) a brief poststimulus refractory-for-recovery period immediately following cessation, or reduction in level, of the sound; and (2) an accelerated recovery that occurs following the poststimulation refractory-for-recovery period.

Two-second Refractory-for-Recovery Period, *i* <2-s Factor

There appears to be a period of ~2 s immediately following the cessation of a sound before poststimulus recovery processes start. This notion is based on the curve shown in Fig. 5.4 showing that separation between a given number of impulses does not appreciably reduce resulting TTS until the separation exceeds ~2 s. This, of course, does not mean that during this 2-s period the ear is refractory with respect to response to stimulation.

The implication of a brief refractory-for-recovery phenomenon is that 2 s of time is removed from the time available for recovery from auditory fatigue for each interruption of that, or longer, duration. Based on this reasoning, and NIPTS data, to be discussed later, from industrial impact and impulse noise, a new term t_e, is substituted for t in the formula for calculating $E'L_{Aeq8h}$:

$$E'L_{Aeq8h} = \mathrm{L}_{A0.5\ \mathrm{s},n_1} - 20\log(57{,}600/t_e),\ e\mathrm{dB}'n_1, \qquad (5.12)$$

where t_e is number of 0.5-s intervals that sound n_1 is present plus the sum of the durations, in 0.5 s intervals of interruptions. The time counted for each interruption is limited to 2 s and only interruptions where intensity level is decreased (>5 dB) level are considered.

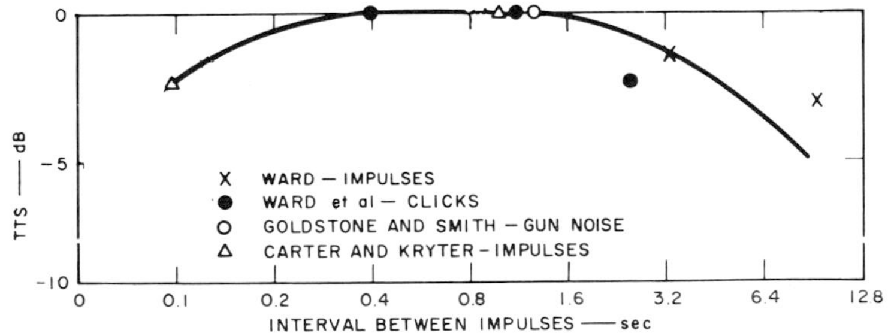

FIGURE 5.4 Note very short or relatively long intervals between impulses reduces amount of TTS, and intervals between ~0.5 and 1.5 s do not reduce TTS from exposures to impulses of noise. (Data from Ward, 1962; Ward *et al.* 1962; Smith and Goldstone, 1961; Carter and Kryter, 1962.)

Accelerated Recovery Period: $i > 15$-s Factor

Following this 2-s interval, recovery from TTS occurs for 30 s or so at an accelerated rate, compared to subsequent longer-term recovery. Figure 5.2 shows this behavior following exposure to white, equal-energy-per-cycle, noise. Somewhat similar TTS recovery functions have been found following exposures to pure tones (Hirsh and Ward 1952; Hirsh and Bilger, 1955).

Empirical data, to be presented later, show that the number of interruptions, as well as the sum of the durations of such interruptions, influenced the amount of TTS accrued by the subjects. Those TTS data were better predicted when the function and mathematical formula given in Fig. 5.5 were applied to measured exposure levels. It is hypothesized that this less-than-expected TTS with such interruptions is due to the accelerated recovery period seen in Fig. 5.2. The minimum interruption duration of 15 s to qualify for this recovery benefit is a midpoint between the about 30-s limit seen in Fig. 5.2 and the 2-s refractory-for-recovery interval. Its choice, of course, is to provide an approximate estimate of the effects on hearing thresholds of this accelerated-recovery phenomenon.

On the basis of the exhibited refractory-for-recovery and accelerated-recovery behaviors, $E'L_{Aeq8h}$ was modified, and labeled EL_{Aeq8h}, where: (1) the daily exposure level is the sum of the effective, 0.5-s, energies over the 8 exposure hours; and (2) the yearly (at 250 days per year) exposure level is expressed relative to one year. The formulas involved in the EE_A model become

$$EL_{Aeq8h,n_1} = L_{Ao.5\,s,n_1} - 20\log(57{,}600/t_e) - (-2.5 + 3.95\log i > 15\text{ s}),\ edBn_1, \quad (5.13)$$

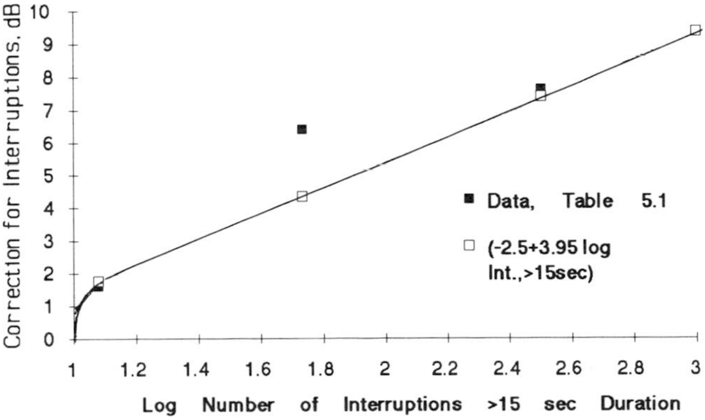

FIGURE 5.5 Correction for overestimation by $E'L_{Aeq8h}$ of TTS from interrupted noise per TTS from continuous noise, as function of log number of interruptions of duration >15 s. Solid curve is function taken to represent approximate relation from a minimum of 10 to more interruptions.

where >15 s is the number of decreasing, >5-dB, interruptions longer than 15 s.

$$EL_{Aeq8h,n_1 - n_x} = 10 \log 10^{(edBn_1 \cdots edBn_x)/10)}, \; edBn_1 - n_x. \qquad (5.14)$$

$$EE_{A,n_1,y,f} = edBn_1 + 8 \log \text{work years exposure [or 8 log days of exposure/250]}, \; edBn_1,y,f. \qquad (5.15)$$

where y = 250 days of exposure; and f = frequency offset adjustment, from Chapter 4, (500 Hz, 12 dB; 1000 Hz, 10 dB; 2000 Hz, 7 dB; 3000 Hz, 2 dB; 4000 Hz, 0 dB; 6000 Hz, 2 dB), and

$$EE_{A,n_1 - n_x,f} = 10 \log 10^{(edBn1,y,f + \cdots edBnx,y,f)/10)}, \; edBn_1,y_1,f \cdots n_x,y_x,f. \qquad (5.16)$$

When only continuous or interrupted steady sounds lasting longer than one second are involved, durations and sound-pressure levels based on pressures averaged over 1 s may, of course, be used with these equations.

Maximum Effects of Interruptions on EL_{Aeq8h}

The magnitudes of L_{Aeq8h} and EL_{Aeq8h}, [Eq. (5.13)] are, of course, numerically equal for exposure to steady noises that are essentially uninterrupted for 8 h. But the magnitudes of EL_{Aeq8h} and L_{Aeq8h} can differ dramatically for exposures to interrupted steady or impulse noises. However, there are maximum amounts each of the terms in general formulas of Eq. (5.13) can change EL_{Aeq8h} relative to L_{Aeq8h}, and to EL_{Aeq8h}. For example:

1. For the off-time term, the maximum difference between EL_{Aeq8h} and L_{Aeq8h} is 53.6 dB. This would occur with -101.2. dB [-20 log (57,600/t)] for a minimum 0.5-s exposure in 8 h, compared to -50.6 dB for the -10 log (T/t) term of L_{Aeq8h} for such an exposure.

2. For the refractory-for-recovery, i <2 s term, in EL_{Aeq8h} the maximum difference is 14 dB. This would occur with a possible maximum of 11,520 interruptions of 2-s-duration exposures to 0.5-s segments of steady or impulse sounds in 8 h {-20 log [(57,600/11,520 on-time in 0.5 s's) + 46,080 rf (refractory) interruption, t_e]} = 0 dB, compared to -20 log (57,600/11,520 on-time in 0.5 s's) = 14-dB increase in EL_{Aeq} compared to $E'L_{Aeq}$ for the same sound.

3. For the accelerated recovery, i >15-sec, term [(-2.5 + 3.95 log i >15 s)], the maximum difference between EL_{Aeq8h} with and without that term is -9.4 dB, a decrease in EL_{Aeq} compared to $E'L_{Aeq}$ for the same sound. This would occur with a suggested maximum of 1000 (or with a maximum possible of 1889) >15-s interruptions in 8 h of exposure to sound events of 0.5-s duration.

These latter two adjustments for interruptions, one retarding recovery and the other accelerating it, will, of course, under some conditions tend to cancel each other.

The EE_A model, as formulated in Eqs. (5.13)–(5.16), is predicated on fundamental data and theory of auditory functions, as well as on data from industrial studies of NIPTS, as given in Chapter 4. Presented in the next sections of this chapter are analyses of (1) additional TTS data relevant to the development of the EE_A model with respect to interruptions in exposures; (2) NIPTS data for exposures to interrupted steady and impulse industrial noises, and the relative accuracy with which EE_A and equal-energy methods predict those data; and (3) TTS from exposure to gun noise, and the question of "overloading" of the ear at intensities above L_A 130 dB.

TTS IN HUMANS FROM INTERRUPTED STEADY NOISES

TTS from Interrupted Octave Band Noise

Table 5.1 gives the amount of TTS2, found by Ward (1960), in young adult male subjects during 8 h of exposure to uninterrupted and interrupted octave bands of filtered white noise. The interruptions were created by imposing on/off ratios from 1/8th to 3/4ths, with those ratios repeated within the 8-h exposure period on duty cycles of 1.5, 9, and 40 min. The intensity level of the interrupted noise was set somewhat differently for different on/off ratios and duty cycles.

The relative abilities of four measures of noise exposure to predict TTS from the interrupted noise, as compared to uninterrupted noise, are also shown in Table 5.1. The four measures of noise exposure are (1) L_{Aeq8h}, equal-energy; (2) $L_{Aeq8h,osha}$; (3) $E''L_{Aeq8h}$ (EL_{Aeq8h} with no terms for interruptions); and (4) EL_{Aeq8h}, calculated with terms for interruptions. Inasmuch as the noises were not impulsive, the common 1-s time unit was used with all the measures of exposure level.

Relative accuracy of prediction was determined by comparing the differences between TTS_2 from the uninterrupted noise versus TTS_2 from an interrupted noise of a given on/off ratio and duty cycle, with the differences between their respective measured exposure levels. If a calculated exposure level is predictive of TTS for uninterrupted noise, the difference between a difference between TTS values for an interrupted and uninterrupted noise, and the difference between their thusly calculated exposure levels should be zero, or nearly so.

As summarized in the bottom section of Table 5.1, TTS from the interrupted exposures is typically overestimated about: 11 dB by L_{Aeq8h}; 7 dB by $L_{Aeq8h,osha}$; 5 dB by $E''L_{Aeq8h}$, with no adjustment for interruptions; and 2 dB by EL_{Aeq8h}, with the interruption factors included. It is also seen that the standard deviation of the underestimations is smallest for EL_{Aeq8h}, 1.9 dB, and largest for L_{Aeq8h}, 3.0 dB.

The overestimates of TTS are, progressively, about 2 dB less from the highest-frequency octave band noise, center frequencies of 250, 1000, and 4000 Hz, with TTS measured at a frequency about 1 octave higher; see lower right-hand section of Table 5.1. No explanation for this can be offered.

TABLE 5.1 Measured TTS_2, and TTS_2 Predicted, by L_{Aeq8h}, $L_{A8h, osha}$, $E'L_{AeqA8h}$, and EL_{Aeq8h} from 8 h Continuous (c) and Interrupted (i) Exposures to Octave-Band Noise

TTS_2 Data from Ward (1976)		1.5-min cycles, 8 h, 320 interrupts						9-min cycles, 8 h, 53 interrupts			40-min cycles, 8 h, 12 interrupts			
Average 500, 700-Hz test frequency, OBN 250 Hz, cf.	Cycle (minutes) =	1.5	1.5	1.5	1.5	1.5	1.5	9	9	9	40	40		
	on/off =	3/4	1/2	1/4	1/2	1/2	1/4	3/4	1/2	1/4	3/4	1/4		
t, s, on-time	28,800	21,600	14,400	7200	14,400	14,000	7200	21,600	14,400	7200	21,600	7200		
L_A dB_A OBN	95	100	105	105	110	115	115	100	115	115	100	115		
L_{Aeq8h} (10 log t)	95	98.9	102.0	99.0	107.0	112.0	109.0	98.8	112.0	109.0	98.8	109.0		
$L_{Aeq8h, osha}$ (16.6 log t)	95	97.9	100.0	95.0	105.0	110.0	105.0	97.9	110.0	105.0	97.9	105.0		
(No interruption adjustment $E''L_{Aeq}$ (20 log t)	95	97.5	99.0	93.0	104.0	109.0	103.0	97.5	109.0	103.0	97.5	103.0		
rf& > 15s interruption adjustment EL_{Aeq} (20 log t) =	95	90.4	92.0	86.3	97.0	102.0	96.3	93.4	105.0	99.4	96.0	101.9		
TTS_2	8.0	7.9	4.7	3.3	5.4	7.5	5.4	8.0	9.5	5.5	9.3	6.6		
(No interruption adjustment $E'L_{Aeq}$ (20 log t)														
$(TTS_i - TTS_c) - (L_{aeq, i} - L_{Aeq, c})$ =		−3.9	−10.3	−8.7	−14.6	−17.5	−16.6	−3.8	−15.5	−16.5	−2.5	−15.4		
$-(L_{A8hosha, i} - L_{A8h, osha, c})$ =		−3.0	−8.3	−4.7	−12.6	−15.5	−12.6	−2.9	−15.0	−12.5	−1.6	−11.4		
$-(E''L_{Aeq, i} - E''L_{Aeq, c})$ =		−2.6	−7.3	−2.7	−11.6	−14.5	−10.6	−2.5	−12.5	−10.5	−1.2	−9.4		
$-(EL_{Aeq, i} - EL_{Aeq, c})$ =		4.5	−0.3	4.0	−4.6	−7.5	−3.9	1.6	−8.5	−6.9	0.3	−8.3		
Average 2000-, 2800-Hz test frequency OBN 1000 Hz,	cycle (min) =	1.5	1.5	1.5	1.5	1.5	9	9	9	9	40	40	40	40
	on/off	1/2	1/2	1/4	1/4	1/8	1/2	1/4	1/4	1/8	1/2	1/4	1/8	1/8
t, seconds, on-time	28,800	14,400	14,400	7200	7200	3600	14,400	7200	7200	3600	14,400	7200	3600	3600
L_A, dB_A, OBN	90	90	95	100	105	105	95	100	105	105	95	100	100	105
L_{Aeq8h} (10 log t)	90	87.0	92.0	94.0	99.0	96.0	92.0	94.0	99.0	96.0	92.0	94.0	91.0	96.0
$L_{Aeq8h, osha}$ (16.6 log t)	90	85.0	90.0	90.0	95.0	90.0	90.0	90.0	95.0	90.0	90.0	90.0	85.0	90.0
(No interruption adjustment $E''L_{Aeq}$ (20 log t)	90	84.0	89.0	88.0	93.0	86.9	89.0	88.0	93.0	86.9	89.0	88.0	81.9	88.4
rf $TTS_i - TTS_c$ > 15 s interruption adjustment, EL_{Aeq} (20 log t) =	90	80.4	85.4	81.3	86.3	81.0	88.4	84.4	89.4	84.0	91.0	86.9	81.6	86.6
TTS_2	16.8	4.3	8.4	5.6	8.1	4.8	10.1	8.2	13.4	6.7	15.0	11.4	8.4	11.9

$(TTS_i - TTS_c)$ –														
$(L_{Aeq,i} - L_{Aeq,c}) =$		−9.5	−10.4	−15.2	−17.7	−18.0	−8.7	−12.6	−12.4	−16.1	−3.8	−9.4	−9.4	−10.9
$-(L_{A8h,osha,i} - L_{A8h,osha,c}) =$		−7.5	−8.4	−11.2	−13.7	−12.0	−6.7	−8.6	−8.4	−10.1	−1.8	−5.4	−3.4	−4.9
$-(E'L_{Aeq,i} - E'L_{Aeq,c}) =$		−6.5	−7.4	−9.2	−11.7	−8.9	−5.7	−6.6	−6.4	−7.0	−0.8	−3.4	−0.3	−3.3
$-(EL_{Aeq,i} - EL_{Aeq,c}) =$		−2.9	−3.8	2.5	−5.0	−3.0	−5.1	−3.0	−2.8	−4.1	−2.8	−2.3	0.0	−1.5
Average 4000-, 5600-Hz test frequency	cycle (min) =	1.5	1.5	1.5	1.5	1.5	1.5	9	9	9	40	40	40	40
OBN 4000 Hz,	on/off =	1/2	1/2	1/4	1/8	1/4	1/8	1/2	1/4	1/8	1/2	1/4	1/8	1/8
t, s, on-time	28,800	14,400	14,400	7200	7200	3600	3600	14,400	7200	3600	14,400	7200	3600	3600
L_A, dB_A, OBN	85	85	90	90	95	95	100	85	90	95	95	90	90	95
L_{Aeq8h} (10 log t)	85	82.0	87.0	84.0	89.0	86.0	91.0	82.0	84.0	86.0	92.0	84.0	81.0	86.0
$L_{Aeq8h,osha}$ (16.6 log t)	85	80.0	85.0	80.0	85.0	80.0	85.0	80.0	80.0	80.0	90.0	80.0	75.0	80.0
(No interruption adjustment) $E'L_{Aeq}$ (20 log t)	85	82.8	84.0	78.0	83.0	76.9	81.9	79.0	78.0	76.9	89.0	78.0	71.9	78.4
rf > 15 s interruption adjustment EL_{Aeq} (20 log t) =	85	75.4	80.4	71.3	76.3	71.0	76.0	78.4	74.4	74.0	91.0	76.9	71.6	75.2
TTS_2	23.3	8.6	14.0	8.5	13.3	8.6	19.7	15.2	14.7	10.5	18.1	18.8	12.5	20.0
$(TTS_i - TTS_c$ –														
$(L_{Aeq,i} - L_{Aeq,c}) =$		−11.7	−11.3	−13.8	−14.0	−15.7	−9.6	−5.1	−7.6	−13.8	−12.2	−3.5	−6.8	−4.3
$-(L_{A8h,osha,i} - L_{A8h,osha,c}) =$		−9.7	−9.3	−9.8	−10.0	−9.7	−3.6	−3.1	−3.6	−7.8	−10.2	0.5	−0.8	1.7
$-(E''L_{Aeq,i} - E''L_{Aeq,c}) =$		−12.5	−8.3	−7.8	−8.0	−6.6	−0.5	−2.1	−1.6	−4.7	−9.2	2.5	2.3	3.3
$-(EL_{Aeq,i} - EL_{Aeq,c}) =$		−5.1	−4.7	−1.1	−1.3	−0.7	5.4	−1.5	2.0	−1.8	−11.2	3.6	2.6	6.5

Summary of results from Table 4.1	Av. over on/off ratios and test frequencies				Average over duty cycles and test frequencies					Average over duty cycles & on/off ratios				
Duty cycle for 8	1.5 min	9 min	40 min	Av.	on/off ratios within each cycle				Aver-	Test Frequency, kHz			Aver-	Overall aver-
Number of interruptions	320	53	12	128	3/4	1/2	1/4	1/8	age	0.5, 0.7	2, 2.8	4, 5.6	age	age
$(TTS_i - TTS_c)$ –														
$(L_{Aeq,i} - L_{Aeq,c}) =$	−12.6	−11.7	−7.8	−10.7	−3.4	−12.0	−13.4	−11.8	−10.1	−11.4	−11.8	−9.9	−11.0	−10.6
$-(L_{A8hosha,i} - L_{A8hosha,c}) =$	−9.3	−8.3	−3.7	−6.0	−2.5	−9.5	−9.7	−6.0	−6.9	−9.1	−7.9	−5.8	−7.6	−6.9
$-(E''L_{Aeq,i} - E''L_{Aeq,c}) =$	−7.9	−6.4	−1.9	−5.4	−2.1	−8.4	−7.8	−3.4	−5.4	−7.7	−5.9	−4.1	−5.9	−5.6
$-(EL_{Aeq,i} - EL_{Aeq,c}) =$	−1.8	−3.1	−1.3	−2.1	2.1	−4.6	−3.1	−0.3	−1.5	−2.7	−3.0	−0.6	−2.1	−1.9

Note: Negative (−) values indicate TTS_i overestimated per TTS_c summary results (also in Table 5.2).

Although the data are rather irregular, there appeared to be no systematic changes in these underpredictions of TTS by the various noise measures as a function of the on/off ratios.

There was a monotomic decrease in overestimation by L_{Aeq8h}, $L_{Aeq8h,osha}$, and $E''L_{Aeq8h}$ of TTS as a function of duty cycle (duty cycles of 1, 5, 9, and 40 mins, which gave, respectively, 320, 53, and 12 interruptions over the 8-h total exposure period). As seen in the lower-left section of Table 5.1, there was, with each of these measures of exposure level, an approximately 1-dB decrease in overestimation of TTS when the number of interruptions was decreased from 320 to 53. There was a further 3–4 dB decrease with a decrease from 53 to 12 interruptions. Shown graphically in Fig. 5.5 are these data and a set of log-linear constants that approximately fit the data.

Application of Interruption Factors

These TTS data were the basis for proposing the interruption factor term, $i > 15$ s, limited to 10–1000 such interruptions in 8 h (rationalized as being related to the accelerated recovery from TTS occurring within 30 s after noise exposure; see Fig. 5.2). This factor contributed to the value of EL_{Aeq8h} as compared to $E''L_{Aeq8h}$ for the interrupted noise. However, the proposed refractory-for-recovery adjustment term [t_e; see Eq. (5.12)] which relates to all interruptions, is such that the number of interruptions of the noises in Tables 5.1, and Table 5.2, are too few, relative to the number of seconds of on-time, to change by more than a fraction of a decibel the value of EL_{Aeq8h} relative to $E''L_{Aeq8h}$.

TTS from Interrupted Broadband Noise

Table 5.2 gives TTS data, also from Ward, for 12–102-min exposures to pink noise when uninterrupted, and when presented with 30-s on- and off-periods. The analyses applied to the TTS data parallel those used in Table 5.1, and, overall, the findings are similar. The lower right-hand part of Table 5.2 shows that L_{Aeq8h} overestimated TTS for the interrupted noise by 8.1 dB, $L_{Aeq8h,osha}$ by 6.0 dB, $E''L_{Aeq8h}$, by 4.8 dB, and EL_{Aeq8h}, by 1.4 dB. With a few exceptions, the relative rankings in accuracy in underestimation of TTS was the same for all durations tested, from 12 to 102 min.

Exceptions to the general overestimation of TTS on the part of all four units of measurement is seen in Table 5.2 to occur for the lowest intensity level, 92 dB_A with, especially, 12 and 22 min of exposure. For the latter conditions, EL_{Aeq8h} overestimates TTS_2 by 5.8 dB. However, the TTS values for continuous noise at this intensity level, 92 dB_A, appear to be inordinately small, respectively: 7, 9, 13, and 18 dB (average of 11.8 dB) for the 12, 22, 47, and 102-minute exposure durations. With the 98-dB_A intensity level of continuous noise, same durations, TTS of 16, 20, 25, and 30 dB (average of

TABLE 5.2 Measured TTS_2 and TTS_2 at 4 kHz, Predicted by L_{Aeq8h}, $L_{A8h,\,osha}$, $E''L_{Aeq8h}$, and EL_{Aeq8h} from Continuous (c) and Interrupted (i) Pink Noise

TTS_2 data from Ward *et al.* (1958)	12-min		Exposure	22-min		Exposure	47-min		Exposure	102-min		Exposure		
Continuous, t, s, on-time	720	720	720	1320	1320	1320	2820	2820	2820	6120	6120	6120		
L_A, dB_A, pink noise	93	99	105	93	99	015	93	99	105	93	99	105		
L_{Aeq8h} (10 log t)	77.0	83.0	89.0	79.6	85.6	91.6	82.9	88.9	94.9	86.3	92.3	98.3		
$L_{Aeq8h,\,osha}$ (16.6 log t)	66.4	72.4	78.4	70.8	76.8	82.8	76.2	82.2	88.2	81.8	87.8	93.8		
(No interruption adjustment) $E'L_{Aeq}$ (20 log t)	61.0	67.0	73.0	66.2	72.2	78.2	72.8	78.8	84.8	79.5	85.5	91.5		
$rf > 15$ s interruption adjustment, EL_{Aeq} (20 log t)	61.0	67.0	73.0	66.2	72.2	78.2	72.8	78.8	84.8	79.5	85.5	91.5		
TTS_2	7.0	16.0	19.0	9.0	20.0	25.0	13.0	[illegible]	32.0	18.0	30.0	41.0		
Interrupted, 30 s on/30 sec off	12-min		Exposure	22-min		Exposure	47-min		Exposure	102-min		Exposure		
t, s on-time	360	360	360	660	660	660	1410	1410	1410	3060	3060	3060		
L_A, dB_A, pink noise	93	99	105	93	99	105	93	99	105	93	99	105		
L_{Aeq8h} (10 log t)	74.0	80.0	86.0	76.6	82.6	88.6	79.9	85.9	91.9	83.3	89.3	95.3		
$L_{Aeq8h,\,osha}$ (16.6 log t)	61.4	67.4	73.4	65.8	71.8	77.8	71.3	77.3	83.3	76.8	82.8	88.8		
(No interruption adjustment) $E''L_{Aeq}$ (20 log t)	54.9	60.9	66.9	60.2	66.2	72.2	66.8	72.8	78.8	73.5	79.5	85.5		
$rf > 15$ s interruption adjustment, EL_{Aeq} (20 log t)	53.7	59.7	65.7	58.0	64.0	70.0	63.3	69.3	75.3	62.3	68.3	74.3		
TTS_2	5.0	6.0	10.0	6.0	8.0	13.0	7.0	10.0	16.0	9.0	12.0	20.0		
													Average	Standard deviation
$(TTS_i - TTS_c) - (L_{Aeq,i} - L_{Aeq,c}) =$	1.0	−7.0	−6.0	0.0	−9.0	−9.0	−3.0	−12.0	−13.0	−6.0	−15.0	−18.0	−8.1	5.8
$-(L_{A8h,\,osha,\,i} - L_{A8hosha,\,c}) =$	3.0	−5.0	−4.0	2.0	−7.0	−7.0	−1.0	−10.0	−11.0	−4.0	−13.0	−16.0	−6.1	5.8
$-(E''L_{Aeq,\,i} - E''L_{Aeq,\,c}) =$	4.0	−4.0	−3.0	3.0	−6.0	−6.0	0.0	−9.0	−10.0	−3.0	−12.0	−15.0	−5.1	5.8
$-EL_{Aeq,\,i} - EL_{Aeq,\,c}) =$	5.2	−2.8	−1.8	5.3	−3.7	−3.7	3.6	−5.4	−6.4	8.2	−0.8	−3.8	−0.5	4.8

23 dB) were found, with an average difference of 11 dB from the average TTS for the 92 dBA level.

For these TTS levels, a rate of about 1 dB TTS per 1 dB intensity is usually found, so that a difference of about 6 dB TTS between the 92 and 98 dB_A intensity levels, rather than the 11-dB difference observed, would be expected. Indeed, for the continuous exposure levels shown in Table 5.2, an average difference of 6 dB in TTS is found for the 98 dB_A (average of 23 dB for the four different durations) vs. 104 dB_A (average of 29 dB for the different durations)

This general rate in growth of TTS with the higher dB_A levels in this study, would suggest that the average TTS from the 92-dB_A level should have been about 4 dB higher than measured, namely, about 15.8 dB rather than 11.8 dB. As a result, the average difference with TTS for the 98 dB_A exposures would have been 4 dB less, and thereby decrease the underestimates of TTS for the 92-dB_A exposures. A factor that could have contributed to the smaller-than-expected TTS from the relatively low-intensity (92-dB_A), exposures would be that the preexposure thresholds for the subjects were somewhat above normal. As will be discussed later, this condition would reduce to below normal the amount of TTS engendered by lower levels of exposure to noise.

The accuracies and variabilities of these four measures of exposure level in predicting the TTS data in Tables 5.1 and 5.2 are graphically shown in Fig. 5.6. It is clear that the EL_{Aeq8h}, which includes the adjustment for interruptions, is the most accurate and least variable predictor of TTS, followed by $E''L_{\mathrm{Aeq8h}}$, $L_{\mathrm{Aeq8h,osha}}$, and, finally $L_{\mathrm{Aeq8h,\ equal\text{-}energy}}$.

It is not surprising that EL_{Aeq8h} better predicts than $E''L_{\mathrm{Aeq8h}}$ the TTS data of Tables 5.1 and 5.2, inasmuch as EL_{Aeq8h} was partly derived from those data. Validation of the EL_{Aeq8h} - EE_A formulations depends, of course, on how well, as will be examined later below, they estimate NIPTS for other data involving exposures to interrupted steady and impulse noise.

NIPTS FROM INTERRUPTED STEADY AND IMPULSIVE INDUSTRIAL NOISES

Studies have been published of NIPTS in the forgery and mining industries that suggest that less NIPTS than expected, on the basis of the equal-energy measurements, is experienced from exposure to impulsive noise. For these studies it was not possible, unfortunately, to precisely specify the level of energy to which individuals or groups of workers were exposed (see, e.g., Sataloff *et al.*, 1969; NIOSH, 1976).

The amount of NIPTS found from exposures to impulses of noise, separated by 20 s or so, in steel mills also qualitatively support the predictions of the $L_{\mathrm{Aeq8h,osha}}$ and the EL_{Aeq8h} measures, rather than the equal-energy L_{Aeq8h} unit (Johansson *et al.*, 1973). That is, less NIPTS was experienced from

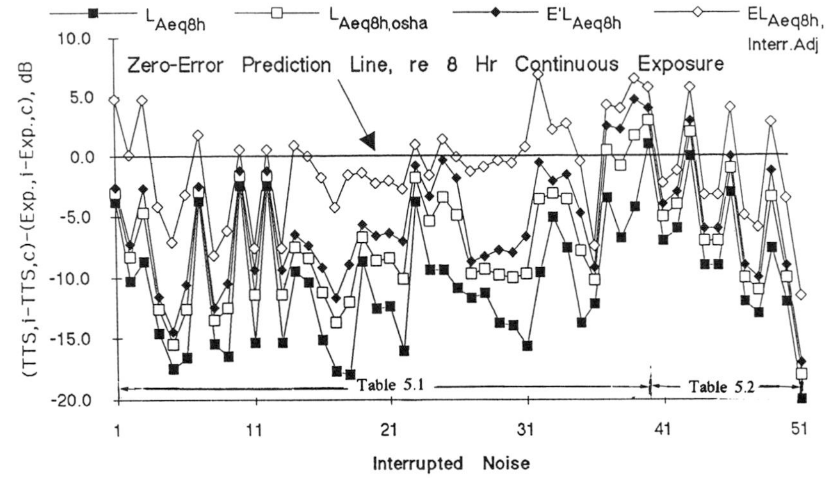

FIGURE 5.6 Differences between TTS_L from interrupted and continuous exposures to different L_A levels of pink and octave-band noises, compared to the differences, for those noise conditions, between their measured energy, or effective energy, by L_{Aeq8h}, $L_{Aeq8h,osha}$, $E'L_{Aeq8h}$, and $ELA_{eq8h,\ interruption\text{-}adjusted}$. See Tables 5.1 and 5.2 for specific noise conditions.

such exposures than expected according to the equal-energy concept. The obvious reason would be that equal-energy, L_{Aeq8h}, levels do not allow for reduced effectiveness for NIPTS due to recovery time between impulses, and lessened effective energy of impusles, when the impulses are separated by more than 2 s or so.

On the other hand, Martin (1976) concluded that NIPTS from exposures to impulsive noise from drop-forge operations (Atherley and Martin, 1971; Guberan *et al.*, 1971 Ceypek *et al.* 1973) was about that to be expected according to Robinson's E_A calculation procedure, which is based on the equal-energy concept. However, as shown in Chapter 4, according to other studies of NIPTS, the E_A formula significantly underestimates high-frequency NIPTS to be expected from the high levels of noise that were involved. Possible reasons for this finding were discussed in Chapter 4.

If those reasons are valid, the agreement between NIPTS as found by Martin (1976), in his analysis of data from drop-forge industries, and that predicted by E_A, could be due to an invalid estimation of NIPTS by E_A. That is, E_A underestimates NIPTS from noise in general, but fortuitously predicted NIPTS from these impulses because their equal-energy E_A levels calculate to be somewhat higher than their truly effective-energy levels. Two wrongs, may here, make a "right." Also, as next discussed, a rather recent study in drop-forge factories provide NIPTS data that are well predicted by EL_{Aeq8h}, but not by the equal energy methods of ISO 1999 and E_A.

NIPTS in Drop-Forge Workers

Taylor *et al.* (1984) published a study of the hearing levels of workers exposed to interrupted impact and impulsive noises found in drop-forge industries. Their hearing-level data, and herein derived NIPTSs per their control group, and per ISO 7029 (1984) are given in Table 5.3. The subjects were medically screened for nosocusis, but were not screened for exposure to military and recreational gun noise. However, because of the very high intensity of the impact and impulse noises, sociocusis, even from exposures to typical gun noise on the part of some of the workers, should not have been a factor influencing the hearing levels of the workers exposed to these impact and impulse noises.

The noise-exposed subjects were audiometrically tested before the start of the workday, or within 2 h of the start of the workday, and then only if the workers had been wearing earmuffs during that time. Noise-exposure time was taken to be those months and/or years when the workers had not worn ear-protective devices.

The physical characteristics of the press-forge impacts of 0.5-s duration (steady, as herein defined), and drop-hammer impulses are shown in Fig. 5.7. The effective duration of the drop-hammer impulses, taken to be that between the 10-dB downpoints from peak level, is estimated to be about 0.05 s. The daily exposure levels, average for 1-s segments, were given by Taylor *et al.* (1984) as being $L_{A1\text{ s,eq8h}}$ 99 for the press-forge impacts, and 108 for the drop-hammer impulses. These levels were determined from dosimeter and other acoustical measurements and analyses.

The daily exposure routines over the workday were 8 cycles of 40 min, 38,400, 0.5-s intervals of working, followed by 20-min breaks in quiet. The noises occurred about every 1–3 s. This is taken, in some calculations, to reflect refractory-for-recovery factors, as giving 9600 impacts or impulses: every 2 s (four 0.5-s intervals), one 0.5-s-duration impact noise, with a 1.5-s duration interruption (three 0.5-s intervals); and one 0.05-s duration impulse, with a 1.95 s duration interruption (three and nine-tenths 0.5 intervals).

EE_A for Exposures to Impact and Impulse Noises

Values of EE_A given in Table 5.3, were calculated for the press-forge impact noise and drop-hammer impulse noises as follows. Press-forge impact (steady noise, see Fig. 5.7, lower-left oscillograph):

$$EL_{\text{Aeq8h}} = L_{A1\text{ s,eq8h}}\ 99, \text{ as given by Taylor } et\ al. \text{ (1984)}, + 3\text{ dB } [10 \log (57{,}600/28{,}800)] = L_{A0.5\text{ s,eq8h}} 102 - 20 \log (57{,}600/38{,}400) = 98.5\ e\text{dB,5s},n + 8 \log \text{years' exposure} = e\text{dB}y \qquad (5.17)$$

where (1) 38,400 = t_e = 9600 impacts + 9600 × 3 [9600 0.5-s impacts + refractory-for-recovery factor [9600 interruptions × 3, where 3 = four

TABLE 5.3 HL and Measured NIPTS per ISO 7029 and Control Groups and Predicted by EE_A; Impact and Impulse Noise

		500-Hz				NIPTS	1000-Hz				NIPTS	2000-Hz				NIPTS
Age/ exp*	EE_A§	Exp HL†	Ctrl HL†	NIPTS ISO	Per ctrl	Predicted by, EE_A	Exp HL†	Ctrl HL†	NIPTS ISO	Per ctrl	Predicted by, EE_A	Exp HL†	Ctrl HL†	NIPTS ISO	Per ctrl	Predicted by, EE_A
Taylor *et al.* (1984): Males Exposed to Impact Noise																
Press-Forge Operators,‡ $N = 211$, $L_{Aeq1s,\ 8h} = 99$ ($L_{Aeq0.5s,\ 8h} = 102$), $EL_{Aeq.5s,\ 8h} = 98.5$ edB*n*																
29/1.3	99.4	8	8	7	0	3.2	3	4	2	−1	4.6	6	3	5	3	7.4
28/2.7	102.0	10	8	9	2	5.1	8	4	7	4	6.9	6	3	5	3	10.2
30/5.3	104.3	11	8	10	3	7.2	8	4	7	4	9.9	12	3	11	9	12.1
37/10.6	106.7	11	9	9	2	9.8	8	8	6	0	12.4	16	7	14	9	14.0
47/19.7	108.9	9	9	6	0	12.6	10	8	7	2	15.4	22	10	16	12	21.2
Taylor *et al.* (1984): Males Exposed to Impulse Noise																
Drop-Hammer Operators,¶ $N = 505$, $L_{Aeq1\ s,\ 8h} = 108$($L_{Aeq0.5s,\ 8h} = 111$), $EL_{Aeq0.5s,\ 8h} = 99.2$ edB*n*																
26/1.3	100.1	10	8	9	2	3.6	7	4	6	3	5.1	8	3	7	5	8.1
28/2.5	102.4	10	8	9	2	5.5	9	4	8	5	7.5	9	3	8	6	10.7
32/5.1	104.9	12	8	11	4	7.9	12	4	11	8	9.5	14	3	13	11	14.0
39/11.2	107.6	15	9	13	6	10.9	20	8	18	12	13.5	40	7	37	33	18.3
49/20.9	109.8	21	9	17	12	13.0	33	8	25	23	16.0	31	10	[illegible]	11	[illegible]
55/36.6	111.7	31	11	26	20	16.9	53	8	47	45	20.9	50	13	41	37	27.8

* Age/years of exposure.

† 50%ile HLs increased by 3 dB for self-recording, midtrace scored audiometer. Data from Tables VIII, XII, XV of Taylor *et al.* (1984). Exp, exposed; Ctrl, controls.

‡ Eigth 40-min work periods, 38,400, 0.5-s intervals of work time with an impact or impulse an average of every 2 s, 9600 impacts or impulses per workday.

§ Press impacts: $EE_A = L_{A0.05s} - 20 \log [57{,}600/38{,}400$ (9600, 0.5-s impacts + 9600 × 3, 0.5-s *rf* periods)] + 8 log years of exposure, *e*dB*n* (see text).

¶ Hammer impulses; $EE_A = L_{A0.5s} - 10 \log(.5/.05) - 20 \log (57{,}600/47{,}040$ [9600, 0.05-s impulses + 9600 × 3.9[2s-0.5s = 3.9,0.5s's)] + 8 log years of exposure, *e*dB*y* (see text).

TABLE 5.3 *Continued*

3000-Hz				NIPTS	4000-Hz				NIPTS	6000-Hz				NIPTS
Exp HL†	Ctrl HL†	NIPTS ISO	Per ctrl	Predicted by, EE_A	Exp HL†	Ctrl HL†	NIPTS ISO	Per ctrl	Predicted by, EE_A	Exp HL†	Ctrl HL†	NIPTS ISO	Per ctrl	Predicted by, EE_A
12	4	10	8	13.2	14	8	12	6	15.7	20	9	17	11	13.2
14	4	12	10	17.1	21	8	19	13	21.4	23	9	20	14	17.1
22	4	20	18	21.9	30	8	29	22	26.2	28	9	25	19	21.9
40	9	35	31	27.6	45	11	39	34	34.7	45	15	35	30	27.6
50	11	40	39	35.0	58	16	44	42	42.7	61	20	55	41	35.0
11	4	10	7	14.2	15	8	14	7	17.3	17	9	16	8	14.2
17	4	15	13	17.7	22	8	20	14	22.0	23	9	20	14	17.7
23	4	21	19	25.6	28	8	26	20	27.6	27	9	24	18	25.6
49	9	43	40	30.2	52	11	44	41	38.0	45	15	36	30	30.2
60	11	48	49	39.0	63	16	47	47	46.5	65	20	47	45	39.0
69	23	53	46	46.8	74	34	52	40	55.0	79	40	54	39	46.8

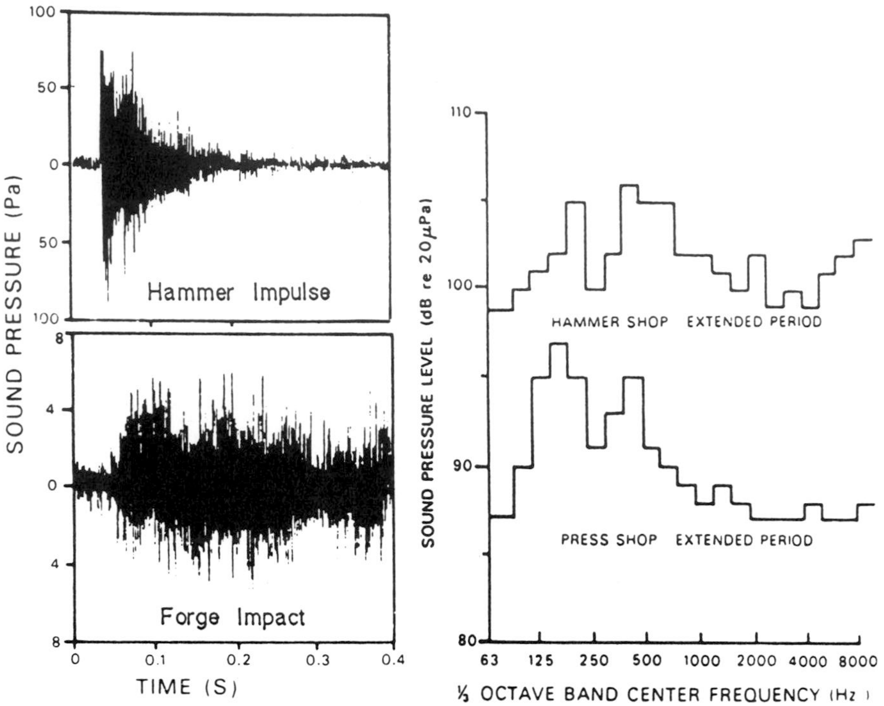

FIGURE 5.7 Oscillographs and ⅓-octave band levels of drop-hammer impulse, and press-forge impact noises. (From Taylor *et al.*, 1984. Copyright 1984 by the American Psychological Association. Adapted by permission of the author.)

0.5-s intervals of allowed maximum of 2-sec refractory-for-recover − 0.5 s taken by impact between successive impact noises]. No adjustments for accelerated recovery in >15-s interruptions are required, inasmuch as only eight interruptions for the eight 20-min rest breaks were involved. As indicated in Fig. 5.5, adjustments are not prescribed when fewer than 10 interruptions of durations >15 s are involved for a given noise condition.

Drop-hammer impulse noise (see Fig 5.7, upper-left oscillograph).

$$EL_{A1\ \mathrm{s,eq8h}} = 108, \text{ as given by Taylor } et\ al. \text{ (1984)} + 3 \text{ dB } [10 \log (57{,}600/28{,}800] = L_{A0.5\ \mathrm{s,eq8h}}\ 111 - 10 \text{ dB } [10\log(0.5\text{s}/0.05\text{s, duration of impulse})] - 20\log(57{,}600/47{,}040) = 99.2\ e\text{dB}_{0.5s,n} + 8 \log \text{years, exposure} = e\text{dB}y \quad (5.18)$$

where, 47,040 = t_e = 9600 0.05-s impulses + refractory-for-recovery factor [9600 interruptions × 3.9, where 3.9 = 4 − 0.05 s, duration of impulse]. No adjustments required for interruptions, as for the forge impact noise.

The term −10 log (0.5/0.05 s), −10 dB is required to convert the reported energy of a hammer impulse to its effective, averaged-over-0.5-s, energy.

The instantaneous pressures measured by Taylor *et al.* (1984), were integrated over a long period of time and then averaged into 1-s-duration levels. As such, they reflect, with a −3-dB, adjustment, the sum of instantaneous pressures of the 0.5-s duration press-forge impact noise, but not the rms average of the instantaneous pressures over a 0.5-s interval that contained an impulse of one-tenth that duration, 0.05 s.

The proper adjustment can be achieved by subtracting 10 dB from the $L_{A0.5s}$ for the hammer impulse of the Taylor *et al.* (1984) study, i.e., 10 log of the ratio of 0.5 s to the actual duration of the impulse, 0.05 s. This technique of converting levels given, or estimated, for brief impulses to 0.5-s effective levels will be used later in the text with impulse noise reported for other studies. Examples of such calculations for 0.012-s-duration impulses were given earlier in the text.

ISO 1999 (1990) and EE_A Predicted NIPTS, Taylor *et al.* Data

NIPTSs, per ISO 7029, for the Taylor *et al.* (1984) data, and NIPTS as predicted by ISO 1999 by EE_A, and by Robinson's (1976) E_A, are shown in Fig. 5.8. As noted before, the ISO 1999 procedures for predicting NIPTS allow the calculation of NIPTS from impulse and impact noise to be done in two ways: (1) as though the noises were continuous, or interrupted, steady noises, and (2) as though the noises were continuous or interrupted, steady noises, but with a 5-dB "penalty" added to their L_{Aeq8h} levels because they are "impulsive/impact" in character.

Figure 5.8A shows that when the optional 5-dB impulse/impact penalty is not applied, ISO 1999 underestimates measured NIPTS per ISO 7029, from exposures to the press-forge impact noise by about 2 to 13 dB, depending on years of exposure. When the penalty is included, ISO (1990) 1999 overestimates NIPTS, per ISO 7029, for the press impact noise by about 2 to 4 dB. Except for the ≤3, years-of-exposure conditions, EE_A is within about 1 dB, on the average, in predicting measured NIPTS per ISO 7029.

Figure 5.8C shows that when the optional 5-dB impulse/impact penalty is not applied, ISO 1999 overestimates measured NIPTS, per ISO 7029, for the hammer impulse noise by about 10–45 dB, depending on years of exposure. When the penalty is included, ISO 1999 overestimates NIPTS, per ISO 7029, for the hammer impulse noise by about 5–15 dB. NIPTS predicted by EE_A is, on the average, within 1 dB of measured NIPTS per ISO 7029.

Data in Table 5.3 show that when NIPTS is measured relative to the industry control groups, the underestimations by ISO 1999 and EE_A would be about 2 dB less, and the overestimations about 2 dB more, than when NIPTS is taken relative to normal hearing specified in ISO 7029. As a result, the magnitudes of the incorrect estimations by ISO 1999 remain large, and those of EEA remain small, about 1 dB on the average.

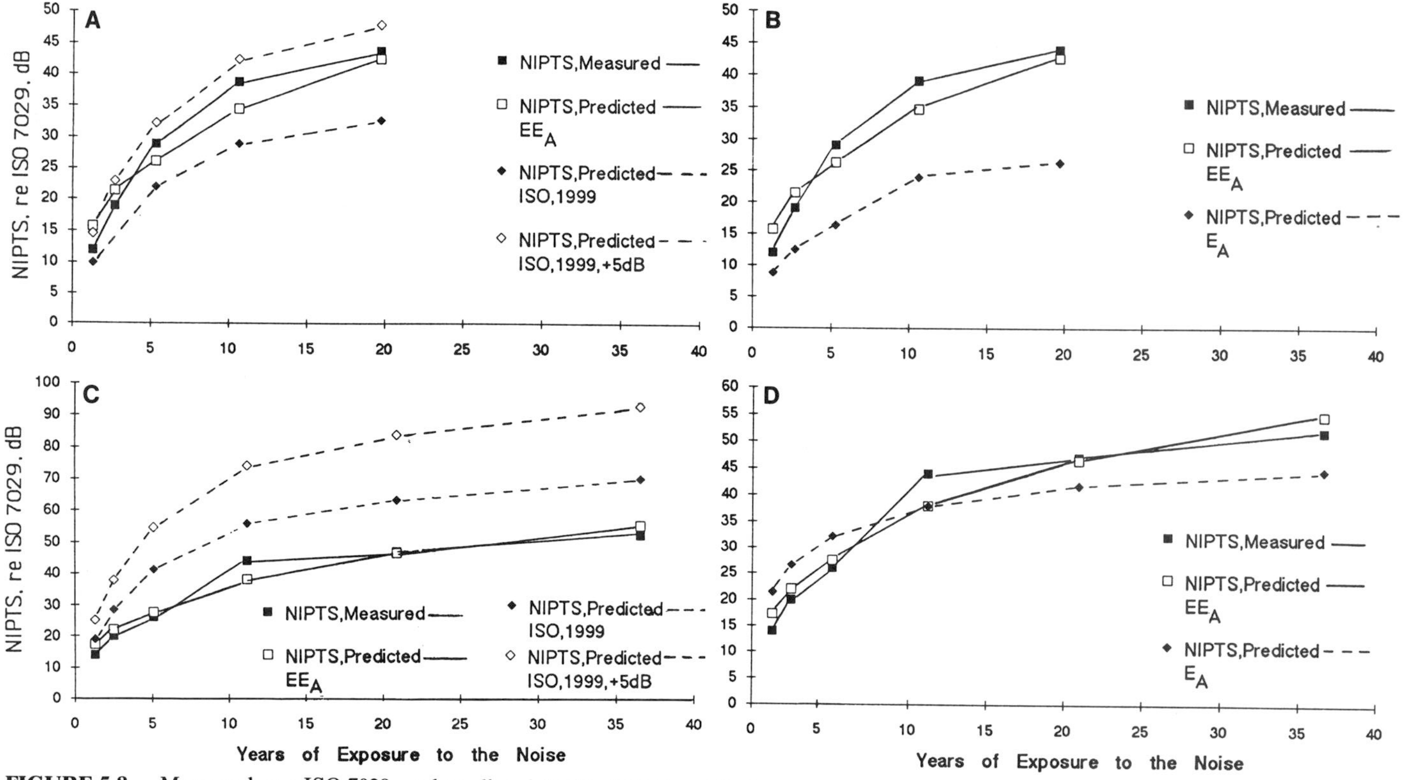

FIGURE 5.8 Measured, per ISO 7029, and predicted 50%ile NIPTS, 4000 Hz, from exposure to (A,B) impact and (C,D) impulse noise. NIPTS predicted by E_A, EE_A and ISO 1999 (steady and impulse noise formulas). Based on Taylor data from Table 5.3.

Even though both the noise exposed and control group subjects in this study were medically screened for ear pathologies, it is believed that the NIPTS found relative to the control group is somewhat less than it should be. The reasons NIPTS relative the industry control groups are considered as questionable are that the control groups (1) were not screened for exposure to gun noise and (2) included personnel from offices and canteens where the noise levels were as high as 85 dB_A.

As seen in Table 5.2, the 50%ile hearing levels of the control group for the Taylor *et al.* (1984) study, exceeded those of the general, normal male population by about 4 dB, on the average. This amount, 4 dB, of extra sociocusis is somewhat less than the 8–10 dB found in the previously discussed studies with screened industrial male control-group subjects. The difference is, no doubt, due to the fact that more than half, 108, of the 189 control subjects in the Taylor *et al.* (1984) study were females, with, presumably, less sociocusis, especially from gun noise, than that typical for males.

E_A Predicted NIPTS, Taylor *et al.* Data

Figure 5.8B shows the EA underestimates by 10-20 dB the NIPTS found for the press-forge impact noise of the Taylor *et al.* (1984) study. Figure 5.8D shows that for exposures of <10 years to the drop-hammer impulse noise, E_A overestimates measured NIPTS by an average of about 5 dB, and underestimates measured NIPTS by about 5 dB for exposures of over 10 years.

This latter finding is somewhat like the results calculated by Martin (1976) for forge impulses. That is, impulse noise causes less threshold shifts than one would surmise from equal-energy measures, such as E_A, and, at the same time, the E_A is believed, as previously explained, to underestimate NIPTS from exposure to noise.

TTS AND PREDICTED NIPTS FROM GUN NOISE

As noted in Chapter 3, the sensation of perceived noisiness (when due to loudness) presumably grows at a somewhat accelerated rate when noise-exposure levels exceed L_{Aex} ~100. It was shown in Chapter 4, and was, and will be further, demonstrated in this chapter, that NIPTS and TTS also appear to continue to grow at an increasing rate as L_{Aex} >100 dB. The apparent similarity of the growth of loudness and threshold shift as a function of exposure level would indicate a common reflection of the magnitude of sensorineural excitation and related auditory fatigue.

To obtain with a single impulse an L_{Aex} ~100, the L_A must be exceedingly intense. Gun noises, with levels ranging from L_A 120 to 180 dB or so, are perhaps the only widespread noises that generate such high L_{Aex} values. However, it has been generally surmised that high-intensity impulses not only cause NIPTS, they may overload and damage the auditory system in special ways. Data pertaining to both of these matters have been obtained from humans and animals as subjects.

Gun Noise

Exposure to noise from sport and military gun usage appears to be a source of significant amounts of NIPTS in industrial workers and the general population (Prosser *et al.*, 1988; Chung *et al.*, 1991; Johnson and Riffle, 1982; Kryter, 1991). Although information as to the intensity, spectra, numbers, and separation times between such impulses was not available for those studies, it was concluded that the typical gun user was exposed to gun noise the equivalent of EL_{Aeq8h} 89.

A number of studies have been conducted (e.g., Coles and Rice, 1965; Elwood *et al.*, 1966; Acton *et al.*, 1966; Goldstone and Smith 1961; Kryter and Garinther, 1965) of TTS from exposure to gun noise in military services. In most of these studies, TTS was taken to be the difference between pre- and postexposure hearing levels of soldier firing rifles on target ranges. The TTS values, but not the acutal hearing levels, of the subjects are available from publications of most of these studies. As will be shown below, without knowledge of the actual hearing levels it is difficult to interpret the significance of the TTS data.

However, pre- and postexposure hearing levels of men firing military shoulder-rifles were published for one of those studies (Kryter and Garinther, 1965). In this study, after preexposure hearing levels were obtained, different groups of five 20–25-year-old soldiers fired various numbers of rounds from military shoulder rifles, with 5-s spacings between each round. A total of 176 men were tested and a given man served as a subject for only one firing condition, one weapon and one session of firing.

Postexposure hearing tests commenced within 15 s for each subject. The tests were administered in separate audiometric test booths in special vehicles located close to the firing line. Hearing levels (HLs) for 500 Hz, which were always taken first during testing, were discarded because they tended to be more variable than those for the higher frequencies and showed no pre- vs. postexposure trends. HLs that were not measured at the different frequencies at exactly 2 min postexposure were adjusted to estimated HL_2 values in accordance with a prescribed set of functions. The maximum time difference between measured HL and 2 min postexposure was 4 min, and occurred for 6000 Hz, the frequency tested last in a session.

The hearing-level data have been corrected to be relative to ISO (1975) 389 audiometric zero, and, because self-recording audiometry was used, the hearing levels have been increased by 3 dB. As discussed earlier in the chapter, these adjustments make possible more valid comparisons of these hearing levels with ISO 7029 (manually obtained) hearing levels.

It was calculated from averaged spectra of the gunfire impulses that the L_A levels were 1 dB higher than their unweighted sound-pressure levels; see Fig. 5.9 and Table 5.4. Numbers of rounds fired per subject, peak L_A, EL_{Aeq8h} and $EE_{A,f,\ 50\ \text{years of exposure}}$, are given in Table 5.5. Also given in Table 5.5 are (1) preexposure HL; (2) 2-min postexposure HL (HL2); and (3) NIPTS at the 25%ile, 50%ile, and 75%ile for the audiometric test frequencies of 1000, 2000, 3000, 4000, and 6000 Hz as predicted by $EE_{A,f,\ 50\ \text{years of exposure}}$. As indicated by footnote to Table 5.5, several data, incorrectly entered in the original published table, have been corrected.

Interpretation of Gun-Noise Data with Respect to Potential for NIPTS

For purposes of discussion, the higher HL_2 levels (those not significantly limited because of preexposure elevated HLs are taken to represent the approximate amount of TTS_2 that would have been found from these exposures in soldiers with normal preexposure hearing levels. It is also postulated that a noise exposure causing a given TTS_2 in normal ears will cause a like amount of NIPTS after a nuimber of years of exposure. These assumptions provide a means of estimating potential NIPTS from the gun-noise data. Bases for the legitimacy of those assumptions, and the single-day-exposure-levels for TTS_2 and work-years of exposure for equal NIPTS, will be presented later.

Acoustical factors in exposures to gun noise suggest that adjustments to their measurements may be needed in order to find a relation between those measurement and NIPTS that is consistent with the relation found with types of noise. One possible adjustment is related to diffractions and resonances around the head and in the ear that differently effect sounds from a lateralized point source, such as a shoulder rifle, than sounds from more typical sources.

Point-Source Gun-Noise Spectra

It is assumed that (1) most of the energy of the industrial noises that were involved in the studies that gave the EE_A-NIPTS function were generally from large, compared to a person's head, sources; and (2) the noise generally came head-on, or from many sources and angles of sound incidence. The general symmetry of bilateral hearing loss in industrial workers indicates that is often the case.

On the other hand, the muzzle of a shoulder-rifle is a point source of sound, about 1.4 cm in diameter, one meter away, and at an approximate 45° angle from the near ear of a rifle-shooter (the left ear of a right-handed shooter). Shaw measured the sound-pressure level for different pure-tone frequencies at the entrance to a person's ear canal, and in free field without the person's head being present. The source and person were in an anechoic chamber, with the orifice of the tube delivering the sound being 1.4 cm in

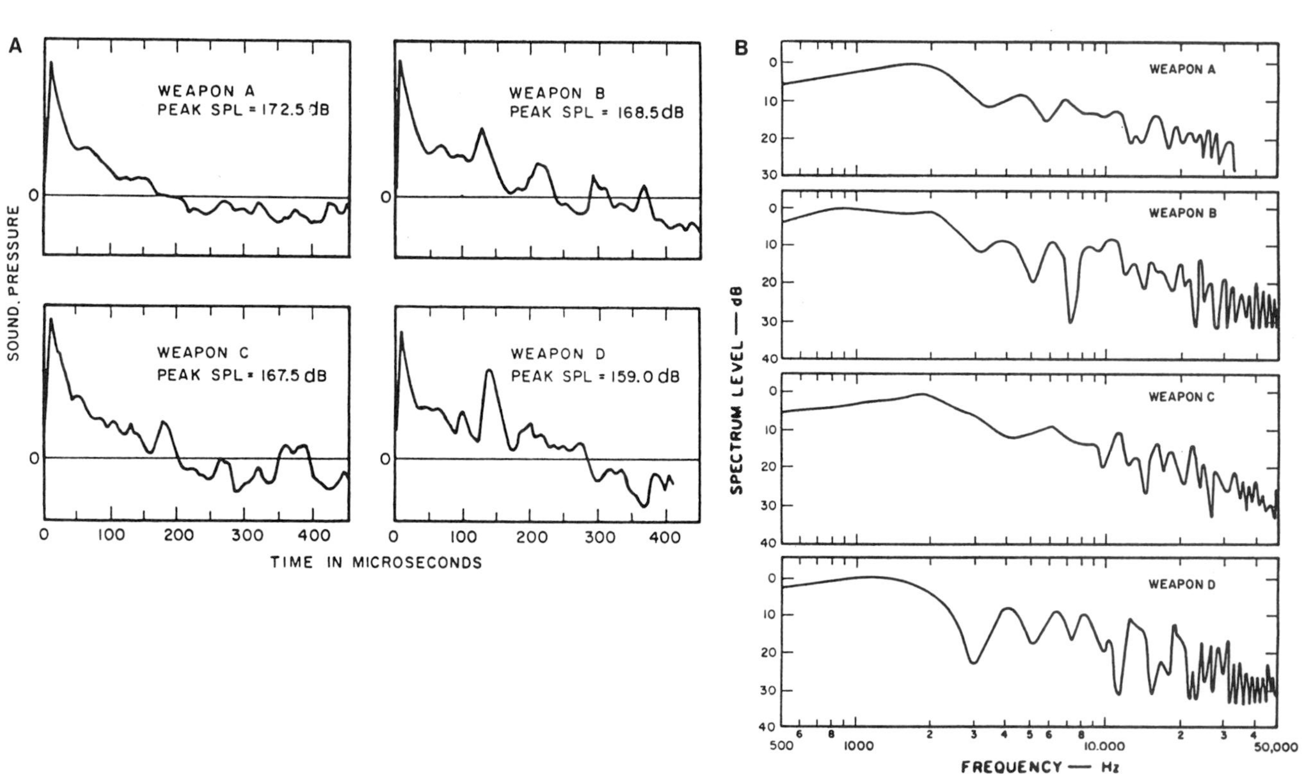

FIGURE 5.9 (A) Pressure waveforms and peak, unweighted, sound-pressure levels of the impulses from the four shoulder-rifle weapons. Estimated duration to timeline of 0.0002 s. Peak levels of the waveform have been adjusted for approximately equal peak amplitude. (B) Relative spectrum levels of the impulses from the four weapons. (From Kryter and Garinther, 1965.)

TABLE 5.4 Unweighted and *A*-weighted Octave Band and Overall Levels of Various Noises

Octave-band center frequency, Hz	*A*-weighting	Gun-noise impulse*		Average factory noise†		Forge hammer impulse‡		Forge press impact‡		Filtered −3 dB/octave		Random noise pink (flat/octave)	
		dB	dB_A	dB	dB_A	dB	dB_A	dB	dB_A	dB	dB_A	dB	dB_A
125	−16	139	120	87	71	101	85	95	79	96	80	90	74
250	−8	142	134	89	81	100	92	91	83	93	85	90	82
500	−4	149	146	90	87	105	102	95	92	90	87	90	87
1000	0	155	155	92	92	102	102	88	88	87	87	90	90
2000	1	164	165	90	91	102	103	87	88	84	85	90	91
4000	1	161	159	90	91	99	100	88	89	81	82	90	91
8000	−1	158	154	88	87	103	102	88	87	78	77	90	89
Overall, 125–8000 Hz		167	168	98	97	111	109	100	96	99	93	98	97

* Military gun noise, Kryter and Garinther (1965). Based on average of field spectra; see Fig. 5.9.

† Average of mostly steady high-level industrial nosies, Gallo and Glorig (1964). Level for 125-Hz band estimated.

‡ Impulse and impact noise from forging industries, Tayler *et al.* (1984).

TABLE 5.5 SPL in Ear Canal per Free Field at Various Azimuths of Source of Sound and Head of Listener; Differences in SPLs in Ear Canals from Shoulder-Rifle Fire and Facing-Source Sound (See Fig. 5.10)

		Shoulder-rifle‡		Gunfire vs. facing-source sound	
Frequency, kHz	Facing source* 0°†	Near ear 45°	Far ear 315°	Near ear	Far ear
5.0	1	5	0	4	−1
1.0	0	5	−5	5	−5
2.0	10	11	3	1	−7
2.5	11	15	5	4	−6
3.0	7	11	1	4	−6
4.0	3	7	−5	4	−8
6.0	6	13	−2	7dB	−8dB
Average	5dB	10dB	−1dB	4dB	−5dB

* SPL at 0° incidence is taken as typical for exposure to noise in industry.

† Azimuth of source to centerline of head-facing source.

‡ For right-handed person: near ear = left ear.

diameter and 1 m from the center of the person's head. Acoustically, these conditions are quite similar to those of the gun-noise study of Kryter and Garinther (1965).

The differences between the levels at the ear canal and those of free field, with various angles of azimuth, relative to the front-centerline of the head, are shown in Fig. 5.10. The free field–ear-canal sound-pressure levels at azimuths of 0°, 45°, and 315° for a number of frequencies were read from enlargements made of Fig. 5.10. Those data and the differences between the levels found for 0° (facing the source), and the 45° and 315° azimuths are given in Table 5.6. The differences are attributed to sound diffraction around the head and resonances of the ear canal.

It is seen in Table 5.6 that the difference between free-field facing the source, and near-ear canal pressures of shoulder-rifle gun noise, averaged about 10 dB. Azimuths of from the source were estimated as being 45° for the near ear, and 315° for the far ear of the shooter. This 10-dB difference undoubtedly explains why the near ear of hunters using shoulder-guns typically has significantly more hearing loss than the far ear. However, in the Kryter and Garinther (1965) study such a difference was not found.

The only explanation that could be offered was that the following factors prevented, or inhibited, the effects of that difference from being manifested in that study: (1) for right-handed shooters, the near-ear–far-ear relationship is nearly reversed for shoulder-rifle firing from that found when hand-pistols are fired; that is, the head is turned so that the right ear of a right-handed

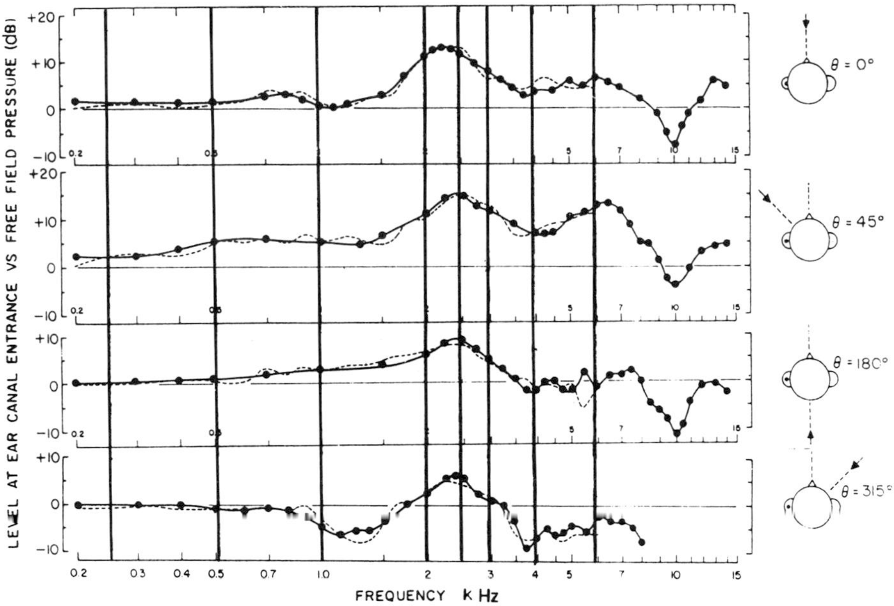

FIGURE 5.10 Differences between sound pressure level at entrance to ear canal and freefield as function of frequency and four angles of incidence from source. (After Shaw, 1966. Copyright 1966 by the American Psychological Association. Adapted by permission of the author.)

shooter is somewhat nearer than is the left ear to, or at least equidistant from, the muzzle of the pistol; (2) a number of the subjects had significant preexposure hearing levels in their far ear, for shoulder-rifle use [their near ear when shooting pistols, see Table III of subject study]; and (3) these far-rifle-ear hearing losses were perhaps due to the firing of hand guns during previous military training. Collins (1948) also found a relatively small difference between the right- and left-ear hearing levels of a sample of military personnel. Be that as it may, when the noise is from a nearby point source that is to the side, or somewhat lateral, to a person's head, like that from a shoulder-rifle, a special assessment of spectrum levels is, acoustically, justified.

Lateralized Point (lp) Source Noise

Table 5.6 shows that the difference in SPL between an ear canal when facing that point source and when at an azimuth angle of about 45° averaged 4 dB for the frequencies 500 Hz to 4000 Hz, and 7 dB at 6000 Hz. These decibel differences were added to the $^1/_3$-octave band levels, at the designated center frequencies, of the rifle-gun noise. The resulting basic unit, labeled *e*dB*n*,lp. was then used to calculate $EL_{Aeq8h}$and $EE_{A,f}$ in accordance with Eqs. (5.13) and (5.16). The results are shown in Tables 5.5.

TABLE 5.6 Exposure to, and 25, 50, and 75%ile pre- and post-HLs, and Predicted NIPTS from, Rifle Fire Data Right and Left Ears, *N*, Averaged

					25%ile			50%ile			75%ile		
Weapon*	Number of rounds	Peak L_A†	EL_{Aeq8h} + lp‡	$EE_{A,f}$ 50 years§	pre-exposure HL	post-exposure HL_2	$EE_{A,f}$ NIPTS	pre-exposure HL	post-exposure HL_2	$EE_{A,f}$ NIPTS	pre-exposure HL	post-exposure HL_2	$EE_{A,f}$ NIPTS
					1000 Hz								
A, *N* = 6	102	174	101.6	105.2	11	13	17	13	29	29	16	39	43
	74	174	99.4	103.0	8	11	14	13	25	24	28	35	35
	32	174	91.5	95.1	10	15	6	14	18	10	23	23	15
	17	174	86.0	89.6	7	14	3	11	18	5	15	21	7
B, *N* = 36	100	170	97.4	101.0	10	8	11	15	12	91	19	23	28
	60	170	93.0	96.6	9	11	7	13	14	12	18	21	18
	30	170	86.9	90.5	12	11	3	13	14	6	18	19	8
C, *N* = 27	97	169	96.1	99.7	15	10	10	17	16	16	20	25	24
	63	169	92.4	96.0	12	18	7	15	20	11	21	24	17
	23	169	83.6	87.2	8	11	2	14	11	3	18	20	5
D, *N* = 30	100	160	88.0	91.6	8	9	4	12	13	7	15	20	10
				Average	10	12	8	14	17	13	19	25	19
					2000 Hz								
A, *N* = 6	102	174	101.6	108.2	9	19	24	14	29	40	21	68	60
	74	174	99.4	106.0	6	9	19	9	37	32	19	62	49
	32	174	91.5	98.1	8	17	9	13	18	14	27	28	21
	17	174	86.0	92.6	6	12	5	12	16	8	19	22	11
B, *N* = 36	100	170	97.4	104.0	8	2	15	13	12	26	17	24	39

	60	170	93.0	99.6	6	10	10	11	14	16	14	22	24
	30	170	86.9	93.5	9	11	5	13	16	9	20	21	13
C, N = 27	97	169	96.1	102.7	12	12	14	12	14	23	19	30	35
	63	169	92.4	99.0	7	12	9	15	17	16	18	24	23
	23	169	83.6	90.2	7	10	3	17	11	5	25	22	8
D, N = 30	100	160	88.0	94.6	5	8	6	9	13	10	13	20	15
				Average	7	11	11	13	17	18	19	31	27
						3000 Hz							
A, N = 6	102	174	101.6	113.2	5	18	37	22	62	62	27	96	92
	74	174	99.4	111.0	3	21	31	18	56	51	35	67	77
	32	174	91.5	103.1	16	17	14	23	32	24	30	39	36
	17	174	86.0	97.6	7	20	8	18	23	14	25	39	20
B, N = 36	100	170	97.4	109.0	10	15	26	15	24	43	21	55	64
	60	170	93.0	104.6	9	12	16	17	20	27	23	34	41
	30	170	86.9	98.5	11	13	9	17	18	15	29	36	22
C, N = 27	97	169	96.1	107.7	12	21	23	13	31	38	22	63	57
	63	169	92.4	104.0	12	17	15	19	22	26	22	50	39
	23	169	83.6	95.2	12	9	6	15	20	10	25	19	16
D, N = 30	100	160	88.0	99.6	5	8	10	9	16	16	19	26	24
				Average	9	15	18	13	29	30	25	47	44
						4000 Hz							
A, N = 6	102	174	101.6	115.2	9	26	44	24	61	73	37	93	110
	74	174	99.4	113.0	6	26	37	20	83	61	29	94	92
	32	174	91.5	105.1	14	23	17	33	39	28	40	69	43
	17	174	86.0	99.6	9	22	10	17	30	16	19	50	24
B, N = 36	100	170	97.4	111.0	11	17	31	15	30	51	29	61	77
	60	170	93.0	106.6	12	11	21	17	21	34	27	34	51
	30	170	86.9	100.5	12	16	11	21	22	18	30	33	27
C, N = 27	97	169	96.1	109.7	9	12	27	12	52	46	23	74	69
	63	169	92.4	106.0	12	16	19	21	44	32	16	64	49
	23	169	83.6	97.2	9	11	8	18	16	13	38	23	20

(*continues*)

TABLE 5.6 *(Continued)*

Weapon*	Number of rounds	Peak L_A†	EL_{Aeq8h} + lp‡	$EE_{A,f}$ 50 years§	25%ile pre-exposure HL	25%ile post-exposure HL_2	25%ile $EE_{A,f}$ NIPTS	50%ile pre-exposure HL	50%ile post-exposure HL_2	50%ile $EE_{A,f}$ NIPTS	75%ile pre-exposure HL	75%ile post-exposure HL_2	75%ile $EE_{A,f}$ NIPTS
D, $N = 30$	100	160	88.0	101.6	8	14	12	19	20	21	23	42	31
				Average	10	18	21	20	38	36	28	58	54
6000 Hz													
A, $N = 6$	102	174	104.7	116.2	13	18	48	20	79	80	65	100	120
	74	174	101.9	114.0	4	5	40	9	85	66	32	99	100
	32	174	94.6	106.1	22	25	20	34	33	33	46	70	49
	17	174	89.2	100.6	11	19	11	24	37	18	28	70	27
B, $N = 36$	100	170	100.5	112.0	12	26	34	16	57	56	40	68	84
	60	170	96.1	107.6	13	18	23	18	28	38	31	42	57
	30	170	90.1	101.5	20	19	12	32	34	20	53	68	30
C, $N = 27$	97	169	99.3	110.7	13	29	30	17	72	51	34	86	76
	63	169	95.5	107.0	10	19	21	22	32	36	42	69	53
	23	169	86.8	98.2	17	20	15	25	25	25	22	40	37
D, $N = 30$	100	160	90.5	102.6	13	17	14	28	39	23	38	58	35
				Average	13	19	24	22	47	40	39	70	61

* Data from Table 4, Kryter and Garinther (1965). HLs corrected to ISO 389; 3 dB added for self-recording audiometer. Three HL_2 entries in original Table 4 corrected: weapon A, 74 rounds, 3 kHz, 75%ile, 5–55; weapon B, 100 rnds, 25%ile, 5 to −5; weapon C, 97 rounds, 6 kHz, 2–12. Data 23 rounds and 97 rounds, weapon C, interchanged.

† L_A, unweighted and L_A SPL calculated from relative spectrum levels. See Table 5.4.

‡ $EL_{Aeq8h + lp}$, $e_{dBn} = L_{A0.5\,s}$ [peak L_A − 10 log(0.5 s/0.00015 s)] − 20 log(57,600/N rounds + 4 = N rounds). [Adjustment for recovery and refractory-for- recovery interruptions] + lp, (lateral point source and incidence factor) (4 dB 1, 2, 3, 4 kHz; 7 dB 6 kHz).

§ $EE_{A,f,}$ 50 years = e_{dBn} + 8 log 50 years' exposure (13.6 dB) − adjusted test frequency NIPTS threshold. 50%ile NIPTS predicted by $EE_{A,f}$ multiplied by 0.6 for 25%ile NIPTS, and by 1.5 for 75%ile NIPTS.

After Kryter and Garinther (1965).

Results of Gun-Noise Study

Figure 5.11A shows, for test frequencies 1000, 2000, and 3000 Hz, the 25%ile, 50%ile, and 75%ile predicted NIPTS, preexposure HL and HL_2, as a function of $EE_{A,f}$, where $EE_{A,f}$ was based on $EL_{Aeq8h,50\ \text{years of exposure}}$, edB,lp,50y. The trend curves are visually fitted to the respective data points. Figure 5.11B shows similar data and trend curves for frequencies 4000 and 6000 Hz. Considering the experimental conditions, it is submitted that there is reasonable agreement at the higher level of exposure between the trend curves for HL_2 and predicted NIPTS for the 50%ile and 75%ile data.

Inasmuch as the soldiers were less than 25 years of age, the 50%ile preexposure hearing levels should have equaled 0 HL had they normal hearing, and HL2 should equal TTS_2. It is clear in Figs. 5.11A and 5.11B that HL_2 can be taken as approximating TTS_2 only when the gun noise exceeded $EE_{A,f}$ of about 104, and then only for the 50 and 75%iles. It appears that the distribution of preexposure hearing losses of the soldiers at least equaled the distribution of TTS_2 that could be caused in normal ears from the lower exposure levels of gun noise.

For example, for the different groups of subjects, 50%ile preexposure level averaged 17 dB at 4000 Hz. This finding, and its misleading effect on deducing a minimum exposure level for inducing threshold shift, is reminiscent of the results of early studies of NIPTS discussed in Chapter 4, where it was found that supposedly non-noise-exposed control groups had 10 dB or so of NIPTS from, apparently, gun noise.

The average ~3-dB increase of postexposure levels, HL_2, for the lower levels of gun noise above preexposure hearing levels would seem to indicate that their effective energies were about equal to the effective energies of previous noise exposures experienced by the soldiers, exposures that caused their elevated-above-normal preexposure hearing levels. As discussed in Chapter 4, and elsewhere in this chapter, if both energies would cause, say, 10 dB threshold shifts, together, or in sequence, they could be expected to cause a $\sim\geq$3-dB shift, for a total of HL 13.

Hypothesis of High-Intensity Overload of the Ear

It has been occasionally hypothesized that there is a level of sound intensity above which NIPTS increases, with increases in intensity, at a faster rate than it does below that critical level. Dieroff (1980) for example, estimated that above a peak level of about 150-dB damage to the inner ear progresses at a more rapid rate than would be expected on the basis of the effects on NIPTS of lower-intensity noise.

Kryter and Garinther (1965) suggested that for gun noise this critical level was about L_A 160. This suggestion was based on the growth of HL_2 (expected TTS_2) above that level of intensity in comparison to the rate of growth below

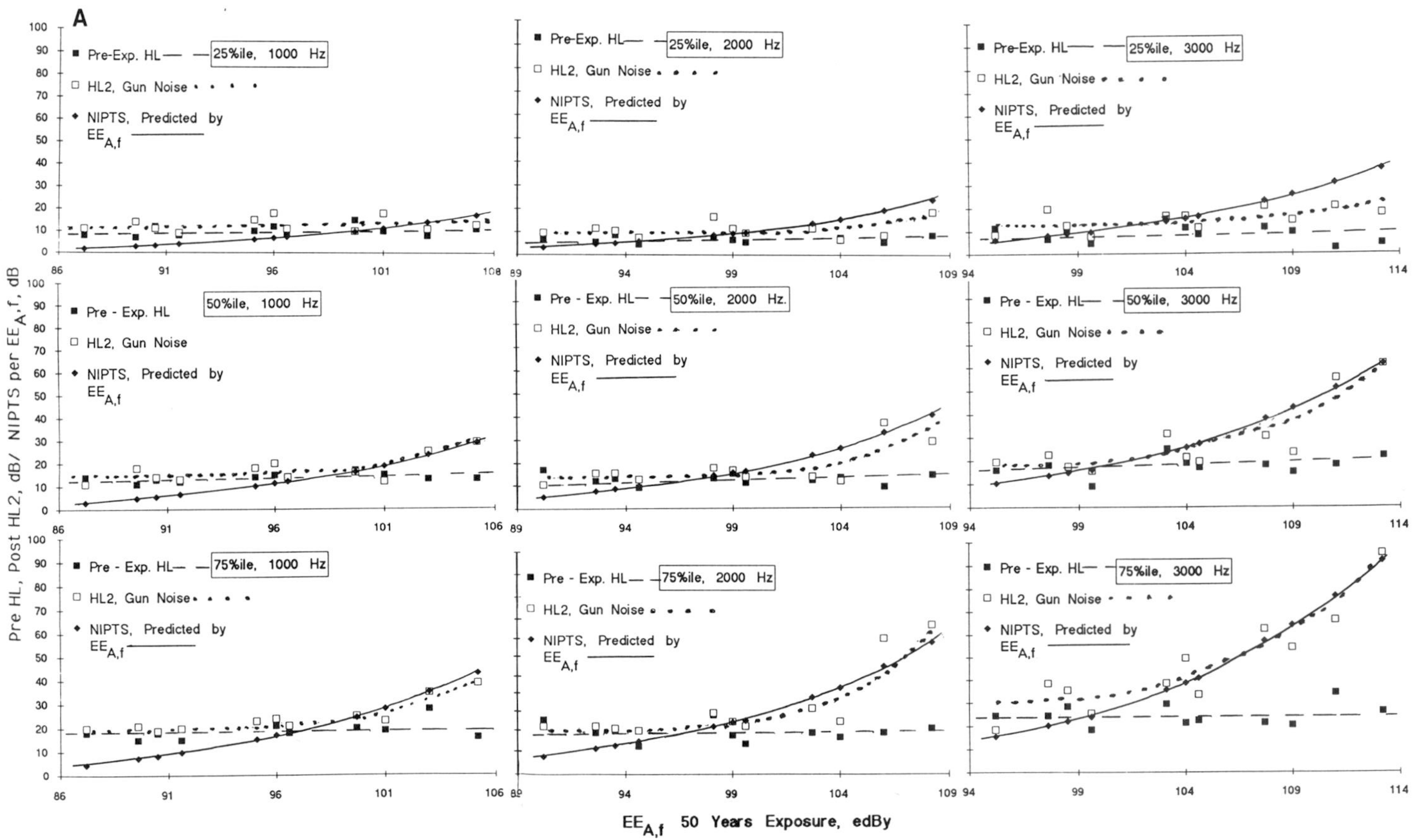

FIGURE 5.11A For 1000, 2000, and 3000 Hz, 25%ile, 50%ile, and 75%ile, preexposure HL, 2-min postexposure HL_2, and NIPTS predicted by $EE_{A,f}$ for soldier-subjects exposed to various numbers (17–102) of rounds, separated by 5 s, of different-intensity rifle fire. Based on data in Table 5.6.

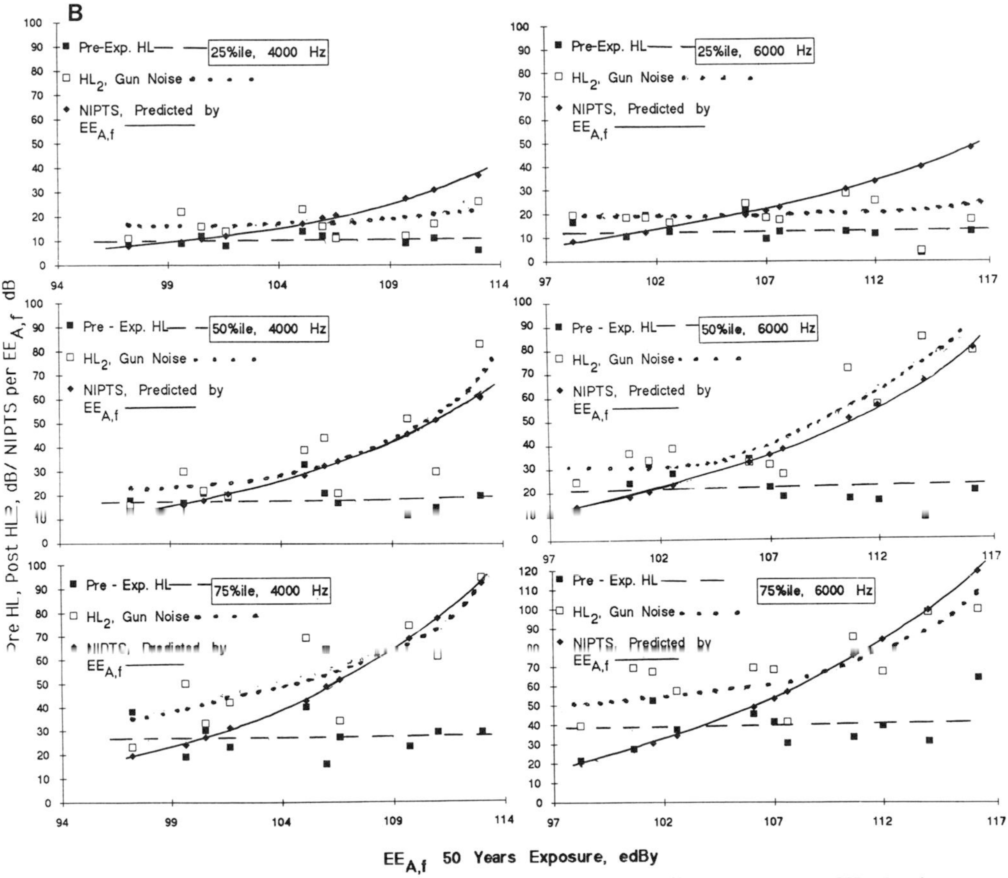

FIGURE 5.11B For 4000 and 6000 Hz, 25%ile, 50%ile, and 75%ile, preexposure HL, 2-min postexposure HL_2, and NIPTS predicted by $EE_{A,f}$ for soldier-subjects exposed to various numbers (17–102) of rounds, separated by 5 s, of different intensity rifle fire. Based on data in Table 5.6.

that level. Unfortunately, as is now noted, TTS_2 for the lower levels of the gun noise was constrained because of elevated preexposure hearing levels of the soldier-subjects.

As was shown in Figs. 5.11A and 5.11B, the estimated rate of growth of HL_2 (TTS_2) with the higher levels of exposure to the gun noise) appears to have about the same shape, except for the 25%ile data, as $EE_{A,f}$ predicted NIPTS. That is, there appears to be no accelerated increase in rate in HL_2 with increasing exposure levels of the ultraintense gun noise, compared to the rate found with for NIPTS with comparable decibel increases in exposure levels of typical industrial noises. A comparative accelerated rate of increase would, of course, be expected, according to the ear-overload theory.

Peak Level of Gun Noise as a Parameter

These gun noise data provide a further means of testing the validity of the high-intensity overload theory. For one session during the study, each of the four military rifles, with peak levels ranging from L_A 160 to 174, were fired about 100 times with 5-s intervals between rounds (weapon A, 102; weapons B and D, 100; and weapon C, 97).

Figure 5.12A shows, for test frequencies 1000, 2000, and 3000 Hz, the 25%ile, 50%ile, and 75%ile predicted NIPTS, preexposure HL and HL_2, as a function of $EE_{A,f,\ 50\ \text{years of exposure}}$, where $EE_{A,f}$ was based on EL_{Aeq8h}, using *e*dB*n*,lp. The trend curves are visually fitted to the respective data points. Figure 5.12B shows the same data for test frequencies 4000 and 6000 Hz. It is seen that, for 50%ile and 75%ile data, there is reasonable agreement, considering the nature of the exposures and other conditions, at the higher level of exposure between the trend curves for HL_2 and predicted NIPTS. In brief, it appears from the gun-noise data that a "critical level of intensity" for causing sensorineural auditory fatigue appears to be L_A >174, if indeed it exists, for humans.

The generality of a similar, and predictive, relation between TTS_2 and NIPTS extending over such a wide range of intensities can be challenged by the threshold shift and histological findings, to be discussed, in some experiments with animals. However, these latter data possibly reflect differences in regard to the structure and sensitivity of the ears of different animal species. It is also perhaps germane to note that critical overloading and damage of physical structures of the ear other than in the cochlea, e.g., the eardrum and ossicles, can in some cases intervene and become involved in hearing at even lower levels of intensity than the L_A 174 dB present in the gun noise.

Sound Transmission by the Ossicles

The human middle ear exhibits nonlinear characteristics in response to high-intensity sounds. The eardrum shows linearity up to about 140 dB SPL, and the ossicular chain to about 130 dB (von Békésy, 1960; Tonnedorf and Khanna, 1967; Tonnedorf, 1976). Above those levels, depending on spectrum, pressure amplitudes are somewhat limited, resulting in some frequency distortion products (Price and Kalb, 1991).

von Békésy (1960) observed that with an input level of about 130 dB there was a vertical displacement in the stapes footplate, and at about 140 dB there was a rotational mode of displacement in the footplate. As a result, according to Bekesy, the fluid displacements in the cochlear fluid would be minimized and, thereby, reduce the efficiency of sound transmission through the middle ear. Both this latter sound attenuation, and the peak amplitude limiting noted above, presumably afford some protection to the inner ear from hazards of ultraintense sounds.

Eardrum

At SPLs in excess of L_A 160, for pulses with slow rise-times and strong low-frequency content, unlike typical gunfire, the eardrum may be ruptured. However, such rupturing appears to provide some protection to the inner ear so that after the drum heals, hearing levels may show less shift than occurs in subjects with unruptured eardrums. (Guild 1944; Perlman, 1945).

Aural Reflex

The aural reflex also provides for some reduction in the transmission of high-intensity sound to the inner ear (see Chapter 2 for further discussion and references to review articles). However, this response recovers in about one second after cessation of a stimulating sound (see Fig. 2.19A), and hence was presumably not a factor in the threshold shifts from the 5-s-separated impulses of gun noise involved in the study discussed above.

While the aural reflex must provide some protection to the inner ear, von Békésy (1960) suggests its main role is to maintain linearity of transmission by the ossicles of high-frequency components in sound when they are associated with intense low-frequency components. von Békésy hypothesizes that (1) the displacement of the ossicles would tend to become progressively larger at lower frequencies, for a given intensity of sound input; (2) this would cause the stapedius muscle (the main muscle attached to the ossicles) to rub against the sides of a bony tunnel through which the muscle passes; and (3) as a result, the ossicles would be forced to "chatter," or, at least, cause distortion in the transmission of higher frequency sounds to the cochlea.

This theory offers a meaningful explanation of why the aural reflex attenuates the lower frequencies (≤1000 Hz; see Fig. 2.18) but not the higher frequencies, frequencies to which the ear is most sensitive. In any event, in the author's opinion, there are insufficient data available to generally quantify the effects of the behavior of the aural reflex in a model for predicting NIPTS.

Delayed TTS from Exposures to Gun Noise

Dancer *et al.* (1991) found that in some soldier-subjects exposed to a mild dosage of gun shots, TTS was larger after 1 h, and in some cases, 4 h, than at 5 min after the exposure. This, of course, is contrary to most TTS data, which typically show a maximum TTS at 2 min postexposure, with some recovery in hearing level thereafter. However, on the average, the differences in the Dancer *et al.* data between TTS, averaged over 10 audiometric frequencies at the different postexposure test times indicated the usually observed trend of decreasing TTS with postexposure interval. The predominate number (~90%) of the averaged threshold shifts were of a negligible size (<5dB). Sixteen of the subjects received 10 shots, with peak level between 156 and

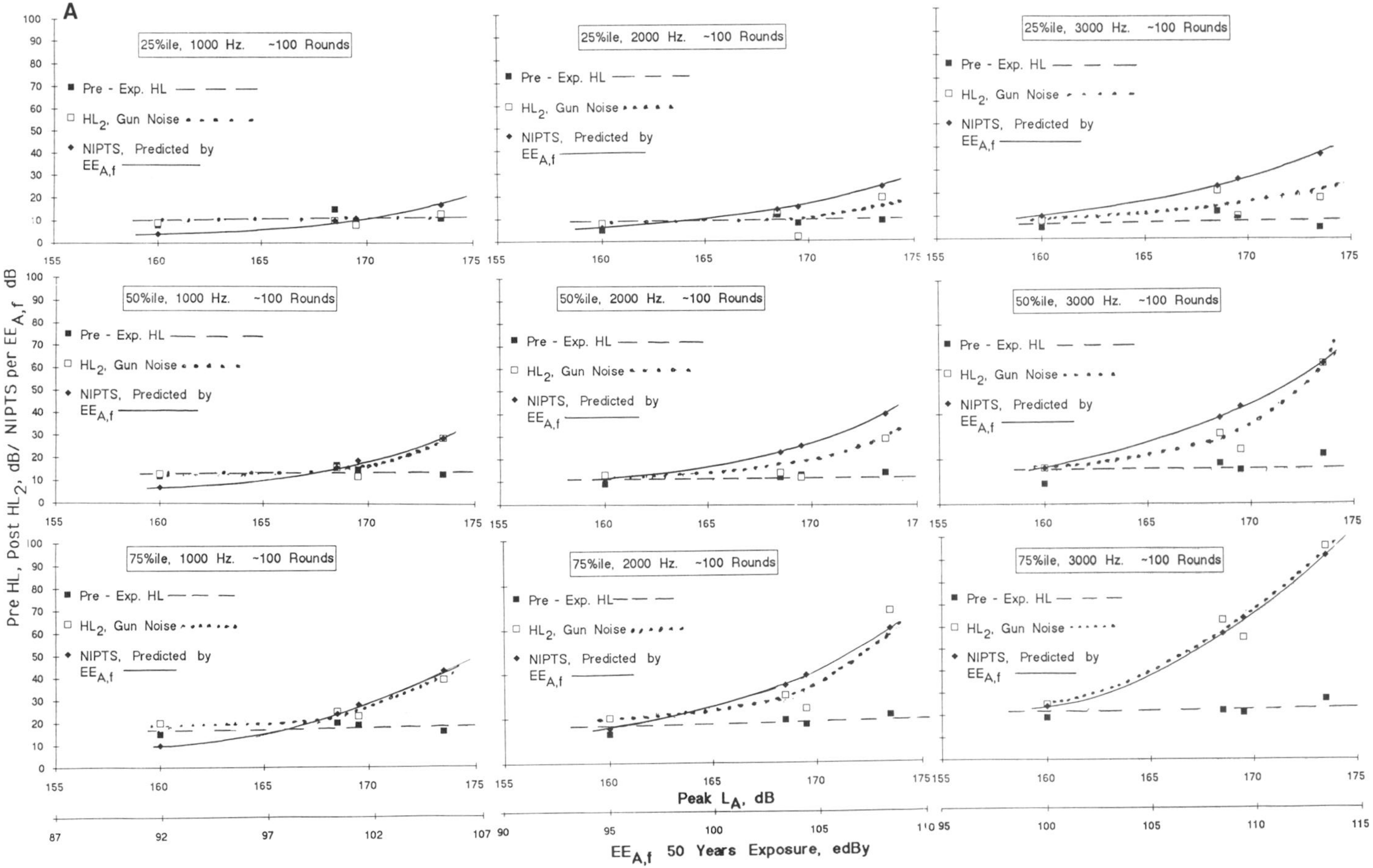

FIGURE 5.12A For 1000, 2000, and 3000 Hz, 25%ile, 50%ile, and 75%ile, preexposure HL, 2-min postexposure HL_2, and NIPTS predicted by $EE_{A,f}$ for soldier-subjects exposed to 97–102 rounds, separated by 5 s, of different-peak-intensity rifle fire. Based on data in Table 5.6.

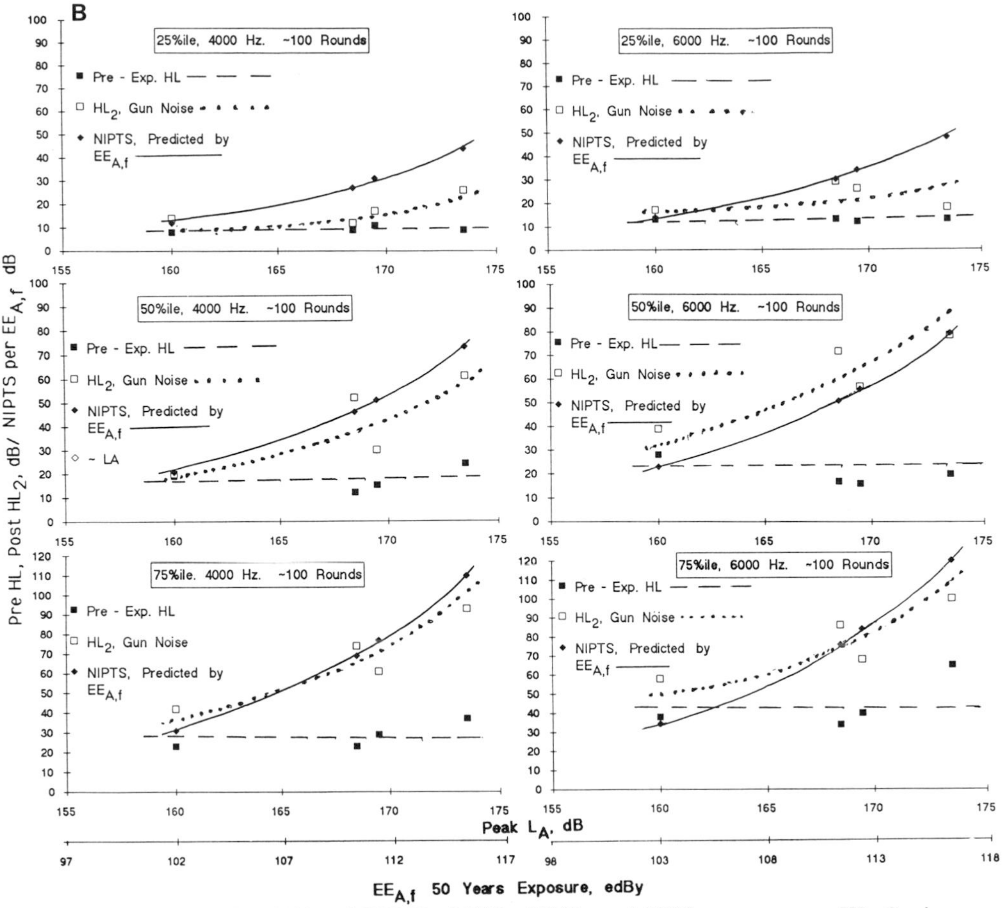

FIGURE 5.12B For 4000 and 6000 Hz, 25%ile, 50%ile, and 75%ile, preexposure HL, 2-min postexposure HL_2, and NIPTS predicted by $EE_{A,f}$ for soldier-subjects exposed to 97–102 rounds, separated by 5 s, of different-peak-intensity rifle fire. Based on data in Table. 5.6.

159 dB, and eight subjects received 100 shots, with peak level of 152 dB, for each of 2 days. Under these circumstances, it is believed that some cases could be expected by chance to show the variability noted by Dancer *et al.*

BEHAVIORAL AND EVOKED POTENTIAL THRESHOLDS OF HEARING IN ANIMALS

Major reasons for the use of animals for experiments of sound-induced loss in hearing sensitivity are, of course, that (1) durations and intensities of exposures to sounds and noises can be set to cause thresholds shifts of magnitudes and durations unacceptable with the use of human subjects; and

(2) the status of the structures in the ears of the animals can be postmortemly examined by histologic and microscopic techniques to determine precise pathological effects, if any, of the sounds. The two primary methods used to measure pure-tone thresholds of hearing sensitivity in animals are behavioral training, and the measurement of electrical potentials generated by neural activity in the auditory system.

Behavioral Thresholds

In this method, the animal is placed in a device that will allow movement by the animal, or contains a lever that can be moved by the animal. The animal is then trained to initiate some movement when it hears a pure tone, and to refrain from making the movement when the tone is not presented. A standard procedure for such training is to apply a brief electric shock to the animal, usually through a grilled floor, if it fails to respond to a tone when it is presented, and to reward it by not shocking it during periods of quiet. The experimenter determines when a tone will be presented, and at what intensity.

A second training technique allows the animal to initiate a trial period, usually about 9 s in duration, by depressing and holding down a spring-loaded response key/feeder-chute. During this 9 s a 2-s period is randomly chosen by the experimenter, or by an automated timer, to be either a stimulus-presented, or a stimulus-withheld, segment. The animal is rewarded with a small pellet of food if it releases the response key when a tone is presented during the 2-s trial period, and, also, if it holds the key down for the 2-s trial periods in which a tone is not presented (Clark *et al.,* 1974).

As with human audiometry, in both of these training methods a threshold is determined by finding the highest intensity of the tone that is apparently inaudible—that level at which, for only some chosen small percentage of trials, the animal will respond as though the tone were present, when, in fact, it was not.

Evoked Potential Thresholds

It is possible to observe and measure auditory system neural activity that is directly related to stimulation of the ear by sound. To do so, time-varying differences in electric potentials between an electrode placed, usually, on the top of the skull and another electrode placed near, or on, the cochlea, auditory nerve, brain stem (inferior colliculas), or brain are monitored. These potentials, which reflect electrical neural activity in the auditor nerve and brian stem, are filtered and analyzed, computer-aided, in ways that show correlations between neural responses initiated in the cochlea with sound introduced into the ear canal. The responses are variously called *brain-stem-evoked response* (BSER); *auditory brain-stem response* (ABR); *auditory evoked potentials* (AEPs); *auditory evoked response* (AER); or, simply, *evoked potential* (EP). (See Moore 1983, for a description of various recording techniques used for these purposes.)

So called cochlear microphonics (CM) are also picked up from electrodes placed near the ear when the ear is exposed to sound. These electrical responses are apparently related to mechanical movement, or stress, of hair cells due to the sound. Cochlear microphonics do not, per se, indicate evoked electrical potentials from sensorineural activity and are not necessarily indicative of auditory nerve activity and actual hearing. CM potentials can be distinguished from neural potentials by, among other things, their sort latency of response to sound stimuli. Their lack of normal presence does indicate, however, abnormal hair-cell function.

TTS and NIPTS Measured by Avoidance-Training Thresholds

The thresholds of hearing at different frequencies for guinea pigs, chinchillas, rats, cats, and monkeys have been found by the shock avoidance-training technique and compared to those for humans. Some of these are shown in Fig. 5.13. Examples of TTS, and recovery therefrom, found in chinchillas following exposure to noise are shown in the graphs of Fig. 5.14.

Animal Studies of "Toughening" of the Ear to TTS and NIPTS

Two somewhat different experimental procedures of exposing chinchillas to a tone and bands of noise have indicated an apparent "toughening," or conditioning process in the ear. As a result, the ear appears to become less susceptible to loss from further exposure to intense sound. The first method is to expose the animal to a moderately intense, relatively long-duration continuous, or interrupted, tone or band of noise, followed by a more "traumatic" tone or nose exposure. For purposes of the following discussion, this method is called *moderate plus traumatic exposure*.

The second method is to follow the actual hearing level (or threshold shift per the baseline level) that occurs following successive equally intense, interrupted exposures. The interruptions may be sufficiently long for considerable, perhaps complete, apparent recovery of any threshold shift to occur between exposures. This method is lableled *successive equal exposures*.

Moderate Plus Traumatic Exposures, 1-kHz Tone

As part of a physiologic–anatomic investigation of acoustic trauma, Canlon (1988) measured the hearing threshold in two groups of guinea pigs. Hearing thresholds were deduced from analysis of brain-stem electrical neural activity recorded from electrodes placed subcutaneously behind the ear and the top

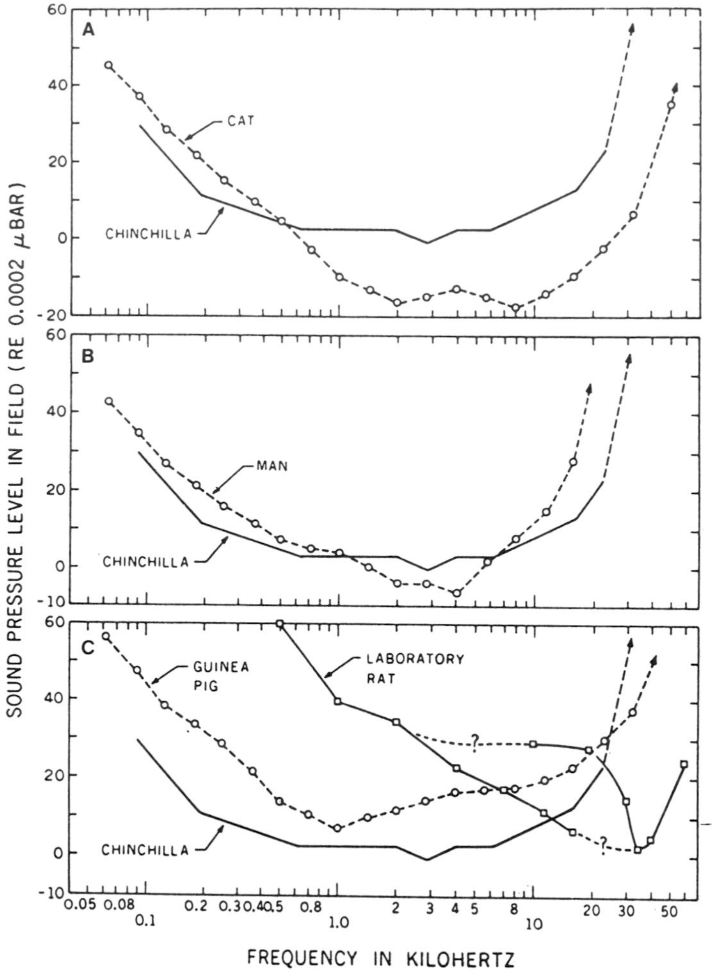

FIGURE 5.13 Threshold of audibility curves of the chinchilla compared to that for (A) the cat, (B) human, and (C) guinea pig and laboratory rat. (From Miller, 1970. Copyright 1970 by the American Psychological Association. Adapted by permission of the author.)

of the scalp. The sound pressure level of the audiometer tones were calibrated as the pressure in the ear canal of the animal.

One group of guinea pigs was exposed for 3 days to a 1000-Hz tone at 105 dB (called the "trauma" noise). The second group was exposed for 24 days to the tone at a level of 81 dB (the "toughening" sound), followed by a 3-day exposure to the tone at the 105-dB level. Canlon had found no threshold shift in a pilot test involving 3 days of exposure to a 1000-Hz tone of 90 dB, and presumed, on an equal-energy assumption basis, that no shift had occurred in the animals from the 24 days of exposure at 81 dB.

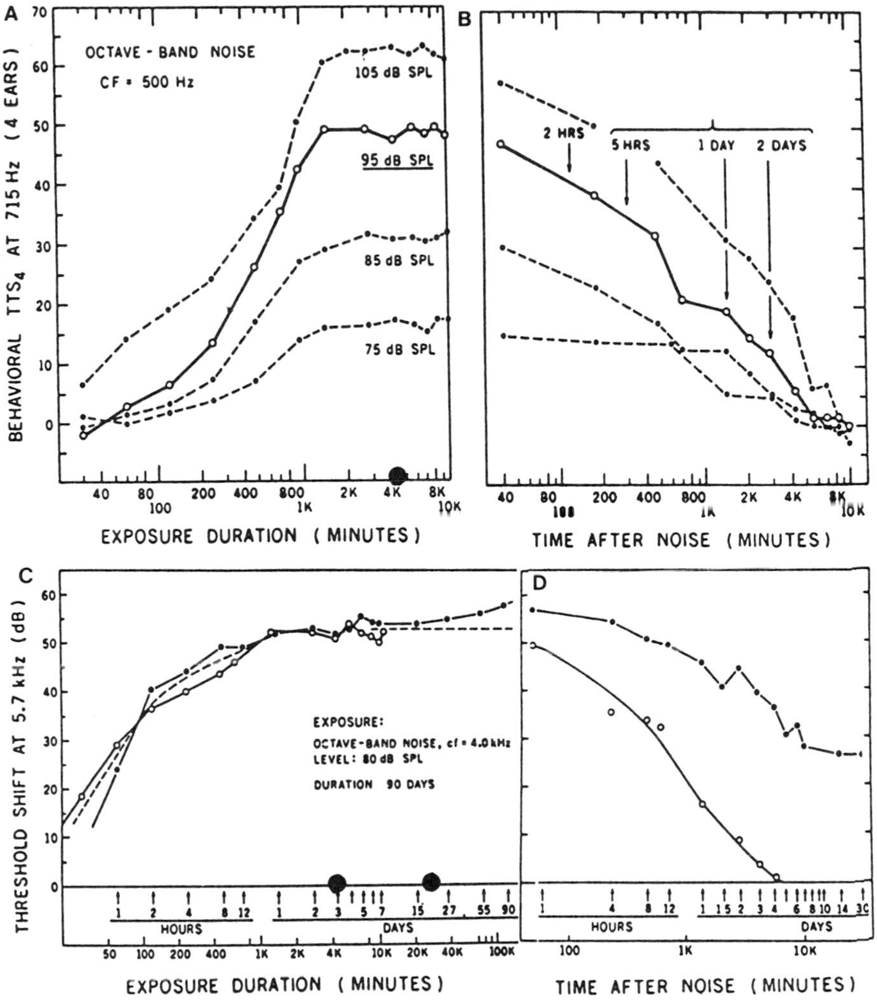

FIGURE 5.14 (A) Growth of threshold shifts to asymptote as a function of duration of exposures to 0.5-kHz octave band of noise with sound-pressure level as the parameter. Dot (●), zero shift found by Canlong (1988) from exposure to 1-kHz tone, 90 dB for 3 days. (B) Recovery from threshold shifts. (After Carder and Miller, 1972.) (C) growth of threshold shifts to asympotote as a function of duration of exposures to 4-kHz octave band of noise. Data from two studies. Dot (●), zero shift found by Canlon (1988) from exposure to 1-kHz tone, 90 dB for 3 days, and 81 dB for 24 days. (D) Recovery from threshold shifts. (After Mills, 1976.)

Figure 5.15A shows the absolute thresholds (filled circles) of the auditory brainstem response of the animals prior to exposure to any noise, and the thresholds (open circles) of the animals 1 h after 3 days of exposure to a 1000-Hz tone at 105 dB. Also shown in Fig. 5.15A, lower row of x's, are the open-field SPLs at thresholds of hearing found in guinea pigs when

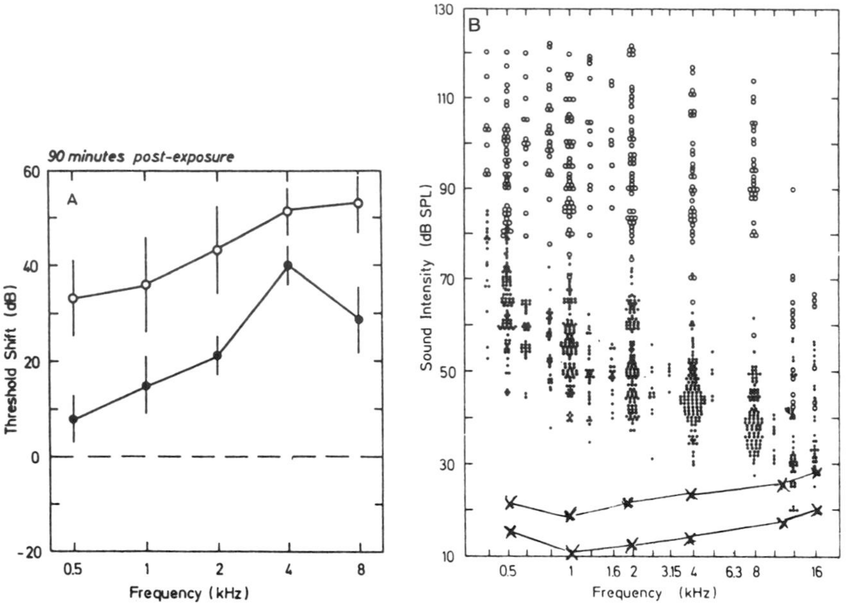

FIGURE 5.15 (A) Evoked-potential thresholds preexposure, filled circles, and 90 min after (open circles) exposure of guinea pigs for 72 h to 1 kHz tone at 105 dB SPL. (From Canlon, 1988.) The lower x's from Fig. 5.13, are open-field, and upper x's are estimated ear-canal SPLs for behavioral thresholds for guinea pigs. (B) Mean evoked potential thresholds shifts relative to mean preexposure hearing levels measured in one group of guinea pigs (open circles) 90 min after exposure to a 1-kHz tone at 105 dB for 72 h; and, in a second group (closed circles) exposure to a 1-kHz tone at 81 dB for 24 days followed by an additional 72 h of exposure at 105 dB. (From Canlon, 1988.)

determined by behavioral, shock-training procedures by other investigators. The estimated approximate comparable ear-canal pressures for the behavioral thresholds are indicated by the upper row of x's in Fig. 5.15.

As clearly seen in Fig. 5.15B, the threshold shift measured 90 min after exposure was greater for the animals in group I, exposed only to the tone at 105 dB for 3 days, than it was to the animals in group II, who were exposed for 24 days to the 1000-Hz tone at 81 dB, then exposed to the tone at 105 dB for 3 days, and then tested 90 min later. This is a most intriguing finding, and is contrary to the relations generally found between noise dosage and threshold shifts. It is usually found that the greater the amount of noise exposure, the greater, not the lesser, the amount of threshold shift.

Canlon, noting that some recent research has shown that isolated outer hair cells can change their length to electrical, chemical, or acoustical stimulation, postulates that this action alters "cochlear sensitivity." Canlon suggested that the 24 days of exposure to the 1000-Hz tone at 81 dB "trained" the cochlea, by exercising the "muscle-like capacity" of the outer hair cells, to be more protective than before to subsequent acoustic stimulation. Figure 5.15B shows an average reduced shift, over the test frequencies 500–8000 Hz of about 20 dB between the animals with "untrained," as compared to "trained" outer hair cells.

Alternative reasons for these findings should be considered. One cause for concern is that behavioral threshold shifts in chinchillas exposed to an octave band of noise at 85 dB reaches an asymptote of 30 dB after only 1–2 days of exposure, and recovery is not complete after several hours in the quiet, as shown in the graphs of Fig. 5.14,. Although guinea pigs apparently have 10 dB or so less sensitive hearing than chinchillas (see Fig. 5.13), the difference is not sufficient, it is believed, to explain the lack of any (0-dB) threshold shift reported by Canlon after exposure of guinea pigs to a 1-kHz tone at 81 dB for 24 days, or 90 dB for 3 days. The filled data-dots in Fig. 5.15A are representative, according to Canlon, of the hearing levels at 0.715 Hz for guinea pigs before and after those exposures.

Another concern (and the possible basis for the first) is the high level of the preexposure, "normal" hearing thresholds in this study. The pre(any)exposure thresholds as measured are approximately 30–35 dB higher than thresholds for guinea pigs measured by other investigators using behavioral training procedures. Those differences are based on comparisons, over the frequency region 500–8000 Hz, of visually estimated means of the closed circles in Fig. 5.15A with the upper row of x's in that graph.

Some of that difference could be due to the apparent lesser sensitivity in threshold measurements by evoked potentials than those obtained with behavioral methods. The evoked potential threshold average, over different studies, to be about 0–15 dB higher than behavioral thresholds in chinchillas, as noted earlier, and a difference of 5–10 dB is sometimes found with humans (McCandless and Lentz, 1968).

In any event, the elevation of evoked potential thresholds above "true," as measured by behavioral thresholds, creates the opportunity of having sensorineural threshold shifts created by exposure to a noise be obfuscated, the amount of obfuscation being equal to the amount of elevation. This is illustrated in Fig. 5.16. That figure indicates that (1) a shift of ~20 dB should, according to other data, be expected after the 81-dB tone for 24 days, but could not have been measured because of the elevated "normal" evoked potential threshold; (2) a shift of ~50 dB relative to "true" preexposure threshold is to be expected, according to other data and theory, 1.5 h after exposure to a tone of 105 dB for 72 h, regardless of whether that noise is preceded by a 24-day exposure to the tone at 81 dB (3) the predicted shift of 50 dB was measured only for the combined toughening and trauma, exposures; and (4) a shift of ~70 dB relative to "true" preexposure threshold was measured 1.5 h after exposure only to the 105-dB tone for 3 days. That 20 dB difference (70- vs. 50-dB shift), which is the same magnitude whether deduced from the estimated "false" EP or "true" preexposure baseline

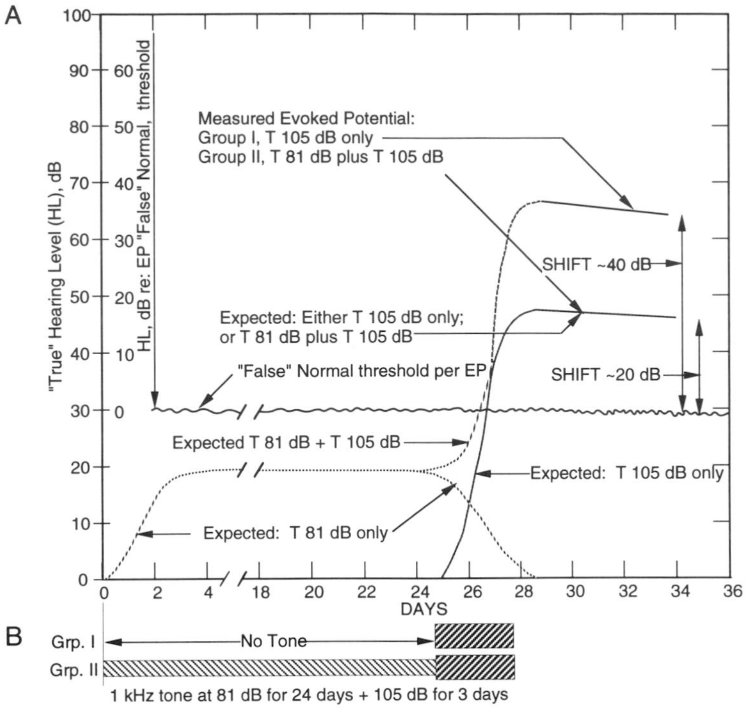

FIGURE 5.16 (A) Evoked-potential threshold shifts for control (group I) and experimental (group II) guinea pigs, measured by Canlon *et al.* (1988), relative to estimated true and false preexposure thresholds; (B) approximate threshold shifts expected according to behavioral data.

threshold, indicates an apparent 20 dB of toughening from the 81-dB, 24-day, pretrauma exposure.

The solid and doted curves on Fig. 5.16 representing the exposure levels of, and hearing levels from, the two regimens of exposure are based on calculations, made in accordance with earlier given formulae, as follows.

Exposure levels: $L_{ex,n1,2}$, = 110.1 dB, and $L_{ex,n2}$ = 110.0, where n_1 is 81-dB tone for 24 days = $L_{ex,n_1 95}$, and n_2 = 105-dB tone for 3 days = $L_{ex,n2}$ 110-dB tone; and L_{ex,n_1}, 95 dB + $L_{ex,n2}$, 110 dB = 10 log $L_{ex}(n_1 + L_{ex,n2})/10)$ = 110.1.

Hearing levels, based on 1.5-h postexposure threshold shifts (TS) relative to estimated true normal hearing level: $HL_{n1,2}$, 1.5 h postexposure = 50.0 dB; and HL_{n2}, 1.5 h postexposure = 50.0 dB, where TS $_{n1}$ is 20 dB, and TS, $_{n2}$ is 50 dB = 10 $\log_{10}$ (TS,$_{n1}$,20 + TS,$_{n2}$,50)/10 + 0 dB, normal HL = 50 dB; and TS_{n2}, = 50 dB + 0 dB, normal HL = 50 dB.)

The apparent abnormally high preexposure thresholds of hearing as measured by the evoked potentials in the Canlon study suggest that some methodological problem may be involved. However, the greater shift found for animals not receiving a toughening exposure prior to a more traumatic noise exposure has also been reported for some other evoked potential and behavioral threshold studies of this question.

Moderate Plus Traumatic Exposures, Octave Band of Noise 0.5 kHz

Campo *et al.* (1991) conducted an experiment similar in exposure-pattern to that used by Canlon (1988). These investigators used chinchillas, obtained evoked potential thresholds with the active electrode placed chronically near an auditory nerve center (the inferior colliculus) in the upper brain stem, and exposed the animals to an octave band of noise (OBN), with a center frequency of 0.5 kHz. (In the text to follow, the frequency designated for an OBN will refer to the center frequency of the designated OBN, not its bandwidth.) Unlike in the Canlon study, the "normal," preexposure, thresholds agreed reasonably well with the sound-pressure levels required for the behavioral thresholds shown in Fig. 5.13.

The experimental group of chinchillas was exposed to the 0.5-kHz OBN of 95 dB for 6 h per day for 10 days, given 5 days of rest, then exposed continuously for 48 h to the 0.5-kHz OBN at a level of 106 dB. A control group was exposed only to the 0.5 OBN at 106 dB for 48 h. The major result are shown in Fig. 5.17, where it is seen that the control group experienced about $\geq$20 less threshold shift, depending on test frequency and postexposure time of measurement, than did the experimental group. It is to be noted that the hearing levels of both groups were at normal prior to the star of the 106-dB, 48-h traumatic exposures; that is, the hearing levels of the experimental group had recovered from any shift experienced from the 95 dB, 6-h day, 10-day conditioning exposures.

These results are clearly supportive of the Canlon findings of a toughening, or increased resistance to threshold shift, from the noise exposures preceding the exposures to the more traumatic noise. Campo *et al.* chose to call this observed effect "conditioning" rather than "toughening."

However, the behavioral threshold shifts found by Carder and Miller (1972), also shown on Fig. 5.17, in chinchillas from exposure to 0.5-kHz OBN, 105 dB, for 48 h, raise some question about the toughening concept. These behavioral data (--○--in Fig. 5.17) are not consistent with the control group (--●--in Fig. 5.17) but are consistent with the evoked potential thresholds of the 'toughened' experimental group (..□..in Fig. 5.17) even showing slightly less shift than the latter. This would be expected from the fact that the latter group had received the 95-dB as well as the 105-dB noises. In brief, one could consider the very large shifts found for the control groups as being

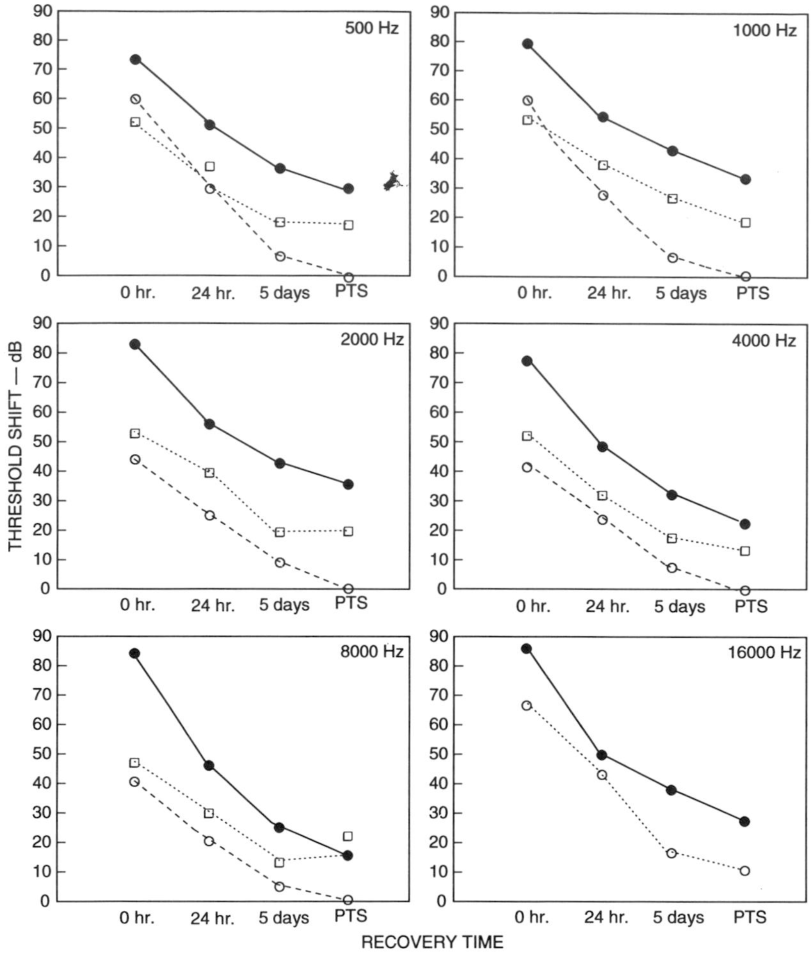

FIGURE 5.17 Recovery of threshold shifts in chinchillas at various test frequencies. Evoked-potential thresholds from Campo *et al.* (1991): (□), experimental group, 0.5-kHz OBN, 6 h per day for 10 days, 5 days rest, 106 dB for 48 h; (●), control group, 0.5 kHz OBN 106 dB for 48 h. Open circles (○) are data points from Carder and Miller (1972) for behavioral threshold from exposures to 0.5-kHz OBN, 105 dB for 48 h.

abberrant, rather than considering the smaller, but normally expected shifts, for the experimental, "toughened" group, as being abnormal.

Accepting the behavioral threshold data on Fig. 5.17 as representing actual hearing, it could then be said that, under some circumstances, evoked potential thresholds may not be indicative of perceived hearing. On the other hand, it is possible that the particular behavioral thresholds involved were for already toughened, or conditioned ears. Indeed, these data are for animals who had been, prior to the exposures represented in Fig. 5.17, exposed for

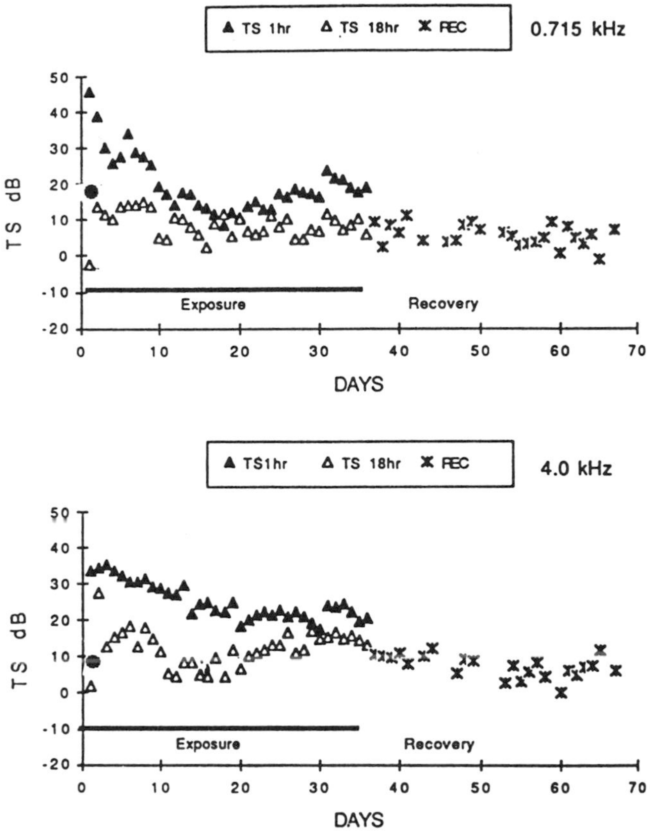

FIGURE 5.18 Mean of threshold shifts (TS), chinchillas, per preexposure baseline, following exposures to 0.5-kHz OBN, 95-dB SPL, 6 h per day for 36 days. Closed triangles: 1 h after each 6-h exposure; open triangles: 18 h after each day's exposure, i.e., prior to start of a following day's exposure. (After Clark, 1991. Copyright 1991 by the American Psychological Association. Adapted by permission of the author.) Added data points (●) show TS 4 min after 6 hr, 1 day, exposure of chinchillas to same noise. (From Carder and Miller, 1972.)

7 days to OBN 0.5 kHz at 75 dB, followed by 27 days of rest, at 85 dB, followed by 27 days of rest prior to 7 days of exposure to the OBN 0.5 kHz at 95 dB. However, the animals showed complete recovery from any TTS during the first few days of the 27-day rest periods following the exposure to the OBN at 75 and 85 dB.

Successive Equal Exposures, OBN 0.5 kHz

Clark *et al.* (1987), using the reward-training method described above, found the pure-tone thresholds of two groups of chinchillas exposed to an OBN 0.5 kHz of 95 dB. Group I (consisting of three animals) was exposed for 6 continuous hours per day for 36 days (a total of 360 min), and group II (four animals), was exposed for 15 min per hour for 144 days (a total of 360 min). A daily session of testing for hearing levels required about 45 min. Hearing levels were measured for group I prior to the first day's exposure and 1 h and 18 h after the termination of each 6-h exposure (i.e, just before the next day's exposure). Group II animals were tested within a 45-min rest periods in each of the 144 days.

Threshold shift data for group I are shown in Fig. 5.18, along with some data from the study by Carder and Miller (1972). The latter data, one large solid dot per graph, represent TTS data from Fig. 3 (see present Fig. 5.14) and Fig. 4 from Carder and Miller. The Carder and Miller data points could be, to make them more comparable, adjusted downward to some extent because they represent TTS 4 min compared to a TTS about one-hour postexposure time for the Clark *et al.* data.

It is seen in Fig. 5.18 that about one hour after the first 6-h exposure, the TTS at 0.715 kHz was around 45 dB, approximately 25 dB higher than the TTS_4 to be expected according to the Carder and Miller study. The data obtained by Clark *et al.* for the four subjects in group II (15-min exposure per hour for 144 days) are qualitative by similar to those of group I, although the shifts are somewhat smaller; the average threshold shift at 0.715 kHz following each of the first several days of exposure was about 35 dB.

Campo *et al.* (1991) also evaluated 'conditioning' from interrupted daily exposures to 0.5-kHz OBN. The noise exposure utilized by Campo *et al.* for 'conditioning' was 6-h exposures at 95 dB on 10 successive days, with evoked potential thresholds measured before and after each exposure. The same noise and pattern of exposure as that used in the Clark *et al.* study. The threshold shift data for those two studies, along with other threshold shift data from single 6-h and 24-h exposures to the same noise, are shown in Fig. 5.19.

The results of the Clark *et al.* behavioral thresholds and the Campo *et al.* evoked potential thresholds are very consistent with each other, indicating that these measures of "hearing" are indeed closely correlated for these conditions. At the same time, it is to be noted that the initial daily threshold shifts found in these two studies are 20–25 dB larger than would be predicted from behavioral threshold shift data for 6-h exposure to 0.5-kHz OBN at 95 dB as found by Carder and Miller.

Indeed they are about equal to the shifts obtained by those investigators and by Bohne and Clark (1982) after 24-h exposure to the same noise. In fact, the postexposure shifts found by Clark *et al.* and Campo *et al.* appear to asymptote after about 10 days (Fig. 5.19) of exposure at about the same value as the Carder and Miller First day of exposure, i.e., 20 dB. About the same, or even an increasing, amount of shift is present in the Clark *et al.* data from the 10th to the 36th day of exposure (exposure days 10–36) (see

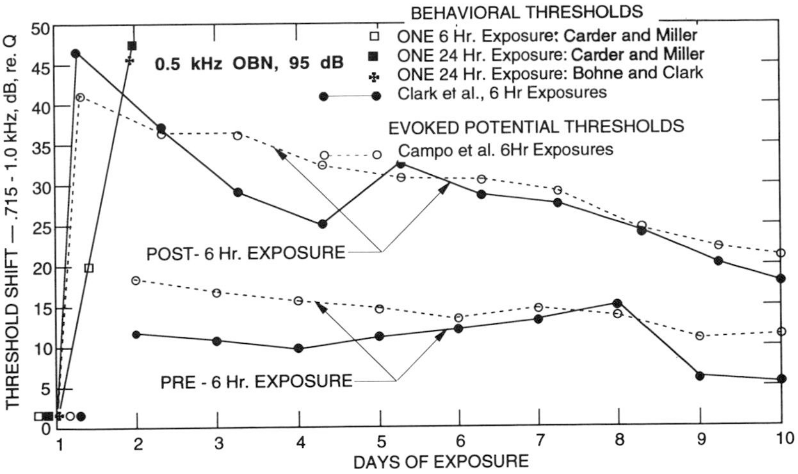

FIGURE 5.19 Comparison of behavioral threshold shifts, per normal baseline hearing levels, found by Clark *et al.* (1987, copyright 1987 by the American Psychological Association. Adapted by permission of the author.), with evoked potential thresholds, found by Campo *et al.* (1991), following exposures 0.5-kHz OBN, 95 dB, 6 h per day for 10 days. Also, threshold shifts found from exposure to 0.5-kHz OBN at 95 dB for 6 h, and for 24 h. Chinchillas.

Fig. 5.18). Again, it is the large shifts found from the initial exposures, rather than the shifts found after toughening, that seem inconsistent with some previous data on TTS and NIPTS.

Moderate Plus Traumatic Exposures, OBN 4 kHz

Subramaniam *et al.* (1991a) conducted two studies in which chinchillas were exposed to traumatic levels of 4-kHz OBN (100 dB for 48 h), with evoked potential thresholds measured before and after exposure. In study 1, a control group was exposed to only the 4-kHz OBN, 100 dB for 48 h; and two experimental groups were exposed to the same noise following: for group A, 18 h of rest; and for group B, 5 days of rest, from 10 successive days of 6-h daily exposure to 4-kHz OBN at 85 dB.

In Study 2, a control group was exposed only to the 4-kHz OBN, 100 dB for 48 h; and an experimental group was exposed to the same noise following 18 h of rest from 10 successive days of 6-h day exposure to a 0.5-kHz OBN at 95 dB. Following collection of the hearing-level data, the animals were dispatched and counts of inner and outer hair-cell losses were made from histological preparations of the cochleas. Major findings are shown in Fig. 5.20.

Figure 5.20 shows that in study 1, when measured immediately after the traumatic exposure, the control group (O) showed (Fig. 5.20A) resistance

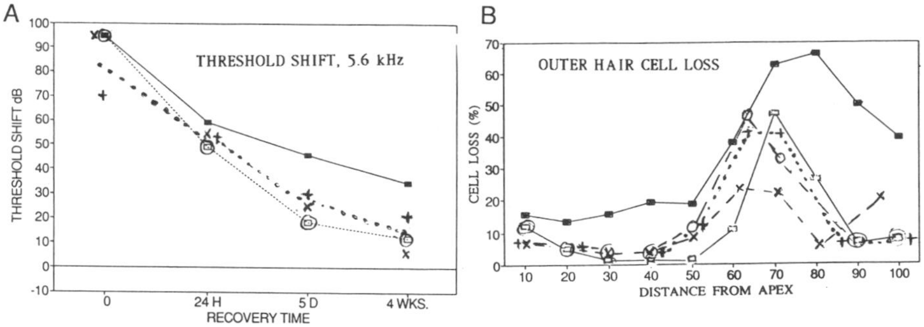

FIGURE 5.20 (A) Recovery in evoked potential hearing thresholds, 5.6 kHz, in chinchillas. (B) Outer hair-cell losses. Study 1 (Subramaniam *et al.*, 1992): control group (O's): 4-kHz OBN, 100 dB, 48 h. Experimental group A (x's): 4-kHz OBN, 85 dB 6 h/day for 10 days, 18-h rest, plus 4-kHz OBN, 100 dB, 48-h; Experimental group B (+'s), same as group A, but with 5 days of rest before start of 100 dB noise. Study 2. (Subramaniam *et al.*, 1993. Copyright 1993 by the American Psychological Association. Adapted by permission of the author.), control group (open rectangles), 4-kHz OBN, 100 dB, 48 h. Experimental group (solid rectangles): 0.5-kHz OBN, 95 dB, 6 h/day for 10 days; 18-h rest; 4-kHz OBN, 100 dB, 48 h. Dashed line, average fit to groups A and B.

to threshold shift from the trauma noise equal to that of experimental group A. Experimental group A (x's, with 1 day of rest between end of conditioning and start of trauma noises) thresholds recovered at a somewhat more irregular rate and (Fig. 5.20B) lost somewhat fewer hair cells than did the control group. When measured immediately after exposure to the traumatic noise, experimental group B (+'s, with 5 days' rest between end of conditioning and start of trauma noises) showed more resistance to threshold shift than the control group, but the thresholds recovered at a slower rate and showed equal hair-cell loss compared to the control group.

Figure 5.20 shows that in study 2, when measured immediately after the traumatic exposure, the control group (open rectangles) showed (Fig. 5.20A) greater resistance to threshold shift from the trauma noise equal to that of the experimental group (solid rectangles). The experimental group (with 18 h of rest between end of conditioning and start of trauma noises) thresholds recovered at a slower rate and lost more hair cells than did the control group. (The investigators also examined inner hair-cell losses, which, while smaller in number, paralleled the relation of outer hair-cell losses among the groups.)

The effects of the 4-kHz trauma noise and 0.5-kHz OBN conditioning noise of study 2, and to a considerable degree the effects of the 4-kHz conditioning and trauma noises of study 1, are contrary for the most part to the toughening process interpretation given the results obtained with the 1-kHz tone and the 0.5-kHz OBN conditioning and trauma exposures discussed above. Subramianium *et al.* (1993), suggest that the mechanism of toughening may be different from exposures to low than high frequencies due to basic anatomic–structural characteristics between the apex and basal portion of the cochlea.

Successive Equal Exposures, OBN 4 kHz

Saunders *et al.* (1977) exposed chinchillas to 4-kHz OBN at a number of levels for 6 h day for 9 days. Behavioral thresholds were measured immediately before and after each exposure. Their findings for exposure to the noise at a level of 86 dB are shown in Fig. 5.21. It is seen that the shift was 50 dB from the first 6 h of exposure, and about 60 dB following each day's exposure thereafter. All the shifts are relative to the hearing level prior to the first day's exposure. The shift is relatively constant after exposure days 2–9 indicates no 'toughening' or conditioning of the ears from the exposures to the 0.5-kHz OBN over this 9-day period.

This is, or course, contrary to the results of Clark *et al.* (1987) and Subramaniam *et al.* (1993) for exposures to 0.5 kHz OBN, as shown in Fig. 5.18. The data point marked on Fig. 5.21 of a shift of 40 dB from exposure to a level of 80 dB is consistent with the 51-dB shift found by Saunders *et al.* from the day of 1 exposure to the 86-dB level, in that a shift or about 1.5 dB per 1 dB of exposure intensity is typical for the hearing levels of this magnitude.

However, Subramaniam *et al.* (1991a) replicated the Saunders *et al.* proto-

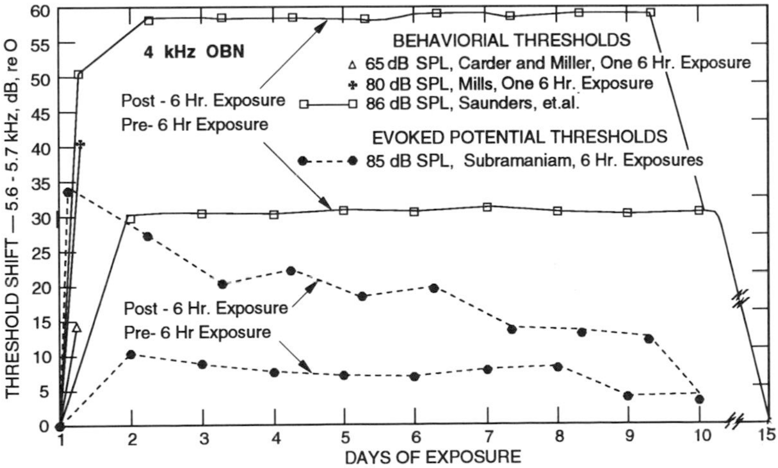

FIGURE 5.21 Comparison of behavioral threshold shifts, per normal baseline hearing levels, found by Saunders *et al.* (1977 with Copyright 1977 by the American Psychological Association. Adapted by permission of the author.) EP thresholds, found by Subramaniam *et al.* (1991b), following exposures to 4-kHz OBN, 86 and 85 dB, 6 h/day for 10 days. Also, threshold shifts found from exposure to 4-kHz OBN at 65 dB and at 80 dB for 6 h. Chinchillas.

col, except they used a 4-kHz OBN at a level of 85, rather than 86 dB, and measured evoked potential, rather than behavioral, thresholds. The results of the Subramaniam *et al.* study, seen in Fig. 5.21, indicate a toughening, or increased resistance to threshold shift, from about 34 to 15 dB, as days of exposure were increased.

Attention is invited to the fact that the threshold shift as measured by evoked potential threshold shifts from the 1st day of exposure to 4-kHz OBN at 85 dB was 34 dB, but was 51–86 dB 4-kHz OBN, and 40–80 dB 4-kHz OBN when measured by behavioral thresholds. If one accepted the Saunders *et al.* and the Mills *et al.* (1979) data as representing the norm, the evoked potential thresholds measured on exposure day 1 by Subramaniam *et al.* would be considered as about 14 dB below expected, the opposite of the trend found for these two types of thresholds from exposure to 0.5-kHz OBN. Thus, method of measuring thresholds and frequency content of the noise appear to be variables differentially, to some extent, affecting the thresholds being measured in these various studies.

Successive Equal Exposures, Impulse Noise

Henderson and Hamernik (1986) obtained, by both behavioral training and evoked potentials, hearing thresholds of monaural chinchillas. All the animals had normal thresholds as found by both measurement techniques. In experiment I, four groups of 3–5 animals each were exposed to 1 s^{-1} impulses (i.e., one impulse per second) for 10 days, at one of four levels: 99, 106, 113, and 120 dB. In experiment II, a single group of 4 animals was exposed to the impulses for a total of 28 days: 7 days at a level of 99 dB (days 1–7); 106 dB (days 8–14); 113 dB (days 15–21); 120 dB (days 22–28).

The protocol of exposures for the two experiments, along with the threshold shifts, relative to pre–day 1 exposure, and recovery following exposure, are shown in Fig. 5.22. It is seen that the groups in experiment I, who received for 7 days impulses only at one specified level, developed shifts, averaged over the different test frequencies, of about the same pattern and magnitude as the shifts developed from 7 days of exposure to a same respective levels in the 4 animals in experiment II.

This would indicate that the successive exposures of the 4 animals in experiment II to impulses at lower levels did not increase resistance to threshold shift from exposures to progressively higher intensity impulses. There is indication, however, that the recovery in threshold shift in group 4 after 7 days of exposure only to the 120-dB impulses was somewhat delayed as compared to the recovery from the shift in the animals who had been exposed to 21 days of impulses at the lower intensities prior to receiving 7 days of exposure at 120 dB. This occurred even though the total shift for the two groups was of about the same initial amount, 68 dB, average for the three test frequencies.

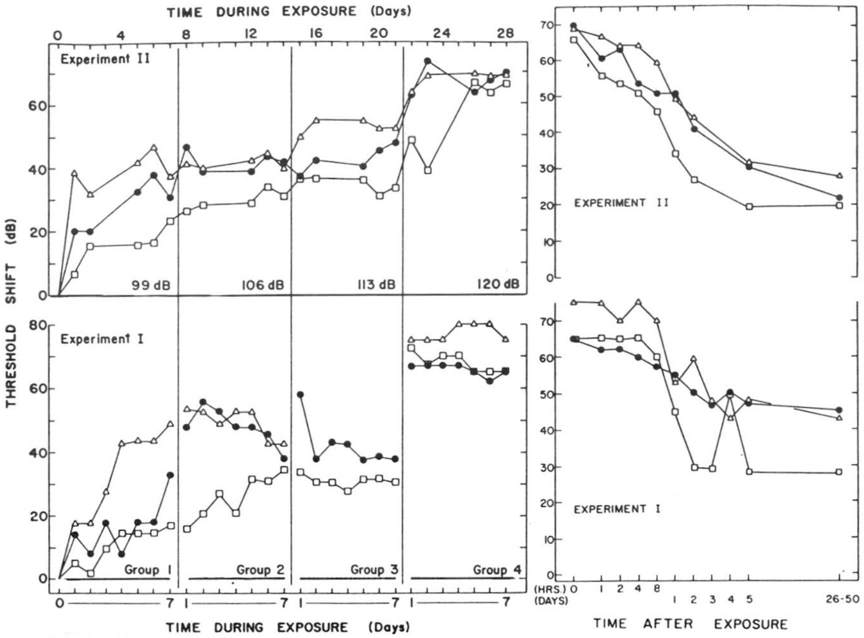

FIGURE 5.22 Comparison of the growth of median threshold shifts in chinchillas, per baseline normal, for 0.5 kHz (squares); 2 kHz (triangle), and 8 kHz (circles). (From Henderson and Hamernik, 1982.)

Summary of "Toughening of the Cochlea" Results and Concept

I. Moderate plus traumatic exposures, EP thresholds:

A. Exposures to 1-kHz tones (Canlon, 1988) and 0.5-kHz OBNs (Campo *et al.*, 1991): About 20–30 dB toughening in Experimental compared to Control subjects reported. However, the initial shifts for control subjects appeared to be abnormally large.

B. Exposure to 4-kHz OBNs: Subramaniam *et al.* (1992), found, for most conditions, no threshold shift toughening, and inconsistent rate of recovery of shift and hair-cell loss in the experimental group compared to control subjects.

C. Exposure to 0.5-kHz OBN conditioning noise, and 4-kHz OBN trauma noise. Subramaniam *et al.* (1993) found no threshold shift toughening, and somewhat greater hair-cell loss and reduced rate of recovery of shift in experimental compared to control subjects.

II. Successive equal exposures:

A. Exposure to OBN 0.5 kHz, 95 dB 6 h per day for 10 days: Clark *et al.* (1987) (behavioral thresholds) and Campo *et al.* (1991) (evoked potential thresholds) found approximately 25 dB of toughening. How-

ever, the threshold shifts found after the first exposure days appear abnormally large.

B. Exposure to OBN 4 kHz, 85 dB, 6 h per day for 10 days: Subramaniam *et al.* (1991b) (evoked potential thresholds) found approximately 20 dB of toughening. However, the threshold shifts found after the first exposure days appear abnormally small, the opposite the finding for exposure to 0.5-kHz OBN.

C. Exposure to OBN 4 kHz, 86 dB, 6 h per day for 10 days: Saunders *et al.* (1977) found no evidence of toughening.

D. Exposure to impulses, 99–120 dB, 7 and 28 days. Henderson and Hamernik (1982) found no evidence of toughening from preceding exposures to impulses at lower levels of intensity.

The 'toughening' of the ear hypothesis is difficult to conceptualize as a general process. Nevertheless, several theories for the sometimes observed apparent toughening, or conditioning, phenomenon have been offered. As noted above, Canlon (1987) suggests the possibility that muscle-like action of outer hair cells can be trained or exercised to tolerate acoustic overstimulation. Evidence for and against the aural reflex and efferent auditory system in this conditioning process have been cited by Campo *et al.* (1991), Fiorino *et al.* (1989), Rajan and Johnstone (1983), Puel *et al.* (1988), Wenthold *et al.* (1990), and Patuzzi and Thompson (1991). Additional recent data from experiments on toughening in the chinchilla are to be found in Hamernik *et al.* (1993) and Henderson and Subramaniam (1993).

A practical question is whether conclusions concerning the susceptibility of the human ear to noise-induced loss in hearing sensitivity have been based on research with ears that have not been toughened, if such a process, beyond that which is normal from typical, real-life, auditory stimulation, exists. As mentioned, in those experiments where a toughening process seems to occur, the thresholds following—rather than preceding—toughening appear more consistent with TTS and NIPTS data that have been involved in the development of models for predicting noise-induced hearing loss in humans.

TTS AND NIPTS IN ANIMALS FROM IMPULSIVE AND NONIMPULSIVE NOISE

Three Studies of Threshold Shifts from Exposures to Continuous and Impulse and Burst Noise

Below are analyzed the results of studies of shifts in evoked-potential thresholds in animals from exposures to uninterrupted and interrupted steady, bursts and impulses of noise. The objectives of these studies were to examine the extent to which energy, temporal variability, and peak intensity of exposures to noise might determine the magnitude of threshold shifts, and, in some cases, damage to structures within the cochlea.

The data for these investigation have been reanalyzed in terms of the equal-energy unit of measurement, $L_{0.5\ s,eq8h}$, and the effective-energy measure, $EL_{0.5\ s,eq8h}$, described earlier in this chapter. The fundamental units of $L_{0.5\ s}$ and $EL_{0.5\ s}$ are frequency-unweighted 0.5 s rms sound-pressure levels. Eight hours (8 h), is used as a reference duration in $L_{0.5\ s,eq,8}$ and $EL_{0.5s,eq,8h}$ formulas to keep the numerical size of the results within the framework of those measures as applied to NIPTS and TTS in studies with humans. The relative waveforms and spectra of the various noises employed in these three studies are shown in Fig. 5.23 (Dunn *et al.*, 1991); Danielson *et al.*, 1991) and Fig. 5.24 (Buck *et al.*, 1984).

The measured threshold shifts and physical exposure data for the three studies cited are given in Table 5.7. Before discussing the threshold shift findings, it is noted that the preexposure thresholds measured by auditory evoked potentials in the chinchilla, and presumably representing normal hearing for that species, are sometimes variable among different studies. For example, the preexposure evoked potential thresholds from 1000 to 8000 Hz

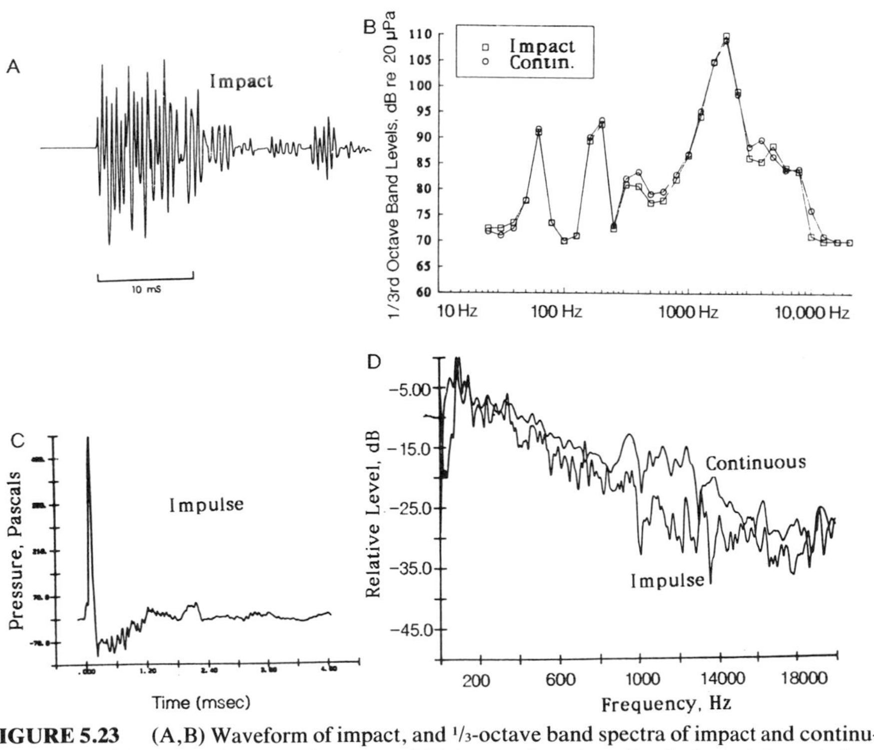

FIGURE 5.23 (A,B) Waveform of impact, and ⅓-octave band spectra of impact and continuous noises of Dunn *et al.* (1991, Copyright 1991 by the American Psychological Association. Adapted by permission of the author.) (C,D) Waveform of impulse, and spectrum levels of impulse and continuous noises of Danielson *et al.* (1991, Copyright 1991 by the American Psychological Association. Adapted by permission of the author.), study.

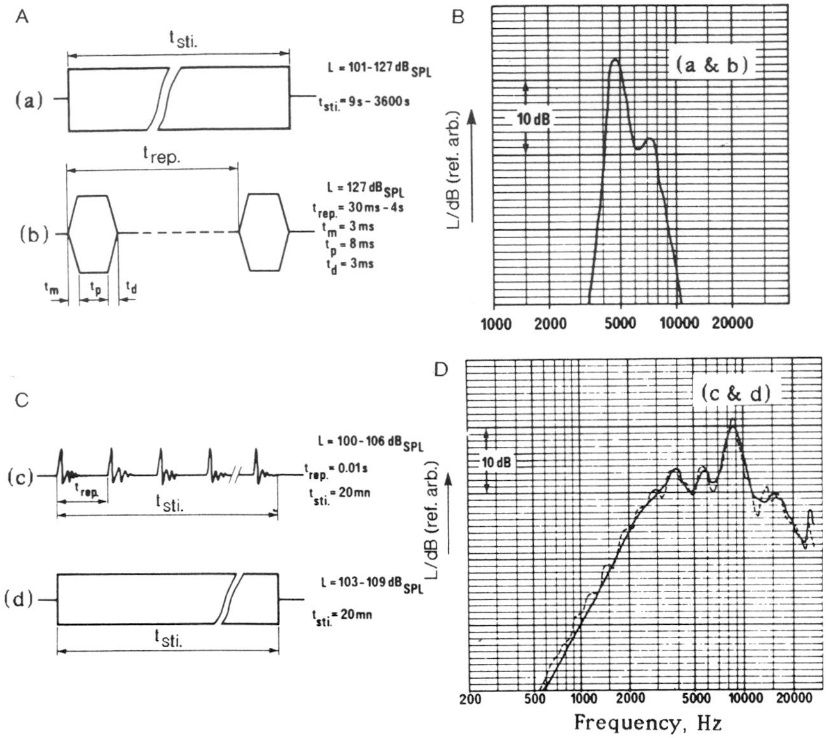

FIGURE 5.24 (A) Waveforms and (B) spectrum levels of continuous and bursts of noise used in experiments 1 and 2, Buck *et al.* (1984, Copyright 1984 by the American Psychological Association. Adapted by permission of the author.), study. (C) Waveforms and (D) spectrum levels of impulse and continuous noises used in experiment 3, Buck *et al.* (1984) study.

ranged from ~20 to 30 dB SPL in the Dunn *et al.* study, and 5–15 dB in the Danielson *et al.* study.

At the same time, behavioral thresholds for chichillas over this frequency region average from 0 to about 10 dB SPL (see Fig. 5.13). However, Henderson *et al.* (1983), found good agreement between shock-avoidance behavioral thresholds and evoked potential thresholds in three normal and noise-exposed chinchillas. As was shown above, Canlon *et al.* (1988) found evoked potential thresholds for guinea pigs classified as being with normal hearing, to be ~35–45 dB higher than the thresholds for guinea pigs found by other investigators using avoidance training behavioral thresholds.

The reason for differences between evoked potential and shock-avoidance behavioral thresholds are possibly due to differences in the placement of electrodes on the animal, and the procedures used in the analysis of the complex neural–electronic signals obtained. Unfortunately, such differences could obfuscate the presence of some amount of preexposure hearing loss that might lead to inappropriate interpretations of threshold shift data. Such occurrences, and possibilities, were previously discussed in relation to the "non–decibel additivity" of TTS and NIPTS.

Study of Dunn *et al.*

Dunn *et al.* (1991) exposed chinchillas for 4 h per day for 5 days to continuous and impulsive noise of similar spectra. Hearing thresholds, at 1000–8000 Hz, were measured by evoked potentials obtained from electrodes inserted under the skin near the ear. The impulse, with a peak level of 136 dB and 0.012-s duration (to the 3 dB downpoints), were presented at a rate of about one every 2.26 s. The frequency-unweighted rms SPL, 1.0 s, was measured as 110 dB for the continuous noise, and calculated by the present writer to be 120 dB for the impulse noises. (A draft "erratum" supplement for the Dunn *et al.* paper, sent in personal correspondence, August 11, 1993, to the writer from R.R. Davis, coauthor of the Dunn *et al.* paper, advised that the peak level of the impulse noise, originally reported in their paper as being about 120 dB, was actually 136 dB, see, also, Davis, *et al.*, 1994. The corrected, and not the originally published, peak level for the impulses is used for the present analysis.)

The average shifts of 24 dB for the continuous, and 51 dB for the impulsive noise, are the reverse of the size of the energy, L_{eq8h}, of those noises, 104 and 98 dB, respectively. The effective, EL_{eq8h} measure, however, of 101 dB for the continuous noise, and 114 for the impulse provides good prediction of the respective shifts in threshold, approximately a 2-dB shift per 1 dB of greater level.

Study by Danielson *et al.*

Figure 5.25 shows that the TTS and NIPTS from exposures to an equal-energy regimen of equally intense impulses is greater for impulses separated by 1 s than when presented in bursts separated by 50 ms. The temporal pattern of the impulses are also shown in Fig. 5.25. The thresholds of hearing were measured by auditory EPs picked up by electrodes implanted in the region of the inferior colluculus on the brain stem of chinchillas.

Danielson *et al.* (1991) suggested that the reduced amount of threshold shift reduction between impulses presented one per second (1 s^{-1}) and (20 s^{-1}) (but for different peak levels and exposure durations so that the exposures were of equal energy) could be attributed to the aural reflex. The average shift for the 135- and 150-dB impulses was 34 vs. 12 dB for the 1 s^{-1} vs. 20 s^{-1} rate, with an average L_{eq8h} of 54.5 for both rates (see Table 5.7). It was hypothesized by Danielson *et al.* that the first impulse of a 20 s^{-1} burst initiated the reflex, which was then maintained by succeeding impulses, whereas the reflex relaxed, affording less sound attenuation, between the 1-s^{-1} impulses. However, note that the effective-energy levels, EL_{eq8h} are,

TABLE 5.7 Threshold Shifts and Calculation EL_{eq8h} and L_{eq8h} for Exposure of Animals to Continuous and Impulse or Burst Sounds

	t_x, 0.5s = day's exposure percen-tile	Number of inter-ruptions,* (N impulses, N bursts)	Duration of impulses	$t = t_x$, or, number of impulses squared (N impulses)^2	rf† = duration of inter-ruptions 0.5 s >4, set4	$t_e = t + rf \times N$ inter-ruptions	L_{pk}/ burst, dB‡	$L_{0.5s}$, dB‡	$E_{Leq,8h}$ $L_{dB0.5-20lg}$ T/t_x or t_e	$L_{eq,8h}$ dB-10lg T/†	Threshold shifts in evoked potentials: Av. ~1–8 kHz: postexposure, 30 days				Aver-age shift
						Dunn *et al.* (1991) Chinchillas, anesthetized, N = 16									
Tested after 5 consecutive days of exposure															
Continuous impulses,	28,800			28,800		28,800		107	101	104				24	24
0.012 s, 32656, 2.26 per s	28,000	32,656	0.0120	391.872	0.8580	28,411	136	120	114	98				51	51
				Danielson *et al.* (1991) Chinchillas, Unanesthetized, N = 42							Av. ~1-8 kHz: postexposure				
												Minutes	Days	Days	Days
Tested after 1 day's exposure.											15	1	10	30	
Continuous impulses,	12,960			12,960		12,960		88	75	82	38	18	1	0	14
0.0002 s., 100, 1 s^{-1}	200	100	.0002	0.02	1.9976	200	150	113	64	48	61	55	28	17	40
0.0002 s., 100, 20 s^{-1}	10	100	.0002	0.02	0.0976	10	150	126	51	61	27	14	9	9	15
0.0002 s., 3200, 1 s^{-1}	6400	3200	.0002	0.64	1.9976	6393	135	98	79	48	61	32	10	7	28
0.0002 s., 3200, 20 s^{-1}	320	3200	.0002	0.64	0.0976	313	135	111	66	61	18	11	1	3	8
					Average of, 150 dB and 135 db, 1 s^{-1}				72	55	Average of, 150 dB and 135 db, 1 s^{-1}				34
					Average of, 150 dB and 135 db, 20 s^{-1}				59	55	Average of, 150 dB and 135 db, 20 s^{-1}				12

Buck *et al.* (1984) Guinea-pigs, Anaesthetized, N = 6, per Condition, Apparently

													Postexposure, 15 min			
													5 kHz	7 kHz	10 kHz	16 kHz
Table I, Continuous, #1		7200			7200		7200		98	80	89	9.7	12.4	20.8	11.8	14
Same spectrum as bursts		3600			3600		3600		101	77	89	14.2	42.5	46.3	15.6	30
of noise in Table II, below		1800			1800		1800		104	74	89	15.8	39.8	44.3	16.3	29
		900			900		900		107	71	89	15.3	39.8	39.8	24.3	30
		450			450		450		110	68	89	14.5	38.5	36.5	23.2	28
		225			225		225		113	65	89	4.2	9.7	22.8	15.8	13
		113			113		113		116	62	89	6.3	6.7	6.1	14.3	8
		57			57		57		119	59	89	3.0	3.6	4.5	4.0	4
Tested after 1 day's epxosure		18			18		18		124	54	89	7.0	5.8	2.5	6.0	5
Table II. 900 bursts, #1 bursts						4.0000										
per second 0.01-s duration	0.25	7200	900	0.0100	9.0		3609	127	101	77	63	11.3	13.8	21.0	12.3	15
Tested after 1 day's exposure	0.50	1800	900	0.0100	9.0	3.9800	3591	127	104	80	66	9.0	15.8	30.0	11.8	17
	1.00	900	900	0.0100	9.0	1.9800	1791	127	107	77	69	20.2	35.5	45.8	19.8	30
	2.00	450	900	0.0100	9.0	0.0900	891	127	110	74	72	9.5	16.3	29.9	12.4	17
	4.00	225	900	0.0100	9.0	0.4800	441	127	113	71	75	8.1	14.8	32.7	15.4	18
	8.00	113	900	0.0100	9.0	0.2400	225	127	116	68	78	5.8	7.0	13.2	10.2	9
	16.00	58	900	0.0100	9.0	0.1000	99	127	119	64	81	8.2	8.8	10.8	10.7	10
	32.00	29	900	0.0100	9.0	0.0445	49	127	122	61	84	7.8	4.0	5.1	5.8	6
Table III. Continuous, #2												11 kHz	16 kHz	22 kHz	32 kHz	
Same spectrum as impulse		2400			2400		2400		03	75	89	9.8	8.6	9.9	5.6	9
noise, Table III below.		2400			2400		2400		06	78	92	21.0	23.7	16.3	10.4	20
Tested after one day's exposure.		2400			2400		2400		09	81	95	29.6	43.3	39.2	22.7	37
Table III. Impulses, #2		2400	120,000	0.0040	480	0.0120	1920	104	00	70	79	2.4	3.1	7.9	5.0	4
Impulse ~0.004 s, 100 s^{-1}		2400	120,000	0.0040	480	0.0120	1920	107	03	73	82	18.3	32.6	35.5	13.8	29
Tested after one day's exposure.		2400	120,000	0.0040	480	0.0120	1920	110	06	76	85	25.0	36.9	42.0	26.4	35

* inter, int (interruptions); imp, im (impulses).

† rf = adjustment for refractory-for-recovery time during interruptions (interruption, with lim.t set at 2.0 s.

‡ $L_{peak/burst}$, dB = [10 log *pi* peak within a 0.5-s segment, measured between 10 dB downpoint; on pressure-intensity envelope].

§ $L_{10.5s,dB}$ 10 log (†/n × ($p2^2$ + ···$p2n^2$/400) = .5dB$_{0.5A}$, where n is number of P^2 sampled in 0.5 s.

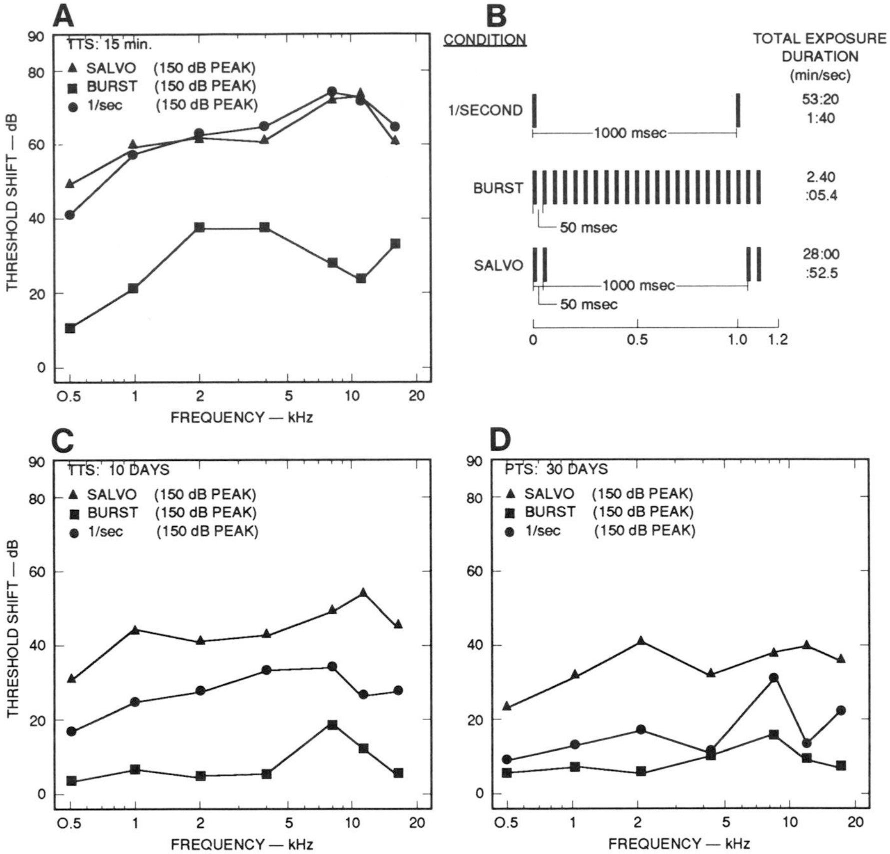

FIGURE 5.25 (A) Schematic of the three temporal patterns of impulses. each bar represents an impulse. The energy was held constant by balancing the number of impulses with duration of exposure. (B,C) Medians of 15-min and 10-day postexposure TTS. (D) Median of 30-day postexposure permanent threshold shift. (From Danielson *et al.*, 1991. Copyright 1991 by the American Psychological Association. Adapted by permission of the author.)

respectively, 71.5 and 58.5 for the two rates, and positively correlated with the threshold shifts.

A suggested alternative explanation of these results to that of a differential action of the aural reflex will be discussed later. An additional feature of these data, also to be analyzed later, is that the threshold shift for the 150-dB peak level exposures are greater than those for the 135-dB exposures for both of their respective 1- and 20-s^{-1} impulse rates.

Study of Buck *et al.*

Auditory evoked potentials were obtained from an electrode placed on the round window of the cochlea of guinea pigs. Preexposure thresholds were not reported. Buck *et al.* (1984) conducted three experiments: (1) with steady noise of different durations and intensity levels such that they were all equal in energy; (2) with "bursts" of noise of 0.01-s duration presented at different rates (see Fig. 5.24B); and (3) impulses of 0.004-s duration, and same spectrum steady noise, at different peak levels of intensity (see Figs. 5.24C and 5.24 D).

Comparison of Threshold Shifts as Functions of $L_{0.5s,eq8h}$ $EL_{0.5s,eq8h}$

Threshold shifts for these three studies are shown in Fig. 5.26 as a function of $L_{0.5s,eq8h}$ top graphs (A, B in Fig. 5.26) and $EL_{0.5s,eq8h}$ (C, D in Fig. 5.26). Figures 5.26A and 5.26 C of the data for continuous, uninterrupted, exposures to steady noise; and Figs. 5.26B and 5.26D, for exposures to impulses and impulsive-bursts of noise.

It is apparent from Fig. 5.26 that within, for the most part, individual studies or overall studies, the equal-energy measure L_{eq8} is not significantly correlated with threshold shift from either impulse/burst (r = .07) or continuous noise (r = .33). However, for both continuous steady and impulse or burst noises, the correlations are positive and much stronger with the effective-energy EE_A measure, EL_{eq} r values of .66 and .65, respectively. An estimated trend curve of the correlation with EL_{eq} is shown by the dotted line in Fig. 5.26. The offsets, or lack of even greater offsets, between the different studies could be due to some extent to differences in animals tested (Buck *et al.*, 1984, used guinea pigs, the other studies were of chinchillas), testing methodologies, postexposure measurement times, etc.

As noted before, the negative relation between L_{eq} and threshold shift for the 1-s vs 20-s^{-1} impulses in the Danielson *et al.* (1991) study becomes positive when compared to their EL_{eq} values. The reason, it is suggested, is that the EL_{eq} measure takes into account the refractory-for-recovery factor that, essentially, makes the 1-s^{-1} impulse effectively continuous in level, and, therefore, a greater cause of auditory fatigue for a given amount of sound energy. The aural reflex hypotheses proposed as an explanation by Danielson *et al.* for this finding can, in the writer's opinion, be questioned, at least for the results obtained at the higher frequencies where the reflex affords little attenuation.

However, the greater magnitude of shift found for 150 dB than the 135-dB peak, but equal effective energy impulses of the Danielson *et al.* study is not understandable in terms of effective energy as calculated. For those impulses, it is seen that both effective energy and peak levels are important variables. An intuitive explanation is that this may be due to a "nonlinear overloading" of the ear by the 150-dB peak intensity, as compared to that from the 135-dB peak level. Also, histological examination of the cochleas clearly show that the noises with a peak level of 150 dB caused a much greater number of missing inner and, especially, outer hairs than did the noises of equal energy, or equal effective energy, of 135-dB peak level (compare graphs on right with those on left of Fig. 5.27).

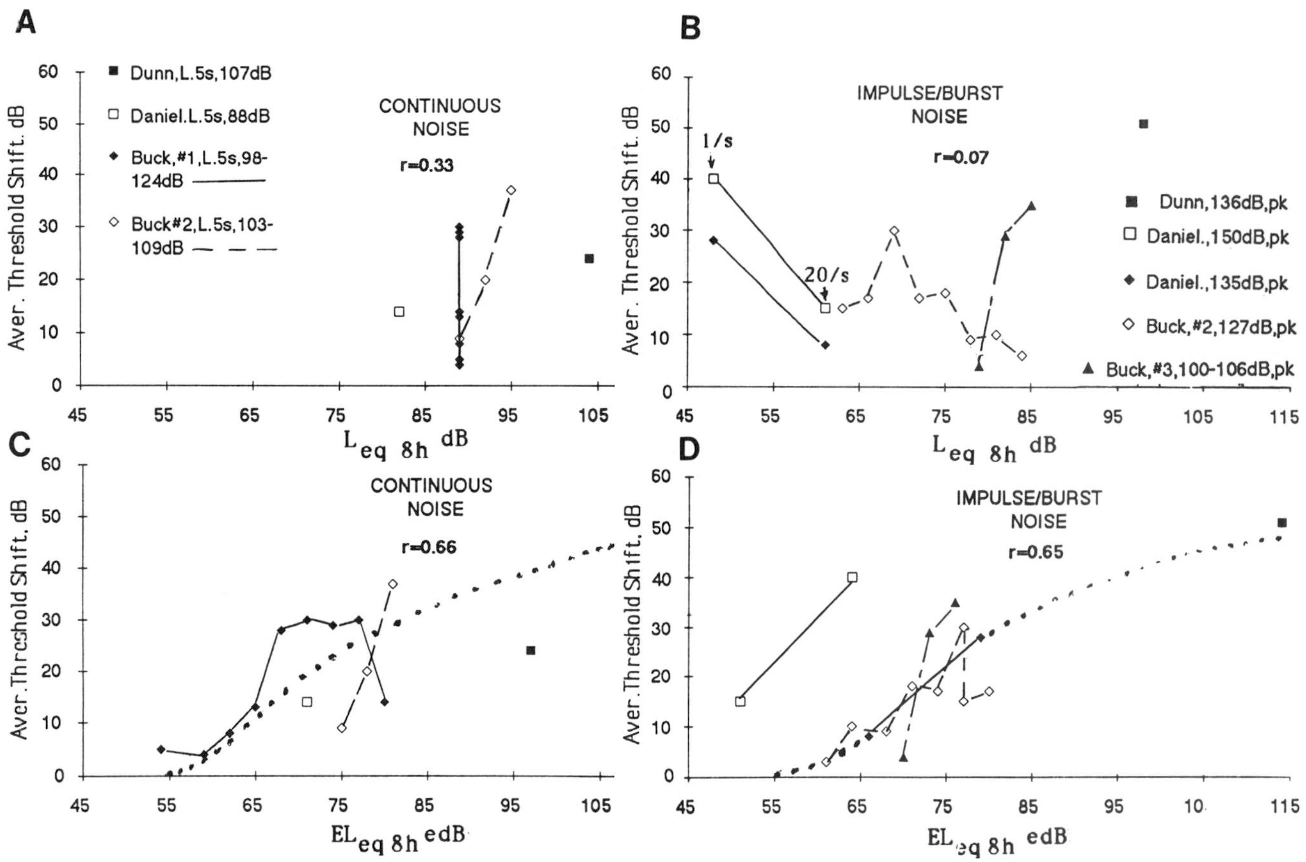

FIGURE 5.26 Average EP threshold shifts in chinchillas and guinea pigs as function of (A,B) $L_{0.5s,eq8h}$ and (C,D) $EL_{0.5s,eq8h}$ from exposures to continuous and impulse or burst noises.

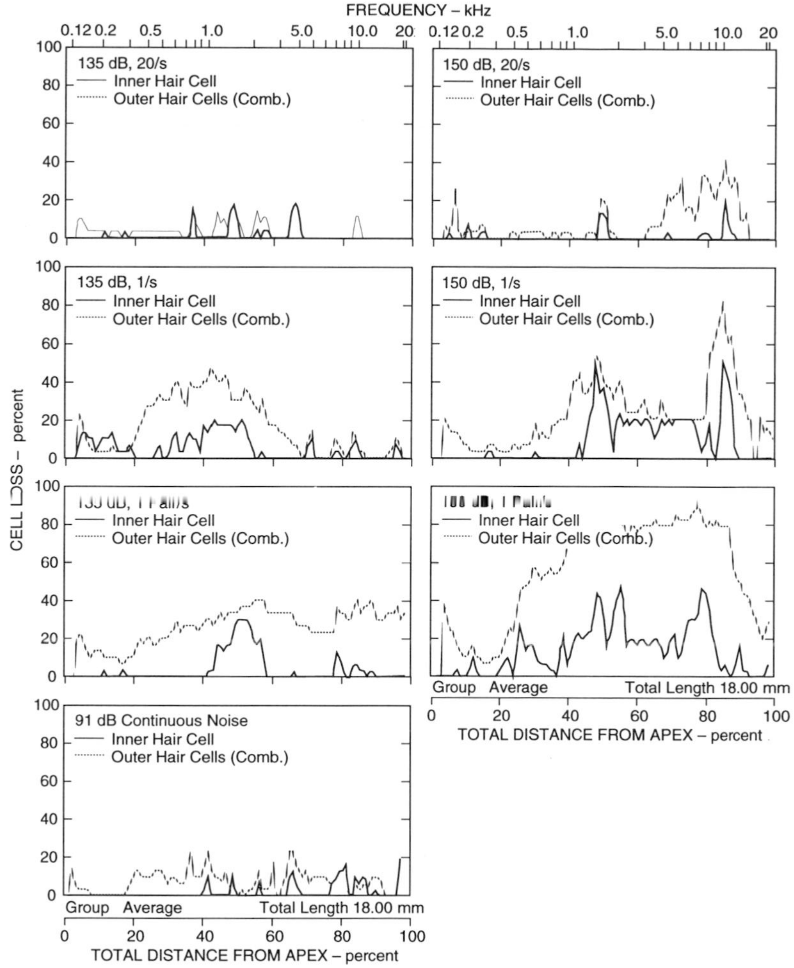

FIGURE 5.27 Median cochleograms (distributions and number of missing hair cells) for seven experimental groups of chinchillas. (From Danielson *et al.*, 1991. Copyright 1991 by the American Psychological Association. Adapted by permission of the author.)

At the same time, the hair-cell loss data in Fig. 5.27 for the 20-s vs. the 1-s^{-1} impulse rate, the top pair vs. the next-to-top pair of graphs in Fig. 5.27, indicate fewer hair cells lost with the 20-s^{-1} rate than with the 1-s^{-1} rate. This is consistent with the effective energy in interrupted impulses, or the aural reflex hypothesis of Danielson *et al.*, as discussed. It would appear that both effective-energy and ear overload phenomena may be involved in these results.

It is seen in Figs. 5.25 and 5.27 that the salvo condition, especially with the level of 150 dB, caused the greatest threshold shift and hair-cell loss.

That condition was a pair of impulses separated by 50 ms, with total exposure time appropriately reduced, to keep total energy the same as for the other impulse conditions. A stepwise increase in threshold shift was not found for salvo impulses at a level of 135 dB. The investigators noted that there may be a brief period of increased vulnerability to damage immediately following a high-intensity impulse (Price, 1976). Whatever the explanation, the 150-dB impulses caused an apparently excessively large increase in damage to the ear when presented at a rate that presumably obviated the protective action of the aural reflex.

A finding of an overload, nonlinearity, threshold at an impulse level somewhere between 135 to 150 dB or so, is not, on the face of it, consistent with gunfire impulse data for humans presented earlier. This may be at least somewhat due to the significantly greater susceptibility to temporary and permanent threshold shifts revealed in these studies in chinchillas and guinea pigs than in the case with human ears. For example, humans exposed to a broadband noise of 91 dB for 108 min could be expected to have a TTS2 min of about 20 dB, and $TTS_{4\ min}$, of 15 dB (see Fig. 5.3), whereas Danielson *et al.* found in chinchillas a $TTS_{4\ min}$, from a 91-dB broadband noise for 108 min of 38 dB. Figure 5.12B shows that humans, 50%ile, exposed to 100 gun impulses, separated by 5 s, of 160-dB peak caused an apparent $TTS_{2\ min}$ (postexposure $HL_{2\ min}$) of only ~20 dB; whereas Danielson *et al.* found in chinchillas a mean $TTS_{4\ min}$ of 61 dB from exposure to 100 "rounds", separated by 1 s, to qualitatively similar impulses of only 150-dB peak.

Thus it appears that, compared to the human ear, the chinchilla ear experiences at least twofold-size threshold shifts from equal exposures to relatively low-intensity continuous noise, and threefold that from impulses of the variety here examined. Whether such differences could be related to differences in the general lifespan of the organisms, structural–functional differences in their auditory systems and built-in protective mechanisms, or insufficient experimental evidence can only be conjectured. Attention is again directed to the graphs of Fig. 5.1, which show that, as a function of exposure duration, TTS increases at about twice the rate for the chinchilla ear as for the human. That damages to elements in the cochlea can dramatically increase above some level of intensity is illustrated in Fig. 5.28.

PREDICTION OF EQUAL TTS_2 AND NIPTS BY EE_A

EE_A-Predicted NIPTS and Equal TTS_2

Figure 5.29 shows that, as a function of EL_{Aeq8h}, the numerical magnitude and rate of growth of threshold shift is about the same for (1) TTS_2 in normal ears from a single 8-h exposure to broadband noise in dB_A, or an OBN that is 6 dB less; (2) NIPTS in nosocusis- and sociocusis-screened personnel from a work career of 50 years in steady and impulse industrial noises of the same level; and (3) NIPTS estimated from TTS_2 due to exposure to high-level gun

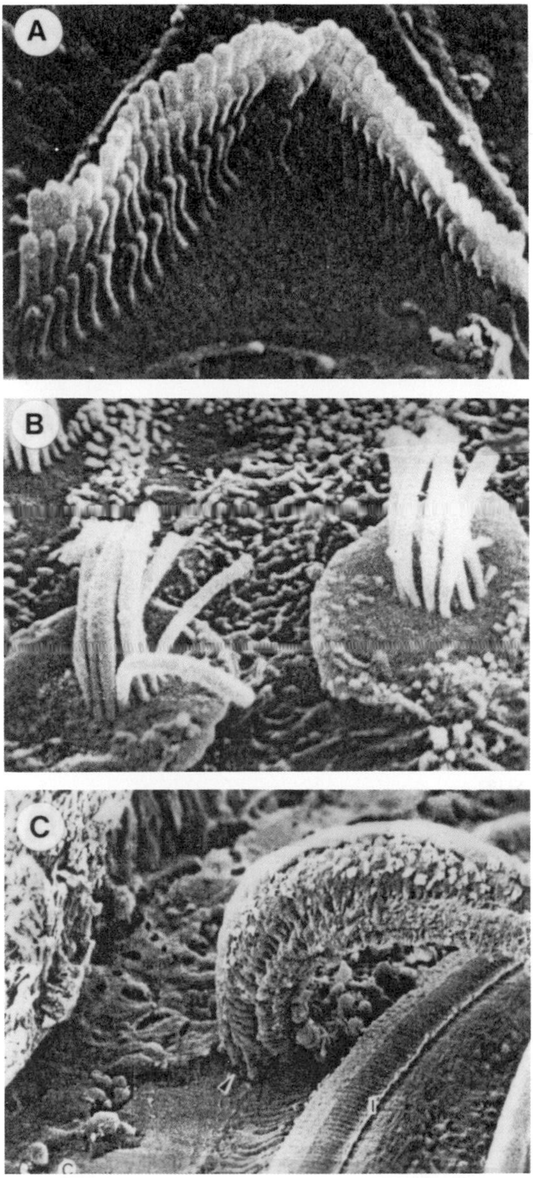

FIGURE 5.28 Scanning electron micrographs of areas in the cochlea.

noise. Accordingly, for noises having the same EL_{Aeq8h}, $EE_{A,f}$ can presumably be used to predict either NIPTS from 50 work-years of exposure, or, in normal ears, TTS_2 from one exposure.

It was estimated in an earlier analysis of some NIPTS and TTS data that their values were about equal to, for TTS_2, one exposure to a given EL_{Aeq8h},

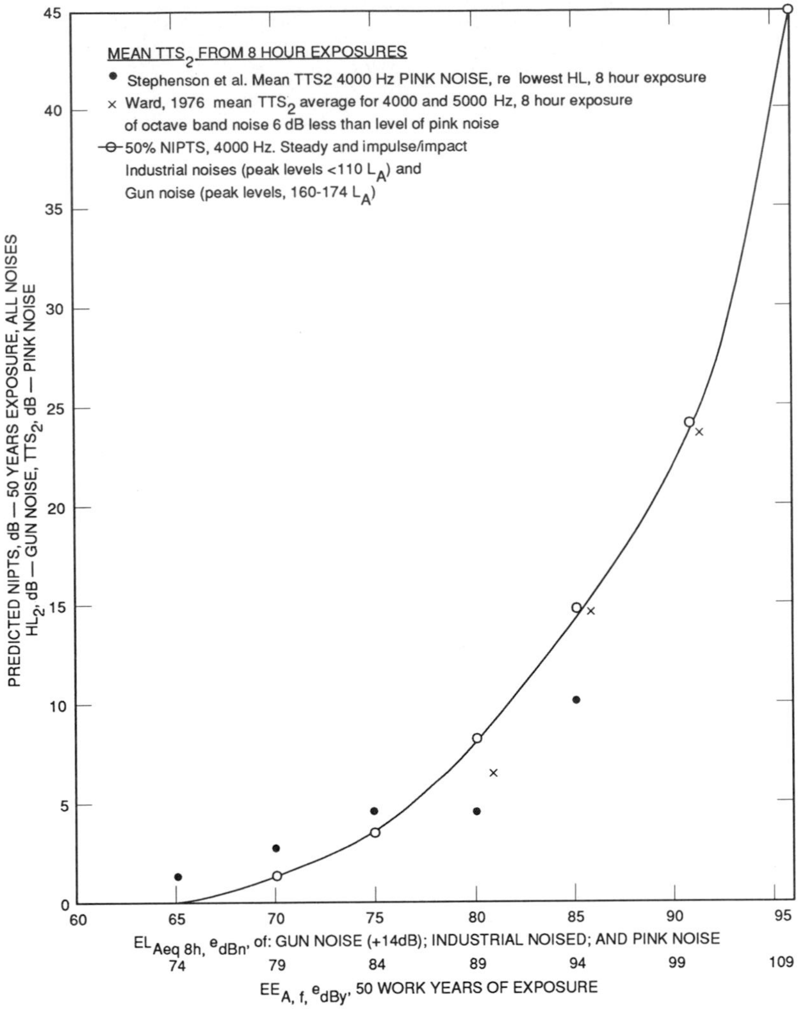

FIGURE 5.29 Note similarity between magnitude of mean NIPTS predicted by EE_A, 50 work-years of exposure ($EL_{A,eq8h}$ 13.6), and mean TTS_2 predicted by EE_A for a single $EL_{Aeq,8h}$ noise exposure, 66–96 e_{dBn}, in normal ears. TTS_2 data points from sources indicated, EE_A function based on variety of industrial noises.

and, for NIPTS, 10–30 years of workday exposures to the same EL_{Aeq8h} (Kryter, 1963; and, in particular, Fig. 7 in Kryter, 1965). Although the difference in number of years estimated seems rather large, the effective difference is small. The earlier estimate of 10 log 20 years exposure, say, gives 13 dB to be added to an EL_{Aeq8h} level for the calculation of EE_A and prediction of NIPTS. The present estimate of 8 log 50 years exposure gives nearly the same amount, 13.6 dB, to be added to an EL_{Aeq8h} level for the same purpose. The present analysis is based on more data and presumably is more accurate.

While TTS is thought to nearly always precede NIPTS, it need not, according to equal-energy proponents, be predictively related to the development of NIPTS (Robinson, 1976). The similarity of the numerical magnitudes of TTS_2, in normal ears, from one 8-h exposure, and predicted NIPTS from 50 work-years of exposure to the same noise, could be a gratuitous coincidence. It is certainly only an empirical finding, and the exact rules whereby NIPTS grows from continuing daily cycles of TTS and apparent near recovery, according to pure-tone threshold measures, is not known.

However, research data and hearing behavior in general support the concept that meaningful correlations exist between TTS and NIPTS. Figure 5.30 from Ahroon *et al.* (1993) illustrates the strong correlation between TTS and NIPTS found in a study of EP thresholds in chinchillas, especially, when

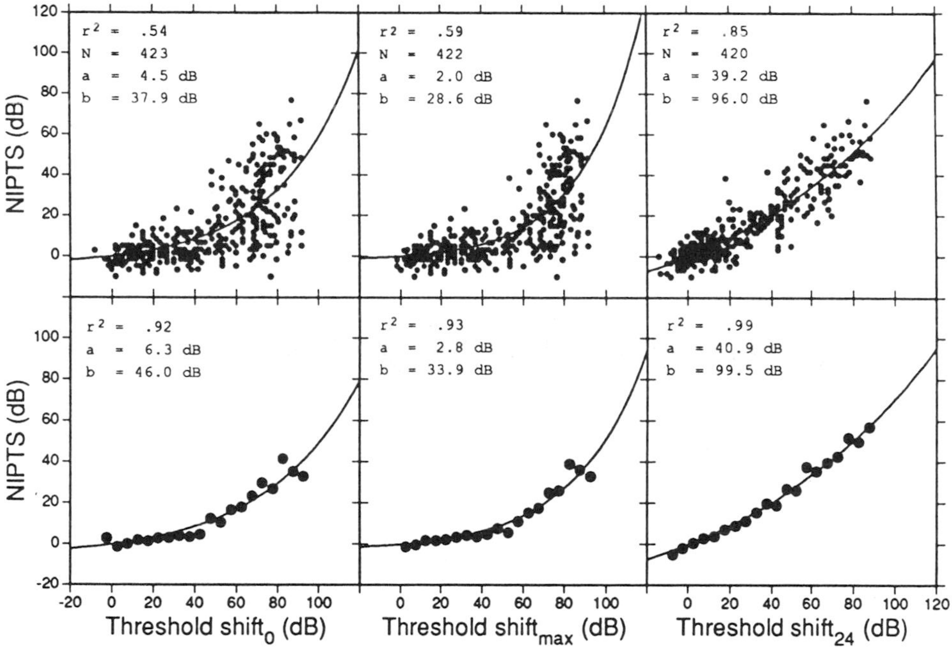

FIGURE 5.30 Scattergraphs for the 2-kHz test frequency. Top panels represent the raw data from 422 chinchillas, while the lower panels represent the mean NIPTS in 5-dB-wide steps of TTS. The left panels depict TTS_0 (taken immediately after first exposure); center panels, TTS_{max} (maximum during the 24-h period after the first exposure); and right panels, TTS_{24} (24 h after the first exposure). PTS mean of 3 days of test starting after 30 days of rest following last day of exposure to noise. The least-squares regression line to the exponential function NIPTS = $a\,(e^{TTS/b} - 1)$ is drawn in each panel. (From Ahroon *et al.*, 1993.)

mean NIPTS is represented by TTS in 5-dB steps, r^2 falls between 0.92 and 0.99. The animals were exposed to broadband impulses, in the range of 150–160 dB, for a fraction of a second up to 16.5 h.

Other examples supporting the hypothesis of a monotonic relation are: (1) when nosocusis and presbycusis factors are taken into account, the relative susceptibilities to TTS and NIPTS at different frequencies from exposure to given spectra noises are generally alike; (2) the ability to make threshold auditory discriminations are similar when thresholds are like amounts elevated by TTS, or NIPTS (also masking and presbycusis, for that matter); and (3) NIPTS and TTS are similarly additive, at the moment in time when they are measured, to presbycusis. As was noted, a predictive ability of NIPTS from TTS is prescribed for EE_A only when the following restriction is met - that the TTS_2 measures no more than ~35–40 dB in normal ears following an ≤8-h, or so, one-day exposure.

A rationale for this restriction, besides the fact that it will cover most industrial, military, and general environmental noise-exposure conditions, is that the courses of recovery from TTS of larger magnitudes and exposure durations cannot be adequately described from present research data. As shown in Figs. 5.3A and 5.3B, recovery from 35–40-dB TTS_2 appears to be generally complete within 16 h, or the typical time between exposures to, at least, workplace noise. Figures 5.3A and 5.3B also indicate that delayed recovery appears to occur only when the TTS_2 exceeds that amount.

Figure 5.14 shows, with some interpolation, that delayed recovery occurs only when the exposure duration exceeds 16 h, or so, the durations of exposure after which TTS therefrom, even of lesser magnitudes than 35 dB, generally becomes asymptotic. The asymptotic leveling off in the magnitude of TTS with continued exposure to low-level noise would seem to portend a break in the proposed fixed relation between TTS_2 and NIPTS, 50 years of exposure. This condition is avoided by the specified restriction of a single 8 or so hours of exposure. Some theoretical interpretations of the implications of magnitudes of TTS, and ATS in the development of NIPTS are given by Mills (1982).

Additivity of TTS and NIPTS Thresholds

Because presbycusis and overstimulation of sensorineural receptors are presumed to progress independently, a given dose of noise should cause a given amount of NIPTS regardless of the age of the person to which it is administered. This principle appeared to be true for TTS in a study that showed TTS in older people was about the same as that found in younger adults from similar noise exposures (Loeb and Fletcher, 1963). Further, the decibel threshold shift from age plus that NIPTS or TTS from noise exposure together indicate the sound pressure level, per audiometric zero, of the just-audible audiometer tone.

However, as discussed previously, it is the sound pressures added together, and not the decibels of the sound pressures, representing an NIPTS and a TTS simultaneously present from exposures to noise, that will indicate the magnitude of the total threshold shift in that ear. That is, the sound-pressure level of the audiometer tone required to reach threshold following two or more noise induced shifts is the sum of the separate sound pressures, squared, converted to decibels. Hearing-level sensitivity thresholds (HL_{meas}), presbycusis shifts (HL_{age}), and noise-induced threshold shifts (NIPTS, TTS), can be generally expressed as follows where the 6-month postexposure period specified in the following period is chosen as a reasonably conservative definition for an established permanent shift):

NIPTS = HL_{meas} >6 months' postexposure noise 1—HL_{age} (ISO, 7029), postexposure noise 1, dB
TTS = HL_{meas} at a moment in time (<6 months) postexposure noise 2—HL_{meas} preexposure noise 2, dB
NIPTS + TTS = 10 log $^{(NIPTS + TTS)/10)}$, $P + T$, at moment in time postexposure noise 2, dB
HL_{meas} = TTS + NIPTS, dB + HL_{age} dB, postexposure noise 2

The following points are noted here:

1. These formulas can be used with more than one known, or estimated, NIPTS for different noise exposures ($NIPTS_{N_1}$ + $NIPTS_{N_2}$. . . + $NIPTS_{N_x}$) = 10 log $^{(NIPTS_{N_1} + NIPTS_{N_2} . . . + NIPTS_{N_x})/10))}$.
2. This process cannot be applied to the estimation of the hearing level when the TTS is the result of more than one preceding noise exposure condition because the rate of recovery from more than one simultaneously present auditory fatigue condition will be a complex function of the rates of recovery post the clock-exposure times for each of the separate noise events causing the summed temporary auditory fatigue. (See discussion in Kryter, 1973, of the problem of adding threshold shifts.) The results of toughening experiments suggest the possible presence of further complications for any efforts to quantify such auditory fatugue.

Figure 5.31 shows the 8 min following a workday noise exposure, the average shift (TTS_8) at 4000 Hz for ears with a preexposure HL of 0 dB is about 27 dB. It is also seen that there was a progressive decrease in the effectiveness of the one day of exposure to cause TTS_8 relative to preexposure hearing level. When preexposure hearing level reached 45–70 dB, depending on test frequency, essentially no TTS_8 was created. As defined by the formulas above, in ears with progressively larger amounts of NIPTS, TTS, from the one day's noise exposure become progressively smaller, while at the same time, assuming about same-aged ears were involved, the hearing

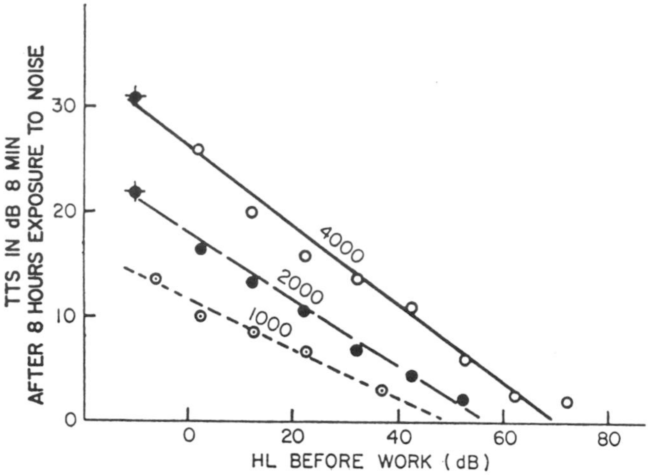

FIGURE 5.31 Relation between average TTS 8 min at 1000, 2000, and 4000 Hz after a day's work in high-level broadband noise and the preexposure threshold for a sample of 81 workers. (From Ward, 1963.)

levels of the workers progressively increased. This phenomenon is not to be interpreted, as also noted by Ward (1976) and Humes and Jesteadt (1991), as indicating a toughening of the ear for hearing loss as the result of continuing exposure to noise.

The same reasoning is presumed to apply also to the accrual of TTS from sound exposures that are separated in time. Illustrated in Fig. 5.32 are the hearing levels, due to TTS, that could be expected to follow during an 8-h workday for two different patterns of noise exposure: (1) when the intensity of the noise is decreased, from L_A 98 for 4 h AM, to L_A 92 for 4 h PM; and (2) when it is increased from L_A 92 for 4 h AM to L_A 98 for 4 h PM.

It is seen that after 8 postexposure hours estimated hearing levels for these two different regimens of equal effective energy (L_A 92 AM + L_A 98 PM and L_A 98 AM + L_A 92 PM) do not coalesce. This is due to the several additional hours of recovery available to the high-intensity AM exposure before the L_A 92 PM exposure starts to cause significant threshold shift. This difference should be compensated for, over days of exposure, because there would be equal time between daily repeats of exposures. For this reason, the long-term residual effects would be the same for both the AM and PM higher-intensity-noise schedule.

Also, it is seen in Fig. 5.32 that recovery from a first, single day's exposure, the L_A 98, 4-h, PM exposure is not as complete at 8 AM the next day as it is for the L_A 98, 4 h, AM exposure, as it is offset by about 4 h of recovery time. However, the long-term residual effects should also be the same for either the only 4-h AM, or 4-h PM, exposure schedule in that each would

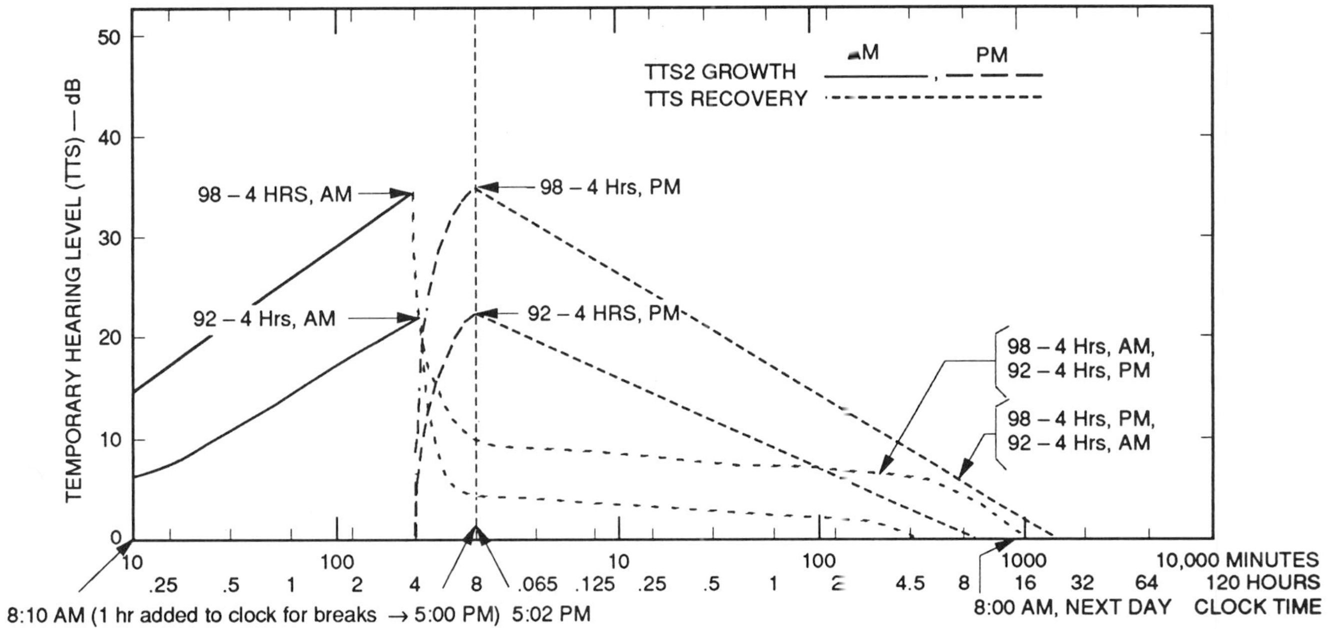

FIGURE 5.32 Idealized growth of, and recovery from, TTS at 4000 Hz, from uninterrupted—except for normal work breaks—exposures to broadband noise for (1) 4 h at L_A 92 followed by 4 h at L_A 98; and (2) 4 h at L_A 98 followed by 4 h at L_A 92.

enjoy a 16-h recovery period between subsequent exposures to the subject noises.

BANDWIDTH AND SPECTRA AS FACTORS IN TTS AND NIPTS

The predictive models that have been described are fundamentally based on L_A levels overall frequencies of broadband noises. As a result, it can be expected that these procedures will tend to underestimate the NIPTS to be experienced in a particular frequency region from exposure to a pure tone or a narrow band of noise. The primary reason for this is the so-called critical bandwidth of the ear.

As discussed in Chapter 2, in experiments on auditory masking, effective sensorineural excitation is proportional to sound energy integrated over a relatively small extent, or region, of sensorineural elements on the basilar membrane. Within limits, the energy in frequencies above and below the critical band do not increase the sensorineural excitation caused by the sound within the critical band. However, the energy over the entire spectrum sound does increase the overall, for example, L_A level of a noise with, as shown in Table 5.4, equal SPL in each octave band (see Table 5.4). Two manifestation of this factor related to the estimation of TTS from overall levels of noises narrow, as compared, to wide spectra, are shown in Fig. 5.33.

Figure 5.33B shows that, when intensity level and exposure time are the same (1) an octave band of noise causes about 5 dB more TTS_2, at 4000 Hz, than does broadband pink noise; and (2) a tone, or a $^1/_3$-octave band of noise of about the same center frequency causes about 3 dB more TTS_2 than does an octave band of noise with the same center frequency. Figure 5.33A shows that within a broadband noise, the energy in octave bands that are above, and below, a given band do not increase the TTS_2 at the test frequency most affected by the given band.

Adjustment to L_A and EE_A for Narrowband Noises and Tones

Prior to the calculation of an *e*dB*n* it is appropriate to increase the L_A measured for ≤ 1 octave wideband noises and tones with center frequencies above about 400 Hz. The adjustment should be the addition of 5 dB to measured L_A if the noise is only $^1/_3$–1 octave wide, and 8 dB if it is less than one-third octave wide, especially if tonal. It is to be understood, that following such adjustments, NIPTS is to be predicted only for frequencies from, and up to one octave or so above, the center frequency of a narrow band of noise.

Locus of Maximum Threshold Shift Relative to Noise Spectrum

Also mentioned in previous chapters was the upward spread, from lower to higher frequencies, of neural excitation, masking and fatigue, due, apparently, to the character of the hydrodynamic waves traveling along the basilar

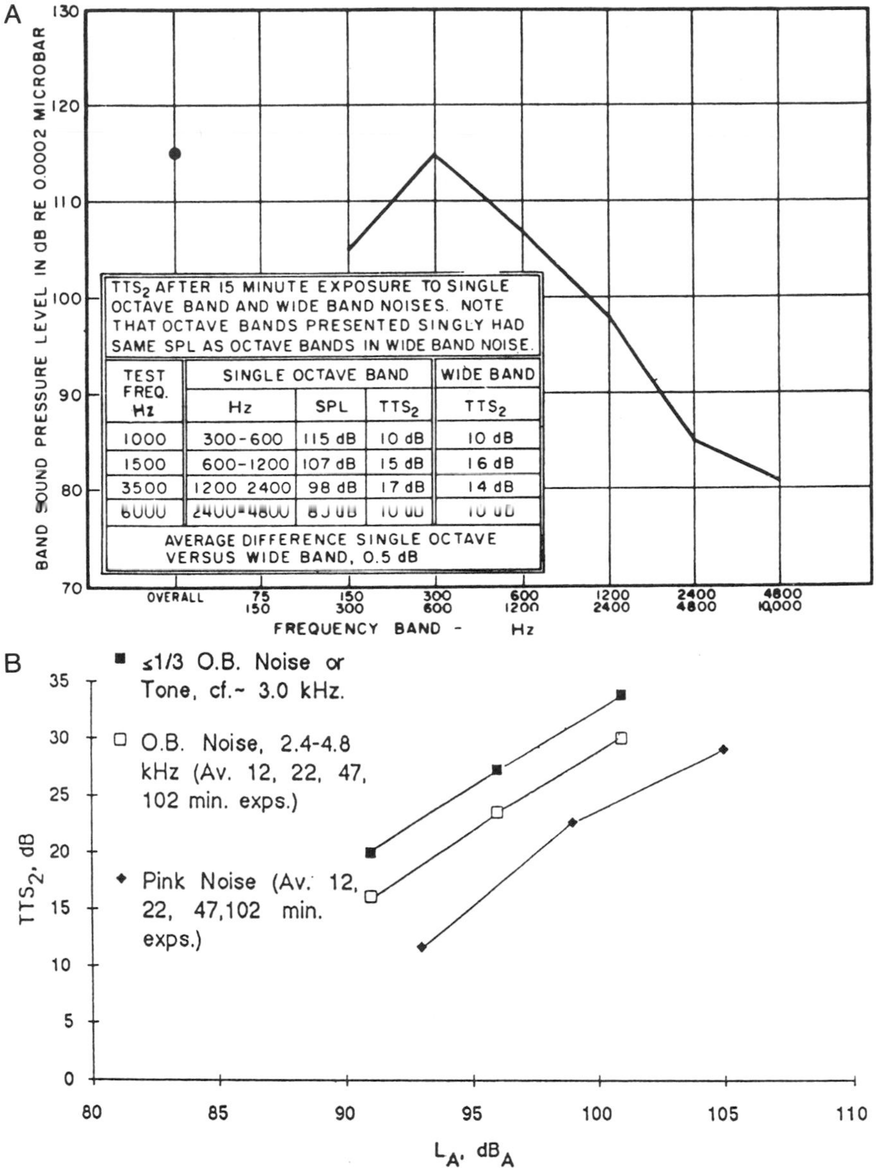

FIGURE 5.33 (A) The octave band of noise ½–1 octave below a given test frequency determines TTS at that frequency, and, within limits, noise energy above and below the OBN does not contribute to TTS at the given test frequency (Kryter, 1963. Copyright 1963 by the American Psychological Association. Adapted by permission of the author.) (B) Mean TTS_2, 4000 Hz, as function of L_A of a ⅓-octave band, or tone (Carter and Kryter, 1962), full-octave band (Ward *et al.*, 1958. Copyright 1958 by the American Psychological Association. Adapted by permission of the author.), and pink noise (Ward *et al.*, 1959. Copyright 1959 by the American Psychological Association. Adapted by permission of the author.)

membrane. The classical study of Davis *et al.* (1943) established the fact that the maximum threshold shift from exposure to a pure tone occurs in the frequency region of about 1/2–1 octave above the frequency of the tone (see Fig. 5.34). That relation has been also found with octave band noises (Ward *et al.*, 1959a; Kylin, 1959, 1960; Kryter, 1963; Shoji *et al.*, 1966).

General Applicability of *A*-Weighting

For greatest accuracy in making estimations of TTS and NIPTS from exposures to sounds of particular spectra, ≤1/3-octave band spectra and specifications of audiometric test frequencies are required.In spite of these requirements, *A*-, *D*-, or phon-weighted sound-pressure levels can be used to fairly accurately predict NIPTS at different frequencies for noises that are broadband. As noted in Chapter 4, most common noises in industry and the living environment are broadband, with energy falling in the range of approximately 125–6000 Hz.

One reason for this practical accuracy is illustrated in Fig. 5.35, where it is seen that the difference between the TTSs from the -6 dB, 0 dB, and the +6 dB/octave slope noises ranged from about 0 dB at the midaudiometric, to a maximum of about 10 dB at the higher- and lower-audiometric test frequencies. Although for some purposes such differences might be considered as significant, overall they seem surprisingly small considering the wide differences in the distribution of sound energy in the different spectra involved (see Fig. 5.35B).

The small differences at 3000 and 4000 Hz are probably due to the rather universally found "4000-Hz dip" in hearing level, and the fact that all the L_A 100 noises in Fig. 5.35 differ in level by only 1–3 dB in the band most effective in causing threshold shifts at 3000–4000 Hz—the octave band 1000–2000 Hz. Wider differences in TTS found at the other frequencies are also consistent with the greater variations seen in industrial-study NIPTS data points for test frequencies other than 3000 and 4000 Hz (see Fig. 4.10).

EFFECTIVE QUIET, EFFECTIVE EVERYDAY NOISE, AND SOCIOCUSIS

Effective Quiet

Several investigators, using human and animal subjects, have found that recovery from TTS is reduced when the level of background noise in periods between exposures to more intense noise was no higher than L_A 40–70 dB (Ward *et al.* 1976b; Hetu *et al.*, 1978; Schmidek *et al.*, 1972). Not until the "noise" in the recovery periods was less than those levels did full recovery continue (see Fig. 5.36). This maximum level, perhaps for humans around L_A 55 for an octave band and L_A 60 for broadband noise, is called *effective quiet*, and presumably indicates a level, perhaps a 24-h, $EL_{Aeq,24h}$, energy

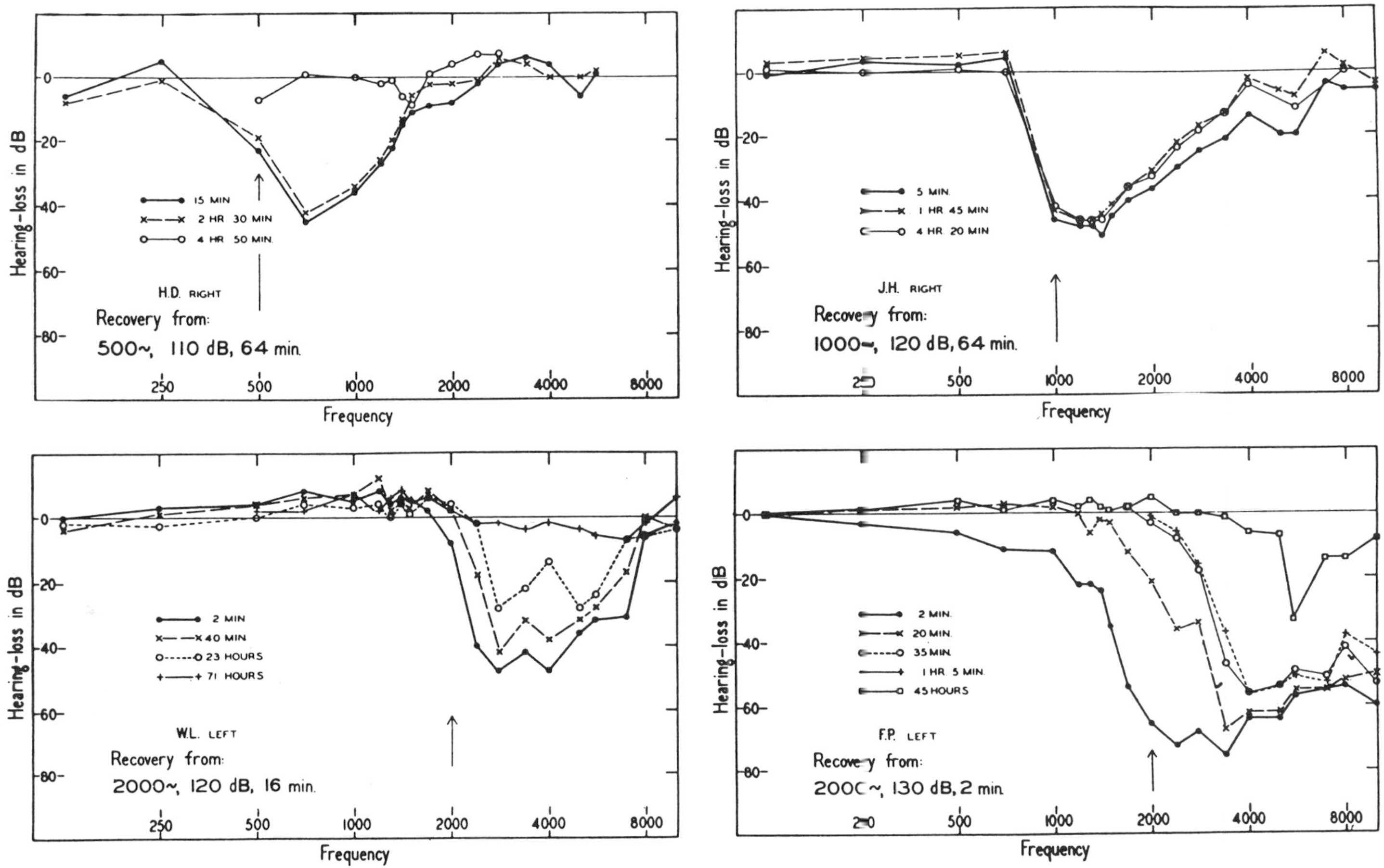

FIGURE 5.34 Recovery from exposures to intense pure tones, showing maximum losses at frequencies about $^1/_2$ octave above that of exposure tone. (From Davis *et al.*, 1943.)

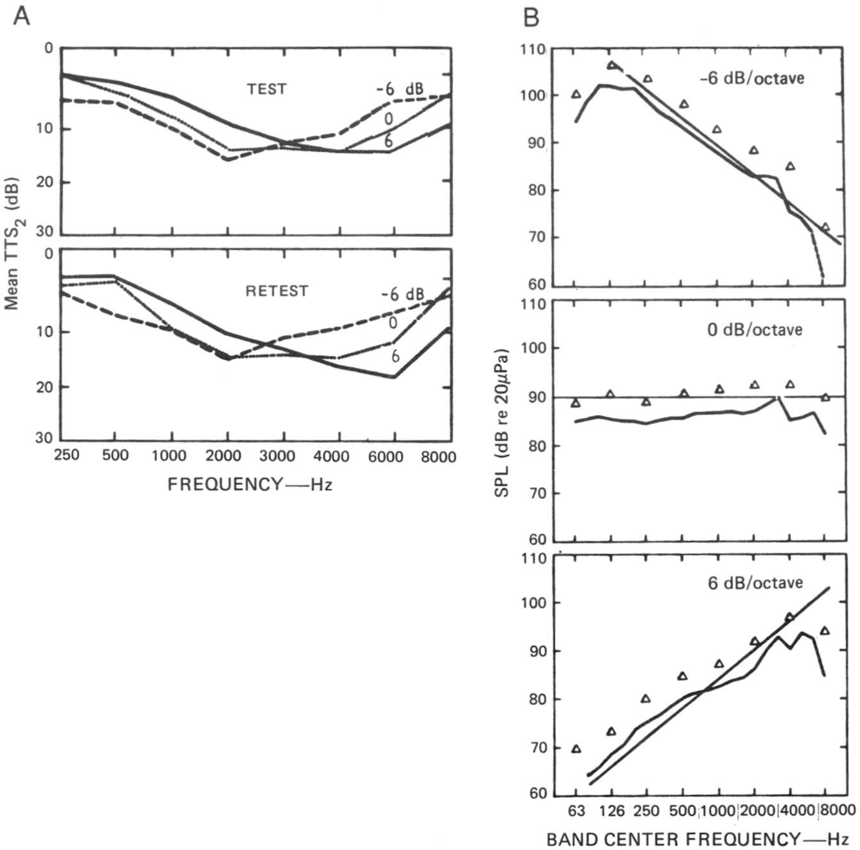

FIGURE 5.35 (A) Mean temporary shift in hearing threshold for different tonal frequencies following exposure to −6-, 0-, and +6-dB/octave spectrum–slope noises (B). (From Cohen *et al.*, 1972. Copyright 1972 by the American Psychological Association. Adapted by permission of the author.)

level, required for complete avoidance by the average, and 50%ile, ear of sound induced permanent threshold shifts during a lifetime.

As shown in Fig. 5.37, Stephenson *et al.* (1980) found TTS_2 at 4000 Hz, after 8 h of exposure to pink noise, to be on the average, relative to preexposure hearing level, left-hand ordinate: 1 dB, for L_A 65; 3 dB for L_A 70, 75, and 80; and 10 dB for L_A 85. TTS_2 values of 3–4 dB were classified by the authors as statistically significant, although not above the .95 level of confidence. TTS_2 relative to the lowest postexposure "rested" hearing level, right-hand ordinate, were about 1–2 dB greater than TTS_2 relative to preexposure hearing level.

The general trend of TTS_2 as a function L_A with 8-h exposure was shown in Fig. 5.29 for the data of Stephenson *et al.* (1980)(exposure to pink noise),

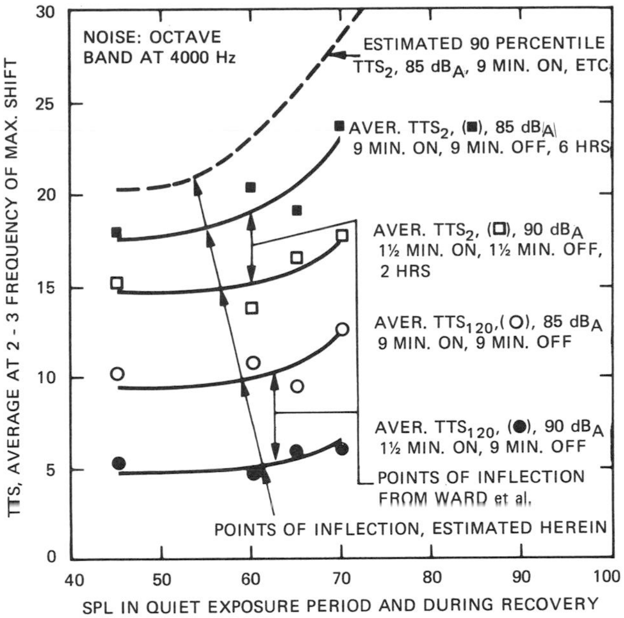

FIGURE 5.36 TTS as a function of lower ("quiet") sound-pressure levels of alternated with higher levels of TTS-producing sameoctave-band noise. Reducing the lower levels down to L_A 55–60 facilitates recovery from TTS. (Data points from Ward, *et al.*, 1976.)

and those of Ward *et al.*, 1976 (plotted against what would be the level of pink noise with the tested, specified OBN; see Table 5.4). As was noted, these effective quiet and TTS_2 results are concordant with threshold of NIPTS preducted by EE_A after 50 work-years of exposure.

However, the precise identification of the threshold level in the average normal ear for TTS_2, and presumed eventual NIPTS, is not possible. First, it involves the measurement of changes of only a few decibels in threshold hearing level, a feat that requires a fairly large sample of subjects to achieve statistical significance. Second, it is important that the subjects tested are not suffering from some TTS before so-called preexposure thresholds are taken, nor from some amount of NIPTS due to sociocusis.

These problems are exemplified by the data of Stephenson *et al.* For example, it is seen from the right-hand ordinate in Fig. 5.37 that the hearing levels, except for the L_A 70 exposures, declined 1–2 dB postexposure compared to their preexposure thresholds. This would indicate that the subjects, on the average, went into the experimental sessions with some small amounts of TTS, and that the true amount of TTS was that much greater than is to be surmised from the left-hand ordinate of Fig. 5.37.

A second factor that may have contributed to an underestimation of TTS in this study is that, although classified as having normal hearing, the ears

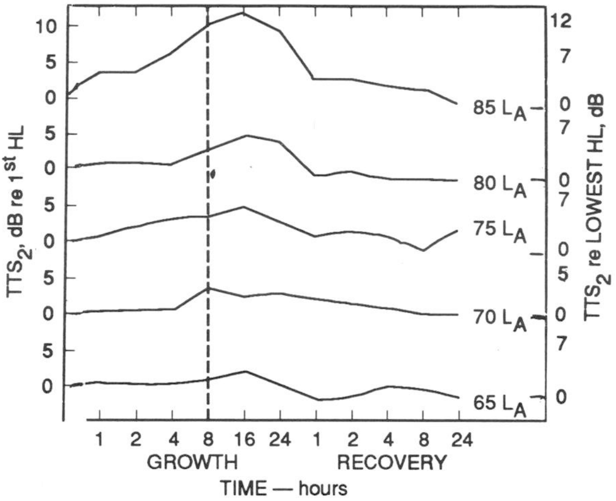

FIGURE 5.37 Mean TTS_2 growth and recovery at 4000 Hz from exposure to pink noise. The effect of decreasing the exposure intensity from 85 to 65 dB_A is demonstrated. (After Stephenson *et al.*, 1980.)

of some of the subjects possibly had some amounts of sociocusis. For example, to qualify for testing, the subjects (12 male college students) in the Stephenson *et al.* study were required to have hearing levels at all test frequencies that were no greater than 15 dB. The actual hearing levels of the subjects were not reported so that we do not know if the average HL for the subjects was actually zero, or normal. It is to be noted that the procedures followed by these investigators were standard for similar studies of TTS, including those Ward *et al.*, used in Fig. 5.29, and elsewhere in this book.

As was noted earlier, with the use of self-recording audiometers, as was the case for the studies being discussed, what should be considered as a normal hearing level is about -3 dB less than specified in present-day standards, ISO (1975) 389 and ANSI S3.6-(1969). This, of course, could be a factor in these studies only with respect to the selection of "normal" subjects for testing. However, the net effect of these test and subject selection procedures is that the thresholds for TTS_2 and effective quiet for the truly normal ear are probably, in the writer's opinion, several decibels lower than deduced in Figs. 5.25, 5.32, and 5.33

Effective Everyday Noise

Twenty-four-hour dosimeter data for a variety of people living in Japanese cities show that L_{Aeq24h} values range from about 60–85 dB_A, with an average overall of ~73 (see Fig. 5.38) (Nimura and Kono, 1980; Kono *et al.*, 1982).

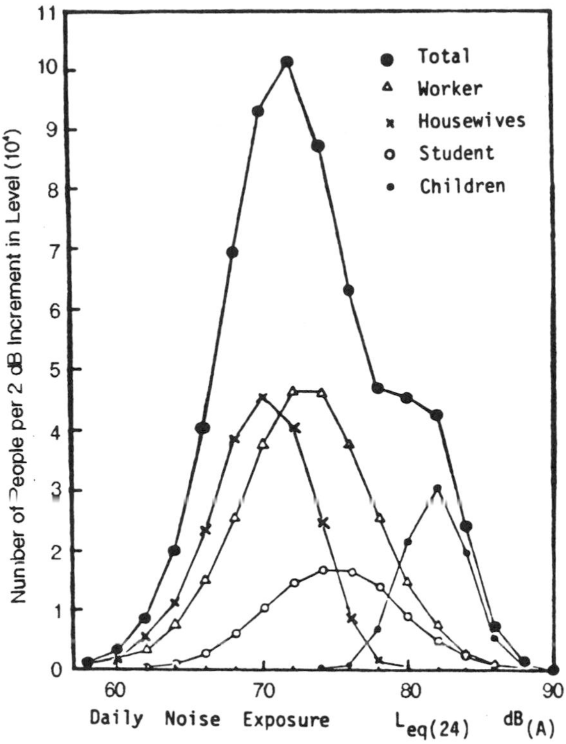

FIGURE 5.38 Distributions of people in a Japanese city (Sendai) experiencing different levels of 24-h day exposures to everyday noise as measured by body-worn dosimeters. (From Nimura and Kono, 1980.)

Those investigators found an average L_{Aeq24h} of 73 dB_A for the 462 workers, and 70 dB_A for 140 housewives.

Garcia and Garcia (1993) conducted a survey in Spain involving 22 people for 137 days of dosimeter monitoring: 4 professors, 2 school teachers, 9 students, 5 clerks-salesmen, 1 soldier, and 1 housewife. The mean L_{Aeq24h} for the entire group was 74 dB_A, standard deviation (s.d.) 4.4 dB_A. Garcia and Garcia also reported the hourly L_{Aeq} for different activity periods: sleeping = 37.9, s.d. 8.2; working = 73,3, s.d. 6.6; home = 66.5, s.d, 7.4; traveling = 76.1, s.d. 4.5; and leisure time = 75.2, s.d. 7.8.

Other 24-h noise exposure dosimeter data have been collected by Johnson and Farina (1977), Fairmen and Johnson (1979), and Schori and McGatha, (1978) in the United States. All these data, in so far as they go, are reasonably consistent with those in Fig. 5.38.

It seems likely that the L_{Aeq8h} period during the daytime dominates these typical 24-h values, and that an L_{Aeq8h} of 75 or so is a reasonable estimate of the equivalent 8-h daytime exposure to sounds for the average adult person. This equivalent everyday exposure is useful for the estimation of sociocusis, and the specification of practical quiet for workers. However, it is important to note that while the cited dosimeter data are equal-energy, L_{Aeq}, values, the everyday sounds and noises to which the average person is exposed are irregular in intensity and of a temporal pattern. As is seen in Figs. 5.39 and 5.40, typical indoor and outdoor sounds from even the same sources range ≥20 dB in level.

For such irregular noise conditions, as discussed earlier, equal-energy L_{Aeq} values significantly overestimate their hazard to hearing, and the effective EL_{Aeq} level could well be approximately 10 dB lower than the L_{Aeq} measured for the same environments; i.e., an EL_{Aeq8h} of about 65 would probably be present, when everyday indoor and outdoor noises, measured L_{Aeq8h} 75. On the basis of present data, it is estimated that an everyday, and a nonnoisy industry level of L_{Aeq8h} 75, as typically measured, would be calculated to have an EL_{Aeq8h} 65. This could be considered as a "practical," but not necessarily "true" threshold level from which to estimate NIPTS for the 50%ile at 4000 Hz from exposure to workplace noise. The levels for the 10%ile and the 90%ile of the population can be estimated by subtracting 8 dB from, for the 10%ile, and adding 11 dB to the 50%ile, or median, levels for both the practical and true threshold levels for NIPTS at 4000 Hz, after 50 years of exposure. This latter rule of thumb is based on the distribution shown on Fig. 4.5 of hearing levels for normal ears at 4000 Hz.

Some discussion will be given in Chapter 7 of the guidelines and policies in the United States, as well as in some other countries, of gearing industrial noise environments to steady noise levels of L_A 90. The relation of those limits to hearing impairment and handicap for speech understanding will be reviewed and new data analyzed in Chapter 7.

Sociocusis

As was discussed in Chapter 4, it seems clear that some of what is considered as presbycusis in ISO (1984) 7029, the standard for normal hearing, is actually sociocusis. What are considered as "normal" hearing levels at 4000 Hz in modern, industrialized societies, ISO (1984) 7029, are ~19 dB higher for 60-year-old males, and 6 dB higher for 60-year old females, than those of like-aged males and females from a nonindustrialized society (see Table 4.2). Table 4.2 showed that by the age 60 in the noise-free society, females had about the same hearing as males, except at 6000 Hz, with 5 dB higher levels at 6000 Hz.

These differences are attributed to the fact that members of industrialized societies are exposed to greater amounts of sound and noise in everyday life. ISO 7029 shows that the hearing levels of males are higher than those of females, e.g., 12 dB at 4000 Hz, age 60 years. If one accepts the hypothesis that there is no basic difference between male and female ears in susceptibility

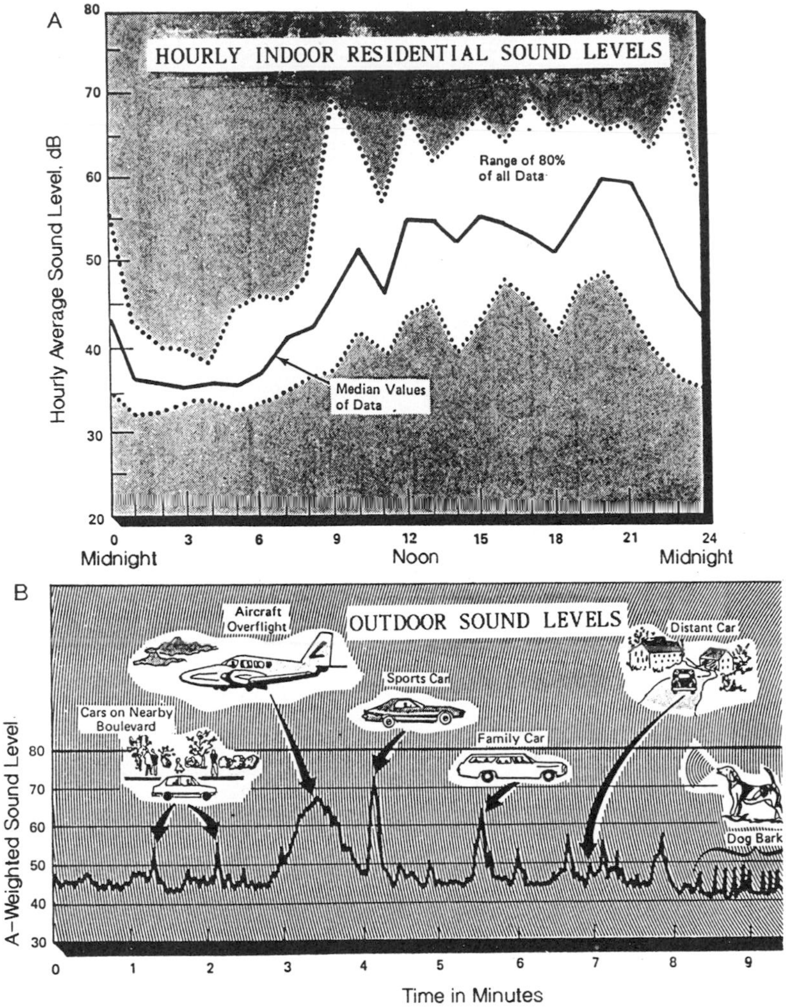

FIGURE 5.39 Time patterns of (A) indoor and (B) outdoor residential *A*-weighted sound-pressure levels. (From EPA, 1978.)

to NIPTS, the conclusion follows that in modern societies males are exposed to more to intense "everyday" noise than are females.

On the basis of a ~6-dB difference between the hearing levels of females of the industrialized and noise-free societies, and the 12 dB between the hearing levels of males and females in industrialized societies, it is guessed that the effective level of everyday noise would have to be decreased by at least 10 dB to remove the effects of sociocusis on hearing sensitivity in modern societies. Accordingly, what was identified as a practical threshold for 50%ile 0 dB NIPTS at 4000 Hz (EL_{Aeq8h} 65, or L_{Aeq8h} 75 for varying-level

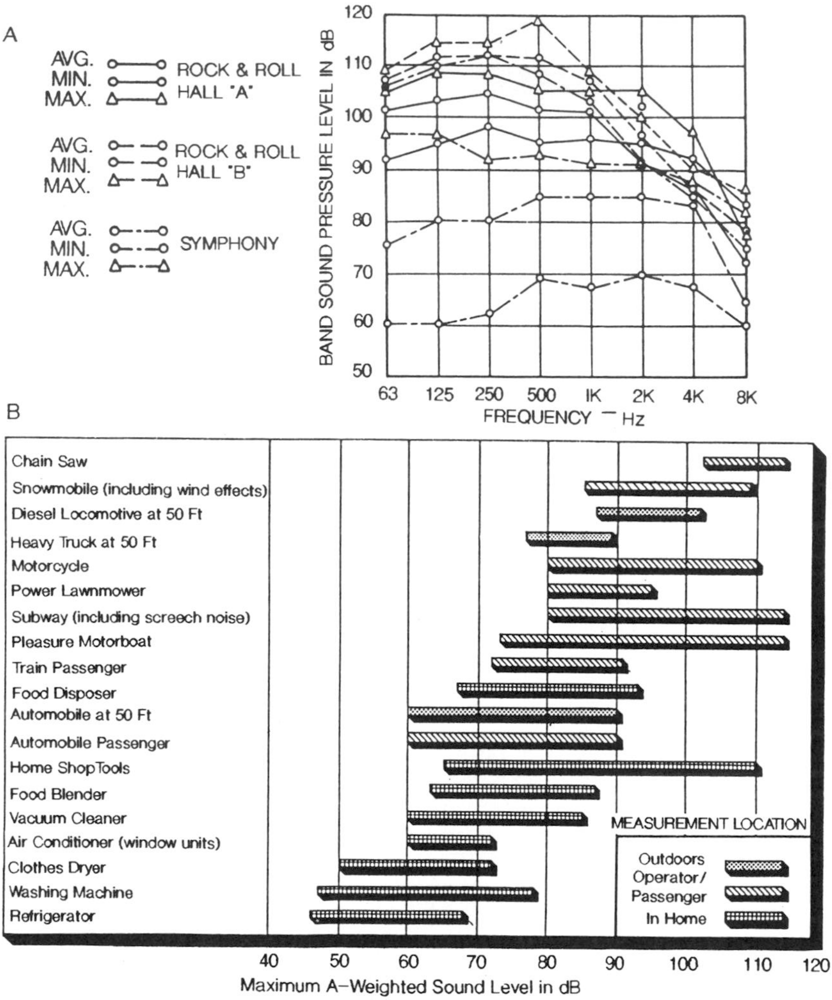

FIGURE 5.40 (A) Variations in sound-pressure level of rock-and-roll and symphonic music. (From Lebo and Oliphant 1968.) (B) Ranges in *A*-weighted levels of some common sounds and noises. (From EPA, 1978.)

noise), would be reduced, for the "true" threshold, to, respectively, EL_{Aeq8h} 55 and L_{Aeq8h} 65, and for 90%ile, most susceptible ears, EL_{Aeq8h} 45 and L_{Aeq8h} 55. These numbers are consistent with the above-noted effective quiet measured under laboratory conditions (see Fig. 5.36). (As will be discussed in Chapter 7, a criterion of hearing loss sufficient to constitute a handicap to the hearing of everyday speech is used for "practical" noise control purposes, rather than the more stringent criterion of NIPTS at 4000 Hz.)

Maximum Allowable Levels for 0 dB NIPTS, 50%ile, from 50-Year, 1-Year, 1-Day, and 0.5-s Exposures

According to the EE_A formulas, the maximum L_A, *e*dB, levels for various once-in-a-lifetime exposures to give, for 50%ile of the exposed population, 0 dB NIPTS at 4000 Hz are

Fifty work-years = L_A 66, steady for 8 h per workday [66 + 14(8 log 12,500 days/250) = EE_A 80]
One work-year = L_A 80, steady for 8 h per workday [80 − 0(8 log 250 days/250) = EE_A80]
One 8-h day = L_A 99, steady for 8 h [99 + 8 log 1 day/250] = EE_A 80}
One 0.5-s exposure = L_A 200, steady for 0.5 s {200 − 89[-20 log (57,600/0.5)] − 19[8 log(1 day/250)] = EE_A 80}

One 0.5-s exposure at a level of L_A 200 would, undoubtedly, be intolerable to the structural integrity of the middle and inner ear. Intensity levels of L_A ~130–135 have been commonly proposed as maximum peak levels for brief, (~1-min)-duration sounds for per day (Kryter *et al.*, 1965).

SUMMARY OF THE *EE* PROCEDURE FOR PREDICTING NIPTS AND TTS

With respect to the prediction of NIPTS, the validation of the EE_A procedure is accomplished primarily by the function relating NIPTS from years of exposures to steady and impulse industrial noises, as described in Chapter 4. In addition to providing a base of fundemental auditory data and theory, Chapter 5 has added specification and quantification of short-term (≤8-h) temporal factors in sensorineural stimulation and recovery from such stimulation. The final EE_A formulation permits the estimation of the effective energy level, as a cause of TTS and NIPTS, of sound in 0.5-s segments of time regardless of whether the sound is impulsive or steady, continuous or interrupted, in character. The predictive accuracy is limited to those sound environments that will cause no more than an average of about 35–40 dB TTS in initially normal ears 2 min after a single daily exposure last no longer than 8, or so, hours.

The prinicpal physiological premises for NIPTS and TTS, as predicted by EE_A, within the magnitude constraint specified, are

1. The amount of response activity of the sensorineural receptors is dependent on the sound energy, as transmitted by the outer and middle ear, and as processed by the inner ear.
2. The amount of functional fatigue, or damage, to the inner ear, as measured by TTS and NIPTS, is proportional to the amount of

sensorineural activity resulting from stimulation by the transformed sound.

3. The amount of recovery from auditory fatigue is a function of the expenditure of metabolic energy.
4. Metabolic energy is a matter of physiological supply and, as such, is neither imported by nor dependent on the acoustic stimulus and therefore is not necessarily proportional to equal temporal-intensity energy in the stimulus.

Measurements and Formulae for Predicting NIPTS, TTS_2, and HL

A-weighted level of 0.5-s interval of noise >60, ±2.5 dB $= L_{A0.5s,n1} = 10 \log (1/x)\ 10^{(pi_A{}^{2}1 \ldots pi_A{}^{2}x)/10}$, dB. (5.I)

Where n is a specified L_A level, ±2.5 dB; x is number of samples, approximately 7500/s; pi is the sound pressure measured per sample; and $L_{A0.5s}$ 60 is taken as a practical exposure threshold level for TTS and eventual NIPTS. Please not the following:

1. Other overall frequency weightings, such as D- and E-, and band calculation methods, such as phons Zwicker and Stevens, and PN_{dB} may also be used for this purpose with, theoretically (see Chapter 3), approximately comparable predictive accuracies for NIPTS and TTS.
2. For a nearby point source with an incidence angle of about 45° lateral to and in front of an ear, such as a rifle fired from the shoulder, the intensity of its free-field spectrum should be increased by 4 dB at frequencies of 500–4000 Hz, and 7 dB at 6000 Hz. The purpose of this adjustment is to help equate such exposures for comparison with the effects on hearing of frontal and/or random incidence noises.

Effective daily exposure level of 8 work-hours per day to a noise, $EL_{Aeq8h,n_1} = L_{A0.5s,n_1} - 20 \log (57{,}600/t_e) - (-2.5 + 3.95 \log i > 15\ s)$, edB$n_1$. (5.II)

where t_e is t, number of 0.5 intervals n_1 is present during 8 h, plus e, the duration, in 0.5-s periods of interruptions of decreased level >5 dB, with a limit of up to four 0.5-s intervals allowed for each interruption; and i >15 s is the number of interruptions of durations >15 s.

Effective daily exposure level to noises, $n_1 \ldots n_x$, $EL_{Aeq8h,n_1 - n_x} = 10 \log 10^{(edBn1 \ldots edBnx)/10}$, edB,$n_1 - n_x$. (5.III)

Effective long-term, or career exposure to a noise, n_1, $EE_{A,n1,y,f}$ = edBn_1 + 8 log work-years' exposure [or 8 log (days of exposure/250)] (5.IV) where 12,500 = 50 years at 250 days/year; work-years = 250 days/year of exposure; and f = frequency offset adjustments, from Chapter 4.

Effective long-term, or career exposure, to noises $n_1 \ldots n_x$ $EE_{A,n1-n,x,f} = 10 \log 10^{(EE_{A,n1,y,f} \ldots EE_{A,nx,y,f})/10)}$, dB. (5.V)

Table 5.8 gives 50%ile NIPTS as a function of frequency-adjusted EE_A, $EE_{A,f}$, and tables for conversion of calculated EE_A to $EE_{A,f}$. Shown are formulas for (1) conversion of 50%ile NIPTS to NIPTS expected at other percentiles and (2) estimation of hearing level for a specified percentile NIPTS and presbycusis age. Table 5.8 also contains a diagram showing the function between NIPTS and number of years of exposure, 250 exposure days per year, for 50%ile NIPTS at 4000 Hz, and constants for a polynomial two-segment fit to the function.

PHYSIOLOGICAL STUDIES OF THE COCHLEA

Significant advances in theory and description of the biomechanics and biochemistry of hearing, and hearing loss have occurred in recent years due to improvements in histological, microscopic, and electrophysiological techniques of observation and analysis of the cochlea and nervous system. Research with animals, particularly guinea pigs, chinchillas, mice, rats, and chickens have shown that overexposure to noise damages the inner ear in two general ways:

1. From the top down, where excessive agitation's of the stereocilia of the hair cells on the basilar membrane causes their tips to become disengaged from the hair cell and, under extreme conditions, mechanical damage to other structures in the cochlea (see Fig. 5.28). This concept of mechanical damage or disarrangements lends itself to the equal-energy concept of hearing loss as being related to structural fatigue and eventual failure from overbending or stress. However, it is also found that some of these apparent structural disarrangements may be reversible during recovery periods.

2. From the bottom up, where the metabolic and electromechanical response activity results in pathological swelling and other conditions in the hair cells, neural connections, and vascular system of the cochlea.. Biochemical investigations have revealed that a wide range of metabolic changes in tissues and fluids of the inner ear take place as the result of exposures to intense noise. These biomechanical and biochemical changes occur, of course, together, as well, perhaps, as interacting with each other at different levels of stimulation.

In many of these studies, cochlear structures have been damaged within a matter of a few hours, or days, of exposure to noise; exposure conditions

TABLE 5.8 Tables and Formulas for Predicting, from EE_A, NIPTS and Hearing Level at Different Percentiles (%ile) and Test Frequencies, and Averages of Frequencies

50%ile NIPTS as function of EE_A, edBy; edBy = edBn + 8 log (days of exposure/250)											
EE_{Af}	NIPTS*	EE_{Af}	NIPTS	EE_{Af}	NIPTS	EE_{Af}	NIPTS	EE_{Af}	NIPTS	EE_{Af}	NIPTS
80.0	0.0	86.5	2.5	93.0	8.0	99.5	15.8	106.0	32.4	112.5	58.6
80.5	0.1	87.0	2.9	93.5	8.5	100.0	17.1	106.5	34.0	113.0	61.1
81.0	0.2	87.5	3.2	94.0	9.1	100.5	18.0	107.0	35.6	113.5	63.8
81.5	0.3	88.0	3.5	94.5	9.6	101.0	18.8	107.5	37.6	114.0	66.4
82.0	0.5	88.5	3.9	95.0	10.2	101.5	20.3	108.0	39.1	114.5	69.2
82.5	0.6	89.0	4.3	95.5	10.8	102.0	21.4	108.5	41.0	115.0	72.1
83.0	0.8	89.5	4.7	96.0	11.4	102.5	22.5	109.0	42.9	115.5	75.0
83.5	1.0	90.0	5.1	96.5	12.1	103.0	23.6	109.5	44.9	116.0	78.0
84.0	1.2	90.5	5.5	97.0	12.7	103.5	24.7	110.0	47.0	116.5	81.1
84.5	1.4	91.0	6.0	97.5	13.4	104.0	25.8	110.5	49.2	117.0	84.2
85.0	1.7	91.5	6.5	98.0	14.1	104.5	26.9	111.0	51.4	117.5	84.5
85.5	2.0	92.0	6.9	98.5	14.8	105.0	28.2	111.5	53.7	118.0	90.8
86.0	2.2	92.5	7.5	99.0	15.5	105.5	29.5	112.0	56.1		Limit

Adjustment to EE_A for predicting, by $EE_{A,f}$, NIPTS at a frequency or average of frequencies

Hz	EE_A, e_{dBy}	Adjustment	$EE_{A,f}$
500	92	−12	80
1000	90	−10	80
2000	87	−7	80
3000	82	−2	80
4000	82	0	80
6000	82	−2	80
Average, 0.5,1,2,3,4	86	−6	80
Average, 1,2,3 kHz	86	−6	80

Hearing level (HL) calculated for a given percentile NIPTS and age

%ile HL; age = [(%ile HL, age, ISO 7029 + 65) + (%ile NIPTS, −65)], db.

Ratio for conversion of 50%ile NIPTS to X%ile NIPTS, any freqeuncy or age

Examples*	Ratio
10%ile	0.4
25%ile	0.1
75%ile	1.5
90%ile	2.0

* X%ile/50%ile =

0.03[illegible]2 + (0.006 × X%ile) + (0.0[illegible]01327) × X%ile^2.

See Fig. 4.13

Years of exposure	8 log Y
1	0.0
2	2.4
3	3.8
4	4.8
5	5.6
6	6.2
7	6.8
8	7.2
9	7.6
10	8.0
15	9.4
20	10.4
25	11.2
30	11.8
35	12.4
40	12.8
50	13.6

(continues)

TABLE 5.8 *(Continued)*

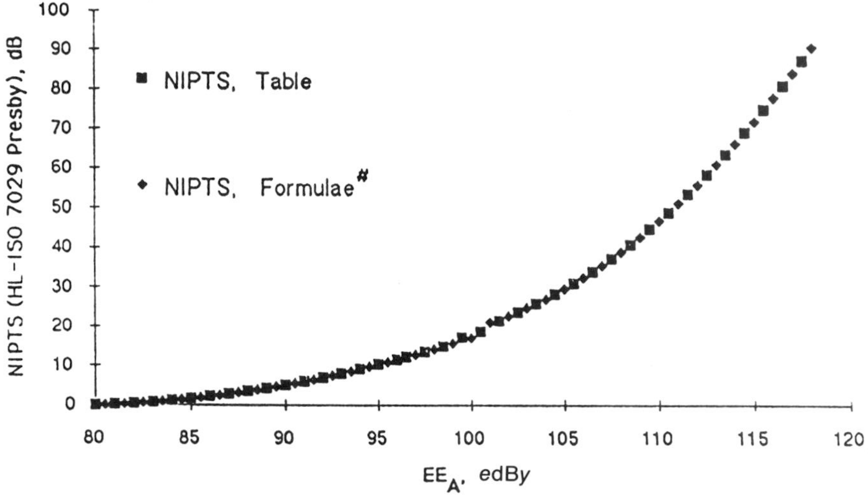

* NIPTS, 80–100, edBy = 206.927 + [(−5.308 × ((edBy + 0.06)] + [0.034 × (edBy + 0.06)^2].

NIPTS, 101–118, edBy = 1418.261 + (−29.186 × edBy) + [0.152 × edBy^2].

generally far in excess of the levels of concern to hearing loss in humans from months and years of everyday living and working environments. The full understanding of behavioral hearing rests, of course, on knowledge of the metabolic functions, and dysfunctions, of the auditory receptor, neural, and vascular system at the biochemical molecular and cytoskeletal levels. One particularly interesting recent finding has been that of regeneration of hair-cell stereocilia, and some other cells, in the cochlea, after being damaged or destroyed by exposure to intense noise. However, to date, no functional recovery of hearing has been demonstrated.

A relatively new approach to the study of NIPTS is the measurement of acoustic emissions from the cochlea. These otoacoustic emissions (that can be heard as *tinnitus,* or ringing in the ear) are apparently due to mechanical actions or *microphonics* of hair cells. As previously mentioned, cochlear microphonics, are electrical potentials generated by a piezoelectric type response, it is believed, occurring from a mechanical pressure being applied to hair cells in the cochlea. Conversely, a mechanical, vibratory reaction of these elements results from application of electrical potentials. Presumably, such neural–electrical activity may be one cause of the otoacoustic emissions, also called *cochlear echoes.* In any event, the nonfunctioning, or abnormal functioning of hair cells due to their damage from exposure to noise or other disease is detectable, relative to normal, from measurements of otoacoustic emissions.

There does not appear to be sufficient data and theory, beyond that already discussed, the review of which would aid in the prediction of sound induced behavioral hearing loss in humans. However, following the references to this chapter, Selected bibliographies are presented for the interested reader of recent papers on (1) cochlear damage from exposure to noise, (2) cochlear regeneration following damage from exposure to noise, and (3) otoacoustic emissions. Some of the references in Chapter 2 are concerned with exploratory research on the basic physiology of the ear and should be referred to.

References

Acton, W. L., Coles, R. R. A., and Forrest, M. R. (1966). Hearing hazard from smallbore rifles. *Rifleman* **74,** 9–12.

AFR (1956). 160-3. "Hazardous Noise Exposure." Dep. Air Force, Washington, D.C.

Ahroon, W. A., Hamernik, R. P., and Davis, R. I. (1993). The relation among postexposure threshold shifts and NIPTS in the chinchilla. *Noise Public Health Prob., Proc. Int. Congr. 6th* (M. Vallet, ed.), Vol. 2, pp. 1–5. l'INRETS, 94114 Arcuil Cedx, France.

Angelborg, C., and Engström, H. (1973). The normal organ of corti. *In* "Basic Mechanisms in Hearing" (A. R. Møller, ed.), pp. 125–184. Academic Press, New York.

ANSI (1969). S3.6. "American National Standard for Audiometers." American National Standards Institutes, New York.

ASA (1951). Z-24.5. "American Standard for Audiometer for General Diagnostic Purposes." Am. Nat. Stand. Inst., New York.

Atherley, G. R., and Martin, A. M. (1971). Equivalent-continuous noise level as a measure of injury from impact and impulse noise. *Ann. Occup. Hyg.* **14,** 11–23.

Bohne, B., and Clark, W. W. (1982). Growth of hearing loss and cochlear lesion with increasing duration of noise exposure. *In* "New Perspectives on Noise-Induced Hearing Loss" (R. P. Hamernik, D. Henderson, and R. Salvi, eds.), pp. 283–302. Raven Press, New York.

Buck, K., Dancer, A., and Franke, R. (1984). Effect of the temporal patter of a given noise dose on TTS in guinea pigs. *J. Acoust. Soc. Am.* **76,** 1090–1097.

Burns, W., and Robinson, D. W. (1970). "Hearing and Noise in Industry" Her Majesty's Stationery Office, London.

Campo, P., Subramaniam, M., and Henderson, D. (1991). The effect of "conditioning" exposures on hearing loss form traumatic exposure. *Hear. Res.* **55,** 195–200.

Canlon, B. (1987). Acoustic overstimulation alters the morphology of the tectorial membrane. *Hear. Res.* **30,** 127–134.

Canlon, B. (1988). The effect of acoustic trauma on the tectorial membrane, stereocilia, and hearing sensitivity: possible mechanisms underlying damage, recovery, and protection. *Scand. Audiol., Suppl. No.* 27, 1–45.

Canlon, B., Borg, E., and Flock, A. (1988). Protection against noise trauma by preexposure to a low level acoustic stimulus. *Hear. Res.* **34,** 197–200.

Carder, H. M., and Miller, J. D. (1972). Temporary threshold shifts from prolonged exposure to noise. *J. Speech Hear. Res.* **15,** 603–623.

Carter, N. L., and Kryter, K. D. (1962). "Studies of Temporary Threshold Shift Caused by High Intensity Noise," Rep. No. 949. Bolt, Beranek, & Newman, Cambridge, Massachusetts.

Ceypek, T., Kuzniarz, J., and Lipowczan, A. (1973). Hearing loss due to impulse noise—A field study. *Proc. Int. Congr. Noise Public Health Prob.* (W. D. Ward, ed.), EPA 550/9-73-008, pp. 219-228. U.S. Environ. Prot. Agency, Washington, D.C.

Chung, D. Y., Gannon, R. P., Willson, G. N., and Mason, K. (1991). Shooting, sensorineural loss, and worker's compensation. *J. Occup. Med.* **23,** 481–484.

Clark, W. W. (1991). Recent studies of temporary threshold shift (TTS) and permanent threshold shift (PTS) in animals. *J. Acoust. Soc. Am.* **90,** 155–163.

Clark, W. W., Clark, C. S., Moody, D. B., and Stebbins, W. C. (1974). Noise-induced hearing loss in the chinchilla, as determined by a positive-reinforcement technique. *J. Acoust. Soc. Am.* **56,** 1202–1209.

Clark, W. W., Bohne, B. A., and Boettcher, F. A. (1987). Effect of periodic rest on hearing loss and cochlear damage following exposure to noise. *J. Acoust. Soc. Am.* **82,** 1253–1264.

Cohen, A., Anticaglia, J. R., and Carpenter, P. L. (1972). Temporary threshold shift in hearing from exposure to different noise spectra at equal dBA levels. *J. Acoust. Soc. Am.* **51,** Part 2, 503–507.

Coles, R. R. A., and Rice, C. G. (1965). High-Intensity noise problems in the Royal Navy and Royal Marines. *J. R. Nav. Med. Serv.* **51,** 184–192.

Collins, E. G. (1948). Aural trauma caused by gunfire. *J. Laryngol. Otol.* **63,** 358–390.

Dancer, A., Grateau, P., Cabanis, A., Vaillant, T., and Lafont, D. (1991). Delayed temporary threshold shift induced by impulse noises (weapon noises) in men. *Audiology* **30,** 345–356.

Danielson, R., Henderson, D., Gratton, M. A., Bianchi, L., and Salvi, R. (1991). The importance of "temporal patter" in traumatic impulse noise exposures. *J. Acoust. Soc. Am.* **90,** 209–218.

Davis, H., Morgan, C. T., Hawkins, J. E., Galambos, R., and Smith, F. (1943). "Temporary Deafness Following Exposure to Loud Tones and Noise" Contract OEMcmr-194. Comm. Med. Res., OSRD, Harvard Med. School, Boston.

Davis, R. R., Franks, J. R., and Pekkarinen, J. O. (1994). Erratum: Hearing loss in the chinchilla from impact and continuous noise exposure. *J. Acoust. Soc. Am.* **95,** 165–166.

Dieroff, H.-G. (1980). Some remarks about differences in mechanisms of damage following exposure to impulse and continuous noise. *Noise Public Health Probl.* (J. V. Tobias, G Jansen, and W. D. Ward, eds.), ASHA Rep. No. 10, pp. 86–91. Am. Speech–Lang.-Hear. Assoc., Rockville, Maryland.

Dunn, D. E., Davis, R. R., Merry, C. J., and Franks, J. R. (1991). Hearing loss in the chinchilla from impact and continuous noise exposure. *J. Acoust. Soc. Am.* **90,** 1979–1985.

Eldred, K. M., Gannon, W. J., and von Gierke, H. (1955). "Criteria for Short Time Exposure of Personnel to High Intensity Jet Aircraft Noise," Rep. WADC-TN-355. Aerosp. Med. Lab., Wright AFB, Ohio.

Elwood, M. A., Brasher, P. F., and Croton, L. M. (1966). A preliminary study of sensitivity to impulsive noise in terms of temporary threshold shifts. *Br. Acoust. Soc. Meet. Impulse Noise, Southampton* Pap.

EPA (1978). "Protective Noise Levels, Condensed Version of EPA Levels Document," Rep. EPA 550/9-79-100. U.S. Environ. Prot. Agency, Washington, D.C.

Fairman, T. M., and Johnson, D. L. (1979). "Noise Dosimeter Measurements in the Air Force," Rep. AMRL-TR-79-52. U.S. Air Force. (Avail. from DTIC as AD A081 284.)

Fiorino, F., Gratton, M., Subbanna, M., Bianchi, L., and Henderson, D. (1989). Physiological mechanisms underlying the progressive resistance to noise induced hearing loss. *Valsalva* **65,** Suppl. 1, 36–41.

Gallo, R. and Glorig, A. (1964). Permanent threshold shift changes produced by noise exposure and aging. *Am. Indust. Hyg. Assoc. J.,* **23,** 237–245.

Garcia, A., Garcia, A. M. (1993). Measurements of noise exposure in daily life. *Noise Public Health Probl., Proc. Int. Congr. 6th* (M. Vallet, ed.), Vol. 2, pp. 367–370. l'INRETS, 94114 Arcuil Cedex, France.

Goldstone, G., and Smith, M. G. (1961). "A Pilot Study of Temporary Threshold Shifts Resulting From Exposure to High-Intensity Impulse Noise," Rep. TM-19-61. U.S. Army. (Avail. from DTIC as AD 269 043.)

Guberan, E., Fernandex, J., Cardinet, J., and Terrier, G. (1971). Hazardous exposure to industrial impact noise: Persistent effect on hearing. *Ann. Occup. Hyg.* **14,** 345–350.

Guild, S. R. (1944). Anatomical changes responsible for blast deafness and the prevention of such damage to the ear. *J. Acoust. Soc. Am.* **16,** 68–70.

Hamernik, R. P., Turrentine, G., and Roberto, M. (1985). Mechanical-induced morphological changes in the organ of corti. *In* "Basic and Applied Aspects of Noise-Induced Hearing Loss" (R. J. Salvi, D. Henderson, R. P. Hamernik, and D. Colletti, eds.), pp. 69–84. Plenum, New York.

Hamernik, R. P., Ahroon, W. A., and Hsueh, K. D. (1991). The energy spectrum of an impulse: Its relation to hearing loss. *J. Acoust. Soc. Am.* **90,** 197–204.

Hamernik, R. P., Ahroon, W. A., Davis, R. I., and Lei, S.-F. (1993). Hearing threshold shifts from repeated six-hour daily exposure to impact noise. *Noise Public Health Probl., Proc. Int. Congr. 6th* (M. Vallet, eds), Vol. 2, pp. 57–60. l'INRETS, 94114 Arcuil Cedex, France.

Henderson, D. and Hamernik, R. P. (1982). Asymptotic threshold shift from impulse noise. *In* "New Perspectives on Noise-Induced Hearing Loss" (R. P. Hamernik, D. Henderson, and R. Salvi, eds.), pp. 265–281. Raven Press, New York.

Henderson, D., and Subramaniam, M. (1993). Toughening: Acoustic parameters. *Noise Public Health Probl., Proc. Int. Congr. 6th* (M. Vallet, ed.), Vol. 2, pp. 65–68. l'INERTS, 94114 Arcuil Cedex, France.

Henderson, D., Hamernik, R. P., Salvi, R. J., and Ahroon, W. A. (1983). Comparison of auditory evoked potentials and behavioral thresholds in the normal and noise-exposed chinchilla. *Audiology* **22,** 172–180.

Hétu, R., Laliberte, L., Filon, J., and St-Cyr, J. (1978). Ambient sound level and recovery from TTS: Conflicting results. *J. Acoust. Soc. Am.* **64,** Suppl. 1, 10. (Abstr.)

Hirsh, I. J., and Bilger, R. C. (1955). Auditory-threshold recovery after exposures to pure tones. *J. Acoust. Soc. Am.* **27,** 1186–1194.

Hirsh, I. J., and Ward, W. D. (1952). Recovery of the auditory threshold after strong acoustic stimulation. *J. Acoust. Soc. Am.* **24,** 131–141.

Humes, L. E., and Jesteadt, W. (1991). Modeling the interactions between noise exposure and other variables. *J. Acoust. Soc. Am.* **90,** 182–188.

ISO (1975). 389. "Acoustics—Standard Reference Zero for the Calibration of Pure-Tone Audiometers." Int. Organ. Stand., Geneva.

ISO (1984). 7029. "Acoustics—Threshold of Hearing by Air Conduction as a Function of Age, and Sex for Otologically Normal Persons." Int. Organ. Stand, Geneva.

ISO (1990). 1999. "Acoustics—Assessment of Occupational Noise Exposure for Hearing Conservation Purposes." Int. Organ. Stand, Geneva.

Johansson, B., Kylin, B., and Reopstorff, S. (1973). Evaluation of the hearing damage risk from intermittent noise according to the ISO recommendations. *Proc. Int. Congr. Noise Public Health Prob.* (W. D. Ward, ed.), Rep. EPA 550/9-73-008, pp. 201-210. U.S. Environ. Prot. Agency, Washington, D.C.

Johnson, D. L. and Riffle, C. (1982). Effects of gunfire on hearing level for selected individuals of the Inter-Industry Noise Study. *J. Acoust. Soc. Am.* **72,** 1311–1314.

Johnson, D. L., and Farina, E. R. (1977). Description of the measurement of an individual's continuous sound exposure during a 31-day period. *J. Acoust. Soc. Am.* **62,** 1431–1435.

Kono, S., Sone, T., and Nimura, T. (1982). Personal reaction to daily noise exposure. *Noise Control Eng.* July-Aug., 4–7.

Kryter, K. D. (1963). Exposure to steady-state noise and impairment of Hearing. *J. Acoust. Soc. Am.* **35,** 1515–1525.

Kryter, K. D. (1965). Damage risk criterion and contours based on permanent and temporary hearing loss data. *J. Am. Ind. Hyg. Assoc.*, **26,** 34–44.

Kryter, K. D. (1970). "The Effects of Noise on Man." Academic Press, New York.

Kryter, K. D. (1973). Impairment to hearing from exposure to noise. *J. Acoust. Soc. Am.* **53,** 1211–1234.

Kryter, K. D. (1985). "The Effects of Noise on Man," 2nd Ed. Academic Press, Orlando, Florida.

Kryter, K. D. (1991). Hearing loss from gun and railroad noise-relations with ISO Standard 1999. *J. Acoust. Soc. Am.* **90,** 3180–3195.

Kryter, K. D., and Garinther, G. R. (1965). Auditory effects of acoustic impulses from firearms. *Acta Oto-Laryngol.*, Suppl. No. 21, 1, 1–22.

Kylin, B. (1959). Temporary hearing threshold shift at different frequencies following exposure to various octave bands of noise. *Acta Oto-Laryngol.* **50,** 531–539.

Kylin, B. (1960). Temporary threshold shift and auditory trauma following exposures to steady-state noise. An experimental and field study. *Acta Oto-Laryngol.*, Suppl. No. 152, 1–93.

Lebo, C. P., and Oliphant, K. S. (1968). Music as a source of acoustic trauma. *Laryngoscope* **78,** 1211–1218.

Loeb, M., and Fletcher, J. L. (1963). Temporary threshold shift for "normal" subjects as a function of age and sex. *J. Aud. Res.* **3,** 65–67.

Martin, A. (1976). The equal energy concept applied to impulse noise. *In* "Effects of Noise on Hearing" (D. Henderson, R. P. Hamernik, D. S. Dosanjh, and J. H. Mills, eds.) pp. 421–456. Raven, New York.

McCandles, G. A., and Lentz, W. E. (1968). Evoked response (EEG) audiometry in nonorganic hearing loss. *Arch. of Otolaryngology* **87,** 1233–1238.

Miller, J. D. (1970). Audibility curve of the chinchilla. *J. Acoust. Soc. Am.* **48,** Part 2, 513–523.

Mills, J. H. (1976). Threshold shifts produced by a 90-day exposure to noise. *In* "Effects of Noise on Hearing" (D. Henderson, R. P. Hamernik, D. S. Dosanjh, and J. H. Mills, eds.), pp. 265–276. Raven, New York.

Mills, J. H. (1982). Effects of noise on auditory sensitivity, psychophysical tuning curves, and suppression. *In* "New Perspectives on Noise-Induced Hearing Loss" (R. P. Hamernik, D. Henderson, and R. Salvi, eds.), pp. 249–264. Raven, New York.

Mills, J. H., Gilbert, R. M., and Adkins, W. Y. (1979). Temporary threshold shifts in humans exposed to octave bands of noise for 16–24 hours. *J. Acoust. Soc. Am.* **65,** 1238–1248.

Moore, E. J., ed. (1983). "Bases of Auditory Brain-Stem Evoked Responses." Grune & Stratton, New York.

Nilsson, P., Erlandson, B., Hakanson, H., Ivarsson, A., and Wersall, J. (1982). Anatomical changes in the cochlea of the guinea pig following industrial noise exposures. *In* "New Perspectives on Noise-Induced Hearing Loss" (R. P. Hamernik, D. Henderson, and R. Salvi, eds.) pp. 69–86. Raven, New York.

Nimura, T., and Kono, S. (1980). Personal noise exposure and estimation of population distributed by Leq(24). *Int. Congr. Acoust. 10th* Vol. 2, Part 1, Pap. 7.7. Aust. Acoust. Soc., Sydney.

NIOSH (1972). "Criteria for a Recommended Standard. Occupational Exposure to Noise," Rep. HSM 73-11001. Natl. Inst. Occup. Saf. Health, Dep. Health, Educ., Welfare, Washington, D.C.

NIOSH (1976). "Survey of Hearing Loss in the Coal Mining Industry, PB-271-811. "National Institute for Occupational Safety and Health, Cincinnati, Ohio.

OSHA (1969). Occupational noise exposure. "Safety and Health Standards." *Fed. Regist.* **34,** 12, Part II (Jan. 17); **34,** 96, Part II (May 20).

OSHA (1981). Occupational noise exposure. "Hearing Conservation Amendment" (20 CFR Part 1910). *Fed. Regist.* **45,** 11 (Jan. 16).

OSHA (1983). Occupational noise exposure. "OSHA Safety and Health Standards" (29 CFR Part 1910) OSHA 2206 (Rev. Mar. 11). U.S. Dep. Labor, Washington, D.C.

Passchier-Vermeer, W. (1974). Hearing loss due to continuous exposure to steady-state broadband noise. *J. Acoust. Soc. Am.* **56,** 1585–1593.

Passchier-Vermeer, W. (1977). "Hearing levels of non-noise exposed subjects and of subjects exposed to constant noise during working hours. Report B367." Research Institute for Environmental Hygiene, Delft, The Netherlands.

Patuzzi, R. B., and Thompson, M. L. (1991). Cochlear efferent neurones and protection against acoustic trauma: protection of outer hair cell receptor current and interanimal variability. *Hear. Res.* **54,** 45–58.

Perlman, H. B. (1945). Reaction of the human conduction mechanism to blast. *Laryngoscope* **55,** 427–443.

Price, G. G. (1976). Effects of interrupting recovery on loss of cochlear microphonic sensitivity. *J. Acoust. Soc. Am.* **59,** 709–712.

Price G. R., and Kalb, J. T. (1991). Insights into hazards form intense impulses from a mathematical model of the ear. *J. Acoust. Soc. Am.* **90,** 219–227.

Prosser, S., Tartari, M. C., and Arslan, E. (1988). Hearing loss in sports hunters exposed to occupational noise. *Brit. J. Audiology* **22,** 85–91.

Puel, J. L. and Pujol, R. (1993). Recent advances in cochlear neurobiology: cochlear efferents and acoustic trauma. *Noise Public Health Probl., Proc. Int. Congr. 6th* (M. Vallet, ed.), Vol. 3, pp. 136–151. l'INRETS, 94114 Arcuil Cedex, France.

Puel, J. L., Bobbin, R. P., and Fallon, M. (1988). An ipsilateral cochlear efferent loop protects the cochlea during intense sound exposure. *Hear. Res.* **37,** 65–70.

Rajan, R. and Irvine, D. R. F. (1993). Reorganization of auditory cortical maps consequent on unilateral cochlear damage in adult mammals. *Noise Public Health Probl., Proc. Int. Congr. 6th* (M. Vallet, eds.), Vol. 2, pp. 437–440. l'INRETS, 94114 Arcuil Cedex, France.

Rajan, R., and Johnstone, B. M. (1983). Crossed cochlear influences on monaural temporary threshold shifts. *Hear. Res.* **9,** 279–294.

Robinson, D. W. (1976). Characteristics of occupational noise-induced hearing loss. *In* "Effects of Noise on Hearing" (D. Henderson, R. P. Hamernik, D. S. Dosanjh, and J. H. Mills, eds.) pp. 383–406. Raven, New York.

Sataloff, J, Vassallo, L., and Menduke, H. (1969). Hearing loss from exposure to interrupted noise. *Arch. of Environ. Health* **18,** 972–981.

Saunders, J. C., Mills, J. H., and Miller, J. D. (1977). Threshold shift in the chinchilla from daily exposure to noise for six hours. *J. Acoust. Soc. Am.* **61,** 558–570.

Schmidek, M., Henderson, T., and Margolis, B. (1972). Evaluation of proposed limits for intermittent noise exposures with temporary threshold shift as a criterion. *J. Am. Ind. Hyg. Assoc.* **32,** 543–546.

Schori, T. R., and McGatha, E. A. (1978). A real-world assessment of noise exposure. *Sound Vib.,* **12,** (9), 24–30.

Shaw, E. A. G. (1966). Ear canal pressure generated by a free sound field. *J. Acoust. Soc. Am.* **39,** 465–470.

Shoji, H., Yamamoto, T., and Takagi, K. (1966). Studies on TTS due to exposure to octave-band noise. *J. Acoust. Soc. Jpn.* **22,** 340–349.

Smith, M. G., and Goldstone, G. (1961). "A Pilot Study of Temporary Threshold Shifts Resulting from Exposure to High-Intensity Impulse Noise," Rep. TM-19-61. Hum. Eng. Lab., U.S. Army Ordnance, Aberdeen Proving Ground, Maryland.

Spieth, W., and Trittipoe, W. J. (1958). Intensity and duration of noise exposure and temporary threshold shifts. *J. Acoust. Soc. Am.* **30,** 710–713.

Stephenson, M. R., Nixon, C. W., and Johnson, D. L. (1980). Identification of the minimum noise level capable of producing an asymptotic temporary threshold shift. *Aviat. Space Environ. Med.* Apr., 391–396.

Subramaniam, M., Campo, P., and Henderson, D. (1991a). The effect of exposure level on the development of progressive resistance to noise. *Hear. Res.* **52,** 181–188.

Subramaniam, M., Campo, P., and Henderson, D. (1991b). Development of resistance to hearing loss from high frequency noise. *Hear. Res.* **56,** 65–66.

Subramaniam, M., Henderson, D., Campo, P., and Spongr, V. (1992). The effect of "conditioning" on hearing loss from a high frequency traumatic exposure, *Hear. Res.* **58,** 57–62.

Subramaniam, M., Henderson, D., and Spongr, V. (1993). Effect of low-frequency conditioning on hearing loss from high frequency exposure. *J. Acoust. Soc. Am.* **93,** 952–956.

Taylor, W., Lempert, B., Pelmear, P., Hemstock, I., and Kershaw, J. (1984). Noise levels and hearing thresholds in drop forging industry. *J. Acoust. Soc. Am.* **76,** 807–819.

Tonnesdorf, J. (1976). Relationship between the transmission characteristics of the conductive system and noise-induced hearing loss. *In* "Effects of Noise on Hearing" (D. Henderson, R. P. Hamernik, D. S. Dosanjh, and J. H. Mills, eds.), pp. 159–177. Raven Press, New York.

Tonndorf, J., and Khanna, S. M. (1967). Some properties of sound transmission in the middle ear and outer ears of cats. *J. Acoust. Soc. Am.* **41,** 513–521.

Ward, W. D. (1960). Recovery from high values of temporary threshold shift. *J. Acoust. Soc. Am.* **32,** 497–500.

Ward, W. D. (1961). Noninteraction of temporary threshold shifts. *J. Acoust. Soc. Am.* **33,** 512–513.

Ward, W. D. (1962). Effect of temporal spacing on temporary threshold shift from impulses. *J. Acoust. Soc. Am.* **34,** Part 1, 1230–1232.

Ward, W. D. (1966). Temporary threshold shift in males and females. *J. Acoust. Soc. Am.* **40,** 478–485.

Ward, W. D. (1963). Adaption and fatigue. *In* "Modern Developments in Audiology" (J. Jerger, ed.), pp. 241–286. Academic Press, New York.

Ward, W. D. (1970). Temporary threshold shift and damage-risk criteria for intermittent noise exposures. *J. Acoust. Soc. Am.* **48,** Part 2, 56–574.

Ward, W. D. (1976). A comparison of the effects of continuous, intermittent, and impulse noise. *In* "Effects of Noise on Hearing" (D. Henderson, R. P. Hamernik, D. S. Dosanjh, and J. H. Mills, eds.), pp. 407–420. Raven, New York.

Ward, W. D. (1991). The role of intermittence in PTS. *J. Acoust. Soc. Am.* **90,** 164–169.

Ward, W. D., Glorig, A., and Sklar, D. L. (1958). Dependence of temporary threshold shift at 4 kc on intensity and time. *J. Acoust. Soc. Am.* **30,** 944–954.

Ward, W. D., Glorig, A., and Sklar, D. L. (1959). Temporary threshold shift octave-band noise: Applications to damage-risk criteria. *J. Acoust. Soc. Am.* **31,** 522–528.

Ward, W. D., Selters, W., and Glorig, A. (1961). Exploratory studies on temporary threshold shift from impulses. *J. Acoust. Soc. Am.* **33,** 781–793.

Ward, W. D., Cushing, E. M., and Burns, E. M. (1976). Effective quiet and moderate TTS: Implications for noise exposure standards. *J. Acoust. Soc. Am.* **59,** 160–165.

Wenthold, R. J., Kim, H. N., and Dechesne, C. J. (1990). Putative biochemical processes in NIHL. *Int. Conf. Eff. Noise Aud. Syst. 4th, Beaune, Fr.*

Selected Bibliographies

1. Cochlear damage from exposure to noise

Bohne, B. A., and Rabbitt, K. D. (1983). Holes in the reticular lamina after noise exposure: implication for continuing damage in the organ of Corti. *Hear. Res.* **11,** 41–53.

Borg, E., Nilsson, R., and Engstrom, B. (1983). Effect of the acoustic reflex on inner ear damage induced by industrial noise. *Acta Otolaryngol.* **96,** 361–369.

Cahani, M., Paul, G., and Shahar, A. (1983). Tinnitus pitch and acoustic trauma. *Audiology* **22,** 357–363.

Cody, A. R., and Robertson, D. (1983). Variability of noise-induced damage in the guinea pig cochlea:electrophysiological and morphological correlates after strictly controlled exposures. *Hear. Res.* **11,** 55–70.

Cody, A. R., and Russell, I. J. (1985). Outer hair cells in the mammalian cochlea and noise-induced hearing loss. *Nature* (*London*) **15,** 662–665.

Cody, A. R., and Russell, I. J. (1988). Acoustically induced hearing loss:intracellular studies in the guinea pig cochlea. *Hear. Res.* **35,** 59–70.

Cotanche, D. A., and Dopyera, C. E. (1990). Hair cell and supporting cell response to acoustic trauma in the chick cochlea. *Hear. Res.* **46,** 29–40.

Cotanche, D. A., Saunders, J. C., and Tilney, L. G. (1987). Hair cell damage produced by acoustic trauma in the chick cochlea. *Hear. Res.* **25,** 267–286.

Dayal, V. S., and Bhattacharyya, T. K. (1986). Cochlear hair cell damage from intermittent noise exposure in young and adult guinea pigs. *Am. J. Otolaryngol.* **7,** 294–297.

Dengerink, H., Miller, J., Axelsson, A., Vertes, D., and Van Dalfsen, P. (1985). The recovery of vascular changes following brief noise exposure. *Acta Otolaryngol.* **100,** 19–25.

Eden, D. (1993). Australian mining industry experience in hearing conservation. *Noise Public Health Prob. Proc. Int. Congr. 6th* (M. Vallet ed.), Vol. **2,** pp. 47–50. l'INRETS, 94114 Arcuil Cedex, France.

Engstrom, B. (1984). Fusion of stereocilia on inner hair cells in man and in the rabbit, rat and guinea pig. *Scand. Audiol.* **13,** 87–92.

Engstrom, B., and Borg, E. (1983). Cochlear morphology in relation to loss of behavioural, electrophysiological, and middle ear reflex thresholds after exposure to noise. *Acta Otolaryngol., Suppl. No.* 402, 5–23.

Engstrom, B., Flock, A., and Borg, E. (1983). Ultrastructural studies of stereocilia in noise-exposed rabbits. *Hear. Res.* **12,** 251–264.

Fredelius, L. (1988). Time sequence of degeneration pattern of the organ of Corti after acoustic overstimulation. A transmission electron microscopy study. *Acta Otolaryngol.* **106,** 373–385.

Fredelius, L., Johansson, B., Bagger-Sjoback, D., and Wersall, J. (1987). Qualitative and quantitative changes in the guinea pig organ of Corti after pure tone acoustic overstimulation. *Hear. Res.* **30,** 157–167.

Fredelius, L., Johansson, B., Bagger-Sjoback, D., and Wersall, J. (1990). Time-related changes in the guinea pig cochlea after acoustic overstimulation. *Ann. Otol. Rhinol. Laryngol.* **99,** Part 1, 369–378.

Goulios, H., and Robertson, D. (1983). Noise-induced cochlear damage assessed using electrophysiological and morphological criteria: an examination of the equal energy principle. *Hear Res.* **11,** 327–341.

Gratton, M. A., and Wright, C. G. (1992). Hyperpigmentation of chinchilla stria vascularis following acoustic trauma. *Pigment Cell Res.* **5,** 30–37.

Grenner, J., Nilsson, P., Sheppard, H., and Katbamna, B. (1988). Action potential threshold elevation in the guinea-pig as a function of impact noise exposure energy. *Audiology* **27,** 356–366.

Hamernik, R. P., Turrentine, G., Roberto, M., Salvi, R., and Henderson, D. (1984). Anatomical correlates of impulse noise-induced mechanical damage in the cochlea. *Hear. Res.* **13,** 229–247.

Hamernik, R. P., Turrentine, G., and Wright, C. G. (1984). Surface morphology of the inner sulcus and related epithelial cells of the cochlea following acoustic trauma. *Hear. Res.* **16,** 143–160.

Hamernik, R. P., Patterson, J. H., and Salvi, R. J. (1987). The effect of impulse intensity and the number of impulses on hearing and cochlear pathology in the chinchilla. *J. Acoust. Soc. Am.* **8,** 1118–1129,

Hamernik, R. P., Ahroon, W. A., and Patterson, J. A., Jr. (1988). Threshold recovery functions following impulse noise trauma. *J. Acoust. Soc. Am.* **8,** 941–950.

Hamernik, R. P., Patterson, J. H., Turrentine, G. A., and Ahroon, W. A. (1989). The quantitative relation between sensory cell loss and hearing thresholds. *Hear. Res.* **38,** 199–211.

Henderson, D., and Hamernik, R. P. (1986). Impulse noise: critical review. *J. Acoust. Soc. Am.* **80,** 569–584.

Henderson, D., Subramaniam, M., Gratton, M. A., and Saunders, S. S. (1991). Impact noise: the importance of level, duration, and repetition rate. *J. Acoust. Soc. Am.* **89,** 1350–1357.

Henry, K. R. (1993). Lifelong susceptibility to acoustic trauma: changing patterns of cochlear damage over the life span of the mouse. *Audiology* **22,** 372–383.

Hillerdal, M., Jansson, B., Engstrom, B., Hultcrantz, E., and Borg, E. (1987). Cochlear blood flow in noise-damaged ears. *Acta Otolaryngol.* **10,** 270–278.

Kaltenbach, J. A., Schmidt, R. N., and Kaplan, C. R. (1992). Tone-induced stereocilia lesions as a function of exposure level and duration in the hamster cochlea. *Hear. Res.* **60,** 205–215.

Liberman, M. C. (1987). Chronic ultrastructural changes in acoustic trauma. *Hear. Res.* **26,** 65–88.

Liberman, M. C., and Dodds, L. W. (1984). Single-neuron labeling and chronic cochlear pathology. III. Stereocilia damage and alterations of threshold tuning curves. *Hear. Res.* **16,** 55–74.

Liberman, M. C., and Dodds, L. W. (1987). Acute ultrastructural changes in acoustic trauma: serial-section reconstruction of stereocilia and cuticular plates. *Hear. Res.* **26,** 45–64.

Lim, D. J. (1986). Effects of noise and ototoxic drugs at the cellular level in the cochlea; a review. *Am. J. Otolaryngol.* **7,** 73–99.

Lonsbury-Martin, B. L., Martin, G. K., and Bohne, B. A. (1987). Repeated TTS exposures in monkeys: alterations in hearing, cochlear structure, and single-unit thresholds. *J. Acoust. Soc. Am.* **81,** 1507–1518.

Mattox, D. E. (1991). Central nervous system changes associated with noise-induced hearing loss: an electron microscopic and freeze-fracture study of the chick nucleus magnocellularis. *Laryngoscope* **10,** 1063–1075.

McFadden, E. A., and Saunders, J. C. (1989). Recovery of auditory function following intense sound exposure in the neonatal chick. *Hear. Res.* **41,** 205–215.

Mulroy, M. J., and Whaley, E. A. (1984). Structural changes in auditory hairs during temporary deafness. *Scanning Electron Microsc.* Part **2,** 831–840.

Nakai, Y., and Masutani, H. (1988). Noise-induced vasoconstriction in the cochlea. *Acta Otolaryngol., Suppl. No.* **447,** 23–27.

Nilsson, P., Rydmarker, S., and Grenner, J. (1987). Impulse noise and continuous noise of equivalent frequency spectrum and total sound energy. *Acta Otolaryngol. Suppl. No.* **441,** 45–58.

Okamoto, A., Hasegawa, M., Tamura, T., Homma, T., and Komatsuzaki, A. (1992). Effects of frequency and intensity of sound on cochlear blood flow. *Acta Otolaryngol.* **112,** 59–64.

Pickles, J. O., Osborne, M. P., and Comis, S. D. (1987). Vulnerability of tip links between stereocilia to acoustic trauma in the guinea pig. *Hear. Res.* **12,** 173–183.

Prince, M. M., Matanoski, G. M., Breyesse, L., Fechter, L. D., and Pena, B. (1993). The joint effects of occupational noise and smoking on changes in hearing acuity, *Noise Public Health Probl., Proc. Int. Congr. 6th,* (M. Vallet, ed.), Vol. 2, pp. 291–296. l'INRETS, 94114 Arcuil Cedex, France.

Puel, J. L., Bobbin, R. P., and Fallon, M. (1989). The active process is affected first by intense sound exposure. *Hear Res.* **37,** 53–63.

Raphael, Y., and Altschuler, R. A. (1991). Reorganization of cytoskeletal and junctional proteins during cochlear hair cell degeneration. *Cell Motil. Cytoskeleton* **18,** 215–217.

Ribeiro, V., Riberio, J., and Cohen, A. (1993). Occupational hearing loss among workers of the steel industry: a computerized survey. *Noise Public Health Probl. Proc. Int. Congr. 6th* (M. Vallet, ed.), Vol. 2, 115–118. l'INRETS, 94114 Arcuil Cedex, France.

Roberto, M., Hamernik, R. P., Salvi, R. J., Henderson, D., and Milone, R. (1985). Impact noise and the equal energy hypothesis. *J. Acoust. Soc. Am.* **77,** 1514–1520.

Roberto, M., Hamernik, R. P., and Turrentine, G. A. (1989). Damage of the auditory system associated with acute blast trauma. (Review, 16 references). *Ann. Otol. Rhinol. Laryngol. Suppl.* 140:23–34.

Robertson, D. (1983). Functional significance of dendritic swelling after loud sounds in the guinea pig cochlea. *Hear. Res.* **12,** 263–278.

Rydmarker, S., and Nilsson, P. (1987). Effects on the inner and outer hair cells. *Acta Otolaryngol. Suppl. No.* **441,** 25–43.

Rydmarker, S., Nilsson, P., and Grenner, J. (1987). Impulse noise of different durations. *Acta Otolaryngol. Suppl. No.* **441,** 3–23.

Saunders, J. C., Dear, S. P., and Schneider, M. E. (1985). The anatomical consequences of acoustic injury: A review and tutorial. *J. Acoust. Soc. Am.* **78,** 833–860.

Saunders, J. C., Cohen, Y. E., and Szymko, Y. M. (1991). The structural and functional consequences of acoustic injury in the cochlea and peripheral auditory system: A five year update. *J. Acoust. Soc. Am.* **90,** 136–146.

Schacht, J. (1986). Molecular mechanisms of drug-induced hearing loss. (Review.) *Hear Res.* **22,** 297–304.

Sliwinska-Kowalska, M., Sulkpwski, W. J., Jedlinska, U., and Rydzynski, K. (1993). Relationship between functional and morphological changes in the cochlea of guinea pigs after exposure to industrial noise. *Noise Public Health Probl., Proc. Int. Congr. 6th,* (M. Vallet, ed.), Vol. 2, pp. 127–130. l'INRETS, 94114 Arcuil Cedex, France.

Stopp, P. E. (1983). Effects on guinea pig cochlea from exposure to moderately intense broadband noise. *Hear. Res.* **11,** 55–72.

Thorne, P. R., Duncan, C. E., and Gavin, J. B. (1986): The pathogenesis of stereocilia abnormalities in acoustic trauma. *Hear. Res.* **21,** 41–49.

Ulehlova, L. (1983). Stria vascularis in acoustic trauma. *Arch. Oto-Rhino-Laryngol.* **237,** 133–138.

Wit, H. P., and Nijdam, H. F. (1984). Relationship of gross cochlear potentials to hair cell pathology in the waltzing guinea pig. *Hear. Res.* **15,** 159–171.

Zhao, Y., Liu, H., Du, D., Zhao, C., and Lu, Y. (1993). Adverse effects of smoking for noise induced hearing loss among workers in Beijing. *Noise Public Health Probl., Proc. Int. Congr. 6th* (M. Vallet, ed.), Vol. 2, pp. 317–320. l'INRETS, 94114 Arcuil Cedex, France.

2. Cochlear regeneration following damage from exposure to noise

Bohne, B. A. (1992). Neural regeneration in the noise-damaged chinchilla cochlea. *Laryngoscope* **102,** 693–699.

Corwin, J. T., and Cotanche, D. A. (1988). Regeneration of sensory hair cells after acoustic trauma. *Science* **240,** 1772–1774.

Cotanche, D. A. (1987). Regeneration of the tectorial membrane in the chick cochlea following severe acoustic trauma. *Hear. Res.* **30,** 197–206.

Cotanche, D. A. (1992). Video-enhanced DIC images of the noise-damaged and regenerated. *Exp. Neurol.* **115,** 23–26.

Marsh, R. R., Xu, L. R., Moy, J. P., and Saunders, J. C. (1990). Recovery of the basilar papilla following intense sound exposure in the chick. *Hear. Res.* **46,** 229–237.

Ryals, B. M., and Rubel, E. W. (1988). Hair cell regeneration after acoustic trauma in adult Coturnix quail. *Science* **240,** 1774–1776.

Saunders, J. C., Adler, H. J., and Pugliano, F. A. (1992). The structural and functional aspects of hair cell regeneration in the chick as a result of exposure to intense sound. *Exp. Neurol.* **115,** 13–17.

3. Otoacoustic emissions

Avan, P., Bonfils, P., Loth, D., Narcy, P., and Trotoux, J. (1991). Quantitative assessment of human cochlear function by evoked otoacoustic emissions. *Hear. Res.* **52,** 99–112.

Bonfils, D., and Uziel, A. (1989). Clinical applications of evoked otoacoustic emissions: Results in normal hearing and hearing-impaired subjects. *Ann. Otol. Rhinol. Laryngol.* **98,** 326–331.

Bonfils, D., Piron, J. P., Uziel, A., and Pujol, R. (1988). A correlative study of otoacoustic emission properties and audiometric thresholds. *Arch. Oto-Rhino-Laryngol.* **245,** 53–56.

Bonfils, D., Piron, J. P., Uziel, A., and Pujol, R. (1988). Screening for auditory dysfunction in infants by evoked otoacoustic emissions. *Arch. Otolaryngol—Head Neck Surg.* **114,** 887–890.

Bonfils, D., Dumont, A., Marie, P., Francois, M., and Narcy, P. (1990). Evoked otoacoustic emissions in newborn hearing screening. *Laryngoscope* **100,** 186–189.

Bray, P., and Kemp, D. (1987). An advanced cochlear echo technique suitable for infant screening. *Br. J. Audiol.* **21,** 191–204.

Collet, L., Gartner, M. G., Marlin, A., Kauffmann, I., Disant, F., and Margon, A. (1989). Evoked otoacoustic emissions and sensorineural hearing loss. *Arch. Otolaryngol.—Head Neck Surg.* **115,** 1060–1062.

Collet, L., Veuillet, E., Chanal, J. M., and Morgon, A. (1991). Evoked otoacoustic emissions: Correlates between spectrum analysis and audiogram. *Audiology* **30,** 164–172.

Harris, F. P., Probst, R., and Wenger, R. (1991). Repeatability of transiently evoked otoacoustic emissions in normal hearing humans. *Audiology* **30,** 135–141.

Kemp, D. T. (1978). Stimulated acoustic emissions from the human auditory system. *J. Acoust. Soc. Am.* **64,** 1386–1391.

Kemp, D. T. (1982). Cochlear echos: Implications for noise-induced hearing loss. *In* "New Perspectives on Noise-Induced Hearing Loss" (R. P. Hamernik, D. Henderson, and R. Salvi, eds.), pp. 189–208. Raven, New York.

Kemp, D. T., Bray, P., Alexander, L., and Brown, A. M. (1986). Acoustic emission cochleography—practical aspects. *Scand. Audiol.* **25,** 71–95.

Kemp, D. T., Ryan, S., and Bray, P. (1990). A guide to the effective use of otoacoustic emissions. *Ear Hear.* **11,** 93–105.

Prieve, B. A., Gorga, M. P., Schmidt, A., Neely, S., Peters, J., Schultes, L., and Jesteadt, W. (1993). Analysis of transient-evoked otoacoustic emissions in normal-hearing and hearing-impaired ears. *J. Acoust. Soc. Am.* **93,** 3308–3319.

Probst, R., Lonsbury-Martin, B., and Coats, A. (1987). Otoacoustic emissions in ears with hearing loss. *Am. J. Otolaryngol.* **8,** 73–81.

Robinette, M. S. (1992). Clinical observations with transient evoked otoacoustic emissions with adults. *Semin. Hear.* **13,** 23–36.

Smurzynski, J., and Kim, D. O. (1992). Distortion-product and click-evoked otoacoustic emissions of normally-hearing adults. *Hear. Res.* **58,** 227–240.

Stevens, J. C. (1988). Click-evoked otoacoustic emissions in normally hearing and hearing-impaired adults. *Br. J. Audiol.* **22,** 45–49.

Vedantam, R., and Musiek, F. E. (1991). Click-evoked otoacoustic emissions in adult subjects: Standard indices and test-retest reliability. *Am. J. Otolaryngol.* **12,** 435–442.

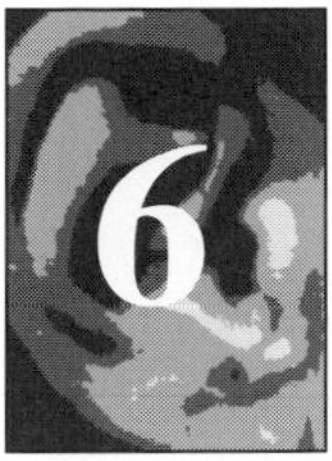

Speech Intelligibility in Quiet and in Noise

INTRODUCTION

Communication by auditory signals, such as speech, is often made difficult because (1) a normally audible signal may be masked by a concurrently present noise; or (2) a loss in hearing sensitivity can have the effect of making parts, or all, of the signal inaudible. In masking, the speech signal cannot stimulate a sensorineural receptor it would normally excite because that receptor is responding to a more intense noise signal. With a sensorineural, or conductive, threshold shift, speech signals, normally sufficiently intense to stimulate sensorineural receptors, may now be insufficient to exceed an elevated threshold.

Inabilities to hear and understand speech can create significant social, economic, and public health problems, as will be discussed in later chapters. This chapter is concerned with (1) the physical characteristics of the speech signal; (2) the relations between speech intelligibility, masking by noise, and hearing loss; (3) ameliorating the effects of noise in speech communication systems; and (4) estimating speech intelligibility from physical measures of the speech signals, background noise, and the hearing levels of listeners.

PHYSICAL CHARACTERISTICS OF THE SPEECH SIGNAL

Figure 6.1 shows that the distribution of the rms (root-mean square) spectrum level (per-cycle level) of speech in 1/8-s intervals encompasses a range of ~20–40 dB, depending on frequency. These data are for speech being uttered at a constant level of vocal effort in an anechoic, nonreverberant, chamber. This variability is a feature of the speech signal that allows portions of it to be momentarily audible in the presence of a noise, or by a person with a hearing loss, even when all parts are not audible.

Variations in Speech Levels as Function of Vocal Effort

Figure 6.2 shows the 1/3-octave-band, 1-s average sound-pressure level (SPL) of speech measured 1 meter (m) from male and female talkers when using various vocal efforts. The average level 1 m from the talker varies from L_A ~50, for causal effort, to L_A 88 for shouting. Data such as shown in Figs. 6.2 and 6.3 are usually collected in terms of so-called *long-time* (or *long-term*) energy of continuous, constant-level-of-effort speech, integrated over at least 10 s and averaged to 1 s, giving L_{Aeq}, if *A*-weighted, or L_{eq}, L_{Ceq}, when unweighted.

The speech material used in the measurements in the anechoic chamber tests in the Pearsons *et al.* (1977) study was: "Joe took father's shoe bench out" and "she was waiting at my lawn"—sentences developed for this purpose at the Bell Telephone Laboratories. These sentences contain most typical vowel–consonant combinations. For the field tests of speech discourse, it is common practice to report the average of the peak L_A levels of

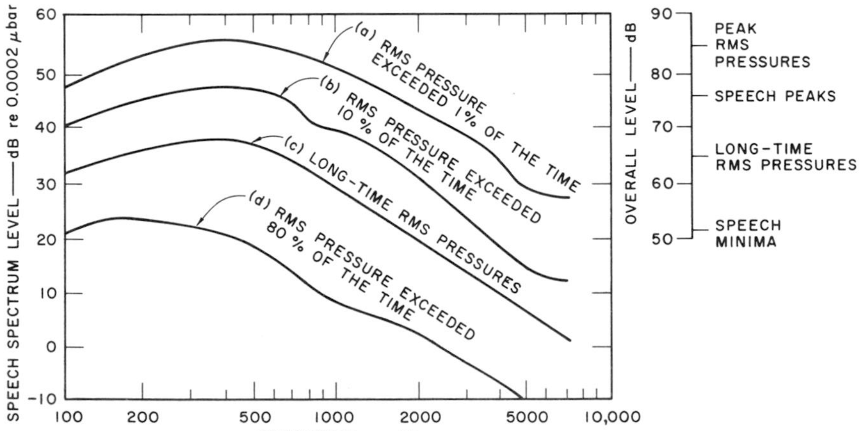

FIGURE 6.1 Percentile distributions of spectrum level of male speech measured in 1/8-sec intervals over a 2-min period. (From Dunn and White, 1940. Copyright 1940 by the American Psychological Association. Adapted by permission of the author.)

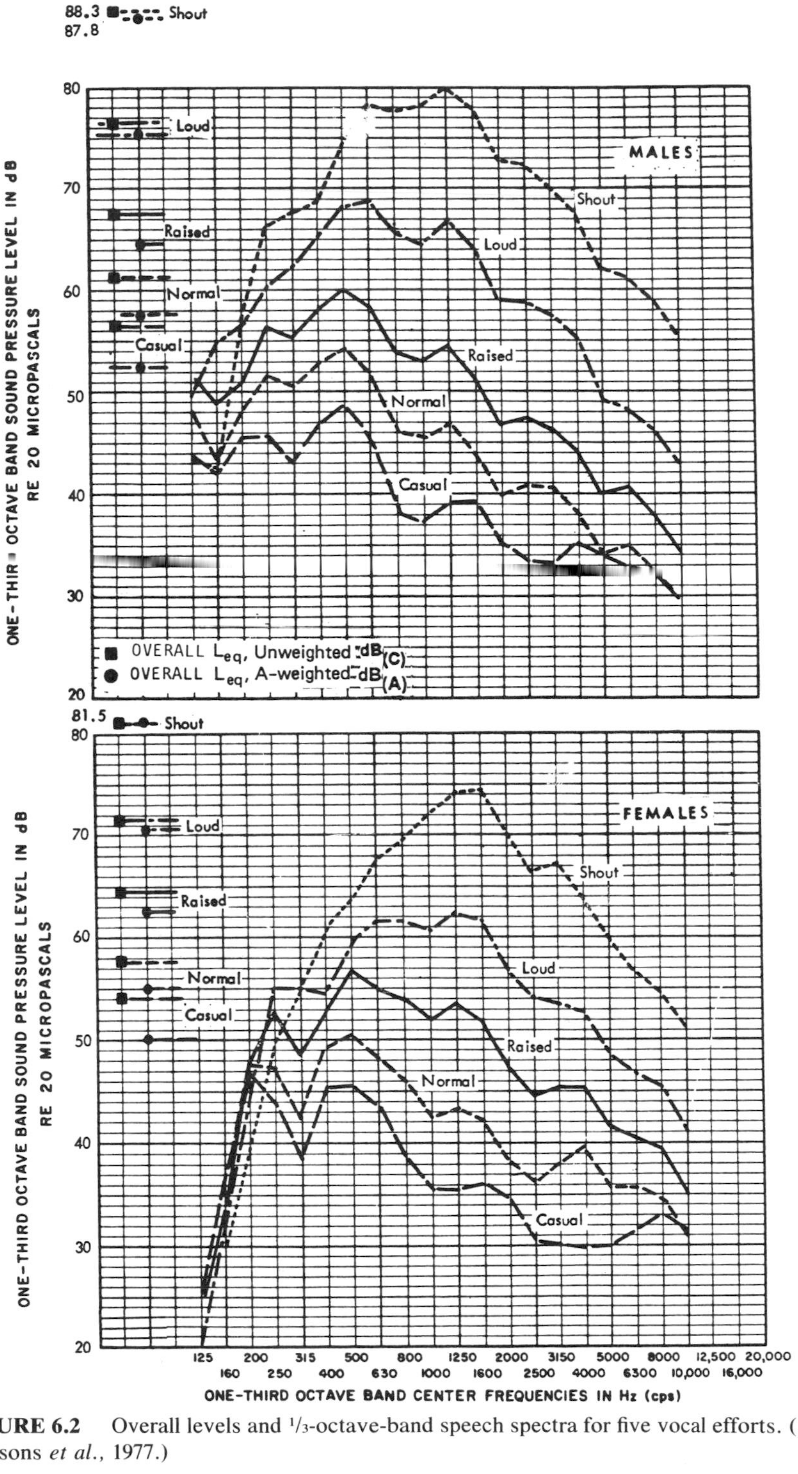

FIGURE 6.2 Overall levels and 1/3-octave-band speech spectra for five vocal efforts. (From Pearsons *et al.*, 1977.)

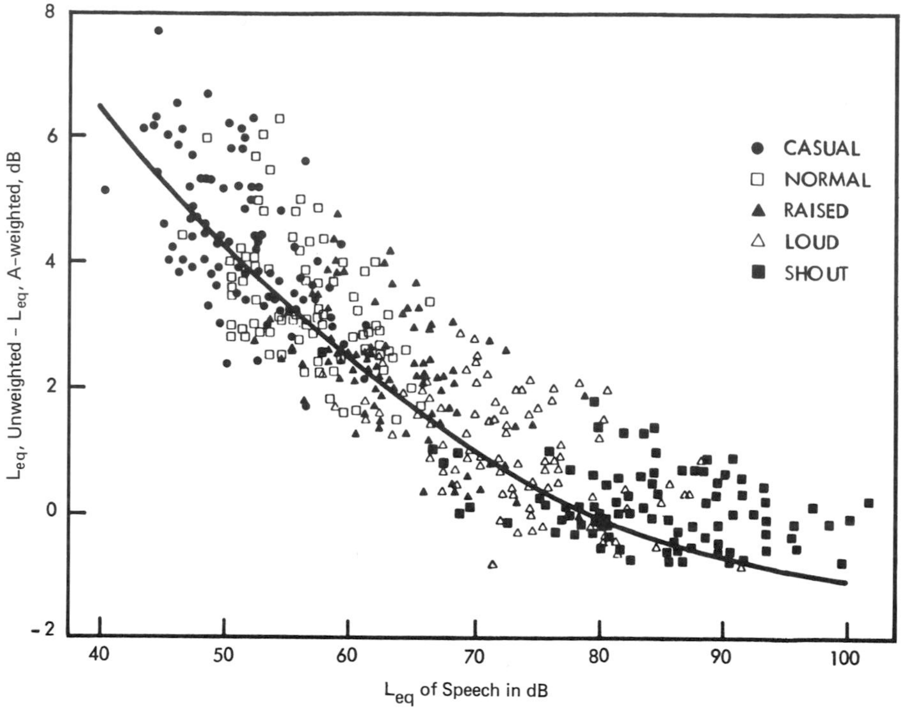

FIGURE 6.3 Differences between unweighted and *A*-weighted L_{eq} (1 s, average) of speech at five vocal efforts. (From Pearsons *et al.*, 1977.)

each word uttered during a conversation. The measurements are usually made with a sound-level meter set on "fast" and the results labeled as "speech level" L_A, or dB_A. To a first approximation, this average L_A level equals, when vocal effort is the same, the L_{Aeq} found by more frequent sampling of the sound pressures of the connected speech discourse, and finding a "true" energy average.

It is seen in Fig. 6.3 that the arithmetic average of the peak *A*-weighted levels, L_{Aeq}, reached by each word are somewhat less than the unweighted, L_{eq}, except when the vocal effort reaches "shout." The reason for this difference is change to the upward shift in the speech spectrum as the level of vocal effort is increased, as seen in Fig. 6.2.

Male and Female Speech Levels

Table 6.1 shows the means and standard deviations of the distribution of speech levels at various vocal efforts by males and females over 13 years and children under 13 years of age when speaking in the quiet. The speech level of males is 2–3 dB greater than that of females at casual to raised levels of effort, and 5–7 dB greater at higher levels of effort.

TABLE 6.1 Mean Speech Levels at Various Vocal Efforts Measured in an Anechoic Chamber

	Speech level, dB*						
	Males		Females		Children		Average
Vocal effort	L_{eq}	σ	L_{eq}	σ	L_{eq}	σ	L'_{eq}
Casual	52.0	4.0	50.0	4.0	53.0	5.0	52.0
Normal	58.0	4.0	55.0	4.0	58.0	5.0	57.0
Raised	65.0	5.0	63.0	4.0	65.0	7.0	64.0
Loud	76.0	6.0	71.0	6.0	74.0	9.0	73.0
Shout	89.0	7.0	82.0	7.0	82.0	9.0	85.0

* Results were rounded to the nearest decibel. Background level L_{eq} = 16 dB.

From Pearsons *et al.* (1977).

Noise and Vocal Effort

Most measures of variations in the intensity of speech have been taken under quiet, laboratory conditions, as were those shown Figs. 6.1 and 6.2 and Table 6.1. In such studies, the talkers were instructed to use different vocal efforts. However, noise in the talker's environment will cause the talker involuntarily to increase somewhat his vocal effort (Korn, 1954, Webster and Klumpp, 1962; Kryter, 1946; Pickett, 1958; Gardner, 1964).

The investigations of Pearsons *et al.* (1977) on this matter are particularly important because some of their measured speech levels were obtained in a variety of real-life circumstances and background noise conditions. Some of their findings are shown in Fig. 6.4 (homes and schools) and Fig. 6.5 (television and various other environments). Figure 6.6 summarizes these data and also shows calculated and estimated regression lines to the data when segmented into three sections.

Figure 6.6 shows that the background noise levels began at about 30 dB_A and increased up to about 80 dB_A. (Pearsons *et al.* reported background noise only in unweight L_{eq}. As shown in Chapters 4 and 5, the L_A level of an environmental noises is typically 5 dB lower than its L_C level.) It appears from Fig. 6.6 that for typical speech communication purposes, a person will utter speech at an average level, 1 m away, of about 50 dB_A, and raise his or her voice about 0.5 dB for each 1-dB increment as background noise increases from about 30 to 65 dB_A, to a speech level, 1 m away, of ~67 dB_A. It is noted that Pearsons *et al.* found that the speech levels measured at the position of listeners was consistent one meter between a talker and listener being typical in real life, except in some transportation vehicles, where the distances were apparently considerably less. Table 6.2 is a statistical summary of the data contained in Figs. 6.5 and 6.6.

It is important to note in Table 6.2 that in trains and aircraft, the speech levels at the listeners' ears were about equal to the background noise level, but in the other situations except the classroom, the speech levels were

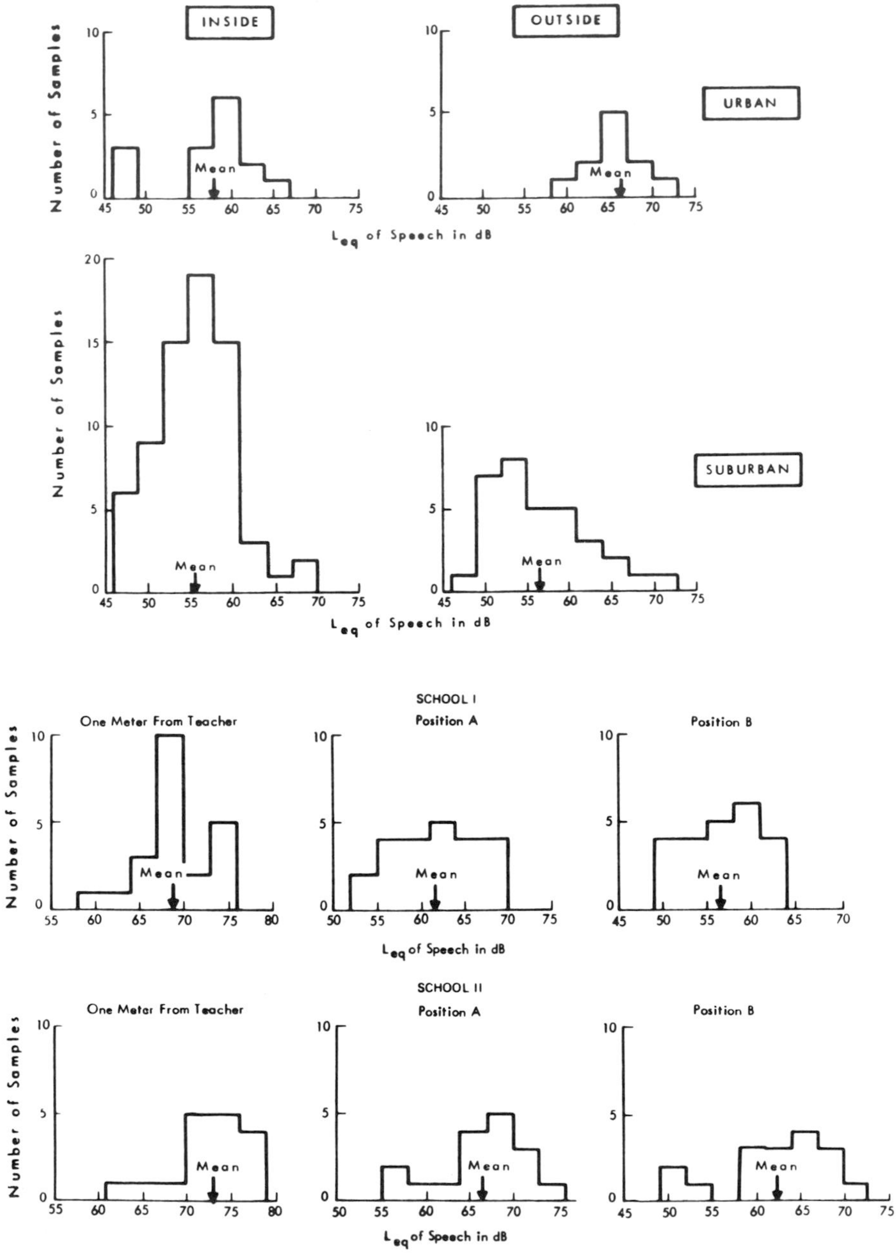

FIGURE 6.4 Distributions of speech levels in homes and schools. *Note:* Levels in $L_{eq,A}$ would be somewhat lower; see Fig. 6.3. (From Pearsons *et al.*, 1977.)

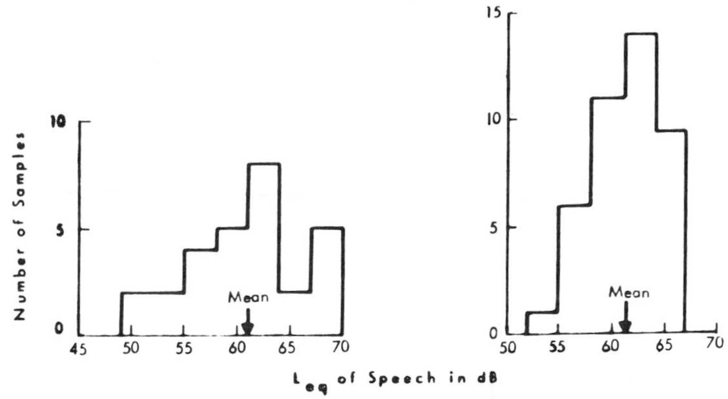

(a) Television speech levels. Measured about 3 m from TV.

(b) Department stores. Measured about 1 m from talker.

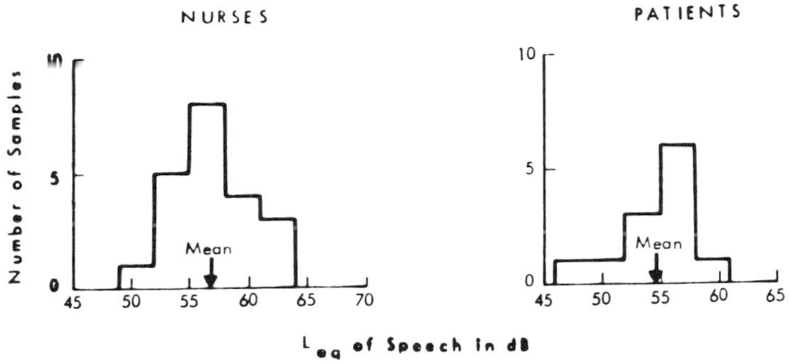

(c) Hospitals. Measured about 1 m from talker.

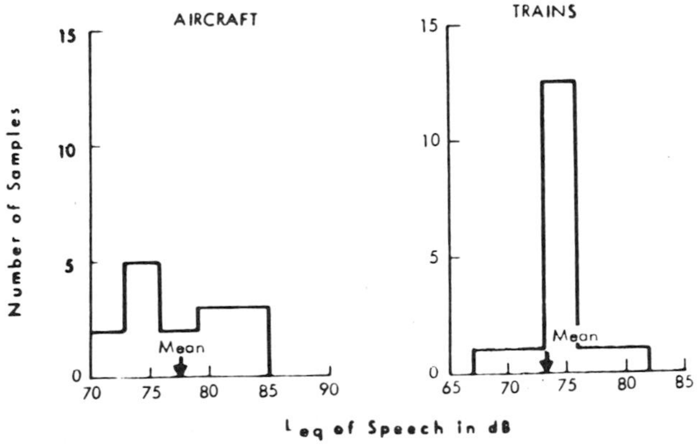

(d) Transportation vehicles. Measured about 0.4 m from talker.

FIGURE 6.5 Speech level in various environments: (A) television speech levels (measured ~3 m from TV set); (B) department stores (measured ~1 m from talker); (C) hospitals (measured ~1 m from talker); (D) transportation vehicles (measured ~0.4 m from talker). *Note:* Levels in $L_{eq,A}$ would be somewhat lower; see Fig. 6.3. (From Pearsons *et al.*, 1977.)

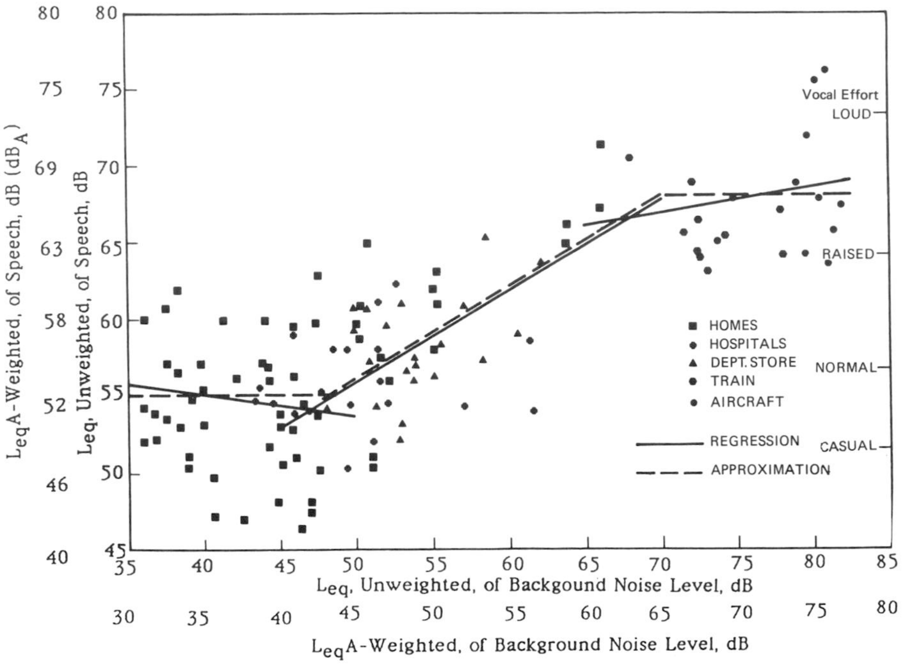

FIGURE 6.6 Conversing speech levels as a function of background noise. The speech levels were measured close to the talker and normalized to 1-m distances. This allowed for the estimation of negative speech-to-noise ratios at 1-m-from-the-talker-positions because the noise level was generally uniform over a large area, but the speech level would be more intense closer than 1 m from the talker. (From Pearsons *et al.*, 1977.)

maintained somewhat above the background noise. In the classrooms the teachers spoke at a level of effort comparable to that used in aircraft, even though the background noise was low. This probably occurred because the classrooms involved were large (about 20 × 35 ft), and a higher-than-normal level of effort was required to have the speech reach all the students at a level sufficient to be properly heard. However, because of reverberation, room acoustics tend to keep the speech level from declining at distances farther than about 12 ft from the talker. The approximate effect is shown in Fig. 6.7.

In summary, there is (1) a ~30-dB range, average over frequencies, in 1/8th-s effective rms levels of constant-effort speech sounds (~42 dB if one considers 'instantaneous' peaks); (2) a ~35 dB range in the long term, but different constant-vocal efforts and levels (see Figs. 6.2 and 6.3 and Table 6.1); and (3) a 15–25-dB range in typical levels used in different real-life listening conditions (see Figs. 6.4, 6.5, and 6.6). These dynamic level variations are features of the speech signals of everyday communications that make it both resistant, and vulnerable, to the effects of noise interference and losses in hearing sensitivity.

TABLE 6.2 Average Speech Levels in Various Environments

Environment	Background level, dB		Distance from talker, m	Speech level, dB*	
	L_{eq}	σ		L_{eq}	σ
Schools					
I	48.0†	2.0	1	69.0	4.0
			2	62.0	5.0
			7	57.0	4.0
II	51.0†	3.0	1	73.0	4.0
			2	66.0	5.0
			7	62.0	6.0
Homes					
Outside, urban	61.0	5.0	≈1	66.0	4.0
	61.0	5.0	Corrected to 1	65.0	4.0
Outside, suburban	48.0	4.0	≈1	56.0	5.0
	48.0	4.0	Corrected to 1	55.0	5.0
Inside, urban	48.0	2.0	~1	57.0	6.0
	48.0	2.0	Corrected to 1	57.0	6.0
Inside, suburban	41.0	3.0	≈1	55.0	5.0
	41.0	3.0	Corrected to 1	55.0	5.0
Hospitals					
Nurses	52.0	5.0	≈1	57.0	4.0
	52.0	5.0	Corrected to 1	56.0	3.0
Patients	45.0	2.0	≈1	55.0	1.0
	45.0	2.0	Corrected to 1	56.0	2.0
Department stores	54.0	4.0	≈1	61.0	3.0
	54.0	4.0	Corrected to 1	58.0	3.0
Transportation vehicles					
Trains	74.0	3.0	≈0.4	73.0	3.0
	74.0	3.0	Corrected to 1	66.0	2.0
Aircraft	79.0	3.0	≈0.3	77.0	4.0
	79.0	3.0	Corrected to 1	68.0	4.0

* Results were rounded to the nearest decibel.

† Measurements were made with typical student activity. Background values of classrooms during the phonetically balanced word test and other "quiet periods" were 47 dB for school I and 43 dB for school II.

From Pearsons *et al.* (1977).

Effect of Noise on Duration of Conversations

It is common for people to increase their vocal efforts when speaking in the presence of the masking noise. A practical question is that of determining how long people can converse in noise without feeling vocal strain. Rupf (1977) studied this question in a simulated small aircraft situation (two persons seated side by side) with aircraft noise present at different levels of intensity during different tests.

The subjects were instructed to engage in conversation during a series of 5-min segments of noise. Among other things, they were asked to assume

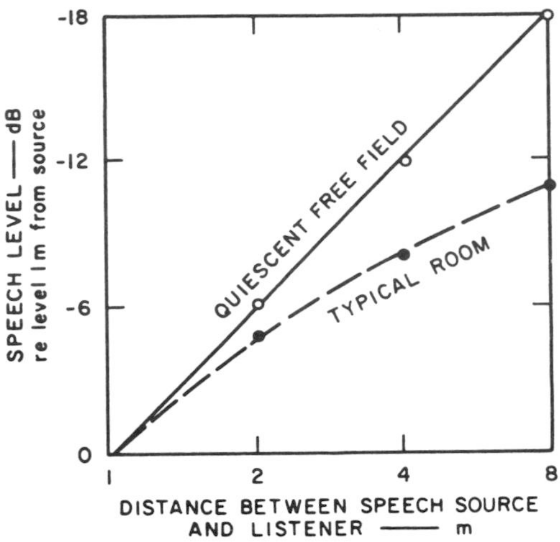

FIGURE 6.7 Approximate effect of acoustic environment and distance, in meters, between speech source and listener on received speech level. (Data points from Beranek, 1954).

that the noises would be present during a trip (with continuous discourse not explicitly stated) and to estimate how long the airplane trip could last without undue strain on their voices. The results are shown in Fig. 6.8.

Fifty percent of the subjects estimated that if the trip lasted more than 1 hr, and the noise level were ~75 dB_A, they would feel undue vocal strain. However, other data collected from the subjects showed that with actual conversation, only 50% of the subjects considered a noise level of 75 dB_A

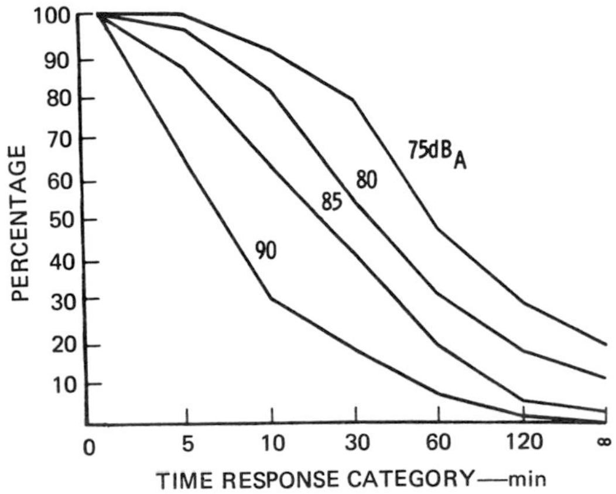

FIGURE 6.8 Cumulative distributions of subject estimates of how long an airplane trip could last without undue vocal strain from conversation in different levels of aircraft background noise. (From Rupf, 1977.)

as being acceptable (without undue voice strain) for only 5 min with a distance of about 1 ft between the talker and listener.

EFFECTS OF MESSAGE SET, NOISE, VOCAL, AND BINAURAL VARIABLES ON SPEECH INTELLIGIBILITY

Tests for the ability of the auditory system to receive, transduce, and transmit to the brain speech signals so they are correctly perceived are called *intelligibility* or *articulation tests*. The distinction is usually made on the basis of how they are scored—if the correct identification of words, phrases, or sentences is of interest, the test is called an *intelligibility test;* whereas if hearing performance is measured in terms of the correct identification of individual phonemes (essentially the consonants and vowels in mono-, or polysyllabic real or artificial words) the test is called an *articulation test*.

It is obvious that if the auditory system, physically and neurally, "articulates" without distortion in its transduction, all the acoustical information in the speech sounds, the system is operating at its maximum possible ability with respect to the understanding of speech. In that sense, an articulation test of all possible nonsense syllables represents the most stringent test of the ability of a communication system, or part thereof, such as the ear, to transmit intelligible speech. This is not to say, of course, that under many circumstances there is not more acoustical information present in speech sounds than is required to understand the meanings of samples of words, phrases, and sentences.

A wide variety of speech tests and test procedures have been developed for two primary purposes: (1) the assessment of the ability of electronic systems and components for transducing and transmitting a speech signal such that the speech is correctly perceived by the listener-receiver and (2) the assessment of the ability of ears with different degrees of hearing sensitivities to correctly perceive speech signals. In that the ear of the listener is part of the transmission–perception system certain principles of speech testing are common to both equipment design and medical evaluation of the ear.

The material in the immediately following section is primarily from studies involving speech understanding by normal ears in the presence of noise. However, the findings are also relevant to the interpretation of the effects of NIPTS on speech understanding. As noted earlier, the effects of masking and loss in hearing sensitivity may, for practical purposes, be considered functionally equivalent.

Message Set

Miller *et al.* (1951) demonstrated that the understandability of speech in noise is a strong function of the probability of occurrence of a given speech sound, word, or phrase. The larger the message set being used in a given communication system, the lower the probability of occurrence of a particular member of the message set and the more susceptible is the communication process to interference from noise. As illustrated in Fig. 6.9, the understandability of the words is as much influenced by the message, information, and set size as by the masking noise. The importance of size of message set in speech communications in noise is illustrated again later in this chapter.

Masking of Speech by Noise

As seen in Fig. 6.10, the masking effectiveness of different frequency bands of noise varies with signal-to-noise ratio. Clearly, by itself the ratio of the speech-to-noise sound-pressure levels is not an adequate indicator of the masking of speech by noise. However, we shall see later that by taking into joint account the type of test material, the speech-to-noise ratios in selected narrow-frequency bands, it is possible to predict fairly well the different kinds of results shown in Fig. 6.10.

The importance of considering the signal-to-noise ratio at a number of points along the frequency scale follows not only from the fact that different frequency regions of speech are somewhat more important than others to speech intelligibility but also because the long-term spectrum level per cycle of speech decreases at the rate of about 8 dB per octave above about 500 Hz (see Fig. 6.1). The spectrum level of the "instantaneous" peaks of speech is flatter than the $\geq 1/8$-s interval rms pressure spectra; however, it appears that the $1/8$th-s pressure spectrum is the effective spectrum with respect to the understanding of speech. For this reason, the lower speech frequencies are the last to be masked by noises whose spectra fall off less

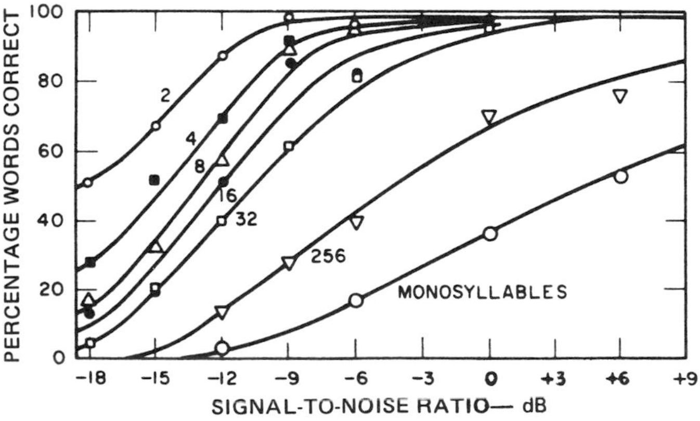

FIGURE 6.9 Word intelligibility scores obtained at various speech-to-noise ratios for test vocabularies containing different numbers of English monosyllables. The bottom curve was obtained with a vocabulary of approximately 1000 monosyllables. (From Miller *et al.*, 1951.)

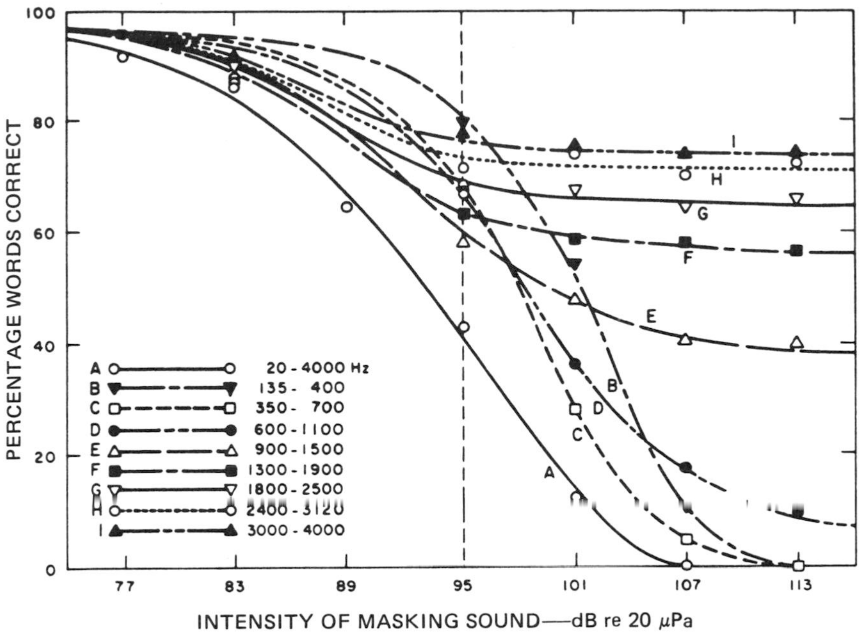

FIGURE 6.10 Percentage of words correct as a function of the intensity of narrow bands of masking noise. This speech was not filtered and its level was held constant at 95 dB. (From Miller *et al.*, 1951.)

steeply than does the speech spectrum as the signal-to-noise ratio is decreased.

Licklider and Guttman (1957) did a study of the masking of speech by pure tones and continuous spectra to show how best, for a given amount of sound energy, one could mask or reduce the intelligibility of speech. They varied the number and relative amplitude of the masking components. The density of spacing between components was varied in accordance with the critical bandwidth function of the ear over the approximate range of 200–6100 Hz, called the "importance function." (The critical bandwidth and the width of bands equally important to intelligibility are proportional to each other, see Fig. 2.7.). Also these investigators masked the speech by means of random noise, with the amplitude as a function of frequency either uniform, negatively exponential, or proportional to the critical bandwidth of the ear.

It appears from the results shown in Fig. 6.11 that (1) 256 components that are separated according to the relative importance function are 2 or 3 dB less efficient in terms of sound power required for masking, than a continuous-spectrum random noise in the 200–6100 Hz band, which has a spectrum that declines as a function of frequency at the rate of 3 dB per octave (so-called pink noise, or negative exponential); and (2) the masking effectiveness of most components and of noises indicates that the upward

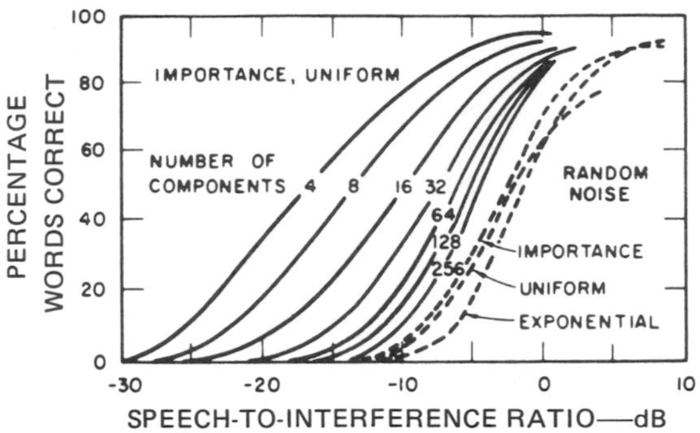

FIGURE 6.11 Masking of unfiltered speech by line-spectrum interference (solid curves) and by continuous-spectrum interference (dashed curves) in regular intelligibility tests. The density of spacing of the line components was governed by the importance function, and the lines were uniform in amplitude. The continuous spectra were shaped by filters. (From Licklider and Guttman, 1957. Copyright 1957 by the American Psychological Association. Adapted by permission of the author.)

spread of masking and remote masking, as found with pure tones, contributes significantly to speech masking. This effect was not found for components containing only a small number of tones.

A similar finding—the importance of the upward spread of masking—is demonstrated by the speech interference effects of pure tones of 50, 100, or 200 Hz shown Fig. 6.12. It is also seen in Fig. 6.12 that pure tones of equal sensation level cause more speech masking than do tones of equal sound-pressure level.

Interrupted Noise

When the speech signal is masked, either partially or completely, by a burst of noise, its intelligibility changes in a rather complex manner, as shown in Fig. 6.13. These functions are explained by Miller and Licklider (1950) as follows:

1. At interruption rates of less than ~2 per second (2 s^{-1}) which, for a noise on-time of 50%, would make the duration of each burst of noise at least 0.25 s), whole words or syllables within a word tend to be masked.

2. At interruption rates between about 2 and 30 s^{-1}, the noise duration is so brief that the listener is able to hear a portion of each syllable or phoneme of the speech signal, and the amount of masking thereby tends to be reduced. This is in good agreement with the temporal masking rcsults shown in Fig. 2.16, where it is seen that appreciable masking occurs for only 5–10 ms before and after an intense 90-dB sound.

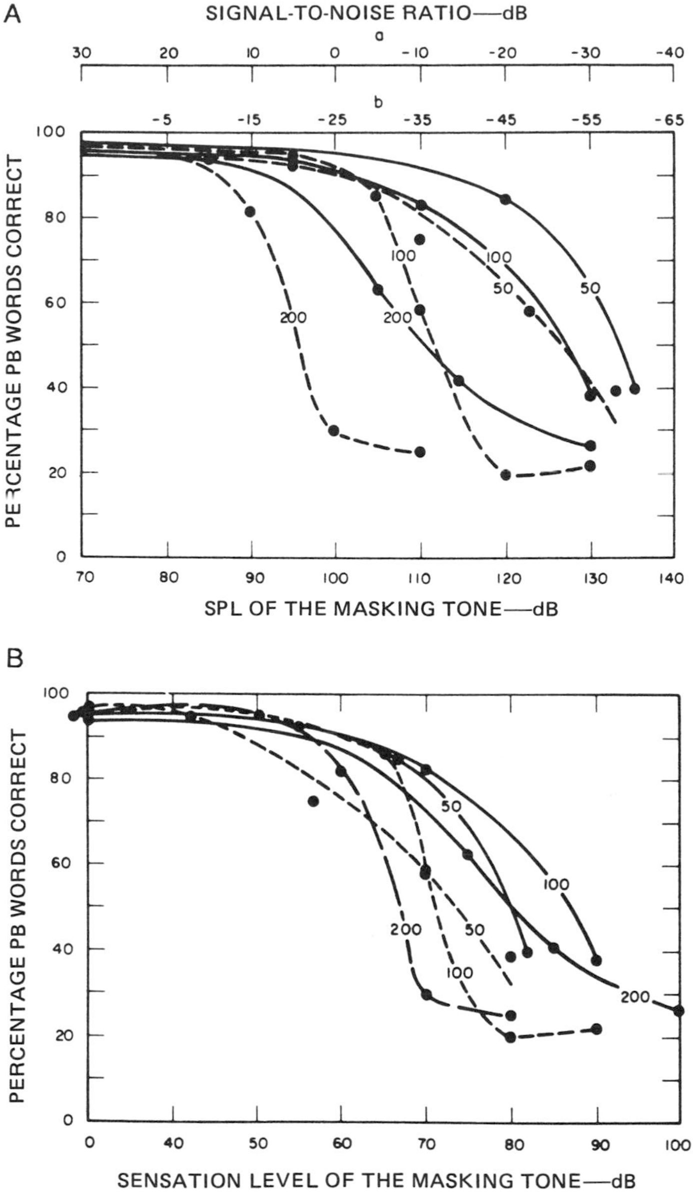

FIGURE 6.12 Percent PB words correct as a function of (A) sound pressure level and (B) sensation level of the masking tone. Solid curves indicate speech at an SPL of 100 dB [upper abscissa (a)]. Dashed curves represent for speech at SPL 75 dB [upper abscissa (b)]. Parameter is frequency in hertz of masking tone. (From Carter and Kryter, 1962.)

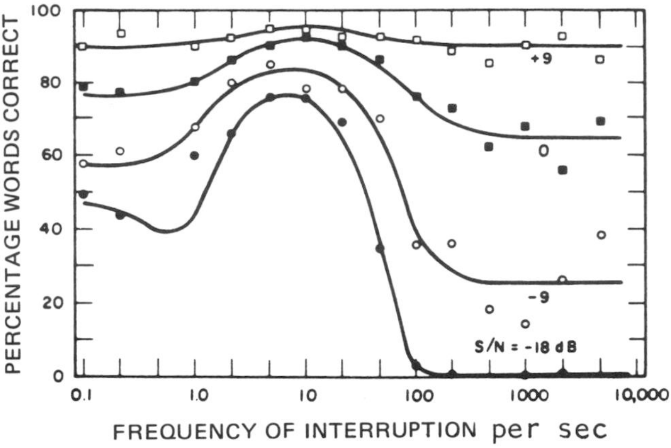

FIGURE 6.13 The masking of continuous speech by interrupted noise. Noise on-time is 50%. (From Miller and Licklider, 1950. Copyright 1950 by the American Psychological Association. Adapted by permission of the author.)

3. When the interruption rate is more frequent than 30 s^{-1}, the spread of masking in time around the moment of occurrence of a burst of noise results in increased masking, until by 100 interruptions per second there is effectively continuous masking.

That the increased masking of speech is due to a spread in time, presumably both forward and backward, is demonstrated in Fig. 6.14, where the intelligibility of speech that is interrupted by turning it "off" and "on" in the quiet can be compared with that of speech that is turned off during noise

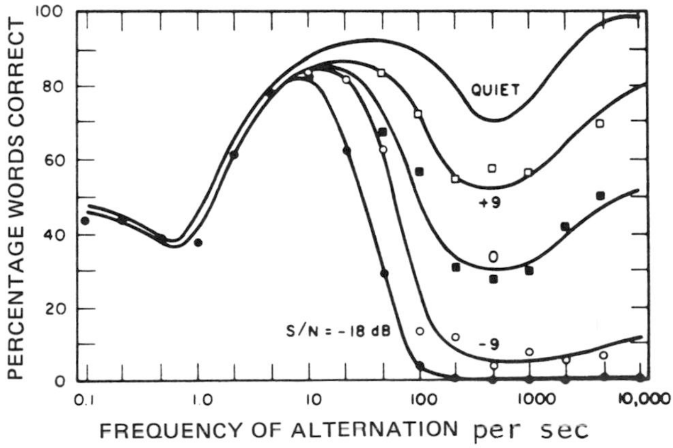

FIGURE 6.14 Word articulation as a function of the frequency of alternation between speech and noise, with SNR in decibels as the parameter. (From Miller and Licklider, 1950. Copyright 1950 by the American Psychological Association. Adapted by permission of the author.)

bursts and on between S/N bursts. Here the term *signal-to-noise ratio* refers to the signal in the quiet versus the noise alone. The temporal masking does not degrade the speech until the interruption rate exceeds 20 or 30 s^{-1}.

Miller and Licklider found that the above effects were the same for random or regularly spaced interruptions and that varying the speech on-time did not appreciably change the nature of the relationship between interruption rate and intelligibility. Pollack (1958a) found that, over relatively wide limits, varying the signal-to-noise ratio at rather slow rates provided intelligibility comparable to that observed with a steady-state signal-to-noise ratio.

One of the most common noises that masks speech is speech itself—the babble of other voices. Figure 6.15 shows how speech intelligibility is affected as a function of the number of competing voices. By the time eight voices are present, the "noise" speech spectrum is apparently effectively steady-state.

Effects of Vocal Effort on Intelligibility

It is of some interest to know what the effect of vocal effort in talking might have on the intelligibility of the speech, with signal-to-noise ratio held constant. Figure 6.16 clearly shows that speech uttered with very weak or very high levels of effort was not as intelligible as speech in the range from about 50 to 80 dB (measured at 1 m from the talker) even when the speech-to-noise ratio was kept constant.

Effects of Speech Intensity on Intelligibility

In many noisy environments, the speech signal is often speech that has been spoken into a microphone at a normal, or near-normal, level of effort and

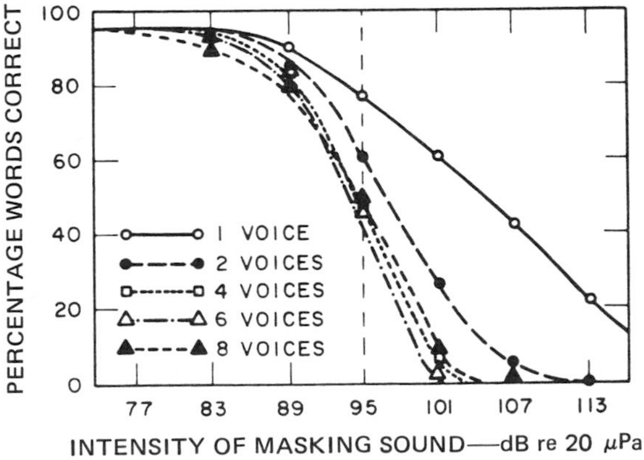

FIGURE 6.15 Word intelligibility as a function of intensity of different numbers of masking voices. Level of desired speech was held constant at 94 dB. (From Miller, 1947.)

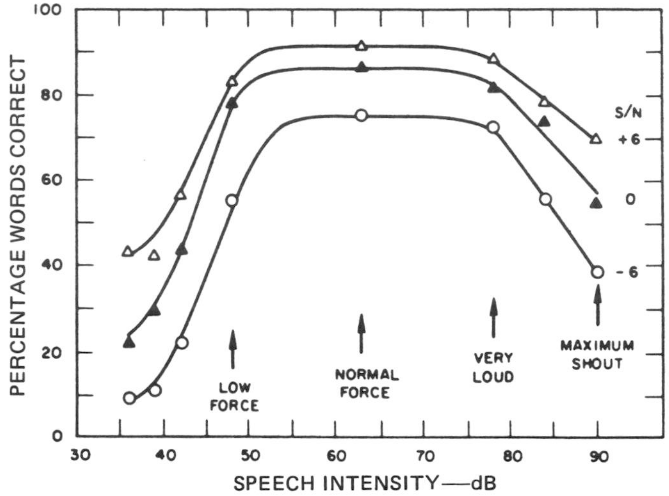

FIGURE 6.16 Intelligibility in noise of speech spoken at different vocal forces. Noise, 70 dB, flat spectrum. The speech was uttered at the level of effort indicated by the abscissa, and then the level of microphone pickup signal was adjusted prior to mixing with the constant level of 70-dB noise to provide the indicated speech-to-noise ratios (S/N) to the listener (e.g., speech spoken at a level of 35 dB, 1 m from the talker and microphone, was heard at a level 76 dB when the S/N was +6 dB, as was the speech spoken at all the levels indicated by the data points on the +6-dB S/N curve). (From Pickett, 1958. Copyright 1958 by the American Psychological Association. Adapted by permission of the author.)

then amplified by electronic means to make it audible above the noise present at the position of the listener. Here the question is how intense the speech can be before it loses intelligibility because of distortion by overloading the linear transmission ability of the ear. Pollack (1958b) found that in the quiet [signal-to-noise ratio (S/N) of 55 dB), there was no loss in word intelligibility even at speech levels of 130 dB, although the speech sounded somewhat distorted. When there was some noise present, however, speech above about 85 dB declined in intelligibility with S/N kept constant (see Fig. 6.17).

These data demonstrate that intelligibility tests are somewhat insensitive indicators of the true fidelity, or undistorted nature, of a given speech signal when nearly 100% of the words are scored as being correct (the case of speech of 130 dB in the quiet). The potentially degrading effects of overloading the ear with very intense speech on intelligibility are, no doubt, actually present when the speech is heard in the quiet, but can be measured only when the test scores have been lowered and rendered more sensitive by some additional stressful condition, such as noise.

It was stated earlier that masking is usually not particularly affected by temporary auditory fatigue in the normal ear provided the S/N remains constant, and the signal consists of pure tones. However, Pollack (1958b) found that the effective masking of speech did increase significantly during

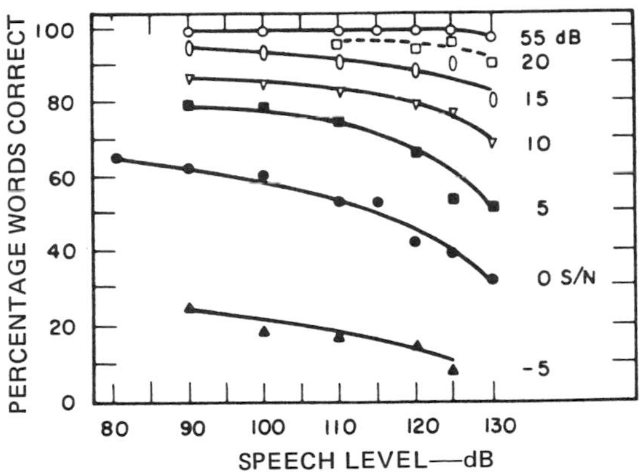

FIGURE 6.17 The deterioration of intelligibility at high levels of intensity. (From Pollack, 1958b. Copyright 1958 by the American Psychological Association. Adapted by permission of the author.)

a 13-min exposure to random broadband noise (flat, 100–5000 Hz) at levels above ~115 dB. This effect (see Fig. 6.18) is presumably due to an inability of the fatigued ear to discriminate among the speech sounds as well as the unfatigued ear.

Binaural Factors in Speech Perception

If there are some temporal or frequency differences at the two ears between the signal and the noise, it appears that listeners may direct their attention to the sounds they wishes to perceive without conscious regard to localization or phenomenal space. This is particularly noticeable when the noise consists of other speech signals—what has come to be called the "cocktail party" effect—and when the competing signals differ somewhat in spectra (Licklider, 1948; Pollack and Pickett, 1958; Weston *et al.*, 1965).

An unusual situation for speech communication, but one that demonstrates the advantages of binaural as compared with monaural listening in the presence of masking sounds, was studied by Pollack and Pickett. They presented, via earphones, a speech signal in phase at the two ears against one background of speech presented to one ear and a different background of speech to the other ear; some of the results are shown in Fig. 6.19. The control condition in Fig. 6.19 was achieved by merely disconnecting one of the listener's earphones. It is clear from Fig. 6.19 that some of the direct masking of the speech (equivalent to about 30 percentage points of words correct) that takes place with monaural listening is appreciably overcome on the basis of cues available with binaural–stereophonic listening.

Experiments conducted by Licklider (1948), clearly revealed the variety of effects of binaural, and monaural, listening on the intelligibility of speech

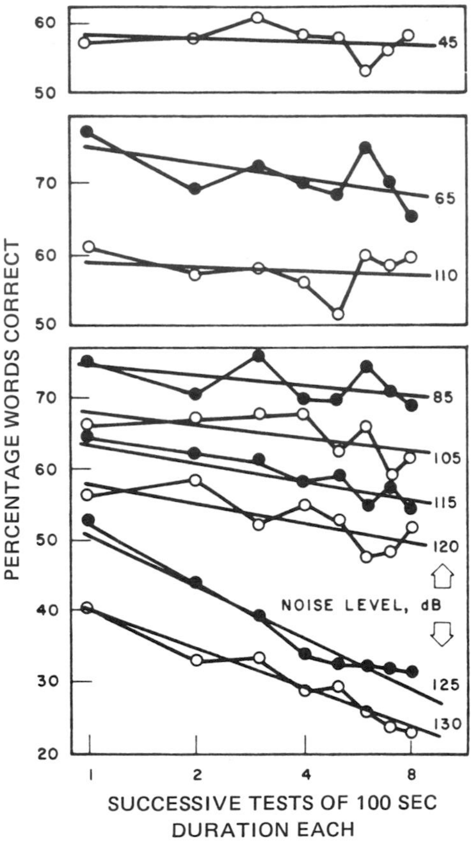

FIGURE 6.18 Speech intelligibility in noise as a function of continuous noise (and speech) exposure. The vertical axis has been broken to avoid overlap among conditions. S/N ratio is 0 dB. Each point represents the average of 500 determinations consisting of one 25-item test list read by each of four talkers to a testing crew of five listeners. (From Pollack, 1958b. Copyright 1958 by the American Psychological Association. Adapted by permission of the author.)

in noise. Table 6.3 shows the effect on intelligibility of all combinations of monaural and binaural listening to speech and noise over earphones. It is seen in Table 6.3 that speech intelligibility is highest with binaural noise and speech, speech intelligibility is highest, when the two signals are of opposite phase, lowest when both are in phase, and midway in intelligibility when they are of random phase at the two ears. For monaural listening, intelligibility is not greatly affected by noise in the opposite ear.

Weston *et al.* also demonstrated that phase and intensity differences between the two ears when listening to noise and speech sources separated in space under free-field conditions were responsible for increased intelligibility. These binaural–stereophonic findings are no doubt due to direct neural con-

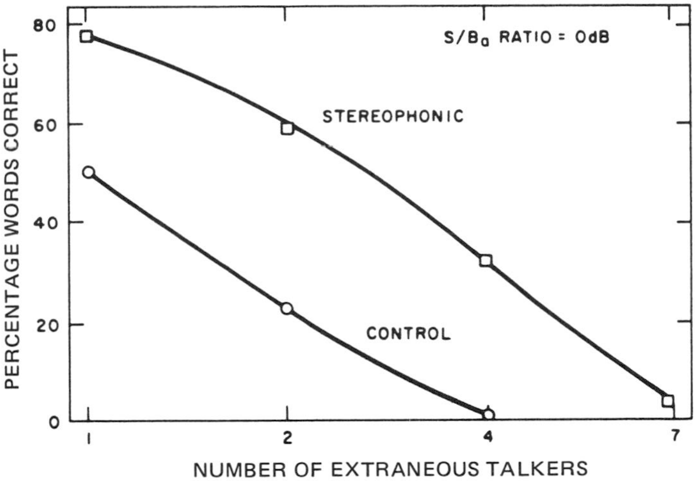

FIGURE 6.19 Comparison between average intelligibility scores of an adjusted speech-to-background noise ratio of 0 dB for a binaural–stereophonic listening (upper curve); and a monaural–control listening condition (lower curve). (From Pollack and Pickett, 1958. Copyright 1958 by the American Psychological Association. Adapted by permission of the author.)

nections between the two ears and to the central nervous system, outlined in Chapter 2.

AMELIORATING THE EFFECTS OF NOISE ON SPEECH INTELLIGIBILITY

Maintaining satisfactory speech communications is obviously of great importance in many business and military operations. Over the years a numer of techniques for overcoming, or reducing, the adverse effects of noise on speech communications in such situations have been developed.

TABLE 6.3 Monaural–Binaural Presentation and Interaural Phase Relations as Factors Influencing the Masking of Speech by White Noise

		Percent PB words correct				
		Binaural noise			Monaural noise	
		+	0	−	R	L
Binaural speech	+	18.0	27.4	35.4	98.0	99.0
	−	43.0	27.3	15.8	98.1	98.8
Monaural speech	R	30.3	13.2	20.1	16.6	98.7
	L	18.1	8.3	15.2	98.4	15.4

Key: +, in phase; −, out of phase; 0, random phase; R, right ear; L, left ear.

From Licklider (1948).

Reducing Size of Message Set

It was mentioned earlier with respect to speech intelligibility testing that, the smaller the size of the set of words to be heard in a given context, the more understandable each word becomes. This principle can be used to advantage in various ways in combatting the masking of speech by noise. The U.S. Air Force and international commercial aviation effects this by prescribing standardized messages and words and procedures (Moser, 1961). This standardization reduces the amount of information with which the listener must cope and thereby improves speech communications in noise (Pollack, 1958a; Frick and Sumby, 1952).

Another technique for overcoming the adverse effects of noise on speech communication is information redundancy; that is, having the talker repeat the words or messages. Thwing (1956), for example, found that the intelligibility of single words increased by about 5–10% (equivalent to a reduction in the noise level of ~3 dB) when each word was repeated once. Further repetition caused little additional improvement.

Increasing the Signal Level Relative to Noise Level

Increasing the level of the signal relative to that of the noise is the most effective way to avoid masking of speech. Methods of alleviating the masking effects of noise under several different conditions have been investigated. Pickett and Pollack (1958) report that a small megaphone improved speech intelligibility relative to the unaided voice by an amount equivalent to a reduction of the noise level by 6.5–11.5 dB, depending on the noise spectrum. The least gain was found with a "flat" white noise; the greatest, with a noise having a −12-dB slope above 100 Hz.

Peak Clipping

As exemplified in Fig. 6.20A, the parts of a speech signal associated with a consonant are less intense than those parts representing vowels. Accordingly, noise will tend to mask consonant at a lower level than that required to mask the vowels. In order to have the consonants override the noise and yet not increase the peak power requirements of a transmission system, the level of the consonant sounds must be increased relative to that of the vowel sounds. This can be achieved by passing the speech through a "peak clipper" and then reamplifying the result to whatever peak power level is available.

This process is illustrated in Fig. 6.20C, where the peak-to-peak amplitude of the consonant "J" is shown to be rendered equal to that of the unclipped vowel "O" by peak clipping and amplifying the speech by 20 dB. Speech thusly clipped has a greater average speech power for a given peak power and is more intelligible in noise than is unclipped speech.

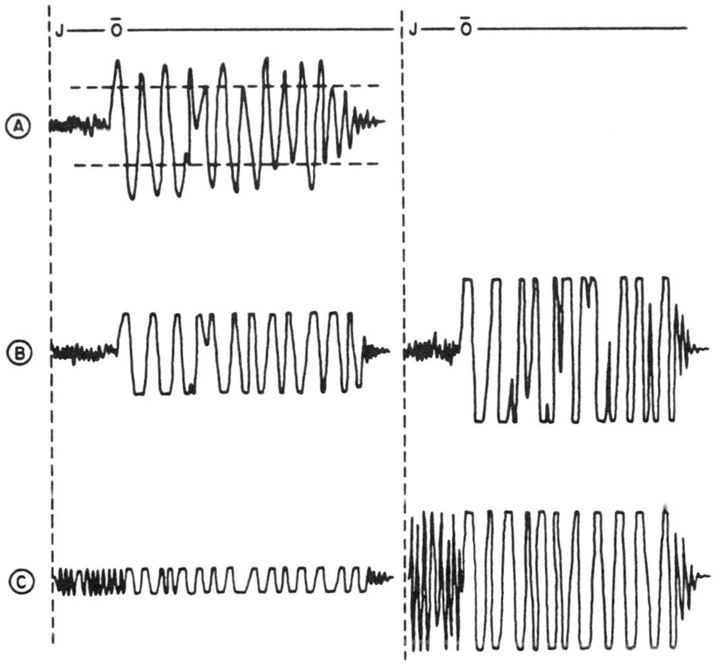

FIGURE 6.20 Schematic oscillographs of word Joe, "J-O". Tracing A is undistorted; tracing B is after 6-dB clipping; and tracing C is after 20-dB clipping. Clipped signals in B and C are shown reamplified until their peak-to-peak amplitudes equal the peak-to-peak amplitude of A. (After Licklider, 1946. Copyright 1946 by the American Psychological Association. Adapted by permission of the author.)

However, certain precautions must be kept in mind when peak clipping is to be used. First, speech peak clipped by more than ~6-dB sounds distorted and noisy when listened to in the quiet due to the clipping of the vowel waveform. (When heard in noise, peak-clipped speech sounds relatively undistorted because the distortion products from the speech signal tend to be masked by the noise.) Second, when there is noise mixed with the speech prior to peak clipping, the amount of clipping that is beneficial is limited. This latter fact is revealed through a comparison of Figs. 6.21A and 6.21B.

Noise Exclusion at the Microphone

One way to keep noise out of a microphone is to attach the microphone directly to tissues of the throat and head so that it will not pick up airborne noise but will pick up the speech signal through the body tissues. Such microphones are reasonably effective in excluding noise when attached to the throat, ear, teeth, or forehead, but they tend to somewhat distort the speech signal (Moser *et al.*, 1956).

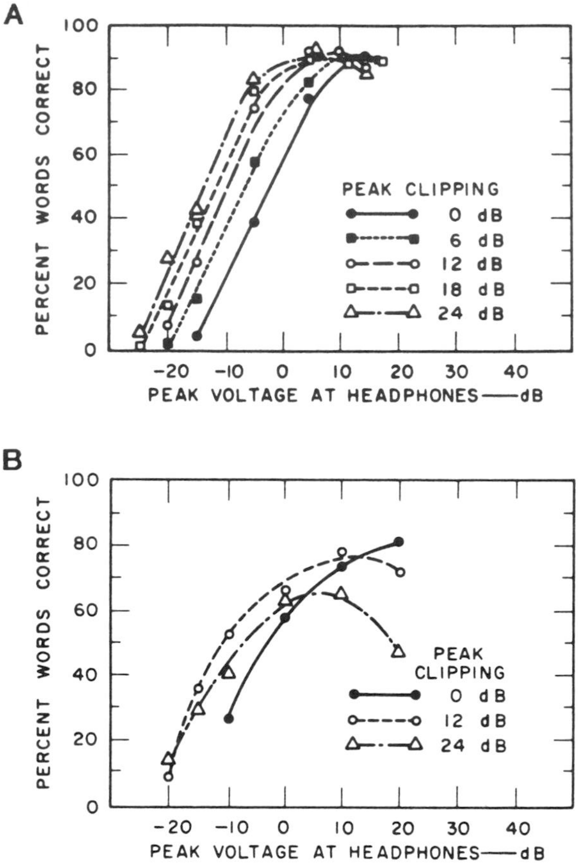

FIGURE 6.21 Results of intelligibility tests with talkers in the quiet and listeners in ambient airplane noise (A); and intelligibility tests with both talkers and listeners in simulated airplane noise (B). Note in B that when the microphone picks up noise, clipping is not always beneficial to intelligibility. A non-noise-canceling microphone was used. (From Kryter *et al.*, 1947. Copyright 1947 by the American Psychological Association. Adapted by permission of the author.)

Placing an air-activated microphone in a shield (usually a cup that forms a seal around the talker's mouth) will typically achieve noise exclusion, as shown in Fig. 6.22. A third method is to use a close-talking pressure-gradient microphone. Here both surfaces of the active element of the microphone are exposed to air. Depending on frequency wavelength, random-incidence sound waves (the noise) will impinge on both sides of the element more or less simultaneously. Thus, they tend to cancel each other; that is, the microphone element does not move.

The speech signal, on the other hand, is highly directional when the microphone is held close to the lips and correctly oriented and, therefore,

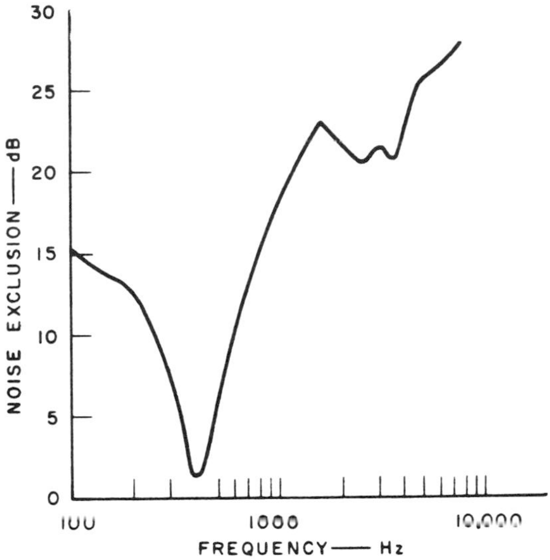

FIGURE 6.22 Noise exclusion with a noise shield. (From Hawley and Kryter, 1957.)

activates the moving element of the microphone. The amount of noise cancellation achieved is shown in Fig. 6.23 as a function of frequency.

Noise Exclusion at the Ear: Ear Protectors

Earplugs and muffs for over the ears (earmuff) have been developed as a means of protecting the ear against auditory fatigue from exposure to intense noise (see Fig. 6.24A). It is to be noted that in practice earmuffs, and especially earplugs give somewhat less protection (sound attenuation) than do these devices when carefully fitted by an experimenter-tester; compare Fig. 6.24A with Fig. 6.24B. Smoorenburg (1982) and Edwards *et al.* (1978) report about 13–34 dB, depending on pure-tone test frequency, less attenuation for the typical military or industrial user of self-fitted earplugs when measured on the job than that afforded by the same devices when tested under laboratory conditions, as is illustrated in Fig. 6.24A.

Ear-protective devices interact in various fortunate, and unfortunate, ways with the reception of speech by users. Because earplugs or earmuffs attenuate equally, at any one frequency, the speech signal and ambient noise passing through them, the S/N at any one frequency often remains constant at the listener's eardrum. Accordingly, speech intelligibility would be expected, if the speech signal is sufficiently intense at all frequencies relative to the noise spectrum, to be the same regardless of whether earplugs or earmuffs were worn.

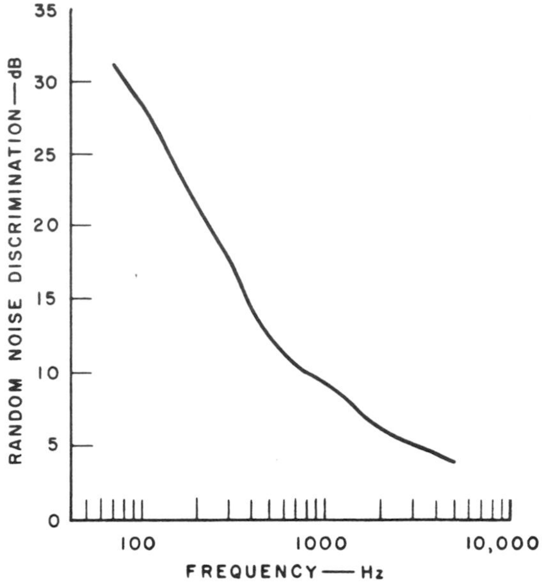

FIGURE 6.23 Random-noise discrimination by a noise-canceling microphone. (From Kryter *et al.*, 1962. Copyright 1962 by the American Psychological Association. Adapted by permission of the author.)

However, what happens in ears with normal hearing is that when earplugs or muffs are worn in (1) very intense noise (> ~90 dB), speech intelligibility is improved because the speech and noise are reduced to a level where the ear is not "overloaded" and discriminates the speech from the noise somewhat better (Fig. 6.25A); (2) moderate-level noise (<85 dB or so), intelligibility is unaffected (Figs. 6.25A and 6.25B); or (3) lower-level noise (<65 dB or so), noise, speech intelligibility is decreased (Fig. 6.25A). On the other hand, the use of ear protectors decreases speech intelligibility in noises at a level of 85 dB for ears with a high-frequency sensorineural hearing loss (Fig. 6.25C).

The fact that ear protectors reduce speech intelligibility under quiet, or relatively quiet conditions, becomes a problem in work situations were the noise may be fluctuating in intensity. Under these conditions, the person with normal ears may be able to understand the speech in the noise as well, or better, with ear protectors. But the person with some hearing loss may have difficulty in understanding speech both in the quiet and in the noise (Alberti *et al.*, 1982; Rink, 1979). The effect of earplugs and muffs on the audibility of speech, or any other auditory signal, in noise can only be predicted from a knowledge of the hearing of the listener, the spectra at a particular moment of the speech and noise at the position of the listener's head, and the sound-attenuation characteristics of the earplugs or earmuffs.

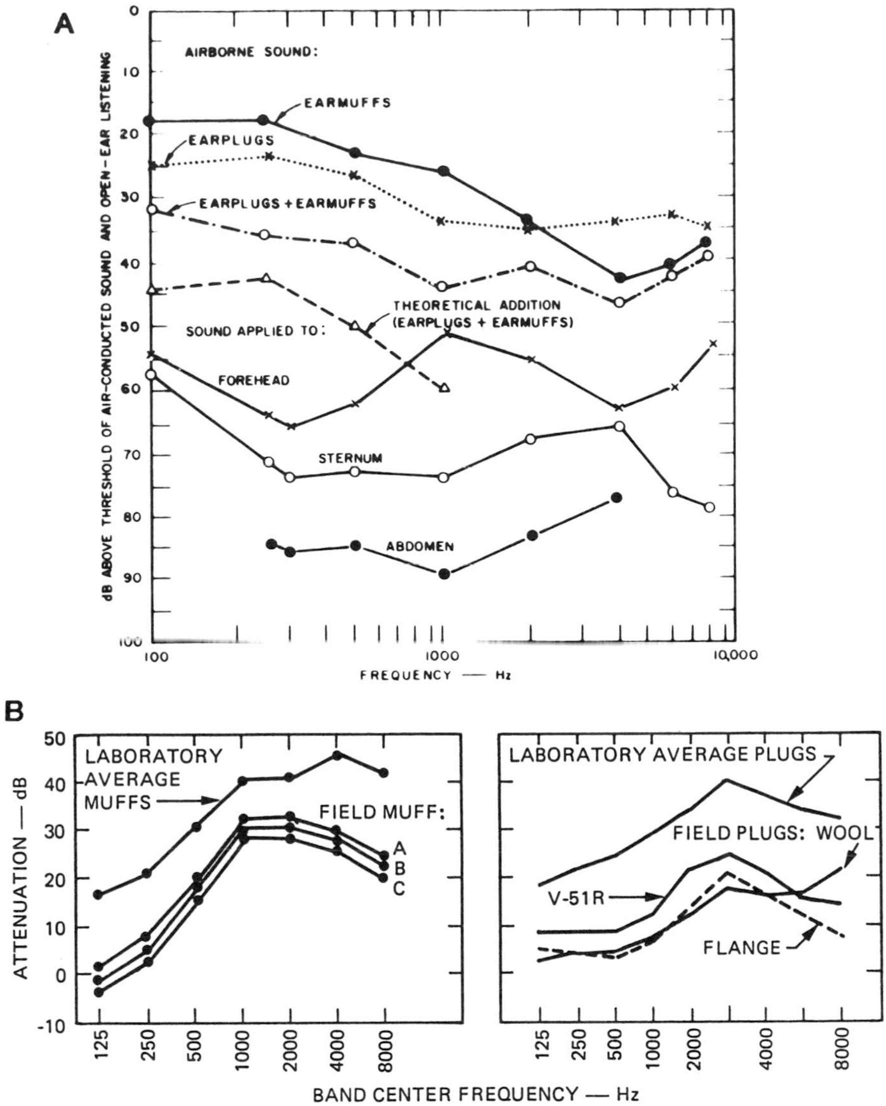

FIGURE 6.24 (A) The top four curves show measured attenuation for earplugs and earmuffs carefully fitted by an experimenter-tester. (Data from Zwislocki, 1957). The bottom three curves show the audibility of sound when applied to different parts of the body and conducted to the ear through body tissues. (From Von Gierke, 1956.) Average attenuation for 10 types of (B) earplugs and (C) earmuffs when fitted by worker-user with no adjustment by the tester. (From Alberti *et al.*, 1982.)

It should also be noted that when a person is in noise, plugging the ears results in a drop of 1–2 dB in voice level (Kryter, 1946; Howell and Martin, 1975). Apparently the earplugs or ear coverings attenuate the ambient noise

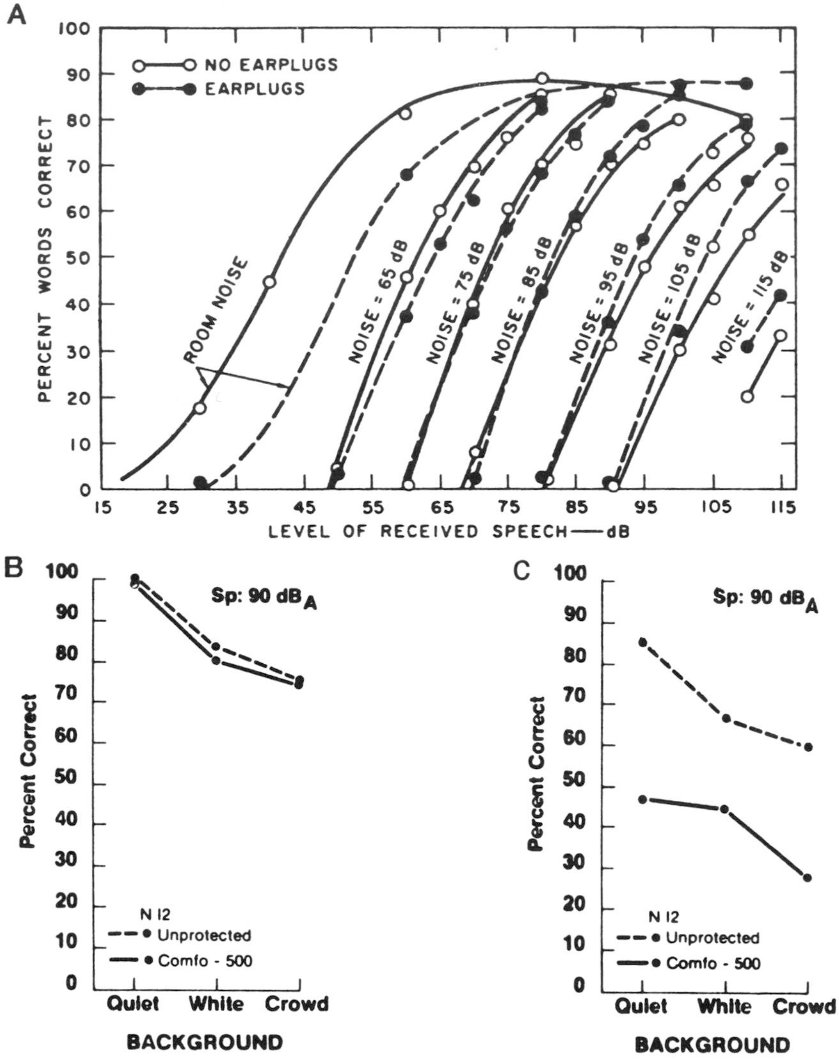

FIGURE 6.25 (A) Relation between intelligibility and speech level for listeners with normal hearing, with noise level as the parameter. (From Kryter, 1946.) (B) Speech intelligibility in quiet and with a background noise of 85 dB; listeners with, and without, ear protectors. Normal hearing listeners, aged 30–35 years. (From Edwards *et al.*, 1978.) (C) Speech intelligibility in quiet and with a background of white noise and recorded crowd noises at 85 dB; listeners with, and without, ear protectors. Listeners with high-frequency hearing loss, aged 30–35 years. (From Edwards *et al.*, 1978.)

without lowering, to as great an extent, the speaker's own speech, which one hears both by tissue and bone conduction through one's head and by airborne sound. For instance, if you were to wear earplugs in the quiet, you would raise your voice level by 3–4 dB, since your own voice now sounds weaker to you because of attenuation of the airborne components of the speech wave (see Fig. 6.26).

Nonlinear Earplugs

Earplugs or earmuffs appear to be counterindicated in military, or other, situations where a high degree of auditory sensitivity is needed in the presence of intermittent, impulsive noise, such as gunfire. The ideal solution would be a nonlinear device that would let weak speech, or other, sounds through at full strength, but would attenuate intense impulse sounds.

Zwislocki (1961) and Collins (1964) have described the theoretical basis for such nonlinear devices and have built and tested models of them. The devices, which are essentially acoustic filters, operate on a frequency selective basis. They afford significant attenuation at frequencies above 1500 Hz but offer little or no attenuation at frequencies below 1500 Hz, the region containing the strongest speech components. Also, the device can be made significantly nonlinear only after the overall sound-pressure level exceeds a certain level.

Noise Cancellation

Olson and May (1953) developed a device for actively canceling ambient noise. In one version of this system, a microphone mounted close to the

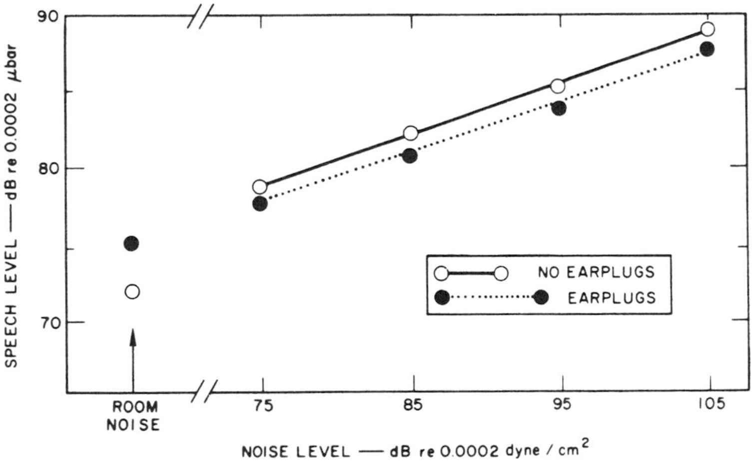

FIGURE 6.26 Effect of noise level on average speech intensity used by eight speakers with and without earplugs. Speech and noise levels were measured at listener's position (7 ft from speaker). (From Kryter, 1946.) Copyright 1946 by the American Psychological Association. Adapted by permission of the author.)

listener's ear picks up environmental noise. The signal from this microphone is then amplified and fed into a loudspeaker (or to the listener's earphones) so that it is 180° out of phase with the noise signal and, therefore, acoustically cancels the noise at the listener's ears. This procedure is effective only for frequencies below ~200 Hz and, for this reason, will generally not help speech communication in noise in the open field.

However, active noise control technology has been developed to the point of its potential use in quieting areas from some low-frequency noise sources, such as in cabins of transportation vehicles (Eghtesadi, 1993). The technique has particular application in the cancellation of field noise that comes to the listener's ears by penetrating the earmuffs and cushions covering headset earphones. A microphone-amplifier on the ear covering detects, tranduces, and inserts the noise, via the earphone in the muff or covering, out of phase with the input noise. This process can not only protect the ear from some exposure to intense noise but also improve the S/N for speech, or other auditory signals, being transmitted to the listeners via the earphone (McKinley and Nixon, 1993; Carme and Roure, 1993a,b).

Enhancement of Speech Signals from Reverberant Speech or Noise Signals

Tohyama discusses the possibilities of microphone and loudspeaker arrays for rooms and auditoria that permit maximizing of the phase coherence of speech signals reaching given room locations and minimizing the phase coherence of reverberant sounds. Involved are the measurement of the effects of exponential and non-exponential reverberation decay-fields, and signal time-delays, upon reverberant-to-direct signal energy, and speech intelligibility. Improvements in signal enhancement for monaural listening are shown for laboratory test rooms and computer simulations.

PREDICTING INTELLIGIBILITY FROM ACOUSTICAL MEASURES OF SPEECH, NOISE, AND HEARING LEVELS: THE ARTICULATION INDEX

Articulation Index

From data of the intelligibility of filtered speech sounds, and certain assumptions regarding the equivalence of bandwidth and signal level, French and Steinberg (1947) developed an index to the intelligibility of speech based on physical measurements of the spectra of speech, thresholds of audibility, and, if present, competing noise. They called this the *articulation index* (AI).

Von Tarnóczy (1971) measured the spectrum level of speech for six European languages and found only small variations among the different languages. Pavlovic (1990) reported similar findings for Danish, German, Italian, English, and French. The similarity between these spectra and the long-term idealized spectrum shown in Fig. 6.1 indicates that AI, as formulated, can probably be applied with accurate predictions of the speech intelligibility of most European languages.

In the calculation of AI, and prediction therefrom of speech intelligibility, the threshold levels of audibility and the masking level of noise are used interchangeably, depending on which is the higher at given points over the audible-speech spectrum. In the discussion to follow, threshold levels of audibility will be generally treated as a form of masking level, consistent with the concept that the former is determined by internal "physiologic noise"; and the latter, by external ambient noise or sound.

Essentially, according to the AI concept, a given speech signal will, within certain limits, be about equally understandable to ears with a given sensorineural loss, expressed as sound-pressure levels over the frequency range of the speech spectrum, when listening in the quiet, and to normal ears listening to the same speech signal in the presence of a noise whose spectrum matches that of the equivalent sound-pressure levels of the thresholds of the ears with the given hearing loss. The AI concept holds that speech intelligibility is proportional to the average of weighted differences between the masking (or equivalent threshold) level, in decibels, of noise and the long-term level, in decibels, plus 12, of the speech signal in each of a number of relatively narrow frequency bands. (It will be recognized that the 12 dB represents the difference between the $^1/_8$th s and the long-time, 1-s rms, speech level (see Fig. 6.1). The masking spectrum of a noise may be somewhat different from the noise spectrum because of the spread of masking and remote masking.

This proportionality holds provided the difference falls between 0 and 30 dB, a negative value is considered as 0, and a value greater than 30 is called 30. Originally, 20 narrow bands were chosen for calulating AI that were found to contribute equally to the understanding of speech. These bands are somewhat similar in width to the critical bands of the ear as determined from studies of loudness and masking (see Fig. 2.7).

Modifications of the calculation procedures for AI, as proposed by French and Steinberg, deal with converting noise spectra to noise-masking spectra, and with methods for calculating using octave and $\frac{1}{3}$-octave-band speech and noise spectra (Beranek, 1947; Kryter, 1962a,b; ANSI, 1969a). Figure 6.27 gives the worksheet used for calculating AI from $^1/_3$-octave-band speech and noise spectra, along with an example of the calculation of an AI.

Studies have shown that different speech materials and test procedures provide bands of frequencies of equal importance for their intelligibility that are somewhat different from those prescribed in the AI standard (Bell *et al.*, 1992; Black, 1959; Pavlovic and Studebaker, 1984; Studebaker *et al.*, 1987; Studebaker and Sherbecoe, 1991). The ANSI S3.5 bands (ANSI, 1969a) were based on those found by French and Steinberg (1947) with articulation tests of nonsense syllables. The differences are, to varying but relatively small

A

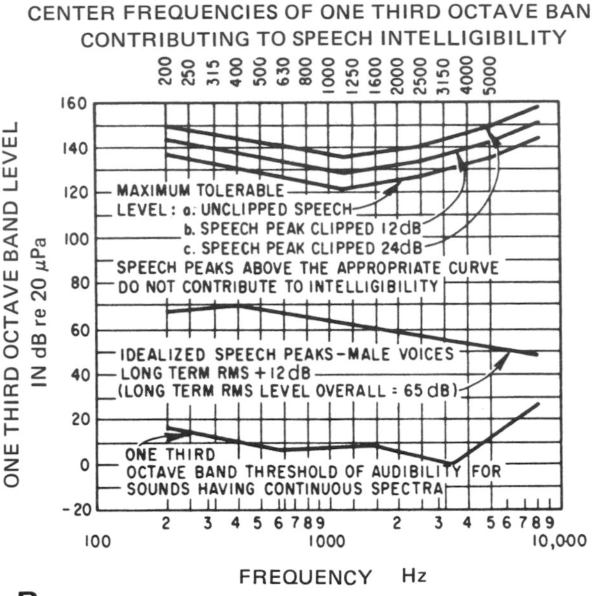

B

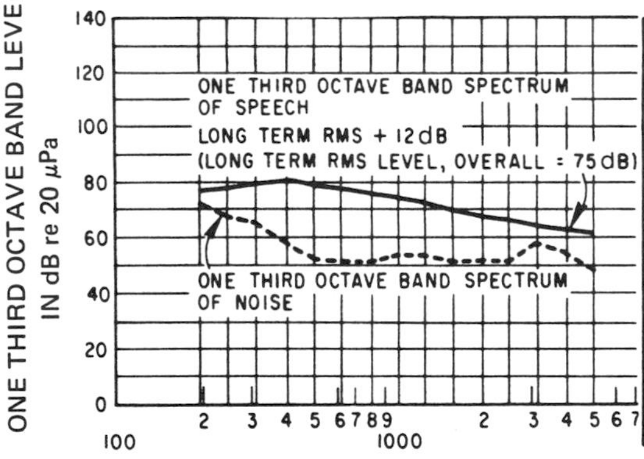

BAND cf	SPEECH PEAKS MINUS NOISE-dB	WEIGHT	CL 2 x 3
200	4	0.0004	0.0016
250	10	0.0010	0.0100
315	13	0.0010	0.0130
400	24	0.0014	0.0336
500	26	0.0014	0.0364
630	26	0.0020	0.0520
800	24	0.0020	0.0480
1000	21	0.0024	0.0504
1250	18	0.0030	0.0540
1600	18	0.0037	0.0666
2000	15	0.0037	0.0555
2500	15	0.0034	0.0510
3150	6	0.0034	0.0204
4000	8	0.0024	0.0192
5000	12	0.0020	0.0240
		AI = 0.5357	

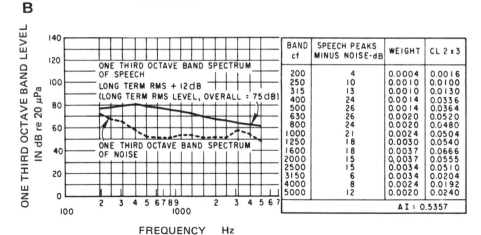

FIGURE 6.27 (A) Worksheet for AI, 1/3-octave-band method. (B) Example of calculation of AI by 1/3-octave-band method. (From ANSI, 1969a.)

degrees, to the effect of shifting more of the weight from the upper to the lower frequencies (about a 1% downward shift). The speech materials used in these later intelligibility tests were, for the most part, materials that are used, or proposed for, clinical speech audiometry.

These intelligibility tests consist of limited sets of words and sentences, and connected discourse from a children's book of knowledge. They are aimed at the screening of persons with hearing loss and the fitting of hearing aids to ears with, generally, large high-frequency losses. The tests are relatively insensitive to differences in hearing loss, much more so than so-called articulation tests. This translation for some different types of speech materials is presently accomplished for AI in accordance with Fig. 6.28.

ANSI Standard S3.5 notes that there are types of communication systems and noise-masking situations that can be evaluated only by direct speech intelligibility or other performance tests. In particular, communication systems that process speech signals in various ways in order to achieve bandwidth compression cannot be directly evaluated by the A1 procedure.

Suggestions are given in ANSI Standard S3.5 (S3.5) for refinements to AI to take into account such things as the vocal effort used by the talker, interruption in the noise, face-to-face talking, and reverberation present in the listening situation. In this regard, it should be noted that other procedures for making allowances for reverberation besides that used in S3.5 have been proposed. Bolt and MacDonald (1949) suggested that reverberation effects could be properly accounted for by adding to the measured noise level an amount that depends on the reverberation time.

More recently, Janssen (1957) recommended that the measured level of the speech signal be reduced to an effective level by an amount that depends on the reverberation time. Also, Levitt and Rabiner (1967) proposed that the effects of binaural phase relations of speech and noise on speech intelligibility, as discussed earlier, can be predicted by AI when certain adjustments are made to measured speech-to-noise ratios present in different frequency bands.

Other AI Procedures

Procedures similar to those used for finding AI have been proposed in several countries over the past 15 or 20 years (Golikov, 1961; Jeffress, 1965; Richards, 1956; Rozhanskaya, 1953). The variations are principally in terms of the width of the frequency bands in which the S/Ns are determined.

Cavanaugh *et al.* (1962) suggested the use of a graphic procedure for estimating AI. In their method, the spectrum of the noise is plotted on the same graph as the peak instantaneous levels reached by speech signals. The area between the noise spectrum and the speech peaks, adjusted for the relative importance assigned to different speech frequencies, is proportional to the AI for that speech and noise condition.

Devices for AI-Type Evaluation of Speech Systems

Tkachenko (1955) proposed a very simple method for estimating the A1 of a speech communication system. He developed an artificial speech signal that consisted of 20 pure tones spaced at the center frequency of the 20

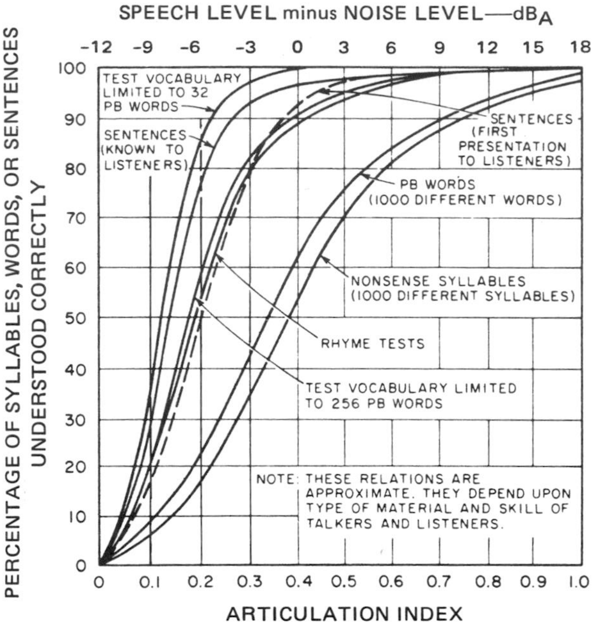

AI	Sentences, Rhyme,& 250 Words	1000 Different PB Words	AI	Sentences, Rhyme,& 250 Words	1000 Different PB Words	AI	Sentences, Rhyme,& 250 Words	1000 Different PB Words	AI	Sentences, Rhyme,& 250 Words	1000 Different PB Words
0.01	01.0	00.5	0.26	70.0	34.0	0.51	95.5	77.0	0.76	98.5	93.0
0.02	02.0	01.0	0.27	73.0	36.0	0.52	96.0	78.0	0.77	98.5	93.5
0.03	03.0	01.5	0.28	76.0	38.5	0.53	96.0	79.0	0.78	98.5	93.5
0.04	05.0	02.0	0.29	78.0	41.0	0.54	96.0	80.0	0.79	98.5	94.0
0.05	07.0	03.0	0.30	80.0	43.5	0.55	96.5	80.5	0.80	98.5	94.0
0.06	09.0	04.0	0.31	82.0	46.0	0.56	96.5	81.5	0.81	99.0	94.5
0.07	11.0	05.0	0.32	83.5	48.0	0.57	96.5	82.5	0.82	99.0	94.5
0.08	14.0	06.5	0.33	85.0	50.0	0.58	96.5	83.0	0.83	99.0	95.0
0.09	17.0	08.0	0.34	86.0	52.0	0.59	96.5	84.0	0.84	99.0	95.0
0.10	20.0	09.0	0.35	87.0	54.0	0.60	97.0	85.0	0.85	99.0	98.5
0.11	23.0	10.0	0.36	88.0	56.0	0.61	97.0	85.5	0.86	99.0	95.5
0.12	26.0	11.5	0.37	89.0	58.0	0.62	97.0	86.0	0.87	99.5	96.0
0.13	29.0	13.0	0.38	90.0	59.5	0.63	97.0	86.5	0.88	99.5	96.0
0.14	32.0	14.0	0.39	91.0	61.0	0.64	97.0	87.0	0.89	99.5	96.5
0.15	35.0	15.5	0.40	92.0	63.0	0.65	97.5	87.5	0.90	99.5	96.5
0.16	38.0	17.0	0.41	92.5	64.5	0.66	97.5	88.0	0.91	100.0	97.0
0.17	41.0	18.5	0.42	93.0	66.0	0.67	97.5	88.5	0.92	100.0	97.0
0.18	44.0	20.0	0.43	93.5	67.5	0.68	97.5	89.0	0.93	100.0	97.5
0.19	48.0	21.5	0.44	94.0	69.0	0.69	97.5	89.5	0.94	100.0	97.5
0.20	52.0	23.0	0.45	94.5	70.5	0.70	98.0	90.0	0.95	100.0	98.0
0.21	55.0	24.5	0.46	94.5	72.0	0.71	98.0	90.5	0.96	100.0	98.0
0.22	58.0	26.0	0.47	95.0	73.0	0.72	98.0	91.0	0.97	100.0	98.5
0.23	61.0	28.0	0.48	95.0	74.0	0.73	98.0	91.5	0.98	100.0	98.5
0.24	64.0	30.0	0.49	95.5	75.0	0.74	98.0	92.0	0.99	100.0	99.0
0.25	67.0	32.0	0.50	95.5	76.0	0.75	98.5	92.5	1.00	100.0	99.0

FIGURE 6.28 Relation between various measures of speech intelligibility and AI (lower abscissa) and approximate speech-to-noise (speech-shaped spectrum) ratio (upper abscissa). (After ANSI, 1969a.)

bands found by French and Steinberg (1947) to be equally important to the understanding of speech. Each tone is audited separately by the listener, who adjusts an attenuator controlling the level of the tone until it is just audible. The level of the tone is read from the attenuator, which is calibrated in terms of equivalent, normal speech level, and 12 dB is added to take into account the speech peak factor. This process is repeated for each of the 20 pure tones, and the average of the levels required for the tones to be just audible is proportional to AI.

Licklider *et al.* (1959) developed an electronic device that, when applied to a speech communication system, will automatically provide a number that is proportional to AI. This machine is actually based on a concept somewhat different from that of AI, although it uses the frequency-importance-weighting and the S/N-weighting functions developed for AI.

The Licklider *et al.* device plays a recorded brief (several seconds) sample of speech over the communication system to be evaluated. At any one moment, the output of the speech system being evaluated is simultaneously compared in a narrow frequency band with the recorded speech input. This process is repeated a number of times, each time the locus of the frequency band in which the input and output speech are to be compared is changed. Suitable integrating circuits average the measured correlations between the input and output signals. Robertson and Stuckey (1961) found that this device predicted speech intelligibility test scores quite well for most, but not all, noise interference conditions tested.

Goldberg (1963) described a machine called a "voice-interference analysis set" that attempts to compute the AI for a communication system. This machine applies an amplitude-modulated tone (1000 Hz) to the system under test. The level of the received signal is compared with the noise level found at the receiver of the system under test in 10 bands that are proportional in width to the 20 AI bands. Certain corrections are electronically determined when the noise present would cause a significant upward spread of masking.

Kryter *et al.* (1964) designed a speech communication index meter (SCIM) that is similar to the Goldberg machine in that it attempts to calculate AI from ongoing measures of S/Ns. The SCIM transmits a broadband signal that simulates normal speech with respect to long-term spectrum shape and, to some extent, amplitude variations. The simulated signal-to-actual-noise ratios are found in nine frequency bands and appropriately averaged to arrive at an approximate AI value. This device takes into account the effects on the speech intelligibility of direct masking (including the upward spread), frequency shifting, frequency distortion, and amplitude limiting of the speech signal. The SCIM has recently been modified to reflect the effectiveness of speech communication systems operating with a signal or noise level that varies with time (Hecker *et al.*, 1968).

Steeneken and Houtgast (1980) devised a computer-aided method for determining the correlations between the signal input and output of a transmission system. A speech-frequency spectrum is applied to the input to a transmission system along with a sinusoidal intensity modulation. The products created by the modulation of the signal plus the products from any distortions introduced by noise, nonlinear frequency, amplitude, and temporal characteristics of the transmission system are compared in a number of frequency bands with the input signal.

The presence of distortion products reduces the correlation possible with linear transmission. The frequency bands can be importance-weighted, as for AI. The result, called the *speech transmission index* (STI), was found in pilot experiments to be predictive of degradations in phonetically balanced (PB) word intelligibility scores resulting from several conditions of noise, bandpass limiting, peak clipping, automatic gain control, and reverberation transmission conditions.

As well as quantitatively indicating any noise and frequency distortion present in a speech transmission system, the correlation approaches of Licklider *et al.* and Steeneken and Houtgast also reflect the presence of distortions in the amplitude and temporal domains during the transmission process. The products of these latter distortions, which are usually ignored in the calculation of A1, are essentially treated as "noise" in these extensions of the AI concept.

Hearing Loss and Noise-at-Listener in Application of AI

It is important to note that the AI procedures, and devices for its estimation, described above are typically applied to the input to an electronic microphone, transmission system, and earphone–headphone transducer operating under ideal, or standard acoustic conditions. The presence of noise in the listener's environment reaching the listener's ears, and/or other than normal hearing on the part of the listener, are not necesarily evaluated.

In such cases, the noise, reverberation, and other effects introduced after the output transducer of the transmission system and—if different from normal—the frequency sensitivity characteristic of the listener's ear(s) must be added to the AI, STI, or similar equations to achieve reasonably accurate estimates of speech understanding. In the next chapter, AI is used for the evaluation of speech understanding on the part of people with sensorineural, including noise-induced, hearing loss when listening under real-life speech and noise conditions.

Validations of the AI Procedure

Data collected by French and Steinberg (1947), Miller (1947), and Egan and Wiener (1946) on the masking of speech by noise of various bandwidths and spectra shapes demonstrate the ability of A1 to predict speech intelligibility for a wide variety of communication systems and noise conditions. Figure 6.29 shows some of these findings.

It should be emphasized that the values of the scores obtained on speech intelligibility tests are influenced by the proficiency and training of the talker

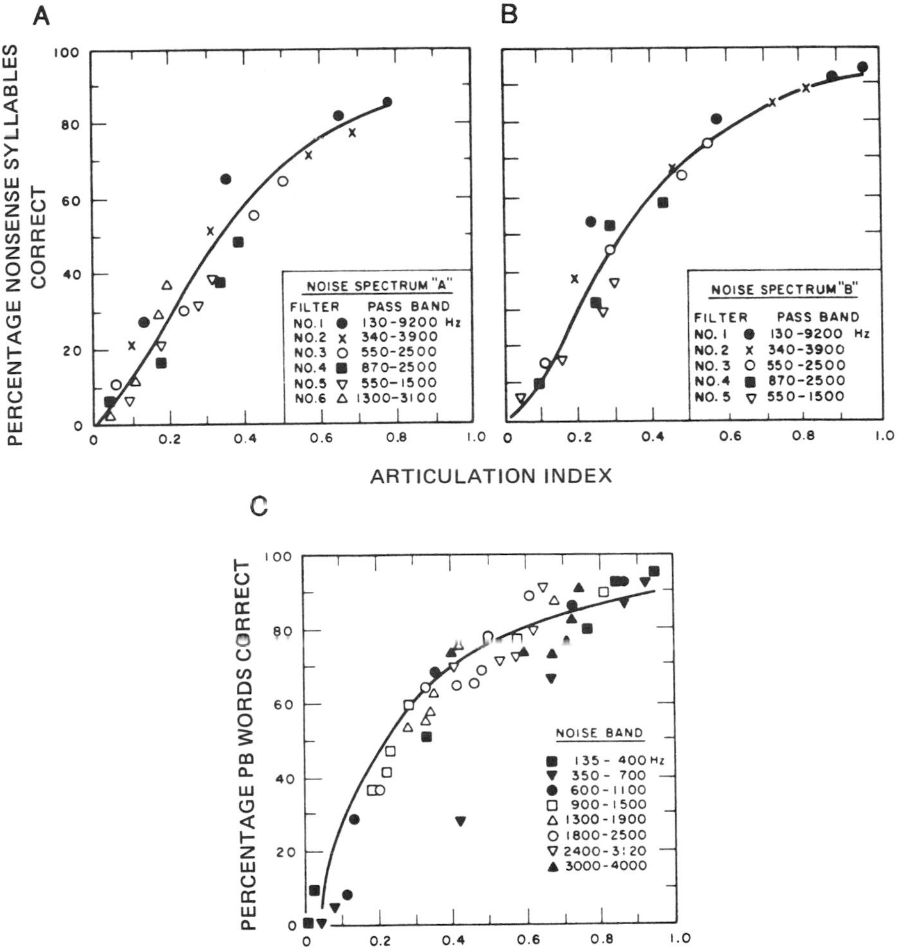

FIGURE 6.29 (A,B) Comparison of obtained and predicted test scores for speech passed through a bandpass filter and heard in the presence of a broadband, negatively sloped spectrum noise set at various intensity levels. (C) Comparison of obtained and predicted test scores for broadband speech in the presence of narrow bands of noise set at various intensity levels. (From Kryter, 1962b. Copyright 1962 by the American Psychological Association. Adapted by permission of the author.)

and listening crew, as well as the difficulty of the speech material being used (see note on Fig. 6.28). Therefore, one cannot expect that a given communication system will provide identical test scores when tested in different laboratories and, particularly, with different groups of listeners and talkers, even though the A1 of the system remains constant. Indeed, the variability in speech intelligibility testing, while not very large when similar test materials and training of the subjects are involved, is recommended with the use of A1 whenever appropriate.

A communications system, that gives satisfactory performance when used with a special vocabulary and trained operators (e.g., air-traffic control by radio) could be judged as completely unacceptable when used by untrained operators or in situations where flexible, nonstandardized speech communication is permitted. Nevertheless, some standards of expected satisfaction with speech communication systems have evolved. Beranek (1947), for example, suggests that a communication system with an AI of <0.3 will usually be found unsatisfactory or only marginally satisfactory; one with an A1 of ≥ 0.3 but ≤ 0.5 will generally be acceptable; one with an A1 of 0.5–0.7 will be good, and a system with an A1 of >0.7 will usually be considered very good to excellent. Richards and Swaffield (1959) proposed, and tested, a method for the assessment of satisfactory usage of telephone communication links.

Relations between AI and Units of Noise Measurement as Means of Rating Speech Communications in Rooms

Beranek (1950) proposed a simplified version of AI to be used in predicting the effectiveness of person-to-person speech communication in the presence of noise. Beranek estimated what the average speech level would be in the octave bands 600–1200, 1200–2400, and 2400–4800 Hz at various distances from a talker using various vocal efforts. Assuming that the noise spectrum was a relatively continuous broadband noise, he estimated what noise levels would be required in these same octave bands to give an A1 of ~0.5. The averages of the decibel levels in the three octave bands from 600 to 4800 Hz were tabulated for this condition, as shown in Table 6.4.

These averages are called *speech-interference levels* (SILs). The SILs listed in Table 6.4, presumably equivalent to an AI of 0.5, should allow sentence intelligibility scores of about 95% correct and PB word scores of about 75% correct (see Fig. 6.28). Various combinations of octave bands other than those between 300 to 4800 Hz have been used to calculate an SIL for different spectra noises (Klumpp and Webster, 1963, 1965; Webster and Klump, 1963).

In addition to SIL, the following methods of noise measurement have been used to estimate the intelligibility of normal speech in the presence of the noise: (1) sound-level meter readings with either *A* or *D* frequency weightings, (2) loudness level in phons and perceived noise level in PN_{dB}, and (3) the noise rating contour (NR, NC, or NCA) procedures. In the NR (noise rating), NC (noise criteria), and NCA (compromise noise criteria) procedures, the octave-band spectrum of a noise is plotted on special graphs (see Fig. 6.30). The highest NC (also called NR) or NCA contour touched

TABLE 6.4 Speech-Interference Levels That Permit Barely Reliable Conversation, or the Correct Hearing of Approximately 75% of PB Words

Distance between talker and listener, ft	Speech interference level, dB — Voice level: Normal	Raised	Very loud	Shouting
0.5	71	77	83	89
1	65	71	77	83
2	59	65	71	77
3	55	61	67	73
4	53	59	65	71
5	51	57	63	69
6	49	55	61	67
12	43	49	55	61

From Beranek (1950).

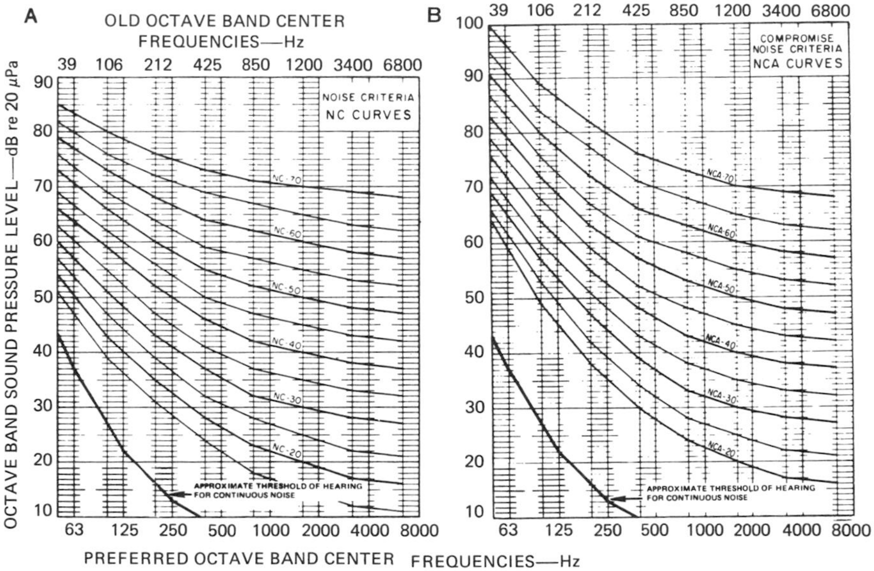

FIGURE 6.30 (A) Noise criteria (NC) curves referred to octave bands of noise. (B) Compromise noise criteria (NCA) curves referred to octave bands of noise. (From Schultz, 1968. Copyright 1968 by the American Psychological Association. Adapted by permission of the author.)

TABLE 6.5 Representative Octave-Band Spectra Used to Evaluate Various Procedures for Estimating Some Effects of Noise on Humans

	SPL, dB, for octave bands, Hz, at								OASPL, dB		
Noise description	53	106	212	425	850	1700	3400	6800	Unweighted	*A*-weighted	*C*-weighted
Thermal noise (−6 dB/octave above 106 Hz)	89	93	87	81	75	69	63	57	95	82	95
Commercial jet landing, 610-ft altitude Kryter and Williams (1966)	81	88	89	91	94	95	92	93	101	100	100
Planer Karplus and Bonvallet (1953)	82	84	85	87	88	88	87	85	95	94	95
Trolley buses Bonvallet (1950)	68	72	74	73	69	64	58	52	79	73	79
Automobiles Bonvallet (1950)	70	73	72	67	62	58	54	50	77	68	77

	SPL, dB, for octave bands, Hz, at								OASPL, dB		
Noise description	63	125	250	500	1000	2000	4000	8000	Unweighted	*A*-weighted	*C*-weighted
Thermal noise, "flat"	60	64	68	69	71	78	75	72	82	82	81
Motor generator Klumpp and Webster (1963)	71	70	71	72	65	71	68	60	79	76	79

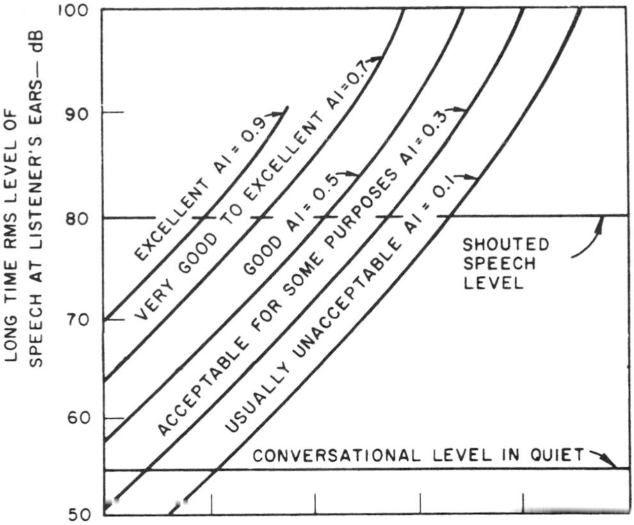

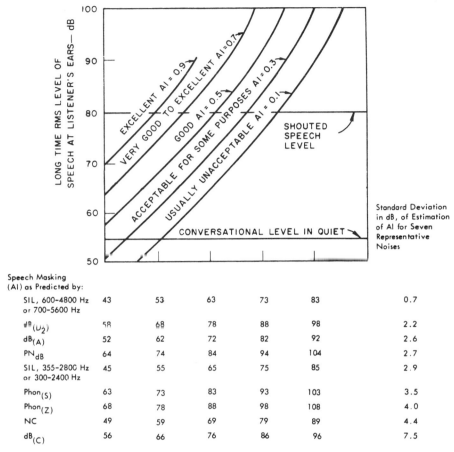

Speech Masking (AI) as Predicted by:						Standard Deviation in dB, of Estimation of AI for Seven Representative Noises
SIL, 600–4800 Hz or 700–5600 Hz	43	53	63	73	83	0.7
$dB_{(D_2)}$	58	68	78	88	98	2.2
$dB_{(A)}$	52	62	72	82	92	2.6
PN_{dB}	64	74	84	94	104	2.7
SIL, 355–2800 Hz or 300–2400 Hz	45	55	65	75	85	2.9
$Phon_{(S)}$	63	73	83	93	103	3.5
$Phon_{(Z)}$	68	78	88	98	108	4.0
NC	49	59	69	79	89	4.4
$dB_{(C)}$	56	66	76	86	96	7.5

NOTE: Percent of word or sentence intelligibility scores for a given noise measurement (SIL, Phons, PN_{dB}, etc.) and speech level approximately correct only when:
(a) Noise has spectrum shaped like the average of the seven spectra given in table
(b) Speech is relatively undistorted

FIGURE 6.31 The average value of each of the noise measures (SIL, dB_{D_2}, dB_A, PN_{dB}, etc.) was calculated when the AI was the same for all seven types of noise listed in Table 6.5. These averages, and their standard deviations, are tabulated on the abscissa. The larger the standard deviations, the greater the disagreement between the unit of noise measurement and AI. These relations are approximately correct for undistorted speech and noise with a speech-shaped spectrum.

by any octave band of the noise that is assigned to that noise. The latter contours have been slightly modified and labeled *preferred noise criteria* (PNC) curves, as discussed by Beranek (1988).

While these various methods, particularly SIL, have been found to be a reasonably accurate method for evaluating speech communication in many noises, unlike AI, they should not be applied to noise spectra that have intense low- or high-frequency components. Other limitations of SIL and these other procedures, compared with AI, are that certain broad assumptions must be made in their use regarding the interactions between room acoustics, vocal effort used by the talker, and level of speech received by the listeners. The applications of NR, NCA, and PNC curves, and other procedures, for the assessment of acoustic conditions for satisfactory speech communications in rooms and halls are discussed by Beranek (1988).

Calculated Comparisons

In an attempt to provide a general estimate of the accuracy with which AI will be estimated by the various measures of noise, seven noise spectra were chosen from the research literature. Five of the spectra represent different, but relatively common, sources of noise, and two of the spectra were tailored from a random-noise generator, as shown in Table 6.5. Figure 6.31 shows how these seven noises are related to A1.

The average deviations of the levels of the seven noises, as measured by each of the units cited when the noises were set to the same AI value, are given in the lower right-hand column of numbers on Fig. 6.31. That column shows that when the AI values of the seven noises were all the same, the standard deviations of the levels of the seven noises were: for SIL 600–4800 Hz, 0.7 dB; dB_D, 2.2 dB; dB_A, 2.6 dB; PN_{dB}, 2.9 dB; and considerably larger, 3.5–7.5 dB, for the other units.

Also indicated on Fig. 6.31 are qualitative statements concerning the acceptability of speech communications systems having certain AIs, when the speech at the listener's ears is of a specified level. The horizontal lines are speech levels 1 m from the talker, or source. The speech levels can be converted to those present at other distances in a room (approximately 15 × 20 ft) by means of Fig. 6.7.

References

Alberti, P. W., Abel, S. M., and Riko, K. (1982). Practical aspects of hearing protector use. *In* "New Perspectives on Noise-Induced Hearing Loss" (R. P. Hamernik, D. Henderson, and R. Salvi, eds.), pp. 461–470. Raven, New York.

ANSI (1969a). S3.5. "American National Standard Methods for the Calculation of the Articulation Index." Am. Natl. Stand. Inst., New York.

ANSI (1969b). S1.8. "American National Standard—Preferred Reference Quantities for Acoustical Levels." Am. Natl. Stand. Inst., New York.

Bell, S. T., Dirks, D. D., and Trine, T. D. (1992). Frequency-importance functions for words in high- and low-context sentences. *J. Speech Hear. Res.* **35,** 1950–1959.

Beranek, L. I. (1947). The design of speech communication systems. *Proc. Inst. Radio Eng.* **35,** 880–890.

Beranck, L. L. (1950). Noise control in office and factory spaces. *Ind. Hyg. Found. Am. Trans. Bull.* **18,** 26–33.

Bernak, L. L. (1954). "Acoustics." McGraw-Hill, New York.

Beranak, L. L. (1988). Criteria for noise and vibration in communities, buildings and vehicles.

In "Noise and Vibration Control" (L. L. Beranek, ed.), Rev. Ed., pp. 554–623. Inst. Noise Control Eng., Washington, D.C.

Black, J. W. (1959). Equally contributing frequency bands in intelligibility testing. *J. Speech Hear. Res.* **3,** 81–83.

Bolt, R. H., and MacDonald, A. D. (1949). Theory of speech masking by reverberation. *J. Acoust. Soc. Am.* **21,** 577–580.

Bonvallet, G. L. (1950). Levels and spectra of transportation vehicle noises. *J. Acoust. Soc. Am.* **22,** 201–205.

Carme, C., and Roure, A. (1993a). A new solution for increasing noise protection. *Noise Public Health Probl., Proc. Int. Congr. 6th,* (M. Vallet, ed.), Vol. 2, pp. 29–32. l'INRETS, 94114 Arcuil Cedex, France.

Carme, C., and Roure, A. (1993b). How to increase a communication intelligibility in a very loud noise. *Noise Public Health Probl., Proc. Int. Congr. 6th* (M. Vallet, ed.), Vol. 2, pp. 149–152. l'INRETS, 94114 Arcuil Cedex, France.

Carter, N. L., and Kryter, K. D. (1962). Masking of pure tones and speech. *J. Aud. Res.* **2,** 66–98.

Cavanaugh, W. J., Farrell, W. R., Hirtle, P. W., and Watters, B. G. (1962). Speech privacy in buildings. *J. Acoust. Soc. Am.* **34,** 475–492.

Collins, G. (1961). "The Design of Frequency Selective Earplugs," Rep. A.R. L./D/R12. Admiralty Res. Lab., Teddington, England.

Dunn, H. K., and White, S. D. (1940). Statistical measurements of conversational speech. *J. Acoust. Soc. Am.* **11,** 278–288.

Edwards, R. G., Hauser, W. P., Moiseev, N. A., Broderson, A. B., and Green, W. W. (1978). Effectiveness of earplugs as worn in the workplace. *Sound Vib.* **12,** 12–18, 20, 22.

Egan, J. P., and Wiener, F. M. (1946). On the intelligibility of bands of speech in noise. *J. Acoust. Soc. Am.* **18,** 435–441.

Eghtesadi, K. (1993). Active control of low frequency noise. *Noise Public Health Probl., Proc. Int. Congr. 6th* (M. Vallet, ed.), Vol. 2, pp. 447–450. l'INRETS, 94114 Arcuil Cedex, France.

French, N. R., and Steinberg, J. C. (1947). Factors governing the intelligibility of speech sounds. *J. Acoust. Soc. Am.* **19,** 901–919.

Frick, F. C., and Sumby, W. H. (1952). Control tower language. *J. Acoust. Soc. Am.* **24,** 595–596.

Gardner, M. B. (1964). Effect of noise on listening levels in conference telephony. *J. Acoust. Soc. Am.* **36,** 2354–2362.

Goldberg, J. M. (1963). The voice interference analysis set, an instrument for determining the degradation of signal quality of a voice communication channel. *J. Audio Eng. Soc.* **11,** 115–120.

Golikov, E. E. (1961). Calculating the articulation in noisy rooms. *Sov. Phys. Acoust.* **6,** 407–408.

Hawley, M. E., and Kryter, K. D. (1957). Effects of noise on speech. *In* "Handbook of Noise Control" (C. M. Harris, ed.), pp. 9.1–9.26. McGraw-Hill, New York.

Hecker, M. H. L., Von Bismarck, G., and Williams, C. E. (1968). Automatic evaluation of time-varying communication systems. *IEEE Trans. Audio Electroacoust.* **AU-16,** 10.

Howell, K., and Martin, A. M. (1975). An investigation of the effects of hearing protectors on vocal communication in noise. *J. Sound Vib.* **41,** 181–196.

Janssen, J. H. (1957). A method for the calculation of the speech intelligibility under conditions of reverberation and noise. *Acustica* **7,** 305–310.

Jeffress, L. A. (1965). "Masking and Binaural Phenomena," Rep. DRL-A-245 (Contract Nos.: NObsr-72627; NE 051247-6; NE 051456-4; Nonr-3579(04); NR 142-190; Fund Transfer R-129. Def. Res. Lab., Univ. of Texas (June 14, 1965). (Avail. as NASA CR-64362.)

Karplus, H. B., and Bonvallet, G. L. (1953). A noise survey of manufacturing industries. *Am. Hyg. Assoc. Q.* **14,** 235–263.

Klumpp, R. G., and Webster, J. C. (1963). Physical measurements of equally speech-interfering navy noises. *J. Acoust. Soc. Am.* **35,** 1328–1338.

Klumpp, R. G., and Webster, J. C. (1965). "Speech Interference Aspects of Navy Noises," Rep. NEL-1314. U.S. Navy (Sept. 1965). (Avail. from DTIC as AD 625 262.)

Korn, T. S. (1954). Effect of psychological feedback on conversational noise reduction in rooms. *J. Acoust. Soc. Am.* **26,** 793–794.

Kryter, K. D. (1946). Effects of ear protective devices on the intelligibility of speech in noise. *J. Acoust. Soc. Am.* **18,** 413–417.

Kryter, K. D. (1962a). Methods for the calculation and use of the articulation index. *J. Acoust. Soc. Am.* **34,** 1689–1697.

Kryter, K. D. (1962b). Validation of the articulation index. *J. Acoust. Soc. Am.* **34,** 1698–1702.

Kryter, K. D., and Williams, C. E. (1966). Masking of speech by aircraft noise. *J. Acoust. Soc. Am.* **39,** 138–150.

Kryter, K. D., Licklider, J. C. R., and Stevens, S. S. (1947). Premodulation clipping in AM voice communication. *J. Acoust. Soc. Am.* **19,** 125–131.

Kryter, K. D., Williams, C., and Green, D. M. (1962). Auditory acuity and the perception of speech. *J. Acoust. Soc. Am.* **34,** 1217–1223.

Kryter, K. D., Ball, J. H., and Stuntz, S. E. (1964). SCIM—A meter for measuring the performance of speech communication systems. *IEEE Trans. Can. Symp. Commun. 3rd, Montreal*

Levitt, H., and Rabiner, L. R. (1967). Predicting binaural gain in intelligibility and release from masking for speech. *J. Acoust. Soc. Am.* **42,** 820–829.

Licklider, J. C. R. (1946). Effects of amplitude distortion upon the intelligibility of speech. *J. Acoust. Soc. Am.* **18,** 429–434.

Licklider, J. C. R. (1948). The influence of interaural phase relations upon the masking of speech by white noise. *J. Acoust. Soc. Am.* **20,** 150–159.

Licklider, J. C. R., and Guttman, N. (1957). Masking of speech by line-spectrum interference. *J. Acoust. Soc. Am.* **29,** 287–296.

Licklider, J. C. R., Bisberg, A., and Schwartzlander, H. (1959). An electronic device to measure the intelligibility of speech. *Proc. Natl. Electron. Conf.* **15,** 1–6.

McKinley, R. L., and Nixon, C. W. (1993). Active noise reduction headsets. *Noise Public Health Prob., Proc. Int. Congr. 6th* (M. Vallet, ed.), Vol. 2, pp. 83–91. l'INRETS, 94114 Arcuil Cedex, France.

Miller, G. A. (1947). The masking of speech. *Psychol. Bull.* **44,** 105–129.

Miller, G. A., and Licklider, J. C. R. (1950). The intelligibility of interrupted speech. *J. Acoust. Soc. Am.* **22,** 167–173.

Miller, G. A., Heise, G. A., and Lichten, W. (1951). The intelligibility of speech as a function of the context of the test materials. *Exp. Psychol.* **41,** 329–335.

Moser, H. H. (1961). "Research Investigations on Voice-Communication in Noise," Rep. CSD-TDR-62-5 (Contract AF 19(604)-6179). Ohio State Univ. Res. Found. (Avail. from DTIC as AD 279 870).

Moser, H. H., Dreher, J. J., O'Neill, J. J., and Oyer, H. J. (1956). "Comparison of Mouth, Ear, and Contact Microphones," Tech. Rep. No. 37, AFCRC TN-56-68. U.S. Air Force. (Rev. 1958).

Olson, H. F., and May, E. G. (1953). Electronic sound absorber. *J. Acoust. Soc. Am.* **25,** 1130–1136.

Pavlovic, C. V., and Studebaker, G. A. (1984). An evaluation of some assumptions underlying the articulation index. *J. Acoust. Soc. Am.* **75,** 1606–1612.

Pearsons, K. S., Bennett, R. L., and Fidell, S. (1977). "Speech Levels in Various Noise Environments," Rep. EPA-600/1-77-025. U.S. Environ. Prot. Agency, Washington, D.C. (Avail. from NTIS as PB 270 053.)

Pickett, J. M. (1958). Limits of direct speech communication in noise. *J. Acoust. Soc. Am.* **30,** 278–281.

Pickett, J. M., and Pollack, I. (1958). Prediction of speech intelligibility at high noise levels. *J. Acoust. Soc. Am.* **30,** 955–963.

Pollack, I. (1957). Speech communications at high noise level: The roles of a noise-operated automatic gain control system and hearing protection. *J. Acoust. Soc. Am.* **29,** 1324–1327.

Pollack, I. (1958a). Message procedures for unfavorable communication conditions. *J. Acoust. Soc. Am.* **30,** 196–201.

Pollack, I. (1958b). Speech intelligibility at high noise levels: Effect of short term exposure. *J. Acoust. Soc. Am.* **30,** 282–285.

Pollack, I., and Pickett, J. M. (1958). Stereophonic listening and speech intelligibility against voice babble. *J. Acoust. Soc. Am.* **30,** 131–133.

Richards, D. L. (1956). A development of the Collard principle of articulation calculation. *Proc. Inst. Electr. Eng.* **103,** 679–691.

Richards, D. L., and Swaffield, J. (1959). Assessment of speech communication links. *Proc. Inst. Electr. Eng.* **106B,** 77–89, 90–92.

Rink, T. L. (1979). Hearing protection and speech discrimination in hearing-impaired persons. *Sound Vib.* **13,** 22–25.

Robertson, D. W., and Stuckey, C. W. (1961). "Investigation and Evaluation of the Gel Speech System Test Set," Rep. RADC TR 61-88. Rome Air Dev. Center, New York.

Rozhanskaya, E. V. (1953). On the question of the mathematical foundation of the theory of intelligibility. *Akad. Nauk SSSR Kom. Akust. Tr.* **7,** 53–60. (Avail. from NTIS as Transl. 62-11581.)

Rupf, J. A. (1977). Noise effects on passenger communication in light aircraft. *SAE* Prepr. No. 770446.

Schultz, T. J. (1968). Noise-criterion curves for use with the USASI preferred frequencies. *J. Acoust. Soc. Am.* **43,** 637–638.

Steeneken, H. J. M., and Houtgast, T. (1980). A physical method for measuring speech-transmission quality. *J. Acoust. Soc. Am.* **67,** 318–326.

Smoorenburg, G. F. (1982). Damage risk criteria for impulse noise. *In* "New Perspectives on Noise-Induced Hearing Loss" (R. P. Hamernik, D. Henderson, and R. Salvi, eds.), pp. 471–490. Raven, New York.

Studebaker, G. A., and Sherbecoe, R. L. (1991). Frequency-importance and transfer functions for recorder CID W-22 word lists. *J. Speech Hear. Res.* **34,** 427–438.

Studebaker, G. A., Pavlovic, C. V., and Sherbecoe, R. L. (1987). A frequency importance function for continuous discourse. *J. Acoust. Soc. Am.* **81,** 1130–1138.

von Gierke, H. E. (1956). Personal protection. *Noise Control* **2**(1), 37–44. Impairment—Problems of Prevention, Diagnosis and Certification Criteria," Rep. TT 7654047. Natl. Libr. Med., U.S. Dep. Health, Educ., Welfare. (Avail. from NTIS.)

von Tarnóczy, T. (1971). Das Durchschnittliche Energie-Specktrum der Sprache (fur Sechs Sprachen). *Acustica* **24,** 57–74.

Thwing, E. (1956). Effect of repetition on articulation scores for PB words. *J. Acoust. Soc. Am.* **28,** 302–303.

Tkachenko, A. D. (1955). Tonal method for determining the intelligibility of speech transmitted by communication channels. *Sov. Phys.—Acoust.* **1**(1/2), 182–191.

Tohyama, M. (1993). Modern techniques for improving speech intelligibility in noisy environments. *In Noise Public Health Probl. Proc. 6th Int. Cong.* (M. Vallet, ed.), Vol. 2, pp. 238–246. l'INTRETS, 94114 Arcuit Cedex, France.

Webster, J. C., and Klumpp, R. G. (1962). Effects of ambient noise and nearby talkers on a face-to-face communication task. *J. Acoust. Soc. Am.* **34,** 936–941.

Webster, J. C., and Klumpp, R. G. (1963). Articulation index and average curve fitting methods of predicting speech interference. *J. Acoust. Soc. Am.* **35,** 1339–1344.

Weston, P. B., Miller, J. D., and Hirsh, I. J. (1965). Release from masking for speech. *J. Acoust. Soc. Am.* **38,** 1053–1054.

Zwislocki, J. (1957). Ear protectors. *In* "Handbook of Noise Control" (C. M. Harris, ed.), pp. 8.1–8.27. McGraw-Hill, New York.

Zwislocki, J. (1961). Acoustic filters as ear defenders. *J. Acoust. Soc. Am.* **23,** 36–40.

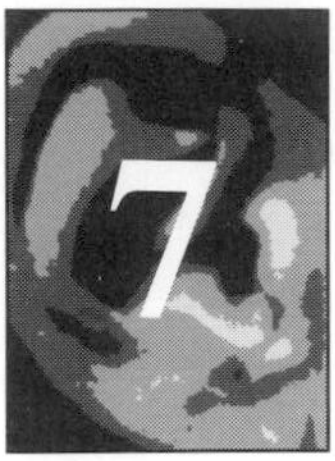

The Assessment of Hearing Handicap and Damage Risk from Noise

INTRODUCTION

People working in intense noise are often unaware of the fact that they are losing some of their hearing because of the noise. This lack of awareness occurs partly because the daily losses during the first years of exposure may last only a few hours, and partly because when working in the noise they do not have any hearing handicap due to any loss that may have incurred from the noise. Even if they have such a loss, their hearing in the noise is as good as that of people with normal hearing.

This happens because the threshold shift, or loss, induced by the noise, whether temporary or permanent, will not prevent the hearing of auditory signals to as large an extent as will the masking afforded by that noise. However, in less noisy situations, the noise-induced loss can become a handicap to hearing not experienced by the person with normal ears.

The adverse effects of noise-induced hearing loss on many daily living activities has made it an industrial and public health problem. Laws requiring the payment of compensation by industry to workers suffering workplace-noise-induced hearing loss is one means of effecting some control of the noise at the workplace. Worker compensation, at least in the United States, is mandated by certain statutes that are based on the principle that some compensation is justified for workplace-noise-induced hearing loss that constitutes a handicap to the hearing of speech outside the workplace. A workplace-noise-induced hearing loss that prevents job performance and continued employment at full wages is considered, for compensation purposes, a separate matter, one unrelated to the present discussion. Reviews of the history and legal aspects of compensation for workplace-noise-induced hearing loss are to be found in Noble (1978) and in Cudworth (1991).

The amounts of compensation to be paid for a general, off-the-job, hearing handicap are a matter of state and federal codes and vary widely. As of 1979, the maximum benefit for total loss in both ears ranged from $8000 in one state, to $135,000 for certain federal jobs (Ginnold, 1979). The average maximum for the 50 states was $21,700 for a total loss in both ears, and the average of all awards, including those for total loss, was around $2250. It was then estimated that state and federal awards together would reach a total of about $156 million annually by the year 1987.

Handicap for speech communication is estimated from medical–legal procedures that are based on clinical tests of pure-tone hearing levels. Recommendations made by medical organizations regarding compensability for noise-induced hearing loss also serve as the basis for the specification of the maximum levels of noise exposure that will cause no more than a specified amount of hearing loss during a work career. Such specifications serve as a basis of government regulations that can require costly noise-control engineering and monitoring procedures in industry, the military services and, to some extent, public situations.

Definitions of what constitutes a hearing handicap for speech understanding, and how to measure it by simple medical procedures, clearly have important economic and social implications. Although these questions have received significant medical and acoustical research over the years, some key issues are matters of continuing controversy and research.

DEFINITIONS OF HEARING HANDICAP, IMPAIRMENT, AND DISABILITY

Hearing Handicap, Impairment, and Disability as Defined by the World Health Organization (WHO)

Handicap is defined by WHO (1980) as "The disadvantage for an individual resulting from an impairment, or a disability, that limits or prevents the fulfillment of a role that is normal (depending on sex, age, and social and cultural factors) for that individual." Stephens and Hetu (1991) note that *handicap,* in the WHO definition, refers to the nonauditory aspects of an individual's life (examples given are "social withdrawal, loss of promotion, marital disharmony"). They argue that such nonauditory behavioral handicaps may flow from "disabilities" a person may have in "localizing sounds, hearing in noisy places," which are, in turn, due to impairments to hearing measurable by pure-tone or speech audiometry. In any event, evaluation of procedures for assessing handicap by observations of nonauditory behavior that may result from impaired hearing falls beyond the scope of this book.

In the United States, these terms are used somewhat differently. In medical–legal context the word *disability* refers, as previously mentioned, to a permanent loss in an ability, because of a (hearing) deficiency, to remain employed at full wages (AMA, 1961). As will be fully discussed below, hearing *impairment* refers to a loss, relative to normal, in hearing sensitivity for pure tones; and hearing *handicap* refers to a loss, relative to normal, in ability to correctly hear everyday speech.

Hearing Impairment and Handicap as Defined by AAOO and AAO

Physiologic impairment is usually defined as a lessening in the ability of a bodily organ or structure to perform with normal, full capacity. Thus, if because of some injury, a limb can be rotated less than its normal arc, or the size of the visual field is less than normal, impairments are said to have occurred. The sense of hearing, however, has not been treated in an entirely similar fashion in guides issued by committees of Academies of the American Medical Association (AMA, 1961).

AAOO 1959 and 1965 Guides

In 1959 the American Academy of Ophthalmology and Otolaryngology (AAOO) published a Guide for the Evaluation of Hearing Impairment (AAOO, 1959). To quote therefrom: "(H)earing impairment should be evaluated in terms of ability to hear everyday speech under everyday conditions. . . . The ability to hear sentences and repeat them correctly in a quiet environment is taken as satisfactory evidence of correct hearing for everyday speech." For estimating the ability to hear speech, "the Subcommittee recommends the simple *average* of the hearing levels at the three frequencies 500, 1000, and 2000 cps (Hz). . . . If the average hearing level at 500, 1000, and 2000 cps is $\leq$15 dB [ASA (ASA, 1951)], usually no impairment exists in the ability to hear everyday speech under everyday conditions . . . however, if the average hearing level at 500, 1000, and 2000 cps is >82 dB, the impairment for hearing everyday speech should be considered total. The "15 dB" and "82 dB" specifications became to be called, respectively, the lower and upper "fences" for impairment to speech reception.

According to this guide, with each decibel, up to 67, the hearing level of the better ear exceeds the fence level is to be multiplied by 5, and added to the number of decibels, up to 67, the poorer ear exceeds the fence level, and the result divided by 6. That sum multiplied by 1.5 represents the binaural percentage evaluation of hearing impairment for everyday speech under everyday conditions.

In 1965, the AAOO published a Guide on the Classification and Evaluation of Hearing Handicap (AAOO, 1965). This Guide discusses, among other ideas (1) the need to express hearing levels relative to the ISO Standard 389 (ISO, 1964) rather than the ASA Z-24.5 Standard (ASA, 1951) (this has the effect of raising, for cases of typical sensorineural hearing loss, the lower fence from 15 to 25 dB, and the upper, from 82 to 92 dB); and (2) the dropping of the word *impairment* in favor of *handicap* when referring to one's personal hearing deficiency. To quote, p. 743: "*Handicap:* the disadvantage imposed by an impairment sufficient to affect one's personal efficiency in the activities of daily living." The guideline also notes that the matter of hearing loss sufficient to prevent work and loss of wages is classified as a *disability,* and is covered by laws other than the worker's compensation statutes for loss in everyday hearing ability, as mentioned earlier. A formula (5 × best ear + worse ear)/6, used for the evaluation of binaural hearing was not changed in the 1965 AAOO guide from the 1959 guide.

The AAOO 1965 guideline is not completely explicit, however, in its definition of *handicap*. Specifically, the statement that a handicap is present only after hearing impairment is sufficient to affect "one's personal efficiency in the activities of daily living" could be interpreted as meaning that this category of handicap should also include some nonauditory behavior, as in the WHO definition. This is ostensibly not the case in that the title of the document is "Guide for the Evaluation of Hearing Handicap," and the only handicapped behavior described in the guideline is the ability to understand sentences under everyday conditions.

This guideline could be made explicit in this regard by adding two phrases, underlined in the following, to the definition for handicap: "*Handicap:* the disadvantage imposed by *losses in pure tone thresholds of sensitivity* sufficient to affect one's personal efficiency in the activities of daily living *involving the hearing of speech.*" In any event, the terminology as defined in the AAO 1979 guide will be followed in the following text.

The adequacy, from a medical measurement point of view, of the 1959 and 1965 guides was discussed by Kryter (1973a,b), with commentary by Cohen (1973), Davis (1973), Lempert (1973), and Ward (1973). For example, the question was raised as to why the noise-deafened individual should not be considered to some degree handicapped when losing some of the ability the normal person has to hear (1) weaker-than-normal sounds of any kind and frequency content—warning signals, tones, music etc.; (2) to understand individual words or phrases when not in sentence form, the unfamiliar name or telephone number; (3) speech at less than normal conversational level 1 meter from a talker; or (4) speech in the presence of everyday noise, or at a meeting when several people are talking.

AAO 1979 Guide

Following a review of related research, the American Academy of Otolaryngology (AAO) published in 1979 a revised guide for the Evaluation of Hearing Handicap. That guide recommended that, p. 2058: "(T)he hearing threshold level at 3,000 Hz should be included (with those at 500, 1000 and 2000 Hz) in the calculation of hearing handicap to provide a more accurate assessment hearing handicap in a greater variety of everyday listening conditions." The 1959 and 1964 AAOO guides served, and for the present time the 1979 AAO guide serves, as a commonly used method and criterion for the evaluation of hearing loss for purposes of worker compensation (AAOO, 1959, 1964; AAO, 1979). These guides are not addressed specifically to the matter of hearing loss due to any particular cause, nor to the noise exposures that may cause hearing loss.

NIOSH-OSHA Definition of "Material Impairment to Hearing"

The National Institute for Occupational Safety and Health (NIOSH), and Occupational Safety and Health Administration (OSHA), U.S. Department of Labor prepared a detailed review of then existing relevant research data and concepts (NIOSH, 1972). That review served as a basis for subsequent OSHA (1981, 1983) regulations specifying allowable noise exposure levels and related hearing conservation programs for industry. In its 1981 regulations, OSHA specifies 25 dB, average hearing levels at 1000, 2000, and 3000 Hz, as the lower fence for material impairment to "people's ability to understand speech as it is spoken in everyday social conditions" (OSHA, p. 4082, 1981).

As will be shown later, the OSHA lower fence can be expected to usually allow for 1–5 dB, depending on years of exposure, less noise exposure before that fence is reached, than will the AAO 1979 fence (25 dB average of hearing levels at 500, 1000, 2000, and 3000 Hz). Later in this chapter, the fences proposed in the AAOO and AAO guides and OSHA regulations for hearing handicap, or material impairment, for everyday speech will be compared with, and their validity somewhat challenged, by recent research data related to this matter.

PURE-TONE HEARING LEVELS AND SPEECH AUDIOMETRY

One major research question related to the procedures of the AAOO and AAO guides has been that of determining which pure-tone hearing levels, and how few, are needed to achieve good predictions of tests of speech reception and understanding. In the 1979 guideline, the AAO committee cited three studies (Carhart, 1946; Harris *et al.*, 1956; Quiggle *et al.*, 1957) as the justification for their recommending the average of hearing levels at

500, 1000, and 2000 Hz to estimate the ability to understand sentences in the quiet.

In their studies, Carhart and Quiggle *et al.* used speech reception threshold (SRT) tests that consisted of individually presented *spondee* words (words of two syllables with each syllable equally accented, e.g., "baseball", "cupcake", doormat"). In the Harris *et al.* study, SRT tests were used that consisted of simple monosyllabic words. The words were presented in the quiet at increasing levels of intensity above being inaudible until the listener could understand about 50% of the words, at which point testing for that individual was usually terminated.

The ability of an individual to understand speech is measured, by SRT test procedures, as the intensity level of speech that is required for that person to correctly understand about 50% of the words in a list. The lower the required speech level, the better the listener's hearing sensitivity is taken to be. However, with the SRT test procedure, the intensity of the speech required to reach that level of performance may be greater than the level of everyday speech; accordingly, no explicit evaluation is made by SRT procedures of the ability of a person to understand speech at "everyday" intensity, or, for that matter, speech at any other specific level of intensity. Another limitation of the SRT procedure is that the 50% words-correct score on the SRT does not necessarily assess the ability of a person with sensorineural hearing loss to understand the more difficult words, or certain sounds of speech.

Some of the persons with sensorineural hearing losses who are able to correctly hear 50% of the words, are unable to understand the other 50%, no matter how intense the words are made to be. However, this is not the case for persons with equal threshold shift due to conductive loss, as is shown in Fig. 7.1. In brief, a similar SRT speech level for subjects with different types of hearing loss does not indicate equal abilities to understand all the speech materials in the test.

As noted above, AAO, in 1979, recommended the addition of the hearing level at 3000 Hz to their formula. This was done on the basis of a conclusion that "quiet", the test condition for speech testing prescribed in the 1959 and 1965 guides, did not fairly represent everyday listening conditions. The following research studies were cited as the basis for this change: Aniansson (1974); Harris (1960, 1965); Harris et al. (1960); Kryter *et al.* (1962); Suter (1978).

Aniansson, Kryter *et al.,* Suter and, also, Kuzniarz (1973), conducted studies of the ability of people with normal hearing, and with different degrees of sensorineural hearing loss, to understand sentence and word tests in the quiet and in the presence of noise. Unlike in the studies conducted with the SRT tests, the actual percentages of words that were correctly heard, when presented singly or in sentences, by the subjects for given speech levels and noise-listening conditions were found.

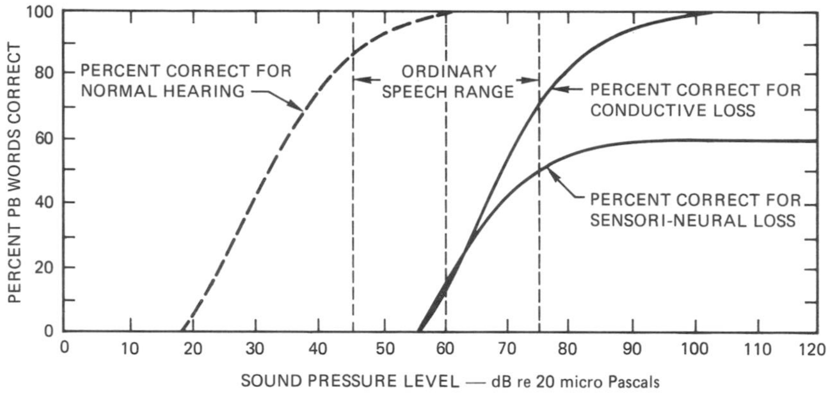

FIGURE 7.1 Speech intelligibility curves (percent PB words correct) at two different levels of amplified speech for normal hearing and for two types of impaired hearing. (After Davis, 1948).

Suter administered via loudspeaker, both sentence and word tests at a level of 60 dB_A at the listener's ear (a level found for speech 1 m from a talker using a slightly raised voice level, and 3 m from a TV set; see Figs. 6.4 and 6.5). The worse ear, according to average pure-tone thresholds, of each listener was blocked by an earplug and one earmuff during the listening tests. Tests were conducted in the quiet and in the presence of background noise (a recording of a babble of 12 voices) at levels, for different test sequences, of 60, 63, and 66 dB_A. The subjects were divided into three groups according to their pure-tone audiograms (see list on lower left in Fig. 7.2D). Group I had essentially normal hearing at all test frequencies. Group II had HLs of $\leq$20 dB up to 2000 Hz, and group III had near normal HLs up to only 1000 Hz.

It is seen in Fig. 7.2D that when the three groups were listening to the speech in the quiet, the mean percent correct responses on the speech tests ranged from 85% correct for group III to 96% correct for group I, the group with essentially no hearing loss at any frequency. However, it is seen that when the speech was heard in the presence of background noise, its understandability rapidly decreases for all groups, falling to near 60% wrong for group I to near 20% wrong for group III. These results are similar to those found in comparable experiments conducted by the other investigators, as shown in Fig. 7.2 (A–D).

FIGURE 7.2 Speech intelligibility (PB words, and words in sentences correct) of persons with normal hearing and sensorineural hearing loss. Investigators indicated on graphs A, B, C, and D.

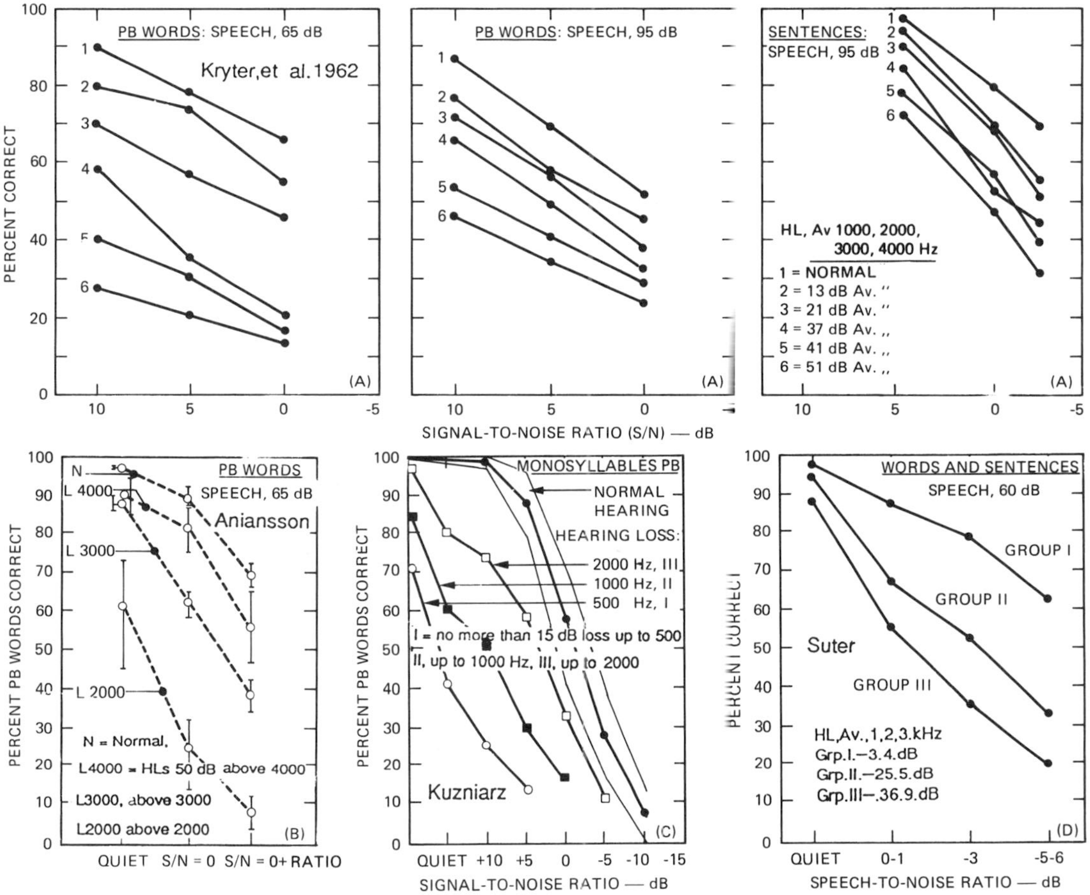
PB WORDS: SPEECH, 65 dB
Kryter,et al.1962
PERCENT CORRECT
(A)
PB WORDS: SPEECH, 95 dB
(A)
SENTENCES:
SPEECH, 95 dB
HL, Av 1000, 2000, 3000, 4000 Hz
1 = NORMAL
2 = 13 dB Av. ''
3 = 21 dB Av. ''
4 = 37 dB Av. ,,
5 = 41 dB Av. ,,
6 = 51 dB Av. ,,
(A)
SIGNAL-TO-NOISE RATIO (S/N) — dB
PB WORDS
SPEECH, 65 dB
Aniansson
N
L 4000
L 3000
L 2000
N = Normal,
L4000 = HLs 50 dB above 4000
L3000, above 3000
L2000 above 2000
(B)
PERCENT PB WORDS CORRECT
QUIET S/N = 0 S/N = 0+ RATIO
MONOSYLLABLES PB
NORMAL HEARING
HEARING LOSS:
2000 Hz, III
1000 Hz, II
500 Hz, I
I = no more than 15 dB loss up to 500
II, up to 1000 Hz, III, up to 2000
Kuzniarz
(C)
PERCENT PB WORDS CORRECT
QUIET +10 +5 0 -5 -10 -15
SIGNAL-TO-NOISE RATIO — dB
WORDS AND SENTENCES
SPEECH, 60 dB
GROUP I
GROUP II
GROUP III
Suter
HL,Av.,1,2,3.kHz
Grp.I.–3.4.dB
Grp.II.–25.5.dB
Grp.III–.36.9.dB
(D)
PERCENT CORRECT
QUIET 0-1 -3 -5-6
SPEECH-TO-NOISE RATIO — dB

Correlations between Pure Tone HLs and Speech Test Scores

Suter calculated the correlations between the speech discrimination scores obtained by groups II and III combined (the groups with sensorineural hearing losses) and their hearing levels averaged for different combinations of test frequencies. The results are shown in Table 7.1, where it is seen that for all listening conditions the average of HLs at 500, 1000, and 2000 Hz has a significantly lower coefficient of correlation than the average HL of any of the other combinations, 0.54, for the average of all conditions, as compared to correlations of .77–.87. Further, it is seen that the AAO 1979 formula, which includes 500 and 3000 Hz, predicts speech discrimination scores slightly less well than do the average of combinations that exclude HL at 500 Hz, but include HLs at 3000 Hz ($r = .80$) or 4000 Hz ($r = .87$).

Kryter *et al.* (1962) found (see Table 7.2) that excluding hearing levels for 500 Hz did not appreciably reduce the magnitude of the multiple correlation of averaged speech intelligibility scores and the averages of hearing levels for the other test frequencies. Of the various combinations examined, the average hearing levels for 1000, 2000, 3000, and 4000 Hz provided, with the fewest number of test frequencies, the highest multiple coefficient of correlation. The tests included frequency filtered and unfiltered speech heard under a variety of noise conditions. The speech was at either 95-dB earphone level (comparable to a 85-dB field level) or 65 dB earphone level (comparable to a 55-dB field level) of intensity.

Acton (1970), on the other hand, found that frequencies above 2000 Hz had no predictive value for speech understanding in a background noise, the spectrum of which peaked at 250 Hz and fell off at the rate of 5 dB per octave to 1000 Hz, and 10 dB per octave above 1000 Hz. However, in terms of speech masking, this listening condition was essentially like the quiet. Because the speech spectrum peaks at about 400 Hz, and declines per octave at about one-half the rates specified for the noise in the Acton study, such

TABLE 7.1 Correlations r between Average of Sentence and Rhyme Test Scores, and Averages of Hearing Levels for Groups Audiometric Test Frequencies

Speech 60 dB_A Test frequency group, Hz	Quiet	Noise 60 dB_A	63 dB_A	66 dB_A	Average scores, all conditions
500, 1000, 2000	.53	.48	.55	.51	.54
500, 1000, 2000, 3000	.62	.74	.77	.75	.77
1000, 2000, 3000	.64	.77	.79	.76	.80
1000, 2000, 4000	.76	.81	.85	.82	.87
2000, 3000, 4000	.65	.83	.85	.84	.86
3000, 4000, 6000	.56	.79	.81	.82	.82

From Suter (1978).

TABLE 7.2 Beta Weights for Hearing Levels at Individual Frequencies and Multiple Correlations *R*, between Average Sentence and Word Test Scores: Audiometric Test Frequencies in Various Groups

Test frequency group, Hz	Beta weight		Hz	Beta weight	
1000	.06		2000	.48	
2000	.41		3000	.26	
3000	.41	R = .806	4000	.17	*R* = .810
1000	.5		500	−.05	
2000	.44		1000	.09	
3000	.27		2000	.44	
4000	.15	R = .813	3000	.27	
			4000	.15	
			6000	.02	*R* = .813

From Kryter *et al.* (1962).

a noise did not provide the interference with speech energy that is common for most everyday noises, such as speech-babble.

Young and Gibbons (1962) administered both SRT and word intelligibility tests to persons with various degrees of hearing loss. Correlations, shown in Tables 7.3–7.4, reveal that hearing level at 500 Hz is more significantly related to the speech reception thresholds than is hearing level at 4000 Hz (correlation coefficients of .90 vs. .38). Furthermore, hearing level at 4000 Hz is more highly correlated with the speech intelligibility test scores than is hearing level at 500 Hz (r = .45 vs. .36).

Harris (1960, 1965) and Harris *et al.* (1960) conducted studies of the ability of subjects with varying degrees of hearing loss at high frequencies to understand sentences that had been uttered at a rate faster than normal, and/or electronically processed, to be somewhat distorted. Table 7.4 shows that the correlations between speech understanding and the audiometric test frequency of 500 Hz are the least (r .03–.14 for the different conditions) for any of the test frequencies, and that the magnitudes of the correlation coefficients with 4000 Hz (r = .18–.57) were nearly equal to those with 3000 Hz (r = .18–.63). In brief, these data indicate that hearing level for 500 Hz is minimally related to the understanding of distorted speech, but

TABLE 7.3 Correlations r between Hearing Levels at Individual Test Frequencies, 1000 PB Words Correct, and SRT Level Score

	Test Frequency, Hz				
	500	1000	2000	4000	SRT
Percent PB words correct	.36	.48	.65	.45	.52
SRT	.90	.92	.66	.38	

From Young and Gibbons (1962).

TABLE 7.4 Correlations *r* between Hearing Levels at Test Frequencies and Sentence Test Scores of Distorted Speech

	Test frequency, Hz					
Type of distortion	500	1000	1500	2000	3000	4000
Speeded maximally	.10	.26	.44	.05	.04	.27
Denasal-speeded	.11	.16	.16	.02	.18	.18
Interrupted 8 s	.14	.17	.28	.33	.34	.32
Reveberation	.03	.05	.01	.22	.63	.57
0% distortion	.19	.32	.52	.34	.09	.10
50% distortion	.19	.31	.05	.48	.38	.36
100% distortion	.16	.24	.39	.50	.53	.49

From Harris (1965).

that hearing level at 4000 Hz is significantly related to the understanding of distorted speech.

Smoorenburg (1992) found tone thresholds and speech levels at 50% speech intelligibility (SRT) for sentences heard in quiet and noise. Two hundred subjects (400 ears) were tested. The tests were administered monaurally via earphone. These SRTs were for a sentence test, developed by Plomp and Mimpen (1979), rather than the spondee and monosyllabic words used in the SRT tests discussed earlier. (In the Plomp and Mimpen test procedure, a set of 13, eight- to nine-syllable sentences is presented to a listener. The first sentence is presented in increasing, 2-dB steps, until the listener can reproduce the sentence without error; the second sentence is presented at that level, and if entirely correct, the level is decreased by 2 dB, and the third sentence presented; if not, the level is increased by 2 dB, etc. for all 13 sentences. The average adjusted level after sentences 4 through 13 is the SRT, and represent the intensity level of the speech at which 50% of the sentences were heard correctly.)

The coefficients of correlation between various combinations of tone hearing levels and SRT speech intensity levels in the quiet, and in a number of different levels of background noise (speech-spectrum-shaped), are shown graphically in Fig. 7.3. Table 7.5 shows magnitude and rank order, from highest to lowest, of the correlations for various combinations of hearing levels separated into those with, versus those without, hearing level at 0.5 kHz. The data are also divided according to whether the tests were conducted in quiet, or in noisy listening conditions, and when averaged over the quiet and noise conditions.

It is seen that for listening-in-quiet conditions, inclusion of hearing level at 0.5 kHz with those at the higher frequencies increased, from an average of 58 to 70, the correlations with the SRT levels, but that for listening-in-noise conditions, the reverse occurred, a decrease in average correlation

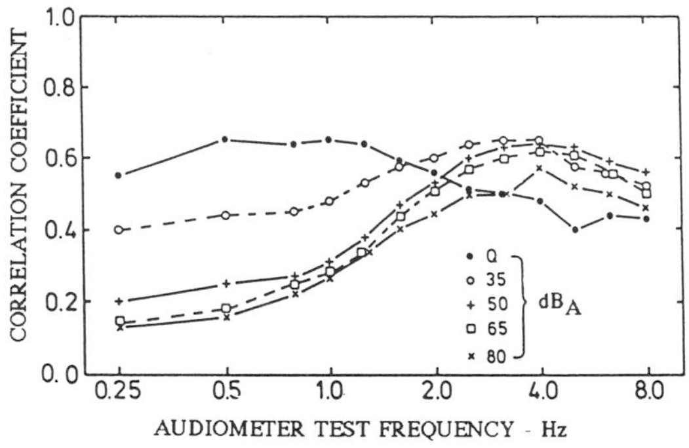

FIGURE 7.3 Correlation coefficients r between pure tone hearing levels and sentence reception thresholds (SRTs) in quiet and in noise of 35, 50, 65, and 80 dB$_A$. Monaural listening, 400 ears. (From Smoorenburg, 1986.)

from 70 to 60. Without hearing level at 0.5 kHz. The highest correlation when the quiet and noise conditions are averaged is r = .68 for the average hearing level at 0.5, 1, 2, and 4 kHz, and the lowest, r = .62, is for the average at 0.5, 1, and 2 kHz. These findings are in agreement with the general trend of the correlations shown in Tables 7.1–7.4.

Kryter and Archer (1994) performed regression analyses of hearing-level and sentence test data obtained from a large random sample of the United States adult population (U.S. Public Health Services, USPHS, 1971—1975

TABLE 7.5 Correlations r between HLs (Grouped with, and without, 0.5 kHz) and SRT (Speech Level, 50% Sentences Correct), in Quiet and Noise at 50, 65, and 80 dB$_A$

Average HL, at frequency, kHz	r, SRT quiet	Group rank	r, SRT, noise	Group rank	Average r Q + N*	All Rank
0.5, 1, 2	.73	1	.50	3	.62	7
0.5, 1, 2, 3	.68	2.5	.63	2	.66	2
0.5, 1, 2, 4	.68	2.5	.67	1	.68	1
Average	.70		.60		.65	
1, 2, 3	.63	1	.66	4	.65	3
2, 3	.57	2	.68	3	.63	6
2, 4	.56	3	.72	1.5	.64	4.5
2, 3, 4	.55	4	.72	1.5	.64	4.5
Average	.58		.70		.64	
N = 400.Ears						

*Q + N = quiet + noise (conditions).

After Smoorenburg (1992).

Health Survey). These particular analyses, and those related to self-ratings of hearing ability in real-life conditions, to be presented later, were based on data furnished to the investigators by the USPHS.

Hearing levels were measured in this USPHS survey at 500, 1000, 2000, and 4000 Hz, but not at 3000 Hz. On the basis of analysis of hearing-level data from other studies, it was concluded that the hearing level at 3000 Hz generally equaled (HL 2000 Hz + HL 4000 Hz) × 0.6. Using this formula, hearing levels for 3000 Hz were calculated for the ears of all the subjects tested. This was done to allow comparison of USPHS data for certain combinations of hearing levels involving 3000 Hz, with similar combinations from other studies. The speech tests consisted of simple five-word sentences administered to each ear monaurally in the quiet. Sentences were given at speech levels of 20, 30, 40, 50, and 60 dB. The percentage of errors shown are the averages for the error scores obtained, or extrapolated in the analysis, for all five speech intensities.

Table 7.6 shows the correlation coefficients between the hearing levels averaged for the left and right ears. These correlations are consistent with the SRT findings of Smoorenburg in that the correlation of speech-in-quiet conditions is somewhat higher for the lower than higher frequencies, individually and in combinations. The individual frequency with highest correlation

TABLE 7.6 Zero-Order (r) and Multiple (R) Correlations between Hearing Levels and Percentage Sentence and Words Incorrect, in Quiet, and Self-Ratings of Ability to Hear Speech Real-Life and Degree of Deafness, Based On U.S. Survey, 1971–1975 (N = 924; 466, left (L) 466, right (R) ears)

Hearing loss, kHz	Sentence tests,† r	Rank, r's sentences	Real-life speech‡ r	Real-life deafness§ r	Average r, real-life r	Rank r's, real-life	Multiple, all three groups, R	Rank R
			Average HL, Right and Left Ears (R,LE)					
0.5	.717	5	.407	.516	.461	7	.753	6
1	.749	3	.475	.571	.523	3	.804	3.5
2	.692	6	.548	.522	.535	2	.768	5
3*	.647	7	.487	.538	.513	4.5	.727	7
4	.534	8	.400	.473	.437	8	.614	8
			Average HL					
0.5, 1, 2	.787	1	.479	.547	.513	4.5	.827	1
0.5, 1, 2, 3	.759	2	.477	.541	.509	6	.804	3.5
0.5, 1, 2, 4	.746	4	.505	.588	.546	1	.813	2

*Hearing levels at 3 kHz not measured in survey. Estimated as 0.6 × (HL 2 kHz + HL 4 kHz/2); see text.

†Average percent words incorrect in sentences. Each ear tested separately in quiet. Speech levels 30–70 dB.

‡Self-rating of binaural ability to understand speech heard at different voice levels in real life.

§Each ear self-rated on scale of good hearing to deafness.

From Kryter and Archer (1994).

in Table 7.6 is 2 kHz (r = .749), and the best combination is 0.5, 1, and 2 kHz (r = .787). On the other hand, as seen in Table 7.1, Suter found the average of HLs at 500, 1000, and 2000 Hz to always, in quiet or noise, correlate the least well with speech intelligibility.

It is to be noted that the opposite relation applies for the corelations of frequencies in combination with the self-ratings of speech understanding and hearing ability in real-life conditions, as perceived by the participants in the survey. This finding, and similar results from other research investigations, will be discussed later.

Robinson *et al.* (1984), for one part of a set of research studies, presented to listeners, via loudspeaker, monosyllabic word tests in a free field. These tests, with the subjects listening binaurally, open-eared, represent a closer approximation to real-life listening conditions than the other studies discussed above, studies in which the tests were presented to the listeners monaurally either by earphone, or by loudspeaker (with one ear blocked; Suter, 1978). The speech tests were scored in terms of errors made on the three consonant–vowel–consonant sounds in each of 20 test words per listening condition.

Results pertaining to the speech intelligibility tests are shown in Table 7.7. It is there seen that for the tests in quiet with speech levels of 35 and 45, and with speech and noise at 70 dB_A, the predictive correlations tended to be somewhat higher for the average HLs at 0.5, 1, and 2 kHz, than when hearing levels for 3 kHz, and particularly 4 kHz, were included to the average. However, for speech at 70 dB_A in the quiet, the correlation was 0.05 lower for the 0.5-, 1-, 2-kHz average than that when the higher frequencies were included (.67 vs. .72). Some of these data seem inconsistent with the general findings of Table 7.1 to 7.6 to the effect that hearing levels above 2000 Hz are helpful for predicting speech understanding in noise, but not in quiet. Perhaps the explanation rests on the wide range of speech levels involved, 30–70 dB_A, in conjunction with the small number of subjects involved, N = 44.

The differences of the average of the r values over the three in-quiet test plus one-noise conditions is nil, less than 0.01, for the average of the 0.5-, 1-, 2-kHz versus the 0.5-, 1, 2-, and 3-kHz combination. These general relations held regardless of whether the data were for the better ear, worse, average, or AAO-weighted average ear. As also seen in Table 7.7, the r values for the average of the quiet and noise speech intelligibility scores were consistently slightly higher with hearing levels of the worse and average ear than with either the better or the AAO-weighted average ear. The average r over the three combinations of test frequencies was .72 for the worse and average of the two ears, and .69 for the better ear and the AAO two-ear-weighted average.

(The results presented in this chapter relative to the Robinson *et al.* study, were reduced by the present author from the Robinson *et al.* data shown in

TABLE 7.7 Correlations of Hearing Levels vs. Percentage Errors CVC Sounds in Words.

Correlation coefficient r Frequency, kHz, average HL	Sentence (word) intelligibility tests 30 dB$_A$ in quiet	45 dB$_A$ in quiet	70 dB$_A$ in quiet	70 dB$_A$ in noise	Average r, Q + N word tests
BE 0.5, 1, 2*	.72	.81	.67	.56	.69
BE 0.5, 1, 2, 3	.71	.80	.72	.56	.70
BE 0.5, 1, 2, 3, 4	.68	.78	.72	.52	.68
					Average = .69
WE 0.5, 1, 2	.73	.85	.72	.64	.74
WE 0.5, 1, 2, 3	.71	.84	.74	.62	.73
WE 0.5, 1, 2, 3, 4	.68	.81	.74	.57	.70
					Average = .72
	(BE + WE)/2; (LE + RE)/2				
0.5, 1, 2	.73	.84	.71	.61	.72
0.5, 1, 2, 3	.72	.83	.74	.60	.72
0.5, 1, 2, 3, 4	.69	.80	.74	.55	.69
					Average = .71
1, 2, 3	.73	.83	.74	.59	.72
	(B × 5 + W)/6 (AAO, weighted average)				
0.5, 1, 2,	.73	.82	.69	.56	.70
0.5, 1, 2, 3	.71	.81	.73	.57	.70
0.5, 1, 2, 3, 4	.69	.79	.73	.53	.68
					Average = .69

Key: BE—better ear, WE—worse ear [44 subjects (88 ears)]; Q + N—quiet and noise conditions. [Based on Robinson *et al.* (1984) data.]

Table 7.8. Robinson *et al.* provide much more detailed statistical, and other, analyses of their data, and for different groupings of the subjects, than are presented herein. The author took the liberty of reanalyzing some of the data of this very important investigation so that the findings would be in formats directly comparable with some of the findings, as examined by the author, of other investigators.)

Glasberg and Moore (1989) administered, binaurally via earphones, Plomp and Mimpen SRT sentence tests, and a number of temporal (gap) and frequency discrimination tests in quiet and in noise. The population of listeners had varying degrees of unilateral and bilateral cochlear hearing impairments. Regression analyses revealed that, particularly in the presence of noise, performance on the gap and other discrimination tasks involved hearing ability were not similarly predicted by the average of the hearing levels at 500, 1000, and 2000 Hz, as were the SRT scores.

Glasberg and Moore did not examine correlations with hearing levels at higher frequencies. However, they found with the impaired ears and noise sufficient to raise the SRT above that measured in the quiet, a significant portion of the variance in the SRTs is not accounted for by variations in the thresholds at 500, 1000, and 2000 Hz. It is perhaps reasonable to presume that threshold impairments at the higher frequencies could account for some of these findings.

SUMMARY OF CORRELATIONS BETWEEN HEARING LEVELS AND SPEECH TESTS

1. It appears from the research discussed, as well as from earlier studies (see, e.g., Mullins and Bangs, 1957; Niemeyer, 1967; Liden, 1965) that the average of the thresholds for pure tones at 500, 1000, and 2000 Hz does not, as a rule, predict the ability of persons with sensorineural hearing loss to correctly understand speech under less than ideal listening conditions as well as does the average of most other combinations that include higher audiometric tests frequencies. However, under idle listening conditions, the average of the levels at 500, 1000, and 2000 Hz is equally, sometimes slightly better, predictive of word intelligibility than when the levels at 3000 and/or 4000 Hz are added. Possible reasons for this listening-in-quiet finding are that (1) the information required to identify different speech sounds redundantly represented in different parts of the speech spectrum, from low to high frequencies; (2) most of the energy in the speech spectrum is in lower-, compared to higher-, frequency regions; and (3) because sensorineural hearing loss occurs predominately at the higher-frequency regions, persons with such loss perceive speech information primarily from lower portions of the speech spectrum. When listening in the presence of noise, or most adverse acoustical conditions, reasons for this finding are that (1) noise spectra (background machinery noise, voice-babble, etc.) tend to be of predominately lower, rather than higher frequencies; and (2) because of greater attenuation by air of higher, than lower, frequencies, and the greater reverberation efficiency of most surfaces of lower, than higher frequencies, the understanding of speech under such listening conditions will at times depend on the perception of higher-frequency components of speech sounds i.e., the noise masks the lower, even though in quiet more audible, speech components. Accordingly, mostly under those conditions does the handicap to speech understanding because of a high-frequency hearing loss manifest itself.

2. The hearing levels for only the worse ear, or for the average for the two ears, is more highly correlated with the intelligibility of speech heard binaurally ($r = .72$) than the hearing levels for those frequencies only in the better ear, or when combined according to the AAOO–AAO binaural-hearing formula ($r = .69$). The issue of which-ear hearing levels, or how

TABLE 7.8 Percentage Error Scores on Word Tests and Speech Information Tasks at Simulated Social Party, Railroad Station, Public Telephone, and Self-Ratings Hearing Disability and Handicap in Various Specified Real-Life Situations [Robinson *et al.* (1984).]

		Average % CVC, errors on test words						Left and right ear HLS kHz									
		quiet, speech					% Wrong info.										
Subject	Age	30 dB_A	45 dB_A	70 dB_A	N & Sp 70 dB_A	% Disability/ handicap	party; RR; public tel	L 0.5	R 0.5	L 1	R 1	L 2	R 2	L 3	R 3	L 4	R 4
1	23	13	0	2	7	15	9	−1	−3	4	4	7	2	16	12	11	12
2	24	13	2	15	22	16	33	−4	0	0	−1	−5	−5	−7	3	0	0
3	20	3	3	0	18	19	11	2	0	−3	−4	−8	−6	−3	−4	−2	−7
4	19	18	3	0	22	21	19	0	4	6	0	−1	−4	4	−2	10	5
5	19	30	3	0	15	24	13	−10	0	15	0	5	10	5	5	4	6
6	21	23	2	5	13	11	12	−1	0	1	2	−8	−5	3	0	5	−4
7	35	20	2	2	27	24	23	−4	−4	1	2	−6	−2	5	0	12	4
8	21	5	7	3	20	19	18	3	7	0	1	−4	−4	−4	0	−6	−5
9	26	30	2	3	32	21	19	8	1	7	3	3	2	4	8	5	−4
10	18	28	2	2	13	24	23	0	−5	−4	−2	−4	−5	−3	−6	−1	−5
11	19	10	0	3	15	17	17	2	0	0	−1	−9	−5	−9	−4	−9	−3
12	19	31	8	3	33	24	25	0	−3	−6	0	−1	0	−4	2	0	−2
13	19	0	2	2	23	12	32	−4	0	−5	3	−6	−4	−6	2	−8	−5
14	21	7	18	3	38	21	19	2	0	10	3	0	8	1	9	−5	5
15	20	26	7	2	27	14	19	0	−1	1	−4	−5	−6	−3	−1	2	−5
16	19	18	2	2	12	17	14	11	15	8	15	8	16	0	5	1	−5
17	23	21	5	2	17	19	19	−5	−5	−5	0	0	0	0	−5	0	0
18	28	10	0	2	23	7	19	0	0	1	0	0	2	2	1	0	−1
19	25	21	5	2	22	14	13	−1	−5	6	6	−5	0	−4	−5	8	5
20	22	10	0	0	18	14	22	−5	−8	−7	−6	−8	−6	−5	−3	−6	−5

21	53	69	8	2	20	14	28	[illegible]	7	4	7	18	20	24	6	27	15
22	49	28	13	2	30	18	46	[illegible]	14	0	5	2	3	12	13	36	35
23	50	15	5	5	28	25	24	[illegible]	3	3	−4	3	2	4	2	0	0
24	59	66	56	17	48	37	57	[illegible]	18	42	35	46	49	58	48	55	38
25	37	53	5	2	30	45	27	[illegible]	2	9	5	8	6	11	20	11	23
26	62	99	84	33	95	51	37	2[illegible]	12	40	15	66	43	70	44	55	40
27	62	58	35	30	45	43	49	2[illegible]	23	37	20	32	25	45	55	66	52
28	52	94	71	18	68	35	36	4[illegible]	30	64	63	63	50	52	35	37	18
29	32	17	2	2	15	30	23	[illegible]	4	8	6	5	3	12	15	6	13
30	23	13	2	12	23	30	30	−[illegible]	3	0	0	10	7	4	0	3	0
31	21	28	7	3	38	29	41	[illegible]	6	8	6	6	0	6	4	2	−1
32	46	12	13	7	30	37	30	13	5	12	4	26	9	42	22	48	38
33	42	48	36	21	35	68	48	1[illegible]	9	17	16	53	53	60	56	60	57
34	39	31	15	15	17	51	49	3	2	6	4	2	3	13	3	26	16
35	30	8	3	2	3	26	25	12	6	6	6	−4	0	6	14	11	18
36	54	20	5	8	23	50	35	[illegible]	5	18	4	43	21	52	30	65	30
37	32	26	7	5	17	29	24	[illegible]	11	2	2	19	6	22	5	29	10
38	30	0	0	7	8	30	21	3	10	−2	5	5	2	3	9	4	10
39	44	21	12	5	48	33	44	5	12	7	16	20	3	10	21	24	17
40	49	2	12	2	23	26	16	[illegible]	0	2	5	−8	15	10	12	17	34
41	57	23	13	7	30	23	40	[illegible]	14	28	18	12	16	32	40	48	52
42	63	12	0	10	13	11	45	[illegible]	13	11	5	23	13	33	31	53	23
43	46	10	5	7	23	53	36	20	17	23	25	12	23	20	25	13	22
44	39	30	13	8	15	28	52	[illegible]	0	−1	6	−6	2	6	2	35	42
Average	34	25	11	6	26	27	28	[illegible]	5	9	7	9	8	14	12	17	13
s.d.†	15	22.5	18.3	7.6	16.3	13.4	12.5	[illegible]	8	14	12	19	15	20	17	22	18

*Subjects 1–20 designated as group YN and subjects 21–44, designated as group NI in Robinson *et al.* (1984). YN = young, mean age 22 years, otologically normal; NI = older, mean age, 45 years, otologically normal.

†Standard deviation.

to combine those of the two ears, in order to predict speech understanding by persons with unequal hearing levels in both ears, is more complicated than the issue of what combinations of hearing levels is the relatively more predictive. In particular, this matter is related to sound-source localization, binaural release from noise masking, and the level of intelligibility, as will be discussed later in this chapter.

"NEW" OBJECTIVE AND SUBJECTIVE DATA RELEVANT TO THE EVALUATION OF HEARING HANDICAP

The appropriateness of the AAO guides as a means for the assessment of noise-induced hearing handicap rests largely on the adequacy of defining what is meant by "everyday speech in real-life listening conditions." In addition, proving the predictive validity of the AAO, or any other, treatment of pure-tone hearing levels, requires a large amount of objective and subjective data of speech understanding under different real-life conditions as it relates to the hearing levels of broad samples of the population.

Discussed below are (1) data showing the range of speech intensities listeners typically receive during real-life voice communications, and the range of intensities of background noise in which the communications typically take place; (2) calculation, by the articulation index (AI) of the word and/or sentence intelligibility to be expected under those everyday speech and listening conditions by persons with different amounts of hearing loss as measured by pure-tone hearing levels; and (3) data pertaining to speech communications and subjective self-ratings of hearing handicap and deafness in real-life conditions.

INTENSITIES OF SPEECH AND NOISE IN EVERYDAY SITUATIONS

Figures 6.4 and 6.5 showed that a wide range in the intensities of everyday speech is found at positions typical for a listener—about 1 m from a talker, or 3 m from a source such as a television set. Figure 6.6 showed samples of these speech levels, and the range of levels of the background noise surrounding, from time to time, the talker and the listener. Those data, which are consistent with other data collected under laboratory and field conditions, appear to adequately describe the approximate speech-level and noise conditions that constitute "everyday speech and noise." The vast majority of the speech levels range from about 45 to 68 dB_A. A level of about 52 dB_A, or 55 dB_C, measured 1 m from the talker, is generally considered typical for everyday conversational speech.

A background babble of voices is a common noise adversely affecting speech communications in social and other everyday situations. As seen in Fig. 7.4, the general shape of the speech spectrum is similar to that of a number of everyday noises in which people must communicate in real life.

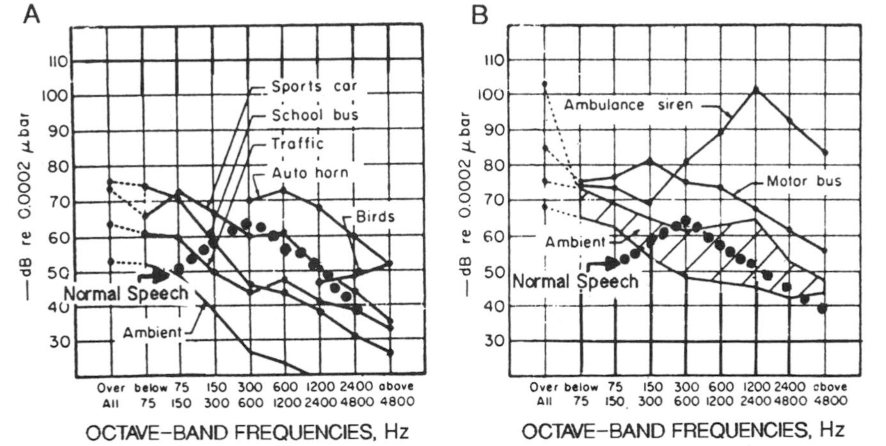

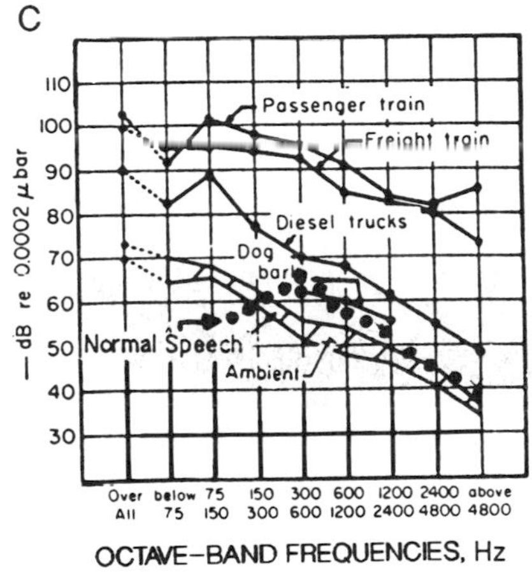

	OA=	dB (A)	dB (C)
A	SC	[illegible]	70
	SB	57	76
	T	52	63
	AB	75	75
	B	54	53
	Amb	36	53
B	AS	103	102
	MB	78	84
	Amb 1	69	76
	Amb 2	54	67
	Speech	62	65
C	PT	97	104
	FT	93	100
	DT	77	90
	DB	64	65
	Amb	58	70

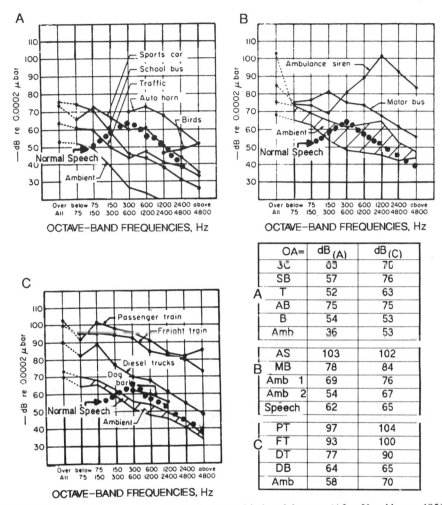

FIGURE 7.4 Noise in residential, business, and industrial areas. (After Veneklasen, 1956.)

CALCULATION OF ARTICULATION INDEX AND THE INTELLIGIBILITY OF EVERYDAY SPEECH

Articulation index values were calculated for a number of everyday speech and noise conditions using a noise spectrum having the shape of a babble of speech. The AIs were calculated for speech at levels of 45 and 65 dB_A (50 and 67 dB_C) with speech-to-noise ratios (S/Ns) of -5 dB; 0 dB; quiet ($>+20$ dB), and for approximate median speech and noise level in homes (speech 52 dB_A, noise 40 dB_A; S/N, $+12$ dB). Patterns of hearing levels at ⅓-octave-band center frequencies, used for the calculation of AI, were estimated from actual, and extrapolated, data for ears with sensorineural losses, average at 1000, 2000, and 3000 Hz, of 5, 15, 35, 40, 50, 60, and 70 dB. The patterns at frequencies other than 1000, 2000, and 3000 Hz are approximations based on examination of the hearing levels of several samples of ears with sensorineural hearing loss.

The speech and noise levels were chosen to represent the typical lower and upper intensities of everyday speech and noise levels, as shown in Fig. 6.6. The S/N ratios chosen are consistent with other data and experiments of speech communication conditions; see for example, the abscissa of studies shown in Fig. 7.2. Negative S/N ratios for speech are not uncommon, and allow for some intelligibility. As previously noted (see Fig. 6.1), the reason is that the dB_A intensity of the speech signal during 10% of 1/8th-s intervals of time will exceed by some 12 dB the average L_{eq}, dB_A, speech level as it, and the noise, is normally measured.

The procedures followed, and examples of the data, in the calculation of AI are presented in Table 7.9A. The AIs calculated for the various conditions outlined above, and the percentage errors on words-in-sentences, and 1000 individual PB word tests predicted by the AIs are given on Table 7.9B.

Equivalent Field and Earphone Hearing Levels

Before discussing these data, the procedure for calulating AI from hearing-level SPLs (measured in the ear canal) and SPLs of speech and noise (measured in an open field) is outlined. As described in Chapter 6, the primary tenet of the AI concept is that the understandability of a given speech signal can be predicted from a weighted ratio of (1) the speech spectrum, or band, levels, plus 12 dB, reaching a listener's ear, versus (2), the hearing levels (internal noise) of the ear, or, if higher, the levels of steady external noise reaching the ear. When the ratio at a given frequency is of equal SPLs, for the speech and either noise, masking of the speech signal at that frequency is presumed, according to AI, to be achieved.

However, the numerical value of the SPL representing free-field speech or noise is a number of decibels less than its effective loudness-masking level, relative to its ear-canal SPL. That is to say, a field measured noise has an effective auditory level, relative to its ear-canal SPL level, that is, about 5–15 dB higher, depending on frequency. This "gain," as previously discussed, is due primarily to ear-canal resonances.

Accordingly, in calculating, for AI, the ratio of masking effectiveness of the ratios of external, open-field SPLs relative to those of ear-canal SPLs, one must adjust upwards the ear-canal hearing levels or SPLs, by the amounts of these gains. As far as the AI calculations are concerned, the adjustment for SPL equivalency could, of course, be made by subtracting the "field" correction from the speech and noise. (This mode of adjustment is used in a later figure showing audibility area of sound expressed relative to ear-canal SPLs.) These adjustments are, of course, not required in the application of

TABLE 7.9A Calculation of AI for Open-Ear Listening to Speech at 65 dB_A in Various Levels of Noise; Typical HL, Average 1, 2, 3 kHz, Losses of 5, 15, 35, 40, 50, 60, 70 dB Example of Calculation of AI for HL <15 dB, and S/N, = 0dB (Speech 65 dB, Noise-Babble 65dB).

Column (C)	Example: speech and noise, 65 dB_A; S/N 0.dB Number	1	2	3	4	5	$6A^e$	Typical patterns of hearing loss[d] $6A^e$	$6A^a$	$6A^c$	$6A^d$	Calculated for example S/N 5dB, EML 6^{**e}	7^f	8	9
1/3-Octave band Hz	Center frequency, Hz	Speech 68 dB_C 65 dB_A[a]	Peaks speech (+12)	Noise babble 65 dB_A[a]	SPL normal HL[b]	Correct for field[b]	1, 2, 3 kHz 5 dB ear, HL	1, 2, 3 kHz 15 dB ear, HL	1, 2, 3 kHz 35 dB ear, HL	1, 2, 3 kHz 40 dB ear HL	1, 2, 3 kHz 70 dB ear, HL	1, 2, 3 kHz S/N odB EML	1, 2, 3 kHz S/N odB C2–3,6	AI Band Weight ANSI S3.5	C7 × C8 1, 2, 3 kHz 5 dB
180–224	200	58	70	58	35	10	0	0	0	[illegible]0	30	45	12	0.0004	0.005
224–280	250	59	71	59	24.5	6	0	0	5	[illegible]0	40	31	12	0.0010	0.012
280–355	315	60	72	60	20	7	0	0	5	[illegible]0	40	27	12	0.0010	0.012
355–450	400	61	73	61	15	5	0	0	10	5	45	20	12	0.0014	0.017
450–560	500	59.5	71.5	59.5	11	5	0	5	10	5	45	16	12	0.0014	0.017
560–710	630	57.5	69.5	57.5	9	5	0	5	15	5	45	14	12	0.0020	0.024
710–900	800	56	68	56	7.5	5	0	5	15	[illegible]0	50	13	12	0.0020	0.024
900–1120	1000	55	67	55	7	5	0	10	25	[illegible]5	55	12	12	0.0024	0.029
1120–1400	1250	53	65	53	6.5	7	0	13	25	[illegible]0	60	14	12	0.0030	0.036
1400–1800	1600	51.5	63.5	51.5	6.5	8	3	14	30	[illegible]5	65	18	12	0.0037	0.044
1800–2240	2000	50.5	62.5	50.5	8.5	10	5	15	35	[illegible]0	70	24	12	0.0038	0.046
2240–2800	2500	49	61	49	8	11	8	18	40	[illegible]0	80	27	12	0.0034	0.041
2800–3550	[3000]	47	59	47	7.5	13	10	20	45	[illegible]5	85	31	12	0.0034	0.041
3550–4500	4000	44	56	44	9	14	10	25	55	[illegible]0	90	33	12	0.0040	0.048
4500–5600	5000	42	54	42	8	15	10	25	55	[illegible]0	90	33	12	0.0020	0.024
															AI total = 0.419

[a] Idealized speech spectrum, male voices, ANSI S3.5 (ANSI, 1969a). Approximate long-term, *C*-weighted, SPL −3 dB, and/or average of dB_A, slow-meter, SPL words in sentences. Conversational-level speech in field approximately 55dB_A, 1 m from talker. Enter, if available, actual equivalent spectra for speech signals reaching open ear or microphone of public address or hearing-aid systems. Noise spectrum = babble of many voices.

[b] ISO 389 (ISO, 1964). Manual audiometry. Correction to SPL (HL) for masking of field-SPL speech, based on Sivian and White (1933) field vs. earphone thresholds. When speech, noise, and HL are all measured in the field, or all measured in the ear, or earphone coupler, do not use column 5.

[c] Estimate HL, at an unmeasured test frequency, by entering the HL measured at the next-higher frequency, at 5.0 kHz, enter HL-measured 4 kHz.

[d] Similar patterns of losses at different frequencies presumed for average HL's of 50-dB and 60-dB.

[e] Column 6 = columns 4 + 5 + 6*A* = equivalent masking level (EML). Do *not* include C_5 if speech, noise, and HLs are all in field levels, or all are in-ear levels and EMLs same as those of their respective 70-dB HLs and EMLs, less 20 and 10 dB, respectively.

[f] Column 7 = column 2, speech peaks, minus column 3 noise band level, or if larger, minus column 6, EML. If resulting difference is less than 0, set to 0; if it is larger than 30 set to 30. Similar column 7s calculated for HLs, average 1, 2, 3 kHz of 15, 40, and 50 dB. Calculations continued in Table 7.9B.

TABLE 7.9B Calculated AI ANSI S3.5 (ANSI, 1969a) and Approximate Percentage of Incorrect Words in First-Time-Presented 10-Word Sentences and 1000 Phonetically Balanced (PB) Monosyllabic Word Tests (See Figs. 6.28 and 7.5 for Choice of Range of Levels)

HL, average at 1, 2, 3 kHz	5 dB	15 dB	35 dB	40 dB	50 dB	60 dB	70 dB
Speech, 45 dB_A/quiet—AI	0.672	0.442	0.231	0.182	0.063	0	0
Sentences, % words wrong	2%	6%	36%	56%	91%	100%	100%
Individual words, % wrong	9%	31%	70%	80%	96%	100%	100%
Speech, 45 dB_A/noise, 45 dB_A; S/N, 0 dB—AI	0.346	0.265	0.151	0.135	0.063	0	0
Sentences, % words wrong	13%	27%	65%	70%	91%	100%	100%
Individual words, % wrong	46%	64%	84%	87%	96%	100%	100%
Speech, 45 dB_A/N 50 dB_A; S/N, −5 dB—AI	0.216	0.168	0.100	0.086	0.063	0	0
Sentences, % words wrong	43%	60%	80%	86%	91%	100%	100%
Individual words, % wrong	74%	82%	91%	93%	96%	100%	100%
Speech, 65dB_A/quiet—AI	0.994	0.846	0.537	0.478	0.326	0.182	0.03
Sentences, % words wrong	0%	1%	4%	5%	16%	55%	90%
Individual words, % wrong	1%	5%	20%	27%	50%	80%	95%
Speech, 65 dB_A/noise, 65 dB_A; S/N, 0 dB—AI	0.419	0.391	0.261	0.235	0.188	0.135	0.063
Sentences, % words wrong	7%	9%	30%	39%	48%	70%	91%
Individual words, % wrong	34%	39%	66%	71%	81%	86%	96%
Speech, 65 dB_A/noise, 70 dB_A; S/N, −5 dB—AI	0.244	0.242	0.162	0.143	0.117	0.086	0
Sentences, % words wrong	35%	42%	61%	68%	74%	84%	100%
Individual words, % wrong	70%	74%	83%	86%	89%	93%	100%
AI and % Incorrect in Approximate Median Speech and Median Background Noise Levels in Homes							
Speech, 52 dB_A/noise 40 dB_A; S/N, +12 dB—AI	0.623	0.471	0.271	0.232	0.108	0.018	0
Sentences, % words wrong	3%	5%	27%	40%	79%	98%	100%
Individual words, % wrong	14%	27%	64%	72%	90%	99%	100%

AI when the speech, noise, and hearing levels are all in terms of ear-canal (earphone-coupler) SPLs, or all are SPLs measured in the field at the position to be occupied by the listener's head.

The amount of gain correction, in decibels, for the field versus earphone thresholds are given in column 5 of Table 7.9A. These corrections are estimates based on data of Sivian and White shown in Fig. 2.21. The physically measured ear-canal resonances and acoustic diffractions around the head, shown in Figs. 2.2 and 5.10, are not entirely consistent with the subjective minimum audible field versus the minimum ear-canal pressure thresholds given in Fig. 2.21. However, hearing threshold data are presumed to be more directly comparable to the hearing behavior in question, and, therefore, are chosen as being more appropriate to use for these adjustments than the purely acoustical measures.

Range of Impairment to Everyday Speech Reception as Function of Hearing Level

The percent of words in sentences misunderstood, as predicted by AI, are shown graphically in Fig. 7.5 as a function of hearing loss, average at 1000, 2000, and 3000 Hz. Figure 6.6 is repeated as Fig. 7.5A to show that the AI functions in Fig. 7.5B fairly encompass the great majority of everyday speech conditions.

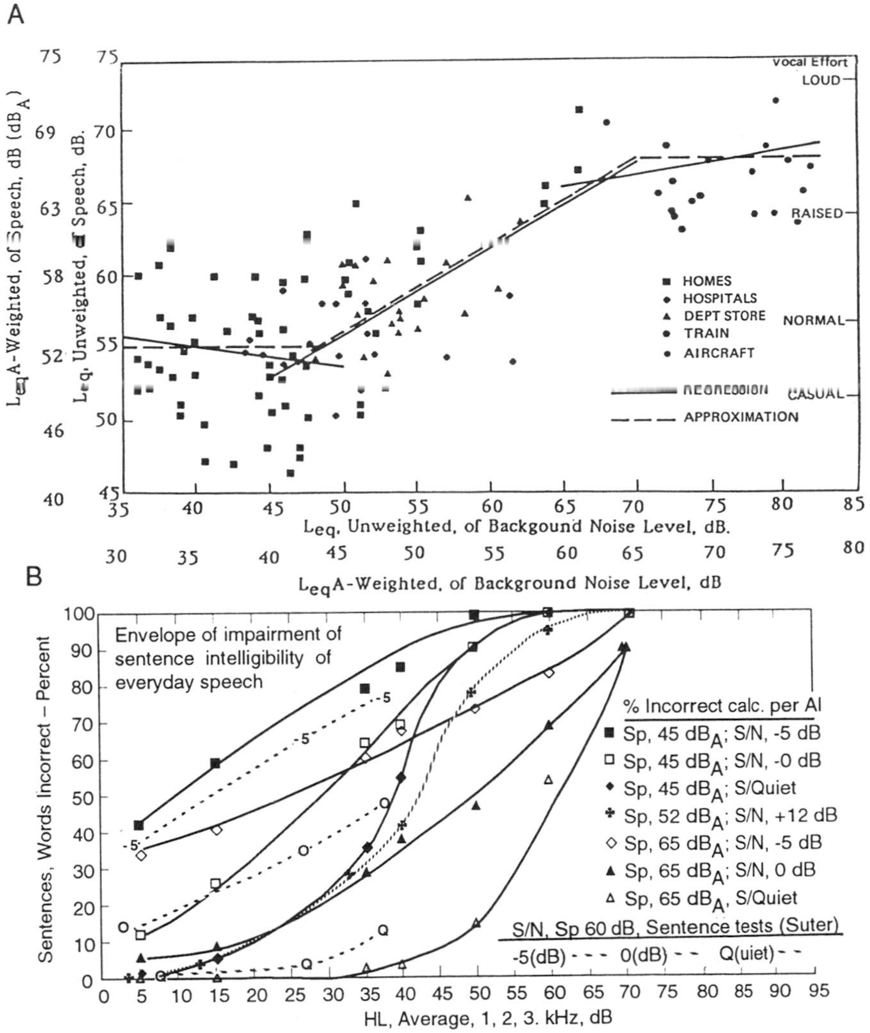

FIGURE 7.5 (A) Speech levels and background noise levels found in various real-life situations. (After Pearsons *et al.*, 1977.) (Repeat of Fig. 6.6.) (B) Percentage incorrect of words-in-sentences for various speech-to-noise ratios, estimated by calculated AI (see Table 7.9), and as measured in tests by Suter (1978).

It is seen in Fig. 7.5B that, when different amounts of hearing loss, average at 1000, 2000, and 3000 Hz, are involved, what might be called "everyday speech under everyday noise conditions" covers a wide range of impairments, or handicap, to use AAO terminology, to speech understanding. It appears that when this hearing loss reaches ~70 dB, impairment, or handicap, for understanding everyday speech is essentially 100%. The reason is, of course, that for those persons the peaks of even raised-voice speech, 65 dB_A, are inaudible, except that speech energy around 500 Hz may occasionally be detected.

Also shown in Fig. 7.5 are the percentages, measured by Suter (1978), of words in sentences misunderstood for speech at 60 dB_A when heard in three different S/N ratios: −5 dB, 0 dB, and quiet. The measured values reasonably closely parallel, for the range of hearing levels of the listeners tested, the intelligibility scores predicted by AI for the −5-dB, 0-dB, and quiet listening conditions. This, it is believed, attests to the general validity of the AI procedure, and the earphone-to-field-level adjustments of hearing levels as employed for calculating AIs for HLs determined with earphones and field-measured and heard speech and noise.

Speech intelligibility as measured, or estimated by AI, represents hearing ability in that regard without any visual aid, such as lip-reading, or the use of electronic hearing aids. It is also customary to evaluate the handicap to hearing due to losses in threshold sensitivity when not using any such aids.

HEARING DIFFICULTIES, HANDICAP, AND DEAFNESS IN REAL-LIFE SITUATIONS (SELF-RATINGS AND TASK ERRORS)

The subjective opinions people have of their own speech communication experiences in real life, and simulated real life, is an important criterion for verifying the validities of (1) a quantitative relation between impairment to pure-tone thresholds and the handicap to understanding everyday speech; and (2) a hearing level ot be identified as the starting point, the "fence," for that handicap, Salomon and Parving, 1985. Results of the following are discussed below:

1. Surveys of the hearing levels of large samples of people who have been asked to indicate real-life situations in which they, retrospectively, typically experienced difficulties in hearing and understanding speech, and the degrees of difficulty, or handicap, they experienced.
2. Experiments showing, as a function of the hearing levels of the subjects, their self-rated handicaps, plus objectively scored errors in speech communication tasks under simulated real-life situations.

3. Surveys of hearing levels of large samples of people who have been asked to self-rate their degree of deafness for sound in general.

Self-Ratings of Speech Communication Difficulties

Nett *et al.* (n.d.) found in a study of "critical incidents" of hearing handicap in a population of 378 hard-of-hearing persons, half of whom had hearing loss of ≤34% as estimated by AAOO (1959) procedures, but 60% of the group estimated their loss as being more than a 60% loss in hearing ability. This suggests, of course, that the AAOO evaluation procedure significantly led to underestimation of hearing handicap in real life as self-rated by persons with measured amounts of pure-tone threshold shifts.

Kell *et al.* (1971) reported data for 96 female weavers whose hearing levels averaged 37 dB, average at 500, 1000, and 2000 Hz; and 96 controls, matched for age, whose average hearing level at those three frequencies was 13 dB (the hearing levels for the two groups are estimated to be, respectively, 17 and 48 dB, average at 1000, 2000, and 3000 Hz). The mean ages of the groups were 64.1 and 64.5 years, respectively. The weavers worked 8 h per day in a noise level of about 100 dB_A.

The results of a questionnaire survey of the subjects were summarized as follows:

The social consequences of this impaired hearing ability were

1. Difficulty at public meetings (weavers 72%, controls 6%)
2. Difficulty talking with strangers (weavers 80%, controls 16%)
3. Difficulty talking with friends (weavers 77%, controls 15%)
4. Difficulty understanding telephone conversation (weavers 64%, controls 5%)
5. 81% of all weavers considering their hearing as impaired (5% controls)
6. 9% of weaver and no controls owning hearing aids
7. 53% of weavers and no controls using a form of lip-reading

The average of the percentages of the weavers and the control subjects reporting "difficulties" with speech communications in the real-life situations is 73% for the weavers and 10% for the control subjects.

Robinson *et al.* (1984) tested 44 otologically normal adult subjects, 24 of whom had histories of exposure to noise. The information collected in that study of interest for the present discussion falls into three categories: (1) pure-tone hearing-level and speech intelligibility tests; (2) errors made on speech communication tasks performed in three simulated real-life situations; and (3) self-assessments, recorded on a questionnaire, of hearing difficulties and handicaps with respect to general real-life situations, as viewed retrospectively, and as judged for nine described real-life-type situations. Correlations between hearing levels and intelligibility tests in the quiet and noise were presented in an earlier part of this chapter (see Table 7.7).

The real-life situations were simulated in a large laboratory room, using electronic (audio and video) signal presentation, measurement, and monitoring equipment. The speech communication tasks were placed in the following three settings: (1) information given at a social gathering, labeled "party" (2) public-address-system announcements in a railroad station concourse, labeled "RR"; and (3) information given on a public telephone, labeled "Public Tel" or "Tel" (see Fig. 7.6 and Table 7.10). In all three situations the speech material to be understood was presented in a simulated, but realistic, background of voices, music, and noise as appropriate for the

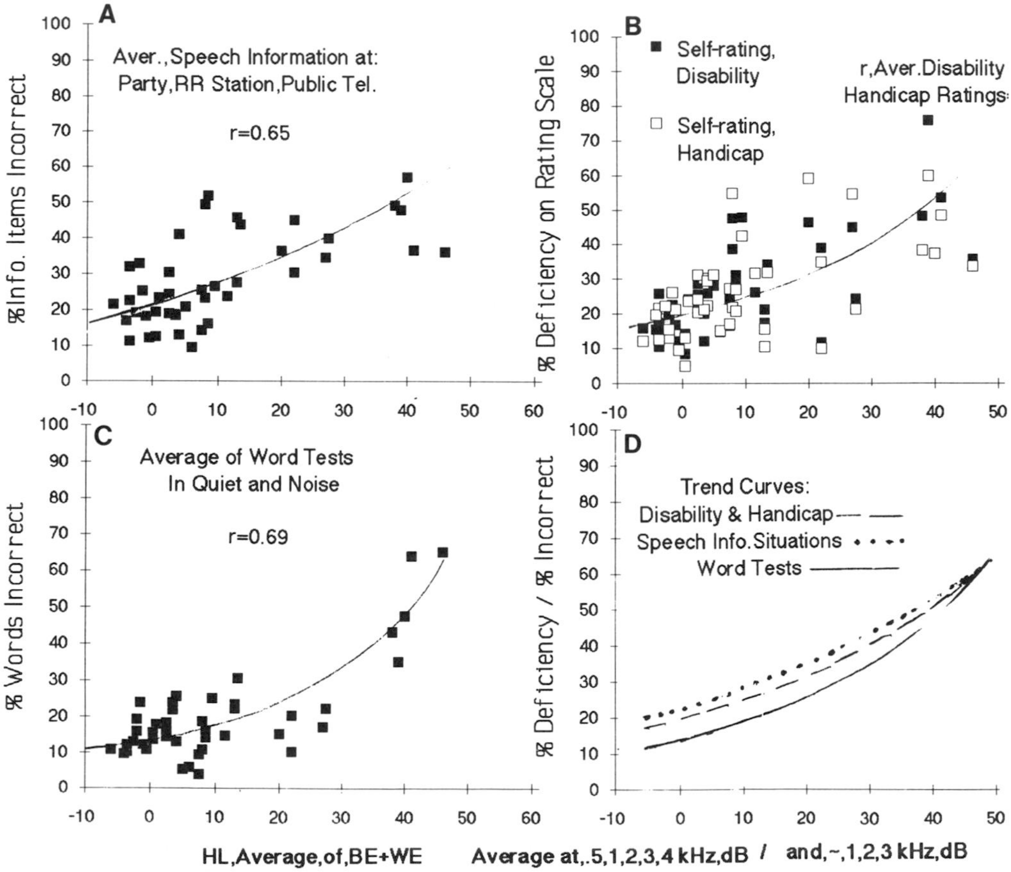

FIGURE 7.6 (A) Percentage items incorrect on speech information tasks; (B) percentage speech sounds incorrect on word tests; (C) percentage deficiency (disability/handicap), self-rated, on real-life situations with speech communications, $r = 0.66$; (D) trend curves from other graphs. (Based on Robinson *et al.*, 1984.)

TABLE 7.10 Correlations *r* of Hearing Levels vs. Self-Rated Disabilities and Handicaps in Understanding Speech in Real-Life Conditions; Errors on Simulated Real-Life Speech Information Tasks; and Word Tests [Based on data in Table 7.8 from Robinson *et al.* (1984)]

	Real-Life conditions				
Correlation coefficient *r* frequency, kHz of average HL	A. Self-rated D/H	B. Sp. Info., P; RR; Tel	Av. r, D/H & P; RR; Tel	C. Av. *r* Q + *N* word errors	Average of average *r* values
BE, 0.5, 1, 2	0.58	0.56	0.57	0.69	0.63
BE, 0.5, 1, 2, 3	0.62	0.61	0.61	0.70	0.66
BE, 0.5, 1, 2, 3, 4	0.65	0.67	0.66	0.68	0.67
		Average =	0.62	0.69	0.65
WE, 0.5, 1, 2	0.59	0.53	0.56	0.74	0.64
WE, .5, 1, 2, 3	0.64	0.57	0.60	0.73	0.66
WE, .5, 1, 2, 3, 4	0.66	0.63	0.64	0.70	0.67
		Average =	0.60	0.72	0.66
	(BE + WE)/2; (LE + RE)/2 (Average ear)				
0.5, 1, 2	0.59	0.55	0.57	0.72	0.65
0.5, 1, 2, 3	0.64	0.58	0.61	0.72	0.67
0.5, 1, 2, 3, 4	0.66	0.65	0.66	0.69	0.68
		Average =	0.61	0.71	0.67
1, 2, 3	0.65	0.59	0.62	0.72	0.67
	(B × 5 + W)/6, (AAO, weighted average)				
0.5, 1, 2	0.58	0.53	0.55	0.70	0.63
0.5, 1, 2, 3	0.63	0.60	0.62	0.70	0.66
0.5, 1, 2, 3, 4	0.66	0.67	0.66	0.68	0.67
		Average =	0.61	0.69	0.65
			Av., r, Q + N Word. Tests		
D/H rates		0.61	0.75*		
Sp. Info., P; RR; Tel			0.53*		

Key: Av, *r*—correlation-coefficient average; BE, WE—better ear, worse ear (B, W—better, worse); D/H—disability and/or handicap; Sp. Info.—speech information; P—party; Q + N—quiet + noise (conditions); RR—public-address-system announcements in a railroad station concourse; Tel—public telephone.

* Average *r*, Q + N word tests.

different situations. For face-to-face voice communications, the talker's face was seen on a video screen. The subjects were asked to write down on special answer sheets the names of people, telephone numbers, street addresses, etc., or, for the RR task, to record the approximate information contained in the public-address-system announcements. Answer sheets were scored for errors, but scores were not changed for spelling, or such noninformational errors.

The self-assessment questionnaires required the subjects to check on a scale, usually a four-point scale, any hearing difficulties or handicap they experienced with respect to some nine real-life social and work situations, with four to five questions per situation. Example:

Situation: You are listening to the sports results or similar factual information on the radio, with the volume control adjusted to your liking. Check your answer: I hear all the information well:
Always ☐ Usually ☐ sometimes ☐ never ☐
Question: Does the state of your hearing interfere with your work? Check your answer: Never ☐ Sometimes ☐ Often ☐ Always ☐

The answers were converted to a percentage of difficulties, or disabilities and/or handicaps, depending on the definitions attached to the different situations and questions. Age, speech intelligibility test error scores, percent hearing deficiency (disability and/or handicap) according to self-rating questionnaire scales, errors on speech information tasks, and left- and right-ear hearing levels of the subjects are given in Table 7.8.

The correlations in Table 7.10 show that speech intelligibility averaged over the three quiet and one noise conditions, as discussed previously, is marginally better predicted by a combination of hearing levels at 0.5, 1, and 2 kHz, or 0.5, 1, 2, and 3 kHz, without the presence of 4000 Hz. However, the inclusion of hearing level at 3 and 4 kHz significantly increases the correlation with the real-life self-ratings and the simulated real-life speech information tasks. For any ear, or average ear, the average of those two real-life hearing-performance measures, the correlation increases from about 0.56, average of the hearing levels of 0.5, 1, and 2 kHz, to 0.61, average for 0.5, 1, 2, and 3 kHz, and 0.66, average for 0.5, 1, 2, 3, and 4 kHz. Indeed, the removal of 0.5 Hz (average for 1, 2, 3, kHz) slightly improves the subject correlation ($r = .62$) for the average ear.

Although some test frequencies better predict retrospective real-life handicap and speech-task performance than do others, no significant differences are seen between the correlations for the hearing levels of different ear or average ear with the self-ratings and performance tests in real-life situations. The correlations "Av. *r*, D/H & P; RR; Tel" are .62, better ear; .60, worse ear; .62, average ear; and .61, AAO-weighted average. As seen in Table 7.10, and as discussed earlier, the hearing levels for the worse ear and average ear best predict word-intelligibility test scores. For the average of the word-intelligibility tests plus the real-life measures, the single highest correlation is .68, that with the average of the hearing levels at 0.5, 1, 2, 3, and 4 kHz for both ears. Although the differences among the various frequency combinations are generally small, the correlations for average of hearing levels at 0.5, 1, and 2 kHz is uniformly less than the others.

Figure 7.6 shows data points and visually drawn trend curves of best fit between hearing level, average at 1, 2, 3 kHz, averaged for left and right ears, and the various performance and questionnaire self-rating scores. Figure 7.6 shows that the trend curves for speech-information tasks and disability/handicap are similar, but indicate somewhat greater hearing deficiency than the intelligibility test scores. However, only one of the speech intelligibility tests was in everyday noise, the other three were administered in quiet.

Lutman *et al.* (1987) administered questionnaires to some 1691 subjects chosen at random from the British adult population. The subjects self-rated the difficulty, on a scale from none to great (or a similar scale depending on the exact question), they had experienced in real-life situations involving hearing. The following four questions (starting with question 5 on the actual questionnaire) were considered as indicative of a hearing "handicap" component: (5) "How difficult do you usually find it to follow somebody's conversation when other people are talking nearby?"; (7) "How often does any hearing problem you may have restrict your enjoyment of social and personal life, compared to others around you?"; (8) "Do you get a feeling of being cut off from things because of difficulty in hearing?"; and (9) "Do any hearing difficulties you may have lead to embarrassment?"

The following four questions were considered indicative of an everyday speech understandability, or, in the investigator's terminology, "disability" component; (1) "Can you follow television news when the volume is turned up only enough to suit other people?"; (2) "Can you follow what is being said on the radio news when the volume is turned up only enough to suit other people?" (4) "If you are in a group of people and someone you can't see starts to speak, are you able to tell where the person is sitting?"; and (5), given in the paragraph above. Answers to question (4) and to question (3): "Do you turn your head the wrong way when someone calls to you?" were taken as indicative of a disability in speech-source localization. The response to one question was used to measure a disability for understanding speech in quiet: (6) "When talking in a quiet room with someone who is a clear speaker, how much difficulty do you have in understanding what they are saying?"

Correlation coefficients were found by Lutman *et al.* that related questionnaire components to monaural and binaural hearing levels, averaged across various combinations for 0.5, 1, 2, and 4 kHz. (Lutman *et al.* do not show correlations with hearing levels at 3 kHz included.) As seen in Table 7.11, within different components, only a few correlations differ from each other in, at best, marginally statistically significant ways, and the averages of the correlations over all components differ by no more than .02. The correlations of hearing levels with the "speech-in-quiet" and "localization" components were, respectively .38 and .32, significantly less than the correlations, .63 and .57, with "everyday speech" and "handicap."

The responses to the first group of cited questions, converted to a "handi-

TABLE 7.11 Correlations Relating Questionnaire Components to Monaural and Binaural Hearing Levels

Frequency, kHz	Everyday speech	Speech in quiet	Localization	Handicap	Average	(Everyday speech + handicap)/2
4BE + WE (0.5, 1, 2)	.64	.39	.32	.57	.48	.61
Better (0.5, 1, 2)	.63	.37	.30	.54	.46	.59
Worse (0.5, 1, 2)	.63	.39	.35	.58	.49	.61
4BE + WE (0.5, 1, 2, 4)	.63	.38	.30	.57	.47	.60
Better (0.5, 1, 2, 4)	.62	.37	.28	.55	.46	.59
Worse (0.5, 1, 2, 4)	.61	.38	.34	.58	.48	.60
Average	.63	.38	.32	.57	.47	.60
BE = better ear		[4BE + WE(0.5,1,2)] + [4BE + WE(0.5, 1, 2, 4)]/2 =				.60
WE = worse ear		WE(0.5, 1, 2) + WE(0.5, 1, 2, 4)/2 =				.60
4BE + WE = (4 × BE + WE)/5		BE(0.5, 1, 2) + BE(0.5, 1, 2, 4)/2 =				.59

Note: In region of $r = .6$, a difference of .03 is significant at .05 level; in region of $r = .4$, a difference of .04 is significant at .05 level ($N = 1691$).

After Lutman *et al.* (1987).

cap'' component, and to the second group, converted to an ''everyday speech'' impairment component, were plotted against various combinations of better-ear hearing levels. The handicap and everyday speech components scale scores were plotted against the average hearing levels at various test frequencies for the better ear multiplied by 4, plus the average for the worse ear, with the sum divided by 5. The functions between hearing levels and the handicap and everyday speech components differed somewhat from each other, but not greatly. Figure 7.7 shows the general function, scaled to 100%, for the handicap component. The investigators found that speech impairment and handicap ratings did not differ for different socioeconomic groups with similar hearing levels.

Comparison of Functions of Hearing Handicap for Everyday Speech

In addition to the speech handicap function from the Lutman *et al.* (1987) study, also plotted on Fig. 7.7, are (1) the connected data points, from the Kell *et al.* (1971) study, of percentages of people with difficulties with speech communications in real life; and (2) the self-ratings and speech-task performance in real-life conditions as studied by Robinson *et al.* (1984).

Except for the endpoints of the vertical scale, and a monotonic growth, there is no necessarily uniform relation among the scalar steps of the different variables plotted on Fig. 7.7. Even so, it is submitted that from present research information, the best estimate possible self-perceived handicap for

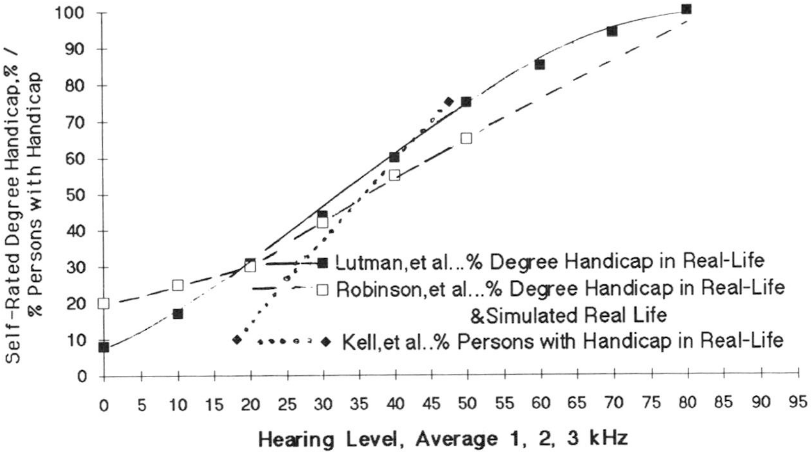

FIGURE 7.7 Self-ratings of percentage difficulty/handicap speech communication in real-life (Lutman *et al.*, 1987; Robinson *et al.*, 1984), and percent of persons indicating difficulties with speech communications in various specified real-life situations (Kell *et al.*, 1971). Hearing levels: Lutman *et al.* (1987), better ear; Robinson *et al.* (1984) and Kell *et al.* (1971), average of left and right ears.

the reception and understanding of everyday speech in real life by people with different degrees of hearing impairment would be a curve approximating that of the average of these functions. As will be shown later in this chapter, the AI–speech-intelligibility curve for typical everyday speech falls along the same general path followed by these functions.

Self-Ratings of Deafness

In several surveys of the hearing levels of groups of people, the participants have been asked to rate, relative to normal, or some standard, their "deafness," if any. The data obtained are believed to be concerned with the disability to hear sounds in general, and not solely to difficulties in the hearing and understanding of everyday speech.

Habib and Hinchcliffe (1978) tested 108 adults with varying degrees of hearing loss at 2000 Hz. The subjects were asked: "Assuming that there is a scale of hearing handicap from 0 to 100 (where 100 is the handicap produced by complete deafness), how much on this scale would you say that your hearing difficulty gives you?" The investigators found that the hearing level for the better ear correlated with the handicap-deafness score at *r* .251; the worse ear, at *r* .311; and the average of the two ears, at *r* .315. They also calculated best-fitting curves for the ratings as a function of the hearing level for two subsamples of the data. The average of those functions is shown in Fig. 7.8.

Lutman and Robinson (1992) obtained self-ratings of hearing disability from 2058 adults in a survey conducted in the United Kingdom. The subjects

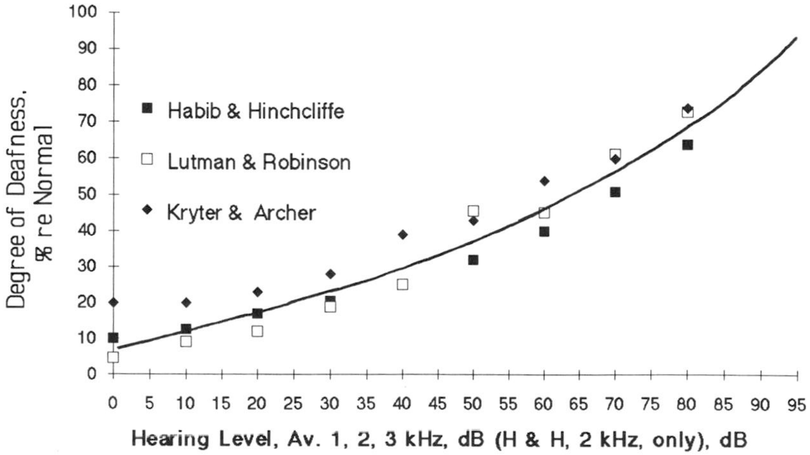

FIGURE 7.8 Self-rated degree of deafness as function of hearing level: Habib and Hinchcliffe (1978) (average left and right ears), and Lutman and Robinson (1992) (better ear), percentage with reference to normal; Kryter and Archer (1994) (average left and right ears), 12.5% = "good."

were asked, by means of a printed questionnaire, to estimate their hearing ability as follows: "Imagine that a normal young adult has a hearing ability of 100 and someone who is totally deaf has a hearing ability of 0. We would like you to circle the number that best indicates the state of your hearing for each ear." The answer sheet provided columns to be checked for left ear, and right ear, each in 10-point steps from 0 to 100.

Hearing level was reported for the better ear of each subject, averaged over 1, 2, and 3 kHz. Figure 7.8 shows the mean percent disability-deafness rating as a function of that hearing level from 0 to 80 dB. The data of 12 subjects with hearing levels that exceeded 85 dB, by some unspecified amount, were excluded from the database because of their small number and range of levels.

Kryter and Archer (1994) analyzed the response to the following question asked of adult participants in the 1971–1975 USPHS hearing survey: How would you rate the hearing in your right (left) ear? Participants selected one of the following replies: (1) good; (2) a little (somewhat) decreased; (3) a lot (significantly) decreased; or (4) deaf. The responses, obtained from 1100 subject for 2200 ears, were scored, somewhat arbitrarily, as indicative of hearing loss, or deafness: good = 12.5%; a little decreased = 37.5%; a lot decreased = 62.5%; and deaf = 87.5%. The distribution of the responses are also shown in Fig. 7.8.

The functions in Fig. 7.8. indicate that persons with hearing levels for an ear in excess of ~80 dB, average 1, 2, and 3 kHz, do not consider themselves as more than ~65–70% deaf. This rating is found even though, according to Figs. 7.5 and 7.7, these persons should would rate themselves as 100% handicapped for hearing speech in real life.

Figure 7.9 shows the normal spectral-intensity area available to the normal ear, divided into the estimated number of "units" of tonal loudness and/or pitch discriminations the normal ear can make (see Chapter 2). That figure also illustrates that ~65–70% of the number of audible discriminations possible are rendered inaudible with a typical loss in hearing sensitivity that averages ~80 dB at 1, 2, and 3 kHz. These losses render inaudible even near-shouted speech, as well as, most of other everyday sounds. At the same time, some intense sounds beyond the major auditory area remain audible to people with even very high degrees of hearing loss.

Underestimation of Hearing Handicap and Deafness in Self-Ratings

It should be noted that retrospective subjective self-ratings of hearing handicap and deafness are generally found to underestimate those hearing deficiencies. This was shown in the Robinson *et al.* (1984) experiments by asking the subjects to (1) retrospectively self-rate their hearing difficulties for speech reception in a number of specified real-life situations, then (2) participate in a number of simulated real-life speech reception tasks, and then (3) reexamine

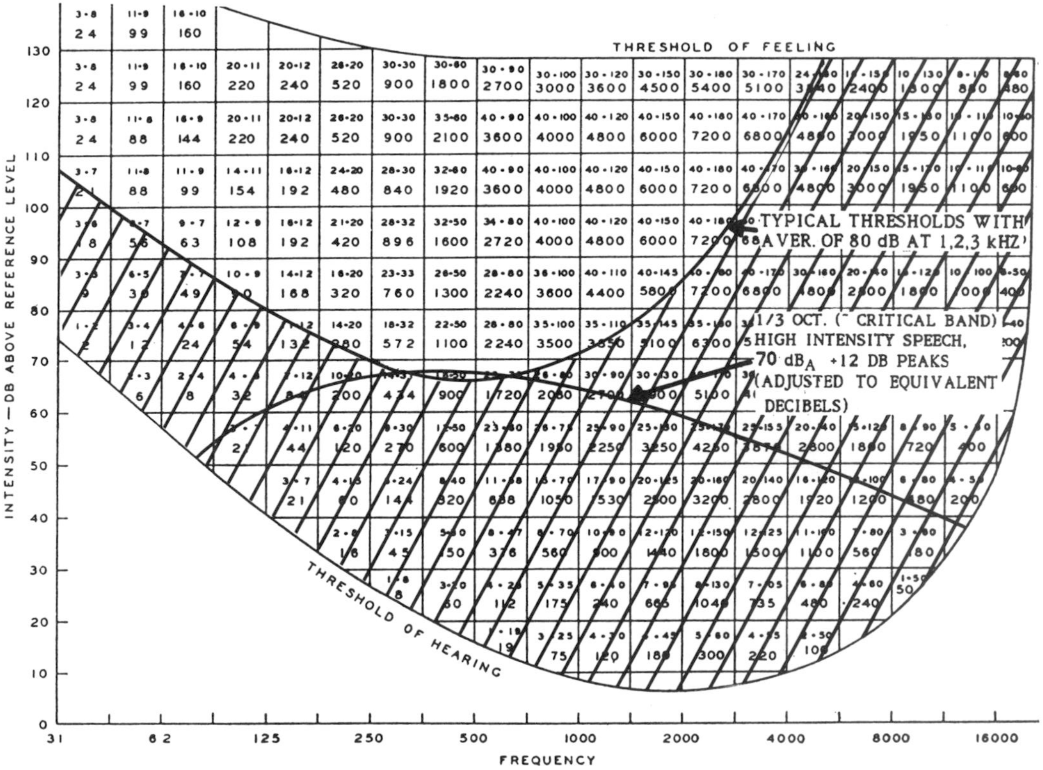

FIGURE 7.9 The shaded area shows, as an example, that with typical hearing level of 80 dB, average at 1, 2, and 3 kHz, about 65% (~225,000) of all possible (~340,000 tonal discriminations from normal threshold to threshold of feeling are inaudible, including practically 100% of high intensity speech sounds. Based on Fig. 2.22.

their first retrospective self-ratings and change their ratings if they so wished. It was found that in light of the immediate actual listening experiences, the subjects lowered their initial retrospective judgments of their speech reception abilities under real-life conditions.

Merluzzi and Hinchliffe (1973) and Lutman *et al.* (1987) also found evidence that subjective retrospective ratings of hearing ability tend to be significantly higher than is measured by performance tests. This can been attributed to (1) some psychological adaptation because of the usual slow, over time, increase in loss of hearing sensitivity, due to either age or noise, or both; (2) some vanity-driven self-denial of a handicap; and (3) some unawareness of many sounds, including speech, that they do not, or cannot, hear but which are perceived by less-deaf persons.

Binaural Hearing

The hearing handicap for everyday speech is evaluated in the AAO procedure with respect to binaural hearing. Unfortunately, most of the research involving pure-tone and speech audiometry has been conducted for monaural listening conditions. In the few studies examined of binaural hearing (Robinson *et al.*, 1984; Lutman *et al.*, 1987) the correlations, in rank order from highest to least, were usually (1) worse ear, (2) average ear, (3) (better ear × 4 + worse ear)/6; and (4) better ear × 5 + worse ear)/5.

Although the differences in correlation values were small, several well-known auditory factors suggest that this rank ordering is to be expected; (1) localization of a talker, or other source of sound; (2) binaural summation of loudness; and (3) binaural release from noise masking. These abilities are adversely affected as a function of increasing disparity in the hearing levels of the two ears. To the contrary, the AAO and British procedures tend to progressively increase the weight given to the better ear as the disparity in hearing levels between the two ears increases.

As seen in Table 7.11, Lutman *et al.*, found that the worse ear hearing levels are more highly correlated with the localization component of the questionnaire than was the better ear or, particularly, the better ear × 4 average. This could, of course, be due to the listener being able to turn toward a talker and visually receive lip and facial movements that can aid in speech understanding. Also, the loudness of the sound when heard with two equal ears is louder than with only one ear.

Colletti *et al.* (1988) examined, by means of a questionnaire, specific aspects of auditory handicap function and degree of education, psychosocial disability, and work performed. The questionnaire was administered to one group of 30–55-year-old adults who had suffered unilateral hearing loss since early childhood, and to a second, matched control group with binaural hearing. The control group clearly demonstrated superiority in sound localization, speech recognition in noise, and appreciation of music. However, the questions asked did not reveal any significant difference between the groups with respect to educational, social, and employment acheivement.

Arkebauer *et al.* (1971) found that speech reception in a free field was less effective when heard monaurally than binaurally, and, further, the more defective the worse ear, the more the monaural, compared to the binaural, degradation in understanding. MacKeith and Coles (1971) also reported advantages, beyond that of an increase in loudness, of binaural, compared to monaural, hearing for the reception of speech.

Two sets of research data provide approximate quantitative estimates of the relative contribution of hearing in the "worse" ear to the binaural understanding of speech. Harris and Myers (1974) presented to listeners with normal hearing binaural and monaural speech in the presence of competing voice signals. For the binaural tests the level of the speech was kept constant in one ear, but reduced in 10-dB steps in the other ear.

The results are shown in Table 7.12 and Figs. 7.10A and 7.10B. It is seen in Fig. 7.10A that when the speech level in one ear remained at 60 dB in one ear, but was reduced from 60 to 10 dB in the other ear, the percentage of incorrect keywords in sentences increased from 10 to 30% incorrect; an increase in percentage of words incorrect of 0.4 percentage point for each 1 dB that the speech level of the weaker ear fell below the level in the louder ear. Figure 7.10B shows that, with monaural listening, there is an increase in 1.2 percentage point for each 1-dB decrease in speech level below the starting level of 60 dB. These results indicate that a decibel difference in level received by the two ears degrades speech intelligibility at about one-third the rate as does lowering the level in an ear monaurally, or, presumably, equally in both ears.

Research results more directly related to binaural speech communications in real life were found in an analysis of the responses made on an item of the 1971–1975 USPHS survey questionnaire. That item asked the subjects to give "yes" or "no" answers to each of the following three questions:

TABLE 7.12 Percentage of Words Wrong in Sentences Heard in Presence of Competing Voice Messages

N	Stereo speech louder ear	Mode level* in weaker ear	Average % words wrong	*N*	Monaural speech level*	Average % words wrong
20	60	60	10.1	36	60	26.6
19	60	50	13.3	32	45	29.3
20	60	40	16.9	—	—	—
18	60	30	23.2	15	30	56.5
18	60	20	28.1	19	20	81.3
36	60	10	30.6	20	10	96.0

* Level above threshold. Subjects with normal hearing.

From Harris and Myers (1974).

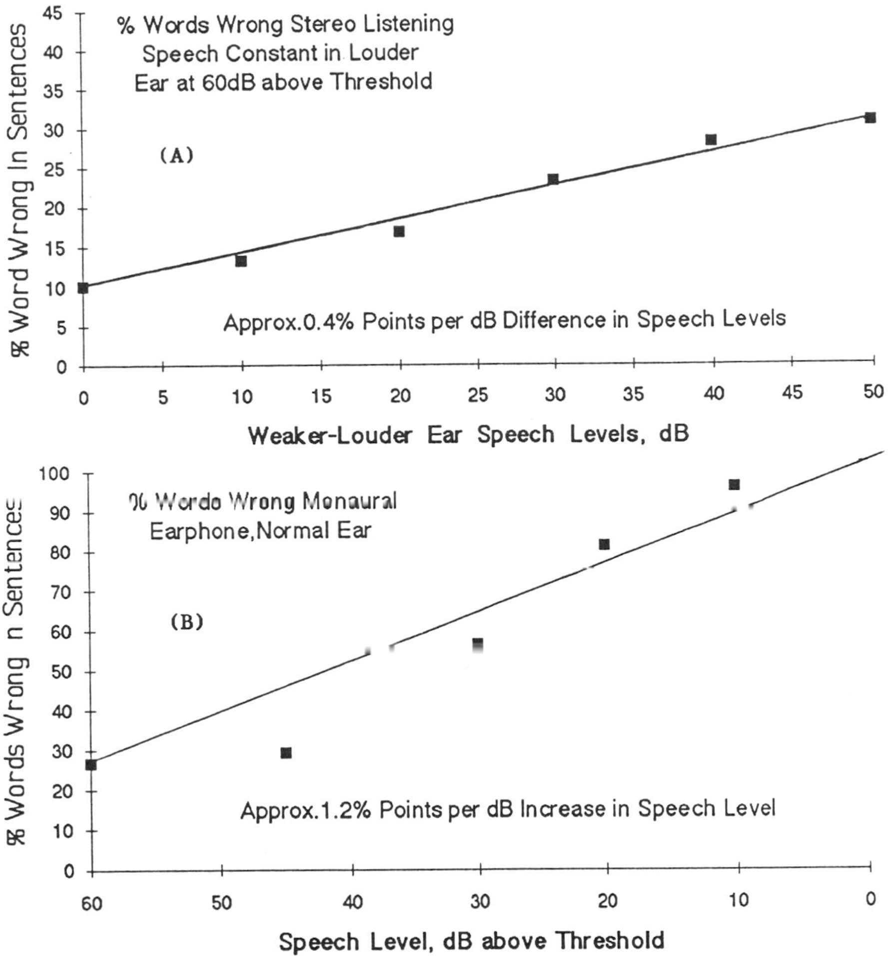

FIGURE 7.10 Percentage words wrong in sentences as function of (A) difference in speech level in two ears and (B) speech level. (Based on data in Harris and Myers, 1974; Table 7.12.)

Without a hearing aid can you usually hear and understand what a person says without seeing the person's face if that person (1) whispers to you from across a quiet room, (2) talks in a normal voice to you across a quiet room, and (3) shouts to you from across a quiet room.

Three Ys ("yes" answer) were scored as 12.5%; one N (no answer) = 37.5%; two Ns = 62.5%, and three Ns = 87.5% hearing deficiency, or handicap. Because of the broad nature of the questions, the lowest and top scores are somewhat arbitrarily truncated. The average percent hearing deficiency, or handicap, for hearing and understanding real-life speech is shown in Fig. 7.11 as a function of better-ear hearing level, average

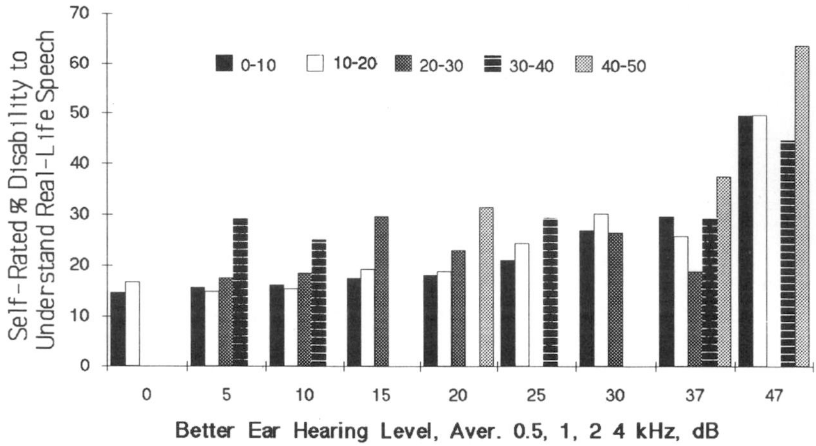

FIGURE 7.11 Percentage self-rated disability to understand real-life speech as function of hearing level of better ear, with difference between worse-ear minus better-ear hearing levels as parameter. (From Kryter and Archer, 1994.)

0.5, 1, 2, and 3 kHz. The parameters of the figure are the differences, in 10-dB steps, between the worse ear minus the better ear hearing levels.

An increase in deficiency rating as the difference between the worse-ear (WE) minus the better-ear (BE) hearing levels increases, within each 5-dB block of better-ear hearing levels, would indicate that the larger the magnitude of that difference the less well does the auditory system perform. As seen in Fig. 7.12A, a change in the WE − BE difference over the range of 5–45 dB results in an increase in percent deficiency rating from about 25% to 45%, or about 0.4 percentage points increase in percent deficiency rating for each 1-dB increase in the hearing level of the worse ear. Figure 7.12B shows that there is about a 0.8% increase in percent deficiency rating increase for each 1-dB increase in the hearing level of the better. These results indicate that a decibel difference in the hearing level of the two ears degrades speech intelligibility at about one-half the rate as does increasing the hearing level, or hearing loss, of the better ear.

These findings, and the results of the Harris and Myers study, suggest that a weighting of about $^1/_3$, rather than a $^1/_6$th (AAO) or $^1/_5$th (British) weighting ratio for the better and worse ears, would be a more appropriate measure of hearing performance for speech understanding. Thus

$$\text{Binaural hearing} = ((\text{BE} \times 2) + \text{WE})/3.$$

RELATIONS BETWEEN DIFFERENT COMBINATIONS OF HEARING LEVELS

It is clear from these research findings that no one combination of hearing levels is always superior as a means of estimating hearing impairment as measured by intelligibility tests, speech-task performance, or self-ratings of

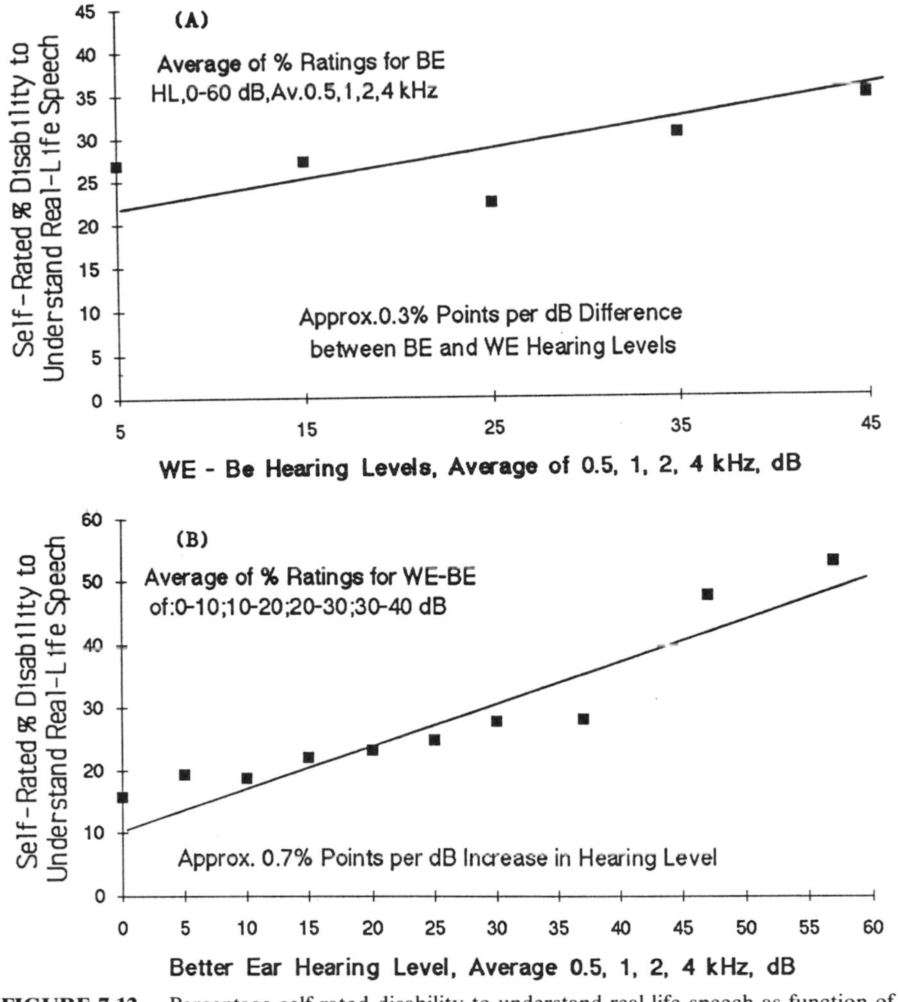

FIGURE 7.12 Percentage self-rated disability to understand real-life speech as function of (A) difference between worse-ear and better-ear hearing levels and (B) hearing level of better ear. Based on Fig. 7.11.

handicap for speech understanding and deafness. Overall, however, the better frequency combinations appear to be 0.5, 1, 2, 3 kHz; 1, 2, 3 kHz, and 0.5, 1, 2, 4 kHz.

In any event, the averages of a wide variety of combinations of pure-tone test frequencies are used in research papers and medical–legal guidelines and regulations to describe hearing threshold sensitivity. Because the shape of audiograms varies as a function of type of hearing problem, and degree of threshold shift, relations among the various averages also varies somewhat at different levels of sensitivity. As a general aid for the interpretation of hearing levels, the average levels for commonly used combinations of test frequencies were found for a large sample of ears.

The results were obtained from an examination of distributions of hearing levels for 6809 left ears and 6809 right ears tested in the USPHS 1971–1975 survey. The hearing levels at 0.5, 1, 2, and 4 kHz were averaged for each ear and sorted in 5-dB steps from 0 (<2.5 dB) to 65 dB (62.5–67.49 dB), and >71 dB. Combinations of hearing levels that included 3 kHz were calculated using estimates of the 3-kHz levels to be expected for each ear, as described earlier in the chapter. The results are shown in Table 7.13, along with the results for the two ears averaged and tabulated in 5 dB, midpoint, steps from 0 to 95 dB, average for 0.5, 1, 2, and 3 kHz. Because of the relatively few ears with hearing levels greater than 71 dB, the data from 70 to 95 dB are extrapolations, and, also because of relatively small numbers of ears, the data for the steps at 40, 50, and 60 dB, average 0.5, 1, 2, and 3 kHz, represent interpolations.

COMPARISON OF PROPOSED AND AAO GUIDES FOR THE EVALUATION OF HEARING HANDICAP FOR EVERYDAY SPEECH

Lower and Upper Fences

Shown on Fig. 7.13A are (1) the recommendation of AAO 1979 guide for the estimation of percent hearing handicap for everyday speech and (2) a function suggested for the same purpose based on the functions shown in Fig. 7.7. It is proposed that the function for hearing handicap for everyday speech be estimated from the average of the hearing levels at 500, 1000, 2000, and 3000 Hz, and that the (better ear × 2) + worse ear]/3 formula be used to represent binaural hearing.

The proposed function specifies a lower fence, average hearing level at 500, 1000, 2000, and 3000 Hz, of 0 dB for 0% hearing handicap, and an upper fence at 72 dB for 100% handicap. The upper fence is placed at the point about between where (1) the reception and understanding of everyday speech is not possible according to physical measures and calculated speech intelligibility and (2) some of the functions representing the data for self-ratings of hearing handicap in real-life conditions extrapolate to 100% handicap. It could be argued that the upper fence should be somewhat lower in that persons with higher hearing levels tend to subjectively overestimate their ability to perceive speech signals in real life.

The proposed lower fence is placed at 0 dB on grounds that there is no sharp break demarcating, as a function of hearing level, a fence between hearing handicap for everyday speech and no handicap. Indeed, for some possible everyday conditions, speech reception is significantly impaired for even persons with normal hearing (e.g., 45-dB_A speech, S/N −5 dB); and for some possible everyday conditions, speech reception is essentially unim-

TABLE 7.13 Average Left (L) and Right (R) Ear Frequency Groups of HLs*

LE + RE, *N* =	917	2393	2794	2153	1649	1188	590	1008	Interp	514	
Test frequency, kHz					Average HL, dB						
0.5, 1, 2, 3	0	5	10	15	20	25	30	35	40	45	
0.5, 1, 2	1	4	9	13	15	20	24	28	33	38	
0.5, 1, 2, 4	−1	5	9	14	19	24	30	36	42	47	
0.5, 1, 2, 3, 4	0	5	11	17	22	28	34	38	43	48	
1, 2, 3	0	4	11	16	21	27	33	39	44	50	
					Average HLs >71						
	Interp	178	Interp	106	Extrp	Extrp	Extrp	Extrp	Extrp	Extrp	N = 144
0.5, 1, 2, 3	50	55	60	65	70	75	80	85	90	95	[88]
0.5, 1, 2	43	48	53	58	63	68	73	78	83	88	[81]
0.5, 1, 2, 4	53	58	61	63	66	71	76	81	86	94	[85]
0.5, 1, 2, 3, 4	53	58	62	66	71	76	81	86	91	95	[88]
1, 2, 3	55	60	64	69	74	79	84	89	93	95	[89]

* Relative to average hearing levels of 0.5, 1, 2, and 3 kHz in 5-dB steps to 95 dB; some interpolations (Interp). Hearing levels in steps >65 dB are extrapolations (Extrp). Based on UPSHS 1971–1975 data.

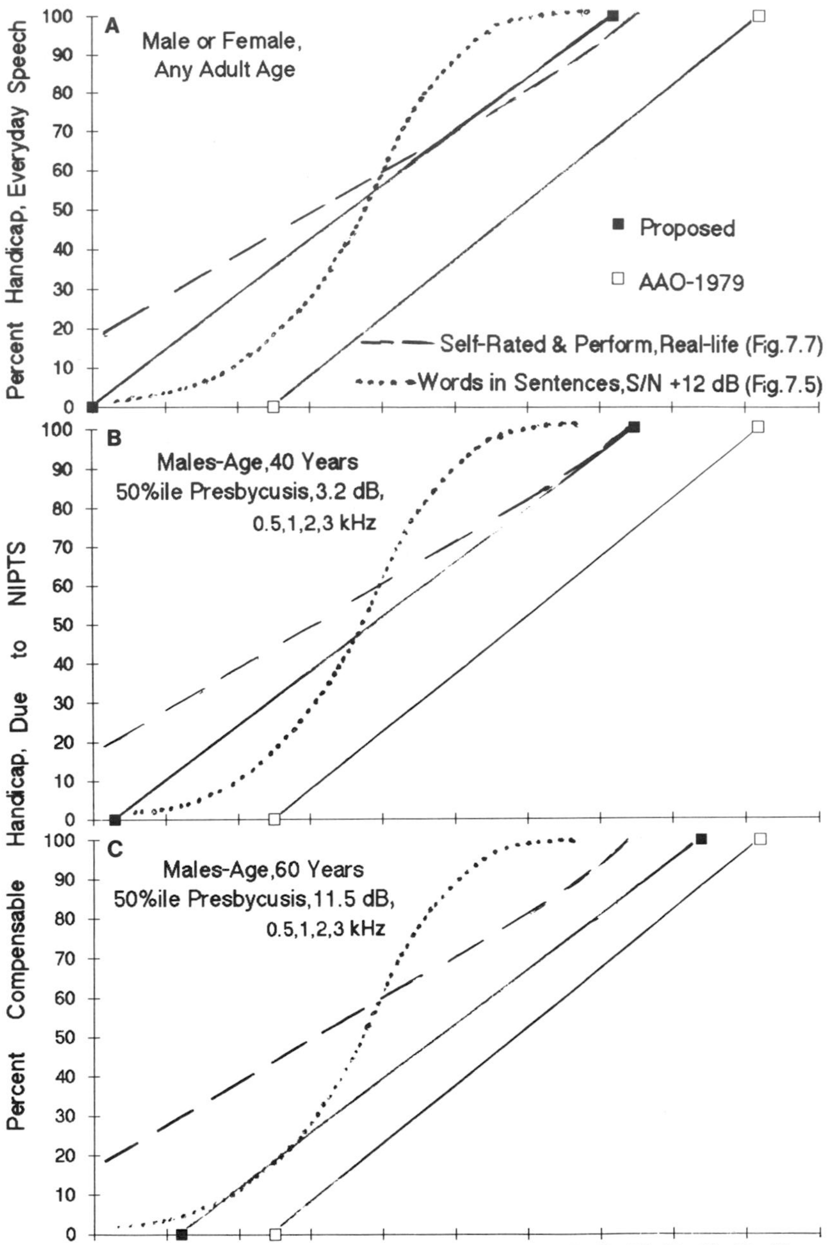

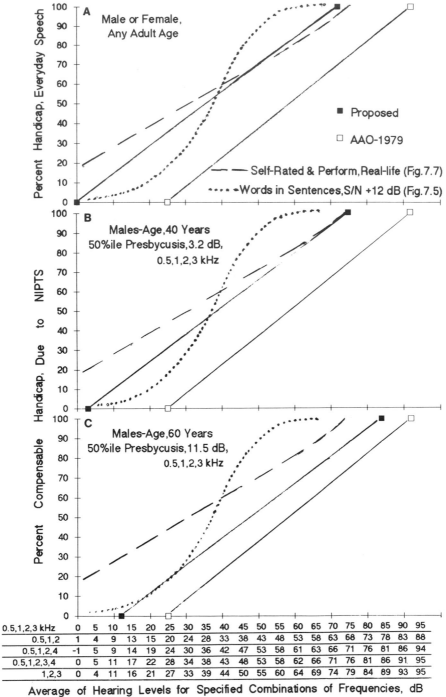

0.5,1,2,3 kHz	0	5	10	15	20	25	30	35	40	45	50	55	60	65	70	75	80	85	90	95
0.5,1,2	1	4	9	13	15	20	24	28	33	38	43	48	53	58	63	68	73	78	83	88
0.5,1,2,4	-1	5	9	14	19	24	30	36	42	47	53	58	61	63	66	71	76	81	86	94
0.5,1,2,3,4	0	5	11	17	22	28	34	38	43	48	53	58	62	66	71	76	81	86	91	95
1,2,3	0	4	11	16	21	27	33	39	44	50	55	60	64	69	74	79	84	89	93	95

Average of Hearing Levels for Specified Combinations of Frequencies, dB

FIGURE 7.13 (A) Percentage handicap for everydav speech: dashed and dotted curves as measured, solid curves, as estimated by herein proposed and by AAO (1979) procedures. (B,C) Percent of compensible handicap due to noise-induced threshold shift (NIPTS), as estimated by herein proposed and by AAO (1979) procedures.

paired for persons with even 25-dB hearing loss (e.g., 65 dB_A speech heard in the quiet). However, as the hearing levels for the average of the specified frequencies increase above 0 dB, much of measured sentence speech intelligibility progressively decreases, and, according to all the different studies, self-rated difficulties of speech communications in real life progressively increases.

The AAOO and AAO guidelines evaluate hearing impairment and handicap with respect to hearing levels, regardless of the whether they reflect hearing losses due to aging, noise, or other causes. In order to equitably apportion responsibility for hearing loss between noise exposure and aging, various methods have been suggested (Coros, 1992; Dobie, 1990). It is suggested that with the fences herein proposed, the nominal amounts of 50%ile presbycusis threshold shift specified in ISO 7029 be subtracted from all measured hearing levels to estimate threshold shifts due to noise, or causes other than that of presbycusis. This process is based on the assumption of the simple additivity of decibels of presbycusis with those of other causes (see discussion in Chapter 4). The use of 50%ile is, of course, driven by the impossibility of knowing the precise percentile represented by the measured hearing level of an individual.

It is proposed that (1) the percentage hearing handicap ascribed to age and other causes be estimated by 1.38 times the average of the average hearing levels in the left and right ears at 500, 1000, 2000, and 3000 Hz up to a total of 72 dB (HL 72 dB); and (2) the percentage hearing handicap due to exposure to noise. other cause (e.g., noise) other than be estimated by 1.38 times the average hearing levels minus presbycusis, in decibels, up to a total of 72. It is assumed that adjustments, if any, for middle-ear, or other, nosocusis causes of hearing loss, such as infections or scarred eardrums, are to be accounted for by otological examinations on an individual case basis.

Figures 7.13B and 7.13C illustrate differences between percentage handicap estimated by the AAO and proposed procedures for males age 40 and 60 years after being exposed for, respectively, 20 and 40 years to workplace noise of $(E)L_{Aeq8h}$ 90 dB_A . It is seen in those graphs that because of the subtraction in the proposed procedure of presbycusis loss from a given hearing level, the amount of compensable handicap due to workplace noise decreases for the older men; and with the AAO procedure, the presbycusis loss is added to any loss due to workplace noise.

COMPARISON OF ASSESSMENTS BY DIFFERENT PROCEDURES OF RISKS OF HEARING DAMAGE AND HANDICAP

In the United States, the AAO 1979 guide is the generally accepted standard method for the evaluation of hearing handicap, and ISO Standard 1999 is the generally accepted procedure for the estimation of risk of noise-induced, threshold-shift, hearing loss. However, the AAO and ISO 1999 procedures differ somewhat from the procedures proposed above for the evaluation of hearing handicap, and the new EE_A method developed in Chapters 4 and 5 for estimating noise-induced hearing loss.

Comparisons follow of the differences to be expected from the application of these different procedures in the estimation of the noise levels to be considered as "safe" with respect to (1) the prevention of the development of hearing handicap for everyday speech, i.e., hearing impairment no greater than a specified fence; (2) the percentage of the population to be at risk of the handicap following 10- and 40-year workday exposures to steady- and variable-intensity noise at L_{Aeq8h} 90 and 100 dB; and (3) the percentages of differently screened, for nosocusis and sociocusis, populations at risk of developing the hearing handicap from specified exposures.

Highest Exposure Levels to Not Exceed Fence

Table 7.14A shows the noise exposures required, according to ISO 1999, with the L_{Aeq8h} equal-energy unit of noise measurement, and the EE_A (with the EL_{Aeq8h} effective-energy unit of noise measurement) to cause hearing losses sufficient to just reach the lower fences specified in the AAO guide and proposed herein. It is seen in the upper part of Table 7.14 that, with 10 or 40 years of exposure, ages 30 and 60 years, ISO 1999, L_{Aeq8h}, allows for a 25–26-dB higher exposure level of steady noise (107 and 101 L_{Aeq8h} vs. 80 and 75 EL_{Aeq8h}). However, the L_{Aeq8h} of variable-intensity noise will generally be about 10 higher than the EL_{Aeq8h} level when causing a specified NIPTS. That is, for many variable and interrupted noises, an EL_{Aeq8h} of 85 *e*dB, for example, will be measured as having an L_{Aeq8h} of 95 dB.

This approximate 10 dB difference between the effective level of steady and variable intensity, or interrupted noises, is a rough estimate. A number of sounds and noises, such as music, speech, and vehicular traffic, of a given L_{Aeq8h} will have an EL_{Aeq8h} that is 10 dB or so less, and, according, that much less a cause of any threshold shift or hearing loss (see temporal distributions of music, Fig. 5.39, and speech, Fig. 6.1, and discussion in Chapter 5.)

NIPTS and Percentage Hearing Handicap from Specific Exposures

The lower section of Table 7.14 shows the 50%ile and 90%ile NIPTS, in decibels, and percent hearing handicap calculated by the AAO ISO and proposed procedures from exposures to steady and variable intensity noise of EL_{Aeq8h} 90 dB following 10 and 40 years of workday exposures. It is seen here that the differences in NIPTS and percent hearing handicap are not as large as might be surmised from the large differences in the exposure levels required to just meet the respective fences.

For the steady noise, the differences in decibels and percentage handicap in estimated threshold shift between the AAO ISO versus proposed procedures are as follows: 10 years—50%ile: 0 vs. 5 dB, 0 vs. 7%; 10

TABLE 7.14 Noise-Exposure Levels According to ISO 1999 and EE_A That Will Result in (A) 50%ile HLs Reaching AAO Guide and Proposed (Prop.) Lower Fences for Hearing Handicap; and (B) NIPTS, Estimated by ISO 1999 and EE_A from Exposure to Steady and Variable-Intensity Noise, and % Handicap as Estimated by AAO and Proposed Procedures

A. Exposures for 50%ile to Reach Fence and 0% Handicap

	Age 30 years	Age 30 years	Age 60 years	Age 60 years
Normal HL,* 50%ile (0.5, 1, 2, 3 kHz)/4	1 dB	1 dB	11.5 dB	11.5 dB
Fence HL (0.5, 1, 2, 3, kHz/4)	25 dB, AAO	0 dB, Prop.	25 dB, AAO	0 dB, Prop.
Allowed NIPTS to reach fence, dB	24 dB, AAO	0 dB, Prop.	13.5, AAO	0 dB Prop.
Years of exposure (YE)	10 YE	10 YE	40 YE	40 YE
Steady L_{Aeq8h}, EL_{Aeq8h} for allowed NIPTS	107, L_{Aeq8h} 107 EL_{Aeq8h}	80, L_{Aeq8h} 80 EL_{Aeq8h}	101, L_{Aeq8h} 101 EL_{Aeq8h}	75, L_{Aeq8h} 75 EL_{Aeq8h}
% handicap, AAO and Prop.	0%	0%	0%	0%
Variable, L_{Aeq8h}, EL_{Aeq8h}, for allowed NIPTS†	107, L_{Aeq8h} 97, EL_{Aeq8h}	90, L_{Aeq8h} 80, EL_{Aeq8h}	101, L_{Aeq8h} 91, EL_{Aeq8h}	85, L_{Aeq8h} 75 EL_{Aeq8h}

B. NIPTS and % Handicap from Exposures

	10 YE, age 30 years		40 YE, age 60 years	
	50%ile	90%ile	50%ile	90%ile
Normal HL* (0.5, 1, 2, 3, kHz)	1.0 dB	10.1 dB	11.5 dB	26.7 dB
NIPTS, ISO 1999: 90 L_{Aeq8h}, steady noise	3	5	5	7
NIPTS, EE_A: 90 EL_{Aeq8h}, steady noise	5	10	10	20
Estimated HL (normal + NIPTS, ISO)	4	15	16	34
Estimated HL (normal + NIPTS, EE_A)	6	20	22	47
Steady noise: AAO-1979, handicap, dB‡	0 dB; 0%	0 dB; 0%	0 dB; 0%	9 dB; 14%
Steady noise: proposed handicap, dB‡	5 dB; 7%	10 dB; 14%	10 dB; 14%	20 dB; 28%
NIPTS, ISO: 100 L_{Aeq8h}, variable noise	11	21	20	32
NIPTS, EE_A: 100 L_A(90, EL_A), variable noise†	5	10	10	20
Estimated HL (normal + NIPTS) ISO	12	31	32	59
Estimated, HL (normal + NIPTS), EE_A	6	20	22	47
Variable noise: AAO-1979, handicap, dB‡	0 dB; 0%	6 dB; 9%	7 dB; 11%	34 dB; 51%
Variable noise, proposed handicap, dB‡	5 dB; 7%	10 dB; 14%	10 dB; 14%	20 dB; 28%

* ISO 389 (1964); ISO 7029 (1984).

† Variable-intensity sounds equal in hazard as steady sounds can be ~10 dB less in EL_{Aeq8h}, than L_{Aeq8h}.

‡ Handicap AAO (1979) Guide = (HL, ISO 7029 + NIPTS estimated by ISO 1999) − 25 × 1.5, to maximum of 100%.

§ Handicap, proposed = NIPTS, estimated by EE_A to maximum of 72 dB − HL, 7029 × 1.38, to maximum of 100%.

years—90%ile; 0 vs. 10 dB, 0% vs. 14%; 40 years—50%ile: 0 vs. 10 dB, 0% vs. 14%; and 40 years—90%ile: 9 vs. 20 dB, 14% vs. 28%. For variable-intensity noise, with a 10-dB difference in effective level, the differences are less, even of the opposite direction for the 90%ile, 40-year exposure condition: 0 vs. 5 dB, 0% vs. 7%; 6 vs. 10 dB, 9% vs. 14%; 7 vs. 10 dB, 11% vs. 14%; and 34 vs. 20 dB, 51% vs. 28%. The reason for these seemingly relatively small differences in estimated percentage hearing handicaps is, of course, the removal of the presbycusis threshold shift in the proposed, but not in the AAO, procedures prior to the calculation of percentage handicap.

Percentage at Risk, Screened Populations

One method of expressing the adverse consequences of a specified exposure to industrial noise is to estimate the increase in the numbers, or percentage, of an exposed population that would exceed some specified hearing level. The increase is calculated relative to the percentage of the same-aged normal-hearing population having the specified hearing level. The method is illustrated in Fig. 7.14 for exposure to a steady workday noise of L_{Aeq8h}, or EL_{Aeq8h}, of 90 dB_A for 40 years. Hearing level is the average at 500, 1000, 2000, and 3000 Hz. Shown are the 10%ile, 50%ile, and 90%ile hearing levels according to ISO 7029 for screened males and unscreened males (Annex B, ISO 1999) plus the NIPTS expected in screened ears as the result of the specified exposure according to the procedures of ISO 1999 and EE_A for estimating NIPTS.

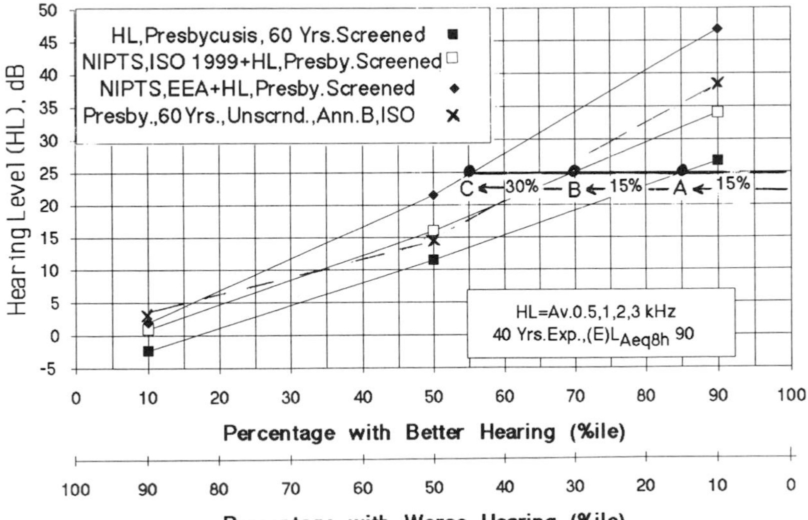

FIGURE 7.14 Example of hearing risk assessment relative to (A) the normal screened population [Annex A, ISO 1999], and (B) an unscreened general population [Annex B, ISO 1999] for male workers exposed to steady noise of EL_{Aeq8h}, or L_{Aeq8h}, 90 dB_A for 40 years with NIPTS predicted by ISO 1999 (ISO, 1991) and by EE_A.

It is seen in Fig. 7.14 that (1) 15% of 60-year-old normal males have worse hearing than the AAO fence of 25 dB; (2) an additional 15%, total of 30%, of the population exposed to the specified noise condition (L_{Aeq8h} 90 for 40 years) will have hearing worse than the 25 dB fence according to ISO 1999, and 30%, total of 45%, according to the EE_A methods for estimating NIPTS. The "percentage risk of incurring handicap" (as defined by AAO) from this exposure would be, respectively, 15%—ISO 1999, and 30%—Effective Energy, EE_A.

Percentage Population at-Risk, Unscreened Populations

As discussed in Chapter 4, Annex B of ISO 1999 provides the hearing levels for a typical unscreened population of an industrialized society (United States). It is proposed in ISO 1999, that, for the assessment of risk of incurring a hearing handicap, Annex B, or the hearing levels of some other reference group typical for the population from which specific industrial workers are drawn, might be used in lieu of the screened population of Annex A. The x's in Fig. 7.14 for 10%ile, 50%ile, and 90%ile represent the hearing levels from Annex B for 60-year-old males. These are essentially the same as the levels predicted by ISO 1999 for the L_{Aeq8h} 90 dB, 40-year noise exposure.

One would conclude from Fig. 7.14 that there is 0% risk of handicap from the specified noise exposure for the entire distribution relative to Annex B, instead of a 15% risk relative to Annex A. The use of Annex B with the ISO 1999 NIPTS predictions indicates that there is essential no NIPTS, whereas relative to the screened population of Annex A, losses in hearing levels are estimated, in conjunction with ISO 1999, to be ~5 dB at 10%ile and 50%ile and 8 dB at 90%ile. It is seen in Fig. 7.14 that the differences in estimations in percentage risk and threshold shifts are considerably larger when EE_A, rather than the ISO 1999 method, is employed to estimate NIPTS.

It is believed that the use of hearing levels from an unscreened reference group, such as Annex B, for estimating hearing handicap can be misleading by underestimating the percentage of exposed persons at risk, and inimical to hearing conservation by underestimating the number of decibels of hearing loss to be expected. The basic reasons are that:

1. Nosocusis, other than sensorineural, may add but a few decibels, on the average, to the distribution of hearing levels of otologically unscreened compared to screened ears. The effects of nosocusis are generally taken into account in otological tests of persons claiming NIPTS, and should, therefore, not be included in the hearing levels of a reference group selected to show the presence of possible NIPTS.

2. The noise exposure that allows the hearing levels of the unscreened workers to reach the distribution of the higher frequency hearing levels of an unscreened reference group, e.g., Annex B, erroneously indicates no damage risk. The random sample of U.S. males in Annex B of ISO 1999

included some workers from noisy industries, which could account for Annex B hearing levels being somewhat higher than those of Annex A. More importantly, as discussed in Chapter 4, exposures to gun noise in hunting and the military services appears to be equivalent to EL_{Aeq8h} of ~89 and the cause of ~15dB NIPTS at 4000 Hz after several years of typical exposures. It is believed that because some segments, of the order of 25%, of the general male population are, or have been, exposed to extensive amounts of gun noise, the entire distributions of hearing levels are ~8 dB higher in the general male population when unscreened, then screened for gun noise. The further addition of 1–2 dB to the hearing levels of a random unscreened sample for the effects of nosocusis, plus ~1 dB for the loss averaged over the small percentage of the total population exposed to high intensity factory noise, is consistent with the difference of ~10 dB seen in Table 4.2 between the screened and unscreened groups at the higher test frequencies.

3. The ~50% of workers who are not exposed to significant amounts of gunfire are vulnerable to accumulating ~15 dB of factory NIPTS before a co-worker who has used guns starts to show any NIPTS from the same amount of factory noise. As discussed, the factory noise does not cause an equal amount of NIPTS, ~15 dB, in the co-worker also exposed to gun noise, because the decibels of NIPTS expected from exposures to each of the workplace and gun noise alone are not additive. It is the sum of the exposure energies that is the determining factor. The ≥50% of the workers who do not, extensively use guns, can be expected to suffer ~15 dB NIPTS from that level of workplace noise. The 50% of the workers, those who have 15 dB NIPTS from gun noise, can be expected to experience 3 dB more loss as the result of the workplace noise, i.e., a total of 18 dB NIPTS, with the gun noise responsible for 3 dB of that rise in the worker's hearing level, and the workplace noise responsible for 15 dB, or vice versa.

Differences in Databases of AAO ISO 1999 (1990) and Proposed Procedures

The databases underlying the ISO 1999 and EE_A procedures were fully examined in Chapters 4 and 5. In brief, the bases of the ISO 1999 procedures appeared to be flawed because of inappropriate use of control-group data, and a possible biased selection of workers exposed to higher-intensity workplace noise.

The differences between the fences identified in the AAO guides, and herein proposed, are attributed to the scarcity of relevant research data available in the preparation of the AAOO and AAO documents. In particular, the scope of the speech and background noise levels for everyday speech necessary for appropriate setting of the lower and upper fences were not then fully appreciated. Both the lower and upper fences are found, by recent objective and subjective data relative to impairment and handicap for speech communications, to be significantly lower than specified in the AAOO and AAO guidelines.

Other Criteria of Hearing Impairment

The guides and procedures discussed above for the assessment of hearing loss and noise limits for the conservation of hearing are all directed toward the criterion of handicap for everyday speech communications. A somewhat overlooked condition of hearing impairment in some cases of permanent noise-induced deafness is that of tinnitus. *Tinnitus* is a persistent "ringing" or noisy sound in the ear that is often very disturbing and bothersome to those suffering from this condition. Although it is experienced in mild forms from time to time by people with normal hearing, it is associated in its acute forms with sensorineural, noise-induced hearing loss, as well as with some other disorders of the ear. Tinnitus is considered a severe handicap by some people (Hinchcliffe and Gordon, 1980; Vernon, 1978). However, Hallberg *et al.* (1993) found, in a regression analysis of self-perceived handicap and tinnitus annoyance in males with noise-induced hearing loss, that tinnitus had no impact of its own on self-perceived handicap.

References

AAO (1979). Guide for the evaluation of hearing handicap, American Academy Otolaryngology. *J. Am. Med. Assoc.* **241,** 2056–2079.

AAOO (1959). Guide for the evaluation of hearing impairment. Report of the Committee on Conservation of Hearing, American Academy Ophthalmology and Otolaryngology. *Trans. Am. Acad. Ophthalmol. Otolaryngol.* **63,** 236–238.

AAOO (1964, 1973). Guide for conservation of hearing in noise, revised ed. 1973, American Academy Ophthalmology and Otolaryngology. *Trans. Am. Acad. Ophthalmol. Otolaryngol.,* AAOO Suppl. (1965). Guide for the classification and evaluation of hearing handicap, American Academy Ophthalmology and Otolaryngology. *Trans. Am. Acad. Ophthalmol. Otolaryngol.* **69,** 740–751.

Acton, W. I. (1970). Speech intelligibility in a background noise and noise-induced hearing loss. *Ergonomics* **13,** 546–554.

AMA (1961). Guide to the evaluation of permanent impairment: Ear, nose, throat, and related structures. American Medical Association Committee on Medical Rating of Physical Impairment. *J. Am. Med. Assoc.* **177,** 489–501.

Anisanson, G. (1974). Methods for assessing high frequency loss in everyday listening situations. *Acta Otolaryngol.* **320,** Suppl., Chapters 3 and 5.)

ANSI (1969a) S3.5. "American National Standard Methods for the Calculation of the Articulation Index." Am. Nat. Stand. Inst., New York.

Arkebauer, H. J., Mencher, G. T., and McCall, C. (1971). Modifications of speech discrimination in patients with binaural asymmetrical hearing loss. *J. Speech Hear. Disord.* **36,** 208–212.

ASA, Z24.5, (1951). "American Standard Specification for Audiometers for General Diagnostic Purposes." American Stand. Assoc., New York.

ASA (1951). Z-24.5. "American Standard for Audiometer for General Diagnostic Purposes." Am. Natl. Stand. Instrum., New York.

Carhart, R. (1946). Speech reception in relation to pattern of pure tone loss. *J. Speech Disord.* **11,** 97–108.

Cohen, A. (1973). Some general reactions to Kryter's paper "Impairment to hearing from exposure to noise." *J. Acoust. Soc. Am.* **53,** 1235–1236.

Colletti, V., Fiorino, F. G., Carner, M., and Rizzi, R. (1988). Investigation of the longterm effects of unilateral hearing loss in adults. *Br. J. Audiol.* **22,** 113–118.

Corso, J. L. (1992). Support for Corso's hearing loss model relating aging and noise exposure. *Audiology* **31,** 162–167.

Cudworth, A. L. (1991). Hearing loss: Legal liability. *In* "Hand Book of Acoustical Measurements and Noise Control" (C. M. Harris, ed.), pp. 20.1–20.11. McGraw-Hill, New York.

Davis, H. (1948). The articulation area and the social adequacy index for hearing. *Laryngoscope* **58,** 761–768.

Davis, H. (1973). Some comments on "Impairment to hearing from exposure to noise" by K. D. Kryter. *J. Acoust. Soc. Am.* **53,** 1237–1239.

Dobie, R. A. (1990). A method for allocation of hearing handicap. *Otolaryngol.—Head Neck Surg.* **103,** 733–739.

Ginnold, R. E. (1979). "Occupational Hearing Loss—Workers Compensation Under State and Federal Programs," Rep. EPA 550/9-79-101. U.S. Environ. Prot. Agency, Washington, D.C.

Glasberg, B. R., and Moore, B. C. J. (1989). Psychoacoustic abilities of subjects with unilateral and bilateral cochlear impairments and their relationship to the ability to understand speech. *Scand. Audiol., Suppl.* No 32, 1–25.

Habib, R. G., and Hinchcliffe, R. (1978). Subjective magnitude of auditory impairment. *Audiology* **17,** 68–76.

Hallberg, L. R. M., Johnsson, T., and Axelson, A. (1993). Structure of perceived handicap in middle-aged males with noise-induced hearing loss, with and without tinnitus. *Audiology* **32,** 137–152.

Harris, J. D. (1960). Combinations of distortion in speech. *Arch. Otolaryngol.* **72,** 227–232.

Harris, J. D. (1965). Pure-tone acuity and the intelligibility of everyday speech. *J. Acoust. Soc. Am.* **37,** 824–830.

Harris, J. D., and Myers, C. K. (1974). "The Contribution of the Poorer Ear to Binaural Intelligibility," Rep. No. 768. Nav. Submar. Med. Res. Lab. Groton, Connecticut.

Harris, J. D., Haines, H. L., and Myers, C. K. (1956). A new formula for using the audiogram to predict speech hearing loss. *Arch. Otolaryngol.* **63,** 158–176.

Harris, J. D., Haines, J. D., and Myers, C. K. (1960). The importance of hearing at 3 kc for understanding speeded speech. *Laryngoscope* **70,** 131–146.

Hinchcliffe, R., and Gordon, A. (1980). Subjective magnitude of symptoms and handicaps related to hearing impairment. *In* "Noise as a Public Health Problem" (J. V. Tobias, G. Jansen, and W. D. Ward, eds.), ASHA Rep. No. 10. *Am. Speech–Lang.–Hear. Assoc.,* Rockville, MD.

ISO (1964). 389. "Acoustics—Standard Reference Zero for the Calibration of Pure-Tone Audiometers." Int. Organ. Stand., Geneva.

ISO (1984). 7029. "Acoustics—Threshold of Hearing by Air Conduction as a Funtion of Age and Sex for Otologically Normal Persons." Int. Organ. Stand., Geneva.

ISO (1990). 1999. "Acoustic—Assessment of Occupational Noise Exposure for Hearing Conservation Purposes." Int. Organ. Stand., Geneva.

Kell, R. L., Pearson, J. C. G., Acton, W., and Taylor, W. (1971). Social effects of hearing loss due to weaving noise. *In* "Occupational Hearing Loss" (D. W. Robinson, ed.), pp. 179–192. Academic Press, New York.

Kryter, K. D. (1973a). Impairment to hearing from exposure to noise. *J. Acoust. Soc. Am.* **53,** 1211–1234. See references Cohen (1973), Davis (1973), Lempert (1973), Ward (1973), and Reply to comments by K. D. Kryter, *J. Acoust. Soc. Am.* **53,** 1235–1252 (1973).

Kryter, K. D. (1973b). Reply to the critiques of A. Cohen, H. Davis, B. L. Lempert, and

W. D. Ward of the paper "Impairment to hearing from exposure to noise." *J. Acoust. Soc. Am.* **53,** 1244–1252.

Kryter, K. D., and Archer, S. (1994). Analysis of hearing data from USPH survey. In preparation.

Kryter, K. D., Williams, C., and Green, D. M. (1962). Auditory acuity and the perception of speech. *J. Acoust. Soc. Am.* **34,** 1217–1223.

Kuzniarz, J. I. (1973). Hearing loss and speech intelligibility in noise. *Proc. Int. Congr. Noise Public Health Probl.* (W. D. Ward, ed.), Rep. EPA 550/9-73-008, pp. 57–72. U.S. Environ. Prot. Agency, Washington, D.C.

Lempert, B. L. (1973). Technical aspects of Dr. Kryter's paper "Impairment to hearing from exposure to noise" with respect to the NIOSH statistics. *J. Acoust. Soc. Am.* **53,** 1240–1241.

Liden, G. (1965). Undistorted speech audiometry. *In* "Sensorineural Hearing Process and Disorders" (A. Graham, ed.), Little, Brown, Boston.

Lutman, M. E., and Robinson, D. W. (1992). Quantification of hearing disability for mediocolegal purposes based on self-rating. *Br. J. Audiol.* **26,** 297–306.

Lutman, M. E., Brown, E. J., and Coles, R. R. A. (1987). Sel-reported disability and handicap in the population in relation to pure-tone threshold, age, sex and type of hearing loss. *Br. J. Audiol.* **21,** 45–58.

MacKeith, N. W., and Coles, R. R. A. (1971). Binaural advantages in hearing speech. *J. Laryngol. Otol.* **85,** 213–232.

Merluzzi, F. and Hinchcliffe, R. (1973). Threshold of subjective auditory handicap. *Audiology* **12,** 65–69.

Mullins, C. J., and Bangs, J. L. (1957). Relations between speech discrimination and other audiometric data. *Acta Oto-Laryngol.* **47,** 149–157.

Nett, E., Doerfler, L. G., and Matthews, J. (und.). "Summary of the Results of Project SP-167—The Relationship Between Audiological Measures and Actual Social–Psychological–Vocational Disability." U.S. Dept. Health, Educ., Welfare, Washington, D.C.

NIOSH (1972). "Criteria for a Recommended Standard. Occupational Exposure to Noise," Rep. HSM 73-11001. Natl. Inst. Occup. Saf. Health, Dep. Health, Educ., Welfare, Washington, D.C.

Niemeyer, W. (1967). Speech discrimination in noise-induced deafness. *Int. Audiol.* **6,** 42–47.

Noble, W. G. (1978). "Assessment of Impaired Hearing—A Critique and a New Method." Academic Press, New York.

OSHA (1969). "Occupational Noise Exposure. Safety and Health Standards," *Federal Register* 34, 12 and 9b, Part II. U.S. Dept. Labor, Washington, D.C.

OSHA (1981). "Occupational Noise Exposure. Hearing Conservation Amendment," 29 CFR Part 1910, *Federal Register* **46,** 11 U.S. Department of Labor, Washington, D.C.

OSHA (1983). "Occupational Noise Exposure. OSHA Safety and Health Standards," 29 CFR Part 1910, OSHA 2206, U.S. Dept. Labor, Washington, D.C.

Pearsons, K. S., Bennett, R. L., and Fidell, S. (1977). "Speech Levels in Various Noise Environments," Rep. EPA-600/1-77-025. U.S. Environ. Prot. Agency, Washington, D.C. (Avail. from NTIS as PB 270 053.)

Plompt, R. and Mimpen, A. M. (1979). Improving the reliability of testing the speech reception threshold for sentences. *Audiology* **18,** 43–52.

Quiggle, R. R., Glorig, A., Delk, J. H., and Summerfield, A. B. (1957). Predicting hearing loss for speech from pure tone audiograms. *Laryngoscope* **67,** 1–15.

Robinson, D. W., Wilkins, P. A., Thyer, N. J., and Lawes, J. F. (1984). "Auditory Impairment and the Onset of Disability and Handicap in Noise-Induced Hearing Loss," ISVR Tech Rep. No. 126. Univ. of Southampton, Southampton, England.

Salomon, G., and Parving, A. (1985). Hearing disability and communication handicap for compensation purposes based on self-assessment and audiometric testing. *Audiology* **24,** 135–145.

Sivian, L. J. and White, S. D. (1933). On minimum audible sound fields. *J. Acoust. Soc. Am.* **4,** 288–321.

Smoorenburg, G. F. (1982). Damage risk criteria for impulse noise. *In* "New Perspectives on Noise-Induced Hearing Loss" (R. P. Hamernik, D. Henderson, and R. Salvi, eds.), pp. 471–490. Raven, New York.

Smoorenburg, G. (1986). Speech perception in individuals with noise induced hearing loss and implications for hearing loss criteria. *In* "Basic and Applied Aspects of Hearing Loss" (R. J. Salvi, D. Henderson, and R. P. Hamerink, eds.), pp. 335–344. Plenum, New York.

Smoorenburg, G. F. (1992). Speech reception in quiet and noisy conditions by individuals with noise-induced hearing loss in relation to their tone audiograms. *J. Acoust. Soc. Am.* **91,** 421–437.

Stephens, D., and Hetu, R. (1991). Impairment, disability and handicap in audiology: towards a consensus. *Audiology* **30,** 185–200.

Suter, A. H. (1978). "The Ability of Mildly Hearing-Impaired Individuals to Discriminate Speech in Noise," Rep. EPA-550/9-78-100. U.S. Environ. Prot. Agency, Washington, D.C.

Veneklasen, P. S. (1956). City noise—Los Angeles. *Noise Control* **2**(4), 14–19.

Vernon, J. A. (1978). The other noise damage: Tinnitus. *Sound Vib.* **12,** 26.

Ward, W. D. (1973). Comments on "Impairment to hearing from exposure to noise" by K. D. Kryter. *J. Acoust. Soc. Am.* **53,** 1242–1243.

Webster, J. C., and Klumpp, R. G. (1962). Effects of ambient noise and nearby talkers on a face-to-face communication task. *J. Acoust. Soc. Am.* **34,** 936–941.

WHO (1980). "International Classification of Impairments, Disabilities and Handicaps—A Manual of Classification Relating to Consequences of Disease." World Health Organ., Geneva.

Young, M. A., and Gibbons, E. W. (1962). Speech discriminations scores and threshold measurements in a non-normal population. *J. Aud. Res.* **2,** 21–33.

Mental and Psychomotor Task Performance in Noise

INTRODUCTION

The methods and results of research on the effects of noise on mental and psychomotor task performance have been, and continue to be, a matter of considerable controversy. Reviews of this problem area include Broadbent (1957, 1979, 1983), Jones (1983), Jones and Broadbent, 1991; Loeb (1980, 1986), Kryter (1985), Smith (1989), Smith and Jones (1992), and Suter (1992).

Much of the initial research on these matters has been concerned with testing the following two theories (in the discussion to follow, unless specifically noted, *work,* and *work performance,* will refer to the performance of either, or a combination of both, mental or skilled motor, so-called psychomotor, work or tasks):

1. Noise above a certain level of intensity causes general physiological overarousal in nonauditory physiological systems of the worker that will enhance some types of work activities but adversely affect others.
2. Noise is psychologically aversive, annoying, or distracting and thereby interferes with work performance.

For this experimentation, noises were defined, as for the sensation of perceived noisiness, as sounds that are unwanted independently of any cognitive meaning they may have, and, further, that the noises supposedly did not mask or interfere with information involved in task performance.

Recent research has also been concerned with questions of whether (1) in the performance of a given task, or tasks, the organism pays a psychological and/or physiological price due to "extra effort" required to overcome the stress, whatever that may be, from the noise; and (2) different types of personality interact differently with the noise and different types and complexities of tasks.

Before discussing the present state-of-the-art findings, some background information is presented. This information illustrates the kinds of difficulties and general concepts historically involved in the early development of this field of research.

Masking Artifacts

A source of inconsistency among the results of research studies on psychomotor task performance in noise has been the role of task-related acoustic cues heard by the subjects when performing the task. These cues can be the slight sounds (clicks or the like) made, for example, by switches, electronic relays, the contact of tracking styluses against metal plates, and the sound of motors that occur when stimuli are presented, or when responses are made. These clicks and sounds can give subjets feedback information as to the presence of stimuli or to the accuracy, quickness, and level of performance in ways that tend to improve performance on psychomotor tasks. When these cues are masked by noise, the results show an apparent decline in the subjects' ability to perform the task.

The presence of such acoustic cues in what were considered definitive studies of the effects of noise on the monitoring and detection of visual signals (Broadbent, 1953, 1954, 1955, 1957, 1958; Broadbent and Gregory, 1963, 1965) was uncovered by Poulton (1976a,b 1977, 1978, 1979, 1980). The implications of these discoveries are discussed and debated by Broadbent (1976, 1977, 1978).

Poulton's initial concern about the possibility of masking artifacts in some of these studies arose over a five-choice visual serial-reaction task in which the subjects were to tap as rapidly as possible one of five small brass disks with a steel-tipped metal stylus; the disk to be tapped depended on which of five neon lamps was turned on at a given moment. Poulton and Edwards (1974) found that a low-frequency noise did not degrade task performance relative to that in quiet at a level of 102 dB_C, although Hartley (1973, 1974) and Hartley and Carpenter (1974) had earlier found that a flat spectrum noise of only 95 dB_C degraded performance on the same task. As Poulton discovered, a plausible reason for these results was that the stylus hitting the brass disks (indicating, in conjunction with a change of lights, a correct response) made a high-pitched click that was not audible in the noise with the flat spectrum, but could be heard in the low-frequency spectrum noise. Thus, the subjects received the same auditory response feedback in the low-frequency noise that was available to them in quiet, but not in the flat spectrum noise.

Poulton next examined the equipment used in Broadbent's "20 dial test" for studies of the effects of noise on vigilance, the results of which served as a base for various generally accepted theories about perceptual task performance in noise (Broadbent, 1953, 1954, 1955, 1957, 1958; Broadbent and Gregory, 1963, 1965). Poulton found that when the subject taking this test turned a control knob in the correct, but not the incorrect direction, a microswitch made a slight click that was audible in the quiet condition (noise at 70 dB) and inaudible in the noisy condition (noise at 100 dB). The experimenters, and probably the subjects, were not aware at the time of the studies of these acoustic feedback cues that were being masked in some conditions of noise and not in others. These data from the 20-dial and the five-choice serial reaction tests served to support the long-held theory of "blinks" that noise above a level of 70–80 dB periodically attracts attention from other sensory perceptions for ~1-s intervals.

Concept of Masking of Internal Speech

To help explain some of the apparent adverse effects of noise on work performance, Poulton (1976a,b, 1977, 1979) hypothesized that noise can interfere with internally generated behavior related to the auditory system. According to this theory, the performance of certain types of ostensibly nonauditory work by some subjects may be affected by the noise internally "masking," or interfering with, internally articulated or rehearsed verbalization of words or numbers involved in the tasks. According to this concept, the noise interferes somewhat with the listener's echoic articulation of words or numbers presented for memorization. This concept perhaps seems, physiologically, very hypothetical. However, recent techniques of scanning brain activity have shown that when a person was having auditory hallucinations there was considerable activity in the brain's speech center, Broca's area, indicating possible incipient verbalizations of visualizations (MGuire *et al.* 1993).

The direct masking by noise of auditory cues helpful to the performance of nonauditory work plus Poulton's theory of the role of internal speech interference by noise explain much of the research findings in this area (Poulton, 1980). There are, however, a number of research studies showing somewhat different interactive effects of noise on performance depending on the type of task involved (such as tasks requiring "focused attention" on a part of a visual screen, as compared to search of the area of a visual screen for targets) that are not readily accounted for by Poulton's composite theory of arousal, internal speech masking, and direct masking of performance-feedback cues.

Concept of Construed Concern

Some of these unexpected effects can perhaps be attributed to beliefs that subjects may have about the nature and purpose of the experimental procedures being followed. This explanation might be called the theory of "construed concern." In particular, subjects may believe (whether or not so instructed) that when the loud noise or sound is present, the noise signifies important information that may be harmful to their hearing, or that the experimental conditions may become overbearing. These concerns may cause some emotion-related physiological arousal or stress. Research findings supporting this concept are presented later in a discussion of measurements of physiological states. Masking of internal speech and construed concern constitute a pseudoauditory factor and a noise-meaning factor that were not considered in the design of most of the early research on the effects of noise on mental and psychomotor task performance.

So much, by way of introduction. The results of number of specific studies and theories relevant to the subjects at hand are discussed below under the following topics:

1. Physiological variables
2. Task variables
3. Aftereffects
4. Information overload
5. Ancillary variables
6. Industrial field studies

PHYSIOLOGICAL VARIABLES

As will be further discussed in Chapter 9, there is no question that intense sound, particularly when it comes as a change in the acoustic environment, can have a general physiologic alerting-arousal effect on an organism—increased respiration rate, blood pressure, heart rate, and adrenal gland secretions. However, some physiologic adaptation or habituation can be expected to take place with repetitions, or long-time continuation, of such noises.

Insofar as task performance depends on alertness, noise might be predicted to have some beneficial effect on work output, at least initially. On the other hand, this physiological arousal could lead to fatigue as well or cause some sensory, perceptual, or motor overactivity that degrades work performance. While this hypothesis is a reasonable one for explaining some variations in work performance in noise, the physiological state of arousal is difficult to measure.

EEG State

Using electroencephalographic (EEG) activity as an index of central nervous system arousal, Gulian (1970) divided subjects into two categories; hyperreactive and hyporeactive. These subjects were exposed to intermittent and continuous noises at various levels of intensity for a number of 1½-h sessions, during which they performed auditory signal detection tasks. The tasks consisted of making discriminations among tonal signals. Some of her findings are shown in Fig. 8.1.

As seen in Fig. 8.1, while the subjects could be ranked as hyporeactive or hyperreactive on the basis of their EEG state in quiet, in the various noise conditions, their states of arousal were not very different from each other. However, relative to their state in quiet, the noise reduced the state of arousal for the hyperreactive and increased it for the hyporeactive. This may be a function of the "law of initial level" (physiological states tend toward a mean level).

Clearly, while the hyperreactive group in general had fewer correct detections than the hyporeactive group, the task performance of neither group was affected by the different noise conditions in any systematic way; however, when in quiet, the hyperreactive group performed exceedingly poorly and were inferior in task performance to the hyporeactive group either in quiet or in noise. A possible argument for this particular finding could be that in quiet the hyperreactive subjects were overaroused and for this reason performed relatively poorly. From these data, noise—intermittent or continuous, weak or intense—does not appear to have had any obvious detrimental effect on task performance or state of arousal as measured by EEG.

Cardiovascular and Adrenal States

A program of research on the effects of noise on physiological stress reactions and task performance was conducted by Glass and Singer (1972, 1973). Some of the performance test results are discussed later, but it is noted here that the skin conductance [galvanic skin response (GSR)], vasoconstriction and muscle tension measures of physiological reaction to noise showed complete habituation to noise presented during the performance of a variety of mental and motor work tasks.

Conrad (1973) studied the effect of 93-dB_A broadband noise on a serial decoding task. Four panel lights were located above a display window on which a four-digit code appeared. The four lights corresponded to the four digit positions in the code. Thus, the light that was illuminated indicated a specific digit in the four-digit code that was to be decoded. The subject responded by using the indicated digit to depress one of the four buttons located under the display window. A trial was given every second. Various physiological measures of muscle tension and vascular changes were taken

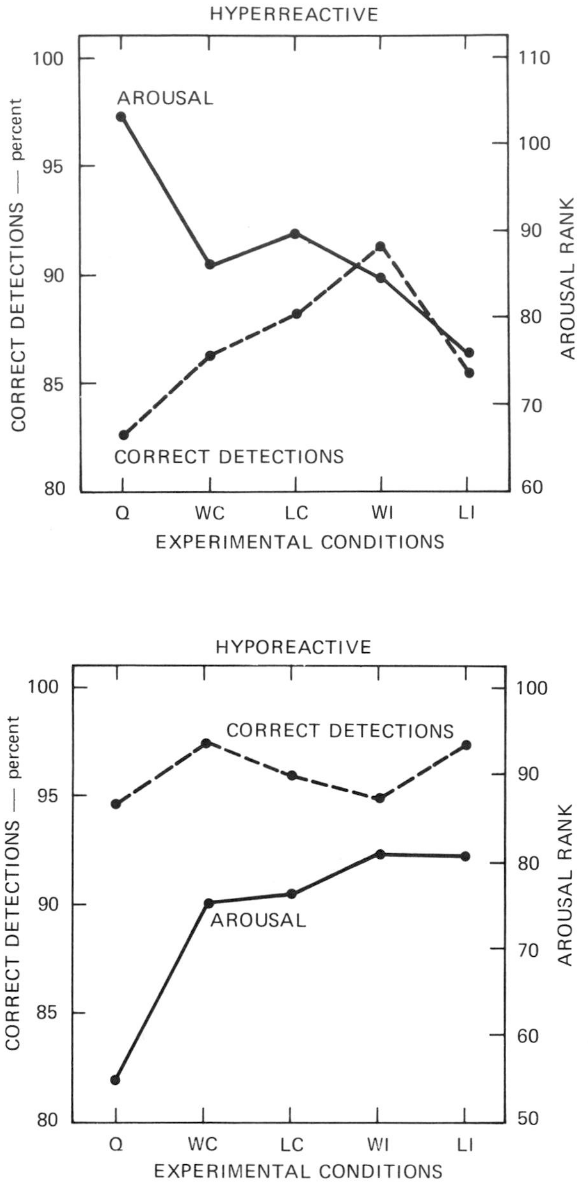

FIGURE 8.1 State of arousal and performance of auditory signal detection tasks during various acoustic conditions: Q = quiet; WC = weak continuous noise (three tones: 100, 300, 400 Hz at 78 dB); LC = loud continuous noise (three tones at 90 dB); WI = weak intermittent noise (3 tones at 71 dB); and LI = loud intermittent noise (three tones at 92 dB. (From Gulian, 1973.)

and the subjects self-rated their sensitivity to noise. Although no effects on task performance were found, there was a significant relation between self-ratings of sensitivity to noise and the vasoconstrictive response.

Becker *et al.* (1971) found that subjects who rated themselves especially sensitive to noise in real life were also the more psychologically sensitive in ratings of noises in laboratory tests. But no significant differences in heart rate and electromyographic responses were found among the less-sensitive than the more-sensitive subjects, according to psychological self-ratings, when in the presence of the laboratory noises. However, it has also been found that subjects who had previously rated themselves as more sensitive to noise were both physiologically more responsive and more adversely affected in the performance of some laboratory tasks conducted in high-intensity noise, than were subjects who had rated themselves as being less sensitive (Bahatia, Shipra, and Muhar, 1991).

Frankenhaeuser and Lundberg (1974) found that aperiodic noise from 65 to 85 dB_A did not interfere with the performance of mental arithmetic, nor affect adrenaline excretion (Fig. 8.2A). After the noise exposure, there appeared to be some relative increase in adrenaline excretion due to the noise compared to the quiet exposure condition, but heart rate showed a relative decline (Fig. 8.2B).

Lundberg and Frankenhaeuser (1978) asked subjects to choose the highest level of white noise between 70 and 108 dB_A that they were willing to endure for 10 min. A second set of subjects was paired to the first set for a subsequent 10-min exposure to the noise level chosen by the first subject of each pair. Comparison of the adrenaline and cortical excretions for quiet control sessions with those for the noise-exposed sessions revealed that the subjects who had selected the noise level were less aroused by the noise than the paired subjects. Further, the self-ratings of discomfort were correlated with the physiological measures. Performance on an arithmetic performance test, however, was not affected by whether the subject had selected the noise level.

Hawel (1975) tested 10 male college students for one 4-h session per week for 10 weeks. Pulse rate, adrenal-gland excretion (catecholamine), and psychological state (anxiety) were monitored. Except for two control sessions (5th and 10th weeks), the Kraepline-Pauli (simple computations) tests were administered. The noise was interrupted (5 s on, 12 s off) pink noise at a level of 90 dB. There were no effects of the nosie on performance, but the noise increased pulse rate and catecholamine excretion and decreased subjective ratings of anxiety. In general, the noise increased general physiological arousal, relative to the control days (when the subjects were in quiet and took no tests), but the state reached did not constitute overarousal detrimental to task performance or to subjective anxiety.

Basow (1974) measured anxiety level (muscle tension) and performance

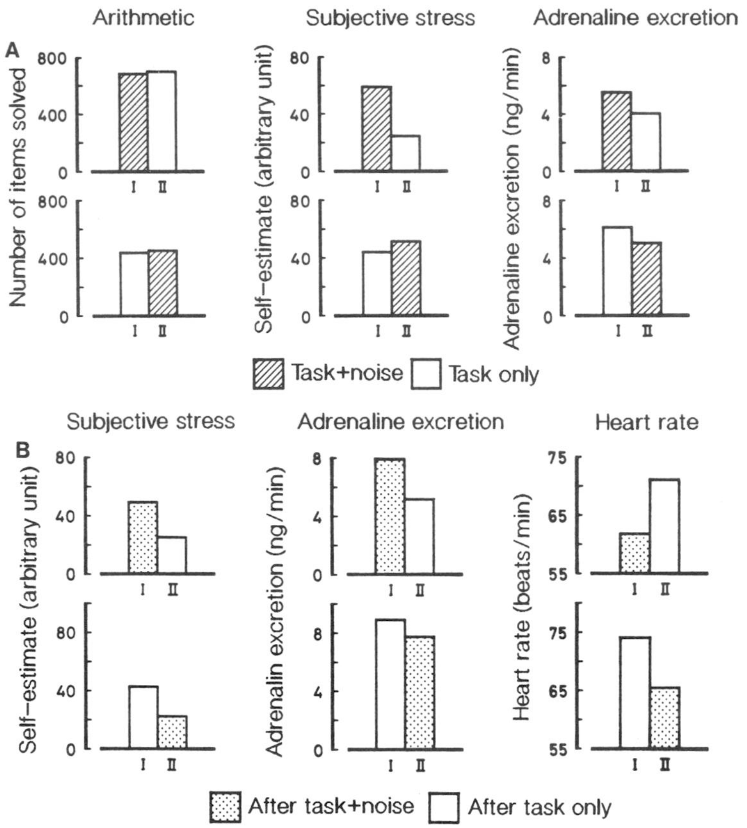

FIGURE 8.2 Effect during and after noise and no-noise periods. (From Frankenhaeuser and Lundberg, 1974.)

on various work and mathematical tasks. There was no average systematic relation between anxiety level, as measured, and task errors.

Cohen *et al.* (1974) found that subjects taking a fast-paced, very complex test involving visual signal decoding and response made a greater number of errors in 100 dB_A of synthesized office machine noise than in quiet. When in the noise, the subjects also revealed the following physiological conditions: "Profuse sweating (particularly in the palmar and armpit regions), muscle tension (back of the neck and shoulders), hand and finger cramps, blanching of the hand and fingers, and feelings of finger coolness or numbness" (p. 30). Cohen *et al.* concluded that the noise in this study when combined with the fast-paced task caused physiological overarousal that interfered with task performance.

However, in a study similar with respect to task and noise conditions, Kryter and Poza (1980) found no reduction in task performance because of the noise (see lower segment of Fig. 8.3). Further, no physiological reactions of the sort reported by Cohen *et al.* were observed in the subjects, nor were there any significant changes in heart rate or blood volume measured as a function of noise condition. However, the typical pulse volume response to broadband noise at an intensity of 100 dB_A occurred (see Fig. 8.3). Because of these contrary findings, as well as the usual fact of physiological habituation to intense noise, it was suggested that the reason for the findings of

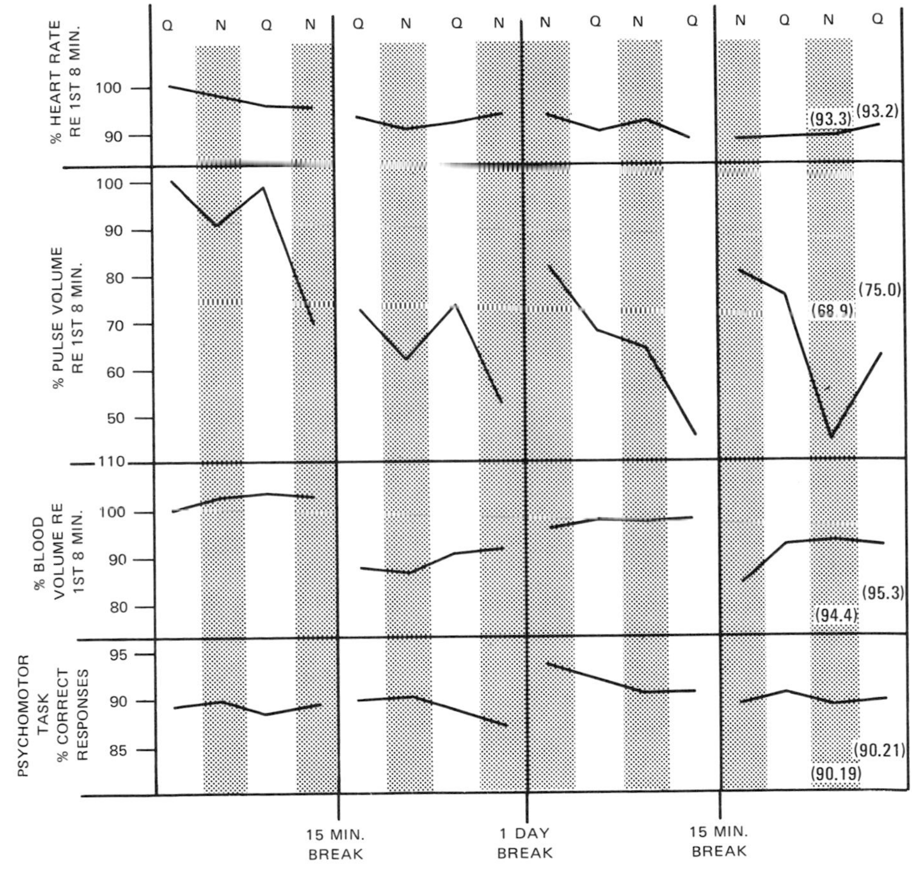

Q = QUIET (50 dB_A STIMULUS NOISE) ON FOR 8 MINUTE SEGMENTS, FOLLOWED BY 2 MINUTES OF NO NOISE.

N = NOISE (100 dB_A) ON FOR 8 MINUTES, FOLLOWED BY 2 MINUTES OF NO NOISE.

FIGURE 8.3 Averaged physiological and task performance results in alternate periods of quiet and noise. The numbers in parentheses in the last N and Q segments are the averages over all test segments for the respective N and Q conditions. (From Kryter and Poza, 1980.)

Cohen *et al.* was possibly overarousal from intense motivation and false anxiety about the effects of the noise on performance and not because of any direct physiological overarousal by the noise per se.

Mosskov and Ettema (1977, 1980) conducted a series of studies on the effects of noise on task performance and physiological arousal. In these studies young men were exposed to a variety of noises at levels from 40 to 100 dB_A and durations from a few minutes to 3 h. Mosskov and Ettema (1980) conclude that the handling of visual information and mental capacity were impaired by the noise, so that the number of mistakes increased and the subjects needed more time to handle information. The physiological overarousal effects of the noise found by these investigators, and the concomitant adverse effects on mental and other task performance, are inconsistent with the majority of other laboratory and field studies on physiological arousal from noise. The most obvious explanation is that for some reason the subjects in the Mosskov and Ettema tests did not show the habituation that normally occurs to such noises.

The aforementioned concept of construed concern is consistent with the lack of habituation to, and overarousal by, the noise that appears to be present in the Cohen *et al.* and the Mosskov and Ettema studies. Also, supportive is a study by Vera *et al.* (1992) showing that subjective tension and physiological (electrodermal) response to high-intensity (85–95 dB) traffic noise was greater when accompanied with negative statements than without the statements.

Carter and Beh (1989) found that performance on a vigilance task of 55-min duration was essentially the same in quiet or in different conditions of intermittent noise. The noise increased diastolic and mean blood pressure, and the variability of heart rate, with no indication of habituation over the 55 min. The results were interpreted to mean that performance was maintained under the noise stress by increased effort on the part of the subjects.

Tafalla and Evans (1993) instructed subjects to exert a low and a high level of effort while completing arithmetic tasks in the quiet, and in the presence of noise. Reaction time was the slower (worse performance) in the noise than quiet, but, for both of those conditions, was shorter for subjects instructed to exert a high, rather than a low, level of effort. It was also found that during high effort, measures of heart rate, noradrenaline, and cortisol indicated some increase in physiological effort, or stress was present. The authors hypothesize that task performance was maintained in the presence of the noise stress by the expenditure of greater physiological "energy."

Belojevic *et al.* (1993) compared the performance on four cognitive tasks taken in the quiet, L_{Aeq} 30 dB_A, and traffic noise of L_{Aeq} 55- and 75-dB_A subjects self-rated for noise sensitivity. No physiological measures were made, but the results are included here on the assumption of a probable correlation between noise sensitivity and physiological arousal by noise. It was found that there were no differences in performance in the noise and quiet conditions on "search and-memory," or a "hidden-figures" tasks among the subjects as a function of subjective noise sensitivity. But lowest performance was found for the more noise-sensitive subjects in the noise condition on "short-term" memory and "mental arithmetic" tasks.

Sleep and Drug States

A number of studies have been done in which the general physiological state of arousal of the subjects was modified by the administration of various substances, or by sleep deprivation, prior to tests of psychomotor task performance in noise. The hypothesis to be tested was that there could be an interaction between the altered state and noise stimulation that could influence task performance.

Strasser (1972) found that noise had no apparent effect on the learning of, or performance on, a visual tracking task but that it did increase heart rate. However, with a sedative medication, the noise had no appreciable effect on either performance or heart rate.

Hartley *et al.* (1977) exposed male college students for 53-min test periods to white noise at levels of 70 and 95 dB_A. Each subject was exposed to two test periods on each of 3 days. The various test conditions were counterbalanced and placebos used as a control for the administration of chlorpromazine (a sedative). No main effects of the drug or noise on a visual target detection (vigilance) task were found. The experimenters also asked the subjects to rate how certain they were of the correctness of their responses on the performance test. The subjects were somewhat more certain of their responses when in noise conditions or when drugged, but these effects were counteracted when both conditions prevailed. All in all, the results indicated no undue arousal from 95-dB_A white noise compared with 70-dB_A noise, and possibly a slight countereffect to the depressive drug.

Hartley and Shirley (1977) tested the hypothesis that the effects of noise and sleep loss on task performance would be counteractive. The task was the detection of slight changes in luminance of lights, and the noise was white noise at a level of 95 dB and, as control, 70 dB. Sleep conditions were 8 h at night, 4 h at night, or 4 h in the afternoon. The subjects were tested for 1 h three times per day. In addition to errors in detection, confidence ratings of responses were obtained from the subjects.

The authors concluded that (1) noise and sleep loss had mutually antagonistic effects (noise decreased performance after sleep, but increased it with sleep loss); and (2) noise made subjects more cautious in their responsiveness, and sleep made them less cautious. However, the variety of conditions and test schedules were complex, and overall there were no main effects of noise or sleep schedules on task (discrimination) performance. In any event, no general overarousal from the noise that would adversely affect task performance was evident.

Colquhoun and Edwards (1975) found that white noise (100 dB) significantly decreased speed of responding to a five-choice serial-response test and increased errors. Doses of alcohol caused no change in speed of responding but increased error rate when in quiet and decreased error rate when in noise. However, note that the noise-effects data per se are suspect because as noted by Poulton (1980), and discussed above, a click made by a response stylus contacting a metal plate could be heard in the control quiet (70-dB noise), but not in the 100-dB noise.

Simpson *et al.* (1974) compared the performance on a tracking task (subjects held a stylus on a rotating visual target) in 50-dB$_A$ noise and in 80-dB$_A$ noise when the subjects had ingested a solution that may or may not have contained glucose. The results showed that the 80-dB$_A$ noise decreased time on target by 20% or so (statistically significant) and that the glucose reduced performance by about 10% for the 50-dB$_A$ exposure condition. These findings seem difficult to relate to arousal–counterarousal effects of noise or glucose (and indeed the investigators do not suggest that this is the case). Possibly because of the use of a tracking stylus, there may have been an audible feedback cue present in this study.

Salame *et al.* (1993) found that, following a 1-hour nap, performance on spatial memory task was slower for 15 min in quiet (45 dB$_A$) than in a continuous 75 dB$_A$ pink-noise condition. This finding was, of course, attributed to the pink noise arousing the subjects from possible aftereffects of sleep.

TASK VARIABLES

The studies presented in the previous section were those in which special effort was made to measure, or control, the physiological state of the subjects. The following material is organized, insofar as possible, in terms of (1) possible interactions between task complexity and its performance in quiet and during and after exposure to noise and (2) possible effects on task performance in noise related to the subjects' psychological aversion to the noise.

Signal Detection Tasks

Numerous simple reaction time studies have been conducted that measure the time required for a subject to press a key or switch whenever a light or sound occurs. Intense noise in the task environment has been found to cause the reaction time to increase, decrease, or remain the same. A decrease in reaction time has generally been attributed to some arousal effect of the noise, and an increase to a physiological or psychological stress effect of the noise. However, these explanations of the effects of noise on reaction time are not very convincing because sometimes, even within the same experiment (same subjects and general procedures), a mixture of all three types of results is obtained.

An example of such varied and conflicting results is shown in Fig. 8.4 from Franszczuk (1973). Relative to reaction time in quiet tones, 1/3-octave and wideband noise at center frequencies of 250 and 1000 Hz either had no special effect or shortened reaction time. However, tones and bands of noise with a center frequency of 4000 Hz and white noise increased reaction time by ~0.02 s. The tones and bands of noise were presented at levels ranging from 80 to 90 dB.

There are at least three possible explanations for the variations in these results: (1) the shortened reaction times in the bands of noise at 1000 Hz are due to some beneficial arousal effect of the noises compared with quiet; (2) because higher frequency noise and tones are generally louder at a given sound pressure level than the lower frequency sounds, the subjects are more

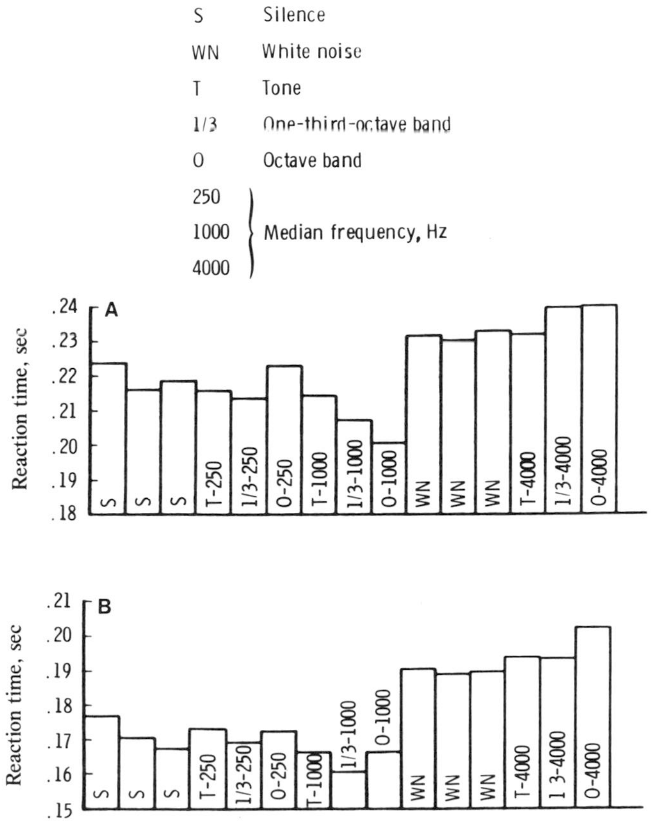

FIGURE 8.4 Comparison of simple reaction time under different acoustic conditions and in silence. Reaction time to (A) light and (B) sound stimuli. (From Franszczuk, 1973.)

stressed by the higher-frequency than the lower-frequency sounds; and (3) the increased reaction times in the white noise and 4000-Hz sounds are due to some artifact. With respect to the third possibility, the response key may have provided a high-frequency detent click or sound related to the amount of pressure placed on the key by the subject, which was masked by the white noise and the 4000-Hz sounds but not by the other noises.

The procedure followed by most subjects in tests of this sort is to complete between signals as much of the switch activation response as possible (pushing the key as far as possible without the final activation) so that the response signal merely serves as a trigger to complete the response act. Possibly, when in the masking noise, the subject refrained, for fear of making a false reaction, from starting to press the response key until the test signal occurred. The average 0.02-s difference involved suggests that this might have been the case.

That such an artifact might have been present in Franszczuk's study is pure conjecture, but it is a condition found in the activation of some switches or keys used in some reaction time tests. Perhaps in support of this conjecture, is that Franszczuk reported in tests of choice–reaction times where the subject must choose which of two keys to touch before responding (thereby obviating the possible partial switch activation artifact), no differences in reaction times were found between performance in noise and quiet.

Osada *et al.* (1971) studied the influence of aircraft, train, and pink noise on both reaction time and time estimation. In the study of reaction time the noises were presented in bursts at levels from 50 to 80 dB_A when the subjects were responding (by pushing different switches) to different-colored signal lamps, one of which flashed every 5 s. The noise somewhat reduced the time required for, and the variability of, the reactions. In the studies concerned with the estimation of elapsed time, the subjects pushed a switch when they believed that 10 s had elapsed after an electric signal light was turned on. No effect on time estimation was observed for the noises except for the "rattling train" noise for which the time estimate was shorter than that given in the quiet listening condition.

Ando (1977) exposed children (boys 13–14 years old) in a classroom to recorded aircraft noise. The noise was of about 60-s duration and repeated 30 times with 60-s pauses between exposures. He found that when the peak level of the noise was around 75 dB_A, time seemed to pass more quickly than during a no-noise session, but when the aircraft noise had peak levels of 90 dB_A, the time seemed to pass more slowly. He also found that subjects who came from an aircraft noise-impacted area tended to judge the test periods to be shorter than did subjects from quiet neighborhoods. The general conclusions from these studies might be that time filled with noise, at least at moderate levels, passes more quickly than it does in quiet and that this effect is stronger for people not accustomed to living in a noisy environment.

Warner (1969) investigated the effect of intermittent white noise at 80, 90, and 100 dB on the time required to detect the presence of an odd (different) letter from a background of 16 homogeneous letters flashed on a viewing screen. This is obviously a more complex target detection task than the task in a simple signal–reaction time test. However, as seen in Fig 8.5, the noise had no apparent systematic overall effect on target detection time. Note in Fig. 8.5 that at 12 and 15 min of time at task, the control (quiet) condition resulted in the fastest detection times. This might be interpreted to mean that the sometimes beneficial (with shorter detection times) effects of noise at 6 and 9 min of time at task could not be sustained by the subjects for longer periods because of increased fatigue. It was suggested that performance in quiet may have been better because of a learning effect, whereas performance in noise may have been better earlier in the session because of an initial arousal effect. These conjectures seem unjustified, however, in view of the general variability of the results and the fact that for the longest time at task, 15 min, the detection times for the quiet and the most intense noise, 100 dB, were almost identical.

In subsequent studies in which the number of letter targets was increased from 8 to 16 and to 32, Warner and Heimstra (1972, 1973) found that the mean detection time was greatly increased in quiet and generally increased in continuous noise at levels of 80, 90, and 100 dB. However, the noise improved performance (reduced detection time) for the more difficult, 32-letter task, relative to that in quiet, but had no such improvement effect on the performance of the 8- or 16-letter tasks (see Fig. 8.6).

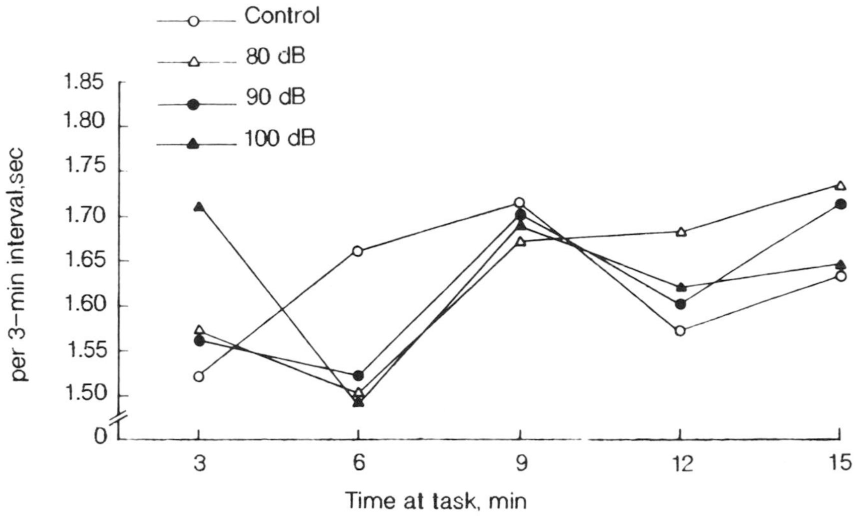

FIGURE 8.5 Mean detection time as a function of time and at the task. [From (*Hum. Factors*, 1969, **11,** 245–250). Copyright 1969 by the Human Factors Society, Inc., and reproduced by permission.]

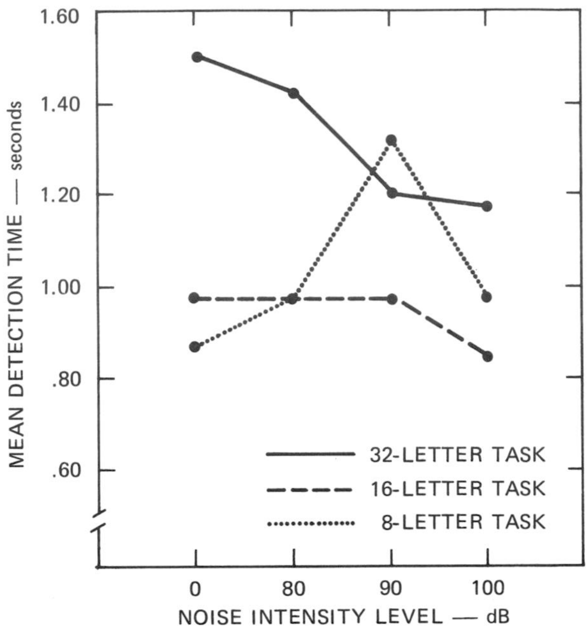

FIGURE 8.6 Detection time as a function of noise intensity and task difficulty. [From (*Hum. Factors*, 1973, **14,** 181–185). Copyright 1973 by the Human Factors Society, Inc., and reproduced by permission.]

Psychomotor Tasks

So-called psychomotor target tracking tests require the subject to manipulate a control level or grip in coordination with the movements of a visual target or display of lights. As reviewed by Eschenbrenner (1971), studies up to 1971 had shown no effect of high-intensity intermittent noise on the ability of subjects to track a moving target on an oscilloscope screen. Some initial decremental effects of noise found in some studies ceased with continued tracking.

Eschenbrenner found that continuous regular periodic and aperiodic noise all reduced performance time on a complex visual tracking task compared with the performance time of a separate control group of six subjects working in quiet. Also, the more intense the noise (levels of 50, 70, and 90 dB of white noise were used), the greater the decrement. Aperiodic noise had more adverse effects than regular periodic or continuous noise. However, as Eschenbrenner notes, a subject received only twenty 40-s trials (a total of ~6.5 min) while exposed to any one noise condition, and perhaps habituation to the noise would occur with more exposure.

Kaltsounis (1973), Davies *et al.* (1973), and Hartley and Williams (1977) compared the performance on various visual tasks (figure completion and target detection) when subjects were exposed to noise and to music at comparable levels (75–95 dB_A), and, by Kaltsounis, to speech and to quiet. Generally, no significant differences were found in task performance for subjects exposed to noise, music, speech, or quiet, although Davies *et al.* found an increase in latency in detection on a difficult task in noise but not in music.

Kunitake *et al.* (1977) assessed the effect of acclimation to aircraft noise on performance of various visual and time judgment tests by students (average age 17.8 years). Half of the subjects came from a residential area exposed to intense aircraft noise and half from a quiet neighborhood. The subjects were exposed in the laboratory for 105 min to recorded aircraft noises (one every 2 min) at a peak level of 95 dB_A and for 105 min to quiet as a control. The investigators found the following: (1) the acclimated subjects, from the noisy residential area, performed as well in the noise as in quiet on the mental tests; (2) the nonacclimated subjects had greater output in noise than the acclimated; and (3) there were no significant differences between the two groups in terms of fatigue or overall performance.

In addition to previously mentioned physiological measurements during a serial decoding task, Conrad (1973) obtained subjective ratings from his subjects regarding their sensitivity to noise. He found, as shown in Table 8.1, that those subjects who rated themselves highly sensitive to noise made fewer errors on the task than did those subjects who rated themselves less sensitive to noise during all test conditions, noise and quiet. There were, however, no significant interactions between overall performances in quiet and in the different noise conditions. As shown more precisely in the table, the main effect of noise condition was not significant ($F = 0.35$) and the main effect of noise annoyance sensitivity was also nonsignificant ($F = 1.53$). No significant interaction effect was found.

Word and Number Search and Memory Tasks

Since 1970 to the present, an increasing number of research studies have been concerned with the effects of noise on the performance of more intellectual tasks, e.g., tasks involving memory of words and numbers and multiple

TABLE 8.1 Mean Error Scores in Various Noise Conditions and Subjective Noise Annoyance Sensitivity

Subjective noise annoyance sensitivity	Noise condition				
	Quiet	Continuous	Periodic	Aperiodic	Mean
High	−7.44	−8.88	−4.97	−7.62	−7.23
Low	−14.09	−13.19	−14.98	−12.93	−13.80
Mean	−10.77	−11.03	−9.98	−10.28	

From Conrad (1973).

simultaneous tasks. Harris and Filson (1971) and Harris (1972) used a difficult search task wherein the subjects scanned pairs of numbers (e.g., 12–61, 41–47, and 56–45) printed on sheets of paper and wrote down those number pairs that were related in specified serial relations (e.g., their sums were an odd number). While taking this serial search task, one group of subjects was exposed to 105-dB broadband noise and a second group, to quiet. Some of the subjects received 3-min rest breaks during 36-min test periods, and other subjects did not receive rest breaks.

The results with the rest group indicated an adverse effect of noise on the first 12 min but no effect on the last 24 min of the test period, a result somewhat contrary to the arousal theory of noise. On the other hand, the rest group performed worse in noise than in quiet and performed worse on the last 2 days of testing in the noise than on the first day; these results are consistent with the arousal theory and could also possibly be related to Poulton's theory of noise interfering with internal, repetitious verbalization of the numbers (Poulton, 1976a).

However, Harris (1980), later reported no negative effects of bursts of predictable and unpredictable noise, modulated and unmodulated at certain interruption rates at levels from 85 to 106 dB_A, on arithmetic serial search (as described above) and proofreading. In these studies, Harris was concerned with both immediate and after effects of the noise. (As will be discussed later, some investigators have found an adverse effect on perseverance on unsolvable puzzles given after exposure to noise.) Harris' conclusions (which differ somewhat from the earlier position of Harris and Filson, that noise can have an adverse effect on the performance of serial search tasks) are as follows (pp. 347–348):

> The results of these series of experiments demonstrate that adverse effects of sound on human performance is not a foregone conclusion. An attempt to degrade performance deliberately in a short time period was unsuccessful. One should not be surprised by this because the literature contains many studies with similar results, and how many unreported studies there are that have failed to find adverse effects is anyone's guess. The effects of noise are so inextricably connected with the motivation of the subjects, the experimental task, and the experimental design, that it will still be a number of years before we begin to understand all of the variables involved.

As mentioned previously, Glass and Singer (1972), found that physiological habituation occurred to their noise with bandwidth from 200 to 5000 Hz (a conglomerate of several people talking in Spanish and English, a mimeograph machine, a mechanical calculator, and a typewriter) at levels as high as 110 dB. This habituation occurred regardless of whether the time of occurrence of the noise was predictable and whether the subjects perceived it as being under their control. The predictable noise consisted of 9-s bursts occurring regularly once every minute;the unpredictable noise consisted of

3- to 15-s bursts occurring randomly in different quarters of 1-min periods (the total amount of noise received during 23-min test periods was the same for the predictable and unpredictable presentations). The subjects' attitudes of having or not having control of the noise were achieved by telling the "control" group that they could choose to terminate the noise at any time by pushing a switch on their chairs, but that the experimenter preferred that they not do so. In these investigations it was found that the noise, both predictable and unpredictable, did not significantly affect proofreading and numerical task performance during exposure to the noise. On the proofreading task given after the termination of the noises, the subjects who were exposed to intense unpredictable noise and felt that they had no control over the noise made more proofreading errors than did the other groups. However, Glass and Singer in other experiments and other experimenters, to be discussed later, did not find similar aftereffects of the noise on proofreading errors.

Wittersheim and Salame (1973) studied the effect of 95-dB pink noise on the learning of a series of six digits displayed one at a time for 500 msec, separated by 140 ms. Overt and covert rehearsal was allowed. They found that the noise reduced memory task performance most when the noise was present during the times of acquisition ("information being taken in") and practice ("edited in storage") than in the reproduction stage of the task. Wittersheim and Salame note that earlier studies on memory tasks performed in noise are highly variable and inconclusive. Their findings that noise has a detrimental effect during the learning of number sequences could perhaps also be explained by Poulton's theory of noise interfering with internal speech rehearsal.

Osada *et al.* (1971) in addition to their previously discussed reaction time and time estimation tests, studied the effect of aircraft and train noise (levels of 60–90 dB) on performance of a test in which the subjects counted dots flashed on a screen. The noise was found to markedly impair figure counting, a task also possibly involving internal speech.

Noise interference with internal speech or verbalizations of words involved in task performance may possibly have a role in performance on the Stroop color interference test. In this test, subjects must name or sort cards according to the hue of the ink used to spell the name of different colors (e.g., the word "red" might appear in blue ink). Hartley and Adams (1974) found small adverse effects (1–3%) on task performance in broadband random noise at 100 dB compared with performance in 70-dB noise. Brief exposure to noise was beneficial to performance, but long (30-min) exposure increased interference with task performance.

On the other hand, O'Malley and Gallas (1977) found that broadband random noise at levels of 75 and 100 dB did not degrade performance on the Stroop test from that achieved in quiet, and that noise at 85 dB improved task performance. O'Malley and Gallas also found no effects of the noise on a "rod-and-frame" test (the subject must set a rod into a vertical position in a nonvertical framework) and a "pathway test" (the subject must trace connections between letters and numbers in some specified pattern).

Weinstein (1977) found that a tape recording of radio news items at 68 dB_A, designated as a noise condition, had mixed effects, compared with quiet, on a proofreading task. The noise impaired the detection of grammatical errors, but did not affect speed or detection of spelling errors. Initially in the noise, proofreading was more accurate than in quiet.

Three studies of the effects of broadband noise at a level of ~85 dB on various word and language tests, including the Stroop word-color naming test, were reported at an international congress on the effects of noise (Smith, 1980; Dornic, 1980; Broadbent, 1980). The results of the Smith study are given in Table 8.2. In the first test week, slightly fewer (18.0 vs. 18.7) words were recalled in the noise than in quiet, but in the second week this was reversed (17.9 in the noise and 17.5 in the quiet). On a *C* score (showing "clustering," defined by the formula given below Table 8.2), there was less clustering in the noise than in the quiet. The significance of this clustering measure to task behavior is not clear to the present author.

Dornic studied the effects of combined white noise with real-life recorded noise on the recall of word lists given in the dominant and subdominant language for each subject. Various types of memory tasks for the two lan-

TABLE 8.2 Results on Recall of Words on Stroop Test in Conditions of Quiet and Noise

Week 1		Week 2	
Quiet	Noise	Quiet	Noise
Mean Number of Words Recalled in Quiet and Noise for Each Session			
18.7	18.0	17.5	17.9
Mean Arcsine-Transformed *C* Scores in Quiet and Noise for Both Sessions*			
2.45	2.19	2.62	2.49

* High scores represent greater clustering. Calculation of the Dalrymple–Alford *C* score (for clustering) as follows:

$$C = \frac{R - \min R}{\max R - \min R}$$

where R = number recalled − observed number of runs
$\max R$ = number recalled − number of categories
$\min R = 0$ (number recalled + 1 ≥ 2 × largest category recalled)
= 2 × (largest category recalled − 1) (number recalled < 2 × (largest category recalled − 1))

From Smith (1980).

guages were administered. Representative findings in Fig. 8.7 show that compared with quiet, the noise has a negligible adverse effect on performance of the dominant language tasks and some adverse effect on the performance of the subdominant language tasks. Dornic concludes that the greater noise effects with the subdominant language are related to covert pronunciation difficulties, a conclusion consistent with Poulton's theory.

Broadbent studied the time taken to read 100 color names printed in black (W), the time taken to name meaningless patches of colored ink (C), the time to name the ink color in which irrelevant color names were printed (CI), and the time to read color names printed in different irrelevant colors (WI). The performance was measured after, rather than during, exposure to noise. Broadbent's findings are given in Table 8.3. The differences between the data after noise and after quiet seem small and variable. However, Broadbent found the C/W ratio after noise to be significantly lower statistically than the ratio after quiet, 1.27 vs. 1.31 (actually from the given data the ratios are 1.263 vs. 1.296, respectively). He concludes (pp. 363–364):

> Thus after noise, people name colored inks relatively faster than they read printed color names. It seems very plausible that effects in the interference condition are secondary to this change; on most theories of the Stroop, interference will be maximal at a particular value of C/W. It may therefore increase or decrease as C/W decreases, depending which side of the maximum one is; or interference may be unchanged as in our results. Notice however the following points: (1) this effect on speech occurs after exposure and cannot be caused by something like masking; (2) the effect is on performance with only one task, not on the interference between two tasks—the effect cannot therefore be included under theories of allocation of attention between stimulus sources; and (3) the effect is not a suppression of speech in general, but of speech in response to one kind of stimulus rather than another—it does not fit any generalization that use of speech as such, is changed by noise.

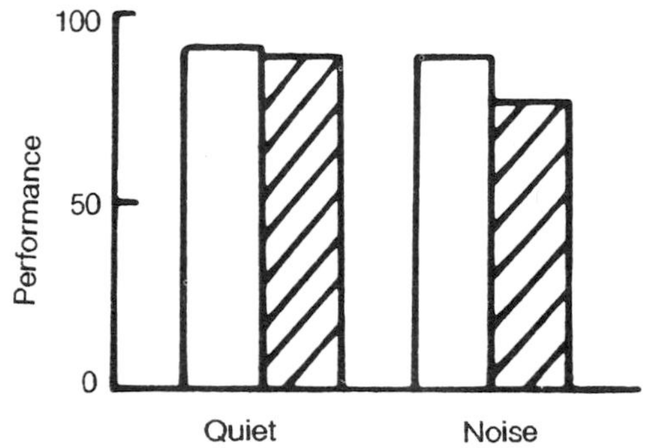

FIGURE 8.7 Performance (combined measure of accuracy and speed) on language tasks in dominant language (open columns) and subdominant language (hatched columns). (From Dornic, 1980.)

TABLE 8.3 Mean of All Subjects' Performance after Noise and after Quiet

Condition	C/W	C	W	CI	WI
After noise	1.27	49.76	39.40	73.54	42.89
After quiet	1.31	50.34	38.85	74.11	42.21

From Broadbent (1980).

Smith found that noise (74 and 78 dB_A, compared to quiet, impaired and slowed performance on a task requiring focused attention, but not on a search task. He also found that subjects who rated themselves as highly sensitive to noise were more distracted than were less-sensitive subjects by irrelevant signals on the periphery of a display.

Breier *et al.* (1987) compared the activity of the glandular–sympathetic nervous system of the body in two groups of subjects during the presence of an adversely loud noise. One group was told that they could control the level of the noise if they wished; the other group was told that they could not. Self-ratings of helplessness, anxiety, and stress, as well as glandular—sympathetic nervous system activity, increased in the subjects who had no control, compared to the subjects believed they had control of the noise.

Santisteban and Santalla (1993a) studied the influence of "silence" (60 dB_A, classical music (75 dB_A) and the noise of an electric drill (85 dB_A) on subjective appraisals of "pleasantness" and performance on word-memorization tasks. The subjects appraised the drill noise as the least pleasant and judged that the music and noise were more disturbing to task performance than was silence. However, task performance was essential the same for all sound conditions. Santisteban and Santalla (1993b) found that, compared to silence (45 dB_A), memorization of scientific text was adversely affected by listening to classical music (55 dB_A), bird singing (75 dB_A), road traffic noise (65 dB_A) and electric drill noise (65 dB_A). However, although their ratings on a scale of subjective pleasantness differed, the adverse effects were not statistically significantly different for the four sounds.

Arnoult *et al.* (1986) conducted three experiments with intermittent and continuous aircraft noise at levels of 60, 70, and 80 dB. No effects of the noise on the performance on a variety of cognitive and perceptual motor tasks were found. In all some 235 college students served as subjects. Although the experimenters suggest the lack of adverse findings may have been due to their use of relatively low-intensity noise, some of the other studies discussed above reported adverse effects from even lower intensity noises.

Foss *et al.* (1989a,b) found that exposure to five noise bursts of 110, 120, or 130 dB during a 15-s aiming of a rifle at a fixed target disrupted aiming for 1–2 s, with amount of disruption increasing with noise intensity. Some adaptation occurred. The acoustic startle reflex appeared to be involved, but was not felt to be the direct cause of the disruptions.

AFTEREFFECTS

As discussed above, Glass and Singer (1972) found that the effects of a noise on performance of a proofreading tasks appear to be negligible, or at least inconsistent. Glass and Singer also measured possible aftereffects from the exposure to the noise on insoluble puzzles and proofreading tests. The insoluble puzzle task, which except possibly for Broadbent's rather tenuous results with certain color naming tests, appears to be of uniquely suited for the detection of an aftereffect of noise exposure. This puzzle task is described by Glass and Singer as follows (pp. 48–49):

> The postnoise task measuring frustration tolerance was adapted from one used by Feather (1961), and consisted of four line diagrams printed on 5 × 7-inch cards arranged in four piles in front of the subject. . . . Each pile was about 1 inch high and contained only one kind of puzzle. Cards were face down so a subject was unable to see the puzzle until he began work on that particular pile of cards. The task was to trace over all of the lines of a diagram without tracing any line twice and without lifting the pencil from the figure. He was informed that he could take as many trials at a given item as he wished. However, he was also told that there was a time limit on how long he could work on a given trial, and the experimenter would inform him when his time was up over a loudspeaker. It was emphasized that such notification did not mean he had to go on to the next pile. That was his decision. It simply meant that he must decide whether to take another card from the same pile or move on to the next item. If the subject wanted another trial he discarded his unsuccessful card into a bin and took another copy of the same item. If he went on to the next pile, however, he could not go back to the previously unsolved item. The subject immediately went on to the next pile following a successful solution.
>
> Two of the line diagrams were mathematically insoluble but sufficiently complex so that subjects were unable to see this. (Post experimental interviews revealed that most subjects believed the insoluble puzzles were potentially soluble.) The puzzles were arranged in front of the subject so that the first pile always consisted of the same insoluble puzzle, the second the same soluble puzzle, the third the same insoluble puzzle, and the fourth the same soluble puzzle."

Glass and Singer found that perseverance in attempts to complete insoluble puzzles in a ~10-min period after exposure to some of the noises was less than after quiet. This effect was the greatest when the time of occurrence of the noise bursts was unpredictable, and the subjects believed the noises not to be under their control. Figure 8.8 shows that the loud noise (108 dB) had about the same aftereffect on number of attempts to solve insoluble puzzles as did soft noise (56 dB), or no noise, when the occurrence of the noise was predictable. When the noise occurrences were unpredictable, the subjects attempted fewer puzzles. Figure 8.8 showed that noise with no perceived control had an adverse aftereffect on perseverance compared with

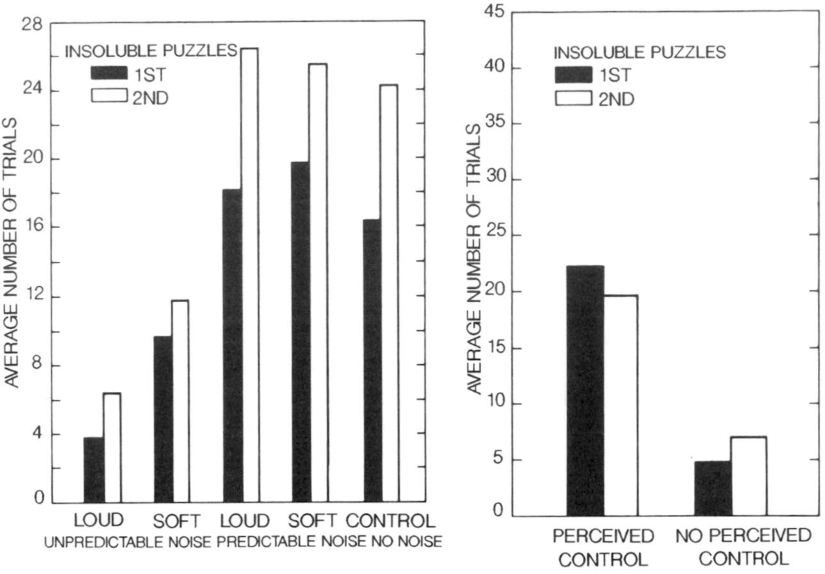

FIGURE 8.8 Relative predictability or perceived control of ambient noise as a factor in perseverance in attempts to solve insoluble puzzles. (From Glass and Singer, 1973.)

noise with the perceived control. Glass and Singer suggest that unpredictable noise conditions with no control levy a psychic cost that results in lower tolerance for frustration after the exposure. Glass and Singer called this condition a "state of learned helplessness."

Wohlwill *et al.* (1976) obtained results consistent with Glass and Singer's findings—namely, that performance on a dial-monitoring task was unaffected by the presence of noise, but that after exposure to the noise, subjects showed less persistence on insoluble puzzles than did the no-noise group. On the other hand, Moran and Loeb (1977), studying the performance of nonauditory and auditory tasks in quiet and in noise, were not able to find any aftereffects on perseverance on insoluble puzzles, even after noise that interfered with the auditory tasks.

Moran and Loeb, in a second experiment that closely replicated Glass and Singer's procedures, again found no aftereffects of the noise conditions on persistence on the unsoluble puzzles. However, Moran and Loeb used recorded aircraft noises and not the conglomerate noise used by Glass and Singer. Percival and Loeb (1980) conducted two experiments aimed at replicating and extending the studies of Glass and Singer on the aftereffects of noise on performance.

In one, subjects were exposed to 24 min of the conglomerate noise (95 dB_A) used by Glass and Singer of either fixed (predictable) or of random (unpredictable) schedule, plus a control quiet condition (46-dB_A background noise). During the test sessions the subjects worked on number comparison, addition, and letter-checking tasks. After exposure, the subjects worked on the insoluble puzzles and proofreading tasks. Persistence on insoluble puzzles was least after the unpredictable noise and greatest after the control condition (see Table 8.4). However, contrary to some of the results of Glass and Singer, there was no evidence in this study of an aftereffect on the proofreading test. Consistent with Glass and Singer, there were no adverse effects of the noises on tasks performed while the noise was present.

In the second experiment, Percival and Loeb used essentially the same tasks and procedures as outlined above, but added some new noise conditions. They used 95-dB_A intermittent white noise, recorded normal aircraft flyover noises, recorded combinations of the peaks of aircraft flyover noises, Glass and Singer's conglomerate noise, and a 46-dB_A background noise (control condition). As in Percival and Loeb's first experiment, the noises had no effect compared with the control condition on any of the performance tasks either during or after noise exposure. In addition, only Glass and Singer's conglomerate noise (GS) and the peaks of aircraft noise (AC), both presented at a random (unpredictable) schedule, significantly affected the number of attempts made on the insoluble puzzles given after exposures (see Table 8.5). Percival and Loeb suggest that the sudden abruptness of the peaks of aircraft noise possibly provided the acoustic characteristics that induced the aftereffect of fewer attempts being made on the insoluble puzzles (an average for both puzzles of about 11 attempts compared with about 19 for the control condition). Glass and Singer's conglomerate noise (GS) probably also contained some sudden, irregular peak levels, which by the same token could account for the average of only a few attempts, about eight, being made after that noise.

Rotton *et al.* (1978) reported that background noise plus meaningful speech (both at a level of 80 dB) presented with tasks requiring memory recall of words reduced an individual's ability to persevere on the insoluble puzzle

TABLE 8.4 Mean and Standard Deviation (in Parentheses) of the Number of Attempts on Insoluble Puzzles after 24 min of Exposure to Glass and Singer's Conglomerate Noise

Noise condition	Sex	Insoluble puzzle 1	Insoluble puzzle 2
Random schedule	Male	7.71 (6.02)	10.71 (5.91)
	Female	7.57 (3.51)	11.14 (7.17)
Fixed schedule	Male	13.00 (7.30)	14.00 (8.06)
	Female	11.00 (4.80)	12.57 (6.13)
Control	Male	14.00 (7.19)	16.29 (4.72)
	Female	15.86 (4.38)	20.00 (0.00)

From Percival and Loeb (1980).

TABLE 8.5 Mean and Standard Deviation (in Parentheses) of Number of Attempts on the Insoluble Puzzles in Second Experiment

	Noise conditions*				
Insoluble puzzle	GS	WN	AC	NA	C
1	8.25 (4.88)	17.67 (7.46)	10.33 (9.27)	16.42 (7.50)	18.83 (6.72)
2	7.60 (4.78)	19.50 (6.71)	11.75 (6.86)	18.08 (7.46)	19.67 (4.31)

* Key: GS = Glass and Singer's conglomerate noise; WN = white noise; AC = peaks of aircraft noises; NA = normal aircraft flyover noises; C = control (46-dB_A background noise).

test. The speech plus noise was somewhat like Glass and Singer's conglomerate noise.

Moch and Maramotti (1993) exposed 20 subjects to 90-dB_A noise (recorded at a racetrack) while taking a visual attention test, followed by administration of a form of the Glass and Singer insoluble puzzles. A control group of subjects was administered the same tests but without the noise. Heart rate was measured on all subjects thoughout the experiment, and the subject's self-rated subjective discomfort experienced during the experiment. Statistically significant difference were found between the noise-exposed and control groups with respect to increased task errors, irregular heart rate changes, and degree of subjective discomfort, all being greater for the noise exposed group.

Evans *et al.* (1993) assessed the aftereffects on the Glass and Singer insoluble puzzle test when taken after (1) listening for 20 min to a relaxing video; or (2) taking 20 min to prepare and present a speech before an audience; plus (3) performing for 20 min a difficult arithmetic task either in the quiet (45 dB_A), or in a 90-dB_A peak level noise (Glass and Singer irregular-level noise). Blood pressure was measured every three minutes before and during the experimental sessions, and the subjects rated their perceived levels of stress.

The blood pressure and aftereffects performance indicated that the stress of the speech preparation and delivery increased the adverse effects of the noise. However, self-reports of perceived stress were to the opposite effect, and performance on the arithmetic task was essentially the same for all prior stress and no-stress conditions. The authors suggest that a more complex task or tasks might reveal that the "cost" of adapting, or coping with the two successive stress could also adversely affect task performance.

Agrawal and Rai (1988) exposed one group of subjects to a noise condition over which they had perceived control, and another group to a noise condition over which they had no control. Difference on the insoluble puzzle test after noise exposure were not significantly different between the two groups of subjects. However, time of perseverance on insoluble puzzles showed more tolerance for frustration by persons who were scored low, rather than high, on a psychological scale rating "dependence-proneness."

The finding, when it occurs, of an apparent reduction in the number of attempts made to solve insoluble puzzles after exposure to some noises irregular in time and spectra attest to the existence of a special noise–task interaction. The possible meaning and significance of this effect, however, is a matter of conjecture.

Glass and Singer's interpretation that the effect represents a reduction of tolerance for frustration and is relatable to learned helplessness is not borne out by the subjective ratings given by the subjects of the irritating, distracting, and unpleasant qualities of the noise. Glass and Singer (1972, p. 54) found that these subjective ratings were more strongly correlated with the intensity of a noise than with its predictability or unpredictability. Percival and Loeb also found no relation between subjective ratings, including ability to cope with the noise, and the aftereffects of the noise. Similar negative findings were cited earlier with respect to subjective ratings of irritation from noise and performance on signal detection, tracking, and other tasks.

The hypothesis that a person's trying fewer times to solve an insoluble puzzle before going to work on another puzzle, represents a degradation in performance due to a "psychic cost" seems debatable. On the face of it, stopping work on an insoluble puzzle seems to be sensible, instead of being a reduction in tolerance for frustration. For some unexplained reason, the insoluble puzzle test was administered only after exposure to noise, whereas the other performance tasks were given both during and after the noise exposures. Conceivably fewer insoluble puzzles might be attempted during and after exposure to the unpredictable and irregular noise than during and after exposure to quiet, or to the other noises tested. But even if this were found, why only this particular type of noise and puzzle task should interact in this way would remain an open question.

In addition to the psychological theories developed by Glass and Singer, a possible explanation could be that judgments of elapsed time are affected (seem shortened) by this type of noise but not by the other noises. Recall that the subjects were instructed to complete as many puzzles as possible during a 10-min period. Also recall that Osada *et al.* (1971) found that during exposure to a "rattling train" noise, but not to other more regular noises, subjects judged the time elapsing after a signal to be somewhat shorter than it was. Perhaps this irregular intense noise makes time seem short and that this effect, not a more complex psychological aspect of frustration tolerance, is involved in the aftereffect data in question.

INFORMATION OVERLOAD

Nearly all the mental and psychomotor tasks that have been employed in laboratory studies of the effects of noise on task performance have required the subject to work at a fast pace. Further, the tasks demanded concentrated attention and repeated mental and psychomotor activities. In brief, the subjects were heavily loaded with a work task on the usually tacit assumption that the noise would constitute an additional physiological and/or perceptual load that would somehow interfere with task performance. Experimenters have taken performance data from subjects on two simultaneous tasks in noise on the theory that the noise might force the subject to concentrate attention on one task, and thereby reduce the ability to perform the other task.

Hockey and Hamilton (1970) and Davies and Jones (1975) required subjects to remember words that were projected in rapid sequence on one of four corners of a screen when in quiet (55 dB_A noise), and when in 95-dB_A noise. They found that, relative to the "quiet" condition, the noise increased the recall of words in their order of appearance (73.75% correct in quiet and 80% in noise; see Table 8.6). The subjects were asked after the word-recall test to try to remember at which corner of the screen the recalled words had been projected. This was designated as a second, and irrelevant, task. As seen in Table 8.6, the subjects correctly recalled fewer of the locations of the words after the noise than after quiet (33.33% vs. 60.12%). The experimenters concluded that their data support the theory that noise forces the attention of the subjects toward high-priority tasks and away from low-priority tasks or irrelevant information. The improvement in performance on the main tasks could be attributed to a beneficial arousal effect of the noise over the quiet control condition.

A study by O'Malley and Poplawsky (1971) supports the concept that noise causes a subject to focus attention on a primary task. The subjects' task was to anticipate words projected on the center of a screen rather than words that were projected onto the periphery of the screen. Fewer peripherally located words (unmentioned to the subjects) were given in free recall after task performance in noise than in quiet.

Loeb *et al.* (1976; Loeb and Jones, 1978) studied possible interactions of noise (recorded continuous industrial noise at 105 dB_A and impact noise at 136 dB) and "quiet" (white noise at 75 dB_A) with performance on two simultaneous tasks. One task consisted of tracking a moving target in the middle of the visual field, and the second task consisted of responding to

TABLE 8.6 Mean Percentage Recall of Relevant and Irrelevant Items (20 Subjects in Each Case)

	Relevant task, percentage of words recalled in correct order	Irrelevant task, percentage of locations recalled
Control (55 dB_A)	73.75 (73.12)	60.12(48.50)
Noise (95 dB_A)	80.00(69.00)	33.33(32.00)

Hockey and Hamilton's (1970) results are shown in parentheses for comparison purposes; for their control condition there were 36 subjects and for their noise condition there were 32 subjects. Data from Davies and Jones (1975).

the onset of lights appearing at the periphery of the visual field. By means of instructions, different groups of subjects were made to give different biases (priorities) and degrees of attention to the two different tasks. The results indicated that regardless of priority instructions, the noise conditions impaired, to a small extent, tracking performance, but not peripheral light monitoring. This result is seemingly contrary to the results cited above from the studies of O'Malley and Poplawsky, Hockey and Hamilton, and Davies and Jones.

Poulton (1980) suggested that the decrement in the tracking task in noise in the Loeb and Jones study was due to the noise masking feedback cues that were audible in the relative quiet. Loeb and Jones listened for such cues and concluded that this was not a factor, however. In any event the lack of an interaction between noise and performance of two tasks of differing priorities, and presumably given different degrees of attention, was not found in the studies of Loeb *et al.*

Finkelman and Glass (1970), Finkleman (1975), Finkelman *et al.* (1977, 1979), and Zeitlin and Finkelman (1975) conducted studies in which, in addition to a no-noise condition, the subjects were presented, via earphones, with bursts of white noise separated by periods of silence. Predictable noise usually consisted of 9-s bursts of white noise separated by 3-s periods of silence; and unpredictable noise consisted of bursts of white noise of random duration (1–9 sec) interrupted with random durations (1–3 sec) of silence. The subjects performed a primary visual tracking task and also a subsidiary task in which they orally repeated a digit previously announced (remembered) over the earphone on the aural presentation of another randomly selected digit. A digit was presented to the subject every 2 s.

Compared with the quiet condition, neither the regularly nor the randomly presented noise, at levels of 80 dB, was found to have any significant effect on the performance of the tracking task in the Finkelman and Glass, and the Finkelman studies. However, on the subsidiary auditory task, the unpredictable noise had a more degrading effect than did the predictable noise; the mean number of incorrectly repeated digits, out of 60 digits, was 0.6 in the quiet, 4.0 in the predictable noise, and 8.0 in the unpredictable noise, Finkelman and Glass. Similar findings were reported by Finkelman *et al.* (1977) in experiments in which the noise was increased to 93 dB_A. These investigators interpreted the results to mean that the information-handling capacity of the subjects was exceeded when in addition to performing a primary task in noise, especially in unpredictable noise, they must also perform a subsidiary task.

Another possible interpretation of these findings, as well as those reported by Finkelman *et al.* (1979), is that the noise masked the digits read to the subjects less in the predictable noise (Finkleman and Glass, 1970; Finkleman, 1975), than in the unpredictable noise, possibly because the regular 3-s periods of silence in the predictable noise allowed at least one of the digits coming at 2-s intervals to occur in silence. The probability of the digits occurring in silence would be less in the unpredictable noise where the periods of silence varied from 1 to 3 s. These investigators believed the speech to be perfectly audible in the presence of the noise, but errors in speech understanding due to slight masking effects can occur without the listener being necessarily aware of the presence of masking. The high levels of noise, 80–93 dB_A, would suggest that components of the speech signals (probably presented at about a comparable level) were masked but seemed intelligible because of the small message set (digits only).

That this was perhaps the case is shown by the Zeitlin and Finkelman study in which as a subsidiary task, the subjects called out digits, from 0 to 9, in random order at a self-paced rate (the subjects were not presented with any aural signals). Task performance was evaluated by determining the randomness of the digits announced by the subjects. There were no interactions between the noise and performance on this nonauditory, subsidiary task.

Similar auditory masking, as well as other artifacts, may have also been involved in a study by Bell (1978). In this study a psychomotor pursuit rotor task (performed with the dominant hand) was considered the primary task, and a subsidiary, concomitant, task (performed by the nondominant hand) consisted of the subject's tapping a telegraph key once if a two-digit number was numerically lower than an immediately previous number and twice if it was higher. The number were heard by the subjects via earphones at a speech level of ~95 dB_A (P. A. Bell, personal communication). White noise at 95 dB_A of randomly determined duration (1–9 s) and intervals of quiet (55-dB_A background noise of 1–9-s duration) and three temperature conditions were present during the performance of the tasks. The results are shown in Table 8.7.

TABLE 8.7 Mean ($\overline{X}$) and Standard Deviations (σ) for Primary and Subsidiary Task Performance for Three Levels of Temperature and Two Levels of Noise

Noise level, dB_A	Temperature 22°C	29°C	35°C
	Primary Pursuit Rotor Task—Time on Target (seconds)		
55	$\overline{X}$ = 398.21	$\overline{X}$ = 392.03	$\overline{X}$ = 389.48
	σ = 151.63	σ = 172.30	σ = 176.16
95	$\overline{X}$ = 383.78	$\overline{X}$ = 357.12	$\overline{X}$ = 341.40
	σ = 165.16	σ = 214.10	σ = 179.34
	Subsidiary Number Task—Number of Errors		
55	$\overline{X}$ = 27.38	$\overline{X}$ = 44.54	$\overline{X}$ = 52.96
	σ = 18.39	σ = 42.49	σ = 64.19
95	$\overline{X}$ = 53.21	$\overline{X}$ = 55.38	$\overline{X}$ = 78.13
	σ = 24.03	σ = 28.97	σ = 48.83

From Bell (1978).

Performance on the audible number task was degraded by the 95-dB_A noise compared with the 55-dB_A background noise, but performance on the pursuit tracking was not significantly affected by the 95-dB_A noise. The temperature effects followed a similar and additive pattern. Bell ascribes the findings to an information overload that forces greater attention on the primary task. However, the audible signals involved in the subsidiary task, as well as feedback clicks from the telegraph key used in that task, might have been masked by the noise. The effects of temperature differences are indeed interesting, but their relation to the information overload theory is, as Bell notes, a matter of further research.

Grether (1972) and Grether *et al.* (1972) conducted studies in which "stress" from broadband random noise at a level of 105 dB, heat of 120°F, and vibration of 5 Hz and 0.30*g* peak acceleration were imposed singly, and in combinations, on human subjects. Control and no-stress conditions were also studied. Tasks performed under these conditions included two-dimensional compensatory tracking, choice reaction time, a voice communication test of logical alternatives, mental arithmetic, visual acuity, and subjective ratings of stress conditions. The subjects rated the subjective severity, but not the intrusiveness, of stress as the number of stressors was increased. There were no additive adverse stress interactions with respect to performance of the various tasks. Indeed, on the tracking task, performance was slightly improved by the addition of noise to the heat and vibration stresses. This was perhaps due to the previously noted ability of noise to mask distracting sounds in the environment and thereby improve concentration on, and performance of, the tracking task.

Multiple Hypothesis Study

Perhaps the tenuous nature of theories that sound or noise has inherent adverse effects on nonauditory task performance is illustrated by the results of a study by Gawron (1982). Five hypotheses were tested. Tasks included classifying into three categories, immediate and delayed canceling of visually displayed digit pairs, and joystick tracking of a moving target. The following is a summarization concerning four hypotheses in that study.

1. The theory that psychological set is a major determinant of the effect of noise on the performance was not supported by the data.
2. Contrary to hypotheses that greater decrements as a result of noise would occur in dual-task rather than in single-task performances, performance at the single-task level and the lowest noise intensity was comparable to dual-task performance at the highest noise intensity. Also, although there was a significant dual-task decrement, there were no significant differences among performance levels at the three noise intensities.
3. The third hypothesis is based on the theory that noise is a distractor to which subjects habituate over time. Thus, performance decrements in the

presence of noise would be expected to occur early in the session and to decrease over time. In this test the opposite effect was found.

4. Arousal theory states that performance in the presence of noise should be a function of intensity and that overarousal should reduce performance. For tracking, and perhaps for percentage-correct scores on delayed digit canceling, there was a linear facilitation of performance associated with increasing noise intensity. The lack of support for this theory may be attributed to the restricted range of noise intensities (55–85-dB_A white noise), and performance decrements may occur at intensities beyond those investigated.

ANCILLARY VARIABLES

It is apparent from some of the studies discussed above, that in addition to noise and task variables, various psychological, physiological, and experimental factors can affect the results of experiments on the effects of noise on task performance. The interactive effects on this performance of a number of seemingly ancillary, but possibly important, factors have been studied to some degree.

Personality

A variety of interactions have been found between physiological and psychological arousal–annoyance by noise and (1) extroversion–introversion and (2) neuroticism. Dornic and Ekehammar (1990) found (1) a strong negative correlation between self-rated sensitivity to noise (Weinstein scale) and extroversion (Eysenck personality inventory), (2) no correlation between noise sensitivity and neuroticism, and (3) a negative correlation between extroversion and neuroticism. However, Matthews (1986) found extroversion was independent of subjective arousal from noise. Campbell (1992) found, as did Dornic and Ekehammar, a negative correlation between extroversion and noise sensitivity, but found no correlation between extroversion and neuroticism. Standing *et al.* (1990) also found a that extroverts were not aroused by noise, 60 dB, as were introverts. These investigators report that noise improved performance on a comprehension task on the part of introverts, but not extroverts.

Gender

Gulian and Thomas (1986) found that noise significantly impaired the rate, but not accuracy, of completion of arithmetic tasks by a group of females, ages 19–30 years. The performance of a similar-age group of males was not affected by the noise. The authors suggest that gender is another factor to consider in the evaluation of the effects of noise on work behavior. However, Madu (1990) found no significant differences between male and female subjects in the number of words recalled in tests conducted in 60-, and 80-, and 100-dB_A noise, that performance increased with increasing noise level, and that younger subjects performed better than older. The experimental groups consisted of 45 males and 45 females, aged 16–30 years.

Viral Infections

Smith and Brockman (1993b) conducted longitudinal studies of equal numbers of males and females who were administered a battery of psychomotor, sustained attention and memory tasks in the quiet and in 70-dB_A "conglomerate noise" (music and speech). The subjects were tested before, during and after they had experience a viral, "cold" infection.

Some of the results are shown in Table 8.8. It is seen that the subjects with colds reported reduced subjective alertness and had poorer reaction time in noise than in the quiet; reaction time was faster in the noise than quiet when the subjects were healthy, but the reverse when with colds. The colds reduced, by 2% points, performance on the serial-response task in both the quiet and noise. Performance on this task was better in noise than quiet for both the healthy and cold conditions. Compared to being healthy, the cold infection improved performance on the repeated numbers task in the noise, but slightly reduce performance in the quiet.

Time of Day

Smith (1987) investigated whether the time during the day that tests were administered in the quiet and in noise affected performance on tests of semantic processing. It was found that (1) time of day (diurnal variation), but not the presence of noise, influenced speed of verifying semantic information; and (2) time of day and noise have different effects on other aspects of semantic processing.

TABLE 8.8 Results of Subjective Judgments of Altertness (Drowsy-to-Alert Scale) and Performance on Mental and Psychomotor Tests

	Healthy		Colds	
	Noise	Quiet	Noise	Quiet
Alertness	27.6	29.7	24.0	19.9
Simple reaction time, ms	365	385	445	380
Detection of repeated numbers, % hits	50.5	59.8	53.9	58.9
Five-choice serial response task, % correct	88.6	86.6	86.6	84.6

From Smith and Brockman (1993).

Focused Attention vs Search Task

Smith (1993) found that noise differently affected performance on tasks that required the subject to focus attention on the center of a display screen than to search for targets on the screen. Noise also had different distractability effects on performance when the subject was engaged in a filtering as compared to a categoric search approach to a task. The effects were not modified by time of day or level of anxiety of the subject.

INDUSTRIAL FIELD STUDIES

There are many practical reasons why it is difficult to conduct research investigations on the possible effects of noise in the workplace on work output and efficiency. Nevertheless, over the years some studies have been published on this question. The following is taken from the author's earlier reviews of these sutdies. The author is not aware of any recently published experimental studies published in this area of research.

Office and Factory Noise

Kornhauser (1927) attempted to determine whether typists working in a relatively quiet office do more work and feel less fatigue than those working in a noisy office. Record was kept of two typists who spent the first 2 days working in a quiet office and then 2 days in the noisy office, and two other typists who worked in the reverse order of noise and quiet. The results showed that wasted lineage was 23% greater in the quiet room than in the noisy room and also that 1.5% more lines were written under noisy conditions. Rating scales revealed that the typists felt that they were working harder in the quiet than in the noise, suggesting a physiological arousal by the noise. The improved performance in the noisy conditions could also possibly be due to the noise masking speech, or other, distracting sounds irrelevant to the office work at hand. If this was the case, the "noise" served as a beneficial masker, sometimes called "acoustic perfume."

However, the differences between the two conditions cannot be accepted as necessarily significant, because of the small number of subjects. The most important criticism against this study, and the one that can be leveled at nearly all the research studies attempted under actual working conditions, is that there may have been differences between the two work offices other than noise level, such as lighting or ventilation, that might account for the results. Also, in this, and some of the experiments subsequently reviewed, "noise" is described only qualitatively, and not by intensity level. This, of course, also limits the accuracy with which comparison can be made among the different findings.

There are some reports that purport to show a deleterious effect from noise. It is claimed (Anonymous, 1928, Laird, 1927, 1930; Lindhahl, 1983) that "moving the assembly department of a regulator company from adjoining a noisy boiler shop to a quiet room resulted in lowering rejections at inspection from 75% to a low figure of 7%." The conclusion drawn was that the reduction in noise level caused the increased efficiency. Changes in lighting, temperature, and facilities were again ignored as possible contributing factors. In spite of the numerous articles published on these results, there are no references to the original study other than the statement (Laird, 1927), that it was done by a "Dr. Sachsenberg" in Germany.

In Great Britain, Weston and Adams (1932, 1935) studied the effect of noise on the work performance of weavers. The looms in weaving sheds generally create noise at a level of ~96 dB. Weston and Adams did three experiments: (1) they had 10 weavers wear earplugs, which reduced the intensity of the noise at the eardrum by 10–15 dB, on alternate weeks and recorded their output over a 26-week period; (2) they equated two groups of weavers, 10 in each group, with regard to past efficiency, and then one group wore earplugs while working for a 6-month period while the second group served as a control, working without earplugs; and (3) they repeated the second experiment, using some different subjects, but extended this experiment over a period of 1 year.

The results of all three experiments were roughly the same, averaging ~12% increase in efficiency for those who wore earplugs with respect to those who did not. The gain amounted to a 1% increase in the amount of material produced. The results of the first experiment were considered suspect by Weston and Adams, however, because of a difference in humidity between the weeks worked with earplugs and the weeks when earplugs were not worn. Figure 8.9 shows the results of the third experiment.

Toward the end of the year the experimental and the control groups were coming closer together with regard to work output. This suggests that an initial difference in motivation between the two groups might have helped make the experimental group superior and the control group inferior. But as the experiment wore on, it might be surmised, the added motivation or interest from being a subject began to wane, bringing the control and experimental groups closer together with regard to the work output. Indeed, the subjective reports of some of the subjects indicate an approval of experiments and attempts to help the worker. Such attitudes alone are known to result in significant changes in work output, in the presence of noise (Baker, 1937). Another critical point has been made by Berrien (1946), who noted that the equality of the control and the experimental groups in the first and second experiments was never demonstrated.

A major American field study was conducted by the Aetna Life Insurance Company in its own offices (Wilson, 1952). Apparently the study has never been published in its entirety, although sample results have appeared in several places. Semimonthly bonus records (reflecting work productivity)

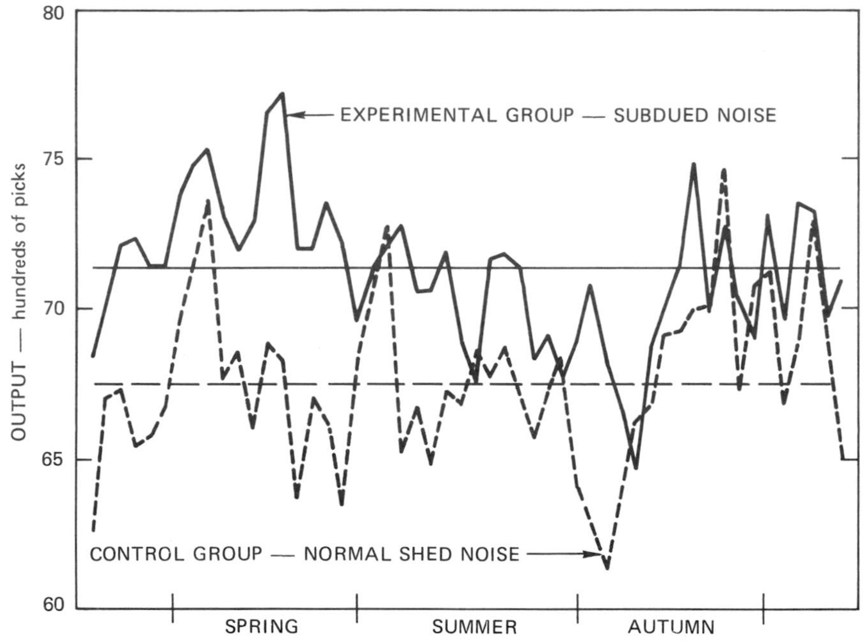

FIGURE 8.9 Weekly variation of output of weavers during 1-year experiment. The experimental group wore earplugs. (From Weston and Adams, 1932.)

for typists, clerical checkers, and punchcard and comptometer operators were compared for a year before, and a year after, sound-absorbing material was installed in all offices. As a result of the quieting, calculating machine operators' errors were reduced by 52%, typists' errors were reduced by 29 percent, health improved by 37.5%, and employee turnover was reduced by 47%, a truly remarkable achievement for absorbent wall board. The sound level was reported at ~41 dB prior to the sound treatment and 35 dB after.

These claims are unrealistically credited to "adjustment of the noise factor alone." It is difficult to criticize this study because of a paucity of relevant facts, but one obvious factor undoubtedly contributing to the differences between the variables recorded was the lapse of time involved. Two years elapsed in which the workers may have improved their efficiency through learning, the ill and nonadept may have changed jobs. One control check was made a year later that should, by itself, provide ample data for negating the conclusion concerning the effects of noise. For this check the sound-absorbing walls were covered with gypsum board, thereby raising the sound level by 6 dB. The bonus efficiency dropped to some extent (not as low as the first year), but within 2 months was as high as the level of the quiet year.

Felton and Spencer (1957) comment that ego involvement in a high-status occupation offsets concern about noise (94–119 dB). Ganguli and Rao (1954) believe, but present no data, that productivity in most workers is not affected by noise of 100 dB or lower. However, De Almeida (1954) found absenteeism from the work room dropped when noise level was reduced.

Broadbent and Little (1960) reported that the reduction in the noise level from 99 to 89 dB in a factory workspace (bay) resulted in fewer numbers of broken rolls of film and equipment shutdowns than were experienced by the same workers when they worked in an untreated bay (the workers moved from one bay to another during the workday). The work performance improved in both the sound-treated and non-sound-treated bays after some of the bays were treated, apparently due to generally improved morale (see Table 8.9).

Broadbent and Little propose that these findings support the conclusions from the serial-search laboratory tests discussed earlier that showed an apparent decline in test performance in noise. However, there may have been an auditory component (as was later found to be the case in some of the laboratory studies) to the work (threading film on spools) that aided the workers threading the film in detecting films slipping from sprockets or malfunctions in the machinery. If this was the case, the reduction of the noise should have led to improved work performance.

Kourigin and Mikheyev (1965) found that increasing the level of noise (given via loudspeakers) in the room used by postal letter sorters decreased the number of letters correctly sorted (see Fig. 8.10). Performance decreased monotonically with increases in noise level. These results cannot be taken to mean necessarily that the noise per se caused the decrease in performance because of some basic physiological or psychological distractive effect; they could be due to personnel viewing the noise as aversive because it bothered their hearing or represented a degradation in the concern of management

TABLE 8.9 Comparison of Performance in Acoustically Treated and Untreated Work Bays before and after Treatment Was Carried Out

	Treated bays		Untreated bays	
	1956/7	1957/8	1956/7	1957/8
Broken rolls (attributed to operator)	75	5	25	22
Other shutdowns (attributed to operator)	158	31	75	56
Calls for maintenance (excluding first 6-week period in each year)	746	597	516	468
Point hour	84.5	89.6	91.2	95.25
Absenteeism (time as % of possible hours worked)	5.18	4.43	2.72	1.556
Labor turnover (mean per 6 weeks)	1956/7 = 6.2%		1957/8 = 0	

The treatment was applied to the "treated bays" at end of 1957; therefore, the 1956–1957 data for those bays are prior to treatment; the "untreated bays" remained unchanged from 1956 to 1958; the workers moved from one bay to the other during normal work procedures.
From Broadbent and Little (1960).

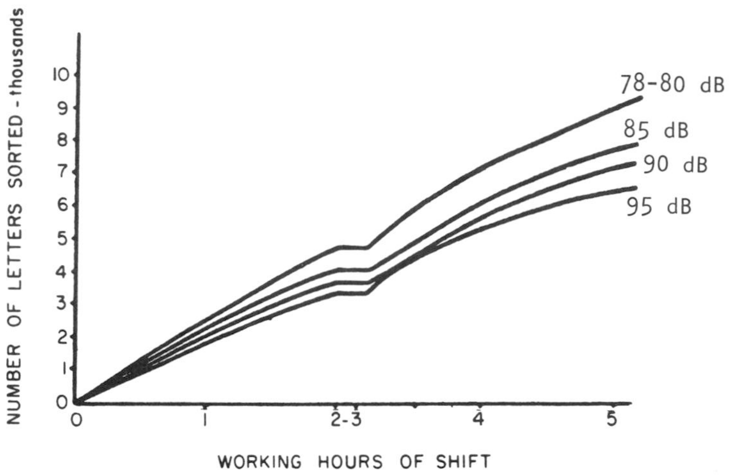

FIGURE 8.10 Effect of change in noise level on working effeciency of postal workers. (From Kourigin and Mikheyev, 1965.)

with their comfort and well-being. Also, the measured effects quite possibly could have disappeared with continued exposure or been due to some masking of sounds helpful to the sorting tasks.

Music

As mentioned earlier, a sound or noise may on occasion mask other sounds or noises that can disturb or distract a worker and thereby reduce productivity. For some purposes, in generally quiet surroundings, a low-level broadband random noise may be introduced to increase a sense of privacy with some possible beneficial effects. Music has also been used in work situations not so much perhaps to mask other sounds as to provide some pleasant stimuli to persons doing nonauditory work. The presumptions have been that work output will be increased because of improved morale or that people are kept more aroused and alert than they otherwise would be in monotonous jobs.

Figure 8.11 shows some data obtained in one study on this matter. That figure shows some, but no consistent, relation between the presence of music and work output. The clearly cyclic characteristics of the work output makes firm interpretation of the data difficult. The beneficial, or adverse, effects of music in industry are difficult to identify and quantify for some of the same reasons that the effects of noise on work output are difficult to demonstrate:

1. The effects may be transitory and related to temporary changes in worker morale.

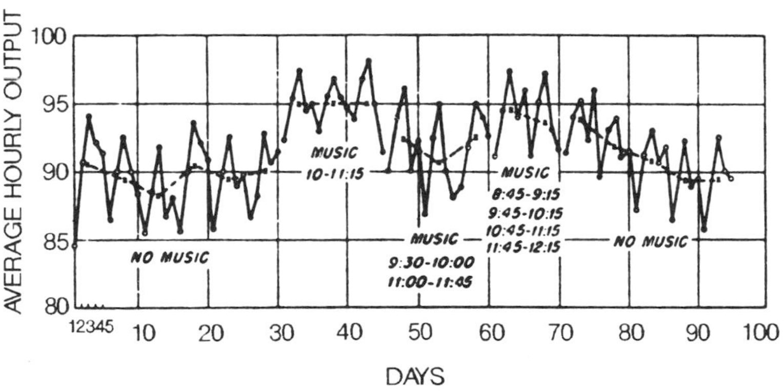

FIGURE 8.11 Output in a light manual task (rolling paper novelties) under various conditions of music presentation. (From Wyatt *et al.*, 1937.)

2. Masking effects of the noise or music on other auditory signals may be beneficial or adverse, depending on task conditions.
3. The effects may be relatively small compared with other task and motivational factors in the situation.

SUMMARY

It is concluded that noise can have a positive effect, no effect, or a negative effect on performance of nonauditory mental and psychomotor tasks. These findings are consistent with, perhaps are the same as, will be discussed in Chapter 9—namely, that there are no significant inherent adverse nonauditory physiological or psychological responses to sound or noise. And, except for some incipient startle response, direct and internal masking by noise of other auditory signals is perhaps the only inherent auditory variable responsible for observed effects of noise on the performance of nonauditory mental and psychomotor tasks.

Adverse effects found in one experiment on the effects of noise on nonauditory task performance have often not been found in repeat or similar experiments. It is clear that, in addition to experimental errors, some of these inconsistencies are due to interactions of basic effects of noise interacting with experimentally uncontrolled motivational and personality variables idiosyncratic to different subjects. Also, adaptation to the noise and other conditions of an experiment may progress at different rates for different subjects; and the opportunity and differential, on the part of some subjects, need for adaptation to those conditions was a variable not well controlled in most experiments.

In any event, experimental results that have been obtained indicated, or can be interpreted to indicate, that noise may:

1. Mask, or interfere with the perception of auditory signals that are needed, or helpful, to the performance of a task
2. Mask irrelevant auditory signals that could distract the worker, and as a result, inadvertently improve work performance
3. Compete for the psychological attention of the worker and thereby distract and interfere with work performance
4. Create a monotonous condition leading to psychological underarousal and less effective task performance
5. Physiologically arouse a worker from a low state of alertness and thereby increase alertness and work performance
6. Physiologically overarouse the worker and thereby decrease work performance
7. Convey meanings not required for performance of a particular task but that create feelings of annoyance affecting performance (e.g., noises from machinery that could cause bodily injury may cause feelings of apprehension that distract from task performance)
8. Create feelings of annoyance, thereby reducing task performance, because the workers believe the noise may be damaging the ear or interfering with the hearing of sounds they wish to hear
9. Create feelings of annoyance, thereby reducing task performance, because the worker feels helpless and unable to control the immediate environment
10. Generate neural impulses that partially preempt the functioning or nonauditory neural pathways or centers involved in the performance of particular nonauditory tasks
11. Preempt the use of some auditory neural pathways or centers that are involved in the internal enunciation and rehearsal of words related to the memory of words required in some mental tasks
12. Differently affect performance on tasks depending on their type and level of difficulty
13. Differently affect coping behavior and task performance on the part of subjects depending on type of "personalities" and emotional reactions to cognitive and motivational aspects of an experimental situation.

References

Agrawal, K., and Rai, S. N. (1988). Post noise frustration tolerance as a function of controllability of noise and dependence proneness. *Indian J. Psychometry Educ.* **19,** 85–89.

Ando, Y. (1977). Effects of noise on duration experience. *J. Sound Vib.* **55,** 600–603.

Anonymous (1928). Increased production resulting from lessening of noise. *Mon. Labor Rev.* **27,** 249–250.

Arnoult, M. D., Gillfillan, G. G., and Voorhees, J. W. (1986). Annoyingness of aircraft noise in relation to cognitive activity. *Percept. Motor Skills* **63,** 599–616.
Baker, K. H. (1937). Pre-experimental set in distraction experiments. *J. Gen. Psychol.* **16,** 471–488.
Basow, S. A. (1974). Effect of white noise on attention as a function of manifest anxiety. *Percept. Motor Skills* **39,** 655–662.
Becker, R. W., Kryter, K. D., and Poza, F. (1971). "A Study of Sensitivity to Noise," Final Rep., Rep. EQ-71-4 (Contract DOT-FA69WA-2211). Stanford Res. Inst., Menlo Park, California.
Bell, P. A. (1978). Effects of noise and heat stress on primary and subsidiary task performance. *Hum. Factors* **20,** 749–752.
Belojevic, G., Öhrstrom, E., and Rylander, R. (1993). Effects of noise on mental performance with regard to subjective noise sensitivity. *Noise Public Health Probl. Proc. Int. Congr. 6th* (M. Vallet, ed.), Vol. 2, pp. 547–548. l'INRETS, 94114 Arcuil Cedex, France.
Berrien, F. K. (1946). The effects of noise. *Psychol. Bull.* **43,** 141–161.
Bhatia, P., Shipra, and Muhar, I. S. (1991). Effect of low and high intensity noise on work efficiency. *Psychologia: Int. J. Psychol. Orient* **34,** 259–265.
Breier, A., Albus, M., Pickar, D., Zahn, T., *et al.* (1987). *Am. J. Psychiatry* **144,** 1419–1425.
Broadbent, D. E. (1953). Noise, paced performance, and vigilance tasks. *Br. J. Psychol.* **44,** 295–303.
Broadbent, D. E. (1954). Some effects of noise on visual performance. *Q. J. Exp. Psychol.* **6,** 1–5.
Broadbent, D. E. (1955). Symposium on noise at work: Noise; its effects on behaviour. *R. Soc. Promotion Health J.* **75,** 541–548.
Broadbent, D. E. (1957). Effects of noise on behavior. *In* "Handbook of Noise Control" (C. M. Harris, ed.), pp. 10.1–10.31. McGraw-Hill, New York.
Broadbent, D. E. (1958). "Perception and Communication." Pergamon, New York.
Broadbent, D. E. (1976). Noise and the details of experiments; a reply to Poulton. *Appl. Ergon.* **7,** 231–235.
Broadbent, D. E. (1977). Letter to the Editor. *Aviat. Space Environ. Med.* **48,** 382.
Broadbent, D. E. (1978). The current state of noise research: Reply to Poulton. *Psychol. Bull.* **85,** 1052–1067.
Broadbent, D. E. (1979). Human performance and noise. *In* "Handbook of Noise Control." (C. M. Harris, ed.), pp. 17.1–17.20. McGraw-Hill Book Co., New York.
Broadbent, D. E. (1980). Low levels of noise and the naming of colors. *In* "Noise as a Public Health Problem" (J. V. Tobias, G. Jansen, and W. D. Ward, eds.), ASHA Rep. No. 10, pp. 362–364. Am. Speech–Lang.–Hear. Assoc., Rockville, Maryland.
Broadbent, D. E. (1983). Recent advances in understanding performance in noise. *Proc. Int. Congr. Noise Public Health Probl. 4th* (G. Rossi, ed.), Vol. 2. Ric. Sudi Amplifon, Milan.
Broadbent, D. E., and Gregory, M. (1963). Vigilance considered as a statistical decision. *Br. J. Psychol.* **54,** 309–323.
Broadbent, D. E., and Gregory, M. (1965). Effects of noise and of signal rate upon vigilance analyzed by means of decision theory. *Hum. Factors* **7,** 155–162.
Broadbent, D. E., and Little, E. A. J. (1960). Effects of noise reduction in a work situation. *Occup. Psychol.* **34,** 133–140.
Campbell, J. B. (1992). Extraversion and noise sensitivity: A replication of Dornic and Ekehammar's study. *Pers. Individ. Differences* **13,** 953–955.
Carter, N. L., and Beh, H. C. (1989). The effect of intermittent noise on cardiovascular functioning during vigilance task performance. *Psychophysiology* **26,** 548–559.
Cohen, H. H., Conrad, D. W., O'Brien, J. F., and Pearson, R. G. (1974). "Effects of Noise Upon Human Information Processing" Rep. NASA CR-132469. NASA Langley Res. Cent. Hampton, Virginia.
Colquhoun, W. P., and Edwards, R. S. (1975). Interaction of noise with alcohol on a task of sustained attention. *Ergonomics* **18,** 81–87.

Conrad, D. W. (1973). The effects of intermittent noise on human serial decoding performance and physiological response. *Ergonomics* **16,** 739–747.

Davies, D. R., and Jones, D. M. (1975). The effects of noise and incentives upon attention in short-term memory. *Br. J. Psychol.* **66,** 61–68.

Davies, D. R., Lang, L., and Shackleton, V. J. (1973). The effects of music and task difficulty on performance at a visual vigilance task. *Br. J. Psychol.* **64,** 383–389.

De Almeida, H. R. (1959). Influence of electric punch card machines on the human ear. *Arch. Otolaryngol.* **51,** 215–222.

Dornic, S. (1980). Noise and language dominance. *In* "Noise as a Public Health Problem" (J. V. Tobias, G. Jansen, and W. D. Ward, eds.), ASHA Rep. No. 10, pp. 326–336. Am. Speech–Lang.–Hear. Assoc., Rockville, Maryland.

Dornic, S., and Ekehammar, B. (1990). Extraversion, neuroticism, and noise sensitivity. *Pers. Individ. Differences* **11,** 989–992.

Eschenbrenner, A. J. (1971). Effects of intermittent noise on the performance of a complex psychomotor task. *Hum. Factors* **13,** 59–63.

Evans, G., Allen, K. M., and Tafalla, R. (1993). The cumulative effects of stress on psychophysiologic and performance responses to noise. *Noise Public Health Probl. Proc. Int. Congr. 6th* (M. Vallet, ed.), Vol. 2, pp. 269–272. l'INRETS, 94114 Arcuil Cedex, France.

Feather, N. T. (1961). The relationship of persistence at a task to expectation of success and achievement related motives. *J. Abnormal and Soc. Psychol.* **63,** 552–561.

Felton, J. S., and Spencer, C. (1957). "Moral of Workers Exposed to High Levels of Occupational Noise." Univ. of Oklahoma Sch. of Med., Norman.

Finkelman, J. M. (1975). Effects of noise on human performance. *Sound Vib.* **10,** 26–28

Finkelman, J. M., and Glass, D. C. (1979). Reappraisal of the relationship between noise and human performance by means of a subsidiary task measure. *J. Appl. Psychol.* **54,** 211–213.

Finkelman, J. M., Zeitlin, L. R., Filippi, J. A., and Friend, M. A. (1977). Noise and driver performance. *J. Appl. Psychol.* **62,** 713–718.

Finkelman, J. M., Zeitlin, L. R., Romoff, R. A., Friend, M. A., and Brown, L. S. (1979). Conjoint effect of physical stress and noise stress on information processing performance and cardiac response. *Hum. Factors* **21,** 1–6.

Foss, J. A., Ison, J. R., Torre, J. P., and Wansack, S. (1989a). The acosutic startle response and disruption of aiming: I. Effect of stimulus repetition, intensity, and intensity changes. *Hum. Factors* **31,** 307–318.

Foss, J. A., Ison, J. R., Torre, J. P., and Wansack, S. (1989b). The acosutic startle response and disruption of aiming: II. Modulation by forewarning and preliminary stimuli. *Hum. Factors* **31,** 319–333.

Frankenhaeuser, M., and Lundberg, U. (1974). Immediate and delayed effects of noise on performance and arousal. *Biol. Psychol.* **2,** 127–133.

Franszczuk, I. (1973). The effect of annoying noise on some psychological functions during work. *Proc. Int. Congr. Noise Public Health Probl.* (W. D. Ward, ed.), Rep. EPA 550/9-73-008, pp. 425–430. U.S. Environ. Prot. Agency, Washington, D.C.

Ganguli, H. C., and Rao, M. N. (1954). Noise and industrial efficiency: A study of Indian jute weavers. *Arbeitsphysiology* **15,** 344–354.

Gawron, V. J. (1982). Performance effects of noise intensity, psychological set and task type and complexity. *Hum. Factors* **24,** 225–243.

Glass, D. C., and Singer, J. E. (1972). "Urban Stress—Experiments on Noise and Social Stressors." Academic Press, New York.

Glass, D. C., and Singer, J. E. (1973). Behavioral effects and aftereffects of noise. *Proc. Int. Congr. Noise Public Health Probl.* (W. D. Ward, ed.), Rep. EPA 550/9-73-008, pp. 409–416. U.S. Environ. Prot. Agency, Washington, D.C.

Grether, W. F. (1972). "Two Experiments on the Effects of Combined Heat, Noise and Vibration Stress," Rep. AMRL-TR-71-113. Wright-Patterson AFB, Ohio.

Grether, W. F., Harris, C. S., Ohlbaum, M., Sampson, P. A., and Guignard, J. C. (1972). Further study of combined heat, noise and vibration stress. *Aerosp. Med.* **43,** 641–645.

Gulian, E. (1970). Effects of noise on arousal level in auditory vigilance. *In* "Attention and Performance III" (A. F. Sanders, ed.), North-Holland Publ., Amsterdam.

Gulian, E. (1973). Psychological consequences of exposure to noise: Facts and explanations. *Proc. Int. Congr. Noise Public Health Probl.* (W. D. Ward, ed.), Rep. EPA 550/9-73-008, pp. 363–378. U.S. Environ. Prot. Agency, Washington, D.C.

Gulian, E., and Thomas, J. R. (1986). The effects of noise, cognitive set, and gender on mental arithmetic performance. *Br. J. Psychol.* **77,** 503–511.

Harris, C. S. (1972). Effects of intermittent and continuous noise on serial search performance. *Percept. Motor Skills* **35,** 627–634.

Harris, C. S. (1980). Effects of predictable and unpredictable sound on human performance. *In* "Noise as a Public Health Problem" (J. V. Tobias, G. Jansen, and W. D. Ward, eds.), ASHA Rep. No. 10, pp. 343–348. Am. Speech–Lang.–Hear. Assoc., Rockville, Maryland.

Harris, C. S., and Filson, G. W. (1971). "Effects of Noise on Serial Search Performance," Rep. AMRL-Tr-71-56. Wright-Patterson AFB, Ohio. (Avail. from DTIC as AD 731 184.)

Hartley, L. R. (1973). Effect of prior noise or prior performance on serial reaction. *J. Exp. Psychol.* **101,** 255–261.

Hartley, L. R. (1974). Performance during continuous and intermittent noise and wearing ear protection. *J. Exp. Psychol.* **102,** 512–516.

Hartley, L. R., and Adams, R. G. (1974). Effect of noise on the Stroop test. *J. Exp. Pscyhol.* **102,** 62–66.

Hartley, L. R., and Carpenter, A. (1974). Comparison of performance with headphone and free-field noise. *J. Exp. Psychol.* **103,** 377–380.

Hartley, L. R., and Shirley, E. (1977). Sleep-loss, noise and decisions. *Ergonomics* **20,** 481–489

Hartley, L. R., and Williams, T. (1977). Steady state noise and music and vigilance. *Ergonomics* **20,** 277–285.

Hartley, L., R. Couper-Smartt, J., and Henry, T. (1977). Behavioural antagonism between chlorpromazine and noise in man. *Psychopharmacology* **55,** 97–102.

Hawel, W. (1975). Investigation of psychological and psychophysiological effects of repeated intermittent pink noise lasting 4 hours. *Z. Exp. Angew. Psychol.* **22,** 613–629.

Hockey, G. R., and Hamilton, P. (1970). Arousal and information selection in short-term memory. *Nature (London)* **226,** 866–867.

Jones, D. M. (1983). Noise. *In* "Stress and Fatigue in Human Performance" (G. R. J. Hockey, ed.), Wiley, New York.

Jones, D. M., and Broadbent, D. E. (1991). Human performance and noise. *In* "Handbook of Noise Control." (C. M. Harris, ed.), pp. 24.1–24.24. McGraw-Hill Book Co., New York.

Kaltsounis, B. (1973). Effect of sound on creative performance. *Psychol. Rep.* **33,** 737–738.

Kornhauser, A. W. (1927). The effect of noise on office output. *Ind. Psychol.,* **2,** 621–622.

Kourigin, S. D., and Mikheyev, A. P. (1965). "The Effect of Noise Level on Working Efficiency." Joint Publ. Res. Serv., Washington, D.C.

Kryter, K. D. (1985). "The Effects of Noise on Man," 2nd Ed. Academic Press, Orlando, Florida.

Kryter, K. D., and Poza, F. (1980). Autonomic system activity and performance on a psychomotor task in noise. *J. Acoust. Soc. Am.* **67,** 2096–2099.

Kunitake, E., Ishinishi, N., and Kodama, Y. (1977). Studies on the effects of aircraft noise in the experimental exposure to the acclimatized and the non-acclimatized students to the noise. *Nippon Eiseigaku Zasshi* **32,** 353–365.

Laird, D. A. (1927). Measurement of the effects of noise on working efficiency. *J. Ind. Hyg.* **9,** 431–434.

Laird, D. A. (1930). The effects of noise: A summary of experimental literature. *J. Acoust. Soc. Am.* **1,** 256–262.

Lindahl, R. (1983). Noise in industry. *Ind. Med.* **7,** 664–669.

Loeb, M. (1980). Noise and performance: Do we know more now? *In* "Noise as a Public Health Problem" (J. V. Tobias, G. Jansen, and W. D. Ward, eds.), ASHA Rep. No. 10, pp. 303–321. Am. Speech–Lang.–Hear. Assoc., Rockville, Maryland.

Leob, M. (1986). "Noise and Human Efficiency." Wiley, New York.

Loeb, M., and Jones, P. D. (1978). Noise exposure, monitoring and tracking performance as a function of signal bias and task prioity. *Ergonomics* **21,** 265–272.

Loeb, M., Jones, P. D., and Cohen, A. (1976). "Effects of Noise on Non-Auditory Sensory Functions and Performance," HEW Publ. No. (NIOSH) 76–176. U.S. Dep. Health, Educ., Welfare, Washington, D.C.

Lundberg, U., and Frankenhaeuser, M. (1978). Psychophysiological reactions to noise as modified by personal control over noise intensity. *Biol. Psychol.* **6,** 51–59.

Madu, S. (1990). Effect of noise on memory and recall among Nigerian students. *J. Afr. Psychol.* **1,** 15–23.

Matthews, G. (1986). The interactive efects of extraversion and arousal on performance: Are creative tests anomalous? *Pers. Individ. Differences* **7,** 751–761.

McGuire, P. K., Shah, G. M. S., and Murray, R. M. (1993). Increased blood flow in Broca's area during auditory hallucinations in schizophrenia. *Lancet* **342,** 703–706.

Moch, A., and Maramotti, I. (1993). Multi-dimensional approach to noise efects and to noise aftereffects. *Noise Public Health Probl., Proc. Int. Congr. 6th* (M. Vallet, ed.), Vol. 2, pp. 543–546. 1'INRETS, 94114 Arcuil Cedex, France.

Moran, S. L. V., and Loeb, M. (1977). Annoyance and behavior aftereffects following interfering and noninterfering aircraft noise. *J. Appl. Psychol.* **62,** 719–726.

Mosskov, J. I., and Ettema, J. H. (1977). 11. Extra-auditory effects in short term exposure to aircraft and traffic noise. *Int. Arch. Occup. Environ. Health* **40,** 165–173.

Mosskov, J. I., and Ettema, J. H. (1980). Experimental investigations into some extra-aural effects of exposure to noise. *In* "Noise as a Public Health Problem" (J. V. Tobias, G. Jansen, and W. D. Ward, eds.), ASHA Rep. No. 10, pp. 337–342. Am. Speech–Lang.–Hear. Assoc., Rockville, Maryland.

O'Malley, J. J., and Gallas, J. (1977). Noise and attention span. *Percept. Motor Skills* **44,** 919–922.

O'Malley, J. J., and Poplawsky, A. (1971). Noise-induced arousal and breadth of attention. *Percept. Motor Skills* **33,** 887–890.

Osada, Y., Hirokawa, A., and Haruta, K. (1971). Effect of intermittent noise on mental tasks—Influence of aircraft- and train-noise on reaction time, time estimation and figure counting test. *Bull. Inst. Public Health, Tokyo* **20,** 163–169.

Percival, L., and Loeb, M. (1980). Influence of noise characteristics on behavioral aftereffects. *Hum. Factors* **22,** 341–352.

Poulton, E. C. (1976a). Continuous noise interferes with work by masking auditory feedback and inner speech. *Appl. Ergon.* **7,** 79–84.

Poulton, E. C. (1976b). Arousing environmental stresses can improve performance, whatever people say. *Aviat. Space Environ. Med.* **47,** 1193–1204.

Poulton, E. C. (1977). Continuous intense noise masks auditory feedback and inner speech. *Psychol. Bull.* **84,** 977–1001.

Poulton, E. C. (1978). A new look at the effects of noise: A rejoinder. *Psychol. Bull.* **85,** 1068–1079.

Poulton, E. C. (1979). Composite model for human performance in continuous noise. *Psychol. Rev.* **86,** 361–375.

Poulton, E. C. (1980). Psychology of the scientist: XLI. Continuous noise can degrade performance when using badly designed equipment: A case history. *Percept. Motor Skills* **50,** 319–330.

Poulton, E. C., and Edwards, R. S. (1974). Interactions and range effects in experiments on pairs of stresses: Mild heat and low-frequency noise. *J. Exp. Psychol.* **102,** 621–628.

Rotton, J., Olszewski, D., Charleton, M., and Soler, E. (1978). Loud speech, conglomerate noise, and behavioral aftereffects. *J. Appl. Psychol.* **63,** 360–365.

Salame, P., Tassi, P., Nicolas, A., Ehrhart, J., Dewasmes, G., Libert, J.-P., and Muzet, A. (1993). Noise, aftereffects of sleep, and cognitive performance, *Noise Public Health Probl. Proc. Int. Congr. 6th* (M. Vallet, ed.), Vol. 2, pp. 519–522. l'INRETS, 94114 Arcuil Cedex, France.

Santisteban, C., and Santalla, Z. (1993a). The effects of everyday noises and their subjective level of pleasantness on recall on categorized lists. *Noise Public Health Probl. Proc. Int. Congr. 6th* (M. Vallet, ed.), Vol. 2, pp. 549–552. l'INRETS, 94114 Arcuil Cedex, France.

Santisteban, C., and Santalla, Z. (1993b). The effects of everyday noise on comprehension and recall of reading texts. *Noise Public Health Probl. Proc. Int. Congr. 6th* (M. Vallet, ed.), Vol. 2, pp. 553–556. l'INRETS, 94114 Arcuil Cedex, France.

Simpson, G. C., Cox, T., and Rothschild, D. R. (1974). The effects of noise stress on blood glucose level and skilled performance. *Ergonomics* **17,** 481–487.

Smith, A. P. (1980). Low levels of noise and performance. *In* "Noise as a Public Health Problem" (J. V. Tobias, G. Jansen, and W. D. Ward, eds.), ASHA Rep. No. 10, pp. 365–368. Am. Speech–Lang.–Hear. Assoc., Rockville, Maryland.

Smith, A. P. (1987). Activation states and semantic processing: A comparison of the effects of time of day. *Acta Psychol.* **64,** 271–288.

Smith, A. P. (1989). A review of the effects of noise on human performance. *Scand. J. Psychol.* **30,** 185–206.

Smith, A. P. (1993). Noise and selective attention. *Noise Public Health Probl. Proc. Int. Congr. 6th* (M. Vallet, ed.), Vol. 2, pp. 535–538. l'INRETS, 94114 Arcuil Cedex, France.

Smith, A. P., and Jones, D. M., eds. (1992). "Handbook of Human Performance." Academic Press, London.

Smith, A., and Brockman, P. (1993). Noise, respiratory virus infections and performance. *Noise Public Health Probl. Proc. Int. Congr. 6th* (M. Vallet, ed.), Vol. 2, pp. 311–314. l'INRETS, 2, Ave. du General Malleret Joinville, 94114 Arcuil Cedex, France.

Standing, L., Lynn, D., and Moxness, K. (1990). Effects of noise on introverts and extroverts. *Bull. Psychon. So.* **28,** 138–140.

Strasser, H. (1972). Effects of noise, tranquillizer and increased delay time on tracking performance and heart rate. *Pfluegers Arch.* **332,** Suppl. No. 332, R82.

Suter, A. H. (1992). "Communication and Job Performance in Noise: A Review," ASHA Monogr. No. 28. Am. Speech–Lang.–Hear. Assoc., Rockville, Maryland.

Tafalla, R., and Evans, G. (1993). Noise, physiology and human performance: The potential role of effort. *Noise Public Health Probl. Proc. Int. Congr. 6th* (M. Vallet, ed.), Vol. 2, pp. 317–320. l'INRETS, 94114 Arcuil Cedex, France.

Vera, M., Vila, J., and Godoy, J. F. (1992). Physiological and subjective effects of traffic noise: The role of negative self-statements. *Int. J. Psychophysiol.* **12,** 267–279.

Warner, H. D. (1969). Effects of intermittent noise on human target detection. *Hum. Factors* **11,** 245–250.

Warner, H. D., and Heimstra, N. W. (1972). Effects of noise intensity on visual target-detection performance. *Hum. Factors* **14,** 181–185.

Warner, H. D., and Heimstra, N. W. (1973). Target-detection performance as a function of noise intensity and task difficulty. *Percept. Motor Skills* **36,** 439–442.

Weinstein, N. D. (1977). Noise and intellectual performance: A confirmation and extension. *J. Appl. Psychol.* **62,** 104–107.

Weston, H. C., and Adams, S. (1932). "The Effects of Noise on the Performance of Weavers," Rep. No. 65. Br. Ind. Health Res. Board, HM Stationery Off., London.

Weston, H. C., and Adams, S. (1935). "The Performance of Weavers Under Varying Conditions of Noise," Rep. No. 70. Br. Ind. Health Res. Board, HM Stationery Off., London.

Wilson, A. (1952). Better concentration reduces employee turnover 47%. *Bankers Mon.* **59,** 254–255.

Wittersheim, G., and Salame, P. (1973). Effects of noise on a serial short-term memory process. *Proc. Int. Congr. Noise Public Health Probl.* (W. D. Ward, ed.), Rep. EPA 550/9-73-008, pp. 417–424. U.S. Environ. Prot. Agency, Washington, D.C.

Wohlwill, J. F., Nasar, J. L., DeJoy, D. M., and Foruzani, H. H. (1976). Behavioral effects of a noisy environment: Task involvement vs. passive exposure. *J. Appl. Psychol.* **61,** 67–74.

Wyatt, S., Landgon, J. N., and Stock, F. G. L. (1937). "Fatigue and Boredom in Repetitive Work," Rep. No. 77. Br. Ind. Health Res. Board, HM Stationery Off., London.

Zeitlin, L. R., and Finkelman, J. M. (1975). Research note: Subsidiary task techniques of digit generation and digit recall as indirect measures of operator loading. *Hum. Factors* **17,** 218–220.

Nonauditory System Responses to Sound and Noise and Relations to Health

INTRODUCTION

The primary purpose of this chapter is to discuss the results, methods, and concepts of research concerned with (1) physiological reactions of nonauditory systems of the body to sound and noise and (2) the possibility that such reactions could constitute physiological stress capable of contributing to some health disorders. These nonauditory system responses include directly activated, reflex-type, alerting-arousal responses to sound, and responses activated as the result of psychological reactions to sound and noise. Also to be presented are the findings of studies of (1) nonauditory sensory systems—pain, cutaneous, vestibular, kinesthesia, and vision—responses to sound; and (2) responses of both auditory and nonauditory sensory systems to so-called infra- and ultrafrequencies of sound, frequencies that are inaudible to the average ear.

NONAUDITORY SYSTEMS AND THEIR RESPONSES TO SOUND

Figure 9.1 illustrates neural connections between the human auditory system and the neural–muscular–glandular systems in the body. Special attention

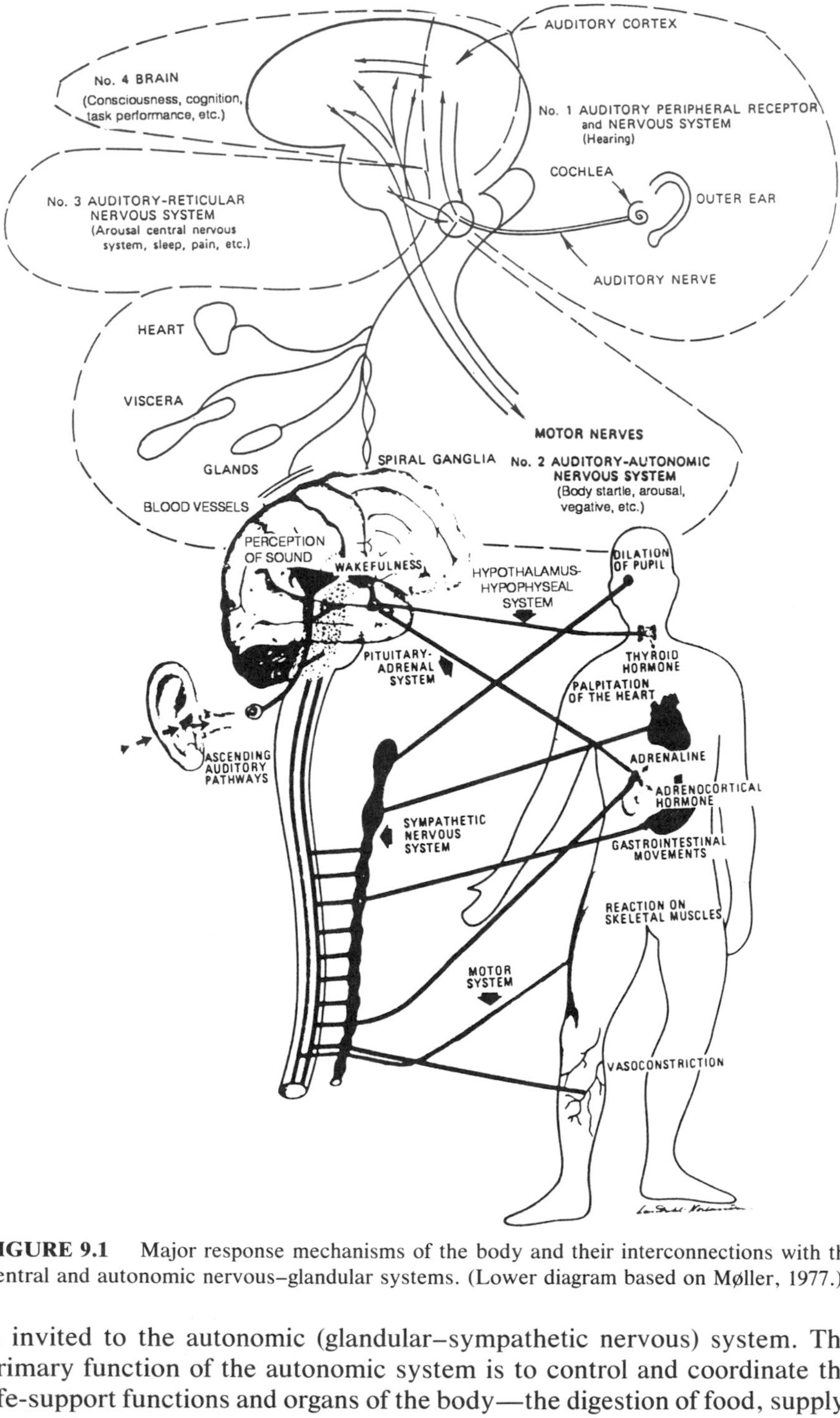

FIGURE 9.1 Major response mechanisms of the body and their interconnections with the central and autonomic nervous–glandular systems. (Lower diagram based on Møller, 1977.)

is invited to the autonomic (glandular–sympathetic nervous) system. The primary function of the autonomic system is to control and coordinate the life-support functions and organs of the body—the digestion of food, supplying blood to all parts of the body, the respiration of air, the control of body temperature, participation in immunity protection from disease-causing agents, and other physiological functions.

The auditory system has some direct neural connections with the sympathetic nervous system at levels below the brain. It is believed that through these connections sounds can cause autonomic-system responses that occur without any conscious processes, and thereby serve as a warning system about the presence of things in the environment. It is considered to be advantageous to have the autonomic system activate the body physiologically in ways that best enable it, if desired, to fight or flee an object or organism creating the sound. In this regard it can be noted that sounds, unlike light, bend around and, to some extent, go through objects, are omnidirectional, and are generated and transmitted as well at night as in the daytime. In brief, sound is generally a more effective warning signal about things, especially moving things, in the environment than is light.

Reflex Theory

It has been proposed that nonauditory-system response to noise can be explained in terms of innate, reflexive responses becoming conditioned into patterns of behavior that depend on reinforcement of some sort (Sokolov, 1963). This reinforcement, or lack thereof, will cause the responses to be modified, habituated, or inhibited in a way that best adapts the organism to its environment. Sokolov postulated that two reflexive types of responses to meaningless sounds are built into humans.

One, Sokolov calls the *orienting response* (OR), wherein the autonomic system responds to any sound stimulus in order to alert and make ready the organism for the purposes of receiving and responding as appropriate to this stimulus. This OR is postulated to get stronger as the noise stimuli become weaker, because the organism would require more effort to react to weaker than to more readily observed stimuli.

The second reflex response of the autonomic system to noise postulated by Sokolov is a *defensive response* (DR), which prepares the organism for fight or flight. This DR becomes stronger as the strength of the noise is increased. These ORs and DRs supposedly occur to meaningless sounds, but as the meaning becomes established through repetition of the noises (e.g., the noise does not warrant either an orienting or a defensive response), the response becomes inhibited or habituated. Research on these, and other relevant concepts has been reviewed by Graham (1973), Jackson (1974), and Ginsberg and Furedy (1974).

Reflex-Nonreflex Theory

An alternative concept is that stimulation of the auditory system by any sound, including noise, causes a reflexive orienting-type response in nonauditory systems, plus slightly delayed, but significantly larger, nonreflexive responses in nonauditory systems. This latter response occurs because the noise conveys meaningful, emotion-arousing information to the person.

The findings of a number of historically important and recent laboratory and field experiments on certain responses to sound and noise of nonauditory life-support and sensory systems are presented next. These are followed by discussion of the concepts and results of studies more directly related to the issue of possible adverse effects of noise on health and well-being. In the discussions to immediately follow, "positive" response or effects refers to measurable, possibly potentially stressful, responses from exposure to sound or noise, and "negative" response or effects refer to no measurable responses or effects from exposure to sound or noise.

LABORATORY STUDIES OF HUMANS AND MONKEYS

Since the early 1940s, numerous laboratory measurements have been made of nonauditory-system responses to sudden, intense sounds or noises, both unexpected and repeated or expected. Davis *et al.* (1955) called the resulting complex of responses to these sounds the N-response, herein called the *alerting response*. The magnitude of this response generally depends jointly on the suddenness of the onset, the intensity of the noise, and the state of quiescence of the organism. A number of physiological responses may be involved.

1. A circulatory response dominated by vasoconstriction of the peripheral blood vessels with other adjustments of the cardio vascular system affecting blood pressure throughout the body
2. A change in heart rate
3. A reduced rate of breathing
4. Galvanic skin response (GSR), a reduction in the electrical resistance of the skin
5. A brief change in skeletal-muscle tension, measured electrically (EMG, electromyograph)

To this list can be added, among others, the changes that occur in gastrointestinal motility, gastric acid secretion; chemical and hormonal changes and excretions in the blood and urine from glandular stimulation by the autonomic nervous system, and suppression of so-called immune-system cells that are responsible for "killing" or "digesting" organisms harmful to the organs of the body.

Heart rate, blood circulation (usually blood volume or pulse in the skin of a finger), skeletal-muscle response (such as from the muscles of the forearm), and electrodermal resistance have been commonly used to measure immediate response of the autonomic system to noise because they can be readily sensed and recorded by electronic transducers without greatly inconveniencing the subject. Although these responses are interrelated, the presence of one does not necessarily mean that other of these responses have occurred. Further, the lack of response may not mean that an alerting reaction should not have occurred; this is because some parts of the nonauditory system, at the time of the noise stimulation, may be somewhat exhausted, or under the domination of other stimulations. These factors can make the collection and interpretation of data in this area difficult (Surwillo and Arenberg, 1965).

Figures 9.2–9.5 show the rather rapid habituation of responsiveness to meaningless sounds or noises that are presented suddenly and unexpectedly to the subjects. It is clear that, although initial responsiveness increases with increases in stimulus intensity, habituation with continued stimulation appears to become nearly complete. That this reduction in response with stimulus repetition is not the result of a fatiguing of the mechanism is shown in Fig. 9.6. It is seen in Fig. 9.6 that following 15 repetitions (15 trials with, for half the subjects, an 80-dB, 200-Hz tone, or with, for the other subjects, a bright light) the autonomic responses were much less than for the 16th trial, when the stimulus was changed from the tone to the light (for half the subjects) or from the light to the tone (for the other subjects). Rossi *et al.*

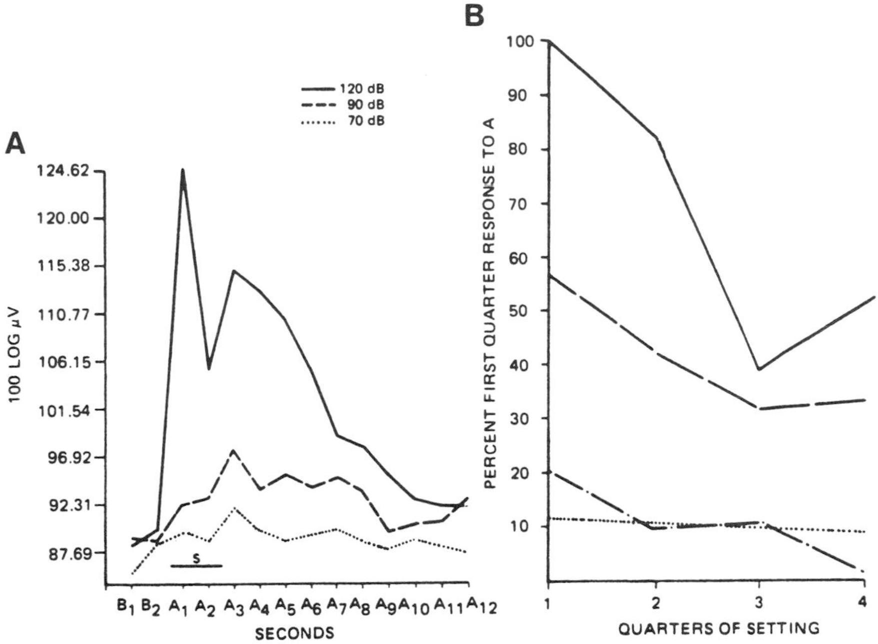

FIGURE 9.2 Mean muscle action-potential response (A) and adaptation of response (B) to 1000-Hz tone. Horizontal line indicates stimulus duration; (A) Brief latency and (B) long latency. (From Davis and Berry, 1964.)

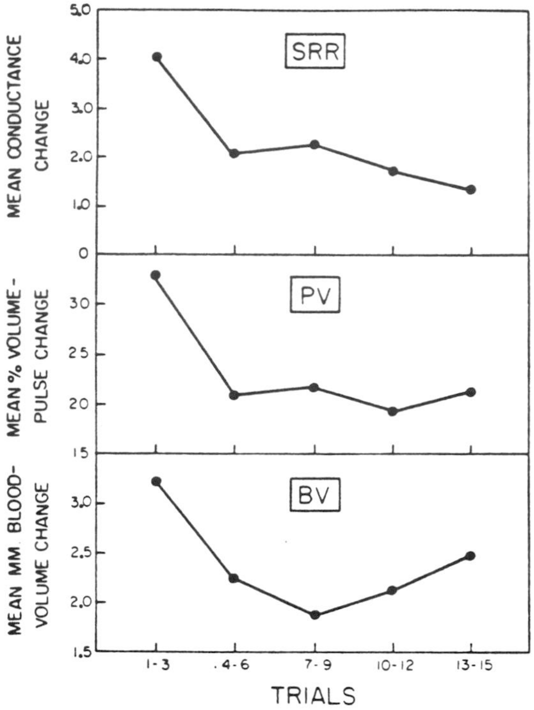

FIGURE 9.3 Mean skin resistance response (SRR), peripheral pulse volume (PV) response, and peripheral blood volume (BV) response to stimulus repetition. (From Ginsberg and Furedy, 1974.)

(1959) found that the habituation of vasoconstriction in subjects exposed to a background noise did not reduce vasoconstriction to superimposed 2000-Hz tones at levels of 80–105 dB.

These responses of the autonomic system probably do not represent any undue stress or health-threatening phenomena. Partly because these responses tend to show rapid adaptation or habituation, and partly because the magnitude of the physiological changes that are associated with these responses are rather small in comparison to the range of physiological conditions or states observed in the human organism during homeostatic operations of the autonomic system normal to daily living. For example, the greatest heart-rate change shown in Fig. 9.5 is about 11 beats per minute, and this change is for only 1 or 2 beats, and the peripheral blood volume changes last only 10–20 s. Changes much greater than these occur from mild exercise, fright, sudden changes in air temperature, laughter, and so forth.

Data Showing Irregular Positive Response of Nonauditory Systems

Glass and Singer (1972) found in their laboratory studies that physiological (GSR and vasoconstriction) habituation occurred in over 90% of their sub-

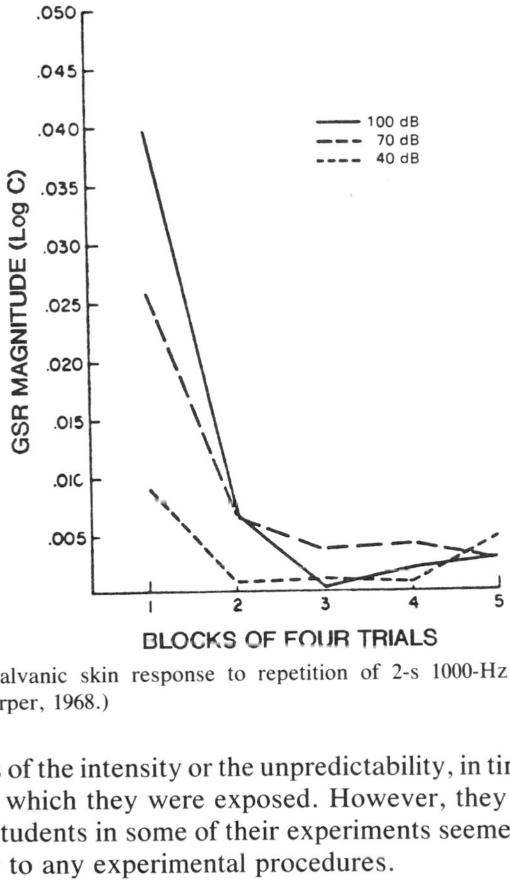

FIGURE 9.4 Galvanic skin response to repetition of 2-s 1000-Hz tones of 40, 70, or 100 dB. (From Harper, 1968.)

jects regardless of the intensity or the unpredictability, in time, of occurrence of the noise to which they were exposed. However, they found that about 4% of college students in some of their experiments seemed unable to adapt physiologically to any experimental procedures.

Table 9.1 shows that either recorded aircraft or street traffic noise caused

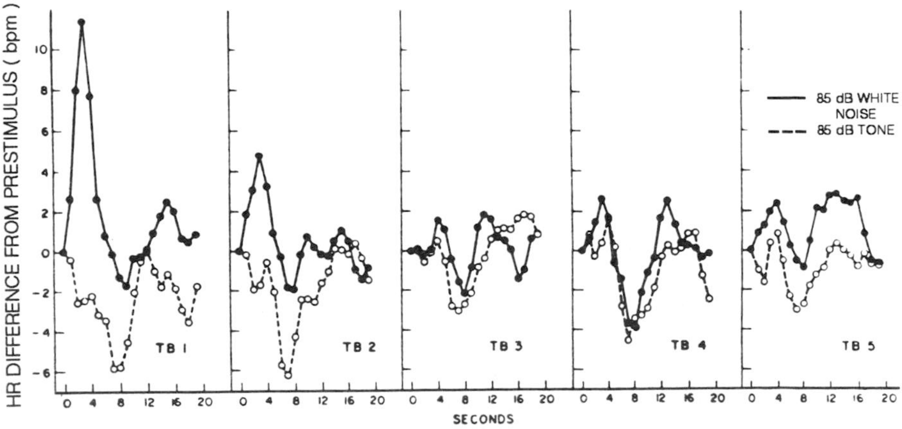

FIGURE 9.5 Heart rate (HR) response to white noise and 1000-Hz tone of 5-s duration on five trial blocks (TB) of two trials each. (From Graham and Slaby, 1973.)

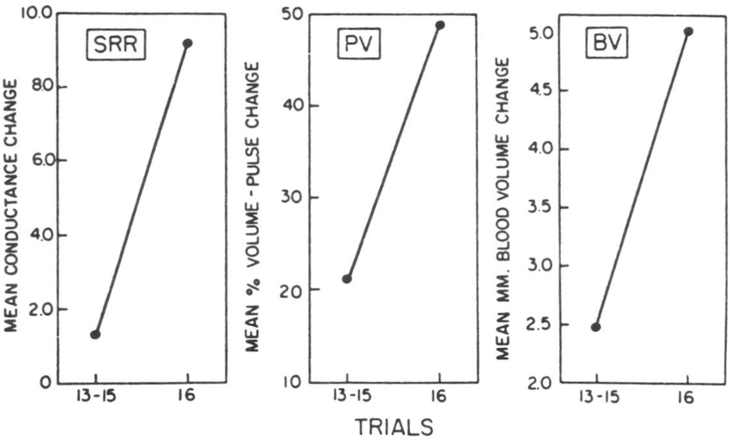

FIGURE 9.6 Mean skin resistance response (SRR), peripheral pulse volume (PV) response, and peripheral blood volume (BV) response to repeated trials and to change trials. (From Ginsberg and Furedy, 1974.)

some statistically significant changes during a 3-h exposure following a 30-min rest period. Adding a mental, two-choice task caused an even greater number of statistically significant changes. Further, there is almost no consistent trend in the changes from the first through the third hour of exposure. The investigators, Mosskov and Ettema (1977), hold that "these results strongly suggest that long-term exposure to noise is a risk factor for cardiovascular disease in daily living and working conditions."

However, one should be cautious in accepting that conclusion. In the first place, the changes noted over the time period could conceivably have occurred with or without the noise being present. Although the authors mention that control data were obtained, these data are not presented. Also, the addition of mental tasks has about the same relation to the rest-period conditions as do the noise data. Again, control data (mental task in the quiet) is required before the significance of these data can be properly assessed. In addition, only the averages for three 4–10-min segments of a total of some eighteen 10-min segments of time were examined. Sometimes in experiments of this kind and duration, such segmentation and infrequent sampling can provide an inadequate picture of the true changes taking place in the physiological responses being examined. Di Cantogno *et al.* (1976) also compared various autonomic-system responses of normal persons and persons with heart disorders to recorded road traffic noise for 1–10 min. the results were too variable to permit interpretation.

Osada *et al.* (1973) conducted an interesting experiment in which subjects were exposed continuously for 2 or 6 h to recordings of road-traffic noise at levels of 40, 50, and 60 dB_A. The noise was presented, via earphones, from

TABLE 9.1 Cardiovascular Responses to Noise (12 Subjects)

	Mean values at condition of				Significance of		Noise with mental load* affecting	
Cardiovascular function	Rest	40th–50th min of exposure	100th–110th min of exposure	160th–170th min of exposure	Difference from rest	Trend for increasing exposure	Mean value	Significance
				Aircraft Noise†				
Heart rate	71	69	64	68			69	
Systolic pressure	117	115	114	115			117	$p < .10$
Diastolic pressure	67	71	72	73	$p < .05$	$p < .10$	75	$p < .01$
Pulse pressure	50	44	42	43	$p < .05$		42	
Sinus arrhythmia	101	102	111	106			82	$p < .01$
Respiratory rate	14	15	16	15			15	$p < .01$
Heart rate/respiratory rate	5.0	4.6	3.8	4.5			4.3	$p < .02$
				Traffic Noise‡				
Heart rate	74	72	68	70			74	
Systolic pressure	117	112	113	113	$p \leq .010$		117	$p < .01$
Diastolic pressure	66	71	75	75	$p \leq .005$	$p < .05$	75	$p < .01$
Pulse pressure	51	41	38	38	$p \leq .005$		41	
Sinus arrhythmia	88	88	102	109		$p < .10$	58	$p < .01$
Respiratory rate	14	15	15	15	$p \leq .020$		17	$p < .01$
Heart rate/respiratory rate	5.3	4.5	4.2	4.5	$p \leq .050$		3.8	$p < .02$

* Presented at 55th–60th min of exposure.

† Twenty flyover noises per hour, with peak levels of 89–100 dB_A.

‡ $L_{eq} = 83.5\ dB_A$.

Data from Mosskov and Eltema, 1977

a small cassette-tape player worn by the subjects. The subjects moved around the laboratory, went out to lunch and so forth, while wearing the cassette player and earphones. For most of the noise conditions, blood and urinary samples revealed a significant increase (relative to control data) in blood cells and hormones, especially the corticosteroids, which would indicate autonomic-system stress reactions. Osada *et al.* concluded that autonomic-system stress activity is caused by noise levels above ~50 dB_A. However, it is suggested that these effects are possibly related to stress caused by the noise masking the hearing of speech and other wanted environmental sounds useful to the subjects in moving about, and not from some direct autonomic system arousal by the noise.

A number of experimenters (see e.g., Grandjean, 1962; Jansen, 1964, 1972; Ohkubo *et al.,* 1976; Osada *et al.,* 1973; Kryter and Poza, 1980) have demonstrated that a constriction of peripheral blood vessels occurs from exposures to rather intense, broadband intermittent or impulsive bursts of noise. This vasoconstriction has been explicitly stated by Jansen (1973) as being related to general activations of the autonomic systems that can have deleterious effects on health. However, as discussed later, it appears that constriction of some peripheral blood vessels may occur in response to noises that are not related to the general activation of the autonomic system, or at least not to activation at a level that could be considered stressful to bodily health.

Data obtained in a study by Jansen (see Fig 9.7) revealed that with each burst of white noise at a level of 95 dB some momentary vasoconstriction (reduction in the amplitude of finger pulse) occurs. Similar results were found by Kryter and Poza with respect to pulse amplitude and blood volume, but other measures capable of showing activation of the autonomic system showed complete habituation to the noise (see Fig. 9.8). Similar patterns of vasoconstrictive responses to noise were found by Jansen (1972) and Froehlich (1975). Accordingly, although there may be little or no habituation of an immediate peripheral vasoconstrictive response to intense, broadband intermittent noises, that response may not always be related to general activation of the autonomic system.

It is seen in Fig. 9.7 that after 30 min in the test room the non-noise-control subjects (lowest panel) had as much reduced peripheral blood flow as did the test subjects. Accordingly, it can be questioned whether the subjects had been "stressed" by the noise. If we assume that the response could be indicative of a state of stress, it follows that sitting in the test room for 30 min with or without the noise was equally stressful.

Jansen (1972) maintains this noise-induced stress response lasts as long as the noise above a certain level of intensity is present. However, as shown in Fig. 9.9, some of these data indicate that following an initial constrictive response, the peripheral blood circulation takes a state apparently appropriate for either the work or the rest phase of activity. Other data on this point, however, are ambiguous (see Fig. 9.8).

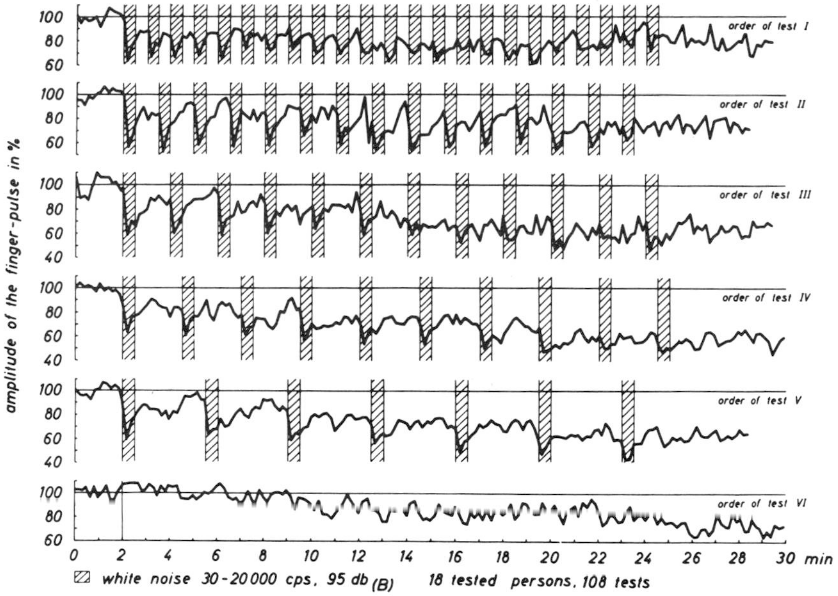

FIGURE 9.7 Autonomic-system reactions during a series of noise exposures. (From Jansen, 1972.)

It is perhaps surprising that there is apparently a complete lack of autonomic-system response to the narrow band of random noise with a center frequency of 3150 Hz, as is seen in Fig. 9.8. At a level of 92 dB, this noise is very loud and obnoxious to the average listener, more so than the wideband noise at 92 dB. Jansen also reported that the narrow band of noise at 3200 Hz at levels around 92 dB has little effect on pulse amplitude during work, whereas a broadband noise of the same intensity and increased low-frequency energy causes a decrease in pulse amplitude during work. The thought that this differential response may somehow be related to a reaction of the auditory system to intense noise without necessarily involving the autonomic system in any general way is reinforced by the fact that noises that most readily elicit aural reflex (lower rather than higher frequencies) also most readily cause the peripheral vasoconstrictive response.

The complex, and sensitive, nature of cardiovascular functions, hormonal effects and their relation to exposure to noise are exemplified in a paper by Andren (1982). This investigator found that exposure to 95- and 100-dB_A noise did not increase blood plasma levels of catecholamines, prolactin, cortisol, or growth hormone in adult male subjects with normal blood pressure. In hypertensive subjects, those with higher than normal blood pressure, this noise caused increased secretion of noradrenaline, but not other plasma constituent. It was found that blood pressure elevation from the noise was caused by (1) vasoconstriction in subjects with hypertension, and in normo-

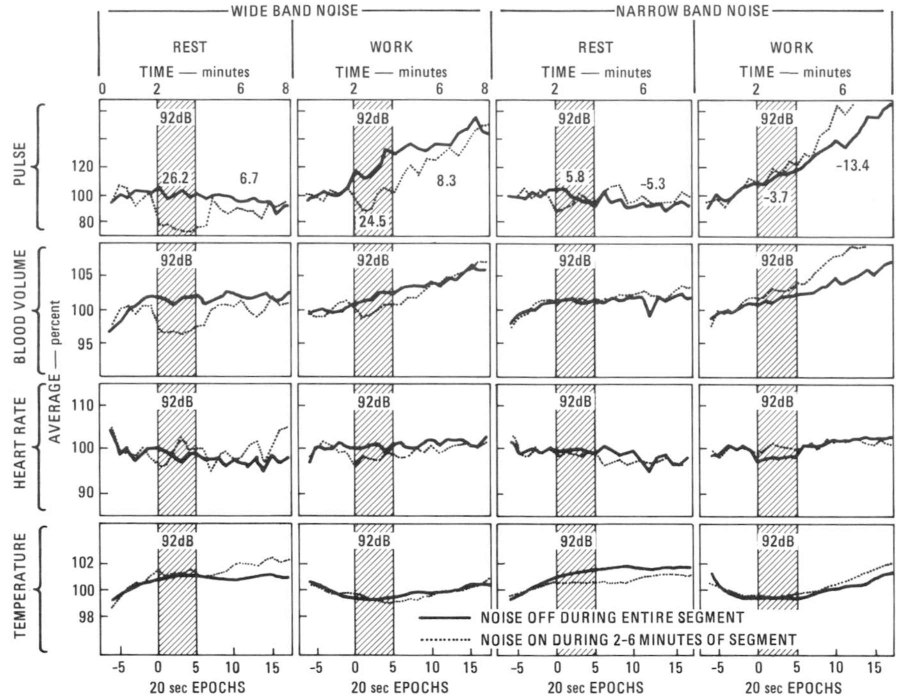

FIGURE 9.8 Pulse amplitude, blood volume, heart rate, and skin temperature changes as a function of noise. High-frequency noise, 1/3-octave band with center frequency of 3150 Hz; wideband, "pink" random noise sloping downward 3 dB per octave. (From Kryter and Poza, 1980. Copyright 1980 by the American Psychological Association. Adapted by permission of the author.)

tensive subjects with a family history of hypertension; and (2) cardiac output in normotensive subjects with no family history of hypertension.

Data Showing Meager or Negative Response of Nonauditory Systems

Finkle and Poppen (1948) exposed 10 men to 120 dB of jet engine noise for 1 h per day for 10 days, followed by 5 days of 2-h exposures. The men wore earmuffs that probably reduced the effective level of noise reaching their ears by 25 dB or so. The men showed complete habituation to the noise following initial responses to the exposures for all the physiological measures taken [cardiovascular output, basal metabolism, electrocardiogram (ECG), EEG, urinary functions, kidney functions, and blood tests].

Slob *et al.* (1973) conducted a study in which periodically obtained urine samples were analyzed for the presence of corticosteroids, adrenaline, and noradrenaline. The Slob *et al.* article also provides a good review of some European studies on this subject. During the hours of 0900–1700

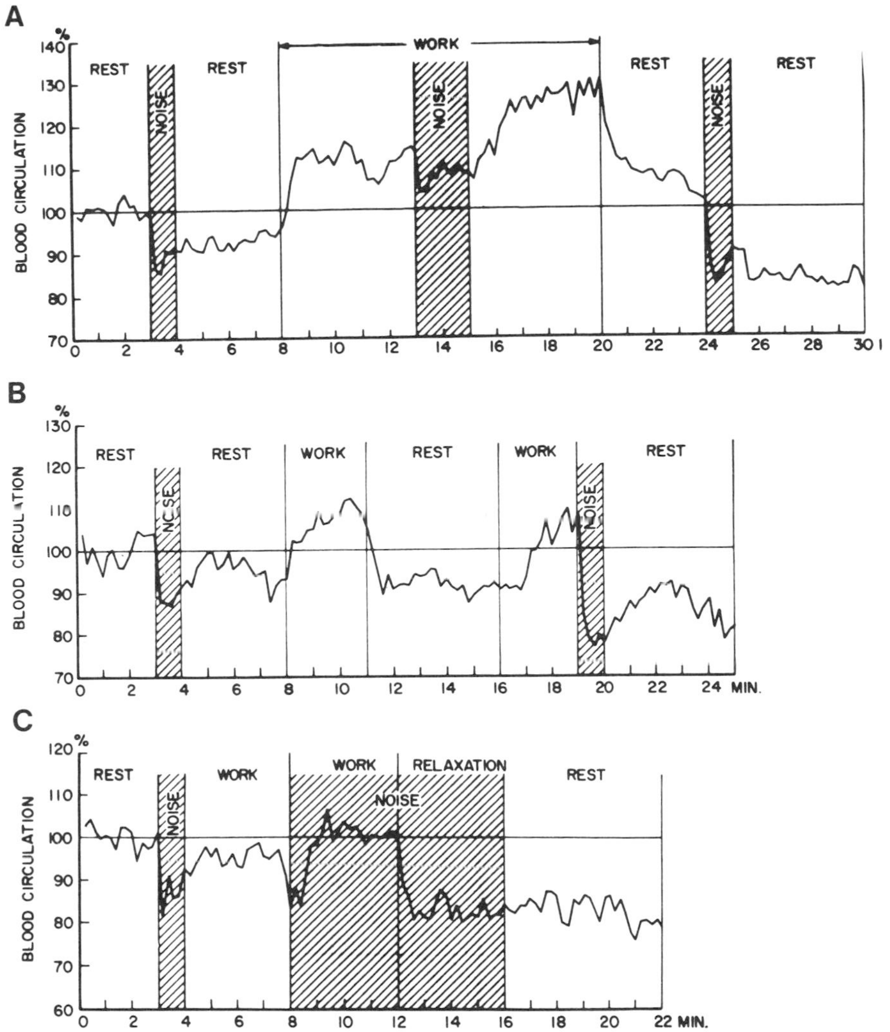

FIGURE 9.9 Effects of combination of work, rest, and noise on blood circulation. Reduces percentage indicates vasoconstriction of the peripheral blood vessels. (From Jansen, 1964.)

(9:00 AM–5:00 PM) urine samples were taken every 4 h on 2 successive days from two groups of 10 male adults. During the second day one group was exposed to a ⅓-octave-band-noise centered at 4000 Hz at a level of 80 dB_C from 1300 to 1500. Comparison of the morning and afternoon excretions between the 2 days showed that the control group experienced the following: (1) a significant drop in adrenaline excretion on the second day compared with the drop between morning and afternoon on the first day, (2) a slightly greater drop in noradrenaline between afternoon and morning on the second day compared with the difference found on the first day, and (3) a similar difference on both days for the corticosteroids. The experimental group showed similar differences between morning and afternoon excretions of all three hormones on both days. The noise seemingly had no effect.

Slob *et al.* conclude, however, that the noise perhaps had some effect because there was no decrease in adrenaline during the afternoon of the second day for the experimental group, whereas there was a decrease in adrenaline on the second day for the control group. Slob *et al.* suggest that these meager or negative results could be because their noise was presented at a level of only 80 dB_C. However, Slob *et al.* seem skeptical and quote Hawel and Starlinger (1967) to the effect that merely taking part in tests produces stress that negates the effects of the agent (in this case, noise) for which the tests are conducted. In such cases the agent may produce no effect at all on the subject.

Brandenberger *et al.* (1977) measured cortisol concentrations in eight human subjects every 10 min from 0800 to 1500 (8:00 AM–3:00 PM). In these experiments, 1 day was a control day and on 1 or 2 other days the human subjects were exposed to a broadband pink noise at levels from 96 to 105 dB_A and to 1/3-octave-band noises centered at 4000 Hz (84 dB_C) and at 8000 Hz (89 dB_C). Some of their findings are shown in Figs. 9.10 and 9.11. Brandenberger *et al.* conclude that noise is not associated with hyperactivity of the pituitary–adrenocortical part of the autonomic system in humans. These findings are also consistent with plasma cortisol and EEG data obtained by Favino *et al.* (1973) from human subjects exposed to a band of noise (700–1000 Hz) at a level of 90 dB. Fruhstorfer and Hensel (1980) exposed 13 young adults to 16-s bursts of white noise for 1 h daily for 10–21 days and measured their heart rate, respiration, cutaneous blood flow, and EEG during exposure. They concluded that certain physiological responses adapt to loud noise but that the time needed for this adaptation is somewhat different for different responses.

As shown earlier, habituation can occur to changes in blood pressure, heart (pulse) rate, and peripheral vascular pulse pressure that follow exposures to noise. This apparent habituation, or negative (no) response to noise has been found in a number of studies in which people and lower animals have been exposed to auditory stimuli. Davis and Van Liere (1949) found habituation in human subjects to repeated loud noises, and Pearsons and Kryter (1965) found similar adaptation of a startle response (heart rate) to simulated sonic booms. Illustrative of the pervasive principle of habituation of organisms to sound is the finding of Bartoshuk (1962) that the acceleration of the heart rate in unborn babies to bursts of acoustic clicks (85-dB level) is adapted out by the end of 40 trials. Also, Ando and Hattori (1970, 1977a) report that babies of mothers from neighborhoods subjected to aircraft noise were much less aroused from sleep by aircraft noise than were babies of women who lived in quiet neighborhoods during pregnancy.

Cartwright and Thompson (1975) conducted a study in which it was found

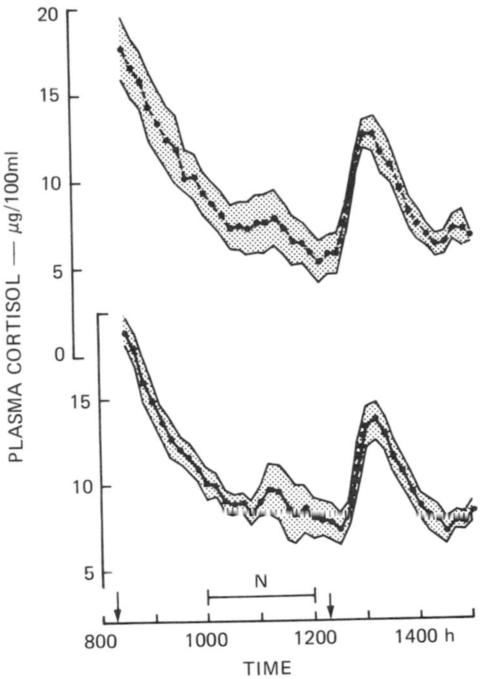

FIGURE 9.10 Mean and standard deviation of plasma cortisol concentration in five subjects during control days (top) and during days with exposure to 96-dB$_A$ pink noise (N) of 120-min duration (bottom). (From Brandenberger *et al.*, 1977.)

that 1-h exposures to white noise at 91 dB$_A$ caused no statistically significant changes in any of the cardiovascular responses from the control data obtained when the noise was not present. Some of their findings are shown in Fig. 9.12. As in the Brandenberger *et al.* study, the need to take frequent samples of data (every 2 min by Cartwright and Thompson) is of obvious importance because of the response variabilities unrelated to the noise stimulation.

As was noted earlier, Glass and Singer found that the peripheral vasoconstriction responses (pulse amplitude) became completely habituated when subjects were exposed to noise at levels of 108 dB$_A$. Also, as seen in Fig. 9.8, Kryter and Poza found that high-frequency, narrowband noise had no effect on heart rate, peripheral pulse pressure or amplitude (vasoconstriction), or peripheral blood volume. However, a broadband noise of the same intensity, 92 dB, consistently caused a vasoconstrictive response.

Laboratory studies of Andren *et al.* (1980) and Andren (1982) support, in general, the hypothesis that the constriction of peripheral blood vessels that occurs because of broadband noise at levels $>\sim 80$ dB$_A$ may be due to a nonstressful reflex response, perhaps associated with the aural reflex or ear protective reaction, rather than being a part of a general, nonspecific stress

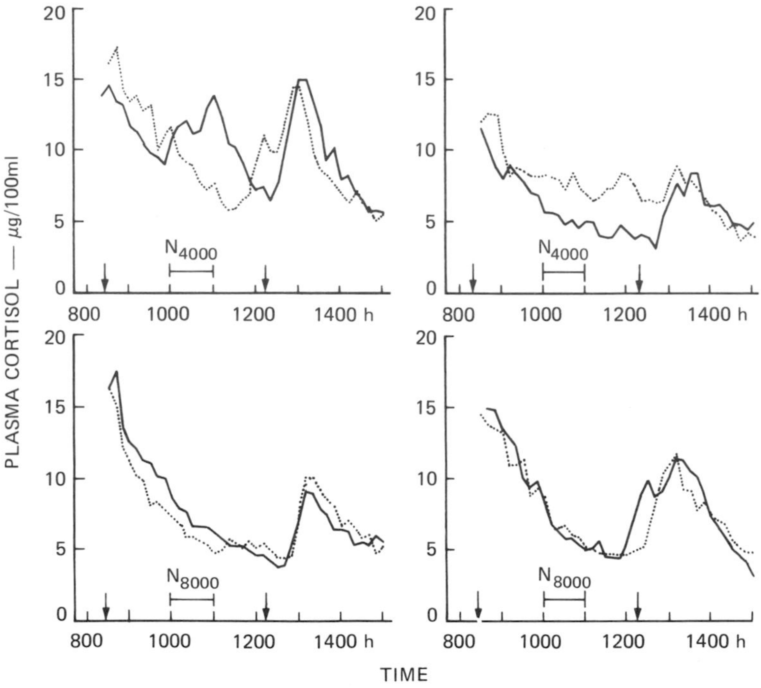

FIGURE 9.11 Plasma cortisol levels during days with exposure to 1/3-octave-band pink noise centered at 4000 or 8000 Hz (continuous line) compared with control-day pattern (dotted line). Arrows locate meal intakes. (From Brandenberger *et al.*, 1977.)

reaction. Andren found that 20-min exposures of adult males to broadband noise at levels of 95 or 100 dB_A caused a significant change in diastolic blood pressure but no changes in systolic blood pressure or heart rate. The increase in diastolic blood pressure was attributed to an increase in constriction of the peripheral blood vessels. No significant changes in cardiovascular behavior were observed from noise at a level of 85 dB_A. The subjects rested comfortably on a bed in a recumbent position during the tests.

Complicating the above-cited study and hypothesis is the fact that the noise at all levels caused no significant changes in the blood plasma levels of so-called stress hormones (adrenaline, noradrenaline, cortisol, prolactin, and growth hormone) in normotensive subjects. In subjects with mild hypertension there was a significant increase only of norardenaline during noise stimulation. Accordingly, it appears that the broadband noise capable of causing a constriction of the peripheral blood vessels did not cause cardiovas-

FIGURE 9.12 Change in various physiological activities for controls (quiet) and test subjects exposed to 91-dB_A broadband noise. (From Cartwright and Thompson, 1975.)

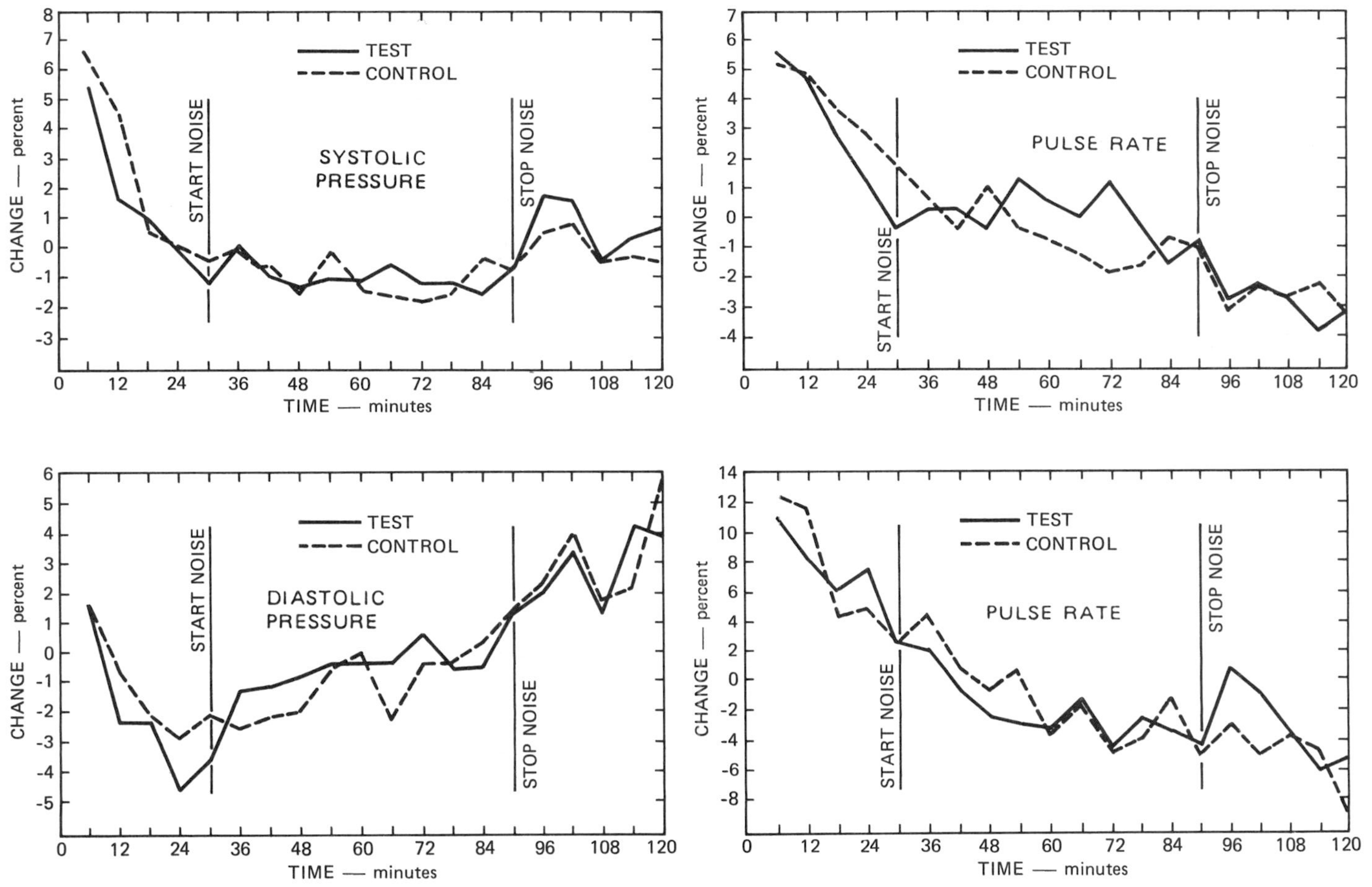

SYSTOLIC PRESSURE
TEST
CONTROL
START NOISE
STOP NOISE
CHANGE — percent
TIME — minutes
PULSE RATE
TEST
CONTROL
START NOISE
STOP NOISE
CHANGE — percent
TIME — minutes
DIASTOLIC PRESSURE
TEST
CONTROL
START NOISE
STOP NOISE
CHANGE — percent
TIME — minutes
PULSE RATE
TEST
CONTROL
START NOISE
STOP NOISE
CHANGE — percent
TIME — minutes

cular or glandular–autonomic nervous system responses associated with psychological or physiological stress (Levi, 1973).

Battig *et al.* (1980) obtained electromyograms, electrocardiograms, and skin conductance and respiration measures from 33 adults in their homes. At times the subjects performed various written tests and at other times engaged in conversation, rest, and so forth. Battig *et al.* found that there was no correlation between noise-exposure level and complaint behavior and the various physiological measures, including the electrocardiograms. However, the physiological measures were related to the activities being engaged in. This study is also interesting in that it was conducted in the homes of the subjects rather than under strict laboratory conditions.

Laboratory Studies of Monkeys

A somewhat similar variety of research results as those found with humans have been obtained with monkeys as subjects. Peterson *et al.* (1975, 1980, 1981) have conducted several experiments with monkeys in which cannulas implanted in the thoracic aorta permitted the continuous monitoring (15 s of each minute) of heart rate and of systolic and diastolic blood pressure. The animals were restrained in chairs within the experimental environment for 24 h per day for 6 to 9 months prior to the experiments proper and for an additional 30 experimental days for one study and 270 experimental days (9 months) for another study. Although some control animals were used, the analyses by Peterson *et al.* (1975, 1980) to show noise effects were done primarily by comparing the mean of the physiological measures for the experimental animals for a few days before they received any noise to the same measures during and after the periods they received noise.

Figure 9.13 shows some of the data from one of the early experiments of Peterson *et al.* (1975). Peterson *et al.* note that prior to the start of the noise (a recording of street and aircraft noises at L_{eq} 78 dB_A), which started at 0600 (6:00 AM), the animals showed heart rate and systolic blood pressure increases in anticipation of the noise. Indeed the levels reached for these two responses prior to the noise were about as great as present at any time during the time the noise was on. The decline in these two physiological activities while the noise is still on shows apparent anticipation of the end of the noise. Accordingly, it would seem logical to conclude that it is the psychological cognitive aspects of the experimental situation and not the noise per se that is eliciting the responses shown in Fig. 9.13.

Somewhat similar deductions can be made from other data published by Peterson *et al.* (1980, 1981). For example, Fig. 9.14 shows that the experimental animals exhibit a sharp increase in blood pressure on the first day or so of exposure to noise and that the increase stays with the animals for the duration of the experiment and beyond. Figure 9.14, which tracks 9-day averages for control and experimental animals, shows the immediate and the lasting effects of the addition of the noise regime to the environment.

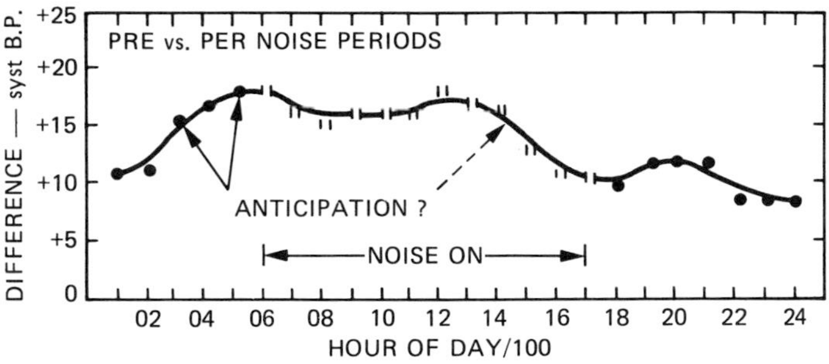

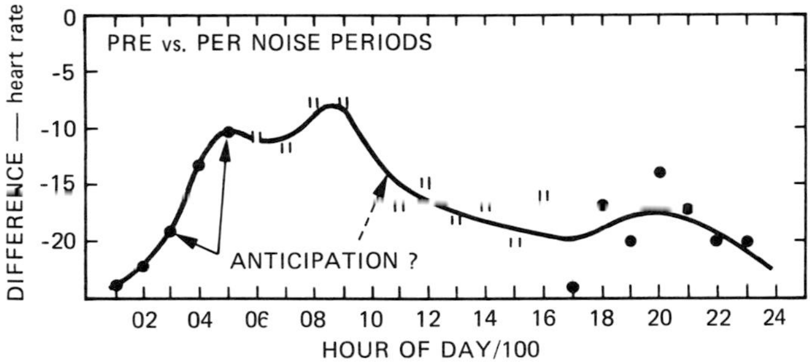

FIGURE 9.13 Hourly effects of noise with diurnal influences removed. "Anticipation?" lines added here. (From Peterson *et al.*, 1975.)

That elevation of blood pressure may be related to the anxiety the monkeys perceive regarding the experimental procedures and situations rather than any direct stress from the noise per se is suggested by the upper graphs in Fig. 9.15. The difference between the lower and the upper graphs in Fig.

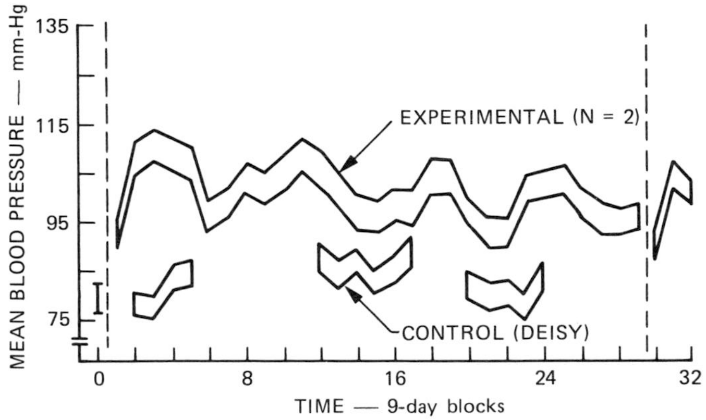

FIGURE 9.14 Comparisons of mean blood pressure for experimental and control animals. Envelopes encompass mean and 95% confidence limit. Dashed vertical lines indicate onset and cessation of noise-exposure period. Thick vertical bar at left represents preexposure values for experimental animals. (From Peterson *et al.*, 1981.)

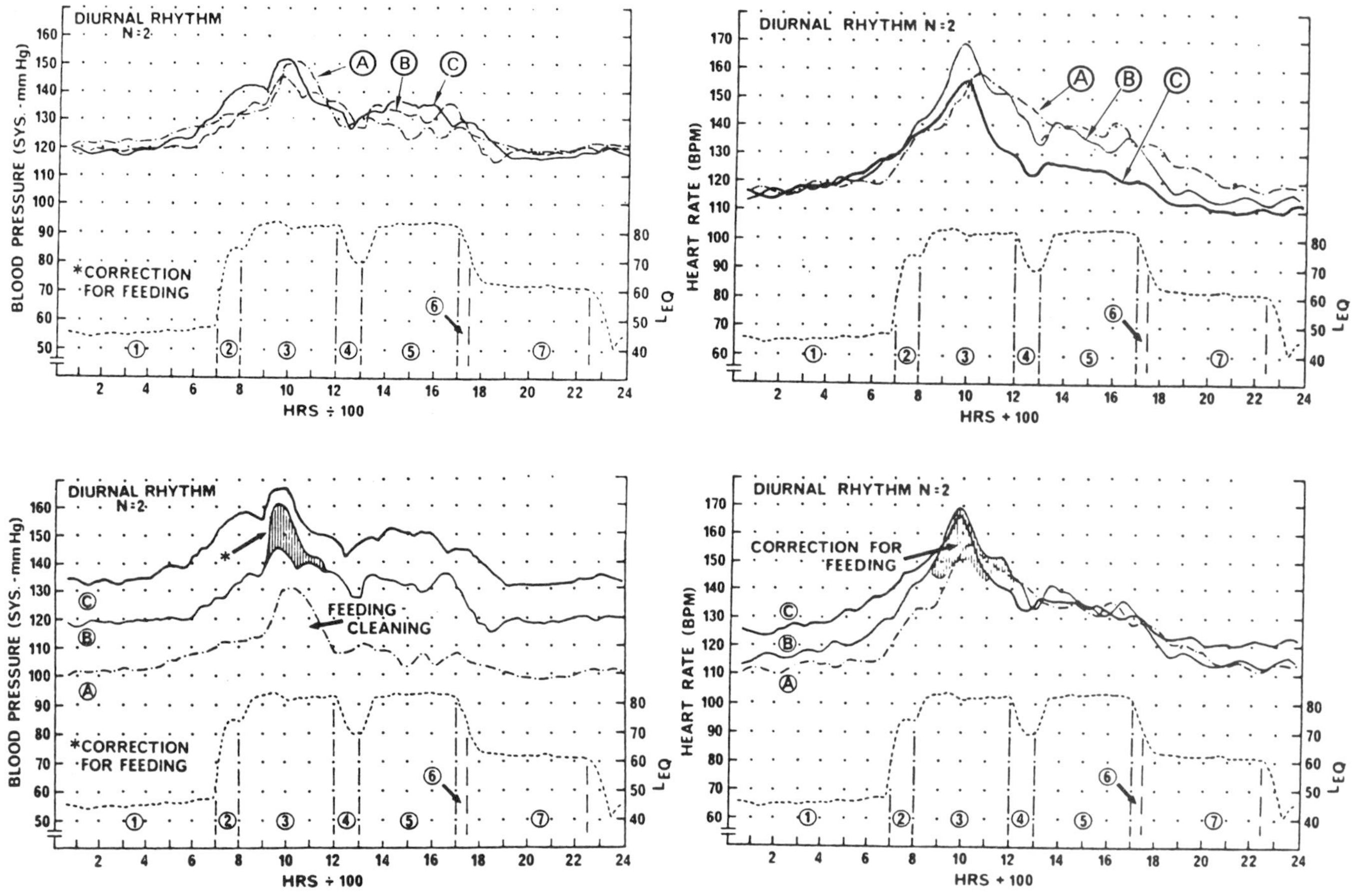

DIURNAL RHYTHM N:2
*CORRECTION FOR FEEDING
BLOOD PRESSURE (SYS. - mm Hg)
HRS ÷ 100
LEQ
DIURNAL RHYTHM N:2
HEART RATE (BPM)
HRS + 100
LEQ
DIURNAL RHYTHM N:2
FEEDING - CLEANING
*CORRECTION FOR FEEDING
BLOOD PRESSURE (SYS. - mm Hg)
HRS + 100
LEQ
DIURNAL RHYTHM N:2
CORRECTION FOR FEEDING
HEART RATE (BPM)
HRS + 100
LEQ

9.15 is that the three curves (*A*—preexposure days; *B*—first 12 days of exposure; *C*—last 18 days of exposure) in the upper graphs have been normalized with the respect to the blood pressure levels for the hours of 12–5 AM before the noise was turned on, whereas the lower graphs represent the raw data. It is shown in Fig. 9.15 that the daily pattern of blood pressure changes appeared to be more related to the time of day than the condition of noise (i.e., the daily preexposure pattern was about the same as the daily exposure patterns). Even if there are some specific noise relations they are minor in magnitude compared with the overall lack of effect of the introduction of noise.

Peterson *et al.* (1981) contend that humans exposed to moderately intense noise can experience sustained elevations in blood pressure without also sustaining hearing losses. (Their animals showed no depression in auditory thresholds measured in the brain stem following the noise exposures.) However, the data indicate that psychological factors (factors probably not relevant to noise-exposure conditions and ways of thinking typical for humans) had more impact than the noise on the nonauditory systems of the monkeys. Further, other experiments with both animals and humans make it clear that noise is not necessarily a cause of increased blood pressure or related nonauditory-system stress responses, and that psychological factors make it somewhat risky to extrapolate positive stress effects found in animals to humans.

In support of this interpretation of Peterson *et al.*'s data is the study of Kraft-Schreyer and Angelakos (1979) in which monkeys were exposed in the laboratory to a 400-Hz sound at a level of 100-dB for 4 months. These investigators found no systematic effects on blood pressure in the monkeys from exposure to the intense sound.

An experiment by Hanson *et al.* (1976) also shows the predominant role played by psychological aspects of the experimental situation in determining the reaction of monkeys to noise. Hanson *et al.* studied the effects on plasma cortisol levels of four 13-min daily exposure periods to 100 dB of noise for 28 days. Each 13-min period was separated by 2 min of quiet. Twelve monkeys were divided into groups and subjected to the following conditions: (1) no noise and no control over noise, (2) control over noises (at the end of each 13-min session the animal was presented a lever that, when pushed, turned off the noise), (3) no control over noise (no lever was presented at the end of each 13-min session), and (4) loss of noise control (animals who had completed the noise-control sessions were given the lever, but pressing

FIGURE 9.15 Diurnal rhythm of cardiovascular responses and noise exposure sequence: $L_{eq,24h}r = 85$ dB_A; 1 = night noise; 2 = morning household noise; 3,5 = work noise; 4 = cafeteria noise; 6 = transportation noise. (From Peterson *et al.*, 1980.) See text for normalization procedure.

the lever now did not turn off the noise). The results showed that blood plasma cortisol levels of animals with noise control did not differ from animals exposed to no noise at all, and that blood plasma cortisol levels were significantly elevated in animals with no noise control and in animals experiencing a loss of noise control. This finding is somewhat reminiscent of the aforementioned (see Chapter 8) findings of Glass and Singer with humans.

LABORATORY STUDIES OF LOWER ANIMALS

Audiogenic Seizures

A large body of literature is available on the effects of sound and noise on mice and rats. The number of studies done no doubt reflects the relative availability of these rodents as laboratory test subjects and the fact that they exhibit marked responsiveness to some intense sounds or noises. However, conjectures and extrapolations about the effects of noise stress in humans from these mice and rat studies have been controversial. [See comments of Falk (1973) and Kryter (1973).] In the writer's opinion, the interpretability of the data from some of these rodent studies is limited for the following reasons:

1. The emotional state of fear engendered in the animals by the experimental conditions, besides that of acoustical stimulation, must be significant. For example, to create neurological overload stress from sensory stimulation, Buckley and Smookler (1970), placed rats in a cage on a shaker in a room $4 \times 4 \times 6$ ft, with loudspeakers in the ceiling and the walls that produced noises such as airblasts, bells, and buzzers at a level of about 100 dB. Spotlights in each corner of the room gave 140 foot-candles of light in the cage. Periods of light and darkness were alternated every 0.5 s. The cage was oscillated at a rate of 140 per minute (140 min^{-1}). There is no question that these conditions should cause stress in the animals, but the interrelationships of psychological and physical stimulation factors can hardly be fathomed.

2. These animals can display stress reactions to some sounds and noises that are peculiar to their species and are pathological within the species. These reactions cover a wide range, from those not detectable from casual observation, to convulsive and hebephrenic behavior. These behaviors, sometimes leading to death, have been called audiogenic seizures.

The mechanisms involved in audiogenic seizures remain something of a mystery and are beyond the scope of this treatise to discuss. Certain facts, however, are clear. For one thing, the seizure response depends on several conditions beyond that of an immediate sound or noise stimulation. Examples of some conditions are the following:

1. When certain strains of rats or mice are exposed to intense auditory stimulation at the age of ~15–25 days, most will be susceptible to audiogenic seizures to intense noises later in life. This is called *priming*, and the sounds used interfere with the normal development of the cochlear and vestibular systems (Henry and Bowman, 1970; Sye, 1970; Saunders *et al.*, 1972; Chen, 1978).
2. Animals suffering from middle-ear infection (otitis media), which a large number of laboratory animals can have without obvious symptoms, are more prone to audiogenic seizures than are noninfected animals (Patton, 1947; Kenshalo and Kryter, 1949), Jensen and Rasmussen (1970). The complexity of audiogenic seizures and interactions among psychological factors, priming, and otitis media is shown by a study done by Niaussat (1977). It was found that in mice genetically nonsusceptible to audiogenic seizures that were primed with exposure to intense noise when 17 days old, 9% became seizure-prone when raised in colonies and only 3.8% became seizure-prone when raised in individual, sound-insulated cages. For mice with otitis media, however, 79% were seizure-prone.
3. The way the animals are handled and the acoustic and other conditions of their living quarters affect their seizure rate (Pfaff, 1974).

Whatever the facts might be, the basis, control, and role of audiogenic seizures in rats and mice is very uncertain from present research information.Seldom in studies of audiogenic seizures or of stress from noise in rats or mice are the animals examined for the presence or history of otitits media or for possible damage to the auditory and vestibular receptor systems from exposures as "pups" to sounds or noises.

Some investigators hold positive views of the value of experiments with rats and mice exposed to noise. For example, Busnel *et al.* (1975) found that mice dropped in a vat of water to swim for their lives with weights attached to their tails had seizures and submerged more quickly when exposed to tones of 50–10,000 Hz at levels ranging from 60 to 115 dB. Busnel *et al.* suggest that the use of these animals avoids the "adaptive" processes that mask the noxious effects of noise in studies with humans. However, it is not clear that their findings are not possibly due to pathological audiogenic seizures rather than normal stress responses to noise, and that in normal mice and rats "adaptive" processes would not, as in humans, also be a factor in controlling their behavior to sounds.

A number of studies clearly showing the deleterious effects of exposure to noise on the cardiovascular, reproductive, endocrine, and neurological functions in rats and mice were presented at a symposium on the physiological effects of noise (Welch and Welch, 1970). In summarizing the symposium, the speaker, Leake (1970) said: "Even though we may have learned both behaviorally and physiologically to ignore noise and thus to reduce the intensity of its emotional response, some of the neurological stimulus may spill into the autonomic nervous system, producing cardiovascular-renal disturbance, together with endocrine, metabolic and reproductive abnormalities." Unfortunately, the methods used in some of these studies, and the use of mice and rats subject to audiogenic seizures, led to results that are not thusly generalizable to the effects of noise on humans or nonpathological animals.

Epilepsy and Audiogenic Seizures

It is sometimes surmised that audiogenic seizures in mice and rats may be somewhat comparable to epileptic seizures in people. Although both apparently involve pathological neurological conditions, the events appear to be quite different. Forster (1970) notes that epilepsy affects about 1% of the population, that about 6.5% of epileptic seizures are evoked by sensory stimulation, and that the vast majority of those are caused by visual stimuli. Forster indicates that sound elicited seizures can result from a sudden loud noise but are usually minor. Some patients will have a seizure only to certain specific sounds (e.g., ringing of a telephone only in their home or a particular song or type of music; see also Rivera, 1978). Forster finds that the rare patients who are stimulated to seizures from sounds, are stimulated by sounds that are not unpleasant or loud to normal people. Apparently sound-induced epileptic seizures are not similar in etiology to audiogenic seizures in mice and rats.

Negative Cardiovascular Response Data

A different situation exists when mice and rats known to be free from audiogenic seizure symptoms or auditory disease are exposed to noise. As shown by Borg and Møller (1978), such animals show habituation to noises that are meaningless in terms of associations with danger.

Borg and Møller divided 130 normotensive (blood pressure <125 mmHg) and spontaneously hypertensive (blood pressure >125 mmHg) rats into the following three main experimental groups: (1) exposed to background noise produced by the rats themselves, approximately 50 dB_A; (2) exposed to noise at 85 dB; and (3) exposed to noise at 105 dB. The noise was a 1640-Hz-wide band of random noise sweeping from 3 to 30 kHz at a rate of once every 2 s. It was interrupted randomly seven times per night with rise and decay times of interruption of 5 ms. Except for random interruptions totaling 2 h during each night, the noise was on continuously for 10 hours each night, which is a normal wake time for the rats. After 1 year in the noise the animals in group (2) showed hearing losses of 10–15 dB at 6 kHz, and those in group (3) showed losses of 40–60 dB. Blood pressure was measured with a cuff attached to the tail of each animal.

Figure 9.16 shows Borg and Møller's major findings. It is seen that mean

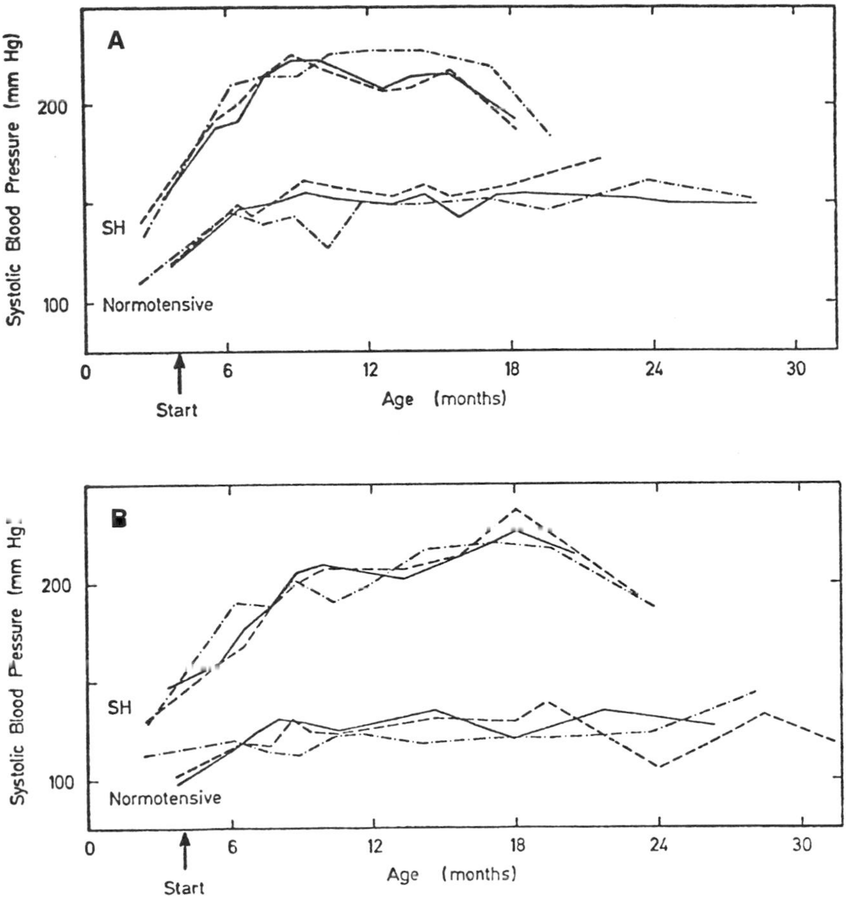

FIGURE 9.16 Mean systolic blood pressure measured indirectly from the tail of spontaneously hypertensive (SH) rats [(A) Males; (B) Females] and normoyensive rats as a function of age for controls (solid curve), 85-dB noise (dashed curve), and 105-dB noise (dash–dot curve). Average of standard error was not more than 11 mmHg for any group. (From Borg and Møller, 1978.)

systolic pressure in rats over a lifetime of daily exposure to different levels of noise did not differ systematically from that of non-noise-exposed rats. There is some suggestion in Fig. 9.16 that the hypertensive animals in group 3 showed a somewhat more rapid initial increase in blood pressure than did the rats in the other two groups. To check the reliability of that possibility, an additional 40 hypertensive rats were tested. As shown in Fig. 9.17, no consistent differences over this initial period were found between the hypertensive animals exposed to the quiet or to the 105-dB-SPL (sound-pressure level) living environments.

Although the noise was sufficiently intense to cause some hearing loss, the losses probably did not reduce the loudness of the noises to the animals

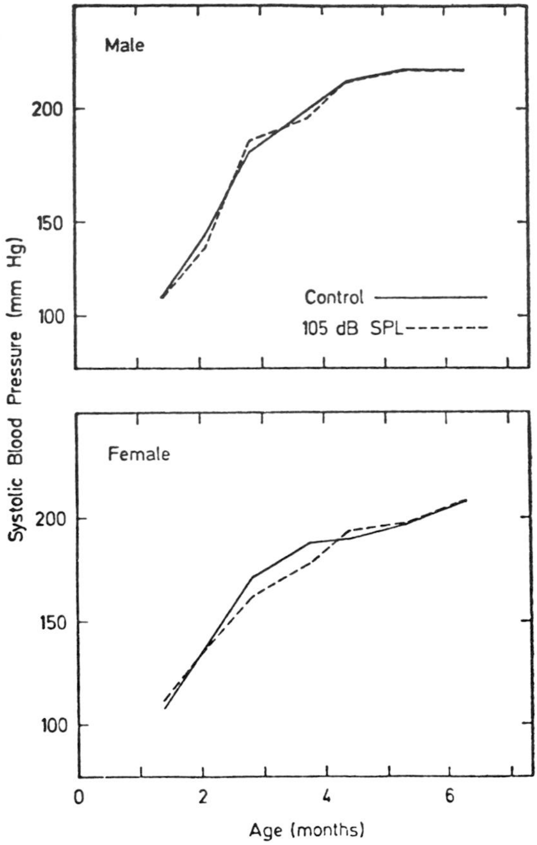

FIGURE 9.17 Average systolic blood pressure for spontaneously hypertensive rats in control environment and 105-dB SPL. (From Borg and Møller, 1978.)

because of recruitment. Further, the animals with only a 10- to 15-dB loss exhibited the same general blood pressure changes as those animals with a 40- to 60-dB hearing loss. Borg and Møller concluded that habituation to the noise environments had occurred in the rats, and that lifelong exposure for 10 hours daily to the 85- or 105-dB levels of the noise used in their study would not alter blood pressure in normotensive or hypertensive rats.

Field Studies of Wildlife

Chesser *et al.* (1975) trapped mice from fields near an airport (noise levels 80–120 dB) and from similar fields away from low-flying aircraft (noise levels 80–85 dB). They found that the mice from the fields close to the airport had larger adrenal glands than did those from the quieter fields but had the same average gross body weight, and that a group of mice from the quieter fields developed larger adrenal glands than a control group of these mice when exposed to 105-dB aircraft noise for 1 min every 6 min for 2 weeks. The authors indicate that population densities of the mice in the two fields were the same, but that air pollution or other factors in the field near the airport could have contributed to the larger adrenal glands found in the mice from that field. It is also possible that the psychological stress or perhaps some incipient audiogenic seizure effects possibly related to ear infections contracted in the laboratory could have contributed to the enlarged adrenal glands in the mice exposed to the aircraft noise in the laboratory experiment.

A possible reason to question the findings of this study is that in another sample of mice taken from the two fields. Pritchett *et al.* (1976) found the control mice to be somewhat heavier, but there were no significant differences in adrenal–pair or in adrenal–body-weight ratios. Pritchett *et al.* removed the adrenal glands from the mice and incubated them in the presence and absence of ACTH (anadrenocorticotropic hormone). They found that the adrenal glands from the noise-exposed mice showed somewhat different responsiveness to ACTH than did the glands from the non-noise-exposed mice.

Busnel and Briot (1980) reported that in land zones near commercial airports in France, wildlife of many forms is abundant. Indeed, it is necessary for the government to mount hunting parties to try to control the bird population because they represent a safety hazard to aircraft. Data pertaining to collisions between birds and aircraft and to numbers of animals and birds bagged per year by hunting parties reveal that the animal populations grew independently of the amount of air traffic. Observations indicated that migratory birds do not hesitate to use airport environs as resting places during migration and do not even necessarily attempt to move because of aircraft noise up to 120 dB. Busnel and Briot conclude that the general absence of humans from the area contributes to the growth of wildlife and that the aircraft noise has little or no effect on the animals. Some habituation no doubt is involved, but it would have to be almost immediate, as evinced the behavior of migratory birds.

Fletcher (1980) reviewed the literature on observations made of wildlife during activities such as the placing of pipelines across wilderness areas and the use of off-road recreational vehicles. Noises such as those from helicopters, blasting, earthmoving equipment, and snowmobiles were involved. For the most part, this literature is ambiguous and impossible to interpret with respect to the effects of the noise on the wildlife. The reasons are primarily that the activities were often threatening to animals (destroyed the flora and fauna of some land areas), that people were present (a usually frightening stimulus to wildlife), and that the noise conditions and operations were for such short periods of time that possible habituation to the noise, as well as to the actions of the machinery and the people, was not adequately studied. In situations where the noise was from fixed structures (e.g., high-voltage lines giving off corona discharge noise levels of ≤63 dB_A when wet) in remote wildlife areas, it was found that coyote, sheep, and many other wildlife species were not disturbed by the noise. Animals fed and "played" in its presence. Some birds built nests and raised their young in the towers supporting the high-voltage lines.

Anderson *et al.* (1993) studied the effects of an increase in noise on the nesting of wild loons, geese, swans, and ducks in areas surrounding a "power-compressor plant" at Prudhoe Bay, Alaska. The change, due to the addition of a large gas-turbine, increased the L_{eq} from ~52 to 55 dB_A in areas near the plant. It was found that spring weather conditions had a greater effect than the increased noise on the number and success of bird nesting. Only two species of birds displayed a shift in distribution that could be attributed to avoidance of the area due to increased noise.

There has been an increase in low altitude, military jet-aircraft training flights over wilderness areas. These operations create noise levels on the ground under the flight path typically ranging from 90 to 125 dB_A. Murphy *et al.* recorded the reactions of herds of caribou, in interior Alaska, to 161 overflights of military jet aircraft. It was found that 76% of the animals showed some sign of behavioral reaction to the noises, moving an average distance of 25 m. Typically, the caribou interrupted their ongoing activity for an average of 20 s, and then resumed an undisturbed activity such as eating.

Harrington (1993) also studied the effect of these military aircraft overflights on caribou in Laborador, Canada. In addition to visual observation, some animals were equipped with satellite-tracked radiocollars. Harrington found that the overflight noise caused a short-lived but relatively intense startle reaction in the animals, that did not appear to have an accumulative effect. A significant finding was that of a negative correlation between the survival of calf was negatively correlated with the level of the mother's exposure to the low-level flyovers.

Krausman *et al.* (1993) monitored over several months the heart rate of six captive desert mule deer and five mountain sheep kept in pens exposed to military jet-aircraft overflights. They concluded that although heart rates of the animals increased during over flights, they quickly returned to normal, these increase are not detrimental.

Studies of Farm Animals

A number of studies and observations (see, e. g., Casady and Lehman, 1967; Espmark *et al.*, 1974; Travis *et al.*, (1972) Bond, 1970; Stephan, 1993) have been made of the effects of sonic booms and other aircraft noise on farm animals. Table 9.2, from a 2-week study of animals on farms near Edwards Air Force Base, shows that the probability of any significant reaction of any of the animals to sonic booms of the order of 1.0–2.0 lb/F^{t^2} is negligible. Young broilers showed the largest reactions. The farms involved in these studies had been regularly exposed to about 8 sonic booms per day for several years. This would suggest that habituation had taken place and that previously nonexposed animals could react differently. However, the fact that the farming operations had continued without apparent problems over the years would suggest that this habituation was a rapid phenomenon.

TABLE 9.2 Animal Behavior Under Sonic Booms at Edwards Air Force Base (Test Period June 6–23, 1966)

A. Poultry Behavior Changes

Parameter	Number of booms	Average effect	0*	1†	2‡	3§
Species						
Broilers	197	1.02	23	158	6	10
Young turkeys	195	0.51	100	91	3	1
Adult turkeys	198	0.52	95	103	0	0
Young pheasants	85	0.81	16	69	0	0
Adult pheasants	125	0.96	7	117	0	1
By farm						
Jones turkeys	187	0.53	90	96	0	1
K-M turkeys	206	0.50	105	98	3	0
Del Mar broilers	106	0.95	9	93	4	0
Ringo broilers	91	1.09	14	65	2	10
Pheasants	210	0.90	23	186	0	1

* Number of booms producing no reaction.

† Number of booms producing a mild reaction.

‡ Number of booms producing a crowding reaction.

§ Number of booms producing pandemonium.

Data from Casady and Lehman, 1967.

B. Dairy Milking Reactions

Date	Number of booms	0*	1†	2‡	Average effect
June 6	12	6	6	0	
7	10	10	0	0	
9	12	6	6	0	
13	7	6	1	0	
14	14	13	1	0	
15	1	1	0	0	
20	12	10	2	0	
21	12	11	1	0	
22	13	13	0	0	
23	11	9	2	0	
Totals	104	85	19	0	0.18

* Number of booms producing no reaction.

† Number of booms producing a mild reaction.

‡ Number of booms producing a severe reaction.

(continues)

TABLE 9.2 (*Continued*)

C. Percentage Changes in Animal Behavior

Animal	Changed	Returned / Changed	Changed to normal / Changed	Changed to abnormal / Changed	Abnormal / Total	Observations	Total changed	Total number of booms
				By Species				
Beef	7.68	24.89	73.79	1.31(3)	0.10	2980	229	168
Dairy	3.38	28.92	70.58	0.49(1)	0.01	6032	204	87
Sheep	2.76	0.00	100.00	0.00	0.00	2750	76	99
Horses	4.52	59.25	33.33	7.40(4)	0.33	1193	54	85
				By Farm				
Beef—1	10.10	25.38	73.09	1.52	0.15	1950	197	65
Beef—10	3.10	21.87	78.12	0.00	0.00	1030	32	103
Horses	4.52	59.25	33.33	7.40	0.33	1193	54	85
Sheep	2.76	0.00	100.00	0.00	0.00	2750	76	99
Dairy	3.38	28.92	70.58	0.49	0.01	6032	204	87

One interesting observation during the Edwards Air Force Base studies is that turkeys that showed some movement in response to the sonic booms did so slightly before the airborne acoustic signal reached them. They were apparently responding to the ground wave of the sonic boom, which travels faster than the airborne wave. In short, the turkeys were being stimulated by vibrations from the ground rather than by the audible sound.

Espmark *et al.* exposed cattle and sheep to 20 sonic booms and 10 subsonic aircraft noises over a period of 4 days. The aircraft noise was at a level of about 94 dB_A and the sonic booms at about 3 lb/F^{t2}. Espmark *et al.* concluded that the effects of the noises were not unusual and that the animals returned quickly to grazing or other normal activities when interrupted.

Besides reports of young chickens being panicked by sonic booms, there are reports that nesting, farm-raised mink would kill their pups when exposed to sudden, intense noises such as sonic booms. Travis *et al.* conducted a study in which farm-raised mink were exposed to three real or three simulated sonic booms at a level of 6 lb/F^{t2} (very intense booms). A group of control animals were not exposed to booms. The effects of the booms were essentially negligible. To summarize from their study: no differences ($p > .05$) were found among experimental treatments for length of gestation, number of kits born per female whelping, number of kits alive per female at 5 and 10 days of age, weight of kits at 49 days of age, and kit pelt value and selling price. A behavioral study showed no evidence that the female mink under observation were sufficiently disturbed by sonic booms to engage in kit packing or kit killing, or to disrupt normal lactation. Results of necropsy examinations showed no mink deaths attributable to real or simulated sonic booms. Likewise, no evidence was found that bacterial disease was induced in the herd following exposure to sonic booms. There were no detectable differences in the overall health of the females at the three sites. The conclusion drawn from these studies was that exposure of farm-raised mink to intense sonic booms during whelping season had no adverse effect on their reproduction or behavior.

Bond summarized research of the U.S. Department of Agriculture and described the following results: (1) milk production in cows was reduced by noise causing fright reactions, but dairy cows exposed to flyover noises of aircraft and sonic booms in real life showed no such effects; (2) swine exposed to loud noises ranging from 100 to 135 dB showed no changes in growth rate, efficiency of food utilization, or reproduction and showed no detectable microscopic changes in ears or in adrenal or thyroid glands; and (3) mink exposed to sonic booms showed no adverse effects.

Stephan reported partial results of an investigation of the effects of noise from low-altitude fixed-wing and helicopter aircraft overflights on horse, cattle, pig, poultry, turkey, mink, and dog. Horses showed flight reactions when the aircraft could be seen and heard approaching, but did not break or jump fences. During hovering of helicopter over horses in small pen, the animals tended to stand motionless. One group of cattle roaming freely in a field showed no flight or stamping movements with either type of aircraft flyover. However, a second group, showed jostling unified movement toward the exit of the pasture when exposed to overflights and helicopter hovering. The investigator states, in summary, that the pig, poultry, mink, and dog when exposed to the same aircraft noise conditions showed species-specific behavior, but mostly as a quite mild expression.

Summary of Effects of Noise on Animals

There are no consistent data from which to conclude that under real-life conditions (or laboratory conditions, for that matter), wild or domesticated lower animals react much differently to sound or noise than do people. When normal animals (excluding those exhibiting audiogenic seizures or symptoms) do react in a stressful manner to "noise," it is probably for the same reasons as in people, namely, the psychological aspects related to the information conveyed by the noise

EFFECTS ON NONAUDITORY SENSORY SYSTEMS

Pain

Gardner and Licklider (1959) developed a device that permitted a dental patient to listen, via earphones, to stereophonic music or filtered random noise. The typical procedure, called *audio analgesia,* was for the patient to relax by listening to the music and to switch to the noise when on feeling any dental pain, increasing the intensity of the noise as necessary to kill the pain. The dosage of noise has to be controlled so as not to cause undue fatigue or stress to the ear (Davis and Glorig, 1962; Kryter *et al.,* 1962).

Since the intensity of the noise is under the control of the patient, this is a potential problem for its general use.

Laboratory experiments conducted by the inventors of the device and by others revealed that pain from things such as heat and cold applied to the hand, electrical stimulation ("tingle" threshold) applied to the teeth, and pressure applied to the arm were not suppressed by the presence of intense random noise, although a reduction in the sensation level of deep-muscle pressure was found (Gardner *et al.*, 1960; Melzack, 1961; Carlin *et al.*, 1962; Camp *et al.*, 1962 Robson and Davenport, 1962). Some observations and tests have reportedly been made of possible pain suppression with noise in people during childbirth, surgical operations (other than dental), and diseased conditions with mixed success.

It is established that hypnotic suggestion can be effective in suppressing pain in some people (Hilgard, 1969), and this may be primary response involved in audio analgesia. However, audio analgesia may involve physiological as well as psychological mechanisms. Beecher has pointed out that analgesic agents, such as morphine, that do not give consistent suppression of pain at its threshold do provide consistent relief at suprathreshold level of pain. It can be concluded that when audio analgesia is effective, one or more of the following conditions prevail:

1. Hypnotic suggestion, enhanced by attention to the music or noise, gives distraction from any pain.
2. In certain cases no pain would actually be felt except that due to the anxiety of the patient, and the music or noise relaxes the patient and reduces anxiety.
3. Neural impulses from the auditory system preempt, to some extent, the activity of centers in the reticular formation of the brain stem that are involved in the processing of pain impulses to the higher nerve centers.

Cutaneous Sensations from the External Ear

Ades *et al.* (1958) and Plutchik (1963) have evoked sensations, other than auditory, from deaf ears exposed to intense noise. They obtained the results for "feeling," "tickle," and "pain" shown in Fig. 9.18. Figure 9.18 is from an experiment in which persons who were totally deaf were exposed to very intense tones and noise. Because of their deafness, the subjects could be exposed to levels that would be harmful to the normal ear. Plutchik reported that three pulses per second were rated as more unpleasant than slower or faster rates. Ades *et al.* found that persons without eardrums reported no pain sensations with levels up to 170 dB. It seems likely that the discomfort or pain thresholds reported for the deaf and normal ear (see Fig. 2.21) are attributable to stimulation of the eardrum, or some middle-ear skin receptors.

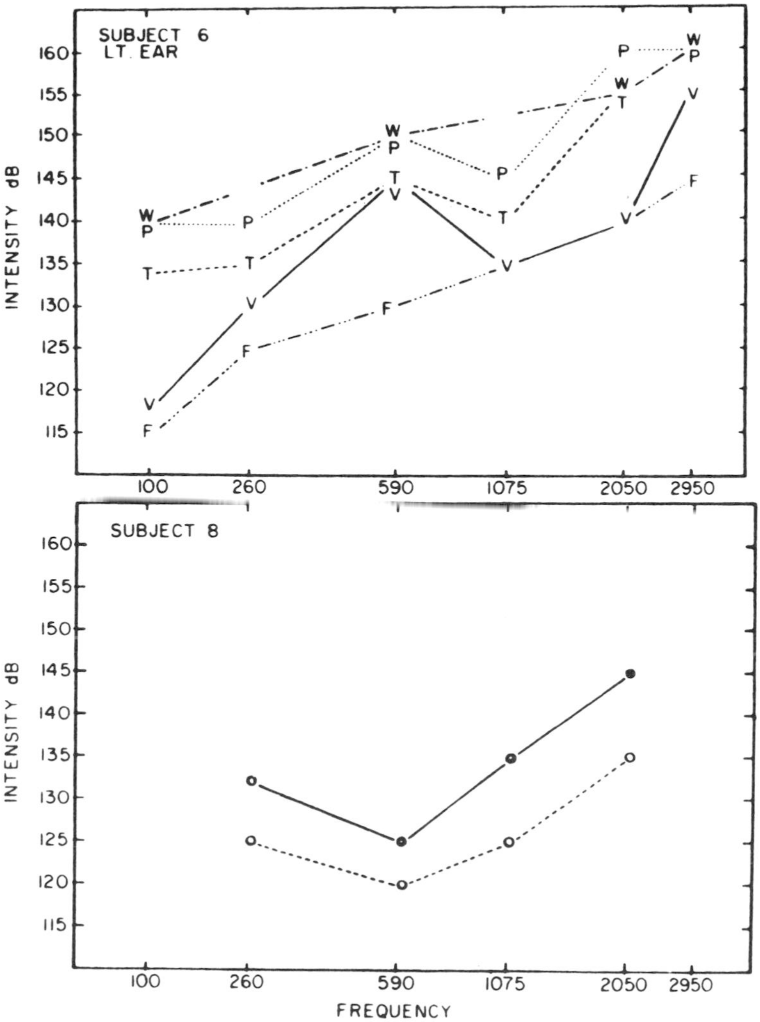

FIGURE 9.18 Threshold curves for vibration (V), tickle (T), pain (P), warmth (W), and feeling (F) for the left ear of subject 6, and threshold curves for small eye movements (broken line) and marked nystagmus (solid line) for subject 8. (From Ades *et al.*, 1958.)

Vestibular System

Connected to the cochlea of the inner ear are the sacculus, the utricle, and the semicircular canals. These structures, called the *vestibular system,* share certain fluids with the cochlea, and their innervations are closely connected (see Fig. 2.1). This vestibular system is involved in maintaining body balance and orientation in space. When stimulated in certain ways, a person may lose the sense of balance or become dizzy, the eyes may show nystagmus movements (a fast movement back and forth of the eyeballs), and, under extreme conditions, the person may become nauseated.

Because of their fluidic connections, it is not surprising to find that intense sounds affect both the cochlea and the vestibular system. The lower graph of Fig. 9.18 shows the intensity required for various tones to reach the threshold of nystagmus in one subject. Dickson and Chadwick (1951) report that for jet-aircraft noise over 140 dB or so, a person may feel a sense of equilibrium disturbance, Roggevsen and Van Dishoeck (1956) note that in persons who experience vestibular reactions to sounds of relatively weak intensity (considerably less than those shown in Fig. 9.18), usually lesions are present in the bony walls of the vestibular system.

If noise can effect the vestibular system, it is possible that this could affect the ability of a person to maintain balance when standing on a narrow rail. Harris and Von Gierke (1971) exposed subjects wearing earmuffs to white noise at levels of 120, 130, and 140 dB while standing balanced on a rail above $1^1/_4$ in. wide with eyes open and on a rail about $2^1/_4$ in. wide with eyes closed. They found that with both ears exposed to the same level of noise, only at 140 dB was there any impairment to balance performance. At the lower levels there was a reduction in balance performance when the noise was louder in one ear than in the other.

Harris (1972) found that an intermittent 1000-Hz tone at a level of 105 dB presented monaurally to an unprotected ear impaired the ability to balance on the rails described above compared with performance with the tone at 65 dB. However, Vanderhei and Loeb (1976), in a later repetition of the experiment, found no effect of the 105-dB, 1000-Hz, monaurally presented tone on the same balance test. These investigators concluded that noise and sound under general field conditions are unlikely to affect equilibrium.

Kinesthesia

Stimulation of the receptors in the muscles and joints of the body by vibrations imposed primarily through contact of the body with physical structures can create sensations of discomfort in the body. Thresholds for these perceptions from body vibrations at different frequencies are shown in Fig. 9.19.

Simultaneous exposure to body vibrations and intense airborne noise is found in a number of types of transportation vehicles, but especially in aircraft. Dempsey *et al.* (1979) have conducted experiments that show the contributions of vibration and noise separately and together to subjective discomfort. They developed a model for the contribution of noise and vibration that shows the tradeoffs available in the design or operation of a vehicle so as not to exceed a given level of ride discomfort (see Fig. 9.20). Interestingly, the magnitude of the noise–discomfort component is dependent on the level of vibration present in the combined environment.

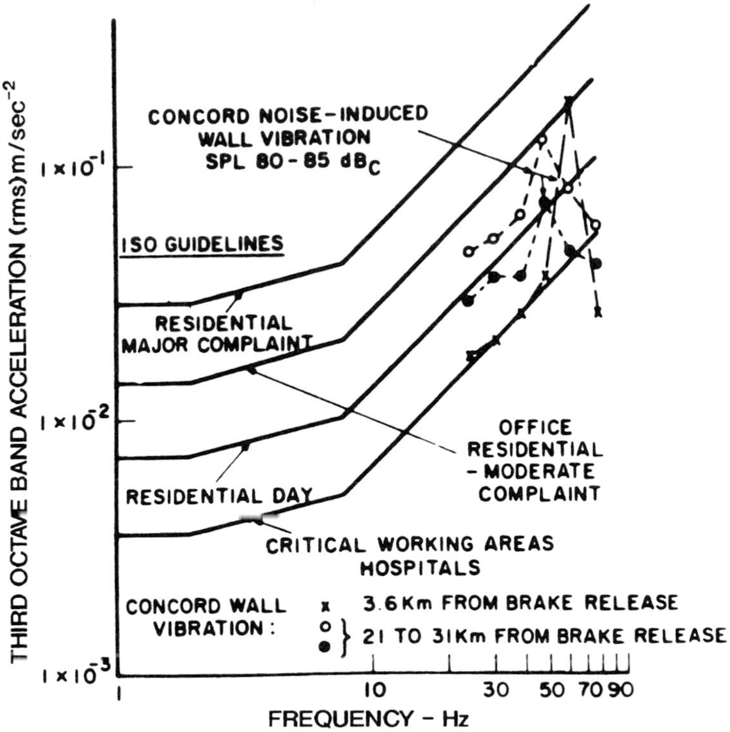

FIGURE 9.19 Acceptability of building vibration to inhabitants. (From Von Gierke, 1980.)

Vision

Noise has been thought to influence visual acuity and field, color vision, and critical flicker frequency (CFF). The last phenomenon refers to the fact that alternating dark and light visual fields will become blurred (cease to flicker) at some frequency of alternation.

Visual contrast thresholds (bright target on less bright field) and minimum visual acuity for lines and discs are apparently not affected by noise levels up to ~140 dB (see Fig. 9.21), although Dorfman and Zajone (1963) found some effect of sound level on perception of background brightness but not on size estimation of objects. Loeb (1954) found that broadband noise at a level of 115 dB had no effect on visual acuity. However, Rubenstein (1954) reported adverse effects from noise at 75–100 dB, and Chandler (1961) reported a shift of verticality of a visual line away from the ear stimulated with noise. Benko (1959, 1962) reported a narrowing of the visual field with noise.

As discussed earlier in the chapter, noises that invariably cause a dilation of the pupil of the eye along with a vasoconstriction of peripheral blood vessels sometimes cause other responses related to autonomic-system activ-

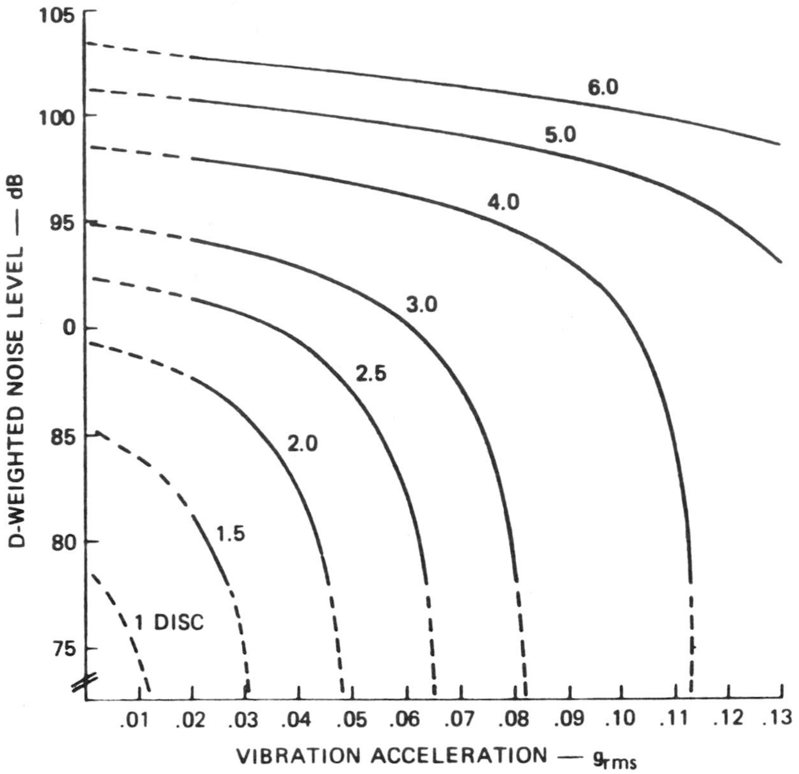

FIGURE 9.20 *D*-Weighted noise level required to produce successive constant discomfort curves as a function of vibration acceleration $g_{\rm rms}$. (From Dempsey *et al.*, 1979. Copyright 1979 by the American Psychological Association. Adapted by permission of the author.)

ity. However, Jones *et al.* (1977) found that although exposure to either continuous or intermittent industrial noise increases pupil size, visual acuity is not adversely affected.

Hermann *et al.* (1978) studied the effect on visual depth perception of several minutes of exposure to broadband white noise at levels ranging from 70 to 115 dB_A. They found that these exposures did not produce any significant changes in stereoscopic depth perception.

McCroskey (1958) reported that random noise at levels from 85 to 115 dB reduced the CFF from 25 to 23 s^{-1}. Ogilvie (1956) found no change in CFF with steady-state random noise of 0 to 90 dB seriation level, an increase in CFF with noise "fluttered" out of phase with the visual flicker, and a decrease in CFF with noise fluttered in phase with the flicker. Walker and Sawyer (1961), however, were not able to duplicate Ogilvie's findings and got negative results except for a small difference in CFF between steady-state out-of-phase and in-phase noise (see Table 9.3).

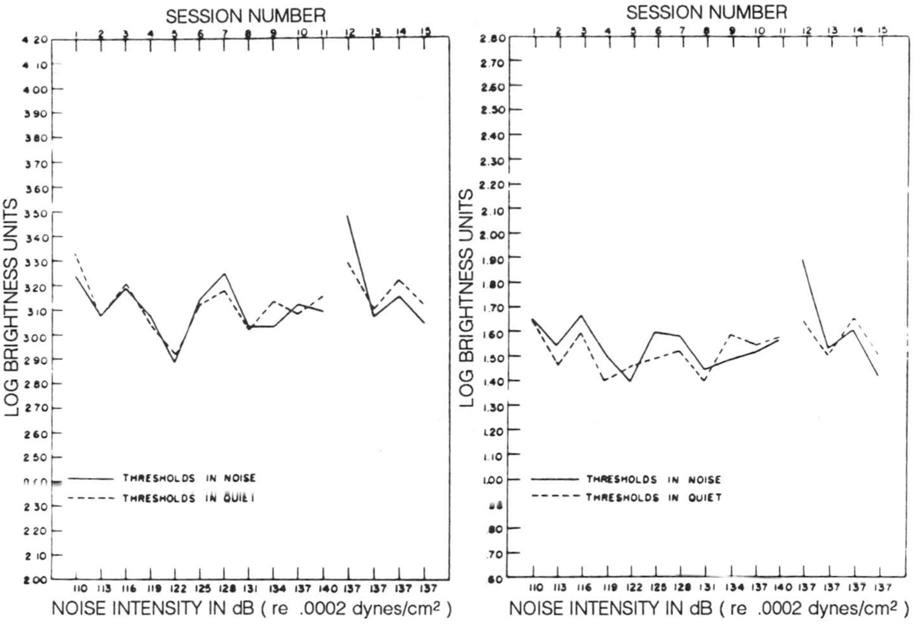

FIGURE 9.21 Threshold of visual acuity in quiet and in noise. (A) Verticle lines and (B) disks. (From Krauskopf and Coleman, 1956.)

The effect of steady-state noise on CFF when the color of the light was varied has also been studied, but the results are very inconsistent. For example, Maier *et al.* (1961) found that CFF decreased with increased loudness when the light was orange-red, but no change occurred with green light. It would appear that noise can sometimes effect about a 10% change (usually a decrease) in CFF from the CFF found in quiet, but the exact effects as a

TABLE 9.3 CFF for Four Conditions

Condition	Sample size, N	Mean CFF, s^{-1}	Standard deviation of CFF, s^{-1}
	With Artificial Pupil		
No noise	13	32.62	6.20
Steady-state noise		31.94	4.75
In-phase noise		32.34	4.78
Out-of-phase noise		32.78	5.44
	Without Artificial Pupil		
No noise	13	38.12	3.43
Steady-state noise		38.01	3.48
In-phase noise		38.42	3.28
Out-of-phase noise		38.72	3.73

Data from Walker and Sawyer, 1961.

function of various noise and light conditions are highly variable and possibly a matter of experimental chance and error.

The converse effects of light on auditory threshold are small and perhaps fortuitous. For example, O'Hare (1956) claimed some colors of light caused a 1–2 dB increase, whereas some caused a 1–2 dB decrease in auditory threshold.

EFFECTS OF NONAUDIBLE ACOUSTIC ENERGY

Infrasonic Frequencies

Intense airborne low-frequency acoustic energy (frequencies below ~20 Hz are generally called *infrasound*) can have adverse effects on nonauditory, as well as auditory, systems of the body. In addition to possible stimulation of the vestibular system and pain in the ear, low-frequency sound can cause resonant vibration in the chest, throat, and nose cavities of the body. The effects from vibrations at low frequencies when imposed directly on the body through mechanical contact are fairly well known (see Figs. 9.19 and 9.20). However, because of the impedance mismatch between airborne acoustic energy and the body, acoustic energy has little or no effect on parts of the body other than the ear until the levels become exceedingly intense.

The effects of very intense airborne sound on the body were determined in a series of tests conducted by U.S. Air Force and NASA research personnel and reported by Mohr *et al.* (1965). The stimuli used in these tests are shown in Fig. 9.22. No nonauditory effects were noted until the spectrum levels exceeded approximatley 125 dB. At various higher levels, decrements in visual acuity, some vestibular-system reactions, and chest, nose, and throat responses occurred, and if no ear protection was worn, ear pain and middle-ear fullness were felt. The observations of the subjects for tests 5–16 are given in Table 9.4. The results of tests 1–4 conducted in levels lower than 125 dB revealed no significant effects of the noise on the subjects.

It is clear from tests 5–14 that the nonauditory and, to some extent, auditory effects of airborne low-frequency and infrasonic-frequency sound become significant only at spectrum levels (single frequency) in excess of 130 dB. Except in the vicinity of unusual sources of noise, such as near heavy rocket engines or special test sirens, one seldom finds steady-state low-frequency acoustic energy at these intensities.

Nixon and Johnson (1973) reviewed research findings on infrasonic-frequency sound with respect to its effect on shifts in thresholds of audibility. Except for one study involving whole-body vibration, little temporary threshold shift was observed from exposure to levels of infrasonic-frequency sound up to 150 dB (see Table 9.5). Figure 9.23 shows the limiting values for exposure to airborne infrasonic-frequency sound.

In regard to these nonauditory-systems effects, smooth muscles will show reduced tension when exposed to very intense low-frequency sound, as

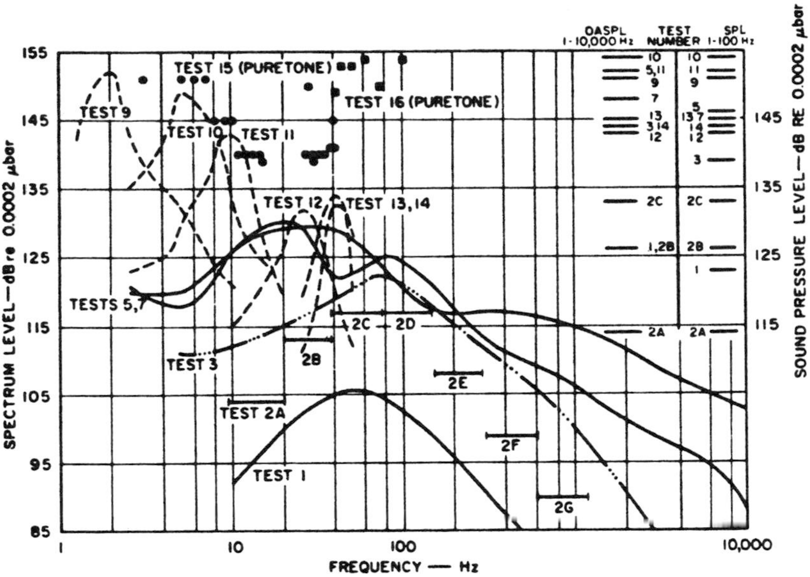

FIGURE 9.22 Summary of test environments for effects of sound on the human body. (From Mohr *et al.*, 1965.)

shown by Doring *et al.* (1980) for in vitro tests with rabbit and pig smooth muscles. Gerd Jansen (personal communication, Johannes Gutenberg University, Mainz, Germany) has found similar effects in humans when exposed to low-frequency engine noise at levels exceeding 170 dB.

Bruel and Olesen (1973) report that some people in intense infrasonic-frequency sound at levels sometimes found in automobiles, in subways,

TABLE 9.4 Summary of Effects of Acoustic Stimuli on a Group of Five Persons

Test 5: *Broadband noise; peak spectrum level 128 dB at 50 Hz.* The speech signals recorded were completely masked despite the noise reduction provided by microphone and shield. Pulse rates were increased 10–40% over resting levels. Two subjects reported mild chest-wall vibration; two others noted mild nasal cavity vibration; and one of these perceptible throat fullness.

Tests 6–8: *Broadband noise of about same levels as in test 5 with relatively less energy in the higher frequencies.* All subjects considered the exposures tolerable for the short durations involved. Speech signals were completely masked, nevertheless, except those of one subject who was stationed inside a vehicle that afforded appreciable attenuation of the high frequencies. His speech was definitely modulated, but the poor intelligibility achieved was attributed to the masking. All subjects reported mild to moderate chest-wall vibration; two subjects noted throat pressure; three subjects experienced perceptible though tolerable interference with the normal respiratory rhythm. Pulse rates measured during test 7 exhibited no significant changes during the exposure.

(*continues*)

TABLE 9.4 *(Continued)*

Throughout these tests visual acuity, hand coordination, and spatial orientation were subjectively normal.

Tests 9–11: *Narrow bands, center frequencies, 2–10 Hz, spectrum level 142–153 dB*. The most prominent effects attributable to the infrasonic noise spectra (tests 9–11) occurred during exposure without ear protection. An uncomfortable sensation reflecting pressure buildup in the middle ear was elicited, which required frequent Valsalva swallowing to relieve. This effect was almost entirely absent when insert earplugs were used. Earmuffs alone helped prevent the middle-ear pressure changes. Three subjects described an occasional tympanic membrane tickle sensation during these exposures without protection, and one subject observed marked nostril vibration. Another noted mild abdominal wall vibration during exposure to the test 10 spectrum (5–10 Hz). No shifts in hearing threshold were detectable one hour following these exposures. When ear protectors were worn to lessen the middle-ear pressure changes, exposures to infrasound of these levels were judged to be well within tolerance.

Tests 12–14: *Narrow bands, center frequencies, 15–50 Hz, spectrum level 140 dB*. The maximum intensity low sonic exposures produced moderate chest-wall vibration, a sensation of hypopharyngeal fullness (gagging), and perceptible visual field vibration in all subjects. Two subjects experienced mild middle-ear pain during brief periods without ear protection, but a third had no sensation of tickle or pain. Recorded speech sounds exhibited audible modulation. Postexposure fatigue was generally present after a day of repeated testing. The exposures as a group were not considered pleasant; however, all subjects concurred that the environments experienced were within the tolerance range.

Test 15: *Pure tones 3–40 Hz, spectrum level 145–155 dB*. Exposures to 24 discrete frequency noise fields showed both objective and subjective responses qualitatively similar to those elicited by the corresponding narrowband spectra. Pressure buildup in the middle ear was not a factor at ≥30 Hz, but the gag sensation was magnified for at least one subject. Although all exposures were judged tolerable, it was noted that the subjective sensations rose to intensity very rapidly as sound pressure levels were increased above 145 dB.

Test 16: *Pure tones 40–100 Hz, spectrum level 150–155 dB*. Voluntary tolerance of the subjects was reached at 50 Hz (153 dB), 60 Hz (154 dB), 73 Hz (150 dB), and 100 Hz (153 dB). The decision to stop exposures at these levels was based on the following subjectively alarming responses: mild nausea, giddiness, subcostal discomfort, cutaneous flushing and tingling occurring at 100 Hz; coughing, severe substernal pressure, choking respiration, salivation, pain on swallowing, hypopharyngeal discomfort, and giddiness observed at 60 and 73 Hz. One subject developed a transient headache at 50 Hz; another developed both headache and testicular aching during the 73-Hz exposure.

A significant visual acuity decrement (both subjective and objective) occurred for all subjects during the 43-, 50-, and 73-Hz exposures. Speech sounds were perceptibly modulated during all exposures. All subjects complained of marked postexposure fatigue. No shifts in hearing threshold were measurable 2 min postexposure; the earplug–earmuff combinations worn are known to provide sufficient protection against the higher harmonics of the noise fields and were apparently effective to an appreciable degree in attenuating the fundamental tones. Recovery from most of the symptoms was complete on cessation of the noise. One subject continued to cough for 20 min, and one retained some cutaneous flushing for approximately 4 h postexposure. Fatigue was resolved by a full night's sleep.

Note: Exposure durations of 1–2 min; ear-protective devices usually worn.
From Mohr *et al.* (1965).

TABLE 9.5 Summary of Studies of Temporary Hearing Loss Following Exposure to Infrasonic-Frequency Sound

Investigator	Exposure	Hearing response	Recovery
Tonndorf (1973)	Submarine diesel room; 10–20 Hz; no level given	Depression of upper limits of hearing as measured by number of seconds a tuning fork was heard; no conversion to maximum audible pressure	Recovery in few hours outside of diesel room
Mohr *et al.* (1965)	Discrete tones; narrowband noise in 10–20-Hz region; 150–154-dB exposures of ~2 min	No change in hearing sensitivity reported by subjects; no TTS measured about ~1 h postexposure	
Jerger *et al.* (1966)	Successive 3-min whole-body exposures; 7–12 Hz; 119–144 dB	TTS in 3000–6000-Hz range for 11 of 19 subjects (TTS of 10–22 dB)	Recovery within hours
Nixon and Johnson (1973)	Piston phone coupled to ear via earmuff; 18 Hz at 135 dB; series of six 5-min exposures in rapid succession	Average TTS of 0–15 dB after 30-min exposures	Recovery within 30 min
Nixon and Johnson (1973)	Piston phone coupled to ear via earmuff; 14 Hz at 140 dB; six individual exposures of 5, 10, 15, 20, 25, and 30 min	Three experienced subjects; no TTS in 1; slight TTS in 1; 20–25 dB TTS in 1	Recovery within 30 min
Johnson, (1973)	Ear only: pressure chamber coupled to ear via tuned hose and muff:		
	171 dB (1–10 Hz), 26 s,1 s;	No TTS	
	168 dB (7 Hz), 1 min, 1 s;	No TTS	
	155 dB (7 Hz), 5 min, 2 s;	No TTS	
	140 dB (4, 7, 12 Hz), 30 min, 1 s;	14–17 dB TTS	Recovery within 30 min
	140 dB (4, 7, 12 Hz), 5 min, 8 s;	8 dB TTS for 1 subject	
	135 dB (0.6, 1.6, 2.9 Hz), 5 min, 12 s;	No TTS	Recovery within 30 min
	126 dB (0.6, 1.6, 2.9 Hz), 16 min, 11 s;	No TTS	
	Whole body: all exposures, 2 s:		
	8 min at 8 Hz at SPLs of 120, 126, 132, 138	No TTS	
	8 min 15 1, 2, 4, 6, 8, 10 Hz at 144 dB	No TTS	
	8 min at 12, 16, 20 Hz at 135–142 dB	No TTS	

From Nixon and Johnson, 1973.

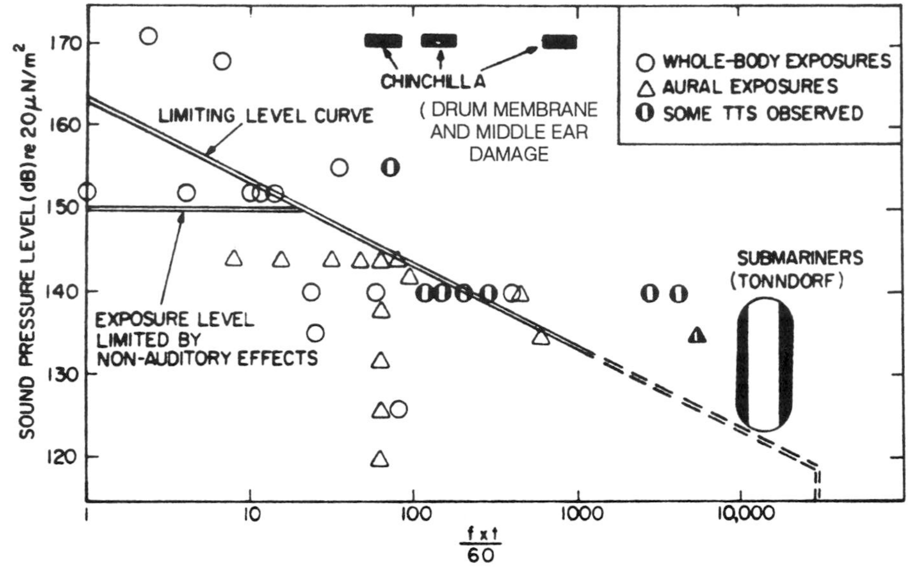

FIGURE 9.23 Various laboratory infrasonic-frequency sound exposures in terms of level and number of cycles $[f(t/60)]$ and a limiting sound-pressure level curve based on the formulation. Limiting SPL $= 10 \log (t/8 \text{ min}) + 10 \log (f/10) + 144$. (From Nixon and Johnson, 1973.)

and during high winds in some high-rise office buildings have feelings of unpleasantness and even loss of balance. To explore these observations, the researchers vibrated flexible walls of a small office to produce intense infrasonic frequencies in the room. Some of their results are shown in Fig. 9.24. That figure clearly shows that some nonauditory sensations can be created by fairly prolonged exposures at relatively high intensities to sound in a narrow region around 10 Hz.

Ultrasonic Frequencies

Acoustic energy in the frequency region above 20,000 Hz is called ultrasonic because it is inaudible to humans. Actually, for most adults, acoustic energy above 15,000 Hz is ultrasonic. As noted in a review of the effects of ultrasound by Parrack (1966), the advent of the jet-aircraft engine, high-speed dental drills, and ultrasonic cleaners provided relatively common sources of high-intensity ultrasounds. Tables 9.6–9.8 show the spectra of the noise from representative samples of these devices.

When there is considerable energy in the bands above 20,000 Hz there is often also energy in the audible-frequency region that may exceed the damage-risk values specified as tolerable for long exposures (see Chapter 5). For this reason, the tinnitus, dizziness, headache, nausea, and fullness of the ears often reported by some persons exposed to these noises are probably

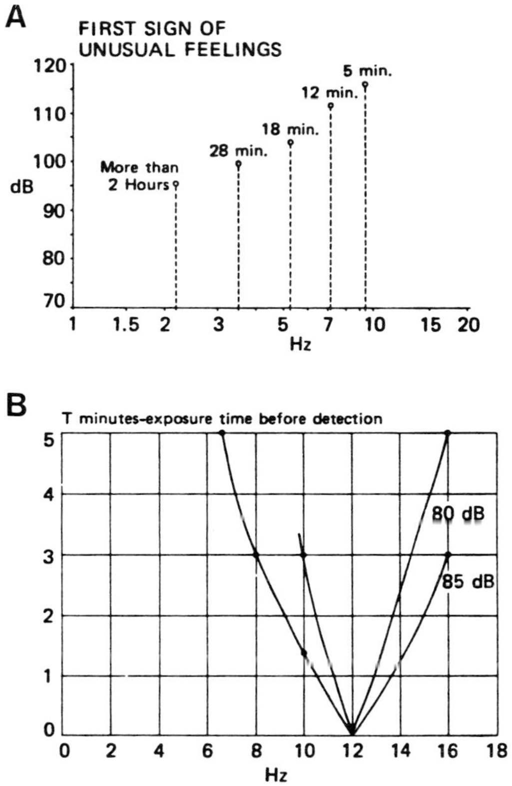

FIGURE 9.24 Thresholds of subjective feelings of "unusualness" from exposure to infrasonic frequency sound in an office space: (A) sensory response of one person to infrasound excitation; (B) threshold–exposure time relationship around most sensitive frequency. (From Bruel and Olesen, 1973.)

because of audible, and perhaps even infrasonic, frequencies in the noise, rather than ultrasonic frequencies. In Parrack's opinion, the reactions of tinnitus, dizziness, nausea, and headache listed above are psychosomatic and are engendered by unwarranted apprehension.

This belief is partly based on the fact that any acoustic energy at high frequencies that significantly affects humans does so only through the inner ear (Davis, 1948; Davis *et al.*, 1949). The physical arguments against ultrasound entering or stimulating humans except through normal stimulation of the inner ear are as follows:

1. The absorption coefficient of the skin for sound >20,000 Hz is <0.1%, and levels at these frequencies that would cause any slightly noticeable local heating effects would have to be in excess of 100 dB. (The absorption coefficient of acoustic energy at 20,000 Hz in small, furry animals is of the order of 21%, so that lethal heating can occur in these animals at levels of ultrasound that go unnoticed by, or are harmless to, humans.)

TABLE 9.6 Sound-Pressure Level around a Jet Aircraft in 1/3-Octave Bands (Aircraft F-102) From Parrack, 1966

Positions and operating conditions	SPL, dB, at 1/3-octave-band center frequencies, kHz, of														
	2	2.5	3.15	4	5	6.3	8	10	12.5	16	20	25	31.5	40	50
100 ft; afterburner	123	122	123	121	119	118	118	115	115	113	112	111	110	107	106
[a]25 ft forward; idle	90	96	94	96	94	92	92	90	90	88	86	84	80	76	73
25 ft forward; military	102	107	104	101	102	100	100	97	96	93	91	89	86	83	80
25 ft forward; afterburner	109	110	107	107	105	104	103	101	100	97	95	93	90	87	87
Maintenance; military	117	115	114	116	112	112	111	108	108	105	103	101	99	96	
Maintenance; afterburner	121	120	120	123	118	117	117	114	113	111	108	106	103	100	

[a] On radius 125° located from nose of aircraft.

TABLE 9.7 Sound-Pressure Levels Measured in Air around the Weber High-Speed Dental Drill From Parrack, 1966

		SPL, dB, for center frequencies of octave bands, Hz, measured at										
Measurement position*	OASPL, dB	31.5	63	125	250	500	1000	2000	4000	8000	16 000	31 500
1	97	46	44	50	48	52	55	64	87	84	93	95
2	89	44	43	47	43	46	47	54	77	82	83	83

* Position 1, patient's ear 6 in. from source; position 2, patient's ear 20 in. from source.

TABLE 9.8 Bendix Model Sec 1825A Sonic-Energy Cleaning System From Parrack, 1966

	SPL, dB, for $^1/_3$-octave-band center frequencies, kHz, of																			
Positions	1.0	1.25	1.6	2.0	2.5	3.15	4	5	6.3	8	10	12.5	16	20	25	31.5	40	50	63	80
Operator,[a] cover closed	56	55	55	57	62	68	70	72	73	83	96	83	83	101	85	91	89	86	85	
Operator,[a] cover open		62	63	63	66	70	74	77	81	91	104	91	93	109	93	102	99	95	95	

[a] Immediately adjacent to one end of cleaner system.

2. Ultrasonic frequencies generated by crystals and applied to bones and tissues of the head resulted (if sufficiently intense) in the person perceiving an audible, high-pitched tone usually ~8000–10,000 Hz, depending on the persons's upper limit of hearing (Haeff and Knox, 1963; Belluci and Schneider, 1962; Deatherage *et al.,* 1954). Deaf subjects in these experiments heard nothing. Crystals have many resonant modes, and the rubbing of the crystal against the skin surface could have created an audible subharmonic that was radiated as an acoustic signal to the ear. Also, it is possible that subharmonics falling in the normal frequency range of audibility may be generated in the middle ear when the ear is exposed to intense ultrasonic frequencies.

Acton and Carson (1967; see also Skillern, 1965) found convincing evidence that unless a person's range of hearing extended to about 17,000 Hz, and unless the energy in that frequency region exceeded 70 dB, no subjective effects (tinnitus, headaches, fatigue, etc.) were experienced from exposure to ultrasonic frequencies. Figure 9.25B shows the results of laboratory tests with ultrasonic signals. The upper curve of Fig. 9.25A shows the spectrum of noise, which did not cause significant complaints. Acton and Carson noted that women had adverse symptoms more often than men and that young men had adverse symptoms more often than older men. This was presumed to be because of the auditory acuity of the people involved and not because of their sex or age per se.

It also appears that hearing in the higher-frequency regions of most industrial workers sooner or later is reduced by the upward spread of a noise-induced permanent threshold shift from lower frequency noise as much as it is by the acoustic energy above 10,000 Hz. It might be conjectured that the upturn in the normal threshold of audibility from 4000 Hz to ~20,000 Hz is severely influenced by everyday noise in the frequency region 2000–8000 Hz. In any event, the subjective effects of ultrasonic frequencies are not due to apprehension on the part of the listener, but are due to sound that exceeds 78 dB in the frequency region of ~16,000 Hz when it is audible to the listener. Continued exposure to sufficiently intense sound at or below 16,000 Hz results in the elimination of the subjective and audible effects apparently because of noise-induced threshold shifts in those frequency regions.

The question remains as to why these adverse subjective effects are more often noticed from ear-damaging exposures to these higher frequencies than from damaging exposures to noise at lower frequencies, for example, below 2000 Hz. Of course, there may be no fundamental difference since some comments regarding headache, unusual fatigue, and certainly tinnitus are also sometimes reported from initial exposures to lower-frequency noise when sufficiently intense and for sufficiently long exposures.

Although the energy above 20,000 Hz (or possibly at any frequency that is inaudible) may not be the direct cause of the tinnitus, dizziness, nausea,

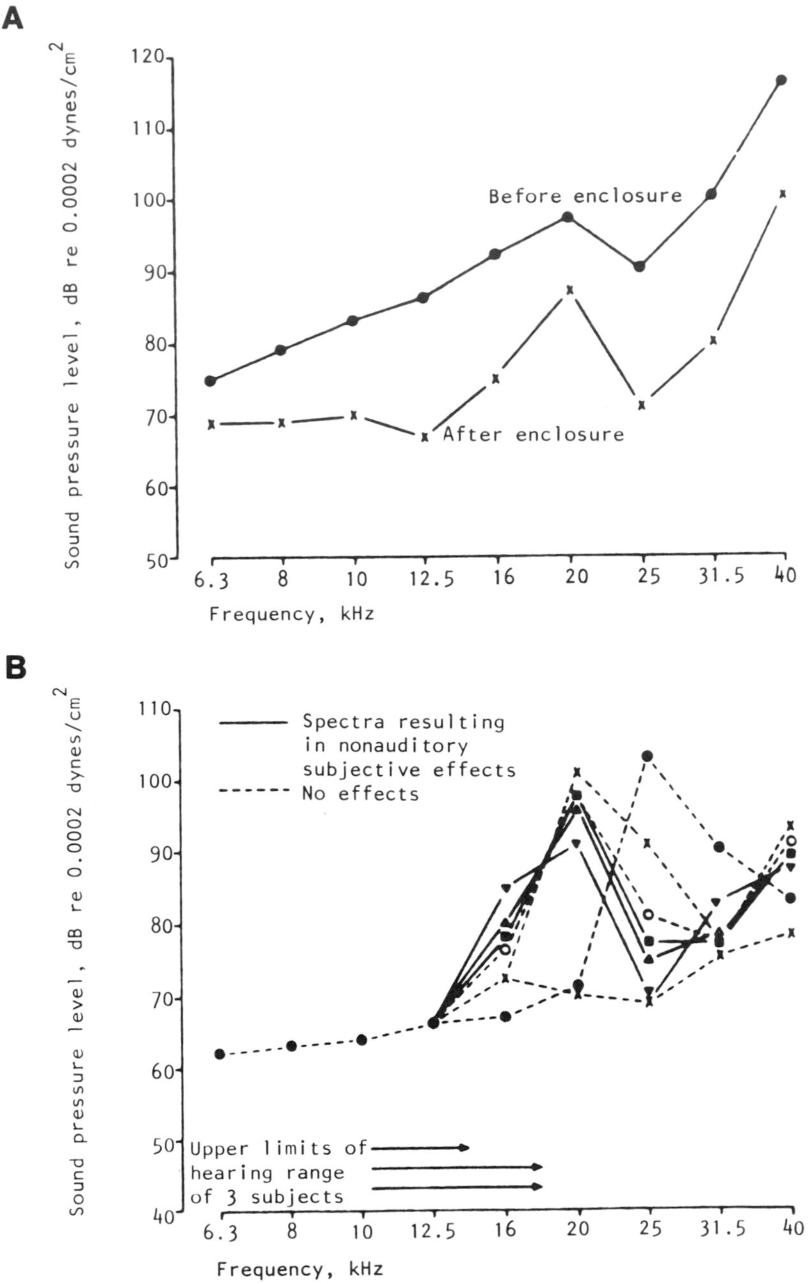

FIGURE 9.25 (A, B) One-third octave band spectra of noise from an ultrasonic washer and that were used in laboratory tests and effects. (From Acton and Carson, 1967.)

and headache experienced by persons exposed to such sound energy, the reactions in question are perhaps not "psychosomatic" in origin either, as presumed by Parrak and others, but are due to trauma occurring in the ear from audible and for inaudible energy in the sounds.

NIOSH Studies

A program of studies was conducted for the National Institute for Occupational Safety and Health (NIOSH) on the effects of noise on nonauditory sensory functions and performance (Loeb *et al.*, 1976). Groups of adult subjects were exposed to continuous noise ranging from 105 to 110 dB_A, to impulsive noise at 136 dB_A, and to quiet. No effects of the noises, relative to quiet, were found for tests of tactile, thermal, or vestibular functions. A few measures of visual functions showed noise-induced effects, but these could not be altogether replicated on retesting.

Conclusion: Nonauditory System Responses

On the basis of the research findings just presented, it appears that other than an arousal effect, sounds and noises have little or no direct neurological-physiological effect on nonauditory organs or systems of the body. In view of the pervasiveness of sound in the environment, it is postulated that if the case was otherwise, the organism could not be biologically successful. However, because of the arousal effect, and the psychological aspects of sensations, and the importance of auditory information and behavior, sound and noise become involved in the nonauditory system processes and conditions of sleep, health, and well-being.

STUDIES OF SLEEP DISTURBANCE

Method of Measurement

The effects of noise on sleep have been measured primarily in three ways:

1. The subject is asked to press a switch when awakened. (behavioral awakening).
2. The state of electrical brain activity measured from an electroencephalogram (EEG) is interpreted by the experimenter to show the stage (or change in stage) of sleep of a subject. It is generally held that a change from a "deep" to a lighter stage of sleep (as measured by the EEG) that is correlated with an exposure to a noise is indicative of some arousal. Some other physiological measures (e.g., heart rate and vasoconstriction in the finger, general body movement) have also been monitored during sleep in noise environments as possible indicators of the arousal effects of noise.

3. Subjects are asked to rate the quality of previous nights of sleep during which noises were present in their sleeping environment.

Habituated and Nonhabituated Responses

It is necessary to allow a number of nights of sleep in laboratory bedrooms before consistent, normal sleep patterns are established. Also, once tests with noises or sounds are started, a further habituation takes place.

Griefahn and Jansen (1978) analyzed the results of a large number of published studies on behavioral awakenings due to noise. They concluded that there was a significant decline in awakenings after the first night of exposure to a noise environment up to about the seventh night (see Fig. 9.26). After about the seventh night, the effects seemed to remain fairly constant at about 35% awakenings.

Thiessen (1980) found this same general habituation for behavioral awakenings, but found it extended to at least 12 nights or so of testing (see Fig. 9.27). However, as seen in Fig. 9.27, there was little indication of habituation of the EEG index of arousal (a change in sleep stage) over the 12 nights. This lack of habituation of a change in EEG stages of sleep from exposure to noise has been consistently found. Vasoconstriction in the finger showed

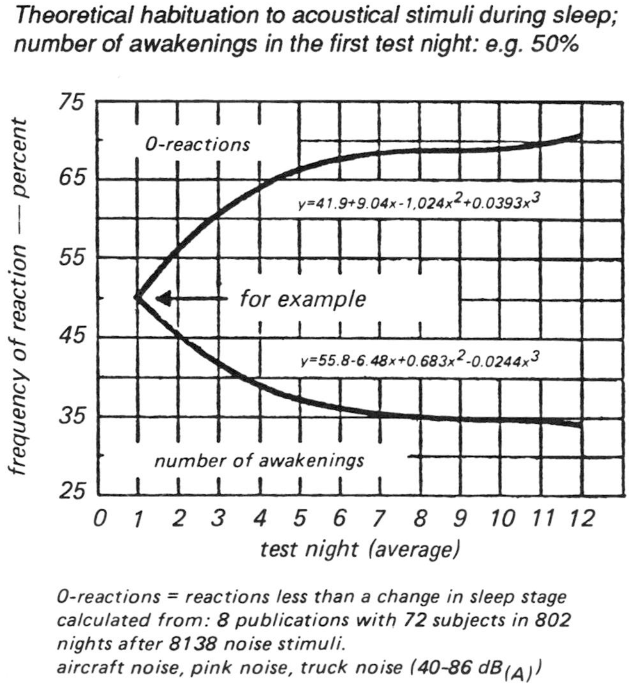

FIGURE 9.26 Sleep disturbances due to noise. (From Griefahn and Jansen, 1978.)

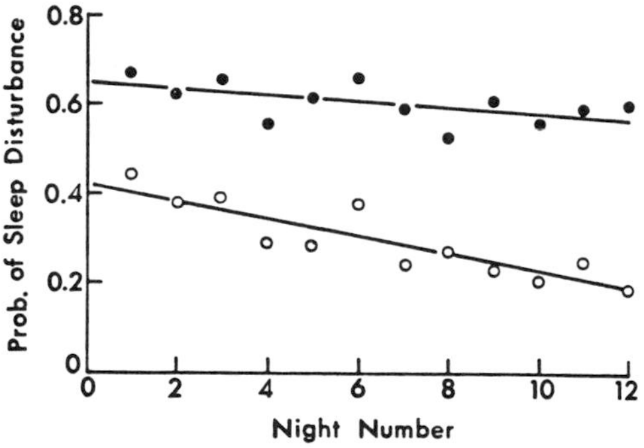

FIGURE 9.27 Laboratory results showing general lack of habituation of shift in EEG level (solid circles) and occurrence of habituation in behavioral awakening (open circles). (From Thiessen, 1980.)

no signs of habituation over 53 nights of exposure to sonic booms (Griefahn, 1975). Muzet and Ehrhart (1980) found in laboratory studies that street traffic noise at a level as low as 45 dB_A (see Fig. 9.28) caused a momentary change in heart rate during sleep that did not habituate over a test period of 15 nights.

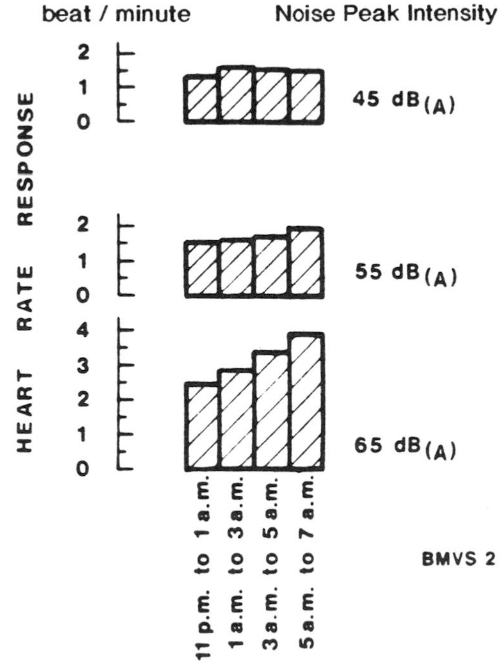

FIGURE 9.28 Changes in heart rate from street traffic noise during sleep. (From Muzet and Ehrhart, 1980.)

Kryter and C. E. Williams (unpublished data) found that although there was no habituation of a change in EEG stages from exposure to some noises over a period of 10 test nights, the intensity level of a 5-s noise had to be higher for deeper stages of sleep than for lighter stages in order to elicit a change in EEG sleep stage. A noise level of ~30 dB relative to a threshold of audibility when awake was needed when the subject was in EEG stage 2 of sleep, ~50 dB was needed when in stage 3, and ~80 dB was needed in stage 4.

Williams *et al.* (1964) found that behavioral awakening also required a higher intensity of sound when in stage 4 and in the dream [rapid-eye-movement, REM] stage of sleep than when in the lighter stages (2 and 3, as classified by Williams *et al.;* see Fig. 9.29). Figure 9.30 shows that the finger vasoconstriction response is marginally differentially responsive in different stages of sleep following sleep deprivation; however, for heart rate (Fig. 9.29) and EEG (Fig. 9.30) the magnitude of change depends somewhat on the intensity level of the noise. Griefahn also found that about the same amount of vasoconstriction seemed to occur for sonic booms of different levels of intensity.

The results of a number of studies of the effects of noise on sleep in which questionnaires for measuring the opinions of the subjects regarding the quality of the previous night's sleep have been reviewed by Lukas (1977). Figure 9.31 shows how the composite Leq for the sonic booms and aircraft noise predicts rated sleep quality.

Ehrenstein and Muller-Limmroth found mood changes at different times

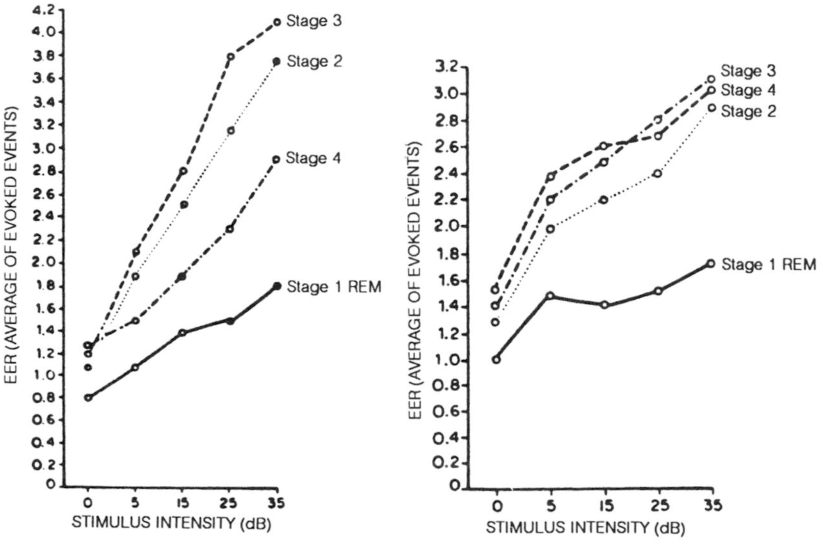

FIGURE 9.29 Effect of stimulus intensity on EER during four stages of sleep after 64 h of sleep deprivation. (From Williams *et al.*, 1964.)

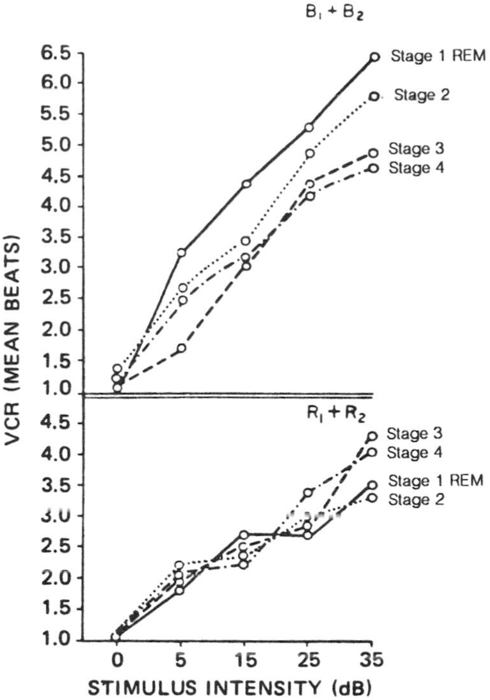

FIGURE 9.30 Effect of stimulus intensity on vasoconstriction response (VCR) during four stages of sleep for baseline nights (B_1 and B_2) and recovery nights (R_1 and R_2) after 64 h of sleep deprivation. (From Williams *et al.*, 1964.)

of the day following exposures to awakening noises. Muzet *et al.* (1973) found that subjective ratings of the previous night's sleep were highly correlated with the amount of sleep disturbance observed in the subjects. Ohrstrom and Rylander (1982) found positive correlations between the levels of exposure to recorded intermittent and continuous traffic noise, sleep arousal (as measured by bodily movements), reduced ratings of sleep quality, and task performance. The continuous noise had a significantly smaller effect than did the intermittent noise. The results of this latter study are difficult to compare with the results of some other similar experiments in that the exposure levels of the different noise conditions are not reported.

On the other hand, LeVere and Davis (1977) found that the correlation between subjective evaluation of subjects regarding their sleep on a previous night and the amount of change in EEG activity measured for that night was zero. However, the aircraft noises used by LeVere and Davis seldom led to any behavioral awakening. It would thus appear that a change in EEG activity that is short of the pattern related to behavioral awakening is not a disruption in sleep to be noticed subjectively by a person but rather that behavioral awakening is associated with subjective ratings of sleep quality.

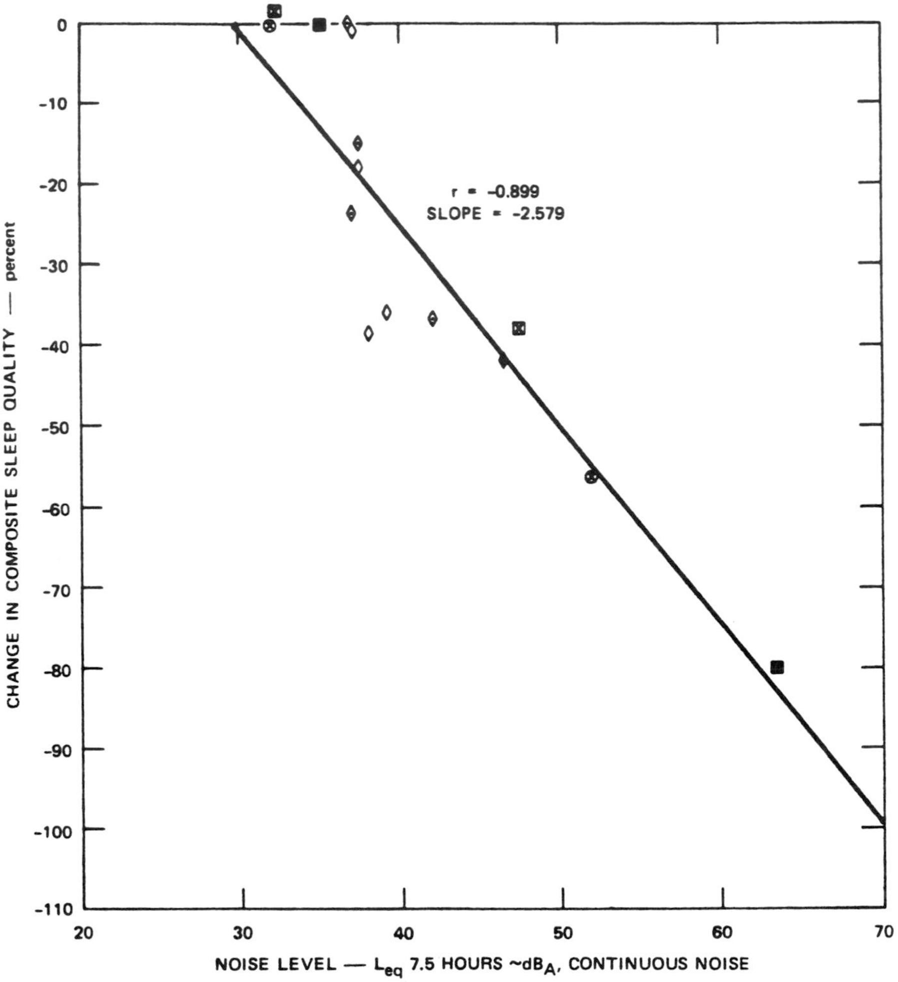

FIGURE 9.31 Relative subjective disturbance of sleep at various total nighttime noise levels calculated in L_{eq}. Solid square represents jet-aircraft noise; open diamond, "clicks"; other symbols, sonic booms. (From Lukas, 1972.)

Johnson *et al.* (1973) studied heart rate, vasoconstriction in the finger, and EEG in young men exposed to 3–4-kHz impulses of 0.75-s duration every 45 s for 24 h per day. The impulses (sonar "pings" in a submarine) were at levels of 80–90 dB. In addition to the physiological measures, records of time asleep and performance on some physiological and psychological tests were obtained. Three experiments were conducted: 1 for 15 days with 20 men, 1 for 55 days with 20 men, and 1 for 7 days with 39 men. Figure 9.32 shows that the experimental subjects experienced increased latency in going to sleep as compared with this latency for the control subjects not exposed to pings. Other behavioral effects related to possible sleep disturbance from the pings were not observed.

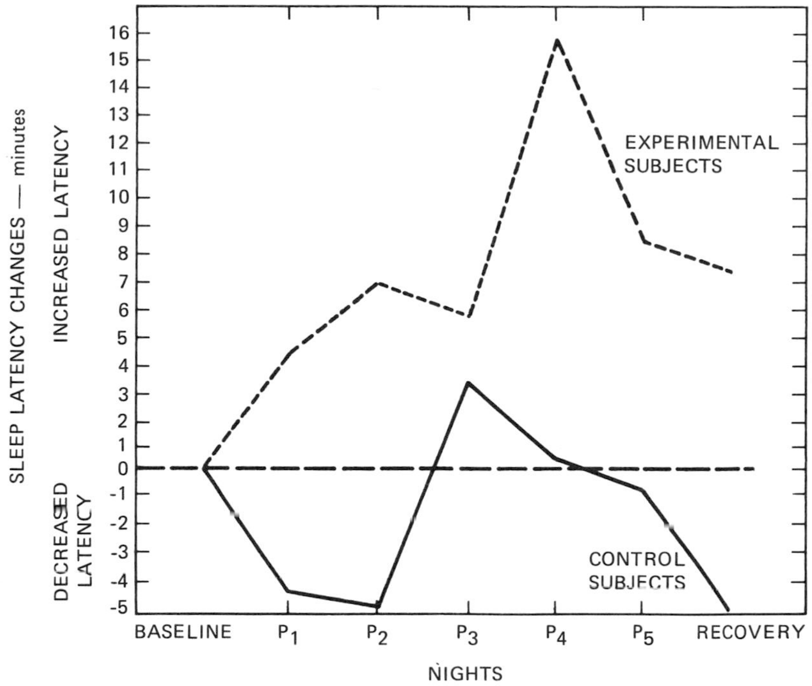

FIGURE 9.32 Changes in sleep latency during 5-day exposure to pings and during recovery compared with sleep latency during baseline. (From Johnson *et al.*, 1973.)

Of particular interest are the findings that throughout each of these experiments, as well as in other similar studies conducted by Johnson and Lubin (1967) and Cantrell (1974), no habituation occurred in vasoconstriction, heart rate, and EEG changes to the pings during certain sleep stages, but none of these changes to the pings occurred when the subjects were awake. These responses are consistent with the concept that there was a cognitive habituation to a startle response when the subjects were awake. The previously discussed alerting response, to which adaptation is presumed to not occur, was measurable when the subjects were asleep, but not when the subjects were awake and in a state of arousal.

Changes in Sleep EEG from Exposure to Noise from Different Sources

Suzuki *et al.* (1993) reported the results of five laboratory experiments of EEG in sleeping subjects when exposed to different intensity levels of pink noise, the noise of a passing truck, and road traffic. It was found that a decrease in REM (deep)-stage sleep may appear when the noise level exceeded L_{eq} 45 dB_A, and a decrease was linearly related to intensity level of the noise.

Hofman *et al.* (1993) exposed seven males (age 20–30 years) to recordings of noise from trucks, airplanes, and trains during sleep. Each subject slept two nights a week for nine weeks, with the first night assigned to adaptation. On separate nights 50 noise stimuli of 45 dB_A, 15 noise stimuli of 65 dB_A, and, on some nights, 15 train and 15 aircraft noises at a level of 75 dB_B (estimated 80 dB_A). The investigators conclude that "Sleep during noise condition showed a significant decrease of total sleep time and an increase in REM sleep," but it was not clear to the present writer that the data were consistent with that conclusion. The Hofman *et al.* data may reflect a nonsensitivity to arousal from sleep associated with young subjects.

Auditory Discrimination during Sleep

It is a common observation that one sleeps better in a familiar environment than in an unfamiliar environment containing unfamiliar sounds. Also, people can apparently be instructed to awaken to certain sounds when they are asleep and to ignore others. Oswald *et al.* (1960) found that persons would awaken more readily to the sound of their own names than to other names. However, research data such as that of Johnson and Lubin suggest the hypothesis that people cannot (1) learn to habituate, or not to habituate, to a noise when asleep unless they can engage in cognition relative to the input stimulus and (2) engage in cognition unless that stimulus exceeds their threshold of cognitive arousal, that is, unless they are awake.

Intuitively, it would seem that a reasonable compromise between the requirements to give the brain a "rest," and yet maintain some reasonable contact between the organism and the world outside, would be for the organism to vary the auditory cognitive–arousal threshold during a night of sleep. This hypothesis is consistent with the studies of Emmons and Simon (1955) and Simon and Emmons (1954) who found that "sleep learning" (information recorded on magnetic tape and played via an earphone under a person's pillow) occurred only when the listeners exhibited brain-wave activity associated with being behaviorally awake. Sometimes the listeners were not consciously aware (particularly the next morning) of the particular times they were awake and capable of hearing and cognitively related behavior.

Other studies supporting this hypothesis were conducted by Williams *et al.* (1964) and by Rechtschaffen *et al.* (1976). Williams *et al.* instructed subjects prior to going to sleep that if they did not awaken to a tone to which they were particularly responsive when awake (called a *critical stimulus*), they would be aroused by a fire alarm and electric shocks to their legs. Furhter, the subjects were told that they would not be thus awakened if they failed to respond to another tone equally loud but at a different pitch (neutral stimulus). They were instructed not to respond to the neutral stimulus even when awake. The results are shown in Fig. 9.33, where it is shown that the arousal (or awakening) effects of the critical stimulus were much greater than those of the neutral stimulus when in the light stages of sleep but not

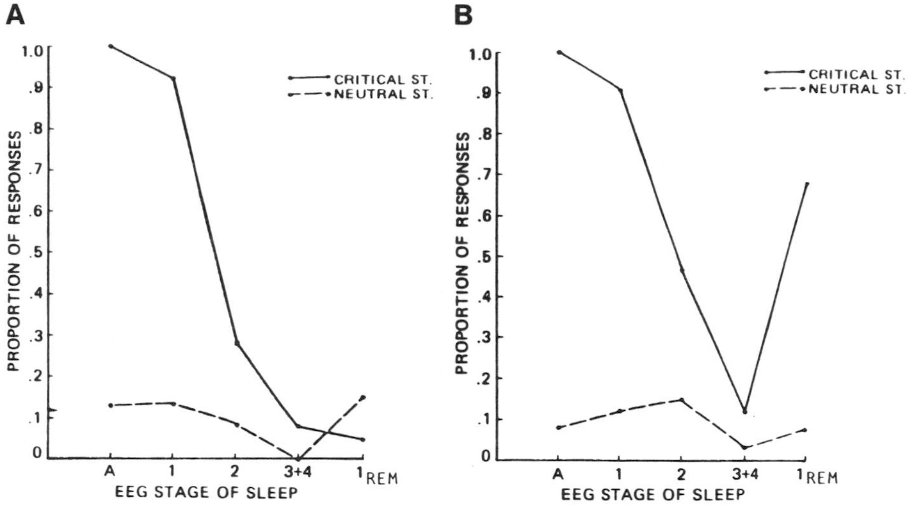

FIGURE 9.33 Responsiveness to a critical stimulus and to a neutral stimulus when awake (symbol A) and when in different stages of sleep. Subjects not punished (A) and subjects punished (B) for failure to respond to the critical stimulus. (From Williams *et al.*, 1964.)

when in the deep stages of sleep. It is also seen that the relative arousal effects of the stimuli remain relatively unchanged regardless of whether the failures to respond were punished, except in the REM stage.

Rechtschaffen *et al.* likewise found that punishing the subjects by shaking them awake when they failed to awaken to a sound did not tend to increase arousal to subsequent exposures to the sound except in the REM stage. Apparently people can be more responsive to sounds that have special meanings when asleep in the brain-wave stages 1 and 2 (light stages of sleep), and people can learn this differential responsiveness only when awake or when in the REM stage. It is possible that persons can, to a certain extent, control their general state of arousal so that they spend more time in "light" stages of sleep than in "deep" stages, thereby increasing the probability of hearing sounds because of their lower threshold of auditory arousal.

Age and Sex Differences

Lukas and Kryter (1970) found in laboratory tests that older persons are much more sensitive, particularly with respect to behavioral awakening, to simulated sonic booms and recorded subsonic aircraft noise than are younger persons (see Fig. 9.34). Indeed, the youngest subjects (ages 7–8 years) were not aroused at all by sonic booms more intense than those that awakened the 67–72-year-old men nearly 70% of the time. It is possible that older people need less deep sleep and are therefore more sensitive to arousal than are younger people, even though their hearing is less acute. Roth *et al.*

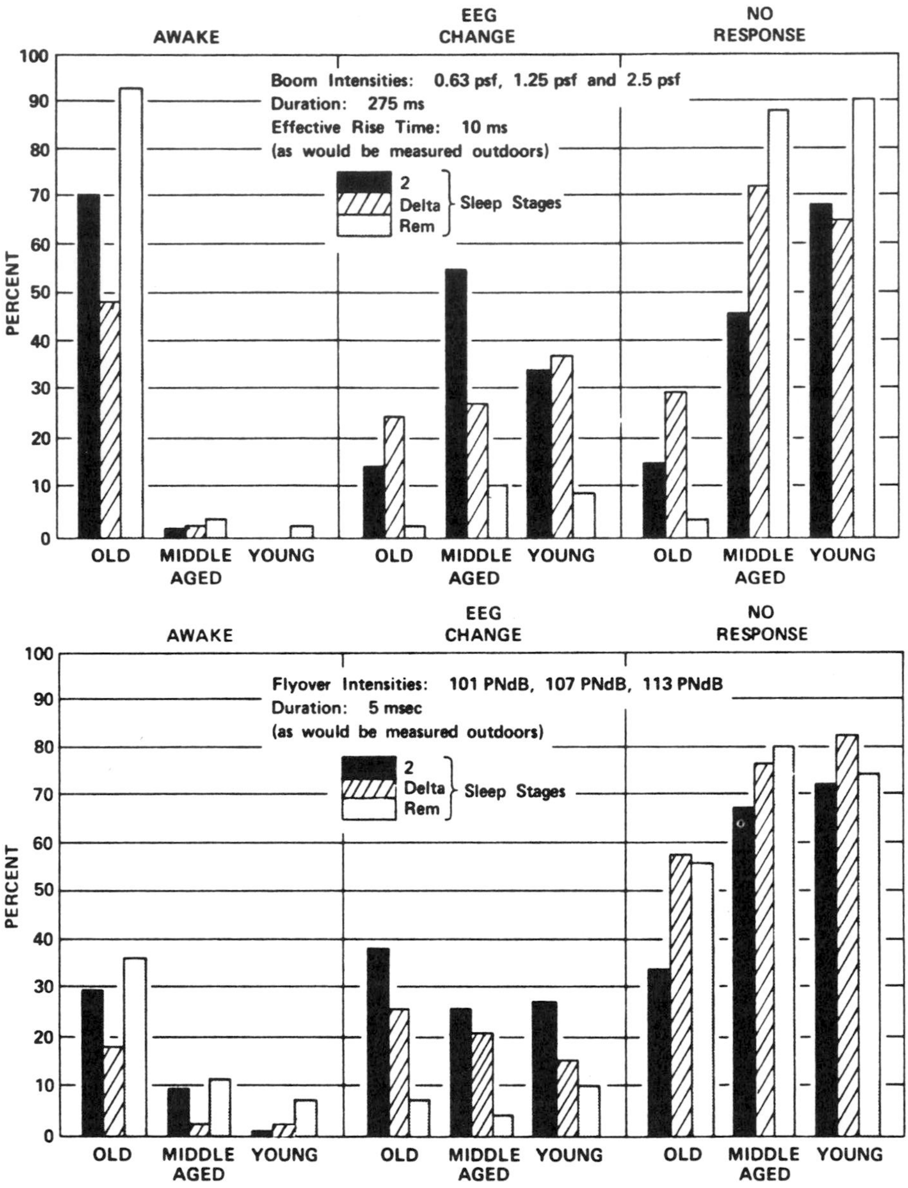

FIGURE 9.34 Effects of simulated sonic booms and subsonic aircraft noise on sleep. (From Lukas and Kryter, 1970.)

(1972), using various noises, also found older people more easily aroused from sleep than younger ones. Griefahn and Jansen (1978) derived the functions shown in Fig. 9.35 on the basis of a number of sleep studies in which age was a variable. The probability of a 70-year-old awakening is shown to be about twice that expected for a 20-year-old.

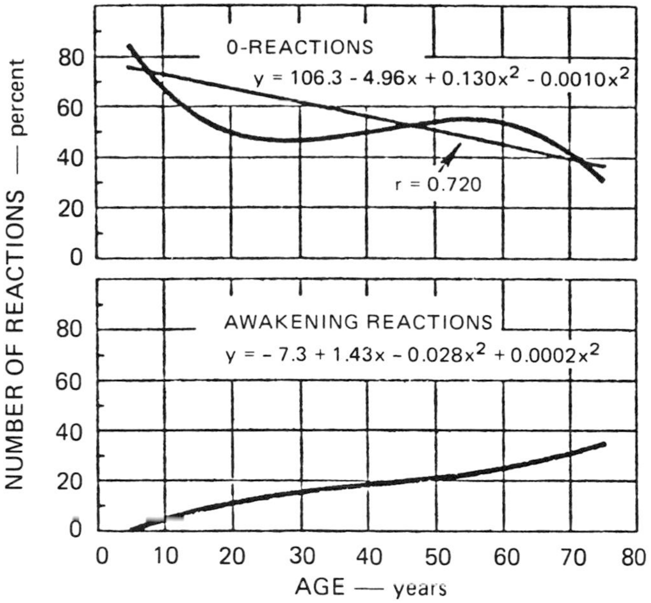

0-reactions = reactions less than a change of one sleep stage
from 3 publications, 26 subjects, 368 nights, 4428 stimuli
(68-85 dB(A), sonic booms and aircraft noises)

FIGURE 9.35 Sleep disturbances by noise, average for a variety of studies. (From Griefahn and Jansen, 1978.)

It is probable that males and females as a group are equally sensitive to being awakened from sleep by noise. Lukas and Dobbs (1972) found females to be somewhat more easily awakened by aircraft noise, whereas Muzet *et al.* (1973) found the opposite.

Sleep Data Collected in Homes

There are obvious reasons for concern about using research data on the effects of noise on sleep collected in the laboratory as the basis for the prediction of what effects are to be expected in the home. One factor is that of "habituation" to the general environment. Another is the disruption of sleep caused by experimental equipment. For example, Johns and Dore (1978) reported that even after 12 nights of sleeping in the laboratory, subjects reported about twice as many spontaneous awakenings as occurred in their homes. One reason was that the EEG electrodes used in the laboratory experiments pulled on their scalps.

There have been several studies conducted on subjects sleeping in their own homes in which EEGs (and occasionally other electrograms) were obtained (see, e.g., Globus *et al.,* 1973; Vallet *et al.,* 1980). In the Globus *et al.* study, six middle-aged couples living in the vicinity of the Los Angeles

International Airport (LAX), and five control couples living in several similar socioeconomic, but aircraft-noise-free neighborhoods had electrodes for EEGs and for electrooculograms (EOGs) attached to their foreheads on retiring for five consecutive nights. EEG, EOG, and acoustic-noise signals were recorded and later analyzed. In the homes exposed to the noise from aircraft approaching the airport the mean noise level was 77 dB_A, compared with a mean level of 57 dB_A in control homes. Some of the results of this study are shown in Fig. 9.36. It is shown there that more minutes of sleep were experienced in the stages of "useful" sleep (EEG stages 2, 3, and 4) and less in "wasted" sleep [waking (W), movement (M), and stage 1] by the couples in the quiet than in the noisier neighborhoods.

Vallet *et al.* conducted a similar study, near Roissy Paris Airport, in which 40 men aged 20–55 years who had been exposed for about 1 year to about 12 aircraft flyovers per night were EEG-monitored when sleeping in their homes. Figure 9.37 shows the percentage of EEG responses that indicated awakening. It is shown that for peak noise levels of ~45–65 dB_A, there is about a 20% probability of an awakening occurring. Above 65 dB_A, the

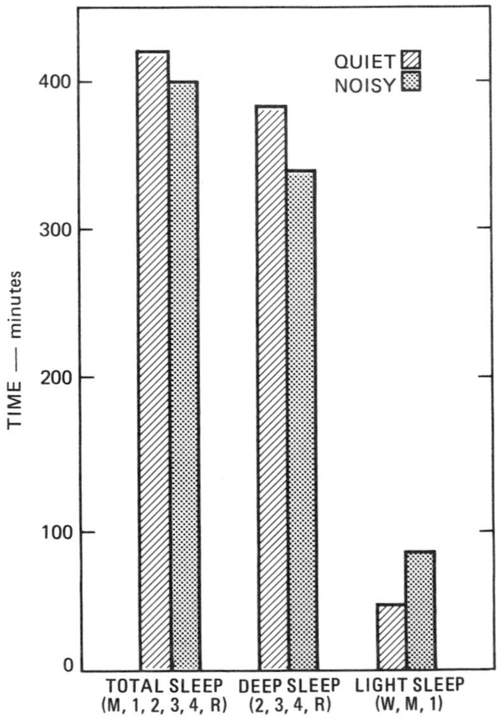

FIGURE 9.36 Average amount of sleeping time in quiet and noisy areas. (From Globus *et al.*, 1973.)

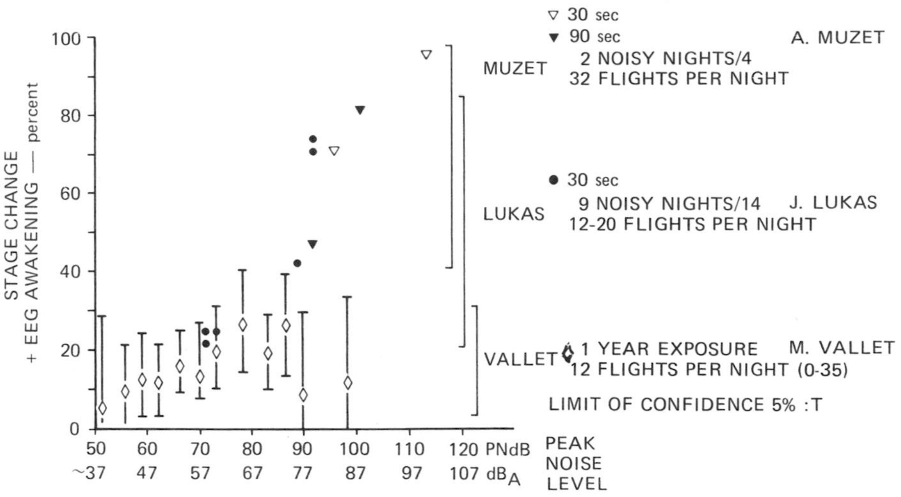

FIGURE 9.37 Comparison of laboratory (Muzet *et al.*, 1973; Lukas, 1972) and field (Vallet *et al.*, 1980) studies of percent of subjects aroused by noise. (From Vallet *et al.*, 1980.)

results show some decline in awakenings. This is contrary to most other such data, as well as the results of attitude surveys that show awakenings generally increasing as the noise level increases.

A study by the British Directorate of Operational Research and Analysis (DORA, 1980), is a particularly important study of sleep disturbance from aircraft noise. Approximately 4400 people were administered an extensive questionnaire about sleep disturbance over a 4-month period (June–September 1979) in areas near London's Heathrow and Gatwick Airports. At the Heathrow and Gatwick Airports, commercial aircraft that create levels of noise above ~90 dB_A in residential areas are not allowed to operate from 11:30 PM to 6:00 AM, as shown in Fig. 9.38. Also shown in Fig. 9.38 are the percentages of people going to bed and arising at particular times.

The extent to which double glazing of windows is present in the houses involved in this study varied from ~20–80% in different areas. The extent to which bedroom windows were generally kept closed because of aircraft noise, and kept closed on a designated night during the period of the study, is shown in Fig. 9.39. Some of the variability in the sleep-disturbance data shown in the text that follows is probably due to variability in the amount of aircraft noise reaching the beds of individual respondents. (Physical factors affecting noise intrusiveness and attitude survey data are discussed more fully in Chapter 10.)

By applying correlation techniques to the data, relations were determined between various physical measures of the aircraft noise and responses to the following three major questions of the survey: (1) percentages of people (respondents) awakened, (2) percentages of people having difficulty getting

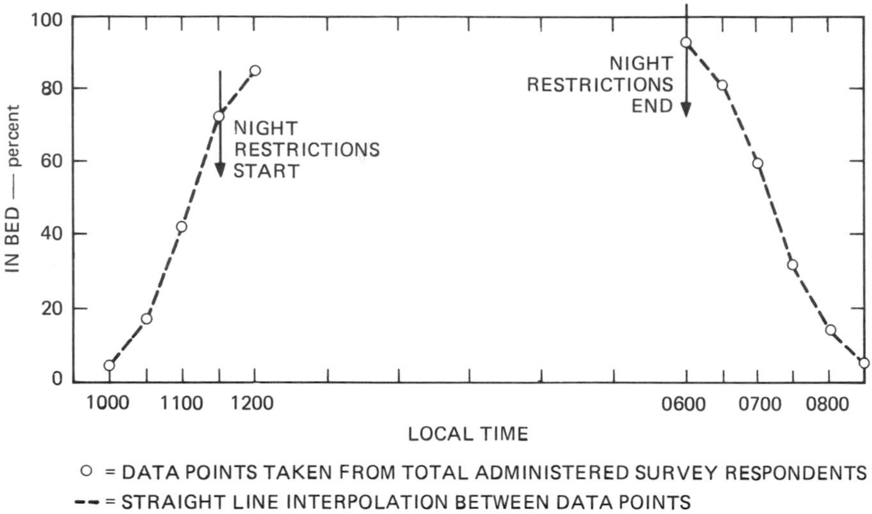

FIGURE 9.38 Times of going to bed and getting up. Noisiest aircraft restricted from operations during times indicated. (From DORA, 1980.)

to sleep, and (3) percentages of people feeling "tired" or "very tired." It was found that an energy type of measure (i.e., *A*-weighted L_{eq}) of aircraft noise correlated best with sleep disturbance from aircraft noise. In support of the appropriateness of the L_{eq} measure of the aircraft noise is the finding that some respondents could not accurately recall the time association between a specific flyover noise event and an arousal from sleep.

The respondents were asked to recollect arousals from sleep and difficulties getting to sleep as a matter of general experience over the past several months and on a recent designated night. Shown in Fig. 9.40 are percentages of the respondents having difficulty in getting to sleep when living in various dosages of L_{eq} of aircraft noise for the hours 10–12 PM. It is shown that at an L_{eq} of ~60 dB about 5% of the respondents on the designated night and about 25% as a matter of general experience, had difficulty in going to sleep because of aircraft noise.

In Fig. 9.41, the percentages of people awakened by aircraft noise from general experience, (A) and on the designated night (B) are shown as functions of L_{eq} from 11 PM to 7 AM. Also shown in Fig. 9.41 are the percentages of people awakened for all reasons. It is shown in the figure that with L_{eq} of ~55 dB_A, about 12% of the respondents, were awakened by aircraft noise on the designated night; and about 25%, by aircraft noise more than once per week as a matter of general experience. Unfortunately, the number of sleep arousals per night were not reported.

It seems likely that the relative amounts of awakenings because of aircraft noise, compared with the number of awakenings for all reasons, would increase if the actual numbers of aircraft operations per night were counted.

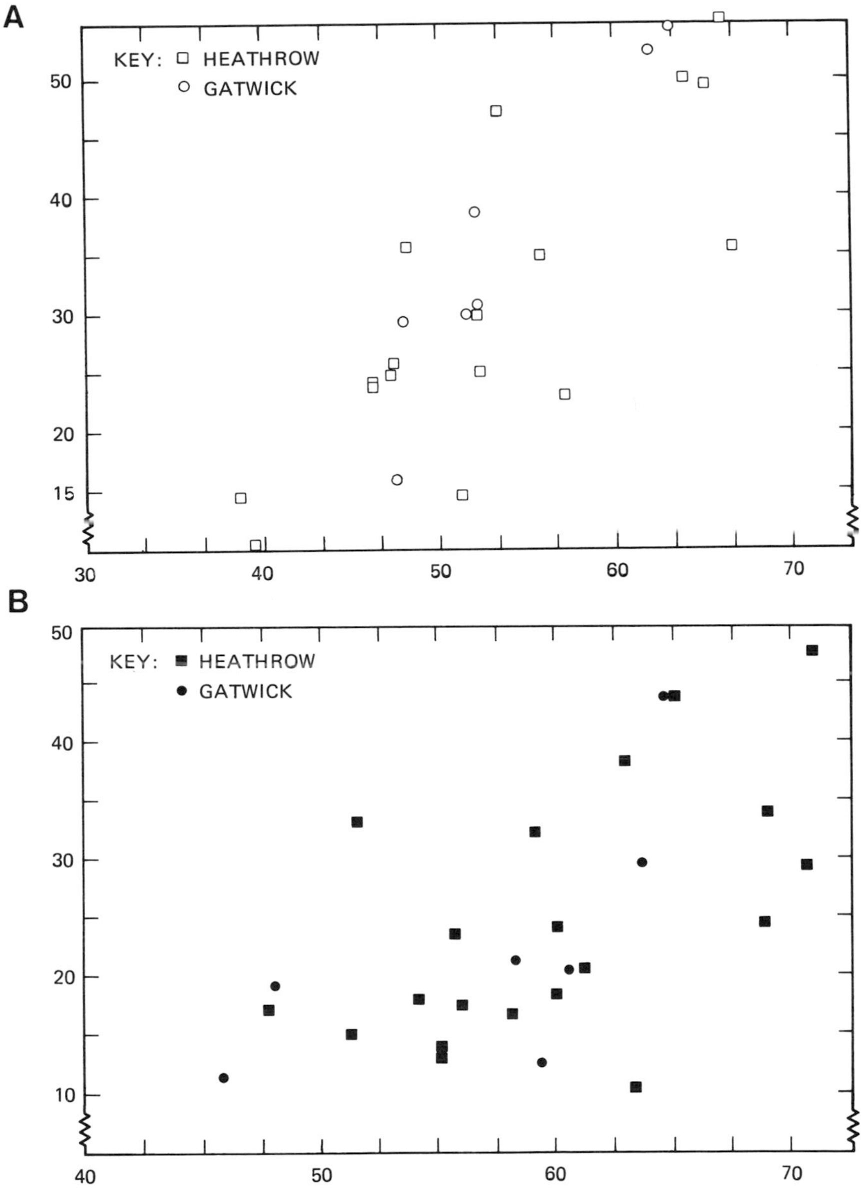

FIGURE 9.39 Percentage of respondents giving aircraft noise as a reason for closed windows (A) and sleeping with bedroom windows closed on designated (B) nights as function of L_{eq} from 11 PM to 7 AM. (From DORA, 1980.)

In the DORA report a "person awoken more than once per week" was counted the same whether awoken by aircraft noise three times per night or only two times per week. Although the sleep disturbances for other reasons

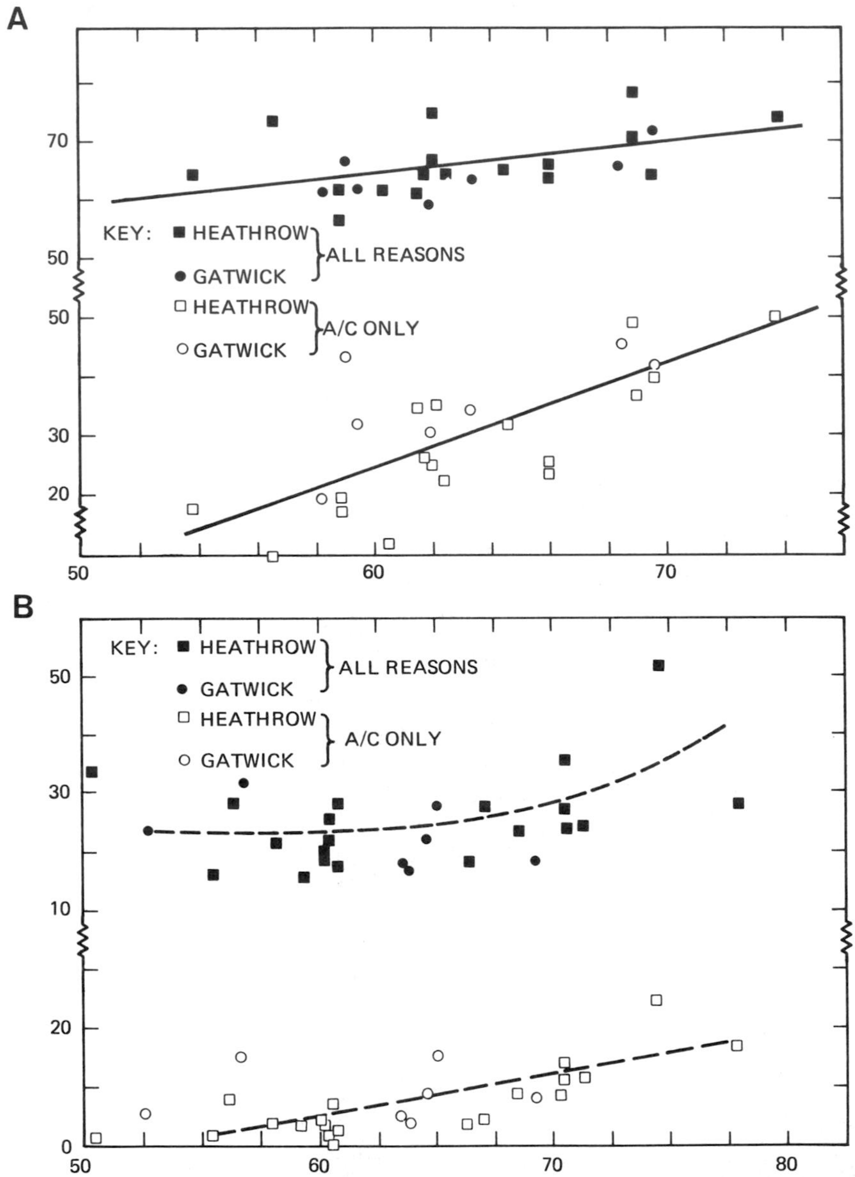

FIGURE 9.40 Percentage of respondents having difficulty in getting to sleep according to general experience (A) and on a designated night (B) as a function of L_{eq} from 10 to 12 PM. (From DORA, 1980.) Dashed trend curves added here.

were scored the same way, it seems likely that the potential for multiple disturbances per night would be greater because of aircraft noise than for other causes. In the DORA study sleep disturbances, no matter what the cause, were considered equally significant. Those awakened by the need to

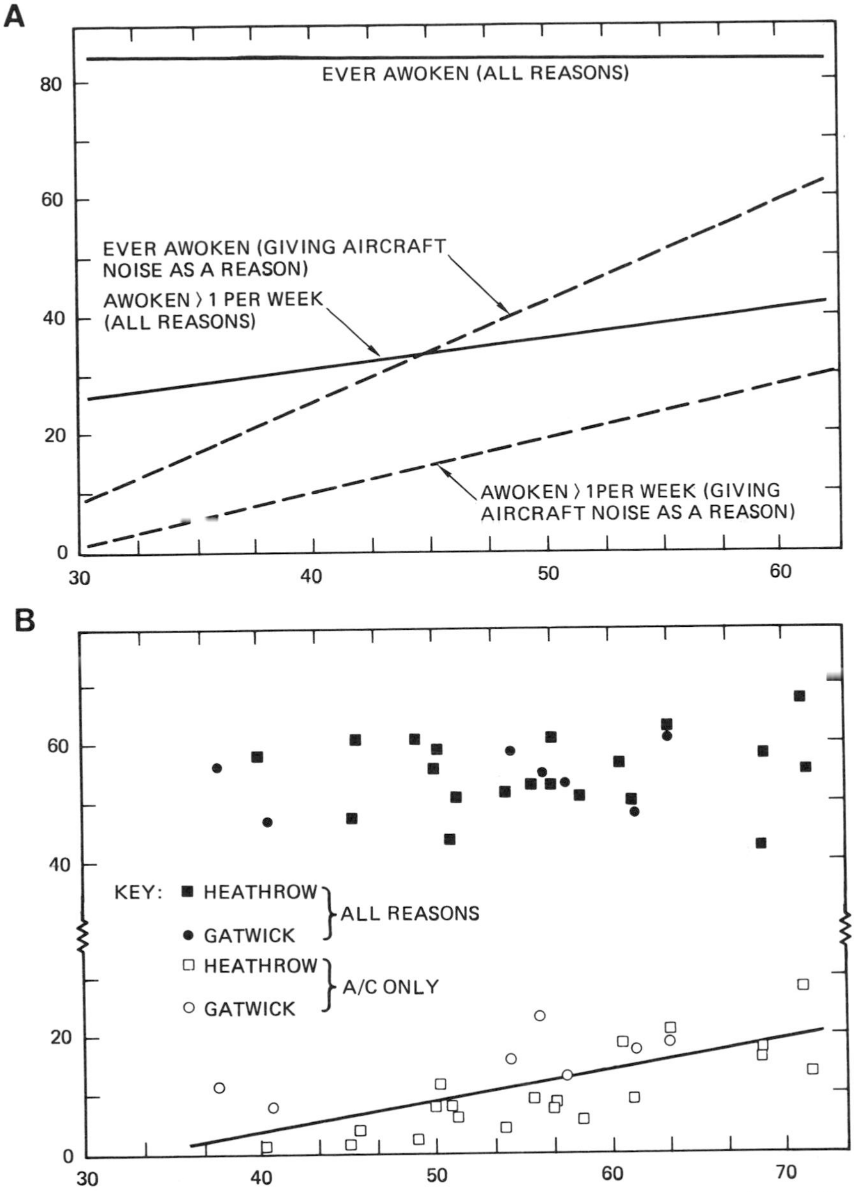

FIGURE 9.41 Percentage of respondents awoken according to general experience (A) and on a designated night (B) as a function of L_{eq} from 11 PM to 7 AM. (From DORA, 1980.)

go to the toilet (found in the study to be one of the major causes of sleep disturbance) would not, it is surmised, have the same the ability to adjust to a other disturbances the same night.

Figure 9.42 shows that with an evening L_{eq} (2, 10–12 PM) of 60 dB_A, about 38% of the respondents in the DORA study, were "very much" or "quite

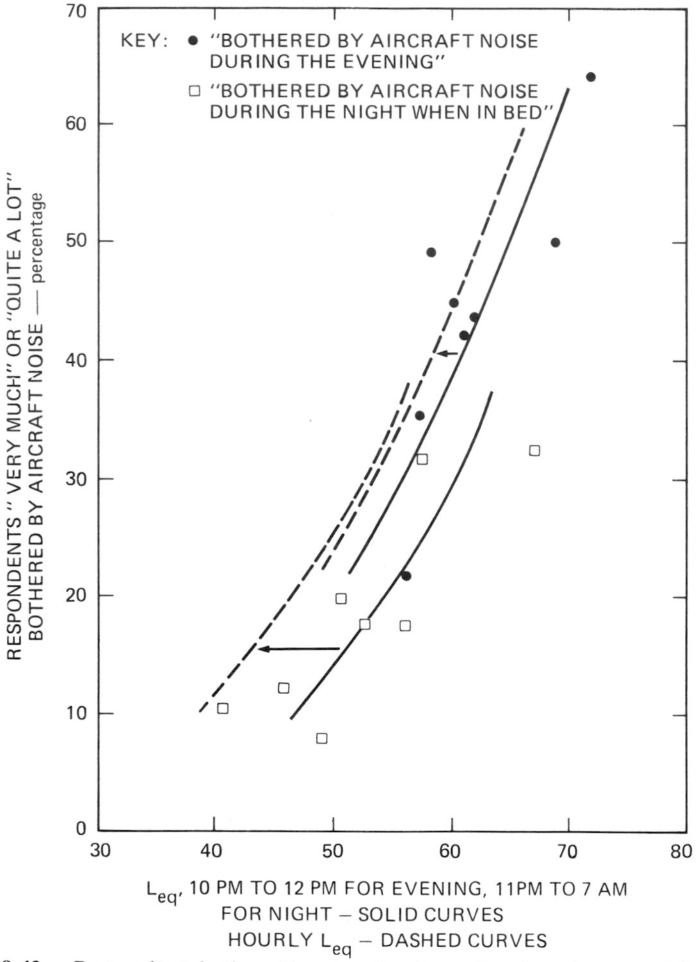

FIGURE 9.42 Respondents bothered by aircraft noise as function of measured L_{eq} for specified time periods and hourly L_{eq}. (Based on data from Fig. 12 and Tables 6c and 6d of DORA, 1980.)

a lot'' bothered by the aircraft noise, and that with a night L_{eq} (8 h, 11:00 PM–7:00 AM) of 60, about 30% were similarly bothered. The respective hourly L_{eq} levels were 3 and 9 dB less.

Figure 9.43 shows the data obtained in response to the question of ''tiredness'' plotted as a function of L_{eq} for 11 PM–7 AM. On the basis of the solid and dashed curves, the DORA report concluded that tiredness from sleep disturbance from aircraft noise does not exceed the amount generally found until the L_{eq} goes above ~65 dB. However, it is submitted that the short–long-dashed curve, added to make Fig. 9.43 realistic, indicates that tiredness from

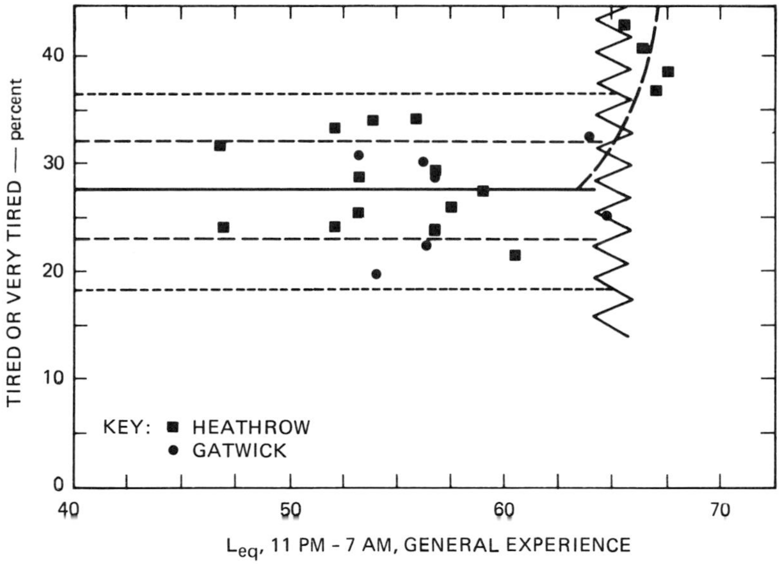

FIGURE 9.43 Respondents "tired" or "very tired" according to general experience as a function of L_{eq} from 11 PM to 7 AM. (From DORA, 1980.) Short-long dashed curve added here.

awakening increases above an L_{eq} of somewhere between L_{eq8h} 55 and 60 dB_A.

In the DORA report, the Civil Aviation Authority posed and answered two "policy-related questions" as follows:

Question: "What is the level of aircraft noise which will disturb a sleeping person?"

Answer: "The study indicates that there is a discernible increase in disturbance for both general experience and designated night results when nighttime noise exposure is about 65 L_{eq}.

Question: "What level of aircraft noise prevents people from getting to sleep?"

Answer: "The proportion of people who report difficulty in getting to sleep for all reasons shows a discernible increase for aircraft noise exposure for sites at about 70 L_{eq} (measured between 10:00 PM and 12:00 AM), although aircraft noise is increasingly quoted as a cause of difficulty as aircraft L_{eq} increases."

However, it would seem that aircraft noise-exposure levels of L_{eq} 65 dB and 70 dB_A, for the start of a discernible increase in disturbing sleep and causing difficulty in going to sleep, are about 10 dB higher than warranted according to the data in Figs. 9.42 and 9.43. These values are also about 10 dB too high to be consistent with other data in this regard presented in this chapter and in Chapter 10.

Fidell and Jones (1975) reported the results of an attitude survey carried out before and after a 1-month period (May 1973) during which normal nighttime (11:00 PM–6:00 AM) aircraft landings over a low-economic residential area were suspended. It was found that this reduction in nighttime landings (50 out of an average of 687 landings in 24 h) did not affect the amount of annoyance measured by the attitude surveys before and after the 1 month of suspended operations. The results were explained as follows: (1) the decrease in the 24-h exposure level as a result of landing reductions is relatively small; and (2) a 1-month period is not sufficiently long for the people to integrate the annoyance reactions, especially as there are always periods when nighttime operations are reduced because of such factors as weather conditions.

Another possible explanation of these findings is that the "before" annoyance survey was conducted in mid-April, so the sleep–arousal attitudes were apparently based on February and March experiences. During this period the weather conditions likely resulted in closed windows, which would tend to reduce the relative amount of noise experienced, and thus reduce the overall annoyance experienced. Further data related to annoyance and complaints about aircraft noise as a function of month of year (weather conditions and climate) will be presented in Chapter 10.

Several ongoing surveys of sleep–arousal, and attendant annoyance, from aircraft noise are being conducted in Great Britain. Hume and Thomas (1993) report that in neighborhoods near the Manchester airport, 18% of the people cited sleep disturbance one of the adverse effects of aircraft noise and that aircraft noise has a greater adverse affect on people than road traffic noise. Hume *et al.* (1993) monitored EEG for a several nights in 46 paid subjects near the manchester airport. They found a 4% increase in number of shifts in stage of EEG activity in periods with aircraft noise events, than in periods no such events.

Ollerhead and Diamond (1993) review the results of repeated social surveys in Great Britain regarding the sleep disturbance from aircraft noise. It appears that total sleep disturbance has a minor dependence on aircraft noise, but the portion that is reported is consistently strongly correlated with L_{Aeq} exposure level. No clear relationships between personal variables and sleep disturbance from aircraft noise are identified.

Ollerhead and Jones (1993) report findings from a field studies in which sleep arousal was measured by recording of movements of a person's arm when sleeping in bed at their homes by means of an actimeter attached to the wrist. The conclusions of the study are that actimetry is a cost-efficient way of measuring arousals from sleep in people at home, and that aircraft noise is a relative minor cause of the movements deemed as arousals. The agreement between measured arousal rates and general self-ratings of sleep quality was poor, but somewhat better for immediate, next-day, ratings.

Öhrstrom (1993) and Hume *et al.* (1993) discuss research findings in which the effects of noise, particularly that from aircraft, upon nighttime sleep as measured by changes in EEG activity. Nicolas *et al.* (1993) found that EEG reactivity to noise during sleep depends not only on sleep stage and type of noise, but also on the period of day in which the sleep takes place. Van *et al.* (1993) measured, by means of EEG response, reactivity to aircraft noise events on the part of 46 males living near airports in the U.K. It was found that 15 subjects responded to more than twice as many aircraft noise events as did the less sensitive subjects.

Maschke *et al.* (1993) found a distinct correlation between sleep stage shifts and exposure to aircraft noise and an increase in adrenaline level in the urine in 40 adult subjects. The experiment was conducted over 200 experimental nights in a laboratory test chamber. On the other hand, Carter *et al.* (1993) found in a similar study no difference between quiet and aircraft-noise nights with respect to excretions of urinary adrenaline, noradrenaline or dopamine, in spite of the decreases in the depth of sleep stage, EEG measured, due to the noise.

An increase in disturbances to sleep compared to other causes of disturbance, has been found to be correlated with the increase in level of road traffic noise, as shown in Fig. 9.44. However, because exposure level for the road traffic noise is expressed in Fig. 9.44 as *A*-weighted level exceeded 10% of the time during a 24-h day, the results are not numerically comparable with the mean L_{eq} levels for the noise in the other figures.

Horonjeff *et al.* (1982) studied sleep arousal from a variety of nonaircraft noises on the part of people when sleeping in the natural setting of their own homes. In this study, 14 subjects (6 females and 8 males, ages 20–59, average 42 years) slept in their homes with a small switch, or response button, on a stand or small table beside their beds. They were instructed to push the button whenever they were awakened for any reason. The experimenter, by

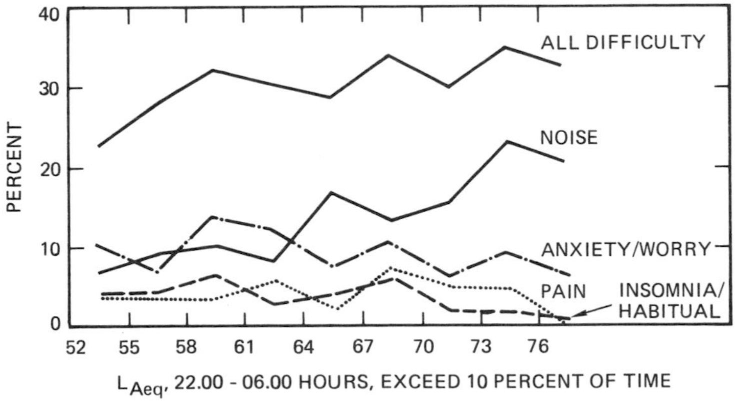

FIGURE 9.44 Reasons given for sleep disturbance compared with level of road traffic noise. (From Langdon and Buller, 1977. Reproduced by permission of the Controller of Her Britannic Majesty's Stationery Office. Crown copyright.)

remote telephone-link control, was able to present noise into the bedroom over a small loudspeaker and to record the awakenings and noise level in the room from a microphone placed near the bed. Some of their results are shown in Figs. 9.45A and 9.45B.

Figure 9.45A shows that the test transmission-line noise was more disruptive to sleep than the other three, which were reasonably similar in that regard. Figure 9.45B shows that as a function of maximum dB_A (*A*-weighted decibel) level the steady, 15 min duration with a 20-dB/min rise–decay times, than the transient "impulse" with a 2-dB/s rise–decay time (see Fig. 9.45C for the temporal patterns of the noise stimuli). The data plotted on Fig. 9.45B for each of these noises as a function of maximum dB_A level, with temporal state as the parameter, clearly indicates that awakening probabilities are a joint function of duration and maximum level.

Noise "Saliency" as Factor in Arousal from Sleep

Krallmann (1962) conducted an extensive experiment of the behavioral awakening of an air-raid siren. In this experiment some 617 male students (ages 16–70, average 44 years) at an air-raid training school in Germany were each tested for four nights. The subjects attended the school for one week, in classes of 24 men. Each subject, when aroused from sleep by the sound of the siren, activated a switch by his bed that caused a number to register for that subject in the experimenter's control room. A recording of a wailing siren of 45-s duration, was programmed to be presented in one of the 15-min periods, from the hours of midnight to 5 AM, at one of five different levels. The levels were randomized among the nights in 5-dB steps from peak 38 to 58 dB_A, (~55–75 L_{Aeq}). (*Note:* L_{Aeq} and L_{Aex} are synonymous when a duration for L_{Aeq} is not specified. They indicate the rms energy summed over a single noise event.)

The percent probabilities of arousal from sleep from the noise of jet aircraft noise, the noises in the Horonjeff *et al.* study, and the sound of a siren are shown in Fig. 9.46A. Krallmann, as have others, as noted earlier, found that arousal was more difficult in younger than older men, and that, as clearly seen in Fig. 9.46A, the deepest sleep—that requiring strongest stimulation to awaken—was during the first 1–1¼ h, and generally declined thereafter. During that period, the siren at a peak level of 38 dB_A (L_{Aeq} 55 dB_A) caused an average of 35% of the subjects to awaken, and with an L_{Aeq} of 75 dB_A, about 60% were awakened.

The transmission-line noise, subjectively characterized as an intense crackling or "frying" sound, was a recording a corona discharge due to rain-moisture in the air being vaporized on an ultra-high-voltage electric power line. One-third-octave-band spectra of the Horonjeff *et al.* noises, that of a siren used in tests conducted by Krallmann, and that of a jet aircraft used in sleep tests of Lukas and Kryter (1970) are shown in Fig. 9.46B.

It is of some interest to note that, as a function of L_{Aeq}, and compared to

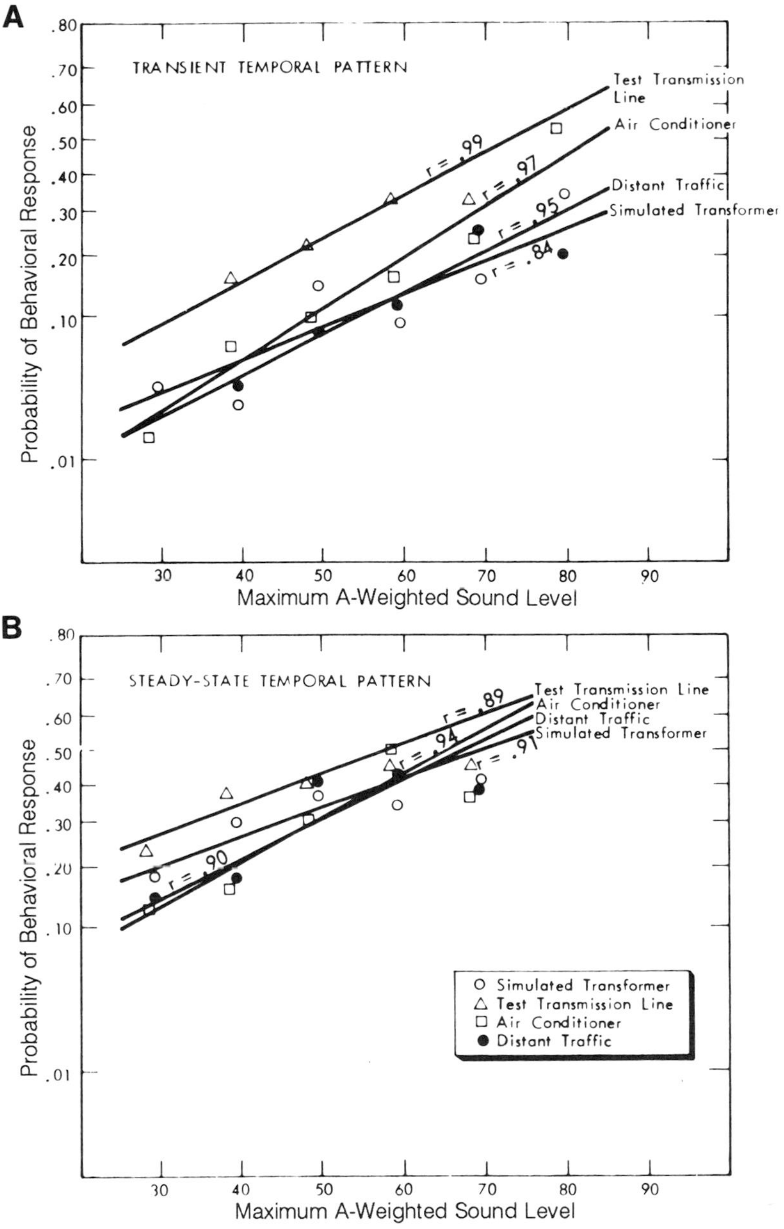

FIGURE 9.45A, B Differing signal sources. Probabilities of behavioral awakenings based on data collected from persons sleeping in own home and exposed to recordings of various types of noises. Temporal pattern as parameter. (From Horonjeff *et al.*, 1982.)

the common low-frequency noises, arousal was a few decibels more effective by the jet-aircraft noise, 12 dB or so by the transmission-line noise, and at least 30 dB by the siren noise. A possible explanation is that these latter

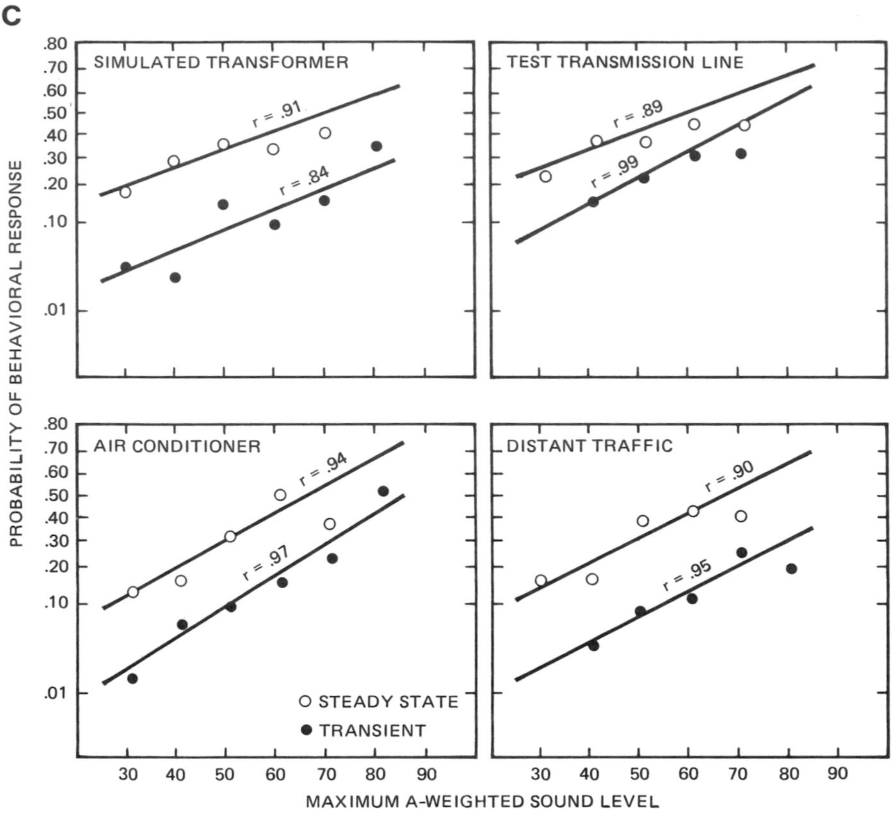

FIGURE 9.45C Differing temporal patterns. Probabilities of behavioral awakenings based on data collected from persons sleeping in own home and exposed to recordings of various types of noises. Type of noise parameter. (From Horonjeff *et al.*, 1982.)

three noises were progressively more salient than the others because of (1) a greater concentration of energy in the mid- to high-frequency, compared to the lower-frequency, region (a smaller mid : low-frequency ratio); (2) temporal irregularities not present in the other noises (the transmission noise had an uneven, ''frying'' character); and (3) the jet aircraft and, particularly the siren noises, contain some pure-tone line spectra. As discussed in Chapter 3, pure-tone components at frequencies above 500 Hz are ''penalized'' up to 13 dB or so, depending of frequency, for enhanced annoyance due to their presence (see Fig. 3.7). These features are, of course, not reflected in the physical measurements made of the noises shown in Fig. 9.46B.

It is suspected also that because of the small number of exposures to the siren (one per night for four nights), the subjects in that experiment were not as adapted to the noise as were the subjects to the noises in the other experiments. The relatively small difference between arousal from the jet aircraft and the low-frequency noises could be due to differences in experimental methods between the two studies involved, rather than saliency.

A

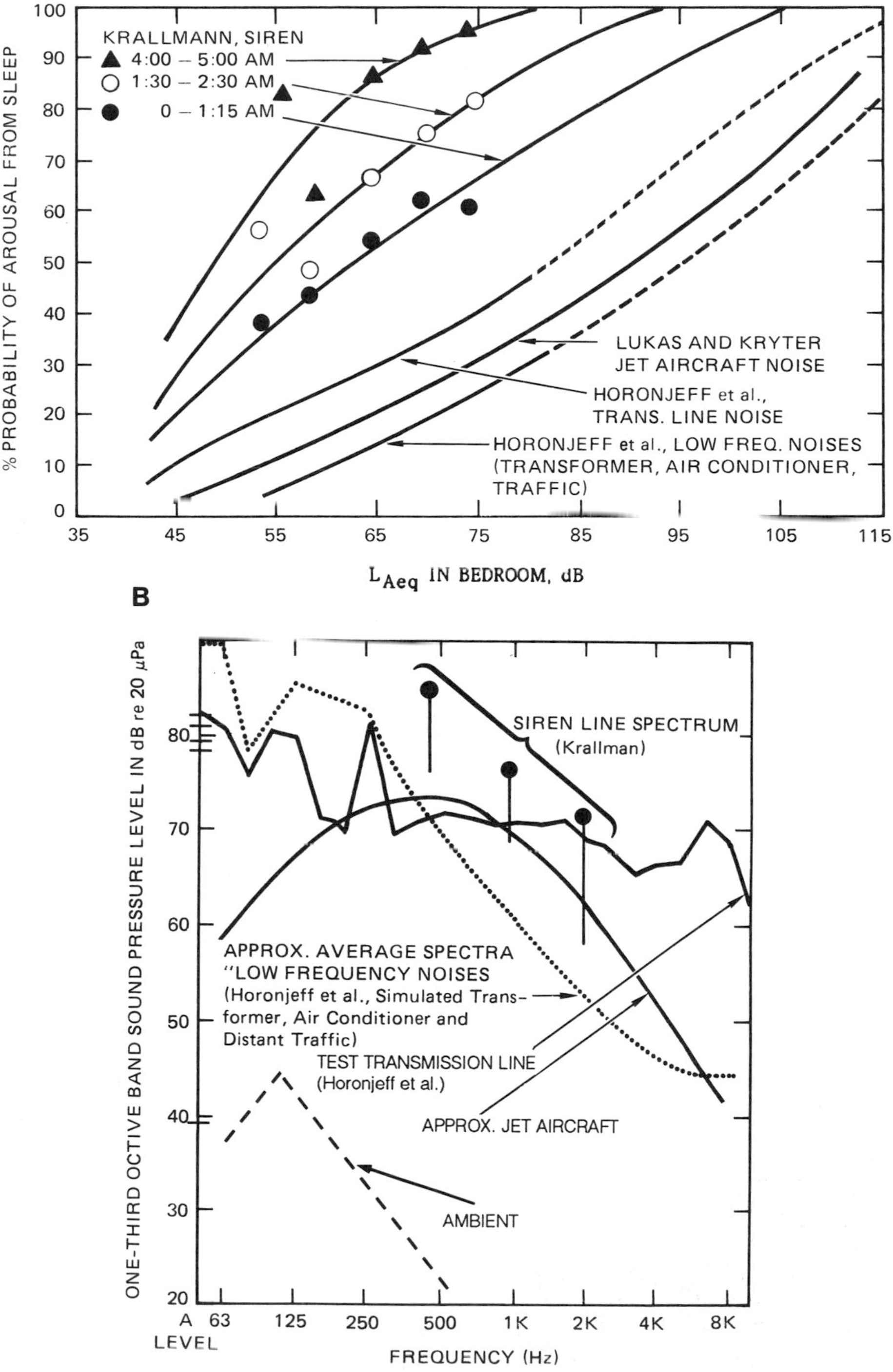

FIGURE 9.46 (A) Percentage probabilities of behavioral arousal from sleep by different varieties of noise. (B) One-third-octave-band spectra of noises. The line drawn down from the siren noise indicates narrowband, line-type spectrum.

Sound-Induced Sleep

Sound can perhaps induce sleep, either because a given sound masks other, more distractive sounds, or serves as a focus for one's attention. Little experimental research seems to have been done on this phenomenon, although Olsen and Nelson (1961) claim a tone of 320–350 Hz calms crying babies and puts them to sleep, and some devices for making soothing sounds to induce sleep are available on the commercial market.

Sleep and Health

Richter (n.d.) observed that a sleeping subject exhibited EEG and vasoconstrictive reactions about every 30 s because of cars, trains, and motorcycles passing the test room, even though the person slept quietly and on awakening had no recollection of any disturbances. Similar results were found, as noted above, by Cantrell (1974), Johnson *et al.* (1973), and Johnson and Lubin (1967) from men exposed to sonar 'pings', and by LeVere and Davis (1977) for persons exposed to aircraft noise that was nonbehavioral awakening. Richter hypothesized that energy from these and other autonomic-system-controlled activities (e.g., gastrointestinal, responses) are withdrawn from the recovery process of sleep and ultimately detrimental to normal health.

However, it is possible that the autonomic-system responses observed are not physiologically stressful. As discussed above, Maschke *et al.* (1993) reported increased, and Carter *et al.* (1993) reported no, overnight effects on output of noradrenaline, adrenaline, and dopamine following a number of EEG-measured sleep arousals due to noise. Carter *et al.* found approximately 25 "arousals" (appearance of Alpha in EEG) during the night from exposure to 50 aircraft or truck noise at levels of 65–72 dB_A. Research findings of Williams *et al.* (1964) suggest that people might develop sleep patterns that would provide some protection for physiological health, i.e., a decrease in arousability. It is shown in Figs. 9.47 and 9.48 that when subjects were deprived of sleep they spent more time in the stages of sleep identified as deep and resistant to arousal than when not deprived.

However, as found in community studies, to be discussed in Chapter 10, as well as in laboratory and field studies just discussed, as noise is increased above certain levels of intensity it will continue to behaviorally awaken people, even after long periods of repeated exposures to the noise. These behavioral arousals can cause feelings of annoyance, not only because of being awakened, but because of fear or some other obnoxious meaning conveyed by the noise as an information-bearing signal. It is surmised that it is only the physiological stress responses to the annoyance that could possibly contribute to some health disorders, rather than any noise-induced EEG and autonomic-system reflex responses that appear to occur prior to all sounds, above certain levels of intensity, but that do not necessarily precede behavioral awakening.

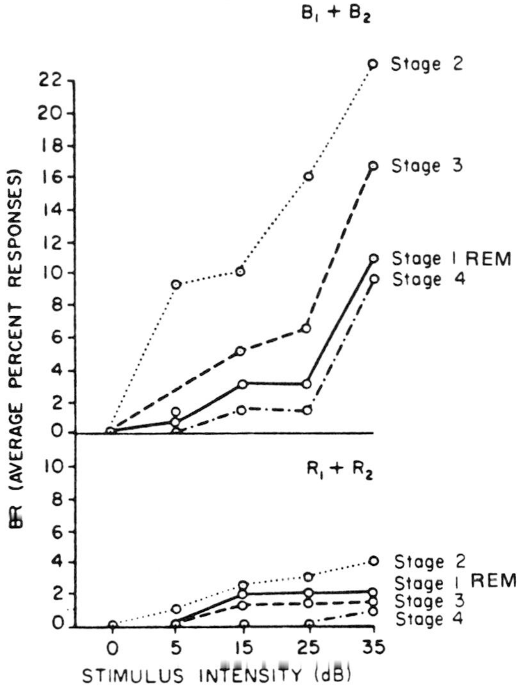

FIGURE 9.47 Effect of stimulus intensity on behavioral response (BR) during four stages of sleep for baseline nights B_1 and B_2 and recovery nights R_1 and R_2 after 64 h of sleep deprivation. (From Williams *et al.*, 1964.)

NONAUDITORY SYSTEM HEALTH DISORDERS

Introduction

As a framework for discussing the associations found between certain health disorders and exposure to noise, it is postulated that:

1. Sound energy does not stimulate or damage, to any significant degree, any part of the body besides the ear.
2. Physiological alerting–reflexive reactions to sound and noise are not of sufficient physiological magnitude to cause health disorders.
3. Diseases, other than those caused by infections and injury from foreign energy or chemical agents, are genetically determined.
4. Brain activities involved in sensations, perceptions, and cognition per se do not cause health disorders, either physical or mental. Sensations, perceptions, and cognition are fundamental to emotional reactions.
5. The glandular and autonomic central nervous systems, when activated by certain emotions, create, for that period, nonhomeostatic conditions in

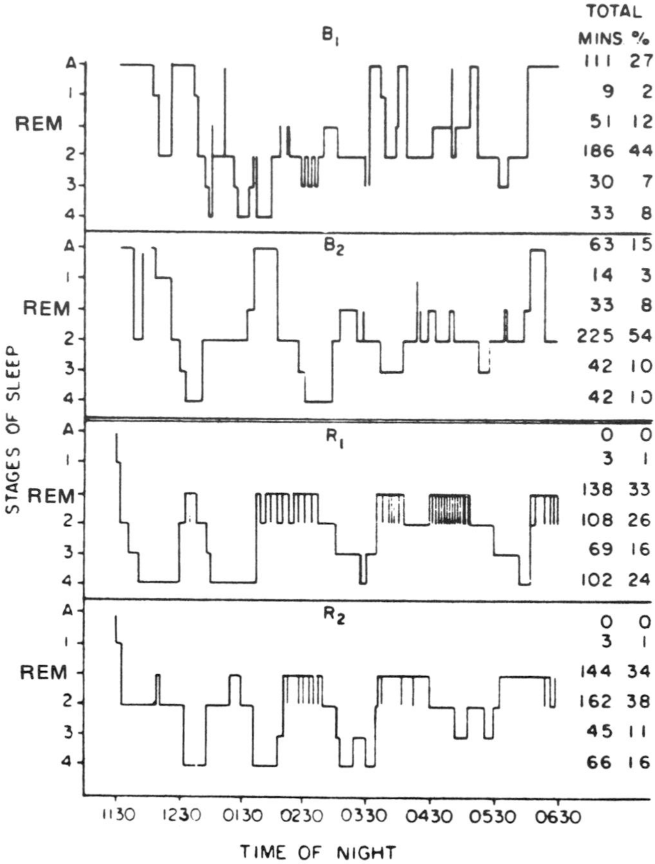

FIGURE 9.48 Effect of sleep loss on the distribution of EEG stages of sleep for one subject. B_1 and B_2 are baseline nights when subject is not deprived of sleep, and R_1 and R_2 are nights after sleep deprivation of 64 h. (From Williams *et al.*, 1964.)

cardiovascular, respiratory, digestive, and cognitive processing systems. Strong degrees of these physiological–emotional responses, although in and of themselves normal and not the proximate cause of disease, are stressful to some disease conditions, such as hypertension; indigestion, asthma, and psychological states of anxiety. (It is ostensibly biologically unreasonable that physiological reactions to emotions would per se cause a disease or pathological condition in organs of the body; just as it was earlier postulated that it would be more or less biologically unacceptable for neurological activity of the auditory system to adversely, stressfully, stimulate a nonauditory organ or system of the body.)

6. Autonomic system disorders, or abnormalities in responses, are genetically present in some percentage of the population and can adversely affect a number of disease conditions (Lamanske and Caliner, 1990).

7. Emotional states may create physiological conditions that can cause manifestations of symptoms of an existing disease [e.g., an asthmatic episode (Caliner and Lamanske, 1992).]
8. Noise engendered emotional states may, under certain conditions and in some people, cause manifestations of the symptoms of certain diseases or health disorders. This does not imply that either the noise or the emotion is the cause of the disease or disorder.

The concept that psychological–emotional responses to events in everyday life can cause physiological activities that in turn may contribute to physical and mental illnesses has been expressed in the medical literature (see reviews in Chrousos and Gold, 1992; Dantzer and Kelley, 1989; Levi, 1973; Kagan, 1980; Peterson, 1991). Kagan for example, states that

> There is much evidence showing that psychological stimuli arising from a large variety of social stressors may cause the catecholamine or corticosteroid stress responses and . . . physiological changes . . . associated with high risk for a large variety of diseases. For example, . . . increased heart rate, raised blood pressure, increased peripheral resistance, increased fat metabolism, decreased glucose tolerance, impaired myocardial uptake of oxygen, cardiac arrhythmias, gastroenteric activity, and possibly effects on the histo-immunological system.

More recently, Dantzer and Kelley (1989) comment that

> Experimental and clinical studies demonstrate that both laboratory and natural stressors alter the activities of lymphocytes and macrophages in a complex way that depends on the type of immune response (and) the physical and psychological characteristics of the stressor. . . . Sensitivity of the immune system to stress is not simply fortuitous but is an indirect consequence of the regulatory reciprocal influences that exist between the immune system and the central nervous system.

Peterson concluded that

> With few notable exceptions, investigations of viral infections in human and in animal models support the hypothesis that stress promotes the pathogenesis of such infections. Similar conclusions can be drawn from studies of bacterial infections in humans and from a small number of studies of parasitic infections in rodent models. While many of these studies have substantial limitations, the data nonetheless suggest that stress is a potential cofactor in the pathogenesis of infectious disease."

Nevertheless, data supporting causal relations between physiological reactions considered stressful and health disorders are not plentiful because large number of variables involved can confound the data (Rabkin and Struening, 1976; Graeven, 1974; van Dijk, 1986) Herd, 1991; Schust, 1993). Bly *et al.* (1993), in a review of laboratory research on immune system responses to noise, found six studies in which noise-induced stress apparently caused moderate suppression of the immune system; three studies suggested immune system stimulation during noise, and contradictory findings in this regard were found in two studies that examined the effects on the immune response of dependence of subject's control of the noise. [These studies were: Sieber *et al.* (1992), Irwin *et al.* (1989), Folch *et al.* (1991), Kugler *et al.* (1990), McCarthy *et al.* (1992), Bomberer and Haar (1992), Weisse *et al.* (1990), Wong (1986).]

Also relevant is the observation that depressed, low-sensitivity subjects were physiologically (heart rate and skin conductance) less responsive to exposure in the laboratory to noise than were nondepressed subjects of matched age and sex (Stansfeld and Shine, 1993), Stansfeld (1993) reviews research showing that subjective measures of noise sensitivity is associated with psychiatric disorders and personality traits such as neuroticism. Other studies showing a positive relation between subjective sensitivity, and physiological arousal, during task performance were discussed in Chapter 8, and it has been found that persons who rate themselves as sensitive to noise in real-life are physiologically more reactive than less-sensitive, self-rated, respondents to noise stimuli presented in a laboratory setting. Discussed below is research relevant to the question of health disorders from exposure to noise in: (1) industry and (2) in residential communities. The practical aspects and implications of the associations of exposure to environmental noises, public health, and noise control are further discussed and quantified in chapter 10.

LONG-TERM EXPOSURES TO INDUSTRIAL NOISES

Studies of the health of people working in noisy industries, compared with workers from quieter industries, are plagued by the problems of adequately equating different groups of workers with respect to socioeconomic and familial health-status variables. There appear to be at least two work-related psychological variables that can have stimulating effects on the autonomic system that can also confound the behavioral results for groups of workers taken from different work situations:

1. The work conditions may be unsafe. Often intense industrial noise is indicative of the operation of moving machinery that must be attended to in order that the worker avoid bodily injury. The noise not only connotes this danger but can also mask or interfere with the hearing of acoustic cues and signals that must be perceived in order to avoid the dangers involved. These conditions contribute to psychological emotions that may be reflected as physiological stress.

2. The work may require the perception of certain sounds (of machinery operating, speech, etc.) in order that the work tasks be properly and quickly performed. The noise may interfere with these perceptions, creating some anxiety about work performance that may also be reflected as physiological stress.

There are obviously other environmental factors, such as air pollution and general physical work conditions, that must also be equated for noise-exposed versus non-noise-exposed workers before valid conclusions on the effects of the noise on health are drawn. For example, Pilawska *et al.* (1977) cited two on-the job factors in shipyards as having decisive significance as causes of illness and absences: (1) improper climatic conditions and (2) excessive intensity of vapors of welding gases, paint and solvent vapors, dust, noise, vibration, ultraviolet radiations, and drafts. Pilawska *et al.* found in a particular industry 1826 persons worked in noise levels of >85 dB_A (group A) and 5825 worked in noise levels of <75 dB_A (group B). A comparison of the medical records of these two groups revealed that hearing disorders were 22 times more frequent, stomach and intestinal ulcers were 5 times more frequent, and high blood pressure was about 2 times more frequent in group A than in group B. Similar types of results were found among workers in noisy environments by Jansen (1961) (see Fig. 9.49), Shatalov and Murov (1970), Zvereva *et al.* (1975), and Cieslewicz (1971). To what extent the findings of these studies may have been influenced by some of the psychological and physical factors noted above is unknown.

Most of the studies of the effects of noise on workers have been concerned with abnormal cardiac conditions as measured by the electrocardiogram (ECG) and by the development of blood pressure, or hypertension, higher than normal for a given age group. Studies, to name a few, of these effects include those of Andriukin (1961), Geller *et al.* (1963), Andrukovich (1965),

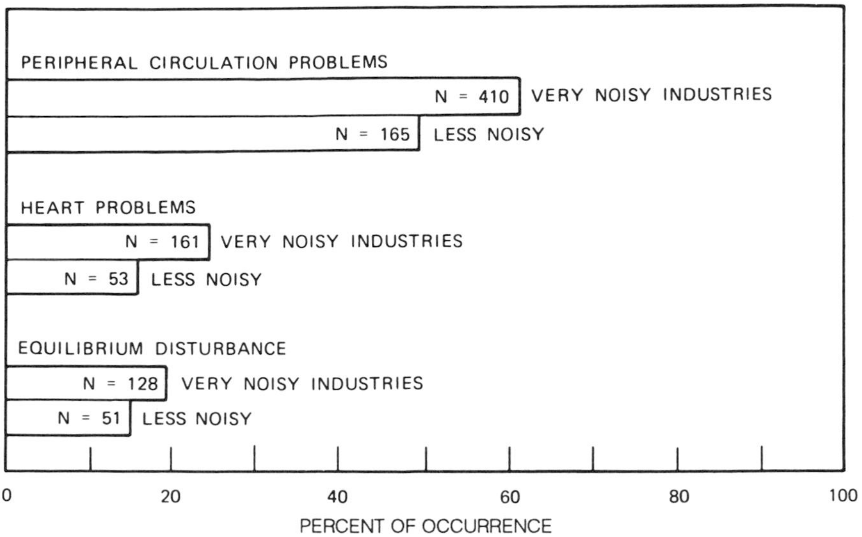

FIGURE 9.49 Differences in percentage occurrence of physiological problems in 1005 German industrial workers. The differences in peripheral circulation and cardiac problems in the two classes of work environments were statistically significant. (From Jansen, 1961.)

Kavoussi (1973), Capellini and Maroni (1974), Parvizpoor (1976), Cuesdean *et al.* (1977), Dega and Klajman (1977), Kachnyi (1977), and Friedlander *et al.* (n.d.). Some more recent investigations will be discussed later, but first the current general controversy regarding the interpretation of these types of studies is examined.

The results for some of these industrial studies are interpreted by some investigators to be mostly positive; that is, persons working in intense noise show a significantly greater incidence of hypertension or heart abnormalities than do persons who work in less noise. It can be pointed out, for example, that Parvizpoor found increased hypertension in weavers in textile mills working in noise above 95 dB_A compared with a group randomly selected from a population matched socioeconomically to that of the weavers (see Table 9.9). Parvizpoor notes, however, that physiological stressors in the mills besides the noise include cotton dust (7.5 mg/m^3, a very heavy dust content), high temperatures and humidity, and other adverse environmental factors. Kachnyi reports that weavers operating smaller, less noisy looms showed more disorders of arterial pressure than did weavers using fewer, noisier looms. In addition, the data are not consistent in showing any uniform relation between noise intensity and cardiovascular functions.

Geller *et al.* found that workers in the Soviet petroleum industry in noise of 115–125 dB and exposed to oil and gas fumes suffered no more hypertension or cardiac neurosis (as determined by ECG, electrocardiograph) than did administrators or laborers working in the quiet. However, petroleum workers in 115–125-dB noise who were not exposed to oil and gas fumes suffered more hypertension and cardiac neurosis than did workers in the quiet. Cuesdean *et al.* found that ECG abnormalities were less for air-

TABLE 9.9 Effect of Noise on Cardiovascular Function of Textile Mill Weavers (95-dB_A Noise Level; Hypertension, >160/90 mmHg Blood Pressure)

	Hypertension, percent, shown by	
Age, years	Weavers	Controls*
20–29	1	0
30–39	7.3	1.2
40–49	12.1	6.5
50–59	27.1	8.6
Total	8.5	2.4

* Socioeconomically matched to weavers.

Data from Parvizpoor, 1976.

compressor operators and stokers in 100–106-dB noise than for mechanics in 95–100-dB noise, and the mechanics showed fewer ECG abnormalities than were found in laboratory assistants in 85–95-dB noise.

Table 9.10 shows that the incidence of hypertension is not related in any systematic way with noise from relative quiet to a noise in the range of 115–125 dB. For example, the percent of people with hypertension is the same, for the "quiet" and the 115–125-dB groups. Obviously these results do not support the notion that intense noise in and of itself is a cause of hypertension or other cardiovascular problems.

Hearing Loss and Hypertension

A working hypothesis of a number of studies has been that hypertension and noise-induced hearing loss should be positively correlated. Jansson and Hansson (1977) examined the prevalence of hypertension in industrial workers who had been exposed to noise at the workplace and had suffered elevated hearing thresholds greater than expected for their age. They found that men with noise-induced hearing losses had a significantly greater incidence of hypertension (systolic/diastolic blood pressure >160/100 mmHg) than did matched groups with normal or nearly normal hearing for their age.

On the other hand, Drettner *et al.* (1975), Hedstrand *et al.* (1977), Takala *et al.* (1977), Brown *et al.* (1975), A. Cohen *et al.* (1980), and Lees and Roberts (1979) found no correlation between noise-induced hearing loss and hypertension. Drettner *et al.*, using one thousand 50-year-old men, also measured other cardiovascular risk factors (serum cholesterol and triglycerides and a glucose tolerance test) with similar results. The results of some of these studies are summarized in Table 9.11.

In the Brown *et al.* study, 22 professional airline pilots were compared over a period of 8 years with 29 males of the same age who did not fly. In

TABLE 9.10 Hypertension as Function of Noise in the Workplace

	Hypertension, percent affected, for noise levels of			
Groups	Quiet	87–102 dB	103–120 dB	115–125 dB
General population*	23	26	17	8
Exposed to little noise†	11	12		20
Administrative workers‡	12			8
Manual workers‡	8			20
Average	14	19	17	14

* Andrukovich, 1965

† Andriukin, 1961

‡ Geller *et al.*, 1963

addition to hypertension, these investigators measured serum cholesterol and glucose. They found that although the pilots developed somewhat more elevated audiometric thresholds compared with the control group (indicating some noise-induced hearing loss from aircraft cockpit noise), there were no significant differences between the groups with respect to the cardiovascular or blood serum tests during the 8-year period.

Figure 9.50 shows the differences in hearing levels for workers with noise-induced hearing loss and for a control group with normal hearing. Table 9.11 compares the systolic and diastolic blood pressures of the NIPTS and control groups found in the various studies discussed above. It is shown in the table that the mean blood pressures and numbers of hypertensives were nearly the same for the NIPTS and control groups in all except the Jansson and Hansson study.

Manninen and Aro (1979) divided a sample of 188 male and 92 female engineering industry workers into 3 groups—those with normal hearing, those with moderate hearing losses, and those with severe hearing losses. It was assumed that the hearing losses were noise induced. The average diastolic and systolic blood pressures were essentially the same between the three categories of hearing level in workers below the age of 41 years. The findings for workers between the ages of 41 and 64 years were somewhat inconsistent: those with moderate hearing losses had about a 15-mmHg elevation in blood pressure above those with normal hearing, but the blood pressure of those with severe hearing losses was only 5 mmHg above those with normal hearing.

Talbott *et al.* (1993) reported the results of blood pressure and hearing level tests of 500 workers randomly selected from each of two metalworking plants. The data for the workers were divided into two groups: group A had

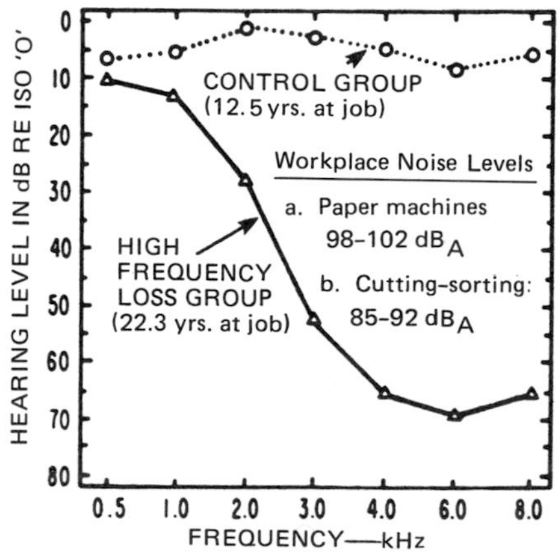

FIGURE 9.50 Mean hearing levels of group with high-frequency hearing loss vs. control group with normal hearing. Only right-ear data are shown. (From A. Cohen *et al.*, 1980.)

TABLE 9.11 Summary of Studies on Hearing Loss and Hypertension

Study	Hearing level	Number of subjects	Mean age, years	Mean blood pressure, mmHg Systolic	Diastolic	Number of hypertensives
Jansson and Hansson (1977)	Normal HL	74	54	133	81	6
	NIPTS*	44	57	145†	89†	10
Hedstrand *et al.* (1977)	Normal HL	376	50	134	84	24
	NIPTS‡	393	50	132	84	26
Takala *et al.* (1977)	Normal HL	67	45	151	95	14
	NIPTS*	32	47	155	99	11
A. Cohen *et al.* (1980)	Normal HL	51	34	122	68	7
	NIPTS*	51	47	123	70	5

* NIPTS = HL >65 dB above 3000 Hz.

† Difference between normal and NIPTS groups statistically significant.

‡ History of noise exposures and a "significant" hearing loss.

been exposed at their job to noise levels <82 dB_A, and group B, to noise >89 dB_A, for 15 years or more. It was found that hypertension was significant, 2–3 mg greater in the workers from the noisier than the quieter plant, and that hyperstension was somewhat more prevalent in men, matched for age, with greater, rather than lesser, hearing losses. Tablott *et al.* (1985) found, from a smaller sample of workers, that the incidence of high blood pressure was the same for men from the noisier (>89-dB_A), than quieter (<81-dB_A) plant, and that there was a stronger relation between amount of hearing loss and blood pressure.

Zhao *et al.* (1993a) found from multiple-regression analysis of data from 1101 textile workers that cumulative, years, of noise exposure was a risk factor for hypertension. However, the contribution to that risk was estimated to be more important than noise by a factor of 3 for age, 2 for parental history, and 1.6 for salt intake.

Hirai *et al.* (1991) obtained data on hearing loss and blood pressure of workers in a noisy factory. The prevalence of hypertension was 10.2%, 10.9%, and 12.5% for those working in, respectively, 85–115 dB noise, <85 dB noise, and "quiet" office noise. No positive relation between the noise level and hypertension is seen, and the higher level in office workers could be related more to the type of job than to noise. It was also found that the prevalence of significant hearing loss was 16.5% in the highest noise group, with 7.5% of those from the <85-dB group, and 2.5% of the office workers.

Kent *et al.* (1986) analyzed records of the hearing levels and cardiovascular function of approximately 2250 U.S. Air Force air crew members. Their analysis failed to indicate any association between degree of noise induced hearing loss and cardiovascular function. A similar finding was reported by Wu *et al.* (1987) for workers in a steel mill.

Other Possible Health-Related Effects

Data pertaining to neurasthenia (headache, giddiness, tiredness, bad memory, dizziness, etc.) were analyzed for 1101 female workers in textile mills (Zhao *et al.* 1993b). The workers were divided into groups exposed for ≥ 5 years to noise at levels of 75–80 dB_A, 86–90 dB_A, 96 dB_A, and 104 dB_A. As with several previous studies done in China on the same general subject, a strong positive relation was found between noise level and percent incidence of neurasthenia. However, contrary to some of these previous studies, the percentage of incidence of neurasthenia was independent of years of exposure. Again, the psychological condition of the subjects could have been related to differences in work task, or other environmental conditions, besides that of the noise.

Meyer-Falcke *et al.* (1993) exposed 552 volunteers to impulsive and continuous noises, ranging from 94 to 175 dB while measuring several pulmonary functions. It was found that with exposures to noises at levels greater than that for a low-flying jet aircraft, (~ 94 dB_A), airway resistance, and lack-of-control of reactions to experimental conditions were reduced.

Injury Rate in Noise

Evidence of the importance of psychological factors in noisy work situations comes from a study by Cohen (1973) of health and accident records in two U.S. industries with both high-noise (>95 dB_A) and low-noise (<80 dB_A) work area. Figure 9.51 shows that in plant complex A the number of medical problems was significantly higher in the high-noise group compared with that in the low-noise group; but in plant complex B the number of problems was about equal. Also, the lower curve in Fig. 9.51 shows the number of accidents in plant complex A to be much greater than in plant complex B in high noise.

Cohen notes that the differential risk of injury in the high-noise work areas (boiler factory) in plant complex A was much greater than in plant complex B (electronics and missile parts plant). He suggests that the greater number of medical problems in high noise in plant complex A was because of anxiety regarding danger of injury or accidents, and not the high-noise level per se. Masking by the higher-level noise of warning signals, and the like, could have also been a factor contributing to accidents and anxiety. These problems included digestive, respiratory, urological, glandular, and cardiovascular disorders, all suggestive of physiological stress elicited by some degree of emotional feelings, such as anxiety.

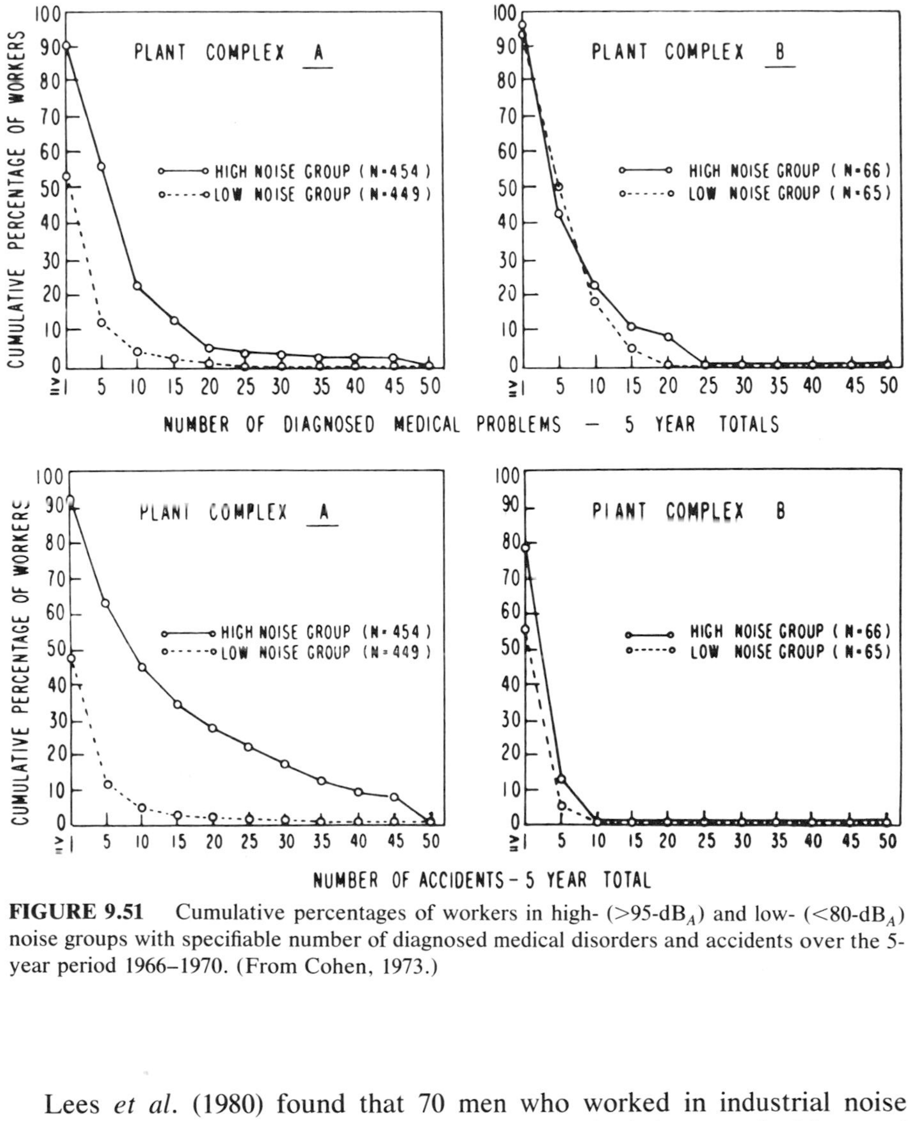

FIGURE 9.51 Cumulative percentages of workers in high- (>95-dB$_A$) and low- (<80-dB$_A$) noise groups with specifiable number of diagnosed medical disorders and accidents over the 5-year period 1966–1970. (From Cohen, 1973.)

Lees *et al.* (1980) found that 70 men who worked in industrial noise levels of 85 dB$_A$ or less for a period of 15 years had the same incidence of absenteeism, headaches, and accident rates (called *indicators of stress*) as 70 matched cohorts who had worked for 3 to 15 years in noise levels exceeding 90 dB$_A$. Lees *et al.* concluded that noise-exposure level was not necessarily a cause of stress in industrial work.

Belojevic and Kocijancic (1993) found that older (35–50 years) textile-mill workers in 104-dB$_A$ noise had higher hearing levels, but a lower incidence and severity of injury rates, than did older workers in 86-dB$_A$ noise. However, younger (20–35 years) workers in the high noise levels had more frequent and more severe injuries than did younger workers in the lower level of noise. The number of subjects in the different groups was small, ranging from 17 to 33.

Melamed *et al.* (1992) studied noise exposure, accident rate, and absenteeism in a broad study among blue-collar workers. Positive relations were found between accidents and absenteeism as functions of noise-related annoyance and job-related psychological stress.

Experiments in Workplaces

Some of the problems of retrospective studies, such as those just discussed, can be avoided in experiments in which the noise environment is controlled or manipulated and the physiological effects on the workers are monitored for any changes. As with the adventitious, retrospective studies, experiments of this type can be divided into two groups—those reporting adverse nonauditory-system effects of the noise and those showing no adverse effects.

In an experiment conducted by Ortiz *et al.* (1974), 18 jet-engine testbench workers who had been at that job for at least 3 years were exposed for one 3-h test period to jet-engine turbine noise at levels from 105 to 115 dB. Various analyses of urine, blood content, and blood pressure were made before, during, and after the exposure to the noise. Of the 18 subjects, 12 showed marked elevation in catecholamine excretions and increases in cholesterol, plasma-free fatty acids, blood pressure, and pulse frequency. The average age of this group was 39 years. Six of the subjects, average age 49 years, showed no significant responses to the noise. Ortiz *et al.* concluded that the blood pressure and catecholamine elevations found in some of the workers might be detrimental to people suffering from arteriosclerosis and other forms of vascular pathology.

The Ortiz *et al.* data should be viewed with caution because of the small number of subjects, the brief duration of the tests, and the lack of controls (no non-noise-exposed periods). Also contrary to the above findings are those from a study by Paolucci (1975), who measured catecholamine excretion in experienced aircraft ground personnel the day before and the day of exposure to different levels of jet-aircraft noise. Ten men were exposed to noise at a level of 120 dB for $1^1/_2$ h in the jet-engine test area; 10 other men were exposed to jet-aircraft takeoff noise at levels of 80–100 dB every 20 min for 5 h. All the men wore earplugs. Neither group of men showed a significant increase in catecholamine excretion for the noise-exposure period of the second day over that found for the same period of the preceding "quiet" day.

If the subjects in the Ortiz *et al.* study did not wear earplugs (whether they actually did was not specified), they received noise at their eardrums about 15–20 dB more intense than did the subjects in the Paolucci study. This could explain the difference in the results between the two studies. However, another possible explanation is found in the aforementioned study of Finkle and Poppen (1948), who exposed, for a period of 1 week, men wearing earmuffs to daily jet-engine noise at a level of 120 dB in a laboratory setting. The subjects showed greatly increased secretions of catecholamine and other related hormones for the first days of exposure, but by the end of the week the noise ceased to cause these or related stress responses (i.e., habituation had occurred). It is suggested that the positive findings for some of the subjects in the Ortiz *et al.* study could be due to a concern of these subjects that the noise was potentially harmful or stressful, and this concern was not habituated out during one 3-h exposure.

Physiological stress responses to noise at the workplace were reported by Ising *et al.* (1979; Ising and Melchert, 1980). Twelve workers in a brewery where the noise was at an average level of 95 dB_A worked for 1 week with earplugs and 1 week without earplugs. The earplugs provided an average daily noise reduction of about 13 dB. It was found that working without earplugs increased the systolic blood pressure by almost 7 mmHg, increased the excretion of vanillyl mandelic acid in urine by 67%, and increased the excretion of noradrenaline by 16 percent over those when working with earplugs. All the differences were statistically significant. After 1 week of work without earplugs, magnesium concentration in the blood of the 12 workers was 5 percent lower than after 1 week of work with earplug protection. The evaluation of the parameters of 26 test subjects showed a negative correlation of −0.52 between the magnesium content of blood sediment and the increase in blood pressure when exposed to noise.

There are, of course, other variables to be mentioned in the interpretation of these findings besides that of the 13-dB reduction in noise exposure reaching the eardrum. One is the well-known Hawthorne effect—that workers respond favorably to changes in their environment that are intended to improve the environment. Why this should cause the particular physiological changes found is not obvious, however. Other possible factors are the following: (1) the workers feel some apprehension in the noise because of fear of auditory fatigue, or damage to hearing, and interference effects of the noise with hearing speech or other auditory cues helpful to job performance—the wearing of earplugs would not only relieve the apprehension but could also improve hearing performance (see Chapter 6); and (2) the higher level of noise provides a greater continuous degree of physiological fatiguing and arousal than does the lower level. Ising *et al.*, postulate that the stress effects elicited by noise can be schematically summarized as follows:

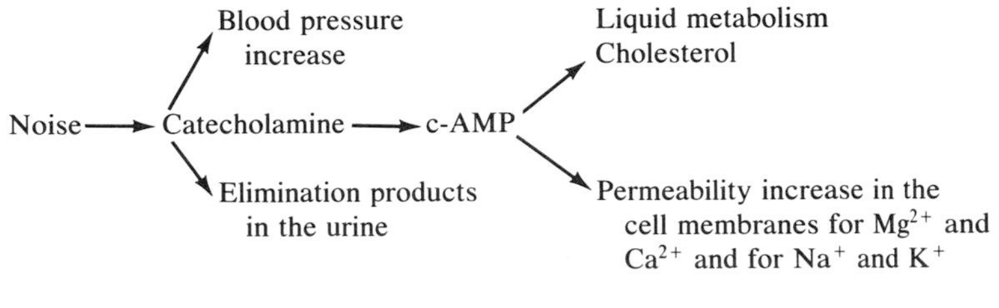

(where c-AMP = cyclic adenosine monophosphate). Whether these effects are related to psychological factors or to some reflexive arousal mechanism, or to both, and are sufficient to be pathogenic in some workers is, of course, a matter of conjecture.

A study previously mentioned was one in which U.S. Naval submarine personnel were exposed to noise (sonar pings) in a simulation of cruising in a submarine (Cantrell, 1974). Twenty healthy young male volunteers were evaluated audiometrically, medically, and psychologically. They were then confined to a dormitory for 55 days. During the first 10 days, audiometric results, mental and motor performance, and sleep patterns were evaluated. The subjects were then exposed to a pulsed, 10-step tone in the 3000–4000-Hz range for 0.66 s every 22 s, 24 h per day for 30 days. The tonal pulses were presented at 80 dB (per 0.0002 dyn/cm^2) for 10 days, 85 dB for 10 days, and at 90 dB for 10 days via 118 loudspeakers hung from the ceiling throughout the building.

The most noticeable physiological effect was a statistically significant rise in plasma cortisol and blood cholesterol levels compared with preexposure levels. The levels decreased after cessation of the noise. Figure 9.52 shows the data for these two physiological measures. However, the results of this study must be taken as inconclusive in demonstrating any causal relation between the 24-h/day exposure to the intense tonal pulses and any noted physiological or psychological responses. The major reason is that the increase in cholesterol and plasma cortisol levels could well be attributed to the prolonged confinement imposed rather than the tonal pulses. Indeed, except for possibly the first period of exposure to the pulses, there was no consistent pattern of these physiological responses as the intensity level (including the cessation altogether) of the pulses was changed. Even the initial increases plotted in Fig. 9.52 are not necessarily related to the onset of the pulses, as clearly indicated by Cantrell; that is, the first increases plotted could have occurred prior to the onset of the pulses.

It is also obvious that in addition to the psychological aspects of confinement per se, with possibly related physiological stress reactions, the subjects could have been apprehensive about the possible effects of the noise on their hearing. Indeed, subjects exhibited varying amounts of audiometric threshold shifts during the study. In a study made of personnel involved, and some not involved, in aircraft launch operations aboard a U.S. Navy aircraft carrier (Davis, 1958a,b), there was a consistent tendency for those most exposed to noise to perform less well on a variety of physiological and psychological tests. Psychiatric examination of the men revealed that the men most exposed to noise had somewhat greater feelings of anxiety than the others. This anxiety may be because their jobs are inherently more dangerous or difficult than those of the men less exposed to noise. (Aircraft launch operations occasionally result in injuries and death to launch operators.) This seems borne out by data showing that the men most exposed to the noise did not

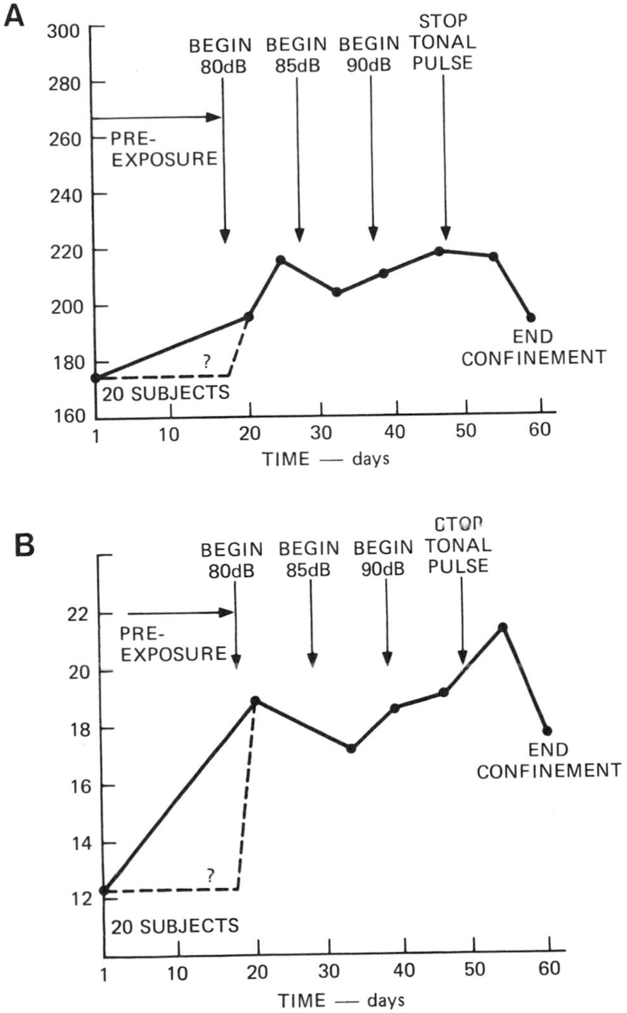

FIGURE 9.52 Mean blood cholesterol levels in milligram-percent (A) and plasma cortisol levels in microgram percent (B) before, during, and after exposure to tonal impulses. (From Cantrell, 1974.)

rate the jet-aircraft noise as more disturbing than did other groups, but did express the most anxiety about their jobs.

Carlestam *et al.* (1973) studied 22 young female IBM operators in their usual work situation. Half of the group was exposed to 6-dB increases in noise of their IBM machines for 4 consecutive days. The noise levels used were 76, 82, 88, and 94 dB_C. The other half was exposed to the same noise levels but in decreasing order (i.e., 94, 88, 82, and 76 dB_C). The normal noise level for the office was 76 dB_C. Each workday started with a 2-h period of rest without noise exposure, followed by exposure to the appropriate noise for three 2-h work periods.

The subjects experienced only minor increases in fatigue and "distress" with increasing noise (see Fig. 9.53). However, the rating differences between those for the highest and lowest noise levels were very small. Adrenaline and noradrenaline excretion levels remained low or moderate (Fig. 9.54), and the changes in these levels were not significant for either control to noise periods or from lowest to highest noise levels. Not even the higher levels of noise seemed to be particularly stressful. Although they indicate that the subjects were familiar with the noise and had positive attitudes about their jobs and the experiment, Carlestam *et al.* question the general validity that noise at work is necessarily a pathogenic agent. To this might be added the comment that the trend toward increased fatigue and distress scores, although small, with increased noise could be due to some masking effects of the noise on hearing wanted sounds in the work environment or concern about auditory fatigue.

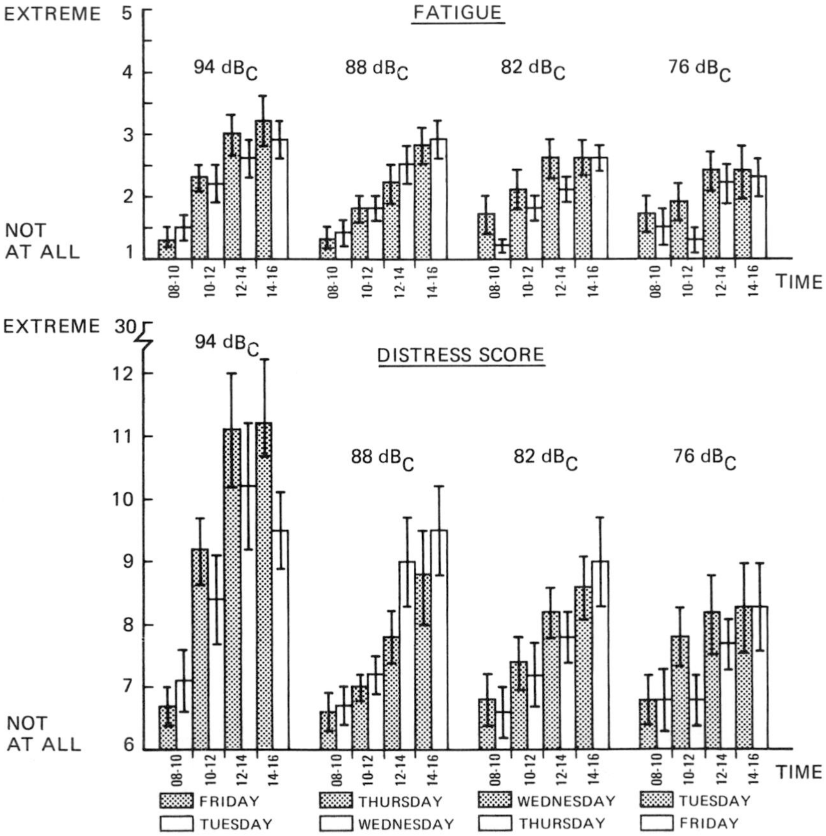

FIGURE 9.53 Self-rated fatigue and "distress" of IBM operators under different noise conditions and during different times of the day. (From Carlestram *et al.*, 1973.)

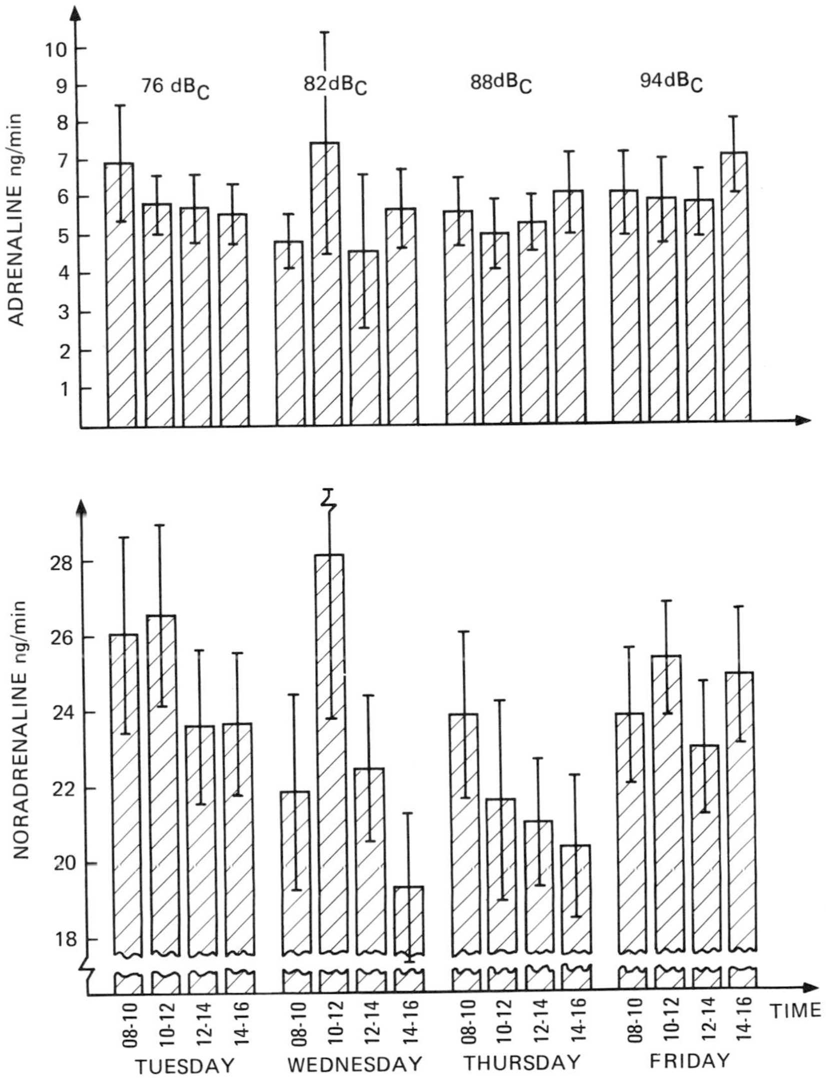

FIGURE 9.54 Urinary excretion of adrenaline and noradrenaline of IBM operators during 4 consecutive days with increasing noise levels. (From Carlestram *et al.*, 1973.)

HEALTH-RELATED EFFECTS IN RESIDENTIAL COMMUNITIES

Introduction

Most laboratory experiments with humans and animals show, except for the reflex alerting response, habituation of significant nonauditory-system stress responses to repeated, meaningless noises. And it is surmised that this alerting response is insufficient in magnitude to be considered as physiologically stressful. For these reasons, it might seem unlikely that adverse effects on health would occur because of noise in the living environment.

There is, however, no habituation possible to the masking by noise of wanted signals, nor, under all conditions, arousal from rest and sleep by noise of sufficient intensity. Also, habituation does not necessarily occur for the annoyance experienced from conern about the effect of noise on health, the "quality" of the environment and property values, fear of accidents from the noisemaker (e.g., aircraft flying overhead), and other meaning-related aspects of some noises. If anything, as will be noted in Chapter 10, some accumulative annoyance with repetitions of some noises may occur.

For these reasons, the degree of psychological accommodation to the effects of noise in residential environments can realistically be measured only by empirical data of the experiences of people in real-life. The results of studies descriptive of the possible liabilities to mental and physical health of individuals as related to environmental noise are presented below. Reviews of research on noise as a possible factor in mental health, physical health, and behavior are also found in papers by McLean and Tarnopolsky (1977) and by Cohen and Weinstein (1981).

AIRCRAFT NOISE AND ADMISSION RATES TO PSYCHIATRIC HOSPITALS

Meecham and Smith (1977) compared admissions to mental hospitals in two groups that were matched to a considerable degree socioeconomically. One group, the control group, came from an area where aircraft noise was considerably below 90 dB_A, and the other group, the maximum-noise-area group, came from an area near Los Angeles International Airport where the aircraft noise reached levels above 90 dB_A, with an average L_{dn} (day–night level; also expressed DNL) of 75 dB_A (L_{dn} and related units will be discussed in Chapter 10; L_{dn} is equivalent to $L_{Aeq,24h}$, with the noise present in the hours of 10 PM–7 AM weighted by an additional 10-dB, "nighttime" penalty).

A 29% increase in mental hospital admissions was found for the maximum-noise-area group over the control group. The chi-square (χ^2) test of statistical significance is at the 90% level of confidence. These findings are in good agreement with those reported by Abey-Wickrama *et al.* (1969) and Herridge and Chir (1972) for similar-type data from a British psychiatric hospital, although Chowns (1970) questioned the methodology of these last two studies.

Gattoni and Tarnopolsky (1973) examined the admission rates to the same psychiatric hospital (Springfield Hospital) from the same areas near Heathrow Airport as analyzed by Abey-Wickrama *et al.* and by Herridge and Chir but for a later period of time (1966–1968 vs. 1970–1972). Gattoni and Tarnopolsky defined the noise areas somewhat differently and also removed some data (those for "old people's care homes") from the high-noise areas that were included in the earlier studies. Table 9.12 shows how the original

TABLE 9.12 Comparison of Two Studies of Admissions to Springfield Hospital

Category	Admission	Abey-Wickrama *et al.* 1959 (1966 to 1968)[a]		Gattoni and Tarnopolsky, 1973 (1970 to 1972)[a]	
		Area with higher admission rates	Statistical significance	Area with higher admission rates	Statistical significance
Both sexes	All	Maximum-noise area	.005	None	Not significant
Both sexes	First	Maximum-noise area	.01	High-noise zone	↓
Females	All	Maximum-noise area	.025	None	
Females	First	Maximum-noise area	.10	High-noise zone	
Males	All	None	Not significant	High-noise zone	
Males	First	None	Not significant	High-noise zone	
Females, age >45	All	Maximum-noise area	.005	None	
Females, age >45	First	Maximum-noise area	.0005	High-noise zone	
Females, married	All	None	Not significant	None	
Females, married	First	None	Not significant	High-noise zone	
Females, other	All	Maximum-noise area	.01	High-noise zone	
Females, other	First	Maximum-noise area	.01	High-noise zone	
Females, Neurotic	All	Maximum-noise area	.05	None	
Females, neurotic	First	None	Not significant	None	
Females, organic	All	Maximum-noise area	.005	High-noise zone	
Females, organic	First	Maximum-noise area	.0005	High-noise zone	↓

[a] Years of admissions to hospitals studied.

analysis of data from the Springfield Hospital compares with that for the 1970–1972 period. It is seen in Table 9.12 that the 1966–1968 data indicate a number of statistically significant greater admission rates for the maximum noise as compared with the lower-noise areas. However, the 1970–1972 data show no statistically significant differences in this regard, but they do show a similar trend in that for 9 of the 16 category comparisons made, the rate of admissions from the high-noise zone was at least 10% greater than that from the lower-noise area.

Taking another time period (January 11, 1969 to December 31, 1972), the same population source (people near Heathrow Airport), and data from several psychiatric hospitals (including Springfield), Jenkins *et al.* (1979, 1981) and Hand *et al.* (1980) made further analyses of hospital admission data for residential areas that were exposed to levels of aircraft noise of L_{dn} <62, L_{dn} 62–74, and L_{dn} >74 dB_A. Figure 9.55 shows that the results obtained are somewhat ambiguous—progressively greater hospital admission rates were generally found for the higher noise zones than for the lower noise zones at Holloway and St. Bernard's Hospitals, but for Springfield Hospital there was a decrease in admissions as a function of noise zone.

This difference between the data for Springfield Hospital and the two other hospitals is as perplexing as the fact that the low-noise-exposure data for Springfield Hospital are so different from those found for the same hospital in the earlier studies, as shown in Table 9.13. Abey-Wickrama *et al.* found a significant difference between admission rates for low-noise and high-noise areas; more hospital admissions were found in high-noise areas. Gattoni and Tarnopolsky's data had a similar, but nonsignificant, trend. Because they found a highly significant difference in the opposite direction, Jenkins *et al.* 1979, 1981 suggest that trends of a positive relationship between psychiatric

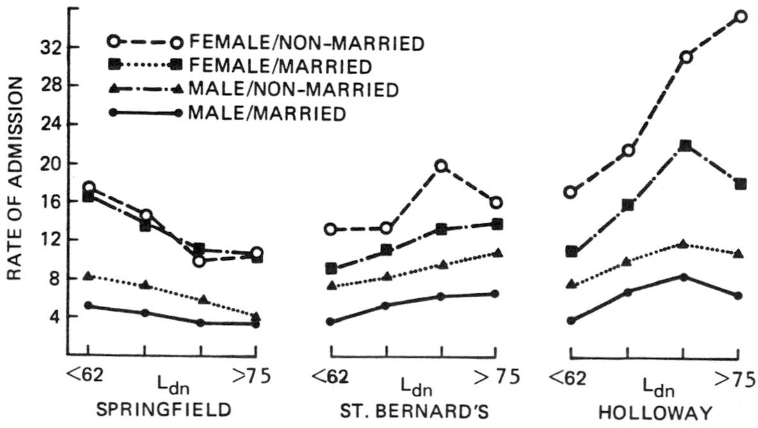

FIGURE 9.55 Age-standardized psychiatric hospital admission rates per 1000 people over a four-year period as a function of noise, sex, and marital status. (From Jenkins *et al.*, 1979.)

TABLE 9.13 Comparison of Springfield Hospital Admission Rates (Rates per 1000 Persons; All Categories of Admissions)

Study	Admission rate of high-noise area	Admission rate for low-noise area
Abey-Wickrama *et al.* (1969) (1966 to 1968)	4.537‡	[c]3.471
Gattoni and Tarnopolsky (1973) (1970 to 1972)	3.462§	3.210§
Jenkins *et al.* (1981) (1969 to 1973)	2.8#	5.3#

‡ Statistically significant difference supporting hypothesis that aircraft noise increases hospital admissions.

§ Difference not statistically significant.

Statistically significant difference supporting hypothesis that aircraft noise decreases hospital admissions. The Jenkins *et al.* (1981) study is for a 4-year period, and the rates they report must be divided by a factor of 2 in order to be roughly compared with the earlier 2-year studies.

hospital admission rates and exposure to aircraft noise found in the other analyses may be due to chance. However, as described below, reanalysis of these, and related socioeconomic data (from 1971 census: percentage of one-person households, percentage of people unemployed, and general level of affluence), indicate that unusual circumstances are associated with data from the Springfield Hospital analyzed by Jenkins *et al.*, 1981

Reanalysis of British Data

The final database developed by Jenkins *et al.* represents psychiatric hospital admission rate and socioeconomic data for nearly one million people exposed to known amounts of aircraft noise (L_{dn} <62, L_{dn} 62–74, and L_{dn} $_{>74 \text{ dBA}}$). As such, it is outstandingly well founded for the assessment of hypothesis of a possible relation between physiological-psychological stress requiring hospitalization and psychological stress from exposure to aircraft noise. For this reason a multiple-correlation analysis was undertaken to examine, as had not been previously applied to these data, the relative contribution of the aircraft noise and socioeconomic variables to hospital admission rates (Kryter, 1985, 1990). Some of the results are shown in Fig. 9.56 and Table 9.14.

It is seen in Table 9.14 that multiple-correlation coefficients R_c (R corrected for small number of areas) are quite large for the different population groups, ranging from 0.978 to 0.999 for the combined groups; see lower section of the table. [In Table 9.14: Im., immigrant; Un., unemployed; Aff, affluent [average of: %home owners + %Exclusive Toilet + %High occupational class − %renters); 1 PH = 1 person household.] It is also seen that the contribution, independently of the other variables, the beta weights, of immigrant status, unemployed, and aircraft noise are generally statistically significant except for not married females and males over 45 years of age.

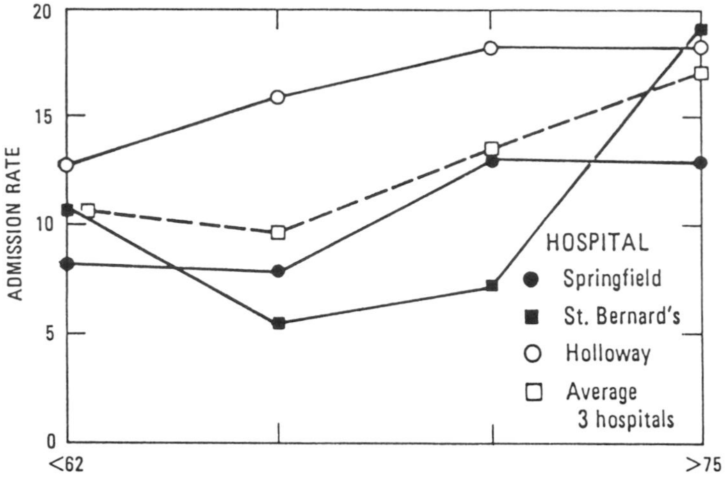

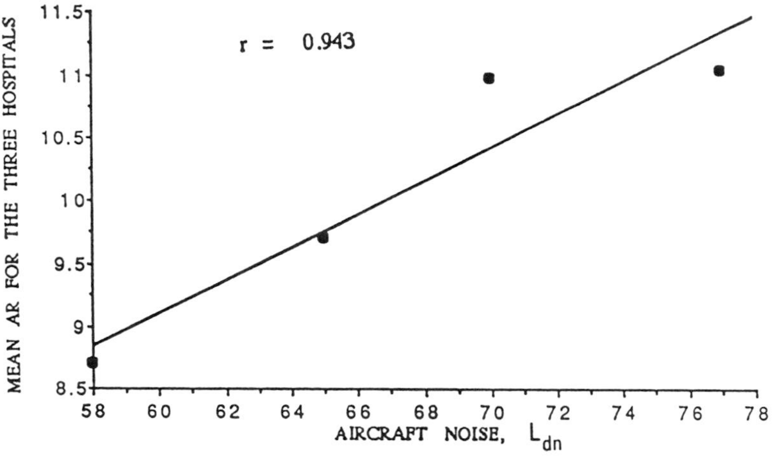

FIGURE 9.56 Regression line and coefficient of correlation between aircraft-noise-exposure level DNL (L_{dn}) and average admission rates (AR) for all three psychiatric hospitals. (From Kryter, 1990.)

The beta weights for affluency, as measured, and 1 person household were generally not significant.

The graph of Fig. 9.56 indicates that the admission rates for the average of these three psychiatric hospitals starts to increase as L_{dn} exceeds L_{dn} about 55, and that by L_{dn} 75 an increase of about two people per 1000 has occurred over a four-year period. Table 9.15 gives the approximate numbers of adult persons living, near London airports 1969–1972, in aircraft noise of L_{dn} <55 to 65 and 65 to 75, the annual rate of admissions to psychiatric hospitals from those residential areas, and the total increase to be expected annually in number of admissions per million people thus exposed. On the basis of these data and analysis, it could be concluded that the aircraft noise apparently increased the number of such hospitalizations by about 160 annually or about 0.7%.

It was further found that the Springfield Hospital areas that provided ambiguous results in the Jenkins *et al.* analysis of their data contained abnormal distributions of immigrants—some 16.9% of the population was in the low noise area, and 33.5% was in the high-noise area. The immigrants were more evenly distributed in the different noise areas of the catchment basins of the other hospitals. The new analysis revealed that a negative correlation of −0.65 for all persons, existed between immigrant status and hospital admission rates. This could, of course, explain the ambiguous results for these Springfield Hospital areas reported by Jenkins *et al.*, 1981, higher admission rates in lower-noise areas.

A possible reason for this negative correlation is that immigrants are screened for health disorders and employment or living arrangements prior to entry into the country, and, as a result, may have had somewhat lower group hospital admission rate. Further, it is conjectured that in the 1969–1973 period, there may have been an influx of immigrants into certain areas near London that provided somewhat different population distributions in this regard than were involved in the earlier analyses cited above of admissions to these psychiatric hospitals.

Caerphilly Study

The preliminary findings of a prospective study of several thousand men in South Wales, U.K. indicate that aircraft and street traffic noise may cause acute psychological symptoms and increased tranquilizer use, but not increased rates of psychiatric morbidity (Stansfeld *et al.* 1993). Much of the noise was from street traffic, and exposure levels were for the front facades of houses.

For two reasons, these results are consistent with the findings just discussed of an increase in psychiatric morbidity, as measured by hospitalization, as a function of exposure level to aircraft noise:

1. As seen in Fig. 9.56, the annualized rate with essentially minimum aircraft noise exposure, DNL, or L_{dn}, of ~58, the rate is about 2.3 persons per 1000 per year (8.9/4); with DNL 68, the rate is about 2.5 (10.1/4), an increase of but 0.2 person per year per 1000 at risk from exposure to aircraft noise at an average level of L_{dn} 68. Accordingly, it will presumably require a much larger sample-population than in the Caerphilly study to detect an increase due to environmental noise in a severe disease such as psychiatric morbidity. (It is believed the data represented in Fig. 10.56 are successful in this regard because they are for an at-risk database of approximately one million persons exposed to known levels of aircraft noise.)

TABLE 9.14 Multiple (R, R_c) Coefficients of Correlation, and β-Weight t Ratios between Admission Rates to Psychiatric Hospitals and Socioeconomic and Aircraft Noise Conditions in the 8 Residential Areas of Springfield and St. Bernard's Hospitals Only, and the 12 Areas for All 3 Hospitals (from Kryter, 1990)

				Socioeconomic and aircraft noise variables; β-weight t-ratios				
	$R_1 \cdots R_m$	$R_{c_1} \cdots R_m$	∂R_c	log% Im.	log% Un.	L_{dn}	log% Aff.	log% 1 PH
Females, married								
(1) Under 45 yr old								
8 areas	0·997	0·989**	0·015	−14·554**	6·196**	7·06**	−6·701**	−1·775
12 areas	0·919	0·869*	0·092	−4·933**	2·430*	2·780*	−1·607	−0·410
(2) Over 45 yr old								
8 areas	0·976	0·913*	0·318	−4·654**	2·261*	3·407*	−1·698	−1·17
12 areas	0·964	0·943**	0·042	−7·234**	3·931**	5·394**	−1·468	−0·131
Females, not married								
(3) Under 45 yr old								
8 areas	0·997	0·989**	0·015	−12·908**	5·095**	9·980**	−8·016**	−0·705
12 areas	0·829	0·713	0·186	−2·516*	2·365*	1·231	−0·741	0·505
(4) Over 45 yr old								
8 areas	0·840	0·560	0·485	−0·357	0·611	0·569	−1·057	−1·065
12 areas	0·789	0·638	0·224	−2·794*	0·802	1·461	0·130	0·658
Males, married								
(5) Under 45 yr old								
8 areas	0·998	0·993**	0·010	−12·099**	8·125**	14·997**	−11·884**	−5·312**
12 areas	0·915	0·863*	0·097	−3·678**	3·813**	3·218**	−0·915	0·533
(6) Over 45 yr old								
8 areas	0·986	0·950**	0·069	−4·964**	3·084*	5·044**	−2·975*	−2·240
12 areas	0·971	0·954**	0·034	−7·442**	5·400**	5·409**	−1·278	−5·550**

Males, not married								
(7) Under 45 yr old								
8 areas	0·988	0·957**	0·059	−[illegible]·884**	1·603	5·559**	−4·637**	−0·736
12 areas	0·966	0·946**	0·040	−[illegible]·718**	3·437**	5·279**	−2·730*	1·404
(8) Over 45 yr old								
8 areas	0·746	0·000	1·000	[illegible]·403	−0·240	−0·028	−0·678	−0·141
12 areas	0·699	0·443	0·304	−[illegible]·136	1·059	0·440	0·431	0·813
Combined population groups								
(9) All under 45 yr								
8 areas	0·999	0·996**	0·005	−1[illegible]·339**	[illegible]9·345**	51·814**	−47·975**	−6·812**
12 areas	0·932	0·891*	0·078	−[illegible]·743**	3·419**	2·090	−1·639	0·779
(10) All over 45 yr								
8 areas	0·994	0·979**	0·030	−[illegible]·820**	5·082**	7·642**	−5·912**	3·532**
12 areas	0·894	0·827	0·119	−[illegible]·259**	1·703	2·622*	−0·055	0·957
(11) All females								
8 areas	0·993	0·975**	0·035	−[illegible]·06**	3·797**	5·664**	−5·344**	2·153
12 areas	0·935	0·896*	0·075	−[illegible]·902**	2·468*	2·982*	−0·633	1·077
(12) All males								
8 areas	0·995	0·982**	0·025	−[illegible]·762**	2·519*	5·472**	−4·581**	−1·094
12 areas	0·936	0·897*	0·074	−[illegible]·141**	3·418**	3·539**	−0·893	1·339
(13) All married								
8 areas	0·978	0·921**	0·108	−[illegible]·734**	1·720	3·512**	−3·511**	−1·112
12 areas	0·979	0·967**	0·025	−[illegible]·749**	6·097**	5·311**	−2·222*	−0.169
(14) All not married								
8 areas	0·998	0·993**	0·010	−[illegible]·971**	8·091**	11·755**	−8·207**	−4·106**
12 areas	0·902	0·841	0·111	−[illegible]·534**	1·891	2·496*	−0·135	1·308
(15) All persons								
8 areas	0·999	0·996**	0·005	−[illegible].207**	10·467**	17·323**	−14·964**	−4·534**
12 areas	0·851	0·922**	0·057	−[illegible]·605**	3·201**	3·697**	−0·767	1·434

$R_c = \sqrt{1 - \{(1 - R^2)[(N - 1)/(N - M)]\}}$, where N = number of areas and m = number of variables, 6 $\sigma R_c = 1 - R_c^2/\sqrt{N - m}$; R_c and t significant at ·05. level, at **0·01 level of statistical probability of error

TABLE 9.15 Estimated Number Per Year of Admissions to Psychiatric Hospitals from One Million People Exposed to Aircraft Noise L_{dn} ~58–78 dB. See Fig. 9.56

L_{dn}	No at Risk	Rate/1000/yr	Increase	No/Yr
<56	X,000,000	2.23		
55–65	~800,000	2.33	0.1	80
65–78	~200,000	2.63	0.4	80
			Total/Yr	160

Numbers at risk based on Table 1, Kryter, 1990.

2. As will be discussed in detail in Chapter 10, the effect of street traffic noise on people in their homes is, effectively, ~10 dB less than that of aircraft noise when the levels are expressed as those present at the front facade of houses in residential areas. The primary reason is because of acoustical-barrier effects afforded the street, but not aircraft, noise to people inside their homes. This factor, of course, significantly diminishes the adverse effects of street, compared to aircraft, noise of supposedly comparable L_{dn} values.

Annoyance and Mental Health

Distinctions can be made between sensitivity to exposures to noise and annoyance from noise as measured in attitude surveys of what bothers people in everyday living. For example, the noise occurrences that interfere with speech communication are likely to do so more frequently and cause greater feelings of annoyance in people who engage most actively in such behavior. Thus, although noise annoyance can perhaps be a burden that creates problems for highly sensitive people, it appears that it creates the most annoyance for persons engaging in normal behavior; that is, it occurs most often in people engaged in normal activities (Broadbent, 1972).

The role of aircraft noise as a contributor to annoyance in people with psychiatric illnesses, and the role of annoyance as a possible contributor to psychiatric illness, were studied in a survey of conducted in aircraft-noise-impacted areas near London Heathrow Airport (Tarnopolsky *et al.*, 1980). In this study psychiatric illness was identified by means of a screening questionnaire, not by admission to a psychiatric hospital. The principal results are shown in Fig. 9.57.

It is shown in Fig. 9.57A that a greater percentage of psychiatrically morbid people suffered the ''highest annoyance'' than suffered any other degree of annoyance, which would seem to suggest that the aircraft noise could contribute to an increased degree of suffering in those who are psychiatrically ill. However, as shown in Fig. 9.57B, there was no general increase in the number of psychiatric cases as a function of the level of aircraft noise

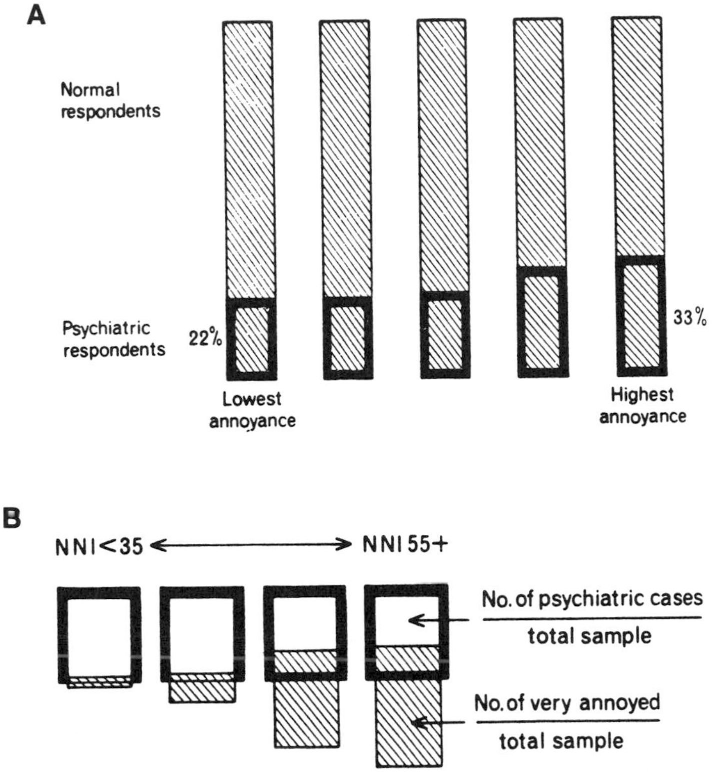

FIGURE 9.57 (A) Proportion of psychiatric cases among persons who report interference with their activities. (B) Relations between noise, psychiatric cases, and extreme annoyance. (From Tarnopolsky *et al.*, 1980.)

exposure. Indeed, the increase in annoyance as the aircraft-noise-exposure level increased occurred predominantly in the normal population. Tarnopolsky *et al.* concluded that most of the people who complain of aircraft noise are psychiatrically normal.

The fact that an average of about 22% of the population was identified as being psychiatrically morbid in each level of aircraft noise exposure would indicate that there were many types of such illnesses revealed by the questionnaire given and that aircraft noise was not a significant cause, if at all, of the total group of illnesses. At the same time, the data, showing an increased degree of annoyance in those psychiatrically ill, would be consistent with the trends in increased psychiatric hospitalization admission rate with increased exposure to aircraft noise.

In summary, the Los Angeles area data, the 1966–1968 and 1970–1972 Springfield Hospital data, and the 1969–1973 Holloway and St. Bernard Hospital data for the London area support, to varying degrees, the hypothesis that intense aircraft noise increases admission rates to psychiatric hospitals.

The 1969–1973 data for the Springfield Hospital indicate an opposite trend, that less aircraft noise increases the hospital admission rate. However, the pattern of admissions to the Springfield Hospital from the "quieter" areas in the 1969–1973 period suggests those particular data were probably biased by a strong population–social (immigrant status) factor. The relatively small size of the populations being studied and levels of noise involved are believed to be insufficient in the Caerphilly study to reveal any psychiatric morbidity due to noise.

OTHER HEALTH DISORDERS ASSOCIATED WITH AIRCRAFT NOISE

If noise can be a cause, direct or indirect, of significant physiological stress, it would seem probable that the effects of some environmental noises would be reflected in more common physical and mental ailments than mental disorders requiring hospitalization. A number of studies have been conducted on that question.

Karagodina *et al.* (1969) conducted a large-scale study of the effects of aircraft noise on, among other things, the physical health of the adult population (over 15 years of age) living near nine formerly Soviet airports. Health statistics (145,000 medical diagnostic records were analyzed) revealed that the populations within about 3.7 statute miles (6 km) had 2–4 times the amount of otorhinolaryngologic diseases (otitis and auricular neuritis), cardiovascular diseases (hypertension and hypotension), nervous diseases (neuritis and neurasthenic states), and gastrointestinal diseases (gastric and duodenal ulcers and gastritis) as those outside that perimeter. These investigators concluded from these, and related laboratory and survey studies, that the maximum permissible exterior peak level of aircraft noise should be set at 85 dB_A during the daytime, and 75 dB_A at night.

The results of an interdisciplinary study of aircraft noise effects in the area of Munich airport were published in 1974 (Fluglarmwirkungen, 1974). As part of that study, 192 men and 200 women were selected from 32 areas in which aircraft noise exposure was measured. These persons were given certain clinical medical tests. It was concluded that there were no major clinical disorders related to the aircraft noise present in the more-or-less healthy population selected, but that there were disorders of sleep and blood pressure reactions to the aircraft noise with an increased risk of hypertension in those more heavily exposed to noise.

Koszarny *et al.* (1981) administered a health questionnaire to 256 residents in an area where the aircraft noise levels exceeded 100 dB_A and to 255 residents in somewhat quieter areas (80–90-dB_A peak noise). No statistically significant differences in complaints about ailments were found in groups of men living in the two areas. However, significantly greater numbers of complaints related to the cardiovascular system, the digestive system, frequency of taking medication for heart problems or headaches, and nervousness were found in women living in the noisier area than in women who lived in the lower-noise-level area. The authors note that the men worked in acoustically unfavorable environments outside their residential area. The results suggest that the health of the women in the noisier area was relatively more adversely affected than the health of the women in the less noisy residential areas, but the health of the men from the two residential areas did not differ because both groups worked in noisy industries and spent relatively less time in their homes than did the women.

Grandjean *et al.* (1976) found a progressive increase in the reported use of tranquilizers and sleeping pills as the exposure level to aircraft noise increased in different neighborhoods (see Table 9.16). The data collected by Grandjean *et al.* that are shown in the table, and other data of theirs discussed later, indicate that the increased use of these sedatives in higher levels of exposure to aircraft noise was due to the interference effects of the noise with sleep and speech communications.

Hiramatsu *et al.* (1993) administered a "health index questionnaire" to 1000 residents living near a large military airbase in Japan. The subjects were random samples of 200 each from aircraft noise areas of approximately L_{dn} 54–58, 59–63, 64–68, 69–73, and ≥74. In addition, a sample of 200 residents living a village not exposed to the aircraft noise were used as a control group. [The aircraft noise exposure was reported as weighted equivalent perceived noise level (WECPNL) = L_{eq}, 7 AM–7 PM + (L_{eq} 7 PM–10 PM + 5) + (L_{eq} 10 PM–7 AM + 10) − 27 = ~L_{dn} − 21.] The questionnaire results indicated that "the residents in the town suffer from psychosomatic effects, especially perceived mental disease, due to the noise exposure of military aircraft and that such responses increase along with the levels of noise exposure." No demographic data were given in the published report of this study.

TABLE 9.16 Effects of Aircraft Noise on Behavioral Reactions [Hours 0600–1800 (6:00 AM–6:00 PM)]

	Percent of people interviewed* responding affirmatively for L_{dn} of						
Behavioral reaction	<47 (223)	47 (485)	55 (460)	63 (1066)	71 (1065)	77 (540)	87 (73)
Use ear protection	2	0.5	2	4	4	7	22
Use tranquilizers + sleeping pills	1	0	2	5	5	10	20
Close windows	2	0.4	13	20	28	46	55
Remain less outdoors	1	0	4	4	11	22	34
Wish to move away	0.4	0	2	9	17	35	33

* Number of people interviewed given in parentheses.

Data from Grandjean *et al.*, 1976.

Cardiovascular Survey

The most substantial body of data concerning a possible relation between exposure to aircraft noise in residential neighborhoods and adverse health effects are those obtained in an integrated program of research studies conducted near the Amsterdam Schiphol Airport in the Netherlands (Knipschild, 1977a,b, 1980; Knipschild and Oudshoorn, 1977). In one of these studies, Knipschild (1977a), about 6000 people were given medical examinations (heart x-rays, ECG, blood pressure, height, and weight) and World Health Organization standard questionnaires for angina pectoris, for medical treatment and drugs for cardiovascular trouble, and for smoking habits. The 6000 people represented about 42% of the people who were invited, by letter from government health agency to participate in the cardiovascular screening study from eight villages near the airport (see Fig. 9.58). All the subjects were screened by the same staff, equipment, and methods.

The main results of this community cardiovascular screening survey are shown in Table 9.17 and Fig. 9.59. The residents of the villages were requested by letter to participate in the cardiovascular study. Table 9.16 shows that the incidence of medical treatment of heart disease, use of cardiovascular drugs, pathological heart shape, and hypertension were all significantly greater (statistically) in people from the higher-aircraft noise areas than in the lower-aircraft-noise areas. The differences were in the same direction with respect to angina pectoris and pathological ECG but were not statistically significant. The most significant statistical difference is that for hypertension (systolic/diastolic blood pressure >175/100 mmHg, antihypertensive drugs regimen, or both). As shown in Fig. 9.59 and the table, the prevalence rate increased from about 10% to 15%. Analyses of the data for age, sex, smoking habits, weight of the subjects, and the size of the villages showed that these variables do not account for the differences.

Rate of Physician Contact for Health Disorders

A second study by Knipschild (1977b) also demonstrated an apparent increase in health problems between the noisier as compared to the quieter areas (see Fig. 9.60). In this study, the records of general medical practitioners serving local villages were examined to determine the physician contacts that had been made for health problems during a 1-week period (March 13–18, 1974). The location of the villages studied are shown in Fig. 9.58B. The respective number of general-practice physicians and the size of the populations at risk were 9 and 17,500 in area C, 4 and 5650 in area EC, and 6 and 12,000 in area E.

The main results are shown in Table 9.18. The data in Table 9.18 are consistent with the cardiovascular survey data in Table 9.17 in that the incidence of hypertension is less in the lower-L_{dn} areas than in the higher-

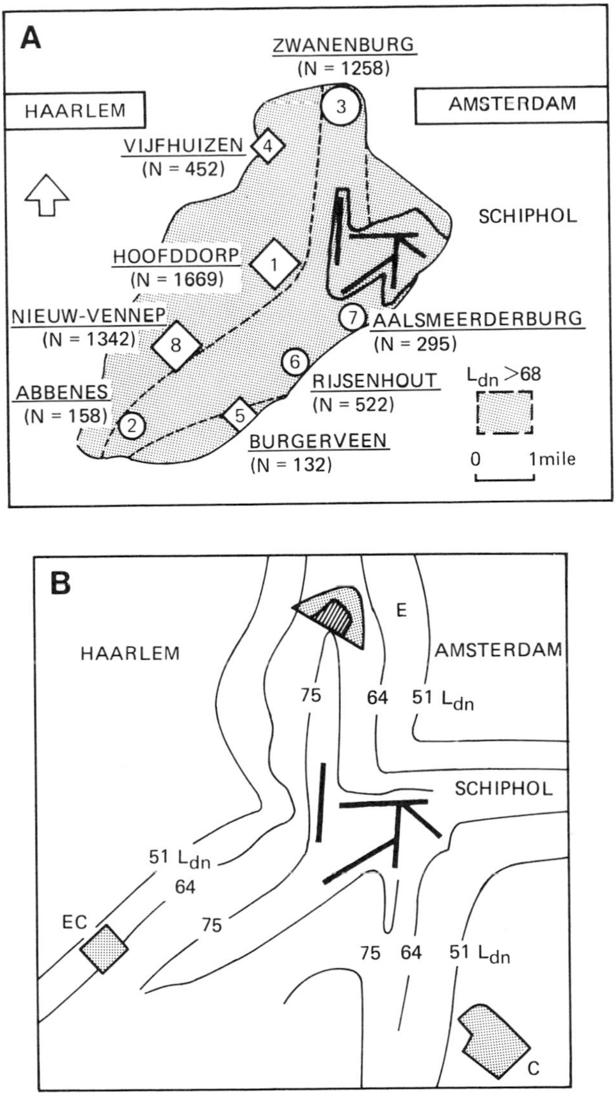

FIGURE 9.58 Location of villages and areas near Schiphol Airport used for surveys. (A) Villages in cardiovascular survey and (B) general-practice survey. (From Knipschild, 1977a.)

L_{dn} areas. For the purpose of further analysis, the four disorders identified in Table 9.18 as psychological problems, psychosomatic problems, cardiovascular disease, and hypertension are grouped together as representing the disorders most likely due to stress from, among other things, exposure to aircraft noise. The remaining physician contacts are, for the present discussion, assumed to be more likely due to non-stress-related causes. Table 9.19

TABLE 9.17 Main Results of the Community Cardiovascular Survey

Cardiovascular conditions	Participants,* %, affected by L_{dn}, dB_A, of <62.5 (3595)	>62.5 (2233)	Fisher's test for significance
Angina pectoris	2.8	3.0	Not significant
Medical treatment of heart disease	1.8	2.4	.04
Use of cardiovascular drugs	5.6	7.4	.003
Pathological ECG	4.5	5.0	Not significant
Pathological heart shape	1.6	2.4	.01
Hypertension†	10.1	15.2	<.001

* Number of participants given in parentheses.

† Blood pressure >175/100 mmHg or use of antihypertensive drugs or both.

Data from Knipschild, 1980.

shows that as the noise level increases (e.g., L_{dn} <60 vs. L_{dn} 60–65), there is an increase in the percent of physician contacts for the non-stress-related health disorders of 36%, 6%, and 44%. Accordingly, there is some indication that the people living in L_{dn} >60 suffer from more health disorders in general than do people in L_{dn} <60.

Table 9.18 also shows that there are greater increases in stress-related disorders than in non-stress-related disorders as noise levels increase (44%,

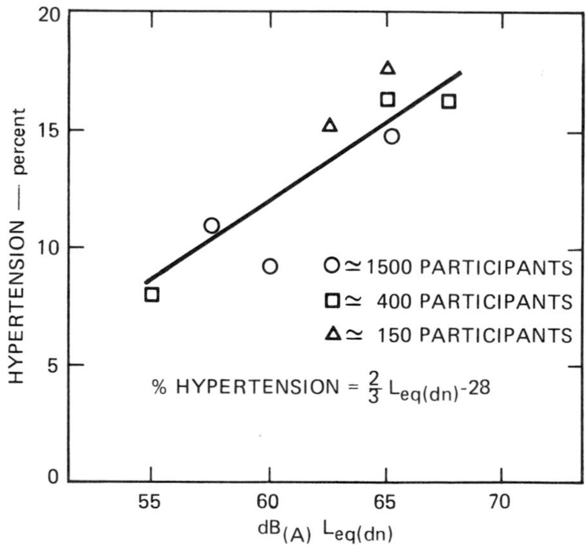

FIGURE 9.59 Aircraft noise and the prevalence rate of hypertension. (From Knipschild, 1977b.)

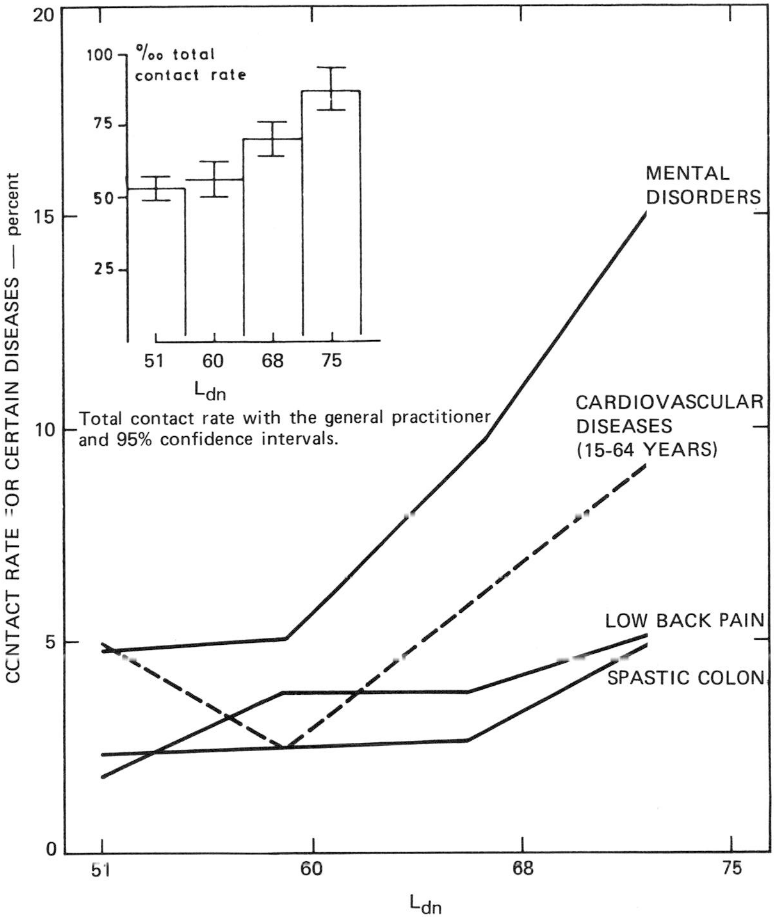

FIGURE 9.60 Physician contact rate for certain diseases in areas with more and less aircraft noise. (From Knipschild, 1977b.)

31%, and 89%, compared with 36%, 6%, and 44%). This greater increase in stress-related health disorders suggests that increasing the level of aircraft noise exposures is at least partially responsible for increases in stress-related disorders. It is, of course, also possible that these findings result from the possibilities that (1) the socioeconomic conditions were significantly worse in the higher- than the lower-L_{dn} and (2) stress-related disorders increase with noise-exposure level at a greater rate than with other types of health disorders because of a stronger correlation between socioeconomic status and stress-related disorders than with other types of health. On the other hand, some of the non-stress-related health disorders were also related to aircraft noise exposure, and Knipschild concluded that the socioeconomic status differences were not large enough to account for such differences.

TABLE 9.18 Main Results of General Practice Survey

Reason for physician contact	Population,* %, contacting physician for L_{dn}, dB_A, <60 (14625)	60–65 (4050)	>65 (3650)	χ^2 test for linear trend
Psychological problems	0.65	1.13	1.75	<0.001
Psychosomatic problems[b]	1.12	1.54	1.69	.001
Cardiovascular disease	.46	.60	.82	.004
Hypertension	.25	.31	.43	.03
Total, stress effects	2.48	3.58	4.69	
Total, contacts	5.71	7.97	9.34	<0.001

* Population at risk given in parentheses.

† Consist of low back pain, spastic colon, stomach complaints, allergic diseases, tinnitus, dizziness, and headache.

Data from Knipschild, 1971.

A total of 43% from the areas least exposed (L_{dn} <62) and 39% from the areas most exposed (L_{dn} >62), to aircraft noise participated in the cardiovascular survey. Possibly fewer did not participate in the most noise-exposed group because they were under a physician's care or on medication for cardiovascular problems (an accepted excuse for not participating). If so, this would also seem to suggest that there were more cardiovascular problems present in the noisier areas, possibly because of the higher level of aircraft noise.

Longitudinal Study of Use of Prescription Drugs

That aircraft noise may be a causal factor in stress-related health disorders is supported by data from a study prosecuted by Knipschild and Oudshoorn

TABLE 9.19 Percentages and Percent Increases of Physician Contact for Stress- and Non-Stress-Related Health Disorders (See Table 9.17 for Basic Data)

Description of parameter	Physician contacts, % for L_{dn}, dB_A, of <60	60–65	>65	Increase in contacts, %, for L_{dn}, dB_A, comparison of— <60 vs. 60–65	60–65 vs. >65	<60 vs. >65
Sum of 4 stress* categories of health disorders	2.48	3.58	4.69	44	31	89
Total contacts, all disorders, minus sum of 4 stress categories	3.23	4.39	4.65	36	6	44

* Stress categories are psychological problems, psychosomatic problems, cardiovascular disease, and hypertension.

(1977). In this study, records of the purchase of certain medicinal drugs for the period 1967–1974 were obtained from pharmacists in village areas C and E shown in Fig. 9.58B. Area C had essentially no exposure to aircraft noise during this period, whereas area E had essentially no aircraft noise until 1969, after which time, because of the opening of a new runway at Schiphol Airport, the noise was of the order of L_{dn} >64. The authors state that there were essentially no changes in age distribution or socioeconomic status within each of the areas during 1967–1974.

Figure 9.61 shows the number of certain drugs obtained per adult per year in the two areas. Clearly, there is a steady increase in the use of most of the drugs after 1967 in area E (the aircraft-noise area), with no systematic change in usage in area C (the no-aircraft-noise area). As shown on Fig. 9.61, coefficients of correlations between years of exposure and prescription drug usage were not statistically significant for any of the drugs in control area C, but were so for all the drugs except sedatives in noise area E. The sedatives showed a decrease in area E after 1972 from a previously increasing trend in their use. In regard to the latter drug, the investigators note that in 1973 nighttime aircraft operations were shifted to the daytime because of a curfew placed on nighttime aircraft operations. This possibly, it is conjectured, then reduced the need for such sedatives to induce sleep during the night.

These data seem to show a causal relation between continuing exposure to aircraft noise and a growth in stress-related health conditions, particularly hypertension requiring medication. This relation cannot be readily attributed to other factors than the aircraft noise in that the health disorders requiring physician prescribed medications steadily increased in more-or-less the same population of people following the onset and continuation of the aircraft noise, whereas in a nearby control population not exposed to aircraft noise, studies over the same period showed no such increase. (The present writer obtained independent opinions from citizens of the Netherlands that one would expect housing and residency in these, and other Netherlands neighborhoods to be relatively stable.)

The Knipschild and Oudshoorn study is unique among studies of the impact of aircraft noise on the health in that it follows the use of physician-prescribed drugs from before and through years of exposure to significant levels of aircraft noise. Further, the study was "blind" in that it was conducted after the fact (retrospectively), so that neither the populations under study nor the pharmacists knew before or during the period of noise exposure that the impact of the aircraft noise on drug usage was to be investigated.

Possible Confounding Factor in Survey and Contact Data

One possible confounding factor in the cardiovascular survey and physician contact studies is that the people from the less noisy areas may be socioeco-

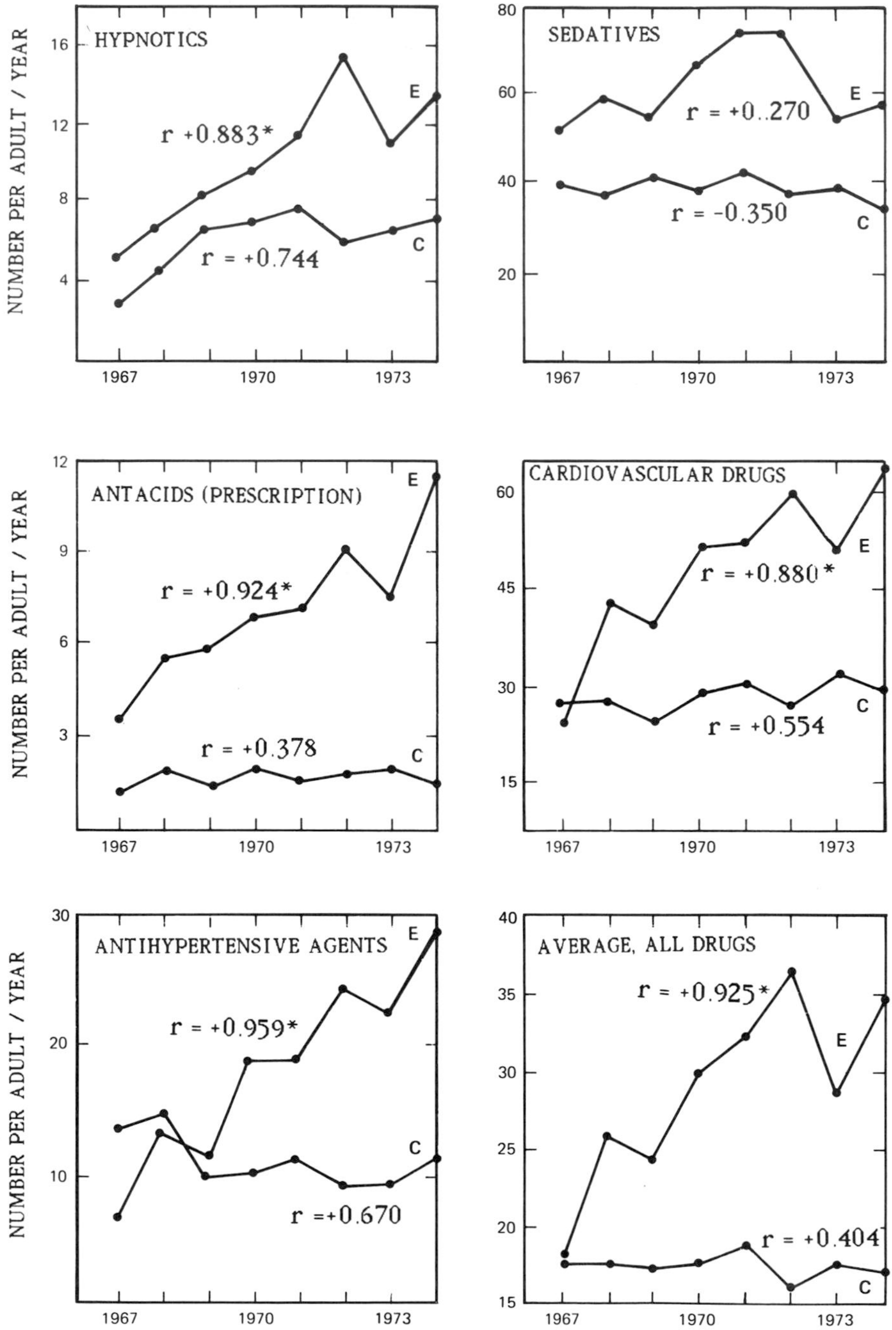

* r coefficients of correlation significant at 99% level of confidence.

FIGURE 9.61 Number of certain drugs per adult per year. Area C—L_{dn} <51: area *E*—L_{dn} <51 (1967–1969) and L_{dn} >64 (1969–1974). (From Knipschild and Oudshoorn, 1977.)

nomically advantaged (and, therefore, perhaps in somewhat better health) than those from the areas with more aircraft noise.

It might be suggested that wealthier (and healthier) people moved from the higher-aircraft-noise area over time and were replaced by generally less wealthy (and less healthy) people. Alternatively, it would seem equally likely that there would be a trend for those most bothered by the noise to move to quieter areas and that this would bias the results in the opposite direction. It can also be argued from some research data that the more affluent and better educated people are more annoyed by aircraft and road traffic noise (and presumably would suffer more stress-related health effects) than would the less affluent and less educated groups of people who more generally live in noise-blighted areas. For example, Ko and Wong (1980) concluded that people with higher education, higher income level, and managerial jobs are more annoyed by road traffic noise. Bradley and Jonah (1979) also found a similar socioeconomic influence on annoyance from traffic noise.

Knipschild (1977a,b; 1980) was of the opinion that overall, although it is arguable, the difference in socioeconomic conditions was not sufficient to explain the differences in health disorders found between the different groups of people. In response to a request of the present writer (September 23, 1983), Dr. Paul Knipschild obtained and furnished to the present writer, some socioeconomic information about the populations of interest collected by Netherlands' government service agencies. The data, as analyzed, are shown in Table 9.20.

In Table 9.20 it is seen that the percentage of one-person households was essentially the same for the higher-noise and lower-noise areas, 10.6% and 10.8%, respectively. The percentage of affluence was about 36% for the higher-noise areas and 23% for the lower, suggesting that, as measured, affluency was negatively related to these health disorders, and does not support a hypothesis that lack of affluence rather than exposure to the higher levels of aircraft noise are responsible for an increase in health disorders. However, the meaning of the affluence data is not clear.

As had been done in the British psychiatric hospital admission rate analysis, *affluence,* for calculation of percent of people affluent in a given area, was defined as the end product of: (% house owners) + (% high occupational class) − (% renting government housing) − (% with no indoor toilet). How to scale the relative value of the different variables, as indicators of some socioeconomic status that is related to susceptibility to health disorders, is unknown. Intuitively, home ownership and high occupational status would seem to be in opposition, in this regard, to renting of government supported housing and with no indoor toilet. In any event, the findings for "one-person household" and "affluence" as variables, as measured, were also found to be not significantly associated with psychiatric health disorders (see Table 9.14).

TABLE 9.20 Socioeconomic and Aircraft Noise Data for Cardiovascular, Physician Contact, and Drug Studies

		Groups*					
Area	L_{dn}	(1)	(2)	(3)	(4)	(5)	(6)
		Cardiovascular Survey, Knipschild (1977a)					
Low-noise	55–65, average 60	33.4	21.5	30.8	0.9	10	23.2
High-noise	60–75, average 68	41.6	16.1	22.8	0.8	10.6	34.1
		Physician Contact Study, Knipschild (1977b)					
Ulthoorn	<55	35.5	N/A†	54.3	0.0	11.3	—
Nieuw-Vernep	60–65, average 63	27.4	21.0	32.6	1.1	6.9	23.1
Zwanenburg	60–75, average 68	40.1	16.1	16.1	0.4	11.2	39.7
		Prescription Drugs, Knipschild and Oudschoorn (1977)					
C. (Ulthoorn)	<55	35.5	N/A	54.3	0.0	11.3	—
E. (high-noise)	60–75, average 68	41.6	16.1	22.8	0.8	10.6	34.7

* *Columns:* (1) % house owners; (2) % high occupational class; (3) % renting government housing; (4) % with no indoor toilet; (5) % one-person households; (6) % affluent. % affluent = Σ (% home owners) + (% high occupational class) − (% renting government housing) − (% with no indoor toilet).

† Data not available.

Mortality and Birth-Defect Rates

Meecham and Shaw (1979) examined mortality rates in aircraft noise-impacted areas versus quiet areas in Los Angeles. They reported greater death rates due to cirrhosis of the liver and strokes in the noisier areas than in the quieter areas. However, a reanalysis by Frerichs *et al.* (1980) of the same data, but taking into account some differences between the two areas with respect to age, race, and sex of the people involved, showed no such differences in mortality rates. Meecham and Shaw (1980) and Frerichs and Coulson (1980) published additional, inconclusive data and comments on this question.

A seemingly startling finding was that birth defects were more prevalent in infants born to women from neighborhoods with high levels of aircraft noise than in infants born to women from areas with lower levels of noise in Los Angeles (Jones and Tauscher, 1978). Jones (1980) suggests that the indirect effects of the noise (interference with communication, sleep, etc.) causes women to be psychologically stressed, resulting in more than normal use of drugs, alcohol, and so forth. However, the small absolute numbers of infants with nongenetically determined birth defects born to women from areas with known levels of noise exposure makes this finding of questionable value (Jones and Tauscher were dealing with tens of cases). Bader points out the variability among hospitals with respect to birth defects is so large that the comparisons made by Jones and Tauscher are not statistically meaningful. In addition, Edmonds *et al.* found no differences in birth defects among children from areas in Atlanta having differing levels of aircraft noise exposure.

Street Traffic Noise

It is shown in Chapter 10 that for a given level of L_{dn}, aircraft noise causes greater annoyance than does street traffic noise (by a factor of ~10 dB). The basis for this difference, as will be discussed, is to a significant extent purely acoustical—when both noises are measured as having equal outdoor levels of L_{dn}, the aircraft noise in the house is physically ~10 dB, on the average, more intense than is street traffic noise in the inside and backyard living areas. There are some additional adverse factors associated with aircraft, as compared with street traffic noise, as will also be discussed in Chapter 10.

Consistent with this 10-dB differential in favor of street traffic noise, is the result of a study by Knipschild and Salle (1979). It was found in that study that women living in areas with high levels of street noise did not have significantly more cardiovascular disorders than did women living in quieter neighborhoods. Also, Mroz *et al.* (1978) reported that a survey of 1901 Warsaw residents found that about one-third were annoyed to some degree because of street traffic noise but that there were no obvious health-related effects. [As noted previously, Koszarny *et al.* (1981) found women living in Warsaw in high-aircraft-noise areas suffered more health disorders than did women living in less noisy areas.]

As discussed earlier Stansfeld *et al.* (1993) related measures, obtained from questionnaires, of psychiatric disorder and noise sensitivity to the levels of street traffic noise to which 2398 men in the small town of Caerphilly, South Wales, U.K. were exposed. Babisch *et al.* (1993) related level of road traffic noise with incidence of heart disease in the British towns of Caerphilly and Bristol and Berlin, Germany. The relative risks of the prevalence of heart disease at the beginning of the study and 3 and 5 years later, for Berlin and the British towns, showed slight, statistically insignificant, differences in shifts in risks toward heart disease for men in the highest daytime road traffic noise levels as compared to men in the lowest levels.

Lercher and Kofler (1993) obtained, by questionnaires, sociodemographic, medical, noise-related behavior, and annoyance information from 1989 citizens living along major transit-traffic road in the Austrian part of the Alps. The noise ranged from $L_{Aeq,24h}$ of 40–70. Regression analysis showed that neither noise levels nor annoyance ratings were associated with blood pressure. A significant link between lower cholesterol levels and closing windows at night was found, but there was no relation of cholesterol level and noise or noise annoyance.

In brief, it would appear that street traffic noise in residential areas is generally not sufficiently intense to be associated with psychiatric or cardiovascular disorders in adults, but aircraft noise can be. As mentioned previously, this is consistent with attitude surveys of annoyance from these two kinds of environmental noise. This is not to say, of course, that street traffic noise cannot—indeed it probably does—cause problems similar to those associated with aircraft noise when sufficiently intense. As will be shown in Chapter 10, it can be a major source of annoyance and disturbance in communities.

Health in Children

Karagodina *et al.* (1969) reported the results of a clinical examination of school children 9–13 years old carried out in 1965 and 1967 in settlements adjacent to Moscow airports and in a control settlement remote from the airport. It was found that those children living near the airports had functional cardiovascular-system and nervous-system changes consisting of increased fatigue, blood pressure abnormalities, higher pulse lability, and cardiac insufficiency (revealed by functional loads and autonomic vascular changes).

Figure 9.62 shows blood pressure levels in high-school children exposed in the classroom to intruding street traffic noise of different intensities. Figure 9.63 shows blood pressure for students in elementary school in Los Angeles that were matched socioeconomically but differed in that three of the schools were in areas impacted by aircraft noise (peak levels of 95 dB_A) and three were in quiet neighborhoods. It is seen in both figures that the students in the higher levels of noise had elevated diastolic and systolic blood pressures compared with the students in quieter areas.

S. Cohen *et al.* (1980) suggested that children are possibly somewhat more susceptible to increased blood pressure from environmental noise than adults. However, tests made 1 year later, Cohen *et al.* (1981b), revealed that the students then in the noisier schools had blood pressure levels similar to those in the quieter schools. The reason was attributed to adaptation, but it appears that the students with higher blood pressure had moved from the area. The fact that those who remained in, or were newcomers to, the higher-noise school did not develop higher blood pressure from that year's exposure to the higher noise, raises the question as to whether the conclusions from the original study were due to chance subject selection rather than the noise. The investigators found no difference in height/weight ratios (a supposed indirect measure of health) between the students from the quiet and from the noisy areas.

Cohen *et al.* (1981b) have reviewed their own findings and those of other investigators concerned with cardiovascular and behavioral effects of community noise. The apparent deleterious effects of aircraft noise in areas

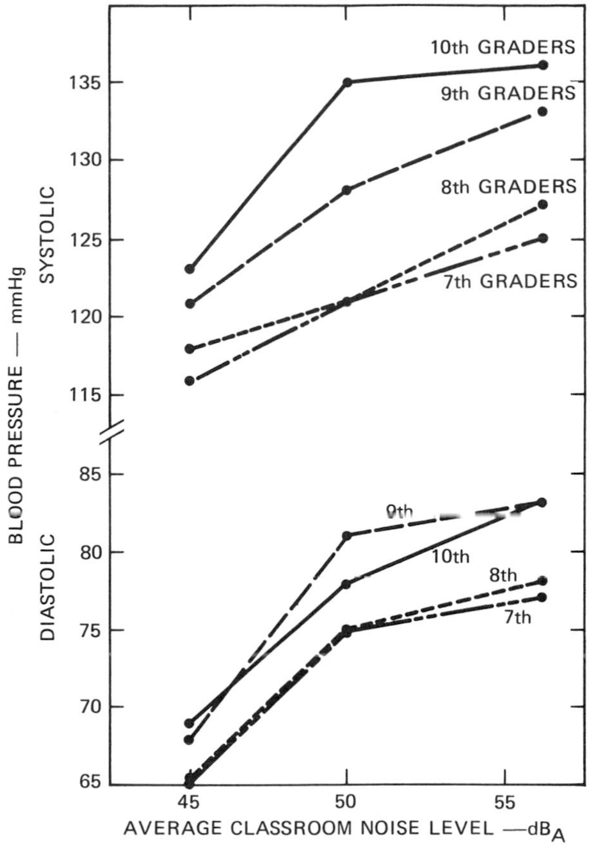

FIGURE 9.62 Blood pressure of students as a function of noise level of intruding street traffic noise. (From Karsdorf and Klappach, 1968.)

around schools and around the home on learning achievement in the school are discussed in Chapter 10.

Fetal and Pediatric Growth

Ando and Hattori (1974) and Knipschild *et al.* (1981) found that infants born to women living in areas exposed to intense aircraft noise had lower average weights at birth than did infants born to women living in quiet neighborhoods. Ando and Hattori also found that aircraft noise increased the number of babies with low birth weights (see Fig. 9.64). In a later study, Ando and Hattori (1977b) found human placental lactogen (HPL) to be lower, which reduces nutrition of the fetus, in the serum of expectant mothers to a greater extent in areas of high aircraft noise than in areas of low noise. If valid, these effects are due to feelings of annoyance and fear engendered in the mothers and are not due to any acoustic energy transmitted to the fetus

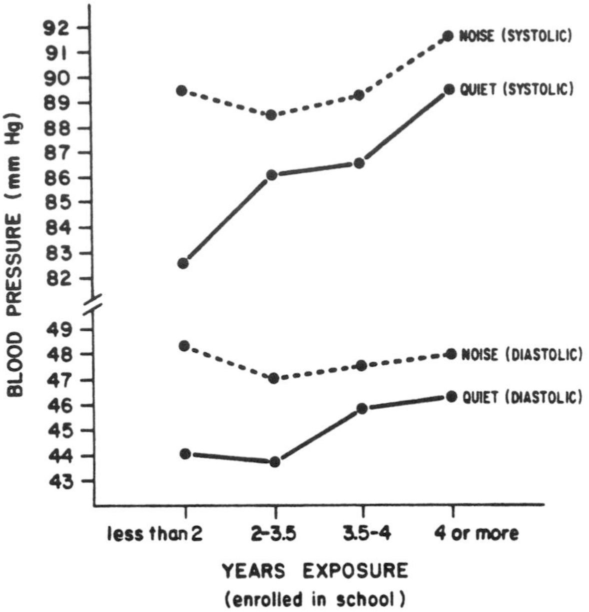

FIGURE 9.63 Systolic and diastolic blood pressure as a function of school noise level and duration of exposure. Each period on the years-of-exposure ordinate represents approximately one-quarter of the sample. (From S. Cohen *et al.*, 1980.)

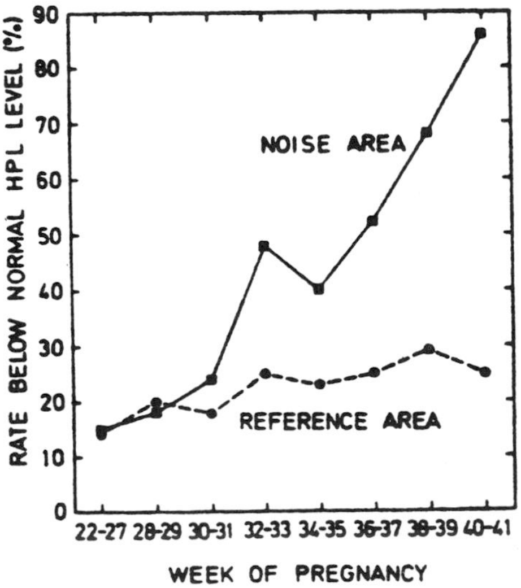

FIGURE 9.64 Rate of women from high-intensity aircraft noise area with placental lactogen (HPL) in serum more that one standard deviation below average for women from area free of aircraft noise. (From Ando and Hattori, 1977b.)

through tissues or fluids of the mother's body, as the acoustic levels are too low in intensity.

Ando (1987) examined the rate of infants weighing <3000 grams in residential areas before and during the introduction of aircraft noise with opening of a new airport relative to the rate in a neighboring low-aircraft-noise area. As seen in Fig. 9.65, as the number of aircraft operations and the noise-exposure level increased, there was a steady increase in birth rate of infants weighing less than 3000 grams in the high aircraft-noise area, compared to the rate in the low aircraft-noise area.

In the Ando and Hattori studies the socioeconomic status and the environmental factors (other than the noise) of those exposed and not exposed to the noise were felt to be reasonably similar. In the analyses of birth-weight data from hospitals in six villages near the Amsterdam airport, Knipschild *et al.* attempted to control the following factors: family income, birth order, and sex of the infant. Only single-birth infants (no twins) were considered. Table 9.21 shows that significantly more female infants whose mothers lived in high levels of aircraft noise (L_{dn} − 65–75) than in low levels of noise (L_{dn} <65) had birth weights below 3000 g. A further division of L_{dn} = 65–75 into

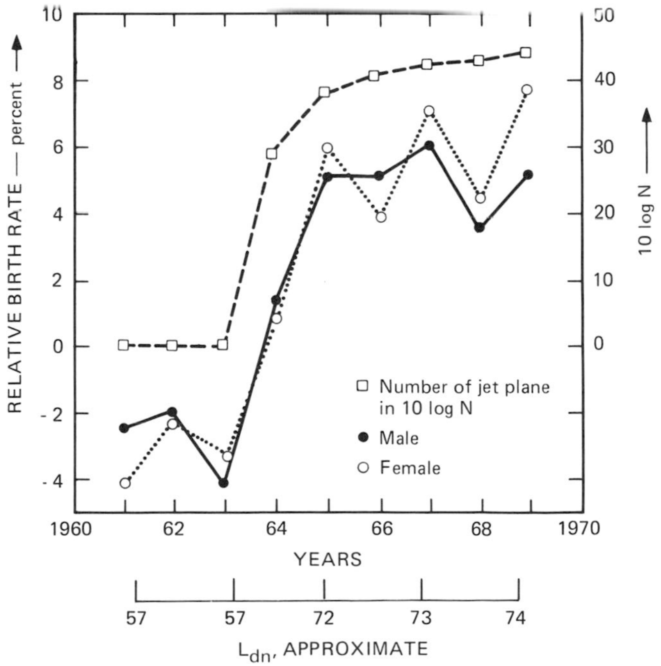

FIGURE 9.65 Percentage, relative to that for noise-free area, of birth of infants <3000 g in residential areas near an airport as a function of increase in exposure level of aircraft noise. (From Ando, 1987.) Estimated L_{dn} added here.

TABLE 9.21 Birth-Weight Statistics as a Function of Noise Level

Socioeconomic category and sex of infant	Infants, percent, with low birth weight* for L_{dn}, dB$_A$, of†		
	<65	65–75	<75
Low income			
Female	17.0 (112)	30.3 (175)	25.1 (287)
Male	21.8 (119)	22.7 (150)	22.3 (269)
High income			
Female	17.9 (84)	24.4 (82)	21.1 (166)
Male	14.6 (89)	14.3 (91)	14.4 (180)
All infants	18.1 (404)	24.1 (498)	21.4 (902)
Adjusted‡	18.1	23.8	

* Birth weights <3000 g.

† Number of infants tested given in parentheses.

‡ Combination of the two populations used as standard population.

Data from Knipschild *et al.*, 1981.

L_{dn} 65–70 and 70–75 found 23% and 29%, respectively, of all infants with birth weights below 3000 g. As shown in Table 9.20, the percentage was 18.1% for all infants from areas with L_{dn} <65.

Rehn, according to Knipschild *et al.* (1981) did not find a significant relation between birth weight and aircraft noise in the city of Dusseldorf. Knipschild *et al.* suggest that the differential age and socioeconomic factors favoring the higher noise areas (an unusual condition for most cities) may have contributed to Rehn's findings.

Schell (1981) studied the effect on the length of gestation and on the birth weight of infants of mothers who were exposed to aircraft noise while pregnant. A multiple-correlation analysis technique was used to partial out the effects of the mother's height, weight, age, and smoking habits, and the father's weight and education. A statistically significant negative correlation between aircraft-noise-exposure level and gestation length was found for female infants but not for male infants. A larger negative correlation was also found between noise-exposure level and birth weights of female than male infants, but neither were statistically significant.

Schell and Ando (1991) obtained data on, among other things, the heights and weights of 6686 three-year-old boys and girls from cities near Osaka Airport in Japan. The children were divided into five groups depending on the level of aircraft noise in the area in which they lived. The data (see Table 9.22), indicate that for each of three criteria of reduced growth in height (less than 87 cm; less than 91 cm; and less than 90.4 cm for males and less than 88.9 cm for females) there was a general monotonic increase in percentage with reduced height as a function of aircraft noise level. A test

TABLE 9.22 Frequency of 3-Year-Old Children (Males and Females, 1972 and 1973 Cohorts Combined) Falling Below Three Criteria of Height as a Function of Level of Aircraft Noise (n) in Their Residential Areas

		Height/n (%)			
Rank	WECNPL*	Males		Females	
		Children <87 cm Tall			
4	85	21/545	(3.9)	18/539	(3.3)
3	80–84.9	26/730	(3.6)	39/733	(5.3)
2	75–79.9	28/799	(3.5)	47/843	(5.5)
1	70–74.9	5/472	(1.1)	11/482	(2.3)
0	69.9	7/827	(1.0)	14/716	(2.0)
	Children <10%ile† for Height (Males <90.4 cm; Females <88.9 cm)				
4	85	54/545	(9.9)	78/539	(14.5)
3	80–84.9	83/730	(11.4)	109/733	(14.9)
2	75–79.9	74/799	(9.3)	118/843	(14.0)
1	70–74.9	33/472	(7.0)	60/482	(12.5)
0	69.9	49/827	(5.9)	80/716	(11.2)
		Children <91 cm Tall			
4	85	137/545	(25.1)	195/539	(36.2)
3	80–84.9	169/730	(23.2)	258/733	(35.2)
2	75–79.9	175/799	(21.9)	263/843	(31.2)
1,0	74.9	241/1299	(18.6)	339/1198	(28.3)

* Weighted equivalent continuous perceived noise level.

† Tenth percentile; local Japanese growth standards (see text).

From Schell and Ando (1991).

for significance of proportions of differences in height with noise indicated statistical significance for both boys and girls. Weight, however, was statistically not significantly related to noise level. (Without more information than provided, it is not possible to precisely translate the WECPNL metric into equivalent L_{dn}. However, usually, and approximately, WCEPNL $- 14 = L_{dn}$.)

The investigators note that socioeconomic status has an important influence on growth in countries where there is significant variation in socioeconomic status (Bielicki, 1986) but that in countries where social services are applied to virtually all socioeconomic strata, there is very little variation in size by socioeconomic status (Tanner, 1986). The average income for the different cities involved were very similar, and a negative correlation of -0.032 was calculated between noise level and average income of a sample of 811 families around Osaka Airport. It was concluded that an association between stature in height of young children and exposure to aircraft noise in the living environment had been found, and that it was independent of socioeconomic status.

References

Abey-Wickrama, I., a'Brook, M. F., Gattoni, F. E. G., and Herridge, C. F. (1969). Mental-hospital admissions and aircraft noise. *Lancet* **ii,** 1275–1277.

Acton, W. I., and Carson, M. B. (1967). Auditory and subjective effects of airborne noise from industrial ultrasonic sources. *Br. J. Ind. Med.* **4,** 297–304.

Ades, H. W., Graybiel, A., Morrill, S., Tolhurst, G., and Niven, J. (1958). "NonAuditory Effects of High Intensity Sound Stimulation of Deaf Human Subjects," Joint Rep. No. 5. Univ. of Texas Southwestern Med. Sch. and U.S. Navl. Sch. of Aviat. Med., Pensacola, Florida.

Anderson, B., Murphy, S., Krugler, B., Barber, D., and Joyce, M. (1993). The effects on waterbirds of increased noise from the expansion of a gas compressor plant at Prudhoe Bay, Alaska, USA. *Noise Public Health Probl., Proc. Int. Congr., 6th* (M. Vallet, ed.), Vol. 2, pp. 247–250. l'INRETS, 94114 Arcuil Cedex, France.

Ando, Y. (1987). Effects of daily dose on the fetus and cerebral hemisphere specialization of children. *Inter-Noise '87* Vol. 2, pp. 941–944. Acoust. Soc. China, Beijing.

Ando, Y., and Hattori, H. (1970). Effects of intense noise during fetal life upon postnatal adaptability (statistical study of the reactions of babies to aircraft noise). *J. Acoust. Soc. Am.* **47,** 1128–1130.

Ando, Y., and Hattori, H. (1974). Reaction of infants to aircraft noise and effects of the noise on human fetal life. *Pract. Otol. Kyoto* **67,** 129–136.

Ando, Y., and Hattori, H. (1977a). Effects of noise on sleep of babies. *J. Acoust. Soc. Am.* **62,** 199–204.

Ando, Y., and Hattori, H. (1977b). Effects of noise on human placental lactogen (HPL) levels in maternal plasma. *Br. J. Obstet. Gynaecol.* **84,** F115–F118.

Andren, L. (1982). Cardiovascular effects of noise. *Acta Med. Scand., Suppl.* No. 657.

Andren, L., Hansson, L., Bjorkman, M., and Jonsson, A. (1980). Noise as a contributory factor in the development of elevated arterial pressure. *Acta Med. Scand.* **207,** 493–498.

Andriukin, A. A. (1961). Influence of sound stimulation on the development of hypertension—Clinical and experimental results. *Cor Vasa* **3,** 285–293.

Andrukovich, A. I. (1965). The effect of industrial noise in winding and weaving factories on the arterial pressure of operators. *Gig. Tr. Prof. Zabol.* **9**(12), 39–42.

Babish, W., Elwood, P., and Ising, H. (1993). Road traffic noise and heart disease risk: Results of the epidemiological studies in Caerphilly, Speedwell and Berlin. *Noise Public Health Probl., Proc. Int. Congr., 6th* (M. Vallet, ed.), Vol. 3, pp. 260–267. l'INRETS, 94114 Arcuil Cedex, France.

Bader, M. (1978). Residence under an airport landing pattern as a factor in teratism. *Arch. Environ. Health* **33,** 214.

Bartoshuk, A. K. (1962). Response decrement with repeated elicitation of human neonatal cardiac acceleration to sound. *J. Comp. Physiol. Psychol.* **55,** 9–13.

Battig, K., Zeier, H., Muller, R., and Buzzi, R. (1980). A field study on vegetative effects of aircraft noise. *Arch. Environ. Health* **35,** 228–235.

Beecher, H. K. (1966). Pain: One mystery solved. *Science* **152,** 840–841.

Bellucci, R. J., and Schneider, D. E. (1962). Some observations on ultrasonic perception in man. *Ann. Otol. Rhinol. Laryngol.* **71,** 719–726.

Belojevic, G., and Kocijancic, R. (1993). Injury rate in textile industry with regard to noise exposure. *Noise Public Health Probl., Proc. Int. Congr., 6th* (M. Vallet, ed.), Vol. 2, pp. 489–492. l'INRETS, 94114 Arcuil Cedex, France.

Benko, E. (1959). Objekt-und Farbengeisichtsfeldeinengung bei Chronischen Larmschaden. *Ophthalmologica* **138,** 449–456.

Benko, E. (1962). Further information about the narrowing of the visual fields caused by noise damage. *Ophthalmologica* **140,** 76–80.

Bielicki, T. (1986). Physical growth as a measure of economic well-being of populations: The twentieth century. *In* "Human Growth" (F. Falkner and J. M. Tanner, eds.), 2nd. Ed. pp. 283–305. Plenum Press, New York.

Bly, S., Goddard, M., and McLean, J. (1993). A review of the effects of noise on the immune system. *Noise Public Health Probl., Proc. Int. Congr., 6th* (M. Vallet, ed.), Vol. 2, pp. 509–512. l'INRETS, 94114 Arcuil Cedex, France.

Bomberger, C. E., and Haar, J. L. (1992). Restraint and sound stress reduce the in vitro migration of prethymic stem cells to thymus supernatant. *Thymus* **19,** 111–115.

Bond, J. (1970). Effects of noise on the physiology and behavior of farm raised animals. *In* "Physiological Effects of Noise" (B. L. Welch and A. S. Welch, eds.), pp. 295–306. Plenum, New York.

Borchgrevink, H., Jenssen, A., Woxen, O., Richmond, D., and Damon, E. (1993). Non-auditory effects on pigs exposed to complex blast pressure waves in enclosures. *Noise Public Health Probl., Proc. Int. Congr., 6th* (M. Vallet, ed.), Vol. 2, pp. 25–258. l'INRETS, 94114 Arcuil Cedex, France.

Borg, E. (1981). Physiological and pathogenic effects of sound. *Acta Oto-Laryngol., Suppl.* No. 381, 68–76.

Borg, E., and Moller, A. R. (1978). Noise and blood pressure: Effect of lifelong exposure in the rat. *Acta Physiol. Scand.* **103,** 340–342.

Bowles, A., McClenaghen, L., Francine, J., Wisely, S., Golightly, R., and Kull, M. (1993). Effects of aircraft noise on the predator prey ecology of the kit fox (*Vulpes macrotis*) and its small mammal prey. *Noise Public Health Probl., Proc. Int. Congr., 6th* (M. Vallet, ed.), Vol. 2, pp. 462–470. l'INRETS, 94114 Arcuil Cedex, France.

Bradley, J. S., and Jonah, B. A. (1979). The effects of site selected variables on human responses to traffic noise. Part II: Road type by socio-economic status by traffic noise level. *J. Sound Vib.* **67,** 395–407.

Brandenberger, G., Follenius, M., and Trémolieres, C. (1977). Failure of noise exposure to modify temporal patterns of plasma cortisol in man. *Eur. J. Appl. Physiol.* **36,** 239–246.

Broadbent, D. E. (1972). Individual differences in annoyance by noise. *Sound* **6,** 56–61.

Broussard, I. G., Walker, R. Y., and Roberts, E. E., Jr. (1952). "The Influence of Noise on the Visual Contrast Threshold," Rep. No. 101. U.S. Army Med. Res. Labs., Fort Knox, Kentucky.

Brown, J. E., III, Thompson, R. N., and Folk, E. D. (1975). Certain nonauditory physiological responses to noises. *J. Am. Ind. Hyg. Assoc.* **36,** 285–291.

Bruel, P. V., and Olesen, P. (1973). Infrasonic measurements. *B & K Instrum., Inc. Tech. Rev.* No. 3, 14–25.

Buckley, J. P., and Smookler, H. H. (1970). Cardiovascular and Biochemical effects of chronic intermittent neurogenic stimulation. *In* "Physiological Effects of Noise" (B. L. Welch and A. S. Welch, eds.), pp. 75–84. Plenum, New York.

Busnel, R. G., and Briot, J. L. (1980). Wildlife and airfield noise in France. *In* "Noise as a Public Health Problem" (J. V. Tobias, G. Jansen, and W. D. Ward, eds.), ASHA Rep. No. 10, pp. 621–631. Am. Speech–Lang.–Hear. Assoc., Rockville, Maryland.

Busnel, R. G., Busnel, M. C., and Lehmann, A. G. (1975). Synergic effects of noise and stress on general behavior. *Life Sci.* **16,** 31–137.

Caliner, M. A., and Lamanske, R. F., JR. (1992). Rhinitis and asthma. *In* "Primer on Allergic and Immuniological Diseases" (R. D. deShazo, ed.), 3rd Ed., pp. 2807–2929. Am. Med. Assoc.

Camp, W., Martin, R., and Chapman, L. F. (1962). Pain threshold and discrimination of pain intensity during brief exposure to intense noise. *Science* **135,** 788–789.

Cantrell, R. W. (1974). Prolonged exposure to intermittent noise: Audiometric, biochemical, motor, psychological and sleep effects. *Laryngoscope* **84**(1), Suppl., 1–55.

Capellini, A., and Maroni, M. (1974). Clinical studies of arterial hypertension and coronary disease and their possible relations to the work environment in chemical industry workers. *Med. Lav.* **65,** 297–305.

Carlestam, G., Karlsson, C. G., and Levi, L. (1973). Stress and disease in response to exposure to noise—A review. *Proc. Int. Congr. Noise Public Health Probl.* (W. D. Ward, ed.), EPA Rep. 550/9-73-008, pp. 479–486. U.S. Environ. Prot. Agency, Washington, D.C.

Carlin, S., Ward, W. D., Gershon, A., and Ingraham, R. (1962). Sound stimulation and its effect on dental sensation threshold. *Science* **138,** 1258–1259.

Carter, N., Crawford, G., Kelly, D., and Hunyor, S. (1993). Environmental noise during sleep and sympathetic arousal assessed by urinary catecholamines. *Noise Public Health Probl., Proc. Int. Congr., 6th* (M. Vallet, ed.), Vol. 2, pp. 388–392. l'INRETS, 94114 Arcuil Cedex, France.

Cartwright, L. B., and Thompson, R. N. (1975). The effects of broadband noise on the cardiovascular system in normal resting adults. *J. Am. Ind. Hyg. Assoc.* **36,** 653–658.

Casady, R. B., and Lehman, R. P. (1967). Response of farm animals to sonic booms. *In* "Sonic Boom Experiments at Edwards Air Force Base. Interim Report, 1-67" Annex H. National Sonic Boom Evaluation Office, Contract AF49(638)-1976, SRI International, Menlo Park, California. (Avail. CFSTI, U.S. Dept., Commerce.)

Chandler, K. A. (1961). The effect of monaural and binaural tones of different intensities on the visual perception of verticality. *Am. J. Psychol.* **74,** 260–265.

Chen, C. S. (1978). Acoustic trauma-induced developmental change in the acoustic startle response and audiogenic seizures in mice. *Exp. Neurol.* **60,** 400–403.

Chesser, R. K., Caldwell, R. S., and Harvey, M. J. (1975). Effects of noise on feral populations of *Mus musculus. Physiol. Zool.* **48,** 323–325.

Chowns, R. H. (1970). Mental-hospital admissions and aircraft noise. *Lancet* **1,** 467.

Chrousos, G. P., and Gold, P. W. (1992). The concept of stress and stress system disorders. *JAMA* **267,** 1244–1252. *Am. Med. Assoc.*

Cieslewicz, J. (1971). Attempt to evaluate the extra-auditory impact of noise upon the workers of a weaving mill in the cotton industry. *Med. Pr.* **22,** 447–459.

Cohen, A. (1973). Industrial noise and medical, absence, and accident record data on exposed workers. *Proc. Int. Congr. Noise Public Health Probl.* (W. D. Ward, ed.), Rep. EPA 550/973–008, pp. 441–454. U.S. Environ. Prot. Agency, Washington, D.C.

Cohen, A., Taylor, W., and Tubbs, R. (1980). Occupational exposures to noise hearing loss, and blood pressure. *In* "Noise as a Public Health Problem" (J. V. Tobias, G. Jansen, and W. D. Ward, eds.), ASHA Rep. No. 10, pp. 322–326. Am. Speech–Lang.–Hear. Assoc., Rockville, Maryland.

Cohen, S., and Weinstein, N. (1981). Nonauditory effects of noise on behavior and health. *J. Soc. Issues* **37,** 36–70.

Cohen, S., Evans, G. W., Krantz, D. S., and Stokols, D. (1980). Physiological, motivational, and cognitive effects of aircraft noise on children: Moving from the laboratory to the field. *Am. Psychol.* **35,** 231–243.

Cohen, S., Krantz, D. S., Evans, G. W., Stokols, D., and Kelly, S. (1981a). Aircraft noise and children: Longitudinal and cross sectional evidence on adaptation to noise and the effectiveness of noise abatement. I. *Pers. Soc. Psychol.* **40,** 331–345.

Cohen, S., Krantz, D. S., Evans, G. W., and Stokols, D. (1981b). Cardiovascular and behavioral effects of community noise. *Am. Sci.* **69,** 528–535.

Cuesdean, L., Teganeanu, S., Tutu, C., Raiciu, M., Carp, C., and Coatu, S. (1977). Study of cardiovascular and auditory pathophysiological implications in a group of operatives working in noisy industrial surroundings. *Physiologie* **14,** 53–61.

Dantzer, R., Kelley, R. (1989). Stress immunity: an integrated view of relationships between brain and immune system. *Life Sci.* **44,** 1995–2008.

Davis, H. (1948). Biological and psychological effects of ultrasonics. *J. Acoust. Soc. Am.* **20,** 605–607.

Davis, H. (1958a). "Project ANEHIN: Auditory and non-Auditory Effects of High Intensity Noise," Joint Rep. No. 7. Central Inst. for the Deaf and U.S. Nav. Sch. of Aviat. Med., Pensacola, Florida.

Davis, H. (1958b). Effects of high intensity noise on naval personnel. *U.S. Armed Forces Med. J.* **9,** 1027–1048.

Davis, H., and Glorig, A. (1962). Audio analgesia: A new problem for otologists. *Arch. Otolaryngol.* **75,** 498–501.

Davis, H., Parrack, H. O., and Eldredge, D. H. (1949). Hazards of intense sound and ultrasound. *Ann. Otol. Rhinol. Laryngol.* **58,** 732–738.

Davis, R. C., and Berry, T. (1964). Gastrointestinal reactions to response contingent stimulation. *Psychol. Rep.* **15,** 95–113.

Davis, R. C., and Van Liere, D. W. (1949). Adaptation of the muscular tension response to gunfire. *J. Exp. Psychol.* **39,** 114–117.

Davis, R. C., Buchwald, A. M., and Frankman, R. W. (1955). Autonomic and muscular responses and their relation to simple stimuli. *Psychol. Monogr.* **69,** No. 405.

Deatherage, B. H., leffress, L. A., and Blodgett, H. C. (1954). A note on the audibility of intense ultrasonic sound. *J. Acoust. Soc. Am.* **26,** 582.

Dega, K., and Klajman, S. (1977). The effect of noise on some indexes of the circulatory system efficiency of shipyard grinders. *Bull. Inst. Marit. Trop. Med. Gdynia* **28,** 143–150.

Dempsey, T. K., Leatherwood, J. D., and Clevenson, S. A. (1979). Development of noise and vibration ride comfort criteria. *J. Acoust. Soc. Am.* **65,** 124–132.

De Young, D., Krausman, P., Weiland, L., and Etchberger, R. (1993). Baseline ABRs in mountain sheep and desert mule deer. *Noise Public Health Probl., Proc. Int. Congr., 6th* (M. Vallet, ed.), Vol. 2, pp. 251–254. 1'INRETS, 94114 Arcuil Cedex, France.

Di Cantogno, L. V., Dallerba, R., Teagno, P. S., and Cocola, L. (1976). Urban traffic noise, cardiocirculatory activity and coronary risk factors. *Acta Oto-Laryngol., Suppl.* No. 339, 55–63.

Dickson, E. D. D., and Chadwick, D. L. (1951). Observations on disturbances of equilibrium and other symptoms induced by jet engine noise. *J. Laryngol. Otol.* **65,** 154–165.

DORA (1980). "Aircraft Noise and Sleep Disturbance," Final Rep. DORA Rep. No. 8008. Civ. Aviat. Auth., London.

Dorfman, D. D., and Zajonc, R. B. (1963). Some effects of sound, background brightness, and economic status of the perceived size of coins and discs. *J. Abnorm. Soc. Psychol.* **66,** 87–90.

Doring, H. J., Hauf, G., and Seiberling, M. (1980). Effects of high intensity sound on the contractile function of the isolated ileum of guinea pigs and rabbits. *In* "Noise as a Public Health Problem" (J. V. Tobias, G. Jansen, and W. D. Ward, eds.), ASHA Rep. No. 10, pp. 288–293. Am. Speech–Lang.–Hear. Assoc., Rockville, Maryland.

Drettner, B., Hedstrand, H., Klockhoff, I., and Svedberg, A. (1975). Cardiovascular risk factors and hearing loss. A study of 1000 fifty-year-old men. *Acta Oto-Laryngol.* **79,** 366–371.

Edmonds, L. D., Layde, P. M., and Erickson, J. D. (1979). Airport noise and teratogenesis. *Arch. Environ. Health* **34,** 243–247.

Ehrenstein, W., and Müller-Limmroth, W. (1980). Laboratory investigations into effects of noise on human sleep. *In* "Noise as a Public Health Problem" (J. V. Tobias, G. Jansen, and W. D. Ward, eds.), ASHA Rep. No. 10, pp. 433–441. Speech–Lang.–Hear. Assoc., Rockville, Maryland.

Emmons, W. H., and Simon, C. W. (1955). "The Non-Recall of Material Presented During Sleep," Rev. Rep. P-619. Rand Corp., Santa Monica, California.

Espmark, Y., Falt, L., and Falt, B. (1974). Behavioural responses in cattle and sheep exposed to sonic booms and low-altitude subsonic flight noise. *Vet. Rec.* **94,** 106–113.

Falk, S. A. (1973). Environmental noise. *Am. J. Public Health* **63,** 833–834.

Favino, A., Maugeri, U., Kauchtschischvili, G., Robustelli, D. C. G., and Nappi, G. (1973). Radioimmunoassay measurements of serum cortisol, thyroxine, growth hormone and luteinizing hormone with simultaneous electroencephalographic changes during continuous noise in man. *J. Nucl. Biol. Med.* **17** (3), 119–122.

Fidell, S., and Jones, G. (1975). Effects of cessation of late-night flights on an airport community. *J. Sound Vib.* **42,** 411–427.

Fink, G. B., and Iturrian, W. B. (1970). Influence of age, auditory conditioning, and environmental noise on sound-induced seizures and seizure threshold in mice. *In* "Physiological Effects of Noise" (B. L. Welch and A. S. Welch, eds.). Plenum, New York.

Finkle, A. L., and Poppen, J. R. (1948). Clinical effects of noise and mechanical vibrations of a turbo-jet engine on man. *J. Appl. Physiol.* **1,** 183–204.

Fletcher, J. L. (1980). Effects of noise on wildlife: A review of relevant literature 1971–1978. *In* "Noise as a Public Health Problem" (J. V. Tobias, G. Jansen, and W. D. Ward, eds.), ASHA Rep. No. 10, pp. 611–620. Am. Speech–Lang.–Hear. Assoc., Rockville, Maryland.

Fluglärmwirkungen (1974). "Eine Interdisziplinäre Untersuchung über die Auswirkungen des Fluglärms auf den Menschen," Hauptbericht. Harald Boldt Verlag KG (West Germany). (Avail. as NASA TM-75819.)

Folch, H., Ojeda, F., and Esquivel, P. (1991). Rise in thymocyte number and thymulin serum level induced by noise. *Immunology Letters* **30,** 301–306.

Forster, F. M. (1970). Human studies of epileptic seizures induced by sound and their conditioned extinction. *In* "Physiological Effects or Noise" (B. L. Welch and A. S. Welch, eds.), pp. 151–158. Plenum, New York.

Frerichs, R. R., Beeman, B. L., and Coulson, A. H. (1980). Los Angeles airport noise and mortality—Faulty analysis and public policy. *Am. J. Public Health* **70,** 357–362.

Frerichs, R. R., and Coulson, A. H. (1980). Frerichs, et al., respond. *Am. J. Public Health* **70,** 543–544.

Friedlander, B., Greberman, M., Wathen, G., and Zeidler, W. H. (n.d.). "An Analysis of Noise and Its Relationship to Blood Pressure in an Industrial Population." Maryland State Dep. Health Ment. Hyg., Baltimore.

Froehlich, G. R. (1975). The effects of ear protectors on some autonomic responses to aircraft and impulsive noise. *In* "Effects of Long Duration Noise Exposure on Hearing and Health" (M. A. Whitcomb, ed.), Rep. AGARD-CP-171, pp. C8 : 1–5 (Nov. 1975).

Fruhstorfer, B., and Hensel, H. (1980). Extra-auditory responses to long-term intermittent noise stimulation in humans. *J. Appl. Physiol.* **49,** 985–993.

Gardner, W., and Licklider, J. C. R. (1959). Auditory analgesia in dental operations. *J. Am. Dent. Assoc.* **59,** 1144–1149.

Gardner, W. J., Licklider, J. C. R., and Weisz, A. Z. (1960). Suppression of pain by sound. *Science* **132,** 32–33.

Gattoni, F., and Tarnopolsky, A. (1973). Aircraft noise and psychiatric morbidity. *Psychol. Med.* **3,** 516–520.

Geller, L. I., Sakaeva, S. Z., Musina, S. S., Kogan, I. D., Belomytseva, L. A., Ostrovskaia, R. S., Volokhov, I. P., Lukianova, E. S., Popova, P. M., and Moskatel'nikova, E. V. (1963). The influence of noise on arterial blood pressure (On the etiology of arterial hypertension). *Ter. Arkh.* **35**(7), 83–86.

Ginsberg, S., and Furedy, J. J. (1974). Stimulus repetition, change, and assessments of sensitivities of and relationships among an electrodermal and two plethysmographic components of the orienting reaction. *Psychophysiology* **11,** 35–43.

Gladwin, D. N., and McKechnie, A. (1993). Case study highlights potential capability of low-altitude aircraft operations with important wildlife resources. *Noise Public Health Probl., Proc. Int. Congr., 6th* (M. Vallet, ed.), Vol. 2, pp. 243–246. l'INRETS, 94114 Arcuil Cedex, France.

Glass, D. C., and Singer, J. E. (1972). "Urban Stress—Experiments on Noise and Social Stressors." Academic Press, New York.

Globus, G., Friedmann, J., Cohen, H., Pearsons, K. S., and Fidell, S. (1973). The effects of aircraft noise on sleep electrophysiology as recorded in the home. *Proc. Int. Congr. Noise Public Health Probl.* (W. D. Ward, ed.), Rep. EPA 550/9-73-008, pp. 587–592. U.S. Environ. Prot. Agency, Washington, D.C.

Graeven, D. B. (1974). The effects of airplane noise on health: An examination of three hypotheses. *J. Health Soc. Behav.* **15,** 336–343.

Graham, F. K. (1973). Habituation and dishabituation of responses innervated by the autonomic nervous system. *In* "Habituation, Vol. I: Behavioral Studies" (H. V. S. Peeke and M. J. Herz, eds.), pp. 163–218. Academic Press, New York.

Graham, F. K., and Slaby, D. A. (1973). Differential heart rate changes to equally intense white noise and tone. *Psychophysiology* **10,** 347–362.

Grandjean, E. (1962). Biological effects of noise. *Proc. Int. Congr. Acoust., 4th, Copenhagen.*

Grandjean, E., Graf, P., Lauber, A., Meier, H. P., and Muller, R. (1976). Survey on the effects of aircraft noise around three civil airports in Switzerland. *INTER-NOISE '76 Proc.* (R. L. Kerlin, ed.), pp. 85–90. Inst. Noise Control Eng., Washington, D.C.

Griefahn, B. (1975). Effects of sonic booms on fingerpulse amplitudes during sleep. *Int. Arch. Occup. Environ. Health* **36,** 57–66.

Griefahn, B., and Jansen, G. (1978). EEG—Responses caused by environmental noise during sleep—Their relationships to exogenic and endogenic influences. *Sci. Total Environ.* **10,** 187–199.

Haeff, A. V., and Knox, C. (1963). Perception of ultrasound. *Science* **139,** 590–592.

Hale, H. B. (1959). Adrenalcortical activity associated with exposure to low frequency sounds. *Am. J. Phsyiol.* **171,** 732.

Hand, D. J., Tarnopolsky, A., Barker, S. M., and Jenkins, L. M. (1980). Relationships between psychiatric hospital admissions and aircraft noise: A new study. *In* "Noise as a Public Health Problem" (J. V. Tobias, G. Jansen, and W. D. Ward, eds.), ASHA Rep. No. 10, pp. 277–282. Am. Speech–Lang.–Hear. Assoc., Rockville, Maryland.

Hanson, J. D., Larson, M. E., and Snowdon, C. T. (1976). The effects of control over high intensity noise on plasma cortisol levels in rhesus monkeys. *Behav. Biol.* **16,** 333–340.

Harper, M. M. (1968). The Effects of Signal Property and Stimulus Intensity on the Skin Resistance Response to Repetition of Auditory Stimuli. M. A. Thesis, Univ. of Wisconsin, Madison.

Harrington, F. H. (1993). The effects of low-level jet fighter overflights on caribou. *Noise Public Health Probl., Proc. Int. Congr., 6th* (M. Vallet, ed.), Vol. 2, pp. 239–242. l'INRETS, 94114 Arcuil Cedex, France.

Harris, C. S. (1972). Effects of increasing intensity levels of intermittent and continuous 1000-Hz tones on human equilibrium. *Percept. Motor Skills* **35,** 395–405.

Harris, C. S., and Von Gierke, H. E. (1971). "The Effects of High Intensity Noise on Human Equilibrium," Rep. AMRL-TR-6761. U.S. Air Force, Wright-Patterson AFB, Ohio. (Avail. from DTIC as AD 737 826.)

Hattis, D., Richardson, B., and Ashford, N. A. (1980). "Noise, General Stress Responses, and Cardiovascular Disease Processes: Review and Reassessment of Hypothesized Relationships," Rep. EPA 550/9-80101. U.S. Environ. Protect. Agency, Washington, D.C.

Hawel, W., and Starlinger, H. (1967). Effect of repeated 4-hr intermittent (so-called) pink noise on catecholaminar separation (in urine) and pulse frequency. *Int. Z. Angew. Physiol. Einschl. Arbeitsphysiol.* **24,** 351–362.

Hedstrand, H., Drettner, B., Kockhoff, I., and Svedberg, A. (1977). Noise and blood pressure. *Lancet* **ii,** 1291.

Henry, K. R., and Bowman, R. E. (1970). Acoustic priming of audiogenic seizures in mice. *In* "Physiological Effects of Noise" (B. L. Welch and A. S. Welch, eds.), pp. 185–202. Plenum, New York.

Herd, J. A. (1991) Cardiovascular response to stress. *Physiol. Rev.* **71,** 305–330.

Hermann, E. R., Hesse, C. S., Hoyle, E. R., and Leopold, A. C. (1978). "Effects of Noise and Hearing Acuity Upon Visual Depth Perception and Safety Among Humans," Rep. IIEQ-77/10. Ill. Inst. Environ. Qual. (Apr.) (Avail. from NTIS as PB 280 365.)

Herridge, C. F., and Chir, B. (1972). Aircraft noise and mental hospital admission. *Sound* **6,** 32–36.

Hilgard, E. R. (1969). Pain as a puzzle for psychology and physiology. *Am. Psychol.* **24,** 103–113.

Hirai, A., Takata, M., Mikawa, M., Yasumoto, K., Iida, S., and Kagamimori, S. (1991).

Prolonged exposure to industrial noise causes hearing loss but not high blood pressure: a study of 2124 factory laborers in Japan. *J. Hypertens.* **9,** 1069–1073.

Hiramatsu, K., Yamamoto, T., Taira, K., Ito, A., and Nakasone, T. (1993). Response to questionnaire on health around a military airport. *Noise Public Health Probl., Proc. Int. Congr., 6th* (M. Vallet, ed.), Vol. 2, pp. 473–476. l'INRETS, 94114 Arcuil Cedex, France.

Hofman, W., Kumar, A., and Eberhardt, J. (1993). Comparative evaluation of sleep disturbance due to noises from airplanes, trains and trucks. *Noise Public Health Probl., Proc. Int. Congr., 6th* (M. Vallet, ed.), Vol. 2, pp. 559–562. l'INRETS, 94114 Arcuil Cedex, France.

Horonjeff, R. D., Fidell, S., Teffeteller, S. R., and Green, D. M. (1982). Behavioral awakening as functions of duration and detectability of noise intrusions in the home. *J. Sound Vib.* **84,** 327–336.

Hume, K. I., and Thomas, C. (1993). Sleep disturbance due to aircraft noise at a rapidly expanding airport (Manchester airport). *Noise Public Health Probl., Proc. Int. Congr., 6th* (M. Vallet, ed.), Vol. 2, pp. 563–566. l'INRETS, 94114 Arcuil Cedex, France.

Hume, K. I. Van, F., and Watson, A. (1993). EEG-based responses to aircraft noise for subjects sleeping at home. *Noise Public Health Probl., Proc. Int. Congr., 6th* (M. Vallet, ed.), Vol. 3, pp. 377–385. l'INRETS, 94114 Arcuil Cedex, France.

Irwin, M. R., Segal, D. S., Hauger, R. L., and Smith, T. L. (1989). Individual behavioral and neorendocrine differences in responsiveness to audiogenic stress. *Pharmacology, Biochemistry and Behavior* **32,** 913–917.

Ising, H., and Melchert, H.-U. (1980). Endocrine and cardiovascular effects of noise. *In* "Noise as a Public Health Problem" (J. V. Tobias, G. Jansen, and W. D. Ward, eds.), ASHA Rep. No. 10, pp. 241–245. Am. Speech–Lang.–Hear. Assoc., Rockville, Maryland.

Ising, H., Gunther, T., Havestadt, T., Karuse, C., Markert, B., Melchert, H.-U., Schoknecht, G., Thefeld, W., and Teitze, K. W. (1979). "Study on the Quantification of Risk for the Heart and Circulatory System Associated With Noise Workers," EPA Transl. TR-79-0857. U.S. Environ. Prot. Agency, Washington, D.C.

Jackson, J. C. (1974). Amplitude and habituation of the orienting reflex as a function of stimulus intensity. *Psychophysiology* **11,** 647–659.

Jansen, G. (1961). Adverse effects of noise on iron and steel workers. *Stahl Eisen* **81,** 217–220.

Jansen, G. (1964). The influence of noise at manual work. *Int. J. Appl. Physiol.* **20,** 233–239.

Jansen, G. (1972). Extra-auditory effects of noise. *Transl. Beltone Inst. Hear. Res.* No. 26.

Jansen, G. (1973). Non-auditory effects of noise, physiological and psychological reactions in man. *Proc. Int. Congr. Noise Public Health Probl.* (W. D. Ward, ed.), Rep. EPA 550/9-73-008, pp. 431–440. U.S. Environ. Prot. Agency, Washington, D.C.

Jansson, A., and Hansson, L. (1977). Prolonged exposure to a stressful stimulus (noise) as a cause of raised blood-pressure in man. *Lancet* **i,** 86–87.

Jenkins, L., Tarnopolsky, A., Hand, D., and Barker, S. (1979).Comparison of three studies of aircraft noise and psychiatric hospital admissions conducted in the same area. *Psychol. Med.* **9,** 681–693.

Jenkins, L., Tarnopolsky, A., and Hand, D. (1981). Psychiatric admissions and aircraft noise from London Airport: Four-year, three hospitals' study. *Psychol. Med.* **11,** 765–782.

Jensen, M. M., and Rasmussen, A. F., Jr. (1970). Audiogenic stress and susceptibility to infection. *In* "Physiological Effects of Noise" (B. L. Welch and A. S. Welch, eds.), pp. 7–20. Plenum, New York.

Jerger, J. B., Alford, A. C., and French, B. (1966). Effects of very low frequency tones on auditory thresholds. *J. Speech and Hearing Res.* **9,** 150–160.

Johnson, D. L. (1973). Unpublished data cited in Nixon and Johnson, 1973.

Johns, M. W., and Dore, C. (1978). Sleep at home and in the sleep laboratory: Disturbance by recording procedures. *Ergonomics* **21,** 325–330.

Johnson, L. C., and Lubin, A. (1967). The orienting reflex during waking and sleeping. *Electroencephalogr. Clin. Neurophysiol.* **22,** 11–21.

Johnson, L. C., Townsend, R. E., Naitoh, P., and Muzet, A. G. (1973). Prolonged exposure to noise as a sleep problem. *Proc. Int. Congr. Noise Public Health Probl.* (W. D. Ward, ed.), Rep. EPA 550/9-73-008, pp. 559–574. U.S. Environ. Prot. Agency, Washington, D.C.

Jones, F. N. (1980). Nonauditory effects of noise on fetal life. *In* "Noise as a Public Health Problem" (J. V. Tobias, G. Jansen, and W. D. Ward, eds.), ASHA Rep. No. 10, pp. 274–276. Am. Speech–Lang.–Hear. Assoc., Rockville, Maryland.

Jones, F. N., and Tauscher, J. (1978). Residence under and airport landing pattern as a factor to teratism. *Arch. Environ. Health* **33,** 10–12.

Jones, P. D., Loeb, M., and Cohen, A. (1977). Effects of intense continuous and impact-type noise on pupil size and visual acuity. *J. Am. Audiol. Soc.* **2,** 202–207.

Kagan, A. (1980). Stress and noise principles of research. *In* "Noise as a Public Health Problem" (J. V. Tobias, G. Jansen, and W. D. Ward, eds.), ASHA Rep. No. 10, pp. 237–240. Am. Speech–Lang.–Hear. Assoc., Rockville, Maryland.

Karagodina, I. L., Soldatkina, S. A., Vinokur, I. L., and Klimukhin, A. A. (1969). Effect of aircraft noise on the population near airports. *Hyg. Sanit.* (*USSR*) **34,** 182–187.

Karsdorf, G., and Klappach, H. (1968). Einflüsse des Verkehrslärms auf Gesundheit und Leistung bei Oberschulerneiner Grossstadt. *Z. Gesamte Hyg.* **14,** 52–54.

Kavoussi, N. (1973). The relationship between the length of exposure to noise and the incidence of hypertension at a silo in Terran. *Med. Lav.* **64,** 292–295.

Kenshalo, D., and Kryter, K. D. (1949). Middle ear infection and sound induced seizures in rats. *J. Comp. Physiol. Psychol.* **42,** 328–331.

Kent, S. J., Von Gierke, H. E., and Tolan, G. D. (1986). Analysis of the potential association between noise-induced hearing loss and cardiovascular disease in USAF aircrew members. *Aviat. Space Environ. Med.* **57,** 348.

Knipschild, P. (1977a). Medical effects of aircraft noise: Community cardiovascular survey. *Int. Arch. Occup. Environ. Health* **40,** 185–190.

Knipschild, P. (1977b). Medical effects of aircraft noise: General practice survey. *Int. Arch. Occup. Environ. Health* **40,** 191–196.

Knipschild, P. (1980). Aircraft noise and hypertension. *In* "Noise as a Public Health Problem" (J. V. Tobias, G. Jansen, and W. D. Ward, eds.), ASHA Rep. No. 10, pp. 283–287. Am. Speech–Lang.–Hear. Assoc., Rockville, Maryland.

Knipschild, P., and Oudshoorn, N. (1977). Medical effects of aircraft noise: Drug survey. *Int. Arch. Occup. Environ. Health* **40,** 197–200.

Knipschild, P., and Salle, H. (1979). Road traffic noise and cardiovascular disease. A population study in the Netherlands. *Int. Arch. Occup. Environ. Health* **44,** 55–59.

Knipschild, P., Meijer, H., and Salle, H. (1981). Aircraft noise and birth weight. *Int. Arch. Occup. Environ. Health* ***48,*** 131–136.

Ko, N. W. M., and Wong, V. L. P. (1980). Responses to road traffic noise: A socio-economic approach. *J. Sound Vib.* **68,** 147–152.

Koszarny, Z., Maziarka, S., and Szata, W. (1981). "The Effect of Airplane Noise on the Inhabitants of Areas Near the Okecie Airport in Warsaw," NASA TM-75879. U.S. Natl. Aeronaut. Space Adm., Washington, D.C.

Kraft-Schreyer, N., and Angelakos, E. T. (1979). Effects of sound stress on norepinephrine responsiveness and blood pressure. *Fed. Proc., Fed. Am. Soc. Exp. Biol.* **38,** 883.

Krallmann, D. (1962). "Untresuchungen über die Wirkung von Wecksignalen auf Schläfer verschiedener Schaftiefen und Dispositionen." (Studies of the effects of waking signals on sleepers with different depths of sleep and dispositions.") Final Rpt. on Research Project. Instut fur Phonetik und Kommunikationsforschung der Universität Bonn, Germany, pp. 1–61.

Krauskopf, J., and Coleman, P. D. (1956). "The Effect of Noise on Eye Movements." U.S. Army Med. Res. Lab., Fort Knox, Kentucky.

Krausman, P., Wallace, M., De Young, D., Weisenberger, M., and Hayes, C. (1993). The effects of low-altitude aircraft on desert ungulates. *Noise Public Health Probl. Proc. Int. Congr., 6th* (M. Vallet, ed.), Vol. 2, pp. 471–478. l'INRETS, 94114 Arcuil Cedex, France.

Kryter, K. D., Johnson, P. J., and Young, J. R. (1967). Psychological experiments on sonic booms. *In* "Sonic Boom Experiments at Edwards Air Force Base. Interim Report, 1.67," Annex B. National Sonic Boom Evaluation Office, Contract AF49(638)-1976, SRI International, Menlo Park, California. (Avail. CFSTI, U.S. Dept., Commerce.)

Kryter, K. D. (1973). Reply to Dr. Falk. *Am. J. Public Health* **63,** 834–836.

Kryter, K. D. (1980). Physiological acoustics and health. *J. Acoust. Soc. Am.* **68,** 10–14.

Kryter, K. D. (1985). "The Effects of Noise on Man." 2nd Ed. Academic Press, Orlando, Florida.

Kryter, K. D. (1990). Aircraft noise and social factors in psychiatric hospital admission rates: a re-examination of some data. *Psychol. Medicine* **20,** 395–411.

Kryter, K. D., and Poza, F. (1980). Effects of noise on some autonomic system activities. *J. Acoust. Soc. Am.* **67,** 2036–2044.

Kryter, K. D., Weisz, A. Z., and Wiener, F. M. (1962). Auditory fatigue from audio analgesia. *J. Acoust. Soc. Am.* **3,** 383–391.

Kugler, J., Kalveram, K. T., and Lange, K. W. (1990). Acute, not chronic exposure to noise periods affects splenic lymphocytes and plasma corticosterone in the mouse. *Internat. J. Neurosci.* **51,** 233–234.

Kull, R. C., Jr. (1993). An overview of USAF studies on the effects of aircraft overflight noise on wild and domestic animals. *Noise Public Health Probl. Proc. Int. Congr., 6th* (M. Vallet, ed.), Vol. 2, pp. 495–582. l'INRETS, 94114 Arcuil Cedex, France.

Lamanske, R. F., Jr., Caliner, M. A. (1990). Autonomic nervous system abnormalities and asthma. *Am. Rev. Respir. Dis.* **141,** S157–S161.

Langdon, F. J., and Buller, I. B. (1977). Road traffic noise and disturbance to sleep. *J. Sound Vib.* **50,** 13–28.

Leake, C. D. (1970). Summary of the symposium. *In* "Physiological Effects of Noise" (B. L. Welch and A. S. Welch, eds.), p. v. Plenum, Press, New York.

Lees, R. E. M., and Roberts, J. H. (1979). Noise-induced hearing loss and blood pressure. *Can. Med. Assoc. J.* **120,** 1082–1084.

Lees, R. E. M., Romeril, C. S., and Wetherall, L. D. (1980). A study of stress indicators in workers exposed to industrial noise. *Can. J. Public Health* **71,** 261–265.

Lercher, P., and Kofler, W. (1993). Adaptive behavior to road traffic noise: Blood pressure and cholesterol. *Noise Public Health Probl., Proc. Int. Congr., 6th* (M. Vallet, ed.), Vol. 2, pp. 465–468. l'INRETS, 94114 Arcuil Cedex, France.

LeVere, T. E., and Davis, N. (1977). Arousal from sleep: The physiological and subjective effects of a 15 dB(A) reduction in aircraft flyover noise. *Aviat. Space Environ. Med.* **48,** 607–611.

Levi, L. (1968). Sympatho-adrenomedullary and related biochemical reactions during experimentally induced emotional stress. *In* "Endocrinology and Human Behaviour" (R. P. Michael, ed.), pp. 200–219. Oxford Univ. Press, London.

Levi, L. (1973). Stress, distress and psychosocial stimuli. *Occup. Ment. Health* **3**(3), 2–10.

Loeb, M. (1954). "A Further Investigation of the Influence of Whole-Body Vibration and Noise on Tremor and Visual Acuity," Rep. No. 165. U.S. Army Med. Res. Lab., Fort Knox, Kentucky.

Loeb, M., Jones, P. D., and Cohen, A. (1976). "Effects of Noise on Non-Auditory Sensory Functions and Performance," HEW Publ. No. (NIOSH) 76-176. U.S. Dep. Health, Educ., Welfare, Washington, D.C.

Lukas, J. S. (1972). Awakening effects of simulated sonic booms and aircraft noise on men and women. *J. Sound Vib.* **20,** 457–466.

Lukas, J. S. (1977). "Measures of Noise Level: Their Relative Accuracy in Predicting Objective and Subjective Responses to Noise During Sleep," Rep. EPA 600/1-77-010. U.S. Environ. Prot. Agency, Washington, D.C.

Lukas, J. S., and Dobbs, M. E. (1972). "Effects of Aircraft Noises on the Sleep of Women," NASA CR-2041. NASA Langley Res. Cent., Hampton, Virginia.

Lukas, J. S., and Kryter, K. D. (1970). Awakening effects of simulated sonic booms and subsonic aircraft noise. *In* "Physiological Effects of Noise" (B. L. Welch and A. S. Welch, eds.), pp. 283–294. Plenum, Press, New York.

Maier, B., Bevan, W., and Behar, I. (1961). The effect of auditory stimulation upon the critical flicker frequency for different regions of the visible spectrum. *Am. J. Psychol.* **74,** 67–73.

Manninen, O., and Aro, S. (1979). Noise-induced hearing loss and blood pressure. *Int. Arch. Occup. Environ. Health* **42,** 251–256.

McCarthy, D. O., Ouimet, M. E. and Daun, J. M. (1992). The effects of noise stress on leukocyte function in rats. *Research in Nursing and Health* **15,** 131–137.

McCroskey, R. L., Jr. (1958). "The Effect of Specified Levels of White Noise Upon Flicker Fusion Frequency," Rep. No. 80. U.S. Nav. Sch. of Aviat. Med., Bur. Med. Surg., Washington, D.C. (Avail. from DTIC as AD 211759.)

McLean, E. K., and Tarnopolsky, A. (1977). Noise, discomfort and mental health. A review of the socio-medical implications of disturbance by noise. *Psychol. Med.* **7,** 19–62.

Meecham, W. C., and Shaw, N. (1979). Effects of jet noise on mortality rates. *Br. J. Audiol.* **13**(3), 77–80.

Meecham, W. C., and Shaw, N. (1980). Comments on "Los Angeles airport noise and mortality—Faulty analysis and public policy." *Am. J. Public Health* **70,** 543.

Meecham, W. C., and Smith, H. G. (1977). Effects of jet aircraft noise on mental hospital admissions. *Br. J. Audiol.* **11**(3), 81–85.

Melamed, S., Lug, J., and Green, M. S. (1992). Noise exposure, noise annoyance, and their relation to psychological distress, accident and sickness absence among blue-collar workers—the Cordis Study. *Israel J. Med. Sci.* **28,** 629–635.

Melzack, R. (1961). Perception of pain. *Sci. Am.* **204**(2), 41–49.

Meyer-Falcke, A., Lanzendorfer, A., Rack, R., and Jansen, G. (1993). Noise and pulmonary function: Is there a correlation? *Noise Public Health Probl. Proc. Int. Congr., 6th* (M. Vallet, ed.), Vol. 2, pp. 485–488. l'INRETS, 94114 Arcuil Cedex, France.

Mohr, G. C., Cole, J. N., Guild, E., and von Gierke, H. E. (1965). Effects of low frequency and infrasonic noise on man. *Aerosp. Med.* **36,** 817–824.

Møller, A. R. (1977). Occupational noise as a health hazard. *Scand. J. Work Environ. Health* **3,** 73–79.

Mosskov, J. I., and Ettema, J. H. (1977). IV. Extra-auditory effects in long term exposure to aircraft and traffic noise. *Int. Arch. Occup. Environ. Health* **40,** 177–184.

Mroz, E., Kopczynski, J., Szudrowicz, B., and Sadowski, J. (1978). Health sequelae of community noise. *Rocz. Panstw. Zakl. Hig.* **29,** 220–227.

Murphy, S., White, R., Kugler, B., Kictcheus, J., Smith, M., and Barber, D. (1993). Behavioral effects of jet aircraft on caribou in Alaska. *Noise Public Health Probl. Proc. Int. Congr., 6th* (M. Vallet, ed.), Vol. 2, pp. 479–486. l'INRETS, 94114 Arcuil Cedex, France.

Muzet, A., and Ehrhart, J. (1980). Habituation of heart rate and finger pulse responses to noise in sleep. *In* "Noise as a Public Health Problem," (J. V. Tobias, G. Jansen, and W. D. Ward, eds.), ASHA Rep. No. 10, pp. 401–404. Speech–Lang.–Hear. Assoc., Rockville, Maryland.

Muzet, A., Schieber, J. P., Olivier-Martin, N., Ehrhart, L., and Metz, B. (1973). Relationship between subjective and physiological assessments of noise disturbed sleep. *Proc. Int. Congr. Noise Public Health Probl.* (W. D. Ward, ed.), Rep. EPA 550/9-73-008, pp. 575–586. U.S. Environ. Prot. Agency, Washington, D.C.

Niaussat, M. M. (1977). Experimentally induced otitis and audiogenic seizure in the mouse. *Experientia* **33,** 473–474.

Nixon, C. W., and Johnson, D. L. (1973). Infrasound and hearing. *Proc. Int. Congr. Noise Public Health Probl.* (W. D, Ward, ed.), Rep. EPA 550/9-73-008. U.S. Environ. Prot. Agency, Washington, D.C.

Ogilvie, J. C. (1956). Effect of auditory flutter on the visual critical flicker frequency. *Can. J. Psychol.* **10,** 61–68.

O'Hare, J. (1956). Intersensory effects of visual stimuli on the minimum audible threshold. *J. Gen. Psychol.* **54,** 167–170.

Ohkubo, C., Miyazaki, K., and Osada, Y. (1976). Response of finger pulse amplitude to intermittent noise. *Bull. Inst. Public Health, Tokyo* **25,** 1–8.

Öhrstrom, E., and Rylander, R. (1982). Sleep disturbance effects of traffic noise—A laboratory study on after effects. *J. Sound Vib.* **84,** 87–103.

Olsen, J., and Nelson, E. N. (1961). Calming the irritable infant with a simple device. *Minn. Med.* **44,** 527–529.

Ortiz, G. A., Arguelles, A. E., Crespin, H. A., Sposari, G., and Villafane, C. T. (1974). Modifications of epinephrine, norepinephrine, blood lipid fractions and the cardiovascular system produced by noise in an industrial medium. *Horm. Res.* **5,** 57–64.

Osada, Y., Ogawa, S., Hirokawa, A., and Haruta, K. (1973). Physiological effects of long-term exposure to low-level noise. *Bull. Inst. Public Health, Tokyo* **22,** 61–67.

Oswald, L., Taylor, A. M., and Treisman, M. (1960). Discriminative responses to stimulation during human sleep. *Brain* **83,** 440–453.

Paolucci, G. (1975). Influence of the noise on catecholamine excretion. *In* "Effects of Long Duration Noise Exposure on Hearing and Health" (M. A. Whitcomb, ed.), Rep. AGARD-CP-171, pp. C9-1–C9-2. Eur. Space Agency, Neuilly-sur-Seine, France.

Parrack, H. O. (1966). Effect of air-borne ultrasound on humans. *Int. Audiol.* **5,** 294–308.

Parvizpoor, D. (1976). Noise exposure and prevalence of high blood pressure among weavers in Iran. *J. Occup. Med.* **18,** 730–731.

Patton, R. A. (1947). Purulent otitis media in albino rats susceptible to sound induced seizures. *J. Psychol.* **24,** 313–317.

Pearsons, K. S., and Kryter, K. D. (1965). "Laboratory Tests of Subjective Reactions to Sonic Booms," NASA CR-187. NASA Langley Res. Cent., Hampton, Virginia.

Peterson, E. A., Augenstein, J. S., Hosek, R. S., Klose, K. J., Manas, K., Bloom, J., Lovett, S., and Greenberg, D. A. (1975). Noise and cardiovascular function in rhesus monkeys. *J. Aud. Res.* **15,** 234–251.

Peterson, E. A., Tanis, D.C., Augenstein, J. S., Seifert, R. A., and Bromley, H. R. (1980). Noise and cardiovascular function in rhesus monkeys: 11. *In* "Noise as a Public Health Problem," (J. V. Tobias, G. Jansen, and W. D. Ward, eds.), ASHA Rep. No. 10, pp. 246–253. Am. Speech–Lang.–Hear. Assoc., Rockville, Maryland.

Peterson, E. A., Augenstein, J. S., Tanis, D. C., and Augenstein, D. G. (1981). Noise raises blood pressure without impairing auditory sensitivity. *Science* **211,** 1450–1452.

Peterson, P. K. (1991). Stress and pathogenesis of infectious disease. *Rev. Infect. Dis.* **13,** 700–710.

Pfaff, J. (1974). Noise as an environmental problem in the animal house. *Lab. Anim.* **8,** 347–354.

Pilawska, H., Mikulski, T., Rusin, J., Soroka, M., and Wysocki, K. (1977). Effect of acoustic microclimate prevailing in shipyards on the health of workers. *Med. Pr.* **28,** 441–447.

Plutchik, R. (1963). Physiological responses to high intensity intermittent sound. *Psychol. Rec.* **13,** 141–148.

Pritchett, J. F., Caldwell, R. S., Chesser, R. K., and Sartin, J. L. (1976). Effect of jet aircraft noise upon *in vitro* adrenocortical response to ACTH in feral *Mus Musculus*. *Life Sci.* **18,** 391–396.

Rabkin, J. G., and Struening, E. L. (1976). Live events, stress, and illness. *Science* **194,** 1013–1020.

Rechtschaffen, A., Hauri, P., and Zeitlin, M. (1976). Auditory awakening thresholds in REM and NREM sleep stages. *Percept. Motor Skills* **22,** 927–942.

Richter, R. (n.d.). "Sleep Disturbances Which We are Not Aware of Caused by Traffic Noise." EEG Stn., Neurol. Univ. Clin., Basel.

Rivera, R. L. (1978). Musicogenic epilepsy. *Bol. Asoc. Med. P.R.* **70**(5), 143–145.

Robson, J. G., and Davenport, H. T. (1962). The effects of white sound and music upon the superficial pain threshold. *Can. Anesthesiol. Soc. J.* **9,** 105–108.

Roggevsen, L. S., and Van Dishoeck, H. A. (1956). Vestibular reactions as a result of acoustic stimulation. *Pract. Oto-Rhino-Laryngol.* **18,** 205–213.

Rossi, L., Oppliger, G., and Grandjean, E. (1959). Neurovegetative effects on man of noises superimposed on a background noise. *Med. Lav.* **50,** 332–377.

Roth, T., Kramer, M., and Trinder, J. (1972). The effect of noise during sleep on the sleep patterns of different age groups. *Can. Psychiatr. Assoc. J.* **17,** Suppl. 2, 197–201.

Rubenstein, M. K. (1954). "Interaction Between Vision and Audition," Rep. No. 151. U.S. Army Med. Res. Lab., Fort Knox, Kentucky.

Saunders, J. C., Bock, G. R., Chen, C. S., and Gates, G. R. (1972). The effects of priming for audiogenic seizures on cochlear and behavioral responses in BALB/c mice. *Exp. Neurol.* **36,** 426–436.

Schell, L. M. (1981). Environmental noise and human prenatal growth. *Am. J. Phys. Anthropol.* **56,** 63–70.

Schell, L. M., and Ando, Y. (1991). Postnatal growth of children in relation to noise from Osaka International Airport. *J. Sound Vib.* **151,** 371–382.

Schmeck, K., and Poustka, F. (1993). Psychiatric and psychophysiological disorders in children living in a military jetfighter training area. *Noise Public Health Probl., Proc. Int. Congr., 6th* (M. Vallet, ed.), Vol. 2, pp. 477–480. l'INRETS, 94114 Arcuil Cedex, France.

Schust, M. (1993). Noise and cardiac infarction—A review. *Noise Public Health Probl., Proc. Int. Congr., 6th* (M. Vallet, ed.), Vol. 2, p. 573. l'INRETS, 94114 Arcuil Cedex, France.

Schwarze, S., and Thompson, S. (1993). Research on non-auditory physiological effects of noise since 1988: Review and perspectives. *Noise Public Health Probl., Proc. Int. Congr., 6th* (M. Vallet, ed.), Vol. 2, pp. 252–259. l'INRETS, 94114 Arcuil Cedex, France.

Shatalov, N. N., and Murov, M. A. (1970). The influence of intensive noise and neuropsychic tension on the level of arterial pressure and the incidence of hypertensive vascular disease. *Klin. Med. (Moscow)* **48**(Mar.), 70–73.

Sieber, W. J., Rodin, J., Larson, L., Ortega, S., and Cummings, N. (1992). Modulation of human natural killer cell activity by exposure to uncontrollable stress. *Brain. Behavior and Immunity* **6,** 141–156.

Simon, C. W., and Emmons, W. H. (1954). "A Critical Review of the 'Learn-While-You-Sleep' Studies," Rep. P-534 (June 14, 1954; rev. Oct. 14, 1954). Rand Corp., Santa Monica, California.

Skillern, C. P. (1965). Human response to measured sound pressure levels from ultrasonic devices. *J. Am. Ind. Hyg. Assoc.* **26,** 132–136.

Slob, A., Wink, A., and Radder, J. J. (1973). The effect of acute noise exposure on the excretion of corticosteroids, adrenalin and noreadrenalin in man. *Int. Arch. Arbeitsmed.* **31,** 225–235.

Sokolov, E. N. (1963). "Perception and the Conditioned Reflex" (S. W. Waydenfeld, transl.). Pergamon, Oxford.

Sonnenberg, A., Donga, M., Erckenbrecht, J., and Wienbeck, M. (1984). The effect of mental stress induced by noise of gastric acid secretion and mucosal blood flow. *Scand. J. Gastroenterol., Suppl.* No. 89, 45–48.

SRI (1967). "Sonic Boom Experiments at Edwards Air Force Base," NSBEO-1-67 (Contract AF 49(638)-1758). CFSTI, U.S. Dep. Commer., SRI Int., Menlo Park, California.

Stansfeld, S. and Shine, P. (1993). Noise sensitivity and psychophysiological responses to noise in the laboratory. *Noise Public Health Probl. Proc. Int. Congr., 6th* (M. Vallet, Ed.), Vol. 2, pp 481–484. l'INRETS, 94114 Arcuil Cedex, France.

Stansfeld, S., Gallacher, J., Babisch, W., and Elwood, P. (1993). Road traffic noise, noise sensitivity and psychiatric disorder: Preliminary prospective findings from the Caerphilly study. *Noise Public Health Probl., Proc. Int. Congr., 6th* (M. Vallet, ed.), Vol. 2, pp. 268–273. l'INRETS, 94114 Arcuil Cedex, France.

Stephan, E. (1993). Behavioral patterns of domestic animals as induced by different qualities and quantities of aircraft noise. *Noise Public Health Probl., Proc. Int. Congr., 6th* (M. Vallet, ed.), Vol. 3, pp. 482–494. l'INRETS, 94114 Arcuil Cedex, France.

Stern, R. M. (1964). Effects of variation in visual and auditory stimulation on gastrointestinal motility. *Psychol. Rep.* **14,** 799–802.

Surwillo, W.W., and Arenberg, D. L. (1965). On the law of initial value and the measurement of change. *Psychophysiology* **1,** 368–370.

Suzuki, S., Kawada, T., Sato T., Naganuma, S., Ogawa, S., and Aoki, S. (1993). Decrease in stage REM, as a most sensitive indicator of all-night noise exposure. *Noise Public Health Probl., Proc. Int. Congr., 6th* (M. Vallet, ed.), Vol. 2, pp. 579–582. l'INRETS, 94114 Arcuil Cedex, France.

Sze, P. Y. (1970). Neurochemical factors in auditory stimulation and development of susceptibility to audiogenic seizures. *In* "Physiological Effects of Noise" (B. L. Welch and A. S. Welch, eds.), pp. 259–270. Plenum, New York.

Takala, J., Varke, S., Vaheri, E., and Sievers, K. (1977). Noise and blood pressure. *Lancet* **ii,** 974–975.

Talbott, E., Helmkamp, J., Matthews, K., Kuller, L., Cottington, E., and Redmond, G. (1985). Occupational noise exposure, noise-induced hearing loss, and the epidemiology of high blood pressure. *Am. J. Epidemiol.* **121,** 501–514.

Talbott, E., Findlay, R., Kuller, L., Lenker, L., Matthews, K., Day, R., and Ishii, E. (1990). Noise-induced hearing loss: A possible marker for high blood pressure in older noise-exposed populations. *J. Occup. Med.* **32,** 690–697.

Talbott, E., Findlay, R., Kuller, L., Day, R., and Ishii, E. (1993). Noise-induced hearing loss and high blood pressure. *Noise Public Health Probl., Proc. Int. Congr., 6th* (M. Vallet, ed.), Vol. 2, pp. 461–464. l'INRETS, 94114 Arcuil Cedex, France.

Tanner, J. M. (1986). Growth as a mirror of the condition of society: secular trends and class distinctions. *In* "Human Growth: A Multidisciplinary Review" (A. Demirjian, ed.), Taylor and Francis, Philadelphia.

Tarnopolsky, A., Hand, D. J., Barker, S. M., and Jenkins, L. M. (1980). Aircraft noise, annoyance, and mental health: A psychiatric viewpoint. *In* "Noise as a Public Health Problem" (J. V. Tobias, G. Jansen, and W. D. Ward, eds.), ASHA Rep. No. 10, pp. 588–593. Am. Speech–Lang.–Hear. Assoc., Rockvill, Maryland.

Thiessen, G. J. (1980). Habituation of behavioral awaking and EEG measures of response to noise. *In* "Noise as a Public Health Problem" (J. V. Tobias, G. Jansen, and W. D. Ward, eds.), ASHA Rep. No. 10. Am. Speech–Lang.–Hear. Assoc., Rockville, Maryland.

Tonndorf, M.D. (1973). The influence of service on submarines on the organ of corti. Personal Notes provided to Nixon and Johnson, 1973.

Travis, H. F., Bond, L., Wilson, R. L., Leekley, J. R., Menear, J. R., Curran, C. R., Robinson, F. R., Brewer, W. E., Huttenhauer, G. A., and Henson, J. B., (1972). "An Interdisciplinary Study of the Effects of Real and Simulated Sonic Booms on Farm-Raised Mink (*Mustela vison*)," FAA-EQ72-2. Fed. Aviat. Adm., Washington, D.C.

Vallet, M., Gagneux, J. M., and Simonnet, F. (1980). Effects of aircraft noise on sleep: An *in situ* experience. *In* "Noise as a Public Health Problem" (J. V. Tobias, G. Jansen, and W. D. Ward, eds.), ASHA Rep. No. 10, pp. 391–396. Am. Speech–Lang.–Hear. Assoc., Rockville, Maryland.

Van Dijk, F. J. H. (1986). Non-auditory effects of noise in industry, II. A review of the literature. *Internt. Arch. Occup. and Environ. Health* **58,** 325–332.

Vanderhei, S. L., and Loeb, M. (1976). Effects of bilateral and unilateral continuous and impact noise on equilibrium as measured by the rail test. *J. Appl. Psychol.* **61,** 123–126.

Von Gierke, H. E. (1980). Exposure to combined noise and vibration environments. *In* "Noise as a Public Health Problem" (J. V. Tobias, G. Jansen, and W. D. Ward, eds.), ASHA Rep. No. 10, pp. 649–656. Am. Speech–Lang.–Hear. Assoc., Rockville, Maryland.

Walker, E. L., and Sawyer, T. M., Jr. (1961). The interaction between critical flicker frequency and acoustic stimulation. *Psychol. Rec.* **11,** 187–191.

Weisse, C. S., Pato, C. N., McAllister, C. G., Littman, R., Paul, S. M., and Baum, A. (1990). Differential effects of controllable and uncontrollable acute stress on lymphocyte proliferation and lekocyte percentages in humans. *Brain, Behavior, and Immunity* **4,** 339–351.

Welch, B. L. (1978). "Extra-Auditory Health Effects of Industrial Noise—Survey of Foreign Literature," Contract No. 16-BB-7. Welch Assoc., Baltimore, Maryland.

Welch, B. L., and Welch, A. S., eds. (1970). "Physiological Effects of Noise." Plenum, New York.

Williams, H. L., Hammack, J. T., Daly, R. L., Dement, W. C., and Lubin, A. (1964). Responses to auditory stimulation, sleep loss, and the EEG stages of sleep. *Electroencephalogr. Clin. Neurophysiol.* **16,** 269–279.

Wong, K. (1986). Quantitation of the respiratory bust induced in human neutrophils by phorbol myritate acetate. *In* "CRC Handbook of Methods for Oxygen Radical Research" (R. Greenwald, ed.), pp. 369–372. CRC Press, New York.

Wu, T., Chou, F., and Chang, P. (1987). A study of noise-induced hearing loss and blood pressure in mill workers. *Int. Arch. Occup. Environ. Health* **59,** 529–536.

Zhao, Y., Zhang, S., Selvin, S., and Spear, R. (1993a). A dose–response relationship between cumulative noise exposure and hypertension among female textile workers without hearing protection. *Noise Public Health Probl., Proc. Int. Congr., 6th* (M. Vallet, ed.), Vol. 3, pp. 274–279. l'INRETS, 94114 Arcuil Cedex, France.

Zhao, Y., Zhang, S., and Spear, R. (1993b). Investigation of dose–response relationships for noise-induced neurasthenia syndrome. *Noise Public Health Probl. Proc. Int. Congr., 6th* (M. Vallet, ed.), Vol. 2, pp.493–496. l'INRETS, 94114 Arcuil Cedex, France.

Zvereva, G. S., Ratner, M. V., and Kolganov, A. V. (1975). Noise of a rolling mill and its influence on the bodies of workers. *Gig. Sanit.* **11,** 104–105.

10

Community Reactions to Environmental Noise

INTRODUCTION

In the 1940s, citizens' complaints to authorities about the noise in residential areas from vehicles of transportation, particularly that from aircraft, started to increase. The reason for this is evidenced in Table 10.1, which shows that the average of samples of primarily single-family-residence areas, approximately 80–90% of the people were not at all disturbed by most of the noises typically found in such neighborhoods; only 65% were not disturbed by noise from automobiles; and only 9% were not disturbed by the noise from aircraft. Indeed, the percentage of people moderately, very, or extremely disturbed by aircraft noise day–night average levels, L_{dn}, as low as 55 dB_A exceeded the percentages thus disturbed by noise from cars, buses, and trucks combined.

For assessment purposes, single-number indices of the effective amount of outdoor noise present in a given residential area were developed that fairly well predicted the average amount of subjective annoyance experienced in that neighborhood. The indices required the measurement, or estimate, of the amount, in a typical 24-h day (annual daily average), of specially weighted noise energy present outdoors at a point on the ground, or in an area, of interest.

TABLE 10.1 Subjective Ratings of Disturbance

A. Environmental Noises

Noise source	Percentage of people rating disturbance as None	A little	Moderately	Very and extremely
Loud neighbors	88	3	3	5
Loud radios	89	3	3	4
Barking dogs	81	5	9	5
Children	94	2	1	4
Lawnmowers	95	3	1	1
Motorcycles	80	6	7	5
Industries	90	3	4	2
Autos	65	11	16	7
Buses	95	2	1	3
Trucks	86	3	6	5
Aircraft	9	16	31	41

B. Aircraft Noise in Different Zones

Aircraft zone, L_{dn}, dB	Percentage of people rating disturbance as None	A little	Moderately	Very and extremely
Less than 55	15	38	38	9
55–60	20	35	35	10
60–65	10	10	53	27
65–70	17	17	39	27
70–75	14	14	18	54
75–80	0	0	50	50

From Department of Aviation (1981)

TABLE 10.1a Annoyance from Aircraft Noise, Percentage of Respondents

Survey question	Level AC noise	Annoyance scale (%) Low	Moderate	High
	Low	59	9	2
TV/Radio	Moderate	15	6	1
	High	26	85	**97**
	Low	65	16	2
Conversation	Moderate	13	8	1
	High	22	76	**97**
	Low	43	9	1
Startle	Moderate	24	10	2
	High	33	81	**97**
	Low	96	72	15

(Continues)

TABLE 10.1a Continued

		Annoyance scale (%)		
Survey question	Level AC noise	Low	Moderate	High
Rest/relax	Moderate	3	8	3
	High	1	20	**83**
	Low	49	25	5
Fears crashes	Moderate	42	40	20
	High	9	35	**75**
	Low	98	84	30
Sleep	Moderate	1	5	2
	High	1	11	**68**
	Low	93	75	28
Rattles/vibrations	Moderate	5	12	4
	High	2	13	**68**
	Low	84	66	25
Affects health	Moderate	9	17	16
	High	7	17	**59**
	Low	50	30	18
Misfeasance	Moderate	22	24	20
	High	28	46	**62**
	Low	12	17	20
AC important	Moderate	25	24	30
	High	63	59	**50**

Source: Borsky (1980).

It is the custom to measure, or estimate, this environmental noise near the facade of a house or building closest to the most intense—if there is only one-noise source. This is done as a practical matter, even though the effects to be evaluated will be due to such noise experienced over time in different spaces in and around the structure. Some form of this procedure is now used in most industrialized countries for land-use zoning, and the enforcement and adjudication of legal issues related to the taking, because of the effects of excessive noise, of property values, health, and well-being.

The unit of noise exposure presently employed for this purpose in the United States is the average of the sum of the A-weighted sound energies in the 86,400 s during, on an annualized basis, a 24-h day, with a penalty of 10 dB added to the energies present during the hours of 10:00 PM to 7:00 AM. This unit is called the "level, day–night," labeled L_{dn}, also DNL, in dB or dB_A. To facilitate comparisons of findings among different research studies to be discussed, noise dosages expressed in other terms will be converted to approximate equivalent L_{dn} values in so far as possible and needed. Although developed primarily for applications to aircraft noise, these measures are now often used for the assessment of environmental noises in general.

$$(L_{dn}\ (\text{DNL}) = 10 \log ((1/54{,}000\ (10^{L_A 1s,7am..L_A 1s,10pm)/10}) + (10(1/32{,}400\ (10^{L_A 1s,10pm..L_A 1s,7am)/10})), \text{dB}.$$

Approximate conversions of some other published measures of daily noise exposures to environmental noise to L_{dn} are: L_{dn} = Composite Noise Rating (CNR) − 35; L_{dn} = Noise Exposure Forecast (NEF) + 40; L_{dn} = Noise and Number Index (NNI) + 25; L_{dn} = Community Noise Exposure Level (CNEL) − 2; L_{dn} = Weighted Equivalent Perceived Noise Level (WECPNL) in dB_A − 2.

The L_{dn} unit has behind it a long history of somewhat different formulations. Its foundations are in reports of Rosenblith and Stevens (1953) and Stevens and Pietrasanta (1957) that describe the CNR scheme. For descriptions of the predecessors of L_{dn}, and similar methods, such as Noise Exposure Forecast (NEF), of measuring environmental noise exposure levels in the United States, and other countries, see Galloway and Von Gierke (1966); Galloway and Bishop (1970), and EPA (1974). Research continues in attempts to provide modifications of the present treatments of noise measurements that will improve the prediction of annoyance of as broad a range as possible of noise levels, types of sources, and listening environments.

Basic Assumptions

The procedures for estimating subjective annoyance and complaints about environmental noise are intended for the assessment of the reactions of large groups or neighborhoods of people, and not specific individuals within a group. The development and application of these procedures requires that a number of formidable, and limiting, assumptions be made. Principal among them are the following:

1. Interference effects of noise with the activities of sleep and resting, and with the reception of speech and other wanted sounds, are significant causes of annoyance reactions to noise.
2. Over a broad range, the interference effects with behavior and perceived loudness–annoyance are correlated with and predictable from frequency and temporal weighted measures of sound energy. A corollary of this assumption is that the source of the noise is not a necessary confounding variable to these effects, even though cognitive meanings associated with the individual sources may also influence complaint behavior in response to annoyances felt because these effects occur; that is, while different meanings held by individuals with respect to given sources of noise may influence complaint behavior about the noise from different sources, the

perceptual and interference effects per se will (1) be, taking into account individual differences with respect to response sensitivities, about the same, provided the noise is equal at the position of the different listeners, and (2) monotonically increase for all normal individuals as exposure level in increased above their respective individual thresholds of response sensitivity.

3. People with different basic psychological and physiological sensitivities to stimulation, and with different idiosyncratic emotion-arousing associations to specific noise sources, are randomly distributed among neighborhoods.

4. The interference effects, and amount of related annoyance, if any, will jointly depend on the activity of an individual when a noise event occurs, and on the intensity level and duration of the event. It is further assumed that over typical days, the number of annoyances experienced averaged over relatively large groups of people in a given L_{dn}, or equivalent, noise area will be about the same; that is, the activities that are affected by the noise are engaged in to about the same extent by the majority of people.

5. A majority of the people in a given neighborhood have been exposed for months or years to the noise(s), so that knowledge of the sources, the psychological effects of unexpectedness, and, within limits, startle, are considered to be nondominant variables determining group reactions to the environmental noises.

In one way or another, basic laboratory research and psychological and physiological principles can perhaps provide a basis for satisfying the first two required assumptions listed above—that annoyance from inherent subjective auditory perceptions and the behavior interference effects of noise are predictable from properly treated acoustical information about environment noise. However, the influences of situation-related acoustical conditions, social and demographic factors, habituation, lifestyle activities, and idiosyncratic attitudes on the reactions of groups to environmental noise can be realistically determined only from information collected from people in real-life conditions.

Discussed in the following section are data on: (1) attitude survey methodology for quantifying community annoyance, (2) reactions of people to community noise as measured by surveys of attitudes and complaint behavior to authorities, including legal actions, (3) the effects of environmental noise on property values; (4) the effects intruding outdoor noise has on pupil and teacher performances in schools, (5) possible modifications for the improvement of the ability of the L_{dn} procedure to predict community reaction to environmental noises; and (6) identifying the kinds and degrees of individual and social/group incompatibilities with living in the presence of different amounts of environmental noise.

METHODOLOGY OF ATTITUDE SURVEYS OF NOISE ANNOYANCE

The primary objective of attitude surveys about noise is, usually, to determine the percentages of people in neighborhoods with different subjective magnitudes of annoyance as a function of the level of exposure to the noise. A secondary goal is to determine what specific effects of noise and related conditions cause such annoyance reactions. The two methods most commonly used in the attitude surveys of annoyance are to ask respondents: (1) to mark the point within numbered steps of a printed line-scale, the point that best reflects the subjective magnitude of their annoyance within the range of "none," at the bottom or start of the line to "extreme," at the top or end of the line. This method directly provides a numerical estimation of the magnitude of the subjective attitude; and (2) which of certain prescribed words, or phrases, describing categories of annoyance, best describes their degree of subjective annoyance, e.g., "(a) not at all, (b) slightly, (c) moderately, (d) very, or (e) extremely." The number and wording of the categories are chosen by the experimenter to be appropriate to the goals of the survey.

Development of Survey Scales for Noise Effects

Data from two early surveys conducted near Heathrow Airport in London were used to derive a general scale of annoyance from noise (Committee on the Problem of Noise, 1963; MIL Research, 1971). In the Heathrow studies, the answers to several questions concerning annoyance and disturbance from aircraft noise were summed in certain ways to arrive at the overall annoyance score. The response scores corresponding, approximately, to the verbal categories "not at all," "a little," "moderately," and "very much annoyed" were identified. On the basis of additional studies and analyses to be described, other verbal descriptors corresponding to different parts of the general annoyance scale have been derived.

Schultz (1978) proposed that respondents to the top 27–29% of the subject magnitude of annoyance be classified as "highly annoyed." The 7- and 11-step numerical magnitude estimation scales used in some French and Swiss surveys lent themselves to such a partitioning. It was argued by Schultz that counting only those marks falling within the top step, or top 14%, of a 7-step scale, as representing those persons who were highly annoyed, must miss some people who are highly annoyed; but that counting the top 3 steps of that scale, 43%, would include almost the entire half of the scale. The top two segments of the 7-step scale, about 29%, or the top three of an 11-step scale, 27%, were proposed by Schultz as encompassing the portion of subjective annoyance, that of "high-annoyance," that is of significance for assessing the impact of environmental noise on communities.

Determining reliable relations between noise exposure level for different noise conditions and "high annoyance" has been a matter of continuing research. However, combining the findings of surveys of noise annoyance in order to achieve "consensus" conclusions has been difficult. One obstacle to reaching that end has been the use, in different studies, of different numbers of steps and different terminologies for identifying degrees of annoyance in categories scales. Some of these difficulties, and proposed resolutions, will be discussed later with respect the findings of recent attitude surveys of annoyance from aircraft and ground-based vehicle noises.

Of course, it does not, within limits, matter exactly what percentage of the annoyance scale is specified to represent the amount of noise annoyance found in different environments. The more important practical issue is the determination of the relation between (1) some attitude survey-measureable criterion or criteria of subjective annoyance, and (2) objectively measurable social and political behaviors and effects in response to environmental noise. This latter issue will be discussed last in this chapter.

Early Attitude Surveys of Aircraft Noise

Figure 10.1 shows, as a function of L_{dn}, the percentage of people who were rated as annoyed to some degree on the scale derived from the Heathrow surveys. Also shown, to indicate further the consistency among the results for some of the early aircraft noise attitude surveys, is a trend curve derived by Alexandre, 1970, from the combined results of surveys in Paris, Amsterdam, and the first Heathrow survey. Grandjean *et al.* (1973, 1976), Grandjean (1980), also showed the general similarity of the results from surveys of annoyance from aircraft noise when the exposure levels for the different studies were all expressed in approximate equivalent levels of exposure.

The data on Fig. 10.1 indicate that 4% of the people will rate the aircraft noise environment as "extremely annoying" no matter how far it falls below an L_{dn} of 50 dB, and that at an extrapolated L_{dn} of 35 dB, 30% of the people will say they are "a little" annoyed. The latter extrapolation may not be too far-fetched for a percentage of supersensitive people in that five daily aircraft noise occurrences at an outdoor peak level of about 71 dB_A, and a 10-s duration above 61 dB_A, would have an L_{dn} of 35 dB. Such noise occurrences conceivably could be sources, on occasion, of some disturbance and annoyance to speech communication or sleep. But the asymptotic slope of the other curves as they approach $L_{dn} < 50$ (at 30–35% of the people responding in the top 70% of the scale) would suggest that there were people probably responding to aircraft noise independently of its intensity or effects on sleep, hearing, or house vibration.

These asymptotic percentages for the given degrees of annoyance represent people who are (1) exposed to aircraft noise events not included in the calculated, or measured, L_{dn}, (2) biased against aircraft operations in general, and (3) confused by the survey questions. This suggestion, while speculative, addresses the question of why aircraft noise at apparently inaudible levels

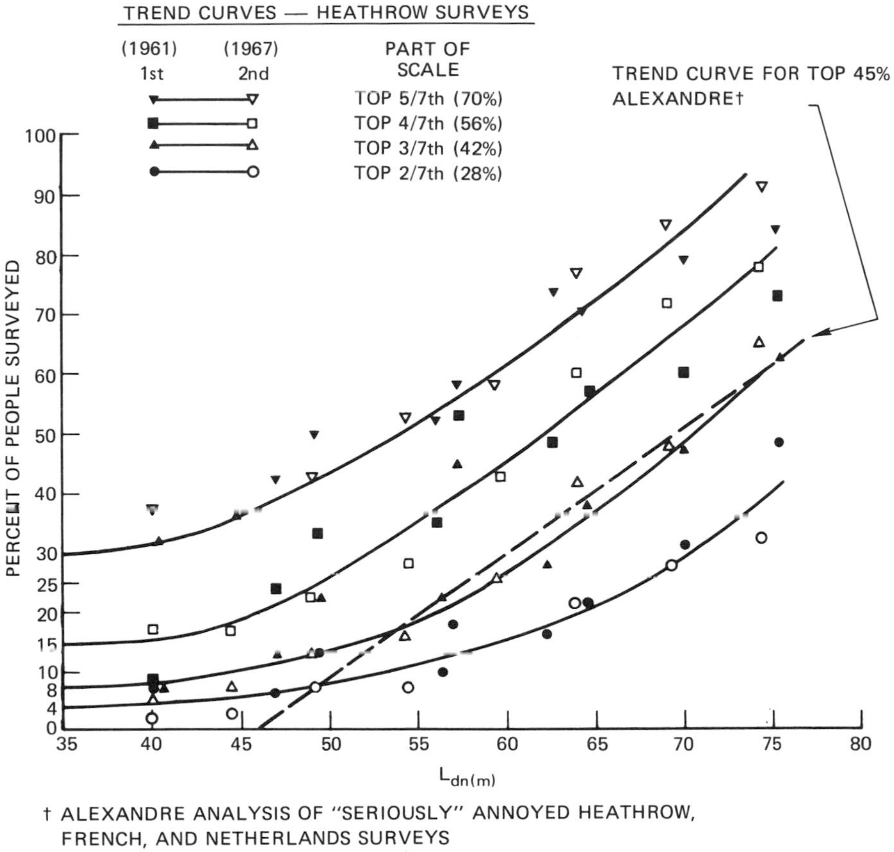

FIGURE 10.1 Percentages of people rated at or above various points of the annoyance scale derived from the Heathrow studies as a function of $L_{dn(m)}$ ($L_{dn(m)}$ calculated from maximum levels, see text), as calculated or estimated in present analysis. [Also shown is trend curve from Alexandre (1970, 1973) and Kryter (1982a). Copyright 1982 by the American Psychological Association. Adapted by permission of the author.]

in typical residential environments appears, from some attitude surveys, to be a cause of feelings of extreme annoyance to some individuals. So-called synthesis and trend functions relating noise exposures to annoyance, to be presented and developed later in the text, tacitly apply such corrections at minimum exposure levels in that they are extrapolated to a zero-response exposure level.

Annoyance-Causing Effects of Aircraft Noise

Examples of the effects of noise that are a cause of annoyance are presented in Fig. 10.2, from surveys conducted in Great Britain, Switzerland, and France. It is to be noted that the terminology used in questions concerned

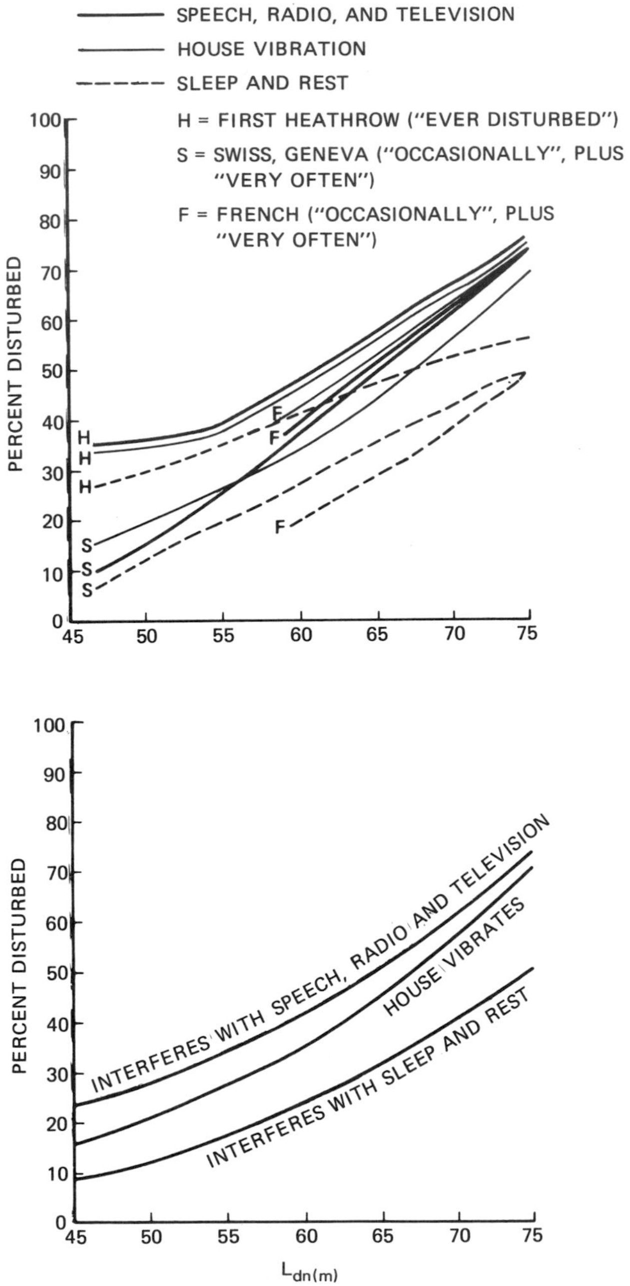

FIGURE 10.2 Disturbances from aircraft noise. Studies: Heathrow (Committee on the Problem of Noise, 1963); Swiss, Geneva Grandjean, et al., 1973); French (Alexandre, 1973).

with disturbances from the noise is somewhat different from study to study (e.g., "ever disturbed," "strongly disturbed," "very often") so that a closer clustering of the results for the various studies is probably not to be expected. Disturbances from house vibration and vibration-induced rattles include cessation of auditory communication, interference with sleep, and, sometimes, concern about possible damage to windows and plaster in the house.

Taylor *et al.* (1981) found that the overall annoyance from aircraft noise in communities with equal L_{dn} exposure was about equal for major airports in Canada and in Japan. At the same time, the relative percentages of people highly annoyed by the noise because of sleep interference compared with speech interference differed in a way commensurate with differences in the number of high-level nighttime operations. (The issue of the "penalty" for sleep arousal by noises occurring during nighttime will be discussed later in a separate section of this chapter.)

One of the major correlates of disturbance from aircraft noise is that of the fear people feel when the noise becomes sufficiently intense. It is seen in Fig. 10.3 that fear becomes increasingly an disturbing effect as the aircraft noise exposure exceeds L_{dn} ~55 dB. For L_{dn} ~70 dB "fright" from street traffic occurs less frequently than the other effects, and dramatically less frequently than "fear" from aircraft. (Because the measurement of exposure levels may have systemically differed somewhat between the two studies

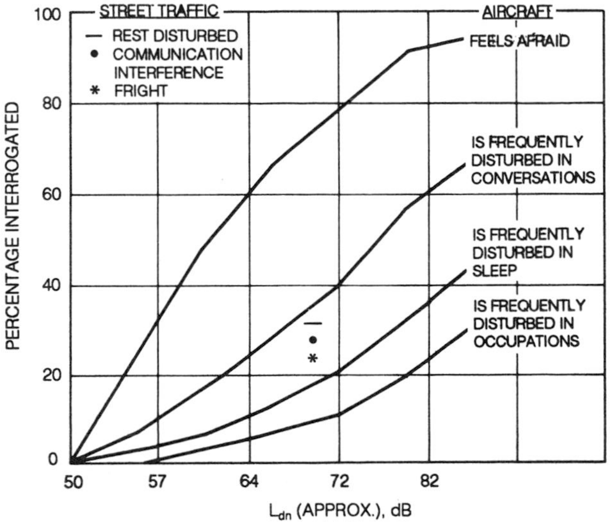

FIGURE 10.3 Results of community survey in the Netherlands on effects of aircraft noise [based on study by Bitter (1968), as reported by Galloway and Bishop (1979), with L_{dn} estimated herein]. Also, effects of street traffic noise in surveys in four Swiss cities. (From Nemecek *et al.*, 1981.)

involved, only the relative percentage differences in the effects within each study can be considered reliable.)

The fear expressed by people in attitude surveys is generally not considered in the assessment of the impact of aircraft noise on people because the sound energy per se is not the source of the fear. Scales of noise annoyance in attitude surveys, as will be discussed in more detail, have been mostly concerned with annoyance from behavior interference effects due to the noises, not emotions due to fear, or the like, nor attitudes that might influence complaint and annoyance behavior—such attitudes as a belief that those responsible for the noise are misfeasant, or that the noise source, on the other hand, is important to the economy, etc.

Although aircraft noise is disturbing because when sufficiently intense, it connotes the possibility an airplane crash, that concern is not as great a source of annoyance as are other effects of the noise. As seen in Table 10.1a, high annoyance is reported by 75% percent of the persons in the highest level of aircraft noise due to fear of crashes, but 83% due to interference with rest and relaxation, and 97% due to interference with conversation, television watching, or radio listening.

Correlations between L_{dn} and Percentage of People Annoyed

As shown in Table 10.2, the correlations between percentages of people "a little or more" annoyed and aircraft noise dosage in L_{dn} are of the order of .90–.95 for the Heathrow studies. This finding would indicate that those factors that contribute to variability in sensitivity to responses to the noise, whether they are demographic, personality differences, acoustical factors, or others, are rather evenly distributed among the different outdoor aircraft noise-level strata in the Heathrow studies. Hall *et al.* (1981) similarily found high correlations ($\geq$.90) between L_{dn} and attitudes of annoyance from exposure to aircraft, or to street traffic noise, when the attitude scores were averaged over neighborhoods exposed to given levels of exposure.

As seen in Table 10.2, restricting the range of noise strata over which the annoyance data are considered from a total range of 35 dB does not greatly reduce the magnitude of the correlations [the r correlations for the lower 23 dB (L_{dn} 40–62.6 dB) range from .88 to .95, and for the upper 20 dB (L_{dn} 55–75 dB) from .77 to .91]. This would indicate that judgments of annoyance to the lower-intensity noise exposures are fairly reliable.

The general reliability of attitude questionnaires is shown in Fig. 10.4. These data were obtained from random-sample surveys (over 3000 different households) independently taken at several different times from the same general neighborhood areas [Federal Aviation Administration (FAA), 1981]. These surveys were administered several times to people in aircraft noise environments with L_{dn} values ranging from about 58 to 69 dB, as shown by the dots in the upper graphs of Fig. 10.4. The surveys were given about

TABLE 10.2 Correlation Coefficients between $L_{dn(m)}$ and Cumulative Percentages of People Having Different Degrees of Annoyance from Aircraft Noise in the Heathrow Studies

		Correlation coefficient			
Study	$L_{dn(m)}$ range, dB	"A little or more annoyed" (scale categories 2–6)	"Moderately or more annoyed" (scale categories 3–6)	"Very much or more annoyed" (scale categories 4–6)	"Extremely annoyed" (scale categories 5 and 6)
First Heathrow	47.7–74.2	.94	.89	.88	.87
Second Heathrow	40.0–75.0	.97	.96	.97	.95
First and second combined	40.0–75.0	.95	.93	.93	.88
	40.0–62.6	.91	.86	.79	.77
	55.0–75.0	.90	.82	.86	.87
Average (first and second)		.93	.89	.89	.87

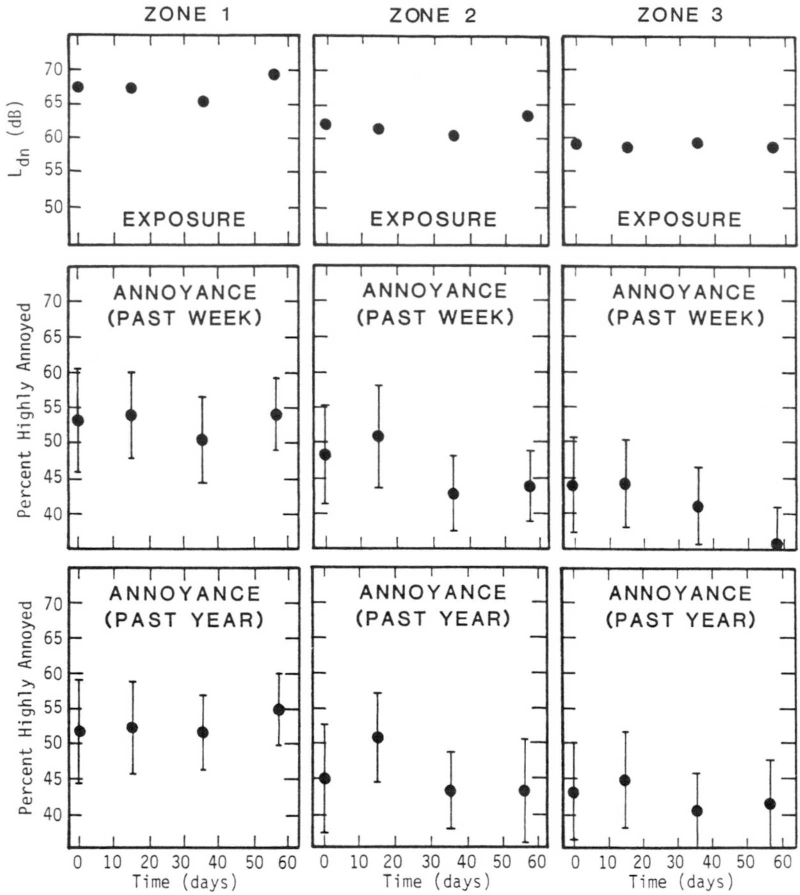

FIGURE 10.4 Results of repeated attitude surveys of annoyance due to aircraft noise in same neighborhood areas near a city. (From FAA, 1981.)

2 weeks apart, over a period of about 2 months. The subjects were asked to rate, on a five-category scale, their annoyance because of street traffic or aircraft noise during the past week, and for the noise from large airliners, during the past year. The percentage of people highly annoyed correlated about .90 with the L_{dn} exposure. The annoyance ratings for the past week were roughly the same as they were for remembrances of the past year (middle row compared with bottom row of graphs). In this investigation, "highly" annoyed referred to those people who rated their annoyance as "very" or "extreme," the top two categories, about 40%, of the five-category annoyance scale employed.

Griffiths and Delauzun (1977) found that much of the variability in predictions of individual annoyance from noise exposure appears to depend on the unreliability of the questionnaires rather than individual differences in sensitivity to noise. Griffiths *et al.* (1980) found that although the correlation coefficient was of the order of .40 between individual ratings of dissatisfaction with traffic and outdoor noise-exposure levels, the correlation became ~.90 when the median of four dissatisfaction ratings (obtained over a period of a number of months) for each of 222 individual respondent was related to noise-exposure level.

It has generally been held (McKennel, 1973; Borsky, 1976; Fields, 1993) that personality characteristics, differences in individual attitudes of misfeasance toward airport and aircraft operators, and fear of aircraft crashes are at the root of the low correlations (usually <.50) between noise exposure and annoyance in individuals. It is also probable that part of the reason for this relatively low correlation of annoyance in individuals in the same aircraft-noise area is that the L_{dn} values used to describe the aircraft noise do not adequately reflect the noise dosages actually received by individuals inside and outside their homes. The person who is more annoyed, suspects more misfeasance, or has more fear than his or her neighbor, may actually be exposed inside his or her house to levels of aircraft noise that are considerably higher than those experienced by his or her supposedly equally exposed neighbor when inside his or her house. Physical data on this point, and the influence of "nonacoustical" and situational-acoustical factors on noise annoyance reactions, will be presented later.

ANNOYANCE FROM AIRCRAFT AND GROUND-BASED VEHICLE NOISE

Schultz compared the results of a number of attitude surveys of annoyance from aircraft and ground vehicle noise conducted in several countries. From that analysis, a single "synthesis" curve, relating exposure level for the noise from any type of transportation vehicle to community annoyance, was prepared; thus, annoyance was predicted to be the same for aircraft and street vehicle noise when measured as being equal at the front facade of houses. This synthesis curve has been adopted by United States governmental agencies as a recommended guideline for the control of environmental noises in general, regardless of source.

An analysis of the findings of the same surveys was made later by Kryter (1982a). The end results of these two analyses are fairly similar with respect to the assessment of annoyance from solely aircraft noise, but differ more significantly with respect to annoyance from solely ground-based vehicle noise; for instance, Kryter found a difference between annoyance of aircraft and ground based vehicle noise, when measured as being equal at the front facade of houses, whereas Schultz did not.

Six major attitude surveys of aircraft noise, all conducted in Europe, were selected for detailed comparative analyses in the Schultz and Kryter reviews. Results of a surveys of aircraft noise conducted in the United States

(TRACOR, 1971; Patterson and Connor, 1973; Connor and Patterson, 1972) were not included because of scale interpretation difficulties. For all except one of the selected studies, the aircraft-noise-exposure levels were based on the noise and number index (NNI), or the peak or maximum level of intensity (L_A or PN_{dB}), reached at a given point on the ground noise event. The formula for NNI was developed in Great Britain for measuring aircraft noise (Committee on the Problem of Noise, 1963): NNI = peak PN_{dB} + (15 Log/N) − 80; or, NNI = Peak L_A + 13 + (15 Log/N) − 80; where N is the average number of flyover noise events per 24-h day.

The L_{dn} values were calculated from given numbers of daily aircraft noise events of given peak levels of intensity, corrected to the estimated "energy" in each flyover event. The formula used for this purpose by Schultz and Kryter was:

$$L_{dn} = \text{Peak } L_A + [10 \log(t/2)] \text{ or, } L_{ex} = \text{Peak PNL} - 13 + 10 \text{ Log}(t/2)] + 10 \text{ dB}_{\text{night time, 10 PM–7AM, penalty,}}$$

where t is the time in seconds between the 10-dB downpoints from the peak level. (Although without knowledge of numbers and times of operation involved it is not possible to do so exactly, usually in midrange of commercial aircraft operations, as afore mentioned, L_{dn} = NNI + 25.)

Figure 10.5 shows trend curves for the six European attitude surveys of annoyance from aircraft noise, as analyzed by Kryter. The average, dotted line, trend curve for aircraft noise is well fitted by the following polynomial expression:

$$\% \text{ Highly Annoyed} = 110.091 + (-5.023 \times \text{Ldn}) = (0.058 \times L_{dn}{}^2).$$

Also shown on Fig. 10.5 is the synthesis curve representing the results as analyzed by Schultz for the average of the same surveys of aircraft noise plus the data from a number of surveys of annoyance from ground based vehicles of transportation—those on streets, roads, and rails. Schultz concluded that the data for all these surveys and vehicles, aircraft and ground surveys and vehicles, aircraft and ground-based, clustered closely around a single curve, his synthesis curve. It is seen that the trend curve indicates considerably more annoyance from aircraft noise than the synthesis curve, the equivalent of 4–8 dB, in exposure level.

The difference between the results of analyses made by Schultz and by Kryter of noise annoyance from ground-based vehicles can be seen by comparing the synthesis curve in Fig. 10.6A with the trend curve in Fig. 10.6B. (The trend curve for the ground-based vehicle noise is well fitted by the following polynomial expression:

$$\% \text{ highly annoyed} = 113.5 + (-4.505 \times L_{dn}) + (0.045 \times L^2{}_{dn}).$$

Worthy of note, with respect to Fig. 10.6A, is that (1) the synthesis curve lies above most of the data points for the highest levels; and (2) there are

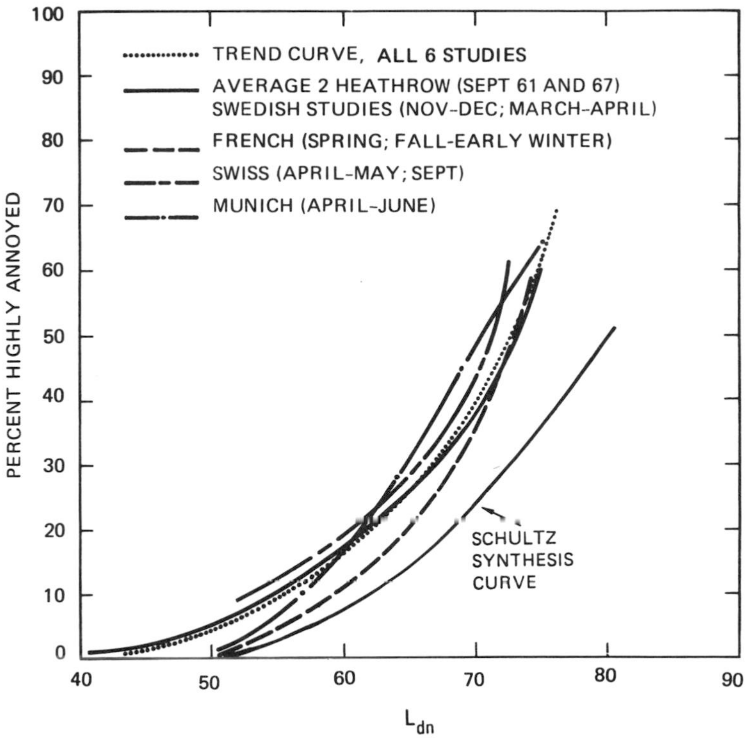

FIGURE 10.5 Results of attitude surveys of aircraft noise and visual-trend fit to the results, from Kryter (1982a, copyright 1982 by the American Psychological Association. Adapted by permission of the author). Percent "highly annoyed" is for the top 27–29% of an annoyance scale. Also shown is synthesis curve developed by Schultz (1978) of combined results of attitude surveys of noise annoyance from aircraft and to ground-based vehicles of transportation.

reasons for questioning, it is believed, the propriety of the inclusion of the data points for the London (L) and Paris (P) ground vehicle noise surveys. It is clear that with these "corrections," a visual fit to the remaining data points would be considerably lower at the higher levels of intensity than is the synthesis curve.

Data from the London and Paris ground-based vehicle noise surveys were not used in Fig. 10.6B, as a basis for the trend curve, for the following reasons:

1. The London survey data were omitted because a bipolar ("definitely satisfied" to "definitely unsatisfied" with the street noise) scale of annoyance was used, whereas a unipolar ("none" to "extreme," or the like) scale of annoyance was used in the other surveys. These two methods could be expected to differently partition the judged annoyance, the bipolar probably showing a higher percentage of people "unsatisfied."

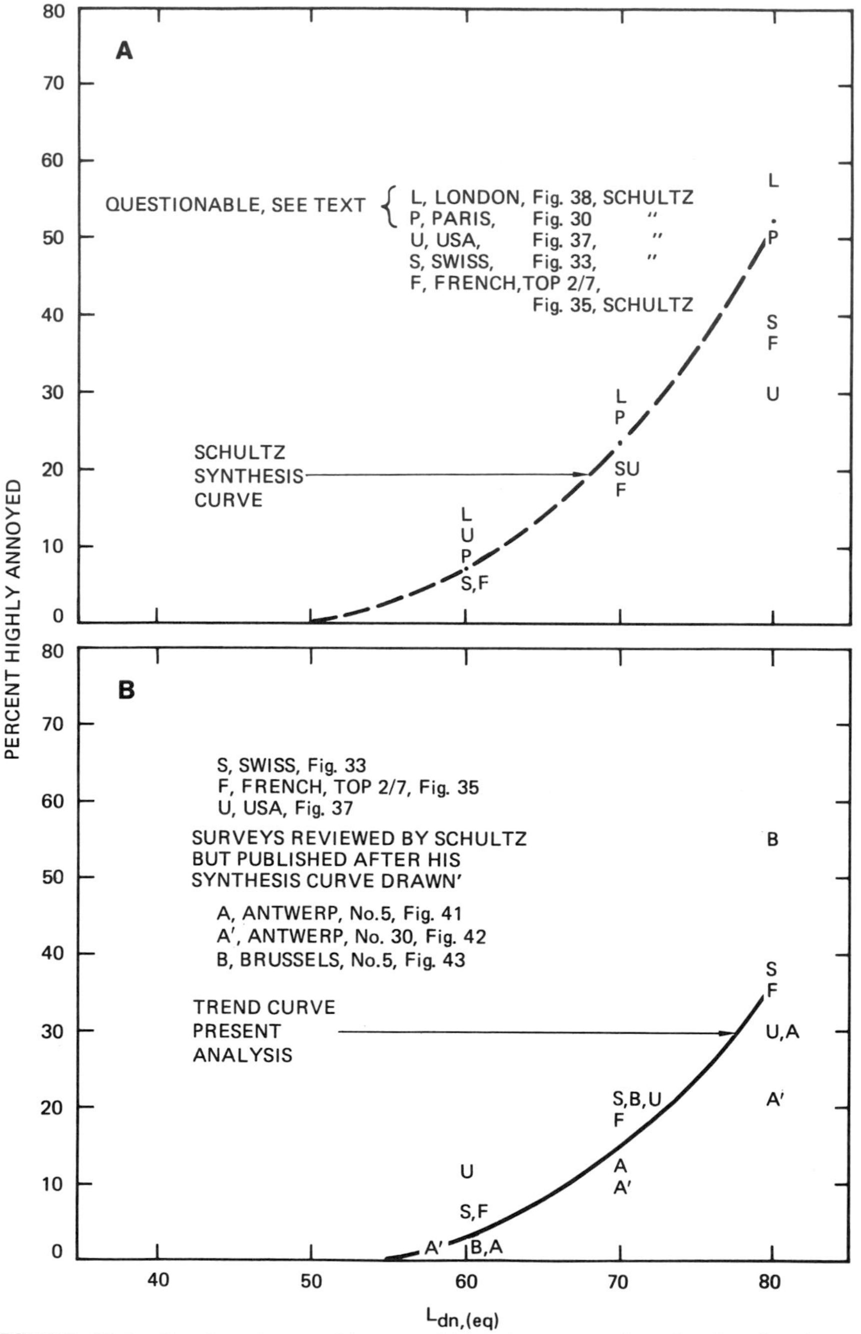

FIGURE 10.6 Results of ground-based vehicles (street, road, and railway) noise surveys, as analyzed by Schultz (A); and by Kryter, used in present analysis (B). "Highly annoyed" refers to top 27–29% of annoyance scale. Trend curve in B = 113.5 + $(-4.505 - L_{dn}) + (0.045 \times L_{dn}^2)$.

2. The Paris data were omitted because no truly comparative noise annoyance-scale questions were asked. Rather, respondents rank-ordered, from 1 to 10, dissatisfaction with amusements, schools, neighbors, shops, public services, etc. in their neighborhoods; those who gave street noise a "10" were called "highly annoyed." However, the number rating of the noise was with respect to the other variables, which could differ widely independently of the street noise, and not the amount of annoyance from the noise per se, e.g., a level of noise exposure rated "8" in an otherwise generally "fair" neighborhood, could be rated as "10" in an otherwise generally "good" neighborhood.

Included in Fig. 10.6B, but not in Fig. 10.6A, are the results of a number of good-quality surveys of attitudes about ground-based vehicle noise. (These results were reported on by Schultz, but were completed too late by him to be include in the derivation of his synthesis curve.) The trend curve of Fig. 10.6B shows considerably less annoyance, for a given L_{dn}, than the synthesis curve, the equivalent of about 2–4 dB.

Results from Comparative Surveys of Aircraft and Ground-Based Vehicle Noises

Figure 10.7A shows that there is about a 10 dB, on the average, difference between the trend curves deduced by Kryter for equal percentages of persons highly annoyed in these early surveys of aircraft, as compared to ground vehicle, noises. Some of this difference could possibly be because different people, houses, locales, and questionnaires were involved in the surveys for aircraft as compared to ground vehicle noise, and/or that experimental errors affected the findings. These experimental–procedural problems are overcome in a study conducted by Hall *et al.* (1981). In their investigation, the same attitude questionnaire was administered to the same people exposed to road vehicle and aircraft noise in their neighborhoods.

As seen in Fig. 10.7B, Hall *et al.* found a greater amount of annoyance from aircraft than road traffic noise of equal L_{dn}. The difference was equivalent to a difference of 8 dB (at aircraft noise of 56 L_{dn}) to 11 dB (at aircraft noise of 64 L_{dn}) in the noise levels, at the fronts of houses, measured or estimated. For both types of noises, the percentages of people "highly annoyed" are somewhat greater in Fig. 10.7B than in Fig. 10.7A. The reason is that in the Hall *et al.* study (Fig. 10.7B), the percentage "highly disturbed" was taken as the percentage of respondents who indicated the top two of five subjective reactions to the noise, reactions restricted to the following categories: (1) "neutral"; (2) "slightly"; (3) "moderately"; (4) "considerably"; (5) "extremely."

The top two categories corresponds to 40% of the subjective disturbed–annoyed scale available to the respondents. Whereas only about the top 27–29%

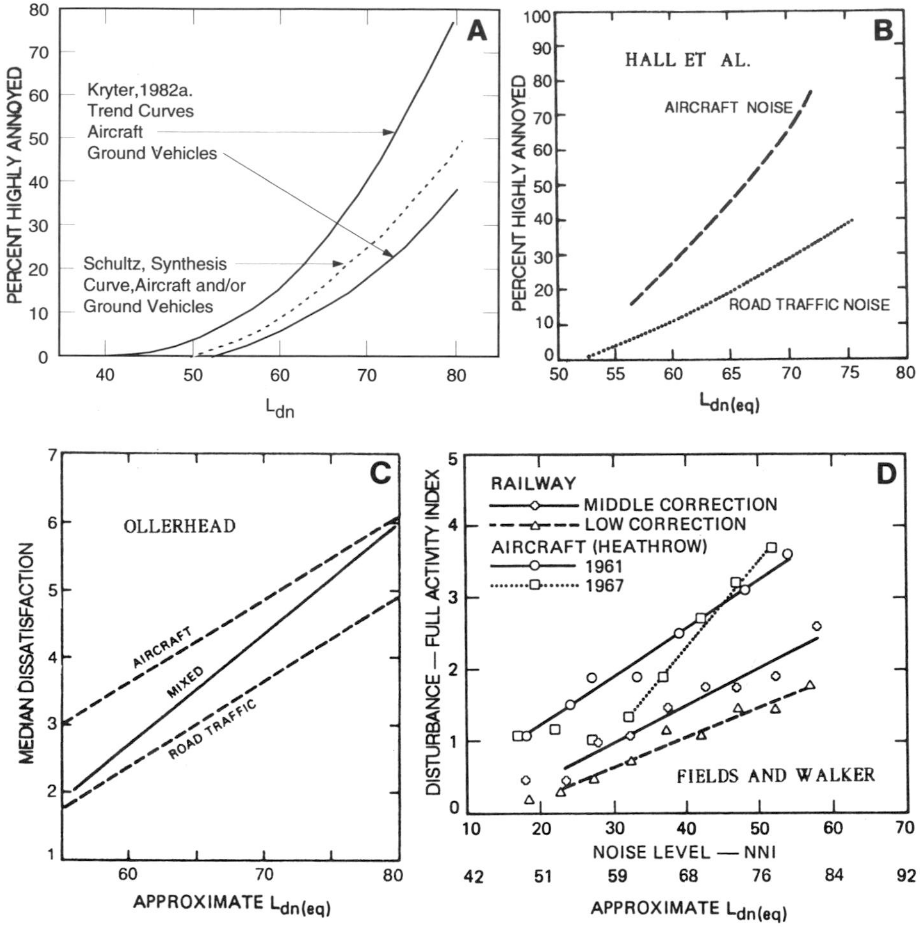

FIGURE 10.7 (A, B) Trend curves of percentage of people highly annoyed from aircraft as compared to ground-based vehicle noise, according to Kryter (1982a) and Hall *et al.* (1981). (C, D) Ratings of disturbance from aircraft as compared to road traffic and railway noise, according to Ollerhead (1980) and Fields and Walker (1980). Also, in (A), Schultz (1978) Synthesis curve of percent "highly annoyed" by either aircraft or ground-based vehicles.

of the highly annoyed magnitude-estimation scale was used for the Schultz and Kryter curves shown in Fig. 10.7A. However, the relative difference between the aircraft and road vehicle noise found by Hall *et al.* would not be affected by this factor, since the same scoring procedure was applied to both the aircraft and the road vehicle noise data. (It is noted that the words "annoyed," "disturbed," and "bothered" have come to be considered as synonyms when used in noise-attitude surveys. Indeed, the question is sometimes put: "How annoyed, disturbed, or bothered are you by the noise?" (Borsky, 1983)).

In Figs. 10.7C and 10.7D, studies by Ollerhead (1980) and Fields and Walker (1980) also show that aircraft noise causes more "dissatisfaction" and "disturbance" than does equal exposure levels of noise from road (Fig. 10.7C) or railways (Fig. 10.7D). Knall and Schuemer (1983) found a 4–5-dB_A difference between the L_{eq} levels of railway and road traffic noise (railway noise the higher) when equally annoying as measured by attitude surveys in 14 different areas in Germany. It appears that tramway (electric street–railway) noise is about equal to street traffic (presumably automobile–truck) noise (Rylander *et al.*, 1977.)

Miedam (1993) found from a compilation of data from a number of European studies that aircraft noise of L_{dn} 60–70 was the equivalent of ~5 dB more annoying than the noise from highways, or ~10 dB more than that from roads, and ~15 dB more than that from railroads. These differences could to some extent possibly be due to differences in acoustic-transmission path and sound-barrier differences for the different sources as associated with the points of noise measurements, as compared to the paths followed by the noises as received by the listeners.

Differences in Behaviors "Disturbed" by Aircraft and Road Traffic Noise

Grandjean *et al.* (1973, 1976; Grandjean, 1980) surveyed nearly 5000 people in the regions of Switzerland with respect to disturbances caused by aircraft and by road vehicle noises. Figure 10.8 shows that it takes an L_{dn} of 5–15 dB higher, depending on L_{dn} level, for road traffic noise than for aircraft noise to cause equal disturbance, averaged over all effects. It should be noted, however, that road noise and aircraft noise cause somewhat different patterns of effects. For example, conversation was less disturbed than was sleep by road noise, with the reverse being true for aircraft noise. Ishiyama (1993) also found that sleep disturbance caused by road traffic noise was considered a more serious problem by residents than that of conversation, watching television, or listening to radio, although the frequency of sleep disturbance was significantly less. This matter will be further discussed later in this chapter.

Reconciliation of Numerical Magnitude Estimation and Category Scales of Noise Annoyance

The variety of numerical magnitude estimation and category scales used in attitude surveys of noise annoyance, and some of the problems created for the interpretation of the data, will be illustrated later. Resolution of some part of those problems is found in the results of an attitude survey of aircraft noise conducted by Hede and Bullen (1982) (see Fig. 10.9). In that survey, some 3500 respondents were interviewed in five cities in Australia. Persons interviewed were asked to mark on a numerical magnitude-estimation scale

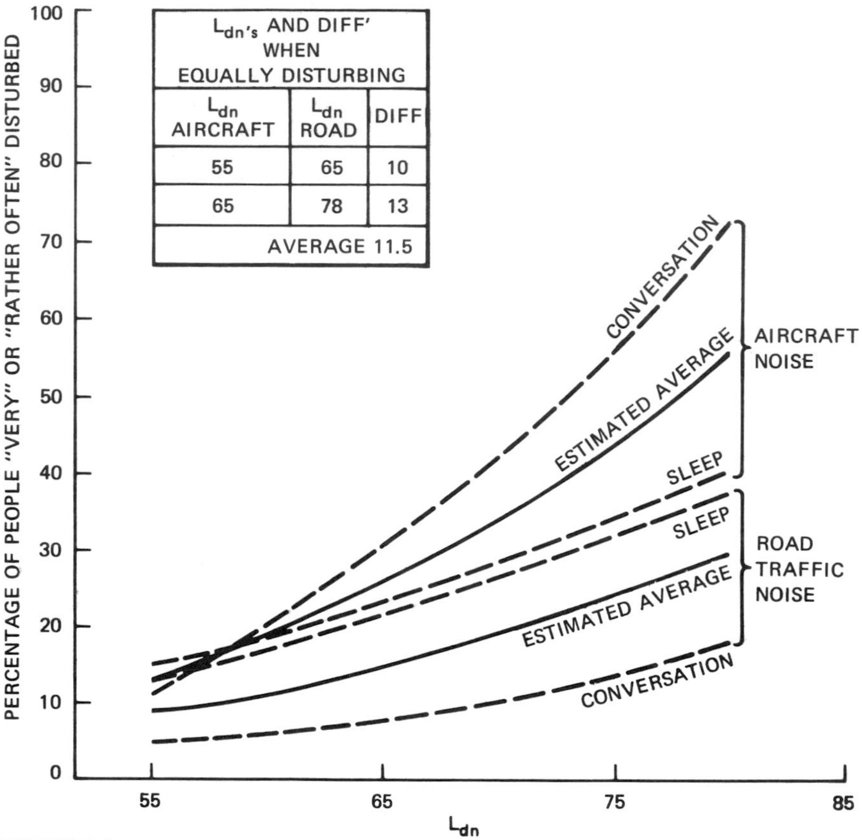

FIGURE 10.8 Average percentage of people disturbed from sleep and conversation by aircraft and by road traffic noise. Based on Grandjean *et al.*, 1973, Grandjean, 1980.)

(a printed "opinion thermometer," ranging from 0 to 10) their (1) subjective reaction as to the effects of, among other things, aircraft noise; (2) choice of category descriptions of noise annoyance describing their subjective annoyance reaction to the aircraft noise condition in their residential area, and reply on the following numerical magnitude scale: (I) "highly annoyed," (II) "considerably annoyed," (III) "moderately annoyed," or (IV) "slightly annoyed." A fifth category, (V) "not annoyed," is assumed as being implied, although not explicitly asked. [This assumption is that made for other similarly worded category scales in which the lowest-named category is "slightly annoyed"; e.g., see Fidell *et al.* (1991) regarding data of Schomer (1983b).]

The significance of this numerical magnitude rating of the category-named levels of annoyance is, of course, that it allows for the "calibration" of the named categories into the approximate percentages each category encompasses on the more finely graded scale of the estimated numerical magnitude of annoyance. The relevant results of the Hede and Bullen surveys are

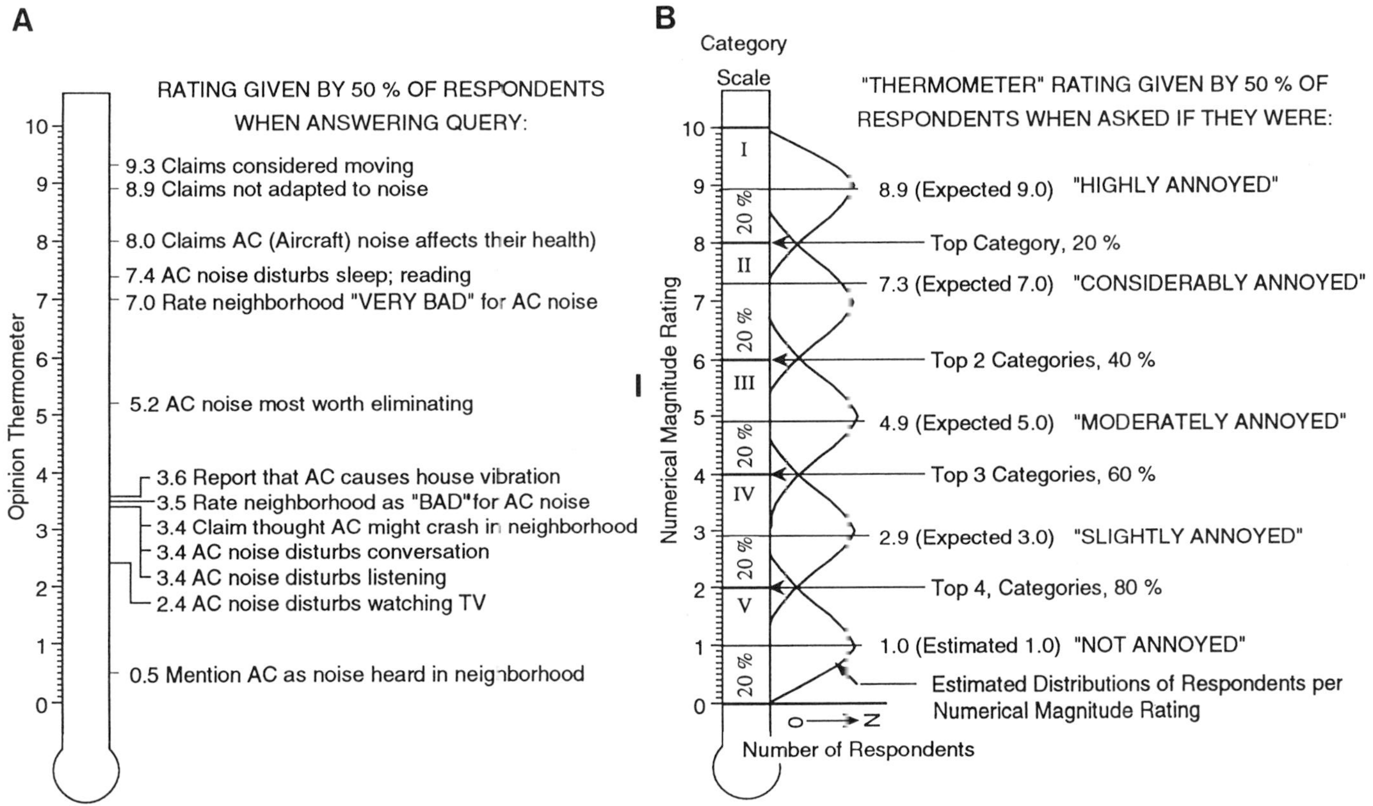

FIGURE 10.9 (A) Numerical magnitude ratings of various reactions to, and effects of, aircraft noise. (B) Numerical-magnitude rating given by 50% of respondents when saying their level of annoyance fell into one of the five designated categories. (After Hede and Bullen, 1982.)

illustrated in Fig. 10.9B, under the heading: "thermometer rating given by 50% of respondents when asked if they were." Sketched on the vertical numerical scale are idealized distributions of persons marking other locations on that scale, when agreeing with a given category phrase. Figure 10.9B was constructed by the writer, but the location of the median, 50% respondents, is that determined by the data at hand.

With amounts of annoyance restricted to five categories, it would be expected that an appropriate choice of word descriptors would provide a linear, subjective numerical partitioning of the annoyance scale. The results in Fig. 10.9 show that this is fairly well the case. It is there seen that, for the different categories, 50% of the respondents marked the "opinion thermometer," the subjective numerical magnitude rating scale, as follows:

"*Highly annoyed*": 8.9 vs. expected, on a linear partitioning, 9.0 (an estimated range to about the top 20% of the subjective scale)
"*Considerably annoyed*": 7.3 vs. expected 7.0 (an estimated range to about the top 40% of scale)
"*Moderately annoyed*": 4.9 vs. 5.0 (an estimated range to about the top 75% of scale)
"*Slightly annoyed*": 2.9 vs. expected 3.0 (an estimated range to about the top 85% of scale)
"*Not annoyed*": expected 1.0 (range, to 100% of scale)

Figure 10.9A shows some of the numerical ratings, from the Hede and Bullen survey, given reactions to noise conditions when 50% of the respondents similarily answered certain queries. It is interesting to note that when 50% of the respondents felt the noise was "considerably annoying," the numerical rating was 7.3, and when 50% felt the noise was "very bad," the rating was 7.0; "disturbs sleep, reading, etc." 7.4; "affects health," rating of 8.0. It is seen in Fig. 10.10A that when moderately, considerably, or highly annoying, aircraft noise created many adverse reactions in the communities.

"Updating" of Synthesis Curve

Fidell *et al.* (1991) undertook a review of suitable survey data of annoyance from general transportation noise published since the Schultz (1978) synthesis curve was prepared. The findings from the different studies were supposedly compared in terms of the percentages of people who could be considered as "highly" annoyed, in accordance with the Schultz criterion, that is, the percentage of respondents who placed themselves, for a given exposure, in the top 27–29% of a unipolar annoyance scale.

"Updating" of Synthesis Curve—Aircraft Noise

Figure 10.10 shows the results of the Fidell *et al.* (1991) analyses of six recent surveys of annoyance from aircraft noise in relation to the synthesis

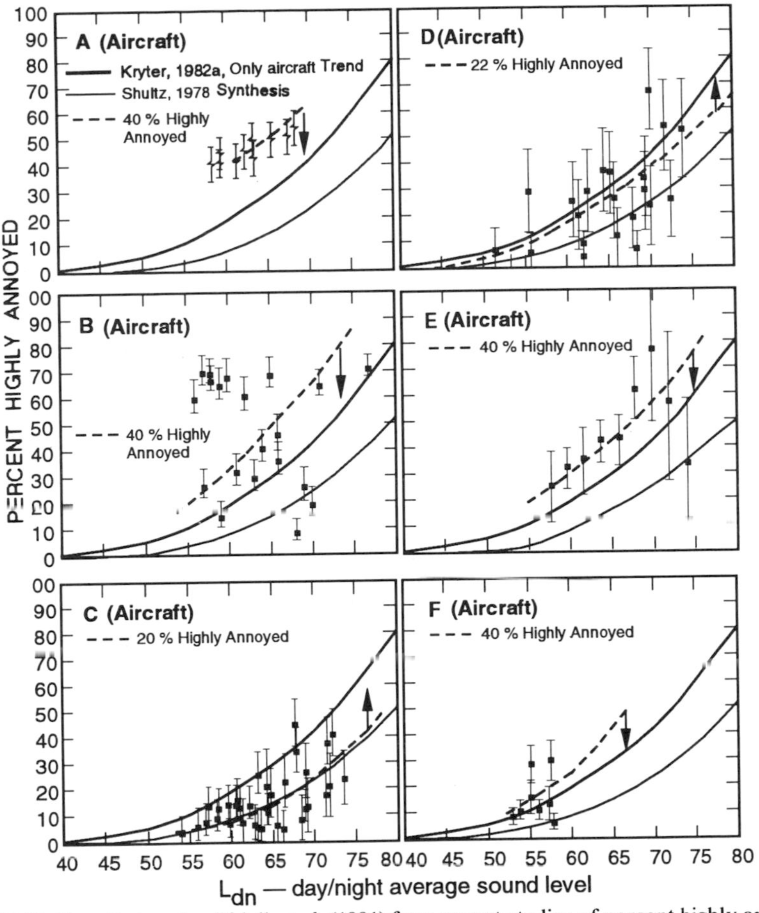

FIGURE 10.10 Data, after Fidell *et al.* (1991) from recent studies of percent highly annoyed by aircraft noise as function of L_{dn}. (A,B,F) Fidell *et al.* (1985); (C) Hede and Bullen (1982); (D) Hall *et al.* (1981); (E) E. Borsky (1985). (After Fidell *et al.*, 1991.) Also shown are the synthesis and trend curves, and estimated adjustments, arrows, to be made to data as plotted for differences in percentages of annoyance scale considered "highly annoyed" among the different studies.

and trend curves. The vertical lines show the 95% confidence intervals that were calculated by the investigators on the assumption that the self-reports of annoyance in the categories of "highly annoyed," and all other categories, were binomially distributed: 1.96 $(PQ/N)^{0.5}$; where P is the proportion of respondents highly annoyed, Q is the proportion not highly annoyed, and N is the number of respondents per exposure level. Also shown on the graphs in Fig. 10.10 are the Schultz synthesis curve for either aircraft or ground-based vehicle noise and the trend curve for aircraft noise derived by Kryter (see Fig. 10.7).

It is seen that, except for the Hede and Bullen survey, panel C of Fig. 10.10, the data are generally closer to the trend curve than the synthesis curve, and that for the studies of panels A, B, E, and F of Fig. 10.10, the data points tend to fall above the trend curve. However, some of the differences between these "new" data and the trend and synthesis curves are, it is suggested, attributable to the method of scoring, by Fidell *et al.*, of the category–response and numerical magnitude estimation data in the newer studies.

As will be explained below, estimates were made of adjustments that appear justified to the response data for these studies as scored by Fidell *et al.* (1991). These adjustments are illustrated in Fig. 10.10, as follows: (1) the dashed curves on each panel are visual best fits, made by the writer, to the sense of the data points plotted by Fidell *et al.* (1991). The attached arrows indicate the direction and estimated approximate extent of expected movement of the points, and dashed curves, had Fidell *et al.* applied an interpretation of the different sets of data that was more consistent with the 27–29% criteria used with the synthesis and trend curves. It is seen that in each case, the data would be moved closer to the trend curve but remain the equivalent of about 10 dB above the synthesis curve.

For the Borsky study, Fidell *et al.* estimated that the percent of the persons marking between 7 and 8 and between 8 and 9 of the numerical annoyance scale running from 0 to 9, fell into the top 30% of the scale. The apparent reasoning being that three points (7, 8, and 9) on the 9-point scale constituted 30% of its extent. However, the number 9 represented the very top of the scale, and not the beginning of a step. Thus, it would follow that the respondents marking 7–8 and 8–9 were in the top two of the nine steps of the scale, or the top 22%.

In the three studies of aircraft noise by Fidell *et al.* (1985) (panels A, B, and F of Fig. 10.10), the respondents were asked to rate their annoyance on a five-part category scale: (1) not at all annoyed (2) slightly annoyed, (3) moderately annoyed, (4) very annoyed, or (5) extremely annoyed. In the Hall *et al.* survey, the respondents were also asked, as previously mentioned, to respond to five categories above "agreeable": (1) neutral, (2) slightly disturbed, (3) moderately disturbed, (4) considerably disturbed, or (5) extremely disturbed. Those describing themselves as "considerably" or "extremely" disturbed were classified as being "highly annoyed." According to the writer's interpretation of Hede and Bullen findings (see Fig. 10.9), this procedure provides, for these four studies, data for the top 40% of the scale, not the 27–29% prescribed for the synthesis and the trend curves.

For the Hede and Bullen study, panel C of Fig. 10.10, Fidell *et al.* took, as did Hede and Bullen, the percentage of people saying that they were "highly" annoyed, the top category of their five-category scale, to be comparable to the top 27–29% criteria of high annoyance found by numerical magnitude estimation. However, as indicated by the Hede and Bullen data for the numerical-scale ratings for that category (see Fig. 10.9), this would probably correspond to an estimated top 20% of the scale, rather than the top 27–29%. Hence the suggested correction shown in Fig. 10.10 to their data, as plotted by Fidell *et al.,* is shown as an upward pointing arrow on panel C. The estimated comparable numerical magnitude rating, in percent of the subjective annoyance scale, for the aircraft noise studies used for the synthesis and trend curves, and in the "updating" review are illustrated in Fig. 10.11.

In summary, when counting those persons "highly annoyed" in the aircraft noise surveys using five-response categories, Fidell *et al.* added together the responses to the top two categories, when the top three categories were labeled either "moderately"; "considerable" and "extremely"; or "moderately," "very," and "extremely." But when, as in Hede and Bullen, these categories were labeled as: "moderately," "considerably," and "highly," only those in the top category where considered as "highly annoyed." In the writer's opinion, respondents would consider the top category of a five-category scale of noise annoyance to be of equivalent meaning whether the label for that category was "highly," "extremely," "strongly," "very," "very much," or the like; provided, however, that an intermediate category

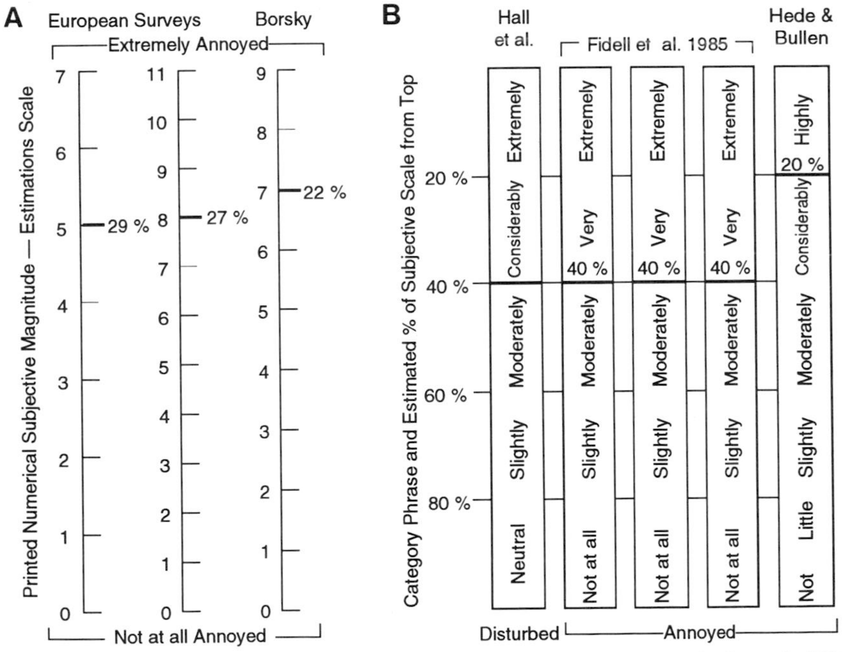

FIGURE 10.11 Percentage (heavy bars) considered highly annoyed by Fidell *et al.* (1991), in attitude surveys of aircraft noise, using methods of numerical magnitude estimation and category scales. (A) The European studies, 27–29% of numerical magnitude scale, used by Schultz as part of synthesis curve and by Kryter for aircraft trend curve: High annoyance for the Borsky (1983) study was for upper 22% of scale, not 30% as deduced by Fidell *et al.*

between the top and a third, ''moderately'' response, category was available to the respondent.

It is suggested that a reasonable approximation of top 27–29% of a numerical magnitude estimation scale would be found from the averaging, rather than the summing, of the responses in the top two categories of five-category, appropriately labeled, scales of noise annoyance; the result would presumably cover about the top 30% of the scale. Unfortunately, the percentages of respondents in each category were not published for these particular attitude surveys, so only an estimated, by the arrows, appropriate adjustment to the data can be indicated. Similar estimated adjustments are illustrated below, as appropriate, for the studies of ground vehicle noise that were reviewed.

''Updating'' of Synthesis Curve—Ground-Based Vehicle Noise

The heavy dot on each vertical data line of Fig. 10.12 shows the percentages of respondents living in specified L_{dn} levels of ground vehicle noise environments who were ''highly annoyed,'' according to Fidel *et al.* (1991). The dotted curve on panel B represents data from a study of street traffic noise by Nemecek *et al.* (1981) data not reviewed by Fidell *et al.* Also shown on the graphs in Fig. 10.10 are the Schultz synthesis curve for either aircraft or ground-based vehicle noise, and the trend curve for ground-based vehicles derived by Kryter (see Fig. 10.7).

It is seen in Fig. 10.12 that the data points for the different studies of ground-based vehicle noise do not consistently cluster, insofar as they do around either the synthesis or the trend curves. However, it should be noted that, except for the study of Nemecek *et al.*, shown on Panel B, the data plotted on Fig. 10.12 are from studies that employed category scales of annoyance. Specifically:

Panel A: In the Hall *et al.* (1981) study, those people in the top two categories were considered by Fidell *et al.* as being ''highly annoyed.''

Panel B: In the Nemecek *et al.* study, a 10-point numerical magnitude-estimation scale of annoyance was employed, with those checking 7 and higher, the top 30% of the scale, taken as being ''highly annoyed.''

Panels B and F: Rylander *et al.* (1977) and *panel D,* Sorensen and Hammar (1983) studies, the categories were, are you (1) ''a little annoyed,'' (2) ''rather annoyed,'' or (3) ''very annoyed.'' ''Very annoyed'' was considered, By Fidell *et al.* as being 'highly annoyed'.

Panel C: Fields and Walker (1980) asked: ''Does the noise of trains bother or annoy you: (1) 'not at all,' (2) 'a little,' (3) 'moderately,' or (4) 'very much.' 'Very much' was considered, by Fidell *et al.* as being ''highly annoyed.''

Panel E: Andersen *et al.* (1983), the categories were (1)''not at all annoyed,'' (2) ''very little annoyed,'' (3) ''slightly annoyed,'' (4) ''some-

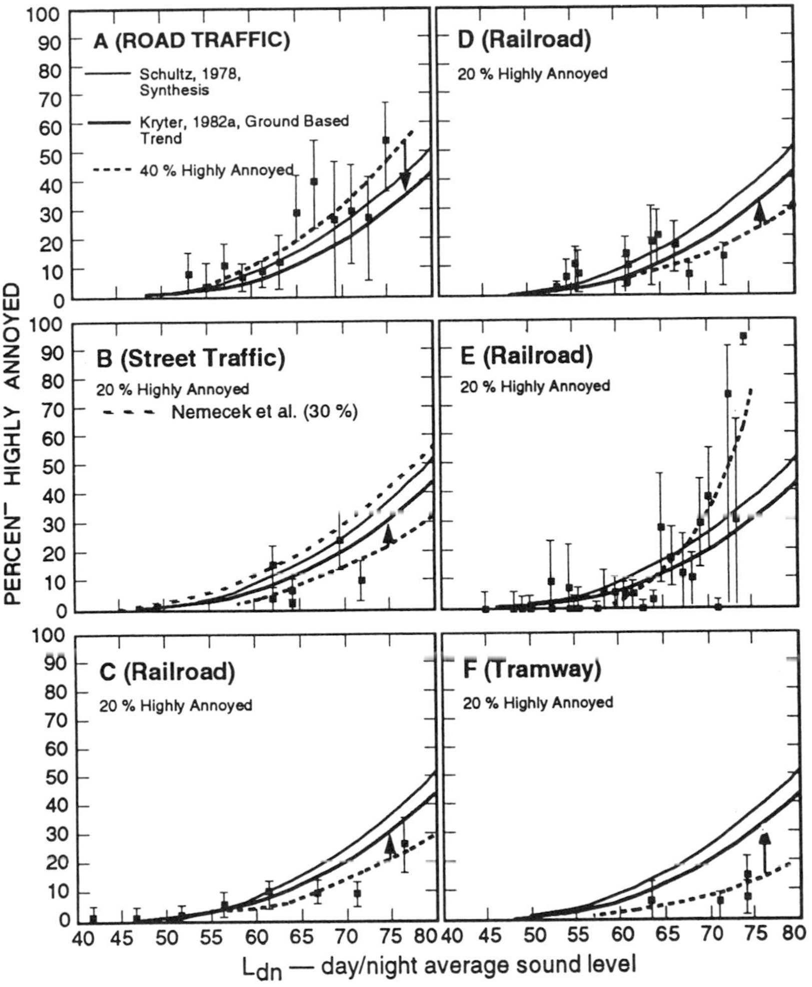

FIGURE 10.12 Data, after Fidell *et al.* (1991), from studies of percentage highly annoyed by ground-based vehicle noise as function of L_{dn}. (A) Hall *et al.* (1981); (B) Rylander *et al.* (1977) and Nemecek *et al.* (1981); (C) Fields and Walker (1980); (D) Sorensen and Hammar (1983); (E) Andersen *et al.* (1983); (F) Rylander *et al.* (1977). Also shown are the synthesis and Kryter trend curves, and estimated adjustments (arrows) to be made to data as plotted for differences in percentages of annoyance scale considered "highly annoyed" among the different studies.

what annoyed," and (5) "strongly annoyed." "Strongly annoyed" was considered, by Fidell *et al.* as being "highly annoyed."

The categories chosed by Fidell *et al.* to represent "high" annoyance for the surveys of ground-based vehicle noise, and their herein-estimated extent on a subjective numerical scale, are shown in Fig. 10.13.

As done in Fig. 10.10, visual fits to the plotted data points are shown by

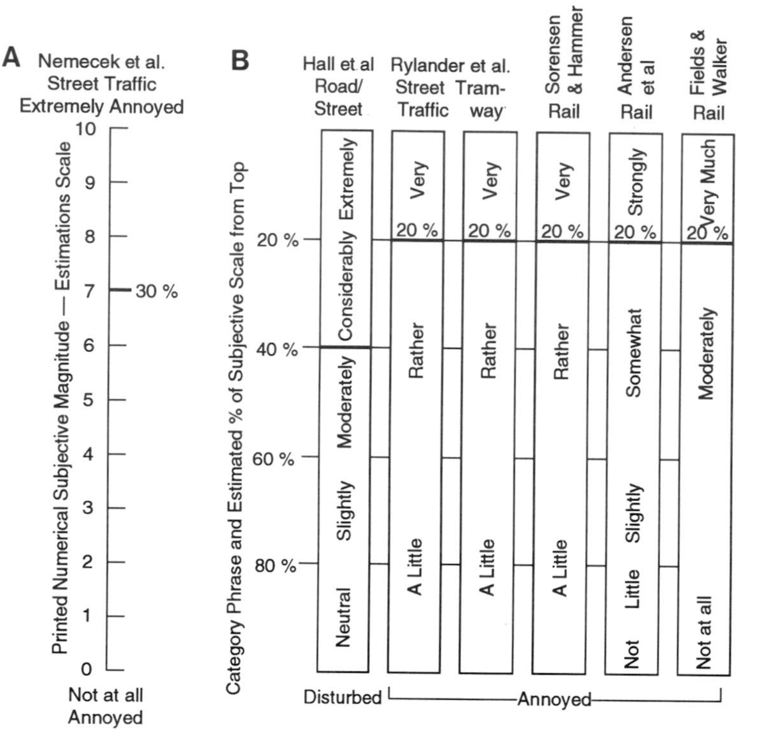

FIGURE 10.13 Attitude surveys of ground-based vehicle noise, using methods of numerical magnitude estimation and category scales (heavy bars indicate percentage considered "highly annoyed).

the dashed curves in the panels of Fig. 10.12, with attached arrows indicating approximate adjustments presumed required to make the category judgment data more comparable to the numerical 27–29% magnitude scale scoring of the synthesis and trend curves. It appears that (1) lowering the Hall *et al.* data (panel A) to account for scoring by 40% of the scale and (2) raising somewhat the data for Rylander *et al.* (panels B and F) Sorensen and Hammar (panel D), and Fields and Walker (panel C), for scoring their top response category as 20% of the scale, would place all those data in approximately the position of the trend curve. However, the numerical-magnitude estimation data obtained Nemecek *et al.* even if lowered slightly for 30%-of-the-scale scoring, would fall closer to the synthesis than the trend curve.

It would seem reasonable to presume that people might divide their subjective scale of annoyance into steps somewhat proportionately to the number of categories they were given to choose from. For the three-category questionnaires of Rylander *et al.* and Sorensen and Hammar, and four-category questionnaire of Fields and Walker, this would suggest that 33% and 25%, respectively, of the scale per category would be covered by each category.

However, it is seen that the results for these studies indicated, overall, fewer respondents than expected in the top category, according to the trend, and particularly, the synthesis curves.

Note that in these studies, an ambiguously specified category ("rather," "somewhat," and "moderately") is the only category of annoyance between a somewhat more definitively specified lower category ("a little") and a top category ("very" or "very much"). It is conjectured that respondents when faced with these categories, as worded, would tend to think that the top category must refer to only extremely annoying conditions, and that the middle category should be used to encompass a much broader range than would a proportional division of the subjective scale.

Partly on the basis of the Hede and Bullen findings, the writer has presumed, for purposes of the estimated adjustments indicated in Fig. 10.12, that the top category for these three- and four-category scales covers about the top 20% of the subjective numerical-magnitude scale of annoyance. Even with this interpretation of these particular scales, the annoyance from ground-based vehicle noise is generally, for a given L_{dn}, below the trend and synthesis curves.

An apparent exception to this are the results of the study by Andsersen *et al.* (1983). The visual-fit curve to the Andersen *et al.* data (panel E, Fig. 10.12) does not follow the slope of either the trend or synthesis curve, rising at a much steeper rate at levels above L_{dn} 65. Perhaps the semantic categories in this study had the effect of partitioning the subjective annoyance scale somewhat differently at different levels of L_{dn}. Note that in this study there was only one category, "strongly," above the four categories of "somewhat," "slightly," "a little," and "not at all" available to the respondents.

From this, it is conjectured, the respondents formed the impression that most noise must cause annoyance that falls within four-fifths (80%), or at least three-fourths (75%), of the noise-annoyance scale. Accordingly, the tendency would be for respondents to place as many responses as possible in those (all except the top), categories. At the same time, there would be no category available between "somewhat" (which seems synonymous with "moderately") and "strongly" to accept responses. It is surmised that when the noises exceeded a certain level of annoyance, this would force an increasing number of responses into the top category, which would normally be rated as between "moderate'" and "strongly." The sharply rising dashed curve in panel C (Fig. 10.12) in consistent with these conjectures.

In any event, it appears clear that both the wording and number of categories of attitude scales of noise-annoyance scales affects the proportioning of subjective annoyance vis à vis that accomplished by numerical magnitude estimation. It is concluded that the category ratings found by Hall *et al.*, adjusted for the 40%-of-scale scoring, and the numerical magnitude-estimation results of Nemecek *et al.*, represent the most readily interpretable findings of recently analyzed attitude surveys of annoyance from ground-based vehicle noise shown in Fig. 10.12.

Annoyance from Small-City Airports

The results of a survey by Schomer of aircraft noise around a small city, general-aviation, airport was also examined by Fidell *et al.* (1991). The findings are shown in Fig. 10.14. It is seen that the exposure levels are very low, as are the percentages of people highly annoyed, even though highly annoyed was taken as those in the top two categories, "very much" and "extremely" annoyed, of a five-category scale. This corresponds to the top 40% of the scale, as compared to the criterion of 27–29% for the synthesis and trend curves; the estimated adjustment for this difference is again indicated by the dashed curve and the arrow.

A possible reason for this lower-than-expected annoyance, according to the trend curve, at least, is that the persons in the highest level of exposure reported hearing an average of only eight aircraft noises per day, and those in the other aircraft noise exposed areas heard an average of only five. This is consistent with the schedule of only six or so flights per day of medium and large aircraft over a given residential area. The L_{dn} levels in these situations are to some extent determined by a large number of general-aviation, relatively low-noise-level aircraft operations. It contrast, large-city residential areas, with similar aircraft L_{dn} levels, are overflown by tens, or more, of such commercial jet aircraft. This finding suggests the possibility that, with very low frequencies of noticeable daily noise occurrences, the predictive accuracy of the L_{dn} energy model is not as reliable as it is with more frequent occurrences of annoyance-causing events.

The reason could be that (1) a noise-annoyance event occurs only when the noise occurs at those moments an individual is engaged in behavior interferred with by the noise; (2) as the frequency of daily noise events decreases beyond a certain number, the probability of a day, or a number of days, passing without a noise–annoyance event occurring increases; and (3) the overall perception of annoyance diminishes at a faster-than-expected rate, as a function of annualized L_{dn}, when the frequency of annoyance occurrences becomes less frequent than daily, or some number of occurrences.

Consistent with the findings of Fig. 10.14 are those of Fig. 10.15, which shows a greater percent, for a given L_{dn}, of people "highly" annoyed in residential areas near large-city, as compared to small-city, airports. In these surveys, the same attitude questionnaires and methods of noise measurement were used for all the cities, so that any differences could not be due to differences in testing methodologies. However, part of the relatively greater annoyance for the large-city surveys could be due the fact that they were administered during summer, whereas those in the small cities where conducted during winter. As will be discussed later, the greater closed-window, indoor living conditions of winter are believed to decrease annoyance from environmental noises.

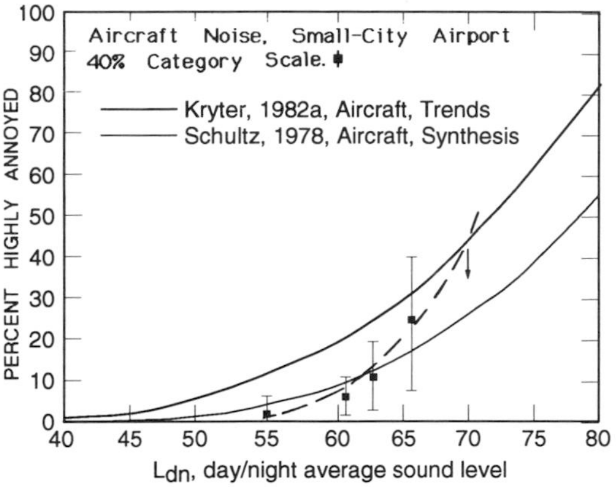

FIGURE 10.14 Annoyance from aircraft noise from operations of a small-city airport (Schomer, 1983b). (After Fidell *et al.*, 1991.) Also shown are the synthesis and trend curves.

Statistical Analysis of Results of Attitude Surveys of Annoyance from Transportation Noise

Green and Fidell (1991) examined the distributions of percentages of people highly annoyed by different levels of noise from different types of transportation vehicles. The studies included in this analysis were those of the Shultz (1978) paper, the Fidell *et al.* (1991) paper just discussed, and several other published investigations, a total of 32. It was found that, with statistical significance, people are more willing to self-report annoyance from aircraft

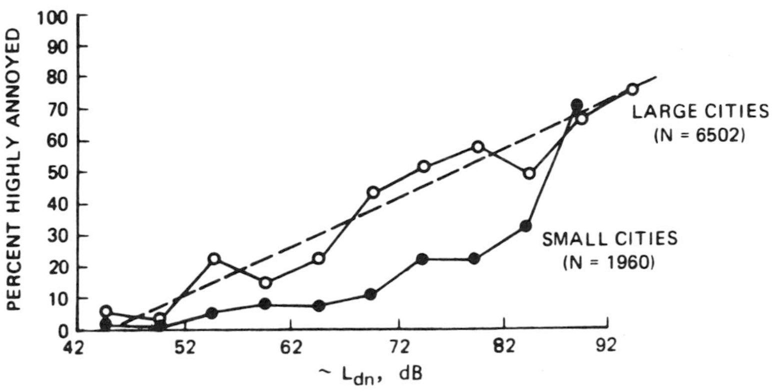

FIGURE 10.15 Percentages of people highly annoyed by aircraft noise. Small cities (Chattanooga, Tennessee; Reno, Nevada) surveyed in winter; large cities (Chicago, Dallas, Denver, Los Angeles, Boston, Miami, New York) surveyed in summer. (After Patterson and Connor, 1973.)

noise than from the noise from other transportation vehicles by a factor equivalent, on the average, to ~5.2 dB in exposure level.

Meta-analyses, such as that of Green and Fidell's, can lead to valid answers to research questions. However, as discussed earlier, Green and Fidell include survey data that were not rigorously analyzed. At the same time, special consideration should be given to studies in which as many as possible of the variables and sources of experimental error are controlled. To the writer's knowledge, the study by Hall *et al.* is the only major investigation of community annoyance from aircraft versus street traffic noise in which the demographic, seasonal, noise measurement and methodological conditions, and, most importantly, respondents and survey questionnaires are the same for both types of noise. That study showed, as previously discussed, greater community annoyance from aircraft than road traffic noise equivalent to 8–11 dB in exposure level (see Fig. 10.7).

ACOUSTICAL AND NON-NOISE FACTORS IN NOISE ANNOYANCE

Whatever the magnitude of the difference may be, 5 or 10 dB, three possible causal factors, acting individually or in part, are suggested: (1) different spectrum–temporal aspects of the different types of noise are not appropriately weighted in the L_{dn} metric for general annoyance; (2) differences in acoustical transmission paths followed by the noises render somewhat invalid the outdoor measures and estimates, as made, of the noises as representing the noises as actually received by the listeners in and around their homes; and (3) a non-noise-related attitudinal bias against aircraft noise that causes people to adopt a more sensitive criterion for self-reporting noise annoyance from that type of noise than from ground-based sources.

Adequacy of Spectral–Temporal Weightings of L_{dn}

As discussed in Chapter 3, attempts are made in the L_{dn} metric to account for any inherent sensation of perceived noisiness due to spectral and temporal characteristics of a sound. As illustrated in Chapters 5, 7, and 9, the weightings chosen, such as *A*, and summed energy over time, are highly correlated with auditory fatigue, the masking of sounds such as speech, and arousal from sleep. Laboratory tests show that noises from different sources that are equal in weighted exposure levels are judged, within noted limits, equally annoying when they are measured at the listerner's ears. This is further illustrated in Figs. 10.16 for the noise from aircraft and ground-based motor vehicles.

The noises in the tests shown in Fig. 10.16A were measured as peak dB_A levels at the position of the listeners, who were seated outdoors with no barriers between them and the sources of the noises. It is seen that the

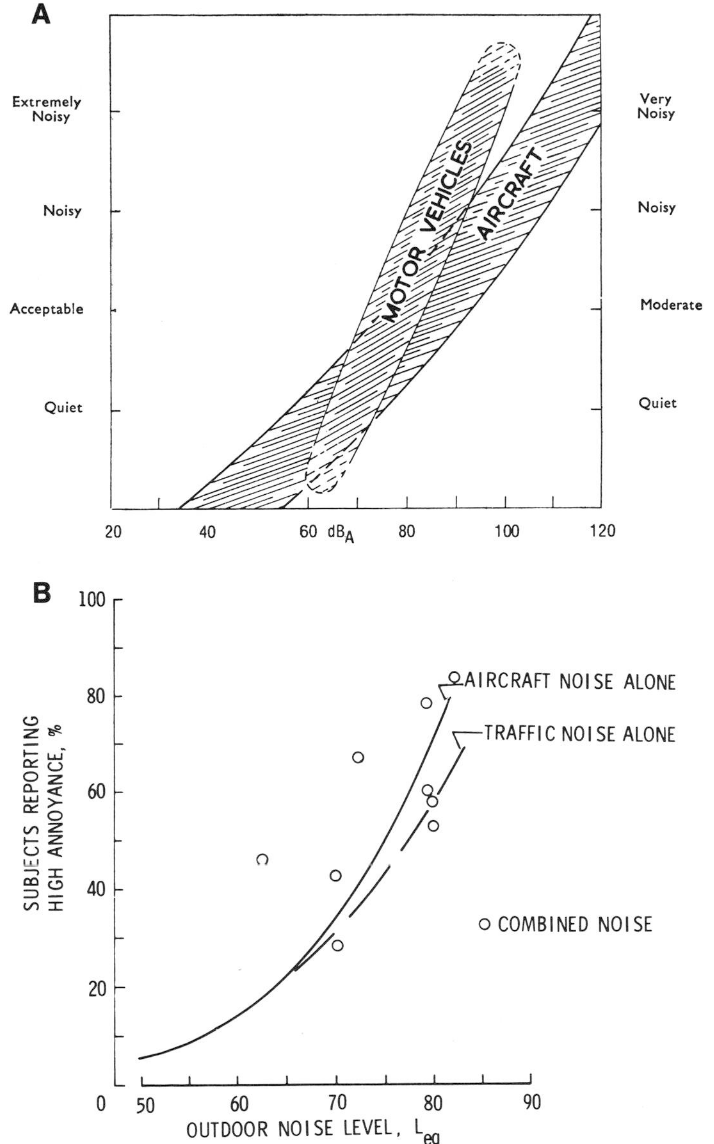

FIGURE 10.16 Judgments of relative annoyance and/or noisiness from exposures to aircraft noise as compared to motor and street traffic noise. Noises measured at position of listeners outdoors. (A) Outdoor field tests. (From Committee on the Problem of Noise, 1963). (B) Recordings heard in a laboratory room. (From Stephens and Powell, 1980.)

ratings for the two types of noise overlap as a function of their peak dB_A levels. The subjective noisiness of the sounds from the motor vehicles and aircraft would have been even more similar if the noise had been measured in L_{Aex}, that is, as an energy sum over the duration of an event. The reason being that for these particular tests the duration of the motor vehicle passbys was kept constant for the tests, whereas the more intense the aircraft noise level, the shorter, in general, was its duration. With shorter durations for the aircraft noise, the relative L_{Aex} exposure levels would have been more in concert with the relative judged noisiness of the two types of noise.

Figure 10.16B shows that about the same percentage of subjects rated jet aircraft traffic noise as street traffic noise as being highly annoying when of equal L_{Aeq}. The tests were conducted with recordings of the noises presented in a special laboratory (Stephens and Powell, 1980).

The data in Fig. 10.17A were obtained from adult subjects listening, in the presence of a continuous background noise of L_{eq} 30 dB_A, to recordings,

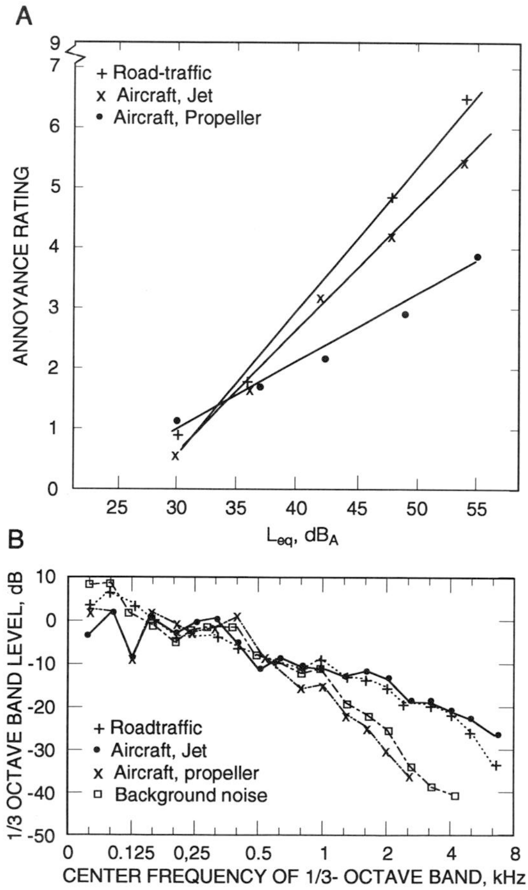

FIGURE 10.17 (A) Annoyance ratings for recordings of noises from road-traffic, jet aircraft, and propeller aircraft. (B) One-third-octave band spectra of background and vehicle noises used in judgment tests of annoyance. (From Vos, 1992.)

presented via loudspeakers, of road traffic and aircraft noises (Vos, 1992). The road noise was recorded 10 m from free-flowing road traffic; and the aircraft noises were recordings of separate flybys of a three-engine (Trident) jet passenger plane, and a two-propeller plane. The durations between the 10-dB downpoints for the two aircraft noises, were, respectively, about 15 s and 40 s. The judgments were made after 45-s segments of time with continuous road traffic noise, or with one aircraft flyover imbedded in the background noise.

It is seen that the road traffic and jet-aircraft noises are rated about equally annoying as a function of equal L_{Aeq}. However, the propeller aircraft noise is judged somewhat less annoying than that of road traffic. This latter finding is, it is suggested, an experimental artifact caused by the similarity in spectra of the background and propeller aircraft noises (see Fig. 10.17B). This similarity probably made it difficult for the subjects to detect the presence of the propeller aircraft noise. Indeed, when at equal L_{Aeq}, the intensity level of the background noise must have been greater than that of the propeller aircraft noise during some portions of its presentations.

Ohrstrom *et al.* (1980) found that judgments in the laboratory of recorded noises from aircraft, trucks, trains, and mopeds were generally predictable from *A*-weighted L_{eq} measured at the position of the listener. However, the noise from trucks was somewhat less disturbing at equal L_{eq} than the other noises. The authors suggest that some "irregularity of the noise or individual experience" could be responsible for this finding.

Thus, it appears that under both laboratory and semilaboratory conditions, unlike the findings of attitude surveys of these noises in real life, aircraft and road traffic noises are judged to be about equally annoying when of equal *A*-weighted exposure levels at the ears of the listeners. As discussed in Chapter 3, this is also the case, within limits, for many types and spectra of noises. Accordingly, while some modifications of frequency and temporal weights may reduce to some extent variance in noise annoyance judgments, it is doubtful that they would be significantly source-specific, or needed for the evaluation of both aircraft and ground-based vehicle noises.

Source-Related Outdoor Acoustical Factors

It was proposed that the lack of correlation between annoyance, found by attitude surveys, from the noise from aircraft, as compared to that from ground-based sources, is due largely to purely acoustical factors (Kryter, 1982a). These factors result in a significant difference in the levels of the noise actually reaching the listeners from these two sources, as compared with the L_{dn} exposure levels as measured or estimated. The acoustical levels normally expressed in attitude surveys for the two sources are those to be found at the front, usually the facade of a house. But the levels that reach the listener, in and around the house, are estimated to be about 10 dB less for noise from ground-based vehicles than from aircraft when the two are measured as being equal, outdoors, at the front facade the house.

There are two principal physical reasons why this should be the case. The first is related to the greater distance between the house and the aircraft than between the house and the ground-based source, The second, and more important, is the greater effectiveness of sound barriers afforded the sound from the ground-based sources than that from the aircraft. Typically, in residential areas fairly close to a commercial airport, the aircraft would be at a slant-range distance of 500–2500 ft (depending on whether a landing or takeoff operation is occurring) from a noise-measurement microphone at the front of a residence. The street or road traffic would be, for many urban areas, only 25–50 ft away from the measurement microphone.

The street-noise levels between the frontyards and backside yards of a house lot will be less solely because of the distance traveled by the noise from the street to the backyard (doubling the 25–50-ft distance results in an air attenuation of about 3–6 dB, depending on the relative size, or ''pointedness,'' of the source). Because of the greater distance from the aircraft source, differences in the noise transmission distance from the aircraft to different points of the yards is negligible, and the level of aircraft noise found at the frontyard is uniform over the entire lot, or yard area. (The fundamental reason for is the relatively greater sound power radiated by the aircraft than, for example, a car or truck. The difference in sound power is proportional to the difference in sound pressure measured for a specified period at the same distance, and over the same area, for the two sources—in the example, the pressure is measured as being equal at the front of the house, but the average distances were roughly 50 ft for the car vs. 1500 ft for the aircraft.)

Because of the usual altitude of the aircraft over residential areas, shielding of the noise by interfering structures tends to be relatively small, except when the aircraft is at low altitudes and rather long distances to the side. The relatively close distance between the front facade of the house and the street or road traffic (coupled with the depth of the house and the relatively small distances between houses—10–20 ft in compact areas) makes for acoustical-barrier shielding of the ground traffic noises from the rear facade and backyard, patio, and porch areas of a house. It is calculated that the noise intruding into the backyard and rooms of one- and two-story houses would typically be about 16 dB less from road traffic than from aircraft flyover operations when the noises are measured as having equal sound-pressure levels in the frontyards of most urban houses. [For formulas and details of these calculation procedures, see Piercy and Daigle (1991).]

To obtain an empirical check on this prediction, the noise from aircraft flying overhead and noise from cars and trucks driving past the same houses were measured. Simultaneous measurements were made from microphones placed in the frontyard (10 ft from the front facade) and in the backyard patio (10 ft from the rear facade). Table 10.3, which summarizes the findings,

TABLE 10.3 Peak L_A Levels of Noises Measured at Two Residences Located Near a General-Aviation Airport in Southern California

Source and date	Residence number	Events/time period	L_A, dB					
			Frontyard		Backyard		Average frontyard—average backyard	
			Average	Range	Average	Range		
Aircraft (general aviation, following takeoff)								
February 27, 1980	1	31/h	77.4	68–91	77.0	68–90	0.4	0.3
February 26, 1980	2	24/h	76.7	63–91	76.5	60–90	0.2	
Street vehicle								
February 27, 1980 (city trash truck)	1	5/10 min*	71	66–75	54	51–57	17.0	19.0
February 26, 1980 (1975 4-cylinder car, manual transmission)	2	11/10 min*	72	68–76	50.9	48–54	21.1	

* Time period is approximate.

From Ortega and Kryter (1982).

shows an average difference in noise level between the frontyard and backyard of 19 dB for the road traffic noise and 0.3 dB for the aircraft noise.

Table 10.4 shows the sound-barrier reductions afforded the noise from aircraft (at an angle of 45° or more to the side and 1350 ft away) by buildings of different heights. At lesser angles, flight paths more directly overhead, the magnitudes of the barrier reductions for the aircraft noise would be even less. These reductions are to be compared with the 16–19 dB or so to be expected for street traffic noise in typical residential areas. Only on the far side of high-rise structures is the aircraft noise reduced to the degree that street traffic noise is reduced by typical one- and two-story dwellings; at the same time, of course, the far-side level of street traffic noise is even further reduced, by the taller structures, than the 16–19 dB typical for one- and two-story houses.

Figure 10.18a shows that the level of traffic noise reaching the front of houses facing a freeway, but located about 100 ft or more from the freeway, is ~20 dB less than expected, in terms of sound attenuation by air, when there is one, or more, house structures between the given house location and freeway. It was deduced that this 20 dB of traffic-noise shielding was attributable primarily to the first intervening house structure between the freeway and more distant houses.

The aircraft noise tends to fall equally over the entire roof structure and, at times, on the sides of the house. Aircraft noise measurement data in 104 rooms in residences (Sutherland *et al.* 1973, Appendix N) revealed the following: "Rooms with windows facing the source (i.e., aircraft in flight) had about 3 dB less noise reduction than for rooms with windows facing 90 degrees to the direction of the source and about 4 dB less noise reduction than rooms which had all windows facing away from the source (e.g., shielded by the house)." This illustrates that the house is able to furnish little shielding

TABLE 10.4 Aircraft Noise Attenuation by 10-ft-Story-Height Buildings

Number of stories	Barrier attenuation, (dBA)*
1	4
2	8
3	12
4	14
5	16.5
6	18
7	18.5

* Aircraft altitude 1000 ft, slant range distance 1350 ft = 48° angle to building. Observer 10 ft out from far side of building.

From Schultz (1982)

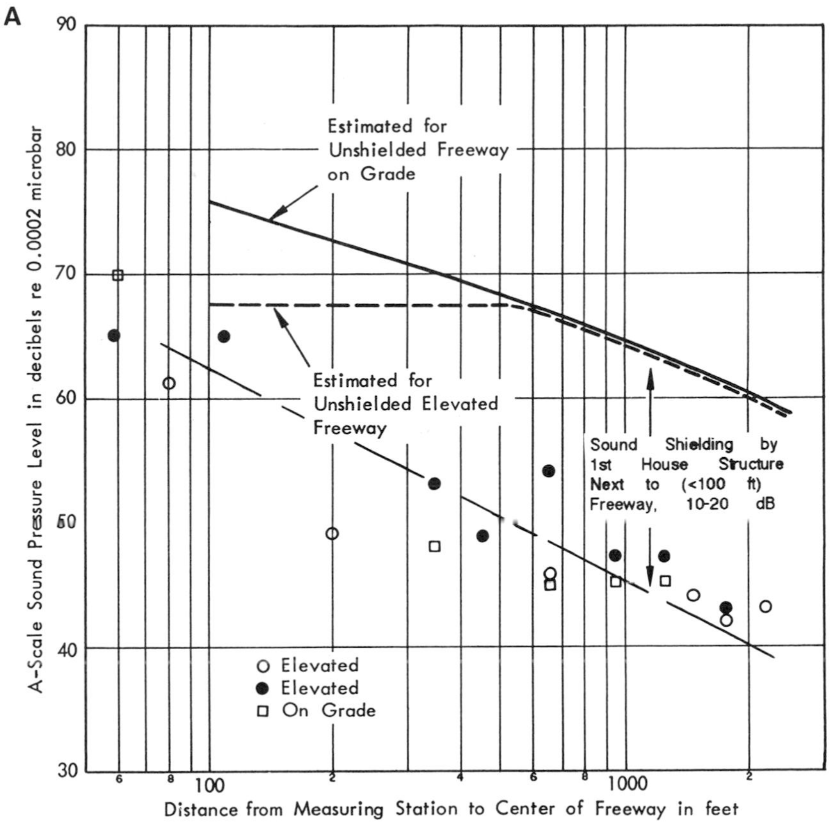

FIGURE 10.18 Schematic diagram of some acoustical factors and their effects of the levels of (A) street traffic and (B) aircraft noises around houses. (See text.)

of the aircraft noise to its different surfaces. The differences in the reduction in the noise from street traffic should be measurably greater in the rooms 90° (side of the house) and, especially, facing away from the source (back of the house).

Although the analogy is somewhat flawed, the sense of the subject acoustical difference is somewhat like the difference between the amounts of water hitting a house from (1) hoses, attached to the top of a car, squirting water as the car is driven by the house; as compared to (2) a cloud, or an aircraft, dropping a blanket of water as it flies over the house. Figure 10.18b more aptly illustrates the acoustical stiuation.

It would appear from these observations and data that the equivalent 10 dB or so less annoyance from street traffic, than aircraft, noise found with apparently equal dosages of the noises (as measured in their frontyards) could—if not must—be to a large extent caused by the differences in the noise dosages actually received by the listeners. If the L_{dn} concept has

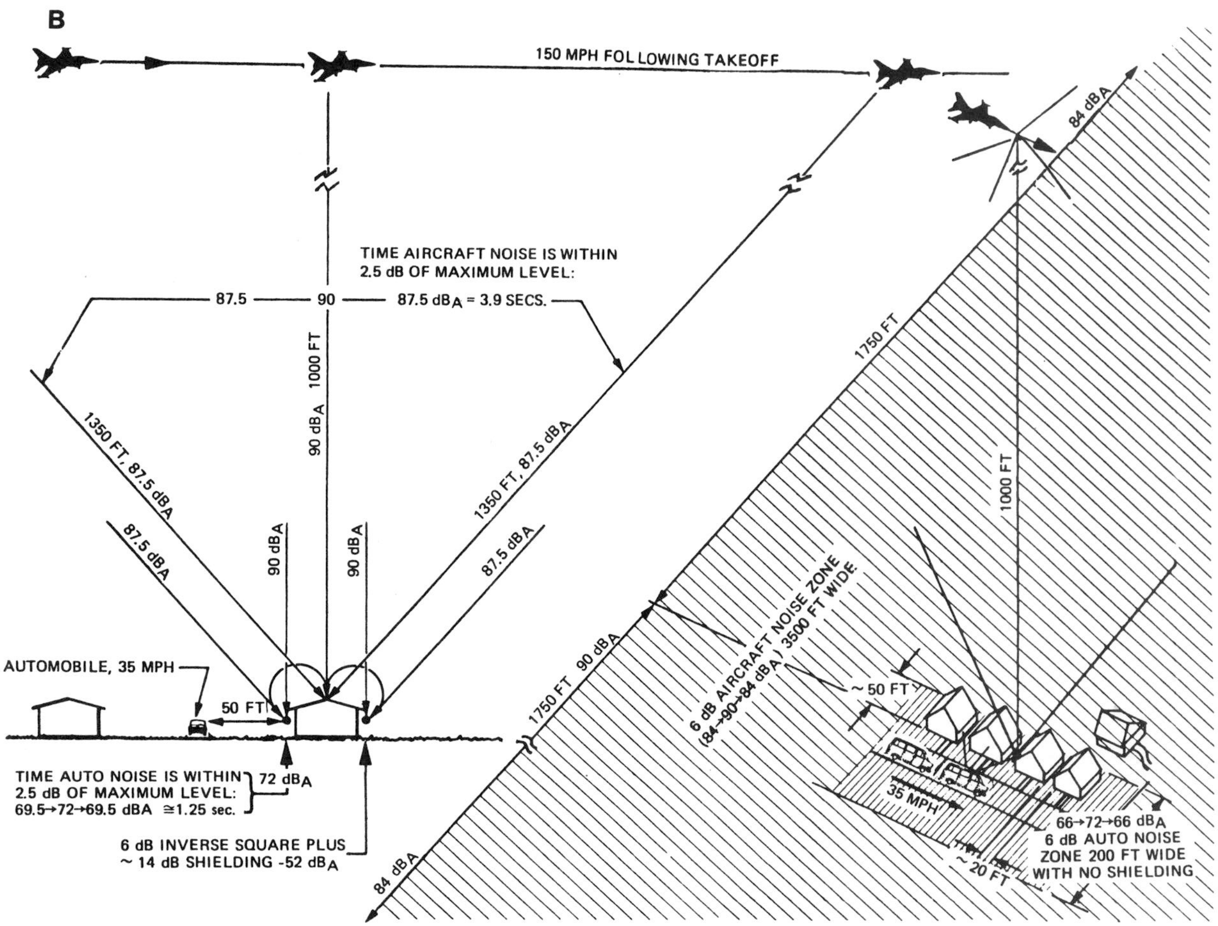
B
150 MPH FOLLOWING TAKEOFF
TIME AIRCRAFT NOISE IS WITHIN
2.5 dB OF MAXIMUM LEVEL:
87.5 — 90 — 87.5 dBA = 3.9 SECS.
1350 FT, 87.5 dBA
87.5 dBA
90 dBA
90 dBA 1000 FT
90 dBA
1350 FT, 87.5 dBA
87.5 dBA
AUTOMOBILE, 35 MPH
50 FT
TIME AUTO NOISE IS WITHIN
2.5 dB OF MAXIMUM LEVEL:
69.5→72→69.5 dBA ≅1.25 sec.
72 dBA
6 dB INVERSE SQUARE PLUS
~ 14 dB SHIELDING -52 dBA
84 dBA
1750 FT
1750 FT 90 dBA
84 dBA
1000 FT
6 dB AIRCRAFT NOISE ZONE
(84→90→84 dBA) 3500 FT WIDE
~ 50 FT
35 MPH
~ 20 FT
66→72→66 dBA
6 dB AUTO NOISE
ZONE 200 FT WIDE
WITH NO SHIELDING

FIGURE 10.18 B

any validity at all, this approximate 10-dB difference between received, or effective, and as-typically-measured noise level for these two types of sources must also result in a significant difference in annoyance reported by people in real-life conditions. The reliabilty and validity of L_{dn} in this regard is amply demonstrated by the attitude survey and other data presented earlier.

It is surmised that differences in annoyance, with equal L_{dn}, found between railway as compared to road, or even highway, noise are possibly due to systematic differences between the noises as measured and as heard because of elevation, location and transmission-path differences. This does not mean, of course, that some additional source-related factors cannot influence general behavior and, to some extent, the noise-annoyance judgments given in attitude surveys.

Indoor Acoustical Factors

Cheifetz and Borsky (1980) found that acoustical factors, rather than individual differences in noise sensitivity, may be the basis of some differences among some people in reported annoyance from environmental noise. For this experiment, people with greatly different feelings of annoyance from aircraft noise, according to an attitude survey, but from similar L_{dn} aircraft noise environments, were brought to a research laboratory at a university. While comfortably seated in a mock living room, with a TV operating, the subjects were asked to rate the annoyance of tape-recorded aircraft noises as though they were in their own homes.

It was found that, in the laboratory, the subjects fairly similarly rated the annoyance level of aircraft noises of given intensities, regardless of differences in noise sensitivity they had, according to the attitude survey, when in their homes. These results suggest that, although the levels were about equal outside their homes, the levels may have actually differed inside different homes and were, therefore, a factor determining the relative magnitudes of in-the-home feelings of annoyance.

Table 10.5 shows that, on the average, the level of an outdoor noise inside different rooms is about 15 dB less, when the windows are open, and 27 dB less, when they are closed, than its level outdoors. More importantly, it is seen that the standard deviation of the differences is about 5 dB, indicating a probable range of some 25 dB in the level in different rooms and different houses from noise of the same level outdoors.

Non-Noise Factors

Green and Fidell cited "fear of crashes, misfeasance, malfeasance, personality factors; novelty and anticipation of exposure; economic dependence on noise source; socioeconomic levels, and so forth" as possible bases for the adoption by people of different criteria for self-reporting annoyance from

TABLE 10.5 Measured Reduction in *A*-Weighted Noise Levels for Residential Structures (Single-Family Detached Dwellings Except for Nine Rooms in Apartments in New York City)

		Windows open			Windows closed		
Climate	Cities	Number of rooms	ΔL_A,* dB	S.D.†	Number of rooms	ΔL_A,* dB	S.D.†
Warm	Miami, Wallops (VA), Los Angeles	14	11.1	4.6	132	26.2	4.8
Cold	Winthrop (MA), Boston, New York	33	18.4	5.1	27	27.7	5.2
	Overall average		14.8	4.85		27.0	5.0

* ΔL_A = average difference between *A*-weighted noise level outside and inside room. The number of measurements per room varies widely from 1 to 46 with an average of 6.0. Almost all sources were jet aircraft.

† S.D. = standard deviation of average ΔL_A over number of rooms measured.

Data from Sutherland *et al.* (1973).

noises from different sources. Such things as travel time to work, as will be shown later, can affect aircraft-noise acceptance, and fear of crashes is indeed a cause of negative attitudes about aircraft. This latter factor does not necessarily mean, however, that it appreciably enhances the annoyance experienced from behavior interferences, when they occur, because of aircraft noise, as compared to that experienced from the interferences caused by street traffic noises. Certainly, respondents in surveys of aircraft noise clearly distinguish among these effects (see Fig. 10.3).

Gunn *et al.* (1981) found, in a field study, that the percentages of subjects having higher ratings, on a scale from "not objectionable" to "unbearable," was somewhat greater when the aircraft was flying directly overhead than to one side. The difference was, on the average, equivalent to about 2 dB in noise level and presumed to be due to greater fear. Hall *et al.* (1980) deduced from an attitude survey conducted near the Toronto, Canada airport that nonacoustical factors such as nearness to flight paths and fear of crashes do affect annoyance responses, but not activity interferences by aircraft noise.

Meta-Analysis of Non-Noise Factors

Fields examined the design, methods used, and results of 282 social attitude surveys of noise annoyance. These surveys were, for the most part, intended to test whether a relation existed between noise annoyance and a nonnoise variable. The surveys, and findings therefrom, were screened first to use only those that are based on contrast within the same survey, or study, i.e., "eliminating speculations based on comparisons between two surveys that differ on not only the explanatory variable of interest, but also in the methods that were used to obtain the data.''

Each selected finding was classified as ''important'' or ''not important'' on the basis of objectively defined criteria relating to size and statistical significance of variances, numbers of sample groups supporting a hypothesis, and strength of verbal assertion of a relation between annoyance and a variable. The nearly 200 findings that met one or more of these criteria were considered as 'standard'. The findings were used to judge whether 22 hypothesis about a possible relation between a nonnoise variable and noise annoyance was supported. The hypotheses fell into the following categories: (1) demographic, (2) attitudinal, (3) situational, and (4) temporal. Major results are presented in Table 10.6.

Fields proposed that (1) when over 50% of the screened and ''standard'' quality evidence supports a stated hypothesis, the nonnoise variable involved should be considered as having an important effect on noise annoyance; and (2) when over 50% of the such evidence does not support the hypothesis, it should be rejected, and the nonnoise variable considered to have no important effect on noise annoyance. The magnitude of these effects, when a hypothesis is supported, were not specifiable in terms of some equivalent amount of noise-exposure level.

It is seen in Table 10.6 that

1. The demographic variables (age, sex, social status, income, education, home ownership, dwelling type, length of residence, benefit) were found to have no important effect.
2. Attitudinal variables (fear of source, preventability of noise, nonnoise annoyance increases noise annoyance, general sensitivity, importance of source) all have an important effect on noise annoyance.
3. Situational variables (exposure time at home, low ambient noise increases intrusiveness) have no important effect on noise annoyance, but insulation from sound around the home has a marginally important alleviating effect on noise annoyance.
4. Temporal variables (change, increase or decrease, in noise environment causes overreaction; new noise is more annoying than old; reducing noise reduces annoyance less than expected; annoyance with a noise decreases in time) have an indeterminant, from present data, importance effect on noise annoyance.

Some of these results, as is annotated by Fields (1993), must be interpreted with caution. For example, fear is certainly a cause of annoyance and is associated with higher levels of aircraft noise; but so is noise-annoyance from the inherent loudness and behavior interference effects of noise. The independence of these variables from each other are not evaluated. The writer is unaware of studies that demonstrate that fear of aircraft crashes

TABLE 10.6 Effect of Non-Noise Variables on Annoyance from Environmental Noise

		Percentage of responses supporting*			
	Variable and hypothesis	Stated hypothesis	No important effect	Opposite hypothesis	Conclusion per hypothesis
Demographic variables	*Age:* older people are more annoyed	19%	52%	29%	Reject
	Sex: women are more annoyed	0%	100%	0%	Reject
	Social status: high-status residents are more annoyed	9%	91%	0%	Reject
	Income: high-income residents are more annoyed	12%	88%	0%	Reject
	Education: high-education residents are more annoyed	11%	89%	0%	Reject
	Home ownership: home owners are more annoyed	33%	61%	6%	Reject
	Dwelling type: single-unit residents are more annoyed	7%	84%	9%	Reject
	Length of residence: longer-term residents are less annoyed	24%	59%	17%	Reject
	Benefit: employees and users of source are less annoyed	19%	81%	0%	Reject
Attitudinal variables	*Fear:* a fear of noise source increases annoyance	100%	0%	0%	Support
	Prevention: belief that preventable noise increases annoyance	100%	0%	0%	Support
	Nonnoise annoyance: nonnoise problems increase noise annoyance	100%	0%	0%	Support
	Sensitivity: a general noise sensitivity increases annoyance	100%	0%	0%	Support
	Importance: a belief that source is important decreases annoyance	71%	29%	0%	Support
Situational variables	*Exposure time:* those at home are more annoyed	40%	41%	19%	Reject
	Insulation: those isolated from sound around home are less annoyed	72%	28%	0%	Support
	Ambient: low ambient, noise increases intrusive noise annoy	16%	74%	10%	Reject
Temporal variables	*Change:* people overreact to any change in noise environment	60%	29%	11%	Mixed
	Newness: a new noise is more annoying than an older one of same level	43%	57%	0%	Mixed
	Change: reducing noise leads to less annoyance than expected	67%	18%	15%	Mixed
	Time since change: annoyance with a noise decreases in time	53%	41%	6%	Mixed

* Based on Fields (1993), Table VII only surveys that met certain quality standards.
After Fields (1993)

significantly increases annoyance from the speech masking, loudness, sleep arousal, etc. due to aircraft noise per se. Also, the independence of nonnoise annoyance from non-noise-problem-sensitivity and specific noise sensitivity is questioned. It is probably, as commented on by Alexander (1976) and Fields (1993), a moot question as to whether feelings about things like misfeasance, malfeasance, and belief of preventability, are the cause of some greater-than-typical annoyance, or the result of annoyance due to individual differences in inherent sensitivities to the effects of noise.

The possible confounding effects of the demographic variables examined by Fields have been frequently cited as reasons to reject, as unreliable, data showing a possible effect of physiological "stress" due to aircraft noise annoyance and fear reactions on some health disorders. The findings that these demographic variables are not important factors for noise annoyance are supportive of the findings of a probable associative role of environmental noise with some health disorders, as discussed in Chapter 9.

It is found in laboratory tests that different "personality" types (e.g., introvert, extrovert, or neurotic, identified by means of psychological tests) differently rate annoyance from expected recordings of aircraft noises presented under varying conditions of room illumination (Shigehisa and Gunn, 1978a,b, 1979a,b). As also shown by research discussed in Chapters 8 and 9, such personality factors, influence sensitivity to annoyance from noises in general. However, from a practical point of view, these personality–sensitivity factors presumably do not distort the group results of social attitude surveys because in real life, except in unusual circumstances, they are probably distributed similarly in different exposure levels of noises.

In summary, it is concluded that

1. There appears to be no basis for believing that annoyance from nonimpulsive noises in general, and aircraft and ground vehicle noises in particular, are not reasonably well estimated by the L_{dn} metric of noise exposure when determined to be about that present, on the average, at the ears of listeners.

2. There are basic acoustical principles, and data, to show that when the noises from aircraft and street traffic are measured as being equal at the front facade of dwellings, there is an average difference of ~10 dB in the levels of the noise reaching people, in and around their dwellings, from the two types of sources.

3. In view of the findings that aircraft noise causes greater community annoyance than does ground-based vehicle noise by the equivalent of 10 dB in L_{dn} exposure level, an adjustment of that magnitude in the assessment of the relative impact of the two types of noise seems required. This adjustment, due, it would appear, to purely acoustical-noise measurement factors may, to some small extent, also be due to some public attitudinal "bias" against aircraft due to fear of crashes.

4. There is no reason to believe, from available data, that demographic, situational, and temporal variables differently influence noise annoyance from aircraft than ground-based vehicles.

5. Attitudinal factors and differences in individual sensitivity to stimulation and annoyance and statistically related to attitude surveys disturbances and annoyance from noise. However, as seen in Table 10.1A, the attitudes of fear and misfeasance are secondary to some behavior interference effects of noise as causes of annoyance. Also, the high correlations between noise exposure and annoyance, as measured by group data indicates that the individual differences in sensitivity and personality are not significantly systematically associated with noise exposure levels, but are fairly randomly distributed among residential neighborhoods.

IMPULSIVE AND "SPECIAL" ENVIRONMENTAL NOISES

Sonic Booms

A special type of noise from aircraft is that of sonic booms created when aircraft fly at supersonic speeds, speeds generally greater than ~700 miles per hour (mph). Some military aircraft and the commercial Concorde are capable of such flight. A great deal of research on the impact of sonic booms on people, animals, and structures was conducted during the 1960s with the advent of the Concorde and other proposed commercial supersonic transports.

As discussed in Chapter 3, to establish the equivalent effectiveness of sonic booms and typical subsonic aircraft flyover noise as causes of annoyance, a series of tests were conducted with subsonic and supersonic jet aircraft. Figure 10.19, based on Fig. 3.15, shows the L_{Aex} value of subsonic aircraft noise judged to be equally as acceptable, or unacceptable, as sonic booms to people accommodated to both sonic booms and subsonic aircraft noise. Using these relations, it is possible to calculate an equivalent, to subsonic aircraft noise, 24-h L_{eq} or L_{dn} for sonic booms of different levels and numbers of daily occurrences. Calculations made for the proposed operations of supersonic transports over the United States indicated that approximately 50 million people per day would be exposed to an equivalent L_{dn} from sonic booms of ~70 dB or greater. Ancillary laboratory experiments and real-life experiences in cities substantiated, in general, this use of equivalent L_{Aex} and L_{dn} for assessing exposure to sonic booms (Kryter, 1969).

Attention is invited to the more rapid growth in annoyance ("unacceptability" rating) to sonic booms as their level is increased compared with ratings for the noise from subsonic aircraft (see Fig. 3.13). For example, for the listener indoors, a sonic boom of 1 pounds per square foot (psf) would be equivalent to a subsonic aircraft noise at an L_{Aex} of about 90 dB (with 50 daytime booms, the equivalent L_{dn} would be 58 dB). However, for a

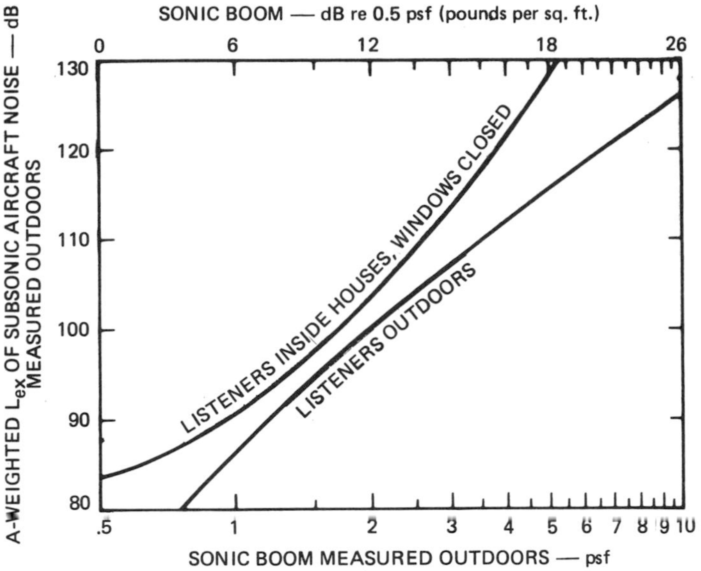

FIGURE 10.19 Graph for converting peak level of sonic-boom (in pounds per square foot) to the L_{Aex} of a subsonic jet-aircraft flyover noise that would be judged about equally annoying. Boom and noise measured outdoors; listeners indoors and outdoors as indicated. Based on Fig. 3.15.

sonic boom of 2 psf (an increase of but 6 dB in psf), the equivalent L_{Aex} is ~103 dB (an increase of 13 dB in L_{Aex}), and the L_{dn} with 50 daily daytime booms would be 71 dB. As shown earlier in this chapter, an L_{dn} of 71 dB for regular aircraft noise represents a very significant source of annoyance in residential areas. It seems likely that the accelerated growth of annoyance from sonic booms relative to subsonic aircraft noise at higher boom levels, shown in Fig. 10.19, is due to the sound of noticeably more "rattles" caused by house vibrations at the higher levels.

Most of the energy in sonic booms, as well as booms from cannon fire and other explosive sources, is generally in the sound frequencies below ~100 Hz. In addition to direct auditory effects of the booms, sound energy in these lower frequencies can cause vibrations and rattles that are a source of annoyance to residents. The relation of the spectra of such booms to judged annoyance is discussed in Chapter 3.

Gun and Helicopter Noises

The L_{dn} procedure can be used with impulse-type noises when their measured levels can be converted to equivalent, effective L_{Aex} values and, if intense low-frequency components are involved, corrected for house-vibration-rattle factors. The impulses from handheld and shoulder-rifles have such a rapid rise time and duration, but the energy in the lower frequency regions is generally not sufficient to cause house vibrations. However, the sound energy in the more audible frequencies, and the impulsive nature of small arms fire, can be a source of annoyance. (See Chapter 7 for information on the spectra of such impulses and their damage risk to hearing.)

Bullen and Hede (1982) measured the noise in a residential area near a rifle range and administered an annoyance attitude survey to a sample of the residents. They found only low correlations between various noise measurements (including *A*-weighted sound-pressure levels) and annoyance. The investigators noted that the noise was very directional and variable from day to day. It was concluded that *A*-weighted energy of L_{eq} was probably the mose useful unit of measurement, even though it did not predict annoyance well. Buchta (1990) found that, relative to road traffic noise, L_{eq}, *A*-weighted, is reasonably predictive of reactions to the noise from small firearms, provided 13 dB penalty is subtracted from the level of the gun noise. Buchta (1993) concludes in a review paper that the magnitude of this penalty is level dependent for small weapon fire, and that C-weighted L_{eq} without adjustment is appropriate for comparing annoyance from large weapon blast with that of road traffic noise. (See discussion in Chapter 3 of present text of the loudness and noisiness of impulses.)

However, L_{dn} in dB_C, (*C*-weighted decibels), or some correction to dB_A, appears to be better suited for assessing community annoyance from impulsive sounds, e.g., from cannon-type weapons that exceed certain levels of intensity; see discussion in Chapter 3 and Schomer (1982). It is worth noting that it is not the structure vibration sensed by the body from these booms and cannon sound, but the associated audible noise and rattling that is particular annoying (Schomer, 1978; Schomer and Averbuch, 1989). It was found that vibration isolating the chairs of subjects inside houses exposed to sonic booms causing vibration and rattling did not reduce their judgments of the amount of annoyance experienced without the isolation (Kryter *et al.*, 1967). Schuemer-Kohrs *et al.* (1993) found that railway-induced vibrations were rated by most people as less annoying than the train noise.

The noise from helicopters is noted for its relatively intense impulsive frequency components, as briefly discussed in Chapter 3. Recent studies [Powell and McCurdy (1982), Ollerhead (1982) [see also review in Molino (1982) of numerous related studies] indicate that *A*-weighting is not as appropriate as *D*-weighting, or PN_{dB}, for assessing judged loudness and noisiness. When L_{Dex} (with greater weighting at low frequencies than *A;* see Chapters 1 and 3) is used as a measure of helicopter noise, it is generally found that no impulse correction is needed. However, it appears in some studies under laboratory conditions, that when helicopter noise is simulated electronically, an impulsive "beating" in the noise increases its noisiness to the extent that some correction to exposure in L_{Dex} is also justified. Some of this effect may be due to acoustical conditions in the field not allowing for as regular a beating at different listening points on the ground as present in the laboratory simulations.

Electric Transformer and Transmission-Line Noise

A study was conducted by Fidell *et al.* (1979) on feelings of annoyance in residents exposed to the "hum" from transformers in ground-based substations in urban areas, and to the "corona" discharge noise, a "crackling, frying" sound that comes from high-voltage power lines when wet from rain, snow, or dense fog. The power lines are usually suspended a hundred or more feet in the air and several hundred feet from backyards of homes along electrical rights-of-way in suburban areas. Those respondents who self-rated themselves as "very" or "extremely" annoyed on a five-category scale (top 40% of the scale) by either the transformer or corona noise were called "highly annoyed" by Fidell *et al.*

The percentages who were "very or extremely annoyed" are shown in Fig. 10.20. The arrows attached to the data points are estimates of the adjustment required to show percent "highly annoyed," defined as the top

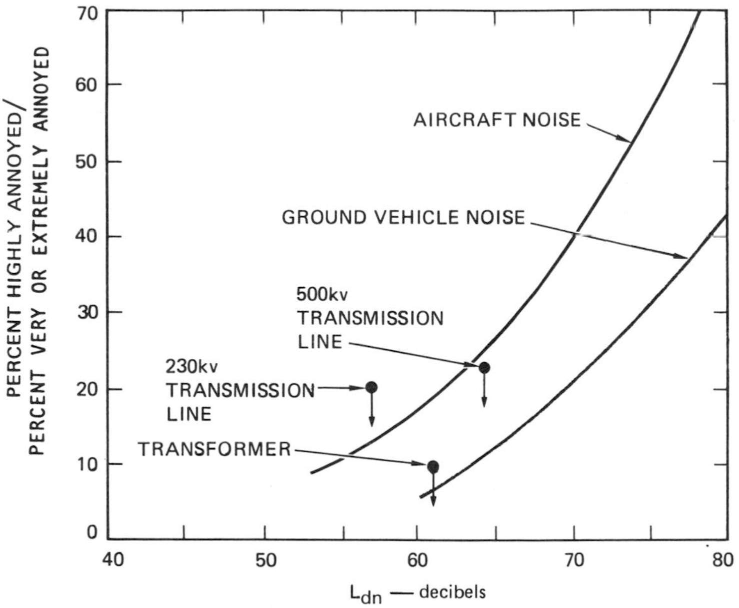

FIGURE 10.20 Percent "very or extremely annoyed" (top 40% of annoyance scale) by electric transformer and transmission-line noise. Data collected from 17 sites in southern California. (From Fidell *et al.*, 1979.) Also shown are trend curves for aircraft and ground vehicle noise, and estimated adjustments (arrows) to be made to data as plotted for differences in percentages of annoyance scale considered "highly annoyed" in this study, and that for the trend curves.

28% of the annoyance scale. Also shown are the trend curves of percentage "highly annoyed" (top 27–29% numerical magnitude scale) for aircraft and ground vehicle noises. It is evident that the transformer noise (from ground-based structures about 20–160 ft from residences) is less annoyance-effective, when of equal L_{dn}, than the noise from 230- and 500-kV transmission lines, but about the same as expected according to the trend curve for ground-based vehicle noise. It is also seen that the transmission-line noise appears to be about somewhat more annoyance-effective, when of equal L_{dn}, than the transformer noise, but less than the noise from aircraft.

It is possible that this difference in the annoyance-effectiveness of the transmission-line noise compared to the ground-based transformer and transportation vehicle noises is related to differences in the altitude of the sources. This difference perhaps allows for acoustical factors that are somewhat similar to, but smaller than, the differences, discussed earlier in these regards, for the noises from aircraft and ground vehicles. However, the considerable differences in the "saliency" characteristic and temporal patterns of exposure to the transmission-line noise may be the primary cause, as will be discussed later, with respect to sleep arousal.

COMPLAINT REACTIONS TO ENVIRONMENTAL NOISE

Complaint Activity

The general scope of reactions and complaints made to local government officials about a variety of transportation, industrial, and other noise are shown in Table 10.7. However, because of a variety of social factors, complaints, or rather lack of complaints, legal and political actions by individuals and citizens are not generally as reliable, or sensitive, a measure of the effects of environmental noise as are attitude surveys (Avery, 1982).

In a survey in the United States, people were asked, among other things, how annoyed they were by aircraft noise and whether they had complained to any authorities about the noise. The results, shown in Fig. 10.21, indicate that some complaints can be expected when 5–10% of the people are highly annoyed by the noise, a percentage typically associated with an L_{dn} of 55 dB. Interestingly, McKennell (1963) found that in Great Britain when 1% of the people had complained about noise, 10% felt like complaining, and when the noise was such that 10% had complained, 40% felt like complaining.

Legal Actions

A special type of complaint that has been used to assess the tolerability of aircraft and other noise-exposure conditions is that of lawsuits filed for relief, or damages, from noise. Figure 10.22 illustrates the range of L_{dn} levels over which threats of, or actual, legal actions occurred in case studies of civic

TABLE 10.7 Summary of Data for 55 Community Noise Reaction Cases

Type of reaction	Case no.	Noise description	$\sim L_{dn}$, dB
Vigorous	A-1	Rocket testing	63
	A-2	Wind tunnel	70
	A-3	Aircraft landing	82
	A-4	Aircraft takeoff	71
	A-5	Circuit-breaker testing	73
	A-6	Auto(mobile) race track	77
	A-7	Aircraft takeoff	69
	A-8	Aircraft landing	84
Threats of legal action	B-1	Rocket testing	57
	B-2	Aircraft ground runup	72
	B-3	Wind tunnel	61
	B-4	Freeway	86
	B-5	Aircraft overflight	57
	B-6	Plant blower	67
	B-7	Asphalt quarry	64
	B-8	Glass-bead plant blower	62
	B-9	Plastics plant	61
	B-10	Target shooting range	54
	B-11	Residential air conditioning	57
	B-12	Unloading newsprint	76
	B-13	Auto body shop	70
	B-14	Motorcycle raceway	65
Widespread complaints	C-1	Transformer substation	49
	C-2	Cement plant	64
	C-3	Aircraft landing	62
	C-4	Paperboard plant cyclone	50
	C-5	Oil refinery	61
	C-6	Milling and grinding metal	66
	C-7	Chemical plant material handling	58
	C-8	Residential air conditioning	56
	C-9	Transformer substation	62
	C-10	Railcar shaker	57
	C-11	Transformer substation	52
	C-12	Positive-displacement blower	55
	C-13	Aircraft takeoff	63
	C-14	Glass manufacturing plant	67
Sporadic complaints	D-1	Factory air pump	71
	D-2	Manufacturing plant	58
	D-3	Chemical plant	56
	D-4	Local automobile traffic	56
	D-5	Plastics plant	51
	D-6	Power station	69
No observed reaction	E-1	Transformer substation	40
	E-2	Aircraft runup	46
	E-3	Asphalt tile shaker	59
	E-4	Asphalt tile reddler	40
	E-5	Power plant	47
	E-6	Aircraft overflight	53
	E-7	Aircraft landing	60
	E-8	City traffic	56
	E-9	Aircraft log and takeoff	57
	E-10	Local traffic	59
	E-11	Auto assembly plant	66
	E-12	Can manufacturing	67
	E-13	Oil refinery	69

Data from Wyle Laboratories (1971).

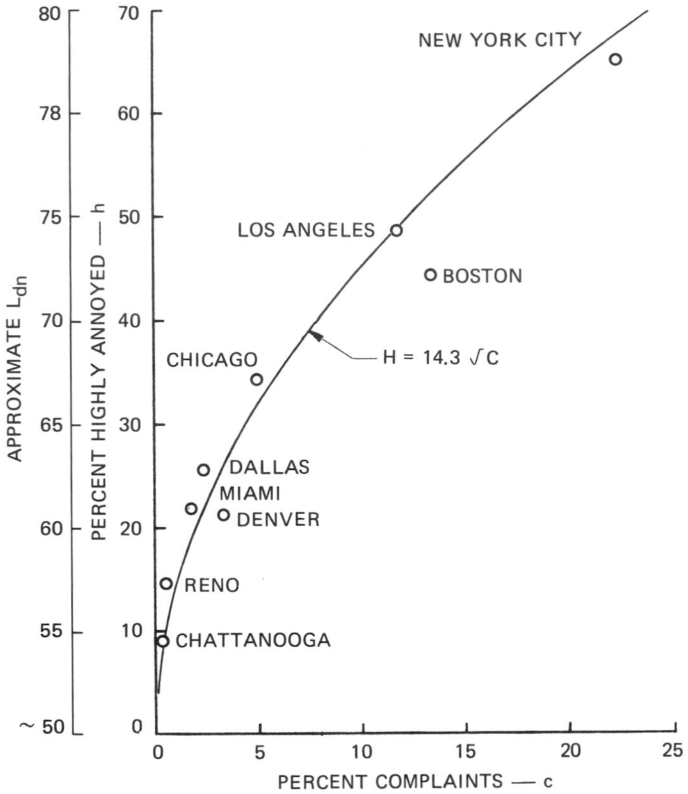

FIGURE 10.21 Percent of people who complained about aircraft noise as a function of percentage "highly annoyed" and approximate L_{dn} (From Connor and Patterson, 1973.)

problems involving aircraft noise. In general, the legal action consisted of lawsuits to prohibit or reduce the level of aircraft noise in specific residential areas, and/or to pay compensation to residents for the 'taking' of property value. It is seen that in relatively warm climate areas, some legal actions started at L_{dn} levels of ~55 dB. It is to be noted that because of legal constraints and codes, statutes of limitations, costs involved, and some societal attitudes, the lack of legal actions is not necessarily indicative of a lack of adverse effects and high levels of noise annoyance in given residential areas.

HOUSE DEPRECIATION DUE TO ENVIRONMENTAL NOISE

One obvious consequence of the presence of environmental noise that is sufficiently annoying is that people do not consider that environment as desirable for residential living. A number of economic investigations have

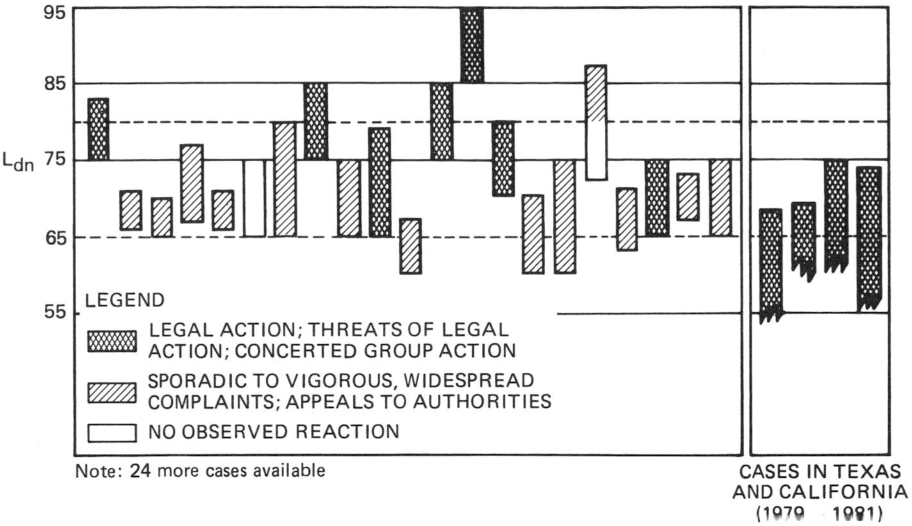

FIGURE 10.22 Reactions of people in communities exposed to aircraft noise environments. The height of the bars represents the approximate range of L_{dn} values found over a given neighborhood. (After Galloway and Von Gierke, 1966.)

been undertaken to measure the degree to which environmental noise depreciates the value of residential property. As far as could be done, the effects on the subjects property values of socioeconomic status of residents, home ownership, population density, age of housing, etc., were taken into account by sampling, and other procedures, in all of these studies.

Researchers examined records of sales, appraisals, and the results of questionnaires administered to panels of real estate experts regarding samples of houses around London's Heathrow and Gatwick Airports (Commission on the Third London Airport, 1970). Some of the findings are given in Table 10.8. The results of the British study and studies conducted in the United States (Nelson, 1978) and Canada (Mieszkowski and Saper, 1978) are shown in Fig. 10.23. Of interest in Fig. 10.23 is the finding in the British study that the rate of depreciation, as a function of exposure to aircraft noise, was significantly related to the general class of house—the higher-priced the dwellings, the greater was the percentage depreciation. The U.S. and Canadian data were not stratified with respect to the cost of the houses.

Also shown in Fig. 10.23 are estimated linear rates of depreciation for the three price ranges of houses, namely, 1% per decibel (L_{dn}) for the high-priced houses and 0.75% per decibel for medium- and low-cost houses. An analysis, conducted for the Federal Aviation Administration of the effects of aircraft noise on residential property values in seven cities indicated that there was about a 0.5% decrease in value for each 1-dB increase in L_{dn} (Nelson, 1979).

TABLE 10.8 Estimated Percent Depreciation in Housing Values

Location	Housing price range	Percent depreciation		
		$L_{dn} \approx 68$ dB	$L_{dn} \approx 75$ dB	$L_{dn} \approx 83$ dB
Around Heathrow airport	Low	0	2.9	5.0
	Medium	2.6	6.3	10.5
	High	3.3	13.3	22.5
Around Gatwick airport	Low	4.5	10.3	15*
	Medium	9.4	16.5	22*
	High	16.4	29.0	39*
Average	Low	2.2	6.6	10.0
	Medium	6.0	11.4	14.0
	High	10.0	21.2	31.0

* Extrapolation.

From Commission on the Third London Airport (1970).

Taylor *et al.* (1982) studied the effect of arterial and expressway road traffic noise on house prices in Ontario, Canada. They found that there was a depreciation of approximately 0.5% per decibel of ground traffic noise in the value of medium-priced houses at a 24-h L_{eq} of ~70 dB (estimated L_{dn} of ~72 dB). This compares roughly with the effect of aircraft noise on house costs at an L_{dn} of ~60 dB as shown in Fig. 10.20. This relative difference between the impact of the two types of noises on house costs is clearly consistent with ~10 dB difference found in the effectiveness between these two noises as a cause of annoyance, as discussed earlier.

Tradeoffs

There is little reason to question the general relations shown in Fig. 10.23 regarding the impact of aircraft noise on housing values. There is at least one factor, however, that may have a compensating effect that offsets, to some degree, the negative effect of the aircraft noise generally associated with closeness to an airport. The factor is the reduction in cost and time to reach the airport for those people working at, or near, the airport, or who use the airport on a frequent basis. In addition, the demand by certain industries to be near an airport may also increase the number of workers who wish to live nearby.

Among other variables, De Vany (1976) studied the relations between distance from an airport, aircraft noise level, and housing costs. He found an interactive effect between distance from an airport (Love Field, Dallas, Texas), aircraft noise level, and house and land values. Figure 10.24 is after Fig. 1 from De Vany's paper. Certain liberties have been taken in preparing Fig. 10.24, especially in regard to quantifying the distance dimensions on the basis of ancillary information regarding typical L_{dn} values.

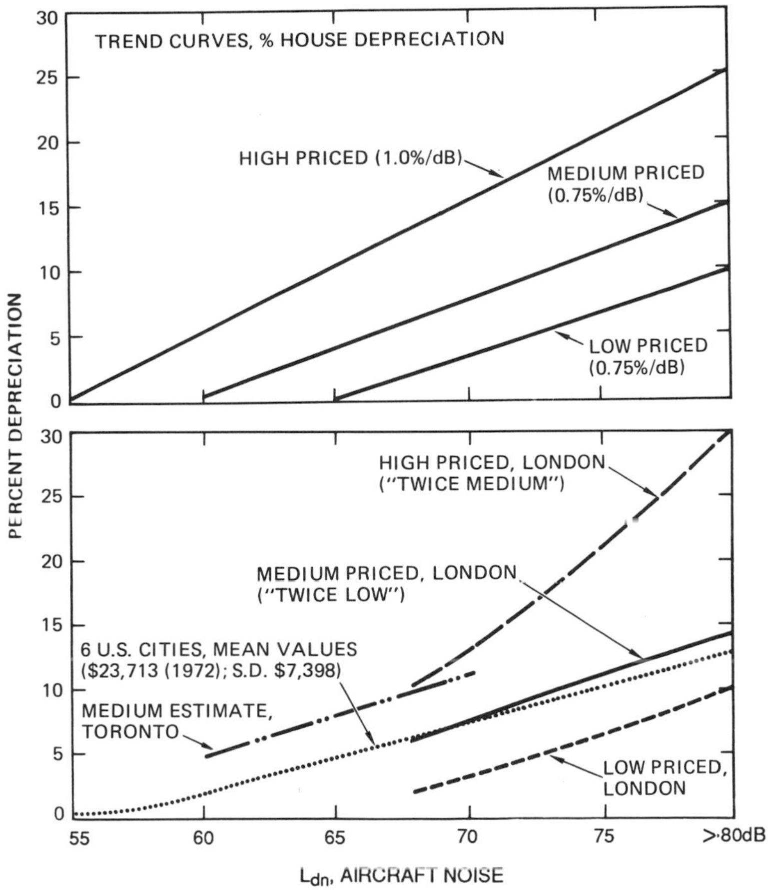

FIGURE 10.23 Depreciation of house values as function of aircraft noise near London (Commission on the Third London Airport, 1970); near U.S. cities (San Francisco, St. Louis, Cleveland, New Orleans, San Diego, and Buffalo) (Nelson, 1970) and near Toronto, Canada (Mieszkowski, and Saper, 1978).

Figure 10.24 can be used to interpret (1) depreciation as a function of L_{dn} for "non–airport workers" and (2) appreciation as a function of closeness and depreciation with L_{dn} for "airport workers" living in a band under the major aircraft flight paths to and from the airport. Figure 10.24 would seem to indicate that at a distance of about 2 miles from the airport (under aircraft flight paths), the interaction between noise costs to residential living and the benefits of nearby ground transportation to airport workplace results in a net increase in house value to those people who work at or near the airport. It is to be emphasized that this figure represents a purely statistical model and simplification of available data. There are, of course, a number of other factors that influence possible depreciation and/or appreciation in the value of a given house.

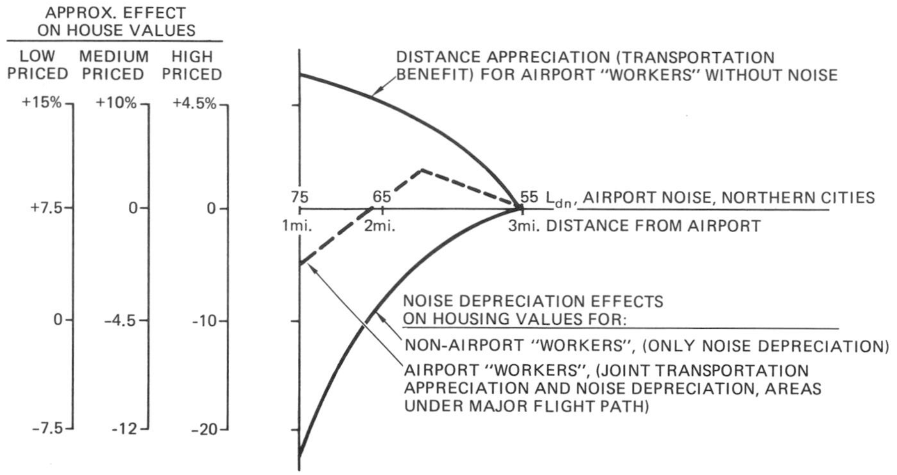

FIGURE 10.24 Model for effects of aircraft noise and transportation distance from airport on approximate housing values. Airport workers are those whose employment location is at or near the airport. (After De Vany, 1976.)

Also, the functions in Fig. 10.24 are not generalizable to all locations around an airport because the relation between distance from an airport and L_{dn} is quite different from that found under the main takeoff, or approach-to-landing, flight paths. A typical example of the L_{dn} levels at different distances from an airport is given in Fig. 10.25, where it is seen that at a distance of only 1 mile to the side of an airport, the aircraft noise is negligible (L_{dn} <55). However, at the end of the runway (on the flight path), an L_{dn} of 55 dB is not reached until about 6 miles from the end of the runway.

EFFECTS OF ENVIRONMENTAL NOISE ON PERFORMANCE IN SCHOOLS

Noise Effects in Schools

Some of the external costs of aircraft noise have been identified in the development of lawsuits brought by city school authorities against city airport authorities for damages to the educational process in schools impacted by aircraft noise. An example of the effects of aircraft noise (having peak levels of ~87 dB_A outdoors and L_{dn} levels of ~70 dB) on various school activities, as observed by the teachers in some schools in San Diego, California, is shown in Fig. 10.26. Comparable data were obtained from teachers in London (Crook and Langdon, 1974) and Hong Kong (Ko, 1979).

It is obvious that some of the activity interferences from aircraft noise are to be expected as a result of masking effects of noise on speech communications. Figure 10.27 shows estimates made by the teachers in the San Diego

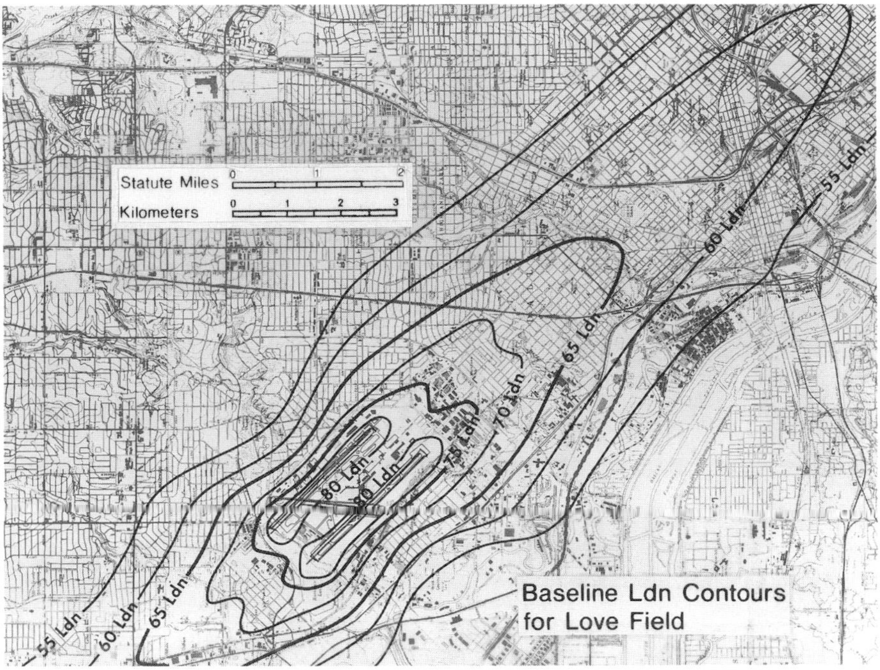

FIGURE 10.25 L_{dn} contours around Love Field, Texas. (From Department of Aviation, 1981.)

study of the duration of interference effects of aircraft noise events. Other studies, unpublished, conducted by the Highline School District (near Seattle, Washington) revealed somewhat longer-duration effects from aircraft noise in schoolrooms than are shown in Fig. 10.27.

Studies in Highline School

In a Highline School District (1976) study (Maser *et al.*, 1978) an analysis of the school achievement test scores over school grades 3–7 and 5–10 revealed that high-academic-aptitude students in schools exposed to aircraft noise did as well as those in quiet schools. Achievement was measured by standardized tests administered to the students each school year. However, middle- and, especially, low-academic-aptitude students in the noisy schools showed progressive deterioration in school achievement tests with continued school attendance as compared with the achievement of cohorts of equal aptitude in quiet schools.

The results of this study are shown in Fig. 10.28. The differences between the test scores of students in the lower third of academic aptitude, in the "noisy" (noise-exposed) schools versus the quiet schools, were statistically

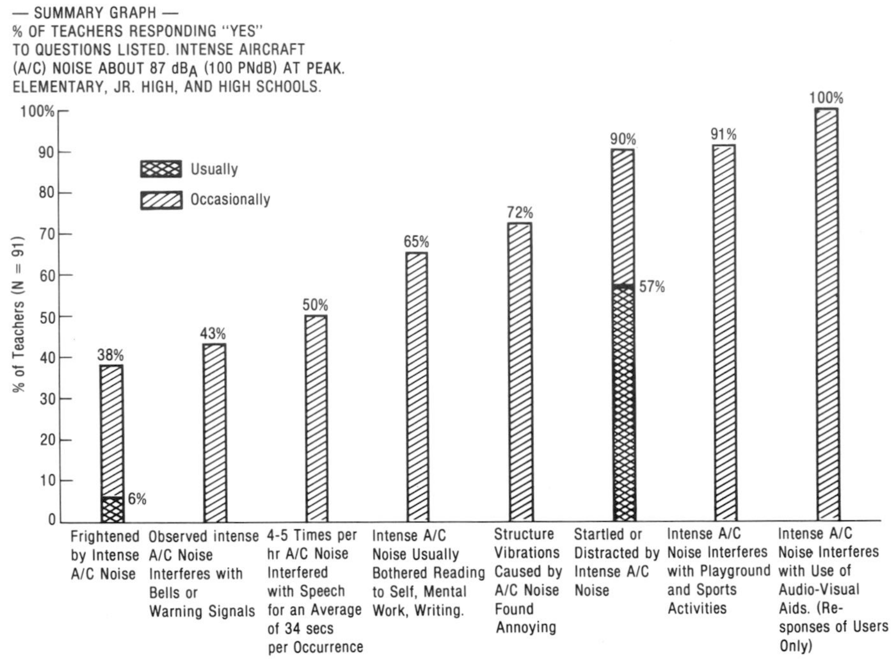

FIGURE 10.26 Results from questionnaire on aircraft noise effects in some San Diego, California, school areas. L_{dn} approximately 70 dB. (From an unpublished report by K. D. Kryter for the City Schools Attorney, San Diego, California, 1978.)

significant for the seventh and tenth grades. The socioeconomic characteristics, according to city and school officials, of the students from the noisy and quiet schools were similar. The most significant difference between the schools was the fact that the noisy schools were exposed 50 times or so on a near-daily basis to aircraft noise reaching peak levels of about 90 dB_A (L_{dn} ~70 dB).

It should be noted that in the San Diego and Seattle studies just discussed, the buildings were typical masonry school structures, but they were not air-conditioned or specially soundproofed. The related lawsuits were settled by the aviation interests paying for the costs of soundproofing certain school structures and/or building new structures in quieter areas.

Cohen *et al.* (1981) also found a generally adverse effect of intense aircraft noise (peak levels as high as 95 dB_A outdoors) on reading and math achievement in grades 3 and 4 (see Table 10.9). Additional evidence of a cumulative adverse effect of freeway noise is seen in Fig. 10.29, from a study by Lukas *et al.* (1981). Some apparent degradation in reading achievement occurred with increased classroom noise in third-graders. This effect was accelerated by the sixth grade. Bronzaft and McCarthy (1975) and Bronzaft (1980) reported that the noise from elevated trains going by grade schools also had

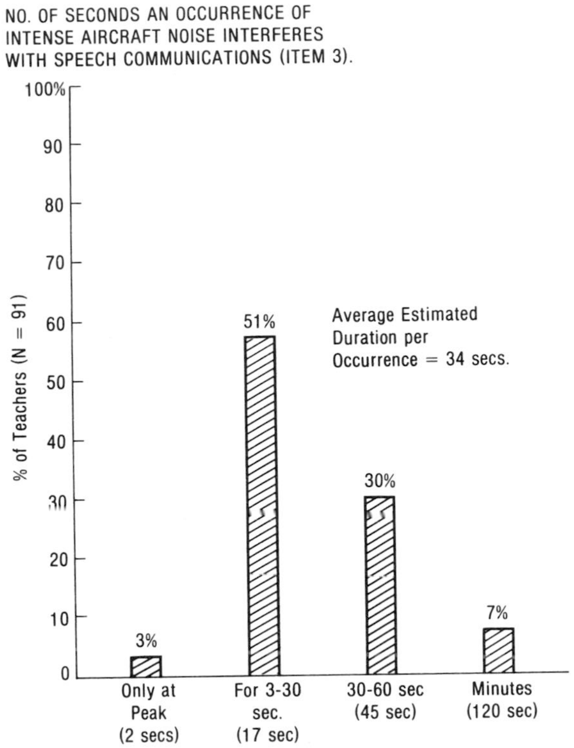

FIGURE 10.27 Estimates made by teachers in some schoolrooms in San Diego, California, of duration of speech interferences by indivdual aircraft noise events. L_{dn} approximately 70 dB. (From an unpublished report by K. D. Kryter for the City Schools Attorney, San Diego, California, 1978.)

more pronounced adverse effects on the reading achievement scores of sixth-graders than on third-graders.

Cohen *et al.*, (1981) found that the amount of aircraft noise around the residences of the children, as well as that at their schools, contributed to a lowering of school achievement scores. This is consistent with an earlier study by Cohen *et al.* (1973) of the effects of freeway noise around high-rise apartment buildings on the reading ability of children measured in the school.

ADDITIONAL RESEARCH QUESTIONS CONCERNING L_{dn}

Several additional issues and questions related to the calculation and interpretation of L_{dn} warrant some further discussion, such as (1) habituation over time, (2) ambient and background noises, (3) practical threshold levels for annoyance, and (4) the combined effects of noise from multiple sources.

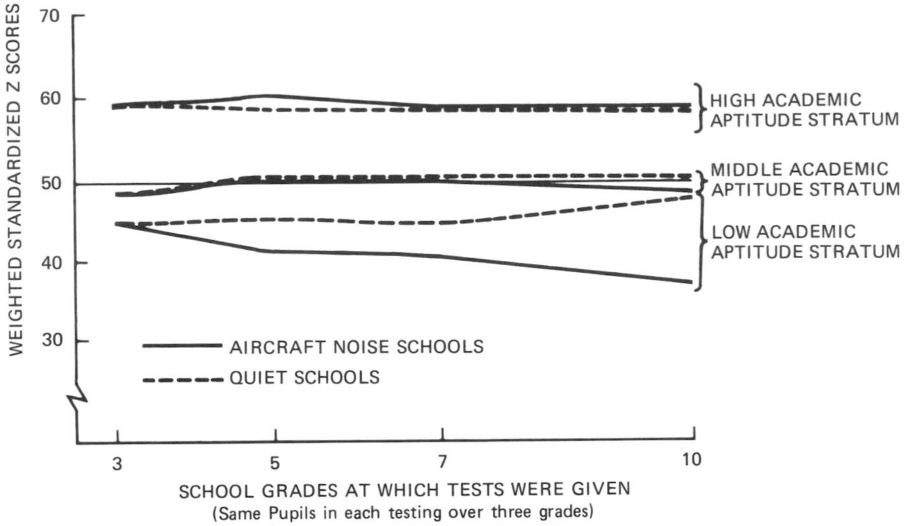

FIGURE 10.28 Standardized Z scores on comprehensive test of basic skills from fall 1970 to fall 1976, for school grades 3, 5, 7, and 10. Scores set to be the same for initial test grade 3. Total 269 students in aircraft noise schools (L_{dn} ~70), and 370 students from quiet (no-aircraft-noise) schools. (From Maser *et al.,* 1978.)

Habituation

The fundamental concept behind the L_{dn}, and similar measures, is that neighborhoods of people exposed to about the same environmental noises nearly day after day, develop reliable attitudes of annoyance about the particular noises in their environment. Comparison of the surveys conducted in 1961 and 1967 around London Heathrow Airport revealed that for each level of loudness intensity present in the two time periods, degree of noise annoyance

TABLE 10.9 Mean (Adjusted) School Achievement Percentiles as a Function of Classroom Noise Abatement and Grade

	Mean achievement percentile			
	Reading		Math	
Classroom condition	3rd grade	4th grade	3rd grade	4th grade
Noise	30.30	35.96	34.35	39.35
Noise-abated	47.36	37.90	56.24	37.54
Quiet	37.85	39.09	36.96	42.76

From Cohen *et al.* (1981).

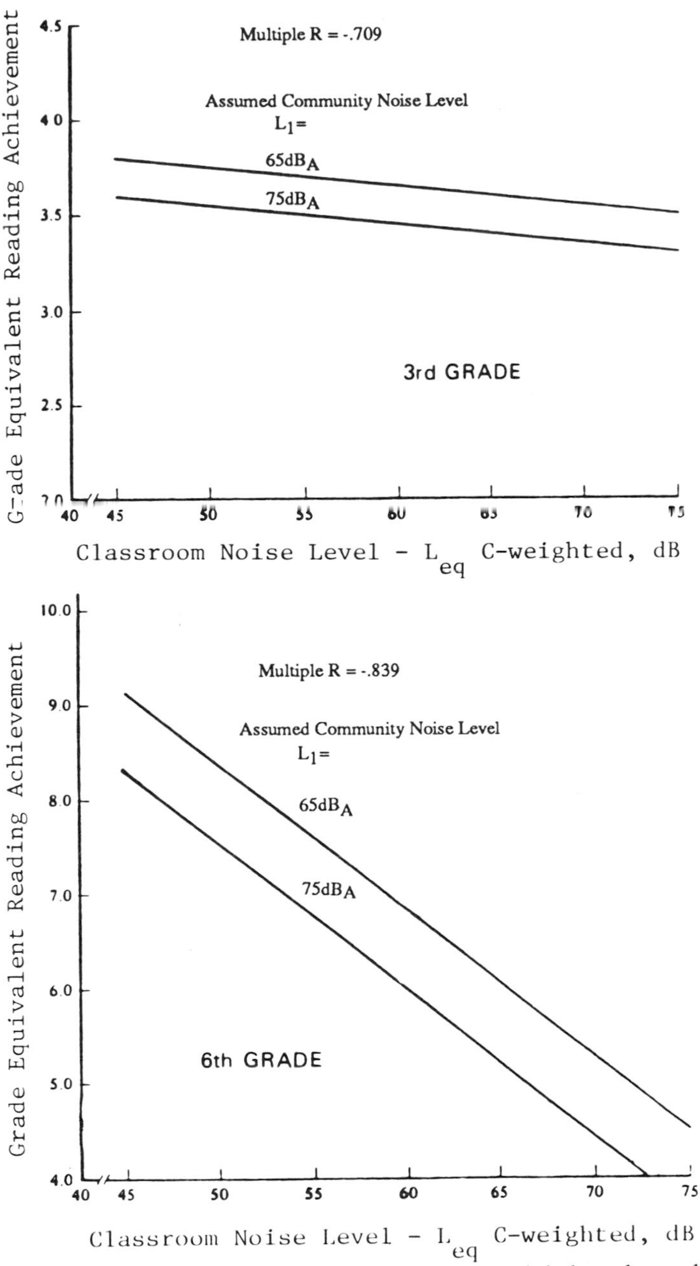

FIGURE 10.29 Relationship between achievement of third- and sixth-graders and classroom noise levels given different noise levels in the community. (From Lukas *et al.*, 1981.)

had stayed the same, but had fallen for each level of number of aircraft noise events. These findings would be expected, relative to L_{dn}, because (1) the noise exposure was measured in terms of NNI, not L_{dn}; (2) the number of noise events increased greatly between the two periods; and (3) the NNI, as previously discussed, adds the "energy" of events as 15 log number of aircraft operations, whereas L_{dn} is calculated on an equal-energy basis, as 10 log number of operations. This would inflate NNI, relative to L_{dn}, as the number, as was indeed the case, of aircraft events increased between the two periods.

Vallet *et al.* (1978) assessed, by attitude surveys, the annoyance of people living near expressways in ten French towns. These investigators found in the second survey, conducted after a lapse of 2 years, that annoyance had not declined during this period. Borsky (1980) found that there may be an initial period, months, of getting used to noises in a new environment. However, the annoyance reported for aircraft and street traffic noise after that does not diminish; if anything, it tends to increase with continued years of exposure. This increased annoyance could perhaps be attributed to some degree to the increase in sensitivity to sound arousal from sleep as people get older (see Chapter 9). Hede and Bullen (1982) found relatively little difference in measured mean annoyance from aircraft noise as a function of the months and years of exposure.

Ambient and Background Noises

In its broadest form, the L_{dn} concept could be used to estimate the annoyance–disturbance impact on people of the total daily dosage of noise regularly received from all sources in a living environment. In this context, the terms *ambient* and *background* noise are sometimes used as labels to distinguish such noise from noise identified as coming from sources such as aircraft, automobiles, or factories.

Exact definitions of ambient and background noise are difficult to make, at least with respect to the calculation of a total L_{dn}. *Ambient* is generally used to mean intermittent sounds at a weak intensity that typify a given area (e.g., the sound of birds, insects, wind, music, and people's voices). Realistically, *ambient noise* is probably a misnomer in that it connotes sounds that are too weak to interfere with speech or other normal behavioral activities. Such sound is not unwanted sound, or noise, and accordingly should not be used in calculating the total L_{dn} of an environment. The same applies, of course, to any sound (speech, music etc.), regardless of intensity, if it is "wanted" by the listeners, i.e., is not considered in a particular context or situation as noise.

Background noise is usually used to describe a continuous condition (e.g., the hum of distant traffic or factory noises) that is less intense than noises, intermittent or continuous, from closer aircraft, street traffic, or other sources. Background noise qualifies for inclusion in estimating a total L_{dn}, provided it is of sufficient intensity to cause some annoyance or disturbance.

In most living environments where noise is a problem, noise occurrences that are readily identified as coming from a particular source determine the value of L_{dn}. Background noise, unless of near-equal intensity, will not contribute sufficient sound energy to increase the decibel value of L_{dn}. It is sometimes surmised that a high background noise level makes an intruding noise less annoying because the increase in noise level above background may seem relatively small compared to the absolute level of the intruding noise. However, a high level of background "sound" can become, in its own right, bothersome.

Laboratory tests and attitude surveys of the effects of continuous background noise level on judged annoyance from aircraft noise have been somewhat inconsistent. Powell and Rice (1975) and Johnston and Haasz (1979) conducted laboratory tests in which subjects judged the annoyance of recorded aircraft noise heard in different levels of recorded background (road traffic noise). It was found that the subjective rating of the aircraft noise decreased when the level of the background noise approached the level of the aircraft noise. However, Taylor *et al.* (1980) found in an attitude survey conducted near Toronto Airport that the effect of background noise level was generally not significant.

It is to be noted that the subjects in these studies were asked to judge the annoyance of the aircraft noise, and not the annoyance of the total environment, background, and aircraft noise. Accordingly, the findings of reduced aircraft noise annoyance in high levels of background noise could be expected as the result of the background noise masking, to some extent, the loudness of the aircraft noise (see discussion of Vos data in Fig. 10.17); at that point the background noise would presumably be the primary cause of noise annoyance.

Threshold Levels of Noisiness of Events for Speech and Sleep Interference

As shown by attitude surveys, it appears that whether a sound in real life is unwanted, independently of any cognitive meaning it may convey, is determined to a large extent by the effective energy level of a noise event that causes interference with the hearing of wanted auditory signals, especially speech, and/or arousal from a state of rest or sleep. Interference with typical-level conversational speech is likely to become noticeable when the noise level exceeds about 45 peak dB_A at the listener's ears (see Chapter 6 and EPA, 1974). But the typical threshold level for most sensitive sleep arousal is around 35 peak dB_A (see Fig. 9.46B). Inasmuch as a house with windows open will offer, on the average, 15-dB attenuation of outdoor noise, it follows that annoyance will start during open-window conditions only when the outdoor noise exceeds (1) about 60 dB_A, for interferences with speech reception; and (2) about 50 dB_A for sleep arousals. As seen in Table 10.5, for closed-window conditions, this outdoor threshold can be about 10 dB higher; i.e., house attentuation of outdoor noise will be about 25 dB.

Interestingly, these threshold differences may account for the results in Figs. 10.5 and 10.8, showing a greater disruption of conversation of speech communication by aircraft than road traffic noise, but the reverse for sleep interruption. The reason could be that the aircraft noise frequently exceeds the threshold for both sleep interruption and speech communications, but while the street traffic can exceed the level for sleep interruption, indoors it seldom reaches the 10-dB higher level for speech communications.

The relatively high threshold level for estimating annoyance from physical measures of noise has been demonstrated by Gjestland (1979) and Gjestland and Oftedal (1980). These investigators found in some laboratory tests that this threshold at the listener's ears was probably at 40 or 50 dB_A, depending on whether quiet or busy daytime activities were involved.

Practical Threshold Levels for Loudness or Noisiness or Events

Figure 10.30 shows the ratings given by 47 adults (19 females, 28 males, average age 34 years) of annoyance felt while listening to recordings of aircraft noises presented, via loudspeakers, in a laboratory "living" room. The ratings were marked on a 16-point scale from completely acceptable annoyance to always unacceptable annoyance. The subjects were instructed to listen and judge as though they were, for some judgment tests (1) engaged in casual activities when in their homes, or, for some tests, on an outdoor patio; or (2) for other tests, indoors engaged in listening to speech from a radio loudspeaker (recordings of Edward R. Morrow's "I Can Hear It Now" and James Whitmore's monologue, "Give 'em Hell Harry"). The speech was played at an average level of 64 dB_A.

If the boundary between acceptable and unacceptable degrees of annoyance is taken as a "practical" threshold of unacceptable annoyance, the threshold level for aircraft noise is (1) peak ~58 dB_A, L_{Aex} 61, when speech is present indoors; (2) peak 76 dB_A, L_{Aex} 79, when no speech is present indoors; and (3) peak 81 dB_A, L_{Aex} 84, with no speech present outdoors. Had the speech been at an average level of L_{Aeq} 55 dB_A, the level of typical conversational speech in the quiet (see Fig. 6.6), presumably the threshold in the presence of speech would have been about 48 dB_A, not too different from the threshold for start of speech-signal masking for such speech. Perhaps more interesting is the tolerance for the flyover noise when the listeners imagined they were not engaged in any particular activities.

Two points to be made with respect to the interpretation of these data are:

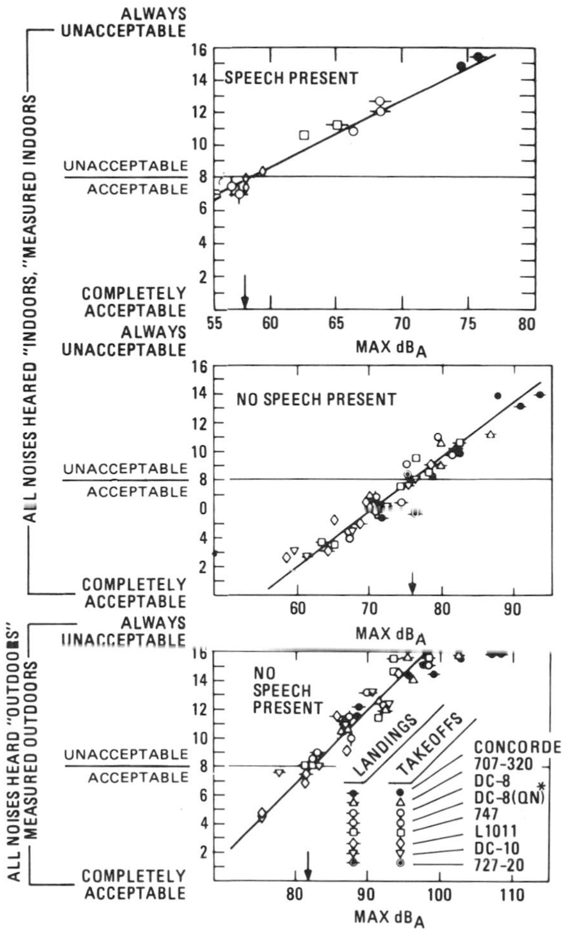

FIGURE 10.30 Mean subjective rating of annoyance acceptability given after each occurrence, and levels of noise at listener's position. (From Kryter, 1977.)

1. With no behavioral activities involved, the "practical threshold" level for a single occurrence of a noise event is of the order of L_{Aex} 82, average of indoor and outdoor, for these particular events. According to these data, at the position of the listener a steady-level sound with a peak level of 62 dB_A, and a duration of about 1.5 min, would be unacceptably noisy; it would be predicted that a steady level of 52 dB_A would be tolerable, under these listening conditions, for about 17 min.

2. When wanted auditory signals are present, the "practical threshold" level, in dB_A, is equal to the peak dB_A level of the signal at the position of the

listener. As noted earlier, the peak dB_A level for "weak" conversational speech is 45 dB_A.

Multiple Source Noises

Another research question facing the L_{eq} or L_{dn} noise energy summation concept is that of whether the annoyance received from different sources (e.g., aircraft and street traffic) is predictable from the total L_{eq} for the two noises. Unlike continuous background noise, the noises may not occur at the same time so that masking does not necessarily, or even generally, occur. As discussed above, it appears that, within limits, the annoyance attributable to either source alone is fairly well predicted from the L_{eq} of different numbers of occurrences.

Taylor (1982) asked people living in residential areas in Toronto to rate on a scale from 0 ("not at all disturbing") to 10 ("unbearably disturbing") the noise in their neighborhood from, among other things, aircraft, main road traffic, and finally, after the ratings to individual noises were given, to "overall" noise. The exposures to the noises were estimated for, or measured at, positions in the fronts of houses facing the street.

The findings for 17 different sites are plotted in Fig. 10.31B. There it is seen that the overall noise at a given L_{eq} (combined noises) is rated somewhat higher than road traffic noise at the same L_{eq}. However, aircraft noise of a given L_{eq} was judged to be much more disturbing than road traffic noise at the same L_{eq}. For equal annoyance, road traffic noise is about 8–11 dB higher than aircraft noise and 2–3 dB higher than overall noise [these same data were reported by Hall *et al.* (1981); see Fig. 10.7, above].

Powell (1979) asked subjects, seated in a simulated living room and engaged in reading or knitting, to rate their annoyance reaction to 15-min sessions during which various exposure levels of recorded aircraft and road traffic noises were presented separately or in combinations. The ratings were made on a scale of 0 ("not at all annoyed") to 9 ("extremely annoyed"). Figure 10.31A shows the data obtained by Powell.

The Powell data, unlike the Taylor data, show that, when of equal L_{eq}, the road traffic and aircraft noise were judged about equally annoying. As also discussed earlier, acoustical factors and noise measurement procedures (at the listener's position by Powell and outdoors in real life by Taylor) would seem to adequately explain the differences found by Taylor.

An unexpected differences between the Powell and the Taylor results is with regard to the "overall" ratings. Taylor's data in Fig. 10.31B indicate that the overall annoyance rating was considerably less than that given the aircraft noise, even though the aircraft noise was the dominant noise in the environment being judged. Powell's data, on the other hand, indicate that

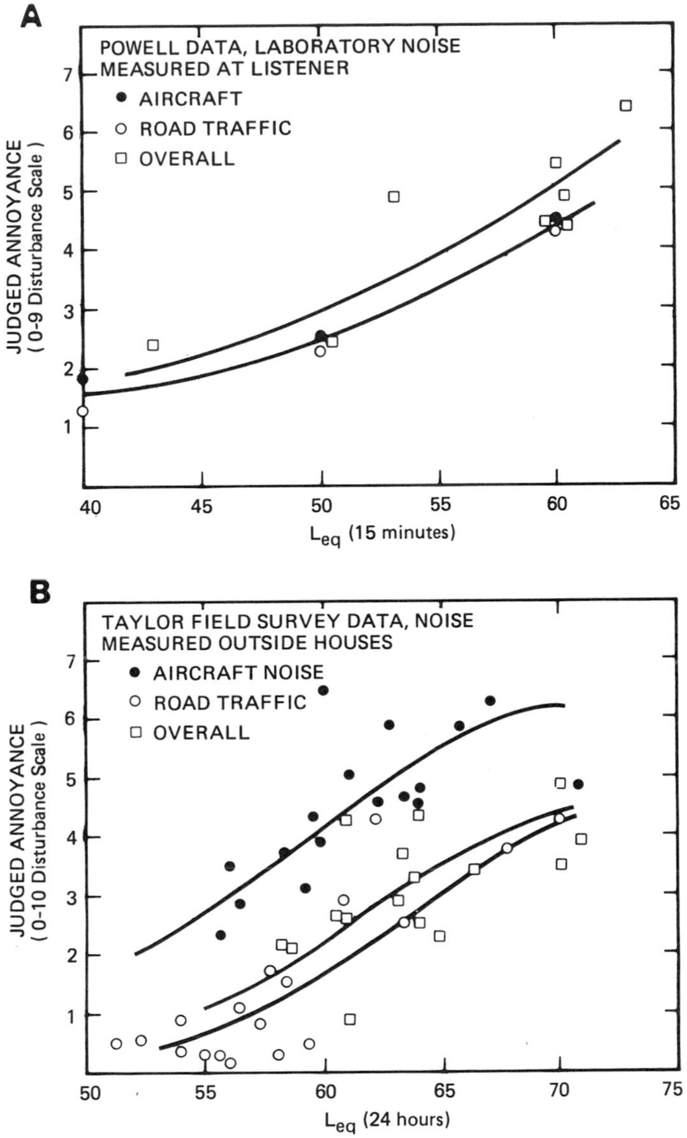

FIGURE 10.31 (A, B) Annoyance ratings given to separate sources (aircraft or road traffic) and overall ratings.

the annoyance from noises from multiple sources summates on about an equal exposure energy basis.

Perhaps the explanation lies in the differences in the questioning procedures used in the two studies. In the Powell study, the subjects rated their annoyance after independent test sessions during which only aircraft noise, only road traffic noise, or a combination of both, were present. For the latter session, the subjects did not rate their feelings of annoyance separately for the two noises. As noted above in the Taylor study, the subjects rated their annoyances first for each type of noise present in their living environment, presumably during a typical day, and, after giving those ratings, for "overall" noise.

It is tempting to think that the respondents in the Taylor study reported for "overall" noise annoyance their impression of the annoyances averaged. For example, if a respondent in the Taylor survey rated for his or her neighborhood the aircraft noise as, say, a "6," and the road traffic noise as a "1," and was then asked to rate the noise "overall," the respondent might well have considered the appropriate response to be somewhere between the two ratings. Indeed, Fig. 10.32 shows that overall annoyance in the Taylor study about equals the average judged annoyance for aircraft and for road traffic noises.

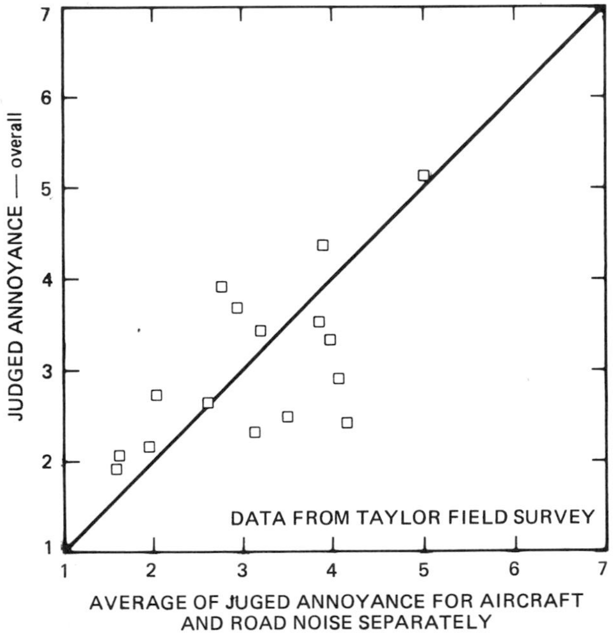

FIGURE 10.32 Relation between judged annoyance overall and the average of judged annoyance for aircraft and road noises given separately. (Data from Taylor *et al.*, 1982.)

POSSIBLE MODIFICATIONS OF L_{dn}

Seasonal Effects

The annualized L_{dn}, especially when expressed in terms of effective, at-the-ear, L_{dn} values, may be practically valid for predicting annoyance from daily occurring, periodic or aperiodic, noises events. However, complaint and attitude survey data indicate that climate has a significant influence on the amount of aircraft noise annoyance experienced as a function of L_{dn}. Because of less open-window and outdoor living conditions, the effective, at-the-ear, amount of aircraft noise can be expected to be less in (1) winter than in summer seasons; or (2) as a year-round average, in a northern–moderate climate (such as New York, London, Geneva, or Amsterdam) than in a warmer climate (such as in southern cities in the United States).

Figure 10.33 shows that higher degrees, equivalent to a difference of 8 PN_{dB} in level, of annoyance were reported for New York City airports during the warmer months than during colder months. Figure 10.15 showed that at a given approximate L_{dn} of exposure to aircraft noise, higher percentages of people were annoyed in the summer than in the winter. However, as discussed earlier, the annoyance reflected in that figure for the small-city (surveyed in the winter) airports may be somewhat disproportionately decreased by the relatively few number of intense jet-aircraft noises, as compared to the number of such events in large city (surveyed in the summer) airports.

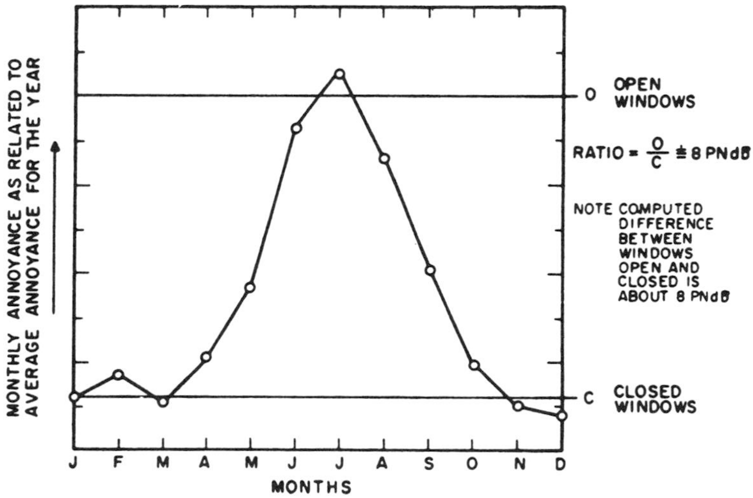

FIGURE 10.33 Total monthly annoyance, as measured by number of complaints registered with airports, as a function of season of the year. Based on 4-year average of four airports in northeastern United States. (From Beranek *et al.*, 1959.)

Surveys in Dallas, Texas (July) by the Dallas Department of Aviation, and in southern California (September–November) by FAA, revealed appreciably more annoyance than that found in attitude surveys conducted in northern–moderate climate cities (April–June; September–November). The latter surveys being those involved in the previously discussed cluster analyses. However, some portion of this difference is attributable to the fact that the trend and synthesis cluster curves, based on northern–moderate climate cities, are for high annoyance defined as the top 27–29% of the annoyance scale, not 40%, as was the case for the studies in warmer-climate cities.

Griffiths *et al.* (1980) found that annoyance ratings of road traffic noise in some London residential areas did not vary significantly for different times of the year even though the proportion of open windows did. It is possible that this apparent lack of a seasonal effect was due to the relatively low effective level of the road traffic noise, as discussed above. It is also possible that people tend to keep the windows facing streets, especially heavily traveled streets, closed during both warmer and colder seasons.

Bertoni *et al.* (1993) studied, by questionnaire, the reactions of a sample of some 908 citizens exposed to urban traffic noise in Modena, Italy. The results showed that the numbers affected and disturbed by traffic noise of L_{dn} ~60–65 was greater when windows were open than closed by the equivalent of about 5 dB in L_{dn} level. These investigators also found that above L_{dn} 60–62 a "moderate degree of disturbance" is manifested, and above L_{dn} 68–70 "situations of constraint" are experienced. These data appear to be indicative of considerably less adverse impact from urban traffic than would be expected on the basis of the amount of "high annoyance" generally found from exposure to aircraft noise of those levels, as discussed earlier.

Figure 10.34 shows that with an L_{dn} of 60–65 dB, about 50% of the people living near a southern California (Orange County) airport believed the aircraft noise to be a serious problem causing decreases in residential property values and danger to health. These percentages are not directly comparable, because of wording, to percentage "highly annoyed" of the other survey data. Nevertheless, they also indicate somewhat greater adverse effects than would be expected on the basis of the annoyance data obtained in the northern climate surveys discussed.

Possible Weight for Outdoor, Open-Window Conditions

Some disparity between the amount of community noise annoyance measured in colder as compared to warmer climates supports, indirectly, the validity of the basic L_{dn} concept. However, it also challenges the present practice of its application on an annualized basis without some regard for the climatic factors. It could be argued that, for example, the increase from 4 months of open-window outdoor living in colder climates, to, for example, 8 months in warmer climates, represents a factor of ~3 dB in increased at-

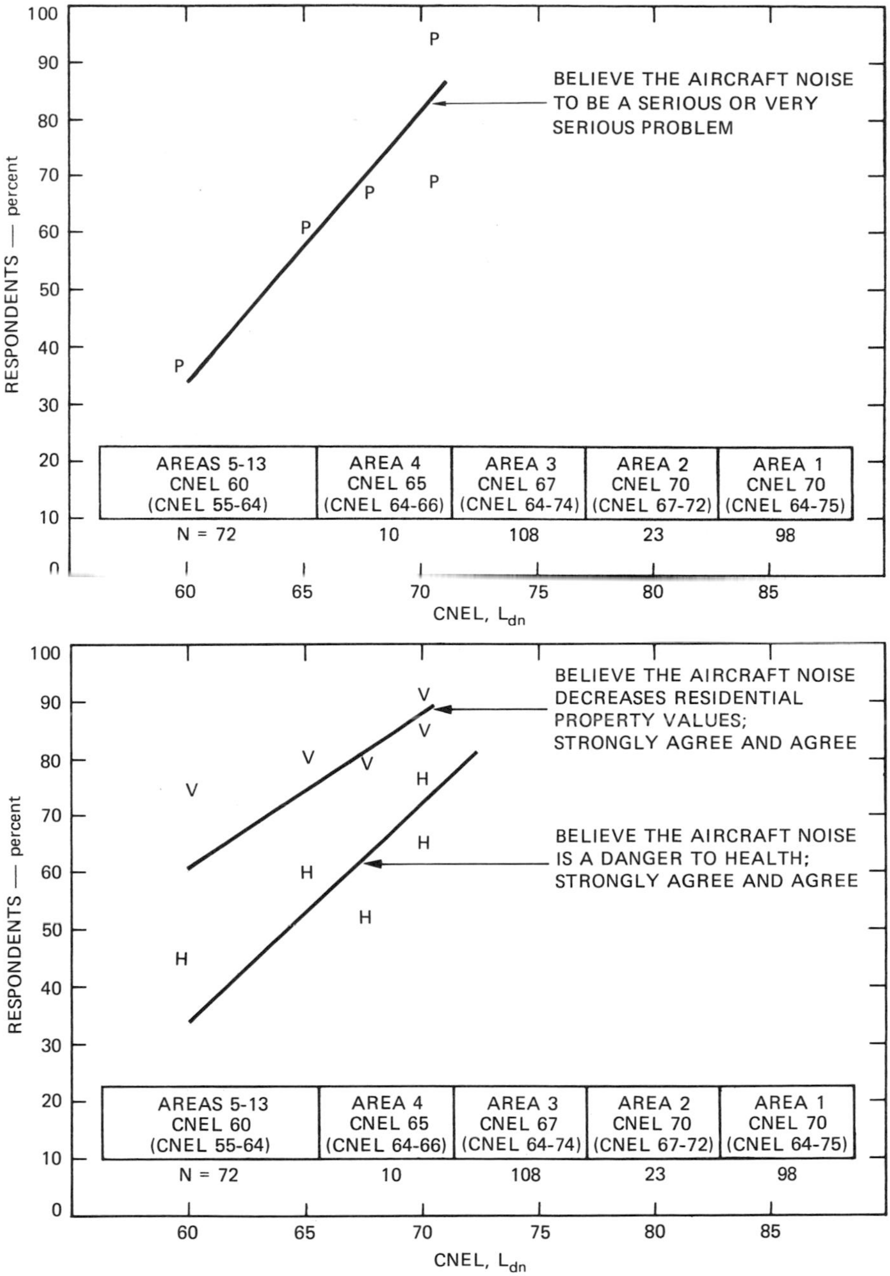

FIGURE 10.34 Percentage of sample of people living near John Wayne Airport (Orange County, CA, 1980), perceiving aircraft noise as a serious or very serious problem, as decreasing the value of their houses, and as a danger to their health. (Based on VTN, consolidated, 1980, Chap. X and Appendix A3.) L_{dn} level of aircraft noise in their neighborhood. Also indicated are the L_{dn} levels at which certain degrees of complaint behavior may be initiated. It is found that, as normally measured, street traffic noise causes approximately similar adverse effects at L_{dn} 10 dB higher than that for aircraft noise.

the-ear noise energy over the year. It is of interest to note that the original CNR procedure, mentioned earlier in this chapter, incorporated a 5-dB correction for a windows-closed-, compared with a windows-open environment.

Daytime and Nighttime Penalties

As noted earlier, the L_{dn} noise measurement procedures involve the addition of a 10-dB penalty to noises occurring during typical hours of sleep, 10 PM–7 AM. The metric, CNEL (community noise-exposure level), used in the state of California, and WECPNL (weighted equivalent perceived noise level, in PN_{dB}, or dB_A), recommended by the International Organization for Aviation, and used in Japan and Elsewhere, for noise-assessment purposes involves, in addition to 10-dB 10:00 PM–7:00 AM penalty, a 5-dB penalty to aircraft noise exposures occurring between 7 PM and 10 PM. These penalties are based on a mixture of laboratory and field research and the general experience of acoustical consultants working on community noise problems. (As noted earlier, for typical commercial-aviation operations, L_{dn} = CNEL -2.)

For example, as discussed earlier, it can be deduced that the level at which a noise will start to interfere with quiet conversational speech is about 10 dB higher than the level at which it will start to interfere with sleep. As shown in Fig. 10.35, the records of a telephone complaint bureau, maintained by the operator of several major airports in the northeastern United States, revealed that, for a given number of aircraft operations, the complaints for nighttime operations were greater than for daytime operations.

An historical review of time-of-day penalties is given in Clevenson and Shepherd (1980). The findings from recent attitude research studies specifically concerned with the question of the magnitude of daily time-period weights for predicting community response to noise are discussed below.

Ollerhead Study

Ollerhead (1977) deduced from interviews of 606 people near London that, during the evening hours of 7–10 PM, the typical person is disturbed about once per each 10 aircraft-noise events, once per each 30 such events during daytime hours of 7 AM to 7 PM, and once per each 100 such events during nighttime hours of 10 PM to 7 AM. These conclusions would translate to an evening exposure penalty, relative to daytime noises of 5 and -10 dB for nighttime.

Although the evening/daytime penalty of 5 dB is probably a valid finding, the -10-dB nighttime/daytime penalty is not at all in agreement with most other research data. It seems probable that the nighttime data may have been influenced by the fact that the operations at London Heathrow Airport were restricted to aircraft operations at night that created noise levels about 10 dB less intense than the peak levels allowed during the evening and daytime.

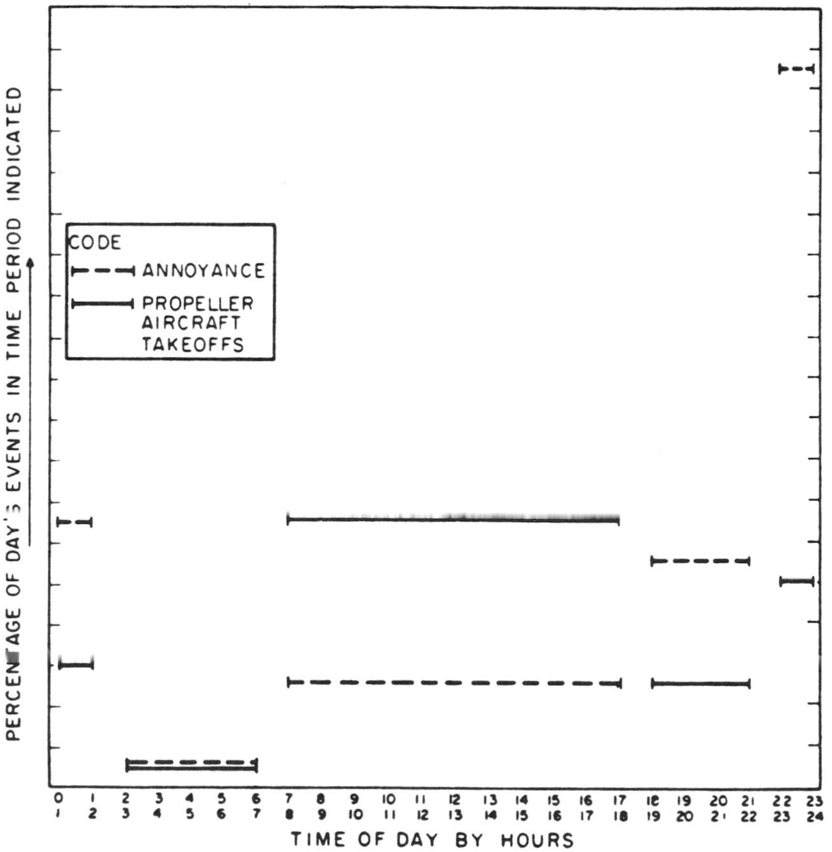

FIGURE 10.35 Annoyance, as measured by number of complaints registered at a major airport, and aircraft takeoff activity at that airport as a function of time of day. Data for 9 months averaged. Complaints and aircraft activity are expressed as the percentage of day's complaint or aircraft activity events occurring in the hour indicated. (From Beranek *et al.*, 1959.)

Borsky Study

Borsky (1976) surveyed approximately 1500 people living near J. F. Kennedy (JFK) International Airport in New York City. In this study the respondents were asked to report on their feelings of annoyance during different time periods. Borsky concluded that each nighttime noise has the equivalent effect of two day or evening flights, which would translate into a 3-dB penalty to nighttime as compared to daytime or evening occurrences. However, Borsky equated in his analysis the average number of flight operations per hour in each time period versus the average annoyance per time period. He did not take into account the differences in the number of hours of flight operations involved in the respective time periods.

Table 10.10 presents the results of calculations of the average annoyance experienced per noise occurrence in each of the designated time periods.

TABLE 10.10 Comparison of Average Annoyance per Aircraft Noise Event in Day (D), Evening (E), and Nighttime (N) Periods*

Time period	Average annoyances per time period	Average number of operations per hour	Average number of operations for time period	Average annoyances per operation	*N/D*	Decibel equivalent	*E/D*	Decibel equivalent
Day (D) 7 AM–7 PM	2.16	6.12, 12 h	74.64	0.029	2.86	5 dB	2.86	5 dB
Evening (E) 7–11 PM	2.76	8.30, 4 h	33.20	0.083	(N/E)/1	0 dB		
Night (N) 11 PM–7 AM	1.95	2.92, 8 h	23.36	0.083				

* Based on data from Table 13 in Borsky (1976).

Also shown are the ratios of the annoyances per noise occurrence for the different time periods and the decibel equivalences. It is seen that the annoyance per noise is equal for the night and evening aircraft noise, but that the daytime noise exposures were the equivalent of 5 dB less effective than the night or evening noises as a source of annoyance.

Bullen and Hede Study

Bullen and Hede (1982) examined the attitude-survey data they collected, near five airports in Australia, with respect to the hour-of-day adverse reactions to aircraft noise occurred. Figure 10.36A shows the percentage of aircraft movements during day (6–9 AM), evening (6–9 PM), and nighttime (9 PM–6 AM) periods for each runway at the five airports.

Bullen and Hede also asked 3575 respondents: "If you could have aircraft stopped from flying over in one of these 3-h periods, which one would you most like to have free from aircraft noise?" The results are shown in Fig. 10.36B for those who also indicated (in response to other questions; see Fig. 10.9) that they were (1) bothered or (2) seriously affected by aircraft noise. As shown on the insert-table to Fig. 10.36B, the sum of the percentages designating the daytime periods (6 AM–6 PM) is about 19%; evening (6 AM–9 PM), 45%; and nighttime (9 PM–6 AM), 26%.

The average percentage per 3-h periods is about 4 for the daytime hours, 45 for the evening 3-h periods, and 12 for the nighttime 3-h periods. The evening periods exceed the day by a factor of 11.3 (10.5 dB), and the nighttime hours exceed daytime periods by a factor of 3 (4.8 dB). Bullen and Hede recommend that, as a practical matter, a penalty weighting of 6 dB should be applied to noise occurrences during both evening and night hours. It is estimated, from the response-data histograms, that had the day–evening–night 3-h segments been defined as, respectively, 7 AM–7 PM, 7–10 PM, and 10 PM–7 AM, the evening/day and night/day 3-h period ratios would have been about 35/7 (7.0 dB) and 14/7 (3 dB).

DORA Study

As was discussed in Chapter 9, the Directorate of Operational Research and Analysis (DORA) administered a questionnaire about sleep disturbance over a 4-month period (June–September 1979) in areas near London's Heathrow and Gatwick Airports. Questions were asked as to the difficulties of going to sleep or being awakened because of aircraft noise during the "evening" (10–12 PM) and during the night (11 PM–7 AM). As is shown in Fig. 9.42, the percentages of people "very much" or "quite a lot" bothered by the aircraft noise is about the same for these two periods given a similar hourly dosage rate of noise. The DORA (1980) study furnishes no data with respect to the relative amount of annoyance, or disturbance, from a given dosage of aircraft noise present during the daytime (7 AM–7 PM) or evening (7–10 PM), the hours differently weighted in L_{dn}, CNEL, and WECPNL.

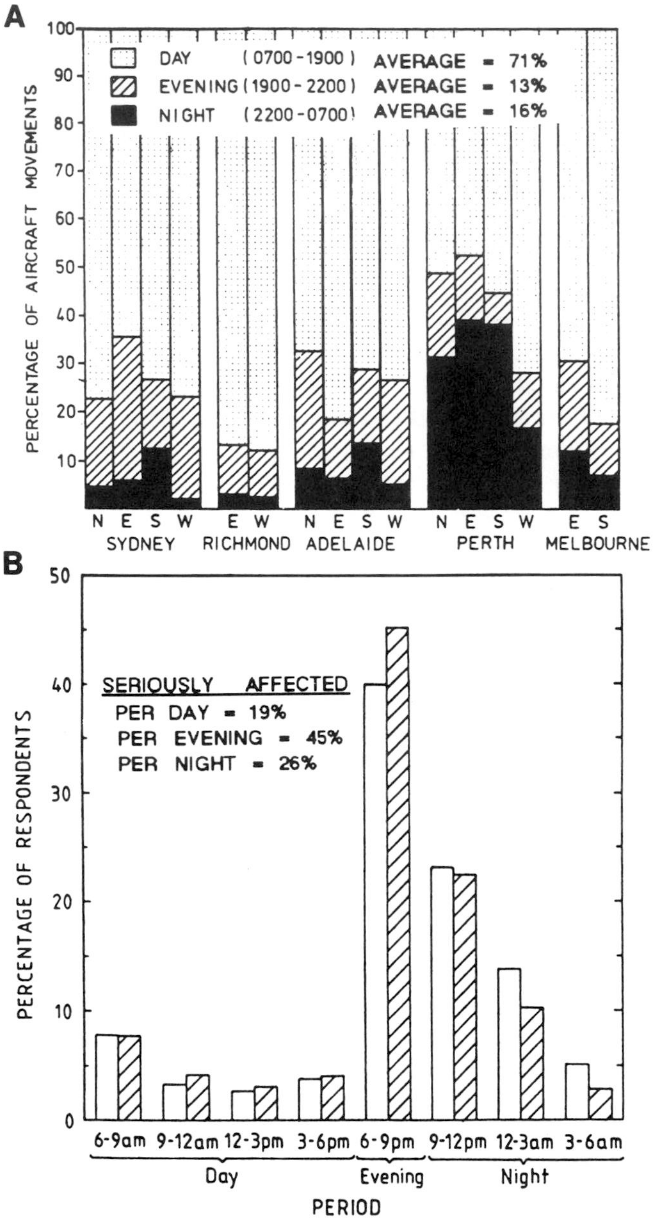

FIGURE 10.36 (A) Percentage distribution of aircraft movements during day, evening, and night hours for the different runways at four cities, and the average percentage by for the four cities. (B) Percentage of respondents choosing each 3-h period as the period they would most like to have free from aircraft noise (excluding respondents not bothered by noise, or who don't know). Unshaded areas—all respondents; shaded areas—seriously affected respondents. (From Bullen and Hede, 1983.)

Schomer Study

Schomer (1983) conducted a survey of disturbance and annoyance from artillery-blast noise and the noises from helicopters, aircraft, children, and pets. The surveys were conducted in civilian residential communities near military installations. Respondents were asked (1) how often they were bothered by the various noise events during the day (7:00 AM–7:00 PM), evening (7:00–10:00 PM), and night (10:00 PM–7:00 AM); and (2) how annoyed they were by a given type of noise during each time period. The annoyance was rated on a five-point scale: not at all, slightly, moderately, very much, and extremely. Estimates were developed of the number of occurrences of each type of noise event during the daytime plus evening (7:00–10:00 PM), and the night (10:00 PM–7:00 AM). The relative impact of the different noises on people was expressed for the day plus evening versus the nighttime periods. It was assumed that the different noise events at a given residence were physically about the same level regardless of the time period in which they occurred.

Table 10.11 shows the number of people "bothered" and "highly annoyed" (HA) during the day-plus-evening and during the night, and the ratio of the night/day-plus-evening of those numbers. The ratio of these ratios, far-right hand column of the table, average ~1.12, indicates that a single nighttime occurrence of a given type of noise caused somewhat more than twice the numbers of people "disturbed" by the noises than were "highly annoyed." (The "highly" annoyed scale was scored as "very much" and "extremely," covering the top 40% of the annoyance scale, not the 27–29% numerical annoyance magnitude scale criterion for "highly" annoyed.)

Although there were about 2–4 times as many people bothered by a given type of noise during the day-plus-evening as during the night (data column 3, Table 10.11, and data column 1, Table 10.12), there were about six to 20 times as many occurrences of the given noises during the night (data column 2, Table 10.12). Dividing the ratios of the number bothered during the day-plus-evening to the number bothered during the night by the ratios of the number of noise occurrences during the respective periods shows that the number bothered per noise occurrence is greater during the night than during the day-plus-evening. This difference factor ranges from 2.5 to 8 or so, the equivalent of 4–9 dB (data column 4, Table 10.12). These decibel values could be interpreted as being appropriate weights to be applied to nighttime noise-exposure levels to account for the greater number of people bothered by the occurrence of a given type of noise during the night as compared to the day-plus-evening periods.

To this penalty weight, an additional 1 dB could be added, according to Schomer, for bothersomeness being intrinsically more "highly annoying" during the night than day-plus-evening, as shown by the >1 ratios of data column 3 in Table 10.11. Schomer concludes that typical environmental noises, including impulsive blast noises, occurring at night are the equivalent

TABLE 10.11 Comparison of Responses for Respondents' Homes at All Times, During Weekdays and Weekends

		Numbered bothered			Number HA*		Percentage HA		
Source	Group	Day-plus-evening	Night	Ratio (day-plus-evening)/night	Day-plus-evening	Night	Day-plus-evening	Night	Ratio (night/day-plus-evening)
Artillery	Weekday	243	94	2.59	102	48	42	50	1.21
	Weekend	317	133	2.38	150	64	47	48	1.02
Airplanes†	Weekday	203	56	3.62	86	28	42	50	1.19
	Weekend	284	97	2.93	130	52	46	54	1.17
Helicopters	Weekday	263	59	4.46	114	31	43	53	1.23
	Weekend	319	97	3.29	167	59	52	61	1.17
Traffic	Weekday	177	63	2.81	91	38	56	60	1.07
	Weekend	377	151	2.50	214	87	57	58	1.02
Children and pets	Weekday	173	111	1.50	99	74	57	67	1.18
	Weekend	333	178	1.87	191	109	57	61	1.07

* HA is an abbreviation for the term ''highly annoyed,'' which is explained in the text.

† Airplanes in this study consisted mainly of single-engine, propeller-driven, general-aviation aircraft, with a small number of jet- and prop-jet-propelled military and commercial aircraft.

From Schomer (1983c).

TABLE 10.12 Rate of Noticing Bothersome Events

Source	Group	Number bothered (day-plus-evening/night)[a]	Actual occurrence (day-plus-evening/night)	Ratio R (column 2/column 1)	10 log(R)
Artillery	Weekday	2.6	6.5[b]	2.5	4.0
	Weekend	2.4	15.0	6.2	7.9
Airplanes[c]	Weekday	3.6	10[d]	2.8	4.5
	Weekend	2.9	13	4.5	6.5
Helicopters	Weekday	4.5	24[d]	5.3	7.2
	Weekend	3.3	24	7.3	8.6
Traffic	Weekday	2.8	12–20[e]	4–7	6–8
	Weekend	2.5	12–20	5–8	7–9
Children	Weekday	1.6	10–20[f]	6–12	8–11
and pets	Weekend	1.9	10–20	6–11	8–11

[a] From Schomer's (1983c) Table X.

[b] Base records.

[c] Airplanes in this study consisted mainly of single-engine, propeller-driven, general-aviation aircraft, with a small number of jet- and prop-jet-propelled military and commercial aircraft.

[d] Records—airfields.

[e] State Highway Department estimate.

[f] Author's estimate.

From Schomer (1983c).

of 5–10 dB in exposure level more annoying than the same noises occurring during the day and evening.

Averaged-Data Weight for Evening–Nighttime Period

Table 10.13 summarizes the penalty weights needed, according to the studies discussed, for the noise events in the time periods to equate the degrees of

TABLE 10.13 Night and Evening Penalties (in Decibels) per Various Investigators and Best Estimate

Survey	Night vs. day-plus-evening*	Evening vs. day	Night vs. day	Night vs. evening
Ollerhead (1977)	—	5	—	—
Borsky (1976)	—	5	5	0
Bullen and Hede (1983)	—	9	4	—
DORA (1980)	—	—	—	0
Schomer (1983)	5–10	(5–10)	(5–10)	—
Best estimate	5	5	5	0

* Day = 0700–1900 (7 AM–7 PM); evening = 1900–2200 (7–10 PM); night = 2200–0700 (10 PM–7 AM) hours. Dashes (—) indicate no data obtained; (5–10 dB), estimated entry.

annoyance and disturbance found in the respective time periods. It is seen that both the nighttime and evening hours are more sensitive periods than the daytime for noise annoyance; if anything, the early evening is a more sensitive time than later nighttime. On the basis of presently available data, it appears that, relative to noise in the hours of 0700–1900 (7 AM–7 PM), a penalty-weight of 5 dB should be added to noises in the period of 1900–0700 hours (7 PM–7 AM). Perhaps this L_{eq} noise metric could be called L_{den}, or DENL (day–evening–night level).

SUMMARY OF OVERALL IMPACTS OF ENVIRONMENTAL NOISE AND SPECIFICATIONS OF COMPATIBILITY WITH RESIDENTIAL AREAS

Figure 10.37 summarizes the subjectively and objectively measured effects that are experienced by specified percentages of people exposed to aircraft noise at given levels of L_{dn}. These relations are based on data for people living in average residential dwellings as present in moderate to cold climates. They are not necessarily fully applicable for structures with special sound isolation and attenuation features, nor for warm-climate conditions. Although an L_{dn} noise dosage of significance is usually dominated, and set, by the

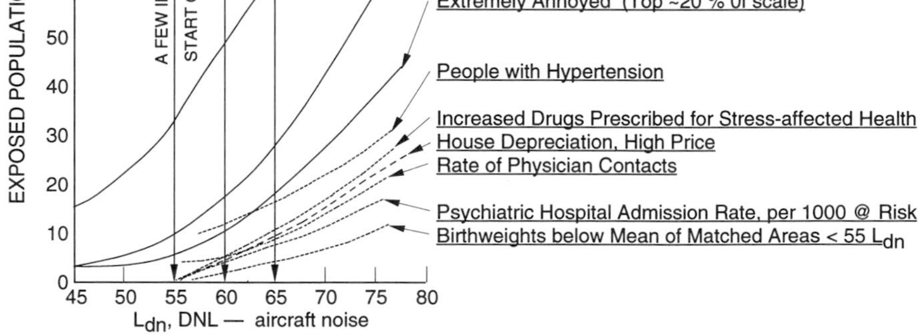

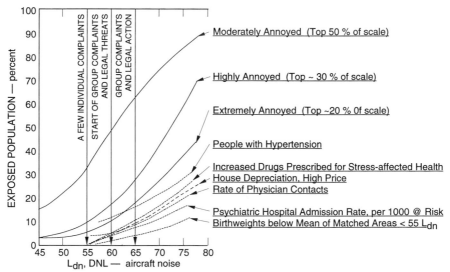

FIGURE 10.37 Percentage of people in moderate climate communities experiencing the designated degrees of annoyance, adverse effects on health and well-being, and loss in property values as a function of the L_{dn} level of aircraft noise in their neighborhood. Also indicated are the L_{dn} levels at which certain degrees of complaint behavior may be initiated. It is found that, as normally measured, street traffic noise causes approximately similar adverse effects at L_{dn} 10 dB higher than that for aircraft noise. Legend: subjective (solid lines) and objective (dashed lines) adverse annoyance, health, and well-being effects.

presence of one particular source (aircraft, street vehicle, or factory), it is believed that the effects of noise from several sources are approximately assessed by effective L_{dn}. [Note that (1) because it is the energy of the individual noise events that are summed, not the decibels values of different L_{dn}s; and (2) in order to intercompare the effective L_{dn} of environmental noises from different sources, the noises from each source are to be referenced to that present at the average position of a recipient in place of residence.]

As discussed, the most extensive information and firmest conclusions as to the effects of environmental noise on people are based on studies of people's reactions to aircraft noise measured in L_{dn}, or comparable measures of exposure. It appears, from data presented, that some improvement in assessment and prediction, with the aid of Fig. 10.37, of the adverse effects noted thereon, would occur with modifications in the calculation of L_{dn} by (1) changing the present 10-dB nighttime (10:00 PM–7:00 AM) penalty to a 5-dB penalty for 6:00 PM–7:00 AM; and (2) the addition of 2–3 dB, to otherwise calculated L_{dn}, for situations with, or during, warm-climate conditions. Such modifications have not been applied for the data in Fig. 10.37.

Noise from Ground-Based Vehicles

The noise from trucks, automobiles, and trains have been a more widely distributed, but generally not as intensely bothersome, source of environmental noise as that from aircraft. As discussed, there are significant acoustical reasons, and possibly some "emotional bias" against aircraft, that are at the source of this difference. The best estimate of the difference in effectiveness, as a cause of high annoyance, from street and road traffic noise as compared to aircraft noise is the equivalent of 10 dB over the range L_{dn} 55–75. It appears that railway noise may be the equivalent of about 5 dB less annoying than aircraft noise, but there conflicting data with respect to railway as compared to street traffic noise in this regard.

Numbers of People Exposed to Street Traffic vs. Aircraft Noise of a Given L_{dn}, and their Relation to Decisions Regarding Noise Compatibility

Schultz (1978, p. 389) recommended that makers of decisions about suitable sites for residential buildings take "into account both the subjective effects of noise on people and the current prevailing noise levels in the United States. It is shown by Schultz (p. 389, Fig. 23), that 20% of the 138 million people in the urban population of the United States were being exposed to transportation noise from aircraft, street, highway, and railroad traffic of $L_{dn} \geq 65$, and 50% to $L_{dn} \geq 60$ or higher. Table 10.14, part of the foundation for those estimations, illustrates that noise in urban residential areas ranges from about L_{dn} ~50–70, with a median of 61 dB.

TABLE 10.14 L_{dn}* at Single- or Two-Family Dwellings from Urban Street Traffic (Cars, Trucks, Buses) in Various U.S. Cities

Site	L_{dn}, dB	Site	L_{dn}, dB	Site	L_{dn}, dB
Atlanta		(Denver—continued)		St. Louis	
401	63.8	1107	59.0	1201	58.5
404	60.7	1109	59.3	1203	62.9
406	67.3	1110	56.6	1204	56.2
Boston		1112	61.3	1206	60.0
0001	61.2	Kansas City		1208	61.0
0003	59.6	1301	60.1	1209	61.5
0004	59.6	1302	53.2	1210	64.2
0005	57.0	1304	61.4	San Francisco	
0006	67.8	Los Angeles		1005	61.9
0007	61.7	1601	56.4	1007	60.5
0008	65.2	1602	57.1	1008	61.2
Chicago		1603	56.1	1010	63.8
502	71.2	1604	61.0	1011	61.1
503	69.6	1605	58.6	1012	61.9
505	59.0	1606	59.2	Seattle	
506	64.4	1607	58.9	1501	55.6
Dallas		1608	55.8	1502	55.1
1401	65.9	Miami		1503	52.4
1402	57.8	0601	66.1	1504	53.2
1403	61.1	0602	58.1	1505	51.0
1404	61.1	0603	63.2	1506	54.7
1405	56.3	0604	64.4	Washington, DC	
1406	61.6	0606	60.9	0102	63.0
Denver		Pittsburgh		0103	62.4
1101	62.6	0301	58.1	0104	64.1
1103	58.3	0302	59.1	0106	64.6
1104	60.7	0303	61.9		
1106	57.3	0305	62.2		

* Microphone located average of 8 ft above ground and 25 ft from street curb; median all sites, 61.0.

Data from Galloway *et al.* (1974).

This information has been used in the past as a basis for interpreting the practical meaning of the findings of attitude surveys about community noise in the following way:

1. The Schultz synthesis curve indicates that the noise from aircraft noise and from ground-based vehicles of transportation causes equal percentages of a community to be "highly annoyed" by the two types of noises when they are of equal L_{dn}, measured in front of residential structures.
2. Since about 50% of the urban population is currently exposed to outdoor transportation noise at a level of $L_{dn} \geq 60$, it follows, according to Schultz,

that 50% of the people should be as annoyed as the 10% who are "highly annoyed" by and, to some extent, threatening legal action against aircraft noise.

3. Such a prediction—that 40% of the people are highly annoyed by, and to some extent threatening to take legal action against, the noise from ground-based vehicles is inconsistent with general complaint and legal activities of the general public. Also, if this were true, 50% of existing residential areas should, presumably, be considered as possibly inappropriate for residential use.

4. Therefore, it can be argued (Galloway, 1982), that some higher exposure level of aircraft noise than L_{dn} 60 should be compatible with residential areas. [Courts of law and local and state government agencies are presently guided by federal housing, aviation, defense, and other regulatory departments that a level of L_{dn} 65, regardless of noise source, should be considered as an upper limit for compatible residential usage without special soundproofing provisions, see Federal Interagency Committee on Urban Noise, (1980).]

However, such an interpretation of this yardstick of public acceptance of environmental noise (number of people exposed to transportation noise of L_{dn} 60) significantly depends on the findings of the relative annoyance and related reactions to street traffic noise as compared with aircraft noise of equal L_{dn} levels at the front of houses. This is particularly true in light of the fact that the numbers of people exposed to noise from ground vehicles of L_{dn} ≥60 at their homes, constitute about 79%, and aircraft only about 21%, of the ~50–58% of the urban population exposed to all transportation vehicle noises of L_{dn} ≥60.

As discussed earlier, the equality deduced by Schultz for noise from those two types of sources in the preparation of his synthesis curve appeared on further analysis and additional data, to be faulty by a factor of about 10 dB (Kryter, 1982a,b; 1983 and as discussed above). The following application of L_{dn} aircraft and effective L_{dn} ground vehicle noise annoyance to the population-exposed data provide significantly different results than have been inferred from the Schultz synthesis function and numbers of the urban population exposed to transportation noise of a given L_{dn}.

Calculation of Numbers for People Exposed to Street Traffic and Aircraft Noise of a Given Effective L_{dn}

Figure 10.38 shows the numbers of the urban U.S. population exposed to aircraft, freeway, and street traffic noise as a function of L_{dn}. Table 10.15 was derived from that figure by finding the percentages of the urban population exposed to L_{dn} 60 and 65 for aircraft noise and ground vehicle noise (the sum of the percentages for street and highway traffic). Percentages were

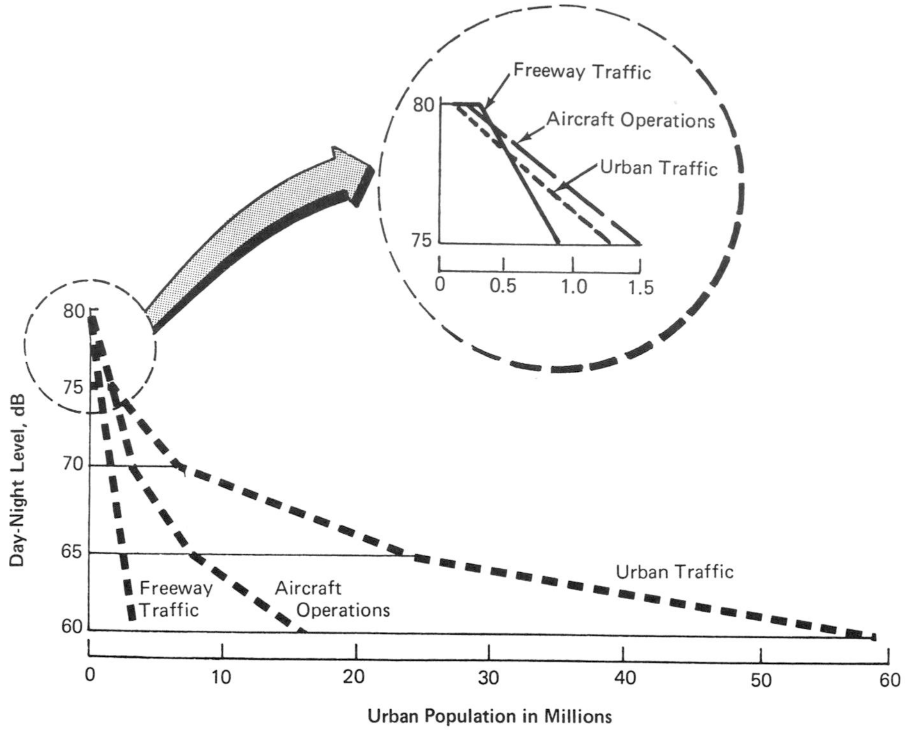

FIGURE 10.38 Cumulative number of people in U.S. urban areas exposed to outdoor day–night (L_{dn}, or DNL) noise level from aircraft operations, and urban street and freeway traffic. Total U.S. urban population estimated to be 138 million. (From EPA. 1978.)

also found for the ground vehicle noises by entering the vertical ordinate at L_{dn} levels 10 dB higher than the specified, measured, L_{dn} values of 60 and 65. It is seen in Table 10.15 that nearly 4-times as many urban people should be, according to L_{dn} as measured, as annoyed by ground vehicle noise as are similarly annoyed by aircraft noise—with L_{dn} 60, 46% for ground-based vehicles vs. 12% for aircraft, a total of 58%. (This finding of a total of 58% exposed to L_{dn} 60 is reasonably similar, as it should be, to the previously noted 50% estimated by Schultz.)

However, Table 10.15 shows that the percentages of the urban population that are exposed to effective levels of ground traffic noise are more commensurate with community behavior as demonstrated by most research data and common observation. Considering that the effective level of L_{dn} ground traffic noise is 10 dB less than measured (primarily because of adventitious acoustical effects not enjoyed by aircraft noise), it would be predicted that with aircraft noise, measured L_{dn} 60, 12% of the urban population would be "highly annoyed," but with ground traffic noise, effective L_{dn} 60, only about 7%. Thus, a total of only 19%, or about 26 million people, are predicted to

TABLE 10.15 Percentage of Urban Population Exposed to Transportation Noise

Vehicle	L_{dn} 60, %	L_{dn} 65, %
Aircraft	12	6
Ground	46	20
Total	58	26
Aircraft	12	6
Ground*	20	3
Total	19	9

* Ground vehicles effective $L_{dn} = L_{dn} - 10$ dB.

be actually highly annoyed by both aircraft and street road traffic noise at their residences.

Table 10.15 indicates that the adverse effects of noise from these vehicles of transportation would be experienced by 26% of the urban people, if one accepts the conclusion that aircraft and ground-based vehicle noise cause, with equal measured L_{dn} exposure levels, equal adverse effects. However, this percentage drops to about only 9% (6% aircraft, 3% ground vehicles) when the effective level of ground vehicle noise is considered to be an average of 10 dB less than that of aircraft noise, as those noises are typically measured or estimated.

L_{dn} Threshold of Residential Incompatibility Based on Noise-Annoyance Data

It is seen in Fig. 10.37 that with aircraft noise, at L_{dn} 55–60, say, 58 dB, there occurs (1) group complaint activity, (2) high annoyance in 13% of the people, (3) a measurable increase in a variety of stress-affected disorders of health and psychological well-being, and (4) property-value depreciation. It would follow that if the general level of tolerability for street traffic noise in urban residential areas is to be commensurate with that for aircraft noise in residential areas, the level of the traffic noise could be 5–10 dB higher, say 8, or L_{dn} 65 as now measured.

In brief, it is concluded that exposure levels of L_{dn} 58 for aircraft, and L_{dn} 65 for ground-based vehicles mark a measurable increase in the amount of objective, adverse effects of noise conditions not compatible with typical residential areas and house structures. At those respective levels for the two types of noise sources, about 15% of those exposed can be expected to report that they are, subjectively, highly annoyed by the noise. This amount of annoyance (15% of the people highly annoyed by noise) is the same as that derived by Schultz for aircraft or ground-based vehicles at L_{dn} 65. This is the same percentage of people and degree of noise-annoyance reaction considered, by the Federal Interagency Committee on Urban Noise, as the upper-level boundary for community noise that is marginally acceptability for typical residential housing.

L_{dn} Threshold of Residential Incompatibility Based on Noise-Interference Effects Data

The Federal Interagency Committee on Urban Noise (1980, Table D-1: "Effects of Noise on People") specifies that at L_{dn} 65, 100%, and at $L_{dn} \geq 75$ and above, 98% sentence intelligibility would prevail indoors. For reasons discussed in Chapters 6 and 7, for typical aircraft noise that is not true, or, at the least, is misrepresentative. For example, 100 aircraft overflights from 7 AM to 10 PM, at a peak level of 84 dB_A, 10 s above 74 dB_A, will have an L_{dn} of 65; and at indoor levels, with windows partly open, ranging from about 59, increasing to 69, then decreasing to 59 dB_A, an average for the 10 s of about 64 dB_A. With a typical indoor speech level at a listener's ears of, say, 52 dB_A (see Fig. 6.6), the speech-to-noise ratio will be less than -12 dB, with 0% sentence intelligibility (see Fig. 6.28) during 10-s duration periods 100 times per day. With windows closed, and/or higher noise intensity, speech-signal intelligibility would, of course, be higher, but would also be less, and continue for longer periods of time, for individual phrases and words, and signals at lower signal levels, such as speech between rooms.

L_{dn} Threshold of Residential Incompatibility Based on Noise Effects on Health and Well-Being

The Federal Interagency Committee observes in its table on the effects of noise that "Research implicates noise as a factor producing stress-related health effects such as heart disease, high blood pressure and stroke, ulcers and other digestive disorders. The relationships between noise and these effects, however, have not as yet been quantified." However, from research discussed in Chapter 9 and this chapter, relationships between L_{dn} exposures to aircraft noise and some stress-affected health disorders can now be quantified. Above $L_{dn} \sim 58$ the prevalence of health disorders progressively increases.

References

Alexandre, A. (1970). "Prevision de la Gene due au Bruit autour des Aeroports et Perspectives sur les Movens d'y Remedier," Doc. A.A. 28/70. Anthropol. Appl., Cent. Etud. Rech., Paris.

Alexandre, A. (1973). Decision criteria based on spatio-temporal comparisons of surveys on aircraft noise. *In* "Noise as a Public Health Problem" (J. V. Tobias, G. Jansen, and W. D. Ward, eds.), ASHA Rep. No. 10, Am. Speech–Lang.–Hear. Assoc., Rockville, Maryland.

Alexandre, A. (1976). An assessment of certain causal models used in surveys on aircraft noise annoyance. *J. Sound Vib.* **44,** 119–125.

Andersen, T. V., Kuhl, K., and Relster, E. (1983). Reactions to railway noise in Denmark. *J. Sound Vib.* **87,** 311–314.

Avery, G. C. (1982). Comparison of telephone complaints and survey measures of noise annoyance. *J. Sound Vib.* **82,** 215–225.

Beranek, L. L., Kryter, K. D., and Miller, L. N. (1959). Reaction of people to exterior aircraft noise. *NOISE Control* **5**(5), 23–31.

Bertoni, D., Franchini, A., Magnoni, M., Tartoni, P., and Vallet, M. (1993). Reactions of people to urban traffic noise in Modena, Itlay. *Noise Public Health Probl., Proc. Int. Congr., 6th.* (M. Vallet, ed.), Vol. 2, pp. 593–596. l'INRETS, 94114 Arcuil Cedex, France.

Bitter, C. (1968). Noise annoyance due to aircraft. *Colloq. Hum. Demands With Respect to Noise, Paris, Nov: 18–19* Pap. Int. Gezondheidtstech., TNO, Netherlands.

Bjorkman, M., and Rylander, R. (1993). The relation between different noise descriptors for road traffic noise and the extent of annoyance. *Noise Public Health Probl., Proc. Int. Congr., 6th.* (M. Vallet, ed.), Vol. 2, pp. 351–354. l'INRETS, 94114 Arcuil Cedex, France.

Borsky, P. N. (1961). "Community Reactions to Air Force Noise, Parts I and II," WADC Tech. Rep. 60-689 (I) and (II). U.S. Air Force, Wright-Patterson AFB, Ohio.

Borsky, P. N. (1976). Sleep interference and annoyance by aircraft noise. *Sound Vib.* Dec., 18-21.

Borsky, P. N. (1980). Review of community response to noise. *In* "Noise as a Public Health Problem" (J. V. Tobias, G. Jansen, and W. D. Ward, eds.), ASHA Rep. No. 10, pp. 453–474. Am. Speech–Lang.–Hear. Assoc., Rockville, Maryland.

Borsky, P. N. (1983). Intergration of multiple aircraft noise exposures over time by residents living near U.S. Air Force Bases. *Proc. 4th Int. Congr. Noise Public Health Probl.* Turin, Italy.

Borsky, P. N., and Leonard, H. S. (1973). A new field survey—laboratory methodology for studying human response to noise. *Proc. Int. Congr. Noise Public Health Probl.* (W. D. Ward, ed.), Rep. EPA 550/9-73-008, pp. 743–764. U.S. Environ. Prot. Agency, Washington, D.C.

Bronzaft, A. L., and McCarthy, D. P. (1975). The effect of elevated train noise on reading ability. *Environ. Behav.* **7,** 517–527.

Bronzaft, A. L. (1980). The effect of elevated train noise on reading ability: Followup report. *J. Acoust. Soc. Am.* **68,** Suppl. No. 1, 591.

Buchta, E. (1990). A field study on annoyance caused by sounds from small firearms. *J. Acoust. Soc. Am.* **88,** 1459–1467.

Buchta, E. (1993). A review of the penalty for impulse noise. *Noise Public Health Probl., Proc. Int. Congr., 6th.* (M. Vallet, ed.), Vol. 2, pp. 420–427. l'INRETS, 94114 Arcuil Cedex, France.

Bullen, R. B., and Hede, A. J. (1982). Assessment of community noise exposure from rifle shooting. *J. Sound Vib.* **82,** 29–37.

Bullen, R. B., and Hede, A. (1983). Time-of-day corrections in measures of aircraft noise exposure. *J. Acoust. Soc. Am.* **73,** 1624–1630.

Cheifetz, P., and Borsky, P. N. (1980). Laboratory study of effects of acoustic and nonacoustic variables on annoyance with aircraft noise. "Noise as a Public Health Problem" (J. V. Tobias, G. Jansen, and W. D. Ward, eds.), ASHA Rep. No. 10, pp. 522–528. Am. Speech–Lang.–Hear. Assoc., Rockville, Maryland.

Clevenson, S. A., and Shepherd, W. T., eds. (1980). "Time-of-Day Corrections to Aircraft Noise Metrics," Rep. NASA CP-2135, FAA-EE-80-3. NASA Langley Research Center, Hampton, Virginia.

Cohen, S., Glass, D. C., and Singer, J. E. (1973). Apartment noise, auditory discrimination and reading ability in children. *J. Exp. Soc. Psychol.* **9,** 407–422.

Cohen, S., Krantz, D. S., Evans, G. W., Stokols, D., and Kelly, S. (1981). Aircraft noise and children: Longitudinal and crosssectional evidence on adaptation to noise and the effectiveness of noise abatement. *J. Pers. Soc. Psychol.* **40,** 331–345.

Commission on the Third London Airport (1970). "Papers and Proceedings," Vol. VII. HM. Stationery Off., London.
Committee on the Problem of Noise (1963). "Noise—Final Report." HM Stationery Off., London.
Connor, W. K., and Patterson, H. P. (1972). "Community Reaction to Aircraft Noise Around Smaller City Airports," Rep. NASA CR-2104. NASA Langley Res. Cent., Hampton, Virginia.
Crook, M. A., and Langdon, F. J. (1974). The effects of aircraft noise in schools around London Airport. *J. Sound Vib.* **34,** 221–232.
Department of Aviation (1981). "Preliminary Report, Noise Control Program." Bolt, Beranek, & Newman to Dep. Aviat., Dallas Texas.
De Vany, A. S. (1976). An economic model of airport noise pollution in an urban environment. *In* "Theory and Measurement of Economic Externalities" (S. A. Y. Lin, ed.), pp. 205–214. Academic Press, New York.
DORA (1980). "Aircraft Noise and Sleep Disturbance: Final Report." DORA Rep. No. 8008. Civ. Aviat. Auth., London.
EPA (1974). "Information on Levels of Environmental Noise Requisite To Protect Public Health and Welfare With an Adequate Margin of Safety," Rep. EPA 550/9-74-004. U.S. Environ. Prot. Agency, Washington, D.C. (Avail. from NTIS as PB 239 429.)
EPA (1978). "Protective Noise Levels: Condensed Version of EPA Levels," Doc. Rep. EPA 550/9-79-100. U.S. Environ. Prot. Agency, Washington, D.C. (Avail. from NTIS as PB 82 138 827.)
FAA (1981). "Evaluation of Three Noise Abatement Departure Procedures at John Wayne Airport." U.S. Dep. Transp., Fed. Aviat. Adm., Washington, D.C.
Federal Interagency Committee on Urban Noise (1980). "Guidelines for Considering Noise in Land Use Planning and Control." Fed. Interagency Comm. Urban Noise, U.S. Dep. Transp., Washington, D.C.
Fidell, S. A., Teffeteller, S. R., and Pearsons, K. S. (1979). "Initial Study on the Effects of Transformer and Transmission Line Noise on People, Vol. 3: Community Reaction," Rep. EPRI-EA-1240-VOL-3. Bolt, Beranek, & Newman, Canoga Park, California.
Fidell, S., Horonjeff, R., Teffeteller, S., and Pearsons, K. (1981). "Community Sensitivity to Changes in Aircraft Noise Exposure," Rep. NASA CR-3490. NASA Langley RES. Cent., Hampton, Virginia.
Fidell, S., Horonjeff, R., Mills, J., Baldwin, E., Teffeteller, S., and Pearsons, K. (1985). Aircraft noise annoyance at three joint air carrier and general aviation airports. *J. Acoust. Soc. Am.* **77,** 1054–1068.
Fidell, S., Barber, D. S., and Schultz, T. J. (1991). Updating a dosage relationship for the prevalence of annoyance due to general transportation noise. *J. Acoust. Soc. Am.* **89,** 221–233.
Fields, J. M. (1993). Effect of personal and situational variables on noise annoyance in residential areas. *J. Acoust. Soc. Am.* **93,** 2753–2763.
Fields, J. M., and Walker, J. G. (1980). Comparing reactions to transportation noises from different surveys: A railway noise vs. aircraft and road traffic comparison. *In* "Noise as a Public Health Problem" (J. V. Tobias, G. Jansen, and W. D. Ward, eds.), ASHA Rep. No. 10, pp. 580–587. Am. Speech–Lang.–Hear. Assoc., Rockville, Maryland.
Fields, J. M., and Walker, J. G. (1982a). Comparing the relationships between noise level and annoyance in different surveys: A railway noise vs. aircraft and road traffic comparison. *J. Sound Vib.* **81,** 51–80.
Fields, J. M., and Walker, J. G. (1982b). The response to railway noise in residential areas in Great Britain. *J. Sound Vib.* **85,** 177–255.
Galloway, W. J. (1980). "Historical Development of Noise Exposure Metrics, in Time-of-Day Corrections to Aircraft Noise," NASA Conf. Publ. No. 2135, FAA-EE-80-3, Mar. 11–12. NASA Langley Res. Cent., Hampton, Virginia.

Galloway, W. J. (1982). *Testimony. In Charles Francis Davison et al. v. Department of Defense et al.,* U.S. District Court, Southern District of Ohio, Eastern Division Case No. C-2-80-871, April 17, 1982.

Galloway, W. J., and Bishop, D. E (1970). "Noise Exposure Forecasts: Evolution, Evaluation, Extensions, and Land Use Interpretations," Rep. FAA-NO-70-9. Fed. Aviat. Adm., Washington, D.C.

Galloway, W. J., and von Gierke, H. E. (1966). "Individual and Community Reaction to Aircraft Noise; Present Status and Standardization Efforts," INC/C4/P9. Am. Stand. Assoc., New York.

Galloway, W. J., Eldred, K. M., and Simpson, M. A. (1974). "Population Distribution of the United States as a Function of Outdoor Noise Level—Vol. 2," Rep. EPA 550/9-74-009-A-VOL-2. U.S. Environ. Prot. Agency; Washington, D.C. (Avail. from NTIS as PB 257 617/1.)

Gjestland, T. (1979). The importance of a threshold level when assessing noise annoyance. *J. Acoust. Soc. Am.* **65,** Suppl. No. 1, 545.

Gjestland, T., and Oftedal, G. (1980). Assessment of noise annoyance: The introduction of a threshold level in Leq calculations. *J. Sound Vib.* **69,** 603–610.

Grandjean, E. (1980). "Socio-Psychological Airplane Noise Investigation in the Districts of Three Swiss Airports; Zurich, Basel, Geneva," Rep. NASA TM-75787. NASA Langley Res. Cent., Hampton, Virginia.

Grandjean, E., Graf, P., Lauber, A., Meier, H. P., and Muller, R. (1973). A survey of aircraft noise in Switzerland. *Proc. Int. Congr. Noise Public Health Probl.* (W. D. Ward, ed.), Rep. EPA 550/9-73-008, pp. 645–660. U.S. Environ. Prot. Agency, Washington, D.C.

Grandjean, E., Graf, P., Lauber, A., Meier, H. P., and Muller, R. (1976). Survey on the effects of aircraft noise around three civil airports in Switzerland. *INTER-NOISE '76 Proc.* (R. L. Kerlin, ed.), pp. 85–90. Washington, D.C.

Green, D. M. and Fidell, S. (1991). Variability in the criterion for reporting annoyance in community noise surveys. *J. Acoust. Soc. Am.* **89,** 234–243.

Griffiths, I. D., and Delauzun, F. R. (1977). Individual differences in sensitivity to traffic noise: An empirical study. *J. Sound Vib.* **55,** 93–107.

Griffiths, I. D., Langdon, F. J., and Swan, M. A. (1980). Subjective effects of traffic noise exposure: Reliability and seasonal effects. *J. Sound Vib.* **71,** 227–240.

Gunn, W. J., Shigehisa, T., Fletcher, J. L., and Shepherd, W. T. (1981). Annoyance response to aircraft noise as a function of contextual effects and personality characteristics. *J. Aud. Res.* **21,** 51–83.

Hall, F. L., and Taylor, S. M. (1977). Predicting community response to road traffic noise. *J. Sound Vib.* **52,** 387–399.

Hall, F. L., Taylor, S. M., and Birnie, S. E. (1980). Spatial patterns in community response to aircraft noise associated with non-noise factors. *J. Sound Vib.* **71,** 361–381.

Hall, F. L., Birnie, S. E., Taylor, S. M., and Palmer, J. E. (1981). Direct comparison of community response to road traffic noise and to aircraft noise. *J. Acoust. Soc. Am.* **70,** 1690–1698.

Hede, A. J., and Bullen, R. B. (1982). *Aircraft Noise in Australia: A Survey of Community Response.* NAL Rep. 88, National Acoustics Laboratories, Commonwealth Department of Health, Australian Government Publishing Service, Canberra, Australia.

Highline School District (1976). *No. 401, King County v. Port of Seattle, 87 Wash. 2d 6, 548 P. 2d 1085,* Seattle.

Ishiyama, T. (1993). A social survey of community responses to road traffic noise. *Noise Public Health Probl., Proc. Int. Congr., 6th.* (M. Vallet, ed.), Vol. 2, pp. 375–378. 1'INRETS, 94114 Arcuil Cedex, France.

Johnston, G. W., and Haasz, A. A. (1979). Traffic background level and signal duration effects on aircraft noise judgment. *J. Sound Vib.* **63,** 543–560.

Knall, V., and Schuemer, R. (1983). The differing annoyance levels of rail and road traffic noise. *J. Sound Vib.* **87,** 321–326.

Ko, N. W. M. (1979). Responses of teachers to aircraft noise. *J. Sound Vib.* **62,** 277–292.

Kryter, K. D. (1969). Sonic booms from supersonic transport. *Science* **163,** 359–367.

Kryter, K. D. (1977). "The Relative Impact of Concorde Aircraft Noise Around J. F. Kennedy Airport." Stanford Res. Inst., Menlo Park, California. (Under contract with Port Authority of New York and New Jersey, New York.)

Kryter, K. D. (1982a). Community annoyance from aircraft and ground vehicle noise. *J. Acoust. Soc. Am.* **72,** 1222–1242.

Kryter, K. D. (1982b). Rebuttal by Karl D. Kryter to comments by T. J. Schultz. *J. Acoust. Soc. Am* **72,** 1253–1257.

Kryter, K. D. (1983). Response of Karl D. Kryter to modified comments by T. J. Schultz on K. D. Kryter's paper, "Community annoyance from aircraft and ground vehicle noise," *J. Acoust. Soc. Am.* **73,** 1066–1068.

Kryter, K. D., Johnson, P. J., and Young, J. R. (1967). "Psychological Experiments on Sonic Booms Conducted at Edwards Air Force Base." SRI, Menlo Park, California. Contract AF49(638)-1758, Natl. Sonic Boom Eval. Off., Washington, D.C. (Avail. from DTIC as AD 689 844.)

Langdon, F. J. (1976). Noise nuisance caused by road traffic in residential areas, Parts I and 11. *J. Sound Vib.* **47,** 243–263, 265–282.

Langdon, F. J., and Griffiths, L. D. (1982). Subjective effects of traffic noise exposure. Comparisons of noise indices, response scales, and the effects of changes in noise levels. *J. Sound Vib.* **83,** 171–180.

Lercher, P., and Widmann, U. (1993). Factors determining community response to road traffic noise. *Noise Public Health Probl., Proc. Int. Congr., 6th.* (M. Vallet, ed.), Vol. 2, pp. 201–204. 1'INRETS, 94114 Arcuil Cedex, France.

Lukas, J. S., DuPree, R. B., and Swing, J. W. (1981). "Effects of Noise on Academic Achievement and Classroom Behavior," FHWA/CA/DOHS-81/01 (Contract I.A.A. 19-7165). Off. Noise Control, California Dep. Health Serv., Sacramento. (Avail. from NTIS.)

Maser, A. L., Sorensen, P. H., Kryter, K. D., and Lukas, J. S. (1978). Effects of intrusive sound on classroom behavior: Data from a successful lawsuit. *West. Psychol. Assoc., Apr., San Francisco* Pap.

McKennell, A. C. (1963). "Aircraft Noise Annoyance Around London (Heathrow) Airport," S.S. 337. Central Off. Inf. (Br.), London.

McKennell, A. C. (1973). Psycho-social factors in aircraft noise annoyance. *Proc. Int. Congr. Noise Public Health Probl.* (W. D. Ward, ed.), Rep. EPA 550/9-73-008. U.S. Environ. Prot. Agency, Washington, D.C.

Miedema, H. (1993). Response functions for environmental noise. *Noise Public Health Probl., Proc. Int. Congr., 6th.* (M. Vallet, ed.), Vol. 2, pp. 428–433. 1'INRETS, 94114 Arcuil Cedex, France.

Mieszkowski, P., and Saper, A. M. (1978). An estimate of the effects of airport noise on property values. *J. Urban Econ.* **5,** 425–440.

MIL Research (1971). "Second Survey of Aircraft Noise Annoyance Around London (Heathrow) Airport." HM Stationery Off., London.

Molino, J. A. (1982). "Should Helicopter Noise Be Measured Differently From Other Aircraft Noise?—A Review of the Psychoacoustic Literature," Rep. NASA CR-3609. NASA Langley Res. Cent., Hampton, Virginia.

Nelson, J. P. (1978). "Aircraft Noise and the Market for Residential Housing: Empirical Results for Seven Selected Airports," Rep. DOT/RSPA/DPB50/78/24. U.S. Dep. Transp., Washington, D.C. (Avail. from NITS as PB 297 681.)

Nelson, J. P. (1979). Airport noise, location rent, and the market for residential amenities. *J. Environ. Econ. Manage.* **6,** 320–331.

Nemecek, L., Wehrli, B., and Turrian, V. (1981). Effects of the noise on street traffic in Switzerland; a review of four surveys. *J. Sound Vib.* **78,** 223–234.

Öhrström, E., Bjorkman, M., and Rylander, R. (1980). Laboratory annoyance and different traffic noise sources. *J. Sound Vib.* **70,** 333–341.

Ollerhead, J. B. (1977). Variation of community noise sensitivity with time of day. *Proc. Inter-Noise '77, Zurich* pp. B692–B697.

Ollerhead, J. B. (1980). Accounting for time of day and mixed source effects in the assessment of community noise exposure. *In* "Noise as a Public Health Problem" (J. V. Tobias, G. Jansen, and W. D. Ward, eds.), ASHA Rep. No. 10. Am. Speech–Lang.–Hear. Assoc., Rockville, Maryland.

Ollerhead, J. B. (1982). "Laboratory Studies of Scales for Measuring Helicopter Noise," Rep. NASA CR-3610. NASA Langley Res. Cent., Hampton, Virginia.

Ollerhead, J., and Jones, C. (1993). Aircraft noise and sleep disturbance: a UK field study. *Noise Public Health Probl., Proc. Int. Congr., 6th.* (M. Vallet, ed.), Vol. 2, pp. 353–358. l'INRETS, 94114 Arcuil Cedex, France.

Opinion Research of California (1977). "Report of Findings—Study Among Residents of Orange County Relative to Operations at Orange County Airport." City of Newport Beach, California.

Orange County, CA (1980). "John Wayne Airport, Orange County for Calendar Year 1979 and Complaint History From 1975 Through March 31, 1980. John Wayne Airport Noise Abatement Program Report for the Periods October 1, 1979 Through October 31, 1979 and January 1, 1980 Through March 31, 1980." Airports Div., Gen. Serv. Agency, County of Orange, Santa Ana, California.

Ortega, J. C., and Kryter, K. D. (1982). Comparison of aircraft and ground vehicle noise levels in front and backyards of residences. *J. Acoust. Soc. Am.* **71,** 216–217.

Patterson, H. P., and Connor, W. K. (1973). Community responses to aircraft noise in large and small cities in the U.S.A. *Proc. Int. Congr. Noise Public Health Probl.* (W. D. Ward, ed.), Rep. EPA 550/9-73-008, pp. 707–718. U.S. Environ. Prot. Agency, Washington, D.C.

Piercy, J. E., and Daigle, G. A. (1991). Sound propagation in the open air. *In* "Handbook of Noise Control" (C. M. Harris, ed.), 3rd Ed., pp. 3.1–3.26. McGraw-Hill, New York.

Powell, C. A. (1979). "A Summation and Inhibition Model of Annoyance Response to Multiple Community Noise Sources," Rep. NASA TP-1479. NASA Langley Res. Cent., Hampton, Virginia.

Powell, C. A., McCurdy, D. A. (1982). "Effects of Repetition Rate and Impulsiveness of Simulated Helicopter Rotor Noise on Annoyance," Rep. NASA TP-1969. NASA Langley Res. Cent., Hampton, Virginia.

Powell, C. A., and Rice, C. G. (1975). Judgments of aircraft noise in a traffic noise background. *J. Sound Vib.* **38,** 39–50.

Rosenblith, W. A., Stevens, K. N., and the staff of Bolt, Beranek, & Newman (1953). "Handbook of Acoustic Noise Control—Vol. 11: Noise and Man," WADC Tech. Rep. 52-204. Wright-Patterson AFB, Ohio.

Rylander, R., Sorensen, S., and Kajland, A. (1976). Traffic noise exposure and annoyance reactions. *J. Sound Vib.* **47,** 237–242.

Rylander, R., Bjorkman, M., and Ahrlin, U. (1977). Tramway noise in city traffic. *J. Sound Vib.* **51,** 353–358.

Schomer, P. (1978). Human response to house vibrations caused by sonic booms or air blasts. *J. Acoust. Soc. Am.* **64,** 328–330.

Schomer, P. (1981). "Community Reaction to Impulse Noise: Initial Army Survey," Rep. CERL-TR-N-100. U.S. Army Constr. Eng. Res. Lab., Champaign, Illinois.

Schomer, P. (1982). A model to describe community response to impulse noise. *Noise Control Eng.* **18,** 5–14.

Schomer, P. (1983a). Noise monitoring in the vicinity of general aviation airports. *J. Acoust. Soc. Am.* **74,** 1764–1772.

Schomer, P. (1983b). A survey of community attitudes towards noise near a general aviation airport. *J. Acoust. Soc. Am.* **74,** 1773–1781.

Schomer, P. (1983c). Time-of-day noise adjustments of "penalties." *J. Acoust. Soc. Am.* **73,** 546–555.

Schomer, P., and Averbuch, A. (1989). Indoor human response to blast sounds that generate rattles. *J. Acoust. Soc. Am.* **86,** 665–773.

Schuemer-Kohrs, A., Sinz, A., and Zeichart, K. (1993). Annoyance caused by railway-induced vibration and noise. *Noise Public Health Probl., Proc. Int. Congr., 6th.* (M. Vallet, ed.), Vol. 2, pp. 299–302. l'INRETS, 94114 Arcuil Cedex, France.

Schultz, T. J. (1978). 1.: Synthesis of social surveys on noise annoyance. *J. Acoust. Soc. Am.* **64,** 377–405; erratum, *J. Acoust. Soc. Am.* **65,** 849 (1979).

Schultz, T. J. (1982). Comments on K. D. Kryter's paper, "Community annoyance from aircraft and ground vehicle noise." *J. Acoust. Soc. Am.* **72,** 1243–1252.

Shigehisa, T., and Gunn, W. J. (1978a). Annoyance response to recorded aircraft noise: I. Effect of intensity of illumination. *J. Aud. Res.* **18,** 175–182.

Shigehisa, T., and Gunn, W. J. (1978b). Annoyance response to recorded aircraft noise: 11. Effect of intensity of illumination in relation to noise spectrum. *J. Aud. Res.* **18,** 183–190.

Shigehisa, T., and Gunn, W. J. (1979a). Annoyance response to recorded aircraft noise: III. In relation to personality. *J. Aud. Res.* **19,** 41–46.

Shigehisa, T., and Gunn, W. J. (1979b). Annoyance response to recorded aircraft noise: IV. Effect of intensity of illumination in relation to personality. *J. Aud. Res.* **19,** 47–58.

Sorensen, S., and Hammar, N. (1983). Annoyance reactions due to railway noise. *J. Sound Vib.* **87,** 315–319.

Stephens, D. G., and Powell, C. A. (1980). Laboratory and community studies of aircraft noise effects. *In* "Noise as a Public Health Problem" (J. V. Tobias, G. Jansen, and W. D. Ward, eds.), ASHA Rep. No. 10, pp. 488–494. Am. Speech–Lang.–Hear. Assoc., Rockville, Maryland.

Stevens, K. N. and Pietrasanta, A. C. (1957). "Procedures for Estimating Noise Exposure and Resulting Community Reaction from Air Base Operations." Rpt. WADC TN 57-10, AD 110705, Wright-Patterson Air Force Base, Ohio.

Sutherland, L. C., Braden, M. H., and Colman. R. (1973). "A Program for the Measurement of Environmental Noise in the Community and Its Associated Human Response, Vol. I—E Feasibility Test of Measurement Techniques," Rep. DOT-TST-74-5. U.S. Dep. Transp., Washington, D.C. (Avail. from NTIS as PB 228 563.)

Taylor, S. M. (1982). A comparison of models to predict annoyance reactions to noise from mixed sources. *J. Sound Vib.* **81,** 123–138.

Taylor, S. M., Hall, F. L., and Birnie, S. E. (1980). Effect of background levels on community responses to aircraft noise. *J. Sound Vib.* **71,** 261–270.

Taylor, S. M., Hall, F. L., and Birnie, S. E. (1981). A comparison of community response to aircraft noise at Toronto International and Oshawa Municipal airports. *J. Sound Vib.* **77,** 233–244.

Taylor, S. M., Breston, B. E., and Hall, F. L. (1982). The effect of road traffic noise on house prices. *J. Sound Vib.* **80,** 523–541.

TRACOR (1971). "Community Reaction to Airport Noise," Vol. I, Rep. NASA CR-1761; Vol. II, Rep. NASA CR-111316, 1970.

Vallet, M., Maurin, M., Page, M. A., Favre, B., and Pachiaudi, G. (1978). Annoyance from and habituation to road traffic noise from urban expressways. *J. Sound Vib.* **60,** 423–440.

Vos, J. (1990). On the level-dependent penalty for impulse sound. *J. Acoust. Soc. Am.* **88,** 883–893.

Vos, J. (1992). Annoyance caused by simultaneous impulse, road traffic, and aircraft sounds: A quantitative model. *J. Acoust. Soc. Am.* **91,** 3330–3345.

VTN Consolidated (1980). "Airport Master Plan/ANCLUC Plan for John Wayne Airport, Orange County, Vol. II: Airport Noise Control and Land Use Compatibility (ANCLUC) Plan Draft Report." Gen. Serv. Agency, Orange County, California.

Wyle Labs. (1971). "Community Noise," Rep. NTID300.3 (Contract 68-040046). El Segundo, California.

Index

A

E

F

G

H

N

ISBN 0-12-427455-2

90018

9 780124 274556